Sale - C

KU-488-420

New Testament Commentary

The Gospel of Matthew

New Testament Commentary

The Gospel of Matthew

William Hendriksen

THE BANNER OF TRUTH TRUST

THE BANNER OF TRUTH TRUST
3 *Murrayfield Road, Edinburgh* EH12 6EL

*

© 1973 *William Hendriksen*
First British edition 1974
Reprinted 1976
Reprinted 1982
Reprinted 1989

Library of Congress Catalog Card Number 54:924
ISBN 0 85151 192 9

*

All rights in this book are reserved.
No part may be reproduced in any manner without
permission in writing from the copyright holder,
except brief quotations used in connection
with reviews in a magazine or newspaper.

No copies of this edition
published and printed in Great Britain
are to be sold in the United States and Canada
either retail or wholesale

*

Printed and bound in Great Britain at the
University Printing House, Oxford

TABLE OF CONTENTS

    The interpretation of each of the Lord's discourses is preceded by
    an introduction and summary. Elsewhere the summary will be
    found at the close of the chapter. By way of exception Matthew
    28 is followed by a "Reflection" on the main theme of that
    chapter.

NEW TESTAMENT COMMENTARY

LIST OF ABBREVIATIONS

The letters in book abbreviations are followed by periods. Those in periodical abbreviations omit the periods and are in italics. Thus one can see at a glance whether the abbreviation refers to a book or to a periodical.

A. *Book Abbreviations*

A.R.V.	American Standard Revised Version
A.V.	Authorized Version (King James)
Gram.N.T.	A. T. Robertson, *Grammar of the Greek New Testament in the Light of Historical Research*
Gram.N.T. (Bl.-Debr)	F. Blass and A. Debrunner, *A Greek Grammar of the New Testament and Other Early Christian Literature*
Grk.N.T. (A-B-M-W)	*The Greek New Testament,* edited by Kurt Aland, Matthew Black, Bruce M. Metzger, and Allen Wikgren
I.S.B.E.	*International Standard Bible Encyclopedia*
L.N.T. (Th.)	Thayer's *Greek-English Lexicon of the New Testament*
L.N.T. (A. and G.)	W. F. Arndt and F. W. Gingrich, *A Greek-English Lexicon of the New Testament and Other Early Christian Literature*
M.M.	*The Vocabulary of the Greek New Testament Illustrated from the Papyri and Other Non-Literary Sources,* by James Hope Moulton and George Milligan
N.A.S.B. (N.T.)	New American Standard Bible (New Testament)
N.N.	*Novum Testamentum Graece,* edited by D. Eberhard Nestle, revised by Erwin Nestle and Kurt Aland
N.E.B.	New English Bible
N.T.C.	W. Hendriksen, New Testament Commentary
R.S.V.	Revised Standard Version
S.BK.	Strack and Billerbeck, *Kommentar zum Neuen Testament aus Talmud und Midrasch*
S.H.E.R.K.	*The New Schaff-Herzog Encyclopedia of Religious Knowledge*
Th.D.N.T.	*Theological Dictionary of the New Testament* (edited by G. Kittel and G. Friedrich, and translated from the German) by G. W. Bromiley

NEW TESTAMENT COMMENTARY

| W.D.B. | *Westminster Dictionary of the Bible* |
| W.H.A.B. | *Westminster Historical Atlas to the Bible* |

B. *Periodical Abbreviations*

ATR	*Anglican Theological Review*
BG	*Bibel und Gemeinde*
BJRL	*Bulletin of the John Rylands Library*
BTr	*Bible Translator*
BW	*Biblical World*
BZ	*Biblische Zeitschrft*
CT	*Cuadernos teológicos*
CTM	*Concordia Theological Monthly*
EB	*Estudios oiblicos*
EQ	*Evangelical Quarterly*
ET	*Expository Times*
Exp	*The Expositor*
GTT	*Gereformeerd theologisch tijdschrift*
JBL	*Journal of Bible Literature*
JR	*Journal of Religion*
JTS	*Journal of Theological Studies*
NedTT	*Nederlands theologisch tijdschrift*
NTStud	*New Testament Studies; an International Journal published quarterly under the Auspices of Studiorum Novi Testamenti Societas*
PTR	*Princeton Theological Review*
RSR	*Recherches de science religieuse*
Th	*Theology: A Journal of Historic Christianity*
ThG	*Theologie und Glaube*
TR	*Theologia Reformata*
TS	*Theologische studiën*
TSK	*Theologische Studiën und Kritiken*
TT	*Theologisch tijdschrift*
WTJ	*Westminster Theological Journal*
ZNW	*Zeitschrift für die neutestamentliche Wissenschaft und die Kunde des Urchristentums*

Please Note

In order to differentiate between the second person singular (see Matt. 26:64: "You said (it)") and the second person plural (same verse: "but I tell y o u,"), the letters in "you sing." are not spaced; those in "y o u pl." are spaced.

Introduction

to

The Gospels

I. Introduction to the Four Gospels: Matthew, Mark, Luke, and John

First of all we should distinguish between "the gospel" and "the Gospels." The first is God's *message* to men. It is the *Godspell,* the spell or story that tells us what God, by means of the incarnation, earthly sojourn, mighty acts, suffering, death, and resurrection of his only Son, has done to save sinners. It is the evangel or "message of good tidings," the glad news of salvation addressed to a world lost in sin. This is the meaning of the term in biblical usage.[1] Not what *we* must do but what *God* in Christ has done for us is the most prominent part of this good news. Nevertheless, what men must do to be saved and thus to live their lives to the benefit of their neighbors and to the glory of God is also definitely included (Matt. 5:16; 11:25-30; Mark 2:17; 8:34; Luke 5:32; John 3:14-18).

According to the second and later (post-biblical) usage of the term, a Gospel—often capitalized to mark the distinction in meaning between this and the first usage—is one of the four books in which this good news is authoritatively set forth.

From the very early days of the recorded history of the New Testament church there have been four, and *only* four, widely recognized Gospels. To emphasize the fact that they set forth one and the same gospel, the term "fourfold Gospel" or "evangelical instrument" is at times ascribed to them. Thus Tertullian, in his work *Against Marcion* (begun about A.D. 207), states:

"We posit as our first principle that the evangelical instrument has apostles as its authors, to whom was assigned by the Lord himself this duty of publishing the gospel. . . . Of these apostles, therefore, John and Matthew first instil faith into us, while the apostolic men, Luke and Mark, renew it" (IV. 2).

Even somewhat earlier, in a work dating from about A.D. 182-188, the great theologian and traveler Irenaeus, sums up what was apparently the consensus of the entire church of his day, in these words:

"It is not possible that the Gospels can be either more or fewer than they are" (*Against Heresies* III.xi.8). We may not be able to accept the validity of some of the grounds upon which he bases this conclusion, namely, that the world is divided into four zones, that there are four principal winds, and that

---

[1] For a word-study of the concept "gospel" see N.T.C. on Philippians, pp. 81-85.

the cherubim are described in Scripture as four-faced; we can, nevertheless, find in this statement confirmation of the position already expressed, namely, that from very early days there have been four, and *only* four widely recognized Gospels.

The superscriptions of the Gospels, as found in the old Greek manuscripts, point in the same direction. Though these headings cannot be dated with absolute certainty and are not part of the original document but were subsequently added by copyists, they do show that probably as early as A.D. 125 *the four books* under discussion were assembled into a collection for use in the churches, and were given the titles: "According to Matthew," "According to Mark," etc. Strictly speaking, such an "according to" ascription does not necessarily indicate authorship. The meaning "drawn up in harmony with the teaching of" satisfies the wording. Yet, there is abundant evidence to show that the early Christians gave a broader connotation to the title, and regarded the person named in it as the actual author. They believed in *one* gospel, proclaimed in written form by four authors in four books.

Now according to tradition it was the apostle John who wrote the last of the four. Says Clement of Alexandria (fl. 190-200):

"Last of all John, perceiving that the external facts had been made plain in the Gospels, being urged by his friends and inspired by the Spirit, composed a spiritual Gospel."[2]

Now in this fourth Gospel the general framework as found in the other three is retained; that is, in all four the coming of Jesus is described in connection with the work and witness of John the Baptist; there follow reports of Christ's entrance into Galilee, the enthusiasm of the crowds and the growing opposition, the miraculous feeding of the multitude, Peter's confession, the departure to Jerusalem, the triumphal entry into the city, a supper of the Lord with his disciples, the experiences in the garden (though the account of *the agony* in the garden is not found in John), the capture, trial and denial, crucifixion, death, and resurrection.

The first three Gospels, taken as a group, and the last (John's) supplement each other. Each requires the other, to be fully understood. Thus it is in the light of Matt. 10:5 ("in the direction of the Gentiles do not proceed") that we can explain Philip's hesitancy in bringing the Greeks to Jesus (John 12:20-22); and it is in the light of John 1:15, 29, 30; 3:30 ("He must increase, but I must decrease") that we can understand what Jesus says with reference to the Baptist's "greatness" (Matt. 11:11). The reason for the trip to Jerusalem (Mark 10:32), though explained even in the Synoptics (for example, the very next verse, 10:33), is made even clearer by John 11:1 ff. Peter's presence in the courtroom of the highpriest's palace (Matt. 26:58, 69 ff.) is explained by John 18:15, 16. Christ's *lamentation*, so filled with

---

2 Quoted by Eusebius, *Ecclesiastical History* VI.xiv.7.

pathos, "O Jerusalem, Jerusalem, *how often* would I have gathered your children together, . . ." (Matt. 23:37-39), and also his *defense* "1 was *daily* with y o u in the temple, teaching" (Mark 14:49), when the Synoptics have said very little about this Jerusalem and temple ministry of Jesus, becomes clear when we study John 2:14; 5:14; 7:14, 28 [8:2] ; and 10:22, 23. The accusation against Jesus, Matt. 26:6 (cf. Mark 14:58), "This man said, 'I am able to destroy the temple of God and to rebuild it in three days,' " becomes clear when read in connection with John 2:19. Moreover, the tone of the reported words and speeches of Jesus as recorded in John's Gospel is not at all inconsistent with the tone of those given in the Synoptics (John 3:3, cf. Matt. 18:3; John 4:35, cf. Matt. 9:37; John 3:35; 10:15; 14:6, cf. Matt. 11:27, 28; etc.).[3]

In spite of allegations to the contrary,[4] no real contradictions between John, on the one hand, and Matthew, Mark, and Luke, on the other, have ever been proved to exist. Yet, both in style and contents the fourth differs in many respects from the three. Thus, John's Gospel describes, with few exceptions, Christ's work in Judea rather than in Galilee, and devotes much space to the Lord's teaching in the form not of parables but of elaborate discourses to—or discussions with—friends and/or enemies. But it is the same Lord who is speaking in all four.

---

[3] The subject of the relation between the Synoptics and John receives fuller treatment in my N.T.C. on John, Vol. I, pp. 12-18, 31-33. See also the discussion devoted to it in F. C. Grant, *The Gospel of St. John*, New York and London, 1956; B. F. Westcott, *The Gospel according to St. John*, Grand Rapids, 1954; and J. E. Davey, *The Jesus of St. John*, London, 1958. The most recent and very thorough elucidation is found in Leon Morris, *Studies in the Fourth Gospel*, 1969; see especially pp. 15-63.

[4] See, for example, the recent attempt by TJ. Baarda, *De Betrouwbaarheid van de Evangeliën*, Kampen, 1967, pp. 12 ff., where, by means of a map (p. 13) he treats the earlier chapters of John's Gospel as if they described consecutive journeys, and states that according to Mark it is from Galilee that Jesus travels to the east side of the Jordan (to feed the five thousand), but according to John it was from Jerusalem (p. 16). Is not Baarda setting up an unfair antithesis between John's Gospel and the Synoptics? He surely knows that John selects certain important events which show that Jesus is the Christ, the Son of God, and that this evangelist is not giving us a *Life of Christ* (see John 20:30, 31). Specifically, John introduces the narrative of the miraculous feeding as follows, "After these things," meaning simply, "At a later time," a very indefinite expression, with no specific chronological or geographical implications. See *N.T.C. on the Gospel according to John*, Vol. I, pp. 187, 188.

The same holds with respect to the so-called contradiction between the Synoptics and John touching the day of Christ's crucifixion. That there is a real conflict here has never been proved. See same work, Vol. II, p. 400-404.

II. Introduction to the Three Gospels:
Matthew, Mark, and Luke (The Synoptics)

A. *Their Origin* (The Synoptic Problem)

The first three Gospels present the same general view of the life and teachings of our Lord; hence are called *The Synoptics* (a viewing together). They are similar, yet also different. As revealed by a detailed study of these Gospels, how extensive is this similarity? This dissimilarity? What problem does the result of our study create? Can it be solved? In accordance with these questions the four main headings will be: 1. Their Similarity, pp. 6-16; 2. Their Dissimilarity, pp. 17-32; 3. The Resulting Problem, p. 32; and 4. Elements Entering into a Solution, pp. 32-54.

1. *Their Similarity*

a. *In material content or subject matter*

One finds, upon examination, that Matthew's Gospel contains, in substance, almost all of the Gospel according to Mark; in fact, of Mark's 661 verses as many as 606 (= about eleven-twelfths) are paralleled in Matthew. Also, slightly more than half of Mark (350 verses - about 53%) is reproduced in Luke.

Stating it differently, the Marcan material that is found also in Matthew is compressed into about 500 of the latter's 1,068 verses; hence, amounts to a little less than one-half of that Gospel. Luke's 1,149 verses have ample room for Mark's 350 verses; in fact, fully two-thirds of Luke's Gospel contains no Marcan material.

It will have become clear that of Mark's 661 verses only 55 are without parallel in Matthew. However, of these 55 not less than 24 are represented in Luke's Gospel. Hence, the resemblance in material content is so great that Mark has only 31 verses which it can call strictly its own. As to contents these 31 verses are as follows:

1:1:	regarding the beginning of the gospel
2:27:	the sabbath made for man, not vice versa
3:20, 21:	the opinion of some that Jesus was beside himself
4:26-29:	the parable of The Good Seed Growing Secretly
7:3, 4:	the parenthetical explanation of Pharisaic ceremonial cleansings
7:32-37:	the cure of the deaf-mute
8:22-26:	the cure of the blind man at Bethsaida
9:29:	the saying, "This kind can come out by nothing save by prayer"
9:48, 49:	the reference to fire that is not quenched and to being salted with fire

13:33-37: the (not altogether unparalleled) exhortation to watch
14:51, 52: the story of the young man who ran away naked.

The following diagrams are added to impress these facts more firmly upon the mind:

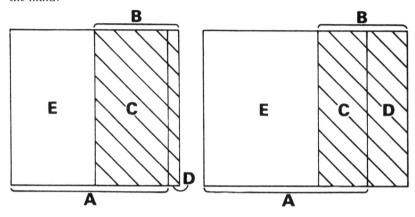

A = Matthew's Gospel
B = Mark's Gospel
C = portion of Mark's Gospel that is paralleled in Matthew
D = portion of Mark's Gospel that is without parallel in Matthew
E = portion of Matthew's Gospel that is without parallel in Mark

A = Luke's Gospel
B = Mark's Gospel
C = portion of Mark's Gospel that is paralleled in Luke
D = portion of Mark's Gospel that is without parallel in Luke
E = portion of Luke's Gospel that is without parallel in Mark

Now the statement that the three Synoptics have much in common must not be misunderstood. It does not mean that in each Gospel equal space is accorded to each topic. On the contrary, the different accounts of the works and words of our Savior are reported with widely varying degrees of fulness. For example, the record of our Lord's temptation is far more detailed in Matthew and in Luke than it is in Mark. The latter simply informs us that the Spirit "drove" Jesus into the wilderness; that he spent forty days there, during which he was tempted by Satan; that he was with the wild beasts; and that angels were waiting on him (1:12, 13). Matthew and Luke, on the other hand, give us a detailed story of three separate temptations (Matt. 4:1-11; Luke 4:1-13). On the other hand, frequently it is Mark's account that is the most detailed. Read, for example, the story of the healing of a demoniac, as recorded in Mark 5:1-20; and compare this with the more condensed coverage in Matt. 8:28-34 and in Luke 8:26-39. Another illustration is Mark 5:21-43; cf. Matt. 9:18-26; Luke 8:40-56.

With this reservation we can affirm that all three present, *each in his own way,* the story of Christ's earthly sojourn; that is, of his ministry particularly in Galilee and its surroundings (in distinction from the Gospel according to John, which places the emphasis on the ministry of Jesus in Judea, as already indicated). Each of the three describes the beginning or inauguration, the progress or continuation, and the climax or culmination of the great task which the Mediator accomplished.

(1) *Its Beginning or Inauguration.* The material common to all three and referring to this opening period of Christ's work on earth is included in Mark 1:1-13; Matt. 1:1-4:11; Luke 3:1-4:13. Purposely we have phrased it "is included in," which means that the indicated references designate the *extent* of the period. It does not mean that everything within the limits of these references is common to all three Gospels, for that would not be true. But we are dealing *now* with what, in the three accounts, is *common* territory. The *differences* will be studied later on.

All three accounts, accordingly, with greater or lesser array of details, describe the coming, preaching, and mode of life of Christ's forerunner, *John the Baptist,* his reception by the crowds, and his testimony concerning Jesus. Also recorded in all three is the story of the baptism of Jesus by John, as well as that of the temptation(s) endured by the Lord in the desert. However, it is but fair to say even at this point that the difference between the space that is devoted to these topics in Mark, on the one hand, and respectively in Matthew and Luke, on the other, is so great that this material can also be considered to belong to the non-Marcan area that is common to Matthew and Luke; see p. 21.

(2) *Its Progress or Continuation.* According to all three accounts Jesus makes Galilee—particularly Capernaum (Mark 1:21; 2:1; cf. Matt. 4:13; 8:5; 11:23; Luke 4:23, 31; 7:1)—his headquarters. Hence, the first phase of this period is often called *the Great Galilean Ministry,* covered in Mark 1:14-7:23; Matt. 4:12-15:20; and Luke 4:14-9:17. All three relate that Jesus bids certain fishermen to be his followers, performs many miracles of healing, stills a tempest, expels demons, and even restores to life a daughter of the ruler of Capernaum's synagogue. He addresses *the multitudes* in parables, a few of which are common to all three Gospels, sends forth The Twelve as his ambassadors, and miraculously feeds the "five thousand." But he has already been rejected by his own people (Mark 6:3; Matt. 13:57; Luke 4:28, 29).[5]

The emphasis now shifts from the multitudes to *the disciples;* from the city to the villages, the countryside, and the mountain. Since Jesus frequent-

---

[5] In Luke the story of Christ's rejection at Nazareth occurs at the beginning (4:16-31); in Mark and Matthew toward the end of this section (Mark 6:1-6; Matt. 13:53-58). In view of John 1:11, Luke's arrangement here does not seem so strange.

ly retires to regions outside of Galilee proper and to places where he can be alone with his disciples, this second phase can be designated *the Ministry of the Retirement*. It is, however, only a shift in emphasis, for even now the Lord never loses interest in the people as a whole (Mark 8:1; 9:14; etc.) nor in Capernaum (Mark 9:33). But it is especially The Twelve who are being gradually prepared for the strange events that are going to happen: the Messiah's suffering, death, and resurrection. The place where, or the day when, any of this teaching is imparted, or where and when a miracle occurs, is often but vaguely indicated: e.g., "the villages of Caesarea Philippi" (Mark 8:27; Matt. 6:13; cf. Luke 9:18), "a high mountain" (Mark 9:2; Matt. 17:1; cf. Luke 9:28), "as they were coming down from the mountain" (Mark 9:9; Matt. 17:9; cf. Luke 9:37).

The final phase of this lengthy period, as described in the Synoptics, finds Jesus going from Galilee to the region beyond the Jordan; i.e., to Perea (see Mark 10:1; Matt. 19:1). It is not strange, therefore, that the term Perean Ministry has been used to describe the locale of Christ's activities and travels at this time. The little band with Jesus as its Leader is heading southward. Next, Christ's wonder-working power is displayed in or near Jericho. Because of the indefinite nature of many of the references to time and place, or at times their complete omission, it is not always possible to tell during which phase (the second or the third) of the long period a saying was uttered or an event occurred. The Gospel writers are not writing a diary. They are far more interested in telling us *what* Jesus did and taught than in giving us a day-by-day continuous chronicle.[6]

What is common to Mark, Matthew, and Luke, in describing Christ's activities during the second and third phases (the Retirement plus Perean Ministries) *is included in* Mark 7:24–10:52; Matt. 15:21–20:34; and Luke 9:18–19:28. However, Luke's section differs so remarkably from the other two that it deserves special treatment; see p. 18. Nevertheless, recorded in all the three indicated sections are such matters as the following: Christ's question addressed to the disciples: "Who do men say that I am?," and his predictions and lessons concerning the cross and the resurrection, imparted on three separate occasions (Mark 8:31; 9:31; 10:33, 34; Matt. 16:21; 17:22, 23; 20:17-19; Luke 9:22, 44; 18:31-34). The stories of the Lord's transfiguration on the mountain and of the cure of the demon-possessed boy in the valley, an epileptic whom the disciples had not been able to cure, are

---

[6] For that very reason it will never be possible to prove the existence of a chronological contradiction between the Gospel according to John, on the one hand, and the Synoptics on the other. There is room for a *Later Judean Ministry* (for which see John 7:2–10:39 and perhaps also Luke 9:51–13:21 as a whole or in part) intervening between *the Retirement Ministry* and *the Perean*, just as there is room for an *Early Judean Ministry* between *the Ministry of the Inauguration* and *the Great Galilean Ministry*. See the brief summary in N.T.C. on the Gospel according to John, Vol. I, p. 36; and see again what was said above, in footnote 4.

also found here in all three Gospels. So are also Christ's dramatically illustrated answer to the disciples' question, "Who among us is the greatest?," and the very comforting saying, "Let the little children come to me, and do not try to prevent them, for to such belongs the kingdom of God." In the story of "the rich young ruler" whose wealth held him captive so that he refused to comply with Christ's demand, the peril of riches is brought vividly to the attention of the disciples. And so the journey, some of whose unforgettable incidents, as here noted, are recorded by all three but never necessarily in complete chronological order, advances toward its dramatic conclusion. In Jericho Jesus once again reveals his power to perform miracles, including that of restoring sight. Thus toward Jerusalem and the cross moves the little company with Jesus as the Leader.

(3) *Its Climax or Culmination.* The events reported by all are found in Mark 11-16; Matthew 21-28; and Luke 19:29-24:53. These large sections describe the happenings that transpired during the week of the Passion, followed by the Resurrection. Luke adds an account of the Ascension. Almost a fifth of Luke's Gospel is devoted to the theme of the Savior's bitter suffering from Gethsemane to Golgotha,[7] and to the events that immediately preceded it. In Mark and Matthew the proportion is even greater, about one-third of each of these Gospels having to do with these happenings. Moreover, what is true with respect to the Synoptics holds no less for John. All four are "Passion Gospels with extended introduction."[8] It is true, indeed, that "Jesus from his throne on high came into this world *to die.*" Accordingly, over against various erring views it cannot be emphasized too strongly that we are not dealing here with Lives of Christ but with *evangels,* books containing good tidings of salvation for men lost in sin and misery.

It is especially in these closing chapters that the three parallel each other most strikingly. Reported by all three are the following events: Jesus enters Jerusalem in triumph, as Prince of Peace. Multitudes, their minds filled with anticipations of earthly glory, welcome him with wild enthusiasm. Arrived in the temple and noticing that its great outer court has been turned into a market-place, a hideout for racketeers, Jesus cleanses it. When his authority is challenged, he very appropriately asks his critics to tell him whether John's baptism—the baptizing practiced by that very John who had borne testimony to the One who just now has driven out the merchants—was of divine or of merely human origin. For good measure he adds the parable of the wicked tenants. He answers the catch-questions of his opponents, and by means of a question addressed to them he clearly implies that David's *Son* is no less than David's *Lord.*

---

[7] The name "Gethsemane" occurs only in Mark 14:32 and Matt. 26:36, not in Luke. Similarly, "Golgotha" is found only in Mark 15:22 and Matt. 27:33.

[8] M. Kähler, *Der sogenannte historische Jesus und der geschichtliche, biblische Christus,* Munich, 1956, p. 591.

10

INTRODUCTION TO THE GOSPELS

In a public discourse—brief in Mark and Luke, but greatly expanded in Matthew—he warns the multitudes against the scribes and Pharisees, denouncing their hypocrisy. This is followed by his discourse about Jerusalem's fall and the end of the world.

The rulers plot his death. For a sum of money Judas agrees to deliver him into their hands. Jesus now sends disciples—according to Mark "two"; according to Luke "Peter and John"—to make preparations for the Passover. At the Passover supper the betrayer is exposed. The Master predicts that he will be deserted by all his disciples, including Peter. In spite of the latter's vehement protest Jesus clings to this prediction. The institution of the Lord's Supper is followed by the agonies in Gethsemane. With a kiss Judas betrays Jesus. The latter allows himself to be seized. He is brought to the house of the highpriest where he is ill-treated and mocked. The story of Peter's three denials follows. Very early in the morning the Sanhedrin condemns Jesus. He is brought before the Roman governor Pilate, who questions him concerning his kingship. Given a choice, the mob asks for the release of the dangerous criminal Barabbas, in preference to Jesus; and, instigated by the chief priests and elders, demands that Jesus be crucified. Pilate at last gives in. On the way to the place of execution Simon of Cyrene is compelled to bear Christ's cross. In all three Gospels something is now said about the superscription, the scoffing that Jesus endured, and the three hours of darkness. With a loud cry Jesus dies. The veil in the temple is rent. The centurion gives his testimony. Women who had been following Jesus in and from Galilee witness all these things and afterward keep vigil at the tomb. It was a new tomb and belonged to Joseph of Arimathea, one of Christ's followers, who had obtained permission from Pilate to remove the body from the cross and to bury it.

On the morning of the first day of the week the women, arriving very early, notice that the tomb-stone has been rolled away. From a heavenly messenger—or: from heavenly messengers ("two men in dazzling apparel," Luke)—they receive the astonishing news, "He is risen."

b. *In the identical or almost identical Greek words employed in parallel accounts*

It is striking how often not only the thought content but even the very words used in the original and reflected in the translation are the same or almost the same in all three accounts. Anyone can see this for himself by placing next to each other the three places in which the story of the cleansing of a leper is told (Mark 1:40-44; Matt. 8:2-4; and Luke 5:12-14); or the parallels in which Jesus defends his disciples for feasting instead of fasting (Mark 2:18-22; Matt. 9:14-17; and Luke 5:33-39); or the triple coverage of the feeding of the five thousand (see especially Mark 6:35-37; Matt. 14:15, 16; and Luke 9:12, 13; also Mark 6:41-43; Matt. 14:19b, 20;

and Luke 9:16, 17). These are only a few of the examples that could be given.[9]

c. *In the order of events as recorded in these three Gospels*

This similarity in sequence is already implied in the summary of the contents of the three, as given above under point 1: a, (1), (2), (3). It has been shown that *in a very general sense* the sequence is the same in all *three* Gospels. This is clear, for example, to anyone who compares the order in Matthew and in Mark, and notes that with respect to the former allowance must be made for his thematic method and for the six discourses. See pp. 26-31. It is especially with respect to Luke's Gospel, however, that *some* see a difficulty.[10] One author who made a study of the Synoptic problem says, "In Luke, as everybody who has tried it knows, it is distinctly harder than in the other evangels to remember the arrangement and order of events and sections."[11] Now it is true that for many people it is indeed difficult to *store*—and especially to *retain*—in the memory the exact order in which the various events in the recorded early sojourn of our Lord, and his many sayings, follow one another in this Gospel, the longest of the four.[12] What makes it all the harder is the circumstance that "twice in this Gospel, in one case for two chapters, and in another for more than eight, he [Luke] turns away from his sources, and then equally neatly and equally unperceived, returns again to his Marcan thread."[13] Last but not least, the order of events and the arrangement of the sayings in Luke's middle section is so loose that it is frequently hard to determine exactly when or where this particular incident occurred or that specific oracle was uttered.

However, when all of this is readily admitted, it is still possible to see a remarkable degree of similarity in the order of events as recorded by Mark and by Luke. Virtually all one has to do is *a.* to commit to memory the general order of Mark's great events; *b.* to bear in mind that chapter 7 and

---

[9] B. H. Streeter, *The Four Gospels*, pp. 160, 161, says that a proportion varying between 30% and 60% of the words in Mark is also found in Matthew and Luke, while many of the remaining Marcan words are common either to Mark and Matthew, or to Mark and Luke. De Solages, in his mammoth work, *A Greek Synopsis of the Gospels* (1,129 pages!), Leiden, 1959, provides detailed lists plus many Tables and Diagrams. See also W. G. Rushbrook's *Synopticon* and A. Huck's *Synopsis of the First Three Gospels.*

[10] Contrast, however, the remark of E. J. Goodspeed, who calls Luke "the delight of the harmonist," but Matthew "his despair," *Matthew Apostle and Evangelist*, Philadelphia and Toronto, 1959, p. 116. (From here on when this author's name is mentioned followed by *op. cit.*, the reference is to this book.)

[11] J. H. Ropes, *The Synoptic Gospels*, Cambridge, 1960, p. 72.

[12] Though in our Bibles Matthew has 28 chapters, Luke only 24, yet, in the English Bible on my desk as I write this, Matthew covers only 37 pages, Luke 39½. Also, as remarked earlier, Matthew has 1,068 verses, Luke 1,149. Here, however, room must be left for the fact that one's decision with respect to variant readings may alter the count very slightly.

[13] Same, p. 73. Ropes refers undoubtedly to Luke 6:17—8:3 and 9:51—18:14.

chapters 10 through 17 in Luke contain little Marcan material; and *c*. to concentrate on the figures **3** and **8**. With certain modifications, to be mentioned in a moment, one can then say that in order to find where in Luke's Gospel a certain topic is treated, for the earlier chapters 3 must be added to the number of the chapter in Mark; for the later 8 must be added. It is not claimed that *everything* that occurs in Mark's Gospel is duplicated in Luke, nor is it implied that when the figures 3 and 8 are used the exact chapter is always *immediately* found. At times one may have to look a little farther in the next chapter. But it remains true that slightly more than 1/3 of what is found in Mark 1 occurs also in Luke 4 (1+3=4); about 3/4 of Mark 2 is reflected in Luke 5 (2+3=5). Now for a few examples where 8 instead of 3 must be added: more than half of Mark 10 is reproduced in Luke 18 (10+8=18); about 2/3 of Mark 11 is echoed in Luke 19 (11+8=19); etc.

Similarity in the order of events even as between Mark and Luke can thus be illustrated as follows:[14]

Parallel between Mark and Luke

Knowing that a subject is treated in MARK Chapter	the subject being	add	and find its parallel in LUKE Chapter
1	Jesus vanquishes the tempter. He performs miracles in Capernaum: healing a demoniac, Simon's mother-in-law, many others	3	4

[14] Naturally column 2 must not be regarded as a complete outline of Mark's Gospel. Certain subjects have been purposely omitted because the rule ("Mark+3" or "Mark+8") does not apply to them, since they are paralleled *elsewhere* in Luke's Gospel, or are omitted from it. In the former case the parallel sometimes occurs in the very neighborhood of the chapter whose numerical indication is the sum of Mark's chapter +3 or +8; for example, Mark 4:1-20 is paralleled not in Luke 7, according to the rule 4+3=7, but in Luke 8:4-15; Mark 11:27-33 is paralleled not in Luke 19 (11+8=19) but in Luke 20:1-8. It is clear, therefore, that had the chapter-division in our Bibles been more consistent, finding one's way in Luke, once Mark is known, would have been even easier, and the full extent of the Synoptics' similarity in material content and in arrangement would have been even more perspicuous. But who will dispute the fact that *on the whole* Stephen Langton, to whom the credit for the chapter-divisions is usually given, performed an excellent and useful task? Who would wish to criticize too severely this very busy man, this champion of law and order, valiant supporter of the Magna Carta? Besides, even as it is, the table will, I trust, perform two useful services: *a.* it will achieve the primary purpose of proving that the Synoptics—in this case Mark and Luke—are indeed very similar in recording the general *order of events*; and *b.* it will aid one in finding his way in the Gospels.

Knowing that a subject is treated in MARK Chapter	the subject being	add	and find its parallel in LUKE Chapter
	at eventide. He departs to a desert place. All seek him. He preaches in the synagogues of Galilee.		
2	He heals a paralytic, calls Levi (=Matthew), and is criticized for associating with publicans. He answers a question about fasting.	3	5
3	He heals a man with a withered hand and choses The Twelve.	3	6
			(No Marcan material in Luke 7!)[15]
4	He tells the parable of The Sower and stills a storm.	4	8
5	He heals the "Gerasene" demoniac, raises the daugher of Jairus, and cures the woman who suffered from hemorrhages.	3	8
6	He sends The Twelve on a preach-	3	9[16]

[15] In the third Gospel, after 6:12-16 (the appointment of The Twelve; cf. Mark 3:13-19) Luke ceases for a while to parallel Mark. At this point the non-Marcan material extends from Luke 6:17—8:3 (or as some see it, from Luke 6:20—8:3). Luke introduces what is popularly known as "The Sermon on the Mount" (6:17-19; cf. Matt. 5:1, 2). Compare, however, Matt. 5:1 ("the mountain") with Luke 6:17 ("on level ground"). He gives his version of the Beatitudes (6:20-26; cf. Matt. 5:3-12), and of the sections whose central themes are "Love your enemies" (6:27-36; cf. Matt. 5:43-48); "Judge not" (6:37-42; cf. Matt. 7:1-6); and "A tree is known by its fruit" (6:43-49; cf. Matt. 7:13-29). Luke 7:1-10 contains that evangelist's account of the healing of the centurion's servant (cf. Matt. 8:5-13); 7:11-17, that of the raising of the widow's son; 7:18-35, that of John the Baptist's question and Christ's answer (cf. Matt. 11:2-19); 7:36-50, that of the anointing of Christ's feet by a sinful woman; and 8:1-3, that of a tour made by Jesus, the twelve, and certain women, "through cities and villages." At 8:4 ff. (the parable of The Sower) the parallel between Luke and Mark is resumed once more. In fact, this "earthly story with heavenly meaning" is found in all three (cf. Mark 4:1 ff. and Matt. 13:1 ff.).

[16] In Luke's Gospel that which follows 9:18 (cf. Mark 6:43; and for Mark 6:44 see Luke 9:14) does not parallel Mark 6:45 ff., but "jumps" to the subject discussed in Mark

INTRODUCTION TO THE GOSPELS

Knowing that a subject is treated in MARK Chapter	the subject being	add	and find its parallel in LUKE Chapter
	ing and healing mission. Herod's perplexity. The Twelve return from their mission. The feeding of the five thousand.		
10	Jesus welcomes the little children. The story of "the rich young ruler" and its application. Jesus predicts what will happen to him at Jerusalem, and imparts sight to a blind man.	8	18
11	Jesus enters Jerusalem in triumph and cleanses the temple. The leaders try to destroy him.	8	19[17]
12	He tells the parable of The Wicked Tenants (or: "The Vineyard"), answers captious questions, and by means of a counter-question affirms that David's Son is no less than David's Lord.	8	20
13	Signs of the end and exhortation to watch.	8	21
14	At the approach of the passover, the leaders plot Christ's death. Preparations are made for the passover. Institution of "The	8	22

8:27 ff.: "Who do men say that I am?," etc. In the ninth chapter of both Mark and Luke such subjects as the following are treated: Christ's transfiguration, the healing of the epileptic boy, "Who is the greatest," and the unknown exorcist. At Luke 9:51 the section peculiar to Luke begins in earnest and extends through 18:14.

Thus Mark's narratives found in 6:45—8:26—Jesus walks on the sea; he answers a question concerning unwashed hands, heals the Syrophoenician woman's daughter, cures a deaf-mute, answers the Pharisees' request for a sign from heaven, and cures a blind man at Bethsaida—are not duplicated in Luke's Gospel. Easy to remember is this: *Mark 7 is not paralleled in Luke, neither is Luke 7 in Mark.*

[17] More than half of Luke 19 is non-Marcan material (story of Zacchaeus and parable of The Pounds).

Knowing that a subject is treated in MARK Chapter	the subject being	add	and find its parallel in LUKE Chapter
	Lord's Supper." The betrayal and denial foretold. The little company departs to the Mt. of Olives (i.e., to Gethsemane). The betrayal, arrest, trial before the Jewish council, and the denial by Peter.		
15	Trial before Pilate. The people ask for the release of Barabbas in preference to Jesus. They demand that Jesus be crucified. Simon of Cyrene. Calvary scenes: the superscription, scoffing, three hours of darkness, loud cry, death, tearing of the temple-veil, centurion's testimony, interest shown by the women, and Joseph of Arimathea's part in taking down the body and placing it in his own tomb.	8	23
16	The women see that the tomb-stone has been rolled away. Explanation: "He is risen."	8	24[18]

The *similarity* that characterizes the Synoptics has thus been established. In addition, finding one's way in these three Gospels has been made a little easier. For Mark this is clear immediately. As to Luke, the fact that chapters 1 and 2 contain the nativity narratives and chapter 3 the story about John the Baptist plus a genealogy of Jesus is well-known. Memorization of the themes of Luke's parables (see p. 23) plus frequent reading of Luke 9:51–18:14 will facilitate mastery of the contents of that Gospel's middle section. For the entire Gospel add the information given in the table above. As to Matthew, see pp. 25-30.

---

[18] Luke 24:9-53 (Jesus' interview with Cleopas and his companion, appearance at Jerusalem, ard ascension) contains very little material that is paralleled in the other Synoptics.

INTRODUCTION TO THE GOSPELS

2. *Their Dissimilarity*
a. *In material content or subject matter*
   For parables see below, under point (7), p. 21-25.

Though, as has been shown, in a general way the material content is the same for all three Gospels, yet certain stories and sayings are found only in Matthew, some only in Mark, some only in Luke, some only in Matthew and Mark, some only in Mark and Luke, and, last but not least, some only in Matthew and Luke, thus exhausting the possibilities.

(1) *Only in Matthew.* Passages and narratives that are peculiar to Matthew are: the line of descent (i.e., the one recorded in 1:1-17; contrast Luke 3:23-38); the birth of Jesus, as Matthew tells it, and the visit of the wise men (1:18–2:23); the Baptist's reluctance to baptize Jesus (3:14, 15); Jesus' settlement in Capernaum in fulfilment of prophecy (4:13-16); his teaching and healing in Galilee (4:23-25 in part); The Sermon on the Mount (5:1–8:1), as far as it is not paralleled in Luke and, to a far lesser extent, in Mark; a quotation from Isa. 53:4 (8:17); the healing of two blind men and of a demoniac (9:27-34); the sending forth of The Twelve (9:35–10:42), to the extent in which the phrases are not reflected in Mark and Luke; the reference to the Baptist as "Elijah" (11:14); preface to woes on impenitent cities (11:20); the invitation, "Come unto me" (11:27-30; but see also Luke 10:22); "I will have mercy and not sacrifice" (12:5-7); the implication that works of mercy are allowed on the sabbath (12:11, 12; see, however, Luke 14:5); a miracle leading to the exclamation, "Could this be the Son of David?" (12:22, 23 in part); "out of his treasures things new and old" (13:51-53); Peter's behavior during a storm (14:28-31); "Every plant which my heavenly Father has not planted will be uprooted" (15:12, 13); "Send her away . . . Lord, help me!" (15:23-25); the healing of great multitudes (15:30, 31); "Can y o u not discern the signs of the times?" (16:2, 3); the leaven of the . . . Saduccees (16:11, 12); "Blessed are you, Simon Bar-Jona" (16:17-19); "This shall never happen to thee" (16:22); the disciples' fear in connection with Christ's transfiguration (17:6, 7); their discovery that "Elijah" is John the Baptist (17:13); the temple tax (17:24-27); Jesus and the Father's attitude toward the little ones (18:3, 4, 10, 14); exhortation to forgive an erring brother, including rules of discipline (18:15-20); remarks with respect to eunuchs (19:10-12); a quotation from Zech. 9:9 in connection with the triumphal entry into Jerusalem (21:4, 5); "This is Jesus the prophet" (21:10, 11); children's praises (21:14-16); "the kingdom of God will be taken away from y o u" (21:43); Christ's final temple discourse, *in part* (chap. 23); certain passages of his discourse on the last things (chap. 24); "all who take the sword will perish by the sword" (26:52-54; cf. John 18:11); the remorse and suicide of Judas the traitor (27:3-10; cf. Acts 1:18, 19); the dream and message of Pilate's wife (27:19); Pilate's attempted self-vindication, including the people's assumption of responsibility for Je-

17

sus' death (27:24, 25); the enemies' unwitting quotation of Ps. 22:8 (27:43); several "miracles of Calvary" (27:51-53); Christ's appearance to the women (28:9, 10); the guard posted, scattered, and bribed (27:62-66; 28:2-4, 11-15); and finally, the departure of the disciples to Galilee, where Jesus meets them (28:16-18, 20).

(2) *Only in Mark.* See above, p. 6.

(3) *Only in Luke.* The third Gospel, in its opening section, contains the following important distinctive accounts: the preamble (1:1-4); the birth of John the Baptist and of Jesus, and the latter's boyhood (1:5–2:52); a chronological note with respect to John's ministry (3:1, 2); questions of various groups ("What must we do?") answered by John (3:10-14); a line of Messianic descent (3:23-38); the return of Jesus to Galilee (4:14, 15; but see Mark 1:14, 15; Matt. 4:17); a miraculous catch of fishes, peculiar to Luke, *mostly* (5:1-11); Christ's sayings concerning the rich, the famous, and the lenders (6:24-26, 34); the raising of the widow's son at Nain (7:11-17); attitude toward Jesus on the part of those baptized by John, and of those not baptized by him (7:29, 30); the anointing of Jesus' feet by a sinful woman at the home of Simon the Pharisee (7:36-39); the company around Jesus (8:1-3); and the sleepy condition of the disciples that were with Jesus on the mount of transfiguration (9:31, 32).

The central section of this Gospel is rich in parables; see (7), pp. 23, 24. Aside from these, it has the following unduplicated narratives or sayings: an example of Samaritan inhospitality (9:51-56); "no man who looks back is fit for the kingdom" (9:61, 62); the mission of the seventy (10:1-24), to the extent in which its phrases are not paralleled elsewhere; Jesus entertained at the home of Martha and Mary (10:38-42); "Blessed is the womb that bare thee"—"Blessed are they that hear the Word of God and keep it" (11:27, 28); Pharisees and lawyers denounced at the home of a Pharisee (11:37-54; but cf. Mark 7:1 ff., and various passages in Matt. 23); "Fear not, little flock" (12:32, 33; but see also Matt. 6:20; 19:21; Mark 10:21); Jesus the divider (12:49-53; but cf. Matt. 10:34-36); rebuke administered to sky-interpreters who cannot interpret the time in which they are living (12:54-59; cf. Matt. 16:1-3); sabbath healings (13:11-17; 14:1-6); "Lord, are those who are being saved only few in number?" (13:22, 23); the warning that once the door has been shut, it will not be reopened (13:25-27; cf. Matt. 25:11, 12); denunciation of "that fox," Herod Antipas (13:31-33); the deriders rebuked (16:14, 15); the cleansing of ten lepers, only one of whom returned to give thanks (17:11-19); and Christ's answer to the question, "When will the kingdom of God come?" (17:20-22, 28, 29, 32, 34). Much of 17:20-37 is duplicated in Matt. 24.

Exclusively—or, in some cases, *almost* exclusively—reported by Luke in the closing section of his Gospel are the following: the call of Zacchaeus (19:1-10); the request of the Pharisees that Jesus rebuke his disciples, and his answer (19:39, 40); Christ's weeping over Jerusalem, and his prediction of its destruction (19:41-44); and several passages of his discourse on "the last things" (21:19, 22, 24, 26, 28, 34-38). Much of chapter 21 is, however, reflected elsewhere, especially in Mark 13 and Matt. 24. Words spoken at the Lord's Table and reported exclusively (or almost so) by the third evangelist are found in 22:15-18 (but see Matt. 26:29); 22:28-32, and 35-38. Luke's distinctive account of Christ's experiences in the garden is found in 22:43, 44, 48, 49, 51, and 53. The *look* that rang the bell of Peter's memory and melted his heart is reported in 22:61. For Luke's version of Christ's confession before the council, see 22:68, 70. In the morning Jesus was brought first before Pilate, then before Herod (23:2, 4-12). He was returned to Pilate (23:13-19; see also Mark 15:6-9). Other mainly Lucan accounts in chapter 23 refer to: Christ's admonition addressed to "the daughters of Jerusalem" (verses 27-36; cf. Mark 15:22, 24; Matt. 27:33-35); the impenitent versus the penitent thief (verses 39-41); the latter's prayer and Christ's answer (verses 42, 43); the seventh "word from the cross" (verse 46); and the crowds going home, beating their breasts (verse 48). There is also a description of Joseph of Arimathea (verse 51); a report on his deed of kindness (verse 53; but see Mark 15:46; Matt. 27:59, 60); a note specifying the exact week-day when Jesus was taken down from the cross and placed in Joseph's tomb (verse 54); and a reference to the women preparing aromatic spices and perfumes (verse 56). Luke's final chapter has the following contents peculiar to that Gospel among the Synoptics: the effect of the women's resurrection message upon the apostles (verses 10, 11); Peter's visit to the tomb (verse 12; cf. John 20:2-10); the risen One's interview with Cleopas and his companion (24:13:25; cf., however, Mark 16:12, 13); the appearance to the disciples on Sunday evening (24:36-49; but cf. Mark 16:14; John 20:19-25); and the ascension (24:50-53; cf., however, Mark 16:19 and Acts 1:9-12).

(4) *Only in Matthew and Mark.* There is, first of all, the reference to the Baptist's audience, food, and clothing (Mark 1:5, 6; Matt. 3:4, 5). According to both Mark 3:7-12 and Matt. 12:15-21 Jesus heals a great many people but forbids publicity. This paragraph, too, is largely confined to Matthew and Mark; see, however, Luke 4:41. Mark's detailed account seems, however, to be merely summarized in Matt. 12:15, 16. On the other hand, Matthew (in verses 17-21) adds the prophecy found in Isa. 12:1-4, which addition can therefore also be subsumed under (1) above. There is, next, a reference to Christ's many parables (Mark 4:33, 34; Matt. 13:34). A well-known narrative which belongs under this exclusive Matthew-Mark heading is that which recounts Herod's wicked birthday party and, in connection with it, the Baptist's gruesome death (Mark 6:17-29; shorter in Matt. 14:3-12).

Attention has already been called to the fact that Mark 6:45–8:26 is "Luke's great omission" (see p. 14). With the exception of two miracles of

19

gradual healing (Mark 7:32-37 and 8:22-26; for which see p. 6) all of this material also belongs to the Matthew-Mark parallel. It begins with the vivid and comforting story of Jesus walking on the sea (Mark 6:45-56; Matt. 14:22-36). But not all of this is parallel; for example, Matt. 14:28-31 belongs under (1). Then there is Christ's teaching concerning ceremonial defilement (Mark 7:1-23; Matt. 15:1-20); the healing of the Syrophoenician woman's daughter (Mark 7:24-31; Matt. 15:21-29); the feeding of the four thousand (Mark 8:1-9; Matt. 15:30-38); the request for a sign (Mark 8:10-12; Matt. 15:39—16:4); and the warning against the leaven of the Pharisees (Mark 8:13-21; Matt. 16:5-12).

The propriety of placing Mark 9:28, 29 (cf. Matt. 17:19) under the present heading[19] is doubtful, but it is true that the question of the disciples "Why could we not cast it out?" (Mark 9:28) is reproduced in Matt. 17:19. In connection with Christ's prediction that the Son of man would rise again, the disciples ask Jesus a question with respect to Elijah (Mark 9:10-13; Matt. 17:10-13). Jesus' teaching regarding divorce and remarriage is also almost completely confined to Mark (10:1-12) and Matthew (19:1-12); see, however, Luke 16:18. Then, there is the request of the sons of Zebedee (Mark 10:35-45; cf. Matt. 20:20-28, but see also Luke 9:48 and 22:25); and the cursing of the barren fig tree (Mark 11:12—14:20-25; cf. Matt. 21:18-22; but see also Luke 11:9; 17:6). Though it is true that Christ's eschatological discourse is found in all three, this statement should be qualified; for example, the prediction concerning false Christs and false prophets is confined to the first two Gospels (Mark 13:21-23; Matt. 24:23-25); so is also that respecting the unpredictability of the day of Christ's second coming (Mark 13:32; Matt. 24:36).

For the anointing in Bethany one consults Luke's Gospel in vain. It is *not* found in Luke 7:36 ff., though many seem to think that it is. As far as the Synoptics are concerned, the story occurs only in Mark 14:3-9 and Matt. 26:6-13. Outside of the Synoptics it occurs also in John 12:1-8. The departure for the Mount of Olives, together with a significant prediction, is also found only in Mark 14:26-28; Matt. 26:30-32.[20] The trial in the highpriest's palace, immediately after the arrest, is largely confined to the first two Gospels (Mark 14:55-65; Matt. 26:59-66), though Luke, as well as the others, report the ill-treatment Jesus received there. On the subject of Christ's silence before Pilate (Mark 15:2-5; Matt. 27:11-14) Luke remains silent! The people's choice of Barabbas, in preference to Jesus, though reported in all three Gospels, is found in fuller detail in the first two (Mark

---

[19] As is done by B. H. Streeter, *op. cit.*, p. 196; but on the preceding page he includes Mark 9:29 in the list of Marcan passages "which are absent from both Matthew and Luke."

[20] It is assumed here that Luke 22:39 has its proper parallel in Mark 14:32 and Matt. 26:36.

INTRODUCTION TO THE GOSPELS

15:6-11; Matt. 27:15-21) than in Luke. Two other important details of the crucifixion story are confined to Mark and Matthew; namely, the crown of thorns (Mark 15:17-20; Matt. 27:29-31) and Christ's cry of agony (Mark 15:34-36; Matt. 27:46-49). Finally, except for Luke 24:47, the Great Commission is confined to the first two Gospels. Though essentially the same, the two statements differ in certain details (Mark 16:15, 16; Matt. 28:19-21).

(5) *Only in Mark and Luke.* Mark's 24 verses that are paralleled only in Luke's Gospel are as follows: a demon-expulsion at Capernaum (Mark 1:23-28; Luke 4:33-37); Christ's purpose to preach (Mark 1:35-38; Luke 4:42, 43); lamps should shine, ears should hear (Mark 4:21-24; Luke 8:16-18); the return of The Twelve (Mark 6:30; Luke 9:10); the strange exorcist (Mark 9:38-41; Luke 9:45, 50); "widows' houses" and "a poor widow's two mites" (Mark 12:40-44; Luke 20:47; 21:1-4).

(6) *Only in Matthew and Luke.* It is estimated that there are about 200 verses common to both. Here are a few examples:

MATTHEW	LUKE	SUBJECT
3:7-10, 12	3:7-9, 17	Specimen of the Baptist's preaching
4:1-11	4:1-13	The story of Christ's temptations
5:3, 4, 6, 11, 12	6:20-23	Some of the Beatitudes
5:18	6:17	Concerning the law
5:39-48 (for the greater part)	6:27-36 (mostly)	Love y o u r enemies, for also God is kind to evil men
6:9-13	11:2-4	The Lord's Prayer
6:19-21, 25-33	12:22-34	Be not anxious
7:7-11	11:9-13	Encouragement to prayer
8:5-13	7:1-10	The story of the centurion's faith
8:19-22	9:57-60	The implications of discipleship
9:37, 38	10:2	Prayer for laborers urged
10:26-33	12:2-9	"Y o u are of more value than many sparrows"
11:2-11, 16-19	7:18-20, 22-28, 31-35	The story of the doubt of John the Baptist, and Christ's testimony concerning John

For the passion and Resurrection narratives there are no parallels peculiar to Matthew-Luke.

(7) *Parables.* Our Lord's parables have been classified in various ways. Also, they have been counted differently. In part this is due to the fact that "The Marriage of the King's Son" (Matt. 22:1-14) and "The Great Supper" (Luke 14:15-24) are by some regarded as variants of what was originally *one*

21

parable. The older text of this parable, so runs the theory, is found in Luke. According to this view Matthew's revision presupposes the destruction of the city of Jerusalem (A.D. 70).[21] Similarly, the parable of The Pounds (Luke 19:11-27) is by some called a variation of that of The Talents (Matt. 25:14-30).[22]

In both of these instances, however, the differences outweigh the resemblances to such an extent that there would seem to be no justification for regarding as *one* that which in the text is presented as *two*.

As to Matt. 22:1-14 and Luke 14:15-24, we are on safe ground when we desist from every effort to "reconstruct," and in both cases take the Greek text as it is presented to us in the best editions of the Greek New Testament. When we do so we notice that there is, indeed, a considerable area of resemblance between the two parables. In both a banquet is prepared, guests are invited, invitations are left unheeded, the underprivileged are then invited, and the house is finally filled with guests. But are not the differences even more striking? The parable of The Marriage—or Marriage Feast—of the King's Son (Matt. 22:1-14) consists of three distinct parts (see on that passage), the last of which is totally lacking from the parable of The Great Supper. In the first of these two parables we are told about a king who prepares a feast for his son's wedding; in the second about a man who prepared a big dinner party. In the first the invited guests simply "make light" of the invitation; in the second they offer excuses. In the first some of the invited guests maltreat and even kill the servants that are sent to them with the invitation; this detail is entirely lacking in the second. So also, naturally, in Luke's parable there is nothing that corresponds to the destruction of the murderers and of their city, an action mentioned in Matthew's parable. Besides all this the historical setting of the two parables differs

---

21 See G. D. Kilpatrick, *The Origins of the Gospel according to St. Matthew*, Oxford, 1946, p. 6. Somewhat similar is the view of G. Bornkamm, *Jesus von Nazareth*, Stuttgart, 1956, pp. 18 ff., and of C. H. Dodd, *The Parables of the Kingdom*, London, 1935, p. 121. R. V. G. Tasker, *The Gospel according to St. Matthew* (*Tyndale New Testament Commentaries*), pp. 206, 207 joins them to the extent that he regards their theory as a possibility. Though he himself considers the *two* parable theory more probable, he views Matt. 22:5, 6 as a marginal addition or gloss which after the fall of Jerusalem was made part of the text.

22 S. MacLean Gilmour has, in fact, produced a narrative which, so he says, "was basic to both versions," *The Gospel according to St. Luke* (*The Interpreter's Bible*), New York and Nashville, 1952, Vol. VIII, p. 327. This view, in one form or another, is shared by many others, among whom are Jülicher-Fascher, Weiss, H. Holzmann, Bultmann, and Klostermann.

A. Plummer, on the contrary, remarks, "It is probable that this [the parable of The Pounds] is distinct from the parable of The Talents. . . . It is more likely that Jesus should utter somewhat similar parables on different occasions than that Matthew or Luke should have made very serious confusion as to the details of the parable as well as regards the time and place of its delivery," *The Gospel according to St. Luke* (*International Critical Commentary*), New York, 1910, p. 437.

widely. Jesus told the parable of The Great Supper when he himself was reclining at table as a guest. The parable of The Marriage Feast belongs to a later date, to Christ's activity in Jerusalem during the week of The Passion.

The situation with respect to the parable of The Pounds as compared with that of The Talents is similar. It is hard to see how the story of a nobleman who gives each of his servants a small and equal sum can have anything to do with that of a man who entrusts incomparably larger amounts to his servants, to each of them a widely different amount!

Another reason for the difference in the final tally, in counting parables, is the fact that as yet no answer on which all can agree has been given to the question, "What is a parable?" Even when it is agreed that "a parable is an extended simile," in distinction from an allegory which is "an extended metaphor"—a helpful but perhaps not altogether correct distinction—unanimous agreement is not attained. The difference of opinion is, however, not very important, and touches only a few of the items included in the following list:

(a) *Peculiar to Matthew*
The Tares (13:24-30, 36-43)
The Hidden Treasure (13:44)
The Pearl of Great Price (13:45, 46)
The Dragnet (13:47-50)
The Unmerciful Servant (18:23-35)
The Laborers in the Vineyard (20:1-16)
The Two Sons (21:28-32)
The Marriage Feast of the King's Son (or The Marriage of the King's Son, The Marriage Feast, The Royal Marriage, 22:1-14)
The Five Sensible and The Five Foolish Girls (25:1-13)
The Talents (25:14-30)
(b) *Peculiar to Mark*
The Seed Growing in Secret (4:26-29)
(c) *Peculiar to Luke*
The Two Debtors (7:40-50)
The Good Samaritan (10:29-37)
The Embarrassed Host (or The Friend at Midnight, 11:5-13)
The Rich Fool (12:13-21)
The Watchful Servants (12:35-48)
The Barren Fig Tree (13:1-9)
The Chief Seats (14:7-11)
The Great Supper (or The Slighted Invitation, 14:15-24)
The Rash Builder (14:28-30)
The Reckless King (14:31-33)
The Lost Coin (15:8-10). In reality it is the parable of A Woman's Search for Her Lost Coin, and Her Joy in Finding It.

The Lost (Prodigal) Son (including his Elder Brother, 15:11-32). Actually it is the parable of The Father's Yearning Love.

The Steward with Foresight (or The Unrighteous Steward, 16:1-13)

The Rich Man and Lazarus (16:19-31)

The Plowing (Unprofitable) Servant (17:7-10)

The Persevering Widow (or The Unrighteous Judge, 18:1-8)

The Pharisee and the Publican (18:9-14)

The Pounds (19:11-27)

(d) *Peculiar to Matthew and Luke*

The Two Builders (Matt. 7:24-27; Luke 6:47-49)

Children Sitting in the Market Places (Matt. 11:16-19; Luke 7:31-35)

The Return of the Unclean Spirit (Matt. 12:43-45; Luke 11:24-26)

The Leaven (Matt. 13:33; Luke 13:20)

The Lost Sheep (Matt. 18:12-14; Luke 15:1-7). It is, of course, the parable of The Shepherd's Search for His Lost Sheep, and His Joy in Finding It.

The Faithful versus the Unfaithful Servant (Matt. 24:45-51; Luke 12:42-46)

(e) *Common to All Three*

The Sower (or The Four Kinds of Soil, Mark 4:3-9, 14-20; Matt. 13:3-9, 18-23; Luke 8:4-15)

The Mustard Seed (Mark 4:30-32; Matt. 13:31, 32; Luke 13:18, 19)

The Wicked Tenants (or The Wicked Sharecroppers, or The Vineyard, or, to use the old title, The Wicked Husbandmen, Mark 12:1-9; Matt. 21:33-41; Luke 20:9-16)

It is clear from all this that, as was true with respect to other elements constituting the material content or subject matter of the first three Gospels, so also with respect to the parables, there is considerable variety in distribution. Mark has only *one* parable that it can call strictly its own, Matthew has 10, Luke 18,[23] and there are nine that appear in more than one Gospel. Thus, as here listed, there are thirty-eight in all. By broadening the concept "parable" some would add several others; such as that of A Lamp under the Peck-measure (Matt. 5:14-16 and parallels), A Piece of Unshrunk Cloth on an Old Garment (Matt. 9:16, etc.), New Wine in Old Wineskins (Matt. 9:17, etc.), and many others. While this usage of the term "parable" is entirely legitimate, so that the total number given by some authors is sixty or even

---

[23] Luke also has six *miracles* not recorded in the other Synoptics; Matthew has only three peculiar to his Gospel; Mark only two. Luke's six are: a miraculous catch of fishes (5:1-11), the raising of the widow's son at Nain (7:11-17), two Sabbath healings (the healing of the woman "bowed together," and of the man afflicted with dropsy, respectively 13:11-17 and 14:1-6), the cleansing of the ten lepers (17:11-19), and the restoration of Malchus' ear (22:51). Cf. (3) above.

eighty, the more general definition of a parable as a story-illustration is here followed.

b. *In vocabulary and style*

Though it is true that often not only the thought content but even the very words used in the original and reflected in the translations are the same or almost the same in all three, this is by no means always the case. Where the accounts are parallel and record the deeds, rather than the sayings, of Jesus, Mark is *generally* (not always!) the most diffuse. Thus, in the story of the stilling of the storm (the one recorded in Mark 4:35-41; Matt. 8:18, 23-27; Luke 8:22-25) Mark, in the original, uses 118 words, Luke 94, Matthew 85. The corresponding figures in the A.R.V. are 151, 135, and 115. As remarked earlier (see p. 6), 606 of Mark's verses (out of a total of 661) are compressed into 500 of Matthew's.

This matter of *words* easily shifts into that of *style*. However, since with respect to Mark and Matthew this subject will come up again,[24] it is necessary in the present connection to point out only this, by way of summarizing, that Mark's style is not only the most diffuse but also the most vivid; Matthew's is more succinct and polished; and Luke's is the most versatile of the three.

c. *In "arrangement" and recorded order of events*

It was pointed out earlier that in a very general sense the sequence in which the great happenings in Christ's earthly sojourn follow one another is the same in all three Gospels (see pp. 8-11). Nevertheless, there are important differences. These come to light when one traces first the course of Mark's narrative, and then, having carefully done this, compares it with the story as it unfolds itself in Matthew and Luke. An illustration will make this clear. The three Gospels can be viewed under the symbolism of three rivers.

The first river is a swiftly flowing stream. Its current rolls on turbulently through rugged terrain. It churns and twists, making sharp turns now to the right, then to the left. Its borders exhibit ever changing scenery. *Such is Mark's Gospel.* Read the first five chapters. Note how quickly the action changes, though, of course, Jesus Christ, mighty in word and deed, is ever in the center of it. The colorful panorama shifts rapidly from one inspiring landscape to another. We catch a glimpse of John the Baptist, clothed with a garment of camel's hair. He is preaching and baptizing. He even baptizes the One whom he confesses to be infinitely greater than himself. The picture changes and we are shown a desert in which Satan is defeated by the Seed of the woman. This scene, too, is gone almost as quickly as it is introduced. We now see the Lord proclaiming "the gospel of the kingdom." Four fishermen

---

[24] For Mark's style see p. 39, for Matthew's pp. 39, 83. As to Luke's style consult commentaries on that Gospel.

appear. They are called to become "fishers of men." There follow scenes in which the Great Physician's might is strikingly revealed, to the amazement of the spectators: a man with an unclean spirit is instantly healed; so is Simon's mother-in-law. And now the sun sets, and this not only on the physical horizon but for many also on their days of grief and misery: "And in the evening, at sundown, they brought to him all that were sick or possessed with demons. . . . And he healed many that were sick with various diseases, and cast out many demons." A beautiful sunset indeed! Next we see "a solitary place," where "a great while before day" the Healer is pouring out his heart in prayer. Praying is followed by preaching, and this once more by healing. Now it is a demoniac from whom the evil spirit is expelled; next a leper who is cleansed; and then a paralytic. Merciful *deeds* are followed by merciful *sayings:* regarding publicans, or in defense of the proposition that the sabbath is made for man, not vice versa. Additional miracles are followed swiftly by the calling of The Twelve, a brief exposition of "the blasphemy against the Holy Spirit," a few parables, the stilling of a storm, and additional exhibitions of healing power, including even a raising of the dead. Thus Mark's Gospel, like a turbulent but scenic river, rushes on and on, until in chapter 16 it reaches the tomb, its huge stone rolled back. Some women, friends of Jesus, are *fleeing away* after they had been told that the tomb's Occupant had left it, having risen from the dead!

The second river is much calmer. It does not twist and swirl nearly as much as the first but flows rather smoothly and majestically. *At times it even takes a rest, as it were, by creating a lake, lingering there for a while,* and then flowing on once more until it again broadens out into a similar expanse of water. This action it repeats several times before it reaches its goal. *Such is Matthew's Gospel.*

That truly beautiful composition, from first to last, is in the habit of dwelling for a while on an important theme, while Mark is already rushing ahead, flashing before our eyes now this scene, then that. Thus, Mark introduces John the Baptist (1:1-6). So does Matthew (3:1-6; cf. Luke 3:1-6). But then, while Mark devotes only two verses to John's preaching, Matthew expatiates upon this theme in no less than six verses; Luke even more, in twelve verses. After a brief account of Jesus' own baptism by John, Mark summarizes the temptation (1:12, 13: again just two verses). Matthew, however, pauses a while, using eleven verses to relate the three separate temptations (4:1-11; cf. Luke 4:1-13). Mark makes mention of the fact that Jesus came into Galilee preaching the gospel of (the kingdom of) God (1:14, 15). But Matthew, having introduced this subject (4:17, 23), devotes three chapters to it, giving us a specimen of this preaching (The Sermon on the Mount; 5:1–8:1). Mark, in his vivid account of Jesus, proceeds from miracle to prayer to preaching to the calling of a disciple, etc., as has already been shown, ever shifting from one kind of topic to another. Matthew, on the other hand, groups his early miracle stories in one almost continuous account that spans sixty-eight verses (8:1–9:34), with two brief interruptions comprising in all only thirteen verses (8:19-22; 9:9-17). It is evident that Matthew has again discovered a theme and dwells on it. The following parallel columns will make this clear. Starting with Matthew, in column 1 notice how this evangelist has bunched together several of the miracles which in Mark are spread over parts of four chapters. He adds one that is also found in Luke (the healing of the centurion's servant), and two others. The second and third columns show that in such cases where Luke parallels Mark, the parallel is generally rather close, so that the rule mentioned earlier (see pp. 13, 14) holds; i.e., here Mark's chapter +3—sometimes +4—equals Luke's chapter.

Theme	Matthew	Mark	Luke
A leper	8:1-4	1:40-45	5:12-16
The centurion's servant	8:5-13		7:1-10
Peter's mother-in-law	8:14, 15	1:29-31	4:38, 39
Many sick at eventide	8:16, 17	1:32-34	4:40, 41
A tempest	8:18, 23-27	4:35-41	8:22-25
Gadarene demoniacs	8:28–9:1	5:1-20	8:26-39
A paralytic	9:1-8	2:1-12	5:17-26
The woman with an issue of blood	9:20-22	5:25-34	8:43-48
Jairus' daughter	9:18, 19, 23-26	5:22-24, 35-43	8:40-42, 49-56
Two blind men	9:27-31		
A dumb demoniac	9:32-34		

This same thematic trait is evident also in Matt. 9:36-38, where the need of laborers is emphasized, followed by chapter 10 which contains the detailed charge to the laborers. Contrast this with the very few verses used by Mark (6:7 f.) in this connection. Jesus is introduced as speaking in parables (Mark 4:1, 2; cf. Matt. 13:1-3a). For a while even Mark becomes thematic, as it were, and actually relates a few of these parables (4:3-32), but he is far too impetuous a story-teller to linger too long. In general it is especially the *deeds* of Jesus, rather than his *words,* on which he loves to dwell. Hence, to his brief reproduction of a few of these parables he quickly appends the summarizing conclusion, "And with many such parables he [Jesus] spoke the word to them" (4:33). Then he returns to the subject of the miracle-working Jesus *in action,* stilling a violent storm and healing an equally violent demoniac. Matthew's parable account, by contrast, is much longer (13:3-53). Similarly in Matt. 18 the question of greatness becomes the occasion for a lengthy discourse on kindness to Christ's little ones, and in general, on the virtue of compassion and the exercise of the forgiving spirit. Here, too, the treatment in Mark 9 and Luke 9 is more compressed. The denunciation of scribes and Pharisees is very briefly summarized in Mark (12:38-40), but again Matthew devotes a whole chapter to it (chap. 23). And even Christ's eschatological discourse is about two and one-half times as long in Matthew (chaps. 24 and 25) as in Mark (chap. 13). When Matthew discovers *a theme,* he dwells on it. When Mark discovers *action* he portrays it, and this in a most interesting manner and with great detail, so that, as already indicated, in several *such* instances it is his account that is the lengthiest. The contrast is, however, by no means absolute. Mark, too, has the highest regard for the words of Jesus, and reports many of them. But *his* emphasis is on action, Matthew's on discourse.

When the basic structure or system of Matthew is grasped—river, lake; river, lake; etc.—it will greatly assist one in finding his way in that Gospel, once the main drift of Mark has been comitted to memory. To begin with, it is a well-known fact that the genealogy and the nativity story are not found in Mark's Gospel, but respectively in Matt. 1:1-17 (cf. Luke 3:23-38) and 1:18-2:23 (cf. Luke 1, 2). Mark begins at once with the account of John the Baptist, which, accordingly, is found in Mark 1 and in Matt. 3. It has already been shown that Matthew, in his characteristic way, stops to give us a rather extensive specimen of John's preaching, while Mark devotes only a couple verses to this subject. It is not surprising, therefore, that Mark's first chapter also has room for the story of Christ's temptation; while, on the contrary, in Matthew's Gospel we must look for this in chapter 4. Similarly, the call of the first four disciples is found in both Mark 1 and Matt. 4. *Matt. 5–7,* as almost everyone knows, *contains the Sermon on the Mount,* with its theme: *the gospel of the kingdom. This discourse, the first of the six,* is represented in Mark by scattered verses only. The contents of Matt. 8 and 9 have just been noted. By means of these wondrous works Jesus reveals his kingly power over the physical universe, over evil spirits, and over the realm of sickness and death. It is not surprising that the preaching of the gospel of the kingdom together with the exhibition of kingdom miracles is followed in *Matt. 10* by the sending forth of the twelve as kingdom ambassadors, *the second great discourse;* in chapter 11 by Christ's words of tribute to the herald of the kingdom, namely, John the Baptist; in chapter 12 by the condemnation of the enemies of the kingdom[25] ; and finally, in *Matt. 13* by *the third great discourse,* the one containing the parables of the kingdom.

This brings us to the fourteenth chapter of Matthew's Gospel. Speaking in general terms—hence, allowing for exceptions—from Matt. 14:13 (cf. Mark 6:32) on, Matthew's account parallels that of Mark rather closely. It will be recalled that in the closing section of Luke's Gospel the key to finding one's

---

[25] In Matt. 16:1-12 (cf. Mark 8:11-21) this theme is continued.

way is "Mark +8." See pp. 15-16. In order to find our way in Matthew we now begin with this same formula. However, as has been pointed out, Matthew stops every once in a while in order to record a discourse of Jesus (the river widens and becomes a lake). He does this far more often and extensively than either Mark or Luke. Accordingly, with reference to Matthew, the formula "Mark +8" must gradually be increased to "Mark +9," "Mark +10," etc. Note, therefore, the following, in which for each chapter only one main event is here indicated:

Knowing that the subject is treated in MARK Chapter	the subject being	add	and find its parallel in MATTHEW Chapter
6	The feeding of the five thousand[26]	8	14
7	The healing of the Syro-phoenician woman's daughter	8	15
8	"Who do men say that I am?"	8	16
9	The transfiguration	8	17

As has been shown—and is generally known—*Matt.'s 18th chapter is the fourth of the six discourses* in that Gospel. In it Jesus emphasizes the necessity of showing kindness to his "little ones," and the forgiving spirit to all. The chapter ends with the parable of The Unmerciful Servant. Certain passages in this chapter are paralleled in Mark and in Luke, but as a single unit it is peculiar to Matthew.

This means, of course, that, beginning with Mark 10, to locate Mark's parallel in Matthew, we will have to use the formula "Mark +9" instead of "Mark +8." In fact, because Mark 10 is a very lengthy chapter (52 verses), while Matt. 19 is relatively short (30 verses), we do well to treat Mark 10 as if it were two chapters (Mark *10a:* verses 1-31; and Mark *10b:* verses 32-52).[27] To locate Mark *10b*'s material in Matthew the formula will then be "Mark +10."

---

[26] In Mark the feeding of the five thousand and that of the four thousand are found, respectively, in chapters 6 and 8; in Matthew, respectively, in chapters 14 and 15.

[27] Note the close similarity between Matt. 19 and Mark 10a: Matt. 19:1-6 cf. Mark 10:1-9; Matt. 19:7-12 cf. Mark 10:11, 12; Matt. 19:13-15 cf. Mark 10:13-16; Matt. 19:16-22 cf. Mark 10:17-22; Matt. 19:23-26 cf. Mark 10:23-27; and Matt. 19:27-30 cf. Mark 10:28-31. Matt. 20:1-16 contains the parable, peculiar to Matthew, of The Laborers in the Vineyard. From that point on the close parallel continues, now between Matt. 19 and Mark 10b, as follows: Matt. 20:17-19 cf. Mark 10:32-34; Matt. 20:20-28 cf. Mark 10:35-45; and Matt. 20:29-34 cf. Mark 10:46-52.

The list, accordingly, continues as follows:

Knowing that a subject is treated in MARK Chapter	the subject being	add	and find its parallel in MATTHEW Chapter
10a	Christ's teaching on divorce, little children, and earthly riches ("the rich young ruler")	9	19
10b	Christ's self-sacrifice ("A ransome for many") versus the sons of Zebedee's request for positions of glory	10	20
11	Triumphal entry into Jerusalem and its temple (the latter's cleansing)	10	21
12	Captious questions and authoritative answers	10	22

Matthew 23 contains Christ's fifth great discourse: The Seven Woes, ending with the stirring climax, "O Jerusalem, Jerusalem." This material, for the greater part, is absent from Mark (see however, Mark 12:38-40). Accordingly, with Mark's Gospel as a starting-point, the formula for locating Matthew's parallel to Mark's *next* chapter (the thirteenth) now becomes "Mark +11." This yields the following:

13	Signs of the end and exhortation to watch	11	24

In Matthew, however, *this general theme of watchfulness*—that is, of faithfulness in the exercise of one's duty, *with a view to the coming of Christ as Judge and Rewarder—is continued in the next chapter, so that together these two chapters (24 and 25) contain Christ's sixth great discourse.* The contents of chapter 25 (the parables of The Ten Virgins and of The Talents plus the majestic portrayal of The Grand Assize) are not paralleled either in Mark or in Luke. This means that for the contents of Mark 14, 15, and 16, as reflected in Matthew, the formula now becomes "Mark +12." The result is as follows:

14	Gethsemane	12	26
15	Calvary	12	27
16	"He is risen"	12	28

The third river is also a most interesting one. It consists of parts that alternate, so that the section that is above ground issues in one that is underground, which, let us suppose, in turn rises to the surface, forming still another section; which then descends again, and so forth. The fact that some of the sections are underground does not make them any less interesting than those above the surface. Nor does it necessarily render them invisible. Do not some of our caverns contain softly illumined streams equipped for boating amid picturesque surroundings?

This river, with its alternating sections, describes Luke's Gospel with its interchanging blocks of material. In this respect Luke differs from Matthew. The latter seems never completely able to forget Mark. It is as if the erstwhile publican, in a manner peculiar to himself, is filling in, or broadening out on, the Marcan outline. With Luke, however, it is different. By and large we can say that his Gospel consists of alternating Marcan and non-Marcan blocks. A Marcan block of considerable extent[28] is Luke 5:12–6:16. It tells us about a leper, a paralytic, Levi, fasting, the disciples in a grainfield on the sabbath, a man with a withered hand, and the calling of the twelve. All of this material is also found in Mark 1:40–3:19, and mainly in that same order.[29] There follows a non-Marcan block (Luke 6:17–8:3); then again a Marcan (Luke 8:4–9:50; cf. Mark 3:31–6:44; 8:27–9:40). Next comes a very lengthy largely non-Marcan section (Luke 9:51–18:14), which in turn introduces a Marcan block (Luke 18:15-52; cf. Mark 10:13-34, 46-52). Luke 19:1-28 (Zacchaeus and the parable of The Pounds) is non-Marcan. Much (by no means all!) of what follows in Luke's closing chapters is paralleled in Mark, but Luke 24:13-52 (the interview on the way to Emmaus, etc., concluding with Christ's ascension) is peculiar to Luke's Gospel (see, however, its very brief summary in Mark 16:12, 13).

Much more could be said about variation in the order in which various events are reported in the Synoptics. But with a view to pointing up the problem it will not be necessary to go into all the details. The following must

---

[28] As to Luke's earlier chapters, a definite and consistently carried out pattern of relationship between Mark and Luke is not in evidence. Luke 1:1–3:2 (nativity of Jesus and chronology of the beginning of John the Baptist's ministry) has no parallel in the other Gospels. In Luke 3:3-22 (the Baptist's ministry) those passages which are not peculiar to Luke resemble Matthew as much as—sometimes even more than—Mark, Luke's genealogy of Jesus has no true parallel in the other Gospels (but cf. Matt. 1:1-17). Luke 4:1-15 (Jesus tempted) is but faintly reflected in Mark, far more extensively in Matthew, but to a large extent peculiar to Luke in phraseology and arrangement. Luke 4:16-30 (rejection at Nazareth) is again predominantly peculiar to Luke (though paralleled to some extent in Mark 6:1-6 and Matt. 13:53-58). Luke 4:31-44 (early miracles in Capernaum) has a definite parallel in Mark 1:21-39. It is followed by largely non-Marcan Luke 5:1-11 (miraculous catch and "fishers of men").

[29] It is true, however, that Mark 1:40–3:19 contains even more material; especially a report about a healing mission (3:7-12; cf. Matt. 12:15, 16), interspersed between the account of the withered hand and the calling of the twelve. It is also true that such a passage as Mark 3:11 is reflected rather in Luke 4:41 than anywhere in Luke 5:12–6:16. But it should be borne in mind that we are here asking the question, "How is Luke reflected in Mark?" rather than, "How is Mark duplicated in Luke?"

31

suffice. Already in Mark 2:23-28 that evangelist relates the incident of the plucking of the ears of grain on the sabbath. Matthew makes no mention of this until he has almost reached the middle of his Gospel (12:1-8; cf. Luke 6:1-5). Similarly, the healing of the withered hand is reported in Mark 3:1-6, but in Matthew not until 12:10-13 (cf. Luke 6:6-10). Christ's rejection at Nazareth is recorded in Luke 4:16-30, but in Matthew not until 13:54-58 (cf. Mark 6:1-6). In Matthew the three temptations are listed in the order: "Tell these stones to turn into bread," "Throw yourself down (from the pinnacle of the temple)," and "Fall down and worship me" (4:3, 6, 9). In Luke, however, the order of the second and the third is reversed (4:7, 9). And as to the sequence in reported *sayings* of Jesus, it should be noted that while in Matt. 5–7 and Luke 6:20-49 The Sermon on the Mount is presented as a unit, Luke *also* scatters its inspired maxims over several of his chapters; e.g., with Matt. 5:13 cf. Luke 14:34; with Matt. 5:15 cf. Luke 8:16; with Matt. 6:22 cf. Luke 11:34; and with Matt. 7:7 cf. Luke 11:9. Something similar happens in connection with Matt. 10; e.g., with Matt. 10:17 cf. Luke 12:11; with Matt. 10:21 cf. Luke 21:16; with Matt. 10:26 cf. Luke 12:2; with Matt. 10:24 cf. Luke 6:40; and with Matt. 10:39 cf. Luke 17:33. Also, in connection with Matt. 18; e.g., with Matt. 18:5 cf. Luke 9:48; and with Matt. 18:6, 7 cf. Luke 17:1, 2. And so it frequently happens that where Matthew *gathers* (groups together) Luke *scatters* (separates). Both were fully justified in doing so. As everyone knows, speakers, especially those who travel, repeat some of the things they have said earlier.

3. *The Resulting Problem*

The facts having now been stated, it will be evident that the Synoptic Problem consists in this, that as to contents, wording, and arrangement there is considerable similarity; yet also noticeable difference. If the resemblance were distant there would be no problem. Again, if the divergence were minimal, there would be a ready answer. But now that neither is true, and both the unity and the diversity stand out, the problem is real.

The aforegoing summary has also shown:

First, that each Gospel has its own distinctive structure.

Secondly, that when the distinctive structure of each Gospel is grasped, finding one's way in the Synoptics will have become far less difficult. What is found on the preceding pages can be helpful to this end. The repeated reading and diligent study of the Synoptics is, of course, even more necessary.

Thirdly, that those who wrote these Gospels were not mere compilers but composers, not mere copyists but authors.

4. *Elements Entering into a Solution*

Note the wording of this heading: not "The Solution," as if a complete solution were possible, but "Elements Entering into a Solution." A *detailed* answer to the question, "How did these Gospels originate?" is impossible for the simple reason that none of the writers has given us a list of his sources, oral and written. Even Luke in his prologue (1:1-4) did not do this. But this is no cause for despair. Whoever approaches these sacred writings with a believing heart, convinced that they were composed under the guidance of the Holy Spirit and reveal to us the Jesus of history who is at the same time the Christ of faith, begins to see that *what* these books teach is far more important than exactly *how* they came into existence. This approach of faith will make it possible to discover at least a *broad* solution, one that, though leaving many questions unanswered, will supply answers to others, thereby considerably limiting the scope of the unknown and unknowable.[30]

a. *Theory of Mutual Dependence*

Traditionally it was assumed that the author of what was regarded as the second written Gospel used the first written Gospel, and that the author of the third used the first and the second. Thus, in his work *The Harmony of the Gospels* I.ii.4, Augustine, having first made some comments about Matthew continues, "Mark follows him closely, and looks like his attendant and abbreviator."

Evaluation: In general, this theory fails to account for the presence of that material in the new Gospel which was lacking in the older one(s). Specifically, as to the relation between Mark and Matthew, if it had been Mark's purpose to give us a summary of Matthew, why would he have left so much beautiful Matthew-material entirely untouched? Besides, is there not a strong early tradition that makes Mark dependent on Peter's preaching rather than on Matthew's written Gospel?[31] Finally, it has already been pointed out (p. 7) that in those paragraphs where Matthew and Mark run parallel it is often Mark which contains the more detailed account. Calvin was aware of this. He states, "Mark's narrative of the same event is sometimes more detailed. It is more probable, in my opinion ... that he had not seen Matthew's book when he wrote his own; so far is he from having expressly intended to make an abridgment."[32]

But though in the form in which the theory of Mutual Dependence was proposed by Augustine and others it is unacceptable, nevertheless in some other form it might be acceptable. For example, unless one is irrevocably committed to the belief that since Matthew was one of The Twelve, and Mark did not belong to that inner circle, therefore Matthew's Gospel must

---

[30] Of the same opinion is S. Greijdanus, who in *Bijbelsch Handboek*, Vol. II, p. 97 (Kampen, 1935) states: "If what is narrated in the Gospels is accepted as being true, the questions regarding the possible relations between the Synoptics not only assume secondary significance but also diminish in number and become easier to unravel."

[31] See pp. 41, 42, 44.

[32] Quoted from the Argumentum of *Commentarius in Harmoniam Evangelicam, Opera Omnia* (Brunswick, 1891), XLV.3; English translation (Grand Rapids, 1949) I.xxxviii.

have preceded Mark's, he might well ask, "If Mark did not make use of Matthew's Gospel, could it be that Matthew used Mark's?" Also, could not Luke have used both Matthew's Gospel and Mark's?

b. *Early Gospel Hypothesis*

G. E. Lessing (in 1776 and 1778) and J. G. Eichhorn (in 1794) argued that all three independently utilized an early Aramaic Gospel, now lost.

Evaluation: This theory, too, may contain an element of value. Yet, whatever may be the truth with respect to an early Aramaic Gospel,[33] and its possible effect on a later Greek revision, the proposed solution is not a complete answer. It does not explain the wide variety in contents, vocabulary, and arrangement, that obtains among the three.

c. *Fragments theory*

F. Schleiermacher (in 1832) called attention to what he considered the artificial links by which the separate units of the Gospels, such units as sayings, discourses, stories, etc., are connected. From this he drew the conclusion that the sources used by the evangelists consisted of ever so many fragments. The Gospel writers had access to a mass of flyleaves on each of which a few items with reference to Jesus were recorded. The different ways in which these fragments were combined resulted in the three widely different Gospels. Due to the fact that many copies were made of the same material, scattered far and wide, and used by all three, these Gospels would, nevertheless reveal a measure of unity amid diversity.

Evaluation: Also this view may be true in part. It is possible, *probable* even, that Matthew, the publican, had taken notes on sayings and deeds of Jesus, and that before any Gospels were written these notes had been translated from Matthew's Aramaic into Greek, copied, and distributed in both languages. Or Matthew himself may have written them in both tongues. Did he also distribute in note-form his own Greek paraphrase of Old Testament passages fulfilled in Christ? And were such early notes used by all three evangelists? Is not a literary connection between the three records evident from the fact that there are quotations from the Old Testament in a form which, though identical in the three Synoptics, differs both from the literally rendered Hebrew Old Testament and from the Greek translation (LXX)? An illustration is Matt. 3:3; Mark 1:3; and Luke 3:4. The quotation is from Isa. 40:3. As found in all three New Testament passages the quoted words are:

> A voice of one crying in the wilderness:
> Make ready the way of the Lord,
> Make straight his paths.

Parallelism (see lines 2 and 3) favors the following translation of the *Hebrew* text:

---

[33] See p. 87.

A voice (is) crying:
In the wilderness make ready the way of the Lord [YHWH],
Make straight in the desert a highway for our God.
And now the LXX:
A voice of one crying in the wilderness,
Make ready the way of the Lord,
Make straight the paths of our God.

But though the literary fragment theory may be true in part, it cannot be considered a complete solution of the Synoptic Problem. It is by no means *adequate* as an explanation. For, first of all, the theory rests upon a gratuitous assumption, namely, that "the links" are artificial. If a saying of Jesus is reported in more than one connection, does this necessarily mean that the words that introduce such a saying or those that connect it with the following passage or paragraph were, for at least one of the reports, created and inserted at a later time? Is it not more natural to suppose that *Jesus repeated himself,* as is done by many traveling speakers even today? Similar *events,* too, may well have occurred in different time-and-place settings. The links, therefore, are not at all necessarily unnatural and artificial. Besides, as has been shown, with all their differences, the three Synoptics nevertheless present *one* story, a narrative of Christ's earthly sojourn in which the *main* sequence of events is the same for all. Would this have been true if the Gospel-writers had nothing but loose fragments to work with?

d. *The Double Source Hypothesis and Its Modifications*

(1) *Brief Description*

This theory was developed by K. Lachmann (in 1835) and H. H. J. Holzmann (in 1863). As they and others after them saw it, Mark was the first to write a canonical Gospel. Matthew and Luke, each independent of the other, made use of Mark *for the narrative portion* of their Gospels. *For the discourse or sayings material* Matthew and Luke used another document. This was known at first as *L* (=Logia). It was described as containing all such non-Marcan material that is common to Matthew and Luke.

Of course, there can be no question about the fact that there is, indeed, such non-Marcan Matthew-Luke material. See the partial list given above, on p. 21. There can be no objection, therefore, to the use of *L* as an algebraic symbol. However, the Double Source Hypothesis, by changing the symbol *L* to *Q* (=Quelle, a German word meaning *Source*), affirms that the material in question was, in some form, an actual written source used by Matthew and Luke in composing their Gospels. It may have been written in Aramaic at first, but if so, in revised form it developed into a very important Greek source underlying the Greek Gospels of Matthew and Luke as we now know them. Such is the theory. This Double Source Hypothesis, with many revisions and modifications, has been accepted by many. Its two elements *a.* priority of Mark and *b.* "Q" deserve to be discussed separately.

35

NEW TESTAMENT COMMENTARY

(2) *The Priority of Mark*

The conviction that Matthew and Luke, each independently, used Mark is shared by scholars all over the world.[34]

In a qualified sense (see pp. 43, 51-54), as concerns the three Synoptics as we have them in Greek, this priority of Mark theory may well be correct. This need not mean that *all* the arguments that have been advanced in

---

[34] From an almost endless list of titles I select only the following:

W. C. Allen, *A Critical and Exegetical Commentary on the Gospel according to S. Matthew* (*International Critical Commentary*), New York, 1910, see especially p. xxxv.

B. De Solages, *A Greek Synopsis of the Gospels*, Leiden, 1959. In this work of 1128 pages the renowned Roman Catholic scholar, by a mathematical process, arrives at the conclusion that Matthew and Luke did indeed use Mark. He states this in spite of the affirmation by the Pontifical Biblical Commission (June 19, 1911) that "Matthew wrote before the other evangelists." However, it should be borne in mind that Roman Catholic leaders draw a distinction between such decrees as are connected with matters of faith and morals, on the one hand, and those that lie outside of that realm, on the other.

F. F. Filson, "Gospel and Gospels" in S.H.E.R.K.; Vol. I of *The Twentieth Century supplement*, Grand Rapids, p. 470.

E. J. Goodspeed, *Matthew Apostle and Evangelist*, Philadelphia and Toronto, 1959; see especially pp. 86, 87, 108, 109.

E. P. Groenewald, *Die Evangelie volgens Markus* (*Kommentaar op die Bybel, Nuwe Testament* II), Pretoria, 1948. On p. 13 he calls Mark's Gospel "grondslag en bron vir Mt. en Lk." (basis and source for Matthew and Luke).

J. C. Hawkins, *Horae Synopticae*, Oxford, 1909.

A. M. Perry, *The Growth of the Gospels*, a chapter in *The Interpreter's Bible*, New York and Nashville, 1951; Vol VII, p. 63.

Herman Ridderbos, "Synoptische Kwestie," *Christelijke Encyclopedie*, Kampen, 1961; Vol. 6, pp. 305, 306.

A. T. Robertson, *Word Pictures in the New Testament*, New York and London, 1930; Vol. I. p. 249.

J. H. Ropes, *The Synoptic Gospels*, London, 1934, pp. 92, 93.

N. B. Stonehouse, *Origins of the Synoptic Gospels*, Grand Rapids, 1963; see especially pp. 73, 76, 115.

B. H. Streeter, *The Four Gospels*, New York, 1925, p. 151.

H. G. Wood, "The Priority of Mark," *ET* (October, 1953).

Among those who do not share this view are the following:

B. C. Butler, *The Originality of St. Matthew*, Cambridge, 1951.

J. Chapman, *Matthew, Mark and Luke*, London, 1937. Contrary to all tradition this writer considers Peter "the real author" of Mark's Gospel. He defends the priority of Matthew by imagining that Peter read from Matthew's Gospel.

John H. Ludlum, Jr., "More Light on the Synoptic Problem" and "Are We Sure of Mark's Priority?" articles in *Christianity Today;* respectively Nov. 10 & 24, 1958; and Sept. 14 & 28, 1959.

To H. Mulder, an ardent proponent of the oral tradition theory, with emphasis on the preaching of Peter, must be given the credit that he treats the priority of Mark theory objectively and regards it as being at least more creditable than the Q hypothesis. In addition to his work *Het Synoptisch Vraagstuk*, Delft, 1952, see his *Gids voor het Nieuwe Testament*, Kampen, 1962, pp. 71-74.

support of this view are valid.[35] But even after subtracting whatever is questionable, that which remains provides rather solid evidence; as follows:

[35] In his valuable work *The New Testament, Its Background, Growth, and Content,* New York and Nashville, 1965, pp. 80-83, B. M. Metzger summarizes the arguments that are found also in the books of earlier writers. It would be hard to find any fault with what he says about this subject on p. 80 or on p. 81 under (a). As to arguments (b) to (h) note the following. He maintains that the view according to which Mark's Gospel is the most primitive of the Synoptics is correct, because:

(b) Mark is decidedly less polished than Matthew and Luke.

Evaluation: That depends upon exactly what is meant by "decidedly less polished." If it means *more simple in style* I agree. I also agree, however, with Cecil S. Emden, who in his instructive article "St. Mark's Use of the Imperfect Tense" *Bible Translator,* Vol. V, Number 3 (July 1954), presents evidence in support of his contention that Mark's style is by no means inelegant and lacking in literary skill and polish. According to J. H. Ropes, *op. cit.,* p. 98, Mark "is in command of an excellent and large Greek vocabulary, and knows how to use the right word in the right place," yet at times his syntax is "most peculiar," manifesting a "barbarous Greek style." On Mark's style see below, p. 39, footnote 37. For an attempt at a solution in a somewhat similar situation see N.T.C. on the Gospel according to John, Vol. I, p. 64.

(c) Matthew and Luke, in passages that parallel Mark, have omitted such difficult phrases as Mark 2:26, contrast I Sam. 21:1-7; and Mark 10:19, contrast Matt. 19:18, 19; Luke 18:20.

Evaluation: Are these Marcan phrases really so difficult that they were omitted by Matthew and Luke for this reason? For Mark 2:26 see on Matt. 12:3; for Mark 10:19 see on Matt. 19:18, 19.

(d) The gradual decrease of respect for the apostles is reflected in Matthew and Luke, as compared with Mark. The latter's blunt statements with reference to the church's leaders are no longer found in the other two Synoptics.

Evaluation: Is it true that Mark's statement about the dispute among the apostles as to who was the greatest is entirely omitted by Matthew? Are not such unsavory quarrels clearly implied in Matt. 18:1-6; 23:1-11? Also, since it cannot be denied that Luke does indeed record these lamentable clashes (9:46-48; 22:24-30), would not the reasoning implied in this argument lead to the conclusion that also Luke's Gospel preceded that of Matthew? Again, when it is said that Mark's reference (9:32) to the inability on the part of the disciples to understand Jesus' teaching reveals a lower degree of respect for the leaders than is found in Matthew and Luke, is not the answer that the disciples' lack of perception is clearly taught in such passages as Matt. 16:5-12, 22, 23; 19:23-26; 26:8, 9; and not only lack of perception but also lack of fully developed faith (14:31; 16:8) and sympathy (15:23; 19:13; 20:24; 26:8, 9)? It is said that Luke omits Mark's reference to Peter as "Satan" (8:33). That reference is, however, also found in Matthew (16:23). To be sure, Luke omits Mark's remark (14:71) about Peter's vigorous cursing, but Matthew has it (26:74). Peter's impudence in rebuking Jesus is recorded in Matt. 16:22; the readiness of "the sons of thunder" (James and John) to call down fire from heaven upon the inhospitable Samaritans, in Luke 9:54, 55. Accordingly, is not this argument in support of the view that Mark's Gospel is the most primitive rather weak?

(e) When Mark's Gospel was written reverence for Jesus was not as yet as high as it became later on when Matthew and Luke, respectively, composed their books.

Evaluation: see the next chapter, pp. 58-60.

(f) The later Gospels omit statements that might be interpreted to imply that Jesus lacked omnipotence (Mark 1:45; others add 6:5) or omniscience (Mark 6:38; 9:16, 21, 33).

Evaluation: Matthew records other questions that can similarly be construed as implying ignorance on the part of Jesus (13:51; 15:34; 16:13, 15). Some questions (Mark 5:9, 30; 14:14), though absent from Matthew, are paralled in Luke (respectively 8:30,

(a) *Agreement in subject matter.* As has been indicated earlier (see pp. 6, 7), almost all of Mark is paralleled in Matthew; slightly more than half of Mark is found also in Luke. It has been shown that neither the Early Gospel Hypothesis nor the Mutual Dependence Theory in the form that would make Mark dependent on Matthew adequately explains this agreement. Besides, as concerns a book taken as a whole, would not subsequent expansion be more probable than contraction?[36] Now all this would certainly seem to point in the direction of Mark's priority. Yet, taken by itself, this argument may not amount to actual proof. One could, for example, argue that the remarkable agreement in subject matter is due not to literary dependence of one document upon another but rather to memorized stereotyped oral tradition. However, as the evidence multiples—see points (b), (c) and (d)—that solution becomes increasingly improbable, and the priority of Mark theory becomes increasingly credible.

45; and 22:11). Moreover, if it were true that references to ignorance on the part of Jesus were consciously omitted by Matthew, why do both N.N. and Grk. N.T. (A-B-M-W) still include *in the text* of Matt 24:36 the words "neither the Son," implying that Jesus did not know the exact moment of his own return? Is not the reason for the inclusion the fact that the variant in support of the omission lacks sufficient textual support? But then this argument for the priority of Mark, as if *he* referred to Christ's ignorance but Matthew did not, collapses.

As to passages according to which man's unbelief is represented as an impediment to the progress of the work of grace, so that *humanly speaking* he cannot receive a blessing, is Mark 6:5 any more surprising than Matt. 23:37? Moreover, does not the fact that Jesus voluntarily accepted the conditions that attended his humiliation imply that he frequently permitted obstacles to be thrown into his path? Thus, instead of asserting his almighty power to suppress the city-multitude's sinful preference for miracles above words, he simply avoided the city (Mark 1:45); just as, instead of miraculously causing the crowds to recede when they pressed upon him, he simply entered into a boat and from that convenient position began to teach the people (Luke 5:1-3). Therefore, when in the presence of certain circumstances Jesus *cannot* do something, it is because he *does not will* to do it. Matthew, Mark, and Luke are in full agreement here.

(g) Matthew is later than Mark, for he heightens the majesty of Jesus' person by more than once insisting that the Master not only *healed* people but healed them *instantly.*

Evaluation: Though it is true that in Matt. 15:28 and 17:18 we are told that those who had been healed were cured "from that hour," and though the very word "instantly" or "immediately" is used by Matthew in comparable connections (8:3; 20:34), Mark frequently employs a similar adverb in connection with miraculous cures (1:42; 2:12; 5:29, 42; 10:52). It is impossible to base any argument for the priority of Mark on such passages, therefore.—For the supposed discrepancy between Mark 11:20, 21 and Matt. 21:19, 20 see on the latter passage; and for Mark 12:8 versus Matt. 21:39 and Luke 20:15 see on Matt. 21:39.

(h) The change in the sequence of clauses—from "killed him and cast him out of the vineyard" (Mark 12:8) to "cast him out of the vineyard and killed him" (Matt. 21:39; Luke 20:15)—reflects a later stage of theological understanding in Matthew and Luke than in Mark.

Evaluation: See on Matt. 21:39.

It will have become clear that not all the arguments in support of Mark's priority are equally valid.

36 Cf. what E. J. Goodspeed says about this, *op. cit.,* p. 142.

(b) *Vocabulary agreement.* With respect to the words that are used note the striking agreement between Mark 1:16-20 and Matt. 4:18-22; also between Mark 2:18-22 and Matt. 9:14-17. Comparing Mark and Luke, see how closely Luke 4:31-37 parallels Mark 1:21-28; and Luke 19:29-35 resembles Mark 11:1-7. These are but a few examples. This does not mean that Matthew and Luke simply copy Mark. On the contrary, amid remarkable agreement one detects certain characteristic *stylistic differences.*[37] Each evangelist has his own way of writing and his own plan. But in parallel sections, except for these stylistic differences, either *a.* both Matthew *and* Luke sedulously parallel Mark, or else *b.* Matthew *or* Luke closely resembles that shortest Gospel. The two never *essentially* support each other against Mark. This would seem to be another rather strong argument in favor of the proposition that Matthew and Luke independently used Mark.

(c) *Agreement in order.* This is, indeed, one of the strongest arguments in favor of the priority of Mark. In order to appreciate it one should see the facts for himself by carefully comparing the Synoptics. It will then become evident that immediately after the description of the preaching of John (Mark 1:3-8; Matt. 3:3-12; Luke 3:4-18), a description which in each of

---

[37] Important among these are the following:

a. Mark frequently uses a tense that differs from the one found in Matthew and/or Luke. Examples: ἐγγίζουσιν (they approach, Mark 11:1) versus ἤγγισεν (they approached, Luke 19:29; in the same verse ἀποστέλλει (he sends) versus ἀπέστειλεν (he sent). So also φέρουσιν (they bring, Mark 11:7) versus ἤγαγον (they brought, Luke 19:35); in the same verse ἐπιβάλλουσιν (they throw on) versus ἐπιρίψαντες (a synonym: having thrown on). In general it may be said that in many instances where Mark uses the present tense Matthew and Luke use the aorist or the imperfect. See J. C. Hawkins, *Horae Synopticae,* pp. 143-153.

b. Another striking difference between Mark, on the one hand, and Matthew and Luke, on the other, is the latter two's preference for the particle δέ over against Mark's strong leaning toward the use of καί. Thus, in the paragraph from which examples showing difference in tense were just cited (Mark 11:1-7 compared with Luke 19:29-35) Luke uses καί five times to introduce a clause or phrase, Mark a dozen times. In these same seven verses Luke uses δέ three times (also once in verse 36 and once in verse 37); Mark only once (also once in verse 8).

c. In connection with Mark's generous use of καί it should also be mentioned that it is characteristic of Matthew and Luke that they frequently substitute a participle for Mark's finite verb with καί. In other words, in such cases the two favor subordination where Mark co-ordinates.

d. Both Matthew and Luke often independently abbreviate Mark's account. They do this by omitting those words, phrases, and (at times) entire sentences from Mark that can be omitted without destroying the main idea that is being conveyed. This, however, must not be interpreted as if Mark's additional words, etc. were superfluous or redundant. The Holy Spirit had his good reason for guiding Mark in the use of words. But this certainly does not mean that Mark's every syllable had to be repeated by Matthew and Luke. These two, under the guidance of that same Spirit, intended to write lengthy Gospels. It was their aim to record many things (stories, discourses, parables, etc.) that are not found, or not as *fully* represented, in Mark. In order to carry out their ambitious plans in the limited space at their disposal the two very properly compressed the Marcan account. See also B. H. Streeter, *op. cit.,* pp. 179-181.

39

these three Gospels starts with a quotation from Isa. 40:3 but otherwise reveals considerable variation, Luke's order of narration begins to differ from that of Mark and Matthew. While the latter two *first* tell the story of Jesus' baptism by John (Mark 1:9-11; Matt. 3:13-17), Luke *immediately* relates John's imprisonment (3:19, 20). His brief account of Christ's baptism follows (3:21, 22). As to the *theme*, Mark and Matthew thereupon continue to parallel each other, for both now present the story of Jesus' temptation. It has already been pointed out, however, that, viewed from a material aspect, the "parallel" is questionable, since breadth of treatment of this temptation narrative differs strikingly. Nevertheless, this does not change the fact that the sequence in which the narrative is presented is the same for Mark and Matthew. Luke, however, departs from the order followed by the other two, and next presents his Genealogy of Jesus (3:23-38). After this he joins the others with his unique coverage of the temptation (4:1-13; cf. Mark 1:12, 13; Matt. 4:1-11). After a brief triple introduction to the story of The Great Galilean Ministry (Mark 1:14, 15; Matt. 4:12 ff.; Luke 4:14, 15) Luke swerves away once more from the sequence found in Mark and Matthew, and relates the rejection at Nazareth (4:16-30). The sequence of narration in Mark and Matthew continues in parallel fashion. Both tell the story of the calling of four fishermen (Mark 1:16-20; Matt. 4:18-22). This may be compared with Luke 5:1-11, which is actually the account of a miraculous catch (see p. 246). When we reach Luke 4:31-37 (cf. Mark 1:21-28) we notice that Mark and Luke are together again, and that *this* time it is Matthew who is following a different sequence. But when we arrive at Mark 1:39—Christ's preaching throughout Galilee and casting out demons—we observe that Matthew, in an expanded account (4:23-25) is with Mark again. Next, Matthew presents The Sermon on the Mount (chaps 5-7). *Very strikingly, immediately afterward he returns to the very point where he had left Mark;* so that both Mark 1:40-45 and Matt. 8:1-4 tell the story of the healing of a leper. This is also found in Luke 5:12-16. In both Mark and Luke this is followed by the account of the healing of a paralytic (Mark 2:1-12; Luke 5:17-26), but it is again Matthew who here follows a different sequence of narration. He now tells the story of the commended centurion (8:5-13; Luke 7:1-10).

The point to note, therefore, is this: *Mark* seems to be "the man in the middle." When Luke departs from him, Matthew generally stays with him; when Matthew leaves him, Luke nearly always remains at his side.

Significance: In *The Fourfold Gospel, Introduction,* Cambridge, 1913, pp. 11, 12, E. A. Abbott, who at one time had been a headmaster, relates how at times three students—whom he calls Primus, Secundus, and Tertius—would hand in papers that resembled each other closely enough to awaken suspicion. Had one of the students furnished help to the others; and if so, which one had done so? Abbott's unfailing experience showed that the answer was not hard to discover. When *P* and *T* were in substantial agreement with each other, they also agreed with *S*. Whenever *P* and *T* differed, *one* of them—sometimes *P*, sometimes *T*—would still agree with *S*. The latter, accordingly, was "the boy in the middle," the one who had furnished help to the other two. Similarly, careful literary comparison would seem to indicate that Matthew and Luke, each in his own way, for his own purpose, with the retention of his own style, and in harmony with his own Gospel-plan, as shown previously, made use of Mark's book.

(d) *The matter of style.* For the facts regarding Mark's style, see p. 39, footnote 37. These facts prove that Mark's manner of writing was the most vivid and sparkling of them all. It was also the most primitive, even repetitious at times, though never to the point of becoming labored, coarse, unmeaningful. Mark wrote as if he had been cupping his ear to the well-nigh breathless report of an enthusiastic eye-witness of Christ's glorious deeds. And he had indeed been listening, namely, to the apostle Peter. Early tradition—as represented by Papias, Irenaeus, Clement of Alexandria, Tertullian, Origen, Jerome, Eusebius and others[38] —agrees that there was a very close connection between Peter and Mark.

"And so great a light of religion shone upon the minds of the hearers of Peter that they were not satisfied with a single hearing or with the unwritten teaching of the divine proclamation [kerygma], but with all kinds of entreaties urged Mark, whose Gospel is extant, seeing that he was a follower of Peter, to leave them, in writing, a record of the teaching transmitted to them orally [by word] ; nor did they cease until they had prevailed upon the man; and so they became responsible for the Scripture that is called the Gospel according to Mark" (Eusebius, *op. cit.*, II.xv.1).

There are those who think that in his second epistle (1:15) Peter promised that he would provide a Gospel. They are of the opinion that Mark's book was the one that redeemed this promise. Other interpreters, however, reject this view. For our purpose it is not necessary to try to decide this question.

The "father-son" relation between Peter and Mark is clear from Scripture (I Peter 5:13; cf. Acts 12:12). In the first of these two passages Peter calls Mark "my son." All the early testimonies assert that Mark, in writing his Gospel, was dependent on Peter, though these sources disagree with respect to the extent of this dependence. It is probably safe to say (with Papias and others) that Mark was "Peter's interpreter." In his Gospel he sets forth the gist of Peter's preaching. Peter and Mark had much in common. Both were men of action, fervor, and enthusiasm. Temporary deviation from the straight and narrow path is recorded in the case of both (Peter's denial,

---

[38] The patristic evidence is given in several encyclopaedias and commentaries; see, for example, J. H. Farmer, "Mark, The Gospel According to," article in I.S.B.E., Vol. III; especially pp. 1989-1991.

Mark's desertion), but both also experienced the wonderful (restoring and transforming) grace of their loving Lord (for Peter see John 21:15-17; for Mark Col. 4:10; Philem. 24; and II Tim. 4:11). Thus, the reader of the Gospel according to Mark feels throughout that he is being brought very close to the scene of action, for back of Mark stands Peter, and back of Peter stands Jesus Christ himself in all his power, wisdom, and love.

This closeness to the original scene is accentuated by one more significant fact; namely, that in several cases Mark has preserved for us the words of Jesus in the very language spoken, whether Hebrew or Aramaic. The contrast in this respect between Mark, on the one hand, and Matthew and Luke, on the other, is striking, especially when in each case in which there is a nearly parallel passage the latter is also examined. Note, accordingly, the following:

Mark	Matthew	Luke
boanerges (3:17), interpreted "sons of thunder"	10:2	6:14
talitha cumi (5:41), interpreted "little girl . . . arise"	9:25	8:54
corban (7:11), interpreted "an offering"	15:5	
ephphatha (7:34), interpreted "be opened"		
Abba (14:36), interpreted "Father"	26:39	22:42

It is not surprising, therefore, that the priority of Mark theory has found such wide acceptance. From the point of view of literary comparison the evidence in its favor would seem to be conclusive. Nevertheless, objections have arisen. The theory, though now accepted by most scholars, has not convinced all. The main objections, together with my answers, are as follows:

(a) If Matthew and Luke both used our present Greek Gospel, why did they omit certain Marcan material? Also, how can it be explained that at times Matthew and Luke, in their phraseology, agree with each other, against Mark? Do not these facts warrant the conclusion that they were not using our present Mark but an earlier edition ("Ur-Marcus")?

Answer: In Matthew the non-used Marcan material is very small indeed, as has already been shown, certainly insufficient as a basis for the postulation of an earlier Mark. And as to Luke's far more extensive "omissions," the idea that the author of the third Gospel intentionally avoids certain Marcan sections in order to leave room, within the compass of a single papyrus roll, for other important material—for example, many beautiful parables which he alone reports—impresses me as far more credible than the supposition of an Ur-Marcus. For the latter there is no historical evidence whatever. As to the so-called "agreements of Matthew and Luke against Mark," when "stylistic variation" is no real solution, could Luke have used Matthew's Gospel?[39]

(b) This theory "degrades Matthew and Luke to the position of slavish compilers, not to say plagiarists."[40]

Answer: Not at all; for, as has been noted repeatedly, Matthew and Luke do not *copy* Mark but *use* his Gospel. As has been shown, the style, purpose, reason for inclusion or exclusion of material, and the basic plan are still their own.

And as to "plagiarism" or literary theft, it should be remembered that today's rules of copyright did not then exist. Besides, if we bear in mind that Mark was Peter's interpreter, the next question would be, "And where did Peter get his material?" Did he depend *entirely* on his memory? Is it not possible—perhaps even probable—that to a limited extent he also made use of notes that had been taken during Christ's life on earth? Who was the logical person to take these notes and to have copies made of them both in Aramaic and in Greek? Was it not Matthew? See pp. 34, 53, 90, 96. If this be kept in mind, it will be seen that judged even by modern standards, the charge of plagiarism would be hard to maintain throughout against Matthew. In some of that which Matthew read from the Gospel according to Mark, the former publican may well have detected an echo of his own notes. Accordingly, when we speak of Mark's priority we should ever bear in mind that this priority is probably not absolute. In comparing the Gospels viewed as a whole, especially as to arrangement of material, that priority, as was shown, is rather convincing, particularly for parallel portions. However, when we enquire more thoroughly into the origin of a particular saying, report, or quotation (often in modified form) of an Old Testament passage, we shall have to leave room for the theory that *to a limited extent* the priority belongs to Matthew! This, as is clear, by no means cancels the use Matthew made of Mark's Gospel.

Matthew, by utilizing Mark, may well have been aiming to present a

---

[39] On the subject of "stylistic variation" see the discussion in B. H. Streeter, *op. cit.*, pp. 179-181; and N. B. Stonehouse, *Origins of the Synoptic Gospels*, pp. 60, 61. On the possibility that Luke used Matthew, see A. W. Argyle's "Evidence" in favor, *JBL* (Dec. 1964), pp. 390-396).

[40] See John H. Kerr, *An Introduction to the Study of the Books of the New Testament*, Chicago, New York, Toronto, 1892, p. 11.

united front to the world, for the confirmation of the faith. We should really rejoice in the fact that the Gospels spring from a common tradition and therefore have so much in common. Was it not rather a tribute to Mark, a real honor conferred upon him, that Matthew and Luke were able to make such good use of his earlier Greek Gospel?

(c) This theory fails to do justice to the work of the Holy Spirit who infallibly guided the authors to write whatever had to be written.

Answer: Could not the Holy Spirit have guided them also in the selection and use of oral *and literary* sources? Is this excluded by what we read in Luke 1:1-4? Is it not true that already in the Old Testament we are repeatedly reminded that the inspired authors were at least acquainted with written materials other than their own? Read Num. 21:14; Josh. 10:13; II Sam. 1:18; I Kings 11:41; 14:19, 29; I Chron. 29:29; II Chron. 9:29; 12:15; 13:22; 20:34; 32:32. Daniel certainly made good use of his written source (Dan. 9:1, 2). Is it not probable that the apostle John had read the Synoptics and that he made use of this fact in the selection of his own material? (See N.T.C. on The Gospel according to John, Vol. I, p. 32.) And does not II Peter 3:16 assume acquaintance with all those letters of Paul that were then in circulation? Certainly, just as predestination by no means excludes human effort and exertion (Phil. 2:12, 13; II Thess. 2:13), so also inspiration by no means bars intelligent research.

(d) In our English (German, French, etc.) Bibles the Gospels follow each other in the order: Matthew, Mark, Luke, and John. In general, the Greek manuscripts and the ancient versions bear testimony to this same sequence. The fathers, as represented, for example, by Irenaeus and Origen, definitely support it.[41] In fact, until comparatively recent times the priority of Matthew was accepted, with very few exceptions, throughout the Christian

---

[41] "Matthew issued a written Gospel among the Hebrews in their own language, while Peter and Paul were preaching in Rome and establishing the church. After their departure, Mark, the disciple and interpreter of Peter, handed down to us in writing what had been preached by Peter. And Luke also, Paul's companion, recorded in a book the gospel preached by him. Afterward John, the disciple of the Lord, who had also leaned upon his breast, himself also published a Gospel during his residence in Ephesus of Asia" (Irenaeus, *Against Heresies* III.i.1).

"In the first of his *[Commentaries]* on the *Gospel according to Matthew*, defending the canon of the church, he [Origen] gives his testimony that he knows only four Gospels, writing somewhat as follows: '. . . having learned by tradition concerning the four Gospels which alone are indisputable in the church of God under heaven, that first was written the one according to the former tax-collector, later apostle of Jesus Christ, Matthew; who published it for those who from Judaism came to believe, composed as it was in the Hebrew language; secondly, that according to Mark, who wrote it in accordance with Peter's instructions, whom also Peter in his general epistle acknowledged as his son, saying, She that is in Babylon, elect together with y o u, greets y o u, as does Mark my son. And thirdly that according to Luke, who wrote for those who from the Gentiles [had come to believe], the Gospel that was praised by Paul. After them all, that according to John'" (Origen, as quoted by Eusebius, *Ecclesiastical History* VI.xxv.3-6).

church. If we regard this order as valid, Matthew cannot have used Mark's Gospel.

Answer: First of all, we find no fault with the arrangement: Matthew, Mark, Luke, John, in our Bibles. It is excellent. However, order of *arrangement* is not necessarily identical with order of *origin*. If it were, we would have to conclude that Isaiah wrote before Amos, Daniel before Hosea, and that Romans was composed before the letters to the Corinthians. Are there any scholars today who would seriously defend this order of origin or composition?

Secondly, the quoted fathers, taken literally, are referring to a Gospel of Matthew written in the language of the Hebrews. On this see the next chapter, pp. 87-91. When we here defend the priority of Mark, the reference is to our *Greek* Gospels.

Thirdly, even upon the assumption that the Gospels to which Irenaeus, Origen and others refer are substantially the same as our present Greek Gospels and their faithful modern translations, the question would still be in order: "Was the opinion that *in order of composition* Matthew's Gospel preceded that of Mark based upon thorough literary comparison? If not, is it of much importance in settling the question at hand?"[42]

Fourthly, the order of arrangement referred to—Matthew, Mark, Luke, John—is by no means unanimous. Tertullian's statement, quoted on p. 3, presupposes a different sequence. According to Eusebius (*op. cit.,* VI.xiv. 5,6) Clement of Alexandria was of the opinion that not only Matthew but also Luke was written before Mark. Whether, in Clement's view Matthew preceded Luke or vice versa is not clear. Codex Bezae has the sequence Matthew, John, Luke, and Mark. In some ancient documents the priority among the four is given to John.

It is clear, therefore, that there is no unanimous tradition defending the order Matthew, Mark, Luke, and John. Moreover, the fathers were not primarily interested in this subject. They were concerned rather with questions touching authorship, apostolic authority, and doctrinal significance. Therefore objection (d) also is of very little value as a ground for the rejection of Mark's priority.

(e) Is it not unnatural to suppose that for information which Matthew, as one of The Twelve, had already received firsthand he would resort to a book written by Mark, a man who did not even belong to the inner circle of disciples?

Answer: This is a kind of two-edged sword. It is used as a premise in two syllogisms, with widely opposite conclusions:

---

[42] Tradition should be carefully sifted. It should neither be accepted uncritically nor rejected hastily. Cf. N. B. Stonehouse, *Origins of the Synoptic Gospels,* p. 56.

Syllogism 1:

a. The apostle Matthew, eye-witness of Christ's deeds and ear-witness of his words, wrote the Gospel that bears his name.

b. A close witness, in composing a Gospel, would not have felt any need to borrow from—or use— a Gospel written by a man whose relation to Christ was not nearly as close.

c. Therefore Matthew did not use Mark.[43]

Syllogism 2:

a. Literary comparison proves that the Gospel which is by tradition ascribed to "Matthew" depends on Mark for a considerable portion of its contents.

b. A close witness, in composing a Gospel, would not have felt the need to borrow from—or use—a Gospel written by a man whose relation to Christ was not nearly as close.

c. Therefore the apostle Matthew, eye-witness of Christ's deeds and ear-witness of his words, cannot have written the Gospel that by tradition is ascribed to him.[44]

It is my belief that in both cases the conclusion is unwarranted, the reason being that the second premise is faulty. It does not do justice to the fact, corroborated by a strong and consistent tradition, that Mark was "the interpreter" of the very apostle whose name is mentioned first in every Biblical list of The Twelve, and for whom Matthew, too, must have had high regard. Moreover, does not Mark's Gospel truly reflect Christ, his person, deeds, and words? And does it not do so in a very lively, interesting manner? E. J. Goodspeed imagines that when a copy of Mark's book fell into the hands of the aged Matthew, the latter, like everybody else, was fascinated with it.[45] It is not hard to believe, therefore, that Matthew, in harmony with his own distinctive plan, used it, enlarged on it, and added much material, both from his own experience and from other sources. And should we not be grateful that such unity of spirit was present among the Gospel writers that both Matthew and Luke were delighted to use Mark's Gospel, each of these two using it in his own way?

It is clear, therefore, that none of the arguments advanced against Mark's priority has succeeded in overthrowing the weight of evidence in its favor.

The qualified endorsement of this theory would seem to be reasonable. This endorsement of Mark's priority might receive support also from a

---

[43] Cf. H. C. Thiessen, *Introduction to the New Testament*, p. 122. My disagreement with Thiessen on this particular point does not detract from my high regard for his book. Even in the treatment of The Synoptic Problem the material with which I am in hearty accord exceeds by far that which I cannot completely endorse.

[44] Cf. J. H. Ropes, *op. cit.*, pp. 37, 38.

[45] *Op. cit.*, p. 110.

world-shaking event that occurred very recently. I refer, of course, to the deciphering by Father O'Callighan of a fragment of Mark's Gospel (part of 6:52, 53). It is one of the "7Q" scraps, that is, scraps found in cave 7 near the Qumran community. At the time of its discovery (1955) the Mark fragment had been dated approximately A.D. 50. *If this date is correct,* then about two decades after Christ's death and resurrection a *copy* (!) of Mark's Gospel already existed, therefore, the original would have been written even earlier.

(3) "Q"

The theory that Matthew and Luke had, in addition to Mark, a second definable source has not met with general approval. Even by some of those who have accepted Mark as a written source for a portion of the contents of Matthew and Luke, "Q" has been rejected or is at least seriously questioned.[46] The reason for this coolness toward "Q" is not that anything in Scripture or in the conservative position would rule out the idea that additional written sources were used by the evangelists. It rests, instead, on reasons such as the following:

(a) We have Mark, but we do not have any independent—separately existing—document containing non-Marcan Matthew-Luke material. Neither has any historical reference to it ever been found.[47]

(b) "Q" is difficult to delineate. For example, does *The Lord's Prayer* belong to it? But if so, which version: Matthew's (6:9 ff.) or Luke's (11:2 ff.)? Do *The Beatitudes* belong to it? But again, in which form: Matthew's (5:3 ff.) or Luke's (6:20 ff.)? Many similar illustrations could be given. To reconstruct "Q" is simply impossible.[48]

(c) Turning now to the partial list (on p. 21) of passages representing non-Marcan Matthew-Luke material, if it be claimed that "Q" consists of "sayings of Jesus," how is it that narrative material is also included (Matt. 4:1-11, cf. Luke 4:1-13; Matt. 8:5-13, cf. Luke 7:1-10; and at least in part also Matt. 11:2 ff., cf. Luke 7:18 ff.)?

---

[46] "In the present state of knowledge, whether such a document ever existed must be regarded as uncertain" (J. H. Ropes, *op cit.,* p. 68; cf. his similar appraisal on p. 93). "There is far less evidence for the second postulate of the double source theory, the existence of 'Q'" (Herman Ridderbos, "Synoptische Kwestie," article in *Christelijke Encyclopedie,* Vol. VI, pp. 305, 306).

[47] As regards "historical reference" the situation re "Hebrew" Matthew is different. See pp. 87-89, 96.

[48] Thus also A. M. Farrer, "On Dispensing with Q," in D. E. Nineham (ed.) *Studies in the Gospels, Essays in Memory of R. H. Lightfoot,* Oxford, 1955, p. 57.

"The very elusive nature of its bounds and the silence of antiquity contribute to the uncertainty of its existence." Thus Lewis Foster, "The 'Q' Myth in Synoptic Studies," in *The Seminary Review,* published by The Cincinnati Bible Seminary, Vol. X, No. 4 (Summer 1964), p. 74. In this excellent article Foster points out that the disharmony regarding Luke's presumed debt to "Q" is so great that among five believers in "Q" there was agreement on less than half the verses that are claimed for "Q."

(d) Again, consulting the same list, how is it to be explained that the order in which the passages were recorded varies so widely in Matthew and Luke that, for example, what in Matthew is found consecutively in chapters 6, 7, and 8 (respectively, "Be not anxious," Encouragement to prayer, and the story of the centurion's faith) occurs in Luke in the reverse order, chapters 12, 11, and 7?

(e) If "Q" is conceived of—as it often is—as having been an early *Gospel,* we may well ask, "What kind of Gospel is this, one that lacks the most essential part of all, namely, the story of the crucifixion and the resurrection?" Streeter's[49] two answers to this objection are certainly very weak: *a.* the Passion story could readily be taught in oral tradition, but ethical teaching necessitated a written document; and *b.* to the apostles, except Paul, the cross was a difficulty. One might counter these answers by saying: *a.* Evidently the composers—or, according to *others* "editors"—of the Gospels in their present form did not think that a written account of Christ's death and resurrection was superfluous; why should the author of "Q" have thought so? Would he not have been shocked by the observation that his product resembled a body without a head, a tree that never bears fruit? And as to *b.* Whatever may have been the degree of difference between Paul and the others in the amount of elaboration which they severally bestowed upon the doctrine of the cross and the resurrection, is it not clear that these others as well as Paul gloried in Christ's accomplished mediatorial work as the sole basis for the sinner's hope (Acts 4:12; I Peter 1:3; 2:24; I John 1:7; Rev. 5:9; 7:14; cf. Heb. 9:22)?

It is understandable, therefore, that so-called document "Q" has not been generally accepted. In order to rescue it, attempts have been made to supplement it by adding other similar sources or modifications. For example, in answer to the objections mentioned above—see especially those under (b) and (d)—, it is claimed that there must have been more than one recension of "Q." Hence, some speak of "Q^{M.}" and "Q^{Lk.}" Or else, before the Gospel according to Luke was written in the form in which we now have it, "Q" had already been combined with "L" into "proto-Luke." Therefore, whoever it was that wrote the Gospel known to us as the one "according to Matthew" had before him one form of "Q," and the writer of Luke made use of another form. In fact each Christian center possessed a different recension of "Q."[50]

---

[49] *Op. cit.,* p. 292.

[50] According to B. H. Streeter's theory someone, perhaps Luke himself, gathered into one document ("L") previously unrecorded materials, especially some narratives and many parables. After Luke had combined "L" and "Q" into "Proto-Luke," he inserted into this document large sections of Mark. Thus arose our third Gospel. Further, a document of Jewish-Christian origin, "M," became one of the sources of our Matthew. The latter's other sources were Mark and "Q." Briefly, therefore, Streeter's theory

But superimposing one uncertainty upon another is no solution. The introduction of hypothetical source-units opens the gateway to the trackless and arid wilderness of unverifiable and often even unlikely hypotheses. It should be freely admitted, therefore, that for more than half of Matthew's Gospel and for considerably more of Luke's—that is, for all such material as is not paralleled in Mark—the theory of definable literary sources has offered no solution. As Ropes says (*op. cit.*, p. 93), this is, indeed, "a little mortifying to scholarship." The one-sided emphasis on the literary analysis of the Gospels has produced what some would call "trivial rewards."

The result has been that of late the interest of scholarship has turned in a different, we might even say in the opposite, direction; that is, away from written sources to oral tradition. What the result has been in *non*-conservative circles will be shown in the next chapter. It is known that among conservatives emphasis on "verbal inspiration" and in connection with it on the words and deeds of Jesus heralded by faithful witnesses and by their associates—that is, "by apostles and apostolic men"—has always been marked. Of late this interest in the spoken word has not diminished. Accordingly, in our attempt to find a solution to The Synoptic Problem we turn next to:

e. *Oral Tradition*

J. C. L. Gieseler (1818) and J. C. Herder (1796, 1797) ascribed the similarities between the Synoptics to oral tradition; that is, they assumed that at a very early date the oral reports concerning the words and works of Jesus had assumed a definitely fixed form. They have had many followers even among those who do not share some of the basic religious convictions of these two men. Thus even today the argument in certain conservative circles runs somewhat as follows: Was not the earliest teaching by word of mouth? Did not Jesus promise that the Holy Spirit would bring to the remembrance of the apostles all the words which their Master had spoken (John 14:26)? Is it any wonder, then, that the Synoptics show such striking

---

amounts to this, that back of Matthew and Luke are four documents: "M," connected with—i.e., embodying the traditions of—Jerusalem, Mark with Rome, "Q" with Antioch, and "L" with Caesarea. The first three—"M," Mark, and "Q"—give rise to Matthew; the last three—Mark, "Q," and "L"—to Luke, but only after "Q" and "L" had already been combined into "Proto-Luke." For the sake of completeness it should be added that according to Streeter's theory, the first two chapters of Matthew were probably derived from oral sources, and the source of Luke 1 and 2 was probably a written document, possibly Hebrew. There is much in Streeter's book that is of value and can be endorsed by even the most conservative scholar. The Four Document Theory itself, however, has been vigorously opposed, as being too speculative. With this judgment I agree. Though Streeter's entire book can be read with profit, I would refer especially to pp. 150, 199-201, 207, 208, 218, 219, and 223-272, as containing the essence of his theory, in summary. In this connection F. V. Filson's article "Gospel and Gospels" in S.H.E.R.K.; Vol. I of *The Twentieth Century supplement*, pp. 469-472, is also very instructive, and ends with an excellent Bibliography.

similarity? If it be true that there are Jewish scholars who know the Talmud throughout and Christian scholars who have committed to memory the entire New Testament, why should it be accounted strange that the earliest witnesses and their immediate followers have transmitted to us these verbally memorized sayings and reports? Is it not true that Matthew was able to record from personal observation almost all of the memorable words and deeds of Jesus which he records in his Gospel, and that he had probably gained from other primary witnesses a knowledge of those vital matters that antedated his own conversion? Is it not true that the apostle Paul treasured very highly the oral teaching of Jesus (Acts 20:35; I Cor. 7:10; 9:14; 11:23-25; and I Thess. 4:15)? And is it not also true that among the earliest disciples of the apostles this interest in the words of Jesus and of his immediate followers was continued, so that, for example, Papias, who according to Irenaeus was a disciple of John, is by Eusebius reported to have written:

"And I shall not hesitate to append to the interpretations all that I ever learned well from the elders and recall well, being confident of their truth. For, unlike most, I did not take pleasure in those who say much, but in those who teach the truth, nor in those who recount the commandments of others, but in those who repeated the commandments given to the faith by the Lord and derived from truth itself. But if ever anyone came who had followed the elders, I enquired into the words of the elders, what Andrew or Peter or Philip or Thomas or James or John or Matthew, or any other of the Lord's disciples had said, and what Aristion and the elder John,[51] the Lord's disciples, were saying. For I did not suppose that information from books would help me so much as the word of a living and abiding voice" (*op. cit.,* III.xxxix.3,4).

On the basis of all this, so runs the theory, while it is admitted that Matthew, Mark, and Luke may have used short written documents—for example, Matthew may have had access to an early collection of Old Testament prooftexts—there is no reason to believe that any one of the three evangelists used either of the other two Gospels.[52]

Evaluation: That there is a great deal of truth in this view cannot be denied. Personal observation (on the part of Matthew and John), memorization, verbal transmission of that which was seen and heard, such factors as these must have played a very important role in the formation of the Gospels. Already during the old dispensation Jehovah demanded that the children should be taught Jehovah's statutes. A definite body of truth had to

---

51 Or "the John already mentioned," see C. S. Petrie, "The Authorship of 'The Gospel according to Matthew': a Reconsideration of the External Evidence," *NTStud* 14 (Jan., 1967), pp. 15-32.
52 An excellent summary of this oral tradition theory, together with quotations from those who have accepted it, is found in H. C. Thiessen, *op. cit.,* pp. 121-129.

be handed down from generation to generation. The Israelites were not afflicted with memorization-phobia. When Moses wrote, "Give ear y o u heavens, and I will speak," he taught this song to the children of Israel (Deut. 31:22). Similarly, the children of Judah were taught The Song of the Bow, the dirge over Saul and Jonathan (II Sam. 1:18). The things which the fathers had taught their children were not hidden from the grandchildren (Ps. 78:1 ff.; see also Exod. 13:8; Deut. 6:7, 20-25; 11:19; Josh. 12:26-28).[53]

It must be admitted, therefore, that the Synoptic Problem is not solved by placing all the emphasis on literary relationships between the Synoptics. As far as we know Jesus never wrote down any of his teachings. He spoke to the people. In turn, he appointed The Twelve, and others too, to proclaim the glad tidings of salvation far and wide. Naturally, at first this transmission was chiefly oral in character (Luke 6:12-16; 9:1, 2). After his resurrection Jesus again addressed his disciples. He told them to be his witnesses to the people by teaching them (Matt. 28:16-20; Acts 1:1-3, 8). That great emphasis was placed on the fulfilment of this task appears from the account of the choosing of Matthias to take the place of Judas (Acts 1:21-26). Other passages which stress the necessity of bearing witness, and the great value of keeping the traditions are Acts 2:32; 3:15; 5:32; 10:39-43; 13:31; 22:15; 26:16; Rom. 6:17; Gal. 1:9; I Cor. 11:2, 23, 24; 15:8-11, 15; Phil. 4:9; I Thess. 4:1; II Thess. 2:15; II Tim. 2:1, 2; 4:1-5; Heb. 13:7, 8; Rev. 1:20 (the churches are light-bearers); 6:9; 11:1-13 (the two *witnesses*); and 20:4. Matthew was himself an eye-witness (so was John). According to all accounts, Mark had received his information from an eye-witness, Peter.[54] Luke also had eye-witnesses as his informants (1:2). He spent some time in Caesarea and in Jerusalem (Acts 21:8 ff.). Therefore he must have enjoyed abundant opportunities to make careful investigations. It should not be forgotten that Luke was living at a time when many of the personal followers of Jesus were still alive (I Cor. 15:6).

The eye-witnesses, in turn, had obtained their message from no one less than Jesus Christ himself. It was he who had spoken the words of life and beauty, and had illustrated them by means of his own earthly sojourn, death, resurrection, and ascension. He had proclaimed *the same* good news in *different* parts of the country, varying the wording as he saw fit. It was from him as "the Light of the world," that light shone forth kaleidoscopically. His disciples, each with a somewhat *different* purpose and in a different style, and each endowed with a different personality, proclaimed this *same* message to the world. It is clear that this factor of personal observation (on the part of some) and oral transmission (on the part of all) must be taken into

---

[53] For a brief summary of education among the Jews, with bibliography, see N.T.C. on I and II Timothy and Titus, pp. 296-299.
[54] See above, pp. 41, 42, 44.

consideration in explaining the unity amid variety that is found in the Gospels, in *all* four, but for our purpose especially in the Synoptics.

All this can be granted, but it offers no excuse for driving the Oral Tradition theory to extremes. It is clear from Luke 1:1-4 that he recognizes both oral and written narrative materials. The results of careful literary comparison should not be ignored. The argument that Matthew and Luke may have used written sources that were small in compass, but that had they used a larger account—say, an entire Gospel—this would have reduced their stature to that of mere compilers, and that this view conflicts with the doctrine of inspiration, is certainly weak. Also, we have shown that the evangelists, each according to his own plan, continually interrupt their main narrative, and afterward resume it again at the very point where they broke off. "The oral theory cannot possibly account for this freedom with which the evangelists vary the order of their record."[55] Moreover, the promise found in John 14:26 by no means implies that miracle memories would be given to the Gospel-writers.[56]

In accounting for the manner in which the Synoptics originated we should never place *oral tradition* over against *written sources,* as if this were an either-or matter. Rather, in a manner suited to each one's own purpose and under the guidance of the Holy Spirit, each Gospel-writer made the wisest use of the best sources, both oral and written. Accordingly, is there not much wisdom in the following quotations?

"It seems then all but necessary to allow for the influence of both of these modes of transmission, even though we may be unable to apportion the amount of influence which is to be ascribed to each" (J. C. Hawkins, *op. cit.,* p. 217).

"Very likely the sources were literary in part (Luke 1:1-4), and in part also oral. . . . These Gospels are not the product of a rather arbitrary compilation of already existing literary pieces, but the purposeful compositions of a richly variegated tradition with respect to the words and works of Jesus, his death, and his resurrection" (Herman Ridderbos, in the article to which reference has already been made).

In the final analysis the question, "Which came first, Matthew's Gospel or Mark's?" is not nearly as important as that other question, namely, "Where did the Synoptists get their material?" Today the apostolic origin of this material is becoming more and more clearly evident.

As to Matthew, he himself was an apostle, and probably obtained the information regarding the events that preceded his "call" from those apostles

---

[55] E. F. Scott, *The Literature of the New Testament,* p. 28.

[56] It is interesting to observe that while many opponents of the Priority of Mark theory emphasize *Matthew's* memory, there is at least one who explains the absence from Mark of the lengthy discourses of Matthew by appealing to the inadequacy of *Peter's* memory! See J. Chapman, *op. cit.,* p. 38.

that had been called earlier and/or from Jesus himself. This by no means excludes his use of Mark's Gospel.

As to Mark, as has been indicated, tradition is unanimous in its testimony that he was Peter's interpreter. Evidence also indicates that for some of his material he was dependent on Matthew's notes. Both Peter and Matthew were among the twelve apostles.

As to Luke, there is good reason to believe that he, in addition to being indirectly dependent on the apostles—the material he presents having traveled from Peter to Mark to Luke—, also, like Mark, received help from Matthew's notes. As some see it, he even received help (cf. footnote 39 on p. 43) from Matthew's Gospel. F. L. Cribbs, "St. Luke and the Johannine Tradition," *JBL*, 90 (Dec. 1971), pp. 422-450, and earlier G. W. Broomfield, J. V. Bartlet, J. A. Findlay, and others, have pointed out verbal parallels between Luke and John, another apostle. However that may be, there can be no doubt about the fact that Luke obtained his material, whether oral, written or both, from those who "from the beginning were eyewitnesses" (Luke 1:2); that is, from apostles—including John—and other witnesses.

Upon *this* fact the emphasis should rest: the material that is found in the Gospels can be traced to the earliest witnesses. All the evidence, including the character of the language that is used, the customs that are described or implied, the places that are named, the vividness of the presentation, points to the fact that we are dealing here with very early material (see also pp. 46, 47). In fact, we can go one step farther: via these earliest witnesses all the evidence points back to the Living Lord, Jesus Christ, himself. It is to him and his Spirit that these writings owe their origin.

f. *Concluding Summary*

On the basis of literary comparison, Luke 1:1-4, and ancient tradition (for example, with reference to the relation between Mark and Peter), the following would seem to be a fair statement embodying a partial solution of the Synoptic Problem:

(1) *Why are the three so similar?*

(a) Because the same Primary Author, the Holy Spirit, inspired them all, and they all record the words and deeds of the same Lord Jesus Christ.

(b) Because the three are based on observation of many of the same facts.

(c) Because the observed facts were transmitted accurately, so that the three Gospels rest upon a thoroughly harmonious oral tradition.

(d) In part also because of literary relationship, both Matthew and Luke having probably used Mark's Gospel; all three having utilized Matthew's earlier notes; Luke perhaps also Matthew's Gospel.

(2) *Why are the three so different?*

(a) Because Jesus himself proclaimed the "gospel of the kingdom" in different ways at different places, and because he performed similar deeds in various places.

(b) Because different witnesses of the works and words of Jesus made different observations. When three intelligent and honest men see the same miracle or hear the same sermon, what they see and hear will generally not be *exactly* the same thing, but will vary in accordance with the respective personality of each of the three witnesses.

(c) Because the oral transmission of these observations, though harmonious, was multiform in character.

(d) Because *more* or *less* extensive use could be made of Matthew's notes (see pp. 34, 53, 90, 96), and their contents could be inserted in various places, according to the judgment of the individual evangelist.

(e) Because in the use of sources, whether oral or written, each evangelist exercised his Spirit-guided judgment, in accordance with his own character, education and general background, and with a view to the realization of his own distinct plan and purpose.

B. *Their Reliability*

1. *Faith and Optimism*

Believers are filled with deep reverence whenever they are confronted with the Word of God, whether oral or written. Instructive in this connection is II Kings 22:8, 10b-13; 23:1-3: "And Hilkiah the high priest said to Shaphan the scribe, I have found the book of the law in the house of Jehovah. . . . And Shaphan read it before the king. And it came to pass, when the king had heard the words of the book of the law, that he rent his clothes. And the king commanded Hilkiah the priest . . . saying: Go, inquire of Jehovah for me, and for the people, and for all Judah, concerning the words of this book that is found; for great is the wrath of Jehovah that is kindled against us, because our fathers have not hearkened unto the words of this book, to do according to all that which is written concerning us. . . . And the king sent, and they gathered unto him all the elders of Judah and of Jerusalem. And the king went up to the house of Jehovah and all the men of Judah, and all the inhabitants of Jerusalem with him, and the priests, and the prophets, and all the people, both small and great: and he read in their ears all the words of the book of the covenant which was found in the house of Jehovah, to walk after Jehovah, and to keep his commandments, and his testimonies, and his statutes, with all his heart, and all his soul, to confirm the words of this covenant that were written in this book: and all the people stood to the covenant."

Another very impressive service is recorded in Neh. 8:1 ff., beginning as follows:

"Now when the seventh month had arrived, the children of Israel were in their cities. And all the people gathered as one man into the square that was before the Water Gate. And they told Ezra the scribe to bring the book of the law of Moses which Jehovah had given Israel. And on the first day of the

seventh month Ezra the priest brought the law before the assembly (consisting of) both men and women and all who were able to understand what they
heard. And he read from it facing the square before the Water Gate, from
early morning until midday, in the presence of the men and women, all who
could understand; and the ears of all the people were attentive to the book
of the law. And Ezra the scribe stood on a wooden platform that had been
made for the purpose, and beside him stood, on his right [there follow six
names], and on his left [seven names]. And Ezra opened the book in the
sight of all the people, for he was above all the people; and when he opened
it, all the people stood. . . ."

Note that in these accounts the audience stands while Scripture is being
read, just as is done in many churches even today. The people stand out of
reverence for God and his inspired Word. This indicates that one's attitude to
this divine message, whether oral or written, is largely determinative of the
blessing he receives or fails to receive.

Whether or not Scripture—and this includes the Gospels—is the very Word
of God is a question that has been decided by God himself: Exod. 20:1; II
Sam. 23:2; Isa. 8:20; Mal. 4:4; Matt. 1:22; Acts 1:16; 7:38; 13:34; Rom.
1:2; 3:2; 4:23; 15:4; I Cor. 2:4-10; 6:16; 9:10; 14:37; Gal. 1:11, 12; 3:8,
16, 22; 4:30; I Thess. 1:5; 2:13; Heb. 1:1, 2; 3:7; 9:8; 10:15; II Peter 1:21;
3:16; I John 4:6; Rev. 22:19; and last but not least II Tim. 3:16, 17: "All
Scripture (is) God-breathed and useful for teaching, for reproof, for correc-
tion, for training in righteousness, that the man of God may be equipped, for
every good work thoroughly equipped." The men who wrote the sacred
writings were "carried along" by the Holy Spirit. That same Spirit bears
witness by and with the Word whenever the latter is accepted by believing
hearts. It is thus that they become convinced of Scripture's authority. Cf.
Westminster Confession, Chapter I, article V.[57]

The fact that a person's basic attitude toward the Word of God—whether
spoken or written—determines, in large measure, the effect which the confrontation with that Word will have upon him is very clear from Luke's
account of Christ's preaching at Nazareth. The attitude of the audience was
one of wonder and . . . disbelief (4:22). The end-result was an attempt to
assassinate the One who had spoken the words of life (4:28, 29). So also,
throughout history, *the prior conviction* that the Gospels cannot be true
leads one to look for errors and discrepancies. Whoever approaches these
books with that inner disposition of heart and mind will cry "Contradiction!" whenever in two parallel accounts he sees something which on the
surface looks like a discrepancy. Often he finds contradictions because he is

---

57 See S. E. Anderson, *Our Dependable Bible,* Grand Rapids, 1960, pp. 129-143; also
The Infallible Word, edited by N. B. Stonehouse and Paul Woolley, Grand Rapids, fourth
printing, 1958, pp. 43, 44.

looking for them. An honest attempt to harmonize the two accounts, without interpreting either in a forced or unnatural manner, is simply *dismissed* as being *unscholarly*. Writes Dr. J. Murray, "Frequently the doctrine of verbal inspiration is dismissed with supercilious scorn as but a remnant of that mediaeval or post-Reformation scholasticism that has tended to petrify Christianity." He calls attention to the fact that this doctrine is often erroneously interpreted as if it involved the theory of mechanical dictation and consequently as if it left no room for "the diversity . . . in those that were the human instruments in the production of Scripture."[58] He concludes by stating: "The rejection of the inerrancy of Scripture means the rejection of Christ's own witness to Scripture. Finally and most pointedly, then, the very integrity of Our Lord's witness is the crucial issue in this battle of the faith."[59] Anyone who will take the time to examine Luke 24:44; John 5:39; 10:34, 35; 14:26; 16:13, as to the nature and contents of Christ's witness to Scripture, will see that Dr. Murray had every right to make this statement.

Unbelief, moreover, breeds *despair*. Faith, on the other hand, produces *optimism*. The Gospels proclaim a Christ who arose from the dead and lives forevermore as the believer's Savior and Friend. Faith is indeed the victory that overcomes the world (I John 5:4).

On the part of those who reject God's Word, oral or written, it has been made the object of *destruction* (Jer. 36:22, 23), *distortion* (Mark 14:57, 58; Rom. 3:8; 6:1; Gal. 1:8, 9), and *disdain* (II Kings 7:1, 2; II Peter 3:4). This was true in Bible times and has continued to the present. Sometimes, however, the rejection seems to be only partial and/or is presented in a refined manner by men of great learning who, in the process of discarding what has long been accepted as true, will here and there even come forth with ideas that are of some value toward the advance of the scientific understanding of the Bible, but whose basic approach, nevertheless, leads them to accept untenable main conclusions. What happens in such cases is this, that what is so confidently affirmed by one famous critic, usually in a setting of seemingly irrefutable arguments, is denounced by the next one, who similarly presents his own theory as the well-established result of scholarly enquiry. When, in turn, this second individual also passes on—or sometimes even while he is still alive!—there follows a third, who with great enthusiasm advocates still another critical view, which for a while enjoys great popularity, and then, after a brief period of incandescence, streaks meteorlike to its doom.

---

58 *The Infallible Word*, p. 39, including footnote 12. That this attack and misrepresentation is still continuing is evident from the otherwise excellent article by Warren Weaver, "Can a Scientist Believe in God?" *Reader's Digest*, May, 1968, p. 131.
59 *Op. cit.*, p. 40.

Since the book you are reading is a Commentary and not a work in Gospel Criticism there is room for only a few illustrations of what the writer has in mind. The main thesis will, I trust be clear, however. It is expressed beautifully in Isaiah 40:6-8, ending with the words, "The grass withers, the flower fades; but the word of our God shall stand forever."

2. Harnack and Liberalism
a. Description

There was, for example, Karl Gustav Adolf Harnack, German Lutheran (1851-1930). Famous as a professor of church history, as librarian (director of the Royal Library in Berlin), and as author, his brilliant lectures delivered at the University of Berlin during the winter semester 1899-1900, attracted a vast audience of students, and were subsequently published, first in German (*Das Wesen des Christentums*) and later in English (*What Is Christianity?*, London, 1901). The amazing effectiveness of these and other lectures, and also many facts about the life and talents of Harnack, are most interestingly, though at times perhaps too sympathetically, portrayed by Wilhelm Pauck, in his book *Harnack and Troeltsch: Two Historical Theologians*, Oxford, 1968. Harnack wrote many other works,[60] including *The Origin of the New Testament* (translation of *Die Entstehung des Neuen Testaments*), London, 1925, and, the most famous of them all, *History of Dogma* (translation of *Lehrbuch der Dogmengeschichte*), 7 volumes, London, 1895-1900.

Now what did this world-renowned scholar teach with reference to Jesus and the trustworthiness of the Gospel accounts? The answer is that Harnack was the "Mr. Liberal" of his day. According to the Liberal view, in the time covered by the Gospels nothing really happened that is incapable of purely scientific explanation. Jesus was a man, definitely not "the Son of God" *in the confessional sense*. He was, however, a most wonderful man, the pure and humble teacher of righteousness, the very embodiment of simple trust in the heavenly Father with whom he was united in spirit. What is needed by everyone, therefore, is not the faith *in* Jesus as Redeemer and resurrected Lord, but the faith *of* Jesus, that is, the faith which he exercised, for he proclaimed not himself but the Father. Said Harnack, "The gospel, as Jesus proclaimed it, has to do with the Father only and not with the Son."[61] According to this view it is men's task, by pondering and especially by taking to heart the example and words of Jesus, to capture his very spirit and, thus ennobled, to reach intimate fellowship with God. It is, accordingly, not the Easter *message*, the report of Jesus' actual, physical resurrection from the grave, that we should be concerned about, but the Easter *faith*. That faith *of* Jesus must become the dominant power in our lives.

---

[60] For an enumeration of titles see S.H.E.R.K., Vol. V, pp. 157, 158, and its Extension, *Twentieth Century Encyclopaedia*, Grand Rapids, p. 492.

[61] *What Is Christianity?*, p. 144.

As to the reliability of the Gospel accounts? As Harnack sees it, the entire New Testament, including the Gospels, is already a tradition that overlies and obscures the actual historical facts.[62] The natural interest in the words and deeds of Jesus and especially in the striking manner of his death, followed by reports of his resurrection, was one of several factors which led the early church to assign a saving significance to that death. However, by doing this it was departing from the central emphasis of Jesus' own teaching. Of course, this new development, according to which the gospel came to mean the good news of the divine plan of salvation, which in fulfilment of prophecy was accomplished through the death and resurrection of Christ, did not arise all at once. It developed gradually. It was pushed to the fore with peculiar force by Paul. Historically the farther the early church was separated from the earthly life of Jesus, the more error began to eclipse the truth.

Now, according to the Liberal view, it is in the Gospel of Mark, which echoes the preaching of Peter, that we catch the most true and vivid glimpse of the life and teaching of *the purely human Jesus.* Not as if *everything* recorded in that Gospel is reliable, but it enables us to penetrate beyond the husk to the kernel of truth regarding the historical Jesus and the faith he lived by. Mark's Gospel, therefore, is mainly historical instead of doctrinal. It pictures Jesus as being himself a believer, not an object of faith.

b. *Evaluation*

The dubious character of Liberalism's reconstruction of sacred history is today admitted on every side. But since its *chief* weakness pertains not only to it but even to those schools of thought that have risen in opposition to certain of its tenets, a discussion of that basic flaw will be postponed until also these conflicting theories have been summarized and evaluated. One serious defect can, however, be mentioned at once; namely this, that the Liberal reconstruction grossly misinterprets Mark; for that Gospel, far from portraying Jesus as if he were merely human, describes him as being, in very truth, the Son of God, the object of adoration and worship. In fact, Mark's Christology is *essentially* the same as that of Matthew, Luke, John, and Paul! It is not denied, of course, that in Mark the *human* side of Christ is throughout clearly taught and presupposed (2:16; 3:9, 31; 4:38; 6:5; 13:32; 15:37). But according to this evangelist the two natures, human and divine (to use later terminology), are in perfect harmony. This is a fact which, in studying certain passages, one can hardly fail to detect (4:38, 39; 6:34, 41-43; 8:1-10; 14:32-41; etc.). And the opinion according to which Mark's Gospel stresses the human side of Jesus at the expense of the divine is certainly erroneous. This evangelist pictures Jesus as being, in truth, *the Son of God.* Moreover, this designation is applied to him not only by Mark

---

62 *The Origin of the New Testament,* pp. 43, 44.

himself (1:1),[63] but also, according to Mark, by the demons (3:11; 5:7), the centurion (15:39),[64] the heavenly Father—and this in connection both with the Son's baptism (1:11) and his transfiguration (9:7)[65] —and even by Jesus himself (14:61, 62), and that in a sense so exalted that those who rejected him considered this claim to be nothing less than blasphemy (14:63, 64).

But in order to reach a conclusion regarding Mark's opinion of Jesus we should not limit ourselves to a consideration of the *titles* which this evangelist ascribes to him who is both "Son of God" and "Son of man." Mark's *narrative* of the words and deeds of this exalted person must also be studied. When this is done it becomes apparent that sonship in the highest sense is indicated here. According to Mark the one whom he describes reigns supreme in the realm of *disease, demons, and death*. As such he heals diseases of every variety, casts out demons (1:32-34), cures the blind, the deaf, etc. (8:22-26; 10:46-52), cleanses the leper (1:40-45), and even raises the dead (5:21-24, 35-43). He exercises power over the domain of nature in general; for he stills winds and waves (4:35-41), walks on water (6:48), causes a fig tree to wither (11:13, 14, 20), and multiplies a few rolls so that they suffice to satisfy the hunger of thousands (6:30-44; 8:1-10). His knowledge of the future is so detailed and comprehensive that he predicts what will happen to Jerusalem, to the world, to his disciples (chap. 13), and to himself (9:9, 31; 10:32-34; 14:17-21). His authority is so outstanding that he pronounces pardon in a manner befitting God and no one else (2:1-12, especially verses 5 and 6). The climax of his majesty is revealed in this that when he is put to death he rises again (16:6)!

As to whether Mark pictures this Jesus as the object of faith, this question, too, must be answered with a vigorous affirmative, really already implied in the foregoing. "Jesus Christ, the Son of God," is immediately introduced as the Lord whose coming, in accordance with prophecy, demands a herald or way-preparer (1:1-3). He is the One to whom the angels minister (1:13). He baptizes with the Holy Spirit (1:8), is Lord even of the sabbath (2:28), appoints his own ambassadors (3:13-19), has a right to be accepted *in faith* even by those of "his own country," (implied in 6:6), has

---

[63] Discussion of the authenticity of the words υἱοῦ Θεοῦ in this passage will be found in commentaries on Mark. Suffice it to say at this point that Grk. N.T.(A-B-M-W) includes these words in the text, though between brackets.

[64] Though it would be wrong to read into this title as uttered by the centurion the full meaning which Christians see in it—as if he were thinking of eternal, essential, co-equal sonship—would it not be equally wrong to interpret it as if his exclamation meant no more than this, "To be sure, there was a spark of divinitv in this man"? The latter explanation disregards both the context (Mark 15:39 *in full*) and the Matthew 27:54 parallel. Did the centurion really think that one who is not even super-human could cause the earth to quake, rocks to split, tombs to be opened, etc.?

[65] The Father, moreover, did not declare that by means of baptism or transfiguration Jesus *had now become* the Son of God. On the contrary, the Father declared him *to be* "my beloved Son," his Son, therefore, in a unique sense.

authority to bid men follow and receive him (8:34; 9:37), is the very One whom David called "Lord" (implied in 12:37), and as "Son of man" is coming again in clouds with power and great glory, when he will send forth the angels to gather his elect (13:26, 27).[66]

3. *Wrede and Skepticism*

a. *Description*

It is not surprising, therefore, that the Liberal view of Mark was unable to maintain itself. Even during the lifetime of its chief advocates it was already being attacked. One of its main opponents was the German New Testament scholar William Wrede.[67] In his brief life (1859-1906) he emphasized again and again that the view according to which Mark's Gospel is mainly historical instead of doctrinal, and fails to present Jesus as an object of worship, is an error. Wrede exposes this error in his well-known book *Das Messiasgeheimnis in den Evangelien,* published in 1901; also in his posthumous publication *The Origin of the New Testament* (translation of *Die Entstehung der Schriften des Neuen Testaments*), London and New York, 1909. This book contains a series of lectures originally delivered to laymen. The style is crisp and lucid. Wrede had the rare gift of expressing himself in language that everyone was able to understand. He defends the view that not only Matthew and Luke but also Mark describes Jesus Christ as the object of faith (pp. 52, 73, etc.).

Now if Wrede had stopped here he might have rendered an outstanding service to the cause of Christian scholarship. He went farther, however, He argued that although it is true that the Gospels picture Jesus as the object of faith, *they are wrong in doing this.* These Gospels, he believed, give us a picture of the subjective opinions of the early Christian community. They do not contain the actual history of Jesus. In *The Origin of the New Testament* (p. 73) he says: "Even our Gospel of Mark, sad as it may seem to us to say, in no way simply depicts the life of Jesus as it was." In his *Messiasgeheimnis* (*Messianic Secret*) he describes Mark's book as being self-contradictory and unreliable. It tells us that Jesus performed the most stupendous miracles, yet forbids people to make these known. To the disciples he reveals himself as the Messiah, yet forbids them to divulge this. Why? Wrede's solution: In the beginning—that is, during Jesus' lifetime—the latter had never been regarded as the Messiah, neither had he himself made this claim. The early Christian

---

[66] Note also the expression "little ones who believe on me" (9:42), though in connection with this there is a textual question with respect to the phrase "on [or "in"] me."

[67] For a list of all of Wrede's principal works see S.H.E.R.K., Vol. XII, Grand Rapids, p. 444. In his *Paul* (translation of *Paulus*), London, 1907, Wrede draws a sharp contrast between Jesus and Paul. The latter, as Wrede saw it, was not a disciple of Jesus but the second founder of Christianity. J. Gresham Machen has refuted this position in his excellent book, *The Origin of Paul's Religion,* Grand Rapids, 1947.

community believed, however, that by means of the resurrection Jesus had been made the Messiah, a belief reflected, according to Wrede, in Acts 2:36; Rom. 1:4. So now, looking back, as it were, from the vantage point of belief in Jesus' Messiahship, the church reasoned that if the Jesus who before his death had walked among men was at that time the prospective Messiah, then even during this earlier period he must already have been aware of, and must have given some evidence of, his future dignity. Thus by Mark (and to a degree also by the other evangelists) Messiahship was read back into those pre-crucifixion days, but in such a manner that by order of Jesus himself it had to be kept a secret at that time. After the resurrection it could be publicly revealed.

It is clear, therefore, that according to Wrede the Gospels are manipulations. They are not reliable.

b. *Evaluation*

Wrede was in the habit of presenting his conclusions as being the result of earnest study and research, uncontaminated by mere theological opinion or prejudice. See his *Origin of the New Testament,* p. 4. Having thus created an attitude of trust on the part of the listeners and/or readers, he proceeds to state a good many mere opinions, presenting them as if they were established facts; for example, (1) that Paul was a man who did not see the brighter side of things, p. 16; (2) that Paul's reasoning in Gal. 3:16 is pure rabbinism, p. 20; (3) that there is a striking difference between the teaching of Jesus and of Paul, p. 23; (4) that Paul wrote a letter to the Laodiceans that has disappeared, p. 26; and (5) that Ephesians, not written by Paul, is merely an extension of Colossians, pp. 40, 43.[68]

When therefore in the same book, in discussing the origin and reliability of the Gospels, he states: (6) that the histories of Jesus' childhood in Matthew and *Mark* [did he mean Matthew and *Luke?*] are to be regarded throughout as myth, p. 61; and (7) that all human tradition implies alteration, p. 70, giving this as one of the reasons why our Gospels, including Mark and his Messianic Secret, cannot be regarded as reliable, we have the right to question the value of such unproved assertions.

4. *Schweitzer and Pessimism*

a. *Description*

Wrede's thoroughgoing skepticism, generally expressed with characteristic clarity and vigor, could not remain unnoticed. There were reactions; some unfavorable, some favorable. A sample of each will now be given.

First of all, then, let us look at what may be regarded as being to a considerable extent an *unfavorable* reaction; namely, that of a Protestant

---

68 I have discussed all these matters in the volumes of N.T.C. Thus, on (1) see the volume on *Philippians,* pp. 20, 21; on (2) the one on *Galatians,* pp. 134-137; on (3), same volume, pp. 94, 192; on (4) the one on *Colossians and Philemon,* pp. 194-197; and on (5) the one on *Ephesians,* pp. 5-32.

theologian who was born at Kayserburg, in the Rhenish province of Upper Alsace, Albert Schweitzer (1875-1965). He is not a stranger to our times. Again and again newspaper and magazine articles have brought his name to the attention of the general public. While those whose specialty is music will always remember him as the author of a great biography and commentary on Johann Sebastian Bach, a work that is still considered a classic, most people knew him especially as a philanthropist, a Nobel Prize winner, the mission-ary-surgeon who virtually sacrificed himself for the cause of the poor and distressed in Africa. It was in the year 1913 that he left his pastorate and professorship to establish the famous hospital at Lambarene, Gabon (former-ly French Equatorial Africa). Except for some lecture and concert tours to raise money for this hospital, he remained among the Africans until the day of his death at the age of 90. The value of the services which he rendered to the distressed of almost every description—including those afflicted with sleeping sickness, malaria, elephantiasis, and leprosy—can hardly be over-estimated. He greatly endeared himself to thousands of Africans, his creed being that every person should sacrifice a portion of his own time for others. In fact, the sacredness not only of *human* but of *all* life was one of the points on which he placed great stress, even to such an extent, it was said, that at the hospital mosquitoes must not be swatted!

For our purpose, however, it is especially Schweitzer *the theologian* who demands investigation. His brief treatise, *The Secret of the Messiahship and the Passion,* appeared in print in the year 1901, on the very day that Wrede's *Messianic Secret in the Gospels* was also published. Schweitzer's shorter work was subsequently expanded into *The Quest of the Historical Jesus* (translation of *Von Reimarus zu Wrede*), 1906. Among his many other writings of special interest to the theologian are: *Paul and His Interpreters,* 1912; *The Mystery of the Kingdom,* 1914; and *Christianity and the Reli-gions of the World,* 1923.[69]

Now, in a sense Schweitzer's forerunner was Wrede. This is true in at least two respects: (1) Both rejected the Liberal reconstruction of the personality of Jesus, described earlier. *That* Jesus of Nazareth, said Schweitzer, "is a figure designed by rationalism, endowed with life by liberalism, and clothed by a modern theology in a historical garb."[70] (2) Both emphasized the eschatological element in the Gospels; that is, both stressed the fact that, *according to the Gospels,* the mind of Jesus was occupied with dramatic events that were yet to be. The difference between the two was, however, this, that while Wrede regarded this prominence of the eschatological ele-

---

69 Fascinating and not without theological interest are his books on more general themes; such as, *On the Edge of the Primeval Forest,* 1922; *The Decay and Restoration of Civilization,* 1923; *Out of My Life and Thought,* 1933; and *Indian Thought and Its Development,* 1936.

70 *The Quest of the Historical Jesus,* p. 396.

ment in the thinking of Jesus as *unhistorical,* Schweitzer viewed it as *historical.* Or, phrasing it differently, what Wrede regarded as *Mark's dogma,* that of the Messianic secret, Schweitzer himself viewed as *Jesus' own belief.*

Schweitzer, in other words, had no patience with Wrede's thoroughgoing skepticism. Though he himself rejected the miracles, he saw no justification whatever for Wrede's refusal to accept the Gospels as being, in the main, historical. What if Jesus was represented by Mark as pre-occupied with what was going to be, was not the very atmosphere of the times saturated with eschatology? Why, then, would it have been so strange for Jesus to speak of his *coming* greatness and of the *future* kingdom? What good reason is there, after all, for regarding Mark's description of the ardent hopes of Jesus as being nothing more than a distortion created by the early Christian community and particularly by Mark?

However, lest we begin to think that Schweitzer's own views regarding Jesus and God's kingdom are more nearly in line with conservative theology than those of Wrede, let it be stated at once that were we to shift our allegiance from Wrede to Schweitzer we would merely be shifting the responsibility for error from Mark to Jesus himself! According to Schweitzer not so much Mark but Jesus himself was committing a tragic error. It was Jesus who was deluded.

From Schweitzer's theological writings—*especially* from *The Mystery of the Kingdom*—we derive the following summary of the life of Jesus, according to the Gospels as interpreted by the surgeon-musician-theologian (or -philosopher):

The public ministry of Jesus covered but a brief period. He began his ministry at the season of the summer seed-sowing and ended it upon the cross at Passover-time of the following year. At his baptism he became aware of the fact that he was going to be the Messiah. However, as such he must remain unrecognized until the new era dawns. In the Sermon on the Mount he teaches that the meek, the peacemakers, etc., are blessed, in the sense that they are destined for the kingdom-to-be. Though, according to Schweitzer, the spirit of this sermon is valuable for all time, for ethics is the very essence of religion,[71] nevertheless, it was not at all the purpose of Jesus to establish a new morality on earth, a gradually developing stable, ethical society. On the contrary, the kingdom of which Jesus was thinking was to arrive very soon, suddenly, supernaturally, and by means of a catastrophic cosmic upheaval through which evil was to be completely overcome. Accordingly, the ethics which Jesus proclaimed was really "interim ethics," that is, ethics with a view to the state of perfection which was to be supernaturally

---

71 Although Schweitzer combated the Liberal view, he remained, nevertheless, in some respects a Liberal at heart, as is evident especially from *The Quest of the Historical Jesus,* p. 397; and from *My Life and Thought,* pp. 73 ff.

brought in. Jesus taught the people to repent as a preparation for this eschatological kingdom, to be divinely established. Its arrival would, however, be preceded by a brief season of affliction in which believers must share. This affliction was to be not only a probation but an atonement, a satisfaction for the sins committed in the present era. Jesus sends his disciples on a mission tour, and expects the sudden, catastrophic dawn of the kingdom before their return. By means of a so-called miraculous feeding he consecrates the multitudes for entrance into this kingdom. On the Mount of Transfiguration he reveals to three of his disciples the secret of his Messiahship. Some had regarded him as the Forerunner. Jesus, however, now indicates that the kingdom is much closer: he himself is the Messiah; the Forerunner was John the Baptist. Through the reading of deutero-Isaiah Jesus discovers that the kingdom will be established without a preceding general tribulation, and that, instead, he himself will suffer for many. By and large Christ's followers, however, are not aware of the secret of the Messiahship. Hence, the entrance into Jerusalem is an ovation to one whom the multitude reveres not as the Messiah, but as the Forerunner. Judas learns the secret of Jesus' claim to Messiahship, and reveals it to the chief priests. They plot his death. "On the afternoon of the fourteenth of Nisan, as they ate the Pascal lamb at even, he uttered a loud cry and died." He died "despairing of bringing in the new heaven and the new earth." His life ended in tragedy, in utter pessimism and disillusionment, for the kingdom had not arrived.

b. *Evaluation*

Now in this presentation there are some items that are worthy of a degree of appreciation: (1) Schweitzer regards as historical many of the Gospel accounts which Wrede rejects. (2) He emphasizes that it is God, not man, who establishes the kingdom; it is "the kingdom *of God*" (cf. Matt. 6:10). And (3) he rightly perceives that in the teaching of Jesus "the kingdom of God" is ultimately an eschatological entity, a future state of bliss in which the will of the entire redeemed society will be in complete harmony with God's will (cf. Matt. 13:40-43; 19:28, 29; 25:34; Mark 9:47; Luke 12:32; 13:28, 29; 21:31; cf. I Cor. 6:9, 10; 15:50; Gal. 5:21; Eph. 5:5; II Thess. 1:5; etc.).

Having said this, however, the erroneous elements should also be pointed out: (1) For the climactic ending of the Gospels Schweitzer has substituted his own thoroughly pessimistic anticlimax; for victory, tragedy. (2) He has failed to show how his eschatological Jesus can be reconciled with his Liberal Jesus. (3) It is a question whether Jesus, as he pictures him, tortured from beginning almost to the very end by an obsession, can even be regarded as being completely sane. It is not surprising, therefore, that for his medical degree Schweitzer wrote a dissertation on the theme, *The Psychiatric Estimate of Jesus* (translation of *Die psychiatrische Beurteilung Jesu*), Boston,

1948. And (4) Schweitzer's one-sided emphasis on the eschatological aspect of the kingdom, as if that is all there is to it, ignores an entire chain of passages in which Jesus stresses the fact that the kingdom (or kingship, royal rule) is a present and continually developing, spiritual reality (Matt. 12:28; 19:14; Mark 4:26 ff.; 10:15; 12:34; Luke 7:28; 17:20, 21).

Like the theory of Harnack and that of Wrede, so also that of Schweitzer has been weighed and, in the light of Scripture, has been found wanting. Moreover, as mentioned earlier, what is probably the chief weakness of this and the preceding views is reserved for later discussion.

5. Bultmann and Radicalism

a. Description

Soon after World War I some German scholars began to concentrate their attention on the word of mouth transmission of Christ's words and of the reports concerning his actions. They began to study the manner in which the teachings of Jesus and the narratives respecting him had been circulated during the period between his death and the time when the Gospels were written. They were encouraged in this pursuit by the fact that the one-sided emphasis on the literary analysis of the Gospels had produced such "trivial rewards," as has been shown in Chapter II A. Among the scholars who undertook this new task two names stand out prominently, Martin Dibelius[72] and Rudolf Bultmann. If Wrede was a skeptic or agnostic, Bultmann may not unjustly be called a radical.

He was born Aug. 20, 1884, in Wiefelstede, in what was then the Grand Duchy of Oldenburg, Germany. Being the oldest son of an evangelical Lutheran minister, he studied theology at Tübingen, Berlin, and Marburg. Among those who strongly influenced him were: at Tübingen Karl Müller, the church historian, and at Berlin the famous Adolf Harnack (discussed earlier) and Herman Gunkel, the renowned Old Testament scholar (1862-1932). It was Gunkel who, in association with J. F. W. Bousset, developed the "history of religion" approach to Biblical literature, as is clear from his writings; in which, for example, he treats Genesis as a collection of sagas or legends. This approach led to what came to be known as Form Criticism, a term which today is by many immediately associated with Dibelius and Bultmann. At Marburg it was Johannes Weiss whose eschatological emphasis is reflected in Bultmann's writings, and who encouraged him to continue his studies toward the doctorate. Other Marburg professors to whom Bultmann

---

[72] Dibelius was a Lutheran theologian (1883-1947), born in Dresden, Saxony. After teaching at Berlin (1908-1915), he accepted an appointment as professor of New Testament in Heidelberg (1915), where he remained until his death. He has been called "the founder of the School of Form Criticism." In addition to Commentaries on the smaller epistles of Paul, books on Jesus and on Paul, and several other volumes, he wrote *From Tradition to Gospel* (translation of *Die Formgeschichte des Evangeliums*), New York, 1935.

himself acknowledges indebtedness were Adolf Jülicher and Wilhelm Hermann.

Preparatory study was followed by teaching. It was while teaching at Breslau that Bultmann wrote the book that deeply stirred the theological world, namely, *The History of the Synoptic Tradition.*[73] A popular abridgment of this work is *The Study of the Synoptic Gospels.*[74] It is in these books that Bultmann sets forth his ideas regarding *Form Criticism.*

From 1921 to his retirement in 1951 Bultmann was professor of New Testament and Early Christian History at Marburg. While there he accepted an invitation to deliver an address at Alpirsbach, Germany, before the Society of Evangelical Theology. His article, "New Testament and Mythology," is based on this address.[75] It is with this article (and later writings) that Bultmann's second approach to the New Testament, namely, *Demythologization,* is generally linked. The two approaches—Form Criticism and Demythologization—are, however, closely related. In fact, in the opinion of several writers the gist of the second approach is already implied in the first.[76]

What, then, is Bultmann's attitude toward the New Testament, particularly toward the Gospels? Revealing is the fact that he calls *Wrede's Messianic Secret in the Gospels* "undoubtedly the most important work in the field of gospel research in the generation now past."[77] In his writings on Form Criticism he develops his own argument as follows. He is convinced that the original tradition consisted for the most part of brief single units, fixed forms; such as, miracle stories (and other stories about Jesus), apothegms

---

[73] German title: *Die Geschichte der synoptischen Tradition,* first published in Göttingen, 1921 (third edition 1957). The English translation was published in New York and Evanston, 1963.

[74] This is found on pp. 5-75 of a volume whose title-page reads: "*Form Criticism, A New Method of New Testament Research,* including *The Study of the Synoptic Gospels* by Rudolf Bultmann, and *Primitive Christianity in the Light of Gospel Research* by Karl Kundsin, Translated by Frederick C. Grant." It was published in Chicago and New York, 1934. The German original of Bultmann's part bears the title: *Die Erforschung der Synoptischen Evangelien.*

[75] The article appeared first in 1941, and was republished in Hans-Werner Bartsch (ed.), *Kerygma und Mythos* I, 1948; English translation *Kerygma and Myth: A Theological Debate,* London, 1953.

[76] For the titles of his other books, for works relating to Bultmann, and for other excellent material on Bultmann, both descriptive and critical, I would refer to R. D. Knudson's contribution in P. E. Hughes (ed.), *Creative Minds in Contemporary Theology,* Grand Rapids, Mich., 1966, pp. 131-159, with Bibliography on pp. 160-162. See also N. B. Stonehouse's valuable accounts in *Origins of the Synoptic Gospels,* pp. 168-175; and in *Paul before the Areopagus,* Grand Rapids, 1957, Chapter 5. For periodical literature see Bruce M. Metzger (compiler), *Index to Periodical Literature on Christ and the Gospels,* Grand Rapids, 1962, pp. 171-177; 188-191, and see Index, p. 559 under Bultmann; and for the most recent literature (both books and articles) see the continuing issues of *New Testament Abstracts.*

[77] *The Study of the Synoptic Gospels,* p. 22.

(short stories that reach their climax in pointed sayings), parables, proverbs, prophecies, sayings about the law, and legends. There is also a more extended Passion Narrative, followed by a Resurrection Account. Further, he believes that many of these units were derived from outside sources; that is, not from the actual, historical words and works of Jesus, but from Jewish apocalyptic and rabbinic originals and from Hellenism. Indications of time and place and other interesting touches were added. The story grew. Thus Mark (9:17) relates that a father brought his demon-possessed son to Jesus. Luke (9:38) adds that this was an *only* son. Again, Mark (3:1) speaks about a withered hand that was healed. Luke (6:6) tells us that this was the *right* hand.

Discussing the units one by one, there are, first of all, *the miracle stories.* Bultmann mentions them in connection with Hellenistic tales, according to one of which an exorcist expels a demon by placing a ring in front of the demoniac's nose so that he might smell a potent root that had been set in that ring; and, according to another, a snake-bitten foot is cured by means of a chip from a virgin's gravestone.

Apothegms may be divided into two classes: (1) those that have been formulated in a Jewish environment, and (2) those that belong to the later Hellenistic period. Those of the first class often consist of a question and a counter-question or brief parable (or both at once). See Mark 2:19; 3:4, 24-26; etc. Those of the second class are introduced by such words as, "When he was asked by" (Luke 17:20, 21). However, at times the loose connection between pointed saying and framework shows that only *the saying* is a word of Jesus, while *the context* was supplied at a later time (Mark 2:15-17; 7:1-23; 10:2-12).

Parables, too, according to Bultmann, owe their origin to the later situation, at least in part. At times what was originally a very brief, real parable, with a single central lesson ("third of comparison"), was changed into an allegory, an extended metaphor in which each of several symbols has a separate meaning. An interpretation, not originating with Jesus, was even added, to suit the needs of the early church. See the parables of *The Sower* (Mark 4:1-20) and of *The Tares* (Matt. 13:24-30, 36-43).

Similarly, many a *proverb* is attributed to Jesus; for example, "Out of the abundance of the heart the mouth speaks" (Matt. 12:34b). See also Matt. 6:34b; 24:28; Luke 12:2, 3; 16-20; etc. As Bultmann sees it, we must reckon with the possibility that many of these, too, were not authentic. They may have been derived from Jewish proverbial lore (wisdom literature).

As to *prophecies,* so the German scholar continues, while some were no doubt authentic words of Jesus, others were probably uttered by Christian prophets that arose in the early church after Christ's death. To the latter type belong such sayings as, "Behold, I stand at the door and knock" (Rev. 3:20); "Behold, I come as a thief" (Rev. 16:15); and thus also in the

Gospels, "Behold I send you forth as sheep in the midst of wolves" (Matt. 10:16a).

Then there are *sayings about the law;* such as, words concerning purity (Mark 7:15) and divorce (Mark 10:11, 12); the antitheses ("Y o u have heard . . . but I say," Matt. 5:21, 22; etc.); and utterances concerning alms-giving, prayer, and fasting (Matt. 6:2-18). Even though also many of these may have originated not with Jesus but with the community, yet their spirit is that of Jesus. According to Bultmann, products of the community and not derived from Jesus were also: "Do not think that I am come to destroy the law or the prophets" (Matt. 5:17); rules of discipline (Matt. 16:18, 19; 18:15-22); and mission regulations (Matt. 10:5-16), including even The Great Commission (Matt. 28:19, 20; cf. Luke 24:49).

Legends are said to abound in *The Passion and Resurrection Narratives.* Jesus really died on the cross but physically he never rose again, says Bultmann. According to him products of pious fancy and apologetic interest are also the story of the weeping women (Luke 23:27-31), that of the death of Judas (Matt. 27:3-10), and that of the watch at the grave (Matt. 27:63-66). Other legends are said to be those concerning Jesus' temptation and transfiguration. The record of his baptism is also not regarded as free from legendary elements.

From all this it appears that for Bultmann the Gospels are not to any great extent a witness to the words and works of Jesus. Rather, they bear testimony to the faith of the early Christian community. They must be viewed as the outgrowth of its "situation-in-life"; particularly, of the needs resulting from its missionary endeavors, discipline, liturgy, and catechetical instruction. By and large, therefore, the historical facts about Jesus himself are beyond our reach. With respect to not a single word of Jesus, says Bultmann, is it possible to produce positive evidence of its authenticity.[78]

Nevertheless, he holds that the historical message of Jesus is evident from a consistent series of passages; for example, "For whosoever will save his life shall lose it; but whosoever shall lose his life [for my sake and the gospel's], the same shall save it" (Mark 8:35). See also Luke 9:60, 62; 11:31, 32; 12:54-56; 14:26, 27; etc.

Bultmann's Form Criticism implies, therefore, that in order to discover what can really be attributed to Jesus himself—the original strands of his teaching, both ethical and eschatological—we must remove from the record not only the editorial elaborations or augmentations but also whatever reflects situations that arose after the crucifixion. A substantial portion of the Gospels is said to have had its origin outside of Palestine.

---

78 Not only the words of Jesus but also his *life* is to Bultmann a question mark. He expressed his doubt in these words, "We can know almost nothing concerning the life and personality of Jesus" (*Jesus and the Word,* p. 8).

INTRODUCTION TO THE GOSPELS

To reach authenticity—the actual words and deeds of Jesus—the Gospels would have to be drastically reduced, therefore. The indicated pruning must be accomplished in accordance with the established laws of folklore and of literary and historical development. It will then become evident that Jesus taught that in the sight of God man is thoroughly unworthy. It is as a little child that he must receive forgiveness and salvation from his Father. God is the final Reality before whom everything fades into nothingness. It is the future alone that can bring salvation to man. In view of this future, man must *now* make a decision for the world or for God.

From Bultmann's writings on Form Criticism to his "New Testament and Mythology" is but a small step. According to this article and several of his later writings, the New Testament expresses itself in mythological terminology. Its myths, moreover, are drawn from Jewish apocalyptic literature and from Gnostic redemption-legends. In harmony with the times in which the New Testament writers were living and the ideas by which they were being influenced, they accept a three-level view of the universe: a heaven above, an earth beneath, and a hell under the earth. Human life on earth, as well as nature itself, is regarded by them as being under the influence of supernatural agents; such as, God, angels, Satan, and demons. A heavenly being is sent to earth to bring about man's salvation. This glorious person, Christ, performs miracles and by rendering atonement for man's sin conquers the evil spirits. Then this Christ, though killed and buried, rises again. He even ascends to heaven, is honored by being exalted to the Father's right hand, from which position of power and authority he governs the universe until he returns in majesty to judge the living and the dead.

Bultmann believes that today it is impossible to regard such items as *history*. Instructed by science, modern man knows that this program runs contrary to the chain of cause and effect. The German scholar is convinced, therefore, that a physical resurrection never took place, and that such a belief probably had its origin in Greek notions about dying and rising gods. To reach historical reality, therefore, it is necessary to penetrate to *the kernel* of New Testament teaching by stripping off *the husk;* that is, by eliminating whatever is mythological; hence, the name *demythologization*. Liberalism, to be sure, started to do this. However, according to Bultmann, it did not go nearly far enough. It was of the opinion that by pruning a little here and there it would be able to arrive at the real "Life of Jesus." That, however, is entirely impossible.

What has been said so far could easily lead to misinterpretation of Bultmann's real position, however, unless two qualifying facts are born in mind:

(1) Demythologization, as Bultmann views it, is not an entirely new discovery. Some of the ancient philosophers already applied it to their own religions. Moreover, it is really not an exegetical tool applied to Scripture

69

"from the outside." On the contrary, the New Testament authors themselves lead the way. Paul makes use of it. So, even more thoroughly, does John.

(2) When we understand the distinction between mere "Historie," the dead past, and "Geschichte," the living present, we see that although the mythological form in which the Gospels are cast fails to recover the past ("Historie") for us, it is of vital importance when it addresses us in this present moment ("Geschichte"), and confronts us with the necessity of making a decision. For, when it proclaims to us the supernatural birth, death, and resurrection of the Son of God, it is really telling us what must happen in our own case. It is *we* who must experience the new birth, must be crucified with Christ, and must rise again with him. It is *we* who must by God's grace and power yield our whole being, our entire *existence,* to him. Theology (the doctrine of God) is therefore really Anthropology (the doctrine of man).

At this point we see the influence upon Bultmann of two men whose names have not as yet been mentioned: Sören Kierkegaard[79] and Martin Heidegger. The last-named taught at Marburg from 1922 to 1928; hence, during part of the period when Bultmann himself was professor there (1921-1951). The philosophical movement or thought system which, among others, these two (Kierkegaard and Heidegger) developed and promoted, is called *Existentialism.* It emphasizes that human *existence* goes beyond that which can be described in purely scientific or in philosophical terms. It stresses such intensely real phenomena as anxiety, suffering, the feeling of guilt, etc., in order to show the need of making a decision or choice into which one enters with his whole *existence.* For example, when we decide

---

[79] He was an influential Danish philosopher who, during his brief and sorrow-filled life (1813-1855), was afflicted with melancholy, the tendency toward which is said to have been inherited from his father. Sören Kierkegaard attacked formal Christendom. In this attack he went to the extreme of not only rejecting dead orthodoxy but every creed as well. Moreover, he wanted to have nothing to do with *organized* Christianity. He described the so-called Christianity of his day as being nothing more than refined epicureanism. Genuine faith as he saw it was inwardness, the proper inner relation of the individual toward his God. In a moment of *crisis* a person chooses for or against God. This *decision* must be constantly repeated. A true Christian's life is one of unrest, anxiety.

The enormous strain brought about by Kierkegaard's attack on the organized Christianity of his day, and particularly on its leaders, left him physically weak and hastened his death. To the extent in which his attack was directed against whatever in religion is merely formal (for example, a prayer that is merely a matter of the lips; a sermon that has no heart in it but is a mere recitation; a church that has lost its love and has become a mere organization; etc.), and to the extent in which he stressed the religion of the heart, his emphasis arouses a sympathetic response. However, when we begin to realize that he subjectivized the objective, and made light of the body of truth as it is revealed in Scripture and summarized in the great creeds of Christendom, we see that he was steering in a dangerous direction; for what is subjective religion without the *truly* objective? See F. Nielsen's article, *Kierkegaard, Sören Aaby* in S.H.E.R.K., Vol. VI, pp. 330, 331; and also V. Hepp's in *Christelijke Encyclopaedie,* Vol. III, pp. 383-387.

whether or not to emigrate, or whether or not to marry a particular person, or how to face death, or what answer to give to the gospel call, in all such cases our thinking is on a different, a higher, plane than when we try to solve a merely theoretical mathematical puzzle. In other words, *existential* thinking ranks higher than *speculative*.

Accordingly, thus influenced, Bultmann teaches that true faith is possible only by means of an existential response, an *encounter* with God. The moment of that encounter is filled with eternity. The salvation-event takes place, as a constantly recurring experience, whenever the Word reaches the heart, and the hearer, by power from above, turns from self to God, from sin to holiness. As Bultmann sees it, this reaveals the great importance of public worship, during which again and again God confronts man with the necessity of making a decision, a choice with *eschatological* import; that is, with significance for the chooser's entire future. It is thus that the Gospels, *even in their mythological form, properly interpreted,* confront the listeners and attain real meaning. It is thus that, in the life of the church, men die with Christ and rise again with him.[80]

b. *Evaluation*

On the positive side the following can be said:

(1) Concentration, within non-conservative circles, of attention upon oral tradition during the period preceding Gospel formation was long overdue. Mouth to mouth transmission is, indeed, deserving of this renewed emphasis, as has always been the conservative position.

(2) Classification of Gospel materials into types or forms, besides being an aid in the study of the possible course of oral tradition, facilitates comparison with "resemblances" in other literature both sacred and secular.

(3) The idea according to which the Gospels are not a tape-recording of all the words of Jesus nor a photographic reproduction of all his mighty acts, but rather a summary composed according to the needs of the church, and with a definite purpose in mind, is confirmed by John 20:30, 31; 21:25.

(4) The statement that true faith is an attitude and activity in which the entire personality is involved, that it is accordingly a complete self-surrender resulting from a decision, reminds one of Josh. 24:15 and of the words of Jesus recorded in Mark 12:29-31.

Had matters such as these been combined with true, childlike faith *in God's entire objective revelation in Jesus Christ, as revealed in Scripture,* they would have constituted a highly valuable contribution. Alas for the

---

80 As to Bultmann's relation to Karl Barth, the two agree in viewing true faith as the proper response to (what they consider) the Word of God. Nevertheless, with the passing of time the thinking of the two began to diverge. Knudsen (*op. cit.,* p. 133) calls attention to the fact that a visit of Barth to Marburg would stir up excited discussion. See also Herman Ridderbos, "Rudolf Bultmann," *Torch and Trumpet,* Vol. XV, No. 9 (November, 1965), pp. 12-15.

movement under discussion, the words in italics reveal what was lacking. Basically, therefore, our evaluation must be sharply negative:

(1) Similarity does not prove descent. Discovery of surface-parallels in the folklore and literature of surrounding nations does not prove that Gospel units were derived from these outside sources or were the same in essence. A certain amount of surface resemblance is altogether natural, for the simple reason that Gospel writers were men of their time. Their writings did not originate in a vacuum. On the other hand, as soon as we penetrate to the inner essence, we begin to see a striking contrast: the miracles performed by Jesus, as recorded in the Gospels, were not acts of magic. The very parallels to which Bultmann refers—such as, a cure brought about by a chip from a virgin's gravestone—refute his theory. It is clear that Bultmann has allowed himself to become unduly influenced by the history of religion school.

(2) Separating a text from its given context without presenting a solid reason for doing this, and then placing it in a new context, is entirely inexcusable. It violates one of the most important rules of sound exegesis.

(3) It is not true that the inclusion in—or exclusion from—the Gospels of certain materials *according to the needs of the early church* implies distortion. Also, *varied application* does not necessarily imply *essential alteration*. On the contrary, the inclusion of so many passages that expose the weaknesses of some of the church's greatest leaders (Mark 8:31-33; 9:34; 10:35-41; 14:37, 66-72; and parallels in the other Gospels) emphasizes the honesty and objectivity of the Gospel writers. The Holy Spirit is in control!

(4) Luke's additions to Mark's account (for example, "*only* son, *right* hand") by no means necessarily indicate legendary snowballing of Mark's simple narrative. According to many interpreters these additions derive from the fact that Luke was a man with a very sympathetic heart and a physician; hence, a person who, more than others, would take note of such details and would report them. There may have been other reasons. What especially reduces the value of Bultmann's remark is the fact that so often it is Mark who gives the more detailed account.

(5) Bultmann fails to present any solid reason for his theory that parables (as well as miracles) were expanded far beyond their originals. Also, he fails to see that even a parable with allegorical traits—a separate meaning for each symbol—can have a single central lesson. See Mark 4:9; cf. Luke 8:8, 18.

(6) Expelling "myths" by the front door and allowing them to re-enter by the back door is strange procedure, indeed!

(7) The idea that the universe is virtually a closed system in which everything is governed by natural law, so that miracles are impossible, is hardly even up-to-date Science. The marked progress in scientific discovery, rather than having reduced the area that must still be explained, is making the realm of mystery, pointing to the Living, omnipotent God, ever greater.

The *real* man of science knows that there are things that are apprehended only by faith in God's infallible special revelation.

(8) After eliminating well-nigh everything that belongs to the supernatural sphere, including the biblical view of God as the sovereign Creator[81] and Redeemer, what is there left of God? Is an "encounter" with such a God *meaningful?* Is it even *possible?* Moreover, as for the true element in such terms as "constantly repeated decision," "encounter," etc., has not the church throughout the centuries, inasfar as it was truly alive, always emphasized the necessity of both basic and daily conversion, of *living* faith, of the constant application of Christ's merits to the hearts and lives of believers; or, changing the phraseology, of the continuous appropriation of the death and resurrection of Christ? Also, this living church did not destroy the validity of this emphasis by rejecting the very God to whom the commitment must be made; that is, God as revealed in Christ according to the inspired record.

(9) According to the Gospels (in fact, according to the entire New Testament) "the Christ of faith" is "the Jesus of history," and vice versa (John 20:31). By what right does Bultmann separate these two?

(10) A philosophy that refuses to render homage to the sinless Christ (John 8:46), who came from heaven (John 6:38); who gave himself as a ransom for sin (Matt. 20:28; Mark 10:45); who rose from the dead on the third day (Mark 16:6), and ascended to the Father's right hand in heaven (Luke 24:51; Acts 2:34), from which position he governs the universe in the interest of his church (Matt. 28:18; Eph. 1:22); and who will come again in glory to judge the living and the dead (Acts 1:11; Phil. 3:20, 21; I Thess. 4:13-18; II Thess. 1:7 ff.; Titus 2:13; Rev. 1:7; 20:11-15), a philosophy that refuses to render homage to this Christ does not deserve the name *Christian* (philosophy, theology, or religion). *Basically Bultmannism and Christianity are opposites.*

6. *The Basic Weakness*

We come now to the basic reason for rejecting all the four theories that have been summarized, beginning with Harnack and Liberalism, and ending with Bultmann and Radicalism. None of them offers a satisfactory explanation of the following facts:

a. The testimony of eye and ear witnesses and their disciples, to the effect that Jesus Christ is really the risen, living Lord.

b. The fact that this testimony is very early, far too early for folklore to have done its work or for pagan myths to have influenced the preaching of those who proclaimed the risen Christ. We have, for example, the four Gospels. The first of the four is by tradition unanimously ascribed to Matthew, one of Christ's twelve disciples.[82] By a host of early witnesses

---

81 On this point see N. B. Stonehouse, *Origins of the Synoptic Gospels,* p. 174.
82 For greater detail see pp. 92-97.

Mark, with whose name the second Gospel is linked, is described as "the interpreter of Peter," an apostle and witness. Peter's name is mentioned first in every list of the twelve apostles (Matt. 10:2-4; Mark 3:16-19; Luke 6:14-16; Acts 1:13). Luke, though himself not an eye witness of the story of Jesus, makes special mention of the fact that he belongs to the number of men who received their information from those "who from the beginning were eye witnesses and ministers of the word" (Luke 1:1, 2). And even the last of the four Gospels, that according to John, was evidently written by a Palestinian Jew, an eye witness, one who possessed a detailed knowledge of Palestinian topography; particularly of Jerusalem and its immediate vicinity and of the temple. The early character of this Gospel has been confirmed by archaeological discoveries. See N.T.C. on this Gospel, Vol. I, pp. 18, 19, 190. Moreover, the Aramaisms present in all four Gospels create a presumption in favor of their early origin.[83] *All four proclaim the risen Christ!* Accordingly, before anyone has the right to reject what these Gospels tell us concerning Jesus Christ--his origin, exalted being, miracles, atoning death, resurrection, etc.--he will have to present proof that the testimony of the earliest witnesses is not reflected in them.

Besides, in complete agreement with the information regarding the risen and ever-living Savior is the testimony of the apostle Paul; for example, that which is found in I Cor. 15. It is commonly agreed that it was indeed the apostle Paul who wrote I Corinthians. In all likelihood this epistle was composed sometime during the period A.D. 53-57; that is, only about a quarter of a century after Christ's death. Nevertheless, even as early as this the apostle already bears emphatic testimony to his faith in the risen Savior (I Cor. 15:20). Not only that, but he refers to a visit to Corinth made earlier still (probably sometime during the period 51-53[84]), at which time the Corinthians had accepted this risen Christ as their own Savior and Lord (15:1). Even more telling is the fact that Paul in this chapter (15:6) informs us that the "appearances" of the risen Christ, of which he mentions several, included also that "to more than five hundred brothers at one time." He adds, "most of whom are still alive, though some have fallen asleep."

c. The additional fact that, according to all the evidence which we possess, none of the earliest witnesses had been expecting Christ's resurrection. At the death of their Master they had all been filled with fear and utter hopelessness. See N.T.C. on the Gospel according to John, Vol. II, pp. 468-471. Yet, a few days later they boldly proclaim the risen Lord.

d. The sudden rise, dramatic growth, and world-shaking power and influ-

---

[83] This is beginning to be recognized more and more. See, for example, R. H. Gundry, "The Language Milieu of First Century Palestine. Its Bearing on the Authenticity of the Gospel Tradition," *JBL* 83 (April, 1964), pp. 404-408.

[84] For verification of this chronology see my *Bible Survey*, pp. 62, 63.

ence of the church, Christ's body (Matt. 28:19; John 11:48; 12:19; Acts 1:8; 17:6; Eph. 3:9; I Thess. 1:8-10; and I John 5:4).

Now all this clearly points to the *one* cause that is able adequately to account for such astonishing results. It points to the fact that there was—and is—actually such a person as Jesus Christ, the Son of God, who came from heaven to seek and to save the lost, and who sent forth his ambassadors, the apostles and those who immediately followed them, to bear witness to the glorious redemption accomplished by God through the suffering and death of his Beloved. It tallies with the fact that it was, indeed, this Christ "who presented himself alive after his passion by many proofs" (Acts 1:3).

Of course, in the final analysis it is entirely true that one must proceed from the assumption of faith. If one refuses to accept the "proofs" of which Acts speaks, their validity cannot be forced upon him. So, too, he who rejects the supernatural—including Christ's deity, wonder-working power, and resurrection—proceeds from a definite assumption; namely, that of unbelief. There is, however, a vast difference between these two assumptions. *On the presupposition of faith* the reports concerning Jesus Christ and the church which he established make sense. *The story is coherent:* the Son of God performs acts in which his divinity is displayed. He even conquers death. With divine power, wisdom, and love he establishes a church, and guides it to its predestined goal. On the other hand, *on the basis of unbelief* the supernatural is ruled out. Accordingly, Jesus, if he lived on earth at all, did not perform a single miracle and did not rise again from the dead. Further, according to this theory, the many witnesses painted a picture of Jesus that was a mixture of history and mythology. The "more than five hundred brothers" who are said to have seen the risen Christ were the victims of mass hallucination or of some other form of mass deception. The sudden rise, dramatic growth, and world-shaking power of the church is left completely unexplained.

It is not surprising, therefore, that the various systems of skepticism and unbelief have vanished one by one. The facts defy the theories. This applies also to Bultmannism. It, too, has had its day. In a most interesting and instructive article[85] Carl F. H. Henry speaks of "the growing disagreement among post-Bultmannians over the significance of the historical Jesus." As he sees it, "classical modernism reigned over the influential formative centers of theological thought from 1900 to 1930, dialectical theology from 1930-1950, and existential theology from 1950 to 1960." God's Word is an anvil that cannot be crushed. On a monument to the Huguenots these words are inscribed:

"Hammer away, ye hostile hands; Your hammers break; God's anvil stands."

---

[85] "Where Is Modern Theology Going?" *Christianity Today*, Vol. XII, Number 11 (March 1, 1968), pp. 3-7.

But is it not true that the Gospels contain many "discrepancies," instances in which one Gospel contradicts another or is in conflict with this or that other Old or New Testament passage? How must we deal with such cases? There are those who say that we should never try to harmonize the Gospels. They maintain that "harmonization is harmful." I answer as follows: harmonization may, indeed, be bad, but it need not be. It is wrong at times, but perfectly natural and legitimate at other times. We must not generalize. If four reliable friends of mine, men with a reputation for integrity, intelligence, and good judgment, have witnessed the same incident, and each brings me his independent report, and I discover that these reports contain items which, on the surface, seem to contradict each other, what is my natural reaction? Do I then immediately charge my friends with error? Do I not, almost instinctively, make an attempt to harmonize the four reports? If, therefore, I consider my friends to be entitled to such deference, shall I treat the inspired documents with less respect? To be sure, harmonization is harmful if it be done in a forced, unnatural manner, without due regard for the respective contexts of the individual passages. The harmonizer is in error if he is never willing to say, "A real solution to this difficult problem has not yet been found." In other cases an honest attempt to seek solutions and to harmonize may well be exactly the proper procedure. The infallibility of the Word must not be rejected, not even by implication.

Introduction

to

The Gospel According to Matthew

I. Characteristics

These may be summarized as follows. This Gospel is:

Methodical; i.e., characterized by orderliness

The author goes to work according to a definite plan, setting forth that Jesus is, indeed, the Christ. The nature of this plan and the manner in which it differs from that of the other evangelists has been indicated on pp. 25-31.

Appealing

This Gospel has been called "the most important book in the world" (Renan), "the most successful book ever written" (Goodspeed). Besides being important and successful it is also truly beautiful. Reading it from beginning to end at one sitting is a thrilling experience. The book is simply irresistible. At the very beginning one is intrigued by the mystery of the three fourteens (chap. 1). There follows the exciting story of the wise men who came "from the east" in order to render homage to a young child (chap. 2). The Sermon on the Mount (chaps. 5–7), with its beatitudes (5:3-12) and Lord's Prayer (6:9-14), and with its many other precious passages—such as 5:13-16, 27 ff., 43-48; 6:19-34; and last but not least 7:24-27—gives us an insight into the very heart of the Master. The charge to The Twelve (chap. 10) is characterized by frankness and tenderness: by the former, for the apostles are plainly told that the faithful discharge of their duties will mean persecution (verse 22); and by the latter, for they receive the assurance of the Father's constant care and of the Son's abiding closeness (verse 40). The kingdom parables of chapter 13 are both interesting and revealing. The rules governing Christian discipline (chap. 18) have been, and are being, quoted again and again and have already resulted in blessings that can neither be counted nor measured. For our instruction chapter 23—the seven woes— shows that the Savior's love is not all sweetness and smiles. It has its stern aspect, for how would it be possible for him who urges men to enter his Father's kingdom to look with special favor upon those who shut that kingdom against men (Matt. 23:13); or for one who helps widows, to take pleasure in those who devour widows' houses (Mark 12:40)? It is also Matthew's Gospel that contains the dramatic portrayal of The Final Judgment (chap. 25). The deeply moving account of the Savior's passion has been given reverential musical expression in Bach's *St. Matthew's Passion*, while Matthew's unique contribution to the account of the resurrection—I refer particularly to his rather lengthy passage about the guard (see on 27:62-66; 28:2-4, 11-15)—still awaits adequate crystallization in music and on canvas.

Turned toward *the past;* i.e., toward the Old Testament, with its many Messianic predictions, and proclaiming their fulfilment in the present, namely, in Jesus Christ.

Matthew contains at least forty formal quotations; that is, quotations that are immediately evident as such, often being introduced by words such as "that what was spoken ... might be fulfilled," "Y o u have heard that it was said," "for so it is written by the prophet," etc. Note the following:

Reference in Matthew	Old Testament Passage	See also
1:23	Isa. 7:14	
2:6	Mic. 5:2	
2:15	Hos. 11:1 (cf. Exod. 4:22)	
2:18	Jer. 31:15	
2:23	Isa. 11:1? (cf. Isa. 53:2, 3)	John 1:46; 7:52
3:3	Isa. 40:3	Mark 1:3; Luke 3:4
4:4	Deut. 8:3	Luke 4:4
4:6	Ps. 91:11, 12	Luke 4:10, 11
4:7	Deut. 6:16	Luke 4:12
4:10	Deut. 5:9; 6:13	Luke 4:8
4:15, 16	Isa. 9:1, 2	
5:21	Exod. 20:13; Deut. 5:17	
5:27 (cf. 19:18)	Exod. 20:14; Deut. 5:18	Mark 10:19; Luke 18:20; Rom. 2:22; 13:9; James 2:11
5:31 (cf. 19:7)	Deut. 24:1	Mark 10:4
5:33	Lev. 19:12; Num. 30:3; Deut. 23:21, 22	
5:38	Exod. 21:24; Lev. 24:20; Deut. 19:21	
5:43 (cf. 19:19; 22:39)	Lev. 19:18	Mark 12:31, 33; Luke 10:27; Rom. 13:9; Gal. 5:14; James 2:8
8:17	Isa. 53:4	
9:13 (cf. 12:7)	Hos. 6:6	
11:10	Mal. 3:1	Mark 1:2; Luke 7:27
12:7 (cf. 9:13)	Hos. 6:6	
12:18-21	Isa. 42:1-4	
13:14, 15	Isa. 6:9, 10	John 12:39-41
13:35	Ps. 78:2	
15:4a (cf. 19:19)	Exod. 20:12; Deut. 5:16	Mark 7:10a; 10:19; Luke 18:20; Eph. 6:2

Reference in Matthew	Old Testament Passage	See also
15:4b	Exod. 21:17; Lev. 20:9; Deut. 27:16; Prov. 20:20; 30:17	Mark 7:10b
15:8, 9	Isa. 29:13	Mark 7:6, 7
19:4	Gen. 1:27	Mark 10:6
19:5	Gen. 2:24	Mark 10:7
19:7 (cf. 5:31)	Deut. 24:1	Mark 10:4
19:18, 19 (cf. 5:43; 22:39)	Exod. 20:12-16; Lev. 19:18; Deut. 5:16-20	For Matt. 19:18, 19a see also Mark 10:19; Luke 18:20; and for Matt. 19:19b see the references listed in connection with Matt. 5:43
21:5	Zech. 9:9	John 12:15
21:13a	Isa. 56:7	Mark 11:17a; Luke 19:46a
21:13b	Jer. 7:11	Mark 11:17b; Luke 19:46b
21:16	Ps. 8:2	
21:42	Ps. 118:22, 23	Mark 12:10, 11; Luke 20:17; Acts 4:11; I Peter 2:7
22:24	Deut. 25:5	Mark 12:19; Luke 20:28
22:32	Exod. 3:6	Mark 12:26
22:37	Deut. 6:5	Mark 12:30; Luke 10:27a
22:39 (cf. 5:43; 19:18, 19)	Lev. 19:18	See the references listed in connection with Matt. 5:43
22:44	Ps. 110:1	Mark 12:36; Acts 2:34, 35; Heb. 1:13
23:38, 39	Ps. 118:26; Jer. 22:5	Luke 13:35
24:15	Dan. 9:27; 11:31; 12:11	Mark 13:14
24:29-31	See p. 862	
26:31	Zech. 13:7	Mark 14:27
26:64	Ps. 110:1; Dan. 7:13, 14	Mark 14:62; Luke 21:27
27:9, 10	Zech. 11:12, 13 (cf. Jer. 32:6-15)	
27:46	Ps. 22:1	Mark 15:34

In addition to the quotations that are definitely designated as such there are others which, though not thus introduced, are immediately recognized as quotations of familiar phrases from the Old Testament. See Matt. 10:35, 36; 11:5, 23; 18:16; 21:9, 33; 26:15, 64; 27:34, 35. Some might not be immediately recognized, and among these there are expressions that may perhaps be better described as allusions than quotations: 8:4; 10:21; 12:4, 40; 27:39, 43, 48.

Turned toward *the present,* and revealing God's will for the here and now; *and toward the future:* his own (suffering, death, resurrection, etc.), that of his people, and that of the world.

In Matthew not only is Jesus the fulfilment of prophecy; he is also himself very definitely *the prophet.* As such he is greater than *Jonah* (12:39-41; cf. Luke 11:29-32), reminds one vividly of *Isaiah* (13:13-15), and answers the prediction given to *Moses.* He is, in fact, the exalted One, who was to come, and to whom the people must give heed (Deut. 18:25-19; Matt. 17:5).[86] As God's prophet he reveals the will of his Father in all he is, says, and does. Whenever we wish to read the great discourses of our Lord and Savior we naturally turn, first of all, to Matthew's Gospel; for whatever parallels the other Gospels contain, it is the former publican who has given us this material in its fullest and most organized form (chaps 5–7; 10; 13; 18; 23; and 24, 25). It is again Matthew who not only has preserved for us Christ's predictions concerning himself—these lessons regarding the cross followed by the crown are found also in the other Gospels—, but who has also left us the Master's most vivid and detailed forecast with respect to the future course of events touching Jerusalem, the church, and the world (23:37–25:30), climaxed by the majestic portraiture of the final judgment, ushering in eternal woe and eternal weal (25:31-46).

Something can be said, therefore, in favor of the view that although in each Gospel Jesus is pictured as the long-awaited Messiah, sent by the Father and anointed by the Spirit to be our Great Prophet, Sympathetic Highpriest, and Eternal King, it is *the prophetic office* that comes into the foreground in Matthew, the kingly in Mark, the highpriestly in Luke. As to Mark and Luke, the argument belongs to commentaries on these Gospels. As to Matthew, it would appear to the present author that F. W. Grosheide was right when he said:

"According to some, Matthew pictures Jesus especially as king. It cannot be denied that we see him rise out of a royal dynasty, that we hear of the adulteration of his kingship by the Jews and by Pilate, that he vindicates himself as Israel's true king, and that at the conclusion he functions as king,

---

86 Cf. R. H. Gundry, *The Use of the Old Testament in St. Matthew's Gospel,* Leiden, 1967, a Ph.D. dissertation accepted by the University of Manchester in the Spring of 1961 and brought up to date in the Summer of 1964, p. 210.

possessing all authority in heaven and on earth. Nevertheless, as we see it, this is not what distinguishes Matthew's Gospel from the others. . . . On the contrary, in no Gospel does the prophetical aspect of Jesus come to the foreground as clearly as it does in the first. Not only is it true that Jesus is the fulfilment of prophecy, but he himself—witness the many connected discourses, more in Matthew than in the others—functions as prophet with respect to his own work, especially as the prophet of his own suffering and death. He is the true prophet, the prophet of Deut. 18:18. . . . In this Gospel, as is shown both by its content and organization, it is the word of Christ, rather than his work, that receives the emphasis" (*Commentaar op het Nieuwe Testament,* Kampen, 1954, pp. 14, 15).

Jesus, moreover, is God's Chief Prophet not only in the *discourses* but even in *the Old Testament predictions* which he fulfils! Is this not clearly taught in I Peter 1:10, 11 and in Rev. 19:10b?

Hebraistic, that is, characterized by the thought patterns and spirit of the Hebrews.

According to some,[87] the four Greek Gospels—with the exception of the last chapter of John and Luke's prologue—are Aramaic documents that were subsequently translated into Greek. The arguments advanced in confirmation of this view are mainly the following: *a.* the Greek is marked by Aramaic—or at least by Semitic—style characteristics; *b.* many passages that are now obscure become clear as soon as they are viewed as mistranslations of the underlying Aramaic, and a correct translation is substituted for the poor one found in the Greek text.

The theory has by no means convinced all scholars.[88] This is not surpris-

---

[87] The theory according to which one or all of our Gospels were originally written in Aramaic, a view already advocated in the nineteenth century by J. T. Marshall and J. Wellhausen, was revived with even stronger emphasis in the twentieth. See especially the following books and articles:

C. F. Burney, *The Aramaic Origin of the Fourth Gospel,* Oxford, 1922.

C. C. Torrey, *The Four Gospels, a New Translation,* New York, 1933
Our Translated Gospels, New York, 1936
Documents of the Primitive Church, New York, 1941
"The Aramaic of the Gospels," *JBL,* 61 (1942), pp. 71-85.

J. A. Montgomery, "Some Aramaisms in the Gospels and Acts," *JBL,* 46 (1927), pp. 69-73

"Torrey's Aramaic Gospels," *JBL,* 53 (1934), pp. 79-99.

[88] The attack on Torrey and his allies was led by the following, among others:

O. T. Allis, "The Alleged Aramaic Origin of the Fourth Gospel," *PTR,* 26 (1928), pp. 531-572.

E. C. Colwell, *The Greek of the Fourth Gospel,* Chicago, 1931.

E. J. Goodspeed, *New Solutions of New Testament Problems,* Chicago; 1927
New Chapters in New Testament Study, New York, 1937, pp. 141-168.

D. W. Riddle, "The Aramaic Gospels and the Synoptic Problems," *JBL,* 54 (1935), pp. 127-138.

A lively debate was carried on between two scholars: one representative of each of the opposing camps: "The Riddle-Torrey Debate," *CC* (July 18-Oct. 31, 1934).

ing. It is not denied that Aramaic is the basis of much or all of the contents of the Greek Gospels. That Jesus generally spoke in Aramaic has already become clear (see p. 42). Is it not probable, therefore, that when his words were first reduced to writing they were written in the language (or at least *also* in the language) in which they had been spoken? Certain idioms that are either characteristically Semitic, or at least occur with greater frequency in Semitic languages than in Greek, also appear again and again in the Gospels.[89]

It cannot be denied that the investigations of Torrey and his allies have brought out clearly the indispensability of the study of Semitic (in this case especially Hebrew and Aramaic) as well as Greek for the proper understanding of the New Testament. The student who specializes in Semitics and is satisfied with a beginner's knowledge of Greek is in danger of seeing Semitisms everywhere in the New Testament. On the other hand, the one who confines himself largely to the study of Greek will fail to see the Semitic style and flavor of the Gospels. A proper balance of interest should be achieved. When this is accomplished, it will also be recognized that the Semitic or Hebraistic atmosphere of the Gospels proves that "they preserve an early, Palestinian, Semitic tradition" (F. V. Filson). They are not late writings that originated during the second century, as rationalistic critics used to affirm with great confidence, but documents that belong to a very early age, a time when Greek-speaking believers were in close contact with those who spoke Aramaic, and when many were conversant with both (or even all three: Hebrew, Aramaic, and Greek) languages. These Gospels, accordingly, were written at a time when the facts concerning Jesus, his

---

[89] Thus, "Jesus answered and said," an introductory formula used even when no question precedes (Matt. 4:4; 8:8; 11:4; Mark 6:37; 7:6; 9:5; Luke 1:35; 4:8; 7:43; John 1:48; 2:19; 3:3), reminds us of the identical expression found in Gen. 18:27; 24:50; 27:37, 39; 31:14, 31; Exod. 4:1; etc. (Hebrew); and in Dan. 2:15, 20, 26, 47; 3:9, 14, 25; 4:19; 5:17; 6:13; etc. (Aramaic). Also, the use of the active third person plural where the Greek and we, too, would more commonly use the passive third person singular, and change the object of the active verb into the subject of the sentence (Luke 12:20) parallels similar usage in the Old Testament. To this may be added the very frequent pleonastic use of καί and also the adversative use; see article on this conjunction in L.N.T. (A. and G.), pp. 392-394. As to presence of Semitic words, in addition to those already mentioned (p. 42) see also Matt. 27:16, 20, 46; John 5:2; 16:20. Parallelisms, abounding in the Old Testament (Ps. 1; 19:2; 93:3; Prov. 14:34; etc.) are also of frequent occurrence in the Gospels (Matt. 7:6; 10:24, 32, 33, 39, 40; 11:28, 29; 20:26, 27; Luke 1:46, 47, 52; 2:32; 15:9, 10; etc.). The Hebraistic formula of transition καί ἐγένετο occurs with great frequency both in Matthew (7:28; 9:10; 11:1; 13:53; 19:1; 26:1) and in Luke (1:23, 41, 59; 2:15, 46; 5:12, 17; 7:11; 8:1; 9:18, 33; 11:1; 14:1; 17:11; 19:15, 29; 20:1; 24:4, 15, 30, 51), where, however, it is often replaced by ἐγένετο δε (1:8; 2:1; 3:21; 6:1; etc.), as we would expect in that Gospel; see p. 37, footnote 39. Finally, another strong reminder of Old Testament usage carried over into the New is *lo* or *behold*, occurring in the form of *hinnēh* or *hēn* in nearly every book of the Old Testament (about 100 times in Gen.), and in the form of ἰδού or ἴδε in the New, profusely distributed throughout all the Gospels (about 60 times in Matt.).

sojourn on earth, miracles, sayings, discourses, atoning death, resurrection, etc., were still fresh in the minds of the disciples and of their immediate followers. Thus God, in his providence, uses the work of one school of higher critics—Torrey and his allies—to combat the theories of another school, the late-daters of New Testament books.

So much for the positive side. The Aramaic theory also has its distinctly negative aspect, as has already been intimated. First, it is now rather generally recognized that this theory has not succeeded in proving that four written Aramaic Gospels underlie our present Greek Gospels. There are, after all, other ways to account for the Semitic flavor of these books. Matthew Mark, and John were Jews, and not only these three but also Luke was in close contact with Jews and used Jewish oral and written sources. When Jews speak or write Greek they do not immediately shed their Hebraistic background. The Semitisms of the New Testament may therefore be partially explained as being *regional variations of Hellenistic Greek.* Intimate knowledge of the Hebrew Old Testament and of its Septuagint (Greek) translation, as well as acquaintance with Aramaic oral and written source-material no doubt contributed their share toward the end-product. And in all this we do not deny that there *may* even have been, at one time, an early Aramaic Matthew. We simply do not know. More about this in a moment.

Secondly, not only did Torrey and his group maintain that our Greek Gospels, etc. are *translations* of Aramaic originals, but in addition they tried to prove that, in many instances, they are *poor translations.* However, that view also has been decisively refuted. It has been shown, for example, that Torrey's contention according to which Matt. 5:48 when translated "Y o u therefore, must be perfect . . ." is an error, and that it should be rendered, "Be, therefore, all-including," *is itself an error.*[90] Even a reader unfamiliar with Greek and Hebrew can see, by comparing Matt. 5:48 with Lev. 19:2 and Deut. 18:13, that the rendering to which he has become accustomed (whether perhaps through the study of A.V., A.R.V., N.A.S.B., R.S.V., or Berkeley) is not wrong, and that, as generally rendered, this passage harmonizes with Jesus' central idea, namely, that as is the Father so should be his children; cf. Luke 6:35. Many similar alleged wrong translations are discussed in Torrey's writings. When carefully examined, they are found to be not wrong at all. The interesting fact is that *in many specific cases the advocates of the Aramaic theory in its extreme form reject each other's conclusions as to mistranslations,* as the literature mentioned on p. 83, footnote 88 indicates.[91]

---

[90] See Torrey, *Our Translated Gospels,* p. 93 ff., and D. Daube's refutation in *BJRL,* 29 (1945), p. 31 ff.

[91] For myself, I can testify that after a rather thorough study of the writings of Torrey and his associates, as well as those of his opponents, a study required as a basis for the writing of a lengthy term-paper on this very subject during my P.G. studies at

How does all this apply specifically to *Matthew's* Gospel? It has been shown that, on the whole, Matthew's Greek is more fluent than that of Mark and contains less Aramaic words. In view of this, the adjective "Hebraistic" is hardly even applicable to this Gospel, *if* one defines this adjective in a narrowly linguistic sense. On the other hand, when the word "Hebraistic" is employed in a broader sense, as having reference to the conceptual world of the Jews, the religious ideas that were prominent among them because of their Old Testament background and the phraseology by means of which these ideas were expressed, the adjective is apt.

The Jewishness of Matthew's Gospel is by no means confined to certain features which, to a greater or lesser extent, it has in common with other Gospels. It reaches much deeper than this. There is, for example, the idea of the divine teleology: God's plan and its realization in history, a stronger emphasis on prophecy and fulfilment than is found in the other Gospels, as has been shown. There is also the delight which Matthew finds in the concept *seven*. Already in the very first chapter he represents Christ as the Beginner of the seventh seven, the climax of the three fourteens. Though the Lord's Prayer, as Matthew records it, has *six* petitions (6:9-13), yet according to him, Jesus uttered a group of seven kingdom parables (chap. 13), and pronounced seven woes upon Pharisees and scribes (chap. 23).[92] All this strongly reminds one of the divine ordinance with respect to the seven-day week (Gen. 2:2; Exod. 20:10; Deut. 5:14), the sabbath of weeks (Pentecost, Lev. 23:15), the festival during the seventh month (Lev. 23:24), the seventh year (Lev. 25:4), and the Year of Jubilee at the end of seven times seven years (Lev. 25:8). For other Old Testament sevens see Gen. 4:24; Exod.

Princeton Theological Seminary, my faith in Scripture's infallibility, reasonably interpreted, was not shaken in the least but rather confirmed. Passages such as Rev. 10:7; 15:2; 18:23; and 19:17, all of which according to Torrey are (or contain) mistranslations, fall into line beautifully and make excellent sense as soon as they are interpreted in the light of the context, as I have tried to do in my book, *More Than Conquerors*, seventeenth printing, Grand Rapids, 1970. None embody mistranslations. The same holds for the Gospels and Acts.

[92] I have purposely left out of consideration the sevens which Matthew has in common with one or both of the other Synoptics; such as seven other spirits (12:45), seven "loaves" (15:34 f.), seven baskets (15:37), forgiveness seven or seventy times seven times (18:21, 22), and seven brothers (22:25). As was indicated, in Matthew there is enough *distinctive* seven material to regard this as one of its peculiar features. I have purposely omitted any mention of Matthew's threes and fives (see the list in W. C. Allen, *op. cit.*, p. lxv. A few items could have been added to that list.) A glance at the appropriate entries in a complete Concordance should convince anyone that these threes and fives are spread rather evenly over the three Synoptics, especially over Matthew and Luke. For the same reason I am not too impressed with Goodspeed's attempt to link the number emphasis which he detects in the first canonical Gospel with the view that it was accordingly probably written by a tax collector, a man who showed ease in handling numbers and figures; see *op. cit.*, pp. 21, 22, 24, 25, 36, 58, 59, 70, 71, 76, 112, 113, 133-135. For that matter, he himself seems to have sensed the weakness of that argument; see p. 58.

INTRODUCTION TO MATTHEW

25:37; Josh. 6:4, 6, 8, 13, 15; Job 1:2; Dan. 4:16, 23, 25; 9:25; Zech. 4:2; to mention but a few.

Matthew also uses the term "kingdom of heaven" instead of "kingdom of God" employed by the other Gospel-writers. To be sure, he does not avoid the latter term (12:28; 21:31), and there is no *essential* difference between the two appellations. However, does not the fact that in his far more usual designation the Greek word translated "heaven" is in the plural (cf. Gen. 1:1 in the original) and that the reference to heaven reminds one of Dan. 2:44; 7:13, 14, point to the conclusion that it is a Hebrew who is writing these things? By him Jesus is represented as "the son of David, the son of Abraham" (contrast Matt. 1:1 with Luke 3:38). The fact that the adverb of time τότε (then) occurs in Matthew about 90 times (contrast Mark 6 times; Luke 15 times; John 10 times) is another link with its Semitic equivalent.

Again, does not this Gospel's constant emphasis on *the law* (see especially the lengthy section 5:17-48; cf. 7:12; 12:5; 23:23) strengthen this conclusion? And if even more evidence is needed, let it be remembered that this is the only Gospel in which the title "king of the Jews," referring to Jesus, is not saved for the closing chapters but is found in the very beginning (2:2). It is also the only Gospel in which Jesus is reported to have issued the command, "Into any road of the Gentiles do not turn off, and into any city of the Samaritans do not enter, but go rather to the lost sheep of the house of Israel" (10:5, 6). It is, again, the only Gospel in which these words are recorded: "I was sent only to the lost sheep of the house of Israel" (15:24). It is the only Gospel that calls Jerusalem "the holy city" (4:5; 27:53; cf. Rev. 21:2). Finally, it is the only Gospel in which Jewish customs do not need to be explained (15:2; contrast Mark 7:3, 4), for the Jews knew their own customs. The statement, "The Gospel of Matthew has a more Jewish aspect than the other Synoptics,"[93] is entirely correct. It is in that sense that we call it "Hebraistic."

Was there ever a Semitic (whether Hebrew or Aramaic) Gospel written by the same author who, according to this view, subsequently produced what is now called the Greek "Gospel according to Matthew"? Eusebius tells us that it was Papias who wrote (in a work[94] now lost): "Matthew arranged the oracles in (the) Hebrew language, and each translated them as he was able."[95]

---

[93] L. Berkhof, *New Testament Introduction*, Grand Rapids, 1915, p. 64.
[94] Title: *Interpretation of the Oracles of the Lord, in five treatises; op. cit.*, III. xxxix. 3-5.
[95] Same, III.xxxix.16. The Greek is as follows:
Ματθαῖος μὲν οὖν Ἑβραΐδι διαλέκτῳ τὰ λόγια συνετάξατο, ἡρμήνευσεν δ' αὐτὰ ὡς ἦν δυνατὸς ἕκαστος.
It would almost seem as if each reader of this statement of Papias has also done with it "as he was able," or, perhaps in some cases, "as suited his view." Renderings differing from the one suggested above are:

87

Various divergent appraisals and interpretations of this statement:

1. Papias was obviously mistaken. He based his opinion upon the fact that Matthew wrote first of all for Jews. Besides, he may have confused our Greek Matthew with another document, as did Jerome, who regarded the apocryphal *Gospel according to the Hebrews* to be the original Hebrew Matthew. An Aramaic Matthew pre-dating Greek Matthew has never been found. Had there been such a Gospel it would, of course, in its quotations from the Old Testament, have followed the Hebrew text. But the very point of Jesus' charge (Matt. 15:6 ff.; Mark 7:8 ff.) against the Pharisees and scribes, denouncing them for making void the Word of God because of their tradition, would have been lost had the Hebrew text (of Isa. 29:13) been followed. It is clear that both Jesus and Matthew are here following the text of the Old Testament *as translated into Greek* (i.e., the LXX). The evidence points, therefore, to a Gospel written originally not in Hebrew (or Aramaic) but in Greek.[96]

2. The same as the one just described, with emphasis, however, on the view that the original language in which, according to Papias, the work which he erroneously ascribed to Matthew was written, was definitely Hebrew, and the several *translations* were into Aramaic, not into Greek.[97]

3. Papias was right. Matthew, after writing his Gospel in the language of the Hebrews—resulting in the fact that in speaking with Greeks each person according to his ability would translate it into his language—having left Palestine to labor elsewhere, produced a Gospel in the Greek language with a view to "the Jews of the Diaspora" (Berkhof), or to "foreign nations" (Thiessen).[98]

4. Papias, in speaking about *logia* was thinking about "Jesus' sayings." Matthew had taken these down in Aramaic. When Mark's Gospel came into the hands of the former publican, he used almost all of it, transposing its materials wherever he found this necessary, and combining it with the sayings, utterances, or teachings of Jesus which he, Matthew, had himself taken down. The result, in the course of time, became the Greek *Gospel according to Matthew*.[99]

5. Papias did not mean that Matthew had written a Hebrew Gospel, but that he had written *in Hebrew style*.[100]

Ἐβραΐδι: "in the Aramaic language," "in the Hebrew dialect," and "in Hebrew style."
τὰ λόγια: "the sayings."
συνετάξατο: "composed," "collected," "noted down."
ἡρμήνευσεν: "interpreted."

[96] For this view see N. B. Stonehouse, *Origins of the Synoptic Gospels*, pp. 87-92.
[97] H. Mulder, "Het Synoptisch Vraagstuk," *Exegetica* (1952), p. 17.
[98] L. Berkhof, *New Testament Introduction*, pp. 66-69; cf. H. C. Thiessen, *op. cit.*, p. 137.
[99] E. J. Goodspeed, *op. cit.*, pp. 16, 108-110, 144.
[100] J. Kürzinger, *BZ* 4 (1960), pp. 19-38.

INTRODUCTION TO MATTHEW

I shall not take the time to comment on all these views separately. A few reflections will have to suffice. First, in speaking about *Mark* and his Gospel [101] Papias clearly defines the word "oracles" (logia) [102] as having reference to "the things said *or done* by the Lord," not only to the "the things said." Papias, therefore, is not thinking of words or sayings apart from works or deeds, when he uses this term. He is thinking of the Gospel as a whole. It is therefore logical to assume that also when he says, "Matthew arranged the oracles," he is speaking about Matthew's *Gospel.*

Secondly, we should carefully distinguish between two questions: *a.* "Is our Greek Matthew a *translation* of an earlier Semitic (whether Hebrew or Aramaic) work?" and *b.* "Was there an earlier work, written in the language of the Hebrews, a writing that preceded Greek Matthew, and stood in some relation to it, being a model for it and/or perhaps even, in a sense however restricted, a source for some of its contents?" These two questions must not be confused. Theoretically it should be considered possible to answer the first question negatively, but the second in the affirmative. As to that second question, the possibility of remaining non-committal must also not be excluded.

As to the first question, the position of those who look upon the Gospels and certain other parts of the New Testament as translations from written Aramaic has already been discussed and refuted (pp. 83-85). Greek Matthew, too, is not a mere *translation* from Aramaic. Throughout, the Greek language and its idioms play too prominent a role in it. The argument based on Matt. 15:8, 9, taken as evidence for the charge found in verse 6 (see above under opinion No. 1), is valid. Though what Jesus is saying may well be *implied* also in the Hebrew, it is certainly far more clearly *expressed* in the Septuagint. The fact that by their tradition the Pharisees and scribes had made void the Word of God because they had substituted for it the precepts of men, precepts which they *teach* the people, reminds one of the Isaiah passage as recorded not so much in the original Hebrew as in the Greek (Septuagint) translation of the Old Testament.

Hebrew (Isa. 29:13):
"Forasmuch as this people draw near with their mouth, and with their lips honor me, but have removed their heart from me, and their fear toward me (is but) acquired precept of men, therefore. . . ."

Septuagint:
"This people draw near to me (and) with their lips honor me, but their heart is far from me. But in vain do they worship me, teaching precepts of men and (their) doctrines."

---

101 Eusebius, *op. cit.*, III.xxxix.15.
102 On λόγιον see Th.D.N.T., Vol. IV, pp. 137-141, especially p. 140, 141.

Matt. 15:8, 9 (cf. Mark 7:6, 7):

"This people honor me with their lips but their heart is far from me. But in vain do they worship me, teaching (as their) doctrines precepts of men."

There is nothing that necessitates the positing of an Aramaic written Gospel underlying Greek Matthew. Such a document has never been found. No ancient witness ever quotes from it. Whether it ever existed cannot now be established with any degree of certainty. The form in which many quotations occur in all three Synoptics indicates a common basis for all. This source could well be Matthew's *notes*.[103] Similar notes written by the same person could very well account also for some of the other (i.e., non-quotation) Gospel material. As has already been shown, Matthew probably also used Mark's Gospel, which, according to tradition, was derived from Peter's preaching, which, in turn, in many instances may have depended on Matthew's notes. Then, there was, of course, Matthew's own memory of what he himself had seen and heard and of that which others had told him (oral tradition). With all this source material at hand, it would be difficult to demonstrate any *necessity* for a written Aramaic Gospel underlying the Greek.

This, however, does not absolutely prove that such a Gospel never existed, and that Papias and those who may have followed his lead were in error. They *may* have been in error, but the final word on this has not been written. The arguments that have been used to prove him wrong have not convinced everyone. Some reason as follows: How the error of Jerome (A.D. 340?-420), a man who lived a very long time after the last of the apostles had died, can be a strong argument against the statement of Papias is hard to understand. This Papias was a *very early* witness (probably writing sometime between 125 and 140); and by Irenaeus described as a hearer of John (the apostle) and a companion of Polycarp.

The fact that an Aramaic Matthew pre-dating a Greek Matthew has never been found nor quoted would be well-nigh annihilating as an argument against the position that there was at one time such a document, were it not for two considerations: *a.* the statement of Papias and others after him vouching for its onetime existence, and *b.* the fact that as time went on there would be less need for such a book, explaining its ultimate disappearance: "The Christian missionaries with an Aramaic book ... in their hands would have been powerless to make propaganda in what was in fact a Greek or rather Hellenized world."[104]

---

[103] See also pp. 34, 53, 96. Reference to Matthew's notes can also be found in A. T. Robertson, *Word Pictures in the New Testament*, New York and London, 1930, Vol. I, p. xii; E. J. Goodspeed, *op. cit.*, pp. 80, 86, 88, 108, 142; W. Hendriksen, *Bible Survey*, Grand Rapids, 1961, p. 384; and R. H. Gundry, *The Use of the Old Testament in St. Matthew's Gospel*, pp. xii, 181, 182.

[104] A. Deissmann, *Light from the Ancient East* (translated from the German by L. R. M. Strachan), New York, 1922, p. 65.

Another objection against the theory that Papias was mistaken has been expressed in these words: "Let us remember also that it is inconsistent to believe Papias when he says that Matthew wrote the Gospel, and to discredit his further testimony that the apostle wrote in Hebrew, as some scholars do. It is indeed almost certain that Pantaenus [see Eusebius, *op. cit.*, V. x, 1-4] was mistaken, when he thought that he had found the Hebrew Gospel in India; and that Jerome labored under a delusion when he imagined that he had translated it at Caesarea. What they saw was probably a corruption of the Hebrew original, known as 'the Gospel according to the Hebrews.' But this possible mistake does not invalidate the other independent testimony of Jerome and that of all the early fathers to the effect that Matthew wrote the Gospel in Hebrew."[105] The same author suggests that Greek Matthew was "a new recension of the Gospel."[106] And in a recent study C. S. Petrie reaches the conclusion that the testimony of Papias regarding Matthew's Gospel rests on firmer ground than the best guesses of today.[107]

It would probably not be too difficult to bring up counter-arguments. It seems to the author of this book that there is no sufficient evidence either to prove or to disprove the onetime existence of an early Gospel according to Matthew in the language of the Hebrews. Did Matthew write a Semitic Gospel? Is Greek Matthew "a new recension"? My answer is, "I do not know." That it is no *translation* of a Hebrew or Aramaic written Gospel is clear. For the rest, one thing I *do* know: Greek Matthew is Hebraistic, in the sense already explained.

Evangelistic, that is having a broad missionary purpose.

Matthew makes it very clear that this Messiah of prophecy stands related to the entire world. In his Family Tree not only a good many direct descendants of Abraham are mentioned but also such "foreigners" as Tamar, Rahab, and Ruth (1:3, 5). Wise men come from the east to worship the Child and to bring him gifts (chap. 2). That the gospel of salvation full and free reaches out even to those outside the boundaries of Israel is evident from the words of Christ: "And I say to y o u that many shall come from the east and from the west, and shall sit down with Abraham, Isaac, and Jacob in the kingdom of heaven, but the sons of the kingdom shall be cast into outer darkness" (8:11, 12). It is this same Christ who healed the centurion's servant (8:5-13), praised the faith of the Canaanitish woman and healed her daughter (15:21-28). It is he who said, "The kingdom of God shall be taken away from y o u, and shall be given to a nation bringing forth its fruits" (21:43). He also said, "As many as y o u shall find, bid to the

---

105 L. Berkhof, *New Testament Introduction*, pp. 69, 70.

106 Same, p. 70. R. V. G. Tasker speaks similarly, *The Gospel according to St. Matthew*, p. 13.

107 C. S. Petrie, "The Authorship of 'The Gospel according to Matthew': a Reconsideration of the External Evidence," *NTStud* 14 (1, 1967), pp. 15-32.

marriage feast. . . . And the wedding was filled with guests" (22:9, 10). What is perhaps the most world-embracing command is found in the final chapter: "Go therefore and make disciples of all the nations" (28:19, 20).

The question might be asked, "But how is it possible for one and the same evangelist—or for Christ, for the gospel (the good tidings of salvation), or for the Gospel (the book ascribed to Matthew)—to be both Hebraistic and evangelistic?" The answer is found in such passages as Acts 13:46 and Rom. 1:16.

After Golgotha, with a foreglimpse even during the period immediately preceding, there is *one* chosen race, consisting of all who are "in Christ," no matter what happens to be their race or nationality. The distinctions that marked the Old Testament era have vanished completely (Rom. 10:12; I Cor. 7:19; Gal. 3:9, 28, 29; Eph. 2:14, 18; Col. 3:11; I Peter 2:9; Rev. 7:9; 22:17).

Written by a man whose qualifications corresponded with these characteristics. Who was that man? This brings us to the next heading:

II. Authorship, Date, and Place

The opinion of many is that the author of the book which opens the door to the treasure-house of the New Testament was "certainly not Matthew the apostle."[108] As far as the doctrine of inspiration is concerned, there can be no objection to this opinion. Nowhere does the author reveal his identity. What he wrote is and remains anonymous. It was different with Paul. When

---

[108] A. H. McNeile, *The Gospel According to St. Matthew*, London, 1915, p. xxviii. The same idea is also expressed by B. M. Metzger, *The New Testament, Its Background, Growth, and Content*, pp. 96, 97. E. J. Goodspeed, *op. cit.*, p. 20, admits that for a long time he also had been of that opinion. His book indicates a complete turnabout. The view is rather widely held that although Matthew was not the author of the finished work, he did have something to do with it. He had provided the basic structure by jotting down the logia of the Lord, etc. Whatever it was that the real Matthew had written was subsequently utilized, enlarged upon, and organized by a compiler or editor whose name has been lost. The whole was then called "The Gospel according to Matthew." According to one author, the reason for this ascription was that "there would be an irresistible tendency to find for it Apostolic sanction," W. C. Allen, *A Critical and Exegetical Commentary on the Gospel according to Matthew (International Critical Commentary)*, p. lxxxi. This reason is not very convincing. If the Gospel in question was ascribed to Matthew "to find for it Apostolic sanction," why was not the longest Gospel ascribed to the apostle Paul instead of to Luke, and the shortest to the apostle Peter instead of to Mark? According to A. Plummer, the author of this Gospel "was not S. Matthew," but "an early Jewish Christian not sufficiently important to give his name to a Gospel." This unknown author used Matthew's earlier *logia* ("collection of facts concerning Jesus, chiefly consisting of his utterances and the circumstances in which they were spoken") as a source (*An Exegetical Commentary on the Gospel according to S. Matthew*, reprint Grand Rapids, 1953, pp. viii-x.

he addressed a letter to Philemon he included these words: "I Paul write it." In fact, in the very first verse of each epistle he names himself as the author. To be sure, Matthew's name occurs in 9:9 and 10:3 but in neither of these passages does he call himself the writer. Moreover, as has been indicated previously, the title, which, as commonly though not strictly interpreted, ascribes the book to Matthew as author, was not added until about A.D. 125. Hence, it does not belong to the inspired book itself.

The possibility that the title of a Gospel might point to the name of a person who, let it be supposed, was responsible for only part of its contents, must be granted. Excellent conservative scholars find no fault with the title although they reject the traditional view according to which the former publican, Matthew, was the composer of the entire Gospel. As they see it, the relation of Matthew to this Gospel must be understood in the sense that, in addition to what it has in common with the other Synoptics, it also contains much that is original in material, purpose, and structure. In this fresh and independent approach they discern the abiding influence of a definite eye-witness, that is, of the apostle Matthew.[109]

Nevertheless, by no means all scholars are satisfied with the idea that the former publican was the author only in the sense that he was responsible for some of its source material. Instead, they believe that in a real sense he was the author or composer of the entire book, though in writing it he made lavish use of sources.[110]

The arguments[111] of those who accept a rather remote connection between the former publican and the book credited to him are as follows:

1. The appeal to early tradition in support of the proposition that Matthew was himself the author of the entire first canonical Gospel is not

---

[109] Thus, for example, H. N. Ridderbos, *Het Evangelie naar Mattheus* (*Korte Verklaring der Heilige Schrift*), Kampen, 1952, pp. 13-15. From here on when this author's name is mentioned followed by *op. cit.*, the reference is to his commentary on Matthew.

[110] As A. T. Robertson sees it, "There is no real reason why the Apostle Matthew could not have written both the Aramaic Logia and our Greek Matthew, unless one is unwilling to believe that he would make use of Mark's work on a par with his own" (*Word Pictures*, Vol. I, p. xi). R. C. H. Lenski considers Matthew the author of the entire book, in which he embodied certain Hebrew logia (*Interpretation of St. Matthew's Gospel*, Columbus, Ohio, 1932, p. 18. From here on when this author's name is mentioned followed by *op. cit.*, the reference is to his commentary on Matthew.) S. Greijdanus considers Matthew the author of the Aramaic Gospel, and believes that someone else translated it into Greek (*Bijbelsch Handboek*, Kampen, 1935, Vol. II, p. 104). N. B. Stonehouse believes that "the apostolic authorship of Matthew is as strongly attested as any fact of ancient church history," (*Origins of the Synoptic Gospels*, pp. 46, 47). As has been stated earlier, this agrees with what Goodspeed has previously written, though not all of the reasons on which the latter based his opinion were accepted by Stonehouse. Finally, R. H. Gundry also defends the view that Matthew was the author of the work ascribed to him (*op. cit.*, pp. 181-185). On p. 182 he gives his estimate of Goodspeed's arguments. With that estimate I am in full agreement.

[111] For these arguments see especially H. N. Ridderbos, *op. cit.*, p. 13.

justified, for tradition refers to an Aramaic writing, and Greek Matthew is not even a translation from written Aramaic.

Answer: If the exponents of early tradition viewed Greek Matthew as a free translation so that by them the supposed Aramaic original and the new document were regarded as *one* book, which they ascribed to Matthew, would not this argument lose its force? If these early witnesses (Papias, Irenaeus, Origen, etc.) did not so regard it, must we not then conclude that some of them, though often quoting Greek Matthew, never discuss its authorship? Besides, does not *the title* "according to Matthew" embody a very early tradition? For evidence of the title's early date see Goodspeed, *op. cit.*, pp. 37, 38.

2. It is very doubtful that Matthew, an eye-witness, would have made such extensive use of a Gospel written by Mark, a man who was not even one of The Twelve.

Answer: This argument has already been answered; see pp. 45, 46.

3. The first canonical Gospel is not nearly as vivid as we would have expected it to be if it had been composed by an eye-witness. In fact, it is not even as vivid as is Mark's Gospel (or John's).

Answer: It is immediately granted that among the Synoptics Mark is generally the most vivid, as we would also expect with reference to a Gospel written by *Peter's* interpreter. However, in order to account for the presence of vivid portrayal, not only proximity to the scene where the action took place must be considered, but also the character or personality of the writer. Peter was probably a more intense and vibrant individual than Matthew. Mark may have resembled Peter in some of his traits (see pp. 41, 42). Matthew may well have been more calm, more deliberate. Also, this probable difference in vividness must not be exaggerated. Matthew's Gospel is not lacking in vivid touches: 1:20; chap. 2; 7:24-27; 8:23-27; 14:28-31; 20:1-16; 22:1-14; 23:1-39; chap. 25; 27:3-10, 19-21, 24, 25, 50-56, 62-66; 28:2-4, 11-15.

What has been discussed just now is a conservative position regarding the authorship of the book known as "the Gospel according to Matthew." Conservatives agree that for one reason or another the title is correct. They also agree in believing that the book is part of the inspired Word of God. The difference among them concerns a relatively minor point. No true conservative, however, will be able to endorse the position of radical scholarship regarding the authorship, character, and content of this Gospel. Since this position is actually an attack upon the reliability of the Gospels, a theme which has already been treated somewhat at length (see pp. 54-76), little need be added here.

A typical example of the radical view with respect to Matthew's Gospel is found in an article by H. H. Koester of Harvard Divinity School.[112] That

---

[112] "Matthew, Gospel according to Saint," *Encyclopaedia Britanica*, Chicago, London, etc., 1969 edition, Vol. XIV, pp. 1117-1118.

author regards some of the material contained in this Gospel as being of a legendary character, flatly denies that an immediate disciple of Jesus could have written the book, and expresses it as his opinion that 22:6, 7 regards Jerusalem's fall as having already occurred. He is also certain that the developed Christological, doctrinal, and liturgical formulations prove that the book was written by a man of the third generation, not earlier than A.D. 75-100.

But rejection of a narrative—for example, the virgin birth—does not prove that the indicated event never happened. The argument based on 22:6, 7 is very weak, as has already been shown (see p. 22). And consistent reasoning would demand that if we are going to reject the possibility of the existence of developed Christological, doctrinal, and liturgical formulations before the year A.D. 75, we would have to deny the authenticity of all of Paul's epistles (and, in fact, of much of the New Testament) along with it!

Arguments in Defense of the Ascription of
"The Gospel according to Matthew" to
Matthew, one of The Twelve

1. Matthew (Matt. 9:9; 10:3; Mark 3:18; Luke 6:15; Acts 1:13), also called Levi (Mark 2:14; Luke 5:27, 29), was, as appears from his very names, a Jew.[113] This may account for the Jewishness of his Gospel.

2. When Matthew received the call to follow Jesus he was a publican, that is, a tax collector in Capernaum. The probability is that he was in the service of Herod Antipas. As he labored in "Galilee of the Gentiles," he had to be at home in Greek as well as in Aramaic.[114] The Gospel according to Matthew shows that its author was, indeed, acquainted with more than one language. Thus, the quotations found here often present a kind of paraphrase in which elements from the Greek Septuagint are combined with Aramaic and derivations from the Hebrew.[115]

---

[113] His father's name was Alphaeus (Mark 2:14). This was also the name of the father of James the Less and of Joses (Matt. 10:3; Mark 15:40). Goodspeed identifies this latter Alphaeus with Matthew's father. As he sees it, the mother in the family was one of the Marys, and was Matthew's step-mother. He even suggests that Matthew's presence in this remarkable family may have been the background of the dramatic call to discipleship he received (*op. cit.*, pp. 2, 6, 7). All this sounds a bit fanciful. I cannot find any support for it in Scripture. Since the Gospels do not indicate any family relationship between Matthew and James the Less (as they do between James and John, and between Peter and Andrew), is it not far more probable that there was no such connection? In all likelihood, therefore, just as the Bible speaks of more than one Goliath, Herod, James, Jeroboam, John, Joshua, Judas, Noah, Philip, Simon, etc., so also it recognizes more than one Alphaeus. In some ways I find Goodspeed's book, *Matthew, Apostle and Evangelist* very stimulating and informative; in other respects, rather repetitious and fanciful.

[114] See E. Schürer, *Geschichte des jüdischen Volkes in Zeitaltar Jesu Christi*, Leipzig, 1901-1909, Vol. I, pp. 57 ff.; 84 ff.

[115] This is made clear by R. H. Gundry, *The Use of the Old Testament in St. Matthew's Gospel*, pp. 174-178.

Again, as a tax collector Matthew was obliged to make written reports of the moneys he collected. He may even have known shorthand.[116] He was therefore the logical person to take notes on Christ's words and works.

3. Not only was Matthew an intelligent Jew; he was also deeply religious, as appears from the fact that when called by Jesus he obeyed immediately. As such we may well believe that he was thoroughly acquainted with both the Hebrew Old Testament and its Septuagint translation. He was certainly well versed in the Scriptures. Hence, led by the Spirit, he was the kind of a man who would be able to interpret Old Testament passages in such a manner that they would apply to new situations. The Gospel according to Matthew tallies with this ability on the part of Matthew. The writers of the other Gospels, we may well assume, were able to make use of Matthew's notes. He, in turn, was able to utilize Mark's Gospel.

4. Tradition is unanimous in pointing to Matthew as the author. It never mentions anyone else:

Eusebius, at the beginning of the fourth century, wrote as follows:

"Matthew, having first preached to Hebrews, when he was on the point of leaving for others transmitted in writing in his native language the Gospel according to himself, and thus, in writing, made up for the lack of his own presence" (*op. cit.*, III.xxiv.6).

A little earlier Origen (fl.210-250) expressed himself similarly, and so, still earlier (about 182-188) did Irenaeus (see above, p. 44, footnotes 41b and 41a respectively). Earliest of all (sometime between 125 and 140) in this series of witnesses, is Papias, whose reference to Matthew and his Gospel has also been quoted and discussed (pp. 87-89). Papias was described by Irenaeus as a hearer of [the apostle] John and a companion of Polycarp.

Use of this Gospel in the earliest patristic writings that have been preserved (those ascribed to Barnabas, Clement of Rome, Ignatius, and Polycarp) is abundantly attested. The Didache also adds its testimony. In fact, one can say without exaggeration that external evidence of the early use of this Gospel, and of its ascription to Matthew as soon as ascriptions were made, is unanimous.

5. It would be hard to explain how within a period of perhaps sixty years since this Gospel was composed the name of its true author could have been lost and a fictitious name substituted.

---

[116] Goodspeed sheds valuable light on this subject, on the basis of discovered papyri, *op. cit.*, pp. 57-76. On the subject of ancient shorthand see also G. Milligan, *The N.T. Documents*, London, 1913, pp. 241-247. That shorthand was well-known and widespread even before Matthew was born is also confirmed by the fact that already in 63 B.C. Marcus Tullius Tiro, a friend of Cicero, had invented a system of shorthand that was widely taught in the schools of the empire and used by the *notarii* in the Roman Senate, to take down the speeches of the orators. And the Greek world was not behind in this, as Milligan and others have shown.

6. The author of a work so beautiful in design, so consistent in style, and so majestic in content could hardly have been lost from view.

7. The fact that this Gospel was ascribed to one of the least conspicuous of the twelve apostles, a man concerning whom hardly anything is known, is another argument in favor of the truthfulness of this ascription.

As to the date and place of origin much is uncertain. Matthew's knowledge of the Hebrew Old Testament and his access to the Hebrew scrolls would seem to call for a *date* when the break with the synagogue where such scrolls were kept was not as yet complete, and for Palestine as the *place* or *general region* where the writing originated. Also supporting the latter are the many references to events and situations in and around Jerusalem, reported exclusively by Matthew (2:3, 16; 21:10; 27:3-8, 24, 25, 52, 53, 62-66; 28:4, 11-15). The date cannot have been later than A.D. 70, for Jerusalem and its temple had not yet been destroyed (24:2, 15-28). Yet, it must be late enough to allow time for Matthew to read and make use of Mark's Gospel. But we do not know exactly when Mark wrote his book. But see p. 46. The variously appraised and interpreted statement of Irenaeus (quoted on p. 44), according to which Matthew published his Gospel "while Peter and Paul were preaching in Rome and establishing the church"[117] would seem to point to a date not much earlier than A.D. 63, and probably before the beginning of the Jewish War. I regard A.D. 63-66 as perhaps not far off. It cannot have been *much* earlier, for 27:8 and 28:15 imply that since Calvary a long time has elapsed.

III. Purpose

In general it can be said that the purpose of this Gospel was *fully to win the Jews for Christ;* that is, to gain those still unconverted and to strengthen those already converted. The Hebraistic character of Matthew's Gospel, as described in the preceding pages, points to this as its goal. In order to achieve it the emphasis throughout is placed on the fact that Jesus is indeed the long awaited Messiah of the Hebrew Scriptures.

Hence, according to God's providential guidance, the Old Testament

---

117 Much is still obscure: *a.* When Irenaeus says that this Gospel was published "among the Hebrews in their own language" is this his own original opinion or is he echoing Papias? *b.* When he states that this writing of the Gospel occurred at the time when "Peter and Paul were establishing the church in Rome," is this an error, in view of the fact that the church in Rome was not founded by Paul? Or must a more figurative meaning be attached to the words "were establishing," for example, "greatly strengthening"? See Phil. 1:12-18. *c.* Was Peter in Rome between Paul's first and second imprisonments there? See I Peter 5:13.

prophetical books are followed immediately by the fulfilment-of-prophecy book, Matthew. Also, in harmony with the rule "to the Jew first, and also to the Greek" (Rom. 1:16); and "Y o u shall be my witnesses in Jerusalem . . . and to the most distant part of the earth" (Acts 1:8; cf. Luke 24:47); the most Jewish Gospel, the Gospel written by a Jew for Jews, is placed first. It is followed by the Gospel according to Mark who, though also a Jew, composed it for the Romans. Luke, not even a Jew, follows with his Gospel directed to the Greeks. Though in all these Gospels Jesus is presented as the sinner's only Redeemer, yet the sublime truth that this Redeemer is "the Savior of *the world,*" that is, of God's elect gathered from *every* nation under heaven, is stressed in *John's* Gospel (1:13; 3:16; 4:42; 10:16; 17:20, 21). Thus the order of the books of our canon proceeds, very beautifully, from the particular to the universal; yet, the particular already includes the universal, and the universal remains, in a sense, always particular: the gospel is the power of God for salvation *to all who believe,* to them *all,* to them *alone.*

In Matthew particular stress is placed on the fact that Jesus is indeed the Christ of prophecy, not only in order that the Jews, by accepting this Son of David as their Savior, may have life in his name, but also in order that they may be able to defend themselves against the attacks of the enemy, and may even gain the Gentiles.

When a person asks, "What is the purpose of this Gospel?" he can best discover the answer by reading and rereading the entire book. *In particular,* the answer, then, is as follows:

1. *Translation* from the realm of darkness to that of light: the conversion of those Jews who have not as yet experienced the basic spiritual change. These must be reminded of the great privileges that had been bestowed on them, and also of the dire consequences of refusing to heed God's call (10:5 ff.; 11:25-29; 23:37-39).

2. *Transformation:* constant renewal of life on the part of those (mostly) Jews who have already, by the power of the Spirit, surrendered themselves to Christ. These are shown how they should conduct themselves in order to be a blessing to others, for the glory of the Father in heaven (4:19; 5:16, 43-48; 6:19 ff.; 7:1 ff., 24-27; etc.).

3. *Vindication* of God's truth against the attack of bitter adversaries (5:17 ff.; 6:2 ff,; chap. 12; 13:10 ff., 54-58; 15:1-20; 16:1-4; chap. 23; etc.).

4. *Evangelization* of all the nations (8:5-13; 15:21-28; 28:16-20).

IV. Theme and Outline

As has been pointed out earlier, the sojourn of Jesus on earth must be viewed not primarily as a series of things that happened to him but rather as the accomplishment of a task assigned to him. Other children are born. They are wholly passive in their birth. He, too, was born, but he also *came*. Moreover, he came with a purpose: not to take but to give, to give his soul as a ransom in the place of many (Matt. 20:28; Mark 10:45), to seek and to save that which was lost (Luke 19:10).

This *design* aspect of the life of Christ on earth is emphasized in all four Gospels: in Matthew with all its fulfilment of prophecy passages (see also 10:34-36; 20:22); in Mark (10:38); in Luke (9:51; 12:50; 22:22, 42); and in John (4:4, 34; 9:4; 17:4; 19:30). Accordingly, a good theme (see John 17:4b) for the story told in any or all of the Gospels is:

The Work Which Thou Gavest Him to Do

The broad divisions, as already indicated, would be the same for the three Synoptics, namely, this work (or this task):

I. Begun
II. Continued
III. Accomplished

Or, in slightly different phraseology:

I. Its Beginning or Inauguration
II. Its Progress or Continuation
III. Its Climax or Culmination

The subdivisions under each heading will, in many cases, be different for each of these three Gospels. For a more detailed outline see Table of Contents and the Outlines at the opening of the chapters.[118]

---

[118] A somewhat similar general plan was followed in the author's N.T.C. on the Gospel according to John; see Vol. I, pp. 66, 68; Vol. II, pp. 2, 134, 218, 260, 374, and 446.

Commentary

on

The Gospel According to Matthew

The Work Which Thou Gavest Him To Do

Its Beginning

or

Inauguration

Chapters 1:1–4:11

Outline of Chapter 1

Theme: *The Work Which Thou Gavest Him to Do*

CHAPTER I

MATTHEW 1:1-17

1 1 Record of ancestry of Jesus Christ, son of David, son of Abraham.
2 Abraham became the father of[119] Isaac, and Isaac became the father of Jacob,
and Jacob became the father of Judah and his brothers, 3 and Judah became the father
of Perez and Zerah by Tamar, and Perez became the father of Hezron, and Hezron
became the father of Ram, 4 and Ram became the father of Amminadab, and
Amminadab became the father of Nahshon, and Nahshon became the father of Salmon,
5 and Salmon became the father of Boaz by Rahab, and Boaz became the father of Obed
by Ruth, and Obed became the father of Jesse, 6 and Jesse became the father of David
the king.

David became the father of Solomon by the wife of Uriah, 7 and Solomon
became the father of Rehoboam, and Rehoboam became the father of Abijah, and Abijah
became the Father of Asa, 8 and Asa became the father of Jehoshaphat, and Jehoshaphat became the father of Joram, and Joram became the father of Uzziah, 9 and Uzziah
became the father of Jotham, and Jotham became the father of Ahaz, and Ahaz became
the father of Hezekiah, 10 and Hezekiah became the father of Manasseh, and Manasseh
became the father of Amon, and Amon became the father of Josiah, 11 and Josiah
became the father of Jechoniah and his brothers, at the time of the deportation to
Babylon.

12 After the deportation to Babylon: Jechoniah became the father of Shealtiel, and Shealtiel became the father of Zerubbabel, 13 and Zerubbabel became the
father of Abiud, and Abiud became the father of Eliakim, and Eliakim became the father
of Azor, 14 and Azor became the father of Zadok, and Zadok became the father of
Achim, and Achim became the father of Eliud, 15 and Eliud became the father of
Eleazar, and Eleazar became the father of Matthan, and Matthan became the father of

---

119 The verb refers here to the father's acquisition of offspring by depositing seed. *Physical* descent is indicated, whether from father to son, as in the case of father Abraham and son Isaac, or father via son to grandson or later physical descendant. It must be considered deplorable that elegant modern English has no easy equivalent for the verb used in the original (ἐγέννησεν). The rendering *begat* (A.V.; A.R.V.) is definitely archaic. The rendering *was the father of* (Beck, Williams, Phillips, R.S.V., N.E.B., etc.) shifts the emphasis from the relation of a past *event*, as in the original, to the description of a past *state*. The German offers: "Abraham zeugete Isaak"; Dutch: "Abraham verwekte—or gewon—Izak." Perhaps the least objectionable renderings into English, though not a single one of them is completely satisfactory, are the following:

"To Abraham was born Isaac" (N.A.S.)

"Abraham begot Isaac" (see, however, the footnote on this in Williams' translation).

"Abraham became the father of Isaac," favored by L.N.T. (A. and G.), p. 154. Between these three it is difficult to make a choice.

Jacob, 16 and Jacob became the father of Joseph, the husband of Mary, of whom was born Jesus, who is called Christ.

17 So all the generations from Abraham to David (were) fourteen genera-tions, and from David to the deportation to Babylon fourteen generations, and from the deportation to Babylon to Christ fourteen generations.

1:1-17 *The Genealogy of Jesus Christ*
Cf. Luke 3:23-38

The Gospel according to Matthew opens with Christ's family tree. Today, by many readers such a list of names is probably considered sufficiently uninteresting to be skipped. We should bear in mind, however, that Matthew was writing primarily for Jews, as has been shown. This also accounts for the fact that he begins the line of descent with Abraham, and does not trace it back to Adam as Luke does. Now, for the Jews genealogy had never been lacking in significance. After the conquest of Canaan it was important in determining a family's place of residence; for, by divine law, the occupation of the land was according to tribes, families, and fathers' houses (Num. 26:52-56; 33:54). If one settled in a territory other than his own he might be called a *deserter* (Judg. 12:4). Under certain circumstances transfer of property required accurate knowledge of pedigree (Ruth 3:9, 12, 13; 4:1-10). Later, in Judah, royal succession was linked with Davidic lineage (I Kings 11:36; 15:4). At the return from Babylon a person who claimed priestly prerogatives was required to prove priestly descent. Otherwise he was excluded from office (Ezra 2:62). At the beginning of the new dispensa-tion, fulfilling one's duty in connection with the general registration or "enrolment" described in Luke 2:1-4 necessitated knowledge of the ances-tral roll.

When we take all this into account we are not surprised that Scripture abounds with genealogical material. In the Old Testament it is found in such chapters as Gen. 5, 10, 11, 22, 25, 29, 30, 35, 46; Exod. 6; Num. 1, 2, 7, 10, 13, 26, 34; Josh. 7, 13; Ruth 4; I Sam. 1, 14; II Sam. 3, 5, 23; I Kings 4; I Chron. 1–9, 11, 12, 15, 23–27; II Chron. 23, 29; Ezra 2, 7, 8, 10; Neh. 3, 7, 10, 11, 12.

As to the New Testament, here in Matt. 1:1-17 we find a *descending* genealogy, one that leads via Joseph to Jesus. In Luke 3:23-38 an *ascending* family tree is presented. When this is read backward, it also ends with Jesus; though, as held by many, via Mary instead of Joseph. These sections in Matthew and Luke do not exhaust the New Testament references to geneal-ogy. Did not Paul (I Tim. 1:4; Titus 3:9) have to issue a warning against excessive interest in such matters, interest stemming from the error of minimizing the fact that with the coming of Christ and the fulfilment of his mission Old Testament regulations had been abolished and prophecies in large measure fulfilled?

The genealogy presented in Matt. 1:1-17 is not just an appendix but is closely connected with the substance of the entire chapter; in a broader sense, with the contents of the entire book.[120] Thus, in the heading of the genealogy (verse 1) Jesus Christ is called "the son of David" (cf. verse 6). This expression recurs in verse 20 where it is applied to Joseph, Jesus' "father" (cf. Luke 2:48). But note the very careful way in which the relationship of Joseph to Jesus is described in verse 16. From this verse it is evident that the evangelist is purposely precluding the possibility that the reader might think of Joseph as being Christ's *physical* father. What he is implying, already here in this genealogy, is that although Mary was indeed Jesus' mother, Joseph was his father not in the natural but only in the legal sense. And it is this very point that receives elaboration in the beautiful account that follows in verses 18-25. We are shown, therefore, that he who is the Son of man is also the Son of God. He is the true seed of David and of Abraham, the fulfilment of prophecy. He alone is Israel's and mankind's Hope.

This central thought, moreover, is by no means confined to chapter 1. Rather, in his entire Gospel the author sets forth the greatness of Christ, as revealed in his exalted origin and in the marvelous manner in which he accomplished the task assigned to him by the Father. Therefore David's *son* is definitely also David's *Lord* (22:41-46)! With this thought in mind we now approach verse 1:

1. **Record of ancestry of Jesus Christ, son of David, son of Abraham.** That here in verse 1 we are dealing with *a caption* is clear. Is it to be construed as the title of the entire Gospel? Evidently it was not so interpreted in very early times when a different title was given to the book, as is known. Is it, perhaps, the heading of the entire first chapter? Probably not, since 1:18, though very closely related to 1:1-17, seems to be another heading. The best procedure, it would appear to me, would be to regard 1:1 as the caption above the entire *genealogy* (1:2-17). It strongly reminds one of several headings or introductory phrases in the book of Genesis, but especially of Gen. 5:1, which similarly introduces a genealogy.

Accordingly, what follows in verses 2-17 is in this heading called *biblos geneseos* of Jesus Christ, son of David, etc. The word *biblos* (cf. Bible) can refer to a *book,* as in Josephus, papyri, etc., or *a sacred book;* for example, "the book of life" (Phil. 4:3; Rev. 3:5). It can, however, also refer to a writing that is less than what we would consider a book. In the present case it refers clearly to a *record* or *list* of names. The next word, *geneseos,* is the genitive of the word with which every English reader is familiar, namely, *genesis;* capitalized *Genesis* when it refers to the Bible's "book of begin-

---

[120] See also M. D. Johnson, *The Purpose of the Biblical Genealogies,* Cambridge, 1969.

nings." The entire expression *biblos geneseos* means, therefore, *record* of *beginning,* or of *origin* or *ancestry.*

It is the record of ancestry of the One who is called Jesus Christ. Our English word *Jesus* is really Latin from the closely resembling Greek *Iesous.* This, in turn, is the hellenized form of the late Hebrew *Jeshua,* the contracted form of *Jehoshua* (Josh. 1:1; Zech. 3:1). The latter means *Jehovah is salvation.* In the shorter form *Jeshua* the stress is on the *verb;* hence, *he will certainly save.* This reminds us of Matt. 1:21, "You shall call his name Jesus, for he will save his people from their sins." Cf. also Matt. 11:27-30; John 14:6; Acts 4:12. For the emphasis on the verb see also Ecclus. 46:1.

To the personal name *Jesus* is added the official name *Christ.* This is the Greek equivalent of the Hebrew *Messiah.* It indicates that the One to whom it refers was by the Holy Spirit anointed (hence, ordained, set apart, and qualified) to carry out the task of saving his people. Cf. Isa. 61:1; Luke 4:18; Heb. 1:9. He was anointed to be our chief prophet (Deut. 18:15; Isa. 55:4; Acts 3:22; 7:37); only highpriest (Ps. 110:4; Heb. 10:12, 14); and eternal king (Ps. 2:6; Zech. 9:9; Matt. 21:5; 28:18; Luke 1:33). Of course, the names Jesus and Christ, as here used, belong together. They really constitute one glorious name given to our Savior.

Now in this genealogical preface Jesus Christ is called "son of David, son of Abraham." That reminds one of prophecy. Interest in genealogy was fortified especially by Messianic prophecy, according to which the coming Deliverer would be the seed of the woman (Gen. 3:15), of Abraham (Gen. 22:18), of Judah (Gen. 49:10), and of David (II Sam. 7:12, 13).

As to the propriety of calling Jesus "the *seed* or *son* of Abraham," it appears to be clearly implied in such passages as John 8:56; Heb. 11:13, 17-19 that Abraham himself did not expect Isaac to be the Hope of mankind. Rather, the friend of God (James 2:23) knew that Isaac's birth would pave the way for the coming of the Messiah. According to the Gospels and epistles, too, the latter was to be "the son of Abraham *par excellence,"* a truth emphasized over against hostile accusations (John 8:39-41; cf. Gal. 3:16); yes, One far greater than Abraham (John 8:58). He was to be the One through whom God would bless all those who by grace exercised Abraham's faith (Gen. 15:6; Rom. 4:3; Gal. 3:6; cf. John 3:16).

As to the prediction that the Expected One would be "the seed or son of David," is it not clear even on the surface that the words, "I will establish the throne of his kingdom forever" (II Sam. 7:13), must refer to One greater than Solomon? Stating it differently, a reference to Solomon does not exhaust the meaning of the passage. It is not surprising, therefore, that, standing as it were on the threshold of the era of Messianic fulfilment, devout people were "looking for the consolation of Israel" (Luke 2:25). Here, in Matt. 1:1, the author points out that Jesus Christ is indeed what his name implies: the divinely anointed Savior, the fulfilment of prophecy, the rightful heir to the throne of David, and—going back even farther—the true seed of Abraham.

Attempts have been made to deny, at least to a certain extent, the connection between Jesus and David. To be sure, it is granted that *Joseph* was of the house of David (Matt. 1:20; Luke 1:27; 2:4, 5), but that Mary was actually a daughter of David is being questioned. [121] Nevertheless, careful study of II Sam. 7:12, 13; Luke 1:32, 69; Acts 2:30; Rom. 1:3; II Tim. 2:8; and Rev. 5:5 should leave no room for doubt.

The very structure of the genealogy, here in Matthew connects Jesus with David. It consists of three groups of fourteen. [122] In the first we are shown the *origin* of David's house; in the second, its *rise and decline;* in the last, its *eclipse.* Yet, even an eclipse need not be total, neither does it mean extinction. Or, to change the figure, a tree is hewn down, but its stump remains in the ground. In the present instance, out of this stump a twig shoots forth, and that twig becomes a great tree (cf. Isa. 11:1; Rom. 15:12). In David the family of Abraham attained royalty (note verse 6a: "David the king"). At the deportation to Babylon this royal power was lost. In Christ it is restored, only in a far more glorious sense.

According to Matthew, therefore, Jesus is the climax of the three four-teens. That these fourteens express a symbolism can hardly be denied. After much reading on this subject I suggest the following interpretation, acknowledging my indebtedness to many scholars who previously have attempted to solve the problem. Seven is the sum of *three* and *four,* each of which, in its own way, suggests *fulness. Three,* when used symbolically, spells that which has beginning, middle, and end, and is therefore complete. In Scripture it is at times associated with God, viewed in the fulness of his glory, the source of blessing for men. Hence, we speak of the *threefold* Aaronitic benediction (Num. 6:24-26); the *thrice* holy of Isaiah's vision (Isa. 6:1-3); the *triad* of blessings pronounced upon God's people at the close of II Corinthians; and the favors emanating from God *Triune,* by which the seer of Patmos comforts the brotherhood (Rev. 1:4, 5).

Four, used symbolically, refers at times to the fulness of the earth and/or of the heavens, with their four winds (Jer. 49:36; Dan. 8:8; 11:4; Zech. 2:6; Mark 13:27; Rev. 7:1).

Now, if even three or four, taken singly, can express fulness, their sum, *seven,* when used figuratively, conveys this meaning no less emphatically. In fact, special meaning was attached to this number not only by the Jews, or

---

[121] Those who question it base their opinion upon what I believe to be an erroneous explanation of Luke 1:5, 36. Cf. Lenski's sharp criticism (*Interpretation of Luke,* p. 49) of Zahn's position. With the main thrust of this criticism I am in agreement.

[122] It is true that, when added, the Hebrew consonants of the name *David* have a numerical value of fourteen (4+6+4). Whether this fact was in the mind of the author we simply do not know.

in Semitic culture generally, but also among the ancient Egyptians, Greeks, and Germans. All of them recognized the seven-day periods of the four phases of the moon.

In Scripture seven frequently indicates the totality ordained by God. *Fourteen,* which is twice seven, also brings out this idea. So, it would seem, does three times fourteen= *forty-two.* This is equal to six sevens, and immediately introduces *the seventh seven, reduplicated completeness, perfection.* Since, in the genealogy as offered by Matthew, Jesus Christ is mentioned at the close of the entire list of three fourteens or six sevens, and since the evangelist does not stop there but continues the beautiful story of this Savior, we cannot be far wrong when we say that he pictures him as the One who not only completes or fulfils the old, but also definitely ushers in the new (9:16, 17; 26:28, 29; cf. John 3:34; I Cor. 11:25; II Cor. 3:6; 5:17; Heb. 9:15; 10:20; 12:24; Rev. 21:5). In him the new and the old meet. He is the Alpha and the Omega, the beginning and the end, the heart and center of all. Apart from him there is no salvation. He is Messiah, David's true Antitype. And in the course of redemptive history, as here symbolized in its three great stages, God's plan from eternity was being perfectly realized. [123]

In Matthew's days and also later, Christ's enemies were constantly making disparaging remarks about Jesus' origin. In essence they were saying that because of his lowly birth he could not be what he claimed to be. Was he not the carpenter's son? Did they not know his father, mother, brothers, and sisters (Matt. 13:54-58; Mark 6:3; Luke 4:22)? Some argued, "We know where this man is from; but when the Christ comes, no one will know where he is from" (John 7:27). Others said, "Surely, the Christ does not come out of Galilee, does he? Has not the Scripture said that the Christ comes out of the seed of David and from Bethlehem, the village where David lived?" (John 7:40, 41). At times his adversaries may even have implied that in his origin he was illegitimate. They said, "We were not born of fornication: one Father have we, even God" (John 8:41); as if to say, "Not *we* but *you* were born of fornication. With respect to *our* parentage there is no legitimate doubt, but it is different with *you.*" Sinister insinuation or innuendo at times changed into open, deliberate, vicious insult: "Are we not correct in saying, 'You are a Samaritan and have a demon'?" (John 8:48). Such antagonistic remarks, in which not only Jesus' Davidic origin but even his legitimate birth were denied, either by innuendo or openly, have continued among the Jews. [124]

---

[123] On the meaning of ἑπτά and its derivatives see especially the following: I.S.B.E., pp. 2157-2163; Th.D.N.T., Vol. II, pp. 627-635); and S.BK., Vol. I, p. 43; IV, pp. 994, 995. Note also what has been said previously regarding Matthew's fondness for the number seven; p. 86 above.

[124] See T. Walker, *Jewish Views of Jesus,* New York, 1931, especially pp. 14-23. Cf. also Laible, *Jesus Christus im Talmud;* Herford, *Christianity in Talmud and Midrash;* Krauss, *Das Leben Jesu nach Jüdischen Quellen.* In a collection of previously unrecorded

Matthew, therefore, by means of this genealogy and its sequel (the narrative of the virgin birth, verses 18-25), aims to show that Jesus, according to his human nature, is indeed the legitimate seed of David, in fulfilment of prophecy. From Joseph, his legal father—and thus from Joseph's ancestor, David—he receives his right to David's throne. From Mary (verse 16)—and via Mary, also from David—he receives David's flesh and blood.

Yet, neither to Joseph nor to Mary belongs the glory. Joseph deserves no credit for his own birth as a descendant of David, and is thoroughly aware of the fact that he had nothing whatever to do with the conception of Jesus. Mary, similarly, knows that what happens in her womb is the work of the Holy Spirit. She is willing to be "the handmaid of the Lord" (Luke 1:34, 35, 38). *The glory belongs to God alone!* It is by grace that man is saved, through faith; and this not of himself; it is the gift of God (cf. Eph. 2:8).

Having written the caption, Matthew now presents the following genealogy: [125]

The Three Fourteens

As introduced in Matthew		in I Chronicles	See also
First Fourteen			
1. Abraham	1:1, 2	1:27	Gen. 11:26
2. Isaac	1:2	1:28, 34	Gen. 21:1-5
3. Jacob	1:2	1:34; 2:1	Gen. 25:26

oral law, called *Tosefta* (pertaining to the tannaitic literature of the Jews) there occurs a story in which Jesus is called "son of Panthera." Pagan philosophers, too, allowed themselves to be influenced by these slanderous representations. See especially Origen, *Against Celsus* I.xxviii. Today, H. J. Schonfield (*The Passover Plot,* pp. 42, 48, 49, 241, 242) follows the example of those who connect the story of Christ's virgin birth with various pagan legends; for example, the one about the god Jupiter Ammon, who in the form of a serpent consorted with Olympias, resulting in the birth of Alexander the Great; as if these two births (Christ's and Alexander's) have in common anything that is essential!

[125] In the majority of instances Matthew's spelling of the names is identical with, or bears very close resemblance to, that found in LXX, I Chron. 1–3. In I Chron. 1:3, where the Hebrew has *Israel,* the LXX has *Jacob.* So does Matthew (1:2). Also, both LXX (I Chron. 3:17) and Matthew (1:12) use the form *Salathiel,* where the Hebrew has *Shealtiel.* Dependence to some extent on LXX, I Chron. 1-3, seems probable therefore, whether it be direct or indirect. Here follows the complete list of names as presented by Matthew. Where the Greek form he uses differs considerably from the Hebrew, Matthew's is indicated between parentheses. The earlier form—i.e., the Hebrew (transliterated into English)—is the one used in this Commentary (as, for example, also in A.R.V.). In the second column, No. 5, Greek Ἰωσαφάτ, naturally refers to Jehoshaphat. Just as obviously, in that same column, No. 7, Greek Ὀζίας, refers to Uzziah (II Kings 15:13, 30; II Chron. 26:1 ff.; etc.); elsewhere called Azariah (II Kings 14:21; I Chron. 3:12; etc.). Finally, the Jec(h)oniah of Matt. 1:11, 12; I Chron. 3:16, 17; Esther 2:6; Jer. 24:1; 27:20; 28:4; 29:2; is the Jehoiachin of II Kings 24:6, 8, etc.; II Chron. 36:8, 9; and Jer. 52:31; the same as the Coniah of Jer. 22:24, 28; 37:1.

As introduced in Matthew		in I Chronicles	See also
4. Judah and his brothers	1:2	2:1, 2	Gen. 29:31-35; 30:1-24; 35:16-18; 49; Exod. 1:1-6
5. Perez and Zerah	1:3	2:4	Gen. 38:24-30; Ruth 4:18
6. Hezron	1:3	2:5	Gen. 46:12; Num. 16:21; Ruth 4:18
7. Ram (Greek: Aram)	1:3	2:9, 25	Ruth 4:19
8. Aminadab	1:4	2:10	Ruth 4:19
9. Nahshon	1:4	2:10	Ruth 4:20
10. Salmon	1:4	2:11	Ruth 4:20
11. Boaz	1:5	2:11	Ruth 4:13, 21
12. Obed	1:5	2:12	Ruth 4:21
13. Jesse	1:5	2:12	Ruth 4:22
14. David the King	1:1, 6	2:15	Ruth 4:22; I Sam. 13:11-13

Second Fourteen

1. Solomon	1:6	3:5	II Sam. 12:24
2. Rehoboam	1:7	3:10	I Kings 11:43
3. Abijah	1:7	3:10	I Kings 14:31
4. Asa (Greek: Asaph)	1:7	3:10	I Kings 15:8
5. Jehoshaphat	1:8	3:10	I Kings 15:24
6. Joram	1:8	3:11	I Kings 22:50
7. Uzziah	1:8	3:12	II Kings 14:21; 15:1
8. Jotham	1:9	3:12	II Kings 15:32
9. Ahaz	1:9	3:12	II Kings 16:1
10. Hezekiah	1:9	3:12	II Kings 18:1
11. Manasseh	1:10	3:13	II Kings 20:21; 21:1
12. Amon (Greek: Amos)	1:10	3:14	II Kings 21:18, 19
13. Josiah	1:10	3:14	II Kings 21:24; 22:1
14. Jechoniah and his his brothers	1:11	3:16	II Kings 24:6, 8, 12; Jer. 22:30

Third Fourteen

1. Jechoniah (for repetition of this name see on 1:12)	1:12	3:17	II Kings 25:27-30
2. Shealtiel (Greek: Salathiel)	1:12	3:17	Ezra 3:2, 8; 5:2; Neh. 12:1; Hag. 1.1, 12, 14; 2:2-4, 20-23

As introduced in Matthew		in 1 Chronicles	See also
3. Zerubbabel	1:12	3:19	Ezra 3:2, 8; 5:2; Neh. 12:1; Hag. 1:1, 12, 14; 2:2-4, 20-23; Zech. 4:6-10
4. Abiud	1:13		
5. Eliakim	1:13		
6. Azor	1:13		
7. Zadok	1:14		
8. Achim	1:14		
9. Eliud	1:14		
10. Eliazar	1:15		
11. Matthan	1:15		
12. Jacob	1:15		
13. Joseph, the husband of Mary, of whom was born	1:16		Matt. 1:18-25; 2:13-15; Luke 2:4, 16, 33, 48
14. Jesus, who is called Christ.	1:16		

2. The first list of fourteen names begins as follows: **Abraham became the father of Isaac, and Isaac became the father of Jacob, and Jacob became the father of Judah and his brothers.**

It has already been shown that it was natural for Matthew, who was writing primarily for Jews, to begin with Abraham. In Abraham's begetting of Isaac there are two elements: a supernatural and a natural. The first is emphasized by Paul in Gal. 4:23; the second here by Matthew. As to the first, Isaac was born "through promise." As a reward for Abraham's faith in the promise, God intervened miraculously, enabling Abraham, though he had become "as good as dead," to deposit seed; and making it possible for Sarah, heretofore barren, to conceive (Rom. 4:19; Heb. 11:11, 12). It is true, therefore, that the family tree, as recorded by Matthew, *begins* with a supernatural birth, that of Isaac, and *ends* with one, that of Christ. However, the two are by no means identical, for in Isaac's case there was no virgin birth, as there was in the case of Christ. With respect to the conception of Isaac there was the usual impregnation of the ovum by a human father, as is true along the entire line of this genealogy, wherever the same verb is used. The two elements in Isaac's conception—*a. supernatural* intervention renewing Abraham's virility, and *b. natural* conception as a result of insemination—must not be confused. Otherwise Matt. 1:2 would clash with Gal. 4:23.

It should be noted that Ishmael's name is not even mentioned here,

113

though he was also a son of Abraham. And Abraham had other offspring (Gen. 25:2). Matthew holds to the Messianic line. In the few cases where collateral relatives are also mentioned (verses 2, 3, 11), there must have been a special reason, though it is not certain that in each instance we know what this reason was.

Isaac became the father of Jacob; and the latter, in process of time, became the father of Judah and his brothers. Judah's name is singled out from all the children of Jacob, for it is in him that the Messianic line is continued. Why did this happen? Was not Reuben the firstborn? Were there not three brothers older than Judah? It is clear that inclusion in, or exclusion from, the line of descent is not determined by age. Neither is it determined by human merit (see verses 8-10). By what then? Only by the sovereign, electing will and grace of God (Rom. 9:16). Yet, even though it is in Judah that the Messianic line is carried forward, the words "and his brothers" are added. The mention of these brothers may have been occasioned by the fact that during the old dispensation Israel as a whole constituted God's people, separated from all the nations of the world, in order *to be,* and especially in Christ *to become,* a blessing to all (Exod. 19:3-6; I Kings 8:41-43; Isa. 53, 54, 60). The entire nation, accordingly, had Messianic significance.

3. The line is extended as follows: **Judah became the father of Perez and Zerah by Tamar, and Perez became the father of Hezron, and Hezron became the father of Ram.** This is the Judah concerning whom it is written, "You are the one your brothers will praise.... The scepter shall not depart from Judah ... until Shiloh come" (Gen 49:8-10); the Judah who, in honoring his pledge to become surety for his youngest brother, delivered that moving address in which he offered to become a slave in Egypt as a substitute for Benjamin. But it is not of such references to Judah that Matthew is thinking but rather of the immoral act that made him the father of Perez and Zerah *by his own daughter-in-law Tamar.* Having mistaken her for a common harlot, for she was veiled when the act occurred, he had made her pregnant. Subsequently, when he was informed that Tamar through harlotry had conceived, he had ordered her burned to death. This command was rescinded when Tamar had furnished proof that her father-in-law himself was the chief culprit (Gen. 38).

Through such a channel of iniquity—"Judah ... Perez ... by Tamar"— the Savior, according to his human nature, was willing to pass on his way from the glories of heaven to the incarnation and to crucifixion in his people's stead. If this be recognized, even the study of genealogy can become a blessing to mind and heart.

We do not know why Zerah, the brother of Perez, is also mentioned. Was it because the brothers were twins, and because, *contrary to human expectation,* Zerah was born last, so that the right of the firstborn was accorded to Perez by an unexpected disposition of divine providence (Gen. 38:29, 30)?

114

The answer to this too ready solution is that Jacob and Esau were also twins, and with respect to them too God had ordained that the humanly unexpected would happen—"The elder shall serve the younger" (Gen. 25:23); yet, in the genealogy Esau's name is never even mentioned!

The line continues: (Perez) Hezron, Ram. Except for their mention in genealogical tables we know nothing about this Hezron and Ram. Does this mean that the names are fictitious? Such a conclusion would be entirely unwarranted. Under the guidance of the Holy Spirit Matthew has carefully studied the registers. Directly or indirectly the information he gathered can be traced to sources such as listed on pp. 111-113. Note, moreover, that the list: Perez, Hezron, Ram, Amminadab, Nahshon, Salmon, Boaz, Obed, Jesse, David (Matt. 1:3-5) is also found in Ruth 4:18-22, in exactly that same order. The evangelist, accordingly, had excellent sources on which to base his genealogy; namely, Genesis, Exodus, Numbers, Ruth, the books of Kings and Chronicles, etc., and perhaps separate genealogical tables [126] both written and oral. His account is entirely reliable.

Hezron and Ram! To us these are merely names. We do not even know whether they were men of untarnished or of spotted reputation. To God, however, they were important for the historical accomplishment of his plan to bring the Messiah into the world for man's redemption. So, too, in the church there are many who never make the headlines. Yet, though unknown here below, they are well-known above (II Cor. 6:9). One day it will become evident that "the last will be first, and the first last" (Matt. 20:16).

4. As the list continues we once again enter somewhat more familiar territory: **Ram became the father of Amminadab, and Amminadab became the father of Nahshon, and Nahshon became the father of Salmon.** As the parallels in Exodus and Numbers indicate, we have now reached the time of the Exodus from Egypt and of the desert journey. Amminadab was the father of Elisheba, who married Aaron (Exod. 6:23). During the desert journey Amminadab's son Nahshon (Num. 1:7; I Chron. 2:10) was the leader of Judah's tribe, which was encamped "toward the sunrise" (Num. 2:3). When the tabernacle had been completed and set up, it was he who, as the representative of his tribe, offered the first oblation (Num. 7:12-17). In marching, the standard of his tribe took the lead (Num. 10:14). Nahshon's son Salmon married Rahab, who figures prominently in the story of the two men sent by Joshua "to survey" the land of Canaan. For this item of genealogical information we turn now to verse 5, 6a. **Salmon became the father of Boaz by Rahab, and Boaz became the father of Obed by Ruth, and Obed became the father of Jesse, and Jesse became the father of David the**

---

[126] There must have been many such lists. *A Genealogy of Priests* was found in Cave 6 of the Dead Sea Scrolls (M. Burrows, *More Light on the Dead Sea Scrolls*, New York, 1958, p. 407).

king. With the new names that are mentioned here every student of the Bible is familiar. Who, brought up in Christian circles, has not been thrilled by the stories about Rahab and the spies (Josh. 2 and 6; Heb. 11:31; James 2:25); Boaz, Ruth, and their child Obed (book of Ruth); Jesse and his sons (I Sam. 16); and, last but not least, David the king (I Sam. 17–31; II Sam.; I Kings 1:1–2:11)?

Nevertheless, Matthew's aim is not primarily to bring these thrilling stories back to mind but to give an enumeration of ancestors, so that, in harmony with prophecy, Jesus Christ may be recognized as David's son and David's Lord. Everything else *cannot have more* than ancillary significance, though it does have that.

This also means that the list must not be used for the purpose of establishing chronological conclusions; for example, to compute the length of the period that elapsed between Rahab and David. If verse 5 is nevertheless used to serve that end, on the assumption that no Messianic link has been omitted, it would follow that Rahab, who lived at the time of Israel's entrance into Canaan (Josh. 2 and 6), was the great-great-grandmother of David; for the sequence presented here is Rahab (wife of Salmon), Boaz, Obed, Jesse, David. This result would be very difficult to harmonize with I Kings 6:1, where, even when the necessary subtractions are made, a considerably longer period is implied for the span Rahab to David. Matthew evidently did not deem it necessary to mention a representative of each passing generation. Neither did other Bible writers (cf. Ezra 7:3 with I Chron. 6:7-9). In Matthew this is clear also from a study of the second fourteen (verses 6b-11) and the third (verses 12-16), as will be indicated. The evangelist is interested in Christology, not in chronology. He is satisfied to show that the three catalogues of Messianic antecedents, logically arranged according to the great turning points in the Davidic dynasty, attain their fulfilment in Christ. In order to achieve this goal neither he nor the inspired author of the book of Ruth deemed it necessary to mention every link in the chain of ancestry.

The origin of the house of David has now been recorded. The next fourteen names, Solomon to Jechoniah, are reminiscent of the glory and the decline of the dynasty. They show us that not even Solomon in all his glory was able to bestow salvation. It is Christ who saves, he alone.

6b. David became the father of Solomon by the wife of Uriah. Among commentators it is customary to point to the all-inclusiveness of the genealogy. It is said, for example, that, contrary to Jewish usage, this list with its three fourteens contains the names of women as well as men. Also, it includes foreigners—Tamar, Rahab, and Ruth [127]—and names of those who,

---

[127] That Rahab was a non-Israelite is clear (Josh. 2:2, 31). Ruth was "a young woman from Moab" (Ruth 2:6). Gen. 38 does not specifically state that Tamar was a Canaanite;

either in a broad or in a more restricted sense, were Jews. Special emphasis is also generally placed on the fact that not only the good are included; for example, Abraham, Isaac, Jacob; but also the evil: Joram, Ahaz, Amon; etc. Wicked almost beyond belief were some of these ancestors!

As I see it, these opinions are true to fact, and warrant the following conclusions:

1. Jewish boasting about Abrahamic descent amounts to unjustifiable glorying in the flesh. It is foolish and wicked. Israel had no reason to be proud of itself. Salvation is not from below, from man; it is from above, from God (cf. II Cor. 11:17; Phil. 3:1-8).

2. Jesus is indeed the long awaited One, sent by God for man's redemption; for it is he who fulfils the prophecy concerning Messiah's lowly origin (Isa. 11:1; 53:2; cf. Matt. 2:23; John 1:46; 7:52).

3. This Jesus Christ is the Savior of *the world* (John 3:16; 4:42), not only of the Jews. There is indeed "a wideness in God's mercy." Those who were destined to be saved through faith were to be drawn from *every* nation.

Verse 6 adds emphasis to all this. As to point 1 (above), the readers are here reminded of the fact that being able to point to the illustrious King David, whether as ancestor or as former king of their nation, offers no ground for boasting; for he was the man who, *by another man's wife,* i.e., by a wife he had stolen by having that other man put to death, had become father of the next king. The first offspring of the adulterous union had died. Later, Solomon was born of this same union. Read about the scandalous manner in which David had plotted and had brought about Uriah's death, so that he might marry that man's wife, Bathsheba, with whom he had already committed adultery (II Sam. 11).

The very reminder of this episode in the life of David also reinforces point 2. With respect to his "father" (in the legal sense only)—also, of course, with respect to his mother (see verse 16, 18-25 and Luke's genealogy, 3:23-38)—Jesus descended from such a great sinner as David. Finally, it also stresses point 3. Even for David there was mercy; hence, there is mercy for all who flee for refuge to David's Antitype.

Accordingly, when we study the entire genealogy (verses 1-17) we are impressed with the fact that even the *good* men stood in need of God's grace; for they, too, were sinners. To be sure, many commendable things are reported with reference to Abraham (Gen. 13:8, 9; 14:13-16; 15:6; 18:22-23; 22:1-19), but so are certain shameful actions (Gen. 12:10-20; 16:1-6; 20). The same holds with respect to Isaac: good (Gen. 24:63, 67; 26:18-25); bad (25:28; 26:1-11). With Jacob the case is no different: good (28:18-22; 32:1, 2, 22-32; 35:1-7; 49:18); bad (Gen. 25:27-34; 27:18-24;

---

nevertheless, this is probably implied in the Genesis context (see verses 1, 2, 6, 11-13). Cf. G. Ch. Aalders, *Genesis (Korte Verklaring)*; Vol. 3, p. 94.

37:3). Judah, too, is an example both to imitate (43:8, 9; 44:18-34) and to shun (Gen. 38). David is a man after God's own heart (I Sam. 13:14; 17; 18:5; 24:1-7; 25:32-35, 39-42; 26; II Sam. 7:18-29; 9; 12:13; 18:5, 33; 23:5; Ps. 51 and many other Psalms); nevertheless, a great sinner (in addition to II Sam. 11, already discussed, see also I Sam. 24:21, 22; II Sam. 5:13; 8:2; 12:31; 21:8, 9; 24). To mention only one more, Hezekiah "did what was right in the eyes of Jehovah, according to all that David his father had done" (II Kings 18:3, and see that entire chapter; also II Kings 19:14-19; 20:2, 3; II Chron. 29:2, and that whole chapter; also chapters 30 and 31); but he, too, was not without flaw (II Kings 20:12-15; II Chron. 32:25).

None was able to save himself. All, even the best in the list, stood in need of redemption by the blood of the promised Reedemer. They also confirmed this by means of their humble and strikingly touching confessions (Gen. 49:18; II Sam. 23:5; II Kings 19:14-19; Ps. 51; cf. Dan. 9:17-19; Luke 18:13; Rom. 7:24, 25).

Continued: 7–11. **Solomon became the father of Rehoboam, and Rehoboam became the father of Abijah, and Abijah became the father of Asa, and Asa became the father of Jehoshaphat, and Jehoshaphat became the father of Joram, and Joram became the father of Uzziah, and Uzziah became the father of Jotham, and Jotham became the father of Ahaz, and Ahaz became the father of Hezekiah, and Hezekiah became the father of Manasseh, and Manasseh became the father of Amon, and Amon became the father of Josiah, and Josiah became the father of Jechoniah and his brothers, at the time of the deportation to Babylon.**

We read that Solomon "loved the Lord" (I Kings 3:3a), but a little later it is reported of him that he "loved many foreign women," who led him astray from the pure worship of Jehovah to idolatry (I Kings 11:1-14). The man whose beginning had been so promising, later did what was evil in the sight of the Lord. Spiritually he did not measure up to his father, whose heart again and again was filled with genuine, poignant sorrow for his sin. As to Solomon, one has to search diligently for evidences of true repentance. Nevertheless, we are not without hope that before his death a return to the Lord actually took place. We are strengthened in this opinion by passages such as the following: II Sam. 12:24, 25; I Kings 3:5-15; 8:22-53; Neh. 13:26; Eccl. 2:1-11; 12:13, 14; cf. John 10:28; Rom. 8:29, 30; and Phil. 1:6. All in all, however, tradition remembered Solomon for the great prosperity which marked his reign, and for his "wisdom," rather than for his piety. When later kings were measured according to a spiritual standard, that yardstick of judgment was always the life of David (II Kings 16:2; 18:3; II Chron. 17:3; 28:1; 29:2; etc.), never that of Solomon. [128] We see, therefore,

---

[128] One of the most delightful and thorough recent studies on Solomon it has been my pleasure to read is that, in the Dutch language, by J. Schoneveld, *Salomo*, Baarn, The Netherlands, no date.

that very soon after the rise to power of David's dynasty it also began to show signs of decline.

This decline, moreover, was not only spiritual but also political and material. After Solomon's death the kingdom was divided. Hence, all the other names mentioned here by Matthew designate kings who ruled over only two of the former twelve tribes. Many good things are reported with reference to Asa, Jehoshaphat, Uzziah, Jotham, Hezekiah, and Josiah. The opposite is true with respect to the others, though it is only fair to state that Manasseh repented in his last days. Finally, with Jechoniah (or Jehoiachin) whatever was left of Judah's glory departed (see on verse 11).

It is immediately evident that between Joram and Uzziah [129] three names are omitted. They are those of Ahaziah (II Kings 8:25; II Chron. 22:1), Joash (II Kings 11:21; 12:1 in the Hebrew text; II Chron. 24:1), and Amaziah (II Kings 14:1; II Chron. 25:1). The reason for such omissions has already been stated (see on verses 5, 6a). Matthew is not giving us a chronological report but a testimony that Jesus is indeed the Christ.

It has been shown that Matthew had abundant source material to draw from. Moreover, as is clearly evident from his entire book, he was thoroughly acquainted with the Old Testament Scriptures. Therefore, for him the names in the list were more than mere *items*. They were *persons* with whom, through Scripture and tradition, he had become well acquainted. And even today anyone who wishes to understand this genealogy in the light of its purpose, should linger over it a while, instead of regarding it of no account. He will soon discover that the more one studies it, the more also he will become convinced that it points, indeed, to the necessity of the coming Redeemer. The way was being paved for his coming.

There was, first of all, the *historical* preparation: God's guidance in the events that were taking place; so that, for example, Solomon's kingdom was divided, two tribes remaining with Rehoboam, ten defecting to Jeroboam. How deplorable, this disruption! Gone was the political unity, the strongly centralized government, which David had labored so strenuously to bring into being. Gone, too, the religious consolidation—*one* temple for *all* the tribes—which Solomon had added. The throne had lost its luster. The glory had departed!

That is one way of looking at it. While fully maintaining the true element in this appraisal we must not forget the *divine* point of view as stated in I Kings 11:12, 13; 12:15, 24b, and especially in 11:36. We read: "*I* . . . will rend . . .; it was a thing brought about of *Jehovah* . . . this thing is of *me* . . . that David my servant may have a *lamp* [posterity, cf. I Kings 15:4] always before me in Jerusalem."

It was God himself who tore asunder . . . in order that he might save. The

---

[129] Not between Uzziah and Jotham, as Lenski states, *op. cit.*, p. 30.

nation was "broken down" that grace might "break through." We have here another instance of that series of *separations* by means of which Jehovah chooses unto himself a certain minority in order that he may use it for the realization of his Messianic program. Solomon's spirit of compromise with respect to many foreign gods was beginning to exert its sinister influence upon the people. Therefore, a separation had again become necessary, just as in the case of Abraham and for the same reason. This separation was to be followed, in course of time, by the Assyrian and the Babylonian captivities. Then Judah will serve one God, and will make propaganda for its monotheistic worship among the Gentiles. For many of the latter the road to salvation will lead from polytheism by way of monotheism to Christianity.

There was also the *symbolical* preparation. Did not the very furniture of Solomon's temple, the building that stood in Jerusalem through nearly his entire first period, point to the fact that "apart from the shedding of blood there is no remission" (Heb. 9:22)? But also, was it not clear to the devout and thinking Jew that animal blood, in and by itself, could never be the true ransom for the souls of men (Ps. 40:6-8)?

Then there was the *prophetical* preparation: the ministry of all the true prophets who labored during this period and pointed forward to the promised Deliverer. Godly kings worked hand in hand with earnest, fiery prophets. Hezekiah and Isaiah were friends (II Chron. 32:20); so were Josiah and Jeremiah (II Chron. 35:25). Among the many Messianic prophecies uttered during this lengthy period were the following: Isa. 7:14; 8:8; 9:1, 2, 6; 11:1-10; 42:1-7; 49:1-9; 50:4-9; 52:13–53:12; 61:1-3; 62:11; Jer. 23:5; 31:15; Hos. 11:1; and Mic. 5:2.

Finally, the *psychological* preparation must not be forgotten. One truth was becoming more and more abundantly clear: no one can achieve righteousness before God. Israel fails, as appears from the lives of the kings and the people. Even the law though in itself perfect, cannot save. Man fails. God alone can save. He will do so by means of the coming Mediator.

Thus considered, it is clear that the Messianic character of Matthew's genealogy is evident not only from the mathematical formula—3x14, as has already been explained, but also from the entire historical context which is represented by the names the evangelist mentions.

As to related lessons, note the following:

Name of king(s)	Character of the man and/or of his reign	One of the lessons to be learned from his life as expressed in the language of the Bible	other literature
Rehoboam	"My father chastised y o u with whips, but I will chastise y o u with scorpions" (I Kings 12:14).	"Like a roaring lion . . . is a wicked ruler over a poor people" (Prov. 28: 15; cf. 20:28).	"Kings seek their subjects' good, tyrants their own" (Herrick).
Abijah and Amon	"Three years he [Abijah] reigned . . . and he walked in all the sins of his father" (I Kings 15:2, 3). "Amon . . . reigned two years . . . and he forsook Jehovah . . . and his servants conspired against him and killed him" (II Kings 21:19-23).	"Surely, thou dost set them in slippery places . . . How are they become a desolation in a moment!" (Ps. 73:18, 19).	"Uneasy lies the head that wears a crown" (Shakespeare).
Asa, Jehoshaphat, and Hezekiah, three reformers and intercessors	"Asa cried to Jehovah, his God" (II Chron. 14:11). "Jehoshaphat prayed: . . . 'Our eyes are on thee'" (II Chron. 20:5, 12). "And Hezekiah prayed . . . 'O Jehovah, our God, save thou us'" (II Kings 19:15, 19).	"Call upon me in the day of trouble; I will deliver you, and you shall glorify me" (Ps. 50:15).	"And Satan trembles when he sees the weakest saint upon his knees" (Cowper).

Name of king(s)	Character of the man and/or of his reign	One of the lessons to be learned from his life as expressed in the language of the Bible	other literature
Joram	"But he walked in the way of the kings of Israel, as the house of Ahab had done; for Ahab's daughter had become his wife" (II Chron. 21:6).	"A worthy woman is her husband's crown; but she who acts disgracefully is like rottenness in his bones." (Prov. 12:4).	"There is no worse evil than a bad wo-man" (Euripides).
Uzziah	"But when he was strong, his heart was lifted up. . . . He went into the temple of Jehovah to burn incense" (II Chron. 26: 16).	"Behold, to obey is bet-ter than sacrifice, and to hearken than the fat of rams" (I Sam. 15:22). See also Prov. 16:18.	"Oh! Why should the spirit of mortal be proud?" (Knox).
Jotham	"He built the upper gate of Jehovah's house, and on the wall of Ophel he built exten-sively. He also built cities . . . and fortresses and towers" (II Chron. 27:3, 4).	"Walk about Zion . . . count her towers. Consider well her defense walls; walk through her cita-dels. . ." (Ps. 48:12, 13).	"Ah, to build, to build! That is the noblest of all the arts" (Longfellow).
Ahaz	"In the time of his distress he—this same king Ahaz—transgressed yet more grie-vously against Jehovah" (II Chron. 28:22).	"Do not be deceived; God is not mocked; for what-ever a man sows, that also will he reap" (Gal. 6:7).	"The mills of God grind slowly, yet surely," (attributed in various forms to various authors).

Manasseh	"And the Lord said, 'Because Manasseh . . . has committed these abominations . . . I am bringing upon Jerusalem and Judah such evil that both ears of those who hear it will tingle" (II Kings 21:11, 12). "And when he was in distress he humbled himself greatly before the God of his fathers" (II Chron. 33:12).	"Remember also your Creator in the days of *your youth*" (Eccl. 12:1).	"For all sad words of tongue or pen, The saddest are, 'It might have been.'" (Whittier).
Josiah	"He did what was right in the eyes of Jehovah" (II Kings 22:2).	"Those who honor me I will honor" (I Sam. 2:30).	"Lives of great men all remind us, We can make our lives sublime . . ." (Longfellow).
Jechoniah	"He did what was evil in the sight of Jehovah . . . and the king of Babylon took him . . . and carried him away to Babylon" (II Kings 24:9, 12, 15).	". . . but those who despise me shall be lightly esteemed" (I Sam. 2:30).	"The thorns which I have reaped are of the tree I planted—they have torn me—and I bleed! I should have known what fruit would spring from such a seed" (Byron).

123

Just as above, in verse 8, the names of three kings were omitted, so in verse 11, between Josiah and Jechoniah (or Jehoiachin), Jehoiachim is left out (see on verses 5, 6a). We read that "Josiah begot Jechoniah and his brothers." The word *begot* is here linked with the grandfather instead of the father. For proof see I Chron. 3:15, 16, where Josiah, his son Jehoiakim, and the latter's son Jehoiachin are mentioned in that order. It is not wrong, in harmony with the preceding verses to translate the passage, "Josiah *begot* or *became the father of* Jechoniah," for in Scripture the term *father* has a very wide use. It does not always refer to "the *immediate* male ancestor," but may indicate one farther removed. Thus in II Kings 18:3 David is called the father of Hezekiah; and for the New Testament see Matt. 3:9; Luke 1:73; 16:24; John 8:39, 53, 56; etc. The same holds with respect to the word *brothers* ("Jechoniah and his brothers"). It will be recalled that Abraham called Lot his "brother" (Gen. 14:14, 16), though the latter was actually his nephew (Gen. 11:27). It is entirely possible that also here in Matt. 1:11 the reference is to relatives in a wider sense; i.e., to Josiah's sons; hence, to Jehoiakim's literal brothers: Jehoahaz (II Chron. 36:2) and Zedekiah (II Chron. 36:10, 11; cf. II Kings 24:17), who were, accordingly, Jehoiachin's uncles. These may have been briefly referred to here because they, too, reigned for a while in Jerusalem; the former three months; the latter eleven years. If Jehoiachin himself had more than one brother in the immediate, literal sense, we cannot derive this information from Scripture.

With the deportation to Babylon, God's promise to the house of David went into eclipse. Dark and dismal was the lot of Jehoiachin. Not only did he not have any seed who sat upon David's throne (Jer. 22:30), but he himself, a mere lad of eighteen, was taken into foreign imprisonment that lasted no less than thirty-seven grim years! (II Kings 24:8-12; cf. 25:27).

As to the nobles, priests, craftsmen, etc., who accompanied him, their forced departure, too, must have been sorrowful. Zedekiah, a third son of Josiah, was Judah's last king. Disregarding the warnings of the prophets Jeremiah and Ezekiel, and placing his trust in Egypt, he rebelled against the king of Babylon. As a result, the Chaldean army came and destroyed Jerusalem, including Solomon's beautiful temple. Zedekiah's tragic end is vividly described in II Kings 25:4-7. The people, except the poorest, were carried away to Babylon (II Kings 25:11). The chief reason for the Babylonian Exile is given in II Chron. 36:44 ff.; in a word: *impenitence* in open and obstinate disregard of every prophetic warning.

The total period of Babylonian oppression, beginning with the deportation that occurred about 605 B.C., including also the removals that took place in 597 and in 586 B.C., and ending in 536 B.C.—hence, "seventy years" in all (Jer. 25:11, 12; 29:10; Dan. 9:2)—may be characterized (in part) as follows:

First, there were years of *false hopefulness*. The early exiles were confident that conditions would change and that they would soon return to their land. Was not Jehovah's temple in Jerusalem still standing? Jeremiah sent a letter to these deluded people, and told them not to trust their false prophets, but to build houses and plant gardens; i.e., to plan for a long stay in Babylonia (Jer. 29; cf. Ezek. 17:11-24).

Secondly, there were years of *hopelessness.* In the year 586 Jerusalem fell, the temple was destroyed, the bulk of the nation deported. Many years passed without any sign of return and restoration, as if Jehovah had forsaken his people. Psalm 137 gives vivid expression to the people's mood.

From David to Jehoiachin, what a decline! How Judah must have yearned for deliverance!—At last the season of *revived hopefulness* arrived. Gloom did not last forever. Though the night was dark and dismal, there were glimmerings of light even during the Exile. Or, to change the figure, though David's sun was eclipsed, the eclipse was not total. This appears from verse 12., which introduces the third series of fourteen, as follows: **After the deportation to Babylon Jechoniah became the father of Shealtiel, and Shealtiel became the father of Zerubbabel.** There is good reason to believe that Jechoniah must be counted twice; first, as the last in the second series of fourteen; then, as the first in the final series. At first glance the decision to count him twice may seem like a totally unwarranted method of getting rid of a Gospel "discrepancy," the latter consisting in this, that otherwise the third list, which like the other two is supposed to contain fourteen names (verse 17), would have only thirteen. [130] However, a little study of what Scripture tells us about Jechoniah soon reveals that two sharply contrasting

---

[130] Some try to solve the problem by means of the conjecture that originally (whether in the Greek autograph or in an earlier Hebrew Matthew, of which the later Greek was supposedly a revision; see pp. 87-91) verse 11 read, "Josiah became the father of Jehoiakim" (instead of "became the father of Jechoniah"). Later in verse 12 the name Jehoiachin was changed to its equivalent Jechoniah; and, since the two names Jehoiachin and Jehoiakim resemble each other so closely, the latter in verse 11 was also changed to Jechoniah. If we now wish to restore the original text, the name Jechoniah in verse 11 must be replaced by Jehoiakim. If this emendation is adopted, Jechoniah's name would not be mentioned until verse 12 is reached. It would have to be counted only once, and the change would result in a series of fourteen names in each of the lists. So runs the argument. Tempting as this solution may seem, especially because of the close resemblance between the names of a royal son and royal grandson of king Josiah, it is beset with difficulties. First, the best textual evidence supports the text as it is; that is, without substituting Jehoiakim for Jechoniah in verse 11. Also, the proposed change in verse 11 would necessitate a far more extensive alteration; for in all the preceding instances, beginning with Isaac in verse 2, and extending to Josiah in verses 10 and 11, *each name is mentioned twice;* first as a son, then as a father. The same holds for the list that follows in verses 12-16, ending with Jacob, Joseph's father. Hence, to be consistent, instead of what we now have, "Josiah became the father of Jechoniah and his brothers," the "restored"(?) text would have to read, "Josiah became the father of Jehoiakim and his brothers, and Jehoiakim became the father of Jechoniah." This would be a change not of just a few letters or merely a word; instead, it would mean the addition of an entire clause. Justification for such a radical emendation would seem to be entirely lacking.

pictures of this king's experiences are drawn. All is dark in II Kings 24:8-12, as has been indicated. The curse of childlessness is pronounced upon Jechoniah (Jer. 22:30). But in his imprisonment matters take a turn for the better: Jechoniah, the exile, has children, in one of whom the Messianic line is continued (I Chron. 3:17, 18). By rereading Jer. 22:30 we now begin to understand that the childlessness predicted with reference to the young king meant no more than this, that none of his offspring would occupy David's earthly throne. Now this favorable change between Jechoniah *before* his deportation and *afterward* is in and by itself probably sufficient to justify the fact that he is counted twice. If more is needed, consider also II Kings 25:27-30. Cf. Jer. 52:31-34. Jechoniah is freed from prison, is treated kindly at the court of Evil-merodach, king of Babylon, at whose table he dines regularly, and is given a continual allowance. He even receives "a seat above the seats of the kings that were with him in Babylon." A sharper contrast is hardly imaginable. Matthew knew all this, of course. Throughout his Gospel he is constantly proving that he is well acquainted with his sources. Is it not natural to suppose, therefore, that it was because of these two sharply contrasting pictures that Matthew counts Jechoniah twice?

Does not the history of the United States of America provide us with a similar instance of counting one man twice? Do we not call Mr. Nixon "the thirty-seventh president"? Nevertheless, beginning with Washington, we soon discover that there were only thirty-six men who were elected to this high position. The solution is: we count Cleveland twice because of his two terms (1885-1889; 1893-1897). Defeated for re-election after his first term, he was subsequently re-elected to office. His circumstances changed. Though, to be sure, the two cases are not identical—for example, Jechoniah never returned to his throne in Judah—yet in both instances the sequence is: *high position-defeat-high position.*

Jechoniah's son in the Messianic line was Shealtiel. The latter's "son" (grandson?; see I Chron. 3:17-19) was Zerubbabel (Ezra 3:2). Both Matthew and Luke (the latter in 3:27) include Shealtiel and Zerubbabel in their genealogical tables. In these two men the ancestral lines of Joseph, as reported by Matthew, and of Mary, as probably transmitted by Luke, converge, and then diverge again. [131]

Shortly before 536 B.C. Babylon fell, and the Persian empire replaced the Babylonian. The new ruler allowed the Hebrew exiles to return to their own land (Ezra 1). When Cyrus issued his decree, only a remnant returned (Ezra 2:64). The highpriest Joshua (or Jeshua) was head of the priesthood. Zerubbabel, the very person mentioned in the two New Testament genealo-

---

[131] The exact manner in which this took place, in connection with Shealtiel and Zerubbabel, is difficult—perhaps impossible—to ascertain. See R. D. Wilson, art. Zerubbabel, I.S.B.E., Vol. V., p. 3147; also my *Bible Survey*, pp. 136-138.

gies, was appointed to be the leader of the civil administration; in other words, *the governor,* and as such the contact man between the Jews and their Persian rulers. Under the direction of these two wonderful administrators the returned built the altar of burnt-offering and laid the foundation of the temple (Ezra 3:1-6). Jealous Samaritans and their allies interrupted the work (Ezra 4). But in the second year of Darius—i.e., about the year 520—the prophet Haggai urged the rebuilding of the temple itself. Zechariah joined him, and greatly encouraged the builders by means of his strikingly beautiful Messianic predictions (3:6-10; 6:9-13; 9:9; 11:12, 13; 12:10). In one of these (6:9-13) we see not only the *prophetical* but also the *typological* preparation for the coming of Christ; for Joshua the highpriest is clearly a type of the One who deserves to be "crowned with many crowns." But the *historical* preparation also is not lacking; for, guiding the hand of the Persian rulers, with their wise policies toward conquered nations, permitting them to return to their own countries, was God's firm decree, according to which Messiah was to be born in Bethlehem of Judea (Mic. 5:2). This accounts for the necessity of the return. Zerubbabel, the descendant of Jechoniah, must make his home in the land from which his ancestors had been driven away, in order that in the line of his seed and on holy soil both Joseph and Mary may be born.

13—16a. The table of ancestry continues as follows: **Zerubbabel became the father of Abiud, and Abiud became the father of Eliakim, and Eliakim became the father of Azor, and Azor became the father of Zadok, and Zadok became the father of Achim, and Achim became the father of Eliud, and Eliud became the father of Eleazar, and Eleazar became the father of Matthan, and Matthan became the father of Jacob, and Jacob became the father of Joseph.**

The period of Babylonian Exile was followed by the Medo-Persian Rule (536-333 B.C.), as has already been indicated. The latter, in turn, was succeeded by the Greco-Macedonian and Egyptian sovereignty (333-200) and its aftermath: Syrian and (after a bitter struggle) Maccabean hegemony (200-63). Then came the Romans. Since most of the period covered in verses 13-16 belongs to inter-testamentary history, it is not surprising that the men whose names are cited are not mentioned elsewhere in Scripture. They lived amid difficult circumstances, under foreign rulers, and among hostile neighbors. At times persecution raged fiercely, especially during the Maccabean struggle. Whether all of the ancestors here listed remained true to the faith we do not know. Even a beautiful name—as, for example, Eliud="God is my praise," or Eliazar="God is my helper,"—does not always necessarily indicate that the one who received it grew up to be a man of sterling trust in the one true God; though frequently it probably embodied the pious wish of devout parents with respect to their newborn child. We *do* know, however, that Zerubbabel, mentioned in verses 12 and 13, receives high praise in Scripture

127

(Ezra 5:1, 2; Hag. 1:12-15; 2:20-23; Zech. 4:1-10). The words "On that day, says the Lord of hosts, I will take you, O Zerubbabel my servant, son of Shealtiel, says Jehovah, and make you like a signet ring, for I have chosen you, says Jehovah of hosts" (Hag. 2:23) place this God-fearing governor of Judea under God's special protection, so that when tumults rage all around, his safety is assured. Do they not also indicate that this chosen servant of God is a type of the Messiah, beloved by the Father?

And as to the last one on the list, Joseph, Matthew is going to show that the husband of Mary was indeed a man of sterling quality, one whose trust was in the Lord, whom he was ever ready to obey.

After what has been said earlier (see pp. 116, 119), it no longer suprises us that, for the period beginning with the one whom Luke regards as the father of Shealtiel and ending with Jesus, this evangelist presents twenty-three names; Matthew, on the other hand, for the same (or approximately the same) period offers only fourteen. He is again intentionally skipping the names of some ancestors. Also, the question, "Where did Matthew obtain his information?" has already been answered (see pp. 111-115). It might be added that further evidence for the preservation of genealogical lists (probably both written and oral) is furnished by the fact that Luke knew that Zechariah, the father of John the Baptist, was "of the course of Abijah," and had a wife who was "of the daughters of Aaron" (Luke 1:5). He also knew that Joseph was "of the house and family of David" (2:4); and that the prophetess Anna was "of the tribe of Asher" (2:36). Similarly, Paul knew that he himself was "of the tribe of Benjamin" (Rom. 11:1; Phil. 3:5). Evidently, therefore, the awareness of a distinction between the tribes continues into the New Testament period, and people know to which tribe and household they severally belong. Priests, and others too, must have kept records, and these had been handed down from generation to generation. [132] Josephus was able to give his own genealogy. He tells us that he had found it in "the public records" (*The Life* I.6). See also his work *Against Apion* I.30.

16b. After the words, "Jacob became the father of Joseph," Matthew adds: **the husband of Mary, of whom was born Jesus, who is called Christ.**

In language simple and clear the truth with reference to the virgin birth of the Savior is introduced. It is *implied* rather than as yet fully expressed. We are *not* now told that Joseph *became the father of* or *begot* Jesus. The marked contrast between the lengthy series of begot . . . begot . . . begot . . . and the abrupt omission of this word here in 1:16b, brings out, as strongly as anything could do, the fact that in connection with the birth of Mary's firstborn son there was no male act of begetting that could be

---

[132] Preservation of such lists was a very ancient custom, by no means confined to the Jews. The Assyrians had their king-lists, and so did the Babylonians; see C. W. Ceram, *Gods, Graves, and Scholars*, New York, 1968, pp. 272; 314, 315.

ascribed to Joseph, or, for that matter, to any other human being anywhere. We are reminded of Gen. 5, where, after a series of "and he died" statements, beginning in verse 5 and repeated every third verse thereafter, six occurrences in all, we suddenly read with reference to Enoch, "and he was not, for God took him" (verse 24).

Joseph is called "the husband of Mary." The manner in which he became the husband is related in verses 18-25. For the present it is sufficient to know that Joseph, a Nazareth carpenter (Matt. 13:55; Mark 6:3), was, indeed, Mary's husband, but had nothing whatever to do with the conception of Jesus. In the physical sense it was "of Mary," and not "to Joseph" that Jesus was born. Joseph was the child's "father" in the legal sense alone. That legal sense, too, was important. Through Joseph, a son of David, the right to David's throne was transferred to Mary's child, *Jesus*, thus named because it was he who would save his people from their sins (1:21). To carry out this task he was set apart and qualified by God, being God's Anointed, the Christ (Isa. 61:1; cf. Luke 4:18-21; and see comments on Matt. 1:1).

17. The record of ancestry is summarized in the words: **So all the generations from Abraham to David (were) fourteen generations, and from David to the deportation to Babylon fourteen generations, and from the deportation to Babylon to Christ fourteen generations.** Since the significance of this triad of fourteen generations each has already been explained, and the legitimacy of the figure *fourteen,* instead of thirteen, even with reference to the third group, has been substantiated, very little need be added. Only this: as always, so also here, the word *all* must be interpreted in the light of its context; hence, the meaning is: all the generations covered in this record of ancestry.

Here, for the first time in Matthew, the word "generation" occurs. It is a "stage" in the succession of natural descent, a "set" of ancestors. "Sum-total of contemporaries" is probably the meaning in 11:16; 12:39, 41, 42, 45; 16:4; 17:17; 23:36. From this meaning the transition to a (Jewish) *nation* or *people* (24:34) is easy. So is that to *time period covered by a generation;* see N.T.C. on Ephesians 3:20, 21.

---

18 Now the birth of Jesus Christ happened as follows: When his mother Mary had been betrothed to Joseph, before they had begun to live together she found herself to be pregnant by the Holy Spirit. 19 Now Joseph, her husband, being intent upon doing what was right and not wishing to expose her to public disgrace, had in view to divorce her quietly. 20 But as he was mulling this over, what happened? An angel of the Lord appeared to him during a dream and said, "Joseph, son of David, do not hesitate to take Mary, your wife, into your home, for what was conceived in her is of the Holy Spirit. 21 She will give birth to a son, and you shall call his name Jesus, for he will save his people from their sins." 22 All this took place in order that what was spoken by the Lord through the prophet might be fulfilled,

23 "Behold, the virgin shall conceive and give birth to a son, and his name shall be called Emmanuel," which, translated, is "God with us."

24 Rising from sleep Joseph did as the angel of the Lord had directed him, and took

his wife into his home, 25 but had no sexual relations with her until she had given birth to a son; and he named him Jesus.

1:18-25 *The Birth of Jesus Christ*
Cf. Luke 21:1-7

18. What was already implied in the genealogy is here clearly taught: **Now the birth of Jesus Christ happened as follows: When his mother Mary had been betrothed to Joseph, before they had begun to live together she found herself to be pregnant by the Holy Spirit.** .

Mary had been "betrothed"—solemnly promised in marriage—to Joseph. The marriage feast and living together was a matter for later date. Matthew makes his point of departure a moment of time shortly after the betrothal. Betrothal among the Jews must not be confused with present-day engagement. It was far more serious and binding. The bridegroom and bride pledged their troth to each other in the presence of witnesses. *In a restricted sense* this was essentially the marriage. So also here, as is clear from the fact that from that moment on Joseph is called Mary's *husband* (verse 19); Mary is called Joseph's *wife* (verse 20). According to the Old Testament regulation unfaithfulness in a betrothed woman was punishable with death (Deut. 22:23, 24). Yet, though the two were now legally "espoused," it was considered proper that an interval of time elapse before husband and wife begin to live together in the same home. Now it was before Joseph and Mary had begun thus to live together, with all this implies both as to domestic and sexual relations, that Mary discovered her pregnancy. She was still a virgin, and not yet "married" in the *full* sense of the term. She knew immediately that the cause of her condition was the powerful life-imparting operation of the Holy Spirit. She knew it because the angel Gabriel had told her that this would happen (Luke 1:26-35). She knew that Joseph had not made her pregnant.

Naturally Joseph became aware of Mary's condition. His reaction is described as follows: 19. **Now Joseph, her husband, being intent upon doing what was right and not wishing to expose her to public disgrace, had in view to divorce her quietly.** Incognizant of the reason for Mary's condition and drawing the natural conclusion, namely, that Mary had been unfaithful to him, Joseph could not see his way clear to take Mary home with him and live with her in the usual marriage relationship. Had she not broken her solemn pledge? Joseph must have agonized about the proper thing to do under these circumstances. He loved Mary and wanted to have her with him as his wife, but, above all, he was a righteous person (cf. Job 1:8; Luke 1:6), a man of principle, one who with his whole heart wanted to live in accordance with the will of God, the God who took so very seriously the breaking of the marriage vow. However, Joseph was also kindhearted. According to the custom of the day, two avenues were open to him: *a.* institute a lawsuit against Mary, and *b.* hand her a bill of divorcement, thus dismissing her quietly, that is, without involving her in any juridical procedure (see Deut. 24:1, 3 and Matt. 5:32). The former alternative, though in practice it would no longer have meant death by stoning, for this law had been modified by so many man-made restrictions that this possibility could be safely dismissed, would nevertheless have exposed Mary to public disgrace and scorn, the very thing which Joseph wanted by all means to avoid. Consequently, he decided upon the latter alternative, namely, to send her away quietly, though even this was not at all agreeable with his strong inner yearning for her, as is clear from verse 20. **But as he was mulling this over, what happened?** [133] **An angel of the Lord appeared to him during a dream and said, Joseph, son of David, do not hesitate to take Mary, your wife, into your home, for what was conceived in her is of the Holy Spirit.**

Though Joseph has decided on the action he must take, he finds it almost impossible to make the transition from resolve to deed. While he is turning these things over in his mind, he falls asleep and begins to dream. With dramatic suddenness, during this dream an angel—his name is not given (nor in 2:13, 19); contrast Luke 1:19, 26—appears, and imparts to him the information that had already been given to Mary (Luke 1:35), namely, that it is by the power of the Holy Spirit, and not in the natural way, that Mary has conceived. To strengthen and comfort him the angel addresses him as *son of David.* In the fulfilment of the Messianic promise Joseph, viewed as legal heir of David and as the one who transmits this honor to Jesus, is not bypassed, neither here nor in the preceding genealogy, which in a sense was really *Joseph's* family-tree. The angel tells Joseph that he must not hesitate or be afraid to take Mary, his wife, into his home. Do not these words, "Do not hesitate" imply that there was something Joseph in his heart of hearts really wanted but did not quite dare to do? Well then, let him shrink no longer from fulfiling his, and Mary's, desire, for the one and only obstacle has been removed: Mary had not been unfaithful after all! Joseph can safely take his wife into his home; in fact, he is even directed to do so.

The contents of this angelic revelation must have been:

---

133 The original ἰδού presents a problem. Many modern translators completely ignore the word. Some consistently reproduce it in English by means of "lo," or "behold." The *very frequent* use of such an interjection, by many considered to be archaic, is probably not the best solution. Yet, the translation loses something of the vividness of the original if it is simply ignored, especially when, as here in 1:20, the sudden appearance of an angel presents a scene full of drama. Could not a safe procedure be this: to translate ἰδού variously, depending upon the degree of vividness implied in any given context? My translation in this instance—the question and answer method—is one way of retaining and reproducing the striking character of the original. It leaves the way open for a variety of different renderings in other passages, including "lo" and "behold." Other possibilities: "lo and behold," "look," "see," "listen," inverted sentence order, "suddenly," "once upon a time," etc., almost anything that arouses interest.

a. *very startling*, for, apart from special revelation, the idea of a virgin birth is found nowhere in old Jewish literature. [134] As to Isa. 7:14, see pp. 133-140. The Jews were firm believers in marriage and the family, with all this implies (Gen. 1:27, 28; 9:1; 24:60; 25:21; 30:1; Ps. 127:3-5; Prov. 5:18). For the notion that the virgin birth idea was borrowed from pagan sources see p. 142. Such a derivation is not supported by any solid evidence. To Joseph, then, this very idea of a virgin conceiving was altogether new. He would never have accepted it had not an angel sent by God conveyed this information to him.

b. *very comforting*. He must have been filled with joy, for the sake both of Mary and of himself. He understood that he could now be Mary's protector, providing for her physical needs and defending her honor over against all malicious slander. The child, too, would now have a "father."

Most of all, involved in this truth of the virgin birth is the guarantee of salvation for God's people, for, apart from this kind of birth it is difficult to understand how Christ could be their Savior. See pp. 143, 144.

The message of the angel continues as follows: **21. She will give birth to a son, and you shall call his name Jesus, for he will save his people from their sins.** All have an interest in the birth of this child: *a.* the Holy Spirit, by the exercise of whose power the child is conceived; *b.* Mary, who, being the willing instrument of the Spirit in conceiving and giving birth to the infant, becomes "blessed among women" (cf. Matt. 1:21 with Luke 1:42); and *c.* Joseph, who, along with Mary (Luke 1:31), is told to give the child a name; not just any name, however, but the name *Jesus*. That name has already been explained (see on 1:1), but even if it had not, no more adequate explanation is possible than the one offered by the angel, namely, "he will save." Whom will he save? Not everybody but "his people" (cf. John 3:16), "his sheep" (John 10:11).

It is ever God, God alone, who in and through his Son, saves his people. While some trust in chariots and some in horses (Ps. 20:7), in physical strength, knowledge, reputation, prestige, position, magnificent and impressive machinery, influential friends, and intrepid generals, none of these, whether operating singly or in conjunction with all the others, is able to deliver man from his chief enemy, the foe that is little by little destroying his very heart, namely, sin; or, as here, *sins,* those of thought, word, and deed; of omission, commission, and inner disposition: all those various ways in which man "misses the mark," God's glory. It takes no less than the atoning death of Jesus and the sanctifying power of his Spirit to cleanse hearts and lives.

The marked and prevailing emphasis which, already in the Old Testament, is placed upon the fact that God is sovereign and that he alone can save is

---

[134] On this see S.BK., Vol. IV, p. 49.

evident from such passages as Gen. 49:18; II Kings 19:15-19; II Chron. 14:11; 20:5-12; Ps. 3:8; 25:5; 37:39; 62:1; 81:1; Isa. 12:2; Jer. 3:23; Lam. 3:26; Dan. 4:35; Mic. 7:7; Hab. 3:18; Zech. 4:6; and a host of other passages equally clear and precious. In the New Testament the emphasis is just as strong, as appears from Matt. 19:28; 28:18; Luke 12:32; 18:13, 27; John 14:6; Acts 4:12; Eph. 2:8; Phil. 2:12, 13; Rev. 1:18; 3:7; 5:9; 19:1, 6, 16; etc.

To be saved means *a.* to be emancipated from the greatest evil: the guilt, pollution, power, and punishment of sin; and *b.* to be placed in possession of the greatest good. Although in the present passage the negative alone is expressed, namely, to save—*from sin,* the positive is immediately implied. One cannot be saved *from* something without also being saved *for* something: true happiness, the peace of God that transcends all understanding, freedom, joy unspeakable and full of glory, answered prayers, effective witness bearing, assurance of salvation, etc. On the concept *salvation* see also N.T.C. on I Tim. 1:15. The promise of the angel to Joseph, then, is this, that this child must be called Jesus—meaning, in brief, Savior—because in the fullest and most glorious sense he will save his people from their sins.

The message of the angel is ended. Matthew himself now resumes his account, showing that the virgin birth of this glorious child who was to be the Savior is a fulfilment of prophecy. He says: **22, 23. All this took place in order that what was spoken by the Lord through the prophet might be fulfilled,**

Behold, the virgin shall conceive and give birth to a son, and his name shall be called Emmanuel, which, translated, is God with us.

This is the first of a long list of prophecies to which Matthew refers in order to show that Jesus is really the long expected Messiah. For the entire list see pp. 80, 81. As has been indicated previously, the evangelist's purpose in bringing these predictions back to the minds of the readers, Jews for the most part, is that they may embrace Jesus with a living faith and may proclaim to Jew and Gentile the good news of salvation through this Mediator.

The introductory formula, "All this took place in order . . .." (verse 22) makes clear that, as Matthew by inspiration sees it, whatever anticipatory fulfilments these predictions may have had during the old dispensation, they attain their consummation in Jesus Christ, in him alone. This does not imply that all these prophecies even had initial as well as crowning or ultimate fulfilments. Each case will have to be decided on its own merits.

The introductory formula also makes clear that the prophecy about to be quoted had its origin in God himself, not in the mind of the prophet. In fact, in the present case the prophet's name is not even mentioned! The words were spoken *by* the Lord *through* the prophet. The latter functioned as God's mouthpiece.

133

The Isaiah Background

Turning now to the quotation itself (verse 23), it is obviously taken from Isa. 7:14. [135] A brief review of the historical background is in order:

A little over seven centuries before the birth of Christ the throne of Ahaz, king of Judah, was being threatened by a coalition of the king of Israel (Pekah) and the king of Syria (Rezin). The threat of these two conspirators was to destroy David's dynasty and to establish a king of their own choice, "even the son of Tabeel" (Isa. 7:6). What was to become of the glorious promise if this plot were to succeed? Of the Messianic prediction found in II Sam. 7:12, 13? Would the coming Redeemer ever be born as the son and legal heir of David? Everything was at stake (see Rev. 12:4).

At this critical juncture Isaiah is sent to Ahaz to admonish him to place his trust in Jehovah, and to ask for a sign of God's protecting care. He is to ask for this sign, this miracle, to take place either in the depth below or in the height above. But wicked Ahaz, who placed his trust in Assyria rather than in Jehovah, feigned a pious excuse and in mock humility refused the sign. The prophet, revealing his indignation (7:13), then gave utterance to the oracle of the Lord in the words, "Therefore the Lord himself will give y o u [136] a sign: behold the [137] *'almah* shall conceive, etc.''

Among those who believe in Christ's virgin birth there are two main groups of interpreters with respect to Isa. 7:14: *a.* those who favor the *double reference* theory, and *b.* those who favor the *single reference* theory. According to the former, the prophecy has *direct* reference only to contemporaneous events and circumstances; i.e., to what happened during the days of Ahaz and Isaiah. *Indirectly* and *ultimately*, however, it is fulfilled in Christ's virgin birth. According to the latter—the single reference view—the passage has only one meaning: it refers directly and immediately to Christ's "virgin birth"; more precisely, to his conception in Mary's womb apart from any sexual union, and to the birth that followed this conception.

---

[135] With the LXX Matthew renders *ha- almah:* ἡ παρθένος. Instead of καλέσεις, "you shall call" of the LXX, and *qara'th,* "she shall call" (unless it be construed as a feminine participle), Matthew writes (according to the best text) καλέσουσιν, "they shall call" = "it [his name] shall be called." Matthew realizes that not only in the estimation of Mary but in that of all believers Jesus is "God with us." Matthew's manner of quoting represents no essential departure from the original Hebrew; unless his use of καλέσουσιν be considered such a departure, which I, for one, do not believe at all.

[136] Note plural: the sign is not just for Ahaz but for the entire "house of David" and, in a sense, for all who read or hear about it.

[137] Whether the article, present both in Hebrew and in the Greek translation (both the Greek of the LXX Isa. 7:14, and of Matt. 1:23), must be reproduced in English by the definite article "the" instead of by the indefinite "a(n)," is hard to determine, because idiomatic usage is not always the same in English as it is in Hebrew or in Greek. From the entire context in Isa. 7:14 and certainly also from Matt. 1:23 it would appear that *one definite 'almah* is meant, not just *any 'almah.* Hence, with several other translators, I would give the preference to "the," without, however, attaching decisive weight to this argument.

Double Reference Theory Stated [138]

According to this theory, in the Isaiah context there is no reference to any miraculous or "virgin" birth. In speaking of an *almah* the prophet was referring to a young woman of marriageable age who, having married, would conceive and give birth to a son and would name him Emmanuel, that is, "God with us." By thus naming the child she would be confessing her trust in God. She would be saying that even in the midst of troublous times she was firmly convinced that the Lord would not forsake his people but would provide for them and protect them against their enemies. It is clear that according to this view the name Emmanuel describes not the child but the mother. It characterizes her as a woman of faith in God.

However, so the theory continues, Matthew was fully justified in applying these words of Isaiah to a more far-reaching event, namely, the miraculous birth of the One who himself is Emmanuel. Or, to phrase it differently, although Isa. 7:14 does not directly refer to the conception and birth of the Messiah, yet in its deepest sense the passage did not come into its own until it was fulfilled in him.

Arguments in Support of The Double Reference Theory

1. Had it been Isaiah's intention to undersocre the *virginity* of the child's mother, he would have used the word *bᵉthulah* instead of *'almah*. An *'almah* is a young woman of marriageable age. We can conceive of this young woman of Isa. 7:14 as being first still unmarried, which is the more usual sense of the term; then, as getting married and in the natural way conceiving and giving birth to a child. Nowhere does Isaiah call the mother a *bᵉthulah* or *virgin*.

2. It is true that Matthew, in translating Isa. 7:14, uses the word *virgin*. It must be borne in mind, however, that the evangelist frequently departs from the literal translation when he quotes or refers to Old Testament prophecies. Compare, for example, Matt. 4:15 with Isa. 9:1, 2. Accordingly, Matthew's use of the word *virgin* does not prove that *Isaiah* had in mind a virgin. Of course, Matthew had a perfect right to apply this passage to Christ's virgin birth. In Christ Isa. 7:14 attains its ultimate fulfilment.

---

[138] Among the many whose names could be listed—for it is a very popular view—I mention only the following as representative. It should be emphasized, however, that on many details these authors present varying viewpoints.

Charles R. Erdman, *Exposition of the Gospel according to Matthew*, Philadelphia, 1920, p. 26.

A. W. Evans, art. *Immanuel*, I.S.B.E., Vol. III, pp. 1457, 1458.

G. H. A. Ewald, *The Prophets of the Old Testament*, London, 1875-81, Vol. II, p. 84 f.

J. Ridderbos, *Jesaja (Korte Verklaring)*, Kampen, 1952, Vol. I, p. 64.

H. N. Ridderbos, *Mattheus (Korte Verklaring)* Kampen, 1954, Vol. I, pp. 35, 36.

R. V. G. Tasker, *The Gospel according to St. Matthew (Tyndale New Testament Commentaries)*, Grand Rapids, 1961.

3. It is natural to assume that the name Emmanuel, as used by Isaiah, is descriptive of the mother's thinking or disposition, her trust in God, rather than of the son's character or role in life. Cannot the same be said with respect to the origin of several other names; such as Reuben, Simeon, Levi, Judah (Gen. 29:31-35), Joseph (Gen. 30:24), Benoni and Benjamin (Gen. 35:18), to mention only a few? In all of them the name describes the giver rather than the recipient. It is clear, therefore, that also in Isa. 7:14 it is not at all necessary to regard the name Emmanuel as being descriptive of the recipient, as if Emmanuel were a synonym of the Messiah, and as if his mother were the virgin Mary. That cannot have been the *primary* meaning of these terms. It is a *later* interpretation or application, namely, that of Matthew, and as such fully justified.

4. Verse 16 shows that Isaiah's prophecy refers not to the distant future but to the days of king Ahaz. It is in his own time and very shortly that the kingdoms or regions whose rulers he abhors will be deserted. Now since verse 16 (and 15 also) stands in the closest possible connection with verse 14, how then can verse 14 refer to the virgin birth of Christ, an event that occurred more than seven centuries later?

Single Reference Theory

This theory does not deny that the words of Isa. 7:14 had meaning for the days of Ahaz. In fact, it insists on this. However, it believes that even in the Isaiah context the son's mother is definitely a virgin, namely, Mary, and that her child is the Messiah.

"This vision of the prophet sweeps far beyond present events . . . and he beholds in this Son that should be born, this child that should be given—who can be none other than the Messianic King—the security for the fulfilment of the promises of David, and the hope for the future of the world." [139]

"If a married woman were referred to in Isa. 7:14, it does seem as though some other word than *'almah* would naturally be used. . . . Why should an ordinary birth be regarded as a 'sign'? . . . But it is not merely the use of this one word [sign] which would lead us to expect something miraculous in that which the prophet proceeds to announce. Equally suggestive is the elaborate way in which the 'sign' is introduced. The whole passage is couched in such terms as to induce in the reader a sense of profound mystery as he comprehends the young woman and her child." [140]

In support of its own position, this second or single reference theory presents the following

---

[139] James Orr, *The Virgin Birth of Christ*, New York, 1924, see pp. 133-136.

[140] J. Gresham Machen, *The Virgin Birth of Christ*, New York and London, 1930, (Grand Rapids, 1965), see pp. 288-291. One can find the same argument, based on the use of the word "sign," in Justin Martyr, *Dialogue with Trypho*, ch. 84, written about the middle of the second century.

Answers to the Arguments of the Double
Reference Theory

Answer to 1. As to '*almah* versus *b*^{e}*thulah:* fact is that while the latter means *virgin* in Gen. 24:16; Lev. 21:3; Judg. 21:12; in Joel 1:8 it probably refers to a *non-virgin,* a *widow* who during the early years of married life had lost her husband, whom she now laments. [141] On the other hand, an '*almah,* in every passage in which this word is indisputably used, means *maiden* (Gen. 24:43; Exod. 2:8; Ps. 68:25; Prov. 30:19; Song of Sol. 1:3; 6:8). It refers to a *girl,* like Rebecca, before she had even seen Isaac, and like Miriam, Moses' sister. The logical inference would seem to be that also here in Isa. 7:14 the meaning is basically the same. Luther's challenge still stands: "If a Jew or Christian can prove to me that in any passage of Scripture *almah* means a married woman, I will give him 100 florins, although God alone knows where I might find them."

Now the fact that a *maiden* becomes pregnant and gives birth to a child is introduced here in Isa. 7:11-14 as something wonderful, unheard of. The readers have been encouraged to expect an announcement of something altogether marvelous. Certainly hardly anyone, in interpreting Isa. 7:14, believes that it was by means of an act of immorality that the maiden here indicated conceived. [142] The conclusion is inescapable that she was a *virgin* when she conceived: no male had brought this condition upon her.

The opinion of two renowned Old Testament scholars may be added for further confirmation of this position:

"The word '*almah* . . . is never used of a married woman, either in the Bible or elsewhere. The new evidence from Ras Shamra is strikingly interesting on this point." With respect to *b*^{e}*thulah* this author writes, "The word in question is ambiguous. Does it mean a virgin, a betrothed virgin, or a married woman? I am convinced that it may mean any one of the three." He continues: "Isaiah [in Isa. 7:14] used the one word in the Hebrew language ['*almah*] which is never employed of a married woman." Further, "In English the word '*almah* is perhaps the most closely approximated by *maid* or *damsel.* The word *virgin,* however, stresses the supernatural character of the birth, and hence is to be preferred. In no case should the word in this passage be translated by the vague and weak term *young woman.*" [143]

---

[141] Thus also R. C. Foster, *Studies in the Life of Christ, Introduction and Early Ministry,* Grand Rapids, 1966, p. 165. In pre-Mosaic literature the two words are at times used interchangeably. See R. H. Gundry, *The Use of the Old Testament in St. Matthew's Gospel,* p. 227.

[142] Even this has, however, been seriously suggested, namely, by Dr. Naegelsbach, Lange's *Commentary on the Holy Scriptures,* New York, 1878, reprint Grand Rapids, no date, volume on *Isaiah,* pp. 123-125. He speaks about "a fallen woman" and "an illegitimate child." Refutation unnecessary!

[143] Edward J. Young, article on "The Virgin Birth" in *The Banner,* April 15, 1955. Cf. his remarks in *Studies in Isaiah,* Grand Rapids, 1954, pp. 161-185.

"Now I wish to state at once that the rendering *young woman* (in Isa. 7:14) is to be rejected." The author of this statement then shows that the word *'almah,* wherever it occurs in the Old Testament indicates those of the female sex who had not yet entered into the relationships commonly associated with marriage. He points out that passages such as the title in Ps. 46 and I Chron. 15:20 do not prove anything to the contrary, because the word used in these passages "is not sufficiently clear." He further shows that the argument according to which *b^{e}thulah* must mean "virgin" fails to figure with the facts. In this connection he refers to Joel 1:8 (already discussed; see above, p. 137). He continues, "For these reasons it is definitely precarious to use the word *young woman* in Isa. 7:14, as a rendering of *'almah.*" [144]

Conclusion: The argument according to which "had it been Isaiah's intention to underscore virginity he would have used *b^{e}thulah* instead of *'almah*" is not convincing. The rendering "virgin" suits the context best.

Answer to 2. As to Matthew's reference to Isa. 7:14, if, as has been shown in the previous answer, Isaiah did indeed refer to a virgin, there is no discrepancy whatever between Isa. 7:14 and Matt. 1:23. On the other hand, if Isaiah was thinking of a young married woman who, with the help of her husband, conceived and gave birth to a child, it is difficult to see how Matthew could regard Christ's birth "of the *virgin* Mary" to be a *fulfilment* of Isa. 7:14. The *'almah* mentioned in Isa. 7:14 cannot have been at the same time virgin and non-virgin. Moreover, it is clearly as an *'almah* that she conceives and gives birth to a child. [145] The interpreter has no right, as is sometimes done, first to introduce her as a young unmarried woman, and then surreptitiously, as it were, to let her get married before she conceives and bears a son.

It is freely admitted that, under the guidance of the Spirit, Matthew and the other New Testament writers at times made a different use of a passage than that to which it had been put originally, but such a fresh application to a new situation is never a contradiction.—As to Matt. 4:15 (in comparison with Isa. 9:1) see on that passage.

Answer to 3. As to the close relation between a name and *a.* its giver, rather than *b.* its recipient or bearer, though the former is often the case, there are also many instances in which the latter holds: Eve (Gen. 3:20), Noah (Gen. 5:29), Abram and Abraham (Gen. 17:5), Sarai and Sarah (Gen. 17:15), Esau (Gen. 25:25), Jacob and Israel (Gen. 27:36; 32:28), Naomi and Mara (Ruth 1:20), Nabal (I Sam. 25:3, 25), Jesus (Matt. 1:21), Peter (Matt. 16:18), and Barnabas (Acts 4:36). The question, then, is legitimate, "To which of these two classes of names [146] does Emmanuel belong? Evidently

---

[144] G. Ch. Aalders, *GTT* No. 5 (1953), pp. 132, 133. See also R. D. Wilson, *PTR* No. 24 (1926), pp. 308-316.

[145] So also R. H. Gundry, *op. cit.,* pp. 226, 227.

[146] These two are by no means the only classes of name-sources. A name may have

to the latter, as the connection between Isa. 7:14; 8:8; and 9:6 indicates. This Emmanuel of 7:14 and 8:8 is the child that is born, the son that is given, upon whose shoulder the government rests, and who is called "Wonderful, Counselor, Mighty God, Everlasting Father, Prince of Peace" (9:6). See also 11:1 ff.

There is also a close connection between these Isaiah passages and Mic. 5:2 (cf. Isa. 7:14 with Mic. 5:3), where the same person is described as the One "whose origin is from of old, from everlasting," and where his birth in Bethlehem is predicted. *Clearly, the name Emmanuel describes the One who bears it, namely, the Messiah!*

"In all the Scriptures names are often given as significant of character, and this is especially prominent in connection with the revelation of God to men, and the revelation of the coming of Messiah as it is gradually unfolded is surely no exception; from the 'seed of the woman' (Gen. 3:15) to the 'Lord Jesus' (Rev. 22:20) the Messiah is constantly revealed by the names which are ascribed to him. With this general trend of revelation in mind, and the connection of 7:14 with 9:6 and 8:8 considered, with the emphatic method of utterance noted as well, it appears that Emmanuel, 'God with us,' has reference to the character of the child, and consequently is yet another name giving testimony to the Deity of the Messiah." [147]

Now if it be true that the name Emmanuel mentioned in Isa. 7:14 refers to the Messiah, as has been established, then is it not also true that the virgin who by the power of the Holy Spirit conceived and bore the child is, indeed, Mary?

Answer to 4. As to the relation between verses 14 and 16, Isaiah can be understood as saying: "Behold, the virgin conceives and gives birth to a son. . . . Before this child, *who before my prophetic eye has already arrived,* shall know to refuse the evil and choose the good—i.e., *within a very short time*—the land whose two kings you abhor shall be deserted."

"This interpretation, we think, is by no means impossible . . . the objections to it largely fall away when one reads the exalted language of the

---

been occasioned by an event (Ichabod), or by circumstances attending the child's birth (Saul, meaning *asked*, or Elishama: God has heard). Patronymics are also of frequent occurrence (Bar-Jesus). There were matronymics (Bath-Shua). Many names, too, expressed a peculiar relation to Jehovah (Joshua, and ever so many others) or to God (Eli). In some El (God) and Jehovah are combined (Elijah: Jehovah is God). In several names the motives underlying origin overlap. It is a vast subject. For more on it see N.T.C. on Philippians, pp. 138, 139. Also J. D. Davis, art. *Names, Proper,* I.S.B.E., Vol. IV, pp. 2113-2117; A. F. Key, "The Giving of Proper Names in the Old Testament," *JBL* (March, 1964), pp. 55-59.

[147] Earl S. Kalland, *The Deity of the Old Testament Messiah, with Special Reference to His Fulfilment in Jesus of Nazareth,* a doctoral thesis submitted to the Faculty of Gordon College of Theology and Missions, 1942 (on file in the Gordon-Conwell Theological Seminary Library), p. 104.

prophet as the language of prophetic vision ought really to be read." [148]
Describing the future as if it were already present is characteristic of Isaiah.
Can anyone read Isa. 53 without being struck by the fact that the prophet,
by divine inspiration, writes as if the details of Christ's humiliation and
consequent exaltation are transpiring before his very eyes, yes as if they have
already taken place?

But even if to some this "Answer to 4" should not seem convincing, it
must be borne in mind that Matthew is not quoting Isa. 7:*16* but Isa. 7:*14*.
Whatever be the correct explanation of verse 16, the conclusion seems
inescapable that Isa. 7:14 clearly refers to the Messiah: the passages with
which it is definitely linked—Isa. 8:8; 9:6; 11:1-5; Mic. 5:2 ff.—so as to form
an unbreakable chain, are too emphatically Messianic to argue otherwise.

The prophecy of Isa. 7:16 was fulfilled. Tiglath Pileser came, within a
very short time after the prediction was uttered. He carried away a portion
of the inhabitants of Pekah's realm and did not at all object when Pekah
himself was murdered by Hoshea (II Kings 15:29, 30). He also advanced
against Rezin's kingdom, took its capital Damascus, deported its people, and
slew Rezin (II Kings 16:9).

Was not this literal fulfilment of prophecy a clear and evident *token*
whereby Ahaz and the whole house of David could assure themselves that
the Lord was standing guard over the realization of his own plan regarding
the Messianic promise? Was not the failure of the two foes, Pekah and Rezin,
to destroy the Davidic dynasty, a clear *sign* that the Davidic ancestry of the
Messiah was being protected, so that the Messianic prediction found in II
Sam. 7:12, 13 and elsewhere could be fulfilled; i.e., so that the coming
Redeemer could indeed be born as the son and legal heir of David? Thus
viewed it becomes clear that the prophecy of verse 14 fits into this context
very beautifully. There is no need whatever to introduce into this passage
any supposed reference to Abi, the wife of Ahaz, and her son Hezekiah (II
Kings 18:2); or to the wife of Isaiah, and one of her children; or to any of
their contemporaries. [149] *The virgin is Mary. Emanuel is Christ.*

Matthew's Quotation of Isa. 7:14

Matthew, then, has every right to appeal to Isa. 7:14, and to state that
Mary's pregnancy by the power of the Holy Spirit, and without assistance

---

148 J. Gresham Machen, *The Virgin Birth*, p. 292. Similarly J. Orr, *op. cit.*, p. 135.

149 Not only would it be very difficult to show that either of these can properly be
called an '*almah*, but there are various other difficulties that beset anyone who tries to
identify the '*almah* of Isa. 7:14 with any contemporary of Ahaz and Isaiah. These
obstacles have been clearly pointed out by J. G. Machen, *op. cit.*, pp. 289, 290; J. Orr,
op. cit., p. 135; and E. S. Kalland, *op. cit.*, pp. 105-107. It is only fair to state that by no
means all the advocates of the double reference theory try to identify the primary '*almah*
and/or her son. Some do, however. Recent illustration of this is R. V. G. Tasker, *op. cit.*,
p. 34, who suggests that Hezekiah is the son.

from Joseph, was in fulfilment of this prediction. That the name of this son would be Emmanuel had also been included in the ancient prophecy and had been reaffirmed in substance in Isa. 9:6: "For to us a child is born, to us a son is given . . . and his name shall be called . . . the Mighty God." There is very little difference in meaning between "to [or: for] us . . . the Mighty God" and "with us God," which is the literal meaning of Emmanuel.

Joseph receives the assurance, therefore, that this child conceived in Mary's womb is *God*. "Veiled in flesh the godhead see." He is God "manifested in the flesh" (I Tim. 3:16). "In him all the fulness of the godhead dwells bodily" (Col. 2:9).

In Emmanuel God has come to dwell with us. "And the Word became flesh, and dwelt among us as in a tent, and we beheld his glory, a glory as of the only begotten from the Father, full of grace and truth" (John 1:14). No one will ever be able to fathom the riches of this grace whereby God, by means of Emmanuel, has come to dwell with sinners. In order to say at least something in the way of further explanation it is probably best to obtain this information from Matthew's own Gospel. It means that, in Christ, God came to dwell

> with the sick, to heal them (4:23)
> with the demon-possessed, to liberate them (4:24)
> with the poor in spirit, etc., to bless them (5:1-12)
> with the care-ridden, to rid them of care (6:25-34)
> with the censorious, to warn them (7:1-5)
> with lepers, to cleanse them (8:1-4)
> with the diseased, to cure them (8:14-17)
> with the hungry, to feed them (14:13-21; 15:32-39)
> with the handicapped, to restore them (12:13; 15:31)
>   and over-arching everything else,
> with the lost, to seek and save them (18:11),

The noble persuasion that, in order to help the downtrodden, one should be willing to live and work by their side and share their lot has moved many a sympathetic person to make heroic sacrifices. Was it not this that prompted Francis of Assisi to embrace the very lepers from whom he had at first turned away in revulsion? William Booth to preach the gospel to London's slum dwellers and to assist them in every way? More than one missionary to literally become a slave himself in order to win slaves for Christ? And Paul to become all things to all men that he might by any and all means save some? These men deserve our most profound admiration. Yet, none of their acts of self-denial can compare with that of Emmanuel who, though he was infinitely rich, became poor, assumed our human nature, entered into our sin-polluted atmosphere without ever being tainted by sin himself, took upon himself our guilt, bore our griefs and carried our sorrows, was wounded for our transgressions and bruised for our iniquities, went to heaven to prepare a

141

place for us, sent his Spirit into our hearts, governs the entire universe in our behalf, not only makes intercession for us but "lives forever to make intercession for us" (Heb. 7:5), and will come again to take us not just "to heaven" but, far more tenderly, "to himself" (John 14:3). Truly, this is the One who became poor, that we through his poverty might become rich. This is Emmanuel, God WITH us!

Origin of the Idea of the Virgin Birth

The truth with reference to Christ's virgin birth having now been expounded, the question arises, "Where did that idea originate?" The unlikelihood that, apart from special revelation, it arose among the Jews has already been pointed out. It may be asked, "Was it derived from pagan mythology perhaps?" We are being told that in the days of the prophets and the apostles the air was full of virgin birth stories, so that the inclusion of one such legend in Holy Writ should not be considered surprising. However, as has been proved by many a writer, from Tertullian and Origen down to the present day, between the foul tales of the heathen and the pure narratives written by Matthew and Luke there is no essential similarity. The former are characterized by gross indecency, squalid inelegancy, and gaudy embroidery; the latter by faultless dignity, charming delicacy, and exquisite simplicity; by reserve and not by the reverse. When a god, inflamed by lust, rapes a girl or commits adultery with a married woman, the result, if conception takes place, is certainly no virgin birth. If the female was a virgin before, she is no longer a virgin when it occurs. To refer once more—see earlier reference on p. 111—to that legend of the so-called virgin birth of Alexander the Great: We are told that a serpent was once seen sharing the couch of Olympias, the wife of Philip of Macedonia. (It must be understood that Zeus, the chief offender in such cases of cohabitation, and other gods also, were able to assume the shapes of reptiles, birds, or even of the foam of the sea.) When Philip discovered what had happened his sexual ardor was dulled. Hence, the product of the strange union, namely, Alexander, was a son not of Philip but of Zeus. At this point the legend splits. According to one version, Olympias, when she sent her son forth upon his great expedition, revealed to him the secret of his begetting, and bade him to be inspired by purposes worthy of his birth. According to another version, she was ashamed of the dirty story and in repudiating it said, "Alexander must cease slandering me to Hera [the lawful wife of Zeus]."[150] Can anyone in his right mind believe that the clean and beautiful story of Christ's virgin birth was derived from—or even suggested by—anything as filthy as this silly tale? Moreover, to top it all, even if the story were true, Olympias was not at all a

---

[150] Plutarch, *Lives* (Vol. VII of *Loeb Classical Library*), *Alexander* II and III.1,2.

"virgin" before she conceived Alexander and could not have become one afterward. The analogy breaks down completely.

What, then, is the real origin of the narrative? There is only one answer: Matthew and Luke tell the story *because it actually happened.* From Mary, either directly or indirectly but in the latter case from a source very close to Mary, the evangelists received the correct information. The Holy Spirit saw to it that it was infallibly conveyed to them, infallibly recorded by them in two completely harmonious accounts (Matt. 1:18-23; Luke 1:26-38), and that also in the rest of the New Testament there is nothing that conflicts with it. Mark introduces Jesus Christ as "the Son of God" (1:1); John, as "the Word who became flesh" (assumed the human nature), "the only begotten of the Father, full of grace and truth" (1:14); and Paul, as "the second man from heaven" (I Cor. 15:47). Cf. also Rom. 8:3; Phil. 2:7. [151]

It was quite natural for Matthew to discover the link between the Isa. 7:14 passage and the information he had received from the family to which Jesus belonged. During the second century B.C., when the earliest extant Greek translation of the prophetical books of the Old Testament was produced, an important portion of which came to be known as the Septuagint, the Hebrew word *ha-'almah* was rendered ἡ παρθένος, i.e., "the virgin." That, in passing, is the *only* pre-Christian rendering of this Hebrew word known to us. Was Matthew influenced by this LXX translation? If so, this cannot be held against him. But it must be borne in mind that in ever so many places it is especially this evangelist who shows that he is by no means slavishly dependent upon the LXX. He is able to read the Hebrew original, and he knows that in the given context *ha-'almah* means "the virgin."

Doctrinal Significance

It is sometimes said that the doctrine of the virgin birth is unessential, since if God had wanted to do so he could have caused his Son to have been conceived and born in some other way. Answer: what God could or could not have done is a speculative question into which it is not necessary to enter. Fact is, however, that Jesus was "conceived by the Holy Spirit, born of the virgin Mary." As has been shown, this article of the Apostles' Creed is firmly rooted in Scripture. Moreover, it blends inextricably with the rest of revealed truth. "The supernatural Christ and the supernatural salvation carry with them by an inevitable consequence the supernatural birth." [152] Moreover, if Christ had been the son of Joseph and Mary by ordinary generation, would he not have been a human *person* and as such a sharer in Adam's guilt; hence, a sinner, unable to save himself, hence also unable to rescue others from sin? In order to save us, the Redeemer must in one person be both God

---

[151] With respect to Gal. 4:4 see N.T.C. on that passage.
[152] B. B. Warfield, *Christology and Criticism*, New York, 1929, p. 452.

and man, *sinless* man. The doctrine of the virgin birth satisfies both of these requirements. It reveals to us Jesus Christ, *one* divine person with *two* natures: *a.* divine, *b.* sinless human.

To account for all the marvelous *works* performed by Jesus without assuming a supernatural origin would be difficult indeed! And then there was that entire sinless *life.* The story is told that an unbeliever once asked a Christian this question: "If I should tell you that a child had been born in this city without a father, would you believe it?" The Christian answered, "Yes, if he should live as Jesus lived."

24, 25. The story is concluded as follows: **Rising from sleep Joseph did as the angel of the Lord had directed him, and took his wife into his home, but had no sexual relations with her until she had given birth to a son; and he named him Jesus.**

The meaning of the words "took his wife into his home" becomes clear when this expression is compared with verse 18: "before they had begun to live together." See on that verse and also on verse 20. Though Joseph and Mary were now together in the same home, they had no sexual relations with each other until Mary had given birth to Jesus. Why this was so is not related. Could this decision have been motivated by the couple's high regard for that which had been conceived? Or did they abstain to be able to refute every allegation that Joseph himself was the father of the child? Whatever it was that prompted the couple to refrain from having sexual intercourse, there is every reason to suppose that after the child's birth the abstention did not continue. This conclusion cannot be based merely upon the negative plus "until." That wording does *not always* introduce an event (in this case: she gave birth to a son) whereby the earlier situation (the couple had no sexual relations) is reversed (they now begin to have sexual relations). [153] Nevertheless, it is also true that *frequently,* in such cases, a complete reversal in the situation is suggested. Each case must be judged on its own merits. In the present instance the case against Mary's *perpetual virginity* is strengthened by these considerations: *a.* According to both the Old and the New Testament sexual intercourse for married couples is divinely approved (Gen. 1:28; 9:1; 24:60; Prov. 5:18; Ps. 127:3; I Cor. 7:5, 9). Of course, even here, as in all things, self-control should be exercised. Incontinence is definitely condemned (I Cor. 7:5; Gal. 5:22, 23). But no special sanctity attaches to total abstention or celibacy. *b.* We are definitely told that Jesus had brothers and sisters, evidently together with him members of one family (Matt. 12:46, 47; Mark 3:31, 32; 6:3; Luke 8:19, 20; John 2:12; 7:3, 5, 10; Acts 1:14). *c.* Luke 2:7 informs us that Jesus was Mary's "firstborn." Though in and by itself this third argument may not be sufficient to prove that Jesus had

---

[153] On "until" see also W. Hendriksen, *Israel and the Bible,* Grand Rapids, 1968, pp. 27, 28.

uterine brothers, in connection with arguments *a*. and *b*. the evidence becomes conclusive. The burden of proof rests entirely on those who *deny* that after Christ's birth Joseph and Mary entered into all the relationships commonly associated with marriage.

Joseph, having risen from sleep, did exactly as the angel had directed him. Not only did he take his wife home with him but when the child was born he named him Jesus. Of course, in doing this, Joseph and Mary acted in perfect harmony (cf. Luke 1:31, 38).

Summary of Chapter 1

This chapter consists of two sections: verses 1-17 and verses 18-25. The first contains a record of ancestry of Jesus Christ. It shows us that Joseph, Jesus' "father" in a legal sense only, was a descendant of David and Abraham. Through Joseph, "son of David" (verse 20) the right to the throne of David was transmitted to Jesus, the far more glorious "son of David" (verse 1).

The genealogy consists of three times fourteen generations. In the first series of fourteen we are shown the *origin* of David's house and royal glory; in the second, its *rise and decline;* in the third, its *eclipse.* But this eclipse is neither total nor lasting. At the close of the third fourteen the sun is shining far more brilliantly than ever, namely, in the person of Jesus Christ, who is both David's son and David's Lord. The Savior is pictured here as the One who not only fulfils the old but also ushers in the new. He both completes the sixth seven, and introduces the seventh. He is both the realization of hope and the incentive to action.

Over against all slander Matthew shows, by means of this family tree, that Jesus is indeed the *legitimate* seed of David. The genealogy contains the names of various kinds of individuals: women as well as men, pagans by birth as well as Jews, those who did what was good in the eyes of the Lord, and those who did not. Jesus Christ has significance not only for Jews but for the entire human race and for all its classes, categories, or subdivisions. He is truly "the Savior of the world" (cf. John 4:42; I John 4:14), the One who saves all who, by sovereign grace, place their trust in him (John 3:16; Eph. 2:8).

In strict harmony with this genealogy, which carefully avoids making Joseph *Jesus' father in the physical sense,* the second section contains the narrative of Christ's virgin birth. We learn that when Joseph and Mary were betrothed, and Mary had not yet been taken to Joseph's home, she found herself to be "with child by the Holy Spirit." Joseph discovers that she is pregnant but does not know the cause. Being righteous he is convinced that the marriage, to the extent that it existed, must now be dissolved. But being also kind-hearted, he immediately dismisses the idea of legal action against

Mary. He decides, therefore, to give her a letter of divorce, thus sending her away privately and not exposing her to public disgrace. Revolving this matter in his mind he falls asleep. While he is dreaming an angel appears to him with the thrilling news that it is by the power of the Holy Spirit that Mary has conceived; that he, Joseph, must not hesitate to take Mary to his home; and that the child to be born must be named Jesus, that is, the One who will save his people from their sins.

Guided by the Spirit, Matthew views this virgin birth of Jesus as a fulfilment of Isa. 7:14: "Behold the virgin shall conceive and give birth to a son, and his name shall be called Emmanuel." In Jesus Christ, God does indeed dwell with his people, imparting to them the joy of salvation, with all this implies; see p. 141.

Rising from sleep Joseph does as the angel of the Lord had directed him. He takes Mary to his home, but has no sexual relations with her until she has given birth to a son, whom he names Jesus.

The rejection of Christ's supernatural origin leaves this supernatural life and deeds unexplained. It also leaves unexplained the very possibility of man's salvation. That salvation is secured only when the initiative is taken by God, not by man!

Outline of Chapter 2

Theme: *The Work Which Thou Gavest Him to Do*

CHAPTER II

2 1 Now when Jesus was born in Bethlehem of Judea in the days of Herod the King, behold, wise men from the east came to Jerusalem, 2 saying, "Where is the (new)born king of the Jews? For we saw his star in its rising and have come to worship him." 3 When King Herod heard this he was frightened, and all Jerusalem with him. 4 And having assembled all the chief priests and scribes of the people he was seeking to learn from them where the Christ was to be born. 5 They told him, "In Bethlehem of Judea; for thus it is written through the prophet:

6 'And you Bethlehem, land of Judah,
Are by no means least among the princes of Judah;
For out of you there shall come a ruler
Who will shepherd my people Israel.' "

7 Then Herod secretly summoned the wise men and ascertained from them the time when the star had made its appearance. 8 And he sent them to Bethlehem, saying, "Go and make careful search for the little child, and when y o u have found him report to me, that I too may come and worship him." 9 So after listening to the king they went on their way, and look, the star they had seen in its rising went ahead of them until it stood still over (the place) where the little child was. 10 At the sight of the star they were overjoyed. 11 Having entered the house they saw the little child with Mary his mother, and they cast themselves to the ground and worshiped him. Next, they opened their treasure-chests and presented him with gifts: gold and frankincense and myrrh. 12 And having been warned in a dream not to return to Herod, it was by a different route that they retired to their own country.

2:1-12 *The Wise Men from the East*

According to God's promise (II Sam. 7:12, 13) Jesus is *the rightful heir* to David's throne. Chapter 1 has made this clear. He is the son whose throne will be "established forever" (cf. II Sam. 7:13 with Luke 1:32, 33). It is fitting, therefore, that royal homage be rendered to him, and this not only by the Jews but also by the Gentiles; for he is Lord of all (Matt. 28:16-20), and the gospel call goes out to all, regardless of race or nationality. Thus we see that there is a close connection between chapters 1 and 2 of Matthew's Gospel: chapter 1 has shown that Jesus deserves royal honor, chapter 2 shows that he receives it. The latter begins as follows: **1. Now when Jesus was born in Bethlehem of Judea in the days of Herod the king, behold, wise men from the east came to Jerusalem.** Two facts thus far unrecorded regarding Jesus' birth are here set forth: *a.* that he was born in Bethlehem,

149

and *b*. that this event took place in the days of Herod the king. The specification that this Bethlehem was the one in Judea serves not so much to distinguish it from the one located west of Nazareth in the tribe of Zebulon (hence, in Galilee) as to make clear that Micah's prophecy was indeed fulfilled in Jesus' birth. See on verses 5 and 6. A comparison between 2:1 and 2:19 lends support to the view that Jesus was born a little while before Herod's death. Since Herod died shortly after a lunar eclipse [154] at the close of March or beginning of April of the year 4 B.C., the date late 5 B.C. for Christ's birth may well be correct. [155]

Shortly after Jesus' birth there arrived in Jerusalem certain "wise men." Their unexpected appearance aroused considerable interest, which Matthew wants his readers to share; hence, he writes, "Behold." [156] Literally the strange travelers from afar are in the Greek original called *magoi* (sing. *magos*), from which the Latin *magi* (sing. *magus*) is derived, which is also found in several English translations, often capitalized. Who, then, were these magi? Where did they come from? The expression "from the east" is rather indefinite. Did they come from the regions inhabited by the Medes and Persians, as some think, or from Babylonia, as others have confidently affirmed?

The Greek word is really a transliteration of an Iranian original. When the word first appears in Herodotus it indicates one of the tribes of the Medes. It would seem that because of the skill which this tribe derived from the study of the stars the name *magi* subsequently began to be applied more generally to the entire like-minded priestly caste among the Medes and Persians. The magus was deeply interested in religion and in several related fields of human interest, including the study of the stars and their supposed influence on human events. Though many of his theories would today not unjustly be regarded as below the level of scientific knowledge and more nearly akin to superstition, and though his religion can scarcely be called even an approach to Christianity—there was no place in it for redemption from sin through an atoning sacrifice—, the magus was by no means merely a nonsense peddler. He generally believed in only one God, in man's duty to practice the good and shun the evil, in the necessity of prayer, and in the nobility of manual, especially agricultural, labor.

But is this also the meaning of the word *magi* as used here in Matt. 2? Some answer in the affirmative. They believe that the wise men who came

---

[154] See Josephus, *Antiquities* XVII.167.

[155] Other arguments in support of this date can be found in W. Hendriksen, *Bible Survey*, pp. 59-62. Since the computation of the year of Christ's birth and that of his crucifixion are, to a certain extent, interdependent, see also M. H. Shepherd's article, "Are Both the Synoptics and John Correct about the Date of Jesus' Death?," *JBL* 80 (June 1961), pp. 123-132.

[156] See footnote 133 on p. 131.

from the east and arrived in Jerusalem were Medes or Persians. In support of this belief they point not only to the Iranian origin of the word *magoi* or *magi* but also to the fact that, as pictured in the earliest Christian art that has been preserved, the travelers from afar are wearing Persian robes. Moreover, such early writers as Clement of Alexandria, Diodorus of Tarsus, Chrysostom, Cyril of Alexandria, Juvencus, Prudentius and others agree that the magi came from Persia. Is it not true also that in the various dispersions of the Jews that took place from the eighth to the sixth centuries B.C. not a few were deported to "the cities of the Medes" and to those of the surrounding country (see II Kings 17:6; cf. I Chron. 5:26; Esther 1:1; 9:2; Acts 2:9-11)? Is it not probable, therefore, that these Jewish monotheists propagandized their Messianic expectation among their equally monotheistic neighbors, with the result that when Messiah's star appeared a few of these Median or Persian magi set out for the land of Judea to honor the newborn "king of the Jews"?

It is an interesting theory with strong support in tradition, but it has not found universal acceptance. Origen believed that the magi came from Chaldea. Many agree with him. One reason for this is that the Chaldeans or Babylonians, too, had their "wise men" (Dan. 2:2, 10, 27, etc.). Through the influence of Daniel and his friends (see Dan. 2:48; 5:11) these wise men and their associates, whether wise or not so wise, were brought into contact with the only true and living God, and, of course, also with the Messianic expectation. Though much of the learning of these counselors of Babylon's king was worthless, as the book of Daniel clearly shows, and though it is true that among the Jews there was even a saying, "Whoever learns anything from a magus is worthy of death, [157] it was, nevertheless, the study of the stars by the Babylonian astrologers—perhaps we should say *astronomers*—which, though faulty in many respects, has been credited with establishing the foundation for the planetary world-system, time computation, and the calendar. [158]

Conclusion: *We know very little about the wise men mentioned in Matt. 2.* We know, however, that, as their actions are here described, whatever they do makes them deserving of the name "wise men." The best course for us to follow would appear to be to adhere strictly to the text, and to agree that these magi came from "the east," in all probability from either the one or the other of the two favored areas. [159]

---

[157] S.BK., Vol. I, p. 76.
[158] C. W. Ceram, *Gods, Graves, and Scholars*, p. 317.
[159] In the sources consulted I have not been able to find any substantiation for Lenski's unqualified statement (*op. cit.*, p. 58), "Medo-Persia is excluded because the magi-caste of this territory were not distinguished by the study of the stars," nor for his categorical assertion, "These magi hailed from Babylon." I have consulted all the paragraphs in *Herodotus* to which reference is made in *Loeb Classical Library;* see

How many wise men there were is not recorded. The fact that they presented the child with three gifts (2:11) has given rise to the theory that there were three men. Whether this inference is justified is doubtful, though there may, indeed, have been exactly three men in the party. We simply do not know. There is no basis whatever, not even in Ps. 72:10 and Isa. 60:3, for the notion that *these* men were "kings." The line "We three kings of Orient are" belongs to the same vast collection of legendary Yuletide lore to which belongs also "But little Lord Jesus no crying he makes," and many similar bits of fancy. Add also the mythical names of these wise men: Melchior, Balthasar, and Caspar; the belief that one came from India, one from Egypt and one from Greece; that they were subsequently baptized by Thomas; and that their bones were discovered by Saint Helena, were deposited in the church of Saint Sophia at Constantinople, were later transferred to Milan and were finally brought to the great cathedral of Cologne. One must be gullible, indeed, to accept all this!

Before leaving this subject it should be pointed out that in the original the word magos (Lat.—*us*) is also used in a different, though closely related, sense, namely *magician,* one who practices *magic.* The relation of these last two English words to the Greek is immediately apparent. The word *magos* is used in this unfavorable sense (magician) in Acts 13:6, 8, with respect to a false prophet, a Jew by the name of Bar-Jesus. The root of the Iranian word of which the Greek *magos* is a transliteration means *great.* It is cognate with the Greek *megas,* Latin *magnus,* as reflected in several English words, one of them being *megaphone:* a cheer-leader's voice-*magnifier.* One can be *great* in one's own estimation and in the eyes of deluded admirers. Such was Bar-Jesus. One can also be *truly great,* that is, great in the eyes of God. Such were the wise men whose story is told in Matt. 2, and with reference to whom we are now told that they were 2. **saying, Where is the (new)born king of the Jews?**

If the sudden *appearance* of these strangers rouses the Jerusalem citizenry, their *question,* repeated over and over, does even more. Not for a moment do the wise men express any doubt with reference to *the fact* as such of the recent birth of the One whom they call "the king of the Jews." For them the birth is real and the title is true. What they desire is an answer to the question, *"Where* is he?" Unless they receive this information they cannot fulfil the purpose of their long and arduous journey. So much is clear from what follows: **For we saw his star in its rising and have come to worship him.** Two questions can hardly be evaded: first, What was the nature of this star?;

Herodotus, Vol. I, Index p. 502; further, the book by C. W. Ceram, mentioned in the preceding footnote; the articles on *Zoroaster & Zoroastrianism* in S.H.E.R.K., Vol. 12, pp. 522-535; and in *Enc. Brit.,* 1969 ed., Vol. 23, pp. 1011-1016; and in the same work also the article on *Magi,* Vol. 14, pp. 469, 470.

secondly, How was it that the magi connected it with the birth of the king of the Jews?

As to the first, various answers are given; namely: *a.* it was a genuine "star" (in the sense in which the sun is also a star) of extraordinary brilliance; *b.* the planet Jupiter, often associated with the birth of kings and therefore called the king-planet; *c.* the conjunction of Jupiter and Saturn in the Sign of the Fish; *d.* a comet acting erratically; *e.* a luminary hanging low in the sky; and *f.* the star of destiny, of hope, one's guiding star within the heart; etc.

Answer *f.* can be dismissed immediately, for it is clear that the remarkable luminary was a physical object that could be seen and observed by the human eye (verses 2, 7, 9, 10). It was not a subjective monitor nor an optical illusion. As to answers *a.* - *e.*, objections can be advanced against each of them, but the general statement should suffice that the nature of the astronomical object is not indicated in the text. Hence, we simply do not know. Even answer *e.* "a luminary hanging low in the sky," though very definitely being in closer harmony with verse 9 than answers *a.* - *d.*, is hard to bring into agreement with verse 2, especially with the phrase "in its rising," which is the common Greek expression for the first appearance of a star upon the horizon. [160] One might say, therefore, that in verse 2 whatever it was that the magi saw acts as we would normally expect a star to act, but in verse 9 (see on that verse) it behaves very differently. We are left in the dark, and should attempt no further explanation as to the identity of this astral phenomenon. Suffice it to say that the wisdom and kindness of God is evident from the fact that he "spoke" to these students of the stars in a language which they could understand, namely, that of a "star."

With respect to the second question we fare no better. Though it is safe to assume that the wise men had been taught by the Jews to expect the coming of a Deliverer, an expectation that was probably rather widely spread in those days and by no means confined to the Jews (cf. John 4:25), [161] their

---

[160] Note that ἐν τῇ ἀνατολῇ (verse 2), which can be translated "in its rising" is not identical with ἀπὸ ἀνατολῶν (verse 1), "in the east."

[161] The fact that, on the basis of numerous prophecies (Gen. 3:15; 9:26; 22:18; 49:10; Deut. 18:15-18; II Sam. 7:12, 13; Ps. 72 and many other psalms; Isa. 7:14; 8:8; 9:6; and many other passages in Isaiah and in the other prophetical books), the Jews expected the Messiah is clear (Matt. 11:3; Luke 1:68-79; 2:25, 30, 38; 3:15; John 7:42). See also passages from pseudepigraphical writings; for example, Similitudes of Enoch, chapters 37-71; Psalms of Solomon 14:2; 18:5; etc. (Some, however, regard the descriptive predictions in the Similitudes to be later Christian interpolations, but this has not been proved.)

As to other extra-biblical sources, see what is said about the Messianic hope in Josephus, *Wars* VI.312; Suetonius, *Vespasian* IV; Tacitus, *Histories* V.13; and Virgil, *Eclogue* IV. All of these are open, however, to more than one interpretation, and the authenticity of some is disputed. On the other hand, it may be regarded as certain that the Jews had not kept their Messianic expectation a secret. Among the non-Jewish

linking of his birth with the appearance of a definite star, called *"his* star," remains unexplained. Had they received some information about the time when, on the basis of someone's interpretation of Dan. 9:25, the One whom the Jews expected would be born; and did this make it easier for them to connect the appearance of the remarkable star with the fulfilment of the Messianic expectation? Did the star appear in that particular sector of the heavens which by them was somehow linked with happenings in Judea? Had they heard about Balaam's prophecy, "There shall come forth a star out of Jacob, and a scepter shall rise out of Israel" (Num. 24:17)? There are those who say that this passage, *if* the magi had heard about it, which is still a question, could not have influenced them in any way, since the word "star" is here used in a metaphorical sense as referring to a person, not to a bright celestial luminary. Is this reasoning sound? It should be borne in mind that expressions which were originally intended to be interpreted figuratively have often been taken literally. The New Testament is full of examples. See

---

population of the world before and at the beginning of the new dispensation the hope of better things to come in connection with a great Deliverer was not the exclusive possession of the Samaritan woman and her neighbors. It must have been rather widespread.

Even among the Jews, however, the character of this hope was by no means the same for all. For many the expected "son of David" was chiefly a Deliverer from earthly oppression and woe (cf. Luke 19:38, 41, 42). Others, however, were looking for the remission of their *sins* through him (Luke 1:77).

This last observation leads to a few brief remarks regarding the Messianic expectation according to the Dead Sea Scrolls. Shortly after their discovery the Qumran monastery in which they had their origin was loudly proclaimed as the very source of the Christian religion. E. Wilson in his book *The Scrolls from the Dead Sea*, New York, 1955, p. 97, stated "this monastery . . . is perhaps more than Bethlehem or Nazareth, the cradle of Christianity." Other appraisals, however, were more cautious; see, for example, Dupont-Sommer's *The Jewish Sect of Qumran and the Essenes, New Studies on the Dead Sea Scrolls* (English Tr.), London, 1954, in which (on pp. 161 f.) the author is careful to indicate that he does not at all equate Jesus Christ and the (Qumran's) Teacher of Righteousness. Of great value, in this connection, are also the books by Millar Burrows, *The Dead Sea Scrolls*, New York, 1956, and *More Light on the Dead Sea Scrolls*, New York, 1958. On p. 60 f. of the latter the author discusses the theory of the possible connection between the Messianic hope in the Qumran Society and this hope in the teaching of John the Baptist.

As to the Qumran's Messianic expectation, it has been definitely shown that its "Teacher of Righteousness" is in no sense whatever a predictive description of Christ. E. J. Young was entirely correct when, in his excellent article, "The Teacher of Righteousness and Jesus Christ," *WTJ* 18 (May 1956), p. 145, he stated, "Whatever formal similarities there may be between Christianity and the Scrolls or between Christ and the Teacher of Righteousness, there are differences so profound that they cannot possibly be explained away. Jesus spake unlike any other man, for the simple reason that he was unlike any other man." To all this may be added the conclusion to which J. Jeremias arrives. In his article (translated from the German), "The Theological Significance of the Dead Sea Scrolls," *CTM* 39 (Aug. 1968), pp. 557-571, he points out that the main difference between the teaching of the Scrolls, on the one hand, and Jesus, on the other, is this, that according to the latter's teaching God is concerned with sinners, not just with those who by human means seek to obtain justification.

N.T.C. on the Gospel according to John, Vol. I, p. 125. The magi, too, might have linked Num. 24:17 with the appearance of a literal star announcing the birth of the king of the Jews. The passage cannot be legitimately used on either side of the argument.

Again, according to a rabbinical legend, in the night when Abraham was born the servants of Terah and the wise men of Nimrod arrived to celebrate the birth. When they left Terah's house that night they saw a brilliant star. On its course through the heavens it devoured four other stars. Seeing this, these men interpreted this to mean that the newborn child would become powerful, etc. [162] Some would argue, therefore that when, many centuries later, another brilliant star appeared to a similar company of wise men, the latter saw in this radiant luminary a definite sign that another majestic person, "the king of the Jews," had been born.

It is obvious, however, that all of these opinions as to how and why the wise men connected the appearance of this star with the birth of the Messiah are mere conjectures. We do not have the answer. We are left in the dark.

This, moreover, is exactly what makes Matthew's story so beautiful and instructive. *Everything else is left out of the picture in order that the full emphasis may be placed on this one thing, namely, "We have come to worship him."* We are not given a detailed description of the star. We are not told how the magi connected this star with the birth. We are not told how many magi there were, how they dressed, how they died, or where they were buried. All that and much more is purposely left in the shade in order that against this dark background the *light* may shine forth all the more brilliantly. These wise men, whoever they were, wherever they came from, *came to worship him!* In the present instance, as is clear from verse 11, this can mean nothing less than that it was their intention to fall down before the Messianic King in humble adoration. Matthew is telling all those who read this story or hear it read that they too must do the same. If even the world of the Gentiles pays homage to him, should not the Jews—who have received the oracles of God—do so? And for the Gentiles there is this encouragement: the king of the Jews desires to be y o u r king also.—Who would dare to criticize Rembrandt for the light-versus-shade contrast (the "chiaroscuro" effect) of that great masterpiece which is popularly known as *The Night Watch?* It was Rembrandt who shows in all of his best paintings that he has caught the spirit of the inspired Gospel-writers!

Continued: **3. When King Herod heard this he was frightened, and all Jerusalem with him.** It is clear from the connection between verses 2 and 3 that the wise men did not immediately wend their way to Herod's palace. The king indirectly *heard* what was happening. It was reported to him that strangers had arrived from afar, inquiring about the whereabouts of a child

---

[162] S.BK., Vol. 1, pp. 77, 78.

recently born, whom they called "the king of the Jews." When Herod heard this he was frightened, terrified. The verb used in the original is very descriptive. *Literally* in the active voice this verb means *to shake, stir up, trouble, agitate,* as when Egypt's king is said to resemble a monster that *troubles the waters with its feet,* thereby contaminating the rivers (Ezek. 32:2). *Figuratively* it has reference to the *upsetting* or *throwing into confusion and alarm* of mind and/or heart; here in Matt. 2:3 the meaning is, of course, *being upset* or *frightened.* Thus the disciples were troubled when they imagined that they were looking at a ghost (Matt. 14:26); Zechariah when he saw an angel (Luke 1:12). See also John 14:1.

That a man with the inner nature and disposition of Herod would become alarmed at the mere mention of a king of the Jews other than himself is not surprising. Was not *he,* even Herod, *the* one and only "king of the Jews"? Had he not received this title from Rome? Had it not taken him months, *years* even, of struggle to make this title come true? Was this, then, another attempt to dethrone him? Would this rumor about another king of the Jews stir up the freedom riots among those fanatics who hated him so thoroughly and had already caused him so much trouble? Herod is *agitated* and *angry.* He is convinced that unless radical measures be taken his worst fears will be realized. But he is not going to take this lying down. In his depraved mind a wicked plot is beginning to develop.

The king was mistaken. It does not appear from Matthew's account that the Jerusalem populace had become deeply impressed by the magi's question. Nothing in the nature of a "We shall overcome" revolt was being planned. Nevertheless, "all Jerusalem" was indeed alarmed, for the people had learned by long and sad experience that there were no limits to the wrath and vengefulness of a thoroughly alarmed Herod. They dreaded to think of what new atrocities were in store for them. As the sequel shows, they had reason to be thus frightened.

This may well be the proper place to answer the question, What was the character of this man who, in order to give him credit for the great talents which he undoubtedly possessed and to distinguish him from all other bearers of the same name, is often referred to as "Herod **the Great**"? Reference has already been made to the Maccabean revolt (see p. 127). In the year 198 B.C. Palestine had become subject to Syria. The ruling nation, in trouble with Rome and forced to pay a heavy penalty for its unsuccessful attempt to meddle in the affairs of the city on the Tiber, had imposed a burdensome tribute upon the Jews. When about the year 175 B.C. Antiochus Epiphanes became king, conditions worsened. While Antiochus was leading an expedition into Egypt the Jews rejoiced when a false rumor of the king's death gained currency. Returned, Antiochus massacred thousands and sold others into slavery. After another attempt to take Alexandria, Antiochus was thwarted by the Romans at the very moment when he regarded the final victory to be within his grasp. Again he decided to vent his wrath upon the Jews. His general Apollonius in 168 B.C. waited for the sabbath; then fell upon the defenseless city and devastated it, killing people right and left. Antiochus Epiphanes and his helpers determined to wipe out the Jewish religion root and branch. They took various measures to accomplish their purpose. By sacrificing swine on the altar of burnt-offering they defiled it, and they destroyed all the holy writings they could lay their hands on.

In this time of sore affliction and distress the saints cried to Jehovah for help. Their prayer was heard. The revolution arrived. At Modein, not far from Jerusalem, there lived an aged priest, Mattathias. When the commissioner of Antiochus requested that he take the lead in offering a pagan sacrifice, the priest not only refused but slew both the commissioner and an apostate Jew who was about to comply with the request. This was the beginning of the revolt which occurred at that time.

After the death of Mattathias his son Judas, a humble child of God and a military genius, achieved victories that constitute a classic in the science of strategy. He was always battling greatly superior forces. His courage was leonine, his swiftness incredible. As a result of his triumphs, about the year 165 B.C. the temple at Jerusalem, which by the wicked Antiochus had been consecrated to Zeus, was cleansed and rededicated to Jehovah. This rededication was the origin of "the Festival of the Lights" (Chanukah) celebrated by the Jews ever since. See N.T.C. on John 10:22a. The Jews regained religious freedom. After the death of Judas his brother Jonathan, just as daring as Judas himself, ruled for a while and gained remarkable victories. In his attempt to outwit the Syrians he was himself outwitted and executed.

Under the next son of Mattathias, Simon, a very wise administrator, a truly glorious period was ushered in. See I Macc., chapter 14. But in the year 135 B.C. Simon was treacherously slain by his own son-in-law. The Maccabean rulers who followed had imbibed the Hellenistic spirit. They placed greater emphasis upon secular than upon spiritual affairs. Simon's son John Hyrcanus was the first of these rulers. Though he was highpriest as well as civil ruler he was a first-class warrior. To the north he conquered Samaria, and destroyed the Samaritan temple built on Mt. Gerizim. To the south he brought Edom into subjection.

If Hyrcanus may be termed a ruler of questionable merit, his son Alexander Janneus (Jonathan) was far worse. His hands reeked with blood. One happening that occurred during his reign must not remain unmentioned for it had far-reaching consequences. Over the country of Edom, conquered, as was indicated, by his father, Alexander appointed a governor, Antipas, whose son, Antipater, was going to play an important role in the history of the Jews. Even more would this be true with respect to Antipater's son, the very *Herod* mentioned in Matthew 2 and Luke 1 and nowhere else in the New Testament.

After the death of Alexander his widow Alexandra assumed leadership. After her death her sons Hyrcanus II and Aristobulus contended for the throne. Some of the people sided with Hyrcanus II, who was the elder; some with Aristobulus, who was the stronger of the two. There was also a third class consisting of those who longed for the abolition of the monarchy and the establishment of a form of government in which the priests should rule the country in accordance with the law of Jehovah. The three parties appealed to Rome.

When Aristobulus became impatient with Rome's delay in reaching a final decision he decided to take matters into his own hands. The result was Pompey's invasion of Judea and the capture of Jerusalem in the year 63 B.C. When Hyrcanus II and Aristobulus were contending for the mastery the aforementioned Antipater, now governor of Edom, took full advantage of the troubled situation. Both Antipater and his son Herod were characterized by slyness. They would court the favor of whoever happened to be on top in Rome. As soon as the government changed hands they would immediately change their allegiance and shower their compliments and presents upon the man whom "until yesterday" they had opposed. And so in course of time it happened that when the Jews were unable to settle their own affairs the Edomite Antipater was by the Romans made procurator of Judea and was allowed to appoint his son Herod tetrarch of Galilee. This happened in the year 47 B.C. In 40 B.C. Palestine was invaded by the Parthians, civil war broke out, and Herod fled to Rome. By the Roman senate Herod was then nominated king of Judea. An army was given him, to enable him to carve out his own kingdom with the sword. This was no easy task. It was, however, his one great ambition. After encountering vigorous and unrelenting opposition from far and near he finally triumphed in the year 37 B.C. Since, according to Josephus, Herod, at his death (in 4 B.C.) was seventy years of age, he must have been born around 74 B.C. He may already have passed his sixty-ninth birthday when the wise men arrived in Jerusalem, but the exact date of their arrival is uncertain.

After the year 37 B.C. Emperor Augustus increased Herod's territory until it included all of Palestine, even the border regions of what is now known as Jordan, Syria, and Lebanon. He had indeed become "the king of the Jews." Amid fierce and protracted struggles he jealously clung to his position of authority until the day of his death.

By race or nationality Herod was not a Jew, though at times, for selfish political reasons, he encouraged the view, proposed by others, that he was of rich and noble Jewish ancestry. But, as stated earlier, his father, Antipater, was an Edomite. Also, his mother, Cypros, was a Nabatean; that is, she hailed from an Arab kingdom to the east and southeast of Palestine. When the Edomites (or Idumeans) had been conquered by John Hyrcanus, the Jewish religion was in a sense forced upon them. It is not surprising, therefore, that it is said at times that Herod "practiced the Jewish religion." If one is willing to interpret this term "Jewish religion" in a sense wide enough to include profound devotion to Hellenistic culture, the statement would probably be correct.

As pictured by Josephus, [163] Herod was *capable, crafty,* and *cruel.* That he was *capable* admits of no doubt. The swiftness with which, even while still a very young governor of Galilee, he destroyed the bands of guerrillas that were making forays against the cities and despoiling the countryside, his efficiency in collecting tribute for Rome, the oratorical ability he revealed when he addressed the troops under his command or the Jerusalem populace, his subtle diplomacy, and the decisiveness with which he turned defeat into victory, were some of the qualities that made him the kind of monarch the Roman emperor admired.

He was also a great builder. As such he gave Jerusalem a theater. Just outside the city he built an amphitheater and a hippodrome. On the city's western edge he constructed a luxurious palace for himself, with three famous towers, called respectively Hippicus, Phasael, and Mariamne. In honor of his benefactor, Emperor Augustus, he instituted and presided over quinquennial games, for he was a lover of sports. It is true that with this phase of his activity Herod by no means ingratiated himself with all the Jews. In fact, his enthusiasm for athletic activities infuriated many of the more devout, who regarded it as an expression of worldly-mindedness, a bad example for the youth, and a flagrant desecration of pure religion. As they saw it, the prominent place accorded to the figure of the emperor in the amphitheater, as well as the many trophies hung on the wall, were in conflict with the divine law forbidding images. An attempt was even made to assassinate the king, but it failed. The ten conspirators were tortured and afterward executed.

In order to add to the luster of his name and, if possible, to win the people to his side, Herod proposed to rebuild and greatly enlarge and beautify Jerusalem's sanctuary, the one at times referred to as *"the second"*

---

[163] For sources on Herod one should read Flavius Josephus, *The Jewish War,* Book I; also by the same author *The Antiquities of the Jews,* books XIV, XV, XVI, and XVII. For a true understanding of Herod the works of Josephus are both indispensable and also at times hard to penetrate, especially in view of the many inconsistencies and inclinations toward tendentious conclusions. See also S. H. Perowne, *The Life and Times of Herod the Great,* New York, 1956; G. J. D. Aalders, *Het Romeinsche Imperium en het Nieuwe Testament,* Kampen, 1936; S. Sandmel, *Herod, Profile of a Tyrant,* Philadelphia and New York, 1967. Though Sandmel's book sheds light on many subjects, is easy to read and nicely arranged, it is *naturally*—the author is a Jew—opposed to the Christian point of view. Sandmel speaks of "the understandable but extravagant aspersion of Herod in Christian lore" (p. 270). Further bibliographical material can be found in the last title and also at the close of the relevant articles in Bible, religious, and general encyclopaedias. I acknowledge indebtedness to all these sources for the summary here given, especially to the works of Josephus.

or "Zerubbabel's" *temple* built in the year 516 B.C., seventy years after the destruction of *the first* (see Ezra 5:2 ff.; Hag. 1:13-15). In an eloquent address to the people the king, if we can trust Josephus, divulged his plan "to make a thankful return, after the most pious manner, to God, for the blessings I have received from him, who has given me this kingdom, and to do this by making his temple as complete as I am able." He began to build it about the year 19 B.C. Long after his death it had not yet been entirely completed. See N.T.C. on the Gospel according to John, Vol. I, p. 126. The grandeur and beauty of this temple which Herod started to build and on which he made very considerable progress is evident from Matt. 24:1, 2; Mark 13:1, 2; and Luke 21:5, 6. See further on 4:5; 21:12, 13, 23; 24:1-3.

The king's building activities were by no means restricted to Jerusalem and its vicinity. He restored and adorned on a magnificent scale the ancient city of Samaria, renaming it Sebaste in honor of the emperor. Its temple, also dedicated to the emperor and containing the gigantic statute of Augustus, crowned the city-summit. On the coast between Joppa (now Jaffa) and Haifa he built the magnificent port of Caesarea, which soon afterward became the capital of Roman Palestine. Within the boundaries of his country he rebuilt and beautified many other cities. Outside of Palestine such places as Antioch, Beirut, Damascus, Tyre, Sidon, Rhodes, and even Athens benefited from his urge and ability to build and embellish.

In speaking of Herod's *capability* as a ruler it is but fair and just to mention one important event that occurred during the thirteenth and fourteenth year of his reign. There was a perpetual drought that affected both Judea and Syria, resulting in a famine that has been described as the greatest since the days of Ahab. The royal treasury was empty because the money had been largely spent on the king's vast building program. Most of the people, never very affluent, lost whatever they had. As a result Herod's ability and obligation to provide relief was taxed to its utmost limit. But here again his resourcefulness was equal to the occasion. Says Josephus, "He cut off the rich furniture that was in his palace, both of silver and gold . . . and sent the money to Petronius, who had been made prefect of Egypt by Caesar." Petronius and Herod were friends. It is remarkable that once again as before (cf. Gen. 41, 42) the relief during a famine came from Egypt. The king provided food for all upon conditions which each family was able to meet, wisely making distinctions according to ability to repay. Inasmuch as because of the drought many of the sheep and goats had perished, so that winter clothing had become hard to obtain, Herod also imported and distributed the necessary garments. Moreover, he saw to it that the farmers had seed. Naturally, he himself benefited from this welfare program. For a while he even gained a measure of popularity. He took care that the people understood that the help came "from himself!" One could expect Herod to do just that.

In addition to being capable he was, however, also *crafty*. He was sly, not to be trusted. The opprobrious epithet "that fox," by the Lord applied to Herod Antipas (Luke 13:32), could have been used also to describe the latter's father, Herod the Great. He knew that the Jews regarded him as a foreigner, since, as already indicated, he was not a Jew. He was painfully aware of the fact that his subjects would far rather be ruled by a Hasmonean, a descendant of the original Maccabees. So he looked upon the very existence of prominent Hasmoneans as a threat to himself and his throne. He had no less than ten wives and more than a dozen children. Outstanding among all his wives was Mariamne I (hereafter simply called Mariamne), [164] a real Hasmonean. In view of what he later did to her it is probably wrong to say, as is nevertheless often done, that he was deeply *in love* with her. It must have been rather a matter of infatuation, emotional fondness, or at best strong sentimental attachment. Marrying her was, moreover, a *clever* move, for by means of this union Herod sought to win status among the Jews and to legitimatize his rule over them. However, when he became aware of the fact that his subjects neither loved nor trusted him he plotted the destruction of the entire Hasmonean house. But he went about it in a very devious manner.

Before entering any further into this subject it may be well to remind the reader of what has already been written on pp. 157, 158, and to give Mariamne's family tree; that is, *only so much of it as is necessary for the understanding of that which follows.*

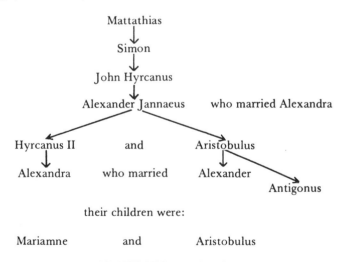

164 She is called Mariamne I to distinguish her from Mariamne II, whom the king married after the death of the first Mariamne. See the chart on p. 189.

When, as a result of the pleading of Herod's wife, Mariamne, and of her mother, Alexandra, the king at last agreed to appoint Aristobulus, the brother of Mariamne, to the highpriestly office, Herod began to take notice of the fact that the comely young man, especially when he was performing his sacred office, was the darling of the people, who "mingled with good wishes their joyful acclamations which they made to him" (Josephus). Herod was exceedingly displeased, and immediately resolved to do away with his brother-in-law. However, the act must be comitted in such a manner that no one would ever be able to prove that the king himself was the murderer. So the young man, along with many others, was invited to a Jordan River swimming party near Jericho. The day was very hot. At first the king and the highpriest remained on the river-bank, as if it were beneath their dignity to mingle in the water with the commoners. But at last Herod prevailed upon Aristobulus to go into the water. After a while some of the young men, appointed by the king for this very purpose (according to Josephus), plunged the highpriest under water, as if it were all in fun. They held him there until he suffocated. Herod provided a magnificent funeral and in public shed copious tears!—Many additional illustrations of the king's treacherous conduct could be given. Deceit was ingrained in his very nature.

The murder of Mariamne's brother Aristobulus also shows what a *cruel* man Herod was. His cruelty was being constantly nourished by his overweening egoism and by his morbid distrust of anyone who, as Herod saw it, might aspire to replace him on the throne. He knew that many of the Jews hated him. They regarded him as the instrument used by a foreign power to keep them under bondage and to rob them of their substance. They thoroughly understood that his Jewishness was a sham and that in heart and mind he was a pagan. He loved *power* more than anything else. Therefore, the least suspicion that someone had arisen who might wish to deprive him of his throne often drew from him the immediate reaction, "He must die!" These dark and sinister drives of his nature grew on him because he did not pray for grace and spiritual energy to crush them. So, as he advanced in age he made progress also in mental and moral depravity until he was completely ruined.

It stands to reason that his wrath was directed especially against the Hasmoneans, for it was to them that the people, whether openly or secretly, looked for deliverance. With the diagram on p. 161 before us, let us see what happened to Mariamne's family tree:

Beginning at the top of the list and working step by step to the bottom, we first meet Mattathias (see p. 157). In the year 167 B.C. he died from the rigors of the revolt which he so nobly initiated. Descending one rung or generation, we note that in 135 B.C. Simon, a son of Mattathias, was treacherously slain by his son-in-law. Still further down, John Hyrcanus, after ruling for nearly three decades, died peacefully in 105 B.C. His son,

Alexander Jannaeus, a cruel and bloodthirsty person—he once ordered the execution of 50,000 of his own people—died in 78 B.C. from an incurable disease. His widow Alexandra ruled for nine years and died in 69 B.C. Next we descend to the days of *The First Triumvirate*. Crassus, Pompey, and Julius Caesar have divided the government of the Roman Empire between themselves. They "go down" in that order: first Crassus, then Pompey, finally Julius. In the year 49 B.C. Aristobulus, a son of Jannaeus, was poisoned by partisans of Pompey. Alexander, a son of Aristobulus, was beheaded.

Herod now appears upon the scene. These are the days of *The Second Triumvirate:* Lepidus, Antony, and Octavian. During the bitter struggle for possession of Jerusalem, Herod, in the year 37 B.C., having sent presents to his friend of long standing, Antony, sees to it that Antigonus, another Hasmonean, is executed. This same Antigonus, son of Aristobulus, had mutilated his uncle (see the chart), the weak highpriest Hyrcanus II, so as to disqualify him for the high-priestly office and to undermine any pronounced political influence he might exercise or others might exert in his behalf. Just a little later, in 35 B.C., Aristobulus the brother of Mariamne (hence, not to be confused with the son of Alexander Jannaeus) meets death by drowning, as has just been related (see p. 162). One can well imagine how Alexandra and Mariamne felt about this. Could the king blame them for distrusting him?

Alexandra writes a letter to Queen Cleopatra, the Egyptian, informing her about the murder of Aristobulus. Cleopatra, in turn, tells Antony, who orders Herod to meet him and give an account. Before departing, Herod instructs Joseph, who was both his uncle and brother-in-law (the husband of Herod's sister Salome) to slay Mariamne if he, the king, should fail to return alive. On Herod's safe return Salome, who had begun to hate her husband, informs her brother that Joseph had bestowed improper attention upon Mariamne. Herod has Joseph put to death. Mariamne denies any guilt and for a while she and her husband are reconciled. But this does not last.

In the year 30 B.C. Herod saw in the aged and mutilated Hyrcanus II a threat to the throne, and had him executed. By this time whatever love Mariamne may have had for her husband had turned into hatred, for she saw him now as the murderer of her brother Aristobulus and of her grandfather Hyrcanus II.

In September of the year 31 B.C. the historic naval battle of Actium takes place. Antony, who had divorced Octavian's sister Octavia, in favor of the bewitching, ruthless, grasping Egyptian Queen Cleopatra (the former mistress of Julius Caesar) whom he married, had been defeated. The following year, August 30 B.C., both Antony and Cleopatra committed suicide. See and/or hear Shakespeare's vivid and imaginative drama *Antony and Cleopatra*. These deaths were a severe blow to Herod, who had consistently taken the side of

Antony and had even offered to help him. The king of the Jews feared that Octavian, now Emperor Augustus, would deprive him of his throne and perhaps even put him to death. So Herod sets out on a trip to make a humble appeal to the one whom he had up to now opposed. Before leaving he instructs an underling, Sohemus, to put to death both Mariamne and Alexandra in the event that he, the king, should meet with death. [165] Before Augustus he very shrewdly does not try to play down his former loyalty to Antony but even emphasizes it, climaxing his appeal with the words, "To you I will be the same loyal friend." This strategy succeeds. In triumph, his royal title having been reaffirmed, he returns, in the expectation that his wife will receive him with open arms. In the meantime, however, she has learned about the instructions Sohemus received with respect to her. So on her part the welcome-back is less than enthusiastic. In striving to discover the reason for this coldness Herod hears that there has been a relation of intimacy between Mariamne and Sohemus. The latter is executed. After a mock trial, in the year 29 B.C. Mariamne is convicted of adultery. She is put to death. Herod's subsequent pathetic remorse does not restore her to life. The next year, 28 B.C., Mariamne's mother, the scheming Alexandra, is also executed. So from the chart on p. 161 the name of every Hasmonean who, either in reality or in the sick imagination of the king, was considered to be a challenge to his power, has been crossed out. But two sons of Herod by Mariamne, namely, Alexander and Aristobulus, are still alive. See the chart on p. 189. Surely, Herod will not harm his own children! Yes, he will even do away with them, if he is convinced that they in any way threaten his title as "king of the Jews." And so, in the year 8 B.C., after many a family plot and counter-plot, these two sons are also put to death. [166] And even this is not the end of the horrors. *Herod goes from bad to worse.* His lust for power, dark suspicion, and almost insane eagerness to avenge himself, enslave him until at last they kill him. Five days before his death there is one more murder of a son. But inasmuch as that occurred *after* the visit of the wise men a more definite reference to it is reserved for later. See p. 186.

By thus describing Herod as a cruel, bloodthirsty tyrant, an increasingly wicked person, more and more as the years rolled along bent on getting rid of anyone who, as he saw it, might wish to deprive him of his power, are we

---

[165] Note the parallel between this and the incident reported in the preceding paragraph. This very parallel seems to have led to some confusion in the accounts given by Josephus. Cf. *The Jewish War* I.441-444 with *Antiquities* XV.62-87. See also S. Sandmel, *op. cit.*, pp. 164, 165. With Sandmel I have assumed that only in connection with Herod's appearance before Emperor Augustus does Mariamne learn about the instruction that she be slain if her husband does not return alive.

[166] It is interesting to note, however, that through Aristobulus the Hasmonean line, now corrupted by the Herodian, regains its lease on life, so that Herod the Great was not as successful as he may have thought. See the chart on p. 189.

not being unjust to him? Were there no extenuating circumstances? From a medical point of view can it not be argued that, especially in his final years, the king was afflicted with a severe case of hardening of the arteries? Did not the reduction in blood-flow to the brain cause him to lose some of his earlier capacity to subdue his wicked traits? Again, is it not true that Herod was by no means alone in his destructive designs? Was he not being constantly prodded by his equally wicked sister Salome, [167] a palace resident as was his mother-in-law Alexandra, another trouble-maker? Was not even greedy Queen Cleopatra guilty of making matters worse by her unauthorized interference? Was not Herod's firstborn son, Antipater, an arch schemer? And Herod's sons by Mariamne, were they not cut from the same piece of cloth? Was not the king's court a veritable hotbed of underhanded plotting? Granted that Herod was a great sinner, was he not also the victim of the sins of others?

Allowance must be made for all this, but it does not blot out or excuse his own accountability. According to Scripture *self-control* is one of the cardinal virtues, the fruit of the Spirit's operation in the heart (Prov. 25:28; Acts 24:25; Gal. 5:23; II Peter 1:6). Strikingly touching and forever valid are the words of Rom. 6:12, "Let not sin therefore reign [or: be king, hold sway] in y o u r mortal body, to the end that y o u should obey its lusts." Herod, who was eager to be and to remain a king, was actually a slave, and this by his own choice!

It is probably the last year of Herod's reign and of his life. He is gravely alarmed because the wise men have arrived, asking, "Where is the (new)born king of the Jews? For we saw his star in its rising and have come to worship him." Understandably, all Jerusalem is also fearfully perturbed. On hearing the bad news the old king stirs up the dying embers of his energy and goes into action. In fact, he becomes very active: he assembles, summons, sends, perceives, is enraged, kills . . . and then dies! See verses 4, 7, 8, 16, 19, and 22. It is immediately clear that the description here given matches that which we find in the extra-canonical sources. Essentially, therefore, the latter must be right! Herod is no laggard. He is a killer. The *thoroughness* he displays is matched only by the awakened wrath of which it is the product. Note also this *hypocrisy:* "that I too may come and worship him" (verse 8), and his *cruelty:* the destruction of Bethlehem's infants (verse 16). With this background in mind we are now ready for verse 4. **And having assembled all the**

---

[167] Not to be confused with her great-niece, the daughter of Herodias, referred to in Matt. 14:3-11; Mark 6:17-28, but not mentioned by name in the Gospels. See Josephus *Antiquities* XVIII.133. *That* Salome was the one who, as a reward for her dancing, obtained the head of John the Baptist. For the latter Salome see the chart on p. 189. There was still another Salome, one who did not at all belong to this company. She is one of the holy women who followed Jesus in Galilee and ministered to him (Mark 16:1, 2; see on Matt. 27:56).

chief priests and scribes of the people he was seeking to learn from them where the Christ was to be born. Since Herod was living in a day when the hope of deliverance through the arrival and work of a promised Messiah was in the hearts and on the lips of many, he realizes that "the king of the Jews" and "the Messiah" are one and the same.

By their question the wise men have greatly disturbed Herod. Yet he is far too shrewd a person not to sense that expelling or killing these men would leave the one whom he regards as the potential pretender to the throne unscathed and even undiscovered. After all, not the *magi* but the Messiah, the king of the Jews, is the one Herod must destroy. To do this he must first of all identify this mysterious individual. He is sufficiently acquainted with the Jewish religion to know that somewhere in the ancient oracles there was a direct prediction of *the place* where Messiah was to be born. So Herod must learn what place this is, for this knowledge will be a stepping stone toward finding the child and killing him.

Herod knows exactly where to go for the desired information. He calls together the official representatives of the Jews, "all the chief priests and scribes of the people," that is probably, *the entire Sanhedrin.* [168] This was the Jewish *Supreme Court.* As long as it did not encroach upon the prerogatives of the Roman government, which, for example, passed the final decision on the death sentences of this court, it was the ultimate authority not only in strictly religious but also in civil and criminal matters. [169]

The *chief priests* consisted of the present ruling highpriest, those who had formerly occupied this high office, and other dignitaries from whose ranks the highpriest was usually chosen. The *scribes* were the men of letters, those who studied and taught God's law, the experts in the Jewish religion. To this body of men, therefore, Herod submits the question as to where, according to Scripture (implied), the Christ was to be born. **5, 6. They told him, In Bethlehem of Judea; for thus it is written through the prophet:**

> **And you Bethlehem, land of Judah,**
> **Are by no means least among the princes of Judah;**
> **For out of you there shall come a ruler**
> **Who will shepherd my people Israel.**

On the part of the high council there is no hesitancy. Among the Jews it

---

[168]The view of E. Johnson, *Interpreter's Bible*, New York and Nashville, 1951, Vol. VII, *on Matthew and Mark*, p. 258, according to which Herod merely consulted a few of the members of the Sanhedrin, does not commend itself. Had it been Matthew's intention to convey this thought he could have done so (cf. John 1:19, 24). The wording sounds very official: it would seem that Herod, via the highpriest, *convenes* the Sanhedrin in *plenary* session. Note "all." Same verb as in John 11:47 where the chief priests and the Pharisees *convene* (or: call together) the specifically mentioned *Sanhedrin*.

[169] See M. Wolff, "De Samenstelling en het Karakter van het groote συνέδριον te Jeruzalem voor het jaar 70 n. Chr." *TT* 51 (1917), pp. 299-320. See also on 16:21.

was a well-known fact that the Messiah was to come from Bethlehem (John 7:42). The words of Matt. 2:6 are taken from Mic. 5:2 (quoted in part).

Though the quotation from Mic. 5:2 is not according to the *letter*—the main change being the one from "who are little to be among" to "are by no means least among"—it is according to the *essence*, for in both cases the meaning is, "Though you, Bethlehem, are but little,[170] yet you are by no means least, for Israel's Ruler shall come forth from you." As Micah saw it, therefore, and as the Jewish authorities now interpret it, Matthew concurring, in the tribal meetings where each city and village was represented by its chief or prince, Bethlehem, though small in population, is very important because Israel's great Leader was destined to be born there.

The final line of Matt. 2:6 bears great similarity to what is found in II Sam. 5:2. According to the context there, the tribes of Israel come to David with the unanimous request that he be their king. To strengthen their appeal they quote the words which God on a former occasion had addressed to David, namely, "You shall be shepherd of my people Israel." By the Sanhedrin—and Matthew is in full agreement—these words are now applied to David's great Son and Lord, namely, the Messiah. According to Scripture, in several ways David was a type of Christ, for example, with respect to *a. birth in Bethlehem:* I Sam. 16:4, 12, 13; cf. Luke 2:4, 7; *b. being "beloved,"* which is the very meaning of the name "David," see also I Sam. 13:14; cf. Matt. 3:17; *c. being God's anointed:* I Sam. 16:13; cf. Ps. 2:2; Isa. 61:1: Luke 4:18, 21; *d. receiving royal position and honor,* already implied in the anointing, see also II Sam. 7:13; cf. Luke 1:32, 33; and *e. the course each had to follow from bitter humiliation to glorious exaltation:* II Sam. 15:23; 22:17-20; cf. John 18:1; Matt. 28:18; etc. Therefore, this application of II Sam. 5:2 to the Messiah was fully justified.

What is often passed by in silence is the fact that neither King Herod nor the Jewish Sanhedrin for a moment doubted that the reference of Mic. 5:2 and the *ultimate* reference of II Sam. 5:2 were to *a person* (not a nation), namely, the Messiah. When anyone reads such precious Old Testament passages—and this includes also Gen. 3:15, 22:18; 49:10; II Sam. 7:12, 13; Isa. 7:14; 8:8; 9:6; and many, many others—without seeing the Christ in them, is he not reading them blindly? See Luke 24:25-27, 32.

Very beautiful and comforting is what is said about Messiah=Christ in the words, "Who shall shepherd my people Israel." The shepherd is here the king. But this king is no cruel tyrant. In the estimation of those whom God tenderly calls "my people" (cf. John 21:5-17) this king is not only *prominent* but also *provident.* To them the word "shepherd" suggests not

---

170 Even in the days of Herod the Great, Bethlehem was only a mere cluster of small dwellings. See L. H. Grollenberg, *Atlas of the Bible,* New York, etc., 1956, p. 125.

only *solemnity* but also *solicitude* (Isa. 40:11; Matt. 18:12, 13; Luke 15:3-7; John 10:11, 14, 27-29; Heb. 13:20; I Peter 2:25; 5:4; Rev. 7:17).

Continued: **7. Then Herod secretly summoned the wise men and ascertained from them the time when the star had made its appearance.** The first meeting, the one of the king and the Sanhedrin, by its very nature could not be kept a secret. But adding a second *public* meeting to the first would have aroused even more suspicion and fear among the people than was already the case. This may well have been the reason why Herod *summoned* the wise men *secretly,* meaning not only that the command that they present themselves before him was issued in secret but also that the actual meeting took place in secret. On the basis of *a.* what has been brought to light previously with respect to the king's duplicity (see pp. 161 f.) and of *b.* what a comparison between verses 8 and 16 reveals, we are fully justified in stating that in his private meeting with the magi Herod concealed his real intention. He did not ask them, "How old do y o u think this child would be by now?" but, "When was it that the star made its first appearance?" For the benefit of the wise men he feigned a deep interest in their specialty, the stars, while his real interest was in the child, that he might destroy him. Naturally, the more he would get to know about this potential competitor, as he saw him, the easier it would be to identify and kill him. He already knew *his birthplace* (verses 4-6). Now, on the basis of the time of the star's appearance he considers himself able to guess the child's approximate *age.* **8. And he sent them to Bethlehem, saying, Go and make careful search for the little child, and when y o u have found him report to me . . .** The king now sends the wise men to Bethlehem as his private detectives, ordering them: *a.* to conduct a thorough search for the child, and, on the presupposition that the search will be successful, *b.* to report back to him. With diabolical but characteristic cunning he adds, **that I too may come and worship him.**

The narrative now turns back to the wise men: **9. So after listening to the king they went on their way, and look, the star they had seen in its rising went ahead of them.** While still in their own country the magi had seen this wonderful star in its rising (verse 2). Now (verse 9) suddenly, dramatically— note: "and look!"—they see it again. Where had the star been between *then* (verse 2) and *now* (verse 9)? We are not told. We indulge in imaginative speculation when we say that by its reappearance every night the star had led these men all the way from the east to Jerusalem. Had this been the case would not the text have read thus, "And look, the star that had led them all the way to Jerusalem," instead of, "And look, the star they had seen *in its rising*"? If any conclusion is valid at all, it would rather seem that the star seen in its rising now reappears *for the first time.*

However this may be, one fact is stated with great clarity: this star now went ahead of them. The luminous wonder was actually moving from north to south, from Jerusalem to Bethlehem! What a strange way for a star to behave. Nevertheless, this is what Matthew says. In their interpretation commentators differ widely. According to some, the star did not really point the way. In an unscientific manner Matthew is simply stating the impression which the stars make upon us. When we travel, they seem to travel along with us. When we stop, they seem to stop also. Not the star but Herod had pointed the way to Bethlehem. [171] Others are of a directly opposite opinion. R. C. H. Lenski writes, "The star moved as a guide, the star arrived, the star stood. It is all perfectly plain, absolutely miraculous, unlike any star that ever was. But what has been done with this star? We are told, it never moved at all . . . the star only appeared to stand still when the magi stood still." [172]

On this point I happen to be in agreement with Lenski. It is entirely true that King Herod had sent the wise men to Bethlehem (verse 8), to which might be added that God, through Micah, as quoted by the Jewish Sanhedrin, had fixed Herod's attention on Bethlehem as the place of Messiah's birth (verses 4-6). But here, as often, God made use of two means: general revelation (the star) and special revelation (the prophecy of Mic. 5:2). When both are present, they always agree.

Further, I do not believe that for the magi the star did exactly what stars are always doing for us. If that were all that was meant would it not be better to say that the wise men, by their traveling, were leading the star? Explain it we cannot, but *this* star actually **went ahead of** the wise men **until it stood still over (the place) where the little child was.** Literally Matthew says, "until, having arrived, it stood still over where was the little child." The star pointed out the very house! As described in verse 9, therefore, at this point the strange and wonderful luminary must have been hanging low. To say that in some other way the magi had discovered the location of the place where the child was [173] fails to do justice to the text, as I see it.

Continued: 10. **At the sight of the star they were overjoyed.** "They rejoiced exceedingly with great joy," thus literally. See Isa. 66:10; John 3:29; and I Thess. 3:9 for similar expressions. Their cup of joy was running over. Possible reasons for this exuberant rejoicing: *a.* they saw their "old friend" once more, the very star they had observed in its rising, the one that, correctly interpreted, had started them upon the journey to greet the newborn king; *b.* they now discerned very clearly that God was guiding them by these two means: the star and the prophetic word; *c.* They knew that very soon they would reach their destination and would pay homage to the Messiah, the king of *the Jews* whose coming concerned *the Gentiles* as well.

The journey of the wise men reaches its climax in verse 11. **Having entered the house they saw the little child with Mary his mother, and they**

---

[171] Cf. Herman Ridderbos, *op. cit.*, p. 42.
[172] *Op. cit.*, pp. 67, 68.
[173] Herman Ridderbos, *op. cit.*, p. 42. Here, too, I agree with Lenski.

cast themselves to the ground and worshiped him. Nativity scenes depict the arrival of the wise men. Often, however, they are shown standing, or kneeling down, in the company of the shepherds, and in a stable. This is obviously incorrect. According to the evangelist Luke, when the *shepherds* arrive the babe is still "lying in the manger" (Luke 2:16). They come at once, that very night (Luke 2:8, 15). The little family, Joseph, Mary, and the child, continues to live in relative poverty for at least forty days, as is evident from Luke 2:22-24; cf. Lev. 12:2-8. If the wise men from the east, bringing precious gifts, had arrived within this period of forty days, then, on the fortieth day Mary's purification offering would probably have been something better than "a pair of turtle-doves or two young pigeons." It is clear that Joseph and his family had left the inn stable, perhaps very soon after the child's birth, certainly before the arrival of the wise men. They are now no longer staying in an animal shelter but living in a building for human beings (with some relatives?). With well-nigh unanimity translators agree with the rendering, (the wise men) "having entered *the house*," [174] or something similar. [175]

Having entered, the wise men see "the little child with Mary his mother." Note that whenever mother and infant are mentioned together (verses 11, 13, 14, 20, and 21) the infant is always mentioned first. It is that little child upon whom the main interest is concentrated. This is as it should be, for in this little one God has become incarnate:

> Veiled in flesh the Godhead see;
> Hail th'Incarnate Deity. (Charles Wesley)

How much of this truth the wise men understood we do not know. We do

---

[174] A. T. Robertson considers this "house" to have been *the inn* in distinction from "the stall where the cattle and donkeys stayed, which may have been beneath the inn in the side of the hill," *Word Pictures*, Vol. I, p. 19. In that case would not Matthew have written "inn" (as did Luke; see 2:7) instead of "house"?

[175] Recently, however, it has been suggested that the Greek word οἰκία, used here in 2:11, should be rendered "village" instead of "house." See S. Bartina, "¿Casa o caserío? Los magos en Belen (Matt. 2:11; 10:12-14)," *EstBib* (March-April, 1966), pp. 355-357. I cannot accept this new suggestion. It would seem far more reasonable to suppose that Matthew wants to tell us that it was when the magi had entered *the house* that they saw the child with Mary his mother than when they had entered *the village*. Also, the homage rendered to the child and the opening of the treasure-chests suggests a home atmosphere rather than a place out in the open. If it be objected that the entrance into the house must be read between the lines, so that the idea would be, "Having entered the village and having been informed about the house they went in and saw. . . ," my question would be, "Would the average reader so interpret the text? If such an able and lucid writer as Matthew had wanted to convey this thought, would he not have spelled it out?" Besides, the usual meaning of οἰκία in the New Testament is *house*, viewed as a *building* (Matt. 7:24-27; 24:43; Mark 10:29, 30; 13:34; etc.); *habitation* or *dwelling* (II Cor. 5:1); or *household, family* (Matt. 12:25; Mark 3:25; John 4:53; etc.). I can see no good reason in the present instance to depart from this general meaning and to adopt, instead, the rendering *village*.

know, though, that on seeing him they cast themselves to the ground and worshiped him; literally, "and having fallen they prostrated themselves before them." They revere him as the Messiah, the king of the Jews.

It is true that the verb used in the original and here rendered "worshiped" does not always indicate an act of reverence paid to God, the Creator and Redeemer. Sometimes it is the creature—Peter (Acts 10:25); or the church in Philadelphia (Rev. 3:9)—rather than the Creator, to whom homage is rendered. But when this is done these are regarded as standing in close relation to God, so that God speaks and operates through them. However, if, in such cases, the worshipper fails to draw this distinction, and begins to regard a mere man as if he were on a par with God, he may well receive a reprimand. Thus, when Cornelius falls down at Peter's feet and worships him, he is told, "Get up; I myself am also but a man" (Acts 10:26). When John, the author of the book of Revelation, falls down in order to worship his angel-guide, he receives a similar warning (Rev. 22:8, 9; cf. 19:10). The magi, however, are not told to desist. They may have made more progress in the true faith than we realize. According to Matt. 2:12 God, who had previously spoken to them by means of a star and (indirectly) by means of Micah, also speaks to them in a dream. Besides, as has been pointed out previously, believers who lived on the very threshold of the new dispensation must have told them about the Messiah to come. Equipped with all this knowledge, sanctified to their hearts as is clear from the entire account, we may well think of them as men who rendered to the Christ-child the type of homage that was in a very real sense acceptable to God. In this child they somehow see God, and worship him!

They have rendered the proper homage. They now offer the appropriate gifts (cf. Ps. 72:10; cf. Isa. 60:3; Ps. 87). We read: **Next, they opened their treasure-chests and presented him with gifts: gold and frankincense and myrrh.** They are pictured here as not only wealthy but also warm-hearted and worshipful. These men offer their treasures to *him:* they are meant for the child to honor him.

In works of exposition *one* use is at times assigned to each of these presents. There is probably a good reason for this. Nevertheless, it may not be amiss *to begin* by showing that *in general* Scripture assigns more than one use to each of these articles.

For example, *gold* was used extensively in the construction of the tabernacle and its furniture (Exod. 25–31; 35–40) and of the temple and its contents (I Kings 5–7; II Chron. 2–5). Yet, it was by no means limited to holy uses. It was also worn in the form of bracelets (Gen. 24:22), necklaces (Num. 31:50), and earrings (Exod. 32:2, 3). We read about "gods of gold" (Exod. 20:23), one of them being "the golden calf" which Aaron made (Exod. 32:4), though he denied that he "made" it: he merely cast the gold into the fire, "and there came out this calf!" (Exod. 32:24). James tells the stingy rich that their gold and their silver are rusted (5:3). In a vision which John saw gold serves the very unholy purpose of decorating the great harlot (Rev. 17:4, 5); Frequently the word gold is used in comparisons, to teach men that there are things that are far more precious than gold (Ps. 19:10; 119:72, 127; Prov. 8:10, 19).

As to *frankincense* (literally meaning *pure incense*), the Old Testament word is derived from a root meaning *white*. An incision is made in the bark of a certain tree of the genus Boswellia, growing on the limestone rocks of South Arabia and Somalia (E. Africa). The resulting fresh juice has a white or milky color; hence the name. [176] Now frankincense, too, has various uses. It is mentioned in connection with meal offerings (Lev. 2:1, 2, 15, 16) and wedding processions (Song of Sol. 3:6). It also occurs in a list of articles of commerce (Rev. 18:13).

Myrrh was probably derived from a small tree with odoriferous wood, namely, the Balsamodendron of Arabia. It was used for the purpose of perfuming a bed (Prov. 7:17) or a garment (Ps. 45:8). It was prescribed for certain young ladies, to make them more desirable (Esther 2:12). It was also used lavishly in bridal processions (Song of Sol. 3:6). Mingled with wine it served as an anaesthetic (Mark 15:23). Finally, it was used in preparing a body for burial (John 19:39, 40).

This list of various uses is somewhat incomplete as any Concordance will indicate. However, it establishes the point to be noted, namely, that according to Scripture (both Old and New Testament) each of the three gifts brought by the wise men serves more than one purpose. Now if this is true, what justification did Origen (and many after him) have for saying that the magi brought "gold, as to a king; myrrh, as to one who was mortal; and incense, as to God"? [177] Does not this representation amount to oversimplification? On the surface it would seem that it does. However, another look at the entire list of passages in which these three items are mentioned proves that, to say the least, there is an important element of truth in Origen's observation. To begin with *gold,* it is striking how often in Scripture this precious metal is indeed associated with royalty: with the king, the queen, the vice-gerent, and the prince. Joseph, a vice-gerent, wears a gold neck-chain (Gen. 41:42). So does Daniel as third ruler (Dan. 5:7, 29). King Nebuchadnezzar, as the first and greatest in a list of earthly rulers, is represented by a head of gold (Dan. 2:32, 38). Rabbah's king wears a crown of gold (II Sam. 12:30). So does the author of Ps. 21, in the superscription identified with David. Princes own gold (Job 3:15). Ps. 45:9 speaks about "the queen, in gold of Ophir." The one who calls himself "king in Jerusalem" is a collector

---

[176] Hebrew root *lbn* as in *Laban* (Jacob's uncle and father-in-law) and in Mount *Lebanon,* so called from the whiteness or the snow on its eastern peak. The Greek word is similar: λίβανος (Matt. 2:11; Rev. 18:13).

[177] *Against Celsus* I.60.

of gold and silver (Eccl. 2:8). And King Ahasuerus holds out his golden scepter to Queen Esther (Esther 4:11, 5:2; 8:4). As if this were not enough, it can be added that King Solomon not only had drinking vessels of gold and an ivory throne overlaid with gold, but was hemmed in by gold to such an extent that in seven verses descriptive of his wealth (I Kings 10:14-18, 21, 22) *gold* is mentioned no less than *ten times!* We see, therefore, that to anyone acquainted with the books of the Old Testament gold would amost immediately suggest royalty.

As to *frankincense,* in by far the most of the cases in which this word occurs in the Old Testament it is mentioned in connection with the service of Jehovah. It was stored in a chamber of the sanctuary (I Chron. 9:29; Neh. 13:5), and is frequently mentioned in connection with meal offerings, as an additive (Lev. 2:1, 2, 15, 16; 6:15). According to Exod. 30:34 it entered as an ingredient into the composition of incense, with respect to which it is specifically stated that it is not for the people but *only for Jehovah* (Exod. 30:37). In the Old Testament the basic word *incense* occurs more than one hundred times. [178] In the New Testament it is found in Luke 1:9-11 and Rev. 8:3, 4. Whenever it occurs it has to do with the service of God. In offering incense, burning coals were taken from the altar of burnt offering and placed on the altar of incense, the golden altar that stood in the holy place immediately in front of the holy of holies. On these coals the incense was then sprinkled. The fragrant smoke rising heavenward was symbolical of the prayers and thanksgivings of the people and the priests. The incense was definitely an offering made to God (see Luke 1:9 f.; Rev. 5:8; 8:3). Frankincense, and also incense in general, immediately suggests God, therefore. It belongs to him, *to him alone.* Even when it is offered to idols, God still calls it "*my* incense" (Ezek. 16:18). It is clear, therefore, that just as *gold and king* go together, so do also *incense and God.*

As to *myrrh,* in the more than a dozen Old Testament passages where the word occurs it is mentioned in connection with the service of Jehovah in only one instance. It enters into the composition of anointing oil (Exod. 30:22-33). For the rest, as has already been indicated, it was a perfume used by and in the interest of *mortal man,* to make his life more pleasant, his pain less dreadful, and his burial less repulsive.

It has been established, therefore, that Origen had good reason to say that the magi brought "gold, as to a king; myrrh, as to one who was mortal; and incense, as to God."

A famous poet said:

> Not what we give, but what we share,—
> For the gift without the giver is bare. (Lowell)

---

[178] However, *l^{e}bhonah,* which A.V. translates "incense" in Isa. 43:23; 66:3; Jer. 6:20; 17:26; 41:5; is correctly rendered "frankincense" in later versions.

173

Here in Matt. 2 we have an illustration of genuine givers. They did not hesitate to make a long and arduous journey (probably more than a thousand miles) to render homage to him who by most people must have been regarded as *merely* a little child. He was, moreover, a child of humble birth, belonging to a nation that had lost its freedom. Yet, these important men not only prostrated themselves before him but presented him with gifts that were not only lavish but also definitely appropriate; *gold,* for he was and is indeed a king—yes, "King of kings and Lord of lords"—*frankincense,* for he is indeed God—the fulness of the godhead dwells in him—and *myrrh,* for he is also man, destined for death, and this by his own choice.

How much of this the wise men understood we do not know. Let it suffice to say that their coming, the homage they rendered, and the gifts they offered were acceptable in the eyes of God. Matthew's main lesson for the Jews who were the first to read his Gospel, or to hear it read to them, must have been to remind them of the fact that salvation, though beginning with the Jews, does not end there. The Gentiles, too, must be won for Christ. The coming of the wise men was indeed a lesson for Jews . . . and for men of every nationality and race, a lesson to be taken to heart: if even the magi, with their limited knowledge, did this for Christ, then why do we, so highly privileged, fall short?

Continued: **12. And having been warned in a dream not to return to Herod, it was by a different route that they retired to their own country.** It is often difficult for thoroughly honest men to understand hypocrites, and for generous people to catch on to the schemes of self-seekers. So it is not surprising that the magi had failed to see what Herod was actually up to when he said, "Report to me that I too may come and worship him." But though the eyes of the wise men are not sharp enough to penetrate the king's disguise, before God nothing is hidden (Heb. 4:13). He does not want any harm to befall the magi, nor does he want the life of his Son to be taken away before the latter has finished the work which his Father had given him to do. So the magi must be warned (verse 12), and so must Joseph (verse 13). In each case the warning arrives during a dream.

Having been instructed not to return to Herod, the wise men retire to their own country by a different route. The one by way of Jericho and the Jordan readily suggests itself, but this is no more than a conjecture.

Matthew's nativity account makes mention of dreams as a means of divine revelation *a.* to Joseph (in 1:20; 2:13, 19, 22) and *b.* to the wise men (in 2:12). The Passion narrative records the dream of Pilate's wife (27:19). The Old Testament relates the dreams of Abimelech (Gen. 20:3, 6, 7); Jacob (Gen. 28:10-17; 31:10, 11), Laban (31:24); Joseph, Benjamin's brother (37:5-11); the butler and the baker (chap. 40); Pharoah (chap. 41); a Midianite (Judg. 7:13-15); King Solomon (I Kings 3:5-15); Nebuchadnezzar

174

(Dan. 2, 4); and Daniel (chap. 7).[179] Frequently that which in the dream was *seen*—i.e., the *vision*—is emphasized.

In view of what we now know about dreams, is it reasonable to believe that the wise men actually "were warned" in a dream? We commonly think of a dream as something for which we ourselves are wholly responsible; that is, the dream reflects, generally in some distorted fashion, what has been on our minds previously. Out of lingering sensations, images, and thoughts a sequence of dream experiences is built up. The dream can be very vivid, a lively experience, whether joyful or alarming. Most dreams are said to occur just after we fall asleep or just before awakening. Since conscious daytime reasoning is no longer in control, and in the state of suspended consciousness and relaxation imaginative guesswork has taken over, the various sensations, images, and thoughts often combine and recombine in a bizarre manner. In many cases the dream, of brief duration, is soon forgotten.[180] This need not bother us. Do not some etymologists maintain that the words träumen, to *dream,* and trügen (to deceive) are derived from the same root? Does not even Scripture teach that "in the multitude of dreams there is futility" (Eccl. 5:7)? If that was true *then,* how much more *today.*

In countering this rather low estimate of dreams some point to the claims that have been made for ESP. For example, a lady dreams that her brother has committed suicide. Late at night she and her husband drive to the brother's house and discover the body.[181] Numerous similar instances have been reported. However, before any conclusion can be based on them, all those people who have had similar dreams which were subsequently proved to be *at variance* with reality should report *their* experiences also. Certainly not every nightmare mirrors reality! Scientifically adequate criteria for judging such reports, without bias in either direction, must first be established.

The question may be asked, "But if dreams were frequently meaningful in Bible times, why not (or: why not as clearly and emphatically) today?" The answer is that since we now have God's full revelation in Jesus Christ, dreams as means of divine revelation are no longer necessary. In a fragmentary manner and in varied ways God spoke of old. One of these fragments and methods by which he revealed himself was the dream. In these last days, especially now that the full revelation in Jesus Christ has been recorded and

---

179 Probably Abraham's experience recorded in Gen. 15:12-16 should be added, but some would prefer not to call this a dream.

180 In substantiation of this point writers will at times refer to Dan. 2:8: "Ye see the thing is gone from me" (A.V.), interpreted to mean, "The dream has slipped away from my mind, I have forgotten it." A better rendering would be, "Y o u see that the decree is firmly resolved on by me, that if y o u do not...." Nowhere in Dan. 2 is there any evidence to prove that Nebuchadnezzar had *forgotten* his dream.

181 J. B. Rhine, *New Frontiers of the Mind,* New York and Toronto, 1937; see especially pp. 10, 11, 255-259.

the Holy Spirit has been poured out, God has spoken to us once for all in his Son (see Heb. 1:1, 2a). It is reasonable to believe, therefore, that the less privileged wise men were indeed warned in a dream, but that for us dreams have lost much of the significance they once had.

To all this one more fact must be added. In by far the majority of the aforementioned interesting dream stories Scripture distinctly adds that the dream, far from being merely the precipitate of a person's daytime experiences, amounted to a divine message. Sometimes the dreamer seems to have been aware of this even during his dream; at other times he recognizes it upon awakening; or else someone tells him this in the course of interpreting the dream. Thus we do not merely read that Abimelech dreamed, but that *God came to Abimilech* in a dream. He is also said to have come to Laban. Jacob, in his dream at Bethel, hears the Lord speaking to him and saying, "I am Jehovah. . . ." By means of Pharaoh's dream God revealed to him what he was about to do. Jehovah appeared to Solomon in a dream, saying, "What shall I give you?" In Nebuchadnezzar's dream of the tree it was the decree of the Most High that was being disclosed to him. It was in all probability an angel who interpreted Daniel's dream to him, showing that also in this case the dream's content was something for which Daniel himself was not *exclusively* responsible. Finally, in no less than three out of the four times a dream of Joseph, Mary's husband, is reported, it was an angel who addressed him in the dream. Thus also the wise men were divinely warned in a dream.

If, in spite of these considerations and in spite of the fulfilment of these *Biblical* dreams a skeptic still insists on regarding them as wholly on the level with our own dreaming, the responsibility is entirely his own. He will have created for himself a problem that is impossible of solution as long as he remains a skeptic.

---

13 Now when they had retired, what happened? An angel of the Lord appeared to Joseph in a dream, saying: "Get up, take the little child and his mother, escape to Egypt, and remain there until I tell you (to leave), for Herod is about to search for the little child, to destroy him." 14 So he got up and in the night took with him the little child and his mother and set off for Egypt, 15 where he remained until Herod's death; that what was spoken by the Lord through the prophet might be fulfilled:

"Out of Egypt I called my son."

2:13-15 The Flight to Egypt

13. **Now when they had retired, what happened?** [182] **An angel of the Lord appeared to Joseph in a dream, saying, Get up, take the little child and his mother, escape to Egypt, and remain there until I tell you (to leave), for Herod is about to search for the little child, to destroy him.**

Joseph and Mary must have been greatly comforted by the coming of the

---

182 On ἰδού see footnote 133, p. 131.

wise men and by what they did. It was a confirmation of all the wonderful things that had been spoken previously concerning the child: by an angel to Joseph (Matt. 1:20, 21), by the angel Gabriel to Mary (Luke 1:26-35), by Elizabeth to Mary (Luke 1:42), by the shepherds when they reported to Mary and Joseph what they had heard from the angels in a field near Bethlehem (Luke 2:8-19), and by Simeon addressing Mary and Joseph (Luke 2:25-33).

But Simeon had also spoken about a sword that was going to pierce Mary's soul (Luke 2:34, 35). This sword was beginning to pierce even now, for *in a dream* (see on the preceding verse, Matt. 2:12) Joseph hears the voice of an angel telling him to get up at once and with child and mother to flee to Egypt; reason: a cruel action on Herod's part was impending, namely, to search for the child with the intention of destroying him.

In this command to get up hurriedly and to escape to Egypt *God's protecting care, Herod's cruelty,* and another stage in *the child's humiliation*—for earlier stages see John 1:14; II Cor. 8:9; Luke 2:7; 2:24—stand revealed. Why must the flight be *to Egypt*? Answer: *a.* Egypt was not too far away, that is, not nearly as far as Babylonia or Persia; *b.* many Jews were living here (Jer. 43:7; 44:1; Acts 2:10), so that the possibility that the holy family could dwell for a while in the midst of acquaintances cannot be overlooked; *c.* Egypt was outside of Herod's domain; and *d.* thus the prophecy of Hos. 11:1 could reach its ultimate fulfilment (see below, on verse 15).

The objection might be raised, "Why did not God use some other means of thwarting Herod's gruesome plan? Why, for example, did he not simply kill Herod?" The answer is, "We have no right to question the ways of God's sovereign providence" (see Rom. 9:19, 20; cf. Dan. 4:35; then turn to Rom. 8:28).

14. **So he got up and in the night took with him the little child and his mother and set off for Egypt.** Here again, as in 1:24, Joseph "did as the angel of the Lord directed him." To get up at night and with the child and his mother to leave for a foreign land, being ordered to stay there until the angel would make his reappearance, must have been difficult. But Joseph is a man who is used to obeying without asking questions. So, in the darkness he makes good his escape from Bethlehem and proceeds toward Egypt. Continued: 15. . . . **where he remained until Herod's death.** The details of the arrival in Egypt, finding a place of lodging there, etc., are not reported. Nor do we know how long the holy family remained there. Of all the opinions that have been expressed with respect to this subject, that according to which the birth of Jesus occurred during the final year of Herod's life, [183] and the return from Egypt very shortly after the king's death ("where he

---

[183] See Sandmel, *op. cit.,* p. 261.

remained until Herod's death"), would seem to be the best. Note that the report of the slaughter of the infants (verses 16-18) which must have occurred very soon after the departure of the wise men, is followed immediately by the statement, "But when Herod was dead."

There follows: **that what was spoken by the Lord through the prophet might be fulfilled, Out of Egypt I called my son.** In a strikingly beautiful manner the prophecy of Hosea sets forth God's marvelous love, a love that reclaims and restores. We are told that the prophet had married a certain woman by the name of Gomer. But his wife was not true to him. She became "a wife of whoredom." She went after other lovers and conceived children in adultery. If the "woman" mentioned in Hosea's third chapter is Gomer, which is a reasonable conjecture, then the rest of the story is as follows. Hosea, instead of completely rejecting his unfaithful wife, slips away to the haunt of shame, buys Gomer back for fifteen pieces of silver and a homer and a half of barley, and mercifully restores her to her former position of honor.

In the prophecy of Hosea the main ideas of the Hosea-Gomer story are applied to Israel. Just as Hosea had married Gomer, so Jehovah had become Israel's Husband. Just as Gomer had become untrue to Hosea, so Israel had become untrue to Jehovah. Just as Gomer had been enslaved by her paramours, so the Israelites would be enslaved by those very nations in which it was putting its trust. Just as in his tender love Hosea restored Gomer, so Jehovah would restore Israel's remnant.

To show the greatness of this love Jehovah, by the mouth of Hosea, reminds Israel that already when it was still groaning under the yoke of Egyptian bondage, he had set his love upon that nation: "When Israel was a child, then I loved him, and called my son out of Egypt" (Hos. 11:1). Other passages in which this marvelous love is beautifully expressed are Deut. 32:8-14, "For Jehovah's portion is his people, Jacob is the lot of his inheritance. He found him in a desert land . . . He kept him as the apple of his eye"; and Isa. 63:9: "In all their affliction he was afflicted . . ." Perhaps most relevant in connection with both Hos. 11:1 and Matt. 2:15 is Exod. 4:22: "Israel is *my son,* my firstborn"; cf. also Ezek. 16:8: "I entered into a covenant with you, says the Lord Jehovah, *and you became mine.*"

When Matthew quotes Hos. 11:1 and applies it to Christ, it is evident that he regards Israel as a type of the Messiah. Jesus Christ, too, is God's Son. This is true in the deepest, trinitarian, sense of the term (cf. John 1:14). Just as Pharaoh, that cruel king, had tried to destroy Israel, so another king, namely Herod, at least equally cruel, was attempting to destroy Christ. But just as on the way to Egypt, during their stay in that house of bondage, and in their exodus Jehovah had protected his people, so God had protected his Son, not only on the way to Egypt and during his temporary residence there

178

but also on the way back. The Messiah was, as it were, recapitulating the history of his people Israel.

Nevertheless, it is hardly enough to say that Israel was a *type* of Christ. The bond between the two is closer than this word "type" would imply. It was Israel out of which Christ, according to his human nature, would come forth. Had Israel been destroyed in Egypt, the Messianic prophecies (Gen. 22:18; 26:4; 28:14; 49:10) would not have been fulfilled. It is therefore very true, indeed, that when Israel was effectually called out of Egypt, Christ, too, was called out. Hence, Matthew has the full right to say, "that what was spoken by the Lord through the prophet might be fulfilled, 'Out of Egypt I called my son.'" Among striking passages in which Christ and his people are drawn very closely together is Acts 22:7, "Saul, Saul, why do you persecute *me*?" See also Matt. 10:25; Mark 13:13; John 15:18-21; II Cor. 1:5, 10; Gal. 6:17; Col. 1:24; Heb. 11:26; and Rev. 3:12, 21; 4:4, cf. 14:14; 12:13; 14:1; 17:14; 19:11, cf. 19:14; 20:4.

---

16 Then Herod, when he saw that he had been tricked by the wise men, became very furious, and had the boy babies in Bethlehem and all the region around it killed, all those who were two years old and under, according to the time which he had ascertained from the wise men. 17 Then was fulfilled what was spoken through Jeremiah the prophet:
18 "a voice was heard in Ramah,
Wailing and loud lamentation,
Rachel weeping for her children,
And she refused to be consoled, because they were no more."

2:16-18 *The Slaughter of the Infants*

In all probability it did not take many days for Herod to conclude that he would never again see the magi. After they had left him he waited a day, two days perhaps. He now realized that his command, "When y o u have found him report to me," was not being obeyed. **16. Then Herod, when he saw that he had been tricked by the wise men, became very furious, and had the boy babies in Bethlehem and all the region around it killed, all those who were two years old and under, according to the time which he had ascertained from the wise men.** Herod is convinced that he has been tricked [184] by the magi. So he flies into a rage. Not having exercised self-control for so many years, he is no longer able to control his passions. In an outburst of violence he orders the boy babies of Bethlehem and environs to be killed, all

---

184 In the Gospels the word ἐμπαίζω usually has the sense *to mock, poke fun of, ridicule* (Matt. 27:29, 31; Mark 10:34; 15:20; Luke 14:29; 22:63; 23:36). However, the meaning *to delude* is represented in the LXX rendering of Jer. 10:15, where idol images are called "works of delusion." Perhaps both ideas are combined here in Matt. 2:16. Since the word *trick* may designate both deception and mockery it is perhaps the best rendering.

those of two years and under. The order is carried out. Herod's soldiers enter the homes and with their sharp daggers cut to death all these little ones.

How sin enslaves men, and how inconsistent it makes them! Herod should have been angry with *himself,* for it was he who had practiced deception. In doing so he may well have chuckled at the simplicity of the magi, who, so he thought, actually believed that *he,* the great King Herod, would go to Bethlehem and prostrate himself before a Jewish baby throne-pretender! Now that his trick has boomeranged—the failure of the wise men to return being an injury to his pride—the cruel tyrant is angry with those whom he himself had tried to trick.

How foolish sin makes men! Is Herod really unable to understand that a Higher Hand is moving the pieces and the pawns on the chess-board of life? Does he not realize that the God who caused the first attempt (verse 8) to fail so that the wise men never returned to him, would do the same for the second (verse 16), so that while the babes of Bethlehem were being slain the real object of Herod's destructive designs was already safely on his way to Egypt? If the king has ever read Psalm 2 he surely has never taken it to heart. Cf. also Rev. 17:14.

In connection with this account of The Slaughter of the Infants several errors or oft debated procedures must not be left out of the discussion:

1. *Questionable Titles?* The caption above this section (Matt. 2:16-18), as it appears in some Bibles, is "The Slaughter of the *Innocents.*" When this word "innocents" is taken in a very broad sense as indicating those who are guileless (cf. John 1:47) and uninjurious, or as those not guilty of the crime charged, it is undoubtedly accurate. In this relative sense we, too, often speak correctly about "innocent children," and this use of the term cannot be disallowed. On the other hand, if the term is intended to indicate those who are free from any sin or guilt whatever, it is contrary to the teaching of Scripture. Infants, too, are guilty in Adam. Sin, both hereditary and actual, cleaves to them also (Job 14:4; Ps. 51:5; Rom. 5:12, 18, 19; I Cor. 15:22; and Eph. 2:3). If infants are to be saved at all, this salvation will have to be granted to them on the basis not of their supposed innocence but of the application to them of *Christ's* merits. [185] Since, therefore, the title "The Slaughter of the Innocents" is rather ambiguous, would it not be better to substitute the word *Infants* for *Innocents?* While the one title may be good, is not the other better?

Worthy of discussion is also another title, "The Slaughter of the First Martyrs." Says Irenaeus, "For this reason also he [the Lord] suddenly removed those children who belonged to the house of David, whose happy lot it was to have been born at that time, that he might send them on ahead

---

[185] On the further question, "Are all those who die in infancy saved?" see the author's book, *The Bible on the Life Hereafter,* Grand Rapids, 1971 (paperback), pp. 100-104.

into his kingdom. Since he was himself an infant he so arranged it that human infants should be martyrs, slain, according to the Scriptures, for the sake of Christ, who was born in Bethlehem of Judea, in the city of David." [186]

At a very early date the church began to regard these children as *the first martyrs*. So, *the Feast of the Holy Innocents* was born, celebrated in the Greek Church on December 29 (O.S.) and in the Latin Church on December 28. However, we generally think of *martyrs* as "those who have suffered or died for their Christian convictions." This word is, accordingly, hardly applicable to infants.

2. *Erroneous Conception*. In the course of history there have been those who held that Herod killed thousands of infants. In fact, their numerous host has even been identified with the 144,000 mentioned in Rev. 14:1. [187] There is no justification for this. In a town as small as Bethlehem was at that time, even when the immediate surroundings are added as they should be (see 2:16) could the total number of those slain have been more than fifteen or twenty?

3. *Wrong Evaluation*. The opinion has been expressed that the death of these infants was a punishment for their parents because the latter had failed to render homage to Christ. Objection: not a word about this is found in the text.

4. *Unwarranted Inference*. From the words, "all those who were two years old and under, according to the time which he had ascertained from the wise men" it has been inferred that Jesus must have been about two years of age when the slaughter of the infants occurred. This conclusion is, however, questionable. Says A. Edersheim, "Our Lord was born *before* the death of Herod, and, as we judge from the Gospel-history, very shortly before that event." [188] This statement is in all probability correct, as the following data will indicate. John 2:20 states that when Jesus attended the first Passover (2:13) and cleansed the temple (2:14-16) that structure had been in the process of building for a period of forty-six years. From Josephus we gather that the work was begun about the year 19 B.C. [189] This would bring us to the Spring of A.D. 27 as the year of the first Passover. But Jesus' baptism and first public appearance occurred a little earlier (see John 1:32—2:12), probably about December of A.D. 26. Luke 3:23 informs us that at that time Jesus was about thirty years of age. Therefore, he may well have been born in December of the year 5 B.C. We cannot allow a margin of error of more than a year. Moreover, as has been stated earlier, the impres-

---

[186] *Against Heresies* III.xvi.4.

[187] See L. M. Sweet, art. "Innocents, Massacre of the," I.S.B.E., Vol. III, p. 1471.

[188] *The Life and Times of Jesus the Messiah*, New York, London, and Bombay, 1898, Vol. II, p. 704.

[189] *Antiquities* XV.380.

sion which Matt. 2 creates is that the birth of Jesus, the coming of the wise men, the flight into Egypt, and the slaughter of the infants took place very shortly before Herod's death on or before April 4 of the year 4 B.C.

This presentation must not be construed as a plea for the unarguable correctness of celebrating Christmas on December 25. [190] It is a well-known fact that this custom did not originate until the third or fourth century. For all we know, Jesus may have been born in some other month. October? November? We do not know. On the other hand, late December should not be ruled out in the belief that at that time of the year there could not have been "shepherds in that same region, out in the field, keeping watch at night over their flock" (Luke 2:8).

In a letter dated January 16, 1967 the New Testament scholar Dr. Harry Mulder of The Netherlands writes (my translation from the Dutch):

"During the brief Christmas vacation my wife and I traveled from Beirut [where he was teaching at the time] to Jerusalem. In this connection I can also answer your question regarding the presence of sheep around Bethlehem in the month of December. On Christmas eve in Shepherd Field a crowd had gathered to sing Christmas carols. We joined this crowd and took part in the singing. Right near us a few flocks of sheep were nestled. Even the lambs were not lacking. It was a moving sight. It is therefore definitely not impossible that the Lord Jesus was born in December. But it is perhaps interesting to mention in this connection that the swarthy Coptic monks whose humble dwellings are located in the heart of the older city celebrate Christmas every month on the roof of the Church of the Holy Sepulchre, because we do not know in which month the Lord was born. The weather in Jerusalem was beautiful, thus also in Bethlehem. We spent a few hours in the fields of Ephrata and were not bothered by the cold or by anything of that kind." [191]

This brings us back to the question, "Does Matt. 2:16 imply that Jesus must have been about two years of age when the slaughter of the infants occurred?" Perhaps this question can best be answered by a counter-question: "Basing our answer upon what we have learned about King Herod

---

[190] Interesting, nevertheless, is the defense of this date made on the basis of the division of the priests into twenty-four courses (I Chron. 24)—Zechariah, the father of John the Baptist belonging to the eighth (Luke 1:5; cf. I Chron. 24:10)—and on the fact that according to the Talmud the destruction of the temple occurred Aug. 4/5 of the year A.D. 70, at the very moment when a sacerdotal cycle of 168 days (24x7) was finished. See A. Fahling, *The Life of Christ*, St. Louis, 1936, p. 732. But perhaps this calculation rests upon one or two unprovable assumptions.

[191] On p. 364 of his most interesting biographical novel *Pontius Pilate*, Garden City, New York, 1968, a book which is a joy to read, Paul L. Maier appeals to Luke 3:1, 2 in contradiction of the chronology I share with many others. Detailed discussion of this passage belongs, however, to a Commentary on Luke. For the present I must limit myself to making a reference to my own attempt at a solution; see *Bible Survey*, Grand Rapids, 1961, p. 415. See also in that same book pp. 59-62.

(see pp. 155-168), the proud, cruel, jealous tyrant who was ever ready to destroy anyone whom he suspected of being a threat to his power, who was rebuked repeatedly by the Roman government for his shocking barbarity, and who right at this very moment was livid with rage, which of the following two interpretations of his command to the soldiers best expresses what he meant?:

a. "Since I have found out from the magi that the so-called 'king of the Jews' is about *two years* of age, therefore kill all the male infants of *two years and under.*"

or

b. "Since I have been informed on good authority that the potential aspirant to my throne is about *two months* old, therefore, in order to make certain that he cannot escape, kill all the boy babies of *two years and under.*"

The answer is obvious. When it came to killing, Herod always allowed himself a very wide margin. There is, accordingly, nothing in Matt. 2:16 that contradicts the chronologically consistent evidence gathered from the rest of Matt. 2 and from Luke 3:23 and John 2:20. [192]

5. *Inexcusable Rejection.* By some the entire story is rejected. It is regarded as a biased portrait of Herod, an expression of the hostile feeling of the early church toward him. [193] However, as must have become evident by now, the account is in every way consistent with the picture of Herod's life as a whole, and especially with the frightful mental and moral disarray that marked the king's last days. Surely, the tyrant who killed some of his own sons when he considered them to be claimants to his throne, would not hesitate to kill the children of other people when he suspected them of having in their midst one who, unless destroyed, might one day become guilty of the same crime!

The section ends with a quotation from Jer. 31:15, as follows: **17, 18. Then was fulfilled what was spoken through Jeremiah the prophet:**

> **A voice was heard in Ramah,**
> **Wailing and loud lamentation,**
> **Rachel weeping for her children,**
> **And she refused to be consoled, because they are no more.**

To understand this quotation it must be borne in mind that in Old Testament times Ramah (modern *er-Ram*) was located on the border between the two kingdoms, Israel and Judah (I Kings 15:17; II Chron. 16:1). It

---

[192] As stated earlier, a margin of a year must be allowed. Hence in question *b.* "two months" might have to be changed to "a year and two months." I do not see how a wider margin than this is possible on the basis of the other scriptural data. And on the strength of the impression which Matthew 2 has made on me as well as on others (see p. 181), I, too, favor "two months" over "a year and two months."

[193] So, for example, Sandmel, *op. cit.*, pp. 261, 262.

was situated five miles north of Jerusalem. It was the place where foreign conquerors ordered the defeated multitude to be assembled for deportation to far away places. Because of its location it was able to represent both kingdoms.

This last statement holds also for Rachel, Jacob's most cherished wife. She, too, having given birth to Joseph, the father of Ephraim and Manasseh, could represent *Israel*, the kingdom of the ten tribes (sometimes simply called "Ephraim"); and having borne Benjamin, could symbolize *Judah*, the kingdom of the two tribes (Judah and Benjamin).

Figuratively Rachel is here in Jer. 31:15 pictured as being still alive. She is, as it were, watching the wretched multitudes gathered in Ramah. She listens to their weeping until she herself also begins to weep. She mourns bitterly because she is being deprived of *her* children: first Israel goes into exile (II Kings 17:5, 6), then Judah (II Chron. 36:17 and 20). She who was so eager to have children—"Give me children or I die" (Gen. 30:1)—sees how some of them are killed, others driven away to foreign soil. How bitter are her tears; how loud and continued is her lamentation. A worldly power—first Assyria, then Babylonia—has robbed her of that which was dearest to her.

Nevertheless, there was reason for rejoicing. In fact, the thirty-first chapter of Jeremiah, from which Matthew quotes these words, [194] is filled with words of consolation. This comfort concerns both Israel and Judah (Jer. 31:27, 31; cf. 33:14), that is, the entire remnant (31:7). Jehovah has loved his people with an everlasting love (31:3). Therefore he who has scattered them will also regather them (31:10). Rachel must therefore refrain from weeping (31:16). Is not Ephraim his darling child? (31:20). Will he not make a new covenant with his people (31:31), forgiving their iniquity and no longer remembering their sin? (31:34). The remnant will indeed return, and for what purpose? Merely to rebuild the cities (31:38)? No, but in order to bring forth "the Branch of Righteousness." It is he who will execute justice and righteousness in the land (33:14, 15).

The parallel drawn by Matthew is very clear. Because of the slaughter of Bethlehem's infants he pictures Rachel as weeping once more, and for essentially the same reason. These children, too, are no more. This time the worldly power that destroyed them was not Assyria or Babylonia but Edom, as represented by cruel King Herod. Bethlehem's infants of two years and under have been killed. The child who was the main object of Herod's wrath has been driven into exile. He is fleeing to Egypt. But also in the present case there is a full measure of consolation, if the one bereft would only take it to

---

194 The quotation is almost literally according to the Hebrew. The main difference is the repetition in the original Hebrew (Jer. 31:*14* in the Hebrew text) of the words "for her children"; hence, "Rachel weeping for her children; she refuses to be comforted for her children." This difference is not essential, for the phrase in question is also *implied* in the last line of Matt. 2:18.

heart. That comfort centers in the same "Branch of Righteousness" of whom Jeremiah spoke. Presently he will return from Egypt in order to save all those who place their trust in him. So, Rachel, be dismayed no longer. Having returned, the Ruler born in Bethlehem will one day utter the comforting words: "Come to me, all who are weary and burdened, and I will give y o u rest" (Matt. 11:28). He will also say, "Let the children come to me; do not try to stop them; for to such belongs the kingdom of God" (Matt. 10:14).

---

19 Now when Herod was dead, what happened? An angel of the Lord appeared to Joseph in a dream in Egypt, saying, 20 "Get up, take the little child and his mother, and go to the land of Israel, for those who were seeking the little child's life are dead." 21 So he got up and took the little child and his mother and came into the land of Israel. 22 But when he heard that Archelaus was now ruling over Judea in the place of his father Herod, he was afraid to go there, and having been warned in a dream, he withdrew to the region of Galilee. 23 Having arrived there he settled in a town called Nazareth, that what was spoken through the prophets might be fulfilled, for he [Jesus] would be called a Nazarene.

2:19-23 *The Return from Egypt and Settlement in Nazareth*

19, 20. Now when Herod was dead. . . . It would seem that the holy family had not been in Egypt very long before Herod died. Josephus in great detail relates the events that transpired during the king's final illness. Since at that time pathology and diagnosis were still in their infancy, it would be rather risky to express in modern terminology the disease or, perhaps better, *complication of diseases,* that caused the tyrant's death. Some remind us of the fact that he had been an enthusiastic athlete, and surmise that cardiac hypertension had something to do with his demise. In close connection with this, others have described his illness as a very advanced case of arteriosclerosis. Some speak of heart disease and dropsy due to malfunctioning of the kidneys. Cirrhosis of the liver has also been mentioned. Josephus, in enumerating the symptoms, speaks of ulcerated entrails, a putrified and maggoty scrotum, foul breath, constant convulsions, etc. Neither physicians nor warm baths led to recovery.

Shortly before his death the king, realizing how intensely he was hated by the Jews, and that the public announcement of his death would be greeted with jubilation, had issued an order that "all the principal men of the entire Jewish nation" should be called to him. At his command as many as came were imprisoned in the Jericho hyppodrome. He then told his fraudulent sister Salome and her husband Alexas that what most troubled him was that he would die without being mourned, and that they must therefore see to it that at his death the imprisoned leaders would all be slaughtered, so that there would indeed be mourning, if not *for,* at least *at,* his death. This was

185

agreed on. Once dead, however, Herod's ability to implement the pact also ceased, so that the massacre did not occur.

Antipater, Herod's oldest son, offspring by his wife Doris (see chart on p 189), had complained to his mother that Herod was stretching out his earthly existence so long that he, Antipater, would be an old man before coming to power. Subsequently testimony was secured according to which Antipater had been deeply involved in a plot to have his father poisoned. Given a court trial, he denied the charge but was convicted. Salome urged her brother to have Antipater executed. Rome gave its permission. All this happened when Herod was approaching death. In the midst of his family troubles, physical agonies, and mental tortures, Herod suddenly threatened to kill himself with the knife with which he was paring an apple. An alert cousin, seeing what was about to happen, prevented it. The cousin's loud outcry, echoing through the palace, had however been misinterpreted to mean that Herod was actually dead. Antipater, hearing the news and believing that it was true, grew bold and tried to bribe the jailer to release him, promising huge rewards. The dying king was informed about this and ordered his son's immediate execution. The command was carried out. Thus Herod added another son to the list of his own offspring whose execution he ordered. Five days later he himself expired.

Archelaus, offspring of Herod and Malthace (see chart on p. 189), saw to it that his father received a gorgeous funeral. His corpse was wrapped in purple. Upon his head had been placed a crown of gold, in his hand a scepter. The bier on which his body rested was of solid gold, lined with precious stones. Five hundred slaves bore perfumes. Along the track leading across the desert from Bethlehem to Jericho the solitary ruin of Herodeion, the place of burial, is still visible.

Josephus sums up Herod's life in these words: "He was a man of great barbarity toward all men equally, and a slave to his passion."

The text continues: (Now when Herod was dead) **what happened? An angel of the Lord appeared to Joseph in a dream in Egypt, saying, Get up, take the little child and his mother.** So far, except for the phrase "in Egypt," here added, the sentence is identical with that in 2:13. In the middle of that verse the angel had promised that he would return when the time had arrived for Joseph to leave Egypt. That promise is now being fulfilled. With respect to dreams as a means of revelation see on 2:12. There follows: **and go to the land of Israel, for those who were seeking the little child's life are dead.** Herod was dead. Let Joseph regard all others who might wish to kill the child also dead. [195] Note the very general character of this command: Joseph

---

[195] The plural "those who were" instead of "he who was" is difficult. "Herod and his soldiers" has been suggested. But were all those soldiers dead? In Gram. N.T. (Bl-Debr), par. 141, the term "allusive plural" is mentioned. Perhaps the angel wishes to emphasize

is not told *where* to go in the land of Israel. That revelation will come a little later (in verse 22b). Continued: 21. **So he got up and took the little child and his mother and came into the land of Israel.** As always Joseph obeys. Arrived in the land of Israel, he probably intended to settle in Bethlehem, where before his flight to Egypt he must have found many friends and relatives and an opportunity to work. Probably, too, he and Mary decided on this because of their child. Was not nearby Jerusalem "the holy city," the center of Jewish religious life, and did not the temple stand here? Something happens, however, that changes Joseph's plans: 22. **But when he heard that Archelaus was now ruling over Judea in the place of his father Herod, he was afraid to go there, and having been warned in a dream, he withdrew to the region of Galilee.**

In order to understand this verse it must be borne in mind that before his death King Herod the Great had made a will which he changed several times. The terms of the final revision were by the Roman government allowed to be carried out. Thus it had come about that at the father's death Herod Antipas, a son by Malthace, became *tetrarch* of Galilee and Perea; Archelaus, another son by the same wife, was made *ethnarch* of Judea, Samaria, and Idumea; and Philip, a son by Cleopatra of Jerusalem (not to be confused with the far more widely known Cleopatra of Egypt) became *tetrarch* of the northern territories: Iturea, Trachonitis, Gaulanitis, Auranitis, and Batanea. The titles: king, ethnarch, and tetrarch, are in this sentence mentioned in the descending order of authority and prestige.

When Joseph heard that Archelaus was now ruling over Judea in the place of his father he was afraid to settle there. The reason for this fear will become clear from the following. While still alive Herod the Great had ordered a huge golden eagle to be erected over the great gate of the temple. To the Jews who took their religion seriously this was an abomination because: *a.* it was a violation of Exod. 20:4, as they interpreted it; and *b.* it was the more repulsive because of the prominence accorded to that bird by the Romans. Roman soldiers bore on their standards images of the imperial eagle. In their temples such images were also displayed. To Greeks and Romans alike was there not a close relation between Zeus=Jupiter and the eagle, in some sense making the latter a partaker of divinity?

Two famous Jewish teachers, Judas and Matthias, men regarded by all pious Jews as experts in the law of God, encouraged their students to destroy this eagle above the temple gate. Some of these young men were eager to comply, no matter what the cost might be to them. At midday they climbed upon the temple's roof and started to pull down the eagle and to cut it to pieces with their axes. The young men were arrested and brought before

---

that there is now absolutely no one left who is seeking to destroy the child. For the meaning of ψυχή ("life") see on 6:25.

Herod. To avoid an insurrection in Jerusalem the ailing king sent them to Jericho for trial. The grievously afflicted king went there himself also. The young men received mild punishment but their teachers were executed and given a dishonorable burial. Herod the Great died. Then, at Passover time, a great rebellion broke out in Jerusalem because of the murder of these two beloved teachers of the law. Archelaus, who was now the ruler, seems to have inherited his father's nature. He used a very harsh method to quell the rebellion, killing about three thousand people, among them many pilgrims visiting Jerusalem to attend the feast.

Before we leave Archelaus it should be mentioned that even after Joseph withdrew to Galilee, Archelaus continued to be a cruel king. As a result the Judean and Samaritan leaders complained to Rome, and the ethnarch was deposed in the ninth year of his reign (A.D. 6). In his place Rome then appointed "governors." The most widely known of these, Pontius Pilate, was the one who sentenced Jesus to be crucified (Matt. 27:2, 26).

This cruelty of Archelaus explains why Joseph had second thoughts about settling in Judea. Nevertheless, as mentioned in the preceding, Bethlehem as a place to live continued to appeal to him. It was probably hard for him to come to a definite decision. His hesitancy is removed in a dream. This time there was no angel as in his three earlier dream experiences. In the present dream he is instructed to go to Galilee. He obeys.

Continued: **23. Having arrived there he settled in a town called Nazareth, that what was spoken through the prophets might be fulfilled, for he [Jesus] would be called a Nazarene.** This can be paraphrased as follows: "Arrived in Galilee Joseph, of his own accord, yet under the direction of divine providence, returned to the place of his former residence, Nazareth (Luke 2:4), for in this act of going to Nazareth to live an Old Testament prediction was fulfilled, namely, that the Messiah would be despised and rejected of men. Nazareth was esteemed of small account, and so were its citizens, the Nazarenes." That the Old Testament does indeed predict the Messiah's low estate and his rejection by men is clear from some or all of the following passages: Ps. 22:6-8, 13; 69:8, 20, 21; Isa. 11:1; 49:7; 53:2, 3, 8; Dan. 9:26. That during his sojourn on earth Jesus was known as the man from despised Nazareth and not as a Bethlehemite is evident from such passages as John 1:45, 46; 7:42. He was, indeed, "scorned and abhorred by men" (Matt. 12:24; 27:21-23, 63; Luke 23:11; John 1:11; 5:18; 6:66; 9:22, 24), as were his followers, the Nazarenes (Acts 24:5).

Here again, therefore, there was a definite fulfilment of prophecy; not, however, of one particular passage, but of "the prophets" in general.[196]

---

[196] Objectionable views:

1. Matthew is thinking of one definite passage, Isa. 11:1, which in its use of the word *netser* points to *Nazareth*.

Answer: no etymological connection between this Hebrew word and Ναζαρέτ can be

Chart of the Family of Herod the Great, to the Extent Necessary for the Study of the New Testament

	HEROD THE GREAT			
by Doris, of unknown origin	by Mariamne I, daughter of Alexander; see Chart on p. 161	by Mariamne II, daughter of Simon	by Malthace, the Samaritan	by Cleopatra of Jerusalem
Antipater	Aristobulus & Alexander HEROD AGRIPPA I & Herodias(1) Acts 12 Matt. 14:3 HEROD AGRIPPA II & Bernice & Drusilla Acts 25, 26 Acts 25:13, 23; 26:30 Acts 24:24	Herod Philip m. Herodias(2) Matt. 14:3 → Salome(1) Matt. 14:6	HEROD ANTIPAS & ARCHELAUS Matt. 14:1 Matt. 2:22 Luke 3:1 m. Herodias(3) Matt. 14:3	PHILIP Luke 3:1 m. Salome(2)

1. Names in bold face type indicate rulers.

2. Only five of Herod's ten wives are represented. Three additional wives, mentioned by Josephus, are of no importance to New Testament history. We do not even know the names of the other two.

3. Meaning of Herodias (1), (2), and (3): She is, first of all, the daughter of Aristobulus. Secondly, she marries Herod Philip. Thirdly, Herod Antipas divorces his own wife, and marries Herodias.

4. The marriages of Herodias are indicated on the chart because the New Testament refers to them. For a good reason, i.e., in order not to make matters too complicated, only the first marriage of Salome is indicated. For a more detailed chart see S.H.E.R.K., Vol. V, p. 245. Herod the Great's marriage to Doris is indicated above because the summary of Herod's life contains a reference to her and her son (p. 186).

5. Meaning of Salome (1) and (2): She is, first of all, the daughter of Herod Philip by Herodias. Secondly, she marries Philip the tetrarch.

189

When we compare Matthew's nativity account with that of Luke we can hardly fail to see the sublime harmony in the two inspired records. Matthew shows how it was that Christ's birth in Bethlehem was gradually forgotten. Herod's act of murder had brought the holy family to Egypt and afterward to Nazareth. So Matthew relates that Jesus, though born in Bethlehem (Matt. 2:1), was called a *Nazarene* (Matt. 2:23; 21:11; 26:71; John 1:45, 46; 17:42). Luke, on the other hand, brings out that Jesus, though brought up in Nazareth (2:4, 51), was born *in Bethlehem* (2:4, 7). Both places (Bethlehem and Nazareth) combine in showing that Jesus is indeed the Christ of prophecy (Matt. 2:5, 6; 2:23).

Summary of Chapter 2

1. *The Wise Men from the East* (verses 1-12)
The journey they accomplish (verse 1)
Wise men from "the east" (Medo-Persia? Babylonia?) arrive in Jerusalem. How many there were is not known, nor how they dressed, their names, later history, date of death, place of burial.
The question they ask (verse 2)
They inquire, "Where is the newborn king of the Jews?" An extraordinary "star," which they had seen at its first appearance upon the horizon, had by them been correctly interpreted as indicating the birth of the Messiah, the king of the Jews. The exact nature of this luminary remains unknown. Also obscure is what had made them connect it with Christ's birth. The one important fact is that the magi had come from afar to worship the newborn king. In order to worship him they must first locate him.
The alarm they incite (verse 3)
King Herod, sly, envious, cruel, suspicious, with a record of murder behind him, one who, though approaching the end of his life, is still with sinister intent on the lookout for those who might wish to dethrone him, is

shown. Besides, Matthew does not say "the prophet," but "the prophets." He does not add the word "saying," as if he were about to quote a definite passage. In all probability, therefore, ὅτι must not here be reproduced by quotation marks or rendered "that," but should be translated "for." All this does not mean that Isa. 11:1 must be excluded from the list of passages to which Matthew refers. It should indeed be included, but not because of any supposed direct reference to Nazareth; rather, because it, too, along with several others, speaks of Messiah's lowly origin. It should immediately be added, however, that calling Jesus "the Nazarene" or "man from Nazareth" does not *necessarily* imply disdain. In fact, in most instances it has no unfavorable connotation, whether in the form of Ναζαραῖος (Matt. 26:71, etc.) or of Ναζαρηνός (Mark 1:24; etc.). Jesus even uses it with respect to himself (Acts 22:8).

2. *Nazarene=Nazirite*, a person specially consecrated to God. See Num. 6.
Answer: the context connects *Nazarene* with Nazareth, not with any idea of special consecration.

alarmed when he hears about the wise men's inquiry. All Jerusalem is also perturbed, wondering who and how many will this time become the victims of the king's mad fury.

The meetings they bring about (verses 4-8)

Not that they themselves arrange these meetings but their arrival and question occasion, or result in, these meetings. Both of them are convened on the initiative of the pathologically frightened king.

The first is a gathering of the king and the Jewish Supreme Court, the Sanhedrin. From that body the king seeks to learn where, according to prophecy, the Christ was to be born.—In order to kill his potential competitor, Herod must know where to find him!—The answer is given, "In Bethlehem." It is taken for granted by king and court alike, Matthew himself concurring, that the Old Testament passage (Mic. 5:2) refers to a definite person, One arriving on history's scene not in the prophet's own days but much later.

Armed with the desired information the king then secretly arranges a meeting of himself with the wise men. Concealing his intention he asks the magi when the star had first made its appearance.—He wants to know the age of the child, for the more he knows about him the better will be his chance to kill him!—Having obtained the necessary data concerning place and time, Herod, turning to the wise men, sends them to Bethlehem and deceitfully adds, "Go and make careful search for the little child, and when y o u have found him report to me, that I too may come and worship him."

The guidance they experience (verses 9, 10)

On their way the magi suddenly rediscover the star and rejoice. It leads them to the very house where the infant is staying.

The homage they render (verse 11)

Having entered the house, they see "the little child with Mary his mother."—Note the order: *first* the little child.—They cast themselves to the ground, rendering homage. Having arisen they open their treasure chests and present the child with gifts: "gold, as to a king; myrrh, as to one who is mortal; and incense, as to God" (Origen).—To what extent the magi themselves understood the nature of the One before whom they prostrated themselves, and in how far they fathomed the appropriateness of their gifts is not revealed. Undoubtedly their homage and gifts were acceptable to God.

The warning they heed (verse 12)

In a dream the wise men are instructed not to return to Herod. They heed the warning and by a different route (Jericho and the Jordan?) retire to their own country.—Question: In so doing did they not break their promise to the king? Answer: *a.* It cannot be proved that they ever made a promise (see verse 9). *b.* If they did, is it wrong to break a bad promise?

Main lesson: Gentiles as well as Jews are included in God's redemptive plan (Matt. 8:11; 28:19; cf. Rom. 10:12).

2. *The Flight into Egypt* (verses 13-15)

Ordered (verse 13)

The sword of which Simeon spoke (Luke 2:34, 35) is even now beginning to pierce Mary's soul, for in a dream an angel tells Joseph to get up at once, to flee to Egypt, with the child and the latter's mother, and to remain there until further notice. Reason: Herod is bent on destroying the child.—Egypt was not very distant. Many Jews lived there. It was outside of Herod's domain.—In this verse God's tender care, Herod's abysmal cruelty, and a stage in the child's vicarious humiliation stand revealed.

Undertaken (verse 14)

The nativity story pictures Joseph as obeying even difficult orders. He gets up in the night, flees with the infant and its mother, and proceeds toward Egypt.

Illumined (verse 15)

In this flight to, and subsequent return from, Egypt, Matthew sees a fulfilment of Hos. 11:1, "Out of Egypt I called my son." At the time of the exodus not only the people of Israel but the Messiah too was, in a sense, being called out of Egypt; for had Israel been destroyed in Egypt, such Messianic prophecies as Gen. 22:18; 26:4; 28:14; and 49:10 would not have been fulfilled. In Christ's return from Egypt (Matt. 2:20, 21), presupposing the escape into, and brief stay in, Egypt (verses 13-15), history was being repeated, now with reference to Christ Incarnate. Israel's Egypt experience was being recapitulated in Christ.

It is comforting to know that in the history of redemption everything proceeds according to God's eternal plan. Hence, salvation rests upon a firm foundation.

3. *The Slaughter of the Infants* (verses 16-18)

The deed itself (verse 16)

The magi's failure to return makes Herod furious. At his command all the boy babies in Bethlehem and vicinity, those two years old and under, are killed. How cruel! How useless, for the chief object of the king's wrath has already escaped.

The historicity of this account is rejected by some, who regard the story as being nothing more than an expression of the early church's hostile attitude toward Herod. Matthew's report is however consistent with the picture of the king's life gathered from other sources.

The deed in the light of prophecy (verses 17, 18)

In this slaughter Matthew sees a fulfilment of Jer. 31:15: Rachel weeping for her children and refusing to be comforted. See the explanation on pp. 183-185.

"The King of the Jews, Herod" contrasted with "the King of the Jews, Jesus"

Herod	*Jesus*
selfish and self-indulgent	self-denying and self-sacrificing (Matt. 16:24; 20:28; cf. John 10:11, 15)
yielding to Satan	vanquishing Satan (Matt. 4:1-11; cf. John 12:31, 32)
destroyer	Savior (Matt. 1:21; cf. Luke 19:10; John 3:16; I Tim. 1:15)
cruel, even to little ones	kind, also to little ones (Matt. 15:32; 19:14; Luke 23:24)
losing all	in control over all (Matt. 11:27; 28:18)

4. *The Return from Egypt and Settlement in Nazareth* (verses 19-23)
The order to return (verses 19, 20)

According to his promise the angel returns, and in a dream directs Joseph to go back to the land of Israel, Herod having died.

The return itself (verse 21)

With his family Joseph enters Judea, is probably headed for Bethlehem.

The settlement in Nazareth (verses 22, 23)

He hears that Archelaus, in cruelty the equal of his father, is now ruling in Judea. So, warned in a dream, he withdraws to Galilee, settling in the place of his former residence. Therefore Jesus would become known as a citizen of despised Nazareth ("a Nazarene"), thus becoming "despised and rejected of men" (Isa. 53:3; cf. 11:1; Ps. 22:6, 7, 13; etc.).

Outline of Chapter 3

Theme: *The Work Which Thou Gavest Him to Do*

3:1-12   The Ministry of John the Baptist
3:13-17   The Baptism of Jesus

CHAPTER III

3 1 Now in those days John the Baptist made his public appearance, preaching in the wilderness of Judea, saying, 2 "Be converted,[197] for the kingdom of heaven is at hand." 3 It was of him that the prophet Isaiah spoke when he said,

"A voice of one crying in the wilderness:
Make ready the way of the Lord,
Make straight his paths."

4 Now this John wore a garment made of camel's hair, and a leather belt around his waist, and his food was locusts and wild honey. 5 Then went out to him Jerusalem, all Judea, and the whole Jordan neighborhood. 6 Confessing their sins they were baptized by him in the Jordan River.

7 But when he saw many of the Pharisees and Sadducees coming for baptism he said to them, "Y o u offspring of vipers! Who warned y o u to escape from the approaching (outpouring of) wrath? 8 Bear fruit therefore in keeping with conversion; 9 and do not presume to say to yourselves, 'We have Abraham as our father,' for I tell y o u that God is able to raise up children for Abraham out of these stones here. 10 Already the axe is laid at the root of the trees; every tree therefore that does not bear good fruit is cut down and thrown into the fire. 11 I on my part baptize y o u with water with a view to conversion; but he who is coming behind me is mightier than I—I am not fit to remove his sandals—he will baptize y o u with the Holy Spirit and with fire. 12 His winnowing shovel is in his hand, and he will thoroughly clear his threshing floor. He will gather his grain into the granary, but the chaff he will consume with unquenchable fire."

3:1-12 *The Ministry of John the Baptist*
Cf. Mark 1:3-8; Luke 3:4-18; John 1:6-8, 15-28 [198]

In chapters 1 and 2 Matthew has revealed to us the greatness of the Christ, the true Son of David, the One to whom even wise men from the east rendered homage. It is proper that a king, especially *such* a king, have a herald to proclaim his approach. This herald was John the Baptist.

1. **Now in those days John the Baptist made his public appearance, preaching in the wilderness of Judea.** The expression "in those days" is very indefinite, probably meaning no more than "in the days of Christ's earthly

---

[197] Or: "Make a complete turnabout in mind and heart." See the explanation.

[198] These cross references to the other Gospels are indicated merely for the purpose of comparison. They do not intend to convey the idea that the entire content of Matt. 3:1-12 is paralleled or even reflected in the other Gospels. The degree or amount of resemblance is not shown.

sojourn." For a more precise chronological note see Luke 3:1, 2. If John, like Jesus (Luke 3:23), was about thirty years of age when he made his first public appearance, then, since the Baptist was about six months older than Jesus (Luke 1:26, 36), and since Jesus probably began his ministry in late A.D. 26 or early 27,[199] it was likely during the summer of that same year that John had begun to address the multitudes.

Everything about John was startling: his sudden emergence, manner of dress, choice of food, preaching, and baptizing. The evangelist Luke first dwells in great detail (1:5-25, 41, 57-79) on the miraculous manner of John's birth to the priest Zechariah and his wife Elizabeth, the latter also of priestly descent. Then, in one brief note Luke covers the entire period between John's birth and the beginning of his ministry: "And the child grew and became strong in spirit, and was in the wilderness until the day when he made his public appearance before Israel" (1:80). On that day suddenly there he was, fullgrown, facing a large multitude, his startling debut reminding men of Elijah (I Kings 17:1).

He was preaching in "the wilderness of Judea," a term indicating the rolling bad lands between the hill country of Judea to the west, and the Dead Sea and lower Jordan to the east, stretching northward to about the point where the Jabbok flows into the Jordan. It is indeed a desolation, a vast undulating expanse of barren chalky soil covered with pebbles, broken stones and rocks.[200] Here and there a bit of brushwood appears, with snakes crawling underneath (see verse 7). It is clear, however, from Matt. 3:5 (cf. John 1:28) that the terrain of John's activity extended even to the east bank of the Jordan. It included *the entire region around*—i.e., on both banks of this part of—*the Jordan.*[201]

He preached, **saying 2. Be converted.** . . . . His message was not prolix but pithy, not soothing but soul-searching, not flattering but frightening, at least to considerable degree. He was a preacher of imminent doom (see verses 7 and 10), a catastrophe that could be avoided only by a radical turnabout of mind and heart. The gist of his message is given here in verse 2. However, the rendering found in many of our translations, namely, "Repent"—thus A.V., A.R.V., R.S.V., etc.—is probably not the best. It has been called *a.* "infelicitous" (W. D. Chamberlain), *b.* a rendering that "does not do justice to the original, since it gives undue prominence to the emotional element" (L. Berkhof), *c.* "a hopeless mistranslation" (A. T. Robertson), and even *d.* "the worst translation in the New Testament" (J. A. Broadus). I agree with *a.* and

---

199 See p. 150.
200 See L. H. Grollenberg, *op. cit.,* map 2 opposite p. 11; also plate 25 on p. 16.
201 Thus literally in the original: ἡ περίχωρος τοῦ Ἰορδάνου. See also R. W. Funk, "The Wilderness," *JBL* LXXVIII, Part III (Sept., 1959), pp. 205-214.

b., but I find *c.* and *d.* too harsh. It is not as bad as all that! The idea of *repentance* is definitely included in the Baptist's terse admonition. Genuine sorrow for sin and an earnest resolution to break with the evil past is even emphasized (see especially 3:6 and Luke 3:13, 14). But repentance, though basic, is only one side of the picture. It might be called the negative aspect. The positive is fruit-bearing (Matt. 3:8, 10). The word used in the original[202] looks forward as well as backward. Therefore the rendering "be converted" is probably better than "repent." Conversion, moreover, affects not only the emotions but also the mind and the will. In the original the word used by the Baptist indicates *a radical change of mind and heart that leads to a complete turnabout of life.*[203] Cf. II Cor. 7:8-10; II Tim. 2:25. Does not this insistence on conversion remind one of Elijah (I Kings 18:18, 21, 37; Mal. 4:5, 6; Matt. 11:14; 17:12, 13; Mark 9:11-13; Luke 1:17)?

It should be stressed that although John attached considerable importance to baptism, baptized many, and was therefore called "the Baptist," he did not consider this rite to have any saving significance apart from the fundamental change of life indicated by conversion. It is on the latter that he placed the greatest emphasis (see especially verses 7, 8).

To the words "Be converted" John adds, **for the kingdom of heaven is at hand.** This "kingdom of heaven" concept will be discussed at greater length in connection with 4:23. For the present it should suffice to state that John meant that the dispensation in which, through the fulfilment of the Messianic prophecies (see pp. 80, 81), heaven's (i.e., God's) reign in the hearts and lives of men would begin to assert itself far more powerfully than ever before, was about to begin; in a sense, had even now arrived. Great blessings were in store for all those who, by sovereign grace, would confess and forsake their sins and would begin to live to God's glory. On the other hand, doom was about to overtake the impenitent. As sovereign Lord, God was about to assert himself most emphatically both for salvation and for damnation. The Baptist emphasized the latter (verses 7, 8, 10-12), though he certainly did not omit the former (verse 12). In order to escape punishment and obtain the blessing men should undergo the radical change already described.

Matthew continues: **3. It was of him that the prophet Isaiah spoke when he said,**

---

[202] μετανοεῖτε, sec. per. pl. present imperative of μετανοέω. The verb occurs five times in Matt. (3:2; 4:17; 11:20, 21; 12:41), twice in Mark, nine times in Luke, five times in Acts, once in II Cor. (12:21), and eleven times in the book of Rev. The cognate noun μετάνοια is also of frequent occurrence, beginning with Matt. 3:8, 11.

[203] See W. D. Chamberlain, *The Meaning of Repentance*, Philadelphia, 1943, p. 22. B. B. Warfield defines μετάνοια as "the inner change of mind which regret induces and which itself induces a reformed life" *Biblical and Theological Studies*, Philadelphia, 1952, p. 366.

A voice of one crying in the wilderness:
Make ready the way of the Lord,
Make straight his paths. [204]

Isa. 40:3-5 symbolically pictures the approach of Jehovah for the purpose of leading the procession of Jews who will be returning joyfully to their homeland after long years of captivity. In the Syrian desert, between Babylonia and Palestine, the way must be prepared for the Lord's coming. So, a herald cries out to the people,

In the wilderness make ready the way of the Lord,
Make straight in the desert a highway for our God.

This figure of the herald is by Matthew applied to John, as Christ's herald. The Baptist, by saying, "I am the voice, . . ." shows that he agrees with this interpretation (John 1:23). So does Jesus himself (Matt. 11:10). This shows that the deliverance granted to the Jews when, in the latter part of the sixth century B.C. and afterward, they returned to their own country was but a type of that far more glorious liberation in store for all who accept Christ as their Savior and Lord. In other words, Isaiah's prophecy regarding the voice that cried out lacked *total* fulfilment until both Messiah's forerunner and also the Lord himself had arrived on the scene. [205]

The appropriate character of the application of Isa. 40:3 to John the Baptist is evident from the following: *a.* John was preaching in the wilderness (verse 1); and *b.* the task assigned to him from the days of his infancy (Luke 1:76, 77), yes even earlier (Luke 1:17; Mal. 3:1), was exactly this, namely, to be Messiah's herald or way-preparer. He was to be the Lord's "voice" to the people, *all of* that but *not more than* (cf. John 3:22-30). As such he must not only announce Christ's approach and presence but also urge the people *to prepare the way* of the Lord, that is, by God's grace and power to effect a complete change of mind and heart (see verse 2). This implies that they must *make straight his paths,* meaning that they must provide the Lord with a ready access into their hearts and lives. They must *make straight* whatever was crooked, *not in line with* God's holy will. They must clear away all the obstacles which they had thrown into his path; such

---

[204] See also p. 34. In the Gospels (Matt. 3:3; Mark 1:3; Luke 3:4) and in the considerably different Septuagint text the phrase "in the wilderness" modifies "of one crying," and not "make ready," as it does in the masoretic accentuation of the Hebrew text of Isa. 40:3, the latter construction being also supported by the parallelism: "in the wilderness make ready" and "make straight in the desert." However, this difference between the Gospels and the Hebrew text is unimportant, for it is natural to assume that the wilderness crier, as the mouthpiece of the One who sent him, wants a way to be cleared in the wilderness.

[205] The fact that what is said of *Jehovah* in the Old Testament is referred to *Christ* in the New should cause no surprise. For similar instances of this transition from Jehovah to Christ see Exod. 13:21, cf. I Cor. 10:4; Isa. 6:1, cf. John 12:41; Ps. 68:18, cf. Eph. 4:8; and Ps. 102:25-27, cf. Heb. 1:10-12. It is in Immanuel that Jehovah comes to dwell with his people.

obstructions as self-righteousness and smug complacency ("We have Abraham as our father," verse 9), greed, cruelty, slander, etc. (Luke 3:13, 14).

It is evident that, both in Isaiah and in John's preaching as recorded by Matthew, "the wilderness" through which a path must be made ready for the Lord is in the final analysis the people's heart, inclined to all evil. Though the literal meaning is not absent, it is subsumed into the figurative. The root idea is indeed the actual desert. "But the very sight of the [literal] wilderness must have had a powerful effect on stupid and hardened men, leading them to perceive that they were in a state of death, and to accept the promise of salvation that had been held out to them" (John Calvin on Matt. 3:3).

The manner of life of John the Baptist is described as follows: 4. **Now this John wore a garment made of camel's hair, and a leather belt around his waist, and his food was locusts and wild honey.** John's long, flowing garment, woven from camel's hair, reminds us somewhat of Elijah's mantle, though there is a difference in the description (cf. Matt. 3:4 with II Kings 1:8). Such rugged apparel may have been regarded as symbolic of the prophetic office. Zech. 13:4 (cf. I Sam. 28:14) seems to point in that direction. At any rate, such rough garb was fit for desert wear. It was durable and economical. Jesus makes special mention of the fact that John did not wear fine clothes (Matt. 11:8). He had not been raised as a Little Lord Fauntleroy, and never became a dandy. The Baptist's rough robe matched his message. Imagine a man "clothed in soft raiment" (Matt. 11:8) being a "Bussprediger"![206] Coarse apparel befitted this stern preacher. The leather belt fastened at the waist not only kept the loose robe from blowing and tearing apart but also enabled it to be tucked up to facilitate walking. In this connection see also N.T.C. on Eph. 6:14.

John's food was as simple as was his clothing. He subsisted on locusts and wild honey, evidently such fare as could be found in the wilderness. Honey, the kind that is found in the wild, presents no problem. It was not just a sweetener (sugar, as we now know it, being then rather rare) but an article of food. In the wilderness it could be found under rocks or in crevices under the rocks (Deut. 32:13). The role which wild honey played in the stories of Samson (Judg. 14:8, 9, 18) and of Jonathan (I Sam. 14:25, 26, 29) is too well-known to need elaboration.

But *locusts!* It is entirely possible that one shudders to think of actually *eating* them, their legs and wings having been discarded, their bodies roasted or baked, a little salt added. Nevertheless, it is clear from Lev. 11:22 that the Lord *permitted*—and by implication *encouraged*—the Israelites to eat four kinds of insects which we in North America would popularly call "locusts."

---

[206] A preacher of repentance. Repentance, as was indicated earlier (p. 197), was certainly *included* in John's message. It was even basic.

Even today certain Arabian tribes relish them. And why not? The Latin saying, *"De gustibus non disputandum est"* ("One should not argue about taste") still holds. Those who enjoy shrimp, mussel, oyster, and frog-leg should not find fault with those who eat the locust. See also p. 218.

It is, however, not necessary to conclude that verse 4 gives us a complete summary of the Baptist's diet. The main point is that by means of his simple mode of life, evident with respect to both food and clothing, he was a living protest against all selfishness and self-indulgence, hence also against that frivolousness, carelessness, and false security with which many people were rushing toward their doom, and were doing this with the judgment so near at hand (see verses 7, 10, 12; cf. Matt. 24:37-39; and Luke 17:27-29).

John's energetic and courageous preaching was effective: **5. Then went out to him Jerusalem, all Judea, and the whole Jordan neighborhood.** In very large numbers the Jerusalem population, the residents of Judea in general, and those living on either side of the Jordan (see on verse 1) went out to see and hear John. "Everybody" took him to be a prophet (Matt. 21:26). Continued: **6. Confessing their sins they were baptized by him in the Jordan River.** Without confession of sins no baptism! For those who truthfully repented of their evil state and wicked conduct baptism, never an independently operating charisma, was a visible sign and seal of invisible grace (cf. Rom. 4:11), the grace of the forgiveness of sins and adoption into God's own family.

Contrary to the opinion of some,[207] who believe that there was no connection between proselyte baptism—i.e., the baptism of non-Jews converted to the Jewish religion—and the baptism of John, the opposite theory would seem to have the weight of evidence on its side. Rabbi Hillel may be confidently dated as having lived during the last half of the first century B.C. and the first quarter of the first century A.D. Rabbi Shammai was his contemporary. Their respective followers gave contradictory answers to the question, "Is it possible for a non-Jew who becomes a proselyte on the evening before the Passover to partake of the paschal meal?" The school of Shammai answered that such a convert "must take a bath" and may then take part. The school of Hillel denied this. Is it not reasonable to believe that these contradictory answers are traceable to the two opposing teachers? It would seem, therefore, that proselyte baptism preceded the baptism advocated and administered by John the Baptist. Also for another reason it is difficult to believe that John's baptism and the immediately following Christian baptism,[208] symbolizing in each case a once-for-all radical change of life, historically *preceded* proselyte baptism. Is it at all conceivable that

---

[207] e.g., Lenski, *op. cit.,* p. 99.
[208] For the relation between the baptism of John and Christian baptism see L. Berkhof, *Systematic Theology,* pp. 623, 624. Aptly F. F. Bruce calls the one that of expectation; the other, that of fulfilment.

the latter, as a Jewish ritual, would be copied by the Jews from something resembling it among the Christians, their bitter enemies? Conclusion: "Proselyte baptism must have preceded Christian baptism."[209]

As already implied, proselyte baptism was not a constantly repeated ceremonial rite but a once-for-all legal act of reception into the religious fellowship of Judaism. Accordingly, when similarly John the Baptist urged upon the Jews that they be converted and be baptized they must have been aware of the fact that such a baptism, if properly received, would symbolize a definite and public renunciation of their former mode of life. What was new and startling for the Baptist's audience was not the rite of baptism as such, as a symbol of radical change, but rather the fact that *such a fundamental transformation and its sign and seal were required* not only as in proselyte baptism, of Gentiles who adopted the Jewish religion, but *even of the children of Abraham! They, too, were filthy! They, too, must acknowledge this openly! They, too, must undergo a basic turnabout in mind and heart!*

Yet, many confessed their sins and were baptized in the Jordan River. What percentage of them accepted baptism in good conscience, and what proportion did not do so with genuine sorrow of heart, we are of course unable to judge. That there was definite danger of hypocrisy is evident from verse 7. **But when he saw many of the Pharisees and Sadducees coming for baptism**[210] **he said to them, Y o u offspring of vipers!**

Pharisees and Sadducees
Their Origin

The exact manner in which, and the exact date when, these parties rose is obscure. There is reason to believe, however, that the Pharisees were the successors of the ḥasidhim, i.e., the Pious or Saints. The latter were those Jews who, during and even prior to the Maccabean revolt (see pp. 127, 157), had opposed the adoption of Greek culture and customs. It is understandable that as long as the Maccabeans in their heroic struggle were chiefly motivated by religious principles they would have the full support of the ḥasidhim; but that when, especially during the days of John Hyrcanus and those who followed him, the emphasis of the Jewish rulers was shifted from the spiritual to the secular sphere, the ḥasidhim would either lose interest and withdraw themselves or else would actively oppose the descendants of the very people whom they had formerly supported. The Pharisees, meaning Separatists, may well have been, in their origin, the reformed or reorganized ḥasidhim, the ḥasidhim under another name. They separated themselves not

---

[209] For this reasoning see Th.D.N.T., A. Oepke, art., βάπτω Vol. I, p. 535; K. G. Kuhn, art., προσήλυτος, Vol. VI, pp. 738, 739.

[210] Or: "for his baptism," but the textual evidence for this variant does not appear to be decisive. Essentially it makes no difference.

only from the heathen, from publicans and from sinners, but even in general, from the indifferent Jewish mutltitudes, whom they derisively dubbed "the people who do not know the law" (John 7:49). They tried hard not to become contaminated or defiled by associating with anyone or anything that would render them ceremonially unclean.

The Sadducees were in many ways the very opposites of the Pharisees. They were the compromisers, the men who, though ostensibly still clinging to the law of God, were not really hostile to the spread of Hellenism. They were the sacerdotal party, the party to which the highpriests generally belonged. It is not surprising that it became popular to derive the name Sadducees from Zadok (LXX:Sadok), an etymology that may be correct. This Zadok was the man who during David's reign shared the highpriestly office with Abiathar (I Sam. 8:17; 15:24; I Kings 1:35), and was made sole highpriest by Solomon (I Kings 2:35). Until the days of the Maccabees the descendants of Zadok had retained the highpriesthood.

Their Mutual Opposition

One important point on which the two parties clashed is clearly brought out in Acts 23:6-8:

"Paul, realizing that one section of the Sanhedrin were Sadducees and the other Pharisees, raised his voice and said to them, 'Brothers, I am a Pharisee and the son of Pharisees. It is with respect to the hope of the resurrection of the dead that I am being examined.' And when he had said this there arose a dissension between the Pharisees and the Sadducees, and the assembly was divided. For the Sadducees say that there is no resurrection or angel or spirit, but the Pharisees accept them all." From Josephus we learn that the Sadducees denied the immortality of the soul along with the resurrection of the body. They held that the soul perished when the body died.

Another point on which the two went in opposite directions had to do with the canon. The Pharisees recognized two criteria or standards for doctrine and discipline: the written Old Testament and the oral traditions. As to the latter, they believed that these additions to—but in reality often rather peculiar interpretations of—the written law had been given by Moses to the elders and had by the latter been transmitted orally down through the generations. They made so much of these traditions that often, by means of their emphasis upon them, they "made the word of God of no effect" (Matt. 15:6; Mark 7:13). The Sadducees, on the contrary, accepted nothing but Scripture. They esteemed the Pentateuch above the prophets, etc.

Finally, if Josephus, who at the age of nineteen had publicly joined the Pharisees, can be trusted, there was still another sharp contrast: the Pharisees believed not only in man's freedom and responsibility with respect to his own actions but also in the divine decree; the Sadducees rejected the decree

(Josephus, *Jewish War* II.162-166; *Antiquities* XIII.171-173, 297, 298; XVIII.12-17).

Their Co-operation

Though they differed so strikingly, yet basically many of these Pharisees and Sadducees were in perfect agreement, for in the final analysis they both tried to attain security by their own efforts: whether this security consisted in earthly possessions on *this* side of the grave, as with the Sadducees, many of whom were rich landowners and/or beneficiaries of the trade carried on in the temple precincts; or, on the *other* side (at least *also* on the other side), as with the Pharisees, who were striving with all their might to work their way into heaven. Religion in both cases was *outward* conformity, through self-effort, to a certain standard.

It should not be a matter of surprise, therefore, that when Jesus, with his emphasis on the religion of the heart and on God as the sole Author of salvation, appeared upon the scene of history he was rejected by both groups: by the Pharisees because he denounced them since they cleansed only the outside of the cup or platter (Matt. 23:25), and, while tithing mint, anise, and cummin, neglected the weightier matters of the law: "justice, and mercy, and fidelity" (23:23); and by the Sadducees because, by means of the temple-cleansing, he exposed their money-grabbing racket, and probably also because they considered his claims to pose a threat to the status quo of the nation and therefore to their own influential position. Besides, it is understandable that both Pharisees and Sadducees envied Jesus (Matt. 27:18).

So at last Pharisees and Sadducees co-operate to bring about his death (16:1, 6, 11; 22:15, 23; 26:3, 4, 59; 27:20). Even afterward they combine in their attempt to prevent belief in his resurrection (27:62). It is not strange, therefore, that Jesus would at times in one breath condemn both groups (16:6 ff).

Now according to our present passage (3:7) Pharisees and Sadducees are approaching John with a request that he baptize them. This may seem strange. Though not all commentators agree, yet in the light of all that has been said about the two groups, their behavior in the present instance can probably best be explained by their selfishness. They did not wish to lose their hold on the multitudes who were flocking to John to be baptized. If this was the place where the action was they wanted to be part of it, in order, if possible, to assume leadership. But did not submission to the rite of baptism imply confession of sin? Well, if necessary they were even willing to "stoop to conquer." Of course, they were not sincere, not really penitent at all nor actually desirous to undergo a radical change of mind and heart. They were deceitful, hypocritical. Cf. Matt. 16:1; 22:15.

It is in this light that we can understand the Baptist's stern rebuke, "Y o u offspring of vipers." John was acquainted with these desert snakes. Though rather small in size they were very *deceitful*. At times it was easy to mistake them for dead branches. Suddenly, however, they would strike and cling (cf. Acts 28:3). The comparison was apt, therefore. [211] Is not Satan, that deceiver (John 8:44), also called a *serpent* (Rev. 12:9; 20:2)? Are they not his tools?

John adds, **Who warned y o u to escape from the approaching (outpouring of) wrath?** In this connection the following ideas deserve attention:

First, this wrath or settled indignation, rests upon unregenerate man by nature (Eph. 2:3). It pertains even to the present (John 3:18, 36; Rom. 1:18).

Secondly, the final outpouring of this wrath is reserved for the future (Eph. 5:6; Col. 3:6; II Thess. 1:8, 9; Rev. 14:10).

Thirdly, this final manifestation of wrath (Zeph. 1:15; 2:2) is connected with the (second) coming of the Messiah (Mal. 3:2, 3; 4:1, 5).

Fourthly, without genuine conversion man cannot escape it: "Who warned y o u to escape. . . .?" This probably means, "Who deluded y o u into thinking that it is possible to evade God, and encouraged y o u to try it?" Cf. Ps. 139; Jonah 1:3.

Fifthly, for the true penitent there is indeed a way of escape: **8. Bear fruit therefore in keeping with conversion.** As pointed out earlier (see on verse 2), repentance, if it is to be genuine, must be accompanied by fruit-bearing. A merely outward confession of sin will never do. A mere desire to be baptized, as if this rite were a wonder-working charm, has no positive value. There must be that inward change which expresses itself outwardly in God-glorifying conduct, fruit-bearing *in keeping with* conversion. According to Luke 3:10-14 this fruit-bearing must include such items as generosity, fairness, thoughtfulness, and contentment; according to Matt. 23:23, justice, mercy, and faith; and in view of the manner in which the Baptist descriptively addresses these Pharisees and Sadducees ("Y o u offspring of vipers"), there must be uprightness. On fruit-bearing see also Matt. 5:20-23; 7:16-19; 12:33; 13:8, 23; 16:6, 11, 12; ch. 23; Luke 13:6-9; John 15:1-16; Gal. 5:22, 23; Eph. 5:9; Phil. 1:22; 4:17; Col. 1:6; Heb. 12:11; 13:15; and James 3:18.

The deplorable lack of fruit-bearing on the part of the addressed is evident also from verse 9. . . **and do not presume to say to yourselves, We have**

---

[211] The idea that these Pharisees and Sadducees were called "offspring of vipers," rather than simply "vipers," because they had entered into the sin of their fathers (Lenski, *op. cit.*, p. 103) is probably an over-refinement. The expression "offspring of vipers" may well be in line with other similar Semitisms; such as, "sons of the prophets," "sons of Belial," "daughters of music," etc. Here in 3:7 the rendering "You snakes" (*Good News for Modern Man*) may not be wrong.

Abraham as our father, for I tell y o u that God is able to raise up children for Abraham out of these stones here. The reason why these Pharisees and Sadducees were headed for damnation was that for their eternal security they were relying on their descent from Abraham. Cf. Gal. 3:1-9 and see N.T.C. on those verses. John the Baptist was fully aware of the fact that physical descent from Abraham did not guarantee being a true son of Abraham. He also knew that entirely apart from such pedigree God could give sons to Abraham. The God who was able to create Adam out of the dust of the ground was also able to make true sons of Abraham out of the desert stones to which John probably pointed. Probable symbolical overtone: He can change hearts of stone into obedient hearts (Ezek. 36:26), entirely regardless of the nationality of these hearts of stone.

As far as salvation was concerned, the old distinctions were gradually disappearing. This does not mean that in the order in which this salvation was being proclaimed and in which the church was being gathered there was no distinction. The historical sequence, a reflection of God's plan from eternity, certainly was "to the Jew first and also to the Greek" (Rom. 1:16; cf. Acts 13:46; Rom. 3:1, 2; 9:1-5). This order is also clear from Matthew's Gospel (10:6; 15:24). But the beginning of a new day, a day in which there would be "no distinction between Jew and Greek" was dawning. See Matt. 2:1-12; 8:11, 12; 22:1-14; 28:19, 20; Acts 10:34-48; Rom. 9:7, 8; 10:12, 13; I Cor. 7:19; Gal. 3:7, 16, 17, 29; 4:21-31; 6:15, 16; Eph. 2:14-18; Phil. 3:2, 3; Col. 3:11; and Rev. 7:9, 14, 15.

As to the impenitent, in verse 10 John the Baptist continues: **Already** [212] **the axe is laid at the root of the trees.** Judgment is at hand. The axe lies right in front of ($\pi\rho\delta\varsigma$) or, as we would say, "at" the root, with sinister intent, ready to hew down one tree after another. *Right now,* therefore, is the proper moment to repent and to believe. In this connection see also Ps. 95:7, 8; Isa. 55:6; Luke 13:7, 9; 17:32; John 15:6; Rom. 13:11; II Cor. 6:2; I John 2:18; Rev. 1:3. Continued: . . . **every tree therefore that does not bear good fruit is cut down and thrown into the fire.** The question might be asked, "But was the day of the final manifestation of God's wrath upon the wicked actually that close? Is it not true that many centuries have passed by since the Baptist spoke these words, and still the Lord has not returned for judgment?" The following facts should be borne in mind:

First, John reminds one of the Old Testament prophet who, in speaking about the last days or the Messianic age would at times look upon the future as a traveler does on a distant mountain range. He fancies that one mountain top rises up right behind the other, when in reality the two are miles apart. The two comings of Christ are viewed as if they were one. Thus we read "A shoot shall come forth out of the stock of Jesse . . . and he shall smite the

---

[212] Note forward position of $\mathring{\eta}\delta\eta$.

earth" (Isa. 11:1-4). "Jehovah has anointed me to preach good tidings to the meek. He has sent me to bind up the broken-hearted, to proclaim liberty to the captives and . . . the day of vengeance of our God" (Isa. 61:1, 2). "I will pour out my Spirit upon all flesh, and y o u r sons and y o u r daughters shall prophesy, y o u r old men shall dream dreams, and y o u r young men shall see visions. . . . The sun shall be turned into darkness, and the moon into blood, before the great and terrible day of Jehovah arrives" (Joel 3:28-31). Cf. Mal. 3:1, 2. This has been called "prophetic foreshortening."

Secondly, Jerusalem's fall (A.D. 70) was drawing perilously near, and foreshadowed the final judgment.

Thirdly, impenitence has a tendency of hardening a person, so that often he is left in his present lost condition. Without genuine repentance death and the judgment are for him irrevocable and "at the door."

Fourthly, "one day is with the Lord as a thousand years, and a thousand years as one day" (II Peter 3:8).

Fifthly, as the references given above (p. 205, beginning with Ps. 95:7, 8) indicate, John was by no means the only one who emphasized the imminence of the judgment and/or the need of becoming converted right now. Therefore, if on this score we find fault with the Baptist we would also have to blame the psalmists, the prophets, the apostles, and even the Lord himself! Surely, no true believer is ready to do this.

Sixthly, all this does not necessarily mean that the Baptist himself always saw the present and the future in true perspective. See on 11:1-3. It only means that the Holy Spirit guided him so that *in his actual preaching as here recorded* he had a perfect right to say what he said.

The "fire" into which the unfruitful trees are cast is evidently a symbol of the final outpouring of God's wrath upon the wicked. See also Mal. 4:1; Matt. 13:40; John 15:6. Jesus spoke about "the Gehenna of fire" (Matt. 5:22, 29; 18:9; Mark 9:47). This fire is unquenchable (Matt. 3:12; 18:8; Mark 9:43; Luke 3:17). The point is not merely that there is always a fire burning in Gehenna but that God burns the wicked with unquenchable fire, the fire that has been prepared for them as well as for the devil and his angels (Matt. 3:12; 25:41). [213]

The question might be asked, "If, then, the Baptist was, to a considerable degree, a preacher of hell and damnation, how was it that by divine direction he was called "John" (Luke 1:13), that is, "Jehovah is *gracious*"? Answer: Warning people that doom is impending and will certainly overtake them unless they repent and believe, is not this a gracious act? Does it not indicate

---

[213] Further questions as to the meaning of Gehenna and of Hades, as to total annihilation or everlasting punishment, as to whether this fire is to be taken literally or symbolically, as to whether God is present in, or absent from, hell, etc., are answered by the author in *The Bible on the Life Hereafter*, pp. 79-87; 195-199. See also below, on 3:12 and on 5:22, 29.

that God is not cruel, not eager to punish, but longsuffering? Did he not show this patience to the antediluvians (Gen. 6:3; I Peter 3:20); Lot (Gen. 19:12-22); David (II Sam. 23:5); the Israelites (Exod. 33:12-17; Isa. 5:1, 2; 63:9; Jer. 8:20; Ezek. 10:19—the lingering of the throne chariot—; 18:23; 33:11); and Simon Peter (John 21:15-17)? Is not that same divine attribute gloriously revealed in the parable of The Barren Fig Tree (Luke 13:8, "Let it alone this year also"); in II Peter 3:9 ("God is longsuffering toward y o u"); in Rom. 9:22 ("God endured with much longsuffering"); in Rev. 2:21 ("I gave her time to repent"); and in Rev. 8:1 ("silence in heaven for about half an hour")?

Turning now to the entire multitude, John continues: **11. I on my part baptize y o u with water with a view to conversion.** But is not this phrase "with a view to conversion" a contradiction of the idea that a man must already have been converted before he can be baptized, a truth clearly implied in verses 6-10? Answer: Not at all, for, by means of baptism, true conversion is powerfully stimulated and increased. The person who in the proper manner—that is, with a pledge to God proceeding from a clear conscience (I Peter 3:21)—receives baptism, understanding the meaning of the outward sign and seal, will *all the more heartily* out of gratitude yield himself to God. Moreover, how could reflection on the adopting, pardoning, and cleansing grace of God, as symbolized by the sign and seal of baptism, have any different effect? For such a person the outward sign and seal applied to the body, and the inward grace applied to the heart, go together. Among Biblical passages that prove this point are: "I will sprinkle clean water upon you, and y o u shall be clean . . . a new heart also will I give y o u, and a new spirit will I put within y o u" (Ezek. 36:25, 26); "Let us draw near with a true heart and fullness of faith, having our hearts sprinkled from an evil conscience, and our bodies washed with pure water" (Heb. 10:22).

This twofold aspect of conversion, *a.* as already present before the actual baptism, and *b.* as augmented by means of it, is also beautifully expressed in several Forms for the Baptism of Adults, from one of which the following words are here quoted:

"It [Baptism] becomes an effectual means of salvation, not from any virtue in it, or in him that doth administer it, but only by the blessing of Christ, and the working of his Spirit in them that by faith receive it" (The Constitution of the Presbyterian Church in the United States of America, Philadelphia, 1941, p. 448).

However, in the final analysis this rich result is not brought about by the person who administers the rite of baptism, not even if that person's name be John the Baptist. All John can do is urge upon his hearers the necessity of conversion. As to baptism, he can supply the sign, but it will take One mightier than John to supply the thing signified. Hence, after saying, "I on my part baptize y o u with water with a view to conversion," he continues, but he who is coming behind me is mightier than I—I am not fit to remove his sandals—; he will baptize y o u with the Holy Spirit and with fire. It was necessary for John to draw this contrast, for the people were already beginning to wonder whether perhaps he might not himself be the Christ (Luke 3:15; cf. John 1:19, 20; 3:25-36). The Baptist, therefore, is saying that the contrast between himself and the One who was chronologically coming behind him was so great that he, John, was not even worthy *to unfasten* (this only in Mark 1:7 and Luke 3:16), *remove and carry away* [214] his Successor's sandals; that is, that to One so great he was not even worthy to render the services of a slave. It was true that on life's pathway, not only in his birth but also in beginning his public ministry, Jesus had come behind John (Luke 1:26, 36; 3:23). But between Christ and the Baptist there was a qualitative difference as between the Infinite and the finite, the eternal and the temporal, the original light of the sun and the reflected light of the moon (cf. John 1:15-17).

John baptizes with water; Jesus will baptize with the Spirit. [215] He will cause his Spirit and the latter's gifts to come upon his followers (Acts 1:8), be poured out on them (Acts 2:17, 33), fall upon them (Acts 10:44; 11:15).

Now it is true that whenever a person is drawn out of the darkness into God's marvelous light he is being baptized with the Holy Spirit and with fire. Thus Calvin in his comments on Matt. 3:11 remarks that it was Christ who bestows the Spirit of regeneration, and that, like fire, this Spirit purifies us by removing our pollution. However, according to Christ's own words (Acts 1:5, 8), remembered by Peter (Acts 11:16), *in a special sense* this prediction was fulfilled on the day of Pentecost and the era which it introduced. It was then that, through the coming of the Spirit, the minds of Christ's followers were enriched with unprecedented illumination (I John 2:20); their wills strengthened, like never before, with contagious animation (Acts 4:13, 19, 20, 33; 5:29); and their hearts flooded with warm affection to a degree previously unheard of (Acts 2:44-47; 3:6; 4:32).

The mention of *fire* ("He will baptize y o u with the Holy Spirit and with fire") fits this application to Pentecost, when "there appeared to them divided tongues as of fire, resting on each one of them" (Acts 2:3). The flame illumines. Fire cleanses. The Spirit does both. Nevertheless, it would appear from the context (both before and after; see verses 10 and 12) and from Joel's Pentecost prophecy (Joel 2:30; cf. Acts 2:19), considered in *its* context (see Joel 2:31), that the ultimate fulfilment of the Baptist's words

---

214 For the various uses of the verb βαστάζω see N.T.C. on Gal., p. 232, footnote 171.

215 Literally "with Spirit." The word πνεύματι like ὕδατι, is anarthrous, to bring out as sharply as possible the contrast between *a*. what John himself was doing, and *b*. what Christ would do through the Spirit, and thus to emphasize the incomparable quality of the Spirit's work.

awaits Christ's glorious return to cleanse the earth with fire (II Peter 3:7, 12; cf. Mal. 3:2; II Thess. 1:8).

Often in Scripture fire symbolizes *wrath*. [216] But fire is also indicative of the work of *grace* (Isa. 6:6, 7; Zech. 13:9; Mal. 3:3; I Peter 1:7). It is not strange, therefore, that this term can be used both in a favorable sense, to indicate the blessings of Pentecost and the new dispensation, and in an unfavorable sense, to indicate the terrors of the coming judgment day. It is Christ who both *purifies* the righteous and *purges* the earth of its dross, the wicked. Moreover, if the Old Testament prophets, as will be shown (p. 467), would often, by means of prophetic foreshortening, combine the events pertaining to Christ's first coming (taken in its comprehensive sense, including even Pentecost) with those of the second, why cannot that same feature be ascribed also to the style of John the Baptist, who resembled these prophets in so many ways? It is clear, therefore, that the case for the interpretation according to which the word *fire* here in 3:11 refers both to Pentecost and to the final judgment is strong. [217]

The reasonable character of the explanation, according to which the baptism with fire includes a reference to the final judgment, is also evident from verse 12, which likewise refers to that great day. **His winnowing shovel is in his hand, and he will thoroughly clear his threshing floor.** The underlying figure is that of a threshing floor where winnowing is taking place. Such a floor is either natural or artificial. If the former, it is the surface of a flat rock on top of a hill, exposed to the wind. If the latter, it is a similarly exposed area, about thirty to fifty feet in diameter, which has been prepared by clearing the soil of stones, wetting it down, and then packing it hard and smooth, causing it to slope slightly upward along the rim, and surrounding it with a border of stones to keep the grain inside. First, the sheaves of grain (barley or wheat) that have been spread out in this area are threshed by oxen, pulling a sled the bottom of which is studded with stones whereby the kernels of grain are separated from the stalks. The chaff (whatever remains of the kernels' hard coat, dust, dirt, small pieces of straw) is, however, still clinging to the kernels. Now the winnowing, to which verse 12 refers, begins. Bunch by bunch the threshed grain is tossed into the air by means of a shovel equipped with two or more prongs, letting the afternoon breeze, generally sweeping in from the Mediterranean from May through September, blow away the chaff. The heavier grain kernels fall straight down upon the

---

[216] See the passages listed on p. 211, beginning with Deut. 9:3.

[217] With respect to this question commentators are divided into three groups: *a.* those who interpret "fire" as a reference to the final judgment only (e.g., F. W. Grosheide); *b.* those who connect it exclusively with Pentecost (e.g., R. C. H. Lenski); and *c.* those who link it with both (e.g., H. N. Ridderbos). As I see it, for the reasons given, the latter position is correct.

threshing floor. *Thus grain and chaff are separated.* The work of winnowing does not stop until the threshing floor has been thoroughly cleared.

Thus also Christ at his return will thoroughly clear the area where the judgment will take place. No one will escape detection. Even now he is fully equipped with all that is needed to perform the task of separating the good from the bad. [218]

Continued: **He will gather his grain into the granary, but the chaff he will consume with unquenchable fire.** Returning now to the underlying figure, the threshed and winnowed grain is brought to the granary; literally, *the place where things are put* (or: *stored*) *away.*

It is *stored away* because it is regarded as being very valuable, very precious. From the underlying figure we proceed to the reality. Even *the death of believers* is described in Scripture in a very comforting manner. It is "precious in the sight of Jehovah" (Ps. 116:15); "a being carried away by the angels into Abraham's bosom" (Luke 16:22); "a going to Paradise" (Luke 23:43); "a blessed departure" (Phil. 1:23); "a being at home with the Lord" (II Cor. 5:8); "a gain" (Phil. 1:21); "better by far" (Phil. 1:23); and "a falling asleep in the Lord" (John 11:11; I Thess. 4:13). Then surely *the final stage* in the glorification of God's children, both body and soul now participating in this bliss, will be most precious: a going to "the house with many mansions" (John 14:2), a being welcomed to the very presence of Christ ("I will come again and will take y o u to be face to face with me, in order that where I am y o u may be also," John 14:3), a living forever in the new heaven and earth from which every stain of sin and every trace of the curse will have been removed; in which righteousness dwells (II Peter 3:13); in which "God will dwell with them, and they shall be his people, and he himself shall be with them and be their God, wiping away every tear from their eyes, etc." (Rev. 21:1-5); and in which the prophecy of Isa. 11:6-9 ("The wolf shall dwell with the lamb, etc.") and of Rev. 21:9—22:5 (the new Jerusalem) will reach its *ultimate* fulfilment.

Back to the underlying figure once more. From the grain we now turn to the chaff. This, having dropped down at a place, or places, away from the grain, is collected and burned. So also the wicked, having been separated from the good, will be cast into hell, the place of unquenchable fire. Their punishment is unending. The point is not merely that there is always a fire burning in Gehenna but that the wicked are burned with unquenchable fire, the fire that has been prepared for them as well as for the devil and his angels (Matt. 25:41). Their worm never dies (Mark 9:48). Their shame is everlasting

---

[218] Some commentators call attention to the fact that the separation does not take place now but at the close of the dispensation. See Matt. 13:30; Rev. 14:14-20. Though in itself this is true, it is not the point on which the Baptist places the emphasis. He rather stresses the imminence of the judgment ("His winnowing shovel is in his hand"), in order that men may repent and believe.

(Dan. 12:2). So are their bonds (Jude 6, 7). They will be tormented with fire and brimstone . . . and the smoke of their torment ascends forever and ever, so that they have no rest day or night (Rev. 14:9-11; cf. 19:3; 20:10).

In which sense is this "fire" to be understood? Answer: though the idea of a fire which in some sense is physical need not be excluded, yet according to Scripture the literal sense does not exhaust the meaning. Everlasting fire has been prepared "for the devil and his angels." Yet these are *spirits* and cannot be hurt by literal fire. Moreover, Scripture itself points the way to the symbolical meaning; i.e., to the divine *wrath* resting upon the impenitent, and consequently, to their anguish (Deut. 9:3; 32:22; Ps. 11:5, 6; 18:8; 21:9; 89:46; Isa. 5:24, 25; Jer. 4:4; Nah. 1:6; Mal. 3:2; Matt. 5:22; Heb. 10:27; 12:29; II Peter 3:7; Rev. 14:10, 11; 15:2).

The Baptist's warning, dire and dreadful though it may seem, is filled with mercy, as has been explained (see p. 206).

---

13 Then Jesus made his public appearance, (coming) from Galilee to the Jordan, to be baptized by him. 14 But John was trying to prevent him, saying, "It is I who needs to be baptized by you, and you come to me?" 15 But Jesus answered him, "Yield to me this time, for it is proper for us in this way to comply fully with every righteous requirement." Then he yielded to him. 16 And immediately, when Jesus was baptized and stepped up out of the water, look, the heavens were opened and he [John] saw the Spirit · of God descending like a dove and lighting on him. 17 And lo, a voice from heaven · saying, "This is my Son, the Beloved, with whom I am well pleased."

3:13-17 *The Baptism of Jesus*
Cf. Mark 1:9-11; Luke 3:21, 22; John 1:32-34

13. Then Jesus made his public appearance, (coming) from Galilee to the Jordan, to be baptized by him. As to both time and place Matthew records the circumstances of Christ's baptism indefinitely: "then . . . the Jordan." In harmony with the preceding context (verses 1-12) and with what is probably the true interpretation of Luke 3:21, the word "then" probably means, "at the height of John's baptizing activity." As to information gained from other passages with reference to the time here referred to see pp. 150, 196. On the basis of those other passages the conclusion seems warranted that it was probably during the latter part of A.D. 26 or in the early days of the year 27 that Jesus went to John to be baptized by him. [219]

Jesus came "from Galilee" (thus Matthew). Mark is slightly more definite

---

[219] There are those, however, who, on the basis of their interpretation of Luke 3:21, believe that they can supply an additional homiletical detail; namely, that Jesus stood patiently waiting until everybody else had been baptized. He purposely chose to be the last in the line, thereby revealing his humility, as a lesson for all. With Phillips they render Luke 3:21 "when all the people had been baptized." This, however, is putting more meaning into Luke's articular aorist infinitive (ἐν τῷ βαπτισθῆναι) than it can conveniently carry.

by saying "from Nazareth in Galilee." John adds that at this time John was baptizing "in Bethany beyond the Jordan" (1:28), which was probably not located near the Dead Sea but farther north. See N.T.C. on the Gospel according to John, Vol. 1, p. 93.

Jesus' public ministry begins here, the verb "makes his public appearance" in 1:13, being the same as the one used in connection with the beginning of John's labors (verse 1). He came to the Jordan with the definite purpose of being baptized by John. So he steps forward, by word and/or gesture requesting to be baptized.

Verse 14 records John's reaction: **But John was trying to prevent him. . . .** John is shocked. His reasoning was probably somewhat along this line: "What! One so high and holy about *to be baptized?* But certainly not by *me,* a person so immeasurably lower in rank and sanctity. It must not, it cannot be! On the contrary, I should be baptized by him!" So John turns to Jesus, saying, **It is I who needs** [220] **to be baptized by you, and you come to me?** John and Jesus were related (Luke 1:36). John's mother, Elizabeth, was well-informed with respect to Mary's first born son, to whom she had referred as "my Lord" (Luke 1:42, 43). It is hard to believe that she had not conveyed her knowledge to her son. The very fact that the Baptist surmises that the person who had now stepped forward to be baptized was the Messiah about whom he had already spoken (verses 11, 12) made him protest so strenuously.

In view of all this, how must we explain John's subsequent report: "I myself did not know him" (John 1:31)? Does it suffice to say that the Baptist, born and raised in Judea, and having spent these many years in its wilderness (Luke 1:80), may never before have met Jesus, who had been brought up in Galilee? Hardly, for though this may indeed enter into the picture, John 1:33 indicates that when the forerunner said, "I did not know him," he was thinking primarily of something else, something higher than mere physical acquaintanceship. In all probability he meant that it had not as yet been divinely disclosed to him that this person was the very Christ. Nevertheless, a promise had been given him, namely, "He upon whom you see the Spirit descending and remaining, he it is who baptizes with the Holy Spirit."

In his attempt to ward off Jesus' request, John, reasoning that the lesser must be blessed by the greater (cf. Heb. 7:7), not vice versa, gives expression to his consciousness of needing to be baptized by Jesus: "It is I who needs to be baptized by you." Though he has already received the Holy Spirit (Luke

---

[220] In the original "I" is spelled out fully as a separate pronoun, and is in an emphatic position at the beginning of the clause; hence, "It is I." As to "I who needs" as compared with "I who need," this is a matter of personal preference. See B. and C. Evans, *A Dictionary of Contemporary American Usage*, New York, 1957, p. 23.

1:15), he wishes to receive the latter's indwelling and gifts in even greater measure. On the other hand, what is there that *Jesus* does not yet possess and that *he* could receive from the Baptist: "and you come to me?"

15. **But Jesus answered him, Yield to me this time, for it is proper for us in this way to comply fully with every righteous requirement.** [221] This passage shows how Jesus overcame John's scruples. But why did he say, "Yield to me *this time*" and "to comply fully *with every righteous requirement*"? The answer has not been specifically revealed to us. In the light, however, of the entire context and also of certain other relevant passages, as will be indicated, could it not be that Jesus had in mind something on this order: "As a general rule what you say is true, but at this particular moment in your and my life, when I am about to begin my public ministry, it is proper that I by means of baptism *reaffirm* my resolution (cf. Ps. 40:6, 8; Eph. 1:4; Heb. 7:22; I Peter 1:20; Rev. 13:8) 'to take away the sin of the world' (John 1:29). Besides, the promise given *to you* (John 1:33) must be fulfilled, so that you will be able all the more persuasively and adequately to *proclaim* me to the people. For the reasons stated it is proper for us in this way to comply fully with *every righteous requirement;* the righteous requirement that I *reaffirm,* and the righteous requirement that you *baptize* and *proclaim.*" Could it not be that this was what the Lord had in mind?

The objection may be raised that the water of baptism symbolized the removal of filth, that is, sin; and that, since Jesus was sinless, he did not need to be, and could not properly be, baptized. The answer is that he did, after all, have sin, namely *ours.* This answer is given in such passages as Isa. 53:6 ("All we like sheep have gone astray; we have turned every one to his own way; and Jehovah has laid on him the iniquity of us all"); Matt. 20:28; Mark 10:45; John 10:11; II Cor. 5:21; and I Peter 3:18. It must not be overlooked either that by means of what was implied in his own baptism (John 1:29) Jesus validated John's baptisms, for the latter would have been meaningless apart from the former.

The Baptist was deeply impressed by the majesty of the Speaker. He had become convinced that Jesus was right. The objections had been surmounted. Hence, there follows, **Then he yielded to him.**

16. **And immediately, when Jesus was baptized and stepped up out of the water, look, the heavens were opened....!** [222] The mode of baptism,

---

221 Literally, "to fulfil all righteousness."

222 I believe there is a sound reason so to construct the Greek original that the adverb εὐθύς, though grammatically pertaining to ἀνέβη, belongs according to the sense, with the opening of the heavens. Reasons: *a.* It is clear both from this verse and from the next, as well as from Luke 3:21, 22, that the emphasis is here no longer on the baptism but rather on the opening of the heavens and the events that occurred in connection with it; and *b.* what would be the purpose in saying that Jesus did not remain in the water a little while

whether, while Jesus was standing in the Jordan so that his feet were covered with water, the Baptist poured or sprinkled water on his head; or whether his entire body was immersed, is not indicated. It is natural to suppose that he had gone down the river's bank and had at least stepped into the water. Verse 16 informs us that, having been baptized, Jesus stepped up out of the water again. That is all we know. It has not pleased the Holy Spirit to give us any specific details as to the mode of baptism practiced during the period covered by the New Testament.

What *is* important, so important that Matthew directs our special attention to it, by introducing it with "look," is that the heavens were opened. This was not merely a subjective experience in the heart of Jesus. It was definitely a miracle, occurring in full view of all who were present there with John and Jesus. Did not Ezekiel also see the opened heavens (Ezek. 1:1)? Did not Stephen (Acts 7:56)? And the apostle John on Patmos (Rev. 4:1; 11:19; 19:11; cf. Isa. 64:1; II Cor. 12:1-4)? Continued: **and he [John] saw the Spirit of God descending like a dove and lighting on him.** Cf. Mark 1:10; Luke 3:22; John 1:32-34. Suddenly the heavens were "rent asunder," and John saw the Holy Spirit! Of course, the Spirit himself has no body and cannot be seen with physical eyes. But we are distinctly told that it was under the symbolism of a dove that the third Person of the Trinity manifested himself to the Baptist. What was seen physically was a bodily form resembling a dove. It was seen descending on Jesus. It is not clear just why God chose the form of a dove to represent the Holy Spirit. Some commentators point to the *purity* and the gentleness or *graciousness* of the dove, which properties, in an infinite degree, characterize the Spirit, and therefore also Christ (cf. Ps. 68:14; Song of Sol. 2:14; 5:2; Matt. 10:16). Thus equipped and qualified, he was able to carry out the very difficult task which the Father had given him to do. To save us from sin he himself needed to be *pure*. To endure torment, to pardon our iniquities, and to exercise patience with our weaknesses, he needed *gentleness, meekness, graciousness*. This, too, he possessed in an abundant measure, and he told his followers that, by the grace and power of God, they should acquire and exercise these same gifts (Matt. 11:29, 30; 12:19; 21:4, 5; Luke 23:34; II Cor. 10:1; Phil. 2:5-8; I Pete 1:19; 2:21-25; and in the Old Testament: Isa. 40:11; 42:23; 53:7; and Zech. 9:9). The Baptist noticed that the form of a dove, symbolizing the Spirit, *remained* for a while on Jesus (John 1:32, 33). It did not immediately disappear. Did this happen in order to fix in the mind of John, and of the entire church throughout the ages, not only that this Jesus was indeed the Christ but also that the Spirit now rested upon him *abidingly*, fully qualify-

---

but got out immediately? The rendering which I have adopted for this passage corresponds with that of H. N. Ridderbos, *op. cit.*, pp. 62, 64.—As to the reading "were opened *to him*," there is considerable doubt that "to him" was in the autograph.

ing him for his most difficult, yet also most glorious, task? It should be constantly borne in mind that, though Christ's divine nature was not in need of, and was in fact incapable of, being strengthened, the same was not true with respect to his human nature. This could be, and needed to be, strengthened (Matt. 14:23; 17:1-5; 26:36-46; cf. Mark 14:36; John 12:27, 28; and especially Heb. 5:8). [223] The fact that the *anointing* by the Holy Spirit (Ps. 45:7; Isa. 61:1-3; Luke 3:22; 4:1, 18-21) was here given to him, in no way conflicts with his earlier *conception* by the power of this same Spirit (Matt. 1:20; Luke 1:35). The two are in beautiful harmony.

So far we have heard about *the Son's* request to be baptized, and his actual baptism, thereby reaffirming his entire willingness to take upon himself and carry away "the sin of the world" (John 1:29); also about *the Spirit's* descent upon him, qualifying him for a task so tremendous and sublime. It is altogether fitting that the voice of *the Father's* wholehearted approval and delight be added, so that it may become clear that in the work of saving sinners, as in *every* divine work, the three are one. Hence, there follows verse 17. **And lo, a voice from heaven saying, This is my Son, the Beloved, with whom I am well pleased.**

The three are always one; for example, the Son dies for "those whom" (literally, according to the better text, for "that which") the Father has given him (John 10:29); and these are the very ones whom the Spirit brings to glory (John 14:16, 17; 16:14; Rom. 8:26-30). So also here: the three are one. The heavens must be opened, so that Jesus himself may hear the voice, as is the representation in Mark 1:11 and Luke 3:22 (*"Thou art* my Son, the Beloved"), but also so that the Baptist may hear it (hence, *"This is. . . ."*), making him a better witness of the things which he saw and heard (cf. John 1:33, 34). As has already been indicated, in connection with the Son's voluntary reaffirmation of his wholehearted commitment to the task of carrying a burden so infinitely heavy, this voice of *delighted approval* was altogether in place.

Whose voice was it? The Speaker is not named. [224] Neither is this necessary, for the very phraseology ("my Son, the Beloved") identifies the Speaker as being, of course, the Father. Moreover, not only in his official Messianic capacity but also as Son by eternal generation, the One who fully shares the divine essence together with the Father and the Spirit, is he the Father's Beloved (John 1:14; 3:16; 10:17; 17:23). No higher love is possible than the love which the Father cherishes toward his Son. According to the

---

[223] Often, in this connection, reference is also made to Luke 22:42, 43. However, there is a textual problem there.

[224] In connection with the subject of *God's good pleasure* the present is by no means the only passage in which the One who exercises this good pleasure is not named; see, for example, also Luke 2:14; Phil. 2:13; and Col. 1:19. Eph. 1:5 makes very clear whose good pleasure is meant. So does the context in each of the other cases.

verbal adjective (*agapetos:* beloved) here used, this love is deep-seated, thorough-going, as great as is the heart of God itself. It is also as intelligent and purposeful as is the mind of God. It is tender, vast, infinite! [225]

Not only that, but this love is also *eternal;* that is, it is timeless, raised far above all temporal boundaries. Though some disagree, the rendering "in whom *I am* well pleased" must be considered correct. [226] In the quiet recess of eternity the Son was the object of the Father's inexhaustible delight (cf. Prov. 8:30). The former's re-affirmation, by means of baptism, of his purpose to shed his blood for a world lost in sin did nothing to diminish that love. That is what the Father is telling his Son. That is what he is also telling John . . . and all of us.

How filled with comfort this paragraph, comfort not only for the Son and for John, but for every child of God, for it indicates that *not only the Son* loves his followers enough to suffer the pangs of hell in their stead, but that also the Spirit fully co-operates by strengthening him for this very task, and that the Father, instead of frowning upon the One who undertakes it, is so very pleased with him that he must needs rend asunder the very heavens, that his voice of delightful approval may be heard on earth! [227] All three are equally interested in our salvation, and the three are One.

Summary of Chapter 3

Verses 1-12 record the sudden emergence, in fulfilment of the prophecy of Isa. 40:3, of Christ's herald or way-preparer. John is pictured as preaching and baptizing in the wilderness of Judea. From Judea and the surrounding country enormous crowds flock to see and hear him. The Baptist's abrupt appearance, ascetic manner of life, and message of impending doom, escapable only by means of basic favorable change of mind and heart ("Be converted. . . ."), evoke a response from many who, confessing their sins, are baptized in the Jordan.

Among those who present themselves for baptism are also many Pharisees (oblique and ostentatious legalists) and Sadducees (wealthy and worldly priests and land-owners). "Y o u offspring of vipers!" John exclaims. The rest of his speech may be paraphrased as follows: "Who deluded y o u into thinking that without a genuine turnabout of mind and heart y o u can evade God's judgment? Bear fruit, therefore, in harmony with real conversion. Do

---

[225] On the difference between ἀγαπάω and φιλέω, and their respective derivatives see N.T.C. on John, Vol. II, pp. 494-500.

[226] This is an excellent example of the timeless aorist. See Gram. N.T., p. 837; thus also in Matt. 17:5; Mark 1:11; and Luke 3:22.

[227] On the entire subject of Christ's baptism read also the following: A. B. Bruce, "The Baptism of Jesus," *Exp,* 5th ser., 7 (1898), pp. 187-201; and W. E. Bundy, "The Meaning of Jesus' Baptism," *JR,* 7 (1927), pp. 56-71.

not rely on your physical descent from Abraham, as if that could save y o u. If God wants *sons of Abraham* worthy of the name, he does not need y o u. He can raise up children for Abraham out of these stones here."

The Baptist emphasizes that the axe is even now lying at the root of the tree; that is, doom is impending. The divine action of bringing about a final separation between precious grain and worthless chaff (the penitent and the impenitent) is imminent. The grain is headed for the granary; the chaff, for the flame.

For the truly converted "the kingdom of heaven" with its numerous blessings is at hand. Meaning: God's rule operating in hearts and lives and in whatever is influenced by them, and affecting even man's physical existence, is about to assert itself more powerfully and gloriously then ever before. However, it must be understood that neither weal nor woe are at John's own personal disposal. On the contrary, all that *he* is able to do (besides preaching) is to baptize *with water.* One far more worthy is about to appear upon the scene; in a sense, has arrived already. It is he who will baptize *with the Holy Spirit and with fire,* a prediction that includes Pentecost and the final judgment in one wide sweep.

Verses 13-17 relate that at the height of the Baptist's activity Jesus makes his public appearance, requesting John to baptize him. When the herald objects, deeming himself unworthy and suggesting that he be baptized by the One for whose coming he has been preparing the way, Jesus overcomes his scruples by saying, "Yield to me this time, for it is proper for us in this way to comply fully with every righteous requirement." It was right that he who had promised to offer himself as a ransom for many ratify this promise by means of submitting to baptism, thereby reaffirming his desire and decision to take upon himself and to carry away the sin of the world. The water of baptism signifies and seals the washing away of sin, and Jesus by means of this sacrament reveals himself as the Sin-bearer. Accordingly, it was also right that John, who was fulfilling his task in obedience to God and in fulfilment of prophecy, should baptize Jesus.

For the performance of his infinitely arduous task the Mediator needed to be anointed by the Holy Spirit, for it must be borne in mind that the Son of God was also the Son of *man.* The second person of the Trinity, being truly divine, has two natures: the divine and the human. The divine does not need strengthening, but the human nature does. All the necessary qualifications are therefore imparted to the Mediator when at his baptism the Holy Spirit, symbolized by the form of a dove, descends upon him *in full measure.*

The Son's present reaffirmation of his desire to take upon himself a task so agonizing elicits an immediate response of love from the heart of the Father, so that the heavens are opened and a voice is heard, saying, "This is my Son, the Beloved, with whom I am well pleased." A more glorious sign and seal of approval is unthinkable.

Thus Father, Son, and Holy Spirit co-operate in bringing about man's salvation.

An additional note on 3:4, "And his food was locusts. . . ." Aversion to eating insects, rich in protein, may be just cultural. In other countries insects are part of the diet. Roasted and salted grasshoppers can be bought in Mexico City. Edible insects keep Australian aborigines from starving. And even in the United States of America there are gourmet food stores that carry chocolate-coated bees and ants. Is it not possible that the Baptist was a little ahead of us, that is, that locusts and other insects may fill a future need?

Chapter 4:1-11

Theme: *The Work Which Thou Gavest Him to Do*

The Temptation of Jesus in the Wilderness

CHAPTER IV:1-11

4 1 Then Jesus was led up by the Spirit into the wilderness, to be tempted by the devil. 2 After going without food for forty days and forty nights he was famished. 3 The tempter came and said to him, "Since you are God's Son, tell these stones to turn into bread." 4 But he answered and said, "It is written,

'It is not by bread alone that man shall live,
But by every word that comes out through the
    mouth of God.' "

5 Then the devil took him along to the holy city, and set him on the pinnacle of the temple,   6 and said to him, "Since you are God's Son, throw yourself down; for it is written,

'He will give his angels instructions concerning you,'
                            and
'On their hands they will bear you up,
Lest you strike your foot against a stone.' "

7 Jesus said to him, "It is also written,

'You shall not put the Lord your God to the test.' "

8 Again, the devil took him along to a very high mountain, showed him all the kingdoms of the world in their splendor,   9 and said to him, "All these I will give you if you will prostrate yourself before me and worship me."   10 Then Jesus said to him, "Be gone, Satan, for it is written,

'You shall worship the Lord your God,
And him only shall you serve.' "

11 Then the devil left him, and behold, angels came and were rendering service to him.

4:1-11 *The Temptation of Jesus in the Wilderness*
Cf. Mark 1:12, 13; Luke 4:1-13

Its Link with the Preceding and the Following

It was the kingship of Christ that was emphasized in 1:1–3:12. At 3:13, however, there is a shift: the king becomes the sin-bearer. By means of his baptism he reaffirms his resolution to offer himself as a ransom for many. Accordingly, *this king is also a priest.* He is "priest forever after the order of Melchizedek" (Ps. 110:4; Heb. 6:17).

Offering himself implies suffering. He suffers *vicariously.* One of the forms assumed by this suffering is temptation (4:1-11): "He suffered being tempted" (Heb. 2:18).

It should be stressed, however, that though the emphasis shifts from the royal to the priestly office, that royal office is by no means ignored or forgotten. In the present paragraph Jesus appears not only as the priest who "suffers being tempted," but also very definitely as the king who gives battle to his chief opponent and overcomes him.

Even the prophetic office is not ignored; for, by his entire reaction and specifically by thrice quoting Scripture, Jesus also functions in this respect. In fact, in this very chapter the emphasis gradually shifts to Christ as not only a healer but also a teacher and preacher (verse 23); and The Sermon on the Mount immediately follows (chaps. 5–7). It has already been pointed out that Matthew's Gospel, more than any other, places stress on Christ as prophet (p. 82). It is impossible, therefore, to separate the three offices in which the Lord functions. They can be viewed as constituting *one threefold* Messianic office.

1. Then Jesus was led up by the Spirit into the wilderness, to be tempted by the devil. The very wording of the present paragraph shows its close connection with the preceding one:

John "saw the Spirit of God descending like a dove and lighting on him" (3:16).	"Then Jesus was led up by the Spirit" (4:1).
"And lo, a voice from heaven saying, 'This is my Son, the Beloved . . .' " (3:17).	"If you are the Son of God . . ." (4:3).

Jesus was *led up* from the Jordan in which he was baptized, to the adjacent highland. It was by the guidance of the Spirit that he was led up, that very Spirit who not only knew that this temptation experience was necessary but whose plenary and active presence also qualified Jesus to triumph over it. He was led "into the wilderness" (see on 3:1), where he was "with the wild beasts" (Mark 1:13). It was here that he was tempted by the *diabolos;* that is, the devil, meaning *slanderer, accuser* (Job 1:9; Zech. 3:1, 2; cf. Rev. 12:9, 10), and (through the influence of the Septuagint which offers *diabolos* as its translation of *Satan*) also *adversary* (I Peter 5:8).

It is clear that Matthew believed in the existence of a personal "prince of evil." So did the other apostles and inspired writers, and so also did Jesus himself. Besides the references in Matt. 4:1, 5, 8; 13:39; 25:41; and the others just mentioned, see also John 8:44; 13:2; Acts 10:38; Eph. 4:27; 6:11; James 4:7; I John 3:8, 10; Jude 9; Rev. 2:10; and 20:2.

Having been cast out of heaven, the devil is filled with fury and envy. His hatred is directed against God and his people; especially against God *as he is about to reveal himself in Jesus Christ unto salvation.* His purpose, accordingly, is to deceive and seduce his great Enemy, the Messiah, in order that, along with the latter, his kingdom (see 4:23) may also be doomed. The

222

devil's methods are very crafty (Eph. 6:11). On this subject see N.T.C. on Ephesians, p. 72.

Its Character

In connection with Christ's temptation certain rather philosophical questions are constantly being asked:

First, "Was it possible for the Savior to succumb to temptation?"

The answer is, "Definitely not." He was without sin, not even able to sin (Isa. 53:9; John 8:46; II Cor. 5:21). In fact, he was filled to overflowing with positive goodness; such as holiness, pardoning love, a yearning to heal and to impart the true knowledge of God; etc. (Isa. 53:5; Matt. 5:43-48; 14:14; 15:2, 3; Luke 23:34; Acts 10:38).

Secondly, "If he was unable to sin, was his temptation real?"

Yes, "he was tempted in all points (or *in every respect*) as we are, yet without sin"; that is, without falling into sin (Heb. 4:15). He experienced the various temptations to which men in general, including even believers, are subjected. In all these experiences he was by Satan urged to believe that he could receive a good thing by committing a bad act.

Heb. 4:15 cannot mean, however, that the psychological process involved in being tempted was exactly the same for Jesus as it is for men in general. For the latter, including believers, there is first, the tempting voice or inner whispering of Satan, urging them to sin. But there is also the inner desire ("lust") goading the tempted one to give heed to the devil's prompting. Thus man, being "drawn away and enticed by his own evil desire" (James 1:14) sins. With Christ the case was different. The outward stimulus—*outward* in the sense that it did not originate in the Lord's own soul but was the voice of another—was there, but the *inner* evil incentive or desire to co-operate with this voice from without was not. Nevertheless the temptation—that is, the sense of need, the consciousness of being urged by Satan to satisfy this need, the knowledge of having to resist the tempter, and the struggle to which this gave rise—was real even for Christ.

The soul of our Lord was not hard as a flint or cold as an icicle. It was a thoroughly human, deeply sensitive soul, affected and afflicted by suffering of every description. It was Christ who said, "I have a baptism to be baptized with, and how I agonize until it be accomplished" (Luke 12:50). Jesus was able to express affection (Matt. 19:13, 14), sympathy (23:37; John 11:35), compassion (Matt. 12:32), anger (17:17), gratitude (11:25), and a yearning for the salvation of sinners (11:28; 23:37; Luke 15; 19:10; John 7:37) to the glory of the Father (John 17:1-5). Being not only God but also *man*, he knew what it was to be weary (John 4:6) and thirsty (4:7; 19:28). Therefore, it should not really surprise us that, after a fast of forty days, he was very hungry, and that the proposal to turn stones into bread was a real temptation to him.

The question will be asked, however, "But did not this very sensitive and searching mind of Christ immediately discern that the three proposals (verses 3, 6, and 9), *as coming from Satan,* were evil?" One author asks, "How could evil be attractive to him? And if it was not attractive, where was the temptation?" (A. Plummer). It must be admitted that it is impossible to answer this question in such a manner that everything will now be entirely clear. The subject of the temptation of the perfect Savior is shrouded in mystery. But is not this true of doctrine in general? In fact, "Mystery is the vital element of Dogmatics. The truth which God has revealed concerning himself in nature and in Scripture far surpasses human conception and comprehension." [228]

We are unable to analyze minutely what occurred in the heart of Christ when he was tempted. But neither do we know how sin originated in the sinless heart of Adam, how guilt can be "imputed" from the sinner to the Savior, how the latter's righteousness can be transferred to his followers, how our Lord can be both omniscient (with respect to his divine nature) and not omniscient (according to his human nature), etc. It ought not to surprise us, therefore, that Christ's temptation, whether here in the wilderness or later, surpasses our understanding. On the basis of the inspired record we believe that it was a real and intense experience. And as to the fact that the deep truths contained in Scripture transcend our comprehension, is not that exactly what can be expected if the Bible is, indeed, *the Word of God?*

Its Progress Step by Step

First Temptation

2. After going without food for forty days and forty nights he was famished. The experiences of Moses on Mount Horeb (Exod. 34:2, 28; Deut. 9:9, 18) and of Elijah on his way to the same mountain (I Kings 19:8) occur to the mind immediately. Luke 4:2 shows that Christ's fast was complete, not partial. Is it not reasonable to believe that the Lord used these forty days to prepare himself, by means of prayer and meditation, for the work which the Father had given him to do, and which he, Jesus himself, had voluntarily taken upon himself? Says Calvin, commenting on 4:1, 2, "There were two reasons why Christ withdrew into the wilderness. First, that, after a fast of forty days he might come forth as a new man, or rather a heavenly man, to the discharge of his office. Secondly, that he might be tried by temptation and undergo an apprenticeship before he undertook an office so arduous and

---

228 H. Bavinck, *The Doctrine of God* (my translation from the Dutch), Grand Rapids, 1955, p. 13.

so exalted." One is reminded of Moses at the burning bush (Exod. 3:1–4:17) and of Paul's retreat to Arabia. See N.T.C. on Galatians, p. 56. [229]

Since Jesus, besides being divine, is also thoroughly human, it is certainly not surprising that at the end of these forty days he is famished. The devil naturally selects this moment as his golden opportunity. So the story continues: **3. The tempter came and said to him, Since you are God's Son, tell these stones to turn into bread.** [230]

It is clear that the temptation came from the outside: "the tempter *came to* him." As has been pointed out, only in this way are we even permitted to think of Christ as being tempted. In I Thess. 3:5, too, the prince of evil is called "the tempter," and so, by implication, also in Matt. 4:1; Mark 1:13; Luke 4:2; and I Cor. 7:5. His meanness consists especially in this, that he first tempts a man into sin. Then, when the tempted one follows his advice, the tempter becomes the accuser! Moreover, he will even continue to accuse the fallen one after the latter's sin has already been forgiven (Zech. 3:1-5; Rev. 12:10).

It must have been in the spirit of derision that the tempter uttered the words, "Since [231] you are God's Son. . . ." He probably meant, "Since that is

---

[229] For a strikingly different view see Lenski, *op. cit.*, p. 136. He believes that Jesus was tempted *throughout the forty days*, that it was this that made him forget about food, and that this period was not a retirement for communion with God. He bases his view, to a large extent, on the use of the present participle πειραζόμενος in Mark 1:13 and Luke 4:2, interpreting this to mean that Jesus was being tempted during the entire forty day period, a view found also in many other commentaries; e.g., J. M. Gibson, *The Gospel of St. Matthew (The Expositor's Bible)*, Grand Rapids, 1943, Vol. 4, p. 700; S. Greijdanus, *Het Heilig Evangelie naar de Beschrijving van Lucas (Kommentaar op het Nieuwe Testament)*, Amsterdam, 1940, Vol. I, p. 193; and E. P. Groenewald, *Die Evangelie volgens Markus*, p. 30. While that explanation of the participle is indeed possible, and would indicate that "the three" recorded temptations came as a kind of climax to a much longer series of temptations, it is not the only one available. The meaning might also be ". . . the wilderness, where he was being tempted by the devil." A reasonable interpretation of the account as presented in the Gospels (greatly abbreviated in Mark) might well be the following: *a.* Jesus is by the Spirit led into the wilderness for the purpose of being tested; *b.* he remains there for forty days during which he fasts; *c.* at the close of this period he is very hungry; and *d.* the devil avails himself of this opportunity (Christ's famished and weakened physical condition) to tempt him.

This interpretation too, it would seem to me, would do full justice to the sense of the present participle. Matthew's account, read by itself, does not suggest that Jesus was tempted during the entire forty day period. The latter theory results from one of two possible interpretations of the report in Mark and Luke, and is then superimposed upon Matthew. Once this has been done, various other thoughts—such as, that the constantly tempted Jesus had no time to think about food or about communion with God in prayer—are then added.

[230] This is a conditional sentence of the First Class (condition assumed to be true to fact): εἰ with the indicative (here the present) in the protasis, and the imperative εἰπέ (used as second aor. of λέγω) in the apodosis. Satan does not deny that Jesus is God's son but challenges him to prove it.

[231] εἰ in causal sense, as frequently (Matt. 6:30; 7:11; cf. Luke 11:13; 12:28; John 12:23; 10:35; etc.).

what the Father told you at your baptism (3:17), and what you believe, make use of your majestic dignity, and no longer be tortured by hunger."— *Son of God . . . hungry.* How ridiculous! If, then, you are God's Son, [232] tell these stones to turn into bread. [233]

It was, of course, a wicked attempt *a.* to cause "the last Adam" (I Cor. 15:45) to fail even as the first Adam had failed, in both cases in connection with food consumption. Was not one of the reasons why the Holy Spirit caused Jesus to be tested exactly this, that, as the Representative and Savior of all his people, he must in their stead triumph over temptation instead of succumbing to it as the first Adam had done? Moreover, on the part of the tempter this was a sinister endeavor *b.* to destroy the Son's confidence in his Father's will and power to sustain him. What the tempter was asking Jesus to do was to distrust his Father, and to take matters entirely into his own hands.

Though, as has been pointed out, there are depths that we cannot fathom, it cannot be denied that this temptation was a very real one for Jesus. He knew that he was clothed with power to perform miracles. Also, here was an opportunity to use that power in his own behalf. He must have been very hungry by this time. The reality of the temptation and the severity of the trial may perhaps become even more clearly evident when *the last Adam's* situation is compared with that of *the first one.* Both were tempted by Satan. But the difference in the gravity of the test appears from the following threefold contrast:

a. Nowhere in Gen. 3:1-7 do we read that the Old Testament Adam had gone without food for any length of time. Jesus, on the contrary, had been fasting for forty days. He was famished.

b. Even had the father of the human race been hungry, he could have easily satisfied that hunger, for he had been told, "Of every tree of the garden you may freely eat" (Gen. 2:17). No such provision had been made for Christ.

c. Eve's husband, when tempted, had, as it were, everything in his favor,

---

[232] The rendering "God's Son" is that of Beck and of Williams. Also correct is "the Son of God" (A.V., A.R.V., N.A.S., R.S.V., N.E.B., etc.). It is true that υἱός is not preceded by the article, but not much can be made of this; for, *a.* even without the article υἱὸς τοῦ Θεοῦ, considered as a title, is definite; and *b.* if, as is generally assumed, Satan is echoing the Father's voice at baptism, he must have had in mind the definite designation, for 3:17 has ὁ υἱός. I do not agree with Lenski, therefore, when he says that, by leaving out the article, Satan "cunningly modifies the Father's word" (*op. cit.*, p. 138).

[233] Or "bread-cakes." The original uses the plural in both cases, so that it is entirely possible that Satan had in mind "stones . . . bread-cakes." In shape there may even have been a resemblance. On the other hand, the context would seem to imply that the emphasis is not so much on form or shape but rather on the substance *bread*, used to appease hunger. Hence, with most translators I still prefer the rendering "bread." "Loaves" is incorrect, as this English word generally has a meaning that is entirely foreign to the original.

for he was living in *paradise*. Jesus, at the time of his temptation, was staying in this horrible wilderness!

Nevertheless, he withstood the temptation: 4. **But he answered and said, It is written,**

> **It is not by bread alone that man shall live,**
> **But by every word that comes out through the mouth of God.**

Note the expression, "It is written," not only here in verse 4 but also in verses 7 and 10, every time with a reference to the same book, Deuteronomy, which, as is clear, Jesus regarded not as "a pious fraud" but as the very Word of God. Other passages that give expression to Christ's exalted view of Scripture are Luke 24:25-27, 44-47; John 5:39; and 10:35. For him the Old Testament Scriptures, as interpreted by himself, were evidently the ultimate touchstone of the truth for life and doctrine, the final court of appeal for the reason.

The first quotation is from Deut. 8:3. It pictures Moses reminding Israel of God's tender care for his people during the forty years of the wilderness journey. Particularly, it shows how the Lord had fed them with manna, heretofore completely unknown to them and their fathers, that he might teach them "that not by bread alone does man live but by everything proceeding out of the mouth of Jehovah does man live."

What Jesus means, therefore, may be paraphrased as follows: "Tempter, you are proceeding upon the false assumption that for a man, in order to appease hunger and keep alive, *bread* is absolutely necessary. Over against this erroneous idea I now declare that not bread but the creative, energizing, and sustaining power of my Father is the only indispensable source of my, and of man's, life and well-being."

The expression "every word that comes out through the mouth of God" [234] refers to the word of his power. It is God's omnipotence exercised in creation and preservation. It is his word of *effective command;* for example, "And God said, Let there be light, and there was light" (Gen. 1:3); "By the word of Jehovah were the heavens made" (Ps. 33:6).

On the part of Jesus this reply to Satan's advice was an expression of filial confidence in the Father's care. Certainly the One who, when there was no bread, had provided manna, and who just a moment ago had said, "This is

---

[234] Clearly a rendering reflecting the Septuagint. Whether this so-called expanded text is to be preferred to the shorter text ("every word of God") is hard to decide. Codex D has the shorter text. Cf. Luke 4:4. Since it is true that the Western text is generally characterized by additions instead of subtractions, it is argued by some that its preference for the shorter text in *this* instance proves that the autograph did not contain the longer reading. *Essentially* the meaning remains the same; for "every word of God," "every word that comes out through the mouth of God," and "everything proceeding out of the mouth of Jehovah" (Hebrew text), all refer to God's omnipotence actively manifested in the creation and preservation of all things.

my Son . . . with whom I am well pleased," would not fail his Beloved in this hour of trial!

Second Temptation

5, 6. "So, you trust your Father?" says the tempter, as it were. "Well, then prove it": Then the devil took him along to the holy city, and set him on the pinnacle of the temple, and said to him, Since you are God's Son, throw yourself down; for it is written,

He will give his angels instructions concerning you,
and
On their hands they will bear you up,
Lest you strike your foot against a stone.

There are those who see a discrepancy between Matthew and Luke, since the order in which Matt. 4:5-10 records the last two temptations is reversed in Luke 4:5-12. The answer is that, while Matthew indeed appears to present a certain historical sequence, as is clear not only from his use of the word "then" (verse 5), and from verse 11, "Then the devil left him," but also, as already noted, from the inner connection between the first and second temptations; Luke, on the contrary, does not even hint such a sequence. He simply connects the three temptations by means of the conjunction "and" (4:5, 9), but neither states nor in any way implies that they followed each other in that historical order. So, there is no discrepancy.

The words, "The devil takes him along," are found also in verse 8, where the question how this must be understood will be considered. We are not surprised that Matthew, the Jew, calls Jerusalem "the holy city" (cf. 27:53). It was intended to be just that (Ps. 46:4; 48:1-3, 9-14; 122; 137; Matt. 5:35). Many cherished memories are associated with Jerusalem or Zion. Was it not the city where David, Christ's great ancestor, had established his throne? Had God not promised to dwell here? Here stood the temple with its "holy place" and "holy of holies." This was the city to which the tribes went up to give thanks to the name of Jehovah.

To this city the devil by God's sufference has brought Jesus, and has set him on the very pinnacle (literally *wing*) of the outer wall of the entire temple complex. The exact spot is not given. It *may* have been the roof-edge of Herod's royal portico, overhanging the Kedron Valley, and looking down some four hundred fifty feet, a "dizzy height," as Josephus points out (*Antiq.* XV.412). This spot was located southeast of the temple court, perhaps at or near the place from which, according to tradition, James, the Lord's brother, was hurled down. See the very interesting account in Eusebius, *Eccl. Hist.*, II.xxiii. [235]

"Since you are the Son of God," says the tempter (exactly as in verse 3), "throw yourself down." His reasoning was probably along this line, "You

---

[235] Acts 12:2 refers to the death of another James, namely, the brother of John. See, however, Lenski, *op. cit.*, p. 144.

will thus be able to prove your confidence in the Father's protection, a confidence which, by implication, you have just now confessed (verse 4). Besides, if Scripture, which you so readily quote, is true, no harm can befall you, for it is written, 'He will give his angels instructions concerning you.' They will not merely *arrest* your fall. No, they will do more. *Very tenderly* they will bear you up on their hands, lest you, wearing only sandals, should hurt yourself by striking your foot against one of those sharp-edged stones present in abundance in the abyss below."

The passage quoted is from Ps. 91:11, 12. As rendered here in Matt. 4:6, it follows the Septuagint (Ps. 90:11, 12). As quoted by the devil, there is, however, an omission, which some regard as being important, others not. According to the Hebrew, Ps. 91:11 ends with the words "to guard you in all your ways." Matt. 4:6 contains nothing that corresponds to this. Luke 4:10 merely has "to guard you." Hence, in both of these Gospels the words "in all your ways" are left out. When these words are *included,* God promises to protect the righteous man in all his righteous ways; for these are the ways of the man who dwells in the secret place of the Most High, abides under the shadow of the Almighty and has found his refuge in Jehovah, upon whom he has set his love. They are, accordingly, the ways of the saint (Prov. 2:8), the good man (Prov. 2:20). It is to such a one that the words apply, "He will give his angels instructions concerning you, to guard you in all your ways." When these words "in all your ways" are *omitted,* does it not become easier to interpret the passage as if it were a promise of Jehovah to protect the righteous *no matter what he does?* So read, the passage would seem to correspond more closely with what the devil wants Jesus to do.

Nevertheless, this point is probably of minor importance, since what Satan omits amounts to far more than a few words in a quotation. He omits any reference to the Scriptural truth that God does not condone but condemns and punishes rashness, a trifling with providence, an impetuous rushing into totally unwarranted danger (Gen. 13:10, 11; Ps. 19:13; Esther 5:14; 7:9, 10; Dan. 4:28-33; 5:22, 23; Rom. 1:30; II Peter 2:10).

Obedience to Satan's proposal was tempting, for what man is there who, when asked to prove a point he has made, does not feel as if he should immediately comply, instead of first asking himself, "What right has my prompter to ask me to prove it?" Jesus, however, does not fall into this trap. He realizes that for him to do what Satan is urging upon him would amount to substituting presumption for faith, effrontery for submission to God's guidance. It would have meant nothing less than to risk self-destruction. The *false trust* in the Father, which the devil demanded of Jesus in this *second* temptation was not any better than the *distrust* he had proposed in the *first.* [236] It would have amounted to *experimenting* on the Father.

---

[236] See the fine remark on this by Lenski, *op. cit.,* p. 146, bottom of page.

A rabbinical tradition reads, "When the king, Messiah, reveals himself, then he comes and stands on the roof of the holy place."[237] On the basis of this tradition some commentators are of the opinion that the tempter was trying to suggest that Jesus, by casting himself from the temple's pinnacle, would establish himself as being indeed the Messiah, for, after a miraculous and safe landing, the crowd, having watched the descent with bated breath, would exclaim, "Look, he is unhurt. He must be the Messiah!" For Jesus, thus the argument continues, this would then be an easy way to success. The cross would be avoided, the crown obtained without struggle or agony.

It is an interesting theory. Nevertheless, there is nothing that would lend any further support to it. No spectators are even mentioned in the Gospel accounts. Moreover, Jesus, in his reply, does not refer to anything of the kind. I believe, therefore, that the entire idea should be dismissed. Luke 16:31 also argues against it.

The reason why Jesus peremptorily rejects the devil's proposal has already been given. It is clearly stated in verse 7. **Jesus said to him, It is also written, You shall not put the Lord your God to the test.**[238] This is a quotation from Deut. 6:16, which reflects the situation of the Israelites described in Exod. 17:1-7, how at a place called Massah and Meribah they made trial of Jehovah and rebelled against Moses because of lack of water. They accused Moses of having cruelly brought them, their children, and their cattle, out of Egypt and into the desert, to destroy them all. They were almost ready to stone him and, instead of in a childlike manner, "making all their wants and wishes known at the Father's throne," they insolently and provocatively challenged God, saying, "Is Jehovah among us or not?" Jesus knows that similar ill behavior on his part, by unnecessarily exposing himself to danger just to see what his Father's reaction might be, whether the latter would be with him or not, would amount to grievous transgression. He knows that it has nothing whatever to do with humbly trusting in the protecting care promised in Ps. 91. He therefore very appropriately answers the tempter by quoting Deut. 6:16.

Daily life all around us affords abundant illustrations of *false confidence,* similar to that which the devil urged Jesus to exercise. A person will earnestly beseech the Lord to bestow upon him the blessing of health;

---

[237] S.BK. Vol. I, p. 151.

[238] After the singulars in verse 6 it is but natural that in verse 7 the quoted verb is also in the singular, instead of in the plural as in Hebrew Deuteronomy. Besides, in the Deuteronomy passage the Septuagint also has the singular.

The verb used in Matt. 4:7 is not the same as the one in 4:1, though the two are very closely related. The verb in verse 1 is the aor. infin. passive of πειράζω; the one in verse 7 is the 2nd, per. sing. fut. indic. act. of ἐκπειράζω. Some translations (A.V., R.S.V., N.A.S. in the text, Phillips) use the identical verb in both instances. Others (A.R.V., Williams, Goodspeed, Weymouth, Berkeley, Beck, N.A.S. in the margin, and N.E.B.) reflect the original more accurately by using a different verb in verse 7 than in verse 1.

however, he neglects to observe the rules of health. Or, he will ask God to save his soul; however, he neglects to use the means of grace, such as the study of Scripture, church attendance, the sacraments, living a life for the benefit of others to the glory of God. Again, someone will plead with the Lord for the spiritual as well as physical welfare of his children, but he himself neglects to bring them up in the way of the Lord. A church member, admonished because at a circus he had eagerly rushed into a corrupt side show, defended himself by saying, "I cannot deny that I went there, but while I was there I was constantly praying, 'Turn away mine eyes from beholding vanity (Ps. 119:37 A.V.).' "—"You shall not put the Lord your God to the test" is the answer to all of this.

Third Temptation

And now the devil drops his mask and, having failed miserably in the first two attempts to conquer his enemy, stakes everything on one final, brutal, desperate attempt to achieve his purpose: **8, 9. Again, the devil took him along to a very high mountain, showed him all the kingdoms of the world in their splendor, and said to him, All these I will give you if you will prostrate yourself before me and worship me.**

How is it to be understood that, in the second temptation, the devil *takes Jesus along* to the holy city, and sets him on the pinnacle of the temple, and that now, in the third temptation, Satan *takes him along* to a very high mountain? Some insist that this must all be taken literally: "The transfer of Jesus to the temple was physical . . . 'takes him with himself' and 'placed him' makes the devil provide the motive power." [239] Just how we must conceive of this is not explained. Did the devil assume a physical body (Gen. 3:1; cf. John 8:44), and did the two—Jesus and the devil—walk side by side through the wilderness, enter Jerusalem, and climb to the pinnacle of the temple? How did they reach a mountain from which the devil could show Jesus "all the kingdoms of the world and their splendor"? In the vicinity of the Judean Wilderness or of Jerusalem, which mountain would that be? Did they glide smoothly through the sky, the devil functioning as a kind of engine? Did they sail along together all the way to Mount Everest? But even then, would not some kind of miracle have been required to enable the devil from there to show Jesus *all* the kingdoms of the world, and this not just in dim outline, but very distinctly, so that "all their splendor (or *glory*)" would be plainly visible; and again, not little by little during a lengthy period of time, but, as Luke adds, "in a moment"?

This is not at all a question of believing Scripture or not believing it. It is simply a question of how best *to interpret* what we fully accept. The writer of this commentary has not been able anywhere to find a solution that

---

[239] Lenski, *op. cit.*, pp. 143, 144; see also p. 149.

satisfies him better than that of Calvin. In his Commentary, reflecting first on the second, then on the third, temptation, he remarks:

"It is asked, was he [Jesus] actually carried to this elevated spot, or was it done in a vision? . . . What is added, that *all the kingdoms of the world* were exposed to Christ's view . . . in one moment . . . agrees better with the idea of a vision than with any other theory. In a matter that is doubtful, and where ignorance brings no risk, I choose rather to suspend my judgment than to furnish contentious people with an excuse for a debate."

Calvin is being very careful. It is clear that he favors the vision idea. On the other hand, he does not wish to press it, leaving room for any other *reasonable* interpretation anyone might be able to offer. I only wish to add that Scripture contains two comparable passages in which we are told that someone is "set on" or "carried to" a high mountain. These two are Ezek. 40:2 and Rev. 21:10. [240] Ezekiel plainly states that this happened "in the visions of God." To the seer of Patmos visions were shown while he was "in the Spirit" (Rev. 1:10). It was "in the Spirit" that he was carried away to a mountain great and high. Calvin's view, accordingly, is worthy of very serious consideration. [241] The objection that if the temptations (whether only the second and the third, or, perhaps better, all three) occurred to Jesus during visions they were not real, is groundless. Was not Ezekiel's experience *real,* even though it occurred in a vision? Is John's description of Jerusalem the Golden bereft of value because it, too, came to him in a vision? Besides, if even a *dream* can be so vivid that there are said to be cases on record according to which people died as a result, shall we then say that the reality of Christ's temptation experiences is diminished in any way because it was in *visions* that the tempter came to him and addressed him?

This view must not be confused with that according to which the temptations were of a merely subjective nature. No, even if it was in a vision that the devil came to Jesus, the great adversary was very real, and it was *he,* not the Lord, who said, "Tell these stones to turn into bread," "throw yourself down," and "prostrate yourself before me." If it was in a vision that the Lord was urged to do these things, we may be sure that what occurred in the vision was as real to his mind as if there had been no vision at all, and everything had taken place with strict literality.

From the top of the very high mountain (whether or not it was in a vision makes no difference) the devil shows Jesus all the kingdoms of the world and (or *in*) their splendor. All this is vividly displayed to Jesus; according to Luke (as we have already seen) in *just one* very significant moment! To gain some conception of what must have been included in the panorama that was

---

[240] Other passages that speak of a high mountain are shown by their contexts to be of an entirely different nature (Isa. 40:9; 57:7; Jer. 3:6; Matt. 17:1; Mark 9:2).

[241] See also the excellent material on this in H. N. Ridderbos, *op. cit.,* pp. 69-72.

spread out before the Lord, would it not be wise to read carefully the following three paragraphs: II Chron. 9:9-28; Eccl. 2:1-11; and Rev. 18:12, 13? All this wealth is by Satan offered to Christ, all for the price of just one genuflection! If Jesus will but *cast himself to the ground and worship* (see on 2:11; cf. 2:2, 8) the devil, he can have it all. He can have it in his possession and under his authority (cf. Luke 4:6).

The question has been asked whether Satan was really the possessor of all these things, and whether he was actually in control of all of them, to such an extent that he could offer them to anyone he wished. Often this question is answered in the affirmative, with an appeal: to Eph. 2:2, where Satan is called "the prince of the domain of the air"; to 6:12, which speaks about "the spiritual forces of evil in the heavenly places"; to I John 5:19, which states that "the whole world lies in (the power of) the evil one"; and even to Luke 4:6, in which the great adversary pictures himself as the rightful owner of, and ruler over, all. Further substantiation is by such interpreters found in the fact that Jesus in his answer (Matt. 4:10) did not in so many words dispute Satan's claim.

Do these passages really prove what those who appeal to them are trying to prove? I do not believe they do. The first three merely prove that Satan exercises a very powerful influence for evil over the lives of all those wicked people and spirits that acknowledge him as their master. But such references certainly do not prove that the devil is the ultimate owner and ruler of the nations, with the right and the might to dispose of them and of their wealth as he pleases, so that Christ himself, at least during the present dispensation, would have to take a back seat to him. The contrary is the truth, as is proved abundantly by such passages as Gen. 3:15; Ps. 2; Matt. 11:27; 28:18; Rom. 16:20; Eph. 1:20-23; Col. 2:15; and Rev. 12; 20:3, 4, 10. If it be argued that some of these passages refer to the power given to Christ in his exaltation, the answer is that even during the latter's humiliation Satan was able to do no more than Christ suffered him to do, as both Matt. 4:11 and also the Gospels in general testify (demon expulsions; Matt. 12:29; Luke 10:18; John 12:31). And as to Satan's boast (Luke 4:6), it is too absurd to merit an answer. But if an answer of a sort be demanded, let it be John 8:44.

On the surface it may therefore seem as if the third temptation was for Christ no temptation at all. Jesus knew that the devil was lying; that is, that the prince of evil had no enchanting kingdoms to give away. No doubt the Lord also knew that even if Satan had possessed them, he would not have fulfilled his promise. In what sense then can we say that also Satan's *third* attempt was a real temptation for Christ? As I see it, only in this way that, although the particular form in which the proposal was made contained nothing that would recommend it to the mind and heart of the Savior, nevertheless the implied suggestion *to try to obtain the crown without enduring the cross* was able to foment a bitter struggle within him. To be sure, it was not a struggle that involved him in sin or could bring him to the point of committing sin, but it was a state of agony, nevertheless. How else can we explain the words uttered in Gethsemane, "My Father, if it be possible, let this cup pass from me; nevertheless, not as I will, but as thou wilt" (Matt. 26:39)? Or, how can we explain Luke 12:50? It is clear, therefore, that for Christ *this* temptation, too, was very real.

Satan received the answer he deserved: **10. Then Jesus said to him, Be gone, Satan, for it is written,**

> **You shall worship the Lord your God,**
> **And him only shall you serve.**

The expression, "Be gone, Satan," a command which was obeyed (see verse 11), not only shows Christ's abhorrence of the devil's proposal, but also his supremacy over him. The answer reflects Deut. 6:3. [242] It also reveals the sharp contrast between Christ, who is ever doing what his Father wants him to do (John 5:30; 6:38), and Satan, whose purpose is the exact opposite (Gen. 2:17, cf. 3:4; Zech. 3:1, 2; John 8:44; I Thess. 2:18; I Peter 5:8; I John 3:8; Rev. 12; 20:8, 9); and who is true to the meaning of the name whereby Jesus here addresses him, *adversary.*

At Christ's command Satan, thoroughly vanquished, leaves him, as is stated in verse 11. **Then the devil left him.** He withheld any further attacks for the time being, waiting until another opportunity would present itself (Luke 4:13). That he did, indeed, resume his attacks afterward is clear from such passages as Matt. 16:23; Luke 22:28. In the light of Heb. 2:18 see also Matt. 26:36-46; Mark 3:21, 31; 8:32, 33.

The visions—if such they were—vanish. Jesus is conscious of being in the wilderness. Continued: **and behold, angels came and were rendering service to him.** Just what this service implied is not stated. Those commentators who reject the vision idea say that, among other things, the angels now assist Jesus in his descent from the very high mountain where the third temptation had just been completed. [243] The general statement that angels were sent by

---

[242] Although the words of Jesus are not a precise rendering of any *single* passage either in the original Hebrew or in the Septuagint, yet they are certainly in complete harmony with the sense of both, for in both the following passages occur: "Jehovah your God you shall fear, and him you shall serve . . ." (Deut. 6:13), followed by verse 14, "Y o u shall not go after other gods"; "You shall not *worship* them [i.e., graven images] nor *serve* them; for I, Jehovah your God, am a jealous God" (Deut. 5:9); to which may be added: "And from there you will seek Jehovah your God and will find him if you search for him with all your heart and with all your soul" (Deut. 4:29). Although in none of these passages the word "only" (of Matt. 4:10) occurs, yet in each case it is clearly implied: in the first two instances because of the context; in the last, because of the phrase "with all your heart and . . . soul." The word "only" does, however, occur in I Sam. 7:3 ("Serve him only"). This, too, may have influenced Matt. 4:10. Note the same sequence *worship . . . serve* in Matt. 4:10 as in Deut. 5:9. Besides, Christ's "You shall worship the Lord your God" is a direct response to Satan's "Worship me."

[243] Lenski, *op. cit.*, p. 154.

the Father to provide for the Son's needs, whatever these may have been, is perhaps the best. That this also included providing bodily nourishment would seem to be a reasonable inference.

Its Lessons

1. Resist the devil by appealing to Scripture, as Jesus did three times in succession.

2. Rest assured that Jesus, as his people's Representative, has vicariously rendered the obedience which Adam, as mankind's representative, failed to render.

3. Derive comfort from the fact that we have a Highpriest who, having himself been tempted, is able to help us in our temptations (Heb. 4:14-16).

4. Note that by *not* giving heed to the devil, Jesus receives the very blessings which Satan had held out to him. However, it is in a far more glorious sense and with the Father's favor resting upon him that he receives the strength to endure physically, the ministry of the angels, and authority over the kingdoms of the world.

Summary of Chapter 4:1-11

Adam, when tempted, failed. So Christ, too, must now be tempted, in order that by his victory over temptation and over the tempter he may, for all those who believe in him, undo the results of Adam's failure. So the Spirit, who when Jesus was baptized had descended upon him never to leave again, leads him into the wilderness to be tempted by the devil.

The three temptations took place at the end of a forty day fast, so that Jesus was very hungry. "Since you are God's Son," says Satan to him, probably meaning, "Since that is what the Father told you at your baptism, and what you believe," "tell these (desert) stones to turn into bread." Why should he trust the Father any longer? Why not, as God's Son, endowed with power, should he not take matters into his own hand? Quoting Deut. 8:3 Jesus answers, "It is not by bread alone that man shall live, but by every word that comes out through the mouth of God." Life does not depend primarily on bread but on the sustaining power and love of God. Jesus is God's own Son; hence, the Father will provide for him and sustain him.

"Prove that you trust him," says Satan, as it were, "by casting yourself down from the pinnacle of the temple." In order to encourage him to do so the devil quotes from Ps. 91:11, 12, as if that passage justified rashness, the substitution of presumption for faith. With an appeal to Deut. 6:16—"It is also written, 'You shall not put the Lord your God to the test,' "—Jesus parries that assault.

Finally, what may well have been the greatest temptation of all: Satan is willing to relinquish his dominion, his powerful influence, over all the kingdoms of the world, and to hand over all these realms together with all their glorious wealth, to Jesus, for him to possess and to control; so, at least, he *says*. He will do this on one condition, namely, that "you will prostrate yourself before me and worship me." The Messiah will not need to suffer at all: no crown of thorns, no shame, no cross.—Like an arrow the answer flies back, "Be gone, Satan, for it is written, 'You shall worship the Lord your God, and him only shall you serve.' "

Then, for the time being, the devil leaves Jesus. Angels came and were rendering service to the Victor.

The lessons to be derived from this temptation account are summarized on p. 235.

The Work Which Thou Gavest Him to Do

Its Progress

or

Continuation

Chapters 4:12–20:34

Outline of Chapter 4:12-25

Theme: *The Work Which Thou Gavest Him to Do*

A. The Great Galilean Ministry

4:12-17   Its Beginning
4:18-22   The Calling of Four Fishermen
4:23-25   Christ's Teaching, Preaching, and Healing

CHAPTER IV: 12-25

4 12 Now when he heard that John had been taken into custody, he withdrew into Galilee. 13 Leaving Nazareth he went and settled in Capernaum by the sea, in the territory of Zebulun and Naphtali, 14 that what was spoken through the prophet Isaiah might be fulfilled:

> 15 "Land of Zebulun and land of Naphtali,
> Toward the sea, beyond the Jordan,
> Galilee of the Gentiles,
> 16 The people sitting in darkness
> Have seen a great light;
> And upon those sitting in the land of the shadow of death
> Light has dawned."

17 From that time Jesus began to preach and to say, "Be converted, for the kingdom of heaven is at hand."

4:12-17 *The Beginning of the Great Galilean Ministry*

Verses 13-16 are peculiar to Matthew; see above, p. 17. For verses 12 and 17 see also Matt. 11:2; 14:3-5; Mark 1:14, 15; 6:17-20; Luke 3:19, 20; 4:14, 15; and cf. John 4:1-3, 43, 44.

12. Now when he [Jesus] heard that John had been taken into custody, he withdrew into Galilee. A new section of Matthew's Gospel begins here. Therefore, a chapter division at this point would have been very proper. Matthew does not indicate any chronological connection between this verse and the preceding material (the account of the baptism and the temptation). There may well have been a time interval of about a year, during which the events related in John 1:19—4:42 occurred. [244] If so, the date when Jesus set out for Galilee to begin the Great Galilean Ministry was probably about December of the year A.D. 27 or a little later.

---

[244] I base this probability on the assumption that the departure for, and entrance into, Galilee, to begin the Great Galilean Ministry mentioned here in Matthew, is the same as that to which John 4:3, 43 refers. In John it was followed soon afterward by what was probably the *second* Passover festival of Christ's public ministry (John 5:1); hence, the Passover of the year A.D. 28, preceded, a year earlier, by the *first* Passover mentioned in John 2:13, 23. See also pp. 181, 196; N.T.C. on the Gospel according to John, Vol. I, pp. 36, 173, 188, 189; and my *Bible Survey*, pp. 61, 62, 69.

But though thus separated in time from the preceding events, yet what Matthew is about to tell us is in material substance closely connected with that which precedes. The preparation for, and inauguration of, the work which the Father gave Jesus to do is ended. The beginning has been accomplished. The identity of Jesus as David's Son who is at the same time David's Lord has been established (chap. 1). From the wise men he has received the honor due to the One who is King of kings and Lord of lords (chap. 2). He has been heralded as sovereign, and by means of his baptism has confirmed his decision to take upon himself the sin of the world (chap. 3). He has proved himself worthy, for in the wilderness he has triumphed over the devil, as our representative succeeding where Adam had failed. Therefore, nothing now prevents him from carrying forward the task assigned to, and voluntarily assumed by, him.

Accordingly, the time has now arrived for Jesus to withdraw from Judea to go to Galilee. This was in fulfilment of prophecy, as Matthew is about to record (verses 14-16). But, as verse 12 shows, it also had something to do with the imprisonment of John the Baptist. The latter, as has been shown, had made his first public appearance in the summer of the year A.D. 26. And now, about eighteen months later, he has been imprisoned for the reason stated in 14:3, 4. The Jewish leaders, especially those in Jerusalem, who in the days of John's great popularity had been filled with jealousy, and about whom John had made some very uncomplimentary remarks (3:7), must have rejoiced. But this joy was of short duration, for other tidings reached the ears of the leaders; namely, that the multitudes surrounding Jesus were more numerous than those which had followed the herald. In fact, even before John's imprisonment Jesus had forged ahead of John in popular favor (John 3:22-26). Hence, from the point of view of the leaders matters were becoming worse instead of better. Now when the Lord knew that John had been imprisoned (Matt. 4:12) and that the Pharisees, with headquarters in Jerusalem, had heard that Jesus was gaining and (through his disciples) was baptizing more disciples than John (John 4:1), he left Judea and started on his way to Galilee. Why did he do this? Was not Galilee ruled by Herod Antipas, the very tetrarch who had imprisoned John the Baptist? Indeed, but it must be borne in mind that this miscarriage of justice was for a very special reason: we do not read that *Jesus* had personally rebuked Herod, as John had done. When, after John's cruel death, Herod becomes convinced that Jesus is "John the Baptist, raised from the dead," Jesus, too, will withdraw himself *to some extent* from that king's immediate attention (Matt. 14:1, 2, 13).

At the time indicated in 4:12 it was not Herod Antipas from whom Jesus needed to withdraw himself, but the Jewish religious leaders in Judea. The question may well be asked, however, "But why did Jesus have to withdraw himself at all? Was he afraid? Did he lack courage?" Perish the very thought!

The real reason was this, that he was well aware of the fact that his own great "popularity" in the country region of Judea would bring about such keen resentment on the part of the Judean religious leaders that this resentment, in the natural course of events, would lead to *a premature crisis.* The Lord knew that for every event in his life there was an appointed time in God's decree. And he also knew that the appropriate moment for his death had not yet arrived. As soon as that moment arrived, he would voluntarily lay down his life (John 10:18; 13:1; 14:31). He would do so *then,* but not before then. Hence, he must now leave Judea.

Just where did Jesus go when he arrived in Galilee? Did he wend his way directly to what had heretofore been his home in Nazareth? Matthew knows that this is what the readers of his Gospel would expect Jesus to do(2:23). Nevertheless, the Lord does the very opposite. Though, to be sure, he has not forgotten Nazareth, and will make a visit to that place when the time is ripe (13:53-58; Mark 6:1-6; Luke 4:16-30), Nazareth will not be his headquarters. It has ceased to be his place of residence. This is indicated in verse **13. Leaving Nazareth he went and settled in Capernaum by the sea, in the territory of Zebulun and Naphtali.** Capernaum can mean *village of Nahum.* Even so, it is not at all certain that the place was named for the Old Testament prophet who predicted Ninevah's overthrow. Originally the reference may have been to some other Nahum. Or, since Nahum, in turn, means *compassionate,* the name may also be interpreted as "village of compassion" or "of consolation." No one knows. What is established, however, is that at one time Matthew, the author of this Gospel, had his office at this place. As has been indicated (Matt. 9:9), he was a "publican," that is, a tax-collector or revenue officer.

It was in the vicinity of this village that Jesus had called his first disciples (John 1:35-42). It was here also that Peter and Andrew, James and John were subsequently invited to become "fishers of men" (Matt. 4:18-22). Capernaum became the center of Christ's activities, his headquarters during the great Galilean Ministry. It was here that Jesus performed many miracles (11:23; cf. 8:5-17; 9:1-8, 18-34; 12:9-13; 17:24-27; Luke 4:23, 31-37; 7:1-10), customarily attended the synagogue, and delivered several messages, including the address on The Bread of Life (John 6:24-65). Matthew even called Capernaum Christ's "own city" (9:1).

The ruins of a Capernaum synagogue have been unearthed. It has been partly restored. That structure dates back to the second or third century A.D. It is thought that an older house of worship, probably the very one that had been provided by the centurion who loved the Jewish nation (Matt. 8:5, 6; Luke 7:5, 6), and where Jesus taught, lies buried beneath the foundation of the one uncovered. It is evident that a detachment of soldiers was garrisoned at Capernaum. The story about the royal officer whose son Jesus healed (John 4:46-54) may indicate that Capernaum was also a center of political administration.

In the year 1905 excavations were started at Tell Hum on the northwestern shore of the Sea of Galilee. They were completed by the Franciscans, who supplied evidence to show that Tell Hum is the site of ancient Capernaum, situated about 2½ miles west of the place where the Jordan River, coming from the north, enters the sea.

For Jesus and his disciples the location was strategic, for from this point in (what used to be) the Zebulun-Naphtali territory, most of the towns and villages of Galilee and surroundings were easily accessible. They could be reached either by land—for Capernaum was situated on the rather thickly populated shore and on the trade route that connected Damascus and the Mediterranean—or else by sea.

Because of the fact that, in spite of all the works of mercy and power that Jesus performed here, and all the gracious words that fell from his lips, the inhabitants of Capernaum on the whole remained impenitent, Jesus predicted their doom, as will be explained (see on Matt. 11:23, 24). As to the destruction of the city itself, what occurred here was so shocking that for centuries even Capernaum's site was a matter of dispute. [245]

By the Spirit's guidance Matthew, giving us his own version of Isa. 9:1, 2, views Christ's settlement in Capernaum as another fulfilment of prophecy; this time 14-16 . . . that what was spoken through the prophet Isaiah might be fulfilled:

> Land of Zebulun and land of Naphtali,
> Toward the sea, beyond the Jordan,
> Galilee of the Gentiles,
> The people sitting in darkness
> Have seen a great light,
> And upon those sitting in the land of the shadow of death
> Light has dawned. [246]

---

[245] The following literature on Capernaum has been consulted: W.H.A.B., p. 86; G. E. Wright, *Biblical Archaeology*, Philadelphia, London, 1957, p. 237, with a picture of the uncovered Capernaum synagogue; E. G. Kraeling, *Rand McNally Bible Atlas*, 1966, New York, Chicago, San Francisco, pp. 373-379; L. H. Grollenberg, *op. cit.*, consult Index, p. 146; W. Ewing, article on Capernaum in I.S.B.E., Vol. I, pp. 566, 567; and J. S. Irvine, article on Capernaum in *Encyclopaedia Britannica*, 1969 edition, Vol. IV, p. 826.

[246] In the Hebrew original of Isa. 9:1, 2 the first two items, "the land of Zebulun and the land of Naphtali" are separated from the other three, "toward the sea, beyond the Jordan, Galîl of the nations." All five are the objects of verbs: the first two, of "brought into contempt"; the last three, of "made heavy," i.e., here probably "made glorious," "caused to be honored." In Matthew, however, the five items form one closely knit group. Here it is probably best to regard all five as nominatives in apposition with "the people sitting in darkness," the predicate being "have seen a great light." The last two lines, beginning with "And upon," are in parallelistic relationship. Here, "light" is the subject, and "has dawned upon, etc." is the predicate. Matthew's rephrasing shows very

In his sovereign grace God did the wholly unexpected. Not mainly to the Jerusalem aristocracy, but especially to the despised, sorely afflicted, and largely ignorant masses of Galilee, a mixed Gentile-Jewish population, did he send his Son. It was in and around Galilee that Jesus spent most of his incarnate life on earth. It was here that he grew up; here also that he subsequently traveled from village to village on his errands of mercy, imparting comfort and healing, and above all else seeking to save the lost. It was here that he walked the shores and addressed the crowds. It was in this general region that he gathered around him a band of disciples. It was from this northern portion of Palestine that his words of life and beauty, of admonition and consolation, were carried far and wide and from father to son.

In all probability the five items mentioned here in verse 15 refer to five different sections of Greater Galilee. See Bible map showing these areas. The *land of Zebulun* was west of the Sea of Galilee, and was bounded on the north by the *land of Naphtali*. The region *toward the sea* was to the west of these, and extended from north to south along the Mediterranean. *Beyond the Jordan* indicates the territory east of the Jordan. The region which because of the strong pagan element in its population is called *Galilee of the Gentiles* (*Galil* in the Old Testament) was the northernmost stretch of what used to be called Naphtali. One of its chief cities during Old Testament times was Kedesh (Josh. 20:7; 21:32). The name of Galil (Isa. 9:1) was changed to Galilee, and thus altered, became the designation of the entire large province ruled by Herod Antipas.

It is evident that the term "land" in verse 5 refers primarily to the people who inhabited it. Cf. Jer. 22:29, "Land, land, land, hear the word of Jehovah." This applies also to the other three designations, "toward the sea. . . ." The entire population of this quintuple northern part of Palestine is described as "the people sitting in darkness," and as "those sitting in the land of death's shadow." For centuries those living in this large territory had been exposed to political and military aggression from the north (Syria, Assyria, etc.) and to the corrosive moral and religious influences of a pagan environment. They had been overrun and imperiled on a scale much larger than had been the case with respect to the people of Jerusalem and surroundings (see II Kings 15:29; Isa. 8:4). No doubt to many of the inhabitants of Galilee the words recorded in II Kings 17:33 with specific reference to the Samaritans would also be applicable: "They feared Jehovah, and served their own gods."

---

little connection with the rather poor rendering found in the Septuagint. Matthew, in his own original way, has very ably reproduced Isaiah's thoughts. Essentially Isaiah and Matthew are in perfect agreement: light dawns (or *shines brightly*) upon those formerly in darkness.

Sitting in *darkness* and in *the land of the shadow of death* indicates a condition of danger, fear, and hopelessness, a pining away, with no human help in sight. In Scripture the designation *darkness,* when used figuratively, refers to one or more of the following features: delusion (blindness of mind and heart; cf. II Cor. 4:4, 6; Eph. 4:18); depravity (Acts 26:18); and despondency (Isa. 9:2; see its context, verse 3). Though all three qualities are probably in the picture here, yet the emphasis may well be on the last of the three (despondency, hopelessness), as has already been explained.

The antonym of darkness is *light,* which, accordingly, refers to genuine learning (the true knowledge of God, Ps. 36:9), life to the glory of God (Eph. 4:15, 24; 5:14), and laughter (gladness, Ps. 97:11). All three may well be included, but here too the emphasis is perhaps on the last of the three.

The real meaning of the quotation, accordingly, is this, that Jesus Christ, by his presence, words, deeds of mercy and power, would fill the hearts of all his Galilean followers with the joy of salvation. No longer would they be pining away in gloom and despair. When Jesus comes into Galilee and begins his great ministry there, the words of a popular hymn go into effect,

> The whole world was lost in the darkness of sin,
> The light of the world is Jesus.

Matthew concludes this paragraph by stating **17. From that time Jesus began to preach and to say, Be converted, for the kingdom of heaven is at hand.** The following points should be noted:

a. In *essence,* though not in detail, Christ's message is the same as that of John the Baptist, witness the fact that in 3:2 the herald's proclamation was summarized in identical words. It is unnecessary therefore to repeat the explanation that has already been given; but see also on 4:23.

b. In connection with the preceding context (4:13-16) the meaning here in verse 17 is that Jesus now begins to bring this gospel of the kingdom into regions which the Baptist had not penetrated to any great extent. The good news is beginning to be spread over a wider territory. The demand that men be converted resounds in regions where it had not been heard before.

c. The fact that the coming of Christ has indeed brought about a tremendous change on earth, so that millions of people have been translated from the realm of darkness into the kingdom of light, shows that the proclamation, "the kingdom of heaven *is at hand*" was fully justified.

d. Not immediately or all at once was this message proclaimed throughout the world. From the beginning its spread was intended to be progressive: it was to reach first the Jew (10:5, 6), then also, step by step, all the nations (24:14; 28:19; Acts 13:46; Rom. 1:16). It is not surprising, therefore, that the announcement "the kingdom of heaven is at hand," found first on the lips of the Baptist, then confirmed by Jesus, is at Christ's command repeated by the disciples (Matt. 10:7), with the intention that it shall at last reach the entire world: every nation. Then shall the end come.

18 While he was walking along the Sea of Galilee he saw two brothers, Simon called Peter and Andrew his brother, throwing a casting-net into the sea, for they were fishermen. 19 He said to them, "Come, follow me, and I will make y o u fishers of men." 20 At once they left their nets and followed him. 21 And going on from there he saw two other brothers, James the son of Zebedee and John his brother, in the boat with Zebedee their father, mending their nets; and he called them. 22 And immediately they left the boat and their father and followed him.

4:18-22 *The Calling of Four Fishermen*
Cf. Mark 1:16-20; and for Matt. 4:19b
and Mark 1:17b cf. Luke 5:10b

18-20. While he was walking along the Sea of Galilee he saw two brothers, Simon called Peter and Andrew his brother, throwing a casting-net into the sea, for they were fishermen. He said to them, Come, follow me, and I will make y o u fishers of men. At once they left their nets and followed him.
As stated in the explanation of verse 17 (see especially *d* above), the wonderful gospel of the kingdom was not intended only for the men living during the time of Christ's earthly ministry. It was intended for the ages. It is not at all surprising, therefore, that at the very beginning of his ministry Jesus chose men who, by means of their testimony both oral and written, would perpetuate his work and proclaim his message. For a teacher to have not only a general audience but also a band of *close companions* or *disciples* was nothing new. Did not Socrates have disciples? Did not John the Baptist? The Pharisees? The rabbis? Christ's disciples were to become the links between himself and his church. They were to be the precious foundation stones for Jerusalem the Golden (Rev. 21:19, 20). Think, for example, of the importance of such men as Matthew, John, and Peter in the formation of the Gospels, which are our chief sources of information about Jesus Christ. Accordingly, while he was walking along the Sea of Galilee Jesus invites certain men to come to him.

There were several calls to discipleship and to closely related apostleship:

a. The one mentioned in John 1:35-51. See N.T.C. on those verses.

b. The one mentioned here (Matt. 4:18-22; Mark 1:16-20).

c. The one mentioned in Luke 5:1-11.

d. The one mentioned in Matt. 9:9-13; Mark 2:13-17; Luke 5:27-32.

e. The one mentioned in Matt. 10:1-4; Mark 3:13-19; Luke 6:12-16.

The five invitations differed; probably as follows (explaining *a* to *e* as listed above):

a. About February of the year A.D. 27 this call was extended to Andrew and an unnamed disciple, in all likelihood John, inviting them to accept Jesus of Nazareth as the Messiah, and to become his spiritual followers. Andrew brought his brother Simon (Peter) to Jesus. John probably rendered the same service to his own brother James. Almost immediately afterward

Philip and (through him) Nathaniel were added to the list. Although occasionally accompanying Jesus on his trips, the disciples continued to pursue their secular occupations.

b. This occurred about a year later; hence, about February of the year A.D. 28. The four disciples referred to in John 1:35-41 (Peter, Andrew, James, and John) now become the Lord's more steady companions, and are made more conscious than ever of the fact that they are being trained for apostleship, that is, for becoming "fishers of men." Even now, however, Matt. 4:20 and 22 can hardly be interpreted to mean that they bade a final farewell to their secular occupation as fishermen. More will be said about *b.* in a moment.

c. This takes place a little later. It comprises the story of the miraculous catch of fishes. Luke 5:10b resembles Matt. 4:19b and Mark 1:17b; that is, "catch men" and "become fishers of men," are similar, though perhaps not identical, the Matthew and Mark passages emphasizing the *effort,* the Luke passage the *success.* Aside from this resemblance, however, the two accounts are entirely different. In the Matthew-Mark account Jesus is walking along the sea; in Luke he is standing. In the former Simon and Andrew, James and John are all mentioned by name. All are also addressed by Jesus. In the beloved physician's account Jesus directs his words to Peter alone. Andrew is not even mentioned, though he may have been present. In the earlier account Simon and Andrew are casting a net into the sea; i.e., they are fishing; James and John are mending their nets. In Luke the fishermen are washing their nets. In the former, Peter and Andrew leave their nets and follow Jesus; similarly, James and John leave the boat and their father and follow the Master. But in Luke the disciples *leave all,* during the entire precrucifixion period of Christ's earthly ministry saying farewell to their occupation as fishermen, and following Jesus permanently.

d. This was the call of Matthew (=Levi) the publican, the writer of this Gospel. It probably occurred very shortly after *c.* Proof: see Luke 5:11, 27. Matthew, too, in following Jesus, "forsook all."

e. This concerns the entire group of twelve. For all of them it is the formal call to discipleship-apostleship. There was probably a brief interval between Mark 3:13-19 (cf. Luke 5:27-32) and Matt. 10:1 ff.

The men who were chosen by Jesus to be his immediate companions needed to be trained for apostleship. Simon the fickle must become Peter the rock. Something similar was true with respect to all. When we first meet these men, and to a certain extent even much later, they manifest lack of deep spiritual penetration (Matt. 13:6; 15:33; 16:7-12, 22, 23; 17:10-13; 19:10-12, 23-30; 24:3); of fervent sympathy (14:15, 16, 23; 19:13-15); of profound humility (18:1-4); of the gladly forgiving spirit (18:21, 22); of persevering prayerfulness (17:16-21); and of unflinching courage (26:56, 69-75). Nevertheless, on their part it required a degree of courage to become

246

Christ's followers and thereby face the opposition of many, including the religious leaders. For further details on The Twleve see on 10:1-4.

In this connection one fact must not be ignored. *Their* decision to side with Jesus exhibits *his* greatness: the impelling force of his influence over the minds and hearts of men, so that when he calls they follow immediately. The breadth of his sympathy and the magnitude of his power are also shown here. Is it not marvelous that he was willing and able to take such common folk, four fishermen, etc., unlettered individuals, and, in spite of all their prejudices and superstitions, to transform them into instruments for the salvation of many; to make them leaders who, by means of their testimonies, would turn the world upside down?

The four mentioned in verses 18-22 are:

Peter, the impetuous (Matt. 14:28-33; 16:22, 23; 26:33-35; John 18:10), who becomes the leader of The Twelve, and is mentioned first in every list of apostles (Matt. 10:2-4; Mark 3:16-19; Luke 6:14-16; and Acts 1:13).

Peter's brother Andrew, who is always bringing people to Jesus (John 1:40-42; 6:8, 9, cf. Matt. 14:18; John 12:22).

Zebedee's son James, the first of The Twelve to wear the martyr's crown (Acts 12:1, 2).

His brother John, who is called "the disciple whom Jesus loved" (John 13:23; 19:26; etc.). To be sure, the Lord loved all "his own" very intensely (John 13:1, 2), but between Jesus and John the tie of attachment and understanding was the tenderest. [247]

A few more details now on verses 18-20. Peter and Andrew were throwing a casting-net into the sea. For *net* Matthew uses three different words. One is *diktuon,* used in verses 20 and 21. It is the most comprehensive or general word of all, and can refer to any net whatever, even a hunting net or a net for catching birds. In the New Testament, however, it is confined to fishing nets of any and every description. The *sagene* is the *seine* or *dragnet.* Very appropriately it is used in Matt. 13:47; see on that verse. The third is the one used here in 4:18 (and Mark 1:16), the *amphiblestron,* i.e., *casting-net.* When skillfully cast over the shoulder it will spread out, forming a circle as it falls into the water, and then, because of the pieces of lead attached to it, will quickly sink into the water, capturing the fish underneath. [248] That was the kind of net with which Peter and Andrew were fishing when Jesus, walking along the sea, said to them, "Come, follow me, and I will make y o u fishers of men." The Lord exercises his sovereignty over these men, not even allowing them to finish their work. They must be ready to follow immediately when he calls them. Cf. 8:21, 22; 10:37.

---

[247] Much can be learned from A. B. Bruce, *The Training of the Twelve,* Garden City, New York, 1928; and from C. E. Macartney, *Of Them He Chose Twelve,* Philadelphia, 1927.
[248] See R. C. Trench, *Synonyms of the New Testament,* Grand Rapids, 1948, par. lxiv.

Peter and Andrew hailed from Bethsaida (John 1:45), but Peter had recently moved to Capernaum (Matt. 4:13; 8:5, 14, 15; Mark 1:21, 29, 30; Luke 4:31, 33, 38). By this time these men had come to know Jesus, because a year had elapsed since the unforgettable event recorded in John 1:35-42. Hence, when he now (Matt. 4:19) said to them, "Come, follow me, and I will make y o u fishers of men," they at once left their nets and followed, encouraged by the promise of their Lord to train them for a task far superior even to the honorable one in which they were now engaged. Instead of catching fish for the table they would recruit men for the kingdom.

It must not escape us that by means of the promise, "I will make y o u fishers of men" Jesus sets the seal of his approval upon the words of the inspired author of the book of Proverbs, "He who wins souls is wise" (Prov. 11:30); confirms Dan. 12:3: "They that turn many to righteousness shall shine as the stars forever and ever"; adds his own authority to Paul's striking statement, "To all I became all, that in one way or another I may save some" (I Cor. 9:22); and anticipates his own glorious invitation, "Come to me, all who are weary and burdened, and I will give y o u rest" (Matt. 11:28).

Two other disciples of Jesus were given the same command and promise: **21, 22. And going on from there he saw two other brothers, James the son of Zebedee and John his brother, in the boat with Zebedee their father, mending their nets; and he called them. And immediately they left the boat and their father, and followed him.** These two are not fishing like Peter and Andrew, but mending their nets. They receive the same call. They too must be ready at this time to enter into a new relationship (stage *b*, pp. 245, 246), that is, a *transition* from *a*. off-and-on fellowship with Christ (the John 1:39 stage) to *c*. permanent discipleship with abandonment of secular vocation (the Luke 5:11 stage). They must immediately leave the boat and their father, to follow Jesus. Doing a little fishing now and then as long as Jesus has his headquarters in Capernaum is not excluded, as Luke 5:10 clearly shows. The time is coming, however, when being fishers of men will be their permanent occupation (Luke 5:11). Even now they must start training in earnest for apostleship.

James and John obey at once. They leave the boat and their father. As to Zebedee's business? It remains intact. Zebedee is not a poor man. He has servants who continue to help him in his business, so that whenever his sons are not able to be with him because of their increasingly closer association with Jesus, these servants can be depended upon to find ways in which to fill the gap (Mark 1:20). Provision has been made for every need.

---

23 And he went through all Galilee, teaching in their synagogues and preaching the gospel of the kingdom, and healing every illness and every infirmity among the people. 24 So the news about him spread throughout Syria; and they brought to him all who

were afflicted, distressed by all kinds of illnesses and torments, demoniacs, epileptics, and paralytics; and he healed them. 25 Huge crowds followed him, from Galilee and Decapolis and Jerusalem and Judea and from beyond the Jordan.

4:23-25 *Christ's Teaching, Preaching, and Healing*
Cf. Mark 1:39; Luke 4:44

23. The type of work Jesus did during his Great Galilean Ministry is now briefly summarized. It was not confined to Capernaum, for we read: **And he went through all Galilee, teaching in their synagogues and preaching the gospel of the kingdom, and healing every illness and every infirmity among the people.** In several ways Jesus' activity differed from that of John: *a.* John preached in the open; Jesus also in the synagogue; *b.* John preached; Jesus also taught; *c.* in his preaching John emphasized the need of repentance in view of the imminent judgment; Jesus, though not neglecting this, placed greater emphasis on the positive message: he proclaimed the kingdom's *gospel* (see N.T.C. on Philippians, pp. 81-85); *d.* "John came neither eating nor drinking; the Son of man came eating and drinking" (11:18, 19); and finally, *e.* John preached and baptized; Jesus preached and performed miracles of healing.

Between preaching and teaching there is a difference, though it is true that good preaching is also teaching. The emphasis, nevertheless, is not the same. The word used in the original for *preaching* means *heralding, announcing, proclaiming* (see N.T.C. on I and II Timothy and Titus, p. 310). *Teaching,* on the other hand, indicates imparting more detailed information regarding the announcement that was made. Jesus made full use of his opportunity to preach and to teach in the synagogue (13:53-58; Mark 6:1-6; Luke 4:16-31).

In the phrase "the gospel of the kingdom," what is meant by "the kingdom"? What has already been said concerning this need not be repeated (see p. 87, also see on 3:2 and on 4:17). In its broadest connotation *the terms "the kingdom of heaven," "the kingdom of God,"* or simply *"the kingdom"* (when the context makes clear that what is mean is "the kingdom of heaven or of God") *indicate God's kingship, rule or sovereignty,* recognized in the hearts and operative in the lives of his people, and effecting their *complete salvation,* their constitution as a *church,* and finally a *redeemed universe.* Note especially the four concepts:

a. God's kingship, rule, or recognized sovereignty. That may be the meaning in Luke 17:21, "The kingdom of God is within you," and is the meaning in Matt. 6:10, "Thy kingdom come, thy will be done...."

b. Complete salvation, i.e., all the spiritual and material blessings—that is, blessings for soul and body—which result when God is King in our hearts, recognized and obeyed as such. That is the meaning, according to the context, in Mark 10:25, 26, "It is easier ... than for a rich man to enter the kingdom of God. And they ... said, 'Then who can be saved?' "

c. The church: the community of men in whose hearts God is recognized as King. Kingdom of God and church when used in this sense are nearly equivalent. This is the meaning in Matt. 16:18, 19. ". . . and upon this rock will I build my church. . . . I will give unto you the keys of the kingdom of heaven."

d. The redeemed universe: the new heaven and earth with all their glory; something still future: the final realization of God's saving power. Thus in Matt. 25:34, ". . . inherit the kingdom prepared for you. . . ."

These four meanings are not separate and unrelated. They all proceed from the central idea of the reign of God, his supremacy in the sphere of saving power. The *kingdom* or *kingship* (the Greek word has both meanings) of heaven is like a gradually developing mustard seed; hence, both present and future (Mark 4:26-29). It is present; study Matt. 5:3; 12:28; 19:14; Mark 10:15; 12:34; Luke 7:28; 17:20, 21; John 3:3-5; 18:36. It is future; study Matt. 7:21, 22; 25:34; 26:29.

Jesus spoke of the work of salvation as the kingdom or reign of heaven in order to indicate the supernatural character, origin, and purpose of our salvation. Our salvation begins in heaven and should redound to the glory of the Father in heaven. Hence, by using this term Christ defended the truth, so precious to all believers, that everything is subservient to God's glory.

Not only did Jesus preach and teach; he also healed. No sickness was too hard for him to cure, no infirmity too difficult to relieve; hence, "every (kind of) illness and every (kind of) infirmity."

Christ's healing miracles had a threefold significance: *a*. they confirmed his message (John 14:11); *b*. they showed that he was indeed the Messiah of prophecy (Isa. 35:5; 53:4, 5; 61:1; Matt. 11:2-6); and *c*. they proved that in a sense the kingdom had even now arrived, for, as has already been indicated, the concept "kingdom" includes blessings for the body as well as for the soul. The Gospels everywhere establish a very close connection between the concepts *kingdom* and *miracles* (Matt. 9:35; 10:7, 8; 12:28; Luke 9:1, 2; and cf. also Acts 8:6, 7, 12).

The universal character of the healings is also brought out by the fact that since Jesus was going through *all* Galilee, the Galilee with its mixture of Jew and Gentile, and healed "every illness and every infirmity among the people," hence he never even asked a sick person, "Are you a Jew or a Gentile?" He healed *all*, regardless of race or nationality. Truly he was, and is, "the Savior of the world" (John 4:42; I John 4:14).

The result of all this healing activity in Galilee is indicated in verse 24. **So the news about him spread throughout Syria.** The news quickly spread, so that Syria heard about it. It is evident that the term "Syria" in this connection cannot mean the entire Roman province, which, until A.D. 70, included Palestine, but rather the region to the north of Galilee toward Antioch and Damascus. Many Jews had settled in these northern cities; some voluntarily, some by forced removal from one region to another. Economic, social, and religious ties bound the hearts of these Jews to those of their relatives and friends in Galilee and Judea. Moreover, there were good road connections between the various cities. We have already seen that Capernaum in Galilee was situated on the highway that came down from Damascus. Antioch and Damascus were similarly connected. And then there was the coast-highway that came down from Antioch and passed through Tyre, Galilee, and Gaza, on its way to Egypt. [249]

It is therefore not at all surprising that from far and near also these northern regions brought to Jesus their afflicted ones, that he might heal them: **and they brought to him all who were afflicted, distressed by all kinds of illnesses and torments, demoniacs, epileptics, and paralytics; and he healed them.**

"Illnesses and torments" is the general term, showing that Jesus was able to cure every illness, no matter what it might be. Pains fled at his touch or even simply at his word of power. Particular mention is made of three groups: demoniacs, epileptics, and paralytics. For the subject of demon-possession see on 9:32-34. For the present it is only necessary to point out that *demoniacs* heads the list, and very properly, for demon-possession was considered the cause of various other afflictions (9:33; 12:22; 17:15, 18; Mark 9:25; Luke 13:10-12, 16).

The word which, in line with many translators and commentators, I have rendered *epileptics,* is etymologically connected with the moon. Accordingly, some prefer the rendering "moon-struck persons" or "lunatics." However, 17:15, where the same word is used and the affliction is graphically described, would seem to make it clear that the reference is to those who suffered from seizures; hence, epileptics. Though word-derivation is important, it should not prevail over detailed description of an illness. The point is that these, too, were immediately healed by the Master, healed once for all. And this was also the case with *paralytics.* Striking examples of such healings are reported in 8:5-13 (cf. Luke 7:1-10) and in 9:1-8 (cf. Mark 2:1-12 and Luke 5:17-26).

It is evident, therefore, that the Son of God was going forth to war. He was destroying the works of the devil, teaching and preaching, casting out demons and healing sicknesses by the power of the Spirit, thus healing both soul and body, and more and more establishing the kingdom of God on earth (Matt. 12:28).

End-result: 25. **Huge crowds followed him, from Galilee and Decapolis and Jerusalem and Judea and from beyond the Jordan.** Naturally, from *Galilee.* Also, however, from *Decapolis,* that is, from the region of *the ten*

---

[249] All of these roads, and many more, are vividly described and mapped in V. W. Von Hagen, *The Roads That Led to Rome,* Cleveland and New York, 1967, pp. 18, 19; see especially the map on pp. 18, 19.

cities, a federation extending, for the most part, northeast of Samaria, and to some extent even northeast of Galilee, and consisting of the cities: Damascus, Kanata, Dion, Hippos, Gadara, Abila, Scythopolis, Pella, Geresa, and Philadelphia. Jerusalem, too, and in fact all of Judea, heard what was happening in the north. So, also from the south people came to swell the crowds that followed Jesus. They heard his words and saw—and in many cases were benefitted by—his miracles. Even Perea, the region east of the Jordan and, mostly, south of Decapolis sent its representatives. The multitude must have been immense!

Summary of Chapter 4:12-25

4:12-17. This brief paragraph describes the beginning of the Great Galilean Ministry. Perhaps about a year after the happenings recorded in 3:13—4:11 (baptism and temptation) Jesus "withdrew into Galilee." He bade farewell to Nazareth, which had been his home until about the age of thirty, and settled in Capernaum situated on the Sea of Galilee's northwestern shore. He did this in fulfilment of Isa. 9:1, 2.

Also, John the Baptist had been taken into custody, and the attention of the Judean population among whom Jesus had been laboring for some time was now wholly concentrated on their great Benefactor whom the Baptist himself had introduced. Jesus, in turn, knew that remaining any longer in the south, with its jealous Pharisees and Sadducees, would lead to a premature crisis. Hence he set out for Galilee. He must not die before the appointed time.

In Galilee he made Capernaum his headquarters, and from there traversed the entire northern territory, teaching, preaching, and healing, so that the light of salvation dawned upon those who were formerly dwelling in the darkness of despair, and the kingdom of heaven began to prosper on earth.

4:18-22. While walking along the Sea of Galilee, Jesus called to himself Peter and Andrew, who were fishing when they heard Jesus say to them, "Come, follow me, and I will make y o u fishers of men." Immediately they obeyed. So did also James and John who a little later were similarly called as they were mending their nets. These four had already known the Master for perhaps about a year, and had been spending some of their time in his company. Now, however, they start training in earnest for apostleship, that is, for being sent out by themselves to proclaim the good news.

4:23-25. The report of Christ's teaching, preaching, and healing spread far and wide. Syria to the north, Decapolis and Perea to the east, and even Judea to the south were represented in the huge crowds that followed Jesus during his Galilean journeys. He healed all the afflicted, including even demoniacs, epileptics, and paralytics. He cured them at once and completely.

No second treatment at some later time was necessary. He restored them because he sympathized with them and loved them.

Among the many art portrayals of Christ's healing power the following deserve special mention: A. Deitrich's painting entitled, "Christ, have mercy on us" (print and description in Cynthia P. Maus, *Christ and the Fine Arts*, New York, 1959, pp. 248-250); J. M. F. H. Hofmann's drawing, "Christ healing the sick" (copy and interpretation in Albert E. Bailey, *The Gospel in Art*, Boston, 1946, pp. 188-192); and, last but not least, centering around the same theme, Rembrandt van Rijn's unforgettably beautiful etching called "the hundred guilder print" (reproduction and explanatory marginal notes in Robert Wallace and the editors of Time-Life Books, *The World of Rembrandt*, New York, 1968, pp. 154-157).

Chapters 5-7

Theme: *The Work Which Thou Gavest Him to Do*

The Sermon on the Mount

The First Great Discourse

CHAPTERS V-VII

5 1 When he saw the crowds he went up into the mountain; and when he had seated himself his disciples came to him.   2 And he opened his mouth and began to teach them, saying:

3 "Blessed (are) the poor in spirit, for theirs is the kingdom of heaven.

4 "Blessed the mourners, for they shall be comforted.

5 "Blessed the meek, for they shall inherit the earth.

6."Blessed those hungering and thirsting for righteousness, for they shall be fully satisfied.

7 "Blessed the merciful, for they shall have mercy shown to them.

8 "Blessed the pure in heart, for they shall see God.

9 "Blessed the peace-makers, for they shall be called sons of God.

10 "Blessed those persecuted for righteousness' sake, for theirs is the kingdom of heaven.

11 "Blessed are y o u whenever people heap insults upon y o u and persecute y o u and, while telling falsehoods, say all kinds of evil about y o u for my sake. 12 Rejoice, yes, be filled with unrestrained gladness, for y o u r reward is great in heaven, for in the same way did they persecute the prophets who lived before y o u r time.

13 "Y o u are the salt of the earth; but if the salt becomes tasteless, what will make it salty again? It is then good for nothing but to be thrown away and trampled underfoot by men.

14 "Y o u are the light of the world. A city situated on a hill cannot be hidden.   15 Nor do men light a lamp and place it under the peck-measure, but on the lampstand, and it gives light to everyone in the house.   16 So let y o u r light shine before men that they may see y o u r good works and glorify y o u r Father who is in heaven.

17 "Do not think that I have come to set aside the law or the prophets. I have not come to set aside but to fulfil.   18 For I solemnly declare to y o u, Until heaven and earth disappears not even the tiniest letter or the tiniest hook on a letter will in any way disappear from the law until all (it calls for) shall have taken place.   19 Therefore, whoever annuls one of the least of these commandments and so teaches men shall be called least in the kingdom of heaven; but whoever practices and teaches them, he shall be called great in the kingdom of heaven.   20 For I tell y o u that unless y o u r righteousness excels that of the scribes and Pharisees, y o u will surely never enter the kingdom of heaven.

21 "Y o u have heard that it was said by the men of long ago, 'You shall not kill,' and 'whoever kills deserves to be punished (with death).'   22 But I say to y o u that (even) anyone who is angry with his brother deserves to be punished (with death). And whoever says to his brother, 'You blockhead!' deserves to be condemned (to death) by

255

the supreme court. And whoever says, 'You idiot' deserves to be cast into the hell of fire. [250]

23 "Therefore if, while you are bringing your offering to the altar, you there remember that your brother has a grievance [251] against you, 24 leave your offering there in front of the altar, and first go and be reconciled to your brother, then come (back) and present your offering. 25 Make friends quickly with your opponent, while you still have the opportunity to deal with him, [252] lest the opponent hand you over to the judge, and the judge to the officer, and you be thrown into prison. 26 I solemnly declare to you, never will you get out of that place until you have paid the last cent.

27 "Y o u have heard that it was said, 'you shall not commit adultery.' 28 But I say to y o u that anyone who looks at a woman in order to lust after her has already commited adultery with her in his heart. 29 So if your right eye lures you into sin, [253] pluck it out and fling it away from you. It is better that you lose one of your members than that your whole body be thrown into hell. 30 And if your right hand lures you into sin, cut it off and fling it away from you. It is better that you lose one of your members than that your whole body go down into hell.

31 "It was also said, 'Whoever divorces his wife, let him give her a divorce certificate.' 32 But I say to y o u that whoever divorces his wife except on the ground of (her) infidelity [254] exposes her to adultery, and whoever marries a divorced woman involves himself in adultery.

33 "Again, y o u have heard that it was said by the men of long ago, 'You shall not break your oath, but shall keep the oaths you have sworn to the Lord.' 34 But I tell y o u, Do not take any oath at all, either by heaven, for it is God's throne, or by the earth, for it is his footstool, or by Jerusalem, for it is the city of the great King. 36 Nor shall you swear by your head, for you cannot make one hair white or black. 37 Let y o u r speech be such that 'yes' is simply 'yes' and 'no' is simply 'no.' Anything beyond that comes from the evil one.

38 "Y o u have heard that it was said, 'An eye for an eye and a tooth for a tooth.' 39 But I tell y o u, Do not resist the evil-doer; but to him that slaps you on the right cheek turn the other also. 40 And if anyone wishes to go to law with you and take your shirt, let him take your robe also. 41 And whoever forces you to go one mile, go with him two. 42 To him that asks (anything) of you give, and from him that wants to borrow of you do not turn away.

43 "Y o u have heard that it was said, 'You shall love your neighbor and hate your enemy.' 44 But I tell y o u, love y o u r enemies and pray for those that persecute y o u, 45 that y o u may be sons of y o u r Father who is in heaven, for he causes his sun to rise on evil (people) and good, and sends rain on righteous and unrighteous. 46 For if y o u love those who love y o u, what is y o u r reward? Are not the tax-collectors doing the same thing? 47 And if, with cordial greetings, y o u approach y o u r brothers only, what are y o u doing that is exceptional? Are not the Gentiles doing as much? 48 Y o u, therefore, must be perfect, as y o u r heavenly Father is perfect.

---

250 In the translation and explanation of verse 21 and 22 I have been aided by the article of J. Jeremias on ῥακά, Th.D.N.T., Vol. VI, pp. 973-976. Nevertheless, a comparison will also reveal differences.

251 Literally "has something against you." However, this rendering can easily lead to a wrong interpretation. See the explanation on this. Therefore, I prefer the rendering favored also by N.E.B.

252 Literally, "while you are on the way with him," i.e., before it is too late.

253 Or: ensnares you, and so also in verse 30.

254 Or: fornication.

6 1 "Take care that y o u do not practice y o u r righteousness before the people, to attract their attention; otherwise y o u will not have any reward with y o u r Father who is in heaven. 2 So, whenever you give to the poor do not publicly announce it with a blast of the trumpet, [255] as the hypocrites are in the habit of doing in the synagogues and in the alleyways in order to win the admiration of the people. I solemnly declare to y o u, they have already received their reward in full. 3 But when you give to charity, do not let your left hand know what your right hand is doing, 4 that your deeds of charity may be (performed) in secret; and your Father who sees in secret will reward you.

5 "Also, whenever y o u pray, do not be like the hypocrites, for they love to say their prayers standing up in the synagogues and at the street corners, that they may be seen by the people. I solemnly declare to y o u, they have already received their reward in full. 6 But whenever you pray, enter into your most private room, and having shut your door, pray to your Father who is in secret; and your Father who sees in secret will reward you. 7 Moreover, in praying, do not babble on and on like pagans, [256] for they imagine that they will be heard because of their flow of words. 8 Do not be like them therefore, for y o u r Father knows what y o u need before y o u (even) ask him. 9 This, then, is how y o u should pray:

'Our Father who art in heaven,
Hallowed be thy name.
10 Thy kingdom come,
Thy will be done,
as in heaven so on earth.
11 Give us this day our daily bread,[257]
12 And forgive us our debts
as we also have forgiven our debtors,
13 And lead us not into temptation
but deliver us from the evil one. [258]
[For thine is the kingdom, and the power,
and the glory, forever. Amen.]'

14 "For if y o u forgive men their trespasses, y o u r heavenly Father will also forgive y o u. 15 But if y o u do not forgive men, neither will y o u r Father forgive y o u r trespasses.

16 "And whenever y o u fast, do not be like the hypocrites, looking glum, for they make their faces unsightly in order that (other) people may see that they are fasting. I solemnly declare to y o u, they have already received their reward in full. 17 But you, when you fast, anoint your head and wash your face, 18 that not men but (only) your Father who is in secret may see that you are fasting. And your Father who sees in secret will reward you.

19 "Do not gather for yourselves [259] treasures on earth, where moth and rust consume, and where thieves dig through and steal. 20 But gather for yourselves treasures in heaven, where neither moth nor rust consume, and where thieves do not dig through and steal. 21 For where your treasure is, there will your heart be also.

22 "The eye is the body's lamp. Therefore if your eye is sound, your whole

---

[255] Or: Do not sound a trumpet before you.
[256] Or: as the Gentiles do.
[257] Or: Give us today our bread for today; or: . . our needful bread.
[258] Or: from evil.
[259] Or: Stop gathering for yourselves.

body will be illumined. 23 But if your eye is in poor condition, your whole body will be dark. If then the (very) light in you is darkness, how great (is) that darkness!

24 "No one can serve two masters; for either he will hate the one and love the other, or he will be devoted to one and look down on the other. Y o u cannot serve God and Mammon.

25 "Therefore I say to y o u, Do not be anxious [260] about y o u r life, what y o u are going to eat or what y o u are going to drink, nor about y o u r body, what y o u are going to wear. Is not life more important than food, and the body more important than clothes? 26 Look at the birds of the air. They neither sow nor reap nor gather into barns, yet y o u r heavenly Father feeds them. Y o u are of more value than they, are y o u not? 27 And who among y o u is able, by being anxious, to add (even) one cubit to his life-span? 28 Moreover, why be anxious about clothes? Consider the lillies of the field, how they grow; they neither toil nor spin; 29 yet I tell y o u that even Solomon in all his splendor was not attired [261] like one of these. 30 Now if God so clothes the grass of the field, which today is alive and tomorrow is thrown into the furnace, will he not much more surely clothe y o u, O men of little faith? 31 So, do not become anxious, saying, 'What are we going to eat?' or 'What are we going to drink?' or 'What are we going to wear?' 32 For all these things the Gentiles crave; besides, y o u r heavenly Father knows that y o u need them all. 33 But seek first his kingdom and his righteousness, and all these things will be granted to y o u as an extra gift. 34 Do not therefore become anxious for tomorrow, for tomorrow will be anxious for itself. Each day has enough trouble all by itself.

7 1 "Do not pass judgment (on others), that y o u may not have judgment passed on yourselves. 2 For in accordance with the judgment whereby y o u pass judgment y o u yourselves will be judged; and in accordance with the measure whereby y o u measure it will be measured back to y o u. 3 And why do you gaze at the speck in your brother's eye, while the beam that is in your own eye you do not (even) observe? 4 Or how can you say to your brother, 'Let me take the speck out of your eye,' and look! a beam in your own eye? 5 You hypocrite, first take the beam out of your own eye, and then you will see clearly (enough) to take the speck out of your brother's eye. 6 Do not give what is holy to the dogs, and do not fling y o u r pearls before the hogs lest they trample on them with their feet, and turn and tear y o u to pieces.

7 "Ask, and it shall be given to y o u; seek, and y o u shall find; knock, and it shall be opened to y o u. 8 For whoever asks receives, and the one who seeks finds, and to him that knocks it shall be opened. 9 Or what man is there among y o u, who, when his son asks him for bread, will give him a stone? 10 Or also (if the son) asks for a fish, will give him a serpent? 11 If, therefore, y o u, evil though y o u are, know how to give good gifts to y o u r children, how much more will y o u r Father in heaven give good things to those who ask him! 12 Therefore whatever y o u want (other) people to do for y o u, do also for them, for this is the law and the prophets.

13 "Enter by the narrow gate; for wide (is) the gate and broad the way that leads to destruction, and many are those who enter by it. 14 For narrow (is) the gate and constricted the way that leads to life, and few are those who find it.

15 "Beware of false prophets, who come to y o u in sheep's clothing, but inwardly are ravenous wolves. 16 By their fruits y o u will recognize them. Grapes are not picked from thorns, or figs from thistles, are they? 17 So every healthy tree bears

---

260 Or: Stop being anxious; or: Stop worrying.
261 Or: did not clothe himself.

good fruit, but the sickly tree bears worthless fruit. 18 A healthy tree cannot bear worthless fruit, neither can a sickly tree bear good fruit. 19 Every tree that does not yield good fruit is cut down and thrown into the fire. 20 Therefore by their fruits y o u will recognize them.

21 "Not everyone who says to me, 'Lord, Lord' will enter the kingdom of heaven, but the one who puts into practice the will of my Father who (is) in heaven. 22 Many will say to me in that day, 'Lord, Lord, in thy name did we not prophesy, and in thy name did we not cast out demons, and in thy name did we not perform many mighty works?' 23 And then will I say to them openly, 'Never have I known y o u; go away from me, y o u law despisers!'

24 "Everyone then who hears these words of mine and puts them into practice will be like a sensible man, who built his house on rock. 25 Down poured the rain, and there came the floods, while the winds blew and fell upon that house, but it did not fall, for it was founded on rock. 26 And everyone who hears these words of mine and does not put them into practice will be like a foolish man, who built his house on sand. 27 Down poured the rain and there came the floods, while the winds blew and beat against that house, and it fell, and the crash it produced was tremendous." [262]

28 Now when Jesus had finished these sayings the crowds were astounded at his teaching, 29 for he was teaching them as having authority, and not as their scribes.

5:1—7:29 *The Sermon on the Mount*
Cf. Luke 6:17-49

As was mentioned earlier (see pp. 26-28) it is characteristic of Matthew to introduce a subject and then to expand upon it. The river broadens into a lake. So also here. Christ's preaching and his healing have been introduced (respectively 4:12-17, 23a and 4:23b, 24). So now a sample of this teaching is given in 5:1—7:29; of the healing, in 8:1—9:34.

First, then, the Sermon on the Mount. It was probably delivered in the spring of the year 28, after Jesus had spent a night in prayer (Luke 6:12). The prayer was followed by the choosing of the twelve disciples (Mark 3:13-19; Luke 6:13-16; on Matt. 10:1-4 see p. 449). This, in turn, was followed by the healing of many sick (Luke 6:17-19). The sermon was next (Luke 6:19, 20).

Introduction to the Sermon

As the popular title indicates, Jesus was on "the mountain" when he preached this sermon: 5:1, 2. **When he saw the crowds he went up into the mountain; and when he had seated himself his disciples came to him. And he opened his mouth and began to teach them, saying. . . .** From Matt. 8:5 and Luke 7:1 it would appear that the mountain referred to was in the general vicinity of Capernaum. The definite article ("the" mountain, not just "a" mountain) probably shows that a well-known mountain is indicated. Was it the *Horns of Hattin*, named thus because its peaks resemble two horns when

---

262 Or: and its fall was great.

seen from afar? This elevation is located about four miles west of the Sea of Galilee and about eight miles southwest of Capernaum. Or was it even closer to, and in the same direction from, Capernaum? If so, the reference could be to the gentle, grassy slope just west of Tabgha. [263]

In connection with the site of the sermon there is this other problem, that according to Luke the sermon was preached "on a level place" (6:17), but according to Matthew "on the mountain." The seeming contradiction disappears either by supposing that Jesus delivered his discourse on a mountain-plain; or that, having chosen his disciples on the mountain top, he with them descended to a plain where he healed the sick, and afterward with the disciples returned to the top (see Mark 3:13; Luke 6:17; and Matt. 5:1, in that order). If the latter view be adopted it would then appear that in the plain he *stood* to heal the sick; on the mountain top he *sat,* according to the then prevailing custom (Mark 4:1; 9:35; 13:3; Luke 4:20), to deliver the sermon. Whichever view one adopts it is clear that a conflict between Matthew and Luke cannot be proved.

Matt. 5:1–7:29 and Luke 6:17-49 clearly convey the impression that all the sayings contained in these two sections were spoken at *one* time and constitute *one* sermon. The entire discourse is preceded by: "And he opened his mouth and began to teach them saying" (Matt. 5:2; cf. Luke 6:20). It concludes with the words, "Now when Jesus had finished these sayings" (Matt. 7:28; cf. Luke 7:1).

It is clear that the sermon recorded by Matthew and the one reported by Luke are one and the same. The historical setting is the same in both; i.e., in both Gospels the sermon is preceded by the account of a great multitude flocking to Jesus to be healed. It is followed—either immediately, as in Luke, or almost immediately, as in Matthew—by the story of the healing of the centurion's servant. Also, the train of thought is to a considerable extent the same in both: the beatitudes, the supremacy of the law of love, and the parable of the two builders. Cf. Matt. 5:3-12 with Luke 6:20-23; Matt. 5:43-48 with Luke 6:27-38; and Matt. 7:24-27 with Luke 6:47-49. It is admitted, nevertheless, that the two reports are by no means identical. In fact, Matthew's coverage is more than three times as extensive as Luke's. This shows that the Gospel writers were not mere copyists. Each wrote in accordance with his own background, character, and endowment. Perhaps even more important: each wrote in harmony with his own specific purpose. Thus it is not surprising that Matthew includes various matters that were of special interest to his *Jewish* readers whom he was trying to reach for Christ (for example, 5:17-42; 6:1-6, 16-18). Since Luke was not primarily writing for Jews he omits such matters. On the other hand Luke's account contains

---

263 See Howard La Fay, "Where Jesus Walked," *National Geographic,* Vol. 132, No. 6 (Dec. 1967), p. 763.

material (6:24-26, 38-40) not found in that identical form in Matthew. (Even here there is at times a resemblance; cf. Luke 6:38 with Matt. 7:2b.) As was pointed out previously (see p. 35) it is not only possible but very probable that many of the sayings found in The Sermon on the Mount were repeated by the Lord as he traveled from place to place.

The Mount of the Beatitudes has often been compared and contrasted with Mount Horeb, where Moses received the law from God. On the one hand, Mount Horeb: cold, bleak, barren, almost inaccessible, situated in the midst of a howling wilderness with its fiery serpents. On the other hand, the Mount of the Beatitudes with its smiling landscapes and grassy slopes, as it were extending a hearty welcome to all and spreading delight by means of its lilies, daisies, hyacinths, and anemones. At Horeb: God appearing in thunder and lightning, and the people overcome with fear. In Galilee: Immanuel, grace and truth proceeding from his lips, sitting down in the midst of his disciples who listen without fear or trembling. Yet we must be careful. Although it is true that from Mt. Horeb Jehovah revealed his greatness and his glory, nevertheless *the law was given in a context of love* (see Exod. 20:2; Deut. 5:2, 3, 6, 28, 29, 32, 33; 6:3-5). Also, what was proclaimed at Sinai is not set aside but is given its deeply spiritual interpretation by Jesus Christ (cf. Matt. 5:17).

There are those who claim that when Jesus delivered this sermon he neither directly nor indirectly had in view the church of today, and that its precepts are unlivable today, "irrelevant" to the conditions prevailing in this modern age. Objection: This view can be maintained only when it is coupled with a crassly literal interpretation of such passages as 5:29, 30, 34. However, the very thrust of the sermon is directed against this error in interpretation (see 5:21-48). Jesus throughout his ministry opposed it. Friend and foe alike were constantly taking literally those precious statements of the Master that were meant to be taken figuratively (John 2:19, 20; 3:3, 4; 4:10, 11, 32, 33; 6:51, 52; 11:11-13; 14:4-6). Besides, even Jesus himself did not carry out all these precepts literally; cf., for example, Matt. 5:34 with 26:63, 64, which shows that under the proper circumstances the Lord did not object to the oath. It is evident that the various teachings here presented must be interpreted in the light of their specific contexts and according to their broad spiritual purpose. When this is done, it will become evident that Christ in this discourse deals with those fundamental principles of conduct which, according to his own testimony, remain the same in every age (Matt. 5:17, 18). Even in his prayers Jesus refused to limit his horizon to the people living during the time of his own earthly sojourn (John 17:20, 21).

The wisdom of Christ applies today as well as yesterday. *Now* as well as *then* the poor in spirit, etc., are, and are pronounced, blessed (5:1-12). Today, too, believers in the Lord Jesus Christ are the salt of the earth and the light of the world (5:13, 14). Also at this present time not only the outward deed of murder but also the inner disposition of hatred that could lead to it are punishable in God's sight (5:21, 22). Now as well as then adultery is a matter not only of the outward act but also of the polluted heart and lustful eye (5:23-26). It is not true that this discourse has meaning only for one age and not for another, or that it can be applied only to a certain class of people—the still unconverted, for example—but not to others. The principles here enunciated are applicable always and to all. The unconverted person should listen in order that he may recognize his total inability to keep these precepts and may flee to Christ for refuge (Matt. 11:28-30; John 3:16). The believer should take to heart the lessons here taught, in order that in the strength of the Lord and by his grace he may begin to obey them "out of gratitude."

The *under*estimation of this discourse, as if it applied only to certain groups or to men living during a certain period of history must be condemned. So, however, must its *over*estimation. It amounts to this, "We do not believe in theology; we believe in the Sermon on the Mount. It contains all we need to know in order to live as Christians. It has no blood theology; no doctrine, only ethics."

Answer: It is surely a very arbitrary procedure *to accept* the Sermon on the Mount but *to reject* those sayings *of the same Jesus* in which he demands faith in himself as present Savior and future Judge (Matt. 16:16-20; 22:42-45; 25:31-46; John 14:1 ff. etc.), and clearly teaches the doctrine of atonement by blood (Matt. 20:28; Mark 10:45; John 6:53, 55; etc.). Besides, does not even the sermon itself declare the majesty of Christ? See especially 5:17; 7:21-23, 28, 29. The reason why the doctrine of the atonement is not here specifically set forth *may be* that even the disciples were not yet ready to receive it. It was reserved for later.

But whatever *was* the reason we have no right to pick and choose between Christ's teachings, rejecting the one and accepting the other. Besides, the way here prescribed and *the way of the cross* do not clash but blend beautifully (cf. Matt. 5:3-5, 10-12 with 16:24-26; John 15:20). Essentially they are the same.

Sermon Summary

The sermon itself is well organized. This is true with respect to *all* the reported discourses of our Lord. Let preachers take note of this in making *their* sermons. Jesus never rambled. He chose a *theme*. In the present case that theme is obviously *"the gospel of the kingdom"* (4:23). Throughout the discourse this kingdom is mentioned again and again (5:3, 10, 19, 20; 6:10, 33; 7:21). The meaning of this concept has already been indicated (see pp. 249, 250).

The sermon also has its well-defined divisions or "points." These are not stiff or formal—"the bones do not stick out"—but organic, so that one subdivision gradually develops into, or merges with, another.

First Jesus speaks about *the citizens of the kingdom* (5:2-16), describing *their character and blessedness* (verses 2-12) and their relation to the world (verses 13-16). They are the salt of the earth, the light of the world.

Secondly the Lord sets forth *the righteousness of the kingdom,* the high standard of life demanded by the King (5:17—7:12). We are shown that this righteousness is in full accord with the moral principles enunciated in the Old Testament (5:17-19), but is not in accord with the current and traditional (rabbinical) *interpretation and application* of God's holy law (verses 20-48). It exceeds the righteousness of the scribes and Pharisees of Jesus' day as well as that of the ancient Jewish interpreters. This contrast is pointed out with respect to several of the Old Testament commandments.

The essence of the righteousness of the kingdom with respect to man's relation *to God* amounts to this: "Love God above all" (chap. 6). Secret (unostentatious) devotion to, and unlimited trust in, God is required. This secret and sincere devotion of the heart, rather than the merely outward deed to attract the attention of the people and to win their admiration, must reveal itself in such matters as giving, praying, and fasting (verses 1-18). And as to unlimited trust in God, it is incompatible with mammon worship and with worry, and is based on the assurance that upon those who seek God's kingdom and his righteousness all things necessary will be graciously bestowed (verses 19-34).

The essence of the righteousness of the kingdom with respect to man's relation *to man* is this: "Love your neighbor as yourself" (7:1-12). This implies absence of censoriousness, discrimination in judgment. Wisdom to judge aright, as well as whatever else one needs, is obtained by prayer. Verse 12 contains Christ's own version of "the golden rule."

Thirdly Jesus concludes his sermon with an earnest *exhortation to enter the kingdom* (verses 13-27). He pictures the beginning of the way (verses 13 and 14), progress upon the way (verses 15-20), and the end of the way: what happens in the end to those who are mere *sayers,* as contrasted with what happens to *doers* (verses 21-23); or, to mere *hearers* versus *doers* (verses 24-27). These last four verses contain the strikingly vivid parable of The Two Builders: the sensible man who built his house on rock, contrasted with the foolish man who built his house on sand.

The effect of the sermon upon the audience is portrayed in verses 28 and 29.

The Setting

During the Great Galilean Ministry Jesus often addressed the crowds. So also here (5:1). The sight of great multitudes of people always filled his heart with sympathy, a desire to help them in their needs (9:36; 14:14; 15:32;

Mark 6:34; 8:2; Luke 9:13). When they were hungry he would feed them. When they would bring their sick to him he would heal all those who were afflicted. So also when, as always, they were in need of teaching he would teach them. Our present passage makes mention of "the crowds" seen by him and of "his disciples" who came to him. Mark speaks of "twelve" (3:14); Luke of "a great multitude of his disciples" (6:17, cf. verse 20). Perhaps we are permitted to picture the scene in this way, that The Twelve formed a circle immediately around the Savior; farther down stood a large company of other disciples; beyond these the great multitude of other interested and inquisitive listeners.

Jesus opens his address with those precious sayings that have imparted comfort and encouragement to the distressed throughout the centuries and, because of the oft-repeated "Blessed," have become popularly known as "The Beatitudes."

The Citizens of the Kingdom: Their Character and
Blessedness (the Beatitudes) and Their
Relation to the World: Salt and Light

The people listening to Jesus that day must have been spellbound from the very beginning. They must have been enthralled by the very opening sentence, for Jesus was telling them things which on the surface seemed absurd. He was actually saying that not the rich, the gay, the well-fed, and the unoppressed were to be accounted well-off, but rather the poor, the mourners, the hungry and thirsty, and the persecuted ones. To be sure here in Matthew—more so than in Luke—some of these descriptions were modified. Hence not necessarily every poor person but the poor *in spirit,* and not without qualification the hungry and thirsty but those hungering and thirsting *for righteousness* are pronounced blessed. But the fact remains that here was a reversal of all human evaluations.

The paradoxical nature of the sayings becomes even clearer when the meaning of the predicate adjective "blessed" is considered. Note that it stands at the very beginning of the sentence and occurs no less than nine times in close succession, yielding *nine* or, if verses 10-12 are combined because of thought similarity, *eight* beatitudes. From here on they will be considered a group of *eight.*

The marked emphasis upon the word *blessed* cannot be questioned. In the spirit of the Old Testament psalmists the Lord is saying, "O the blessedness of the poor in spirit, the mourners, the meek!" etc. Think of David's exuberant exclamation in Ps. 32:1, "Blessed (is he whose)—or "O the blessedness (of him whose)—transgression (is) forgiven, (whose) sin (is) covered!"

The sayings of Matt. 5:1-12 must have resounded from the mountain with

264

tremendous emotional force. What the Speaker is doing is nothing less than this: he is stating that though everybody may consider his followers to be most wretched and unfortunate and though they themselves are by no means always filled with optimism regarding their own condition, in the sight of heaven and by the standards of its kingdom they are happy indeed; yes, "happy" in the most exalted sense of the term; hence, superlatively blessed. [264] Not only is this true because of the blessings in store for them in the future—that, too, is implied; see especially 5:12: "y o u r reward in heaven is great"—but even because of their present state. *Already* heaven's favor is resting upon them. Right at this moment the light of their future bliss is beginning to engulf them. Even now, no matter how despised they may be, this is true, for the Spirit of glory and of God rests upon them (I Peter 4:14).

Each beatitude consists of three parts: *a.* an ascription of blessedness ("Blessed"), *b.* a description of the person to whom this ascription applies, that is, of his character or condition ("the poor in spirit," "the mourners," etc.), and *c.* a statement of the reason for this blessedness ("for theirs is the kingdom of heaven," "for they shall be comforted . . .").

Those who are always looking for contradictions and discrepancies in Scripture see a conflict between Matthew's and Luke's account of the beatitudes. Now it is true that there are *differences*. Thus Matthew 5 records (at least) eight beatitudes; Luke 6 only four, followed by four woes. Also, in Matthew the sayings, with the exception of the last, are in the third person; in Luke in the second. Finally, where Matthew has "poor in *spirit*" (5:3) Luke simply reads "y o u poor" (6:20; cf. also Matt. 5:6 with Luke 6:21). One might say, therefore, that in Matthew's version the emphasis is on the spiritual quality of the citizens of the kingdom; in Luke the external condition is brought more into the foreground.—But are such differences tantamount to contradictions? Not in the least. Luke nowhere tells us that Jesus uttered *only* four beatitudes. Again, it is entirely possible that Jesus used both the third and the second person; or that, while using the third person, he was looking at his immediate disciples ("and he lifted up his eyes on his disciples and said," Luke 6:20), so that this very gesture indicated that this comfort was intended especially for them. In either case was not Luke fully justified in using the second person ("y o u poor")? Finally, Jesus certainly did not mean and could not have meant that every person who is poor in earthly possessions is for that very reason to be accounted "blessed." The implication even in Luke's account is that although with respect to earthly possessions people may be ever so impoverished, yet because of their

---

264 Cf. Ps. 1:1; 2:12; 32:2; 33:12; 34:8; 40:4; 41:4; etc. The emphasis and fulness of meaning of the opening predicate adjective is expressed beautifully in the Dutch (*Statenvertaling*) rendering *Welgelukzalig*. A great deal of useful information is found in the article on μακάριος by F. Hauck, Th.D.N.T., Vol. IV, pp. 367-370.

faith in "the Son of man" (Luke 6:22) theirs is the kingdom of heaven. Conclusion: there is no real conflict. See also what has been said earlier about these alleged contradictions and discrepancies (pp. 75, 76).

It is hardly necessary to state that when Jesus speaks about the poor in spirit, the mourners, the meek, etc., he does not refer to eight different classes of people: some poor in spirit, others mourning, still others meek, etc., but to one and the same group. Moreover, in describing those who belong to this group he is at the same time giving a description of the kingdom to which they belong showing that it is not an earthly realm but a heavenly; not a physical but a distinctly spiritual empire, in which the one and only true God, the Father of Jesus Christ, is acknowledged and worshiped as Sovereign. Cf. Luke 17:21; John 18:36; Rom. 14:17.

It has been argued that the qualities mentioned in these beatitudes are far too passive and self-renunciatory to meet the requirements of the age in which we are living. Is not the world sinking into a morass of moral and spiritual degradation? Has not scientific progress left religious advancement far behind? Therefore, instead of the life of privation here set forth, is it not rather intense Christian activity, deep involvement in mission programs and in social reform, that is called for today? Is not energetic enterprise instead of tame, uncolorful, rather sheepish poverty in spirit, mournfulness, meekness, purity of heart, etc., the real answer to our problem?

Answer: The world of Elijah, too, was very, very wicked. Nevertheless, Jehovah was not in the wind, nor in the earthquake, nor in the fire, but in "a still small voice" (literally "a sound of gentle stillness"). To Zechariah came the message, "Not by might nor by power but by my Spirit says Jehovah of hosts" (Zech. 4:6). Through Isaiah the word of the Lord comes to us, "In quietness and confidence shall be y o u r strength" (Isa. 30:15). He who thinks lightly of the qualities mentioned in these beatitudes must be consistent. Let him never again speak of "stooping to conquer," about "the quality of mercy . . . blessing him that gives and him that takes," and about "the pen being mightier than the sword." Also, let him never again wax enthusiastic about the contents of I Cor. 13. Involvement in programs of Christian action? By all means, as long as the main purpose is the glory of God (Matt. 5:16; I Cor. 10:31)! Extending help toward the needy and underprivileged of any and every race, whether by individual or group action? Definitely, with the same proviso. Read Gen. 47; Prov. 14:21; 19:17; Matt. 25:34-40; II Cor. 8:1-9; Eph. 2:10; James 2:6, 8, 13; 5:1-6, to mention only a few of the long list of passages in which such endeavor is prescribed and even emphasized. However, only when "the heart is right," that is, when such effort is being expended for the benefit of others and thus to the glory of God, and not to win men's approval or to build up one's ego, will heaven reward it. It is the spirit of hypocrisy, the doing of so-called *good* works from *bad* (ulterior) motives, that is condemned in the Sermon on the

Mount (see especially Matt. 6:1-18). It is *preaching* what one does not *practice* that is denounced (see Matt. 23:4; Luke 11:46).

We should never forget that when Jesus here pronounces a blessing upon the meek he does it as the One who himself was the meekest of all men (Matt. 11:29; 12:17-21, cf. Isa. 42:1-4; Matt. 21:5, cf. Zech. 9:9). So also when the merciful are promised mercy it is the supremely merciful One (Luke 23:34) who makes that promise. When the pure of heart receive the assurance that they shall see God the One who conveys this assurance is also the very One who is able to ask, "Who of y o u convicts me of sin?" (John 8:46). And when the peacemakers are honored with the title "sons of God" it is the chief Peace-maker (Isa. 9:6; John 14:27; 20:19-21; Eph. 2:14) who confers this title upon them. The qualities which the Lord demands of others he himself possesses in infinite degree. That is one reason why his teaching was and is so dynamic. This holds also for Christianity. A Christianity (?) devoid of the qualities held before us in these beatitudes lacks vitality. On the other hand, a Christianity that treasures and displays these graces in all that it is and does is a channel of blessing for mankind.

A final question demands an answer: Must we conceive of these beatitudes as so many separate grains of sand, or are they more like a chain of events in which each link, or at least each group of links, is organically connected with the others? Is the sequence in which they follow each other of such a nature that No. 8 might as well be No. 1, and No. 6 could trade places with No. 2, or is there a discernible orderly arrangement? In some commentaries this question is not even discussed. Now it must be granted that a certain amount of overlapping may well be present; compare, for example, "the poor in spirit" with "the meek." It may indeed be impossible to prove that there is here a rigid step by step progression so that each beatitude (after the first) would indicate an ascending stage in the development of Christian character and/or experience. Though it *might* be true, it is perhaps impossible to prove that merciful, pure in heart, and peace-making represent a climactic sequence. Nevertheless, a general group by group onward trend is not difficult to detect.

Thus we observe that both here in Matthew and also in Luke a blessing is pronounced *first* on "the poor in spirit" (thus Matthew) or simply "y o u poor" (Luke). Also, in both of these Gospels the entire series *ends* with an exhortation that the maligned and persecuted children of God should rejoice. Moreover, elsewhere too the Lord, in his description of man's state and condition, begins where the beatitudes begin. Jesus consistently pictures the sinner as being at the outset dead by nature (Matt. 8:22; Luke 9:60; 15:24, 32; John 6:53; 11:25, 26), utterly lost (Matt. 10:6; 15:24; 18:11; Luke 15:4, 6, 9, 24, 32; 19:10), and in need not merely of re*form* but of re*birth* (John 3:3, 5). He must repent (Matt. 4:17; Luke 13:3, 5), in the sense already explained (see pp. 196, 197). Is it then strange that the first three

267

beatitudes are those in which *that* man is pronounced blessed who recognizes his own poverty and lack; as did, for example, the prodigal in the parable popularly known as that of The Prodigal Son (see Luke 15, especially verse 17)? Next, when the prodigal recognizes his wretched condition and is filled with regret as he reflects on the fact that he himself is to blame for it, does he not hunger and thirst for an opportunity to say, "Father, I have sinned against heaven and before you"? Is not the re-establishment of the *right* relation with God the chief object of his yearning? With this longing for righteousness compare the fourth beatitude. And now having received mercy, will he not be merciful in return and thus the recipient of even more mercy than he has already received (Matt. 5:44-48; 18:21-35; Luke 6:36)? And will he not also, by God's grace and power, strive to be pure of heart, trusting God with singleness of purpose (Matt. 6:22; Luke 11:34)? And, having himself received the peace that passes all understanding, will he not become a peace-maker (Mark 9:50; Luke 10:5, 6; Phil. 2:1 ff.)? In other words, will not the fifth, sixth, and seventh beatitudes apply to him?

Finally, note that the blessing pronounced upon those who for Christ's sake endure *persecution* is placed *at the close* of the entire series, as the eighth and final beatitude. Is not also this true to life? Generally it is not the person who has just "come to himself" that is persecuted, but rather the one who has already begun to reveal himself outwardly as a new man. Thus also in the parable of The Prodigal Son the displeasure of the self-righteous elder brother toward the returned penitent is mentioned near the end of the story (Luke 15:30). Similarly, Christ's Upper Room Discourse *ends* (just before the touchingly beautiful highpriestly prayer) with the words, "In the world y o u have tribulation; but be of good courage. I have conquered the world" (John 16:33). Cf. Matt. 10:13b-42 *after* 10:1-13a.

It is clear, therefore, that at least in their general trend the beatitudes follow the actual course of the developing new life, and that, in broad outline, the sequence found here parallels what is found elsewhere in the sayings and discourses of the Lord. But though these pronouncements reveal the beginning and the further progress of the faith of the citizens of the kingdom, and the persecution to which this faith is subjected, showing us the various features of Christian character in their (to some extent) successive development, yet, as the flower-bud already contains the flower, so the earliest grace, consciousness of spiritual poverty, already contains all the others in its bosom and is itself never lost but rather enhanced in beauty and winsomeness through its blending with all the other virtues.

The First Beatitude

3. **Blessed (are) the poor in spirit, for theirs is the kingdom of heaven.** The world says the exact opposite, "Blessed are the rich," etc. Jesus says, "Blessed are the poor, mourners, meek." Reason: one's outward condition

may be ever so enviable; in the end it vanishes like a dream. God never made a soul so small that the whole world will satisfy it. But the inner state and character of the soul abides. Cf. Luke 12:15; I Cor. 7:31.

However, Jesus does not pronounce these people blessed because they are poor in material goods, though for the most part they are that also. They are called blessed as being poor *in spirit,* not in spirituality but "with respect to" their spirit; that is, *they are the ones who have become convinced of their spiritual poverty.* They have been made conscious of their misery and want. Their old pride has been broken. They have begun to cry out, "O God, be thou merciful to me, the sinner" (Luke 18:13). They are of a contrite spirit and tremble at God's word (Isa. 66:2; cf. 57:15). [265] They realize their own utter helplessness (Rom. 7:24), expect nothing from self, everything from God.

Theirs, theirs *alone,* right now is the kingdom of heaven, that is complete salvation, the sum-total of blessings that result when God is acknowledged as King over heart and life. See definition on p. 249, under point *b.* It is theirs even now *in principle.* Therefore they are pronounced *blessed.*

The book of Revelation contains two vivid passages that respectively show *a.* how one can be poor though deeming himself to be rich, and *b.* how a person can be rich indeed in the midst of his poverty. The risen and exalted Church Visitor, Jesus Christ, addresses lukewarm Laodicea as follows:

"So because you are lukewarm, neither hot nor cold, I am about to spew you out of my mouth. For you say, 'I am rich and have become richer right along and have need of nothing whatever,' but you do not know that you are the one who is wretched and pitiable and poor [or: beggarly] and blind and naked" (3:16-17).

But he gladdens the church of Smyrna by saying:

"I know your tribulation [or: affliction] and your poverty, but you are rich" (2:9).

---

[265] If the word used here for *poor* (πτωχός) is used in its primary or basic sense, as may well be the case, it would indicate not the pauper, one so poor that he must daily work for his living (πένης), but the beggar, one who is dependent on others for support. Think of Lazarus in the parable of The Rich Man and Lazarus (Luke 16:19-31; note especially verses 20, 21). On this distinction between πτωχός and πένης see R. C. Trench, *op. cit.,* par. xxxvi. However, the possible difference in meaning must not be pressed, since πτωχός can also simply mean *poor* without necessarily implying that the person so designated is a *cringingly poor beggar* (Matt. 26:11; Mark 14:7; Luke 14:13, 21, etc.). Besides, πένης occurs only once in the entire New Testament (II Cor. 9:9); πτωχός, on the other hand, more than thirty times. This, *taken by itself,* would hardly furnish sufficient material on which to base a distinction in meaning. On the other hand, because of Christ's view of the sinner in his natural state (see above, p. 267), he may, after all, here (Matt. 5:3) have used the term πτωχός in its primary sense: one who is completely destitute, deprived of every means of self-support, with the additional idea in the present case that he *knows* himself to be such. In the spiritual sense (note "poor *in spirit*") this meaning certainly fits the context.

How, then, can the poor be called rich? The answer is found in such meaningful passages as, "I have everything" (Jacob to Esau, Gen. 33:11); and "To them that love God all things work together for good" (Rom. 8:28). For further confirmation of this glorious truth see Ps. 23; 63:1; 73:23-26; 81:10; 116; Prov. 15:16; 16:8, 19; 19:1; John 1:16; 14:1-3; 17:24; Rom. 8:31-39; I Cor. 3:21-23; II Cor. 4:8; Eph. 1:3; I Peter 1:3-9; I John 5:4; Rev. 7:9-17; 17:14; 21:1-7.

The Second Beatitude

4. The poor in spirit are also the mourners. It is this aspect of their life and behavior that is brought to the fore in the second beatitude: **Blessed the mourners, for they shall be comforted.** Blessed indeed is the person who, having said, "I perish here with hunger," continues by saying, "Father I have sinned." People mourn for many reasons: sickness, pain, bereavement, material loss, wounded pride, etc. In the present context, however, a basically different kind of mourning is in view. It is the mourning of those who recognize their spiritual bankruptcy (first beatitude) and are—or are presently going to be—hungering and thirsting for righteousness (fourth beatitude), that is emphasized. To be sure, when a person bemoans his sin he also laments sin's consequences (Rev. 21:4). From the many distresses of life, including the physical, none need be excluded. But they are included only in their character as the results of sin. Accordingly, by no means all mourners are here called blessed. Cf. II Cor. 7:10.

It is not necessary, however, to limit this mourning to that which takes place because of a person's own individual sins: those whereby he himself has grieved his God. That type of sorrow can be poignant indeed (Ps. 51:4). More, however, is undoubtedly included. The regenerated learn to love God to such an extent that they will begin to weep because of "all the deeds of ungodliness which the ungodly have committed in such an ungodly manner" (Jude 15). Their mourning therefore is God-centered, not man-centered. They "sigh and cry" not only over their own sins, nor only over these plus the power of the wicked to oppress the righteous (Hab. 1:4; II Tim. 3:12), but "over *all* the abominations that are done in the midst of Jerusalem" (Ezek. 9:4). It grieves them that God, *their own* God whom they love, is being dishonored. Cf. Ps. 139:21. This type of grief "to the glory of God" is also strikingly expressed in Ps. 119:136, "Streams of water run down my eyes because *they* do not observe thy law." See also Ezra 10:6. In a most touching chapter Daniel, in mourning over and making confession of sin, combines his own personal sins and those of his people (Dan. 9:1-20; see especially verse 20). In doing so he pleads, "O Lord hear, O Lord forgive, O Lord hearken and do; defer not, for thine own sake, O my God, because thy city and thy people are called by thy name" (verse 19).

The powerful surge of emotion that characterizes the outpouring of heart expressed in Ps. 119 and in Dan. 9 fits the present context, because the word for *mourning* in the second beatitude indicates a sorrow that begins in the heart, takes possession of the entire person, and is outwardly manifested. [266]

The blessedness of these people consists in this, that *they shall be comforted.* Godly sorrow turns the soul toward God. God, in turn, grants comfort to those who seek their help from him. It is he who pardons, delivers, strengthens, reassures (Ps. 30:5; 50:15; Isa. 55:6, 7; Mic. 7:18-20; Matt. 11:28-30). Thus tears, like raindrops, fall to the ground and come up in flowers (Ps. 126:5; Eccl. 7:3; John 14; see N.T.C. on that very comforting chapter; I Cor. 10:13; II Cor. 1:3, 4; Rev. 7:14-17; 21:4).

At times the comfort consists in this, that the affliction itself is removed (II Chron. 20:1-30; 32:9-23; Ps. 116; Isa. 38; Acts 12:5 ff.; etc.). Often, however, the affliction remains for a while but a weight of glory outbalances the grief (II Cor. 4:17; 12:8, 9). Think also of Rom. 8:28; even better, of 8:28-39. Most beautifully is this "comfort" summarized in Lord's Day 1 of The Heidelberg Catechism:

"Question. What is your only comfort in life and death?

"Answer. That I, with body and soul, both in life and death, am not my own, but belong unto my faithful Savior Jesus Christ; who with his precious blood has fully satisfied for all my sins, and delivered me from all the power of the devil; and so preserves me that without the will of my heavenly Father not a hair can fall from my head; yea, that all things must be subservient to my salvation, wherefore by his Holy Spirit he also assures me of eternal life, and makes me heartily willing and ready henceforth to live unto him." Add to this II Tim. 1:12; 4:7, 8; Rev. 17:14; 19:7.

The Third Beatitude

5. Blessed the meek, for they shall inherit the earth. There is very little difference between being "poor in spirit" and being "meek." Nevertheless, there is a slight distinction, namely this, that the first designation describes the man more as he is in himself, namely, broken-hearted; whereas the second pictures him more definitely in his relation to God and the fellow-man.

What is said here about the meek individual is an echo of Ps. 37:11 (see also verses 22, 29, 34 of that same psalm). In order therefore to learn what is meant by the expression "the meek" we do best to derive the content of this concept from that psalm. It describes the person who is not resentful. He bears no grudge. Far from mulling over injuries received, he finds refuge in the Lord and commits his way entirely to him. All the more does he do this because he has died to all self-righteousness. He knows that he cannot claim

---

[266] On πενθέω see R. C. Trench, *op. cit.*, par. lxv.

any merit before God (cf. Ps. 34:18; 51:17). Since God's favor means everything to him he has learned to take joyfully "the plundering of his possessions, knowing that he has a better possession and an abiding one" (Heb. 10:34). Yet *meekness is not weakness*. Meekness is not spinelessness, the characteristics of the person who is ready to bow before every breeze. It is submissiveness under provocation, the willingness rather to *suffer* than to *inflict* injury. The meek person leaves everything in the hand of him who loves and cares.

The blessedness of those who are meek consists in this, that "they shall inherit the earth." In a sense they inherit it even now, and this for several reasons: *a.* by *not* paying undue attention to enriching themselves but rather to doing their duty before God and fulfilling their task on earth; in other words, by first and most of all seeking God's kingdom and his righteousness, "all these things" (food, clothing, etc.) are graciously bestowed upon them as an extra gift (Matt. 6:33). The law of indirection is by no means a dead letter. *b.* Their very meekness makes them a blessing to their fellowmen, some of whom will bless them in return (Mark 10:30; Acts 2:44, 45; 16:15; Phil. 4:18). *c.* They may possess only a small portion of this earth or of earthly goods, but a small portion with God's blessing resting upon it is more than the greatest riches without God's blessing.

Except in a very formal or legal sense, does a man whose soul is racked by the fear of the coming judgment really *possess* his earthly goods? Does he possess them in the sense of enjoying them? Of course not! It is not *he* who has *them: they* have *him!* A comparison of two passages from the book of Isaiah shows who are really the ones that inherit the earth:

"Thou wilt keep him in perfect peace whose mind is stayed on thee, because he trusts in thee" (26:3).

"There is no peace, says Jehovah, for the wicked" (48:22). Not the men of the world but the meek are those who know that Rom. 8:28 is true. Therefore, they, and they alone, are the ones who possess the earth.

But the most complete fulfilment of the promise is reserved for the future, when at Christ's return in glory the meek will inherit the new heaven and earth, the rejuvenated universe from which every stain of sin and every remnant of the curse will have been removed and in which righteousness will forever dwell (Rev. 21:1 ff.).

To *inherit* the earth indicates the following:

a. By grace the citizen of the kingdom has a *right* to this possession;

b. He will certainly receive it as an *inalienable* treasure;

c. He will not need to—*cannot* even—*earn it* himself.

The Fourth Beatitude

Out of the depths of conscious spiritual poverty, mourning over sin, and meekness the citizens of the kingdom cry to God for fulfilment, that is, for righteousness, the complete satisfaction of their basic spiritual need. The fourth beatitude therefore follows very naturally: 6. **Blessed those hungering and thirsting for righteousness, for they shall be fully satisfied.** This righteousness consists in perfect comformity with God's holy law, that is, with his will. It is first of all a righteousness *of imputation:* "Abraham believed in Jehovah; and he reckoned it to him for righteousness" (Gen. 15:6). Man is unable to earn this right standing with God. No amount of good works will ever be able to atone for his sin. In fact, "All our righteousnesses are as a polluted garment" (Isa. 64:6). No human cleansings of any kind, be they ceremonial or other, can ever wash away sin, "For though you wash yourself with lye and use abundant soap, the stain of your guilt is still before me, says the Lord Jehovah" (Jer. 2:22). No amount of sacrifices is able to wipe out human guilt: "Sacrifice and offering thou hast no delight in . . . burnt-offering and sin-offering hast thou not required" (Ps. 40:6). No mere human being can ever atone for the sin of his brother: "None of them can by any means redeem his brother, or give God a ransom for him" (Ps. 49:7). In fact, as far as man himself is concerned the situation is entirely hopeless. His chief, basic, and irreplaceable need is to be in perfect accord with God; and this is also the goal that he can never attain: "How can a man be just before God?" (Job 9:1).

Into this hopeless and horrifying situation God's Son in his glorious and sovereign grace entered. It was he (together with the Father and the Spirit, the one only true God) who came to the rescue when all other means failed. "Then said I, Lo, I am come; in the roll of the book it is written of me; I delight to do thy will, O my God; thy law is within my heart" (Ps. 40:7, 8). The manner in which the sinner's rescue was to be accomplished and salvation provided is clearly depicted in Isa. 53: "He was wounded for our transgressions; he was bruised for our iniquities; the chastisement of our peace was upon him; and with his stripes we are healed. All we like sheep have gone astray; we have turned every one to his own way; and Jehovah has laid on him the iniquity of us all" (verses 5 and 6). And so the Immanuel was destined to become "Jehovah our righteousness" (Jer. 23:7). Through him as a ransom the sins of his people were freely pardoned, so that David could sing, "Blessed is he whose transgression is forgiven, whose sin is covered" (Ps. 32:1).

All of this, of course, was known to Jesus when he said, "Blessed those hungering and thirsting for righteousness." Even while on earth he was fully cognizant of his function as *Substitute.* Was it not in order to perform that office that he had left his heavenly home (II Cor. 8:9)? See also on Matt. 20:28 (cf. Mark 10:45). And was it not *for his people* that he was going to pour out his blood (Luke 22:19, 20; I Cor. 11:24, 25; cf. John 10:11, 28; Acts 20:28; Eph. 1:7, 14; Col. 1:14; Heb. 9:12; I Peter 1:19; Rev. 5:9)? Moreover, the fact that man's righteousness is based on God's mercy and not on human merit or works is a truth that did not need to wait for Paul (Rom. 4:3, 9; Gal. 3:6) to be discovered. Not only did Moses know it (Gen. 15:6), and David (Ps. 32:1), but certainly also Jesus. He clearly taught it in the unforgettable parable of The Pharisee and the Publican (Luke 18:9-14; see especially verses 13 and 14). It is true that the teaching of the Old Testament and of Jesus paved the way for the broader and far more detailed exposition of this doctrine by the apostle to the Gentiles.

That here in Matt. 5:6 Christ, nevertheless, refers to a righteousness not merely by imputation but also *by impartation*, not merely of legal state but also of ethical conduct, seems to follow clearly from such a passage as Matt. 6:1, "Take care that y o u do not practice y o u r righteousness before the people," and see also Matt. 5:10, 20-48. *The two are inseparable.* Though it is impossible for good works to justify anybody, it is just as impossible for a justified person to live without doing good works. The term "righteousness" as used by Christ is therefore very comprehensive, embracing both the forensic and the ethical.

Relation between "righteousness" as pictured by Christ and the "righteousness of the Pharisees": the former is internal, the latter generally external; the former is of the heart, the latter predominantly of outward appearance; the former is genuine, the latter all too often a manufactured article. Cf. Matt. 5:20-6:18.

"For they shall be fully satisfied" (literally: "filled"). [267] Note, however, that not those who merely feel that "something is wrong," but only those who "hunger and thirst" after righteousness shall be filled. The righteousness imputed and imparted by God must be the object of intense desire, earnest yearning, and relentless pursuit. Cf. Ps. 42:1, "As the hart pants for the water-brooks. . . ." Cf. Isa. 55:1; Amos 8:11; John 4:34; 6:35; 7:37; Rev. 22:17.

How does this hunger and thirst for righteousness become fully satisfied? By the imputation of Christ's merits. Thus we obtain a righteousness of state. By the sanctifying work of the Holy Spirit. Thus we obtain a righteousness of inner condition and outward conduct. Cf. Rom. 8:3-5; II Cor. 3:18; II Thess. 2:13. These two are inseparable: those for whom Christ died are sanctified by the Holy Spirit. Therefore, those whose sins are forgiven render the sacrifice of thanksgiving. [268]

---

[267] The verb χορτάζω [here 3rd per. pl. fut. indic. pass.: χορτασθήσονται), though used at first with respect to the feeding and fattening of animals (of which meaning there is an echo in the clause: "all the birds *gorged themselves* with their flesh," Rev. 19:21), and applied to men chiefly by the Comic poets, was gradually losing its deprecatory sense and is here simply used as a synonym for *to have plenty, to be(come) fully satisfied.* Cf. Matt. 14:20; 15:33, 37; Mark 6:42; 7:27, 8:4, 8; Luke 6:21; 9:17; 15:16; 16:21; John 6:26; Phil. 4:12; James 2:16.

[268] Others define the righteousness here referred to differently; for example, as "the revelation of God's royal right, which puts an end to all power, injustice, and untruth,

The Fifth Beatitude

The fifth, sixth, and seventh beatitudes describe the fruits of the work which God through his Spirit performs in the hearts of his children. They are therefore very closely connected with that which immediately precedes. Those who, according to the fourth beatitude, have become "filled" or "fully satisfied" as the result of God's mercy shown to them, now in turn exercises mercy towards others (fifth beatitude). Those who have experienced the purifying influence of the Holy Spirit become pure in heart (sixth beatitude). And, of course, these same people, having been saved by the Prince of Peace, now become peace-makers (seventh beatitude).

As was indicated earlier, it is impossible to prove that merciful, pure in heart, and peace-making represent a climactic sequence or are the manifestations of a step by step gradually ascending development in the believers' life. It is conceivable, to be sure, that the relation is as follows: those who have become merciful become conscious of the fact that their mercy is still mingled with sin, and thus all the more strive after purity of heart. Also it is possible that peace-making is mentioned next according to the rule stated by James, namely, that "the wisdom which is from above, is first pure, then peaceable" (3:17). However, as A. Plummer, followed by A. T. Robertson, has stated, the order in which James mentions these two is probably more logical than chronological. [269] Accordingly, since the reason for the sequence in which the fifth to the seventh beatitudes are reported is not clear they will simply be regarded as parallel responses to God's redeeming grace. First, then, the fifth beatitude: **7. Blessed the merciful, for they shall have mercy shown to them.** Mercy is love for those in misery and a forgiving spirit toward the sinner. It embraces both the kindly feeling and the kindly act. We see it exemplified in the parable of The Good Samaritan (Luke 10). and especially in Christ, the merciful Highpriest (Heb. 2:17).

Although it would be unrealistic to deny that, due to God's loving disposition, remembered and unremembered acts of sympathy and kindness are in evidence all around us, even in the world of the unregenerate (Acts 28:2), the mercy spoken of in this beatitude grows "out of the personal experience of the mercy of God" (Lenski). As such it is a peculiarly Christian virtue, which holds also for the other characteristics mentioned in the beatitudes. All indicate qualities of the citizens of the kingdom. For that

---

and vindicates the oppressed" (H. N. Ridderbos, *op. cit.*, Vol. I, p. 94). Lenski's remark in this connection is to the point, I believe: " 'Righteousness' here cannot mean the power of right in the world of men generally in human affairs; for the passive 'shall be filled' denotes a gift of God to certain persons rendering them 'righteous' in his sight" (*op. cit.*, p. 184). On the other hand for reasons that I have indicated I do not go along with Lenski in limiting this righteousness so exclusively to that of imputation.

[269] A. T. Robertson, *Studies in the Epistle of James*, New York, 1915, p. 185.

matter, it should never be forgotten that while the Romans spoke of four cardinal virtues—wisdom, justice, temperance, and courage—mercy was not among them. And to obtain a balanced view of the semblance of this grace in the world at large it is but fair to balance Acts 28:2 with Prov. 12:10, "The tender mercies of the wicked are cruel."

It is worthy of note that again and again Scripture exhorts believers to show mercy out of gratitude for the mercy with which they themselves have been treated. The parable of The Unmerciful Servant (Matt. 18:23-25) is a striking example. See also Matt. 25:31-46; Rom. 15:7, 25-27; II Cor. 1:3, 4; Eph. 4:32; 5:1; Col. 3:12-14. This mercy must be shown to those who belong to "the household of the faith," but must not be confined to them (Gal. 6:10). In fact, it must be shown to "all men," not even excluding those who hate and persecute believers (Matt. 5:44-48). It is immediately apparent that if the implication of the fifth beatitude were put into practice with greater zeal and consistency the preaching of the gospel would be far more effective! What a blessing for mankind this would be!

"For they shall have mercy shown to them." They, they alone, who exercise mercy can expect to receive from the Lord the reward of mercy, as is evident not only from some of the passages mentioned in the preceding paragraph but also from II Sam. 22:26; Matt. 6:14, 15; and James 2:13. When this golden seed is sown an abundant harvest is gathered in (Matt. 7:2; Luke 6:38).

The Sixth Beatitude

8. Blessed the pure in heart, for they shall see God. It is often said that the pure in heart are the *sincere* and *honest* people, the men of *integrity*. A reference to Ps. 24:3, 4 would seem to confirm this:

> Who shall ascend the hill of Jehovah?
> And who shall stand in his holy place?
> He who has clean hands and a pure heart;
> Who has not lifted up his soul to falsehood
> And has not sworn deceitfully.

Purity in heart is also commended in Ps. 73:1. Similarly, in I Tim. 1:5 *pure* is a synonym for *unfeigned.* And see also II Tim. 2:22 and I Peter 1:22. All this could easily lead to the conclusion that the people who in the sixth beatitude are pronounced blessed are without any further qualification the sincere individuals, the men who think, speak, and act without hypocrisy.

Now there can be no doubt about the fact that sincerity, honesty, the condition of being without guile, is indeed the emphasis here. Over against all human duplicity, be it Pharisaic or otherwise, Jesus pronounces his blessing upon the persons whose outer manifestation is in harmony with their inner disposition.

Nevertheless, a study of the context in each of the aforegoing references makes clear that something must be added. Sincerity or integrity is not sufficient in and by itself. A man may be *sincerely right* but he may also be *sincerely wrong.* No doubt, the prophets of Baal were very sincere when from morning until noon they were leaping about the altar, cutting themselves with knives, and constantly crying out, "Hear us Baal" (I Kings 18:26-28). But they were sincere in the wrong direction. So also, in a passage to which reference is often made in the explanation of the sixth beatitude (Gen. 20:6) Jehovah himself testifies that Abimelech, *in the integrity of his heart,* had taken Sarah away from Abraham. Nevertheless, the Lord did not approve what the king had done but threatened him with death unless he would restore Sarah to her rightful husband (verse 7). Similarly, the "pure in heart" of Ps. 73:1 are those who in all sincerity are guided by "God's counsel" (verse 24). The *faith unfeigned* of I Tim. 1:5 adheres to "sound doctrine" (verse 10). And the people to whom Peter refers (I Peter 1:22) are those who have purified their souls "in obedience to the truth."

It is clear, therefore, that the blessing of the sixth beatitude is not pronounced without qualification upon all people who are sincere, but rather upon those who, in the worship of the true God in accordance with the truth revealed in his Word, strive without hypocrisy to please and glorify him. These, these alone, are "the pure in heart." They worship God "in spirit and truth" (John 4:24) and love to dwell on and practice the virtues mentioned in I Cor. 13; Gal. 5:22, 23; Eph. 4:32; 5:1; Phil. 2:1-4; 4:8, 9; Col. 3:1-17; etc. Their *heart,* the very mainspring of dispositions as well as of feelings and thoughts (Matt. 15:19; 22:37; Eph. 1:18; 3:17; Phil 1:7; I Tim. 1:5), is in tune with the heart of God.

Hence, it is not really surprising to read that the pure in heart "shall see God," and that this is the essence of their blessedness. The man whose delight is not *truly* in the things pertaining to God is unable to appreciate the love of God in Christ toward sinners. *Resemblance is the indispensable prerequisite of personal fellowship and understanding.* To know God one must be like him. Just as to the hunter devoid of musical knowledge and appreciation the voice of the wind roaring through the forest meant no more than that a hare might be startled from his hiding place and become an easy victim, while to his companion Mozart this same loud deep sound signified instead a majestic diapason from God's great organ, so also to the impure, God remains unknown but to those who "imitate God as beloved children and walk in love" he reveals himself.

Now the beauty of this vision of God, this spiritual perception of and delight in his being and attributes, is that it is transforming (II Cor. 3:18). Here on earth, however, it is still a "seeing in a mirror darkly," but in heaven and in the renewed universe, in which the conditions of heaven will also be found on earth (Rev. 21:10), so that "the earth shall be full of the knowledge of Jehovah as the waters cover the sea" (Isa. 11:9), this beatific vision will amount to the sinless and uninterrupted fellowship of the souls of all the redeemed with God in Christ, a seeing "face to face" (I Cor. 13:12).

> When I in righteousness at last
> Thy glorious face shall see,
> When all the weary night is past
> And I awake with thee,
> To view the glories that abide,
> Then, then shall I be satisfied.
> (F. F. Bullard,
> based on Ps. 17:15)

Thus will be fulfilled the prayer of Jesus, "Father, I desire that they also whom thou hast given me, be with me where I am, in order that they may gaze on my glory which thou hast given me, for thou lovedst me before the foundation of the earth."

The Seventh Beatitude

9. Blessed the peace-makers, for they shall be called sons of God. A blessing is here pronounced on all who, having themselves received reconciliation with God through the cross, now strive by their message and their conduct to be instrumental in imparting this same gift to others. By word and example such peace-makers, who love God, one another, and even their enemies, promote peace also among men.

In a world of peace-*breaking* this beatitude shows what a thoroughly "relevant," vital, and dynamic force Christianity really is. Aspersions are frequently cast upon "the church" as if its influence in this direction is pitifully insignificant. If, when the word "church" is used, the reference is to an institution in which nought but dead orthodoxy prevails, the charge is probably valid. On the other hand, if the reference is to "the army of Christ," that is, the sum-total of all true Christian soldiers, redeemed men and women of all generations, religions, and races who wage the Lord's battle *against* evil and *for* right and truth, the reply, in the form of a counter-question, is, "Without the influence of this mighty army how much worse would not world conditions be today? Is not the church the very cork on which the world remains afloat (Gen. 18:26, 28-32)?"

True peace-makers are all those whose Leader is the God of peace (I Cor. 14:33; Eph. 6:15; I Thess. 5:23), who aspire after peace with all men (Rom. 12:18; Heb. 12:14), proclaim the gospel of peace (Eph. 6:15), and pattern their lives after the Prince of Peace (Luke 19:10; John 13:12-15; cf. Matt. 10:8).

The gospel of peace is, however, at the same time the preaching of Christ Crucified (I Cor. 1:18). By nature man, wishing to establish his own righteousness, is disinclined to accept this gospel (I Cor. 1:23). Therefore its proclamation initiates a struggle in his heart. If, by God's grace, the sinner finally yields and welcomes the Prince of Peace as his own Savior and Lord he may face another battle, namely, within his own family. It is for this reason that Jesus, who called the peace-makers blessed, was not inconsistent when he said, "Do not think that I have come to bring peace on earth. I have not come to bring peace but a sword . . . a man's foes will be those of his own household" (Matt. 10:34-36). However, this situation is not Christ's fault but man's. It is God in Christ who continues to urge men to find in him reconciliation and lasting peace (Matt. 11:27-30; II Cor. 5:20).

This, moreover, is not a peace at any price. It is not brought about by compromise with the truth, under the guise of "love"(?). On the contrary, it is a peace dear to the hearts of all who speak *the truth* in love (Eph. 4:15).

Those who by word and example are promoters of this peace are called blessed. Their title is "sons of God," a designation of high honor and dignity, showing that by their promotion of peace they have entered into the very sphere of their Father's own activity. They are his co-workers. By their trustful attitude and many good works, performed out of gratitude and to the glory of God, they have become their Lord's agents who are everywhere engaged in the business of crowding the evil out of human hearts by filling them with all that is good and noble (Rom. 12:21; Phil. 4:8, 9). They are, as it were, God's own "peace corps." *Already* they are the sons of God (I John 3:1). In the day of judgment their glorious adoption as sons will be publicly revealed (Rom. 8:23; I John 3:2).

The Eighth Beatitude

10. **Blessed those persecuted for righeousness' sake, for theirs is the kingdom of heaven.** When the faith of God's children has developed sufficiently to be outwardly manifested so that those who do not share it with them begin to take notice, persecution results. The persecution to which Jesus refers does not spring from purely social, racial, economic, or political causes, but is rooted in religion. It is distinctly a persecution "for righteousness' sake." It is because the men to whom reference is made wish to be and to live in harmony with God's holy will that they endure persecution and continue to hold out under it no matter what happens to them. [270] There is no need to change the definition of the word "righteousness" here: it is the same as in verse 6. The wicked cannot tolerate those who in the eyes of God are accounted "righteous." Their very character is a constant protest against the character of their opponents. For that reason the "world" *hates* the children of God (Matt. 10:22; 24:9; John 15:19; I John 3:12, 13). This hatred underlies the persecution of which 5:10 speaks.

The Lord assures the persecuted ones that they are *blessed.* By constant

---

[270] The original has δεδιωγμένοι, perf.pass. participle: they have endured under persecution.

reading of this beatitude, having probably already committed it to memory in our childhood (in whatever language), we have become so accustomed to it that it has lost its original impact. The impression upon those whom Jesus was addressing must have been tremendous, for it was a rather common idea among the Jews that all suffering, including persecution (see Luke 13:1-5), was an indication of God's displeasure and of the special wickedness of the one thus afflicted. Christ here reverses this view, but only with respect to those who endured persecution for the sake of *righteousness* (verse 10), *himself* ("for my sake," verse 11), *the kingdom of heaven* (19:12).

We might add that the meaningfulness of this beatitude is not lost either upon those who *today,* while this commentary is being written or read, are being persecuted because of their allegiance to Christ. May we never forget them in our prayers and in every other way in which they can be benefitted by us! "Theirs is the kingdom of heaven," says Jesus, returning thus to the pronouncement of bliss found at the conclusion of the first beatitude (verse 3). All the grace and the glory that results when God in Christ is recognized and obeyed as Soveriegn is theirs even now, and will be theirs in ever increasing measure.

11, 12. **Blessed are y o u whenever people heap insults upon y o u and persecute y o u and, while telling falsehoods, say. all kinds of evil against y o u for my sake. Rejoice, yes, be filled with unrestrained gladness, for y o u r reward is great in heaven, for in the same way did they persecute the prophets who lived before y o u r time.** Note the change from the third person to the second, beginning here and continuing (with either *y o u* or *you*) for most of the rest of the sermon. In substance, nevertheless, this is a continuation of the eighth beatitude. Not only are those who suffer abuse for the sake of their abiding faith in Jesus called "blessed," but they are told to rejoice, yes, not only to rejoice but to be filled with (or: leap forth with) unrestrained (exuberant) gladness.

The imperative that is added to "rejoice" has been well rendered by A.V.: "be exceeding glad"; Phillips: "be tremendously glad"; and Williams, "keep on . . . leaping for ecstasy." It is the type of exultation with which, according to Peter's address on Pentecost, David reacted to the fact that Jehovah was constantly at his right hand (Acts 2:26); with which the converted jailer and his entire household praised God (Acts 16:34); with which Abraham greeted the welcome news that he was to see Christ's day (John 8:56); with which Peter, contemplating the grace and the glory of the *now* unseen Jesus Christ, described his readers, who shared this contemplation with him, as "rejoicing greatly with joy unspeakable and full of glory" (I Peter 1:8); and with which the great triumphant heavenly multitude will one day respond to the coming of the Bridegroom to take his bride to himself, "Let us rejoice and be exceeding glad, and let us give him the glory; for the marriage of the Lamb is come, and his wife has prepared herself" (Rev. 19:7).

MATTHEW

The persecution referred to takes various forms:

a. *Reproach:* heaping insults upon believers; for example, "You were wholly born in sin, and you would teach us?" (John 9:34). Surely, those who did not hesitate to address Jesus as follows, "Are we not correct in saying, You are a Samaritan and have a demon," would not hesitate to heap insults upon his disciples also (cf. John 15:20).

b. *Slander:* "while telling falsehoods, (they) say all kinds of evil against y o u for my sake." "They shall cast out y o u r name as evil" (Luke 6:22). With reference to those who had been deeply impressed with the words of Jesus and had the courage to admit this, the Pharisees were going to say, "This rabble that does not know the law, accursed are they" (John 7:49). Similarly, a little later, during the early persecutions of the church, Christians were going to be called *atheists* because they did not worship a visible God; *immoral* because perforce they would frequently meet in secret places; and *unpatriotic* because they confessed loyalty to Christ as their King and refused to worship the emperor.

c. *Persecution in deed.* Though no mention is made of this here, see on 10:16-36.

Reasons why those who are persecuted for Christ's sake are urged to rejoice greatly:

a. Because this persecution indicates the genuine character of their faith: "for in the same way did they persecute the prophets who lived before y o u r time." Cf. Luke 21:13; I Peter 4:13. Justin Martyr in his *Dialogue with Trypho* accuses the Jews of having sawn Isaiah asunder with a wooden saw. There may be a reference to this in Heb. 11:37. [271] Jeremiah was repeatedly subjected to ill treatment (see Jer. 12; 20; 26; 36; 37; 39; 43). If tradition can be trusted, he was finally stoned to death by the people who had forced him to go down to Egypt with them. [272] Ezekiel fared little better (see Ezek. 2:6; 20:49; 33:31, 32). Amos was told to flee away and deliver his prophecies elsewhere (Amos 7:10-13). The labors of Zechariah were not appreciated according to their true worth (Zech. 11:12). Such rejection of the prophets was the rule, not the exception. This follows not only from the words of Jesus here in 5:12 but also from his words as reported by Matt. 23:31, 37; Luke 6:23; 11:49-51; 13:33, 34; John 12:36-43 (cf. Isa. 53:1). [273] And were not such men as Moses, Samuel, Elijah, and Elisha "prophets" also? Had they been treated differently?

---

[271] See also TB *Yebamoth* 49b; *Sanhedrin* 103b; Tertullian, *On Patience* 14: "Isaiah is cut asunder, and does not cease to speak concerning the Lord."

[272] Tertullian, *Antidote for the Scorpion's Sting* 8.

[273] Cf. Acts 7:52; and see C. C. Torrey, *Legendary Lives of the Prophets*, Philadelphia, 1946; and H. J. Schoeps, "Die jüdischen Prophetenmorde," *Aus frühchristlicher Zeit* (Tübingen, 1950), pp. 126 ff.

b. Because Christian character is purged and made mature through suffering (Rom. 5:3, 5; James 1:3, 4; book of Job).

c. Because persecution is followed by great reward in heaven; not a wage won by human merit, but the reward of grace. This reward is in proportion to, yet much greater than, the sacrifice (Rom. 8:18; II Cor. 4:17, 18).

When Jesus spoke the words of verses 11, 12 he clearly implied that his own teaching was not a contradiction of prophetic utterances but was in line with them. He had not come to destroy or annul. He had come to fulfil (5:17).

Salt and Light

In the beatitudes the character and blessedness of the citizens of the kingdom were described. The final beatitude was transitional in character. It described the attitude of the world toward believers in the Lord Jesus Christ. The "two emblems," salt and light, now introduced, describe the opposite, namely, the influence of the kingdom upon the world, the response of Christ's followers to those who persecute them. By means of these two emblems or metaphors the important truth is revealed that those people whom the world—including even the quasi-pious world of scribes and Pharisees—hates most are exactly the ones to whom it owes most. The citizens of the kingdom, no matter how despised they are and how insignificant they may seem to be, *they alone,* not the scribes and the Pharisees, are *the salt* of the earth and *the light* of the world.

The words of 5:13-16 show both how totally different from the world and yet how closely related to the world believers are. Worldly-mindedness or secularization is here condemned, but so is also aloofness or isolationism. Salt is a blessing when it remains truly salt; light, as long as it is really light. But salt must be sprinkled over, better still, rubbed into, the meat. Light must be allowed to shine into the darkness. It must not be put undercover.

As to salt, Jesus says: **13. Y o u are the salt of the earth.** Though salt has many characteristics: whiteness, pungency, flavor, preservative power, etc., it is probably especially the last quality, the potency of salt as an antiseptic, a substance that prevents and retards decay, upon which the emphasis falls here, though the subsidiary function of imparting flavor must obviously not be excluded (see Lev. 2:13; Job 6:6; Col. 4:6).

Salt, then, has *especially a negative* function. It combats deterioration. Similarly Christians, by showing themselves to be Christians indeed, are constantly combating moral and spiritual decay. How often does it not happen that when a believer suddenly steps into a crowd of worldly individuals the off-color joke by which someone was about to entertain his companions is held back, the profanity is left unspoken, the wicked plan remains unexecuted? To be sure, the world is wicked. Yet God alone knows how *far more* corrupt it would be without the restraining example, life, and prayers of the saints (Gen. 18:26-32; II Kings 12:2).

Salt acts *secretly*. We know that it combats decay, though we cannot see it perform its task. Its influence is very real nonetheless.

Continued: **but if the salt becomes tasteless, what will make it salty again? It is then good for nothing but to be thrown away and trampled underfoot by men.** The salt from the marshes and lagoons or from the rocks in the neighborhood of the Dead Sea easily acquires a stale or alkaline taste, because of its mixture with gypsum, etc. [274] It is then literally "good for nothing" but to be thrown away and trampled underfoot (cf. Ezek. 47:11). Jesus, as he walked on earth, saw many Pharisees and scribes, people who advocated a formal, legalistic religion in the place of the true religion proclaimed by the ancient prophets in the name of the Lord. Thus by and large the salt had lost its flavor in the religious life of Israel. Many "sons of the kingdom" would be cast out (Matt. 8:12).

The implication is clear. Just as salt having lost its flavor cannot be restored, so also those who were trained in the knowledge of the truth but who then resolutely set themselves against the exhortations of the Holy Spirit and become hardened in their opposition are not renewed unto repentance (Matt. 12:32; Heb. 6:4-6). Therefore, let that which is named salt

---

[274] This very common observation is set forth by many, among whom are: Hauck, art. ἅλας, Th.D.N.T., Vol. I, pp. 228, 229; and A. Sizoo, who remarks, "It stands to reason that salt was also obtained from the Dead Sea. But this salt was of an inferior quality and more readily subject to spoiling than was the salt from the Mediterranean Sea," *De Antieke Wereld en Het Nieuwe Testament*, Kampen, 1948, p. 28. See also art. *Salt*, W.D.B., p. 525.

Others, however, maintain that since pure sodium chloride does not deteriorate the passage (Matt. 5:13) contains an obvious inaccuracy. So ran the statement of a certain professor of chemistry at a meeting of a science club which this author attended many years ago. Others, though not willing to admit an inaccuracy, think that Jesus is purposely "using a figure of something impossible in nature" (thus Lenski, *op. cit.*, p. 194, adding, "The very idea of salt losing its saltness!"). J. Schniewind, *Das Evangelium nach Matthäus* (*Das Neue Testament Deutsch*, Vol. II), Göttingen, 1960, p. 51, is of the same opinion. F. W. Grosheide leans toward this view (*op. cit.*, p. 51).

I respectfully disagree. My reasons are as follows:

a. Not only is it true that grammatically the modifier "if the salt become(s) tasteless" is not a contrary to fact condition, but it also differs rather sharply from such formulations as "What man is there among y o u. . . ." (Matt. 7:9), in which case the implication, "There is no such man" is immediately clear.

b. The conclusion, "It is then good for nothing but to be thrown away and trampled underfoot by men" certainly sounds as if this was what actually happened in such cases. Moreover, in this last expression, namely, "trampled underfoot by men," the underlying figure definitely refers to salt. It can hardly refer directly to people.

c. As has been shown (see the articles in Th.D.N.T., etc., above referred to), the spoilage of the "salt" to which reference is made here is a well-attested fact. To be sure, "*pure* salt remains salt," but the reference with respect to salt becoming tasteless is to a process of adulteration, contamination, or infiltration: the salt becomes tasteless because foreign substances had become mixed with it.

be salt indeed! Ever so many people who never read the Bible are constantly reading us! If in our conduct we are untrue to our calling our *words* will avail very little.

We have seen that in the main salt has a negative function and acts secretly. Light, on the other hand, has a *positive* function and shines *openly, publicly*. The two metaphors therefore complement each other. As to light Jesus says: **14a. Y o u are the light of the world.** Light in Scripture indicates the true knowledge of God (Ps. 36:9; cf. Matt. 6:22, 23); goodness, righteousness, and truthfulness (Eph. 5:8, 9); joy and gladness, true happiness (Ps. 97:11; Isa. 9:1-7; cf. 60:19). It symbolizes the best there is in learning, love, and laughter, as contrasted with *darkness*, that is, the worst there is in dullness, depravity, and despair. When light is mentioned, sometimes one quality—for instance, revealed knowledge—is emphasized; then again another, depending on the context in each case. In certain instances the meaning of the word "light" may even be broader than any *one* quality would indicate. It may be sufficiently comprehensive to include all the blessings of "salvation" (cf. Ps. 27:1; Luke 1:77-79). So, perhaps, also here in 5:14.

The statement, "Y o u are the light of the world" probably means that the citizens of the kingdom not only have been blessed with these endowments but are also the means used by God to transmit them to the men who surround them. The light-possessors become light-transmitters. Collectively believers are "the light." Individually they are "lights" (luminaries, stars, Phil. 2:15). Both ideas may well have been included in the words as spoken by Jesus, though the emphasis is on the collective.

However, Christians are never a light in and by themselves. They are light "in the Lord" (Eph. 5:8). Christ is the true, the original "light of the world" (John 8:12; 9:5; 12:35, 36, 46; II Cor. 4:6; cf. Ps. 27:1; 36:9; 43:3; Isa. 49:6; 60:1; Luke 1:78, 79; 2:32). Believers are "the light of the world" in a secondary or derived sense. He is "the light lighting" (John 1:9). They are the light lighted. He is the sun. They resemble the moon, reflecting the sun's light. Apart from Christ they cannot shine. The electric bulb does not emit light all by itself. It imparts light only when connected and turned on, so that the electric current generated in the power-house is transmitted to it. So also as long as Christ's followers remain in living contact with the original light they are a light to others (cf. John 15:4, 5).

Now since it is the business of the church to shine for Jesus, it should not permit itself to be thrown off its course. It is not the task of the church to specialize in and deliver all kinds of pronouncements concerning economic, social, and political problems. "The great hope for society today is in an increasing number of individual Christians. Let the Church of God concentrate on that and not waste her time and energy on matters outside her providence."[275] This is not to say that an ecclesiastical pronouncement revealing the bearing of the gospel upon this or that not specifically theological problem is *always* to be condemned. There may be situations in which such an illuminating public testimony becomes advisable and even necessary, for the gospel must be proclaimed "in all its fulness" and not narrowly restricted to the salvation of souls. But the *primary* duty of the church remains the spreading forth of the message of salvation, that the lost may be found (Luke 15:4; I Cor. 9:16, 22; 10:33), those found may be strengthened in the faith (Eph. 4:15; I Thess. 3:11-13; I Peter 2:2; II Peter 3:18), and God may be glorified (John 17:4; I Cor. 10:31). Those who, through the example, message, and prayers of believers, have been converted will show the genuine character of their faith and love by exerting their influence for good *in every sphere*.

Continued: **14b-16. A city situated on a hill cannot be hidden. Nor do men light a lamp and place it under the peck-measure, but on the lampstand, and it gives light to everyone in the house. So let y o u r light shine before men that they may see y o u r good works and glorify y o u r Father who is in heaven.** In connection with the symbol of light two ideas are combined here: The followers of Christ must be both *visible* and *radiant*. They must be "in the light" and must also send out rays of light. The first idea is conveyed by the city situated on a hill. Such a city, with its walls and fortresses, "cannot be hidden." It is clearly visible to everybody.

The second idea is set forth by the figure of the lamp set on the lampstand (not "a candle put on a candlestick," A.V.). Such a lamp "gives light"; it "shines." The lamps of that day can be seen today in any large museum and in many private collections. The author at this moment is looking at one of these terra cotta saucer-shaped objects. This one happens to be about five and one-half inches long, four wide, and one-and-a-half high. It has a handle on one end; on the other a nozzle-shaped extension with a hole for a wick. In the top of the lamp's upper surface there are two holes, one for adding oil, the other for air.

What Jesus is saying, then, is this, that no one would be foolish enough to light such a lamp—evidently for the purpose of illumining the surroundings— and then immediately place it under the peck-measure.[276] Any sensible person would of course set the lit lamp on the lampstand. Such a lampstand was generally a very simple object. It might be a shelf extending from the pillar in the center of the room (the pillar that supported the large cross-

---

[275] D. M. Lloyd-Jones, *Studies in the Sermon on the Mount*, Grand Rapids, Mich., 1959, Vol. I, p. 158. The two volumes of this excellent series should be in everyone's library!

[276] Greek μόδιος, from Latin *modius*, a capacity measure = 16 sectarii, about 8.75 liters or almost exactly a peck.

beam of the flat roof), or a single stone projecting inward from the wall, or a piece of metal conspicuously placed and used similarly. The point is that the lamp, already lit and placed on the stand, would give light "to everyone in the house." This is understandable when it is remembered that the houses of the poor, the very people whom Jesus was addressing (Luke 6:20), had only one room.

Now what a lamp is to a house the follower of Christ should be to the world. A lighted lamp should be given the opportunity to send out its rays. Similarly the followers of Jesus should "let their light shine" in order that men may see their conduct, their "good works." It is on these works, considered as products of faith (see on verse 17) that the Lord places the emphasis, for "actions speak louder than words."

It is not at all necessary nor even advisable in the present connection to make a separation between works done in obedience to the first table of the law and those performed in conformity with the second. In the teaching of Jesus these two go together even though it is true that the first is basic (Matt. 22:34-40; Mark 12:30, 31; Luke 10:25-28). When such excellent works, of whatever nature, are done out of gratitude for salvation obtained by grace through faith they are pleasing to God. This is true whether they consist of taking hold of God in prayer (Matt. 6:6; cf. Isa. 64:7) and trusting him (Matt. 6:24-34); or of helping those in need (25:34-40) and loving even one's enemies (5:44).

That some of these good deeds are seen by men is unavoidable. Even unbelievers will at times hear the songs of praise sung by God's children. Worldly people will take note of the quiet trust in God manifested by believers in times of trial and distress. They will at times express astonishment about the manner in which Christians will go out of their way, risking danger and even death, in order to extend help to the sick and dying. Tertullian (fl. about A.D. 200) wrote: "But it is mainly the deeds of a love so noble that lead many to put a brand upon us. 'See,' they say, 'how they [the Christians] love one another,' for they themselves [the non-Christians] are animated by mutual hatred; 'see how they are ready even to die for one another,' for they themselves will rather put to death" (*Apology* XXXIX).

It is a fine thing that these good works are seen by men. That is exactly what Jesus wants. Rightly considered, it is even what those who perform them want, but not in order to gain honor for themselves, in the sense of 6:1, 5, 16. On the contrary, Jesus says, ". . . and glorify y o u r Father who is in heaven." The *end*, therefore, and also to a certain extent the *result*, of seeing such good works, will be that men, influenced by God's Spirit, will ascribe to God the reverence that is his due for having caused the light to shine forth from human lives (Isa. 24:15; 25:3; Ps. 22:23; cf. I Cor. 10:31). [277]

A word must be added about this phrase, in the Gospels here used for the first time, "y o u r Father who is in heaven" (literally "in the heavens"). A highly respected author writes, "It is true indeed that even in the Old Testament God is sometimes addressed as Father, but then not to express the personal relation between God and the individual believer but as an indication of the relation between God and the covenant people Israel; compare, for example, Isa. 63:16." [278] I fail to see the correctness of this statement. Even in the Old Testament God is recognized as the Father not only of the nation (besides Isa. 63:16 see also 64:8; Mal. 1:1, 6; and cf. Num. 11:12), but even of individual believers, holding them in his tender embrace and caring for them: "A Father of the fatherless and a Judge of widows is God in his holy habitation" (Ps. 68:5). "He will cry to me, Thou art my Father, my God, and the Rock of my salvation. . . . My lovingkindness will I keep for him forever" (Ps. 89:26, 28). Although it is true that in Ps. 103:13 God is not directly addressed as "Father," yet the idea of his fatherhood in relation to individuals is clearly implied: "As a father pities his children, so Jehovah pities those that fear him." To them he is more precious than any earthly father: "Though my father and my mother have forsaken me, yet Jehovah accepts me" (Ps. 27:10). See also II Sam. 7:14, 15 (cf. I Chron. 28:6). Jesus, then, builds on this Old Testament foundation—was it not his own Spirit that inspired this book?—and in the Gospels causes the term as applied to God, to stand out in all its *tenderness* ("Father") and *majesty* ("who is in heaven"). See further on Matt. 6:9. All those, whether of Jewish or Gentile origin, who have accepted Jesus as their Lord and Savior, are privileged, in addressing God, to say, "Our Father who art in heaven."

The Righteousness of the Kingdom

The high standard of life demanded by the King is now set forth. First we are shown that

This Righteousness Is in Full Accord with the
Moral Principles Enunciated in the Old Testament

Jesus just now has been admonishing his hearers to let their light shine by performing good works to the glory of the Father in heaven. Now such works are those that are in harmony with God's holy law. The scribes and the Pharisees were reputed to be the guardians of the law. Yet Jesus was about to expose these men as being hypocrites (5:20; 6:1, 2, 5, 16; see

---

277 For the concept *glory* see N.T.C. on Philippians, pp. 62, 63, footnote 43.
278 H. N. Ridderbos, *op. cit.*, Vol. I, p. 100.

further 15:1-9; 16:1-4; 22:15-22; chap. 23). Did this mean then that he had come to undermine the authority of the law, and of the prophets reaffirming the law? He answers: **17. Do not think that I have come to set aside the law or the prophets. I have not come to set aside but to fulfil.** Christ's opponents even now had begun to regard him as a destructive revolutionist, an iconoclast who wanted to break every tie with the past (John 5:18). This attitude toward Jesus never left them but rather grew on them (Matt. 26:59-61). See Acts 21:21 for a similar attitude toward Paul.

The opponents were wrong. Did the scribes and Pharisees demand good works? So did Jesus (5:16). Did they hold Moses in high regard? So did he (8:4; Mark 7:10, Luke 16:31; 24:27, 44; John 5:46). The righteousness which he proclaimed was not a novelty. It was in thorough harmony with that enunciated in the Old Testament; that is, in "the law and the prophets" (cf. Luke 16:16). [279] Here in 5:17, however, in order to emphasize each in its own right, the term used is "the law *or* the prophets," the Pentateuch or the rest of the Old Testament.

Jesus, then, as he begins to set forth "the righteousness of the kingdom," immediately dismisses the charge of his enemies that he is a proclaimer of novelties, and shows that his ministry was not in collision with the Old Testament but in harmony with it; in fact, that without him the Old Testament was incomplete, unfulfilled. Peter, too, on Pentecost interpreted the strange things that were transpiring round about him as a fulfilment of prophecy (Acts 2). And Paul also links the new with the old, making clear that his doctrine of justification by grace through faith was not something altogether new but was firmly rooted in Old Testament teaching (Rom. 3:21; chap. 4; 7:7 f.; chaps. 9–11; Gal. 3:6-22; 4:21-31; etc.).

Calvin, commenting on Matt. 5:17, makes this application: "If we intend to reform affairs that are in a state of disarray we should always exercise such prudence and moderation as will convince the people that we are not opposing the eternal Word of God, or introducing any novelty that is contrary to Scripture. We must take care that no suspicion of such conflict shall injure the faith of the godly, and that rash men shall not be emboldened by a pretence of novelty."

Actually the honor which Jesus bestowed on "the law or the prophets" was higher by far than that in which it was held by scribes and Pharisees.

---

[279] Another term for "The Old Testament" is "the law of Moses and the prophets and the psalms" (Luke 24:44); still another, "Moses and the prophets" (Luke 16:29, 31; 24:27). The shortest of all, as a designation of the entire Old Testament, is "the law" (see next verse, i.e., Matt. 5:18; cf. John 12:34). Similar to this is "y o u r law," which, in John 10:34, though it covers as much territory as do the preceding designations, refers directly to Ps. 82:6. In I Cor. 14:21 "the law" refers to Isa. 28:11 f. And in Rom. 3:19 the reference is to an entire series of quotations from the psalms and the prophets. These facts prove that the term "the law" is used at times where we would say "The Old Testament."

They buried the divine oracles under a load of tradition and regarded the doing of the law to be the only way to obtain salvation. Therefore in reality *they* were the ones who were setting aside the Old Testament. With Jesus the case was entirely different. When he (5:16) demands good works he address-es this exhortation to those who had previously been pronounced "blessed" (Matt. 5:2-12; Luke 6:20-23). According to the beatitudes these people, convicted of their spiritual poverty, had mournfully confessed their sins and had received from God the righteousness of imputation and impartation. In such a context "good works" are works of gratitude for salvation already received. Thus the law was in principle being fulfilled, and so were the prophets, in which the demand of the law was reaffirmed. It is clear therefore that it was Jesus—not the opponent—who had the right to affirm, "I have not come to set aside but to fulfil." It was his aim that *in the lives of his true followers* the spiritual requirement of the Old Testament would receive its due, that is, that in these lives the vessel of the law's (hence also of the prophets') demand would become filled to the brim.

However, it does not appear to the present author that the explanation given so far *fully* satisfies the meaning of the passage. It is hard for him to believe that in saying, "I have not come to set aside but to fulfil" Jesus was thinking *only* of fulfilment *in his followers*. It would rather seem that he was referring to the law's fulfilment "both in his own experience and increasingly in the experience of his followers" (C. R. Erdman, *op. cit.*, p. 48). Note: also "in his own experience." This brings the passage in harmony with such other sayings of Jesus in which he presents himself as the fulfilment of the Old Testament; not only with the words uttered at a much later time (Matt. 26:56; Luke 18:31; 24:25-27, 44), but also and especially with those who probably belong to the very year when this sermon was delivered.

It is hard to believe that he who had very recently revealed himself to the woman of Samaria as the realization of mankind's hope (John 4:25, 26, 42), and who very shortly would describe himself to John the Baptist and to the people of Nazareth as the fulfilment of prophecy (respectively Matt. 11:1-6 and Luke 4:16-30), would in this sermon have been able, without thinking of any realization *in himself,* to speak about fulfilling the Old Testament.

Now if the fulfilment was to be in relation to himself also, then was it to be with respect to his teaching *only,* setting forth the true meaning of the law and revealing himself as the fulfilment of the Old Testament types and predictions, so that he would stand out as *the chief prophet* (Deut. 18:15, 18)? Or with respect to his vicarious suffering and death *alone,* by which through his active and passive obedience he would satisfy the demand of the law as his people's *sympathetic highpriest* (Ps. 40:6, 7; Jer. 23:6)? Or *exclusively* with respect to his royal rule, thereby delivering his people from the power of the enemy and holding sway over their lives as their *eternal king* (Gen. 49:10; II Sam. 7:12, 13; Ps. 72)? But why not all three? Does not the Old Testament itself lead the way to a fuller interpretation of the concept "Messianic Fulfilment" when in describing the coming Redeemer it does not always restrict itself to the manner in which he would function in *one* office? See Ps. 110:4; Isa. 53; Zech. 6:13. Conclusion: in *all* he was and was to do he had come not to set aside or annul the Old Testament but to fulfil it. The context does not require—perhaps it is not erroneous to say, "does not even permit"—any restriction to be made as to the meaning of this majestic statement (5:17). Moreover, the passage itself, by means of its disjunctive "or" ("the law *or* the prophets" instead of "the law *and* the prophets") emphasizes breadth of meaning, causing the mind to linger a little longer on the two distinct parts, and probably indicating that Jesus had not come either to lift the demand of the law or to invalidate the words, including the predictions, of the prophets. He had come to fulfil both.

"I have come," said Jesus. This indicates that he was fully conscious of his Messianic mission, and in close connection with it, of his pre-existence. This doctrine of pre-existence is therefore not peculiar to John (1:1-14; 3:17; 5:36, 43; 6:38; 8:58; 16:28; 18:37) and Paul (II Cor. 8:9; Gal. 4:4, 5; Eph. 4:9, 10; Phil. 2:5 ff.; etc.). Though not as abundantly it is nevertheless taught clearly also in the Synoptics (Matt. 5:17; Luke 12:49; 19:10).

On the basis of the explanation given of verse 17 what follows is easier to understand: **18. For I solemnly declare to y o u, Until heaven and earth disappears not even the tiniest letter or the tiniest hook on a letter will in any way disappear from the law until all (it calls for) shall have taken place.** A strictly literal rendering, one which would make little sense to the reader unacquainted with Hebrew and Greek, would be: "For Amen I say to y o u, until the heaven and the earth pass away, one iota or one keraia will not at all pass away from the law until all come to be."

As to "Amen," in Hebrew it refers, in general, to ideas of *truth* and *faithfulness*. In its *simple (Qal)* form, the verb means *to be faithful, secure.* In the *simple reflexive* (Niph'al): *to be made firm; to be confirmed, established.* In its *causal* (Hiph'il) form: *to stand firm, consider as trustworthy, believe.* It occurs in statements which affirm or confirm a solemn truth. In the Old Testament the single Amen is found in Deut. 27:15, 16-26; I Kings 1:36; I Chron. 16:36; Neh. 5:13; Ps. 106:48; and Jer. 28:6. The double Amen is found in Num. 5:22; Neh. 8:6; Ps. 41:13; 72:19; and 89:52. In the New Testament the word Amen, as an adverbial accusative, combines the ideas of truthfulness and solemnity. The rendering "verily"="in very truth" of the A.V. was certainly not bad, but today is considered somewhat archaic. Whether "truly" (R.S.V., N.A.S.) conveys that same fulness of meaning or whether, through association with such phrases as "yours truly," it has lost some of the strength or solemnity usually associated with "verily," is a matter with respect to which opinions differ. In every case—let the reader examine this for himself with the use of a Concordance—in which this word occurs in the New Testament it introduces a statement which not only expresses a truth or fact—as, for example, 2x2=4 would be a fact—but an *important,* a *solemn* fact, one that in many cases is at variance with popular opinion or expectation or at least causes some surprise. It is for that reason that I personally prefer the translation "I solemnly declare" [280] to "Truly I say."

Just why it is that John in his Gospel always uses the double Amen (Greek "Amen, Amen"; A.V.: "Verily, verily") but the Synoptics always the single Amen is not clear. Some surmise that John's double Amen literally reproduces what Jesus, speaking Aramaic, said, and that Matthew, Mark, and Luke, giving the Greek equivalent, regarded the single Amen to be all that was necessary to reproduce the solemnity of Christ's words. As long as Christ's meaning is fully conveyed—and it was in every case!—this makes no material difference.

In connection, then, with the immediately preceding verse, in which Jesus had said that he had not come to set aside the law or the prophets but to fulfil them, he now, sharply contradicting what the opponents must have been saying about his attitude, reaffirms his complete loyalty to the sacred oracles. Not until the universe in its present form disappears (Ps. 102:25, 26; Isa. 34:4; 51:6; Matt. 24:35; Rom. 8:21; Heb. 1:12; II Peter 3:7, 10-13; Rev. 6:14; 21:1-3) [281] will even the smallest part of the Old Testament that requires fulfilment fail to be fulfilled. Every type will be exchanged for its antitype. Every prediction will be verified. The law's demand will be fully met.

Not even an *iota* (A.V. "jot") or a keraia (A.V. "tittle") will disappear from the law, that is, from the Old Testament, until its mission has been accomplished. The Old Testament was originally written in Hebrew letters, the smallest of which was the *yodh,* sounded "y" as in "young." In Greek it was represented by the similarly tiniest letter in that tongue, the *iota.* The *keraia* is a very small projection, a little hook that distinguishes one Hebrew letter from another. Thus the second letter of the Hebrew alphabet, the one called *beth,* in English corresponding to "b" or "bh," has a slight extension at the lower right hand corner, to distinguish it from the letter *kaph,* corresponding to English "k" or "kh." *Beth* is written ב, *kaph* is כ. The meaning, then, is this, that not even in the slightest respect will the Old Testament remain unfulfilled. It is as if we were to say that with respect to its fulfilment "not a 't' will remain uncrossed and not an 'i' undotted."

As Jesus was speaking, some parts of the Old Testament had already been fulfilled, for example, the incarnation. Other parts were being fulfilled. Still others were to be fulfilled soon, that is, in the crucifixion and the resurrec-

---

280 Cf. Williams: "I solemnly say."
281 Heaven and earth will not "go out of existence" but will be gloriously transformed. See the author's *The Bible on the Life Hereafter,* Chap. 48, pp. 205-207.

tion; or were to be fulfilled later, in the ascension, at and after Pentecost, and finally at Christ's return in glory.

In the new heaven and earth "the law" as a written book will no longer be necessary. In fact, the written Bible—Old and New Testament—will have become superfluous. Until that time arrives, however, nothing whatever will remain lacking as to fulfilment. God's program with respect to Christ, the church, mankind in general, and the universe, will be carried out in full (Isa. 40:8).

It is evident from this that our Lord regarded the law of God very highly. Hence, we are not surprised that he continues: **19. Therefore, whoever annuls one of the least of these commandments and so teaches men shall be called least in the kingdom of heaven; but whoever practices and teaches them, he shall be called great in the kingdom of heaven.** Although all is of grace and nothing whatever is *earned* by the citizen of the kingdom, yet his rank or position in that kingdom will depend on and be commensurate with his respect for God's holy law. Not every commandment of that law is of equal significance. The rabbis divided the law into 613 commandments. They considered 248 of these to be positive, 365 negative. They carried on lengthy debates about heavier and lighter commandments. Some rabbis considered Deut. 22:6 ("You shall not carry off the mother-bird together with her young") to be the "lightest" (least significant) of them all. [282] As to the heaviest or greatest of all commandments, the question as to its identity was answered by a scribe (Luke 10:27). That Jesus agreed with him is clear from his response (Luke 10:28; cf. Matt. 22:34-40; Mark 12:28-34).

Now, though it is certainly true that Christ's teaching as to the law was far removed from the trivial hairsplitting arid legalism and torturing scrupulosity of the rabbis, yet he too regarded some requirements of greater importance than others. Not only is this clear from verse 19, quoted above, and from what he said concerning the greatest commandment, it also follows from his statement regarding "the weightier matters of the law: justice, mercy, and faithfulness" (Matt. 23:23). Nevertheless, he insists that *every* commandment of that which is truly God's moral law—the very law which he is about to discuss in greater detail in 5:21 ff.—must be kept. Nothing must be annulled or canceled.

Anyone, no matter how excellent he may be in other respects, who wilfully disregards even the law's least commandment and teaches others to copy his example will be least "in the kingdom of heaven" (see pp. 249, 250); whereas, on the other hand, whoever practices and teaches these commandments (as interpreted by Christ) "shall be called"—implying "and shall actually be" (cf. I John 3:1)—great in that kingdom. As Scripture confirms, this principle holds with respect to Christ's rule both on earth (cf.

---

[282] See S.BK. I, p. 249.

Matt. 18:1-4) and in heaven. It is true now and will apply also in the day of judgment and afterward. Salvation is not only *by* grace and *through* faith, it is also *according to* works. For more on the last point see Eccl. 12:14; Matt. 25:35-45; Rom. 2:16; II Cor. 5:10; and Rev. 20:12, 13. In degree of faithfulness God's children differ even here. Therefore, in degree of glory they will differ in heaven and at the time of the resurrection (I Cor. 15:41, 42).

It follows from verse 19 that keeping the law and teaching it to others in the manner in which it should be taught is very important. This is also shown in verse 20, the introductory conjunction "for" indicating that what Christ's audience was about to hear was in confirmation and further elucidation of what had just been said.

However, though there is this connection between verses 19 and 20, there is also a transition at this point to a new, though closely related, subject. Jesus has been showing that the righteousness of the kingdom is in full accord with the moral principles enunciated in the Old Testament. Now he is going to show that

This Righteousness Is Not in Accord with the Current and
Traditional Interpretation and Application
of God's Holy Law

So Jesus said, 20. **For I tell y o u that unless y o u r righteousness excels that of the scribes and Pharisees, y o u will surely never enter the kingdom of heaven.** Note the emphatic introduction, "For I tell y o u." Jesus is about to make a very important statement regarding the reprehensible righteousness of the scribes and Pharisees, as contrasted with another righteousness, one in which God delights. Immediately after making this statement he is going to become very specific. He is going to show what "You shall not kill" has been interpreted to mean by the rabbis, and what it *really* means; next, how "You shall not commit adultery" has been explained by the ancients, whose explanation had been adopted by the scribes and the Pharisees, and what was its original intention and is its proper application. So he is going to continue to contrast the false and the true interpretation of the law, discussing one by one the oath, retaliation, and love toward the neighbor. This discussion will go on until the end of chapter 5. But even much of chapters 6 and 7 will reflect the indicated contrast.

Accordingly, the statement made in verse 20 is definitely basic for what follows. The righteousness demanded by Jesus is nothing less than *complete* conformity with God's holy law (cf. Matt. 22:34-48, especially verse 48) in all that a person *is* and *does*. Such a righteousness means that the heart, not only the outward deed, is right, yes right as the holy God himself views it. This righteousness, moreover, is God-given, here below in principle, hereafter in perfection. On the contrary, the scribes and Pharisees accepted a righteousness of outward compliance, and they believed or pretended to believe that by strenuous exertion they would be able to achieve their goal, and that they were in fact on the way to its realization.

It is natural that Jesus groups together *a profession* (the scribes) and *a sect* (the Pharisees). The scribes were the acknowledged expounders and teachers of the Old Testament. The Pharisees were those who tried very hard to make everybody believe that they were adhering to this teaching.

Briefly, the two kinds of righteousness, as sharply contrasted in the Gospels, may be described as follows, the corroborative evidence being appended in each case:

a. That of the scribes and Pharisees *fails to satisfy the heart.* It is formal, external, and shallow. It falls far short of perfection. That commended by Jesus *satisfies the heart.* It is genuine, internal, and deeply rooted. It is complete.

"Blessed the pure in heart, for they shall see God" (Matt. 5:8).

"Y o u are those who justify yourselves before men, but God knows y o u r hearts" (Luke 16:15).

"Woe to y o u, scribes and Pharisees, hypocrites!, because y o u clean the outside of the cup and of the dish, but inside they are full of extortion and intemperance" (Matt. 23:25).

b. That of the scribes and Pharisees *fails to satisfy the mind.* It is based upon reasoning that is deceptive, misleading, and merely "clever," and proceeds from a mind that is not at rest. That commended by Jesus *satisfies the mind.* It is in line with reasoning that is honest, reliable, and sound, and proceeds from a mind that has found, or is in the process of finding, rest.

"Come to me all who are weary and burdened and I will give y o u rest" (Matt. 11:28). Note the *sound* reasoning of the "prodigal son" after he had come to himself (Luke 15:17-19).

An example of specious reasoning is found in Matt. 15:3-5. Jesus comments, "Y o u have made the word of God null and void for the sake of y o u r tradition" (15:6).

c. That of the scribes and Pharisees *is self-made.* These men were "self-righteous." That commended by Jesus *is God-given.*

"Blessed those hungering and thirsting for righteousness, for they shall be fully satisfied" (Matt. 5:6).

"To some who trusted in themselves that they were righteous and who despised all others Jesus told this parable: Two men went up into the temple to pray, the one a Pharisee and the other a tax-collector. The Pharisee took his stand and began to pray with himself as follows: 'O God, I thank thee that I am not like the rest of the people. . . . But the tax-collector, standing far off . . . said, 'O God, be merciful to me, the sinner.'. . . I tell y o u, it was this man and not the other who went home justified" (Luke 18:9-14, in part).

d. That of the scribes and Pharisees *glorifies self.* It is ostentatious and proud. That commended by Jesus *glorifies God.* It is unpretentious and humble. This too is clear from the passage just quoted (Luke 18:9-14). It is proved also by the following:

"So let y o u r light shine before men . . . that they may glorify y o u r Father who is in heaven (Matt. 5:16).

"Take care that y o u do not practice y o u r righteousness before the people, to attract their attention; otherwise y o u will not have any reward with y o u r Father who is in heaven. So, whenever you give to the poor do not publicly announce it with the blast of the trumpet, as the hypocrites are in the habit of doing. . ." (Matt. 6:1, 2).

Having then laid down the underlying principle (verse 20: in a sense verses 17-20), that basic truth is now going to be applied to various commandments. Six times Jesus is going to place his own authoritative pronouncement over against the teaching of scribes and Pharisees, and, going back beyond them, over against the misinterpretations of the sages of long ago. Six times he is going to say, "It was said . . . but *I* say" (5:21, 27, 31, 33, 38, and 43). We may call these The Six Antitheses.

The First Antithesis: The Sixth Commandment, Murder

It will become evident that Jesus sharpens the edge of every precept. He does this by pointing out and condemning the evil disposition of the heart that lies at the root of the transgression, and then placing over against it the positive commandment. This is immediately apparent from his interpretation of the sixth commandment. The introduction is as follows: 21. **Y o u have heard that it was said by the men of long ago, You shall not kill, and Whoever kills deserves to be punished (with death).** The formula, "Y o u have heard that it was said" presents a difficulty, since the following phrase, considered by itself, can be translated either *"to* the men of long ago" (R.S.V.: "to the men of old") or *"by* the men of long ago." Many translators and commentators prefer *to.* Several others favor *by.* [283] According to the first view Jesus meant that Moses in the law said something *to* the fathers, and that Jesus now "assumes a tone of superiority over the Mosaic regulations" (A. T. Robertson, *Word Pictures,* Vol. I, p. 44). J. Jeremias, in the article to which reference was made on p. 256, footnote 250, expresses the same view in even stronger language when he states that "Jesus establishes a new divine law when he opposes his 'But I say to y o u' to the Word of Scripture."

According to the second view Jesus meant that *by* the men of long ago, that is, *by* the expounders of the law, the rabbis, an interpretation had been

---

[283] "by them of old time" (A.V.; similarly also F. W. Grosheide, *op. cit.,* p. 57; H. N. Ridderbos, *op. cit.,* Vol. I, pp. 107, 108; and D. M. Lloyd Jones, *op. cit.,* Vol. I, pp. 211, 212).

presented with which he disagrees or which he considers as being dangerously incomplete, even though the scribes and Pharisees of his own day were in agreement with it (as is clearly implied in verse 20).

Reasons for rejecting the first interpretation ("to") and accepting the second ("by"):

a. It would be very strange that Jesus, having just affirmed in most emphatic terms that he had not come to set aside the law or the prophets, would now suddenly turn around and do this very thing.

b. Had Jesus been referring to what Moses in the law had commanded he would have used different language; for example, "Moses commanded" (Matt. 8:4), or "It is written" (Matt. 4:4, 7, 10; Luke 2:23; 4:4).

c. In later Jewish writings such famous rabbans as Hillel and Shammai were called "fathers of antiquity." [284] The designation "the men of long ago" is accordingly an excellent designation for those who had orally interpreted the written Old Testament.

d. The expression "it was *said*," though possible even as a reference to something written, is more readily associated with oral teaching and tradition than with that which had been put down in a document.

e. It is clear that when Jesus says, "Y o u have heard . . . but I say" (5:22, 28, 32, 34, 39, 44) he is drawing a contrast between two positions that are sharply opposed. This contrast is clearer when the two opposing clauses are "It was said *by* the men . . . but *I* say," meaning "*They* said . . . but *I* say," than it would be if they were, "It was said *to* the men . . . but I say," meaning, "They heard . . . but I say."

The ancient interpreters, then, in quoting the sixth commandment had said, "You shall not kill." What was wrong with this? Was not this, after all, exactly what God in his law had written on tablets of stone (Exod. 20:13; Deut. 5:17)? They had added, "Whoever kills deserves to be punished (with death)." And what was wrong with that? It is true that strictly speaking this was an addition of their own. One does not find it in Exod. 20:13 or in Deut. 5:17, but the substance of this addition or interpretation is certainly found in Gen. 9:6, A.V. "Whoso sheddeth man's blood, by man shall his blood be shed. . . ." From that verse it also follows that the punishment to which the men of long ago referred was capital punishment. [285]

On the surface, therefore, it would seem that no fault whatever can be found with the manner in which the men of long ago had interpreted the sixth commandment. In the present instance what was wrong was not what they had said but what they had left unsaid, or at least unemphasized. This

---

[284] See, for example, Mishna, Eduyoth I.4. See B. Pick, *The Talmud, What It Is*, New York, 1887, p. 23.

[285] Thus also in Josephus, *Antiquities* I.102, "I exhort y o u . . . to keep yourselves pure from murder, punishing those comitting such a crime," the meaning, since the reference is again to Gen. 9:6, must be "punishing with death."

applied also to the scribes and Pharisees of Jesus' day, for, as already indicated, they endorsed the tradition of the ancients. Accordingly, they too were not giving a full summary of the law regarding murder. Their interpretation, though correct as far as it went, did not go nearly far enough. It was woefully inadequate. Imagine a present-day minister of the Gospel preaching on this commandment and limiting his exhortations to a warning to be very careful when using fire weapons, clubs, or automobiles. He might even warn against peddling drugs. As long as he fails to point out *the spiritual cause that produces murder,* and warns against *that,* has he not missed the mark? Is the law of God nothing but a penal code?

This *one* lesson, namely, that a person cannot expect a healthful drink from a polluted fountain, summarizes what Jesus teaches in verse 22. **But I say to y o u that (even) anyone who is angry with his brother deserves to be punished (with death). And whoever says to his brother, You blockhead, deserves to be condemned (to death) by the supreme court. And whoever says, You idiot, deserves to be cast into the hell of fire.** Note the emphatic and fully spelled out *I* (ego) at the very beginning of each of the statements in which Jesus contradicts the traditional interpretation (see verses 22, 28, 32, 34, 39, and 44). Here in verse 22 what Jesus is as it were saying is *Principiis obsta,* that is, "Resist beginnings." The beginning of the outward act of murder is sinful anger, hatred. Cf. James 4:1. Such a surly and ill-natured attitude toward a brother is actually sin against the sixth commandment, says Jesus, and deserves to be punished (with death). When in this spirit of contempt and utter disgust anyone says to his brother, "Raca," probably Aramaic and meaning, "You blockhead" (or "You empty-head") he is worthy of being condemned to death by the (Jewish) supreme court (the Sanhedrin). Similarly, when in that same frame of mind and heart he says, "You idiot" (or "You moron," "You fool") he deserves to die. Moreover, that the Lord is not just thinking of physical death but of eternal death is clear from the wording, "he deserves to be cast into the hell (Gehenna) of fire." For more on Gehenna see on 10:28.

If this explanation of the passage is adopted everything is quite simple. Jesus is teaching just *one* lesson, a very important one. He is saying that sinful anger—the kind that leads to bitter words—is in its very nature murder. It is murder committed in the heart. Unless he repents, the person with this kind of attitude faces everlasting punishment in hell. Whatever he may be in human eyes, before God he stands condemned and is on his way to never-ending death. Thus, while the scribes and Pharisees placed the emphasis on the outward deed, as if that alone were reprehensible, Jesus traced the deed to the underlying evil disposition of the heart.

There is, however, another interpretation. In part, it amounts to this: Jesus is saying that for being angry with his brother a man must be sentenced by "a local court"; for doing something worse, namely, in anger calling his

297

brother a blockhead or a good-for-nothing he must be punished by the supreme court; and, worst of all, for calling him an idiot he deserves the extreme penalty, everlasting perdition. [286]

Objections:

a. That the rabbis might resort to making hairsplitting distinctions between the degree of guilt implied in calling a man a blockhead as compared with that implied in calling him an idiot would be understandable; but that Jesus himself resorts to anything of this nature would not be. This is all the more unlikely in a discourse in which he severely criticizes the interpretations of the men of long ago and of their followers.

b. The view that the Greek word *krisis*, here in verse 22, or in verses 21 and 22, means "local court," [287] is probably erroneous. Such a definition is burdened not only by the objection mentioned under *c.* but also by the fact that, aside from 5:21, 22, in none of the well over forty instances of its widely distributed use in the New Testament can it have this meaning. Often it indicates decision, judgment, verdict. Sometimes this amounts to a decision *against,* hence condemnation, punishment. See N.T.C. on John 3:17-19.

c. It is hard to understand how being angry with a brother, without revealing this anger in word or deed, could get a man in trouble with a "local court."

d. This "three gradations of sin and of punishment" theory obscures the fact that not only here, in his teaching about murder, but also in what follows in the rest of the chapter, Jesus is emphasizing one central lesson, namely, that the root of evil lies in the heart, where love must be substituted for hatred and indifference, and sincerity for hypocrisy and selfishness.

There was no excuse for the fact that in their interpretation of the sixth commandment the scribes and Pharisees of Jesus' day, in agreement with the men of long ago, were omitting the main lesson. "Moses" had emphasized love for God (Deut. 6:5) and for man (Lev. 19:18). Not only that but the very first domestic quarrel narrative, the story of Cain and Abel, had in a very impressive manner pointed up the evil of jealous anger, as being the root of murder (Gen. 4:1-16; see especially verses 6 and 7). The same lesson had been re-emphasized in the later writings (Prov. 14:17; 22:24; 25:23; Eccl. 7:9; Job 5:2; Jon. 4:4). Accordingly Jesus, in interpreting the sixth com-

---

[286] F. W. Grosheide, *op. cit.,* p. 58, says that Jesus is presenting gradations in sin, and that a fool (cf. Μωρέ) is worse than a good-for-nothing (cf. 'Ρακά). Similarly, C. R. Erdman says that "Jesus suggests three expressions of this evil and intimates for each an increasing severity of punishment" (*op. cit.,* p. 49). A Plummer, *op. cit.,* p. 79, makes a similar suggestion: "unexpressed hatred, expressed contempt, and expressed abuse," but is not entirely satisfied with it, and says, "Possibly Christ is ironically imitating the casuistical distinctions drawn by the rabbis. . . ." Calvin, too, commenting on 5:22 says that Christ assigns three degrees of condemnation.

[287] An opinion also favored by L.N.T. (A. and G., p. 54).

mandment as he does, far from annulling it, is showing what it had meant from the very beginning.

But what happens when in a person's daily conduct this principle of love does not receive its full due? What must be done by the man who is not living in harmony with his brother? Would this strained relationship in any way affect his worship of God? Or are we dealing here with two separate domains? A very practical question indeed, not only then but also today! How often has not the excuse been heard, "This (action or attitude with respect to my neighbor, my family, my business, my country, etc.) has nothing to do with my religion"?

Jesus, differing sharply, answers: **23, 24. Therefore if, while you are bringing your offering to the altar, you there remember that your brother has a grievance against you, leave your offering there in front of the altar, and first go and be reconciled to your brother; then come (back) and present your offering.** There is an important change here from the (second person) plural to the singular, a change retained in the A.V. (from "you" to "thou") and in the translation as given above from "y o u," in "Y o u have heard" and in "But I say to y o u," to "you," in "Therefore if, while you, etc."). Modern English translations, in making no provision for this transition from the plural to the singular, lose something of the vividness of the original. When the change is recognized it gets to be clear that Jesus is becoming very personal now. He is addressing each individual in particular. Let each man examine his own heart.

The very word "Therefore" shows that what the Lord is about to say follows directly from what he has just stated. It is a positive application of the rule that the heart must at all times be filled with love, not with anger and hatred. It also shows that loving God and therefore bringing him an offering, yet not loving the brother but remaining unreconciled to him, cannot go together. "If a person does not love the brother whom he has seen he cannot love God whom he has not seen" (I John 4:20b).

The illustration Jesus presents is that of a person who, according to Jewish custom, is bringing an offering to the altar (cf. Gen. 4:3-5; Exod. 25:2; Lev. 1:2 ff.; Ps. 66:13). Naturally, if he is doing this in the proper manner he is meditating upon the goodness of God toward him. In the midst of his musings the idea occurs to him, "Since God has been so good to me how should I treat my brother?" Suddenly the thought shoots into his mind, "Brother Jonathan (or whatever the name may be) and myself are no longer on speaking terms. Between him and myself there is something which he considers to be a rightful reason for blaming me. What, if anything, must I do about it?"

In this situation Jesus, in thorough harmony with the principle to which he has just now given expression, says, as it were, "Do not finish your act of devotion. Having left your offering at the altar, immediately go and see that man who has this grievance against you. *Between* the two (διά) bring about *another*, a totally different and better (ἄλλος) relationship; that is, *be reconciled* [288] to your brother. Then return and finish bringing your offering."

Strictly according to the original Jesus said, "If . . . you remember that your brother has *something* against you. . . ." What is meant by "something"? Does it mean that if you know of anyone who even in the minutest degree finds fault with you, you cannot bring that offering until you have succeeded in getting him to approve of you and of all your ways? If that were true how few would be the acts of worship and devotion! I do not believe that anything as impractical as that can have been intended. The "something" must be of a nature important enough to be called *a grievance*.

The next question is, "Must it be a *righteous* grievance, that is, must the other man have *just* cause for complaint before you need to spend your efforts on him for the purpose of reconciliation?" Lenski may be taken as a representative of those who answer in the affirmative (*op. cit.*, p. 214); Ridderbos of those who reply in the negative (*op. cit.*, Vol. I, p. 110). My inclination is to agree with Ridderbos. If I know that my brother even *thinks* that he has a right to be dissatisfied with me, should I not strive to be reconciled to him? How easy it is to find a reason (an excuse?) not to do this!

Also in connection with verses 23 and 24 Jesus is re-emphasizing the true spiritual meaning of the commandment. The Old Testament everywhere teaches that under certain circumstances offerings are *not* acceptable to God (Gen. 4:5; I Sam. 15:22; Isa. 1:11; Jer. 6:20; Amos 5:22; Mic. 6:6, to mention a few of a much longer series of passages). The gift derives its value from the *heart* of the giver (Mark 12:41-44; Luke 21:1-4; Heb. 11:4; cf. John 3:16!).

Does the illustration found in verses 23, 24 mean that reconciliation can wait until a person is bringing an offering to the altar, or is entering the church? Not at all. The time for reconciliation is always *right now*. Tomorrow may be too late. This is clear from verses 25, 26. **Make friends quickly with your opponent, while you still have the opportunity to deal with him, lest the opponent hand you over to the judge, and the judge to the officer, and you be thrown into prison. I solemnly declare to you, never will you get out of that place until you have paid the last cent.** The picture changes a little. In the preceding application of the sixth commandment (verses 23, 24) the brother to be reconciled was one described as having "something (a grievance) against you." Here (verse 25, 26) the opponent is contemplating, in fact may already have started, legal proceedings. [289] As in the previous

---

[288] διαλλάγηθι from διαλλάσσομαι.
[289] For the word ἀντίδικος see also Luke 12:58; 18:3; and I Peter 5:8. The *concept*

instance so also here, whether this opponent is morally in the right is not indicated. Neither is the nature of the matter in dispute definitely stated, though verse 26b ("until you have paid the last cent") may point in the direction of a financial debt. In any event "you," the person whom Jesus addresses, must do your utmost to become "well-disposed" (thus literally) toward your opponent. You must try to make friends with him. You must make every attempt to settle the matter "out of court," while you still have the opportunity to deal with him; hence privately, without involving the judge or court. Unless you do this, when the suit is prosecuted the decision may go against you. The result would be that the judge will hand you over to his "underling" or assistant, "the officer" who carries out the judge's orders. You will then be thrown into prison and will stay there until you have paid the last *penny,* [290] that is, you will never, never get out!

It is clear that the words of the Lord have a deeper meaning. In the final analysis he is speaking not about an earthly but about the heavenly Judge; nor about an earthly jail but about hell. That this is the meaning is clear from a comparison not only with verse 22b but also with 18:30 and 35. It is *the heart* that must be right. It is *the inner disposition* that must be one of love toward all others. That is the only way to fulfil the sixth command- ment.

To summarize, in verses 25, 26 it is as if Jesus were saying, "Be not surprised about the urgency of my command that you be reconciled; for, should it be that you were to pass from this life with a heart still at variance with your brother, a condition which you have not even tried to change, that wrong would testify against you in the day of judgment. Moreover, dying with that spirit of hatred still in your heart, you will never escape from the prison of hell."

The question may be asked, "Does the burden rest on me alone, not at all on the person who opposes me?" Or, wording it differently, "Granted that I am the sinner—so at least my opponent views me—is it not *his* duty to forgive?" The answer is given in such passages as Matt. 6:12, 14; 18:21-35. These same passages also imply that when I have done all in my power to

---

applies also to Satan (Job 1:6 ff.; Zech. 3:1; I Peter 5:8; cf. Rom. 8:31). For more information on the word see my dissertation, *The Meaning of the Preposition ἀντί in the New Testament,* Princeton Seminary, 1948, pp. 67-69.

[290] The original has the word κοδράντης, a loanword from the Latin *quadrant.* A quadrant is a "quarter" of an "as" or "assarius." The latter is worth one sixteenth of a denarius. The denarius is a laborer's average daily wage (Matt. 18:28; 20:2, 9, 13; 22:19). Due to constantly changing monetary values it is impossible to indicate with any degree of accuracy what such coins would be worth today in American or in English money. *If* the denarius be viewed as the equivalent of 16-18 American cents, then the assarius would be worth about a cent, and the quadrant, only about ¼ cent. However, it is not necessary to estimate what would be the exact modern equivalent. The point is: the person who refuses to make an earnest attempt at reconciliation will never be able to pay his debt.

bring about a reconciliation, and the opponent still refuses to be fair, and where necessary to be forgiving, the guilt will rest on himself alone.

The sixth commandment, then, is a matter that involves the heart, not merely the outward act. And so it is with every commandment, also the seventh; as

The Second Antithesis: The Seventh Commandment, Adultery

will show: **27, 28. Y o u have heard that it was said, You shall not commit adultery. But I say to y o u that anyone who looks at a woman in order to lust after her has already committed adultery with her in his heart.** The men of long ago, as also the scribes and Pharisees of Jesus' day, were certainly correct in quoting the seventh commandment as they did. But here again, just as was shown in connection with the sixth commandment, they stopped short of giving a full exposition of the matter. As in the previous case, it was not the law but the rabbinical explanation that was at fault.

The seventh commandment should have been explained in the light of the tenth, "You must not covet your neighbor's wife" (Exod. 20:17; Deut. 5:18). Had that been done, it would have been abundantly clear that "out of the heart come evil deliberations, murders, adulteries, immoralities . . ." (Matt. 15:19). Christ's enemies condemned the outward act. At least it was that upon which they placed the emphasis. When it suited their purpose they could be very severe toward those who committed literal adultery (John 8:1-11). Jesus, however, views *the evil lust of the heart* as adultery, just as he views the hatred of the heart as murder.

It is hardly necessary to add that what holds for the married *man* applies also to the married *woman*. Unfaithfulness in the marriage-bond is always wrong. This implies, of course, that any tendency to arouse such unfaithfulness—for example, the attempt by an unmarried person to disrupt a marriage—is equally a sin against the seventh commandment.

Upon closer examination we notice that there is nothing innocent about the man described in verse 28. He is not one who, without any evil intentions, happens to *see* a person of the opposite sex. No, he *is looking*, gazing, staring at a woman in order [291] to lust [292] after her, to possess and dominate her completely, to use her for his own pleasure. To be sure, the expression "anyone looking," taken by itself, is entirely neutral. The verbal form used in the original is very general in its use. But what we have here in verse 28 is a looking *to lust after*. There is nothing innocent about that. It is

---

[291] Note πρὸς τό with inf.

[292] See word study of ἐπιθυμία in N.T.C. on I and II Timothy and Titus, pp. 271, 272, footnote 147. As it is with the noun ἐπιθυμία so also with the verb ἐπιθυμέω, it can have a favorable sense: to desire (eagerly), long for, aspire to (Matt. 3:17; Luke 22:15; I Tim. 3:1; Heb. 6:11; I Peter 1:12). Here, however, in connection with "adultery" it must mean "lust after."

selfish. See Matt. 7:12. In the proper setting sex is a wonderful gift of God. However, for lewdness and vulgarity there is no excuse. It is wrong always and everywhere, for the unmarried as well as for the married.

What, then, is to be done with respect to the lustful heart and eye? The answer is found in verses 29, 30. So if your right eye lures you into sin, [293] pluck it out and fling it away from you. It is better that you lose one of your members than that your whole body be thrown into hell. And if your right hand lures you into sin, cut it off and fling it away from you. It is better that you lose one of your members than that your whole body go down into hell. This command must not be taken literally, for even if a person should literally pluck out his right eye he would still be able to sin with his left eye. Jesus has himself supplied us with the key to its interpretation, namely, in Matt. 18:7-9, where in slightly different form this command is repeated. From that passage it follows clearly that the eye and the hand that lead a person into sin symbolize and represent "occasions of stumbling," or if one prefers, *enticements to do wrong, beguiling allurements.* The general meaning of the passage, then, is this: "Take drastic action in getting rid of whatever in the natural course of events will tempt you into sin." In the present connection it is especially the sin against the seventh commandment that is in view.

More in detail, it would seem that the following lessons are taught here:

a. The present is not our only life. We are destined for eternity. Note: ". . . than that your whole body be thrown into—or go down into—hell."

b. Nothing, no matter how precious it may seem to us at the moment—think of the *right* eye and the *right* hand—should be allowed to doom our glorious destiny.

c. Sin, being a very destructive force, must not be pampered. It must be "put to death" (Col. 3:5). Temptation should be flung aside *immediately* and *decisively.* [294] Dillydallying is deadly. Halfway measures work havoc. *The surgery must be radical.* Right at this very moment and without any vacillation the obscene book should be burned, the scandalous picture destroyed, the soul-destroying film condemned, the sinister yet very intimate social tie broken, and the baneful habit discarded. In the struggle against sin the believer must fight hard. Shadow-boxing will never do (I Cor. 9:27).

Of course, these destructive, and in that sense negative, actions will never succeed apart from the powerful sanctifying and transforming operation of God's Spirit in heart and life. Throughout the sermon therefore Jesus

---

293 Greek σκανδαλίζετε. The σκάνδαλον is the bait-stick in a trap or snare. It is the crooked stick that springs the trap; hence, *snare, temptation to sin, enticement* (Matt. 18:7; Luke 17:1); also, object of revulsion, the stumbling-block of the cross (I Cor. 1:23; Gal. 5:11). Similarly the verb basically means *to ensnare, lure into sin, lead astray* (Matt. 5:29; 18:6; etc.).

294 Note the crisp aorist imperative actives ἔξελε, βάλε, and ἔκκοψον.

emphasizes the positive. He has done it just now (see verses 23-26), previous-ly in the beatitudes (5:1 ff.), and will continue to do it (5:37, 39-42, 44-48; etc. See also Luke 11:24-26). The beautiful passage found in II Cor. 6:17, 18, a composite quotation from the Old Testament, gives the sense as follows:

"Wherefore come out from among them and be separate, says the Lord, and touch no unclean thing; and I will receive y o u. And I will be to y o u a Father; and y o u shall be to me sons and daughters" (II Cor. 6:17, 18; see also verses 14-16).

By saying, "It is better that you lose one of your members," etc. Jesus emphasizes how incomparably more necessary and far better it is to prepare for eternity than to enjoy (?) the sinful pleasures of this life. Without in any way encouraging or even permitting anyone literally to mutilate himself he is saying that it is surely better to go through the present life maimed in body than, with the whole body still sound and unharmed, to be thrust into Gehenna ("hell"). See also on 10:28 and 16:26.

"Y o u were bought with a price. Therefore glorify God in y o u r body" (I Cor. 6:20).

Continuing his teaching on the seventh commandment Jesus discusses the important subject of divorce. By implication he defends the inviolability of the marriage bond. Countering what was wrong in the traditional teaching Jesus states in

The Third Antithesis: The Seventh Commandment, Divorce

31, 32. It was also said, Whoever divorces his wife, let him give her a divorce certificate. But I say to y o u that whoever divorces his wife except on the ground of (her) infidelity exposes her to adultery, and whoever marries a divorced woman involves himself in adultery. Here, then, are the two contrasted positions: the first, about which the scribes and Pharisees, on the basis of opinions expressed by the men of long ago, were always talking and debating, amounted to this, that when a wife was to be dismissed a certificate of divorce had to be properly drawn up and given to her. As if a piece of paper could dissolve a marriage! The second position was that of Jesus. He as it were asks the question, "Why a divorce at all?" He stresses the fact that the violation of the sacred marriage contract is nothing less than infidelity and adultery.

It is clear that here again, as previously, Jesus goes back, beyond rabbini-cal opinions, to the original intention of the law (Gen. 2:24; 24:67; Exod. 20:14; Deut. 5:18; and Mal. 2:14-16). With all this compare Eph. 5:31, 32 and Heb. 13:4. This appears even more clearly when Matt. 5:32 is studied in connection with 19:3-9. Notice the phrase "from the beginning" in 19:4, 8, and see on that entire passage. The law had made it very clear that in marriage *one* man is joined to *one* woman, the implication being that death alone is able to part them. Cf. Rom. 7:2; I Cor. 7:39. The exception to which Jesus refers in Matt. 5:32 ("except on the ground of infidelity") permits divorce only then when one of the contracting parties, here the wife, [295] by means of marital unfaithfulness ("fornication") rises in rebellion against the very essence of the marriage bond.

The objection might be raised, however, "But did not Moses leave room for the exercise of a greater measure of freedom? Does not the regulation found in Deut. 24:1-4 amount to this, 'If you wish to divorce your wife, go right ahead, but be sure to give her a divorce certificate?' " Such seems to have been the opinion of scribes and Pharisees, though not of all of them in equal degree, as the explanation of 19:3-9 will indicate.

Actually, however, Moses had not at all encouraged divorce but, while not completely forbidding it, had greatly discouraged it. Indeed, whatever be the meaning of the much debated Hebrew phrase `erwath dābhār ("some uncleanness," thus A.V., Deut. 24:1; see on Matt. 19:3), Deut. 24:1-4, taken as a unit, most definitely discouraged divorce. The regulation of the first four verses of that chapter may be summed up as follows: "Husband, you better think twice before you reject your wife. Remember that once you have put her away and she has become the wife of another you cannot afterward take her back; not even if that other husband should also have rejected her or should have died." Moses did mention the giving of a "bill of divorce" (Deut. 24:1), but only in passing, that is, by way of assumption, included in the warning. Scribes and Pharisees, however, as Matt. 5:31 indicates, placed all the emphasis on that certificate. Jesus (verse 32) placed the emphasis where it properly belongs. *They* greatly exaggerated the importance of *the exception,* that which made divorce possible. About that they were always debating (cf. 19:3-9). *He,* on the other hand, stresses *the principle,* namely, that husband and wife are and must remain *one.*

With respect to the translation of Christ's answer commentators differ rather widely, particularly with respect to the words generally translated "causeth her to commit adultery" (A.V.) or "maketh her an adulteress" (A.R.V., cf. R.S.V.). The reader must often have wondered how the act whereby the husband divorces his *innocent* wife could make *her* an adulteress! As if the disgrace of having been unjustly rejected by her husband and being forced to face the struggle of life alone were not enough, must she now in addition be branded an "adulteress"? In reply, it is generally pointed out that the statement when thus read is being misinterpreted. It must be read proleptically: she is called an adulteress because she may easily become one. Will the average reader actually so interpret the words, "Every one that

---

295 Matthew was writing primarily to Jews, among whom the rejection of a wife by her husband was well-known, but not vice versa. Mark, writing to Gentiles, includes both possibilities (10:11, 12). But naturally Matt. 5:32 *applies* to the wife who "puts away" her husband as well as to the husband who does the same to his wife.

putteth away his wife, saving for the cause of fornication, *maketh her an adulteress*"? Is not the real solution a better rendering of the original? The Greek, by using the passive voice of the verb, states not what the woman becomes or what she does but what she undergoes, suffers, is exposed to. She *suffers* wrong. He *does* wrong. To be sure, she herself also may become guilty, but that is not the point which Jesus is emphasizing. Far better, it would seem to me, is therefore the translation, "Whoever divorces his wife except on the basis of infidelity exposes her to adultery," or something similar. [296]

What Jesus is saying, then, is this: Whoever divorces his wife except on the ground of infidelity must bear the chief responsibility if as a result she, in her deserted state, should immediately yield to the temptation of becoming married to someone else. The erring husband should be given an opportunity to correct his error, that is, to go back to his wife. This also explains the closing clause, according to which anyone who rushes in to marry the deserted wife is involving himself in—hence, is committing—adultery.—It was thus that Jesus counteracted the looseness in morals prevailing in his day.

The more we study Christ's teaching as presented to us in this passage the more we begin to appreciate it. Here, by means of a few simple words, Jesus discourages divorce, refutes the rabbinical misinterpretation of the law, reaffirms the law's true meaning (cf. Matt. 5:17, 18), censures the guilty party, defends the innocent, and throughout it all upholds the sacredness and inviolability of the marriage bond as ordained by God!

And now:

The Fourth Antithesis: The Commandment Concerning the Oath

33-37. Again, y o u have heard that it was said by the men of long ago, You shall not break your oath, but shall keep the oaths you have sworn to the Lord. But I tell y o u, Do not take any oath at all, either by heaven, for it is God's throne, or by the earth, for it is his footstool, or by Jerusalem, for it is the city of the great King. Nor shall you swear by your head, for you cannot make one hair white or black. Let y o u r speech be such that yes is simply yes, and no is simply no. Anything beyond that comes from the evil one. Here again, as previously, what was said by the men of long ago was not incorrect. It was a fair summary of the letter of the law concerning the oath

---

[296] The Greek, according to the best reading, is ποιεῖ αὐτὴν μοιχευθῆναι. L.N.T., p. 417, entry μοιχάω, comments, "passive of the wife, to suffer adultery, be debauched, Matt. 5:32a." Of the same nature, though with slight variations, are the renderings suggested by F. W. Grosheide and H. N. Ridderbos in their respective commentaries. These, too, indicate that it is what this woman suffers, what she is exposed to, that is expressed. So also H. Bouwman in his article *Echtscheiding* (Divorce) in *Christelijke Encyclopaedie*, Kampen, 1925, Vol. II, p. 4.

(Lev. 19:12; Num. 30:2; and cf. Deut. 23:21). Only, from the words of Jesus it is very obvious that the ancients, and thus also the scribes and Pharisees of Jesus' day, misplaced the emphasis. As is clear from the context in every case, the divinely intended emphasis (note italics) was as follows:

"*Y o u shall not swear* by my name *falsely*" (Lev. 19:12).

"When a man makes a vow to Jehovah or swears an oath . . . *he shall not break his word*" (Num. 30:2).

"When you shall make a vow to Jehovah your God, *you shall not be slack to pay it*" (Deut. 23:21).

Or, using the phraseology of the interpreters:

"*You shall not break your oath, but shall keep the oaths* you have sworn to the Lord."

In each case the emphasis is on truthfulness: a person must be truthful when he solemnizes his promise with an oath. He must really mean it. He must also be faithful in keeping the oath; that is, he must carry out his promise. Even in connection with the promises which God himself confirmed with an oath it is truthfulness that is stressed, "Jehovah has sworn to David in truth; he will not turn from it" (Ps. 132:11). And in connection with "the two immutable things" (the promise and the oath) from which believers derive strong encouragement (Heb. 6:18) it is emphasized that "it is impossible for God to lie."

Now this emphasis on truthfulness "in the heart" or "in the inward parts," absence of "falsehood and deceit" (respectively Ps. 15:2; 51:6; and 24:4) is well distributed in the writings of the Old Testament. In addition to the references already given from the Pentateuch and from the Psalms, see also Prov. 8:7; 12:19; Jer. 5:3; Hos. 4:1; Zech. 8:16; Mal. 2:6; and cf. Mic. 6:8.

It is evident from the words of Jesus in Matt. 5:34-36 that the traditionalists had shifted the emphasis, so that the Pentateuch passages now began to read as follows:

"You shall not swear *by the name* falsely" (Lev. 19:12).

"When a man makes a vow *to Jehovah* or swears an oath . . . he shall not break his word" (Num. 30:2).

"When you shall make a vow *to Jehovah your God,* you shall not be slack to pay it" (Deut. 23:21).

Summary: "You shall not break your oath, but shall keep the oaths you have sworn *to the Lord.*"

In other words, in the thinking of scribes and Pharisees and their forerunners an oath sworn "to the Lord" must be kept; on the contrary, an oath in connection with which the name of the Lord was not expressly mentioned was of lesser significance. One did not need to be quite so conscientious about keeping it. And so in daily conversation oaths began to multiply "by heaven" and "by the earth" and "by Jerusalem" and, according to 23:16,

18, even "by the temple" and "by the altar." In order to make an impression a person might utter such an oath, "talking big" and dispensing enormous promises. If the affirmation which he had made was a lie or if the promise was never even meant to be kept, that was not so bad, as long as he had not sworn "to the Lord."

Jesus forbids this hypocrisy. He shows that the subtle, hair-splitting distinctions by means of which the rabbis, etc. were classifying the oaths into those which were absolutely binding, those not quite so binding, and those not binding at all, or whatever their groupings may have been, were completely devoid of reason. He tells them that an oath "by heaven" must be truthful and must be kept, for was not heaven God's throne? The man who swears such an oath is invoking *God* therefore. And so also for the oath "by the earth"; for, was not the earth God's footstool (Isa. 66:1)? And as to the oath "by Jerusalem," was not Jerusalem the city of the great King (Ps. 48:3)? In other words, when oaths were sworn with an appeal to any of these objects they were as definitely binding as if the name of the Lord had been expressly invoked in connection with them.

There were even those who swore "by their heads," meaning, "May I lose my head—hence, may I lose my life—if what I am telling you is not the truth, or if I do not fulfil my promise." Jesus points out, however, that nobody is able to change the intrinsic color of his hair. It is God, he alone, who determines whether at any given moment a hair is to be white or black. Since this is true, even swearing by one's head is swearing by God and is as binding as is a different type of oath.

The real solution of the problem is in the heart. In that heart truth should reign supreme. Hence, in daily conversation with his fellowmen a person should avoid oaths altogether. Instead, let him become so truthful, so thoroughly dependable, that his words are believed. When he wishes to affirm something let him then simply say, "Yes"; and when he desires to deny something let him simply say, "No." Anything "stronger" than that is from the evil one.

It is characteristic of certain individuals who are aware that their reputation for veracity is not exactly outstanding that the more they lie the more they will also assert that what they are saying is "gospel truth." They are in the habit of interlacing their conversations with oaths. Such perjurious conduct, says Jesus, stems "from the evil one," the creator of falsehoods (Gen. 3:1, 4; Job 1:9-11; Matt. 4:6, 10, 11; John 8:44; Acts 5:3; and II Thess. 2:9-11. [297]

---

[297] It is true that ἐκ τοῦ πονηροῦ can also be neuter and thus can mean "comes from evil." Those who favor this rendering interpret the words "whatsoever is more than these cometh of evil," (A.V., and similarly A.R.V., R.S.V. text, and N.A.S.) to mean that oaths owe their origin to evil, that is, to untruthfulness, present on such a large scale in our society. "In a world without sin the oath would be unnecessary but now it is necessary"

Does this mean now that by saying, "Do not take any oath at all" Jesus forbids even those oaths that are made in court? Does he teach that nowhere in the entire realm of human relations is there any room for the solemn invocation of the name of God in substantiation of an important affirmation or promise? Not at all. Such a view would be contrary to the teaching of Scripture. It was with an oath that Abraham confirmed his promises to the king of Sodom and to Abimelech (Gen. 14:22-24; 21:23, 24). Abraham also required an oath of his servant (24:3, 9). The oath is mentioned also in connection with Isaac (26:31), Jacob (31:53; cf. 28:20-22), Joseph (47:31, 50:5), "the princes of the congregation" (Josh. 9:15), and the children of Israel (Judg. 21:5). See also Ruth 1:16-18; II Sam. 15:21; I Kings 18:10; and II Chron. 15:14, 15.

With respect to God's own oaths, to the references already mentioned (p. 307) can be added Gen. 22:16; 26:3; Ps. 89:3, 49; 110:4; Jer. 11:5; and Luke 1:73. Finally, it was under oath that Jesus declared himself to be the Christ, the Son of God (Matt. 26:63, 64). In this world of dishonesty and deception the oath is at times necessary to add solemnity and the guarantee of reliability to an important affirmation or promise. Nothing either here in Matt. 5:33-37 or anywhere else in Scripture forbids this. Heb. 6:16 confirms this practice without a word of adverse criticism. What we have here in Matt. 5:33-37 (cf. James 5:12) is the condemnation of the flippant, profane, uncalled for, and often hypocritical oath, used in order to make an impression and to spice daily conversation. Over against that evil Jesus commends simple truthfulness in thought, word, and deed.

The Fifth Antithesis: The Commandment
Concerning Retaliation

38-42. Y o u have heard that it was said, An eye for an eye and a tooth for a tooth. But I tell y o u, Do not resist the evil-doer; but to him that slaps you on the right cheek turn the other also. And if anyone wishes to go to law with you and take your shirt, let him take your robe also. And whoever forces you to go one mile, go with him two. To him that asks (anything) of

---

(G. Brillenburg Wurth, *De Bergrede en Onze Tijd*, Kampen, 1933, p. 73). So also H. N. Ridderbos, *op. cit.*, Vol. I, p. 115. Though I believe that this explanation of the necessity of the oath is correct and even important, I question whether in the present context it adequately accounts for the phrase in question. To me the phrase thus construed seems somewhat out of context. Besides, to the consciousness of Christ, the devil was very real (see temptation references in Matt. 4 and parallels; Matt. 12:27; 13:19, 39; 16:23; 25:41; Mark 8:33; Luke 10:18; 11:18; 13:16; 22:31; John 12:31; 14:30; and 16:11). Finally, as has been shown, untruthfulness is a very salient characteristic of Satan, so that deriving flippant and (generally) lying oaths from the devil as their source is after all quite natural. The rendering "the evil one" or "the devil" is also favored, among others, by The Amplified New Testament, Beck, Berkeley, Goodspeed, N.E.B., Weymouth, Williams, and the new Dutch translation (*Bijbel, Nieuwe Vertaling*).

you give, and from him that wants to borrow of you do not turn away. In Exod. 21:24, 25 we read, ". . . eye for eye, tooth for tooth, hand for hand, foot for foot, burn for burn, wound for wound, stripe for stripe." Lev. 24:20 adds "fracture for fracture"; Deut. 19:21, "life for life." This was a law for the civil courts, laid down in order that the practice of seeking private revenge might be discouraged. The Old Testament passages do not mean, "Take personal revenge whenever you are wronged." They mean the exact opposite, "Do not avenge yourself but let justice be administered publicly." This is clear from Lev. 24:14, "Take the blasphemer out of the camp; and let all who heard him lay their hands upon his head, and let all the congregation stone him." Cf. Deut. 19:15-21.

The Pharisees, however, appealed to this law to justify personal retribution and revenge. They quoted this commandment in order to defeat its very purpose. Cf. Matt. 15:3, 6. The Old Testament repeatedly forbids personal vengeance: "You shall not take vengeance, nor bear any grudge against the children of your people; you shall love your neighbor as yourself; I am Jehovah" (Lev. 19:18). "Do not say, I will repay evil. Wait for Jehovah, and he will save you" (Prov. 20:22). "Do not say, as he has done to me so will I do to him; I will pay the man back according to what he has done" (Prov. 24:29).

What then did Jesus mean when he said, "Do not resist the evil-doer; but to him that slaps you," etc.? When Christ's words (verses 39-42) are read in the light of what immediately *follows* in verses 43-48, and when the parallel in Luke 6:29, 30 is explained on the basis of what immediately *precedes* in verses 27, 28, it becomes clear that the key passage, identical in both Gospels, is "Love y o u r enemies" (Matt. 5:44; Luke 6:27). In other words, Jesus is condemning the spirit of lovelessness, hatred, yearning for revenge. He is saying, "Do not resist the evil-doer with measures that arise from an unloving, unforgiving, unrelenting, vindictive disposition."

Once this is understood it becomes evident that "to turn the other cheek" means to show in attitude, word, and deed that one is filled with the spirit not of rancor but of love. Rom. 12:19-21 presents an excellent commentary.

Something similar holds with respect to the person who threatens by means of a lawsuit to take away someone's "shirt," the tunic worn next to the body, as payment for an alleged debt. Note that not the person whom Jesus is addressing is suing but his opponent is (cf. I Cor. 6:1). Rather than *resentfully* to contest this lawsuit, says Jesus, allow the plaintiff to have the outer robe also. This robe was considered so indispensable that when taken as a pledge it had to be returned before sunset, since it also served as a cover—often the poor man's only one—during sleep (Exod. 22:26, 27; Deut. 24:12, 13; Ezek. 18:7; and Amos 2:8). In summary: we have no right to hate the person who tries to deprive us of our possessions. Love even toward him should fill our hearts and reveal itself in our actions.

The first verb in "Whoever forces you to go one mile. . . ." refers to the authority to requisition, to press into service. It is a loanword from the Persian language, which in all probability borrowed it from the Babylonian. The famous Persian Royal Post authorized its couriers whenever necessary to press into service anyone available and/or the latter's animal. There must be no delay in the dispatch and delivery of the king's decrees, etc. Cf. Esther 3:13, 15; 8:10. As happens frequently, so also here, the verb gradually acquired the more general meaning of *compelling* someone *to render any kind of service.* It is used in connection with Simon of Cyrene who was compelled to carry Christ's cross (Matt. 27:32; Mark 15:21). Now what Jesus is saying is that rather than to reveal a spirit of bitterness or annoyance toward the one who forces a burden upon a person, the latter should take this position with a smile. Did someone ask you to go with him, carrying his load for the distance of *one* mile? [298] Then go with him *two* miles!

Similarly, when someone in distress asks for assistance, one must not turn a deaf ear to him. On the contrary, says Jesus, give, not grudgingly or gingerly but generously; lend, not selfishly, looking forward to usury (Exod. 22:25; Lev. 25:36, 37), but liberally, magnanimously. Not only *show* kindness but *love* kindness (Mic. 6:8; cf. Deut. 15:7, 8; Ps. 37:26; 112:5; Prov. 19:17; Acts 4:36, 37; II Cor. 8:8, 9).

Biblical illustrations of the spirit which Jesus here commends:

a. Abraham, rushing to rescue his "brother" Lot (Gen. 14:14 ff.), though the latter had earlier revealed himself to be a rather avaricious nephew (Gen. 13:1-13).

b. Joseph, generously forgiving his brothers (Gen. 50:19-21), who had not treated him very kindly (37:18-28).

c. David, twice sparing the life of his pursuer King Saul (I Sam. 24 and 26).

d. Elisha, setting bread and water before the invading Syrians (II Kings 6).

e. Stephen, interceding for those who were stoning him to death (Acts 7:60).

f. Paul, after his conversion, writing Rom. 12:21; I Cor. 4:12; and I Cor. 13; and putting it into practice!

g. Above all, Jesus himself, praying, "Father, forgive them, for they do not know what they are doing" (Luke 23:24; cf. Isa. 53:12, last clause; Matt. 11:29; 12:19; and I Peter 2:23). [299]

This brings us to

---

298 Original μίλιον, a Latin loanword (*mille*), meaning literally a thousand paces=eight stadia, approximately .92 of a British, American, etc. statute mile.
299 Whatever be the textual merits of Luke 23:34, do not the other passages reveal the same spirit?

*The Sixth Antithesis: The Summary of the
Second Table of the Law*

43-47. Y o u have heard that it was said, You shall love your neighbor
and hate your enemy. But I tell y o u, love y o u r enemies, [300] and pray for
those that persecute y o u, that y o u may be sons of y o u r Father who is in
heaven, for he causes his sun to rise on evil (people) and good, and sends rain
on righteous and unrighteous. For if y o u love those who love y ou, what is
y o u r reward? Are not the tax-collectors doing the same thing? And if, with
cordial greetings, y o u approach y o u r brothers only, what are y o u doing
that is exceptional? Are not the Gentiles doing as much? "You shall love
your neighbor and hate your enemy" must have been the popular way in
which the average Israelite during the days of Christ's ministry summarized
the second table of the law and regulated his life with respect to friend and
foe. [301] He must have learned it from the scribes and Pharisees, though not
necessarily from all of them without exception. We know at least that the
scribe whose summary is reported in Mark 12:32, 33 and the *lawyer* (an
expert in the Jewish law) who speaks in Luke 10:25-27 were careful not to
omit "as yourself" when they quoted Lev. 19:18. What was even worse than
this omission (see 5:43) was the addition "and hate your enemy." Nowhere
in the Old Testament do we find anything of the kind. In fact, by means of
this addition the emphasis was again shifted away from the original intention
of the law as happened also in connection with the commandment
concerning the oath (see p. 307). Lev. 19:18, "You shall not take vengeance,
nor bear any grudge against the children of your people; you shall love your
neighbor as yourself; I am Jehovah" emphasized *love* over against *vengeance.*
Its perversion in the popular summary drew a sharp contrast between
neighbor and *enemy,* as if the purpose of the commandment had been that
the former be loved and the latter hated. The result was the question, "And
who is my neighbor?" (Luke 10:29). Was it only the Israelite? Or was it the
Israelite and the proselyte? See Lev. 19:34. But if so, what kind of proselyte,
only the genuine proselyte, that is, the non-Israelite who through baptism
and circumcision had become a Jew in every way except for the fact that he
was not literally a son of Abraham? Or must the other proselytes also be
included? Some of these questions were already being asked during the time
of Christ's sojourn on earth. Others were to demand attention a little
later. [302]

It stands to reason that as a result of this woeful misinterpretation of the
law a wall of separation was built between Jew and Gentile; the former to be

---

[300] The words ". . . bless them that curse you, do good to them that hate you," A.V.,
were probably inserted from Luke 6:27, 28, where they occur in reversed order.
[301] Cf. S.BK., Vol. I, p. 353.
[302] See the lengthy discussion in S.BK., Vol. I, pp. 553-568.

loved, the latter to be hated. But it was hard to stop here. Another barricade must be erected between *good* Israelites, such as the scribes and Pharisees, and *bad* Israelites, such as those renegades, the publicans (see verse 46) and in general the entire rabble that did not know the law (John 7:49). In such an atmosphere it was impossible for hatred to starve. It had plenty to feed on.

It was in the midst of this intensely narrow-minded exclusivistic and intolerant environment that Jesus carried on his ministry. All around him were those walls and fences. He came for the very purpose of bursting those barriers, so that love—pure, warm, divine, infinite—would be able to flow straight down from the heart of God, hence from his own marvelous heart, into the hearts of men. His love overleaped all the boundaries of race, nationality, party, age, sex, etc.

When he said, "I tell y o u, love y o u r enemies," he must have startled his audience, for he was saying something that probably never before had been said so succinctly, positively, and forcefully. Thorough research of all the relevant sources resulted in the statement: "The conclusion remains that the first one who has taught mankind to see *the neighbor* in every human being, and therefore to encounter every human being in love was Jesus; see the parable of The Good (literally, the Compassionate) Samaritan."[303] Without in any way denying that statement one might add, Jesus taught the people that one should not even ask, "And who is my neighbor?" but should prove himself neighbor to the man in need, whoever that might be (see Luke 10:36).

Although in the form here expressed ("Love y o u r enemies") Christ's teaching was new, it did not contradict the law. Rather, it was the fruition of the seed planted earlier. As has been shown, the Old Testament forbade revenge. But it even went beyond that, teaching that whenever necessary one should render assistance to his enemy:

"If you happen upon your enemy's stray ox or donkey, you must bring it back to him. If you see the donkey of one who hates you lying (helpless) under its pack, you must refrain from leaving him with it. You must help him to lift it up" (Exod. 23:4, 5).

From "Assist your enemy" to "Love him" was but a step. Jesus took that step. He added, "And pray for those that persecute y o u." On persecution of believers see 5:10-12. Jesus does not require that his disciples do the impossible. He does not ask them to be fond of their persecutors. But he does definitely ask that those for whom he was to die while they by nature were still God's enemies (Rom. 5:8, 10) shall pray for the salvation of *their* enemies, meaning "for the salvation of those who hate them."

By means of loving their enemies and praying for them Christ's followers will prove to themselves and to others that they are true sons of the Father

---

[303] S.BK., *op. cit.*, Vol. I, p. 354.

in heaven. It stands to reason that by saying, "that y o u may be sons," etc. Jesus could not have meant, "that y o u by so doing may become sons or earn sonship." By grace they were sons already, but their son-like or childlike behavior would confirm this fact, for children imitate their father (Eph. 5:1, 2). This is true in the heavenly family even more definitely than in the earthly, for while in the latter case by no means every son is endowed with the "spirit" of his father, in the former every true "son" (one saved by grace through faith, Eph. 2:8) receives the Father's Spirit. It is to that Spirit that he owes his new birth (John 3:5), as well as his growth in Christian virtues and his final perfection.

When Jesus exhorts those whom he addresses to prove their kinship to the "Father who is in heaven" (on this term see pp. 326, 327) by loving and praying even for their enemies, he illustrates the implied primordial and active love of the Father by calling attention to the fact that "he causes his sun to rise on evil (people) and good, and sends rain on righteous and unrighteous." This statement is remarkable in more than one respect:

a. It is far more meaningful to say "*He* causes *his* sun to rise" and "*He* sends rain" than "the sun rises" and "it rains." The way Jesus says it we are made to look beyond the action to the One who causes it, and also beyond the fact as such to the reason that brings it about, namely, the Father's love for mankind.

b. The definite articles are omitted; hence probably *not*, with most versions, "on *the* evil and on *the* good . . . on *the* just and on *the* unjust," but "on evil and good . . . on righteous and unrighteous." Thus special emphasis is placed on the character of these people, as if to say, "Though the Father is the spotlessly Holy One, yet he does not shrink from pouring out his blessings on both evil and good."

c. In order to make the marvelous nature of the Father's love stand out all the more conspicuously the two pairs of objects are arranged chiastically (X-wise), the emphasis falling neither on the evil nor on the good.

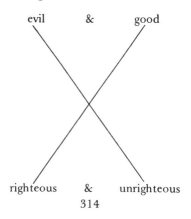

evil   &   good

righteous   &   unrighteous

In the first pair "evil" (people) are mentioned first, in the second "righteous" (people) are. Sunshine and rain descend on all alike, and in so doing reveal the Father's love of which all are the objects.

Now it is certainly true that men respond differently to the blessings by means of which the Father reveals his love. There is no common gratitude. It is therefore also true that those who reject the gospel use God's blessings to their own hurt. However, all this cannot cancel the fact that the love of God for earth-dwellers, good and bad, is impartially revealed in the blessings of sunshine and rain and all their beneficial results. This love of God for those whom he created is also clear from Gen. 17:20; 39:5; Ps. 36:6; 145:9, 15, 16; Jon. 4:10, 11; Mark 8:2; Luke 6:35, 36; Acts 14:16, 17; Rom. 2:4; and I Tim. 4:10. To single out just one of these passages, Jonah 4:10, 11—God's tenderness toward the Ninevites, to their little ones and even toward their cattle—, can anyone read this without being overcome with emotion? Read what G. C. Berkouwer says about this, *De Voorzienigheid Gods (Dogmatische Studiën)*, Kampen, 1950, p. 97.

None of this should be regarded as a denial of the fact that there is indeed a love of God that is not shared by all. Such passages as Gen. 17:21; Ps. 103:17, 18; 147:20; Matt. 20:16; Luke 12:32; Rom. 8:1, 28-39; and a host of others prove this beyond any doubt. But just as a human father, in addition to uniquely loving his own sons and daughters, has room in his heart for his neighbor's children, yes even for all the children in the world, so also the Father in heaven, in addition to sustaining an altogether peculiar relationship of tender concern and intimate friendship toward those who by his grace are his very own, loves mankind in general. See N.T.C. on John 3:16.

Those, on the other hand, who refuse to include their enemies and their persecutors in their love are putting themselves on a moral and spiritual level with the very people whom they so thoroughly despise, namely, in Christ's day the tax-collectors ("publicans") and the Gentiles. Matthew, the man who records all this, having himself been a tax-collector (see pp. 95-97 and on 9:9), was no stranger to the intense hatred with which especially the scribes and Pharisees regarded the people who belonged to this class. The tax-buyers or "farmers" had paid a fixed sum of money to the Roman government for the privilege of levying tolls upon exports and imports as well as upon whatever merchandise passed through the region. The main tax offices were located at Caesarea, Capernaum, and Jericho. The farmers would sublet their rights to "chief publicans" (Luke 19:2) who employed "publicans" to do the collecting. These charged what the traffic would bear, huge sums. So the "publican" had the reputation of being an extortionist. If he were a Jew, he was regarded by his fellows as being also a renegade or traitor, for he was in the service of the foreign oppressor. The low esteem in which publicans were held appears from such passages as Matt. 9:10, 11;

11:19; 21:31, 32; Mark 2:15, 16; Luke 5:30; 7:34; 15:1; 19:7. Publicans and sinners were mentioned in one breath, the two designations being regarded as synonyms.

If tax-collectors were disdained, so also were the Gentiles. This had not always been the case. In Old Testament times the Israelites had been commanded to love the "sojourners," (Deut. 10:19), and to remember that they themselves too had at one time been sojourners in the land of Egypt (Exod. 23:9). However, when during the time of the Exile the Israelites suffered indescribable woes at the hands of their captors, and when even later, during the inter-testamentary period, Antiochus Epiphanes threatened to blot out their religion root and branch, the attitude of the Jews toward the Gentiles changed. Besides, were not the Gentiles idolaters? And was not idolatry the evil that had led the Israelites into captivity? Were not the Romans also Gentiles, and were not they the foreign oppressors? Were they not also trying to lead Israel astray religiously? During New Testament times, therefore, the Gentiles, like the publicans, were treated with extreme antipathy and scorn. By "pious" Jews they were regarded as "unclean" (John 18:28), in fact as "dogs" (reflected in Matt. 15:26, 27). For a Jew to have dinner with an uncircumcised Gentile was unthinkable (Acts 11:2).

It is understandable that this hatred was mutual. If the Israelites treated those unclean Gentiles with scorn, they themselves received similar treatment (John 18:35; Acts 16:20; 18:2). So, barring a few notable exceptions, with respect for example to a non-Israelite who showed a deep interest in Israel's religion (Luke 7:1-5), publicans, Gentiles, and Jews formed separate groups. So did also the Samaritans. The Samaritan woman was astonished that Jesus, being a Jew, would ask her to give him a drink of water (John 4:9; cf. Luke 9:52, 53; John 8:48). Fragmentation all around. Hatred everywhere! And as to love? Well, tax-collectors loved tax-collectors. Gentiles cordially greeted [304] Gentiles.

We now understand the background of Christ's saying (in brief) "If y o u love those who love y o u, what is y o u r reward? Are not the tax-collectors doing the same thing. . . . And do not Gentiles fondly greet Gentiles?" The Lord is telling his hearers therefore that by imitating the tax-collectors and the Gentiles in their exclusivism, they are simply showing that they themselves are not any better than those whom they have been regarding as being far below them in moral and spiritual worth. They are doing nothing that is exceptional, that overflows or is extraordinary. Yet, in order to receive a reward the righteousness of those who desired to be Christ's disciples must "excel" that of the scribes and Pharisees (see verse 20). [305]

---

[304] Evidence for the fact that ἀσπάσησθε means more than simply "y o u greet" is furnished by L.N.T.(A. and G.), p. 116. The word suggests cherishing, being fond of, here perhaps: approaching with cordial greetings.

[305] The word περισσόν used here in verse 47, and περισσεύσῃ used in verse 20 are cognates.

There is nothing wrong with the idea of looking forward to a *reward*, provided, however, that it be understood *a*. that the work that is done for the Master must be done spontaneously, in the spirit of Matt. 25:37, 38; and *b*. that the reward is not out of merit but of grace" (Heidelberg Catechism, Lord's Day 24). See especially Matt. 6:1, 4, 5, 6; Luke 17:10; I Cor. 3:8; 4:7; 9:17; Phil. 3:14; and Heb. 12:2.

Jesus summarizes this entire paragraph (verses 43-47) by saying: **48. Y o u, therefore, must be perfect, as y o u r heavenly Father is perfect.** This, too, was in harmony with the law: "Speak to all the congregation of the children of Israel, and say to them, Y o u shall be holy, for I Jehovah y o u r God am holy" (Lev. 19:2). "You shall be perfect before Jehovah your God" (Deut. 18:13). See also Lev. 11:44; 20:7, 26; Eph. 5:1; and I Peter 1:15, 16. Does this mean that Jesus was a perfectionist in the sense that he taught men that they could reach sinlessness before death? Not at all, as the beatitudes clearly show and as the petition that he taught his disciples to pray, namely, "And forgive us our debts" (Matt. 6:12) reaffirms. He never even hinted that there might be a time before death when this petition could be omitted! Against perfectionism in the sense indicated see also I Kings 8:46; Job 9:1; Ps. 130:3, 4; Prov. 20:9; Eccl. 7:20; Rom. 3:10; 7:7-26; Gal. 5:16-24; James 3:2; and I John 1:8.

If the question be asked, "Then why even try to become perfect?" the answer would be, "Because that is what God commands," as has been shown. Also, a follower of Jesus cannot do otherwise. He, with Paul, yearns for perfection (Phil. 3:7-16). Even here and now he has received the righteousness of imputation. Also the righteousness of impartation (see above, pp. 273, 274), but the latter is not complete in this present life. The struggle for perfection also in the latter sense will not go unrewarded. It is exactly to those who strive to attain the goal that the victory is assured. When they reach the glorious shores of eternity their ideal will be realized. It will be God's gift to them (Ps. 17:15; Phil. 1:6; 3:12b; II Tim. 4:7, 8; Rev. 21:27, cf. 7:14).

In the present connection, however, "perfect" means "brought to completion, full-grown, lacking nothing."[306] Jesus is saying to the people of that day, as well as to us now, that they and we should not be satisfied with half-way obedience to the law of love, as were the scribes and Pharisees, who never penetrated to the heart of the law. Though in a sense Jesus is here repeating the admonition implied in verse 45 ("that y o u may be sons of y o u r Father who is in heaven"), he now (here in verse 48) indicates even more definitely that it is the Father's *perfection* that we should strive to imitate; that is, perfection here specifically (as the preceding context indicates) in the love he shows to all. Is he not the One who causes his sun to rise

---

[306] For the meaning of τέλειος in Paul's epistles see N.T.C. on Philippians, p. 176, footnote 156.

317

on evil and good, and sends rain on righteous and unrighteous? Is he not also the One who gently admonished Cain (Gen. 4:6, 7)? The One who all the day spread out his hands toward a disobedient and contrary people (Isa. 65:2; Rom. 10:21)? Similarly, therefore, the love of all those for whom his words were intended must not stop short of embracing everybody, including even the haters and persecutors! Not only that, but in its *quality* or *character*, too, it must be a love patterned after the Father's; for example, in patience, tenderness, earnestness, etc.

Let it be granted immediately that the love of even the most mature believer is and will always remain finite, whereas God's love is infinite. Let it be added, therefore, that such finite love can never be anything more than a shadow of his marvelous love. This *kind* of finite love is, nevertheless, attainable. How do we know? Because of the very fact that he is *our heavenly Father,* who will, for that very reason, not withhold this gift from his children.

Between chapters 5 and 6 there is a close connection. This is evident especially from two facts: *a.* Jesus continues to speak about the righteousness of the kingdom (cf. 5:6, 10, 20 with 6:1); and *b.* he continues for a while to contrast genuine righteousness with that which he associates with the scribes and Pharisees (5:20), the hypocrites (6:2, 5, 16).

Nevertheless, there is also a definite transition to a new subdivision. In chapter 5 true religion was contrasted with that which the scribes and Pharisees, on the basis of rabbinical tradition, *were teaching;* in 6:1-18, it will be contrasted with what they *were practicing.* Beginning with 6:19 the hypocrites recede into the background. Though it would probably be wrong to say that they drop from view entirely, in this sermon they are no longer specifically mentioned.

Beginning with 6:1 and continuing through 7:12 Jesus, more positively than before, directs the attention of his audience to what is meant by the righteousness of the kingdom. Briefly, living the righteous life consists in spontaneous obedience to the rule, "Love God above all and your neighbor as yourself." Note the two parts: *a.* love God; *b.* love the neighbor. Chapter 6 deals chiefly with the first of these two; 7:1-12 with the second. As to chapter 6, in it Jesus demands the sincere devotion of the heart to God (verses 1-18), and undivided trust in this heavenly Father amid all circumstances (verses 19-34); for, if man is to love the Father sincerely, then *to* him he will surrender everything, and *from* him he will expect everything.

The gradual shift of attention, away from scribes and Pharisees, and toward "y o u r heavenly Father" is clear from the fact that while this appellation or the similar "y o u r Father who is in heaven" occurs only three times in chapter 5 (verses 16, 45, and 48), in the considerably shorter chapter 6 the Father is mentioned no less than a dozen times, in slightly varied ways ("y o u r Father," "your Father," and "our Father"). See verses 1, 4, 6 twice, 8, 9, 14, 15, 18 twice, 26, and 32. The transition from chapter 5 to chapter 6, also in this respect, is gradual, as 5:45, 48, and 6:1 indicate. Accordingly, the new subdivision (chapter 6) may be given the title:

The Essence of This Righteousness with Respect to
Man's Relation to God

First in order is

The Sincere Devotion of the Heart (6:1-18)

Speaking, then, about righteousness in the ethical sense (included in 5:6), that is, the practice of the true religion—here particularly as expressed in the religious exercises of giving to charity, prayer, and fasting—Jesus says, **6:1. Take care that y o u do not practice y o u r righteousness** [307] **before the people, to attract their attention; otherwise y o u will not have any reward with y o u r Father who is in heaven.** But is not this exhortation in conflict with 5:16, "So let y o u r light shine before men that they may see y o u r good works"? It is not, for the purpose commended in 5:16 was to secure praise for the "Father who is in heaven" (see 5:16b). On the other hand, the purpose of the hypocrites, referred to in 6:1 ff., is to obtain praise for themselves. They perform their religious acts in order "to attract the people's attention," [308] so that the latter will carefully inspect and closely examine them, while they are engaged in almsgiving, prayer, and/or fasting. Hopefully the spectators will then say, "How devout, how remarkably pious are these scribes and Pharisees!"—Naturally, a public display, *so motivated,* must be avoided.

The point in ". . . otherwise y o u will not have any reward with y o u r Father who is in heaven" is, "Y o u will then *already have* y o u r reward, yes, y o u r reward *in full,* namely, from *men,* the very people from whom y o u expected the reward of honor, admiration, and praise. Since in y o u r innermost being y o u never meant to please and glorify *God, he* will not reward y o u. All the more is this true because such religious (?) exercises are fraudulent. If y o u engage in them, y o u are trying to cover up y o u r real motive. Y o u are putting on an act. Y o u are dissimulating, for under the guise of giving glory to God y o u are seeking glory for yourselves, as if y o u could deceive the Omniscient!" In such cases (verses 1, 2, 5, and 16) the one reward, from men, cancels the other, from God. For the expression "y o u r Father who is in heaven" see pp. 287, 326; for "reward," pp. 316, 479.

---

[307] Another reading has ἐλεημοσύνην (A.V. "alms," cf. 6:3, 4). But δικαιοσύνην (righteousness) has the strongest textual support.

[308] Greek θεαθῆναι, aor. inf. passive of θεάομαι, on which see N.T.C. on the Gospel according to John, Vol. I, p. 85, including footnote 33.

The general principle having been enunciated (verse 1), the three expressions of "righteousness" that are here considered—namely, charitable giving, prayer, and fasting—are now taken up one by one.

Charitable Giving

As to this, Jesus begins by saying, 2. **So, whenever you give to the poor do not publicly announce it with a blast of the trumpet, as the hypocrites are in the habit of doing in the synagogues and in the alleyways in order to win the admiration of the people.** Giving to the poor is demanded by the laws of God (Exod. 23:10, 11; 30:15; Lev. 19:10; Deut. 15:7-11), the exhortations of the prophets (Jer. 22:16; Dan. 4:27; Amos 2:6, 7), and the teaching of Jesus (Matt. 7:12; Luke 6:36, 38; cf. 21:1-4; John 13:29; Gal. 6:2). It also pertains to the expression of gratitude for benefits received. In this very sermon Jesus has already pointed out that it is exactly the merciful who "shall have mercy shown to them" (5:7). We are not surprised therefore when here in 6:2 he takes such charitable giving for granted. He assumes that it is being done.

Almsgiving was by no means confined to the disciples of Jesus. Even those Jews who refused to accept Jesus as their Lord and Savior took pride in it. In fact, in Christ's day "relief" for the underprivileged was provided by the "religious" community, each person being taxed according to his ability. [309] This amount was supplemented by voluntary gifts. The latter welfare contributions were announced publicly in the synagogues, and, as here indicated, even in the alleyways, the places where the poor were accustomed to gather, near where they lived. That such doles were literally announced by means of trumpet-blasts cannot now be ascertained. It seems unlikely that in the synagogues this would be allowed. Besides, since in his sayings and discourses Jesus again and again makes use of symbolical language, it is probable that he does this also in the present case, and that he is simply referring to the fact that the Pharisees did everything in their power to advertise their gifts. It is this practice that the Lord condemns. No wonder, for it was hypocrisy, and the men who were guilty of it were therefore rightly called "hypocrites." They were hypocrites (cf. 15:1, 7; 23:1 ff.) because while they *pretended to give,* they really *intended to receive,* namely, honor from men.

Continued: **I solemnly declare to y o u, they have already received their reward in full.** No future reward awaits them. See on 6:1. In all kinds of ways, sometimes bold, at other times subtle, people are still advertising their deeds of benevolence and in the process of doing so are depriving themselves of any real reward.

Not only is it wrong, however, to seek praise from others, it is also wrong

---

[309] S.BK. Vol. I, p. 388.

to praise oneself: 3. **But when you give to charity, do not let your left hand know what your right hand is doing.** The two hands almost always act in unison. Together they often lift, carry, and catch things. They are together in work and in play. They can therefore be viewed as being thoroughly acquainted with each other. Whatever the one does, the other knows. Symbolically speaking therefore, for the left hand *not* to know what the right hand is doing means total lack of acquaintance, utter ignorance. And since the hands are part of the person, the expression probably refers to the fact that as much as possible a person must keep his voluntary contribution a secret not only to others but even to himself; that is, he should forget about it, instead of saying in his heart, "What a good man, woman, boy, girl, am I!" This explanation receives support from 25:37-39, where the righteous are represented as being totally unaware of their own past benevolent deeds. Continued: 4. **that your deeds of charity may be (performed) in secret; and your Father who sees in secret will reward you.** [310] It is God who keeps the account. Nothing escapes him (Gen. 16:13; Ps. 139; Heb. 4:13; cf. John 21:17). It is he who on the judgment day will grant the reward (Matt. 25:34-36) to the surprised well-doers. And are there not anticipatory rewards even now, such as a good conscience and rejoicing along with the recipients?

As far as grammar is concerned, the correct Greek text can also be rendered, ". . . and your Father, the seeing One, will reward you in secret." Objections to this construction: *a.* After the introduction, which refers to hypocrites who do their best to have men admire their good works, and in which Jesus admonishes his hearers that these works must not be advertised but must be kept as secret as possible, we rather look for a statement to the effect that unadvertised deeds will, nevertheless, be seen and rewarded, namely, by "your Father who sees in secret." The sudden introduction of the Father as "the seeing One," without modifier, would make little sense here. *b.* Scripture everywhere proclaims that all of men's words, actions, etc., including what occurred in secret, will become public (Eccl. 12:14; Matt. 5:3-12; 10:26, 27; Mark 4:22; Luke 8:17; 12:2, 3; Rom. 2:16; I Cor. 3:13; 14:25; Rev. 20:12, 13). The idea that deeds of kindness toward the poor, done in secret, will remain secret forever, even the reward being bestowed in secret, clashes with this prevailing teaching.

Prayer in General

Turning, then, to this subject (verses 4-15) Jesus says, 5. **Also, whenever y o u pray, do not be like the hypocrites, for they love to say their prayers standing up in the synagogues and at the street corners, that they may be**

---

[310] The modifer "openly" (A.V.) is based upon an inferior Greek text. So also in verse 6.

seen by the people. The reference here is to prayer in general, including thanksgiving, praise, adoration, confession of sin, personal petition, intercession for the needs of others, etc. Among the Jews, though prayers were always appropriate, there were set times for prayer, when the pious were expected to attend to their devotions. Thus, there were morning, afternoon, and evening prayers (Ps. 55:17; Dan. 6:10; Acts 3:1). According to Josephus (*Antiquities* XIV.65) sacrifices, including prayers, were offered in the temple "twice a day, in the early morning and at the ninth hour." There was also a sunset service. [311] Naturally, if one were living or staying in or near Jerusalem and could get to the temple in time, that would seem to the devout Israelite to be the best place to pray (Luke 18:9, 10; Acts 3:1). Otherwise, the synagogue would do, or even the street.

Now Scripture nowhere condemns public prayer (II Chron. 6:14-42; Neh. 9; Acts 4:24-31), nor individual prayer offered in a public place. Neither the Pharisee nor the publican sinned by praying in the temple (Luke 18:9, 10). What the Lord condemns here is *ostentatious praying,* that is, having one's private (?) devotions in the most public place, with the intention of being seen and honored by the people. That was, however, exactly what the hypocrites were in the habit of doing. When the Pharisee of Christ's famous parable (Luke 18:9-14) entered the temple, he took care *not* to be standing in some corner or at a considerable distance from the front, like the publican. He stood up in front, in full view of everyone who might be present. What happened in the temple took place also in the synagogue. And even at the street corners! Note: here not alleys or alleyways as in 6:2, but the corners of the busiest streets. Did the hypocrites just happen to reach the most conspicuous place at exactly the right moment? However that may be, their motive and purpose was "to be seen by the people" and to be admired by them. It is this that Jesus condemns.—From this it appears clearly that in the teaching of Jesus it is the inner disposition that counts. It is the heart truly and humbly devoted to God upon which the divine approval rests (John 4:24).

As to the hypocrites and their vain display, Jesus repeats the words spoken just a moment ago (see on verse 2): **I solemnly declare to y o u, they have already received their reward in full.**

The negative condemnation of the wrong practice is followed by the positive exhortation to follow the right practice, just as in verses 2 and 3 in connection with giving to charity, and in verses 16-18 in connection with fasting. From start to finish the sermon is arranged in a very orderly, systematic, and logical manner. 6. **But whenever you pray, enter into your most private room, and having shut the door, pray to your Father who is in**

---

[311] E. Schürer, *History of the Jewish People in the Time of Jesus Christ,* English translation Edinburgh, 1892-1901, Vol. II, pp. 290 f.

secret. The idea is not that there must be a separate prayer room. As was pointed out earlier, the houses of many in the audience had only one room. The sense is this: if there be a private room [312] then use that for your private prayer; otherwise choose the most hidden corner. Do not try to make yourself conspicuous. The main emphasis, however, is not even on *the place* of prayer but on *the attitude of mind and heart.* Not the secrecy is the real underlying thought but the sincerity. The reason for mentioning the secret place is that the sincere and humble worshiper, one who is not interested in making a public display for the sake of enhancing his prestige, will find the secluded nook or den to be most appropriate for his devotions. It is there that he can shut out the world and be alone with his God.

The shutting of the door (cf. II Kings 4:33; Isa. 26:20) makes the secret place even more secret. As to the Object of the prayer, namely, the Father, he not only *sees* in secret (verse 4), but also *is* in secret: he fills every secret (as well as public) place with his presence, yet transcends all spatial limitations (I Kings 8:27; Ps. 139:7-10; Isa. 66:1; Jer. 23:23, 24; Acts 7:48, 49; 17:27, 28).

Here again it is necessary to add that the purpose of entering the secret place and shutting the door can be defeated if one begins to advertise this practice, as some ministers are in the habit of doing, when at the beginning of the worship service—sometimes even in the pastoral prayer—they assure the congregation that before they sat down to prepare the sermon they had locked the door of their study and spent so many minutes in earnest prayer!

The one who prays with the proper disposition of heart and mind is blessed, as in verse 4: **and your Father who sees in secret will reward you.** The man who so prays will have peace of heart and mind. He will know that the Father, in his infinite love, will give the supplicant whatever is best both for himself and for all concerned. He will also know that this same Father "is able to do infinitely more than all we ask or imagine" (see N.T.C. on Eph. 3:20, 21).

A sincere prayer does not have to be wordy: 7. **Moreover, in praying, do not babble on and on like pagans, for they imagine that they will be heard because of their flow of words.** Is it possible that, in saying this, Jesus was also thinking of the scribes, who "for a pretense make long prayers" (Mark 12:40; Luke 20:47)? However that may be, the Lord condemns this practice as being pagan in character. Not as if a lengthy prayer is always wrong. Such a position would immediately condemn the prayers found in II Chron. 6:14-42; Neh. 9; and Ps. 18, 89, and 119. The *motive* must be kept in mind. Pagans pray on and on because they imagine that the longer and the louder

---

312 Greek ταμεῖον, probably related to the verb τέμνω: to cut, to distribute. Related nouns are: distributor, treasurer, treasury room, storeroom. Such rooms where precious objects were kept would naturally be found in the most secluded places. So, in course of time the noun ταμεῖον began to be used to indicate any very private room or place.

they pray, the greater also will be their chance of success in receiving what they desire. The prayer of the priests of Baal (I Kings 18:25-29) offers a striking example: "They called on the name of Baal from morning even until noon." Another example is the prayer-wheel of the Tibetan Buddhists, a cylinder revolving on an axis, and inscribed with written prayers. Is not the rosary, used for example to keep count of five decades of Ave Marias, each preceded by a paternoster and concluded with a Glory Be, another illustration? As if the acceptability of our prayers depends, at least in part, upon the number of words we use or the number of prayers we rattle off!

Many of the most striking and fervent prayers recorded in Scripture are brief and pithy; such as that of: Moses (Exod. 32:31, 32), Solomon (for an understanding heart, I Kings 3:6-9), Elijah (I Kings 18:36, 37), Hezekiah (II Kings 19:14-19), Jabez (I Chron. 4:10), Agur (Prov. 30:7-9), the publican (Luke 18:13), the dying thief (Luke 23:42), Stephen (Acts 7:60), and Paul (for the Ephesians, Eph. 3:14-19). To this class belong also the many sentence prayers or ejaculations of Nehemiah (Neh. 4:4, 5; 5:19; 6:9; 13:14, 29, 31). Christ's highpriestly or intercessory prayer, too, can hardly be called lengthy (John 17), and the Lord's Prayer, which he taught his disciples to pray, is certainly marked by brevity (Matt. 6:9-13; Luke 11:2-4). Continued: **8. Do not be like them therefore, for y o u r Father knows what y o u need before y o u (even) ask him.** What Jesus means is, "Y o u must not approach y o u r Father with the idea that he is uninformed, totally unaware of y o u r needs, so that y o u have to explain to him in every detail just what y o u r (or: your) situation happens to be. On the contrary, before y o u even begin to pray, y o u r Father already knows y o u r need."

Some might object, "Then, why pray at all?" The objector, however, misses the point. Jesus was not condemning the outpouring of the heart to God, not even when of necessity such an outpouring contains a brief statement of certain facts already known to the Lord (see, for example, many of the Psalms). In fact, it is just because an earthly father or mother understands a child so thoroughly and knows its needs better than any stranger does, that the child will go with his needs to him and/or to her, which is exactly what loving parents want him to do. So, *far more* so, it is also with the heavenly Father (Ps. 81:10; Matt. 7:7, 8; John 15:7; Heb. 4:14-16; James 4:2). What Christ condemns is the spirit of fear and distrust, which causes pagans, who recognize no heavenly *Father,* to babble on and on, in the belief that otherwise their gods will not be thoroughly informed nor sufficiently placated to grant the requests.

The Model ("Lord's") Prayer

Jesus introduces this prayer as follows: **9a. This, then, is how y o u should pray.** Before entering into the contents of this prayer a few introductory remarks may be in order:

a. *Christ's Reason for Teaching His Disciples This Prayer*

Literally, according to the original, the sentence reads: "Thus (or: in this manner), therefore, y o u should pray." Some stress the fact that the second person plural imperative verb is in the present tense. They interpret this present as having continuative force (y o u should keep on praying), and on this they base their conclusion that Jesus wants his very prayer to be prayed again and again and again. Now it certainly is not wrong to make frequent use of this prayer if the worshiper, when he does this, is able to do it with heart and mind. On the other hand, *very* frequent use may easily lead to the sin of formalism which the Lord has been condemning. Besides, it must be borne in mind that Jesus said, "Thus" or "In this manner" or "This is *how*." He did not say, "Use exactly these words, and no other." The so-called "Lord's Prayer" is really *the model prayer;* meaning: it should serve as a pattern for our devotions. Its characteristics should mark also our prayers. Some of these qualities will now be mentioned:

b. *Its Brevity*

The prayer consists of two parts: an invocation ("Our Father who art in heaven") and six petitions; or, if the conclusion ("For thine is the kingdom, etc.") be considered as belonging to it, then three parts, approximately seventy words in all.

c. *The Priority to Which It Points*

In harmony with the fact that, according to both Old and New Testament, the glory of God is important above everything else, the first three petitions have reference to *the Father's* name, kingdom, and will. *Human* needs—bread, pardon for sin, and victory over the evil one—take second place.

d. *Its Breadth or Scope*

There are six petitions, [313] as follows,

Petitions with reference to

God's			
	name	first petition	verse 9b
	reign	second	...10a
	will	third	...10b
Our			
	bread	fourth	11
	debts	fifth	12
	foe	sixth	13

The comprehensive or universe-embracing nature of these petitions appears from the fact that they bear reference not only to God's glory, etc.

---

[313] Not seven. "And lead us not into temptation but deliver us from the evil one" should be viewed as *one* petition. As I see it, the idea that the first three petitions symbolize the Holy Trinity, the last "four" the universe with its four dimensions, is rather fanciful.

(first three petitions), but also to our needs (last three); not only to our physical needs (fourth petition), but also to our spiritual (fifth and sixth); not only to our present need (fourth petition), but also to our need with reference to the past (fifth), and even to our future need (sixth). Finally, in this prayer the worshiper carries to the throne of grace the burdens that are not only his own but also his brothers' ("our," "us"). All of this is included in the six brief requests. This is indeed the perfect pattern for our prayers!

The Invocation or Words of Address

9b. Our Father who art in heaven. It is immediately clear that not everyone is privileged to address God thus. That is the exclusive prerogative of those who are "in Christ" (John 1:12; Rom. 8:14-17; Gal. 4:6; II Cor. 6:18; I John 3:1, 2). To be sure, there is a sense in which God can be correctly referred to as the Father of all men. He has created all, and provides sustenance for all (Mal. 2:10; Ps. 36:6). But that is not the usual sense in which in Scripture the term "Father" can be interpreted. In "the Sermon on the Mount," too, the term is used in a definitely soteriological or redemptive sense, a sense in which God is the Father *not* of all (though he is kind to all, 5:45; Luke 6:35, 36) but of some. He is called "y o u r (also: your) Father" (5:16; 6:18, etc.), the Father of the peacemakers (5:9) and of those who love even their enemies (5:44, 45). Similarly, according to Christ's teaching recorded elsewhere, those who reject him are children *not* of God but of the devil (John 8:44; I John 3:10).

Once this is understood it becomes clear that this model prayer is for believers in the Lord Jesus Christ, for them alone. It also follows that the objection of those who say that "the Lord's Prayer" is not a Christian prayer because it does not even mention the name of Jesus, and/or because it does not end with the phrase, "for Jesus' sake," is groundless. The name and the atoning work of the Lord are clearly implied in the very words of the invocation. Apart from Christ no one can come to the Father (John 14:6).

As to the words of address themselves, first of all see what has been said earlier (pp. 286, 287). The striking fact, of which we should never lose sight, is that he who is King of the kingdom of heaven is at the same time the Father of its citizens. The citizens are the children. The kingdom is the Father's Family. See N.T.C. on Eph. 3:14, 15. Note also the combination of immanence and transcendence, of condescension and majesty. "Our Father" indicates his nearness. He is near to all his children, infinitely near. Therefore with confidence they approach the Father's throne, to make all their wants and wishes known to him, that is, all those that are in harmony with his revealed will. They need not be afraid, for God is their Father who loves them. Yet, he is the Father *in heaven* (literally "in the heavens"). Therefore, he should be approached in the spirit of devout and humble reverence. The chumminess or easy familiarity that marks a certain type of present day "religion" is definitely antiscriptural. Those who indulge in this bad habit seem never to have read Exod. 3:5; Isa. 6:1-5; or Acts 4:24!

Also, whereas the words "Our Father" indicate God's willingness and eagerness to lend his ear to the praises and petitions of his children, the addition "who art in heaven" shows his power and sovereign right to answer their requests, disposing of them according to his infinite wisdom. Finally, reflect again on those words, "Our Father . . . *in heaven.*" They make the Father's children feel that they are pilgrims here below, and that their real home is not here but in heaven. It is comforting to know that not only do the children wish to be where the Father is, but the Father also desires that his children be where he is (Ps. 73:23, 24; Jer. 31:3; cf. John 17:24). Does the child sing Ps. 42:1? With slight change of wording ("O my child" for "O God") Ps. 42:1 can be (shall we say "is being"?) sung also by God himself.— The idea of a God who sings, rejoicing in his children's salvation, has scriptural support (Zeph. 3:17).—Then in glory these children will forever address God as their Father, but nevermore will they have to add "who art in heaven," for they will be with him.

The First Petition

9c. **Hallowed be thy name.** In ancient times the name was not generally regarded as a mere appellation to distinguish one person from another, but often rather as an expression of the very nature of the person so indicated, or of his position, etc. This was true to such an extent that frequently when in some important respect the facts concerning a man had undergone a change, he was given a new name. See pp. 132, 138. The name was to some extent identified with the person. This is especially true with respect to the names of God. God's name is *God himself as revealed in all his works.* This is not so difficult to understand, for also among us the same holds with respect to the name *Jesus,* as is clear from the poetic line, "That beautiful Name, that beautiful Name from sin has power to free us!" (from the hymn "That Beautiful Name," by Jean Perry). We immediately recognize the fact that a mere vocal cannot free or save anybody, but a person can—and does!

Now since God's names reveal who he himself is, it is necessary for us to know them. This, moreover, is very rewarding. In the Old Testament the Supreme Being is called *'El,* that is, God, viewed as the Mighty One. This name occurs in various combinations. *'El-Shaddai* is God Almighty, the source of salvation for his people (Gen. 17:1; Exod. 6:3). *'Elohim* (Gen. 1:1) is a plural, and refers to God in the fulness of his power. *'Elyon* indicates the Most High (Num. 24:16). *'Adonai* points to God as Master (properly "my Master") or Lord; cf. "O Lord, I am not a man of words" (Exod. 4:10). The meaning of the name *Jehovah* is to some extent explained in Exod. 3:13, 14; cf. 6:2, 3. It is a form of the verb *to be,* and has been interpreted to mean "I am that I am," or "I shall be what I shall be." In the original

327

Hebrew this name consists of the four letters YHWH, and is therefore called the *tetragram(maton)*. There came a time, perhaps about 300 B.C., when the Jews, owing to *a.* their reverence for God, *b.* their interpretation of Lev. 24:16, and *c.* their resulting fear of becoming guilty of the sin of desecration, ceased to pronounce this name. In reading Scripture they substituted for it 'Adonai or, less frequently, 'Elohim. The Masoretes, those Jewish textual experts who flourished between the destruction of Jerusalem (A.D. 70) and the tenth century, but whose activity in a more general sense antedated the period of the Maccabees and extended to the year A.D. 1425, attached to the four consonants (YHWH) the vowels of 'Adonai (or of 'Elohim).[314] It is sufficiently clear from such passages as Exod. 6:2-4; 15:1-3; Ps. 83:18; Isa. 42:8; Hos. 12:5; and Mal. 3:6 that the name Jehovah, however it be vocalized or transliterated, emphasizes God's unchangeable covenant faithfulness toward his people.

Various combinations occur in connection with this name. Probably most familiar are the designations "Jehovah of hosts" (Ps. 46:7, 11), and "Jehovah our righteousness" (Jer. 23:6). Other combinations are "Jehovah will provide" (Gen. 22:14), "Jehovah (is) my banner" (Exod. 17:15), "Jehovah heals you" (Exod. 15:26), "Jehovah (is) peace" (Judg. 6:24), and "Jehovah (is) my shepherd" (Ps. 23:1).

To hallow God's name means to hold it in reverence; hence, to hold *him* in reverence, to honor, glorify, and exalt him. To do this, far more than a merely intellectual knowledge of the meaning of the divine names is required. Humility of spirit, gratitude of heart, earnest study of God's works until observation changes into rapturous astonishment and worship is certainly implied. The composers of the Psalms knew what this meant. Everywhere—in the work of creation and in the events of history—they observed and took time to meditate upon God's majesty. They viewed their God as the One who delivered them from their enemies and constantly protected them. As such he was a God filled with wrath aimed at those who rejected him and who persecuted his people. This very wrath was, as it were, the proof of his tender love for his own (Ps. 3; 4; 5; 7; 11; 13; 14; 18; 48; 50; 63; 97; 135; etc.). As to the latter (the tender love), the Psalms are filled to overflowing with the idea that for those who trust in him the Lord is the hearer of prayer, the refuge in the time of storm, the one who daily cares,

---

[314] Originally only consonants were used in writing Hebrew words. When the knowledge of Hebrew decreased, the absence of vowels began to hamper the understanding of the text, since the mental insertion of the wrong vowel would result in misinterpretation. For this reason there were several early attempts at vowel-insertion or vocalization. The one that finally triumphed was that of the Jews who belonged to the Masoretic school in Tiberias. The standard text of the Old Testament was prepared in the first half of the tenth century A.D., by Aaron ben Moses ben Asher. The well-known R. Kittel edition of *Biblia Hebraica* was checked against the Leningrad copy of this Asher text.

who blots out transgression, and never forsakes his children, not even at the moment of death (Ps. 16; 17; 23; 42; 73; 81; 89; 91; 92; 103; 111; 116; 118; 146; to mention but a few).

"Hallowed be thy name" means, therefore, that the one who has been brought into fellowship with this tenderly loving Father now calls upon everyone to share this experience with him, and to exalt this glorious God. This means far more than that the petitioner does his utmost to fight profanity. It has a positive content. The supplicant calls upon the entire creation and especially upon the world of men to praise his God. He exclaims, as it were, "O magnify Jehovah *with me*, and let us exalt his name *together*" (Ps. 34:3). He traces God's steps in history (Pss. 76–80, especially 78; further 106; 107; 118; 124; 126; 136), and wants his children and everyone to adore and glorify God because of his wondrous deeds. He also is filled with gratitude and amazement when he observes God's wisdom and goodness in nature, and he desires that his own thrilling observations and lasting impressions shall be shared by others, so that they too may see the reflection of God's glorious attributes in the sky above as well as in the earth below, and may exult in the One whom he calls "my God" (Ps. 8; 19; 29; 63; 65; 104; 139; 145; 147; 150).

So also today the person who knows what it means to pray "Hallowed be thy name" will joyfully magnify the Lord when he beholds the blue of the starlit sky, full of silent beauty and majesty, with its myriads of stars, scintillating like so many dewdrops upon the meadows of the heavens. He praises God when he sees his glory reflected in the softly blending hues of the rainbow, in wooded hills, fruited groves, murmuring brooks, sparkling lakes, and meandering rivers, as well as when he listens to the richly variegated, almost continuous song of the mockingbird. He marvels when he contemplates the wisdom of God revealed in the construction of the human body (Ps. 139:15, 16). And when from general revelation he ascends to special revelation, and ponders the implications of such passages as Isa. 53; John 3:16; Rom. 5:8-11; 8:31-39; and I Cor. 8:9, is it any wonder that he falls in love with the matchless name of him who through Christ is his Father, that he pours out his heart in fervent doxologies (II Cor. 9:15; Eph. 1:3 ff.; I Peter 1:3 ff.; Rev. 19:16, 17), and urges others to do likewise?

Style and grammar help us to enter into the spirit of this prayer. Not only is the contrast between the three imperative passives, all in the *third* person, of the first three petitions (literally, "Let be sanctified thy name, let come thy kingdom, let be done thy will") in striking and pleasing contrast with the *second* person verbs of the last three requests, but also these three crisp, opening third person imperatives, being aorists and in each case heading the petition, stress *urgency*. With respect to the first petition this means that the worshiper is so completely filled with unrestrained eagerness that the Father's name be adored, honored, and glorified, that he cannot wait to communicate his consuming desire that it receive this honor from the lips, hearts, and lives of everyone.

The Father's name will not be hallowed throughout the world unless his royal rule be acknowledged. This leads to

The Second Petition

10a. Thy kingdom come. For the meaning of the concept "kingdom of heaven" or "of God" see pp. 249, 250. The second petition implies the following:

1. It is only when the heavenly Father, on the basis of the Son's atonement, and through the operation of the Holy Spirit, rules in men's hearts that true and lasting betterment in individual, family, social, national, and international conditions can be expected (Ps. 20:7; Zech. 4:6).

2. This is a *prayer*. In the history of missions it has been demonstrated again and again that the coming of the entrance of the reign of God into human hearts requires earnest prayer (Matt. 7:7; Mark 9:29; Acts 4:31; 13:3).

3. Until the moment of the second coming there is need for this prayer; for, though the kingdom is here already (Luke 17:21), it is still absent from many hearts. In fact, there is every reason to doubt that progress in evangelization is keeping pace with progress in iniquity.

4. The transforming grace and power of God is required before a man changes from the ardent yearning, "*My* kingdom come," and from the boast, "By my own effort I am already on the way to the realization of this goal," to the humble petition, "*Thy* kingdom come." As to the boasters and their fall, think of Korah and his company (Num. 16), Sennacherib (Isa. 37:10-13, 37, 38), Nebuchadnezzar (Dan. 4:30-33), Edom (Obad. 1-4), Haman (Esther 3-7; especially 5:11, 12), Herod Agrippa I (Acts 12:21-23), and "the rich fool" of the parable (Luke 12:18-20).

5. Prayer for the establishment of the kingship of Christ in human hearts does not exclude the necessity of work. There must be preaching, visits to the homes, Bible translation and distribution, follow-up work, etc. Cf. Acts 20:17-38; I Thess. 2:9-12.

6. "Thy kingdom come" is clearly a prayer for the progress of missionary activity (Rev. 6:2);

> Jesus shall reign where'er the sun
> Does his successsive journeys run;
> His kingdom stretch from shore to shore
> Till moons shall wax and wane no more.
>
> (Isaac Watts)

7. The desire of the supplicant is, however, not only that the kingdom may come extensively but also that it may more and more be established

intensively, that is, that he himself and all those already converted may increasingly acknowledge God in Christ as their sovereign Ruler:

Fill thou my life O Lord my God
In every part with praise,
That my whole being may proclaim
Thy being and thy ways.
Not for the lip of praise alone,
Nor e'en the praising heart
I ask, but for a life made up
Of praise in every part.

(Horatius Bonar)

Just as the first petition already implied the second, so the second implies the third, for God's kingdom will not come unless his will be done. So we proceed to

The Third Petition

10b. Thy will be done, as in heaven so on earth. The will of God to which reference is made is clearly his "revealed" will, expressed in his law. It is that will which is done in heaven, but not yet to any great extent on earth. On the other hand, the will of God's "decree" or "plan from eternity" is always being realized both in heaven and on earth (Dan. 4:35; Eph. 1:11), and cannot be the subject of prayer. (Incidentally, the statement that God's revealed will is being perfectly obeyed in heaven—hence not only by heaven's angels but also by the hosts of the redeemed—implies that the very moment a soul is translated from this sinful earth to heaven it has been freed from every vestige of sin.) It is the ardent desire of the person who sincerely breathes the Lord's Prayer that the Father's will shall be obeyed as *completely, heartily,* and *immediately* on earth as this is constantly being done by all the inhabitants of heaven.

As to "completely," the story of King Saul shows that incomplete obedience, in which man sets his own will over against the divine, does not receive God's approval and may have serious consequences (I Sam. 15:1-3, 7-9, and note especially verses 22 and 23). As to "heartily," note the words of Deut. 26:16 and Matt. 22:37. And as to "immediately," the cherubim in Ezekiel's vision of the throne-chariot, each cherub being equipped with four faces, and the chariot itself with wheels within wheels, so that its "drivers" were always ready to take it wherever the Lord wanted it to go, furnish a vivid illustration of the kind of obedience in which heaven delights (Ezek. 1; 10). Examples of human obedience: Noah (Gen. 6:22), Abraham (Gen. 11:28-32, cf. Acts 7:3; Gen. 12:1, cf. Heb. 11:8; Gen. 22:2 ff., cf. James 2:23); Joshua (Josh. 5:13-15); Samuel (I Sam. 3:1-10); Simon (Peter) and Andrew (Matt. 4:19, 20); Simon (Peter) once more (Luke 5:5); James and John (Matt. 4:21, 22); Peter and the apostles (Acts 5:29); Mary of Bethany

(John 11:28, 29); Paul (Acts 16:6-10; 26:19); and the Philippians (Phil. 2:12). The greatest example of all is Jesus Christ himself (Luke 2:51, 52; John 15:10; 17:4; Phil. 2:5-8; and Heb. 5:8). It was he who in the garden said, "Not as I will, but as thou wilt" (Matt. 26:39). As to the manner in which obedience is rewarded, from a host of passages that could be listed the following few should suffice: Josh. 1:8; Matt. 7:7, 8; John 7:17; 8:29; 14:21, 23; 15:10; Phil. 2:9, 10; Heb. 12:1, 2; and Rev. 3:20.

The petitions for the fulfilment of human needs follow. Although it is true that between the first three petitions, pertaining to God, and the last three, pertaining to man, there is a rather sharp division, the two are not to be regarded as wholly separate. If the believer is to take an active part in the hallowing of God's name, the coming of his kingdom, and the doing of his will—such an active part being certainly implied in the first three petitions— he must have bread (Luke 10:7, cf. I Tim. 5:18; Gal. 6:6; Eph. 4:28; Phil. 4:15, 16). Jesus, accordingly, is not forgetful of the physical needs of his disciples (see Matt. 6:25-34; 25:34-40; Mark 10:29, 30; cf. Acts 24:17; II Cor. 8:8 f.; James 2:15, 16), both in order that they may live and be happy, and that they may be able vigorously to support kingdom causes. This introduces

The Fourth Petition

11. **Give us this day our daily bread.** What did Jesus mean by "daily"? In Greek literature the word which it translates is very rare; in fact, so rare that it used to be thought that it was coined by the evangelists. In Scripture it occurs only in the Lord's Prayer (here and in Luke 11:3). Although it has now become clear that the word did not originate with the Gospel writers, there is no unanimity in explaining it. All kinds of guesses have been ventured, among them being "continuous," "supersubstantial," "ready at hand," "for future use," "for sustenance," etc. The explanation "sufficient for the next day" has been strongly defended.[315] As I see it, a good argument can be made in favor of: *a.* "Give us this day our bread for (or: belonging to) the current day (the day in being),"[316] and of *b.* "Give us this day our needful bread," that is, "our bread necessary for existence."[317] The two ideas (*a.* and *b.*) combine easily. In any case we must make sure that our interpretation does not run counter to the teaching of Jesus in this very chapter (verses 31-34), the warning against worry about food. See especially

---

[315] It is favored by J. H. Thayer, L.N.T., entry ἐπιούσιος. His argument to the effect that this view is not contradicted by Matt. 6:34 impresses me as being rather ingenious, not entirely convincing. For different reasons A. T. Robertson, *Word Pictures*, Vol. I, p. 53, also defends this explanation.

[316] This would amount to a substantivizing of ἐπὶ τὴν οὖσαν (ἡμέραν). See the entry ἐπιούσιος in L.N.T.(A. and G.). That entry also furnishes an abundant bibliography on this subject.

[317] On the theory that ἐπιούσιος is derived from ἐπί and οὐσία.

verse 34. Personally I see no reason, therefore, to depart from the translation to which many people have become accustomed, namely, "daily." The meaning then would be, "Give us today the portion that is needed for any one day." [318]

What has been said so far indicates that by means of this petition Jesus teaches his disciples to be moderate in their desires and requests. This is brought out even more strikingly in the original, where the words "our daily bread" occur at the very head of the petition; hence, "Our daily bread give us this day." Christ's disciples must ask for bread, not for luxuries. "Neither poverty nor riches give thou me. Feed me with the bread that is appointed to me, lest, being full, I deny thee and say, 'Who is Jehovah?' Or, lest, being poor, I steal and profane the name of my God" (Prov. 30:8, 9, taken from the prayer of Agur). It is clear, of course, that the term "bread" should not be taken too literally. Whatever is necessary to sustain physical life is meant.

Not only a. *moderation* is here taught, also b. *trust* in the heavenly Father, who loves and cares, the childlike confidence expressed so beautifully in Ps. 37:25. Yet, it is not "making provision for the future" (Gen. 41:33-36; Prov. 6:6-8) that is here condemned, but "anxiety about the future," as if there were no heavenly Father. And well may the conviction of c. *total dependence* fill the heart, for all men, including even the richest, in order to have, consume, and enjoy food, are dependent upon the condition of soil, water, weather, and health of body. Moreover, in order to eat, men of slender and those of average means need to work, that they may earn their bread. Therefore, all men are dependent upon the general state of the economy, together with all its contributing factors, ecological, social, political, etc., which in the final analysis means that all are dependent upon the sovereign God, who is in control of the universe. Then, too, d. *humility* is required; hence, "*Give* us. . . ." Although the supplicant is making a living in the sweat of his brow and besides has even paid for his groceries, he must still accept what is on the table as a gift from God, a product of grace; for, not only is God the ultimate source of every blessing (James 1:17) but also, by reason of sin man has forfeited all! e. *Willingness to work* is also presupposed. Else how would one dare to pray for daily sustenance (cf. II Thess. 3:10)? To all this add one more quality, namely, f. *generosity;* hence, not "Give *me*," but "Give *us* . . . *our* daily bread." The needs of believers all over the world are included, for together they constitute one family (Eph. 3:14). And, in the spirit of Gal. 6:10, are not the supplicant's horizons extended even beyond "the camp of the saints, the beloved city"? [319]

---

318 So also H. N. Ridderbos, *op. cit.,* pp. 124, 134, and 135, retains, "*Geef ons heden ons dagelijks brood.*"
319 The believer's duty as a Christian citizen is also very important in this connection. Hungry nations should be given assistance. Yet, this must be done wisely. In this connection much can be learned from W. and P. Paddock, *Hungry Nations,* Boston and

Man has been endowed by the Creator with body and soul (Gen. 2:7). So, from a petition for the fulfilment of the needs of the body the prayer now advances to a request for the satisfaction of the soul's requirements, that what is spiritual may be both first (see the first three petitions) and last (see the last two, or the last two plus the doxology).

The Fifth Petition

12. **And forgive us our debts as we also have forgiven our debtors.** In connection with this petition, which sounds so simple, a few questions are in order:

1. What is the difference between "debts" (verse 12) and "trespasses" (verses 14, 15)?

Answer: see on verse 14.

2. Why should we pray for forgiveness, since we no longer sin?

Answer: We do, indeed, sin daily. See p. 317.

3. Granted that we sin, why must we still daily pray for forgiveness, since through Christ's atonement we are already cleansed (justified) from every sin?

Answer: It is true that the basis of our daily forgiveness has been established once for all by means of Christ's atonement. Nothing need be and nothing can be added to that. But this total, objective cleansing needs daily application for the simple reason that we sin every day. A father may have bequeathed a large inheritance to his son. It now very definitely belongs to the son. Nevertheless, this does not mean that the latter is immediately allowed to withdraw the entire huge amount from the bank and spend it all within one week. Very wisely the father included a stipulation limiting the withdrawal privilege to a certain generous amount each month. So also when a person receives the grace of regeneration, this does not mean that all of that which Christ merited for him is immediately experienced by him. If it were, would it not overwhelm and crush his capacities? Rather, "He [God] giveth and giveth and giveth again." See also John 13:10.

The prayer for *forgiveness* implies that the supplicant recognizes that there is no other method by which his debt can be wiped out. It is, therefore, a plea for grace.

However, a totally different difficulty arises in connection with "Forgive us our debts *as we also have forgiven our debtors.*" This certainly cannot mean that our forgiving disposition earns God's pardon. The forgiveness of

---

Toronto, 1964. These authors, experienced in this field, point out that so-called "help" is often wasted, because those charged with helping the hungry nations forget that the latter must be shown how to carry forward their own development based on their own resources.

our debts is based not on our merits—how could we have any?—but on Christ's, applied to us. Consequently, from our point of view, forgiveness is based on God's unmerited (not merited by *us*) favor, that is, on divine grace (Eph. 1:7), compassion (Matt. 18:27), and mercy (Luke 18:13). Nevertheless, our own forgiving disposition is very important. In fact, without it we ourselves cannot be forgiven. For us it is the indispensable condition of receiving the forgiveness of sins. That fact is stated clearly in verses 14 and 15, which, together with 18:21-35, is the best and simplest explanation of 6:12 one could ask for. It is with this as it is with salvation in general. We are not saved on the basis of our faith, as if faith had earning power. We are saved by grace (Eph. 2:8). Yet faith must be present if we are to be saved (hence, "by grace through faith"). Faith and one of its manifestations, namely, the disposition to forgive, are conditions that must be met and exercised if salvation and its component, pardon, are to be received. *We* must believe, *we* must forgive. God does not do these things for us. Nevertheless, it is *God* who plants in our hearts the seed of faith and of the forgiving disposition. Moreover, the power to believe and the power to forgive are from God. At every step—beginning, middle, and end, all along the way— God is both present and active. "With fear and trembling continue to work out y o u r own salvation; for it is God who is working in y ou both to will and to work for his good pleasure" (Phil. 2:12, 13). See also N.T.C. on Eph. 2:8 and on Phil. 2:12, 13. It is exactly as Greijdanus observes, in commenting on the parallel passage, Luke 11:4 ("And forgive us our sins, *for* we ourselves also forgive every one indebted to us"). He writes, "In spite of *for*, this clause does not indicate the ground upon which God bestows forgiveness, but that which must be complied with for us to enjoy God's forgiveness of our own sins." [320]

To be genuine, this forgiveness that we ourselves bestow upon our fellow men must be given gladly, generously, and with finality; not in the spirit of, "I'll forgive, but I'm telling you that I'll never forget." Lord's Day 51 of the Heidelberg Catechism gives a correct, succinct, and beautiful explanation of the fifth petition: "Be pleased, for the sake of Christ's blood, not to impute to us, miserable sinners, any of our transgressions, nor the evil which always cleaves to us; as we also find this witness of thy grace in us that it is our full purpose heartily to forgive our neighbor."

A possible objection to the explanation given must be briefly answered: "Does not this mean, then, that our act of kindness toward the one who has injured us precedes Christ's act of kindness toward us?"

Answer. In the circle of salvation the beginning is always with God, never with us. See I John 4:19; cf. John 13:15; Eph. 4:32; and I Peter 2:21.

---

[320] *Het Heilige Evangelie naar de Beschrijving van Lucas* (*Kommentaar op het Nieuwe Testament*, Vol. I), p. 523.

Nevertheless, the forgiving love of Christ not only precedes but also accompanies and even follows the love with which we love him and the neighbor. Our sincere purpose to forgive those who have injured us, and thus also our experience of the pardoning love and grace of God in Christ, can be enhanced by the following considerations:

Extend forgiveness to others, for

1. God so commands. Vengeance belongs to him, not to us (Deut. 32:35; Rom. 12:19).

2. We should follow the example Christ himself has given us (Luke 23:34; John 13:12-15; Eph. 4:32; 5:1, 2; Col. 3:13).

3. We cannot be forgiven unless we forgive, as has been shown.

4. The man who injured us needs our sympathy and love. We owe him this love (Rom. 13:8).

5. Harboring a grudge and planning revenge is not only wicked but also foolish, for it deprives us of the strength we need to do effective work. We should have the forward look (Phil. 2:13).

6. Forgiving others will impart peace of heart and mind to us, the peace that passes all understanding (Phil. 4:7, 9).

7. Thus, thus alone, will God be glorified, which should be our aim in all we do (I Cor. 10:31).

The fourth petition is linked to the fifth, and the fifth to the sixth, by the conjunction *and.* All three represent human needs, and are closely connected. The connection between the fourth and fifth has already been indicated. Very close is also the relation between the fifth and the sixth, and this in at least the following respect: we are in need not only of forgiveness of past sins, but also of God's protecting care so that in the future we may not fall into the clutches of Satan.

Between "And lead us not into temptation" and "deliver us from the evil one" there is no conjunction *and.* On the contrary, the conjunction *but* shows that the petition simply continues, the negative request being balanced by the positive in one petition. These two are, as it were, the two sides of the same coin. Accordingly, I am in agreement with all those who accept six, not seven, [321] petitions.

The Sixth Petition

13. or 13a. [322] And lead us not into temptation but deliver us from the evil one. Probable meaning: "If it be thy will do not permit us, weak as we are by nature and prone to sin, to enter into situations which in the natural

---

[321] Hence, on this point I do not agree with Lenski (*op. cit.*, p. 263), but with Calvin. See his commentary on this verse.

[322] 13a if the conclusion ("For thine is the Kingdom. . . .") is regarded as authentic, as in A.V.

course of events would expose us to temptation and fall (cf. 26:41), but, whatever be thy way with us, deliver us from the evil one." Though it is true that here as before (5:37) both the neuter "from evil" and the masculine "from the evil one" are possible, and, as Calvin points out, "There is no necessity of raising a debate on this point, for the meaning remains nearly the same," nevertheless, both because in the consciousness of Christ the devil was very real (see proof on p. 309), and because one naturally associates *temptation*, mentioned in this petition, with the *tempter* (see especially 4:1), I, along with many others, [323] give the preference to the rendering "the evil one." Though it is true that God himself never tempts man to sin (James 1:13), it is also true that there is good reason to ask him not even to permit us voluntarily to run into temptation; for example, by establishing a dangerously close alliance with the world, becoming "unequally yoked" with unbelievers (II Cor. 6:14-16); or by going into the opposite extreme and withdrawing ourselves entirely from society (contrary to Matt. 5:14; Phil. 2:15); by becoming so absorbed in our daily affairs that the spiritual atmosphere which should characterize our home is neglected; by serving on so many good-cause committees that matters even more important are not attended to; etc. It is God alone who knows how many tests of faith, and how severe, each saved sinner can endure, as he is constantly being assaulted by the devil (Eph. 6:12; I Peter 5:8), the world (John 15:19), and his own "flesh" (that is, whatever in himself is not a fruit of redeeming grace, Rom. 7:23; Gal. 5:17). Instead of going down to defeat in this struggle, may he remain watchful at all times, and in any event, may he triumph completely over the evil one (Rom. 16:20; I Thess. 5:23).—For more with respect to Satan and his crafty methods see N.T.C. on Ephesians 2:2 and 6:11, 12.

The logic of the petition is clear. An analogous request would be, "Lord, grant that I may be so careful in observing the rules of health that I may not become ill, but whatever in thy providence befalls me, keep me close to thy side that my faith may not fail." Here, too, however, "we," "our," and "us" should be substituted for "I," "my," and "me." The supplicant is constantly including others in his prayers.

The Conclusion

13b. [For thine is the kingdom, and the power, and the glory, forever. Amen.] It is commonly held that, since these words are absent from the leading manuscripts, the rules of textual evidence do not favor their inclusion in the Lord's Prayer. Without disputing the correctness of this view it is but fair to point out, however, that, in one form or another, the doxology is

---

323 A.R.V., The Amplified New Testament, Berkeley, Goodspeed, Grosheide, N.E.B., Ridderbos (H.N.), Weymouth, Williams, and the Dutch translations, both old (*Statenvertaling*) and new (*Bijbel, Nieuwe Vertaling.*).

found in some rather ancient versions. Moreover, the *Didache* or *Teaching of the Twelve Apostles* (VIII.2), by many regarded as having originated in the first half of the second century, contains the conclusion in the abbreviated form "for thine is the power and the glory forever." A defense of the authenticity of the Greek words upon which the A.V. form of the conclusion is based is found in E. F. Hills, *The King James Version Defended,* Des Moines, 1956, pp. 97-102. His main argument is that from the earliest times in the worship of the church the conclusion was separated from the rest of the Lord's Prayer. The body of the prayer was repeated by the people, the conclusion, exclusive of "Amen," by the priest, after which the people responded, "Amen." [324] Because of this liturgical separation, so he argues, this conclusion "began to be regarded by some Christians as a man-made response and not part of the original prayer as it fell from the lips of Christ."

Now it is true that even during the gatherings for worship, whether regular or on special occasions, both in ancient Israel and in the apostolic church, the scene was more lively and responsive, less formal, than in much of later Christendom (except for the modern trend). To be sure, the services were generally orderly. If they were not, the membership was apt to be duly admonished (I Cor. 14:23-40). The control was definitely in the hands of the leader. There were, however, responses by the congregation (Deut. 27:15-26; I Chron. 16:36; Neh. 5:13; 8:6; I Cor. 14:16; cf. Rev. 5:14). Nevertheless, whether an argument of this type, based to a large extent on ancient liturgical practices, is sufficient to offset the considerable lack of manuscript support for the retention or insertion of the words in question ("For thine is, etc.") is debatable. The evangelist Luke, in reporting the Lord's Prayer, omits any mention of a concluding doxology.

On the other hand, it must be admitted that the A.V. conclusion reflects the spirit of both the Old Testament (I Chron. 29:11; Neh. 9:5; the conclusions of Pss. 145-150) and the New (John 8:50; 17:4; I Cor. 10:31; II Tim. 4:18; Rev. 1:6; 4:11; 5:12, 13; 19:1 ff.). It would be difficult, indeed, to frame or devise a more fitting close. [325] Is it not entirely appropriate that we, the supplicants, having concluded our humble *petitions,* as it were turn our eyes upward again (as in the beginning of the prayer) in adoration, and concentrate heart and mind on God's majesty and love, which constitute the basis of our confidence that the prayer will be heard? [326]

---

[324] Dr. Hills bases this information on a volume by C. A. Swainson, *The Greek Liturgies,* London, 1884. Interesting and instructive is also the article, "Liturgics" in S.H.E.R.K., Vol. VI, pp. 498-505; and see the articles "Liturgical Movement" and "Liturgical Worship, Recent Trends In" in the Twentieth Century extension of S.H.E.R.K., pp. 669-671.

[325] So also H. N. Ridderbos, *op. cit.,* p. 136.

[326] See D. A. Schlatter, *Erläuterungen zum Neuen Testament,* Stuttgart, 1908, Vol. I, p. 71.

Viewing the words of the doxology, therefore, as being in any case in thorough harmony with the rest of the Bible, and as constituting an eminently suitable conclusion of this prayer, a few words of interpretation are in order. The phrase "For thine is the kingdom" can be regarded as pertaining to each of the preceding petitions, as if to say, "Hallowed be thy name, for thine is the kingdom," that is, "for it is thy sovereign right as King that thy name be hallowed"; so also, "Thy kingdom come, for thine is the kingdom," that is, "for it is proper that thy divine authority over hearts and lives be reverently acknowledged"; "Thy will be done, for thine is the kingdom," that is, "for since thou art King thy will should be obeyed by us and by everyone"; and so on through the rest of the prayer.

Not only the Father's *right* to grant the requests, since he is King over all, but also his *power* to do so is recognized ("and the power"), and this, too, is basic to each of the preceding petitions. Those who pray this prayer acknowledge that all power belongs to the Father, not only the power *over* the entire universe and all it contains, but even the power that resides *within* all: in the sun to glow, in winds to blow, in rivers to flow, in plants to grow, etc. Even the power exercised by sinister forces is his, though *they* are responsible for its evil use. If it were not his, how would he be able to overrule it for good?

Finally, since all of God's virtues are reflected in his work of creation and redemption, in each according to its own nature, the children of this heavenly Father, deeply impressed with the manifestations of his power, wisdom, and goodness, add, "and the glory," [327] joyfully ascribing to the Father all these three—the kingdom, the power, and the glory—not only now but "forever." With a reverend "Amen," in attestation of the sincerity of their words and of their conviction that the Father will attend to their needs, they conclude the prayer.

Though the Lord's Prayer is ended, Jesus regards it necessary to append to it a clarification of the fifth petition, "And forgive us our debts as we also have forgiven our debtors." Since in the explanation of the petition I have already touched on verses 14 and 15, little need be added here. **14, 15. For if y o u forgive men their trespasses, y o u r heavenly Father will also forgive yo u. But if yo u do not forgive men, neither will y o u r Father forgive y o u r trespasses.** Though in the teaching not only of Paul (Rom. 3:24; Eph. 2:8; Titus 3:5) but certainly also of Christ (Matt. 5:1-6; 18:27; Luke 18:13) salvation rests not on human accomplishments but solely on the grace and mercy of God, this does not mean that there is nothing to do for those who receive it. They must believe. Included in this faith is the eagerness to

---

[327] See footnote 277 on p. 287.

forgive. Unless the listeners forgive men their trespasses, they themselves will remain unpardoned.

In verse 12 sins were called *debts,* that is, that which we owe, and for which we must suffer punishment unless payment is made, satisfaction rendered, by ourselves or by another. Here, in verses 14 and 15, these sins are called *trespasses,* deviations from the path of truth and righteousness. [328] Now whether these deviations are of the milder character, as in Gal. 6:1 and perhaps also in Rom. 5:15, 17, 18, or whether they are far more serious, as in Eph. 1:7; 2:1, they must be forgiven. Moreover, as far as it is in his power to do so a follower of Jesus should make not only his brothers in the Lord but also men in general the objects of his forgiving love, as is clear from the fact that the very word "men," that is, human beings, is spelled out in full, and this both in verse 14 and in verse 15.

The question might be asked, "But in the process of bringing about forgiveness and reconciliation, does the entire obligation rest upon the person who has been sinned against? Does not the offender also have an obligation?" The answer is, "Indeed, he does." He must repent and with the message of this repentance he must gladden the heart of the one whom he has injured (Luke 17:3, 4). But this does not remove the latter's obligation to do all in his power to open wide the gate toward reconciliation. If in that case there is no co-operation from the other side, the blame will rest not on the offended person but on the offender, who originally inflicted the injury.

Of the three manifestations of "righteousness" here reviewed two have been discussed: charitable giving and prayer. There remains

Fasting

Prayer and fasting are often combined (I Sam. 7:5, 6; II Sam. 12:16, 21-23; II Chron. 20:3, 5 ff.; Ezra 8:21-23; Neh. 1:4; 9:1 ff.; Isa. 58:6, 9; Jer. 14:12; Dan. 9:3; Luke 2:37; Acts 13:2, 3; 14:23). **16. And whenever y o u fast, do not be like the hypocrites, looking glum, for they make their faces unsightly in order that (other) people may see that they are fasting.** Fasting, as here meant, refers not to a condition that is forced upon a person (II Cor. 6:5; 11:27), but to voluntary abstinence from food as a religious exercise. It served various purposes, either singly or in any combination. Thus, it might be an expression of *humiliation,* that is, sorrow for, and in connection with confession of, sin (Lev. 16:29-34; 23:26-32; Num. 29:7-11; Deut. 9:18; I Kings 21:27; Neh. 9:1 ff.; Dan. 9:3, 4; Jonah 3:5), or of *lamentation* over ill, either already experienced—defeat in battle (Judg. 20:26), bereavement (I Sam. 31:13; I Chron. 10:11, 12; II Sam. 1:12), the arrival of sad tidings (Neh. 1:4), a plague (Joel 1:14; 2:12-15)—or threatened (II Chron. 20:3,

---

[328] On παράπτωμα see R. C. Trench, *op. cit.,* par. lxvi.

5 ff.; Esther 4:3; 9:31). In the case of David, when the threatening death of the child becomes a reality he ceases to fast (II Sam. 12:16, 21-23). There was a natural basis for the fasts mentioned so far, since overwhelming grief or distress produces loss of appetite (cf. I Sam. 1:7).

Sometimes a fast was ordered and/or observed in order to promote *concentration* on an important religious act or event, such as the commissioning of missionaries (Acts 13:2, 3), or the appointment of elders (Acts 14:23). See also Exod. 34:2, 28; Deut. 9:9, 18. In this connection, what is perhaps the most beautiful chapter on fasting in the entire Bible (Isa. 58) deserves special mention (especially verses 6-12). It may well be that here in Matt. 6:16-18 Jesus had that chapter in mind, as a comparison will show. In both cases the wrong kind of fast (cf. I Kings 21:9, 11; Zech. 7:3-5) is condemned and the right kind commended.

The law of God suggests only one fast in an entire year, namely, on the day of atonement (Lev. 16:29-34; 23:26-32; Num. 29:7-11; cf. Acts 27:9). In course of time, however, fasts (not always total; see the text in each instance) began to multiply, so that we read about their occurrence at other times also: from sunrise to sunset (Judg. 20:26; I Sam. 14:24; II Sam. 1:12, 3:35); for seven days (I Sam. 31:13); three weeks (Dan. 10:3); forty days (Exod. 34:2, 28; Deut. 9:9, 18; I Kings 19:8); in the fifth and seventh month (Zech. 7:3-5); and even in the fourth, fifth, seventh, and tenth month (Zech. 8:19). The climax was the observance of a fast "twice a week," [329] the boast of the Pharisee (Luke 18:12).

As an expression of *lamentation* over sorrowful circumstances Jesus did not encourage fasting on the part of his disciples. On the contrary, he wanted them to rejoice because of his own presence among them (Matt. 9:14-17; Mark 2:18-20; Luke 5:33-35). He himself, as has been indicated, observed a fast of lengthy duration, probably for the purpose of *concentration* on the work which the Father had given him to do, and which he, Jesus himself, had voluntarily taken upon himself (see the explanation of Matt. 4:2).

Here in Matt. 6:16-18, however, it is the fast as an expression of *humiliation,* whether feigned (verse 16) or genuine (verses 17 and 18), that is in view. The hypocrites, that is, the scribes and Pharisees (5:20; 15:1, 7; 23:13), put on a dismal look, making their faces unsightly, perhaps by covering them with ashes (I Kings 20:38), in order that to the people round about them they might look O so sorry for their sins; hence, O so pious! They were putting on an act.

Jesus continues, **I solemnly declare to y o u, they have already received their reward in full.** For explanation see on 6:1 and 2. They tried hard to look glum so as to impress the fickle crowd. Well, they attained their goal!

---

[329] On Mondays and Thursdays, according to *Didache* VIII.1.

As if to say, "How utterly ridiculous, such a *reward!*" [330] How absurd to prefer it to the real reward (6:1)!

Continued: 17. **But you, when you fast, anoint your head and wash your face.** Jesus does not say that his followers must fast, neither does he forbid them to fast if that is what they wish to do. In certain circumstances he seems to regard fasting as entirely proper. Did he not himself fast also, though, as has already been indicated, for an entirely different reason? The point Jesus stresses is that when his followers think they ought to fast they should, by anointing their head and washing their face, make this voluntary observance of a religious exercise as inconspicuous as possible. This admonition parallels that with respect to giving to charity (6:2-4) and praying (6:5, 6). All such practices should take place "in secret," that is, away from the eyes of men. They should be sincere acts of devotion to God, to him alone. Concluded: 18. **that not men but (only) your Father who is in secret may see that you are fasting. And your Father who sees in secret will reward you** (for explanation see on 6:4).

With the passing of the day of atonement, fasting is no longer a religious requirement (Col. 2:14). Are there, nevertheless, lessons here that hold today as well as they did yesterday? I suggest the following:

1. Intemperance in eating, as well as in everything else, is warned against in Scripture. See N.T.C. on I and II Timothy and Titus, p. 122. The lazy gluttons of Crete, sluggish and sensual gormandizers, do not remain unrebuked (Titus 1:12). A mark of the enemies of the cross is that "their god is their belly (Phil. 3:19; cf. Rom. 16:18)." Instead of striving to keep their physical appetites under control (Rom. 8:13; I Cor. 9:27), realizing that our bodies are the Holy Spirit's temple, in which God should be glorified (I Cor. 6:19, 20), these people surrendered themselves to gluttony and licentiousness. They worshiped their sensual nature. The Bible forbids this. In this connection it is interesting to note that the physical advantage in cutting down the intake of animal fats is not a modern medical discovery (see Lev. 3:17; 7:22-25). [331]

2. Nevertheless, in Scripture it is not the salutary effect which a moderate amount of fasting may have on a person's physical welfare that is especially in view. It is rather the spiritual benefit that is basic. As has already been indicated, often fasting was an expression of sorrow for sin or was observed in order that mind and heart might concentrate not on material matters but wholly on God and on the tasks which he assigns. That there is a close connection between fasting and spiritual meditation and contemplation is widely recognized.

---

[330] See E. Trueblood, *The Humor of Christ*, New York, Evanston, and London, 1964, pp. 15, 58.
[331] See S. I. McMillen, *None of These Diseases*, Westwood, New Jersey, 1963, pp. 85-89.

3. The indispensability of sincerity in worship is, however, the main thrust of this entire section (6:1-18).

As to the relation of 6:19-34 to the sermon as a whole, and specifically to the immediately preceding verses 1-18, see pp. 263, 318. Righteousness in relation to God requires not only the sincere devotion of the heart to the heavenly Father (6:1-18) but also unlimited trust in him under all circumstances. We turn, therefore, to the sub-theme:

Unlimited Trust (6:19-34)

This truth is made clear, first of all, by the condemnation of its opposite, namely, lack of trust in God, that is, feverish anxiety. The latter:

a mounts to idolatry,

for its accompanying attachment to mammon means detachment from God (verse 24);

b lurs vision,

for, by being preoccupied with piling up material wealth, it obscures the real goal of our existence (verses 22, 23);

c onfuses values,

for it attaches primary significance to that which is secondary, and vice versa, as if food were more important than life, and clothing than the body (verse 25); and

d efies all reason,

for it barters away heavenly for earthly treasures, the imperishable for the perishable (verses 19-21); forgets that it cannot even add one cubit to a person's life-span (verse 27); borrows tomorrow's troubles as if today's were inadequate (verse 34); and, worst of all, refuses to consider that if, even as *Creator*, God feeds the birds and clothes the lilies, then certainly, as *heavenly Father*, he will care for *his children* (verses 26, 28-32).

Secondly, this truth (the necessity of unlimited trust in God) is also stated positively; for over against the negative commandments ("Do not gather. . . . Do not be anxious. . . . Do not become anxious") of, respectively, verses 19, 25, and 31, 34, stand the positive ("But gather. . . . Look at. . . . Consider") of, respectively, verses 20, 26, and 28, climaxed by the powerful and very comforting words of verse 33, "But seek first his kingdom and his righteousness, and all these things will be granted to y o u as an extra gift."

19, 20. Do not gather for yourselves treasures on earth, where moth and rust consume, and where thieves dig through and steal. But gather for yourselves treasures in heaven, where neither moth nor rust consume, and where thieves do not dig through and steal. First the negative command is issued, then the positive (cf. verses 5, 6; 7-9; 16, 17; 19, 20; 25, 26, 28; 31,

33; and 7:1, 5). How absurd (see *d* above), Jesus is saying, to "treasure up" for oneself perishable earthly "treasures," and while doing this to lose the imperishable heavenly riches! Earthly treasures are vulnerable because of deterioration and defalcation.

As to the first, deterioration, the *moth* consumes them. Moths, skippers, and butterflies belong to the large order of insects called *Lepidoptera,* that is, insects with scale-covered wings. In distinction from butterflies, moths *a.* constitute the largest division of this order, *b.* are largely nocturnal, and *c.* have antennae that are not club-shaped. [332] The reference here in 6:19-21 is to the tiny insect that deposits its eggs in woolens. It is in the larval stage that it feeds on the cloth until the garment, etc., becomes moth-eaten and is destroyed (Isa. 51:8; Luke 12:33; James 5:2). *Rust* probably indicates the corrosion of metals, their being gradually gnawed into by the action of chemicals.

In all probability, however, the terms "moth" and "rust" represent *all* those agencies and processes that cause earthly treasures to diminish in value and finally to cease completely to serve their purpose. Thus, bread becomes moldy (Josh. 9:5), garments wear out (Ps. 102:26), fields (particularly neglected ones) become weed-infested (Prov. 24:30), walls and fences break down (Prov. 24:31), roofs cave in so that houses begin to leak (Eccl. 10:18), and gold and silver become tarnished and perish (I Peter 1:7, 18). Add the havoc brought about by termites, hurricanes, typhoons, tornadoes, earthquakes, plant diseases, soil erosion, etc. The list is almost endless.

As to the second, defalcation, thieves break through and steal. Through the clay wall of the houses of which Jesus was thinking the thief rather easily digs an entrance and steals the ill-guarded treasures. Inflation, oppressive taxation which may amount to confiscation, bank failures, stock market slumps and crashes, expenses in connection with prolonged illnesses, these and many similar woes have the same effect. Besides, man's body, including that of the strongest, gradually wears away (Ps. 32:3; 39:4-7; 90:10; 103:15, 16; Eccl. 12:1-8). When he dies, all the earthly treasures on which he had pinned his hopes vanish with him.

Completely different are "the treasures in heaven" (cf. 19:21), that is, those blessings that are reserved for us in heaven (I Peter 1:4), that are heavenly in character, but of which we experience a foretaste even now. Beginning, as is proper, with the enumeration of some of these as Jesus himself describes them, one thinks of our standing with God as being fully pardoned (Matt. 6:14), answered prayer (7:7), the enrolment of our names in heaven (Luke 10:20), the Father's love (John 16:27), a welcome not only to the "mansions" of heaven but to the Savior's own heart (John 14:2, 3), a

---

[332] See the article "Butterfly and Moth," in the 1969 edition of the *Encyclopaedia Britannica*, Vol. 4, pp. 487-501.

full share in Christ's own peace (John 14:27), his own joy (John 15:11), and his own victory (John 16:33), and the Holy Spirit's permanent indwelling (John 14:16, 26; 15:26). See also all the spiritual blessings mentioned in the beatitudes (Matt. 5:1-12). Paul is thinking of these same treasures, and describes them sometimes in the same, sometimes in his own terms: our "being justified by faith" (Rom. 5:1), "answered prayer" (II Cor. 12:8, 9), "the love of God shed abroad in our hearts" (Rom. 5:5), "the crown of righteousness" with which the Savior will welcome us (II Tim. 4:8), "the peace of God that passes all understanding (Phil. 4:7), "rejoicing in God through our Lord Jesus Christ" (Rom. 5:11), "the victory" (I Cor. 15:57), and "his Spirit in the inner man" (Eph. 3:16; cf. Rom. 8:14, 16, 26, 27). The enumerations are merely illustrative, not exhaustive.

There is a degree of difference with which spiritual (as over against material) blessings are emphasized in the New Testament as compared with the Old. With the coming of Christ heaven as it were touches the earth. See N.T.C. on Fphesians, p. 73.

That the heavenly treasures are moth-proof, rust-proof, and burglar-proof (verse 20), in other words, that they endure forever in all their sparkling luster, as the irremovable possession of the children of the heavenly Father, is the teaching of Scripture throughout, for it tells us about:

a faithfulness that will never be removed (Ps. 89:33; 138:8),

a life that will never end (John 3:16),

a spring of water that will never cease to bubble up within the one who drinks of it (John 4:14),

a gift that will never be lost (John 6:37, 39),

a hand out of which the Good Shepherd's sheep will never be snatched (John 10:28),

a chain that will never be broken (Rom. 8:29, 30),

a love from which we shall never be separated (Rom. 8:39),

a calling that will never be revoked (Rom. 11:29),

a foundation that will never be destroyed (II Tim. 2:19),

and an inheritance that will never fade out (I Peter 1:4, 5).

The following questions may well be asked, however, "But if it is wrong to gather treasures on earth, does this mean, then, that making provision for future physical needs is always and absolutely wrong?" "Must all trade, commerce, and industry, carried on for the purpose, at least in part, of making a profit, be condemned?" "Are all rich people to be considered reprobates?" To all three questions the answer is, "No." God did not condemn Joseph for advising Pharaoh to store up grain for future use (Gen. 41:33-36). Nor were Solomon and Agur wrong in pointing to the ant as an example of the common sense revealed in providing during the summer for the needs of the winter (Prov. 6:6; 30:25). Nor did Paul make a mistake when he wrote II Cor. 12:14b and I Tim. 5:8. Business and banking are encouraged, by implication, in Christ's parables (Matt. 25:14-30; Luke 19:11-23). The rich man Abraham (Gen. 13:2) was a friend of God (Isa. 41:8; II Chron. 20:7; James 2:23). Rich Zachaeus (Luke 19:2) was accounted worthy to be called "a son of Abraham" (Luke 19:9); and wealthy Joseph of Arimathea was a follower of the Lord (Matt. 27:57).

Nevertheless, the accumulation of wealth is fraught with spiritual danger (Matt. 19:24; Luke 12:16-21; I Tim. 6:10). To be sure, money can be a great blessing, if it is not an end in itself but a means to an end, namely, *a.* to prevent one's own family from becoming a burden to others (I Tim. 5:8), *b.* to help those who are in need (Prov. 14:21; 19:17; Acts 4:36, 37; 11:27-30; 24:17; Rom. 15:25; II Cor. 8:4, 9; Gal. 2:10; 6:10; Eph. 4:28), and *c.* to encourage the work of the gospel both at home and abroad (Mark 15:41; Luke 8:2, 3; Acts 16:15, 40; I Cor. 9:9; Phil. 4:15-17; I Tim. 5:17, 18), all to the glory of God (I Cor. 10:31). However, money can also be a snare (Mark 14:11; Luke 22:5; Acts 8:18, 20).

Naturally, if a person's real treasure, his ultimate aim in all his striving, is something pertaining to this earth—the acquisition of money, fame, popularity, prestige, power—, then his heart, the very center of his life (Prov. 4:23), will be completely absorbed in that mundane object. All of his activities, including even the so-called religious, will be subservient to this one goal. On the other hand, if, out of sincere and humble gratitude to God, he has made God's kingdom, that is, the joyful recognition of God's sovereignty in his own life and in every sphere, his treasure, then *there* is also where his heart will be. Money, in that case, will be a help, not a hindrance. Something of this nature Jesus must have had in mind when he said, **21. For where your treasure is, there will your heart be also.** The "heart" cannot be in both of these places at the same time. It is an either-or proposition! See verse 24.

Piling up earthly treasures blurs vision (see *b* above, p. 343). With a figure of speech that amounts almost to a parable Jesus says, **22, 23. The eye is the body's lamp. Therefore, if your eye is sound, your whole body will be illumined. But if your eye is in poor condition, your whole body will be dark. If then the (very) light in you is darkness, how great (is) that darkness.** Jesus does not mean that the eye is *the source* of light for our body, but that it is, as it were, the light-bringer, the guide on which the entire body depends for illumination and direction. It is because of the eye that a man is able to make use of the light. Therefore, in this secondary sense, the eye may itself also be called the body's light or lantern.

This implies, however that the eye must be *single,* that is, in this connection, *without any speck,* hence, *sound.*[333] It must be able to see clearly. If

---

[333] The basic meaning of the adjective ἁπλοῦς, is *simple, single, uncomplicated.* However, as is true of words in general, various shades of meaning develop from this primary sense. Thus, for example, the noun ἁπλότης in Eph. 6:5 and Col. 3:22 refers to

the eye is diseased, the body will be full of darkness and thus not able to function properly. It is a well-known fact that lack of sufficient light from sun, moon, stars, lamps, etc., makes it difficult to see things. Yet, a sound eye quickly adjusts to the darkness. But if the eye itself, the very organ of light (in the sense already explained), is in poor condition, the darkness will be great indeed. In that case, even if the sun were shining, not much would be gained. At best, everything would be indistinct, a huge blur.

Implication on the basis of verses 19-21: Just as a person has a natural eye (the *one* eye representing both eyes here) to illumine his physical existence and to bring him into contact with his earthly environment, so he has a spiritual eye, namely, the mind, to brighten his inner life, to guide him morally and spiritually, and to keep him in contact with the heavenly Father. But if the "light" that is in him be darkened—for example, by means of his inordinate yearning for earthly treasure—, then how great must be that darkness, the very organ of light-reception having been obscured by sin. By missing what should have been his goal, namely, the promotion of God's glory, this person misses everything!

The impossibility of combining two opposite goals (glorifying God and satisfying the yearnings of the flesh) is stated very tersely and unambiguous-ly in verse 24. **No one can serve two masters; for either he will hate the one and love the other, or he will be devoted to one and look down on the other. Y o u cannot serve God and Mammon.** The man with the misplaced *heart*

---

singleness of heart; hence, *sincerity, integrity, uprightness* (cf. I Chron. 29:17). See also II Cor. 11:3: *sincere devotion.* It is not difficult to understand that the disposition of heart and mind that is "single," in the sense that it is unmixed with ulterior or selfish motivations, would be "generous." Hence in Rom. 12:8; II Cor. 8:2; 9:11, 13 the meaning is *generosity, liberality;* and in James 1:5 the adverb ἁπλῶς means *generously.*

So also the transition from "simple" or "single" to "unmixed with any defect," "speckless," hence *clear, sound, healthy,* is easy to understand. See L.N.T. (A. and G.), entry ἁπλοῦς, p. 85. And the evident contrast here (in Matt. 6:22, 23) indicated between the adjectives ἁπλοῦς and πονηρός is probably best interpreted by *sound* versus *in poor condition* (or *bad*). Lenski, however, insists on "single" versus "wicked," and denies that these adjectives describe the natural eye (*op. cit.,* p. 269). The text clearly states, however, that it is the eye as *the body's* lamp that is being described. The word σῶμα, "body," occurs no less than three times in verses 22, 23. I agree, therefore, with the vast majority of translators and commentators who render the contrasted pair of adjectives as follows: "clear ... bad" (N.A.S.), "sound ... unsound" (Williams), "healthy ... bad" (Beck), "sound ... not sound" (R.S.V.), "sound ... defective" (Berkeley), "sound ... bad" (N.E.B. and Ridderbos). Calvin, commenting on 6:22, 23, states that the eye is here regarded as the torch or lamp of the whole body. He continues, "If the hands and feet are foolishly and improperly directed, the blame ... ought to be ascribed to the eyes, which do not perform their duty." He also clearly discerns that this reference to the natural eye is here used as a figure: "We must now apply this comparison to the mind. . . ." As I, along with most others, see it, that is the only reasonable interpretation. Jesus, in describing the physical eye, and calling it either sound or bad, leaves the application of this illustration to be inferred by the audience. In the light of the context the "point" was easy to grasp.

(verse 21) and misdirected *mind* (verses 22 and 23) also suffers from a misaligned *will*, a will not in line with God's will (verse 24). He imagines, perhaps, that he can give his full allegiance to the two goals of glorifying God and acquiring material possessions, but he errs. He will either hate the one and love the other, or vice versa. By "God" is meant the heavenly Father, as representing the Trinity, and as revealed to us by Jesus Christ. By "Mammon," a word of uncertain derivation, is meant wealth, property, as Luke 16:5, 9, 11 clearly indicates. Think of money, real estate, victuals, clothes, etc. Here in Matt. 6:24, as well as in Luke 16:13, wealth of property is, however, personified: it is presented as a master to whom a person is devoted and whom he loves. Today also people will say, "He has become the slave of his holdings."

If a person loves God he will show this by being devoted to him, placing everything—money, time, talents, etc.—at his disposal, serving him. It is clear, therefore, that *loving* God is not merely a matter of the emotions but of heart, soul, mind, and strength (Matt. 22:37; Mark 12:30). To love God requires service and even sacrifice (Matt. 10:37-39). So described, it becomes all the more evident that this supreme, self-sacrificing, enthusiastic allegiance cannot be rendered to two parties. Whoever renders it becomes a *worshiper*, and the One to whom it is rendered becomes his *God*. Moreover, since there is only one true God, it follows that Mammon-worship is idolatry (see *a* on p. 343).

The psychological tension that is built up in the soul of a person who imagines for a while that he will be able to love and serve both masters becomes so severe and unendurable that in attitude, word, and deed he will sooner or later begin to show where his real allegiance lies. Either the one master or the other will win out, actually has been "on top" all the while, though, perhaps, the individual in question was not fully aware of this. In the crisis the agitated soul, out of love for the one master, will begin to show that he hates the other, perhaps even to the point of being willing to betray him. Think of Judas Iscariot. Was it not Mammon that led him to deliver Christ into the hands of the enemy? See Matt. 26:14-16; John 12:6. And on the other hand, think of Paul. There came a time in the life of this former persecutor when he began to look down on whatever of personal merit, earthly possessions, and prestige he at one time had prized so highly. Whatever used to be gain had now become loss (Phil. 3:7 ff.).

Another point, already implied in the preceding, is now brought to the foreground more definitely, namely, that the person who, because of his lack of trust in the heavenly Father, devotes his time and talent to the piling up of earthly treasures, hence to the worship of Mammon, confuses values. He is "all mixed up" with respect to priorities. He attaches primary significance to that which is secondary, and vice versa (see *c* on p. 343). Says Jesus, **25. Therefore I say to y o u, Do not be anxious about y o u r life, what y o u** are going to eat or what y o u are going to drink, nor about y o u r body, what y o u are going to wear. Is not life more important than food, and the body more important than clothes?

The word "Therefore" shows the connection with the preceding. On the basis of what has gone before and in connection with what follows, the meaning is probably this: Since transitory earthly treasures do not satisfy, and setting the heart on them implies forfeiting the enduring pleasures of heaven (verses 19-21), and since the yearning for such earthly riches blurs mental and moral vision (verses 22, 23), and finally, because a choice must be made between God and Mammon (verse 24), do not continue to set y o u r heart on the latter, that is, on earthly things, such as food and drink, to keep alive, or on clothes, to keep dressed. After all, it is y o u r heavenly Father who gave y o u y o u r life and y o u r body and will sustain them. He who has provided the greater, namely, life and body, will he not also furnish the lesser, namely, food, drink, and clothes? Is not life [334] more important than food, and the body than clothes? Do not, then, confuse priorities!

What we have here, therefore, is an argument from the greater to the lesser, somewhat on the order of Rom. 8:32, "He who did not spare his own Son but delivered him up for us all, how shall he not with him also graciously give us all things?"

'"Do not be anxious," says Jesus. Since the present imperative is used here, the meaning seems to be, "Do not have this bad habit." It may, however, also mean, "If y o u have already fallen into it, then break this habit: stop being anxious." Compare with verse 31, where the exhortation is, "Do not *become* anxious." The word used in the original for being anxious means being *distracted,* as was, for example, Martha, whose attention was *divided* to such an extent that she, for a while, forgot about "the one thing needful" (Luke 10:38-42; note verse 41, "you are *anxious* and troubled about many things").

Anxiety must also be avoided because it is unreasonable (see *d* on p. 343). Jesus has just now (verse 25) warned about being unduly concerned about the means of sustaining life, namely, food and drink. So, pointing upward, perhaps, to a flock of birds, he continues: 26. **Look at the birds of the air. They neither sow nor reap nor gather into barns, yet y o u r heavenly Father feeds them. Y o u are of more value than they, are y o u not?** The sky above

---

[334] In verse 25a and 25b the word ψυχή has the meaning *life*, the animating principle of the body (cf. 2:20; 16:26; Mark 3:4; Luke 6:9). At other times, as used in the Gospels, it refers to the sum total of life that is above the physical, especially the seat of *emotional* activity (Matt. 26:38; Mark 12:30); or it may indicate the self, the person (Matt. 11:29; 20:28; Mark 8:36; 10:45).

For a fuller statement showing the various uses of ψυχή and πνεῦμα in the New Testament and their relation to each other (in how far they can be distinguished, and to what extent they overlap) see N.T.C. on I and II Thess. pp. 148 and 149; also the author's book, *The Bible on the Life Hereafter,* pp. 36-39.

Palestine and neighboring countries is full of birds. Scripture mentions many of them. In the small compass of seven verses (Lev. 11:13-19) no less than twenty kinds are listed: eagle, ossifrage, osprey, kite, falcon, raven, ostrich, nighthawk, sea gull, hawk, owl, cormorant, ibis, water hen, pelican, vulture, stork, heron, hoopoe, and bat. [335] In the old dispensation all of these were considered "unclean." The pigeon and the turtle-dove are mentioned in Lev. 12:6 (cf. Luke 2:24); the sparrow and the swallow in Ps. 84:3; for the former see also Matt. 10:29, 31; Luke 12:6, 7. In addition to turtle-dove and swallow Jer. 8:7 mentions the crane. In the passage parallel to Matt. 6:26 Jesus calls the attention of his audience to the (already mentioned) raven (Luke 12:24). The barnyard with its domestic fowl is not neglected; note the strikingly beautiful passage about the hen and its chicks (Matt. 23:37), and the part the rooster plays in the story of Peter's denial (Matt. 26:34 ff., and parallels). The eagle, referred to not only in Lev. 11 but in several other Old Testament passages (including such well-known ones as Deut. 32:11; Ps. 103:5 and Ezek. 17:3, 11) returns in the pages of the New Testament (Matt. 24:28; cf. Luke 17:37; Rev. 4:7; 12:14). We have already become acquainted with the dove in our study of the baptism of Jesus (see p. 214).

For a complete list and description of the birds mentioned in Scripture one should turn to the delightfully interesting work by A. Parmelee, *All the Birds of the Bible,* New York, 1959. That author calls the country in which the Sermon on the Mount was delivered "the cross-roads of bird-migrations." [336] Was a thick swarm of winged travelers cleaving the air at the very moment when the Lord spoke the words of 6:26? It is entirely possible.

What Jesus is saying here is that the birds of the air neither sow nor reap nor gather into barns, yet are being fed and kept alive by their Creator. This passage must not be misinterpreted as if it were an encouragement to idleness. It could not have been that, for the Lord knew well enough that his audience was conscious of the fact that adult birds are by no means lazy. They work for their living. They do not just settle themselves on some twig and wait for food to drop into their mouths. No, they are very busy. They gather insects and worms, prepare their nests, care for their young and teach them how to fly, etc. A certain degree of "care" for impending contingencies can be ascribed to them, especially to the migrants among them; for, as the season may dictate, these travel to warmer or cooler regions. Nevertheless, two things must be borne in mind. First, birds are not guilty of overdoing a good thing. They are not like the rich fool of the parable (Luke 12:16-21). Secondly, when these birds prepare their nests, train their young, migrate, etc., they are acting "instinctively." When we say this, are we not really

---

[335] These are the names according to R.S.V. However, authorities are by no means in agreement with respect to the correctness of some of them.

[336] p. 183.

affirming that it is their Creator who, by endowing them with these instincts, is caring for them, while they themselves are merely responding to certain stimuli?

With men the story is entirely different. It is they, not the birds, who not only sow and reap and gather into barns, but who, while engaged in all this, are often filled with dreadful forebodings, in large measure ignoring God's promises! While the birds are "carefree," men are "careworn."

Christ's argument—from the less to the greater, contrast verse 25—amounts to this: If the birds, who cannot in any real sense plan ahead, have no reason to worry, then certainly y o u, my followers, endowed with intelligence, so that y o u can take thought for the future, should not be filled with apprehension. Again, if God provides even for these lower creatures, how much more will he care for y o u, who were created as his very image. And especially, if the One who feeds them is "y o u r heavenly Father" but *their* Creator, then how thoroughly unreasonable y o u r anxiety becomes. "Y o u are of more value than they, are y o u not?" asks the Lord, in a question so worded in the original that it expects an affirmative answer.

The senselessness of anxiety is also evident from the following: 27. **And who among y o u is able, by being anxious, to add (even) one cubit to his life-span?** The word translated "life-span" (Greek: *hēlikia*) may refer either to *age* or to *height* or *stature*. Thus Zachaeus was small in *stature* (Luke 19:3), but Sarah was long past the *age* of conceiving (Heb. 11:11). The man born blind, healed by Christ, had reached the *age* of legal maturity (John 9:21, 23). Here in Matt. 6:27 (cf. the parallel passage, Luke 12:25). A.V. has "stature." But in the present context this cannot be correct, for two reasons: *a.* adding this amount is represented as being "a small thing" (Luke 12:26), but actually becoming taller by about eighteen inches or forty-six centimeters can hardly be considered an altogether insignificant accomplishment; and *b.* who, except perhaps an abnormally small person, would impatiently desire to add that amount to his stature?

The true meaning, then, is this: "Who among y o u is able, by means of worrying, to lengthen the pathway of his life by ever so little?" On a birthday a person will sometimes say, "I have reached another mile-post." On his seventieth birthday this individual will have reached his seventieth mile-post. Adding a cubit to seventy miles, or even to ten miles, would certainly be hardly worth mentioning. It would be "a small thing," but even such a small thing, says Jesus, no one is able to accomplish by means of worrying. A man may "worry himself to death"; he cannot worry himself into a longer span of life. See also Ps. 39:4-6.

The Lord now turns to another example from nature. Paralleling what he has said about the birds (verse 26) he now refers to the lilies (verses 28-30). In line with his teaching regarding the divine provision of food so that a person may keep alive, he now shows that God will also provide clothes so

351

that this person's body may be covered. It will be noticed that in verses 26-30, taken in their entirety, we therefore have an orderly elucidation and elaboration of verse 25. Jesus, then, continues to speak about the senselessness of worry (see d. on p. 343), in order that men may place their full trust in the heavenly Father.

He says: **28, 29. Moreover, why be anxious about clothes? Consider the lillies of the field, how they grow; they neither toil nor spin; yet I tell y o u that even Solomon in all his splendor was not attired like one of these.**

"Consider"—that is, notice carefully, study closely—"the field-lilies," says Jesus, as he asks his audience, "Why be anxious about clothes?". Exactly what kind of flower the Lord had in mind when he said "field-lilies" cannot be determined. Some guesses are: irises, narcissi, Turk's cap lilies, [337] and gladioli. Goodspeed translates "wild flowers" ("See how the wild flowers grow"). In the light of the context (note "the grass of the field. . . .") it is very well possible that Jesus, instead of referring to any particular kind of flower, was thinking of all the beautiful flowers that were adding their splendor to the landscape at this time of the year.

"How they grow" must mean, as the context indicates: without any toil whatever on their part, nor any care being bestowed on them by any human individual, "how *easily* and *freely,* and yet how *gorgeously.*" Though the "lilies" do not spin a single thread, yet even Solomon in all his splendor—to which extensive reference has already been made; see p. 118 and p. 173—was not arrayed like one of these. Is not this true in at least this respect, namely, that Solomon's finest apparel was at best but a mimicry and derivative of that which in nature comes fresh from the hand of God? *Pristine beauty cannot be matched!*

Yet the simultaneous outburst of flowers in the spring of the year just as suddenly vanishes: today these flowers are fully alive and adorn the fields; tomorrow this "grass of the field," that is, this sum-total of uncultivated (in contrast with cultivated) plants, serves as fuel for the domestic oven, in a land where fuel was not plentiful.

The lesson is as follows: **30. Now if God so clothes the grass of the field, which today is alive and tomorrow is thrown into the furnace, will he not much more surely clothe y o u, O men of little faith?** There is a double argument here, as follows:

a. from the less to the greater: If God provides for the short-lived *grass,* he will surely provide for *his children,* destined for eternal glory.

b. from the greater to the less: If God decks the wild flowers with such

---

[337] It is with this tall and very beautiful flower, with its "radiant, nodding blossoms," rapid growth, and presence in great abundance, that Mrs. W. Starr Dana, in her fascinating book, *How To Know the Wild Flowers,* New York, 1922, pp. 260, 262, 263, connects Matt. 6:28, 29. She is careful to point out, however, that the term "lily" was freely applied by many Oriental poets to any beautiful flower.

very beautiful garments, then he will certainly clothe his children with the *ordinary garments* which they need.

Jesus calls his worrying followers "men of little faith." The various passages in which he makes use of this description, in their contexts, are as follows:

Matt. 6:30 and its parallel Luke 12:28 (worry about clothes)

Matt. 8:26 (the disciples' fear of drowning during a storm at sea)

Matt. 14:31 (Peter's similar fear)

Matt. 16:8 (the disciples' failure to remember the lesson they had received in connection with Christ's miracle-working power).

Based upon these passages, it would seem that the description refers to the fact that those so characterized were not sufficiently taking to heart the comfort they should have derived from the presence, promises, power, and love of Christ.

In verse 31. Jesus summarizes the lesson with reference to the sinfulness and senselessness of anxiety regarding food and clothing: **So, do not become anxious, saying, "What are we going to eat?" or "What are we going to drink?" or "What are we going to wear?"** As noted earlier (see on verse 25) there is a slight change. Not only must habitual anxiety be avoided, but even the first step leading to this habit should be shunned; hence, "Do not become [or: Do not grow] anxious." [338]

In verse 32 to the exhortation, "Do not become anxious" two reasons are appended. [339] They are as follows: **32. For all these things the Gentiles crave; besides, y o u r heavenly Father knows that you need them all.** Naturally the Gentiles, who do not acknowledge any heavenly Father and are in complete ignorance concerning the promise of far superior spiritual realities (see Eph. 1:3; 2:11, 12), set their hearts on and worry about food and clothing. Material things are the objects of their consuming desire. [340] Since Christ's followers are entirely different (Matt. 6:7; Eph. 4:17-24) they must also pursue a different course: they must be distinctive and not sink down to the level of the Gentiles. They must trust and not be afraid.

Closely linked with the first is the second reason for the admonition "Do not become anxious," namely, "Y o u r heavenly Father knows that y o u

---

[338] The form μεριμνήσητε is sec. per. pl. aorist subjunctive of μεριμνάω.

[339] Note the use of γάρ introducing both clauses; hence πάντα γὰρ ταῦτα, and οὐδεν γάρ. By reproducing both of these by "for" the impression can easily be created that the second clause states the reason for the first, which makes little sense. Better, therefore, it would seem to me, is it to follow R.S.V., which in verse 32 translates "for . . . and." I reach the same result with "for . . . besides." The fact that not every γάρ has to be rendered "for" is well-known. See H. E. Dana and J. R. Mantey, *A Manual Grammar of the Greek New Testament,* New York, 1950, pp. 242-244. See also N.T.C. on Galatians, p. 43, footnote 25.

[340] Note the emphatic position of πάντα γὰρ ταῦτα at the very beginning of the sentence.

need them all," yes, he knows this "even before y o u ask him" (verse 8). That is all that is necessary, for so loving is this Father toward his children that his very *knowledge* of their needs makes it certain that he will also provide (cf. Eph. 3:20).

A climactic positive command reinforces the lesson that one should place his trust entirely in the heavenly Father: **33. But seek first his kingdom and his righteousness, and all these things will be granted to y o u as an extra gift.** Over against the Gentiles, who crave food, drink, garments, etc., Christ's followers are urged to seek first his kingdom and his righteousness. The verb *seek* implies a being absorbed in the search for, a persevering and strenuous effort to obtain (cf. 13:45). The form of the verb that is used also allows the rendering, "Be constantly seeking" (cf. Col. 3:1). Note: seek *first;* that is, give God the priority that is his due (II Cor. 4:18).

The object of this seeking is "his kingdom and his righteousness." The listeners are exhorted, therefore, to acknowledge God as King in their own hearts and lives, and to do all in their power to have him recognized as King also in the hearts and lives of others, and in every sphere: education, government, commerce, industry, science, etc. For the concept "kingdom of heaven" see pp. 249, 250. It stands to reason that when God is recognized as King, righteousness will prevail. For this concept see pp. 274, 317. These two (*kingdom* and *righteousness*) go together. In fact, "the kingdom of God is [means, implies] righteousness" (Rom. 14:17), a righteousness both imputed to men and imparted to them, both of legal standing and of ethical conduct.

Now it is true that the kingdom and its righteousness are gifts, graciously bestowed. They are *his* kingdom and *his* righteousness. [341] They are, however, also objects of continuing, diligent search; of ceaseless, strenuous effort to obtain. These two are not contradictory. An example from nature will clarify this. Of itself a tree has no power to maintain itself. Its roots are, as it were, empty hands stretched out to the environment. It is dependent on the sun, the air, the clouds, and the soil. It does not even have the strength to absorb the nourishment it requires. The sun is the source of its energy. But does this mean that the tree is therefore inactive? Not at all. Its roots and leaves, though completely receptive, are enormously active. For example, it has been estimated that the amount of work performed by a certain large tree in a single day to raise water and minerals from the soil to the leaves was equal to the amount of energy expended by a person who carried three hundred buckets full of water, two at a time, up a ten-foot flight of stairs. The leaves, too, are virtual factories. They, too, are tremendously active.

The same holds also with respect to the citizens of the kingdom. They

---

[341] There may also be an allusion here to the righteousness of scribes and Pharisees; as if to say, "*his* righteousness, not *theirs*. See 5:20.

receive the kingdom as a gift. Yet, after the new principle of life has been received, the recipients become very active. They work very hard, not by means of anything in themselves but by the power that is being constantly supplied to them by the Lord's Spirit. They "work out their own salvation," and are able to do this because "it is God who works in them both to will and to work for his good pleasure" (Phil. 2:12, 13. See also Matt. 7:13; cf. Luke 13:24; 16:16b). They trust in God's promises, pray, spread the message of salvation, and out of gratitude perform good works to benefit men and to glorify God.

The reward of grace: "all these things will be granted to y o u as an extra gift." While *they* are concentrating their attention on the kingdom and its righteousness, God's gift to them, *their heavenly Father* sees to it that they have food, drink, and clothing. For further elucidation see I Kings 3:10-14; Mark 10:29, 30; and I Tim. 4:8.

The conclusion, based on all that precedes, is: **34. Do not therefore become anxious for** [342] **tomorrow, for tomorrow will be anxious for itself. Each day has enough trouble all by itself.** See *d.* on p. 343. *Providing for* tomorrow is one thing. To a certain extent this cannot be condemned. See Luke 16:8, 9, but note also verse 13. *Becoming anxious for* tomorrow is always wrong. The only right way to provide for tomorrow without at the same time being anxious is to take care that *today* the admonition of verse 33 ("But seek first his kingdom and his righteousness") is obeyed.

Jesus has given all the reasons that prove why worrying about tomorrow is wrong and senseless. See the summary on p. 343. *Today* has been given to us. On this day, therefore, we should, out of gratitude, do what God demands of us. *"Today,* O that y o u would hear his voice" (Ps. 95:7). As to tomorrow, here personified, let that rest. Allow it to be "anxious for itself," says Jesus, shall we say "with a touch of humor"? When tomorrow arrives, there will be new troubles, but also renewed strength. God has not given us strength today for tomorrow's difficulties. When we reflect on the fact that "each day has enough trouble all by itself" (or: "Sufficient unto the day is the evil thereof," the more literal A.V. rendering, retained by A.R.V.), let us also immediately be reminded of Lam. 3:22, 23, "His compassions fail not. They are new *every morning;* great is thy faithfulness!"

---

[342] I do not agree with Lenski (*op. cit.*, p. 278), when he translates, "Do not therefore worry into the morrow." The Greek preposition εἰς does not always mean *into*, not even in this type of context. It can very well mean "for," as L.N.T. (A. and G.), p. 228, shows, Cf. Eph. 4:30; Phil. 2:16; Rev. 9:15.

The ten commandments were written on two tables (Deut. 5:22). Jesus summarized this law in the familiar words of Matt. 22:37-39, "You shall love the Lord your God with all your heart . . . and you shall love your neighbor as yourself." Similarly, the Lord's Prayer contains two sets of petitions, the first set of three has to do with God, the second with man. So it is also with the Sermon on the Mount viewed as a whole. Having summarized man's duty toward God (chap. 6), it then states his obligation toward the neighbor (7:1-12).

The two duties are related, for man is God's image (Gen. 1:27).

Accordingly, we have now reached the subdivision dealing with:

The Essence of This Righteousness
with Respect to Man's Relation to Man

Jesus begins this section by saying: 7:1. **Do not pass judgment (on others)** . . . As in 6:1, 19, 20; 7:7; etc., a principle is first stated, then explained. Just what did the Lord mean when he said, "Judge not" (A.V.)? Did he mean that all manner of judging is absolutely and without any qualification forbidden, so that with respect to the neighbor we are not allowed to form and/or express any opinion whatever, at least that with respect to him we must never voice an adverse or unfavorable opinion? In the light of what Jesus himself says in this very paragraph (verse 6), where he implies that we must regard certain individuals as being dogs and hogs, and of John 7:24; cf. I Cor. 5:12; 6:1-5; Gal. 1:8, 9; Phil. 3:2; I Thess. 2:14, 15; I Tim. 1:6, 7; Titus 3:2, 10; I John 4:1; II John 10; III John 9, and a good many other passages that could be added, it is clear that no such wholesale condemnation of forming an opinion about a person and expressing it can have been intended.

Jesus himself had arrived at certain conclusions regarding scribes and Pharisees, and he did not hesitate to express them (Matt. 5:20; 6:2, 5, 16; 15:1 ff.; 23:1 ff.). Though it is true that we, on our part, cannot read what is in our neighbor's heart, as Jesus was able to do (John 3:24, 25), so that *our* judgment must be more reserved and can never be final, there is nothing in the teaching either of Christ himself or of the apostles after him that relieves us of the obligation to form opinions about people and to act upon the basis of these opinions, which also implies that at times it will be our duty to express our judgments. Matt. 7:1 has been used at times as an excuse for laxity in exercising church discipline, but in the light of its context, and also of 18:15-18 and John 20:23, such use of this passage is without any justification.

What, then, did Jesus mean? He means (see verses 3-5) that it is wrong for anyone to concentrate his attention on the speck in his brother's eye and, while thus occupied, to ignore the beam in his own eye. The Lord is here condemning the spirit of censoriousness, judging harshly, self-righteously, without mercy, without love, as also the parallel passage (Luke 6:36, 37) clearly indicates.

To be discriminating and critical is necessary; to be hypercritical is wrong. One should avoid saying what is untrue (Exod. 23:1), unnecessary (Prov. 11:13), and unkind (Prov. 18:8). One of the best, and also one of the most interesting, expositions of this truth I have come across is that by L. B. Flynn, in his book, *Did I Say That?*, Nashville, 1959; see especially chapter 3, which bears the title, "A Keen Sense of Rumor."

That the sin here condemned was very common is clear, for example, from the fact that David condemned to death the rich man who, so the king had been made to believe, had stolen and killed the poor man's little ewe lamb, not realizing that in thus condemning him he (David) was passing sentence on himself (II Sam. 12:1-7)!

This inclination to discover and severely condemn the faults, real or imaginary, of others, while passing lightly over one's own frequently even more lamentable violations of God's holy law, was common among the Jews (Rom. 2:1 f.), especially among the Pharisees (Luke 18:9; John 7:49), and is common always and everywhere. According to the words of Jesus here in 7:1, that y o u may not have judgment passed on yourselves, the habitual self-righteous faultfinder must remember that he himself can expect to be condemned, and this not only by men but also and especially by God, as 6:14, 15 has already indicated. Cf. 18:23-35.

For the sake of emphasis the thought expressed in 7:1b is repeated in somewhat different phraseology: 2. **For in accordance with the judgment whereby y o u pass judgment y o u yourselves will be judged; and in accordance with the measure whereby y o u measure it will be measured back to y o u.** Meaning: The standard of judgment that y o u apply to others will be applied to y o u. If y o u judge without mercy, y o u will be judged without mercy. Similarly, if y o u judge kindly, y o u will be judged and treated kindly. There will then be poured into y o u r lap "good measure, pressed down, shaken together, and running over." Y o u will be thus judged and rewarded by God, to be sure (6:14, 15; cf. Rom. 2:16, 3:6), but the human agents are not excluded (Luke 6:34, 38).

A figurative description of, and a warning to, carping critics follows in verses 3-5. **And why do you gaze at** [343] **the speck in your brother's eye,**

---

[343] This passage (verses 3-5) contains four different words that belong to the general area of observation or contemplation. They are as follows:

a. βλέπεις sec. per. sing. pres. indic. active of βλέπω, here probably with continuative force: *gaze at* or *keep looking at*. It is a very common verb (cf. 5:28; 6:4, 6, 18; etc.).

b. διαβλέπεις sec. per. sing. fut. indic. of διαβλέπω, an intensification of βλέπω; hence, *see clearly, look through, penetrate.* Cf. Luke 6:42. In Mark 8:25 probably: *open one's eyes wide.*

while the beam that is in your own eye you do not (even) observe? Or how can you say to your brother, Let me take the speck out of your eye, and look! a beam in your own eye? You hypocrite, first take the beam out of your own eye, and then you will see clearly (enough) to take the speck out of your brother's eye. The beam is a heavy piece of timber fit to be used for the rafter or joist of a building. The "speck" or "mote" is a small piece of straw or of wood, a tiny chip from a beam, perhaps. Now in the figure which Jesus uses he asks the average listener how it is that he is gazing at a mere speck in his brother's eye, and that he even requests permission to remove that speck, while at the same time he completely overlooks the incomparably larger beam in his own eye. Cf. John 8:7!

The question is: Who is this would-be eye-doctor? Answer: he is called a "hypocrite," a word which Jesus generally uses to characterize the scribes and Pharisees of his day (5:20, cf. 6:2, 5, 16; 15:1, 7; 23:13), a class of individuals whom the Lord describes as "those who trusted in themselves that they were righteous and who despised all others" (Luke 18:9). Any person with a Pharisaic disposition is meant, therefore. Since in the hearts of all, including even Christ's followers to the extent in which grace has not yet fully transformed them, there houses a Pharisee, the conclusion follows that this passage applies to all, in the sense that all need to examine themselves (I Cor. 11:28), lest without self-examination and self-discipline they find fault with and strive to correct someone else. A person may be ever so good in his own eyes (Cf. Luke 18:11, 12); yet, if he is not humble, then, as God sees him, there is a beam in his eye, the beam of self-righteousness. This makes him a blind eye-doctor who tries to perform an operation on someone else's eye! However grievous the other man's error may have seemed to the eye of the would-be corrector, was it not a mere "speck" compared with his own self-righteousness, a defect so glaring that in the sight of God it amounts to a beam in the critic's eye?

When by sovereign grace this beam has been removed, the former fault-finder will be able to see clearly enough to take the speck out of his brother's eye; that is, he will then be able to "restore such a person in the spirit of gentleness," and, examining himself in the light, let us say, of I Cor. 13, will look to himself lest he also be tempted (Gal. 6:1).

It is clear from the last clause, in which mention is made of removing the speck from the brother's eye, that it was not Christ's purpose in verses 3-5 to discourage mutual discipline. On the contrary, both self-discipline and mutual discipline are encouraged in this saying. Moreover, to prevent any notion from taking root that the hypercritical attitude denounced in verses 3-5

---

c. ἰδού, discussed on p. 131, footnote 133.

d. κατανοεῖς, sec. per. sing. pres. indic. of κατανοέω; here (and in the parallel Luke 6:41), *take careful notice of, observe.* Cf. Acts 27:39.

might mean that in dealing with errorists patience must be endless, the Lord now adds: **6. Do not give what is holy to the dogs, and do not fling y o u r pearls before the hogs** . . . "Brothers" (see verses 3-5) and "dogs" or "hogs" (verse 6) must not be treated alike. Believers must discriminate carefully.

In order to understand this saying it is necessary, first of all, to discover what is meant by "dogs" and "hogs." Among the Jews the dogs of the street were held in low esteem. The reference here is not to little pet dogs but to pariahs, large, savage, and ugly. One could see them almost everywhere, prowling about the garbage and the rubbish thrown into the streets. They were considered unclean and filthy (Prov. 26:11; cf. II Peter 2:22; Rev. 22:15). They threaten (Ps. 22:16, 20), howl and snarl (Ps. 59:6), are greedy and shameless (Isa. 56:11). In brief, they are contemptible (I Sam. 17:43; 24:14; II Sam. 9:8; 16:9; II Kings 8:13). To be eaten by dogs was a sign of God's special curse resting upon a person (I Kings 14:11; 16:4; 21:24; cf. I Kings 21:19; 22:38).

As to hogs or pigs (in Matt. 8:30-32 and parallel passages, the chosen refuge of demons), these are here viewed as being similarly contemptible and filthy. The Old Testament mentions swine among the unclean animals (Lev. 11:7; Deut. 14:8). In Isa. 65:4; 66:3, 17 the eating of swine's flesh is called an abomination. For the prodigal son to be sent into the fields to feed the pigs must have added to his misery (Luke 15:15, 16). Dogs and hogs are mentioned together not only here in Matt. 7:6 but also essentially in II Peter 2:22: "The dog returns to its own vomit, and the sow has bathed herself, only to wallow in the mud again."

It is clear that by Jesus the expression "what is holy"—that is, set apart from the common sphere, standing in close relation to God and consecrated to him [344] —and "pearls" are here used synonymously. The Greek word for *pearl* is *margaritēs*, from which the given names Margaret and Reta (or Rita) have been derived. Pearls, obtained from the Persian Gulf or from the Indian Ocean, were fabulously priced, way beyond the purchasing power of the average person. In order to obtain a pearl of great value a merchant might have to sell all his possessions (Matt. 13:46; cf. I Tim. 2:9; Rev. 17:4; 18:12, 16; 21:21).

Combining all this, we are now able to conclude that here in 7:6 Jesus is saying that whatever it is that stands in special relation to God and is accordingly very precious should be treated with reverence and not entrusted to those who, because of their utterly wicked, vicious, and despicable nature, can be compared to dogs (see also Phil. 3:2) and hogs. This means, for example, that Christ's disciples must not endlessly continue to bring the gospel message to those who scorn it. To be sure, patience must be exercised,

---

[344] For a more detailed explanation of the concept "holy" see N.T.C. on Philippians, p. 46.

but there is a limit. A moment arrives when constant resistance to the gracious invitation must be punished by the departure of the messengers of good tidings.

Christ's further sayings and also his actions serve as a commentary on Matt. 7:6. How patient he was with Thomas (John 20:24-29) and with Peter (John 21:24-29), but for Herod Antipas, who often had been warned (Mark 6:20) but had disregarded all of these admonitions, Jesus had not a single word (Luke 23:9). He pronounced a curse upon Capernaum, which had failed to take his messages to heart and to apply to itself the lesson taught by his mighty works (Matt. 11:23). He instructed his disciples not to remain too long in those places that would reject their preaching (Matt. 10:14, 15, 23). In the parable of The Barren Fig Tree (Luke 13:6-9) he showed that God's patience, though prolonged, is not endless. Cf. Prov. 29:1.

The apostles took this lesson to heart, as we see, for example, in the case of Paul (Acts 13:45, 46; 18:5, 6; cf. Rom. 16:17, 18; Titus 3:10). Staying on and on in the company of those who ridicule the Christian religion is not fair to other fields that are waiting to be served, especially in view of the fact that the harvest is plentiful but the laborers are few (Matt. 9:37; cf. John 4:35). Besides, the capacity of the disciples to endure persecution so that they will be sufficiently vigorous to continue the work elsewhere has its limits; note the words of the Lord (Do not fling y o u r pearls before the hogs) **lest they trample on them with their feet, and turn and tear y o u to pieces.** In the illustration Jesus pictures the hogs in the act of trampling on the pearls with their feet, thereby treating them with utter disdain. The suggestion may be correct [345] that, since pearls resemble peas or acorns, these hogs, having greedily tasted a few and having discovered that they can do nothing with them, in anger trample the pearls underfoot and turn and tear to pieces those who had flung such non-edibles in front of them. "Let this not happen to the pearl of gospel proclamation nor to yourselves," says Jesus as it were.

As to specific reference, the terms "what is holy" and "pearls" are rather indefinite. They undoubtedly apply to other things besides the gospel message. The office of the ministry, the eldership, and the diaconate must not be entrusted to the unqualified. The *Didache* or *Teaching of the Twelve Apostles* (IX.5) makes still another—I believe legitimate—application, as follows, "But let no one eat or drink of y o u r eucharist [Lord's Supper] except those who have been baptized in the Lord's name. For concerning this also did the Lord say, 'Do not give what is holy to the dogs.' "

Jesus continues: **7, 8. Ask, and it shall be given to y o u; seek, and y o u shall find; knock, and it shall be opened to y o u. For whoever asks receives, and the one who seeks finds, and to him that knocks it shall be opened. Is**

---

[345] See A. T. Robertson, *Word Pictures*, Vol. I., p. 61.

there a connection between these verses and verses 1-6? There are those who see no connection at all. This, however, would be strange. In the entire sermon up to this point we have witnessed a very logical development of ideas, an easy thought transition from one paragraph to the next. Must we suppose that here at 7:7 we are face to face with a sudden break in continuity? I cannot believe it. In the preceding verses Christ has been speaking about man's relation to man. In verse 12 he again—shall we say, "he still"?—dwells on this. Is it not reasonable to assume that also the intervening lines (verses 7-11) refer to a phase of this same theme?

The connection, as I see it, is not difficult to establish. The Lord has been admonishing his listeners to abstain from judging others (verses 1-5), yet also to judge (verse 6); not to be hypercritical, yet to be critical; to be humble and patient, yet not too patient; etc. After a detailed examination of the entire preceding paragraph (verses 1-6) the question cannot be suppressed, "And who is sufficient for these things?" (II Cor. 2:16 A.V.). This question Jesus answers by urging the necessity of persevering prayer accompanied by earnest effort. To be sure, the threefold exhortation ("ask . . . seek . . . knock") is general. It pertains not only to asking for wisdom in the matter to which reference has just been made, but in all matters. In fact, it refers to asking for the fulfilment of every need, particularly every *spiritual* need. Hence, the same threefold exhortation occurs also in a different context (Luke 11:9 f.). And why not? It surely takes but little imagination to understand that an authoritative advice, so singularly precious and so thoroughly practical, would not be spoken just once and then forever laid at rest. Do present-day speakers (including ministers!) never repeat themselves? Accordingly, though the content of verses 7-11 is much broader than any link with the preceding would indicate, it is natural to assume that verses 1-6 *occasioned* the present beautiful little paragraph. Certainly Christ's audience, having listened carefully to Jesus as he urged them to undo habits of long standing and to adopt a mode of life entirely different, and having noticed besides that what he asked of them seemed to be almost self-contradictory, was looking for a solution of this complicated problem. The Lord does not fail them.

Let us, then, first of all examine *the threefold exhortation;* next the promise that accompanies the exhortation and that shows that our obedience to the command will not be in vain. The simplest form of the command is:

Ask

Note the rising scale of intensity, which may be presented thus: "Ask, *seek*, KNOCK." Asking implies humility and a consciousness of need. The verb is used with respect to a petition which by an inferior is addressed to a superior. The Pharisee of the parable (Luke 18:10-13) asks nothing. He *tells* the Lord how good he is. The publican *aks*, that is, *pleads*, "God be merciful to me, the sinner." Asking also presupposes belief in a personal God with whom man can have fellowship. When one asks, he expects an answer. Hence, this implies faith in a God who can, does, and will answer, that is, faith in God the Father. Having such a faith makes the prayer warm and personal. Such a supplicant would not be able to say, "O God, if there be a God, save my soul if I have a soul."

Seek

Seeking is *asking plus acting*. It *implies* earnest petitioning, but that alone is not sufficient. A person must be active in endeavoring to obtain the fulfilment of his needs. For example, one should not only *pray* for a deep knowledge of the Bible but should also diligently *search* and *examine* the Scriptures (John 5:39; Acts 17:11), attend the services (Heb. 10:25), above all strive to *live* in harmony with God's will (see this very section: Matt. 7:21, 24, 25; cf. John 7:17).

Knock

Knocking is *asking plus acting plus persevering*. One knocks again and again until the door is opened. In reality, however, perseverance is probably already implied in all three imperatives, since all are in the present tense; hence, a possible rendering would be "continue to ask, to seek, to knock." This all the more in view of Luke 18:1, 7; cf. Rom. 12:12; Eph. 5:20; 6:18; Col. 4:2; I Thess. 5:17. But what is probable for all three is a certainty with respect to the last, the very idea of biblical knocking already implying perseverance. One continues to knock at the door of the kingdom-palace until the King, who is at the same time the Father, opens the door and supplies whatever is needed (Luke 11:5-8).

As to *the promise* that is fulfilled when the command is obeyed, in each instance the correspondence between command and promise is exact: hence, *ask* is followed by *given; seek* by *find;* and *knock* by *opened.* Note that in verses 6 and 7 this promise, in one form or another, occurs no less than six times. The first three promises, those of verse 7, are virtually repeated in verse 8, and even strengthened by the introductory word *whoever,* the inclusiveness of which is re-emphasized by *the one who* and *to him that,* as if to say, of those who obey the command not a single one will be disappointed. An answer to the kind of prayer that is accompanied by seeking and knocking is promised to every sincere follower of the Lord.

The certainty that persevering prayer accompanied by the activity of faith will be rewarded is strengthened by an argument from the less to the greater, verses 9-11. **Or what man is there among y o u, who, when his son asks him for bread, will give him a stone? Or also (if the son) asks for a fish, will give** him a serpent? If, therefore, y o u, evil though y o u are, know how to give good gifts to y o u r children, how much more will y o u r Father in heaven give good things to those who ask him! Meaning: If even an earthly father—note the words "what *man*"; the supposition is very general—though evil (Ps. 51:1-5; 130:3; Isa. 1:6; Jer. 17:9; John 3:3, 5; Rom. 3:10; Eph. 2:1), will satisfy the reasonable desires of his son, then surely y o u r heavenly Father, who is the source of all goodness, will give good things to those who address to him their humble petitions.

Details of the interpretation:

1. If the son asks for bread (the staff of life, the main dish), his father will not give him a stone, perhaps resembling a cake of bread. He will not deceive his child. Similarly, if the son will ask him for a fish, as a side-dish, which would be very natural in *this* region where fish was abundant, the father will not give him a serpent. Was Jesus thinking of a snake as an ersatz eel? At any rate, for a real father such an act of base deception would be unthinkable.

2. All the more, then, the *heavenly* Father will not disappoint his children. This, however, does not mean that he will always give them whatever they ask. It means that he will not give them anything that is bad for them. He will give "good things" to those who ask him. On the basis of Luke 11:13 the conclusion is valid that the heavenly Father will give his children the Holy Spirit and all his benefits. He will supply whatever they need.

3. Note the importance of prayer in this connection. The Father loves his children and cares for them, but he wants them to *ask* for the things they need.

Christ's followers may rest assured therefore that in answer to their prayers the Father will also day by day provide solutions for the problems with respect to man-to-man relationships, the difficulties arising from the earnest attempt to follow the instructions given in verses 1-6. As far as the *succeeding* context is concerned, could anything be more appropriate as an introduction to the command to treat our neighbors as we like to be treated by them than the admonition "Ask . . . seek . . . knock"? Is it not true that in matters such as these the Father's constant help is definitely needed?

As a very appropriate conclusion not only of 7:1-11 but of the entire large division beginning at 5:17 (and see also 5:5, 7, 9, 13-16) Jesus now presents his own version of

The Golden Rule

12. **Therefore whatever y o u want (other) people to do for y o u, do so also for them. . . .**

In order that the believer may be ready for any emergency, that is, in order that he may know at any definite moment how to conduct himself toward his neighbor, the Lord here in verse 12 lays down a rule which, as it consists of measuring one's duty by one's self-love, is like a pocketknife or carpenter's rule, always ready to be used, even in a sudden emergency when there is no time to ask for the advice of a friend or to consult a book. How does this Golden Rule compare with similar rules outside of Christianity? Is it true, as some seem to believe, that Matt. 7:12 furnishes common ground upon which the believer and the unbeliever can together rear their palace of peace, goodwill, and brotherhood?

There are those who contend that the difference between Christ's rule and that of others, for example, the one laid down by Confucius, consists in this, that the latter rule is merely negative, while Christ's rule is positive. Jesus said, "Whatever y o u want (other) people [literally: men] to do for y o u, do so also for them," but Confucius said, "Do nothing to your neighbor which afterward you would not have your neighbor do to you" (*Mahabharata* XIII.5571). As I see it, however, the difference on this score has been exaggerated. To be sure, when the worst possible interpretation is given to the negative rule, as if it meant no more than, "Do not kill your neighbor and do not steal his marriage partner or his property, for you would not like to have him do this to you either, so, leave your neighbor severely alone," then it must be admitted that in its positive form the rule is far better. However, even in its negative form this rule can be interpreted far more favorably. It can also mean, "Do not treat your neighbor with anything less than genuine love, for you yourself would not want to have him treat you with anything less than genuine love." Thus construed, the negative implies the positive. And must we not in fairness to Confucius grant that he had at least something of this positive implication in mind? Are not his words that were quoted preceded by the line, "This is the sum of all true righteousness, Treat others as you would yourself be treated"? That surely is positive.

Similarly, Jesus teaches that the law with its *negative* commandments ("You shall not kill; you shall not commit adultery," etc.) is fulfilled in obedience to the *positive* rule, "You shall love your neighbor as yourself" (Matt. 5:21 ff.; 19:19; 22:39). Rom. 13:9 is conclusive on this point, "For this, 'You shall not commit adultery, You shall not kill, You shall not steal, You shall not covet,' and if (there be) any other commandment, is summed up in this one rule, 'You shall love your neighbor as yourself.' " Now it is true that in Christ's teaching the emphasis on love for the neighbor, not merely kind treatment, a love, moreover, that is bestowed even upon the enemy, receives greater emphasis than it does outside of Christianity. But it will not do to declare that a rule expressed negatively is, because of that very fact, necessarily inferior to one stated positively.

Nevertheless, there are important differences between Christ's truly Golden Rule and somewhat similar rules that have come to us from the non-Christian religions or are favored by religious liberals. That such rules have a *relative* value must be admitted. There is a sense in which unbelievers do good (I Kings 21:27-29; Matt. 5:46; Luke 6:33; Acts 28:2; Rom. 2:14). Yet, there are important differences between Christ's Golden Rule and whatever may resemble it. These differences are as follows:

1. The non-Christian religious prophet views his rule as a requirement which man is able to fulfil in his own strength, or at best in the strength of someone or something other than the true God, who revealed himself in Jesus Christ. Scripture emphatically denies that he has this ability (John 3:3, 5; II Tim. 3:2; Titus 3:3; etc.). Apart from the operation of the Holy Spirit in the hearts and lives of God's children obedience (even in principle) upon which God's approval can fully rest is impossible (Rom. 7:24; 8:3-8; Phil. 2:12, 13; II Thess. 2:13).

2. The religious liberal has a tendency to separate the rule of love for *man* from the commandment of love for *God*. He generally minimizes the latter's importance. According to his view the Golden Rule is the sum and substance of all ethics. The one important thing in life, as he sees it, is rendering service to fellowmen. It is in support of this contention that an appeal is made to Christ's Golden Rule. But such an appeal is unjustified, for in the sermon the Golden Rule is preceded by a lengthy discourse in which Jesus, by clear implication (cf. Matt. 22:37), teaches us to love God above all. This, as has been shown, implies the inner devotion of the heart to God and undivided trust in him amid all circumstances of life. Now it is in the light of that attitude toward our heavenly Father that we, as his children, are exhorted to love our neighbor, whom God created as his image. To be sure, the rule of the modernist resembles Christ's Golden Rule. Its music is the same in pitch, but not in quality, just as a note played on the piano differs very much in quality from the same note played on an organ. The musical instrument behind the note—that is, the background—is different.

3. The same people who commit the error stated in point 2 generally also misconceive the purpose of the rule, as if it meant, "Therefore whatever y o u want (other) people to do for y o u, do so also for them, *for in the end that will pay.*" Just like honesty, it is "the best policy." In this way the rule's gold degenerates into the pyrite of utilitarianism. Christ's truly Golden Rule is different. It ends with the words **for this is the law and the prophets.** It is that, indeed, for the summary of the law and the prophets (that is, of the Old Testament; see p. 288, including footnote 279) is *love* (Matt. 22:37-40); and love, honest and true, implies self-denial and outgoingness, expressed so beautifully in such passages as Isa. 53:4-6, 12; Matt. 20:28; Mark 10:45; John 3:16; 10:11; Rom. 8:32; II Cor. 8:9; Gal. 2:20; Eph. 5:2; I Tim. 1:15, 16 (climaxed by the doxology of verse 17); and I Peter 2:24.

Notice again the word "Therefore" at the beginning of verse 12. Not only does it link the present passage with the entire large division introduced by 5:17, for through Christ's work in human hearts "the law and the prophets," mentioned both in 5:17 and here in 7:12, attains fulfilment, but it also connects closely with the immediately preceding verses; as if to say, "How much more will y o u r Father in heaven give good things to those who ask him. Therefore—that is, out of gratitude for the Father's continuing gifts—y o u should love y o u r neighbors even as y o u desire that they love yo u, in order that the stream of love toward the undeserving may flow on and on, not only *to* y o u r hearts, but also *through* and *from* y o u r hearts until it reaches even the most unworthy. Thus, indeed, y o u will be sons of y o u r Father who is in heaven, who causes his sun to rise on evil (people) and good, and sends rain on righteous and unrighteous (5:45)." This, indeed, and this alone, is *The Golden Rule.*

Exhortation to Enter the Kingdom

The final main division of the sermon begins at this point. First Jesus says something about

The Beginning of the Way: The Narrow Gate and the Constricted Way versus the Wide Gate and the Broad Way

Jesus has described the citizens of the kingdom, their blessedness and their relation to the world (5:1-16); and also the righteousness which the King grants to and demands of them (5:17—7:12). Hence, it is natural that now in this final division of the sermon he urges all who are reached by his message, whether at the time it was delivered or later, to enter into the kingdom (7:13-27). If they have already done so, then let them enter it more•fully than ever before, or, to change the figure somewhat, let them make sure that they continue stedfastly on the way to which the gate has admitted them. In due order the Lord describes the beginning of the Christians' path, urging his listeners to choose it rather than the unbelievers' boulevard (verses 13, 14); tenders warnings with respect to his followers' progress upon this "way" (verses 15-20); and last of all contrasts the two final destinations (verses 21-27).

Accordingly, Jesus begins by saying: **13, 14. Enter by the narrow gate; for wide (is) the gate and broad the way that leads to destruction, and many are those who enter by it. For narrow (is) the gate and constricted the way that leads to life, and few are those who find it.**

It should be noted that Jesus has already, by way of implication, pictured entrance into his kingdom as being both inviting and difficult, that is, as attended by circumstances both favorable and unfavorable. Favorable, for those who enter are signally blessed. They are the possessors of the kingdom they have entered, are comforted, inherit the earth, shall be fully satisfied, etc. Unfavorable, in the sense that they will be persecuted, insulted, and slandered; and that they are burdened with heavy obligations; for example, they must practice a righteousness that excels that of the scribes and Pharisees; must love even their enemies and pray for their persecutors; must not be hypercritical but must nevertheless be discriminating, etc. Such things are "unfavorable" in the sense that they clash with men's natural tendencies.

It is clear, therefore, that our Lord does not follow the method that is used by certain self-styled revivalists, who speak as if "getting saved" is one of the easiest things in the world. Jesus, on the contrary, pictures entrance into the kingdom as being, on the one hand, most desirable; yet, on the other, not at all easy. The entrance-gate is narrow. It must be "found." And the road with which it is linked is "constricted." J. M. Gibson's remark is to the point, "[Christ's] appeal is made in such a way as shall commend it, not to the thoughtless, selfish crowd, but to those whose hearts have been drawn and whose consciences have been touched by his presentation of the blessedness they may expect and the righteousness expected of them." [346] It is not true that the really great evangelists—think of Whitefield, Spurgeon, and their worthy present day followers—stressed and are stressing this same truth? Was this not also the lesson that Joshua was trying to teach the Israelites (Josh. 24:14-28; see especially verses 14-16; 19)? Cf. Acts 14:22.

The passage speaks of *a.* two gates and two ways, *b.* two kinds of travelers, and *c.* two destinations.

First, then, the two gates and the two ways. It is clear from the description that these—gate and way—should be combined: narrow gate and constricted way, wide gate and broad or roomy way. *Which is first, the way or the gate?* Does a person enter the gate in order to be admitted to the way, or does he follow the way in order to reach and go through the gate? If it be true that Jesus, in mentioning the gate, was thinking of what happens when a person dies or at the second coming, then obviously the way precedes the gate. This presentation has become rather popular; for example, on the basis of Scripture we speak of entering Jerusalem the Golden through its pearly gates (cf. Rev. 21:21; 22:14). In this connection one might also refer to Luke 13:23-30, where entrance through the narrow "door" brings one into "the kingdom of God" in its final or eschatological phase.

On the other hand, however, Matt. 7:13, 14 in each case mentions first the gate, then the way. The question is legitimate, therefore, "Which is first, the way [347] or the gate?

Among the commentators who have struggled with this question—some apparently have not, for they ignore it—the following positions have been taken:

---

[346] *The Gospel of Matthew* (*Expositor's Bible*, Vol. IV), p. 721.

[347] Instead of "way" some prefer the rendering "road." Much can be said in favor of either. Neither is wrong. My slight preference for "way" is based on the fact that it makes the intended thought transition from the physical to the moral-spiritual realm a little easier, since we, too, speak of a "way of life," "way of self-denial and sacrifice," ". . . of obedience, . . . of sanctification," etc.

1. "Possibly Christ's precept was simply, 'enter through the narrow gate,' all the rest being gloss." [348]

Objection: The available manuscript evidence does not warrant such a radical excision.

2. "Each of the two ways leads up to and passes through a gate." According to this view the way is first. So R. V. G. Tasker. [349] So also J. Jeremias, who appeals to Luke 13:23 f., which he regards as a parallel, and which, as he sees it, "makes it plain that the image of the gates has an eschatological character." He, accordingly, views the sequence *a.* gate and *b.* way as "a popular hysteron-proteron" (later-earlier), that is, a figure of speech in which the real order is reversed, like "thunder and lightning." [350]

Objection. The context, and to a certain extent even the wording, of Luke 13:23 f., is so different from what is found in Matt. 7:13, 14 that it is questionable whether the problem can be solved by this appeal. Moreover, calling the figure used by Jesus in the Matthew passage a hysteron-proteron is begging the question.

3. *Gate* and *way* mean substantially the same thing, namely, the obedience demanded by Christ. Viewed as a unit this obedience can be called a *gate;* considered in its multiplicity, a *way.* Therefore one should not even ask, "Which is first, the gate or the way?" [351]

Comment. Inasfar as this solution stresses the very close relation between "gate" and "way" I agree with it, for the text is clear on this. Nevertheless, the text says "gate *and* way," not "gate *or* way," and this not once but twice. Unless this is hendiadys (gateway?), it would seem best to distinguish, however slightly, between the two.

4. "The gate is first. It is followed by the way. . . . In these verses Jesus is not thinking of death but of the choice that must be made right now, and exhorts us to choose, since only by making a conscious choice does one arrive on the right way." [352]

Comment. If a selection should have to be made between theories 1, 2, and 3, I would, without hesitancy, select 3. Nevertheless, I personally prefer the very closely related 4 as being the most natural. The gate is mentioned first, then the way. Also, is it not true that in nearly every case a "gate" admits to a "way," be it a highway or a byway, a street, avenue, boulevard, or path? A gate admitting to nothing is rare indeed. On the other hand, a "way" or "road" does not necessarily lead to a gate. The order "gate"

---

[348] A. B. Bruce, *The Synoptic Gospels* (*The Expositor's Greek Testament,* Vol. I), Grand Rapids, no date, p. 132.

[349] *The Gospel according to St. Matthew* (*The Tyndale New Testament Commentaries*), p. 82.

[350] See the entry πύλη in Th.D.N.T., Vol. VI, especially pp. 922, 923.

[351] H. N. Ridderbos, *op. cit.,* p. 154.

[352] Grosheide, *op. cit.,* p. 91.

followed by "way" is therefore very natural and makes good sense, especially in view of what is probably the intended meaning: right initial choice (conversion) followed by sanctification; or else, wrong initial choice followed by gradual hardening.

The one gate is called "narrow." It has, not unjustly I believe, been compared to a *turnstile* that admits one person at a time. [353] In the New Testament the word *narrow*, with reference to a gate, occurs only in Matt. 7:13, 14. In Luke 13:24 the same adjective is used with reference to an eschatological "door." Cf. Matt. 25:10.

In order to enter by the narrow gate one must strip himself of many things, such as a consuming desire for earthly goods, the unforgiving spirit, selfishness, and especially self-righteousness. The narrow gate is therefore the gate of *self-denial* and obedience. On the other hand, "the wide gate" can be entered with bag and baggage. The old sinful nature—all it contains and all its accessories—can easily march right through. It is the gate of *self-indulgence.* So wide is that gate that an enormous, clamorous multitude can enter all at once, and there will be plenty room to spare. The "gate," then, indicates the choice a person makes here in this life, whether good or bad.

The "way" to which the narrow gate admits is "constricted," or, as we might say today, "It is so confining." [354] The path on which the believer is traveling resembles a difficult pass between two cliffs. It is hemmed in from both sides. So also even in the case of the person who has already spiritually entered through the narrow gate, whatever still remains of the old nature rebels against laying aside evil propensities and habits. This old nature is not completely conquered until the moment of death. So, a bitter struggle develops. Read about it in Rom. 7:14-25. But total victory is assured, for *the narrow gate* has been found and entered, and *the way* of sinners has been exchanged for *the way of the righteous* (see Ps. 1); that is, a conscious choice has been made, a *good* decision. Basic conversion, in turn, has become daily conversion or, if one prefers, sanctification. On the other hand, the "way" to which the wide gate admits is broad and roomy. One might call it Broadway. The signs along this wide avenue read, "Welcome to each of y o u and to all y o u r friends, the more the merrier. Travel as y o u wish and as 'fast' as y o u wish. There are no restrictions." However, "The way of the wicked shall perish."

The contrast is clearly between "the way of life" and "the way of death." The first way was constructed according to the specifications of the Supreme Architect (Heb. 11:10). The building directions are found in his holy law. The other "way" was built by the devil. His followers travel on it.

---

[353] D. M. Lloyd-Jones, *op. cit.*, Vol. II, p. 221.
[354] Greek τεθλιμμένη, nom. sing. fem. perf. pass. participle of θλίβω, *to press upon, crowd.* Hence, the participle here used means *constricted.* Rom. 2:9 has the combination θλῖψις καὶ στενοχωρία, that is, "tribulation and anguish."

Secondly, the two kinds of travelers. Those who have chosen the wide gate and the spacious way are called "many"; those who have entered the narrow gate and are traveling on the constricted way are called "few." This corresponds with Matt. 22:14, "Many are called, few chosen," and with such "remnant" passages as Rom. 9:27; 11:5; etc. [355] Nevertheless, the entire company of the chosen ones are spoken of as an innumerable host (Rev. 7:9).

From what has been said on the preceding pages the erroneous conclusion must not be drawn that the tremendous crowds streaming through the wide gate and now traveling on Broadway are free and happy; while, on the other hand, those individuals who have found the narrow gate and are now proceeding on the constricted way are to be pitied. Actually this "freedom" and "happiness" of the majority is of a very superficial nature. "Everyone who is living in sin is a slave of sin" (John 8:34). He is as truly chained as is the prisoner with the iron band around his leg, the band that is fastened to a chain which is cemented into the wall of a dungeon. Every sin he commits draws tighter that chain, until at last it crushes him completely. Since the wicked have no inner peace (Isa. 48:22), how can they be truly happy?

On the other hand, "Great peace have they that love thy law" (Ps. 119:165; cf. Isa. 26:3; 43:2). Though, as has been pointed out, entering by the narrow gate and walking on the constricted way implies self-denial, difficulty and struggle, pain and hardship, this is especially true because the sinful nature has not yet been completely conquered. For "the new man" (the regenerated nature) there is joy unspeakable and full of glory (I Peter 1:8; cf. Rom. 7:22; Phil. 2:17; 3:1; 4:4; etc.). The "few" who have entered through the narrow gate are "afflicted but not crushed, perplexed but not despairing" (II Cor. 4:8 f.), "sorrowful yet always rejoicing, poor yet making many rich, having nothing yet possessing all things" (II Cor. 6:10). And in addition to the treasures which they possess even now, they know that riches greater by far await them, for "Our light and momentary affliction is producing for us an everlasting weight of glory, far beyond all measure and proportion" (II Cor. 4:17; cf. Rom. 8:18).

Thirdly, the two destinations. Those who have entered through the wide gate and are now walking upon Broadway are headed for destruction, that is, not for annihilation but for *everlasting* perdition (Dan. 12:2; Matt. 3:12; 18:8; 25:41, 46; Mark 9:43; Luke 3:17; II Thess. 1:9; Jude 6, 7; Rev. 14:9-11; 19:3; 20:10). On the contrary, "The way of the cross leads home." It is the way of self-denial that "leads to life" in its full, eschatological sense: *a.* fellowship with God in Christ, first in heaven, subsequently in the new heaven and earth; plus *b.* all the blessings resulting from such fellowship. For

---

[355] I have discussed this "remnant" doctrine in greater detail in the paperback *Israel and the Bible*, pp. 49, 50.

a fuller description examine such passages as Ps. 16:11; 17:15; 23:6; 73:23-36; John 14:2, 3; 17:3, 24; II Cor. 3:17, 18; 4:6; Phil. 4:7, 9; I Peter 1:4, 8, 9; Rev. 7:15-17; 15:2-4; 20:4, 6; 21:1-7; etc. [356]

A twofold reason [357] is given for the exhortation "Enter by the narrow gate." A "twofold" reason rather than two separate reasons, for basic to the entire argument of verses 13 and 14 is this unifying thought: men should choose the gate and the way that lead to life, that is, the narrow gate and constricted way, not the gate and the way that end in destruction, that is, not the wide gate and broad way. Constantly bearing this in mind note the two subordinate arguments: *a.* It is natural to prefer what is wide and broad, easy of access, to what is narrow and constricted; and *b.* It is also natural to follow the crowd rather than the few. Beware!

The exhortation is an earnest plea, a very tender invitation issuing from the most loving heart of all. It is substantially the same as that found in 4:17, "Be converted, for the kingdom of heaven is at hand." It will be repeated in the words of 11:28-30, of John 7:37; and of II Cor. 5:20, to mention but a few passages. It was anticipated or foreshadowed in Isa. 1:18; 55:1, 6, 7; Ezek. 33:11; Hos. 11:8; etc., and is climaxed in Rev. 22:17b. And the wooing heart from which it proceeds was laid bare in Matt. 23:37, on the cross, really throughout Christ's earthly sojourn, and even before (II Cor. 8:9; cf. John 1:14). That heart is beating still!

Warning with Respect to the Believers'
Progress on the Way

This warning is found in verses 15-20. The principle, as usual, is stated first: **15. Beware of false prophets, who come to yo u in sheep's clothing, but inwardly are ravenous wolves.** Does entrance through the narrow gate and proceeding upon the path to which it admits mean that any further caution can now be thrown to the winds? Not at all. To be sure, God preserves his children, but he does this by means of their own God-given perseverance. The enemies are many and shrewd. They are called "false prophets."

A *true* prophet is God's mouthpiece. He was commissioned by God and conveys God's message to men. For the present we may conceive of the false prophet as being self-appointed and as being a person who, though pretend-

---

[356] See my book *The Bible on the Life Hereafter,* pp. 49-78; 205-217.

[357] That is, if, with A.V., A.R.V. (in the text), R.S.V., Berkeley, N.A.S.. and many others we read not only ὅτι πλατεια η πύλη (verse 13) but also ὅτι στενὴ ἡ πύλη (verse 14). Although Grk. N.T. (A-B-M-W) gives the preference to τί (instead of ὅτι) in verse 14, which suggests the exclamatory rendering, "How narrow (is) the gate and constricted the way. . . !", and the *possibility* that this was the original text must be granted, the textual evidence has not convinced me that there is a definite and solid basis for this preference. Besides, reading ὅτι in both cases produces a pleasing balance of clauses.

ing to proclaim God's truth, actually proclaims his own lie. Such a tentative description, though incomplete, as verses 16-20 and especially verses 21-23 will show, fits the requirements of verses 15-20.

The word used in the original for "false prophets" is *pseudo-prophets* (cf. Matt. 24:11, 24; Mark 13:22; Luke 6:26; Acts 13:6; II Peter 2:1; I John 4:1; Rev. 16:13; 19:20; 20:10). In formation it is similar to *pseudo-brothers* (II Cor. 11:26; Gal. 2:4), *pseudo-apostles* (II Cor. 11:13), *pseudo-teachers* (II Peter 2:1), *pseudo-speakers* (liars, I Tim. 4:2), *psuedo-witnesses* (Matt. 26:60; I Cor. 15:15), and *pseudo-Christs* (Matt. 24:24; Mark 13:22). In each case *pseudo* means *false* or *sham.*

Jesus warns his hearers, "Beware of—literally, Hold (y o u r minds) away from—false prophets." Reason: although they "come in sheep's clothing," dressed up in wool as if they were sheep, yet *on the inside* they are savage, rapacious wolves (cf. 10:16; Luke 10:3; John 10:12; Acts 20:29). They are evidently pretenders, hypocrites. That the scribes and Pharisees were included among those of whom Jesus was thinking is well-nigh certain (cf. Matt. 6:2, 5, 16; 15:7; ch. 23). However, in view of 7:21 ff.; John 10:8, 12, it is clear that the description fits many others besides. It applies, in fact, to all those whose influence tends to lead God's children astray, especially to those who *selfishly* and *maliciously* lead astray. The Gospels, book of Acts, epistles, the book of Revelation are full of examples of false prophets (Matt. 27:20; 28:12-15; John 7:41, 42; 9:29; Acts 2:13; 8:18, 19; 15:1; Rom. 6:1; 16:17, 18; I Cor. 15:12; II Cor. 10:10; Gal. 1:6, 9; 3:1; 4:17; 5:2-4; Eph. 5:3-14; Phil. 3:2, 17-19; Col. 2:4, 8, 16-23; II Thess. 2:1, 2; 3:6, 14; I Tim. 1:3-7, 18-20; 4:1-5, 7; 6:20, 21; II Tim. 2:14-18; 3:1-9; 4:3, 4; Titus 1:10-16; 3:9, 10; Heb. 6:4-8; 10:26-28; James 2:17; II Peter 2:1 ff.; 3:3, 4; I John 2:18; 4:1; II John 10; III John 9, 10; Jude 4 ff.; Rev. 2:9, 14, 15, 20-24; 3:9). In fact, one of the dragon's (Satan's) allies is "the beast out of the earth" (Rev. 13:11), who is also called "the false prophet" (16:13; 19:20; 20:10). It is worthy of note that Christ's description of the false prophet, the one who comes in sheep's clothing but inwardly is a ravenous wolf, and the picture presented in Rev. 13:11, "the beast with two horns like a lamb but speech like a dragon," closely resemble each other. In both cases inner essence is in conflict with outward manifestation. False prophets are the representatives of the power of *darkness* (Col. 1:13; cf. Luke 22:53; Acts 26:18; Eph. 6:12) masquerading as an angel of *light* (II Cor. 11:14).

The characterization of the false prophet as the man who lacks divine authorization and brings his own message, generally telling people what they like to hear, is rooted in the Old Testament (Isa. 30:10; Jer. 6:13; 8:10; 23:21). This is the kind of prophet who, when defeat is actually imminent, will say, "Go up and triumph" (II Chron. 18:11). He will shout, "Peace, peace!" when there is no peace (Jer. 6:14; 8:11; Ezek. 13:10). His words are "softer than oil" (Ps. 55:21; cf. John 10:1, 8).

The warning of Jesus against false prophets is "relevant" now as well as when it was first spoken. Today the following are among the slogans used by the modern representatives of this cult of deceit:

"Heaven and hell are myths."

"The God of love will not permit anyone to be punished everlastingly."

"Satan is a myth."

"Sin is sickness. It has nothing to do with guilt. Get rid of your guilt-complex."

"An individual is not responsible for his own so-called sins. The blame, if there is any, rests on the parents or on society."

"In many situations what used to be considered *sin* is not really that at all." Is this what is meant by "situation ethics"? Is it a handy device for condoning extramarital sexuality and other evils?

The destructive intention of the operations of these workers of evil is indicated by the term Jesus uses to describe them: "ravenous wolves." Wolves, with their strong jaws, sharp fangs, and fiendish cunning, mercilessly attack, seize, and kill their prey. The adjective *ravenous* stresses their greed and cruelty. It is related to the verb *to snatch* or *seize* (cf. John 10:12: "And the wolf snatches them"). This word "ravenous" or "greedy," now used as a noun to describe grasping individuals ("extortioners"), also occurs in Luke 18:11; I Cor. 5:10, 11; and 6:10. The church of Jesus Christ, in every age, should be on its guard against those who distort the Word of God for their own selfish purpose. Though their speech may be ever so smooth and oily, they constitute a real peril against which believers must arm themselves (Eph. 6:10 ff.).

In order to do so it is necessary to know who they are. Accordingly, Jesus continues: **16-20. By their fruits y o u will recognize them. Grapes are not picked from thorns, or figs from thistles, are they? So every healthy tree bears good fruit, but the sickly tree bears worthless fruit. A healthy tree cannot bear worthless fruit, neither can a sickly tree bear good fruit. Every tree that does not yield good fruit is cut down and thrown into the fire. Therefore by their fruits y o u will recognize them.** As true as it is that grapes (noble fruit) are not picked from thorns (weeds) nor figs (very precious) from thistles (a nuisance), so true it is also that what is God-glorifying does not issue from a false prophet. Good fruit proves that the tree from which it came is healthy. Worthless fruit shows that the tree from which it fell is sickly. This cannot be otherwise. What a man is in his inner being comes to expression outwardly, especially in words and deeds. Says Luke (6:45) in a similar context (see 6:44), "The good person out of the good treasure of his heart produces good, and the evil person out of his evil (treasure) produces evil; for out of the abundance of the heart his mouth speaks." *Character reveals itself.* To be sure, the false prophet may be able *for a little while* to deceive people, and to hide his real face behind a mask of

373

seemingly pious words and deeds. This cannot last. "Nothing is more difficult than to counterfeit virtue" (Calvin). The fruit will show the true character of the tree.

The question is asked, however, "Just what is meant by this *fruit?* Does it refer to what a person teaches or to how he conducts himself?" That the former is included is clear from the passage just quoted (". . . his mouth speaks"), as well as from such other passages as Matt. 15:9 (see on that passage); Isa. 8:20; Titus 1:9-12; Heb. 13:9; I John 4:1-3; II John 9-11. Calvin may well be right when he says that among the fruits "the manner of teaching holds the first place." By diligently comparing with Scripture the teachings of the man who presents himself as a prophet it will generally not be difficult to detect whether he is a servant of God or of the devil. Cf. Deut. 13:1-5. Nevertheless, the term "fruit" generally includes more than teachings. As used by John the Baptist, by Jesus himself, by Paul, etc., it also indicates a person's life or behavior, as a careful examination of the following passages will show (Luke 3:8-14; John 15:8-10; Gal. 5:22-24; Eph. 5:9-12; Phil. 1:11; Col. 1:10; and James 3:17, 18). [358]

From ever so many passages we learn that "every tree that does not yield good fruit is cut down and thrown into the fire," a text that occurs also in the teaching of John the Baptist. For explanation see on Matt. 3:10. Cf. Ps. 1; 37:20; 73:18-20; Prov. 29:1; Isa. 66:24; John 15:6.

For the sake of emphasis Jesus repeats the important statement, "By their fruits y o u will recognize them," (verses 16 and 20), as if to say, "On y o u r way to glory take careful note of these fruits, whatever they be, that y o u may not be deceived, and y o u r progress may be assured."

The End of the Way: Sayers versus Doers

That the sermon is tending toward the conclusion is clear from the fact that Jesus begins to speak about "that day" (verse 22), a term which in the present connection (note verses 25, 27) is an obvious reference to the great day of the final judgment. Cf. Isa. 2:11, 17; Zeph. 1:15-18; Zech. 14:6; Mal. 3:17; Matt. 24:36; Mark 13:32; Luke 10:12; 21:34; I Thess. 5:4; II Thess. 2:3; II Tim. 1:12, 18; 4:8.

The section, verses 21-27, consists of two brief paragraphs. The first of these (verses 21-23) draws a contrast between *a. mere talkers* or *sayers*, and *b. doers*. The talkers (implied in verse 21a) are those who say, "Lord, Lord," without putting the Father's will into practice. The doers (verse 21b) are those who both say and do what is pleasing to God. The emphasis is clearly on the merely nominal confessors (described again in verses 22-23). The

---

358 While I agree with Lenski's emphasis on teaching, I find his virtual exclusion of conduct a bit extreme (*op. cit.,* p. 293), Calvin's view, it would seem to me, is more well-balanced, as the lists of passages to which I refer would seem to indicate.

second paragraph (verses 24-27) fixes the attention on the same two groups, this time treating them in reversed order, and describing them as *doers* versus *hearers.* The reward that awaits the doers and the ruin in store for the mere hearers are pictured under the vivid symbolism of the house built on rock versus the one built on sand.

The first paragraph begins as follows: 21-23. Not everyone who says to me, Lord, Lord, will enter the kingdom of heaven, but the one who puts into practice the will of my Father who (is) in heaven. Many will say to me in that day, Lord, Lord, in thy name did we not prophesy, and in thy name did we not cast out demons, and in thy name did we not perform many mighty works? That there is a connection between these words and the immediately preceding warning against false prophets (verses 15-20) is clear. Jesus had told his audience to be on guard against false prophets, those who, while telling lies, pretended to be speaking the truth. Did this mean that if a man proclaims the truth he thereby proves himself to be a true prophet? "Not necessarily," says Jesus as it were. A man who speaks the truth but acts the lie is also in a sense a false prophet. Let every person therefore examine not only his neighbor but also himself. As has already been shown, the "fruit" that indicates whether a man is reliable or untrustworthy relates not only to doctrine but also to life. Thus with tremendous force the message is driven home to every heart.

The people whom Jesus condemns are branded as false because in their case life and lip had not been in harmony. Their exclamation "Lord, Lord" had been deceitful. By means of it they also now, on this day of the Great Assize, present themselves as Christ's loyal servants; yet in their previous life they by their actions had constantly been claiming lordship for themselves (Mal. 1:6 ff.; Luke 6:46). But on this day of the last judgment they discover that, whatever may have been their previous success in deceiving others, and perhaps while on earth even *themselves,* they cannot fool the Judge. From the kingdom in its final phase they are excluded.—The lesson is clear: let everyone examine himself! What makes introspection important is that there will be many "sayers" who have not been "doers." Jesus says they have not practiced the will of "my Father. . . ." See p. 215.

As in Matt. 25:34-46 so also here (7:22, 23) what happens on the judgment day is represented under the figure of a dialogue between those who have refused to carry out the will of the Father, on the one hand, and Jesus the Judge, on the other. Even before the verdict is pronounced those about to be doomed realize, as is clear from their words, that it is not going to be in their favor. In this connection it must be remembered that with respect to their souls the great majority of these people have already spent some time in hell. Cf. Ps. 73:12-19; Luke 16:23, 26; Acts 1:25. [359] So now

---

[359] See the author's *The Bible on the Life Hereafter,* pp. 79-82.

that with soul and body they are arraigned before the Judge what else but further doom can they expect? Besides, the very manner in which *their* ranks, in sharp contrast with those of the righteous, have been arranged before the Great Tribunal confirms their fears (25:32, 33). Nevertheless they argue with the Judge.

They address him as "Lord, Lord." Trembling with fear they pronounce this title with awe and reverence, pouring into it far more meaning than they had ever done before the arrival of this crisis of deepest despair. Cf. Ps. 66:3; Mic. 7:17; Phil. 2:11.

Three times, and in each case at the very beginning of the clause, as is clear from the original and from my translation, they appeal to *the name* of Jesus ("in thy name"), as if genuinely intimate union with Christ had been the conscious source both of their preaching and of their miracle-working power. *Actually* they had degraded that very name, having used it merely as a kind of magic formula. But now they appeal to their former use of it, desperately hoping that it may still prove the God-glorifying character of their former words and deeds and may even now secure for them a place in the kingdom of heaven. Cf. 25:11, 12.

In their appeal these false prophets state that in the name of Jesus they had prophesied, driven out demons, and performed many mighty works. Jesus does not deny the claim that they had indeed represented themselves as his ambassadors and that in connection with the invocation of his name they had indeed performed astounding deeds. The question that divides commentators is, "Were these deeds genuine products of supernatural power or were they fraudulent?" II Thess. 2:9, 10 teaches that in connection with the coming of "the lawless one" there will be a mighty display of power, signs, and wonders, all of them false. Acts 19:13, 14 shows that when the seven sons of Sceva, a Jew, tried to imitate Paul's exercise of miraculous power their attempt at exorcism failed miserably. There was also the similar failure of Egypt's magicians to reproduce the third plague, which failure, as many see it, sheds doubt on the genuine character of their earlier "successes" (Exod. 7:22, 8:7, 18, 19). Does not all this point to the possibility that also the demon expulsions and other mighty works of which the false prophets of Matt. 7:22 boast had been nothing but sham? Have not investigations proved again and again that among false prophets illusions, trickery, sleight of hand, etc., abound, and that what is presented as genuine is very often nothing but deception? *Populus vult decipi* ("The people wish to be deceived").

All this, however, must not blind us to the fact that *by God's permission* Satan at times exerts influence upon the physical (as well as upon the moral-spiritual) realm, as is clear from the book of Job (1:12; 2:6, 7). Is it not possible that, by God's power and/or permission, Egypt's magicians had been enabled to change rods into serpents (Exod. 7:11, 12a)? Note, however, that in each case—the one recorded in the book of Job and the one described

376

in Exodus—the end result was a victory for the Lord and for his people (Exod. 7:12b; Job 19:23-27; 42:5, 6). It is unnecessary to exclude the possibility that among the feats of which the false prophets are now boasting there had been some that were accomplished by the aid of supernatural power, whether divine or Satanic. Similarly, it is entirely possible—*probable* even—that the men whom Jesus condemns had actually spoken many a true word when they prophesied in the name of Jesus. Is it not true that the Lord at times makes use of the wicked to proclaim marvelous truths (Num. 23:8-10, 18-24; 24:5-9, 17; Rev. 2:14; Acts 16:16, 17)? Demas may have preached many a fine sermon (Col. 4:14; II Tim. 4:10). And was not even Judas Iscariot among those who were commissioned to heal the sick and to cast out demons (Matt. 10:1)? The reason why the men described here in Matt. 7:22 are condemned is not that their preaching had been wrong and/or their miracles spurious but that they had not practiced what they preached!

It is for that reason that the Lord continues: **And then will I say to them openly, "Never have I known y o u; go away from me, y o u law despisers!"** "Never," that is, not a single moment. Just what does Jesus mean when he says, "Never have I known y o u"? There is a knowledge of the mind. That according to his divine nature Jesus possessed this knowledge in unlimited degree is clear from John 1:47, 49; 2:24, 25; 21:17. It was exactly because he knew the false prophets so thoroughly that he was so completely justified in condemning them. There is, however, also a knowledge of the heart, that is, of electing love, acknowledgment, friendship, and fellowship (Amos 3:2; Nah. 1:7; John 10:14; I Cor. 8:3; Gal. 4:9; and II Tim. 2:19). The connection makes plain that it is this knowledge that is referred to in our passage. The false prophets speak as if Jesus had been their friend. Jesus replies, as it were, "Not for a single moment have I acknowledged y o u as my own, or known y o u to be my friends." When he now forever expels the law-despisers (literally "workers of lawlessness"), he is dooming them to eternal destruction, in body and soul, away from his loving presence (Matt. 25:46; Luke 13:27, 28; II Thess. 1:9).

Before leaving this little paragraph (verses 21-23) attention should be called to the honors to which Jesus here lays claim. He is *Lord* of the universe and all it contains, the sovereign ruler of all men and of all things (cf. 11:27; 28:18; Phil. 2:11; Rev. 17:14). Though, to be sure, it would be wrong to attach to the title "Lord, Lord," uttered by the false prophets during the days of Christ's sojourn on earth (verse 21), the same exalted significance which they attach to it on the day of the final judgment (verse 22), nevertheless even in the former case it must have implied paying lip service to the fact that Jesus was their superior, the One to whom they owed honor and obedience. Again, though during Christ's sojourn on earth the term *kurios* (Lord) with reference to him can hardly have attained to the fulness of meaning which it reached when applied by loyal disciples to the One exalted at the Father's right hand in glory (I Cor. 12:3), yet even when this appellative was used by the men described in 7:21 it must have meant more than simply "Sir" (the meaning which the vocative of this title has in John 12:21, with reference to Philip). When used by true disciples it meant no less than that Jesus was regarded, in an ever ascending measure, as the object of their faith, love, and devotion. [360]

Jesus also claims to be the One who is coming to judge all men. Note: "Many will say to me in that day. . . . Then will I say to them." Cf. 25:31, 32; 26:64; 28:18; John 5:22, 27; Phil 2:9, 10. God through the Lamb, Jesus Christ, will be the Judge (Rev. 20:11-15). Already here in 5:21, 22—hence, rather early in Christ's ministry—we have a clear testimony to the effect that Jesus laid claim to nothing less than being the One to whom the entire world, believing and unbelieving, would be answerable. In a far more detailed manner this tremendous fact will be set forth in 25:31 ff.

Finally, Jesus claims to be *in a unique sense* "God's Son." He says "my Father" (verse 21). Just what does he mean when he says this? In which sense does he call himself, by inference, the Son of God? In the sense in which believers can all say, "Our Father"? Answer: The very fact that he never includes himself when he uses the term "our Father," and, of course, never includes any others when he says "my Father" or "my own Father," shows that he viewed himself as Son of God in a very special sense. He enjoys community of essence with the Father. See John 10:30; also Matt. 11:25-28; 14:33 (Jesus accepted the testimony of the disciples); John 1:18 ("the only begotten God," according to the best reading); 3:16; 5:18 (Jesus called God "his own Father"); etc. Now if, as has been proved, Jesus was conscious of his natural, essential, divine, trinitarian sonship, then is it not reasonable to believe that whenever he used the term "my Father," a reference, direct or indirect, to this divine sonship is never wholly excluded? See the following passages: Matt. 7:21; 10:32; 12:50; 15:13; 16:17; 18:10, 19; 20:23; 25:34; 26:39, 42, 53; Luke 10:22; 22:29; 24:49; John 5:17, 43; 6:32; 8:19, 49, 54; 10:18, 29, 37; 14:7, 12, 20, 21, 28; 15:1, 8, 10, 15, 23, 24; 16:10; 18:11; and 20:17. To be sure, Jesus was God's Son in a fourfold sense: *a.* ethical sonship, being "a child of God"; *b.* official sonship, being the Messiah; *c.* nativistic sonship, being virgin-born, so that God is the Father of his human nature; and *d.* trinitarian sonship, being eternally begotten by the Father, and partaking of the divine essence equally with the Father and the Holy Spirit. But these four are not separate. Do not the first three relationships rest upon the fourth? On "Father in heaven" see pp. 287, 326.

---

[360] See J. G. Machen, *The Origin of Paul's Religion*, pp. 293-317.

The End of the Way: Doers versus Hearers
The Parable of the Two Builders

In close connection with the preceding little paragraph, as has already been shown, Jesus concludes his sermon with the parable [361] of The Two Builders. He said: 24-27. Everyone then who hears these words of mine and puts them into practice will be like a sensible man, who built his house on rock. Down poured the rain, and there came the floods, while the winds blew and fell upon that house, but it did not fall, for it was founded on rock. And everyone who hears these words of mine and does not put them into practice will be like a foolish man, who built his house on sand. Down poured the rain and there came the floods, while the winds blew and beat against that house, and it fell, and the crash it produced was tremendous.

Both of the men mentioned in this parable are *builders*, for to live means to build. Every ambition a man cherishes, every thought he conceives, every word he speaks, and every deed he performs is, as it were, a building block. Gradually the structure of his life rises. Not all builders are the same, however. Some are sensible, some foolish.

Jesus speaks first about the manner in which the sensible man built his house, namely, on rock; secondly, about the test to which this house was subjected; and thirdly, about the result of this test and the reason for this result. He follows the same sequence with respect to the foolish man and the house he built. It is worthy of note that there are only two kinds of builders, not three, four, or five; and that these two form a striking contrast. The Lord is constantly dividing men into two classes. So also in 6:22, 23; 7:13, 14; 7:17, 18; 10:39; 13:11, 12, 14-16, 19-23 (good soil versus soil that is not good, though for various reasons), 24-30, 36-42; 47-50; 22:1-14; 25:2, to mention some of the more striking examples.

Nevertheless, though the two builders differ strikingly, on the surface they have much in common. Each builds a house. The "houses" of which Jesus speaks were not constructed as sturdily as many a present day strict building code would require. Thieves were able to dig through the walls (6:19). The roof, of earth and grass, could easily be "opened up" (Mark 2:4; cf. Ps. 129:6). Everything therefore depended on *the foundation!* Now the two builders also have this in common that both erect their house in a valley containing the bed of a water-course. During the dry season this bed is dry or nearly so, with the result that there is no harm to either house. So far so

---

[361] Though the word *parable* is not used in the text of verses 24-27, we should not hesitate to call it that. When a parable is defined as "an extended simile," or as "an illustrative story in which a comparison is drawn and the word or phrase indicating this comparison (in this case *will be like*) is included," or simply as "an earthly story with a heavenly meaning," it becomes clear that we have every right to call this a *parable.* So also H. N. Ridderbos, *op. cit.,* p. 158.

good.—Is it not true that also among people, including those who were listening to Christ's discourse or those who today read it, there is much surface resemblance?

Essentially, however, how radical is the contrast between the two builders! The first builder is sensible. He has foresight. He figures with the fact that the dry season will not last. Soon the sky will become dark and the black winged legions of the storm will arrive. His house will be deluged by the rains, battered by the winds, and, unless precautionary measures are taken, will be washed away by the rising, swirling tide. So he provides for this imminent peril. Before constructing his house he removes the loose gravel, digging down to rock bottom (cf. Luke 6:48). Then he lays a foundation on rock. [362] —The foolish man does nothing of the kind. He erects his house on the loose gravel, as if bright and sunny days will never cease.

In his explanation of the parable Jesus points out that the figurative meaning of the foundation is "these words of mine," that is, this entire Sermon on the Mount, and, by an extension of the figure, all the words that proceed out of my mouth and are directed to men. Since by means of what he says and commands he reveals his own heart, his very being, it is certainly also correct to say that, as far as the interpretation or spiritual meaning of the parable is concerned, Christ himself is the Rock (Isa. 28:16, cf. I Peter 2:6; Rom. 9:33; I Cor. 3:11; 10:4). What is said about God as the believers' Rock (Deut. 32:15, 18; Ps. 18:2; 89:26; and Isa. 17:10) is also applicable to Christ. See N.T.C. on Ephesians, p. 190. According to the teaching of Jesus here in verse 24 (cf. verse 26) *building one's house on rock means not only listening to the Lord but, out of gratitude for salvation received (certainly implied in 5:1-16), putting his commands into practice.* By the grace of God the sensible man does this; the foolish man, trusting in self and refusing to think about the future, does not. He is a hearer but not a doer. He follows the promptings of his own sinful will.

The day of testing arrives. It comes for *both* houses. Down pours the rain, on and against the house, certainly on top of *the roof.* It is one of those terrific storms which in this region the sudden winds bring up from the Mediterranean. There is cloudburst upon cloudburst. As a result the bed of the water-course is dry no longer. It begins to fill with water, first a brook, shallow and sluggish; then a torrent, deep, swift, and furious, threatening the

---

362 Matt. 7:24 reads τὴν πέτραν. The word πέτρα refers in this context to rocky ground, a rocky foundation. Because of the presence of the article many prefer the translation "the rock" (A.R.V., N.A.S., R.S.V., etc.). This, however, can easily lead to misunderstanding, as if even in the *illustration* a particular rock is meant. Therefore, the translation "on rock" (N.E.B.) or "on rocky foundation" (Williams) is probably better. The contrast is between "rock" and "sand." In Greek we probably have a generic use of the article; hence, it may be omitted in translation: "upon rock," "upon sand."

very *supports* of the walls, whatever it is on which the house stands. And all the while the western gale pommels and pounds against the top and *the walls,* particularly the latter.

So also for every hearer of the gospel, whether he be sensible or foolish, the test or crisis is surely coming. It comes in various forms: trial (Gen. 22:1; book of Job), temptation (Gen. 39:7-18; Matt. 26:69-75), bereavement (Gen. 42:36; Job 1:18-22; Luke 7:11-17; John 11:1 ff.), death (Acts 7:59, 60; 9:37), and in the present context (note verse 22: "in that day") especially the judgment day. Its coming cannot be prevented. Often it arrives with dramatic suddenness (Matt. 24:43; 25:6; I Thess. 5:2).

What is the outcome of this test? The sensible man's house did not fall. Note the play on words: "the winds . . . *fell* upon that house, but it *fell* not." The swirling waters that threatened it were not even able to shake it (Luke 6:48). It braved the tumultous cloudbursts. It withstood the enormous force of the onrushing flood. It defied every furious blast. When the force of the storm was completely spent, there stood that house, none the worse for the elements of nature that had raged against it. Reason: it had been built on rock!

On the other hand, it took hardly any effort for the angry floods to undermine the walls of the other house and to carry away the very sand or gravel on which it had been erected. Moreover, the rain and the wind easily finished whatever was left undone by the tide. All the wind had to do was give the tottering structure a little push. [363] Then, with a tremendous crash, it fell into the water and was washed away, pieces of wreckage strewn about everywhere. Its ruin was complete.

The sensible man, who shows by his very deeds that he has taken to heart the words of Christ, and is therefore building upon the Rock, will never be put to shame. See p. 345. Even the day of judgment will be for him a day of triumph (I Thess. 2:19, 20; 3:13; 4:16, 17; II Thess. 7:10; II Tim. 4:8; Titus 2:13, 14):

> The soul that on Jesus has leaned for repose,
> I will not, I will not desert to his foes;

---

[363] This is clear from the entire picture. It is also possible that the difference in the verbs used in the original to describe the action of the wind against the house built on rock as compared with its action against the one built on sand confirms this fact. In the former case the verb is προσέπεσαν (fell upon, struck against, beat upon with great force); in the latter it is προσέκοψαν (beat against; in John 11:9, 10 stumble). The very fact that the description of the various elements of the storm in their raging against these houses is exactly the same in each case *except* for these two different verbs to indicate the action of the wind would seem to strengthen the possibility that a difference in meaning ("beat upon with great force" over against "stumbled against") is indicated. See also Lenski, *op. cit.,* p. 304.

That soul, though all hell should endeavor to shake,
I'll never, no never, no never forsake.
Stanza from "How Firm a Foundatin," by "K"
in John Rippon's *Selection of Hymns,* 1787.

The theory that Jesus here teaches the doctrine of *works* as the means whereby salvation is achieved is certainly wrong, for the very point of the parable is that *the foundation* of man's everlasting weal is not to be sought in man but in Christ and his utterances, as has been shown. It is upon that foundation that man must build his life, including his hope for eternity.

The ruin in store for those who are building on sand is described at the very close of the sermon, probably in order all the more to impress upon the listeners and on those who afterward would be brought into contact with this earnest message that their reaction to these words of the Lord has significance for all eternity. In reality, therefore, the announcement of the unbelievers' tragic end is a manifestation of Christ's mercy, an implied serious invitation to repent (cf. 4:17), extended to all who are still living in the day of grace.

Matthew appends the following words in order to show the sermon's effect upon the audience: **28, 29. Now when Jesus had finished these sayings the crowds were astounded at his teaching, for he was teaching them as having authority, and not as their scribes.** When Jesus stopped speaking, the large crowd that had been listening spell-bound was left in a state of amazement. In English it is very difficult, perhaps impossible, to reproduce the exact flavor of the picturesque verb used in the original to describe the people's state of heart and mind. In addition to "were astounded" the following have been offered: "were awed," "amazed," "filled with amazement," "dumbfounded," "astonished." The Amplified New Testament has "were astonished and overwhelmed with bewildered wonder." These renderings are all very helpful. The literal meaning of the original is "were struck out of themselves." "Struck out of their senses" has been suggested. Compare also the German "ausser sich gebracht sein" (Lenski, *op. cit.,* p. 305) and the Dutch idiom *"uit het veld geslagen."* The tense of the verb [364] shows that this state of astonishment was not just a momentary experience but lasted for a while.

The question may well be asked, What were some of the reasons for this feeling of wonder and astonishment? Matt. 13:54, 55 may supply part of the answer. Nevertheless, on the basis of the sermon itself and of 7:28 ("not as their scribes") the following items are worthy of consideration:

a. *He* spoke the truth (John 14:6; 18:37). Corrupt and evasive reasoning marked the sermons of many of *the scribes* (Matt. 5:21 ff.).

---

[364] ἐξεπλήσσοντο, third pers. pl. imperf. pass. of ἐκπλήσσω.

b. *He* presented matters of great significance, matters of life, death, and eternity (see the entire sermon). *They* often wasted their time on trivialities (Matt. 23:23; Luke 11:42).

c. There was system in *his* preaching. As their Talmud proves, *they* often rambled on and on.

d. *He* excited curiosity by making generous use of illustrations (5:13-16; 6:26-30; 7:24-27; etc.) and concrete examples (5:21—6:24; etc.), as the sermon shows from beginning to end. *Their* speeches were often dry as dust.

e. *He* spoke as the Lover of men, as One concerned with the everlasting welfare of his listeners, and pointed to the Father and his love (5:44-48). *Their* lack of love is clear from such passages as 23:4, 13-15; Mark 12:40; etc.

f. Finally, and this is the most important, for it is specifically stated here (verse 28), *he* spoke "with authority" (Matt. 5:18, 26; etc.), for his message came straight from the very heart and mind of the Father (John 8:26), hence also from his own inner being, and from Scripture (5:17; 7:12; cf. 4:4, 7, 10). *They* were constantly borrowing from fallible sources, one scribe quoting another scribe. *They* were trying to draw water from broken cisterns. *He* drew from himself, being "the Fountain of living waters" (Jer. 2:13).

Outline of Chapters 8 and 9

Theme: *The Work Which Thou Gavest Him to Do*

CHAPTERS VIII–IX

8 1 When he came down from the mountain large crowds accompanied him. 2 And, lo and behold, a leper came up to him, knelt before him, and said, "Lord, if you will, you can cleanse me." 3 So he stretched out his hand, touched him, and said, "I will; be cleansed"; and immediately his leprosy was cleansed. 4 Jesus said to him, "Be sure not to tell anybody, but go, show yourself to the priest, and, for a testimony to them, bring the offering Moses prescribed."

5 When he entered Capernaum a centurion came up to him asking for help, 6 saying, "Lord, my servant-boy is at home, bed-ridden with paralysis, suffering terribly." 7 And he said to him, "I will come and heal him." 8 But the centurion answered, "Lord, I am not worthy for you to come under my roof, but simply speak the word and my boy will be cured. 9 For I myself am a man under authority, with soldiers under me; and I say to one, 'Go,' and he goes; to another, 'Come,' and he comes; and to my slave, 'Do this,' and he does it." 10 Now when Jesus heard this he was amazed and said to those accompanying him, "I solemnly declare to y o u, with no one in Israel have I found such faith. 11 Many, I tell y o u, shall come from east and west and recline at table with Abraham, Isaac, and Jacob, in the kingdom of heaven, 12 but the sons of the kingdom shall be cast out into the most distant darkness. There shall be weeping and grinding of teeth." 13 And Jesus said to the centurion, "Go home; as you believed, so let it be done for you." And his boy was cured that very moment.

14 And on coming into Peter's house Jesus saw Peter's mother-in-law laid up with fever. 15 So he touched her hand, and the fever left her, and she got up and began to wait on him. 16 And when evening had come they brought to him many who were demon-possessed, and he cast out the spirits with a word, and healed all who were sick; 17 in order that what was spoken through Isaiah the prophet might be fulfilled:
"He has taken our infirmities upon himself,
And carried our diseases."

18 Now when Jesus saw a crowd around him he gave orders to go over to the opposite side. 19 And a certain scribe came up and said, "Teacher, I will follow you wherever you go." 20 Jesus said to him, "The foxes have holes, and the birds of the air roosts, but the Son of man has nowhere to lay his head." 21 Someone else, one of his disciples, said to him, "Lord, allow me first to go home and bury my father." 22 But Jesus said to him, "Follow me, and let the dead bury their own dead."

23 When he stepped into the boat his disciples followed him. 24 Suddenly a violent storm shook the sea, so that the boat was being swamped by the waves; but he was sound asleep. 25 So they came and woke him up, saying, "Lord, save (us), we're perishing." 26 He said to them, "Why are y o u frightened, O men of little faith?" Then he got up and rebuked the winds and the sea; and there was a deep calm. 27 The men were amazed and said, "What kind of person is this, that even the winds and the sea obey him?"

28 And when he came to the opposite side, to the country of the Gadarenes, he was met by two demon-possessed men, coming out of the tombs. So violent were they that no one could pass by along that road. 29 All at once they started screaming, "Why do you bother us, you Son of God? Did you come here to torture us before the appointed time?" 30 Now at some distance away from them a large herd of pigs was feeding. 31 So the demons were begging him, saying, "If you cast us out, allow us to enter that herd of pigs." 32 He said, "Go ahead." So they came out and went into the pigs, and the whole herd rushed headlong down the cliff into the sea and perished in the water. 33 The herdsmen fled, went away to the city, and reported everything, including what had happened to the demon-possessed. 34 Lo and behold, the whole city came out to meet Jesus; and when they saw him they begged him to leave their district.

9 1 So he got into a boat, crossed over, and came to his own city. 2 And behold, they were bringing him a paralyzed man, lying on a bed. When Jesus saw their faith he said to the paralytic, "Take courage, son; your sins are forgiven." 3 At this some of the scribes said within themselves, "This fellow blasphemes." 4 Jesus, knowing their thoughts, said, "Why are y o u thinking evil in y o u r hearts; 5 For, which is easier, to say, 'Your sins are forgiven,' or to say, 'Get up and walk'? 6 But in order that y o u may know that the Son of man has power on earth to forgive sins," (then he said to the paralytic) "Get up, take up your bed, and go home." 7 And he got up and went home. 8 When the crowds saw this they were filled with awe, and glorified God for giving such power to men.

9 As he was passing on from there Jesus saw a man named Matthew, sitting at the tax office, and he said to him, "Follow me." He got up and followed him. 10 In the house, as Jesus was reclining at table, what happens? Many tax collectors and (other) people of low reputation came and reclined at table with him and his disciples. 11 The Pharisees took notice of this, and said to his disciples, "Why is it that y o u r teacher is eating with tax collectors and sinners?" 12 When he heard this he said, "It is not those who are healthy that need a doctor but those who are ill. 13 Go and learn what is meant by:

'I desire mercy and not sacrifice.'

For I did not come to call righteous people but sinners."

14 Then the disciples of John came to him, saying, "Why is it that we and the Pharisees fast often, but your disciples do not fast?" 15 Jesus said to them, "As long as the bridegroom is with them is it possible for the bridegroom's attendants to be mourning? But days will arrive when the bridegroom shall be taken away from them. Then they shall fast. 16 No one puts a patch, made of a piece of new cloth, on an old garment, for then the patch pulls away from the garment, and a worse tear results. 17 Nor is new wine poured into old wine-skins; otherwise the wine-skins burst, the wine is spilled, and the skins are ruined; but new wine is poured into fresh wine-skins, and both are preserved."

18 While he was still saying these things look, a ruler came, knelt before him, and said, "My daughter has just died, but come, lay your hand upon her, and she will live." 19 At once Jesus began to follow him, and so did his disciples. 20 Immediately a woman who had suffered from hemorrhages for twelve years, having come from behind, touched the tassel of his garment; 21 for she said within herself, "If I but touch his garment I shall get well." 22 But Jesus turned, saw her, and said, "Take courage, daughter; your faith has made you well." Instantly the woman recovered. 23 And when Jesus came to the ruler's house and saw the flute-players and the noisy crowd 24 he said "Go away, for the girl is not dead but asleep." But they were laughing in his face.

25 When the crowd had been expelled he entered and took her by the hand,. and the girl got up. 26 The news about this spread throughout that entire region.

27 And as Jesus passed on from there, two blind men followed him, constantly crying out, "Take pity on us, Son of David." 28 And when he had gone inside the house the blind men came up to him, and Jesus said to them, "Do y o u believe that I am able to do this?" They said to him, "Yes, Lord." 29 Then he touched their eyes and said, "According to y o u r faith let it be done for y o u." 30 And their eyes were opened. And Jesus sternly warned them saying, "See that no one finds out!" 31 But when they had departed they spread the news about him throughout that entire region.

32 As they were departing there was brought to him a demon-possessed man who was unable to speak. 33 When the demon had been cast out the dumb man spoke. The crowd was filled with amazement and said, "Never has anything like this been seen in Israel." 34 The Pharisees, however, were saying, "By the prince of the demons he casts out the demons."

8:1—9:34 *A Series of Early Miracles. Follow Me. Fasting versus Feasting*

Cf.

Matthew	Mark	Luke
8:1; cf. 7:29		
8:2-4	1:40-45	5:12-16
8:5-13		7:1-10
8:14-17	1:29-34	4:38-41
8:18, 23-27	4:35-41	8:22-25
8:19-22		9:57-62
8:28-34; 9:1	5:1-20	8:26-39
9:2-26	2:1-22; 5:21-43	5:17-39; 8:40-56
subdivided:	subdivided	subdivided:
9:2-8	2:1-12	5:17-26
9:9-13	2:13-17	5:27-32
9:14-17	2:18-22	5:33-39
9:18-26	5:21-43	8:40-56
9:27-34		
subdivided:		
9:27-31		
9:32-34		

The arrangement of Matthew's material, so that a specimen of the preaching of Jesus (chaps. 5—7) is here followed by a group of miracle narratives, has already been examined. See pp. 26-28. Matthew's arrangement, accordingly, is topical rather than chronological. Room must be left for the possibility that while 8:2-4; 8:14-17; and 9:2-13 refer to events that preceded the Sermon on the Mount, 8:5-13; 8:18—19:1; and 9:14 ff. record what happened afterward.

That 4:16 is indeed true, so that those who sat in darkness saw a great light, has been shown in the Sermon on the Mount; and cf. 4:23a. That this light shone also in *deeds* was indicated in 4:23b-25, and will now be proved in greater detail.

A Leper Cleansed

Matthew begins this section as follows: **8:1. When he came down from the mountain large crowds accompanied him.** The state of astonishment recorded in the immediately preceding verses (7:28, 29) accounts for the fact that the people did not immediately forsake Jesus when the sermon was ended. When he descended from the mountain they continued to follow and surround him, and may well have been joined by others who had not heard him speak; note the plural: "large crowds." He was now on his way to Capernaum (5:1; cf. Luke 7:1). However, *exactly* when and where the miracle, about to be studied, occurred is not stated in the Gospels, not even in Mark 1:40 or in Luke 5:12. It is enough for us to know that this deed of sympathy and power "was not done in a corner" (cf. John 11:47; Acts 4:16; 26:26). There were ever so many eye-witnesses.

Continued: **2. And, lo and behold, a leper came up to him knelt before him, and said, Lord, if you will, you can cleanse me.** The disease which we today call leprosy generally begins with pain in certain areas of the body. Numbness follows. Soon the skin in such spots loses its original color. It gets to be thick, glossy, and scaly. In fact, the affliction is called *leprosy* because it makes the skin *scaly,* the Greek word *lepos* or *lepis* meaning *scale.* [365] As the sickness progresses, the thickened spots become dirty sores and ulcers, due to poor blood supply. The skin, especially around the eyes and ears, begins to bunch, with deep furrows between the swellings, so that the face of the afflicted individual begins to resemble that of a lion. Fingers drop off or are absorbed; toes are affected similarly. Eyebrows and eyelashes drop out. By this time one can *see* that the person in this pitiable condition is a leper. By a touch of the finger one can also *feel* it. One can even *smell* it, for the leper emits a very unpleasant odor. Moreover, in view of the fact that the disease-producing agent frequently also attacks the larynx, the leper's voice acquires a grating quality. "His throat becomes hoarse, and you can now not only feel, see, and smell the leper, but you can hear his rasping voice. And if you stay with him for some time, you even imagine a peculiar taste in your mouth, probably due to the odor. All the senses of the well person are engaged in the detection of the leper." [366]

---

365 In connection with Matt. 6:19 it has already been observed that a term formed, in part, from a similar stem, namely, the term *lepidoptera*, indicates the insects, including moths, with *scale*-covered wings. Acts 9:18 reports that there fell from Paul's eyes, as it were scales (λεπίδες).

366 L. S. Huizenga, *Unclean! Unclean!*, Grand Rapids, 1927, p. 149. Having read Dr. Huizenga's book, listened to some of his lectures, and benefited by his answers to my

The Old Testament references to leprosy can be summarized as follows:

Exod. 4:6, 7: The hand of Moses, placed in his bosom, becomes leprous, as is evident when it is taken out. When the action is repeated, the leprosy has disappeared. This is a sign for the Egyptians.

Lev. 13: Method described whereby the priest can detect leprosy. Ordinance for the isolation of the leper (Lev. 13:46; cf. Num. 5:1-4; II Kings 15:5; and II Chron. 26:21).

Lev. 14: Offerings prescribed in connection with the cleansing of the leper.

Num. 12:10: Miriam's effrontery punished with leprosy. See also 12:13-15.

Deut. 24:8, 9: The previous commandments respecting leprosy reaffirmed, with reminder of Miriam's punishment.

II Sam. 3:29: David's curse on the house of Joab, including the stipulation "May it never be without a leper."

II Kings 5 (especially verses 14 and 27): Naaman cured of his leprosy; Gehazi punished with it.

II Kings 7: The four lepers of Samaria: their peculiar situation, courageous resolution, surprising discovery, and exemplary response to duty.

II Chron. 26:19-23 (cf. II Kings 15:5): Uzziah follows Miriam's example, and is similarly punished.

As some see it, the "leprosy" mentioned in the Old Testament is not equivalent to what today is called leprosy. Others disagree. Dr. Huizenga, basing his conclusion upon a detailed study of all the pertinent biblical material and on his own experience with lepers, states: "I believe that Moses describes a definite disease—a disease which corresponds to what we today call leprosy, although the symptoms may not be the same." [367]

The New Testament references are as follows:

The present passage, Matt. 8:1-4 (cf. Mark 1:40-45; Luke 5:12-16).

Matt. 10:8: "Cleanse the lepers."

Matt. 11:5 (cf. Luke 7:22): "The lepers are cleansed."

Luke 4:27: "There were many lepers in Israel . . . none of them was cleansed except Naaman the Syrian."

Luke 17:11-19: The ten Samaritan lepers who were cleansed, only one of whom returned to give thanks.

---

questions, I hereby acknowledge my debt to him. I have had somewhat similar personal contact with another famous Christian doctor, namely, E. R. Kellersberger. Both of these great medical missionaries, during their earthly careers, in a very remarkable way fulfilled their task: "Preach . . . heal the sick, cleanse the lepers." See Kellersberger's article, "The Social Stigma of Leprosy," reprinted in pamphlet form from *The Annals of the New York Academy of Sciences*, 54 (1951), pp. 126-133. Add to this articles on Leprosy in various encyclopaedias, including I.S.B.E. and Britannica (1969 edition); and S. I. McMillen, *op. cit.*, pp. 11-14.

[367] *op. cit.*, pp. 145, 146; see his entire argument, pp. 143-147.

Matt. 26:6-13 (cf. Mark 14:3-9): Jesus is anointed at the home of Simon the (former) leper.

Is leprosy contagious? The authorities consulted agree that leprosy is *not very* contageous. Many missionaries have worked among lepers for years and have never been infected with this dread disease. There are exceptions, however. The contageous character of leprosy is confirmed by *a.* the fact that it frequently happens that the Japanese baby who is carried in a sling on its mother's back, in such a manner that his forehead is in habitual contact with the nape of its mother's neck, "catches" the disease from the infected parent, the first evidence of the transmission appearing on the infant's forehead; and *b.* the well attested gradual spread of the scourge once it has entered a region. As Dr. McMillen sees it, this infectuous character of leprosy shows the wisdom of the legislation found in Lev. 13, according to which the leper was to be isolated from the community. [368]

Nevertheless, it is not the contagious character of leprosy that is emphasized in Scripture but rather the fact that it renders the afflicted person ceremonially "unclean" and shuts him off from social and religious contact with his people.

Can leprosy be cured? The fact that in ancient times it was regarded as virtually incurable is confirmed by the following incident: Syria's ruler sent a letter to Israel's king, in which he said, "When this letter reaches you, know that I have sent to you Naaman my servant, that you may heal him of his leprosy." The result? Israel's king tore his clothes and exclaimed, "Am I God, who can kill or restore to life, that this fellow has sent a man to me that I may cure him of his leprosy?" (II Kings 5:7). Though today it is admitted by specialists in this field that there are sporadic cases in which persons afflicted with the dread disease recover without treatment, and though in modern times sulfone and even newer drugs have had favorable results, the fact remains that until recent times leprosy was generally regarded as an incurable affliction. The rabbis considered the healing of a leper as difficult as raising the dead. Yet, God is able to cleanse the leper, as Num. 12:13-15; II Kings 5:14; Matt. 8:2-4 (and parallels); 11:5; Luke 7:22; and 17:11-19 clearly prove; but at the moment when Jesus was confronted with the leper mentioned in our passage, Matt. 8:2-4, the healings recorded in the New Testament had not yet occurred, and the Old Testament cures were known to have been very few indeed. All in all, therefore, from a purely human standpoint the prospects did not look at all favorable.

Not only this, but a leper might well shrink from the very suggestion of even approaching someone for help, for leprosy was by most people regarded with superstitious horror, as it is also today. "There is one fact that makes leprosy different from all other diseases, and that is the social stigma

---

[368] *op. cit.*, pp. 12-14.

connected with it. . . . This mark of infamy or disgrace . . . sets its victims apart from all other people. I have found this to be universally true as I have traveled around the world ferreting out these unfortunates from their hiding places. . . . Everywhere the social stigma of leprosy is the same." [369]

From Job 4:7; 8:20; 11:6; 22:5-10; Luke 13:1-5; and John 9:2 we gather that the erroneous but almost universal notion (cf. Acts 28:4) according to which a bitterly afflicted person must be notoriously wicked, a superstition refuted by Jesus, was prevalent also among the Jews. We can well imagine, therefore, that if the leper, mentioned here in Matt. 8:2-4, should have attempted to approach the average Jew, the latter, unwilling to become ceremonially "unclean" or to be seen near an individual upon whom the dreadful curse of the Almighty was thought to rest, would have rushed for shelter, meanwhile drawing the folds of his outer garment together in order not to become contaminated. Most lepers, accordingly, would have despaired of ever being cleansed. Even those few who dared to hope would have "stood afar off" (Luke 17:12) as they cried out for help.

But, "lo and behold," [370] *this* leper steps right up to Jesus, drops to his knees right in front of him, and, even more humbly, falls on his face (Luke 5:12), putting his whole soul into this act of reverence and adoration. [371] As he does this he says, "Lord, if you will, you can cleanse me."

He is sure of Christ's *power* to heal, to heal even a leper, in fact a man *full* of leprosy (Luke 5:12), that is, afflicted with leprosy in a very advanced stage! As to the Master's *will* to effect the cure, to this *will* the leper submits himself completely. After all, Jesus knows what is best. Naturally, he fervently hopes that the One before whom he is prostrating himself will indeed rid him of this dreadful illness. His statement, in the form of a confession of faith, implies an urgent request.

Where did he get this trust in the Savior? Is it not altogether probable that he had heard about the earlier miracles performed in this general region (Matt. 4:23, 24; Mark 1:21-32, 39; Luke 4:31-41; and John 2:1-11; 4:46-54)? The Lord had applied this knowledge to his heart. Whether or not the leper already saw, however faintly, that by means of Christ's words and miracles Messianic prophecies were being fulfilled we do not know. It should suffice to honor his memory by stating that his touching confidence in the power of Jesus to heal even him, whose condition was probably by everybody else considered to be hopeless, should serve as a model for all. We may be sure that when this man called Jesus "Lord" (see on 7:21-23), he meant far more than "Sir."

Continued: **3. So he [Jesus] stretched out his hand, touched him, and said, I will; be cleansed.** Repeatedly the Gospels speak about the healing

---

[369] Kellersberger, *op. cit.*, p. 126.
[370] See footnote 133 on p. 131.
[371] For προσκυνέω (here προσεκύνει) see on Matt. 2:2, 8, 11.

touch of Christ's hand (to 8:3 add 8:15; 9:18, 25, 29; 17:7; 20:34; Luke 7:14; 22:51). Sometimes the sick would themselves touch Jesus (Matt. 9:20-22; 14:36). Either way the afflicted ones were healed. Evidently in connection with such physical contact healing power issued from the Savior and was transmitted to the person in need of it (Mark 5:30; Luke 8:46). This, however, was no magic! The healing power did not originate in his fingers or his garment. It came straight from the divine and human Jesus, from his almighty will and infinitely sympathetic heart. There was healing power in that touch because he was, and is, "touched with the feeling of our infirmities" (Heb. 4:15). It should not escape the reader that according to Mark 1:41 Jesus was "moved with compassion" when he stretched out his hand and touched the leper. The leper's need and faith found an immediate response in the Savior's eagerness to help. And this readiness was one in which his power and his love embraced each other.

It is sometimes said that between the words of the leper and those of Jesus there is perfect correspondence. This is correct in the sense that the two statements do not clash but are in full harmony, revealing even a partial identity of phraseology. One could also say, however, that the words of the Lord excel mere "correspondence." To be sure, the leper's "you can cleanse me" is answered by Christ's "I can, indeed!" implied in his act of healing. But the leper's "*if* you will" is superseded by the Master's swift and splendid "I will." Here the *will* joins the *power,* and the subtraction of "if" conjoined with the addition of "Be cleansed" transforms a condition of hideous disease into one of hardy health. **And immediately his leprosy was cleansed.** The restoration was immediate and complete. The forehead, the eyes with brows and lashes, the skin, the mucous membrane of nose and throat, the fingers and toes, whatever parts of the body had been infected and damaged by the leprosy bacillus (mycobacterium leprae) were in an instant completely restored! Better still: the door of thorough social, cultic, and religious restoration was opened wide for this man, as is shown by what follows, namely, verse 4. **Jesus said to him, Be sure not to tell anybody, but go, show yourself to the priest, and, for a testimony to them, bring the offering Moses prescribed.**

What was the reason for the restraint placed on this man? The context does not plainly state the reason. Wrede's very speculative "Messianic secret" idea, discussed and refuted earlier (see pp. 60, 61), can be dismissed without any further consideration. The following suggested reasons for commanding the cleansed leper to be silent deserve mention:

a. The man is ordered to rush to the temple at Jerusalem, so that an examination by the priesthood, in accordance with the laws of Moses (Lev. 14, as noted above), can at once be conducted, and he can be pronounced cured of his leprosy and qualified to bring the required offerings. When it is subsequently discovered by the priests that it was Jesus who had healed this man, the clean bill of health already given to him will serve as a testimony regarding Christ's respect for the Mosaic law (cf. Matt. 5:17) and regarding his love and power employed for the benefit of those in need. By means of this testimony the priests who nevertheless reject him will be condemning themselves, for such rejection will be in conflict with the evidence based on their own findings. This presupposes, of course, that as soon as the leper was healed by Jesus he must *immediately* go to Jerusalem. He must not delay, for in that case the news that it was *Jesus* who had restored him to health might reach the priests before the former leper himself did, with the result that the Jerusalem hierarchy, hating Jesus, would probably refuse to pronounce the applicant cleansed. Accordingly, the leper must not take any time to first tell the neighbors, etc., about the miracle. [372]

b. Jesus must not become known chiefly as a miracle-worker, "a mere thaumaturgist," but rather as the Savior from sin. [373]

c. Too much publicity with reference to Christ's miracle-working power would have so fanned the flames of enthusiasm about him as a potential Deliverer from the Roman yoke that the opposition and envy roused by such widespread attention might have brought his public ministry to an untimely end. [374]

d. It would not have been proper for Jesus, *during the days of his humiliation,* to encourage widespread acclaim. [375]

The reason why it is so hard to choose between these possibilities is not that they are so bad or unreasonable, but rather the opposite. Theory *a.* looks like an ingenious attempt to honor the context. Theory *b.* is in line with the fact that again and again Jesus himself rebuked the yearning for signs and miracles (Matt. 16:1 ff.; Luke 4:23 ff., John 4:48; etc.). Theory *c.* agrees with the fact that Jesus was indeed very conscious of the fact that he had been appointed to carry out the work which his Father had given him to do, every detail of which task had been definitely marked off in the eternal decree, so that for each act there was a stipulated moment (John 2:4; 7:6, 8; 7:30; 8:20; 12:23; 13:1; and 17:1). And theory *d.* can and does appeal to Matt. 12:15-21.—It is possible that any *one* of these considerations (whether *a* or *b* or *c* or *d*) may have been the one Jesus had in mind when he said, "Be sure not to tell anybody," etc. Is it not also possible that a combination of two or more of the reasons given, and perhaps even others besides, prompted him to say it?

The man's disobedience to the command, though understandable, cannot

---

[372] Along this line Lenski, *op. cit.,* pp. 311, 312.

[373] Cf. N. B. Stonehouse, *The Witness of Matthew and Mark to Christ,* Philadelphia, 1944, p. 62.

[374] Stonehouse, same page.

[375] Cf. H. N. Ridderbos, *op. cit.,* p. 162. The same thought is expressed more than once in his *Zelfopenbaring en Zelfverberging,* Kampen, 1946; see especially p. 76.

be condoned. Its results for Christ are noted. But this is Marcan material (1:45; see, however, also Luke 5:15), and requires no discussion in the present connection.

A Centurion's Servant Healed

The record of this miracle is found in Matt. 8:5-13 and Luke 7:1-10. It should not be confused with the event reported in John 4:46-54. *That* story has to do with a royal officer's *son;* this one with a centurion's *servant.* John 4:46-54 places Jesus in Cana; in Matt. 8:5 ff. he is entering Capernaum. The supplicant mentioned in the former could not immediately conceive of Jesus' power to heal at a distance; the centurion himself took the initiative in declaring that Jesus had this power.

There are also several important differences between the miracle recorded here in Matt. 8:5-13 and the one covered in the immediately preceding paragraph. The leper was able to come to Jesus, not so the paralytic. His master intercedes for him. In both cases the main interest centers in Jesus, in what *he* says and does. As to focus of interest, next in order in the former story is the afflicted one himself; in the latter, the afflicted person's master. The former was living under the regime of the Jews (see Matt. 8:4). The latter, that is the centurion, was a Gentile by race, an officer in the Roman army of occupation. The former was healed by Christ's word plus the touch of his hand; the centurion's servant, solely by the word of power. We cannot say that *everything* reported in the Gospels regarding the leper is favorable (see Mark 1:45); the centurion, on the contrary, receives nothing but exuberant praise. Finally, verses 2-4 end with a command addressed to the healed leper; verses 5-13, with a prediction regarding the salvation of many Gentiles versus the rejection of a host of Jews, and with the mention of Christ's word and act of healing.

The present paragraph opens as follows: **5, 6. When he entered Capernaum a centurion came up to him asking for help, saying, Lord, my servant-boy is at home, bed-ridden with paralysis, suffering terribly.** The centurion was an officer in the pay of Herod Antipas, whom we have met before (see pp. 189, 240). This officer had heard what Jesus had done for others (Luke 7:3). So now he pleads that the same mercy be shown to his own slave (Luke 7:2), whom he affectionately calls "my boy."[376] The latter's condition was indeed deplorable. Being bed-ridden with paralysis, he was "suffering terribly," "fearfully tortured." Was this a case of progressive paralysis with muscular spasms dangerously affecting his respiratory system, bringing him to the very portals of death, as Luke suggests?

---

[376] It is true that "boy" (Greek παῖς) for "slave" or "servant" (δοῦλος) was not itself exceptional terminology. Yet, the present context—note the centurion's manifest concern here in Matthew, and "was dear to him" in Luke—shows that the appellation is here used in its most favorable sense, as a term of endearment.

The centurion's heart was in his plea, for the boy "was dear to him." The words of the officer amounted to a *statement* rather than a request. It was a statement describing the lad's condition, and trustfully leaving the disposition in the hands of Jesus. Nevertheless, *implied* was a request for help: "He came up to him asking for help." [377]

According to Matthew it was the centurion himself who informed Jesus about his need. Luke, on the other hand, says that the officer sent some elders of the Jews with this request. This involves no contradiction, for it was through these elders that the centurion's plea was made known to Jesus. When Matt. 27:26 reports that Pilate scourged Jesus this does not mean that the governor applied the scourge with his own hand. Even today we frequently make use of abbreviated diction. See N.T.C. on the Gospel according to John, Vol. I, p. 206.

However, according to Luke's account (7:4, 5) the elders were more than mere transmitters of a message. As, through them, the centurion was interceding for his "boy," so the elders, in turn were interceding for the centurion. They said, *"He is worthy* to receive this favor from you, for he loves our nation, and he built the synagogue for us."

The Lord's answer was all that anyone could have wished, and far more than the centurion had dared to expect. It was not, "Why did you wait so long?" Nor, "Since you represent the oppressor I can do nothing for you." Nor even, "I will see what I can do." It was the thrilling, unequivocal, concise, and positive assurance found in the next verse: 7. **And he said to him, I will come and heal him.** According to the original that pronoun "I" is very emphatic, as if to say, "I myself," "I without any doubt."

Continued: **8, 9. But the centurion answered, Lord, I am not worthy for you to come under my roof, but simply speak the word and my boy will be cured. For I myself am a man under authority, with soldiers under me; and I say to one, Go, and he goes; to another, Come, and he comes; and to my slave, Do this, and he does it.** "He is worthy," the elders had said. But the centurion, on hearing Christ's answer, becomes overwhelmed with the sense of unworthiness. After all, who is *he* in comparison with this Exalted One, this personal embodiment of majestic authority, all-embrasive power, and condescending love, a love that bridges every chasm and overleaps every obstacle of race, nationality, class, and culture? Who is *he* to cause this kind Master to commit an act that would put him in conflict with the time-honored custom of his own people, according to which a Jew does not enter the house of a Gentile lest he be defiled (John 18:28; Acts 10:28; 11:2, 3)? Let Jesus therefore not enter the house nor even approach too closely but let

---

[377] For the meaning of παρακαλέω and παράκλητος see N.T.C. on the Gospel according to John, Vol. II, pp. 276, 277.

him simply speak the word of healing. That is all that will be necessary to bring about a complete cure.

The centurion reasons: If, though I am but a military officer with very limited authority and power, an officer who must himself obey his superiors, even *my* orders are immediately carried out by both soldier and slave, then certainly *he*, this Great One, exercising independent authority and holding the universe in his all-powerful grasp, can command, and whatever it is that he desires will be done. When he says "Go," sickness will go, and when he says, "Come," health will arrive.

Here, again, the fact that according to Luke this message was not spoken to Jesus directly but was on the Lord's approach conveyed to him by the centurion's friends, can, with Augustine and many after him, be explained as in the previous instance; see above, on verses 5 and 6; compare Matt. 8:5 with Luke 7:3, and then Matt. 8:8 with Luke 7:6. We are justified, perhaps, in assuming that the centurion, having gone outside, and having seen Jesus approaching, hurriedly sent his friends to him. The message was in any case the centurion's own answer to Jesus, which is what both Matthew and Luke are saying. [378]

10. **Now when Jesus heard this he was amazed and said to those accompanying him, I solemnly declare to y o u, with no one in Israel have I found such faith.** Jesus was astonished, and for a reason contrary to that mentioned in Mark 6:6. The words "I solemnly declare" (see on 5:18) are a fitting introduction to the expression of this amazement. To the large crowds that accompanied him (see verse 1), including undoubtedly the centurion's friends just now arrived (Luke 7:6), he revealed that the faith of this man of Gentile origin surpassed in excellence anything he had found even among the Jews, in spite of the latter's special privileges. To be sure, also in Israel Jesus had found faith (Matt. 4:18-22; 5:1-16; 7:24, 25), but not a combination in one person of a love so affectionate, a considerateness so thoughtful, an insight so penetrating, a humility so outstanding, and a trust so unlimited. In many cases was not what Jesus had found *"little* faith" (6:30)? It had taken the court officer whose story is told in John 4:46-54 a long time to grasp the fact that Jesus was able to heal even at a distance. The centurion of Matt. 8:5-13 grasped this fact immediately!

As Jesus sees it, this faith of the centurion affords a foreglimpse of events that are to occur in the world of the Gentiles as contrasted with that of Israel. He says, 11, 12. **Many, I tell y o u, shall come from east and west and recline at table with Abraham, Isaac, and Jacob, in the kingdom of heaven, but the sons of the kingdom shall be cast out into the most distant darkness.** As was pointed out earlier (see pp. 91, 92, 98, 191), the Gospel of Matthew

---

[378] Not only Matthew but also Luke presents this view. See Luke 7:6 in the original; note the present participle *singular:* λέγων ("he saying").

has a braod missionary purpose. The evangelization of all the nations is one of its outstanding objectives. The passage now under discussion fits into this scheme. The fact that many shall come from east and west, that is, from everywhere, to share the blessings of salvation with the patriarchs, in other words that the church will be extended among the Gentiles, was predicted by the prophets. Again and again they dwelt on this theme (Isa. 2:2, 3; 11:10; 45:6; 49:6, 12; 54:1-3; 59:19; Jer. 3:18; 31:34; Hos. 1:9, 10; 2:23; Amos 9:11 ff.; Mic. 4:1, 2; and Mal. 1:11).

The blessings of salvation in which all the saved shall share are here pictured under the symbolism of together reclining (according to the prevailing custom) on couches at a table loaded with food, enjoying sweet fellowship with each other and with the host, in a spacious banqueting hall flooded with light. See also Ps. 23:5; Prov. 9:1-5; Isa. 25:6; Matt. 22:1 ff; 26:29; Mark 14:25; Luke 14:15; Rev. 3:20; 19:9, 17. It is not surprising that here, as so often in Scripture, Abraham, Isaac, and Jacob are mentioned in one breath, for it was to them that the promises had been made. Cf. Gen. 28:13; 32:9; 48:16; 50:24; Exod. 3:16; 6:3; 32:13; Deut. 1:8; 9:5, 27; 29:13; 30:20; I Chron. 29:18; Matt. 22:32, Mark 12:26; Acts 3:13; 7:32.

This sharing of the Gentiles in the blessings of the Jews started to happen already during the old dispensation (I Kings 8:41-43; 10:9; Jer. 38:7-12; 39:16-18), has been taking place on a much larger scale during the entire new dispensation, and will become evident especially when the countless multitude gathered out of every nation will be standing before the throne (Rev. 7:9).

On the other hand, the "sons of the kingdom," that is, the Jews, called thus because of the many kingdom privileges they had enjoyed (Ps. 147:20; Isa. 63:8, 9; Amos 3:2; Rom. 9:4; Eph. 2:12), shall be cast into the *most distant* darkness, that is, symbolically speaking, far away from the banqueting hall flooded with light. Reason: see Luke 12:47, 48. O(pportunity) plus A(bility) = R(esponsibility). The large scale rejection of Christ by the Jews is clear from Scripture (Matt. 27:25; John 1:11; I Thess. 2:14-16; and Rev. 2:9). This does not mean that God is finished with the Jews. Was not this very prediction (Matt. 8:11, 12) intended to win also them? The Lord has his elect remnant among them as well as among other nations and peoples (Rom. 11:1-5). Salvation is for *all* those who accept the Lord Jesus Christ by personal, living faith. It has nothing to do with nationality or race. In line with Matt. 8:11, 12 are the following passages: John 3:16; Rom. 10:12, 13; I Cor. 7:19; Gal. 3:9, 29; Eph. 2:14, 18; Col. 3:11; and I Peter 2:9. Abraham is the father of "all believers." National origin makes no difference (Rom. 4:11, 12). [379]

The punishment for the highly privileged rejectors of the King who had a

---

379 This is explained in greater detail in my paperback *Israel and The Bible.*

special claim on them is further emphasized by the words: **There shall be weeping and grinding of teeth.** As to this *weeping:* it is not here a shedding of tears because of true sorrow for the sins one has committed (Matt. 26:75; Mark 14:72; Luke 7:38; cf. II Chron. 34:27), or for transgressions by means of which others have dishonored God (Ps. 119:136; II Cor. 2:4; Phil. 3:18). Nor does it occur because of impending separation from dear ones (Acts 20:37, 38), or because of being the object of unjust treatment by other people (I Sam. 1:7, 8). It is not a result of wounded pride because of not getting one's way (I Kings 21:5-7). The present weeping is not brought about by temporal calamity (Gen. 27:38; Lam. 1:16), by bereavement (Deut. 34:8; II Sam. 1:17 ff.; Matt. 2:18), or by deep yearning and sympathy (Gen. 21:16, 17; 43:30). As far as God's people are concerned, there will come a day when every tear will have been wiped away (Isa. 65:19; Rev. 7:17; 18:15, 19). The tears of which Jesus speaks here in Matt. 8:12 are those of inconsolable, never-ending wretchedness, and utter, everlasting hopelessness. The accompanying *grinding or gnashing of teeth* (cf. 13:42, 50; 22:13; 24:51; 25:30; see especially the very similar Luke 13:28; occurring, however, in a different context) denotes excruciating pain and frenzied anger. This grinding of teeth, too, will never come to an end or: cease (Dan. 12:2; Matt. 3:12; 18:8; 25:46; Mark 9:43, 48; Luke 3:17; Jude 6, 7; and Rev. 14:9-11).[380]

The words of verses 10-12 were meant not only for the centurion but for all—centurion, his friends, the entire accompanying multitude—in order that all might rivet their main attention on a matter far more important than physical healing, namely, on being saved and living lives to the glory of God. What now follows is meant specifically for the centurion: **13. And Jesus said to the centurion, Go home; as you believed, so let it be done for you.** The officer had said that it would not be necessary for Jesus to enter his home. As he believed, so it is done, that is, Jesus does not enter his home. The centurion himself, who, let us assume, from outside his home had seen Jesus approaching, is told to re-enter, and the friends, too, must return. **And his boy was cured that very moment.** Literally, "from that hour," but, as is clearly evident from Luke 7:6, 10, it did not take the friends an hour to return to the *nearby* home, and upon their arrival they found the dear servant-boy *already* recovered! Such a context justifies the rendering "from that very moment."

The Healing of Peter's Mother-in-law and of Many Others

Not only the centurion but Peter too was now living in Capernaum (see on 4:18-20). The miracle that was performed in his home occurred on a

---

[380] For more on the subject of the final state *a. of the wicked,* see my book *The Bible on the Life Hereafter,* pp. 195-204; *b. of the righteous,* same title, pp. 205-217.

sabbath, after a synagogue service (cf. Mark 1:21, 29). One receives the impression that what is recorded here in Matt. 8:14-17; Mark 1:29-34; and Luke 4:38-41 (the healing of Peter's mother-in-law, etc.) and what is related in the immediately preceding paragraph, namely, in Matt. 8:5-13; and Luke 7:1-10 (the healing of the centurion's servant) took place not very far apart in time, but see also p. 387.

Matthew writes: **14. And on coming into Peter's house Jesus saw Peter's mother-in-law laid up with fever.** Peter was a married man. At a later period his wife accompanied him on his evangelistic journeys (I Cor. 9:5). During Christ's earthly ministry Peter's wife's mother was living with her daughter and son-in-law. Peter's brother Andrew was also living in that same house, as Mark informs us. That same evangelist also tells us that James and John were with Jesus when he now entered that home. Had the three been invited for dinner? [381] This is possible, though not stated in the text. Besides, is it not also possible that the three had come to make a sick-call (Luke 4:38) and/or a customary social call on friends with whom they were closely associated? Matt. 8:15b ("she began to wait on him") does not rule out these possibilities, for the hospitality practiced in this region and the great blessing of healing about to be bestowed upon this home would certainly explain such cordial attention, even apart from any definite dinner invitation.

However this may have been, Jesus saw that Peter's mother-in-law was laid up with fever. Though Peter was a disciple, and we may well assume that all the others who dwelt in this home were also among the Lord's friends (Andrew, too, being one of The Twelve), affliction had been allowed to enter. Yes, in God's providence believers, too, become ill (Elisha, II Kings 13:14; Hezekiah, II Kings 20:1; Dorcas, Acts 9:36, 37; Paul, Gal. 4:13; Epaphroditus, Phil. 2:25-27; Timothy, I Tim. 5:23; Trophimus, II Tim. 4:20). They even die! The passage, "With his stripes we are healed," does not mean that they have been exempted from the infirmities of the flesh. Often, to be sure, it pleases God to heal them, a blessing which frequently arrives in answer to prayer (James 5:14, 15). But even if God's will be otherwise, theirs is ever the comfort of such passages as Ps. 23; 27; 42; John 14:1-3; Rom. 8:35-39; Phil. 4:4-7; II Tim. 4:6-8; Heb. 4:16; 12:6, to mention only a few among many references.

In view of the many sacrifices and acts of self-denial implied in Christian service, as Peter himself states (Matt. 19:27), it must have been a real comfort for Peter's wife that her mother was living with her. But now mother is sick, *very* sick, indeed. Luke, the physician, informs us that she was "suffering with a severe attack of fever." Jesus saw her thus laid up, for his help had been called in (Mark 1:30; Luke 4:38).

Continued: **15. So he touched her hand, and the fever left her, and she**

---

381 Thus Lenski, *op. cit.*, p. 324.

got up and began to wait on him. A mere touch of the hand was all that was necessary, but what a power and what a sympathy there was in that touch (see on 8:3)! So immediate and complete was her recovery that she not only got up but started to wait on the Healer. What a blessing and what a joy, not only for her, but for all concerned!

Sabbath over, and the news of healing, both in the synagogue (Mark 1:21-28) and in the house, having spread, people came from all around to see Jesus: **16. And when evening had come they brought to him many who were demon-possessed, and he cast out the spirits with a word, and healed all who were sick.** This reminds us of 4:23, 24. The demon-possessed were cleansed, the evil spirits that were in control over them being driven out by Christ's word of power. Was not this a sign that the kingdom of God was asserting its claims in a very special way, that Satan's power was being curtailed now as never before, that is, that "the strong man" was being *bound?* See Matt. 12:29; Luke 10:18; Rev. 20:2, 3. Note also: *all* the sick. No matter what the sickness and no matter how severe or, humanly speaking, "incurable" or "terminal," *all* were healed.

In this work of casting out demons and healing the sick, Matthew, by divine inspiration, sees a fulfilment of Isaiah 53:4, which he quotes not according to the Septuagint ("He bears our sins," etc.) but more faithfully according to the sense of the Hebrew original: **17. in order that what was spoken through Isaiah the prophet might be fulfilled:**
> **He has taken our infirmities upon himself,**
> **And carried our diseases.**

Isaiah had been lifted to the very top of the mountain of prophetic vision, and uttered things which transcended his own understanding. He stood, as it were on Calvary, and pictured the substitutionary suffering of Christ as if it had already occurred. It was *voluntary* suffering. Apart from this voluntary character it would have had no atoning value. So Isaiah said: "Surely, our diseases he has borne, and our pains [or: sorrows] he has carried." On the surface it might seem as if Isaiah and Matthew were talking about two different matters, for the New Testament evangelist has just been speaking about Christ as the One who delivered people from their sicknesses and sorrows; whereas, on the other hand, the royal prophet of the Old Testament describes the Suffering Servant as the One who takes these burdens upon himself. Actually, however, there is no difference, because it is exactly by means of the latter that the former is accomplished.

The question might be asked, however, "In what sense is it true that Jesus took the infirmities and diseases upon himself, and thus off the shoulders of those whom he befriended?" Certainly not in the sense that when, for example, he healed a sick person he himself became afflicted with that very sickness. The true answer can be reached only by examining what Scripture itself says about this. Two things stand out: *a.* He did so by means of his deep *sympathy* or *compassion,* thus entering fully and personally into the sorrows of those whom he came to rescue. Again and again this fact is mentioned. Jesus healed because he pitied. See the following passages: Matt. 9:36; 14:14; 20:34; Mark 1:41; 5:19; cf. 6:34; Luke 7:13. This note of compassion enters even into his parables (Matt. 18:27; Luke 10:33; 15:20-24, 31, 32). At least just as important is *b.* He did it by means of his *vicarious suffering for sin,* which—and this, too, he felt very deeply—was the root of every ill, and dishonored his Father. Thus whenever he saw sickness or distress he experienced Calvary, *his own* Calvary, his own bitter, vicarious suffering throughout his life on earth but especially on the cross. That is why it was *not easy* for him to heal (Mark 2:9; Matt. 9:5). That also accounts for the fact that at the tomb of Lazarus he was deeply moved and agitated in the spirit.

It was in this twofold sense that the Lord took our infirmities upon himself and carried our diseases. Our physical afflictions must never be separated from that without which they never would have occurred, namely, our sins. Note how very closely the Isa. 53:4, 5 context connects these two; for verse 4—"Surely, our diseases he has borne. . . ."—is immediately followed by: "He was wounded for our transgressions; he was bruised for our iniquities."

Implications of Discipleship

At this point there is an interruption in the series of miracles which Matthew is recording. It is, however, hardly comparable to the brief, charming interlude between two dramatic acts in a play, a kind of pleasant intermezzo to relieve tenseness. On the contrary, the theme of suffering and self-denial, clearly implied in verse 17 as has been shown, is underscored here in verses 18-22. Although Jesus himself is the only one who suffers *vicariously,* his disciples must also suffer, and this for the very reason that they identify themselves with him and his cause (John 15:20). Their path is not a bed of roses, and this must be well understood. It is clear therefore that there is a rather close material connection between the little paragraph about to be studied and the immediately preceding passage. There is also a connection between verses 18-22, on the one hand, and verse 23, on the other, a chronological link, for a comparison between verse 18 and verse 23 shows that the events with reference to the scribe (verse 19) and the disciple of Jesus (verse 21) immediately precede the story of the violent storm (verses 24 ff.).

18. Now when Jesus saw a crowd around him he gave orders to go over to the opposite side. Again a large crowd surrounds Jesus. It is evening, though, as the context of Mark 4:35 makes clear, not the evening mentioned in Matt. 8:16. Chronologically Matt. 8:18-22 links with the following, not with the immediately preceding context.

Jesus was often surrounded by crowds. Often, too, he would after a while dismiss those multitudes. Why was this? Being not only thoroughly divine but also thoroughly human, he needed time for prayer, for rest, and for sleep. So did his disciples (8:24; cf. Mark 6:31). Besides, the enthusiasm of the crowds must not reach too high a pitch too early (see above, on 8:4).

The order to cross over has been given, namely, to the disciples (Mark 4:35). Just previous to departure, however, two men [382] come up to Jesus. They desire to join the inner circle of his disciples, and to accompany the Master on all his journeys. As to the first of these two we read: **19. And a certain scribe came up and said, Teacher, I will follow you wherever you go.** A remarkable declaration indeed, especially as coming from *a scribe,* a member of a group generally hostile to Jesus (5:20; 6:2, 5, 16; 15:1 ff.; chap. 23). Moreover, the scribes were themselves teachers; yet this teacher acknowledges Jesus as *his* teacher and so addresses him. Finally, of his sincerity there can be no doubt. At the particular moment when he uttered his promise he actually meant it: he wanted to be a constant follower of Jesus.

There is something very attractive about the words, "I will follow you wherever you go." Who can read them without being immediately reminded of Ruth's glorious resolution, "Wherever you go, I will go. . ." (Ruth 1:16, 17)? Nevertheless, as Christ's answer clearly indicates, this man's intentions were not altogether honorable. He saw crowds, miracles, enthusiasm, etc. It seemed so good to be closely associated with the One who was in the very center of all this action. So, he wanted to be Christ's disciple, but he failed to understand the implications of discipleship, namely, self-denial, sacrifice, service, suffering! **20. Jesus said to him, the foxes have holes, and the birds of the air roosts, but the Son of man has nowhere to lay his head.** Foxes were plentiful in the country of Christ's travels (Judg. 15:4; Neh. 4:3; Ps. 63:10; Song of Sol. 2:15; Lam. 5:18; Ezek. 13:4). Their holes, dens, or lairs were often burrows in the ground. From these they would make their nightly raids, not only hunting frogs, rabbits, mice, poultry, and birds, but also devouring eggs, fruits, etc., and devastating the fields, orchards, and vineyards. The point Jesus emphasizes is, however, that these animals have their definite dwelling-places, their homes to which they return again and again. The same is true also with respect to birds. Ecological conditions (weather, food supply) permitting, they have their definite roosts, temporary lodging places, the place where they, as it were, pitch their tents. [383] If "enemies" try to intrude, they drive them away if they can at all do so.

For "the Son of man," things are entirely different, however. In his

---

[382] Really three (Luke 9:57-62), but the incident in connection with the third is omitted by Matthew.
[383] Note the original: κατασκηνώσεις.

wandering from place to place he, for whom there was no room in the inn, has no place on which he can figure to spend the night. As the story develops, Judea rejects him (John 5:18), Galilee casts him out (John 6:66), Gadara begs him to leave its district (Matt. 8:34), Samaria refuses him lodging (Luke 9:53), earth will not have him (Matt. 27:23), and finally even heaven forsakes him (Matt. 27:46). Therefore let the scribe figure the cost before he builds the tower. Let him consider that permanent discipleship implies struggle and warfare.—It is said that at the time of the Civil War (U.S.) there were many volunteers who eagerly joined the ranks, as if going to war meant nothing more than taking part in parades, drills, and reviews, and receiving medals and honors! To be sure, there are glorious rewards for all true followers of the Lord, but it is ever the way of the cross that leads home (Matt. 10:24; Luke 14:26; John 16:33; II Tim. 3:12; Heb. 13:13).—Whether this scribe ever became a steadfast follower is not recorded. After all, that is not nearly as important as is the lesson itself.

This is the first place in the Gospels where the term "Son of man" occurs. The literature on this subject is enormous. [384] The first question that is generally asked is, "What is the origin of this expression?" In this connection the following points deserve comment:

---

[384] See, for example the following:

Aalders, G. Ch., *Korte Verklaring, Daniel*, Kampen, 1928, pp. 133-135.

Bavinck, H. *Gereformeerde Dogmatiek*, Kampen, 1918, third edition, Vol. III, pp. 259-264.

Berkhof, L., *Systematic Theology*, Grand Rapids, Mich., 1949, fourth edition, pp. 313, 314.

Bouman, J., art. "Son of man," in *ET* 59 (1948), pp. 283 ff.

Burrows, M., *More Light on the Dead Sea Scrolls*, New York, 1958, pp. 71, 72.

Campbell, J. Y., "Son of man," in *A Theological Word Book of the Bible* (edited by A. Richardson), New York, 1952, pp. 230-231.

Colpe, C., on the same subject, in Th.D.N.T., Vol. VIII, pp. 400-477.

De Beus, C. H., "Achtergrond en inhoud van de uitdrukking 'de Zoon des Menschen' in de synoptische evangeliën," *NedTT*, 9 (1954-55), pp. 272-295.

De Beus, C. H., "Het gebruik en de betekenis van de uitdrukking 'De Zoon des Menschen' in het Evangelie van Johannes," *NedTT*, 10 (1955-56), pp. 237-251.

Greijdanus, S., *Het Evangelie naar de Beschrijving van Lukas*, Amsterdam, 1940, Vol. I, p. 253 (and the literature indicated on that page.).

Parker, Pierson, "The Meaning of 'Son of Man,' " *JBL*, 60 (1941), pp. 151-157.

Stalker, J., art. "Son of man," in I.S.B.E.

Stevens, G. B., *The Theology of the New Testament*, New York, 1925, pp. 41-53.

Thompson, G. H. P., "The Son of Man: The Evidence of the Dead Sea Scrolls," *ET*, 72 (1960-61), p. 125.

Vos, G., *The Self-Disclosure of Jesus*, New York, 1926, pp. 42-55; 228-256.

Young, E. J., *The Prophecy of Daniel*, Grand Rapids, 1949, pp. 154-156.

For further titles of periodical literature on "Son of man," see Metzger, B. M., *Index to Periodical Literature on Christ and the Gospels*, pp. 437-442; and for both books and journals see the continuing copies of *New Testament Abstracts*.

1. In Ps. 8:4 the term "son of man" simply means *man,* as the parallelism indicates:

> What is man that thou art mindful of him?
> And the son of man that thou visitest
> [or: thinkest of, carest for] him?

The reference is to man in all his weakness and dependence. To stress these same qualities of frailty, powerlessness, lowliness, and utter dependence on God, Ezekiel is repeatedly addressed as "son of man" (Ezek. 2:1, 3, 6, 8; 3:1, 3, 4, 10, 17, 25; etc.).

Somewhat similarly, the expression "sons of wickedness" (II Sam. 3:34) means wicked people; "son of a foreigner" (Exod. 12:43), foreigner; and "sons of thunder" (Mark 3:17), thunderites, that is, men characterized by fiery zeal. Even the word "daughters" must at times be interpreted similarly. Thus, as some see it, "daughters of music" (Eccl. 12:4) indicates musical notes.

Based on such examples the opinion might arise that when Jesus calls himself "Son of man" he means no more than that he is simply a man, that is, that he is thoroughly human; or even, if one prefers, that he is "the ideal man," man as the Creator intended him to be. *Evaluation:* Examination of the passages in which the term occurs immediately indicates that this view will never do. It surely is unreasonable to suppose that Jesus meant that either *mere* man or even the *ideal* man is Lord of the sabbath, gives his life as a ransom in exchange for many, is going to rise again from the dead, will send forth his angels, etc. From the more than eighty instances in which the New Testament uses the term "Son of man" it is clear that the reference is never to man in general but always to *one* particular, unique person, namely, Jesus Christ.

2. Can Christ's use of the term "Son of man" be traced to pseudepigraphal literature; for example, to the earlier part of the Book of Enoch? It must be admitted that there the term is indeed used with reference to the Messiah. This usage is not original, however, but is based on Dan. 7:9 ff. Besides, all evidence that at the time when Jesus began his ministry the term "Son of man" was a then current designation of the Messiah, thus understood by the people in general, is lacking. [385] And as to the possibility that Jesus might have derived his use of the designation from Qumran literature, according to Millar Burrows the term "Son of man" does not occur at all in that literature and the idea has not been found in the Qumran texts. [386] Nor can it be traced to Ugaritic texts about Baal.

3. The true origin of the term is undoubtedly Dan. 7:13. Note the resemblances, here underscored:

---

[385] S.BK., Vol. I, p. 486.
[386] *More Light on the Dead Sea Scrolls*, pp. 71, 72.

Dan. 7:13: "I continued to watch in the night visions, and behold, *with the clouds of heaven* there was one *coming* like a *son of man;* and he advanced toward the Ancient of Days and was presented before him.

Matt. 26:64: "But I tell y o u, from now on y o u shall see *the Son of man* seated at the right hand of Power and *coming on the clouds of heaven.*"

In addition to the resemblances that are immediately evident note also the similarity between "he advanced toward the Ancient of Days and was presented before him" and "seated at the right hand of Power [some prefer: of the Almighty]." The idea of heavenly dominion, glory, and power, implied in "seated at the right hand of Power" (Matt. 26:64), is also clearly derived from Dan. 7:14: "And there were given to him dominion and glory and royal power, that all peoples, nations, and tongues should serve him. His dominion is an everlasting dominion that shall not pass away, and his kingdom [or: kingship] one that shall never be destroyed."

It is not true that the designation "one like a son of man" in Daniel represents the Hebrew people, and that the transference of the title from a collective body ("the saints of the Most High") to an individual was mediated through extra-canonical literature (e.g., the book of Enoch). The *one like a son of man* appears on the clouds of heaven, but *the saints of the Most High* (Dan. 7:18, 21, 22, 25, 27) are found on earth. Also, in Daniel's vision the former does not make his appearance until the day of judgment, but the saints are contemporaneous with the little horn (verses 21 and 25). [387] Also in the book of Revelation (1:13; 14:14), which employs the same expression ("one like a son of man") the reference is very distinctly to one person, namely, the exalted Christ. Too much is often made of the fact that we read "one like (unto)," as if this meant that the designated individual is not really the Son of man himself but some vague, symbolic, representative figure. The truth is that the figure, as it appears in the vision, *resembles* the man for the simple reason that *it designates and describes him.* The *description* in Daniel becomes the *title* in the Gospels (see also Acts 7:56), but the same *person* is indicated in both.

In order to arrive at the meaning of the title "Son of man" as found in Matthew, Mark, and Luke (the Synoptics) each passage in which it occurs must be studied in its own individual context. When this is done it appears that in several of these passages the term indicates the Savior's *humiliation.* He has no permanent abode on earth (Matt. 8:20), is going to be subjected to bitter suffering (17:12), shall be betrayed and put to death (26:24), shall be buried (12:40). Other passages just as clearly predict his *exaltation.* He

---

[387] See the detailed argument in G. C. Aalders and in Young; for titles and page references see above, footnote 384.

shall rise again (17:9); having left the earth he shall return, in the glory of his Father and accompanied by angels (16:27), and shall sit on the throne of his glory as Judge (25:31; cf. several references in 24:27-44, adding 26:64).

In the following columns the letter "H" indicates that the reference to which it belongs clearly speaks of Christ's *humiliation*. Similarly, "E" indicates *exaltation,* and "HE": humiliation followed by exaltation (the latter at times in the immediately following context of the designated verse). Similarly "EH" means exaltation preceded by humiliation. When neither humiliation nor exaltation is *clearly* and *immediately* indicated, the reference is left unmarked. It is true, of course, that although for the sake of clarity and ease of reference the passages are listed in the order in which they occur in the three separate Gospels, in several cases a passage in one Gospel has a parallel in another; for example, Matt. 8:20, cf. Luke 9:58; Matt. 9:6, cf. Mark 2:10 and Luke 5:24; Matt. 12:8, cf. Mark 2:28 and Luke 6:5; Matt. 20:28, cf. Mark 10:45; Matt. 26:64, cf. Mark 14:62; etc.

MATTHEW		MARK	LUKE	
H 8:20	E 19:28	E 2:10	5:24	HE 18:31
9:6	H 20:28	2:28	6:5	19:10
E 10:23	E 24:27	HE 8:31	6:22	E 21:27
11:19	E 24:30a	E 8:38	7:34	E 21:36
12:8	E 24:30b	E 9:9	HE 9:22	H 22:22
12:32	E 24:37	H 9:12	E 9:26	H 22:48
H 12:40	E 24:39	HE 9:31	H 9:44	E 22:69
13:37	E 24:44	HE 10:33	H 9:58	HE 24:7
E 13:41	E 25:31	H 10:45	11:30	*******
16:13	H 26:2	E 13:26	E 12:8	
E 16:27	H 26:24a	H 14:21a	12:10	
E 16:28	H 26:24b	H 14:21b	E 12:40	
E 17:9	H 26:45	H 14:41	E 17:22	
H 17:12	E 26:64	E 14:62	EH 17:24	
HE 17:22	*******	*******	E 17:26	
18:11 (A.V., probably			E 17:30	
an interpolation from Luke 19:10)			E 18:8	

Humiliation is probably basic in most unmarked references. The matter is, however, not quite as simple as this. Several of the passages are difficult to classify, for they indicate that even during his humiliation the Son of man was definitely not an ordinary man. On the contrary, he was Lord of the sabbath (Matt. 12:8 and parallels), had authority to forgive sins (Matt. 9:6 and parallels), "came" into this world with a definite purpose, namely to give his life as a ransom in exchange for many (Matt. 20:28; Mark 10:45); and, in line with this purpose, "came" to seek and to save the lost (Luke

19:10). Woe to the man by whom this Son of man is betrayed (Luke 22:22)! The Son of man is therefore at one and the same time "a man of sorrows" and "the Lord of glory!"

That Jesus, in using the term "Son of man," and never declaring (predicatively) "I am the Son of man," is, nevertheless, always referring to *himself,* is clear from Matt. 16:13-15, where "Son of man" is obviously equal to "I"; from 26:62-64, where the charge of blasphemy would otherwise have been impossible; and from the fact that the title "Son of man" in Mark 8:31 (cf. Luke 9:22) is in Matt. 16:21 replaced by the simple "he," with "Jesus" as antecedent. In fact, in every passage the context clearly shows that when Jesus employs this title he is referring to himself.

By using this title in speaking to *the Jews,* Jesus was able to reveal himself gradually, not all at once. Had he, in his work among them, immediately called himself the Messiah, would not his ministry have been brought to an untimely end? Besides, would not the carnal, materialistic, and political interpretation of the Messianic office, the type of conception accepted by the masses, have compounded the error? It is entirely possible that at first many of those who were in Christ's audience took the designation to mean no more than *man,* as in Ezekiel. Gradually, however, as Jesus continued to describe what he was doing, facing, and planning *as Son of man,* they began to wonder and to ask the question, "Who is this Son of man?" (John 12:34, in the Gospels the only passage in which anyone other than Jesus himself uses this term). Thus gradually the minds of the listeners were being enlightened. The climax came when, without any qualification whatever, Jesus identified himself (Matt. 26:62-64) in his coming glory, with the august Person who in Daniel's prophecy (7:13, 14) was introduced to the Ancient of Days!

Use of the self-designation "Son of *man*" emphasized the fact that the bearer of this title was not the nationalistic Messiah of Jewish expectation but (in a sense) "the Savior of the world" (John 4:42; cf. I Tim. 4:10). His well-meant invitation of salvation by grace through faith goes out to all men. He himself is unique among men. He is *the* Son of man. He is the man of sorrows, but this very path of suffering leads to the crown, to glory. Moreover, this glory is revealed not only eschatologically, when he comes with the clouds, but reaches back, as it were, through his entire life on earth and through every redemptive act. He is *always* the glorious Son of man! [388]

As has been shown, the scribe mentioned in verses 19 and 20 was *too ready* to become a steady follower of Jesus. The next individual who comes

---

[388] For the Johannine passages in which this title is used see N.T.C. on John, Vol. II, pp. 205, 206, and the summary on p. 207; also the commentary on each passage, presented in the two volumes of that work.

up to Jesus before the latter's embarkation and departure was, it would seem, *too unready.* We read: 21. **Someone else, one of his disciples,** [389] **said to him, Lord, allow me first to go home and bury my father.** This man evidently belongs to that large group of people that had been impressed by the words and works of Jesus. Frequently this aspirant was to be found in Christ's audience. When he reported his experiences to others he spoke favorably and enthusiastically about Jesus. In the wider sense of the term he was therefore a disciple of Jesus. His desire is to become a disciple in the more narrow sense, a steady follower, one who belongs to the inner circle. However, he does not seem to be quite ready to take this step immediately. If he does not exactly impose his own terms for joining the group, he at least enquires about the possibility of making a time reservation. His father has just died. So this aspirant asks Jesus to allow him first to go home and bury his father. [390]

According to custom, burial generally took place very soon after death (John 11:1, 14, 17; Acts 5:5, 6, 10). In Israel giving an honorable burial to the dead was considered a duty and a kindness (Mic. 6:8) that ranked higher than any other service requiring attention. Filial piety obliged a son to attend to this bestowal of the final act of devotion. Cf. Gen. 25:9; 35:29; 49:28–50:3; 50:13, 14, 26; Josh. 24:29, 30; etc. [391] It is not surprising therefore that Jesus was asked by this man for permission to *first* bury his father. On the surface the request for delay seemed to be reasonable.

At first glance the answer he received comes as somewhat of a surprise: 22. **But Jesus said to him, Follow me, and let the dead bury their own dead.** What Jesus means is clear enough, namely, "Let those who are spiritually dead tend to the funeral of one who belongs to their own company." The question might be asked, however, "Why did not Jesus consent to this request, especially since this aspirant, having performed his functions in connection with the funeral of his father, could then immediately return, to be with Jesus?" Various possibilities occur to the mind:

1. As customarily conducted, funeral ceremonies were not exactly condu-

---

[389] Literally, according to what is probably the best reading, "and another of his disciples." Here, too, however, we must figure with the possibility of abbreviated expression. The preceding context, concerning the scribe, who is *not* called a disciple of Jesus (in Luke 9:57 he is called "a certain man"), makes it clear that the meaning here in verse 21 is, "someone else, one of his disciples." *This* man is a disciple, the scribe was not.

[390] The suggestion that the father had not really died, and that what the disciple meant was this, "Let me stay home with my father until he dies and I provide for his funeral," does not impress me as being very valuable. In that case Jesus would be implying that at that future point of time those whose duty it would then be to provide for the funeral would still be spiritually dead, that also the father would have died in unbelief, etc. The words of Jesus clearly apply to a *present* situation.

[391] Cf. S.BK., Vol. I, pp. 487-489.

cive to spiritual growth and edification. They were noisy affairs, often characterized by excessive and hypocritical mourning. See Matt. 9:23, 24; Mark 5:38-40; Luke 8:52, 53: vociferous wailing suddenly changes into derisive laughter. Jesus wanted to spare the man this agony. He wanted him to receive a blessing for himself and to be a blessing to others by spending much time with the Savior, so that, thus strengthened in the faith this "disciple" would be able to "proclaim the kingdom of God" (Luke 9:60).

2. Jesus had already issued the order to leave (verse 18) and was about to embark (verse 23). If this man wanted to be in Christ's immediate company he must therefore join right now. Others could attend to the funeral.

3. The fact that Jesus is sovereign Lord, and that following him means doing whatever he commands, without any qualification, condition, or reservation, must be deeply impressed upon the mind and heart of this man (cf. John 15:14). Jesus knew that the aspirant was the kind of individual who stood in special need of being reminded of this.

4. Jesus wishes to teach him that in the kingdom of heaven the ties pertaining to earthly family life are superseded by those that knit together the members of the heavenly or spiritual family (cf. Matt. 10:37; 12:46-50; and see N.T.C. on Eph. 3:14, 15).

Mentioning these four points does not mean endorsing them all! We do not know which and how many of the suggested answers were present in the mind of Christ when he said, "Follow me. . . ." There may even have been other reasons. I trust, however, that those suggested will have shown that the *mashal* (veiled and pointed remark) here uttered, far from being unreasonable, was filled with wisdom. As given, it suited this particular person, as, for example, Matt. 19:21 answered the needs of "the rich young ruler." Occasions and personalities differ, and to conclude from the answer Jesus gave that believers must never help to provide for, or attend, funerals of unbelievers, including those of members of their own family, would be completely unwarranted. It would be just as unjustified as to declare that Matt. 6:34 (see on that passage) condemns every oath. Nevertheless, enough has been said to show that also this passage (8:21, 22) is full of meaning and value for all times (see especially items 3 and 4 above).

A Tempest Stilled

This story is found in Matt. 8:23-27; Mark 4:35-41; and Luke 8:22-25. In Matthew its beginning is connected logically with verse 18: "He gave orders to go over to the opposite side," and so now 23. **When he stepped into the boat his disciples followed him.** The disciples, no matter what the cost, follow Jesus; compare this with the mental attitude of the two aspirants (verses 19-22). According to Mark 4:37 other vessels left shore at the same time. **24. Suddenly a violent storm shook the sea, so that the boat was being swamped by the waves.** Literally, "And behold a great shaking [or: sea-

409

quake, storm] occurred in the sea. . . ." On "behold" see p. 131, footnote 133. The word that describes the storm is *seismos;* cf. "seismograph," a meter that indicates the amount of shaking or vibration. The word *seismos* elsewhere indicates an earthquake (Matt. 24:7; 27:54; Mark 13:8; etc.). In the present case, however, it has reference to a violent storm on the sea, caused by high winds. Mark 4:37 and Luke 8:23 speak of a *lailaps,* that is, a whirlwind or a storm that breaks forth in furious gusts.

The water above which this tempest occurred was the Sea of Galilee. It is located in the north of the valley of the Jordan, is about thirteen miles in length and seven and one-half miles in width. It lies approximately six hundred eighty feet below the level of the Mediterranean. Its bed is a depression surrounded by hills, especially on the east side with its precipitous cliffs. It is understandable that when the cool currents rush down from Mt. Hermon (9,200 feet) or from elsewhere and through narrow passes between the steep hills collide with the heated air above the lake basin, this downrush is impetuous. The violent winds whip the sea into a fury, causing high waves that splash over bow, side rails, etc., of any vessel that happens to be plying the water surface. In the present instance the small fishing craft, swamped by towering billows, was becoming the toy of the raging elements. **But he was sound asleep.** The tense used in the original pictures Jesus slumbering peacefully. He had been working hard and was very tired. Besides, it was not difficult for him to fall into a deep sleep, for his trust in the heavenly Father—*his own* Father—was unfaltering. Neither the roaring of the wind nor the dashing of the waves nor even the rolling and pitching of the boat was able to awaken him.

As the storm increased its fury the disciples who were with Jesus in the boat, experienced seamen though they were, appeal to him for help. Having now been with him for some time and having witnessed his astonishing miracles, they are beginning to see in him far more than a carpenter. Yet, they do not fully believe that even he can accomplish anything against such a tempest (see verse 27). Theirs was a mixture of faith and fear, the latter predominating (Luke 8:25). They were well-nigh desperate, but decided to try nevertheless. They went to the stern of the boat, where Jesus was sleeping "on a cushion" (Mark 4:38). **25. So they came and woke him up, saying, Lord, save (us), we're perishing.**

There is a slight difference in the manner in which the evangelists report the cries of these fear-stricken men: Mark has: "Master, don't you care that we're perishing?" Luke: "Master, master, we're perishing." Commentators call attention to the fact that this is one of many evidences that prove the independence of the authors; amid essential unity there is personal variety. True, and is it not also a fact that in a situation of terrified distress this disciple would cry one thing, another something else? One should read all three accounts to get the entire picture.

What the elements of nature were unable to bring about, namely, awaken Jesus, the disciples' agonizing appeal and his own eagerness to minister to human need accomplish. Roused from sleep: 26. **He said to them, Why are y o u frightened, O men of little faith?** Jesus reminds them that there was no valid reason for their bewildered panic. Very recently these men had been selected to be Christ's disciples, with a view to apostleship (Mark 3:13-19; Luke 6:12-16) and all this implied. Would the One who had chosen them allow them now to perish in the angry deep? Was not his very presence reassuring?

Matthew's account is the most dramatic of the three (Matthew, Mark, and Luke). As he pictures it, Jesus did not immediately still the storm. On the contrary, while the tempest was still raging and the boat being tossed to and fro by the billows, "majestic calmness" sat enthroned upon Christ's brow. It was in the thick of all the confusion that he asked the disciples why they were frightened. It was then, even before he got up, that he, with perfect serenity and self-composure, addressed them as "men of little faith," that is, men who were not sufficiently taking to heart the comfort they should have derived from the presence, promises, power, and love of their Master (as in 6:30; 14:31; 16:8).

When a forest fire rages, it frequently happens that for days in succession the newspapers report that the destructive holocaust is still spreading. It is not yet "under control." Finally the bulletin for which everyone has been waiting arrives: though the flames have not yet been completely extinguished, the fire is now "under control." The danger to life and property has been sufficiently checked to justify an optimistic report. On the other hand, as Matthew pictures it, Jesus has this storm "under control" even while the winds are still roaring and the waters seething! The storm is his instrument for the strengthening of the disciples' faith, as is clear from verse 27.

> God moves in a mysterious way
> His wonders to perform;
> He plants his footsteps in the sea
> And rides upon the storm.
> Ye fearful saints, fresh courage take;
> The clouds ye so much dread
> Are big with mercy and shall break
> In blessings on your head.
> —William Cowper

Then he got up and rebuked the winds and the sea; and there was a deep calm. There are those who assume that the verb "rebuked" [392] implies an

---

[392] ἐπετίμησεν, third person sing. aor. indic. of ἐπιτιμάω. It has the sense *rebuke* in such passages as Matt. 8:26; 16:22; 17:18; 19:13; Luke 4:39; 9:42, 55; 19:39; 23:40; but at times means *warn* (Matt. 12:16; 16:20; Mark 3:12; Luke 9:21).

animate object. They say that this inference is strengthened by Mark 4:39, which is then translated, "Peace! Be muzzled!" But, to begin with the latter, a word does not always retain its basic or primary connotation. "Hush! [or: Peace!] Be silent!" is the more usual and better rendering of Mark 4:39. As to the expression, "He rebuked," it should be borne in mind that Matthew does not say, "Jesus rebuked the devil," or "the demons," or "the evil spirits that were in the winds and the sea." He simply says, "He rebuked the winds and the sea." It would seem, therefore, that this is simply a figurative or poetic manner of speaking (cf. Ps. 19:5; 98:8; Isa. 55:12; etc.). So also in Luke 4:39, where we are told that Jesus "rebuked" the fever by which Peter's mother-in-law was being afflicted. The really important fact conveyed by the expression "He rebuked the winds and the sea" is that in a very effective manner Jesus asserted his authority over the elements of nature, so that there was a deep (literally "great") calm. What is striking is that not only the winds immediately quiet down, but so do even the waves. Generally, as is well-known, after the winds have perceptibly diminished, the billows will continue to roll for a while, surging and subsiding as if unwilling to follow the example of the now subdued air currents above them. But in *this* instance winds and waves synchronize in the sublime symphony of a solemn silence. Something comparable to an evening stillness of the starry heavens settles upon the waters. Suddenly the surface of the sea has become smooth as a mirror. Are we surprised that even *after* the miracle had been performed (thus Mark 4:40 and Luke 8:25) Jesus reproves the disciples because of the weakness of their faith? Was it not rather natural that he would return to this all-important subject?

That the faith of these men was indeed strengthened appears from verse **27. The men were amazed and said, What kind of person is this, that even the winds and the sea obey him?** I take it that the expression "the men" refers to the disciples in *this* boat. To be sure, "other boats" had left the shore at the same time (Mark 4:36). Also, after Jesus and his disciples landed, the miracle may well have become "the talk of the town." But these matters are not in the present context. Here the antecedent of "men" is clearly "his disciples" (verse 23), "they" (verse 25), "them" and "men of little faith" (verse 26). These men are astonished. They begin to realize that Jesus is greater by far than they had previously imagined. He exercises control not only over audiences, sicknesses, and demons, but even over winds and waves.

It often happens that those who are most closely associated with a great or famous person are far less enthusiastic about him than are strangers, who eagerly imbibe glowing reports. The intimate friends are less outspoken in their praise, for the simple reason that they see not only the strong but also the weak points of the celebrity. When Jesus is the center of attention the story is different. The closer the association with him, the greater is also the admiration and the amazement. In this connection see N.T.C. on the Gospel according to John, Vol. I, pp. 3 and 4.

Much that is wrong on earth can be corrected. There are mothers who dry tears, repairmen who fix machines, surgeons who remove diseased tissues, counselors who solve family problems, etc. As to correcting the weather? People talk about it, to be sure. But it takes deity to change the weather. It is Jesus who commands the winds and the sea, and they obey him!

In the Land of the Gadarenes:
Helpfulness over against Heartlessness

It was evening when the Lord and his disciples crossed the sea. Night must have fallen when the events recorded in Matt. 8:28-34; Mark 5:1-20; and Luke 8:26-39 began to occur. This is clearly implied in Mark 4:35; 5:1, 2. Is it not reasonable to assume that at verse 33 or 34 Matthew relates what happened on the following day?

The present account begins as follows: 28. **And when he came to the opposite side, to the country of the Gadarenes, he was met by two demon-possessed men, coming out of the tombs.** The original as represented by Grk. N.T. (A-B-M-W) has *Gadarenes* in Matt. 8:28; *Gerasenes* in Mark 5:1; and *Gergesenes* in Luke 8:26. In each case variant readings are recognized in the footnotes. In order to locate the place where Jesus landed, a description as given in the Gospels (Matt. 8:28, 32; Mark 5:2, 13; and Luke 8:27, 33) is helpful. We learn that it was a region of caves used as tombs, and that a steep hill descended sharply to the very edge of the water. This description does not fit Gerasa, a town situated at least thirty miles to the south-southeast of the Sea of Galilee. It does, however, suit *Khersa,* which could very well be indicated as the town inhabited by the Gerasenes or Gergesenes. If it be assumed that the larger city of Gadara, mainly located a few miles southeast of the sea but extending all the way to the shore, was, as it were, the capital of the entire district to which Khersa belonged, the various geographical designations begin to make sense. Moreover, at Khersa, situated on the northeastern shore, about six miles diagonally (oversea) southeast of Capernaum, there is indeed a hill descending sharply to the edge of the water. There are also many caves—evident even today—suitable for tombs. [393]

The place where the party landed was predominantly Gentile. See on Matt. 4:12-16. When Jesus and his disciples stepped ashore they were suddenly confronted by two demoniacs, who came down from among the tombs. They are described as violent or fierce, and may have shown this trait in the impetuous manner in which they rushed to the attack. Why Matthew mentions *two* demoniacs, while Mark and Luke tell the story of *one* [394] is

---

[393] See A. M. Ross, art. "Gadara, Gadarenes,," *Zondervan Pictorial Bible Dictionary,* Grand Rapids, 1963, p. 293; and L. H. Grollenberg, *Atlas of the Bible,* p. 116, map 34.

[394] Cf. also Matt. 20:29 ("two blind men") with Mark 10:6 and Luke 18:35.

not known, but such a variation in reporting is not uncommon even today. It has been suggested that the demoniac to whom Mark and Luke refer was the leader and spokesman, but this opinion is merely a guess. It should be noted, however, that these other evangelists do not say that *only* one demoniac met Jesus that day. No one, therefore, has a right to speak about a Matthew versus Mark-Luke "contradiction."

Continued: **So violent were they that no one could pass by along that road.** For a more detailed description of the wild character and behavior of these men see what is said about one of them in Mark 5:2-6 and in Luke 8:27. These pitiable human wrecks were in the power of an entire legion of demons, who were in control of their thinking, speaking, and general behavior. The people of the surroundings, cognizant of the dangerous situation, purposely by-passed the road that led through this territory. As to the demoniacs—*really* the demons who spoke through them—**29. All at once they started screaming, Why do you bother us, you Son of God? Did you come here to torture us before the appointed time?** Literally, what they screamed was, "What (is there) to us and you?" meaning, "What have you to do with us?" and so, "Why do you bother us?" [395] They recognize Jesus as being the Son of God, and they know that on the day of the coming judgment their relative freedom to roam about on earth and in the sky above it (see N.T.C. on Ephesians 2:2; 6:12) must cease forever, and that their final and most terrible punishment is destined to begin at that time. They seem to sense the difference between Christ's first and his second coming, a fact not always fully recognized even by the Lord's followers (see on 11:1-6). The demoniacs know that right now they have come face to face with their great Antagonist, the One to whom the final judgment has been committed, and they are afraid lest even now—that is, "before the appointed time" [396] —he might hurl them into "the abyss" or "dungeon" where Satan is kept (cf. Rev. 20:3). What adds to their fear is the fact that almost immediately upon meeting, Jesus had ordered the demons to depart from these men (Mark 5:8; Luke 8:29).

Continued: **30, 31. Now at some distance away from them a large herd of pigs was feeding. So the demons were begging him, saying, If you cast us out, allow us to enter that herd of pigs.** The demons are keenly aware of the fact that without the permission of Jesus they can do nothing. The presence of a large number of pigs, "about two thousand" (Mark 5:13), feeding on a hillside some distance away from the place where the meeting between Jesus and the demoniacs occurred, prompts the demons to request permission to

---

[395] On τί ἡμῖν καὶ σοί see M. Smith, "Notes on Goodspeed's 'Problems of New Testament Translation,' " *JBL*, 64 (1945), pp. 512, 513.

[396] Note πρὸ καιροῦ. In distinction from χρόνος, time viewed as the succession from past to present to future, καιρός indicates the proper moment or season for this or that event to take place; see Eccl. 3:1-8, where LXX uses καιρός consistently.

enter that herd. What was the reason for this request? Simply a yearning to destroy? The sinister desire and hope that the owners of the herd, seeing their property thus destroyed, would become filled with antagonism against Jesus? That certainly is possible, but there may have been other reasons. We do not know. What we do know is that Jesus granted their request: **32. He said, Go ahead. So they came out and went into the pigs, and the whole herd rushed headlong down the cliff into the sea and perished in the water.** Why did Jesus allow this to happen? Was it, as has been suggested, [397] because Jews were not allowed to have swine, so that these Jewish owners were being punished for disobeying a regulation regarding unclean animals? Neither the context nor the character of the region where all this occurred (see on verse 28 and on 4:12-16) favors this explanation. As I see it, the reasons were these: *a.* negatively: Jesus knew that the demons were right in implying that the time of their final consignment to hell had not yet arrived; and *b.* positively, he also knew that there was one lesson which the inhabitants of this region needed to learn more than any other, namely, that people—in the present case the two demoniacs—are of more value than pigs, that is, that human values surpass material values by far. That the men of this region were actually in need of this lesson is shown in verses 33, 34. **The herdsmen fled, went away to the city, and reported everything, including what had happened to the demon-possessed.** Though the men who had been tending the pigs were some distance removed from Jesus (verse 30), they had apparently witnessed the meeting between him and the demoniacs, and had also observed that the wildness of these two men had left them and had been transferred to the pigs. They drew the correct conclusion that it was Jesus who had driven the demons out of the men and had permitted these evil spirits to enter the pigs, with the result that the entire two thousand perished in the water. The loss of the pigs was therefore not the fault of the herdsmen. They wanted everybody to know what had really happened. Result: **Lo and behold, the whole city came out to meet Jesus; and when they saw him they begged him to leave their district.** On "Lo and behold" see p. 131, footnote 133. This is one of those passages that says as much by means of its silence as it does by its actual words. The people of this region were heartless. They did not rejoice with those who were rejoicing. They did not praise Jesus for having bestowed an unfathomable blessing on two shockingly distressed individuals. They did not even bring their sick to Jesus that he might heal them, nor did they ask him to heal their souls. They could think of only one thing, namely, the loss of these pigs. It was this that filled them with great fear. So they asked Jesus "to depart from their border." He did: **9:1. So he got into a boat, crossed over, and came to his own city** (Capernaum; see p. 241).

---

[397] Lenski, *op. cit.*, p. 342.

But, as Mark and Luke report, the Lord's helpfulness triumphed over the people's heartlessness. He did not completely cast them aside. Just before leaving he gave them a missionary! See Mark 5:18-20; Luke 8:38, 39.

The Healing of a Paralytic

The story of the cleansing of the leper (see above, Matt. 8:1-4) is in Mark's Gospel, and also in Luke's, immediately followed by that of the healing of the lame man who by four companions was lowered through the roof of the house where Jesus was teaching. Cf. Mark 1:40-45 with 2:1-12; and cf. Luke 5:12-16 with 5:17-26. There follows the call of Levi (=Matthew). From Mark and Luke one certainly receives the impression that this cure of the paralyzed man and this call of Levi occurred previous to the preaching of the Sermon on the Mount and the calling of the twelve disciples (Mark 3:13-19; Luke 6:12 ff.). Now Matthew, here in 9:2 ff., parallels Mark 2:1 ff. and Luke 5:17 ff., but the place which this material has in his Gospel, namely, the *ninth* chapter, so far removed from the *fifth to the seventh* chapters, in which the Sermon on the Mount is recorded, might cause the unwary reader to think that this miracle and this call took place long after the preaching of the sermon. However, since Matthew's arrangement is topical rather than chronological, and since a call of Matthew subsequent to the calling and commissioning of The Twelve in which he was included would make little sense, it is surely reasonable in broad outline to follow Mark's historical sequence. Doing this involves no contradiction, since Matthew's account here in 9:2 ff. is not introduced by any specific time reference. He simply states, "And behold they were bringing. . . ." Mark and Luke, though leaving no doubt as to the question which occurred earlier, *a.* the selection of The Twelve and preaching of the sermon, or *b.* the healing of the paralytic and call of Levi, do not satisfy our curiosity as to *exactly* when this healing, etc. occurred. Mark has, "after some days"; Luke, "on one of those days."

Does this mean now that Matthew, in departing from the historical order of events, presents his material in a haphazard manner, without rhyme or reason? Not at all. In recording the miracles Matthew shows that he loves variety and a kind of climactic arrangement. By a touch of the hand Jesus cleanses the leper. Without so much as a touch he heals the centurion's servant. He banishes a fever, but, as if such miracles of healing are not sufficient to show his power and glory, he even stills the winds and the waves. Moreover, not only over the physical universe does he sway his scepter; also over demons. They too must obey his will. Nevertheless, all these benefits bestowed upon the children of men are largely of a physical nature. As described, they do not, at least not primarily and emphatically, go down to the root of misery: human guilt and pollution, the evil that separates man from his Maker. Sin unforgiven is Satan's best friend, man's chief enemy. The section about to be studied proves that the Great Physician is a Healer also in this respect. While ridding man of physical illness, he also wields the power to deliver him from sin, the greatest of all evils: **2. And behold, they were bringing him a paralyzed man lying on a bed. When Jesus saw their faith he said to the paralytic, Take courage, son; your sins are forgiven.**

Before attempting to explain Matt. 9:2-8 it may be well first of all to furnish a brief harmonized story, one that with a minimum of comment includes all the main features of the three reports: Matt. 9:2-8; Mark 2:1-12; and Luke 5:17-26.

Jesus has entered a private home in Capernaum. The news spreads quickly, so that the place where he is becomes overcrowded. Included in the throng are Pharisees and scribes (doctors of the law) from every village of Galilee and Judea. Some have even come all the way from Jerusalem. The Master begins to bring the message.

Now toward this house four people (relatives, friends?) are carrying a paralyzed man. They desire to bring him to Jesus that he may heal him, but their search for a normal means of entrance is futile. So, on a "bed" or sleeping pad they carry the man to the roof, remove some of the tiles, and lower and deposit him in front of Jesus. The latter, seeing their faith, says to the paralytic, "Take courage, son; your sins are forgiven." In their hearts the scribes are now saying, "This is blasphemy! Who but God alone can forgive sin?" When Jesus perceives in the spirit what is happening he says to his opponents, "Why are y o u thinking evil in y o u r hearts? For, which is easier, to say, 'Your sins are forgiven,' or to say, 'Get up and walk'? But in order that y o u may know that the Son of man has power on earth to forgive sins," (then he says to the paralytic) "Get up, take up your bed, and go home." The man gets up, takes up that on which he had been lying, and goes home. Everybody is seized with amazement. All—including the man who has been cured—glorify God. On every side exclamations such as the following are heard, "We have seen strange things today." "Never have we seen anything like this."

Turning now to Matthew's own account, the shortest of the three, we note first of all that he merely mentions that a paralytic was being brought to Jesus. Just how he got to the place in front of Jesus is not here indicated. The degree of severity of the illness is not specified in any of the three accounts; contrast Matt. 8:6; Luke 7:2. That the case must have been rather serious is however implied in the circumstance that the afflicted one was unable to move about and had to be carried. He is pictured as lying on a pallet or a sleeping pad. Jesus, on the basis of what he could observe with his eyes, namely, that this man was being brought to *him,* and also because of his power to read the secrets of men's hearts (John 2:25), "saw" the faith of the entire little company, that is, of the paralytic himself and of those who had brought him. The friends or relatives had carried him to Jesus. The sick man himself had consented (perhaps even suggested?) to be thus conveyed. There had been a mutual agreement, and this had been carried out. Did the faith of these men consist only in their belief that Jesus was willing and able to bestow physical healing? Or did it include also the confidence that the Master would relieve the paralytic from the burden of his guilt? Though the latter cannot be definitely proved, does it not seem probable in the light of the fact that before Jesus does anything else he assures him of pardon?

A peculiar thing happens. Generally when Jesus is confronted with a sick or handicapped person it is the latter who opens the conversation, or else his friends or relatives do, with a request for healing (8:2, 5; 9:18, 27; 15:21; 17:14, 15; 20:30; Mark 1:30; etc.). In the present case, however, nothing of the kind is reported. The audience is hushed. The men who have carried the paralytic to this house and have deposited him in front of Jesus are silent, and so is also the afflicted one himself. But not a word from any of them is necessary. The Master fully understands. It is he who loves and cares and now addresses the afflicted one. The very first thing Jesus says to him is "Take courage, son." As to "son" or "child" (somewhat more literal), either way this is a term of endearment. Combined with "take courage" we witness here the warmheartedness and tenderness of the Good Shepherd. He dispels the sick man's embarrassment and gloom and as it were embraces him with the arms of his protecting love and care. As far as the record is concerned, in the New Testament, with a single exception, the only one who says "Take courage" or "Be of good cheer" (A.V.) is Jesus. In addition to 9:2 see verse 22; 14:27; Mark 6:50; 10:49 (the one exception) [398]; John 16:33; and Acts 23:11. And the reason for the cheer? It is this: "Your sins are forgiven." They are blotted out, completely and forever. [399] For this comforting truth see also Ps. 103:12; Isa. 1:18; 55:6, 7; Jer. 31:34; Mic. 7:19; and I John 1:9.

The inference seems altogether justified that the matter about which the paralytic was concerned more than about anything else was not the paralysis of his body but the perilous state of his soul. Hence, before making any other pronouncement Jesus absolves him from guilt. Is the further conclusion also justified, namely, that in this man's case sin and sickness stood to each other in the relation of cause and effect, in the sense that loose living had brought this illness upon him? That there was this relation is generally assumed. Nevertheless, there is nothing in the text or in the context that

---

[398] And even this does not necessarily have to be viewed as an exception, for it is the friends' reaction to Christ's command that the blind man be called. It is almost as if Jesus by the mouth of these friends were saying to the blind man, "Be of good cheer."

[399] A. T. Robertson, *Word Pictures*, p. 71, calls the present passive indicative ἀφίενται (the preferred text) an "aoristic present." That it is a kind of past-present, meaning "have been, and therefore are at this very moment, and remain, forgiven," would seem to follow also from the use of the perfect passive indicative ἀφέωνται in the parallel passage, Luke 5:20.

proves it. All we know is that the afflicted one was a paralytic deeply concerned about his sin. That this sin had resulted in his sickness is not stated and probably not even implied. See also Luke 13:1-5; John 9:1-3. [400]

Continued: 3. **At this some of the scribes said within themselves, This fellow blasphemes.** "Who can forgive sins but God alone?" they reason (Mark 2:7; Luke 5:21). Only he knows what is going on in the heart of man, whether or not he has truly repented. Basically, therefore, no one else has the right and the power to grant absolution. The scribes were right in considering the remission of sins to be a divine prerogative (Ps. 103:12; Isa. 1:18; 43:25; 55:6, 7; Jer. 31:34; Mic. 7:19). To be sure, there is a sense in which we, too, forgive, namely, when we earnestly resolve not to take revenge but instead to love the one who has injured us, to promote his welfare, and never again to bring up the past (Matt. 6:12, 15; 18:21; Luke 6:37; Eph. 4:32; Col. 3:13). But *basically,* as described, it is God alone who forgives. It is he alone who is able to remove guilt and to declare that it has actually been removed. Hence, as the scribes see it, Jesus by saying to the paralytic, "Your sins are forgiven," is claiming for himself a prerogative that belongs to God alone. Here again the scribes were right. But now their thinking arrives at the fork in the road, and they make the wrong turn. Either: *a.* Jesus is what by implication he claims to be, namely, God; or *b.* he blasphemes, in the sense that he unjustly claims the attributes and prerogatives of deity. The scribes accept *b.*

Not only do they commit this tragic error, but, as the following context indicates, they compound it by reasoning somewhat as follows, "It is an easy thing for him to say, 'Your sins are forgiven,' for no one is able to disprove it, since no one can look into his neighbor's heart or enter the throne-room of the Almighty and discover his judicial decisions as to who is, and who is not, forgiven." As they see it, therefore, Jesus is both blasphemous and flippant.

In what Jesus now says and does he annihilates both of these false conclusions: 4-6. **Jesus, knowing their thoughts, said, Why are y o u thinking evil in y o u r hearts? For, which is easier, to say, Your sins are forgiven, or to say, Get up and walk? But in order that y o u may know that the Son of man has power on earth to forgive sins, (then he said to the paralytic) Get up, take up your bed, and go home.**

He knew their thoughts (John 2:25; 21:17). Had he not been God he would not have known them (Ps. 139). By questioning the scribes he sharply reprimands them. Their cogitations were wicked, "for" (elucidary) they were *falsely* accusing him. Jesus asks why they are doing this. Let them examine their own hearts. Was it not in order to find fault with them that they had come here today, with the ultimate purpose that they might destroy him (cf.

---

[400] As to John 5:14 see N.T.C. on that passage.

12:14; Mark 3:6)? As to which was easier, to say, "Your sins are forgiven," or to say, "Get up. . . .," do not both in an equal measure require omnipotent power? Therefore, if Jesus can do the one, then can he not also perform the other? In order that they may know that he, the humble yet all-glorious Son of man (see on 8:20), has the divine right and power on earth—hence, before the door of grace is closed (25:10)—to forgive sins . . . here parenthetically Matthew adds, "then he said to the paralytic," the words addressed to the latter being, "Get up, take up your bed, and go home." The first two actions indicated in the command are in the nature of the case performed in a moment, the third (going home) is pictured as taking a little while, proceeding step by step. [401]

Continued: 7. **And he got up and went home.** By means of the power and love of Jesus a complete cure was immediately brought about, for, because of the operation of these attributes, the man believed that he was able to do what he was told to do. So he acted on the basis of this faith, was healed, and started on his way, finally reaching home.

Thus, in the realm of the visible Jesus performed a miracle which simultaneously proved that also in the universe of the invisible he had exercised his divine power and love. He had given this man a healthy body but also, and this first of all, a healthy soul ("Your sins are forgiven"). He had thoroughly refuted the accusations of his enemies. Moreover, as to the charge that it was easy for him to pronounce absolution, well, he was *able* indeed to do it and he actually did it, as he here proved; but as to it being *easy,* was it not exactly this granting of pardon that required all the suffering he endured during his earthly sojourn, climaxed by the bloody sweat of Gethsemane, the scourging of Gabbatha, and the cross of Golgotha? And similarly, as to the granting of physical recovery, does not 8:17 apply here also? See on that passage.

Did the scribes admit their defeat? Did they at least acknowledge that Jesus had justified his claim? On this point Matthew is silent. So are also Mark and Luke. The sequel would seem to indicate that they admitted nothing and became more and more hostile (Matt. 9:11, 34; 12:2, 14, 24; Mark 2:16, 24; 3:2, 5; 3:22; 7:1 ff.; Luke 5:30; 6:2, 7, 11). As to the people in general, their reaction is described as follows: 8. **When the crowds saw this they were filled with awe, and glorified God for giving such power to men.** According to Matthew (the best reading) the people were "filled with awe," or "awe-struck"; Mark has "astonished" or "astounded"; Luke, "seized with astonishment . . . and filled with awe." All report that the people "glorified God." Matthew adds, "for giving such power to men." It

---

[401] The original uses two aorists (ἐγερθείς, aor. pass. participle, having arisen; and ἆρον, aor. imper. active, take up); then ὕπαγε, sec. per. sing. pres. imperative, go or be going.

will hardly do to interpret this to mean that the people in general now understood that in a unique sense Jesus was divine, and that they, filled with a sense of their own sinfulness and unworthiness in *his* presence, now did what on one occasion Peter is reported to have done (Luke 5:8). The true interpretation is probably that they ascribed glory and honor to God because, as they saw it, he had imparted such power to a member of the human race, the very race to which they themselves also belonged. It is very well possible that we have here an echo of the words that had just now been uttered by Jesus himself, namely, "But in order that y o u may know that the Son of man has power, etc." Note the word "power" (or "authority") in both cases; also compare "Son of man" with "men." If this be correct, they were equating "Son of man" with "man" (as in Ezekiel), and by doing this they missed the term's deeper meaning. To be sure, for a moment the glory of Jesus flashed before their consciousness, but they caught only a glimpse of it. They missed seeing him as "the effulgence of God's glory and the very image of his substance" (Heb. 1:3, A.R.V.).

The Call of Matthew

In all three Gospels the story of Matthew's call is related next (Matt. 9:9-13; Mark 2:13-17; and Luke 5:27-32). Moreover, in a rather general way a time and place connection is established between the healing of the paralytic and this call. Both obviously took place in Capernaum and, as Matthew remembered it, the two events followed each other closely in time, for the author says, 9. **As he was passing on from there Jesus saw a man named Matthew, sitting at the tax office, and he said to him, Follow me.** Much of the material relating to Matthew—his occupation, place of residence, call to discipleship, qualifications, style, etc.—has already been presented; see pp. 92-97; 241; 315, 316. According to Mark 2:13 it was in the vicinity of the seashore that Matthew received his call to become one of the disciples of Jesus. The future evangelist was sitting at the tax collector's booth or customhouse, the place where the tariff was collected on the traffic in goods passing along the international highway between Syria and Egypt.

Jesus said to Matthew, "Follow me." **He got up and followed him.** Thus soberly and without taking any credit for himself the man who was most deeply concerned records this unforgettable experience. For more detail, with emphasis on the greatness of the sacrifice, we must turn to Luke's Gospel, which informs us that in getting up to follow Jesus, the publican "forsook all." It is well-nigh certain that Matthew, who lived and worked in Capernaum, the very place which Jesus had chosen as his headquarters, had had frequent previous contacts with the Master and that when the call came he had already surrendered his heart to him and the cause he represented. Nevertheless, when he now not only makes a clean break with his occupational past and joins the One who called him, declaring to the whole world

421

that it is to Jesus that he has unreservedly dedicated himself, he performs an act of devotion whose sacrificial character must not be minimized.

In passing, it should be observed that since Matthew was a minor official, not the chief tax collector and certainly not the tax farmer or lease holder, the business of collecting the tariff at Capernaum did not cease when he left all to follow Jesus.

Was it at this time that the man whom Mark (2:14) and Luke (5:27) call *Levi* (for explanation of that name see Gen. 29:34) received and/or adopted the name *Matthew*, meaning "gift of Jehovah" (cf. Theodore: "gift of God")? If so, Jesus himself may have given him this name (cf. Mark 3:16; John 1:42). It is also possible that from the very beginning the one who now joined the little group of closest followers had two names. Double names were not uncommon among the Jews: Thomas was called Didymus (John 11:16); and in all probability Bartholomew (Matt. 10:3; Mark 3:18; Luke 6:14; and Acts 1:13) is Nathanael (John 1:45-49; 21:2). The identity of Levi and Matthew can hardly be questioned, as a comparison of the three Synoptic accounts of this call immediately proves. Moreover, Luke calls Levi "a publican" (5:27), and in the list of The Twelve as recorded in what in our Bibles is the first Gospel there is mention of a "Matthew the publican" (10:3). In all the lists of the twelve the name Matthew has replaced Levi (Matt. 10:2-4; Mark 3:14-19; Luke 6:13-16; Acts 1:13).

It has already been pointed out that as a tax collector, experienced in writing and in keeping records, and of necessity versed in more than one language, the services of Matthew would be very valuable to Jesus and to the cause of the gospel. To the Mediator this man was indeed a gift of God. He was destined to write and preserve for his contemporaries and for posterity a record of Christ's words and deeds. Moreover we receive the impression from the very brevity with which Matthew records his call, omitting any mention of the cost to himself, that he was modest and humble. He may well have been a man of few *spoken* words. Nowhere in the four Gospels is he ever introduced as *saying* anything. In this respect he ranks with two other "obscure" disciples: James the Less [402] and Simon the Zealot. Peter speaks with great frequency (Matt. 14:28; 15:15; 16:16, 22; 17:4; etc.). Andrew, at times (Mark 13:3; John 1:41; 6:8, 9; 12:22). So also do the brothers James (Mark 10:35-39; Luke 9:54) and John (Luke 9:54; John 13:23-25). So do Philip (John 1:45; 12:22), Thomas (John 11:16; 14:5; 20:24-29) and Judas the Traitor (Matt. 26:14-16, 25; 27:3, 4; John 12:4, 5). Even Nathanael is not completely silent (John 1:46-49), nor is Judas the Greater (John 14:22). But from the lips of Matthew we hear never a word. All the more brilliantly does he let his light shine in this glorious Gospel!

---

[402] As to the idea that Matthew and James the Less were brothers see footnote 113, p. 95.

Nevertheless, to think of Matthew as being only a writer would be doing him an injustice. We see in him a (shall we say *rare?*) combination of writing ability and hospitality, in his case both of these being the product of deep spirituality. Matthew had caught the Master's spirit. He knew that it was to seek and to save sinners, definitely including publicans!, that Jesus had come to dwell among men. So, as Luke records but Matthew modestly refrains from saying, it was this same publican, now disciple, who "made a great banquet *for him* [that is, for Jesus!] in his [Matthew's] house," a banquet to which Matthew's friends, the publicans, were welcomed (Luke 5:29). Matthew merely says, 10. In the house, as Jesus [403] was reclining at table, [404] what happens? [405] Many tax collectors and (other) people of low reputation came and reclined at table with him and his disciples. This may be considered a kind of farewell banquet, arranged by Matthew and at his house, in honor of Jesus, bidding farewell to the old life, ringing in the new, and beckoning all to become spiritual followers of the Lord. Many "tax-collectors and sinners" (thus literally) attended and were reclining at table with Jesus and those disciples who by this time had become his steady followers.

The tax-collectors have been described earlier (see on 5:46). The reasons why they were held in low esteem, as being dishonest, greedy, and unpatriotic, have been discussed. However, these "publicans" had company. See John 7:49; cf. 9:24. "Publicans *and sinners*" had at least this in common that none of them paid much attention to the rules and regulations which by the rabbis had been superimposed upon the law of God. Of these "traditions" Pharisees and scribes made everything. It remains true, however, that even the law of God itself was often grossly violated or at least disregarded by publicans and their friends. The low reputation which they had acquired in the eyes of the Jewish religious leaders and their followers was partly undeserved, partly deserved. The main point is this, that Jesus had come to deliver them from their sins and miseries. Matthew understood this. The Pharisees did not. They were too proud and too self-righteous to understand. But they did take cognizance of the fact that Jesus was associating familiarly with "such bad characters": 11. The Pharisees took notice of this, and said to his disciples, Why is it that y o u r teacher is eating with tax-collectors and sinners? In all probability it was when the banquet had ended and the guests

---

[403] With most translators and commentators (but against Lenski, *op. cit.*, p. 353) I believe that the first αὐτοῦ (as well as the last) in verse 10 refers to Jesus, to whom the preceding αὐτῷ (in ἠκολούθησεν αὐτῷ) also points. This furnishes an easy thought transition: "as he [Jesus] was reclining at table, many . . . reclined at table with him [Jesus]. . . . Why is it that y o u r teacher is eating with tax-collectors and sinners?"

[404] Literally, "And it came to pass while he was reclining at table that. . . ." This "and it came to pass" or "happened" is a construction of frequent occurrence in Hebrew (way^ehî) and its Septuagintal equivalent.

[405] On ἰδού see footnote 133 on p. 131.

were departing that the Pharisees, ever ready and eager to find fault with Jesus (12:2, 24; 15:1; 19:3; etc.), but at times lacking courage to criticize him directly, vent their bitterness upon the disciples who had chosen *such* a person to be their teacher. The real and final object of their disgust was, of course, Jesus himself. The words, "Why is it that *y o u r teacher*. . . ." are full of stinging reproof, as if to say, "Shame on y o u for having accepted such a man as y o u r teacher!"

Was there merit in this thinly veiled accusation, a charge in the form of a question? Is it not true that eating with a person implies friendship and fellowship? See on 8:11. How then was it possible for Jesus to recline at table in the company of such disreputable people? What the Pharisees, because of their legalistic and unsympathetic hearts, fail to understand is that there are times and occasions when such fellowship is entirely proper and justified. Jesus, by means of this close association, is meeting a need, as he himself now declares: **12. When he heard this he said, It is not those who are healthy that need a doctor but those who are ill.**

The slur of the Pharisees and the resulting embarrassment of the disciples had been duly noted by Jesus. He himself, by means of what may have been a current proverb, flings back a clinching answer. When he associates on intimate terms with people of low reputation he does not do this as a hobnobber, a comrade in evil, "birds of a feather flocking together," but as a physician, one who, without in any way becoming contaminated with the diseases of his patients, must get very close to them *in order that he may heal them!* Moreover, it is especially the Pharisees who should be able to understand this. Are not they the very people who place their trust in their own righteousness while they despise all others (Luke 18:9)? If, then, in the eyes of the Pharisees, publicans and sinners are so very sick, should they not be healed? Is it the business of the healer to heal the healthy or the sick? The sick, of course.

We see, therefore, that it is on the basis of their own reasoning that Jesus is condemning the attitude of the Pharisees and justifying his own. Implication: could it be that the Pharisees are neglecting their duty? Are these carping critics extending to those in need the hand of healing and kindness? We now understand why Jesus continues: **13. Go and learn what is meant by:**

I desire mercy and not sacrifice.

Here, as once before (see on 2:15), we have a quotation from the prophecies of Hosea. This time, however, it is Jesus himself, not the evangelist, who quotes. The background and general outline of this Old Testament book have been presented in connection with the earlier quotation. Among the sins committed by the adulterous nation were, besides the transgressions against the first table of the law (Hos. 6:7; 7:10, 11, 14; 8:1-7, 14; etc.), such abominations as robbery and murder (6:9; 7:1, 7). It is easily understood that in such a context of iniquity bringing sacrifices amounted to sheer mockery. The manifestation of "goodness" with respect to both God and man [406] was what God desired, rather than merely burnt-offerings. That is the essence of the Hosea passage (6:6) quoted here in Matt. 9:12. When without a genuine change of heart and conduct sacrifices were nevertheless brought, this amounted to dead ritualism, loathsome to the Lord (8:13, 14). "Religion" without goodness or kindness is worthless. Jesus tells the Pharisees to go and learn that lesson, that is, to reflect on it and take it to heart. Let them ponder and apply to themselves the lesson taught in Hos. 6:6; Amos 5:21-24; Mic. 6:8; cf. Matt. 23:23-26. A religion that tithes mint, dill, and cummin but leaves undone the weightier matters of the law: justice, mercy, and fidelity, is nothing but a sad distortion of the genuine article.

To this quotation from Hosea Jesus adds, **For I did not come to call righteous people but sinners.** Substantially this is the reading also in Mark and Luke, though "for" is found only in Matthew, and Luke ends the sentence with "to repentance." The "for" may be called "explanatory" or "continuative." In the present context it means something like: *"In line with* this fact that as a physician I came to answer need and to show mercy, the kind of mercy which y o u, Pharisees, should also show, is the fact that I did not come to call righteous people but sinners." The fact that the calling is "to repentance," though expressed only in Luke, is implied also in Matthew and Mark (see Matt. 3:2; 4:17; Mark 1:4, 15).

The *calling* to which there is reference in these Gospel passages (Matt. 5:13; Mark 2:17; Luke 5:32) is the earnest invitation extended to sinners to accept Jesus Christ as their Lord and Savior. That this calling is not always effectual is clear from Matt. 22:14, "For many are called, but few chosen." In the epistles, on the other hand, calling is that act of the Holy Spirit whereby he savingly applies the gospel invitation to certain definite individuals among all those to whom, in the course of history, that invitation is extended (Rom. 4:17; 8:30; 9:11, 24; Gal. 1:6, 15; Eph. 1:18; 4:1, 4; Phil. 3:14; I Thess. 2:12; 4:7; II Thess. 1:11; II Tim. 1:9). Does this mean that the way of salvation proclaimed in the Gospels differs from that set forth in the epistles, so that, for example, in the former, salvation ultimately depends on the will of man, but in the latter on the grace of God? Not at all, the difference is only one of terminology. The doctrine is the same in both. According to the Gospels too it is only by the grace and power of God that sinners are able to accept the invitation and along with it the salvation held out to them by God; as is clear from Matt. 7:7; 19:25, 26; Luke 11:13;

---

[406] As the parallelistic construction indicates, the *ḥesedh* of Hos. 6:6 refers not only to love toward the neighbor but also to "knowledge" of—hence, covenant fellowship with—God. Here in Matt. 9:13 the emphasis on ἔλεος is obviously on the former: kindness extended even toward publicans and sinners.

12:32; 22:31, 32; John 3:3, 5; 6:44; 12:32; 15:5. With all this compare James 1:17, 18; I Cor. 4:7; Eph. 2:8; Phil. 2:12, 13; and II Thess. 2:13, 14.

Here in Matt. 9:13 the glorious purpose of Christ's incarnation and mission receives beautiful expression. The passage makes clear that not to those who consider themselves worthy but rather to those who are in desperate need the invitation to salvation, full and free, is extended. It was sinners, the lost, the straying, the beggars, the burdened ones, the hungry and thirsty, whom Jesus came to save. See also Matt. 5:6; 11:28-30; 22:9, 10; Luke 14:21-23; ch. 15; 19:10; John 7:37, 38. This is in line with all of special revelation, both the Old Testament and the New (Isa. 1:18; 45:22; 55:1, 6, 7; Jer. 35:15; Ezek. 18:23; 33:11; Hos. 6:1; 11:8; Rom. 8:23, 24; II Cor. 5:20; I Tim. 1:15; Rev. 3:20; 22:17). It is a message full of comfort and "relevant" to every age!

The Question about Fasting

It is held by some [407] that the incident reported here in 9:14-17 (cf. Mark 2:18-22; Luke 5:33-39) occurred in very close chronological connection with the one just discussed (Matt. 9:9-13). This opinion is based not so much on the word "then" or "thereupon" at the beginning of Matt. 9:14—this word is very indefinite, and can mean "in those days" as well as "at that very time" or "shortly afterward"—as on the parallel passage in Mark 2:18, "Now John's disciples and the Pharisees were fasting, and they come and say to him, 'Why do John's disciples and the disciples of the Pharisees fast [or: Why are . . . fasting] but your disciples do not fast [or: are not fasting]?' " When this close temporal connection between the two incidents is accepted, the dramatic character of the account is heightened: at the very time when Jesus, his disciples, and many publicans are *feasting* at Matthew's house, the Baptist's disciples and the Pharisees with their followers are *fasting*, with the immediate result: the question of Matt. 9:14.

By no means is it true, however, that this exegesis has found favor with all commentators. Even among those who do favor it reservations in stating this position are not uncommon. Several interpreters do not even touch the question at all. [408] The simple fact is that none of the evangelists definitely indicate when this questioning about fasting occurred. [409] Besides, those

---

[407] For example, by A. T. Robertson, *Harmony of the Gospels*, New York, 1922, footnote on p. 40; also by H. N. Ridderbos, Lenski, and Grosheide in their respective commentaries on this Matthew passage.

[408] See the comments on Matt. 9:14 by W. C. Allen (*I.C.C.*), A. B. Bruce (*Expositor's Greek Testament*), John Calvin, C. R. Erdman, S. E. Johnson (*Interpreter's Bible*), and R. V. G. Tasker (*Tyndale New Testament Commentaries*).

[409] The periphrastic imperfect ἦσαν νηστεύοντες (Mark 2:18) does not decide the issue in either direction. It describes or pictures but does not necessarily indicate that what is being described coincided in time with the event related in the preceding paragraph. It

who nevertheless accept the chronological concurrence of the feast and the inquiry about fasting may run into difficulty when they arrive at Matt. 9:18. See on that verse; especially footnote 413 on p. 429.

But though there may not have been a close *chronological* connection between the two events, there may very well have been a *logical* relationship. Fellowshipping with publicans and sinners, and this on more than one occasion (11:19; Luke 7:34; 15:1, 2; cf. 19:1-10), while the disciples of John and the Pharisees abstained from such convivialities and even practiced a measure of austerity, was sooner or later bound to lead to what is reported in verse 14. **Then the disciples of John came to him, saying, Why is it that we and the Pharisees fast often, [410] but your disciples do not fast?**

It is clear from this question that even after John's imprisonment (see on 4:12) some of his disciples continued as a distinct group. In view of John 3:25, 26 this is not very surprising. It appears from John 3:30 that he who had been their leader gave no encouragement to this separatistic movement and would not have supported "Disciples of John the Baptist" outgrowths that persisted for centuries. Encouraged, perhaps, by the fact that in spite of the Baptist's witness to Jesus as the Christ (Matt. 3:11; John 1:29-36) and the many things which Jesus and John had in common, there were also some sharp differences (Matt. 11:18, 19), these "disciples of John" inquire why it is that while they and the Pharisees fast often, Jesus' disciples do not fast. In favor of these inquirers it must be said that they do not bypass Jesus but approach him directly and frankly (contrast the Pharisees, verse 11), and also that their question, though perhaps not entirely free from a tinge of criticism, is probably rather an honest request for information than a veiled but bitter accusation.

In reality, however, there was no justification for this question. Had these men been better students of Scripture they would have known *a.* that the only fast that could by any stretch of the imagination be derived from the law of God was the one on the day of atonement (Lev. 23:27), and *b.* that according to the teaching of Isa. 58:6, 7 and Zech. 7:1-10 it was not a literal fast but love, both vertical and horizontal, which God demanded.

There was an important reason why for the disciples of Jesus the kind of fasting in question would have been inappropriate: **15. Jesus said to them, As long as the bridegroom is with them, is it possible for the bridegroom's attendants to be mourning?** The question is so phrased that the answer must be, "No." Jesus here compares his blessed presence on earth with a wedding-

---

simply is a fact that in Mark's Gospel 2:18-22 is one of those sections that lack any specific reference to time or chronological order. See also N. B. Stonehouse, *Origins of the Synoptic Gospels*, p. 66.

410 Whether we read πολλά or πυκνά, the rendering "often" is allowable in either case. See L.N.T. (A. and G.), pp. 695 and 736. There is also strong support for the reading which omits the adverb altogether. See textual apparatus N.N.

feast. Again and again Scripture compares the relationship between Jehovah and his people, or between Christ and his church, with the bond of love between bridegroom and bride (Isa. 50:1 ff.; 54:1 ff.; 62:5; Jer. 2:32; 31:32; Hos. 2:1 ff.; Matt. 25:1 ff.; John 3:29; II Cor. 11:2; Eph. 5:32; Rev. 19:7; 21:9). [411] Verse 15 speaks about "the sons of the bridal chamber" (thus literally), meaning "the bridegroom's attendants." These were friends of the groom. They stood close to him. They had been invited to the wedding, were in charge of arrangements, and were expected to do everything possible to promote the success of the festivities. [412]

Bridegroom's attendants fasting while the feast is in progress! How absurd, says Jesus as it were. Disciples of the Lord mourning while their Master is performing works of mercy and while words of life and beauty are dropping from his lips, how utterly incongruous! Jesus adds, however, **But days will arrive when the bridegroom shall be taken away from them. Then they shall fast.** This, of course, is an early prediction of Christ's death on the cross. That the mourning in connection with it would not be of long duration is pointed out in John 16:16-22. By means of Christ's resurrection it was going to be replaced by joy.

By two illustrations taken from daily life Jesus makes clear how inappropriate it would be for the disciples *now* to be fasting, as if with the coming of Christ a great calamity had descended upon them. The main lesson conveyed is that the new order of things which Jesus by his coming has ushered in, bringing healing to the sick, liberation to the demon-possessed, freedom from care to the care-ridden, cleansing to lepers, food to the hungry, restoration to the handicapped, and above all salvation to those lost in sin, does not fit into the old mold of man-ordained fasting. The first figure is as follows: **16. No one puts a patch, made of a piece of new cloth, on an old garment, for then the patch pulls away from the garment, and a worse tear results.** If a patch of unfulled wool is placed on a garment that has seen better days, the result will be that when this unshrunk piece becomes wet and shrinks, it will pull to pieces the bordering cloth of the badly worn garment. The patch which was supposed to take care of the original tear will now produce an even bigger tear. The second figure reinforces the first: **17. Nor is new wine poured into old wine-skins; otherwise the wine-skins burst, the wine is spilled, and the skins are ruined.** The wine-skin was usually made of the skin of a goat or a sheep. After being removed from the animal it was tanned, and after the hair had been cut close the skin was turned inside out. The neck opening became the mouth of the "bottle." The other

---

[411] For a more detailed account of this relationship see my *More Than Conquerors*, Grand Rapids, seventeenth edition 1970, pp. 214-217.

[412] These "bridegroom's attendants" must not be confused with "*the* friend of the bridegroom" (John 3:29) whose duty it was to bring the bride to the bridegroom and who rejoices when he hears the groom's voice in welcoming the bride.

openings, at the feet and the tail, were closed with cords. Naturally an old wine-skin is no match for new, still fermenting wine, for such wine tends to stretch the container. A new wine-skin would be sufficiently elastic to stand the pressure, but under similar conditions an old one, stiff and rigid, would crack. The wine would spill out and the skin would be of no further use. Continued: **but new wine is poured into fresh wine-skins and both are preserved.**

It is hardly correct to say that while the new wine represents salvation by grace, the old wine-skins symbolize salvation by the works of the law. What Jesus taught with reference to the law is found in such passages as 5:17-20 and 22:34-40. Not the law of God as such was in question here, for, as previously stated, the frequent fast was a purely human institution. What Jesus did show was that the salvation which he brought was out of line with fastings from which the note of joy was completely excluded, and that this was especially true with respect to his disciples, the men who stood in the closest relation to him. The new wine of rescue and riches for all who were willing to accept these blessings, even for publicans and sinners, must be poured into the fresh wine-skins of gratitude, freedom, and spontaneous service to the glory of God.

The Restoration to Life of the Ruler's Daugher
and
The Healing of the Woman Who Touched Christ's Garment

18. While he was still saying these things. . . . Having explained the incident that is reported in verses 14-17 as belonging to a time later than the preaching of the Sermon on the Mount, we encounter no difficulty with this chronological note at the beginning of verse 18. [413] The obvious meaning is that while Jesus was still answering the question regarding fasting, **look,** [414]

---

[413] Both Mark and Luke leave the impression that the two intertwined miracles about to be studied occurred *after* the preaching of the Sermon on the Mount and the calling and commissioning of The Twelve (cf. Mark 5:21-43 with 3:13 ff.; and cf. Luke 8:40-56 with 6:12 ff.). Those who accept this view but nevertheless ascribe an earlier date to the question about fasting get into a difficulty, because Matt. 9:18 chronologically links verses 14-17 with verses 18-26. Let the reader judge whether their attempts to solve this puzzle are successful. In my opinion they are not. F. W. Grosheide gets rid of the sequence problem by rendering verse 18a as follows: "Once while he was teaching such things." See his *Kommentaar op het Nieuwe Testament,* p. 115. A. T. Robertson, in his *Harmony,* p. 74, a footnote, remarks, "Broadus felt that the language of Matt. 9:18 compelled him to place 9:18 after 9:17. I [Robertson] do not think so, for 'While he spake' may be merely an introductory phrase for a new paragraph." A striking illustration of what can happen when one refuses to arrive at a decision with respect to the lateness or earliness of the question about fasting is furnished by the Berkeley Version which ascribes two different dates to what is clearly the same incident. Above Matt. 9:14 ff. it places the date "Autumn, 28 A.D." and above its parallel, Mark 2:18 ff., the date "April-May, 28 A.D."

[414] For ἰδού see p. 131, including footnote 133.

a [415] ruler came, knelt before him, and said, My daughter has just died, but come, lay your hand upon her, and she will live.

The synagogue was ruled by a board of elders. One of its responsibilities was to maintain good order at the synagogue meetings. The man who came to Jesus and whom Matthew does not mention by name but whom Mark and Luke call Jairus was a member of such a board. Since he was probably living in Capernaum we may assume that he had heard about, and perhaps even witnessed, some of the miracles performed by Jesus.

Matthew's report of the double miracle is very brief, nine verses; Luke's covers seventeen verses; Mark's twenty-three. We are perhaps justified in interpreting the ruler's behavior (as reported by Matthew; cf. Mark 5:21 ff. and Luke 8:40 ff.) as an expression of high respect for Jesus ("he came and knelt before him"), of intense stress ("but come"), and of great faith ("lay your hand upon her, and she will live"). According to Mark and Luke, Jairus had first asked Jesus to heal the child; then, when informed about her death, had been urged by the Lord not to despair but to believe. So he now renews his request in modified form, namely, that Jesus may lay his hand upon the dead girl, adding, "and she will live." This conviction on the part of the ruler is all the more remarkable in view of the fact that the Gospels do not report a restoration-to-life miracle performed by Jesus previous to this time. As to "lay your hand upon her" see on 8:3.

Continued: **19. At once Jesus began to follow him, and so did his disciples.** The rendering, "Jesus rose and followed him," though true to the basic meaning of the participle used in the original, [416] is confusing. It might suggest that the Lord was either still reclining at table in Matthew's house when the grieving father of the dead child asked him to come along with him, or that he had been sitting by the roadside. In view of the preceding context in Matthew and of the accounts in the other Gospels neither of these ideas seems to be within the realm of probability. A far more reasonable interpretation is that at the ruler's request Jesus went into action *at once*. Compare such colloquial expressions as, "He up and married," "up and bought." Such a verbal "up" describes abrupt action. And so it is here. Without any delay Jesus as it were quickened his steps in following the ruler toward the latter's home. So did Christ's disciples. Cf. Mark 5:31. From Luke 8:51 we learn that of the total number of these disciples Jesus suffered only Peter, James, and John to be with him when he performed his astounding miracle. Cf. Mark 5:37.

Suddenly there is an interruption: **20, 21. Immediately** [417] **a woman who had suffered from hemorrhages for twelve years, having come from behind, touched the tassel of his garment; for she said within herself, If I but touch**

---

[415] εἰς used indefinitely. See Gram. N.T., p. 292.

[416] ἐγερθείς: having arisen.

[417] For ἰδού see footnote 133 on p. 131.

his garment I shall get well. Again and again during his earthly ministry Jesus was interrupted; namely, in his speaking to a crowd (Mark 2:1 ff.), conversing with his disciples (Matt. 16:21 ff.; 26:31 ff.; Luke 12:12 ff.), traveling (Matt. 20:29 ff.), sleeping (Matt. 8:24, 25), and praying (Mark 1:35 ff.). The fact that none of these intrusions floor him, so that for the moment he would be at a loss what to do or what to say, shows that we are dealing here with the Son of man who is also the Son of God! What *we* would call an "interruption" is for him a springboard or take-off point for the utterance of a great saying or, as here, for the performance of a marvelous deed, revealing his power, wisdom, and love. What for us would have been a painful exigency is to him a golden opportunity.

A sermon based on Mark's or on Luke's account of the theme "The woman who touched the border of Christ's garment" might have the following points: Her Faith Concealed (Mark 5:25-28; Luke 8:43, 44a), Rewarded (Mark 5:29; Luke 8:44b), and Revealed (Mark 5:30-34; Luke 8:45-48). But, as already indicated, Matthew's account does not contain all of this material. It is very brief. We are given to understand that this woman was in great distress. No wonder, for she had suffered from hemorrhages for a period of twelve years. There are those who believe that the phrasing of verse 20, especially in light of Mark 5:29 and Luke 8:44, makes it certain that the drain of blood was constant, that is, without ever any intermission. Another view would be that throughout the twelve years an excessive loss of blood, occurring periodically, made it impossible for her ever to feel strong and healthy, and that at this particular moment she was again being afflicted by one of these hemorrhages. Mark reports that this woman had "suffered much from many physicians, had spent all she had, and had not improved but rather grown worse." Without in any way contradicting Mark, it is certainly not surprising that Luke—Dr. Luke, remember! (Col. 4:14)—informs us that she "*could not* be healed" by any physician. The doctors did not cure her, for, humanly speaking, her sickness was incurable! Whether or not the drain of blood was constant, on either view her condition was now such that it would make her ceremonially unclean and would similarly affect anyone she touched (Lev. 15:19 ff.).

It does not surprise us therefore that she is afraid to come out into the open. She is not going to come into physical contact with Jesus himself. She will merely touch his garment, and even then, only one of the four wool tassels which every Israelite was ordered to wear on the corners of his square, outer robe (Num. 15:38; cf. Deut. 22:12) to remind him of the law of God. See also the explanation of Matt. 23:5. [418] Naturally the quickest and easiest way to bring oneself into physical contact with a garment without being noticed was to come from behind and touch the tuft swinging freely from

---

[418] Cf. S.BK. IV, p. 277.

the back of the robe. The wearer, so this woman thought, would never even notice what was happening. [419] So, she came from behind and touched the tassel.

The greatness of her faith consisted in this, that she believed that the power of Christ to heal was so amazing that the mere touch of his garment [420] would result in an immediate and instant cure. That this faith was nevertheless by no means perfect appears from the fact that she thought that such an actual touch was necessary and that Jesus would never notice it. But he did notice it, praised her for her faith, encouraged her, and healed her: **22. But Jesus turned, saw her, and said, Take courage, daughter; your faith has made you well. Instantly the woman recovered.** So, she had not escaped Christ's notice after all (for Christ's knowledge see above, on verse 4; cf. John 1:48; 2:25; 21:17).

Jesus now turns around and addresses her. Affectionately he calls her "daughter," and tells her to "take courage" (see on 9:2, 3). When he adds, "Your faith has made you well," we may perhaps detect a threefold purpose: a. to reward her for her conviction that he would cure her instantly and completely; b. to stress that it was his *personal* response to her *personal* faith in him that cured her, thereby removing from her mind any remnant, however small, of superstition, as if the garment as such had contributed in any way to the cure; and c. to open the way for her complete reinstatement in the social and religious life and fellowship of her people.

The recovery was instant. In one brief moment the hemorrhage stopped completely. Health and vigor were surging through every part of her body. Mark and Luke report that, by inducing her to give a public testimony, Jesus provided also for her soul. In the process of testifying was she not also a blessing to others?

After the interruption Jesus continues on his way to the ruler's house. The usual mourning ceremonies then prevailing were in full swing: **23, 24. And when Jesus came to the ruler's house and saw the flute-players and the noisy crowd he said, Go away. . . .** Both Matthew and Mark picture the noisy, clamorous, disorderly crowd of people in the house of the ruler. As, according to custom, burial followed soon after death, this was the crowd's only opportunity, and everybody, especially the professional mourners (cf. Jer. 9:17, 18), made the most of it, perhaps all the more because a ruler of the synagogue was a very important man! Here then was moaning and groaning at its loudest.

Matthew makes mention of flute-players. Because flutes were very easy to

---

[419] On this passage see A. Schlatter, *Erläuterungen zum Neuen Testament*, Stuttgart, 1908.

[420] By touching *the tassel* she was, of course, touching *the garment*. Mark 5:27, 28 does not even mention the tassel, only the garment.

make, and could be constructed of a variety of material—reeds, cane, bone, etc.—they were very popular. As ancient pictures have shown, such flute-playing was often accompanied by the clapping of hands. In the New Testament the word flute-player occurs only here and in Rev. 18:22, in the latter passage in connection with merriment.

Jesus, realizing a. that much of this ostentatious display of grief was insincere and therefore improper, and b. that in this particular case death was not to have the last word, commanded the noise-makers to leave the room where the dead child lay. He added, **for the girl is not dead but asleep.** Those who heard him say this took this literally, as if Jesus meant that soul and body had not actually separated. Even today there are interpreters who make allowance for the possibility that the ruler's daughter was merely in a coma. [421] But John 11:11-14 presents a striking parallel. When Jesus told the disciples, "Our friend Lazarus has fallen asleep," the disciples interpreted this saying literally. They should have paid more attention to what the Lord had told them a few moments earlier, "This illness is not unto death. . . .," that is, "Death will not be the final outcome of this illness." Again and again the New Testament exposes as error the tendency to interpret every word of Christ literally (John 2:20, 21; 3:3, 4; 4:14, 15, 32, 33; 6:51, 52; 7:34, 35; 8:51, 52; 11:11, 12, 23, 24; 14:4, 5). So also here in Matt. 9:24 what Jesus says must not be interpreted literally but means that death would not have the final say.

Matthew records the crowd's reaction as follows: **But they were laughing in his face.** Literally the Greek says, "They were laughing him down." The reference is probably to repeated bursts of derisive laughter aimed at humiliating him. [422] It seems that these mourners were endowed with the dubious gift of shifting (automatically?), in one sudden moment, from dismal moaning to uproarious mirth.

25. **When the crowd had been expelled he entered and took her by the hand, and the girl got up.** Jesus has entered the room in which the body is lying. The noise-makers have been expelled. In addition to the Lord himself and the dead child there are present the child's parents and, as already

---

421 Thus, for example, R. V. G. Tasker, *op. cit.*, p. 100, states that the girl may have been in a deep coma which her relatives not unnaturally mistook for death. It is only fair to add that he also gives reasons in support of the opposite view, namely, that the child had actually died.

422 I believe this description does justice both to the imperfect tense, the meaning of the uncompounded verb (see Luke 6:21), and the sense of the prefix. A somewhat similar compound verbal form occurs in German: *"Sie lachten ihn aus,"* Dutch: *"Zij lachten hem uit"* (they were laughing him out). It is difficult, perhaps impossible, to find an English term that will convey exactly the same meaning. "They were laughing at him" and "They were ridiculing him" are hardly adequate. As I see it, the best is still, "They laughed him to scorn" (A.V.), or else, with retention of the descriptive flavor of the imperfect, "They were laughing in his face."

indicated, Peter, James, and John. The astounding happening is related in simple language. With the exception of the resurrection of Jesus himself (28:6) and of those who were raised in connection with his death and resurrection (27:52, 53), this is the only bringing back to life from the dead that is recorded by Matthew.

The ruler has asked Jesus to lay his hand upon the child (verse 18). The Lord does even better: with authority, power, *and tenderness* he takes the child by the hand. According to Mark, as he does this he says, "Talitha cumi" ("Little girl arise," cf. Luke 8:54; see p. 42). Immediately her spirit returns and she gets up.

26. **The news about this spread throughout that entire region.** It is clear that with the recording of this miracle Matthew has reached a climax. See above, p. 416. He has borne testimony to the manifestation of Christ's power at its zenith. It is not surprising that, in spite of the charge Jesus gave to the parents (Luke 8:56), the news of this miracle spread throughout that entire region or country.

Combining the accounts in the three Gospels the entire story can be summarized under the following theme and headings:

The restoration to life of Jairus' daughter

A word of encouragement: "Fear not, only believe" (Mark 5:36; Luke 8:50)
A word of revelation: "She is not dead but asleep (Matt. 9:24; Mark 5:39; Luke 8:52)
A word of love and power: "Little girl arise" (Mark 5:41; Luke 8:54)
A word of tender concern: "Give her something to eat" (Mark 5:43; Luke 8:55)

The Healing of Three Handicapped Persons

27. **And as Jesus passed on from there, two blind men followed him, constantly crying out, Take pity on us, Son of David.** To the list of miracles reported in chapters 8 and 9 Matthew adds two more, probably because they happened on the same day as those described in 9:18-26. They round out that busy day. In the first of these two the Lord imparts sight to two blind men; in the second, the power of speech to one who lacked it. If it should seem as if Matthew's story thus descends from the climax of verses 25 and 26 to an anticlimax, the answer is that in reality he is preparing for a second climax. Next to the climax of Christ's wonder-working power he, in verse 34, is going to describe that of the hostility of the Pharisees.

As Jesus is walking away from the ruler's house he is being followed by two blind men who are constantly yelling, "Take pity [or: have mercy] on us, Son of David." As far as is known, in pre-Christian literature the designation "Son of David," as a title for the Messiah, occurs only in the pseudepigraphical Psalms of Solomon 17:21. [423] Though there are those who deny that the two blind men in Matthew's story are using the term in the Messianic sense, the probability is that they did indeed so intend it, for on the basis of Matt. 21:9; 22:41-45 (see on those verses) it is clear that during Christ's ministry on earth "Son of David" and "Messiah" had become synonyms. Otherwise how can one satisfactorily explain the indignation of the chief priests and scribes when the children were honoring Jesus with the title "Son of David" (21:15, 16)?

Apparently Jesus paid no attention to the cries of the two blind men. His reaction, though not specifically recorded, seems not to have been one of unmixed elation. This is not surprising, for to the people in general the Messiah would be an earthly, political deliverer.

It is not surprising, therefore, that Jesus does what Matthew describes him as doing: **28. And when he had gone inside the house** . . . As some see it, this means "his own house in Capernaum." Matt. 4:13 is generally quoted in support of this view. To disprove this interpretation 8:20 is frequently cited. However, neither passage is entirely conclusive. The first passage does not *necessarily* mean that Jesus owned or even had rented a house in Capernaum; this may be implied, but it is not certain. Friends may have provided a home for him. The second passage may simply mean that during his travels from place to place Jesus had no fixed place of residence, no definite place to stay that he could figure on. So also here in 9:28 the reference may be to a house which some kind follower had invited him to use. Do we not perhaps have a parallel in the home of Mary and Martha at Bethany, sometimes referred to as "Christ's Judean home" (Matt. 21:17; Mark 11:11)?

However this may be—and of the various possibilities none should be aprioristically excluded—when Jesus had gone inside the house **the blind men came up to him, and Jesus said to them, Do y o u believe that I am able to do this?** Among the inferences that must be avoided are the following:

a. Faith is necessary before Jesus can perform a miracle.

Answer: Matt. 8:28 ff.; 11:20-24; and Luke 17:17 prove that this is not true.

b. Since the blindness of these men was self-induced—they were blind because they believed that they were—all they needed in order to have their sight restored was faith.

Answer: There is nothing in the text to indicate that this blindness was without physical cause. Besides, Jesus does not merely demand faith, but distinctly faith *in himself* as the Healer.

It has been said at times that what Jesus demanded was faith in the Father, not faith in himself. It is clear from the present passage that this theory is contradicted by the facts. That Mark's Gospel does not so picture

---

[423] S.BK. I, p. 525.

him has already been shown. See pp. 59, 60. But the same is true with respect to Matthew. As the present passage shows, Jesus does indeed fix the attention upon himself as the object of faith. See also 7:21 ff.; 10:37, 38, 40; 11:25-30; 16:13-20; 19:28; 26:64; 28:18 ff.

When Jesus asks the blind men whether they believe that he is able to do this, that is, to cure them of their blindness, very respectfully **They said to him, Yes, Lord.** For the meaning of "Lord" see on 7:21 and 8:2. **29. Then he touched their eyes and said, According to y o u r faith let it be done for y o u.** For this marvelous and tender "touch" see on 8:3. The act of Jesus is in thorough correspondence with their faith; cf. 8:13. To bring about faith in himself and to preserve this faith is the very purpose of the miracles. **30. And their eyes were opened.** At Christ's touch sight entered into their eyes, so that in one glorious moment they saw everything distinctly. **And Jesus sternly warned them, saying, See that no one finds out.** The original has only three words; cf. "See none discover." For "sternly warned" see also Mark 1:43; 14:5; John 11:33, 38; especially Mark 14:5, "They censured [or: scolded] her." In view of what has already been said (verse 27) it is not very surprising that Jesus issued this warning. To be sure, the miracle could not remain a secret. Relatives and friends could not be kept in the dark. But was it not altogether reasonable that Jesus, knowing that the people would draw wrong deductions from his miracle-working power, ordered these men not to give needless and dangerous further publicity to the matter? See further on 8:4. Did the men heed the warning? The answer is found in verse 31. **But when they had departed they spread the news about him throughout that entire region.** What they did was definitely wrong, yet understandable. Jesus, so it appears, could not remain hid.

32. As they were departing there was brought to him a demon-possessed man who was unable to speak. Jesus was being kept very busy. When one group leaves, another enters upon the scene. This time a demoniac deprived of the power of speech is brought to Jesus.

Demon-Possession [424]

What the New Testament teaches with respect to this subject may be briefly summarized as follows:

1. It is not true that the New Testament writers, in common with all

---

[424] In addition to the entries on this subject in the various religious, and Biblical encyclopaedias, and the sources mentioned in them (see, for example, S.H.E.R.K., Vol. III, pp. 401-403; I.S.B.E., Vol. II, pp. 827-829) I wish to call attention to the following: Foerster's article on δαίμων and related words, Th.D.N.T., Vol. II, pp. 1-20; J. D. Mulder's articles on "Mental Disease and Demon Possession," *The Banner* (a weekly published by the Christian Reformed denomination, with headquarters in Grand Rapids, Mich., issues of March 24, 31, April 7, 14, 1933); and, in the same periodical, Sept. 2, 1921 issue, the article on "Demon Possession" by H. Schultze.

primitive people, ascribed all *physical* illnesses and abnormalities to the presence and operation of evil spirits. It is clear, for example, that Matt. 4:24 distinguishes between demoniacs and epileptics. Some afflicted persons are demon-possessed, blind and dumb (Matt. 12:22); others lack the power of sight or of speech but are not demon-possessed (15:30). Other passages showing that the Gospel writers carefully distinguish between diseases caused by demons and diseases not so caused are Matt. 8:16; 10:8; Mark 1:32-34; 6:13; 16:17, 18; Luke 4:40, 41; 9:1; 13:32; and Acts 19:12.

2. It is not true that demon-possession is simply another name for *insanity.* The fact is that in only two of the many reported cases of possession does the latter very definitely affect the mind (Matt. 8:28 ff. and parallels; and Acts 19:14-16).

3. Though there is resemblance, it is not true that demon-possession is simply another name for multiple personality or dissociation (for example, Dr. Jekyll and Mr. Hyde; or the young lady who was divided between three distinct personalities: the Saint, the Realist, and Sally). Differences between multiple personality and demon-possession: *a.* demons are spiritual beings who are able to depart from a man and to enter the swine; *b.* they are always evil; and *c.* they are not driven out by psychological treatments applied over a longer or shorter period of time, but by the word and power of Christ, instantly. None of this (*a., b.* and *c.*) applies to multiple personality.

4. The term demon-possession describes a condition in which a distinct and evil personality, foreign to the person possessed, has taken control of an individual. This evil personality or demon is able to speak through the mouth of the possessed individual, and to answer when addressed (Mark 5:7-10; Luke 4:41; Acts 16:18; 19:13-15).

5. Demons are the agents of Satan. Jesus came on earth in order to crush the power of Satan. He came to bind "the strong man" (Matt. 12:29; Luke 11:21, 22; cf. Rev. 20:1-3) by means of his victory over him in the desert of temptation, and also by means of demon-expulsions and especially the cross (Col. 2:15). This "binding of the devil" points forward to the latter's ultimate and complete defeat in connection with Christ's second coming (Rev. 20:10; cf. Rom. 16:20).

6. Convincing evidence of present-day demon-possession has not been furnished. Demonic influence, yes; demon-possession, not necessarily.

It is clear that in the case mentioned here in 9:32 demon-possession had resulted in a serious handicap: loss of the power of speech.

33. When the demon had been cast out the dumb man spoke. The manner in which the spectators were affected by this miracle is stated in these words: **The crowd was filled with amazement and said, Never has anything like this been seen in Israel.** Though this expression of astonishment is linked with this one miracle, and is also very appropriate in this connection—for who would not be filled with wonder if, in his very presence, a person known to be without the power of speech suddenly starts to talk—it may very well be viewed as the people's reaction to all the miracles that took place that day (verses 18-33). The words and the works of Jesus aroused surprise and wonder (Matt. 7:28, 29; 9:8, 26; 15:31; Mark 7:37; 4:41; Luke 4:15, 36, 37; 5:26, etc.).

That the reaction was not unanimously favorable is brought out in verse 34. **The Pharisees, however, were saying, By the prince of the demons he casts out demons.** It is to be observed that the Pharisees did not try to deny the reality of these mighty works. Cf. Acts 4:16. They did something even more wicked. It was to the enabling influence of Satan, the prince of the demons, that they ascribed Christ's power to perform miracles. The hostility revealed already in verses 3 and 11 reaches a very high point here in verse 34. Since 12:24 dwells in greater detail with this same Pharisaic accusation further discussion will be postponed until that passage is reached.

The sin of the Pharisees was terrible indeed. They should have combined the evidence of the mighty works with the equally powerful testimony of the Messianic prophecies that were being fulfilled before their very eyes. In connection with the events recorded in Matt. 9:30, 33 ("and their eyes were opened"; "the dumb man spoke") they should have thought of Isa. 35:5, 6 ("Then the eyes of the blind shall be opened . . . and the tongue of the dumb shall sing").

---

35 And Jesus went through all the cities and the villages, teaching in their synagogues and preaching the gospel of the kingdom, and healing every illness and every infinity. 36 Now when he saw the throngs he was moved with compassion for them, because they were fatigued and forlorn like sheep without a shepherd. 37 Then he said to his disciples, "The harvest (is) plentiful, but the laborers (are) few. 38 Pray therefore the Lord of the harvest to thrust laborers into his harvest."

9:35-38 *"The harvest is plentiful, but the laborers are few"*
Cf. Mark 6:6, 34; Luke 10:2

35. And Jesus went through all the cities and the villages, teaching in their synagogues and preaching the gospel of the kingdom, and healing every illness and every infirmity. Here Matthew pauses, as it were. He looks back and repeats, almost word for word, what he has previously written (cf. 9:35 with 4:23), but substitutes "all the cities and the villages" for the earlier "all Galilee," by means of this substitution probably adding emphasis to the comprehensive scope of Christ's ministry. For the rest, see on 4:23.

At this point, however, the character of the narrative changes somewhat. The terrain remains the same: the Great Galilean Ministry continues, and will continue until 15:20. But whereas until now the main interest has been centered in Christ's words of wisdom and his works of power, to which the crowds respond with enthusiasm but the scribes and Pharisees with growing antagonism, from this point on the deeply emotional forces motivating each of the leading actors in this drama of salvation become more sharply defined. Thus we are now told, for the first time *specifically* (already *implied* in 8:17), that Jesus' helping and healing missions result from sympathy or compassion; that the base accusation of the Pharisees—"By the prince of the demons he casts out demons," 9:34—is not about to be dropped but is to be repeated (10:25; 12:24, 27), with murderous intent (12:14); and that the people's enthusiasm regarding the prophet of Nazareth is to a large extent of a carnal nature, so that when their earthly expectation is not satisfied they turn against him (11:20 ff.). So do his own brothers (12:46 ff.; cf. Mark 3:21, 22), and his own townspeople (13:57).

Consequently Christ's ministry becomes a bitter struggle. Gradually the cross comes into view; for him uniquely, but in a broader sense for his disciples also, because of their connection with him (10:25, 38).

In line with these introductory remarks is verse 36. **Now when he saw the throngs he was moved with compassion for them, because they were fatigued and forlorn like sheep without a shepherd.** We may perhaps picture Jesus as standing on an elevated place. He sees many people coming toward him. Are some perhaps seeking physical healing for themselves, while others carry their sick to Jesus? One thing is clear: few, if any, have found the peace that passes all understanding. How can they discover it when their leaders are always burdening them with legalistic niceties about sabbaths, fasts, phylacteries, and tassels? These poor people are oppressed by the burdens which the Pharisees place upon them (Matt. 11:28; 15:14; 23:4).

Jesus, whose emphasis is upon "the weightier matters of the law: justice, mercy, and fidelity" (Matt. 23:23), takes their condition *to heart.* He is deeply moved with compassion or sympathy,[425] both of these English words being identical in origin and referring to "something—whether sorrow or joy, though mostly the first—which someone experiences along with another." The sorrows of the people are Christ's own sorrows, for he dearly loves these burdened ones. He feels deeply for them, and is eager to help them. On the subject of the Lord's sympathy see also 8:17; 14:14; 15:32; 18:27; 20:34; Mark 1:41; 5:19; 6:34; Luke 7:13.

Jesus sees them as only he, with his marvelously sympathetic heart, is able to see them, namely, as sheep whose shepherd has abandoned them, and who are therefore perishing on the barren, windswept steppe. Such sheep are "fatigued and forlorn," "dejected and deserted."[426] They are thoroughly

---

425 The verb is ἐσπλαγχνίσθη, third per. sing. aor. indic. pass. of σπλαγχνίζομαι. For a discussion of its basic idea, particularly in connection with the cognate noun σπλάγχνα see N.T.C. on Philippians, p. 58, footnote 39.

426 Note verbal similarity: in the original each of the two words has ten letters, begins with the same letter, ends with the same five letters, is a perf. pass. participle, and has

exhausted and are exposed to ravenous beasts, wind and weather, hunger and thirst. What domestic animal is more dependent, hence more helpless when left to itself, than a sheep? Sheep untended, unprotected, and unsought, what a picture of sinners left to themselves or harassed by the rabbis of that day. The people, like sheep, were in need of true guides and shepherds.

The figure of sheep without a shepherd is rich in Biblical references. In addition to the passages based on Zech. 13:7, namely, Matt. 26:31 and Mark 14:27, see also Num. 27:17; I Kings 22:17; Ezek. 34; Zech. 10:2; 11:5; and John 10:12. For a more favorable situation—the shepherd seeking his lost sheep and finding it—see on Matt. 18:12-14; cf. Luke 15:3-7. For a lengthy discussion of the relation between the Good Shepherd and his sheep, see N.T.C. on the Gospel according to John, Vol. II, pp. 97-132.

The disciples, who as a group of twelve were chosen by Jesus about the time when he preached the Sermon on the Mount, have now been with him for a while, and have received initial training toward apostleship. In their own small way they must share with their Master the burden of responsibility for men's salvation to the glory of God. It is therefore not surprising that we now read: **37, 38. Then he said to his disciples, The harvest (is) plentiful, but the laborers (are) few. Pray therefore the Lord of the harvest to thrust laborers into his harvest.** Jesus knows that every guilt-laden person in these large crowds is headed for the day of death and for the final judgment. These multitudes suggest a deplorable lack and the necessity of evangelistic labor to make up for this lack. They suggest the imperative need of something similar to the hard work that is required when without delay a crop must be harvested (cf. Josh. 24:15, "*this* day"). The huge crowds are therefore very appropriately called "the harvest," the very extensive field in need of immediate attention. By a legitimate extension of the figure one can say that this harvest, as here viewed, consists of the sum-total of "the lost sheep of the house of Israel" (10:6). The application to present (twentieth century) conditions would, without doing violence to the basic idea, enlarge the scope of the interpretation, so that the reference would be to all those who can be brought within the reach of the gospel (Matt. 28:16-20; cf. Mark 16:15, 16).

Essentially this is the explanation favored by most commentators. [427] I believe it to be the correct view. There is, however, a different explanation. There are those who limit the figure of the harvest to those who are

---

four syllables. The first participle ἐσκυλμένοι, from σκύλλω, basically means *skinned*, then *completely worn out, fatigued, exhausted.* The second, ἐρριμμένοι, from ῥίπτω, means *thrown* (here: on the ground), and so *lying down in an utterly helpless and forsaken condition.*

[427] See, for example, the remarks of C. R. Erdman, H. N. Ridderbos, and A. T. Robertson, in their respective comments on this passage. Many names could easily be added to the list.

"gathered into the heavenly garner," that is, to "all those in whom the work of God's grace succeeds"; [428] or, using different phraseology, to "the limited number of the elect, who were mixed with unbelievers." [429] But so to limit the figure, as used here in Matt. 9:37, would seem hardly to be doing justice to the context, in which there is no mention of a separation between two groups: the ultimately saved and the ultimately lost. Matt. 9 regards the approaching throngs, with their burdens and needs, as living in this present moment, the moment when Jesus sees them and is moved with compassion because of them. To all of these people the gospel of salvation must be brought. What will happen in the end, at Christ's return, is not now being emphasized. It is true that in connection with that solemn and tremendous future event there will indeed be a twofold harvest (Matt. 13:24-30, 36-43; Rev. 14:14-20; cf. Matt. 3:12; 25:31 ff.), but that is not the context *here*. Here "the harvest plentiful" of verse 37 indicates *at least* the approaching "crowds," "throngs," or "multitudes" of verse 36.

Jesus fixes the attention of the disciples upon the sharp contrast between the large number of people that constitute the harvest and the scarcity of the laborers who must try to gather them in. It is for this reason that he urges the disciples to pray that God, who is the "Lord"—that is, the Owner and Supreme Ruler—of the harvest, may send laborers into his harvest. Besides, in encouraging them to pray in this manner, is Jesus not also emphasizing the fact that more than the mere *number* of the laborers is at stake, namely, also their *quality?* They must be God-sent, not self-appointed. They must be men of love for God and love for souls.

It is clear that Christ's intense desire for laborers and still more laborers to be thrust into the soul-harvest springs from his deep and infinite compassion. Verses 37, 38 must not be separated from verse 36 ("He was moved with compassion for them"). This surely shows that "as many as are called by the gospel are unfeignedly called. For God has most earnestly and truly declared in his Word what is acceptable to him, namely, that those who are called should come to him. He also seriously promises rest of soul and eternal life to all who come to him and believe" (Canons of Dort, Heads of Doctrine III and IV, article 8). Among the many passages which support this doctrine of the well-meant presentation of the gospel to sinners, and of God's delight in their conversion and salvation, are the following: I Kings 8:41-43; Ps. 72:8-15; 87; 95:6-8; Prov. 11:30; Isa. 1:18, 5:1 ff.; 55:1, 6, 7; 61:1-3; Jer. 8:20; 35:15; Dan. 12:3; Hos. 11:8; Mic. 7:18-20; Mal. 1:11; Matt. 22:9; 23:37 ff.; 28:19, 20; Luke 13:6-9; 15; 19:10; John 3:16; 10:16; Acts 2:38-40; 4:12; Rom. 10:1, 12; 11:32; I Cor. 9:22; II Cor. 5:20, 21; I Tim.

---

[428] R. C. H. Lenski, *op. cit.*, pp. 373, 374.
[429] Calvin, *Commentary on a Harmony of the Evangelists, Matthew, Mark, and Luke*, English translation, Vol. I, p. 421.

1:15; Rev. 3:20-22. See also the treatment of this subject in connection with 18:14, and note the additional references mentioned there. For verses 36-38 see also N.T.C. on John 4:35.

Summary of Chapters 8 and 9

These chapters are mainly devoted to the narration of a series of miracles performed by Jesus. It is by means of them that the Lord reveals his omnipotence. By a mere touch of the hand (8:3, 15; 9:29) he heals immediately and completely. In fact such a touch is not even needed (8:8, 13). His power to heal extends not only to man's body but comprises also his soul (9:2). He not only delivers from physical illness; he also drives out demons (8:16, 28 ff.; 9:32, 33). In fact, there is no limit to his power to restore (8:16; 9:35). He even stills the storm (8:26) and raises the dead (9:25).

Not only does he by means of these marvelous works reveal his power, also his infinite love. He carries men's diseases by taking their infirmities upon himself (see the explanation of 8:17). His tender compassion, implied already in 8:17 and 9:13, receives its fullest expression in 9:36. His sympathy overleaps the boundaries of race and nationality (8:10-12). He is a friend of publicans and sinners (9:10).

Those who would follow him must do so without any reservation, the lesson which the two aspirants (8:19-22) had not learned, but Matthew had taken to heart (9:9). Though as concerns man's weak and sinful nature discipleship implies painful self-denial, nevertheless for those who are experiencing the grace of renewal, be it only in its initial stage—think of Christ's disciples, "men of little faith (8:26)—close association with the Lord means joy. Why then should they observe man-made fasts (9:15)?

Matthew draws a sharp contrast between *a.* the hatred toward the Lord shown in increasing measure by the Pharisees (9:3, 11, 34) and *b.* the love of the Savior. The latter is moved with compassion when, on beholding approaching multitudes, he realizes that their Pharisaic leaders, always majoring on minors (23:23), have in reality left their charges as sheep without a shepherd (9:36). In view of this, Jesus says to his disciples, "The harvest (is) plentiful, but the laborers (are) few. Pray therefore the Lord of the harvest to thrust out laborers into his harvest."

Chapter 10

Theme: *The Work Which Thou Gavest Him to Do*

The Charge to The Twelve
The Second Great Discourse

CHAPTER X

10 And he called to himself his twelve disciples, and gave them authority over unclean spirits to cast them out, and to heal every sickness and every infirmity.

2 Now the names of the twelve apostles are as follows:

first, Simon called Peter, and Andrew his brother; and

James the son of Zebedee, and John his brother;

3 Philip and Bartholomew;

Thomas and Matthew the tax collector;

James the son of Alphaeus, and Thaddaeus;

4 Simon the Cananaean, and Judas Iscariot, the one who betrayed him.

5 These twelve Jesus sent out after giving them the following charge:

"Into any road of the Gentiles do not turn off, and into any city of the Samaritans do not enter, 6 but go rather to the lost sheep of the house of Israel. 7 And as y o u go, preach, saying, 'The kingdom of heaven is at hand.' 8 Heal (the) sick, raise (the) dead, cleanse (the) lepers, cast out (the) demons; freely y o u received, freely give.

9 "Don't supply yourselves with gold or silver or copper (money) to put into y o u r belts, 10 nor with a traveler's bag, two tunics, or (extra) sandals, or a staff, for the worker is entitled to his support.

11 "Whatever city or village y o u enter, look for someone there who is deserving, and stay at his house until y o u leave (the place). 12 When y o u enter a home pronounce y o u r greeting upon it; 13 and if that home is deserving let y o u r peace come upon it, but if it is not deserving let y o u r peace return to y o u. 14 And if anyone will not receive y o u and listen to y o u r words, in going out of that house or of that city shake the dust off y o u r feet. 15 I solemnly declare to y o u, in the day of judgment it will be more tolerable for the land of Sodom and Gomorrah than for that city.

16 "Look, I am sending y o u out as sheep in the midst of wolves. Therefore be keen as the serpents, guileless as the doves. 17 And beware of men, for they will hand y o u over to councils, and in their synagogues they will flog y o u. 18 On my account y o u will be dragged before governors and kings for a testimony to them and to the Gentiles. 19 Now whenever they hand y o u over (to the authorities), do not worry as to how or what y o u should speak, since what y o u should say will be given to y o u in that hour; 20 for it is not y o u who speak, but it is y o u r Father's Spirit (who is) speaking in y o u.

21 "Brother will deliver up brother to death, (the) father (his) child, and children will rise up against (their) parents and will kill them. 22 And y o u will be hated by all for my name's sake; but he that endures to the end, he will be saved. 23 Now whenever they persecute y o u in this city, flee to the next one; for I solemnly declare to y o u, y o u will certainly not finish (going through) the cities of Israel before the Son of man comes.

24 "A pupil does not outrank his teacher, nor a slave his master. 25 Let the pupil be satisfied to share his teacher's lot, and the slave to share his master's. If (even) the master of the house was called Beelzebul, how much more the members of his household!

26 "Therefore do not be afraid of them; for there is nothing covered that will not be uncovered, or hidden that will not be made known. 27 What I say to y o u in the dark, tell it out in broad daylight; what is whispered into y o u r ear, proclaim it on the housetops. 28 And do not fear those who kill the body but are unable to kill the soul; rather fear him who is able to destroy both soul and body in hell.

29 "Are not sparrows sold two for a cent? Yet not one of them shall fall to the ground without (the will of) y o u r Father. 30 And as for yourselves, the very hairs of y o u r head are all numbered. 31 Therefore do not fear. Y o u are worth more than many sparrows.

32 "Whoever therefore shall confess me before men, I will also confess him before my Father who is in heaven. 33 But whoever shall deny me before men, I will also deny him before my Father who is in heaven.

34 "Do not think that I came to bring peace on the earth. I did not come to bring peace but a sword. 35 For I came to set a man against his father, a daughter against her mother, and a daughter-in-law against her mother-in-law. 36 A man's enemies (will be) the members of his household.

37 "He who loves father or mother more than me is not worthy of me; he who loves son or daughter more than me is not worthy of me; 38 and he who does not take up his cross and follow after me is not worthy of me. 39 He who finds his life shall lose it, and he who loses his life for my sake shall find it.

40 "He who receives y o u receives me, and he who receives me receives him who sent me. 41 He who receives a prophet because he is a prophet shall receive a prophet's reward; and he who receives a righteous person because he is a righteous person shall receive a righteous person's reward. 42 And whoever gives to one of these little ones even so much as a cup of cold water because he is a disciple, I solemnly declare to y o u, he shall certainly not lose his reward."

10:1-42 *The Charge to The Twelve*
Cf. Mark 3:13-19; 6:7-13; Luke 9:1-6

This chapter, from verse 5 to the end, contains one of the Lord's instructive discourses, the second of the six. For all six see pp. v, vi, 846. Here, as in the preceding chapters, Christ's prophetic, priestly, and royal offices are inextricably intertwined, as follows:

In sending his disciples out on a mission tour Jesus shows them how they should conduct themselves. Accordingly, he appears here as teacher or prophet, revealer of the Father's will. But this title "prophet" applies to him also in the more restricted sense of predictor of coming events. A single reading of the charge shows that, especially from verse 16 to the end, the One who addresses The Twelve is predicting the future. He is describing what is going to happen when the church brings Christ's message to those lost in sin.

The Lord's priestly office, with its implication of vicarious suffering, is also foreshadowed (see verse 38), though as yet very dimly. The disciples, in taking up their cross, must follow after their Master. *They* will be hated because *he* is hated (cf. verses 22, 24, 25).

Finally, it is as king—"Lord of lords and King of kings" (Rev. 17:14)—that Jesus sends out his ambassadors. He arms them with authority (10:1) because he himself is clothed with supreme authority.

Summary

Matthew first gives the setting of the charge-discourse. In reality the background material begins at 9:35-38 (see on these verses). In 10:1 the evangelist makes mention of the summoning of the disciples and of the power Jesus delegates to them. Then (verses 2-4) the roll of The Twelve is called. The actual charge follows (verses 5-42).

As was true in connection with the Sermon on the Mount so also here in this Charge to The Twelve there is no rambling but a very orderly progression of thought. The specifics of the charge are given in what may be considered the first part of the address (verses 5-15). The "disciples," who may now properly be called "apostles," are told where they should go, what they have to proclaim, what they must do, in what condition they are to set out on their tour, and with whom they must lodge. In what may be viewed as the second portion of the address (verses 16-42), where the charge, though continuing, begins to blend with prophetic discourse, Jesus describes what will be the people's sharply contrasted response to the apostle's mission: some will accept it; many will reject it. For the missionaries this rejection will mean bitter persecution, probably already *implied* in verses 13b-15. Jesus shows them how they should respond to this treatment, namely, with courage and with trust in the Lord who is going to reward them for their loyalty.

The reading of verses 13-16 would seem to indicate, however, that what may be considered Part I of the address (verses 5-15) blends into Part II (verses 16-42) so gradually and exquisitely that the entire charge-discourse (verses 5-42) can be treated as a unit; hence verse by verse or paragraph by paragraph without any sub-topics. Result: a division of *the chapter* into two parts: *a.* the setting (verses 1-4); and *b.* the charge (verses 5-42).

However, the gradual character of the transition from verses 5-15 to verses 16-42 is not universally admitted. As some see it, Christ's warning that the disciples would not be welcomed everywhere but would be rejected by many is not an adequate introduction to the predictions of the persecution in store for the church. Thus the conclusion is reached that what is found in 10:5-42 is not really a *unit* but is a *combination*. Jesus, so it is argued, did not at *this* time deliver the entire address. On the contrary, when, sometime after Christ's resurrection, persecution began to raise its head the Gospel composer combined an early address of Jesus with some of his later sayings, particularly with those found in his eschatological address (cf. Matt.

447

10:17-22 with Mark 13:9-13 and with Luke 21:12-17). According to this view the result of the combination is what is found in Matt. 10:5-42. To bolster this combination theory it is further pointed out that the dire prediction of martyrdom (verses 21, 28) was not fulfilled during the apostles' first missionary tour; rather, the very opposite occurred (Luke 22:35). But since the earliest readers of this Gospel knew very well that the predicted afflictions did not take place before Christ's resurrection but afterward, they would experience no difficulty in understanding the composite nature of that which is here presented as if it were one charge. [430]

Objections:

a. The discourse is presented as if it was delivered as a unit. It is preceded by the words, "These twelve Jesus sent out after giving them the following charge" [literally, "after commanding them, saying"] (10:5). It is followed by, "Now when Jesus had finished instructing his twelve disciples he went on from there . . ." (11:1).

b. Jesus had already dimly referred to his own approaching death (9:15). Was it not natural, therefore, that he would even at this time begin to tell the disciples, and through them the church, what would happen after his departure? Though before Christ's resurrection, none of The Twelve was martyred, strong opposition must have arisen immediately (10:14, 15, 23-25), with martyrdom following later (John 21:18, 19; Acts 12:1, 2; cf. Rev. 6:9). It is not clear why both of these links in the chain of persecution could not have been predicted at the same time.

c. Even in his eschatological discourse (Matt. 24, 25) Jesus *himself* (not merely the evangelist) blends into *a single* discourse a chronologically far removed event (the second coming), a closer and long continuing transaction (the preaching of the gospel to all the nations), and an imminent tragedy (the fall of Jerusalem). So why may he not have done something similar here in Matt. 10?

d. As has been pointed out before, it is not at all unusual for speakers to repeat earlier important sayings or remarks. Why, for example, would it be unnatural for Jesus to allude to Mic. 7:6 both here in Matt. 10:21, 35 and also in Luke 21:16? Besides, the difference between the discourse found in Matt. 10 and any of Christ's other discourses is far greater than the similarity.

---

[430] Along this line H. N. Ridderbos, *op. cit.*, Vol. I, p. 203. It is but fair to add that he grants the possibility of the correctness of the opposite view. For a view similar in some respects to that of Ridderbos see W. C. Allen, *op. cit.*, p. 101. F. W. Grosheide in his preliminary summary of Matt. 10:17-42 states that we are compelled to believe that Matthew combined two pieces spoken at different occasions. R. V. G. Tasker presents a fine summary of the arguments that have been presented in favor of the combination theory. He himself leans toward the single unit view, *op. cit.*, pp. 104, 105. Finally, see the discussion in D. J. Chapman, *Matthew, Mark, and Luke*, London, 1937, pp. 236-242.

e. The fact that the phraseology, "In their synagogues they will flog y o u" (10:17; cf. 23:34) occurs only in Matthew's Gospel would seem to indicate an early, Palestinian origin for this expression, rather than a later time of persecution. [431]

I shall proceed on the assumption, therefore, that the address recorded in Matt. 10:5-42 was delivered as a unit, as Matthew indicates.

The Setting

10:1. **And he called to himself his twelve disciples, and gave them authority over unclean spirits, to cast them out, and to heal every sickness and every infirmity.** Matthew seems to take for granted that the readers of his Gospel already know that The Twleve, taken as a group, had been chosen earlier, though he himself does not record this call. According to Luke 6:12, 13, 20 this company of twelve had been called just previous to the preaching of the Sermon on the Mount (cf. Mark 3:13, 14). *Now,* perhaps somewhat later (during the same summer, namely, of the year A.D. 28?), Jesus sends these men out on a mission tour. They were to be his official ambassadors or "apostles," clothed with authority to represent their Sender. That exactly twelve men, no more and no less, were chosen for this task must mean that the Lord designated them to be the nucleus of the new Israel, for the Israel of the old dispensation had been represented by the twelve patriarchs (Gen. 49:28).

Very interesting and instructive surely is the fact that the very men who had been urged to pray that the Lord of the harvest might thrust out laborers into his harvest (9:38) are now placed in the forefront of these laborers (cf. 18:18). They are, moreover, given authority over "unclean spirits" (cf. Rev. 6:13), probably designated by that name because not only are these spirits themselves filthy but among men they are also the instigators of filthy thoughts, words, and deeds. [432]

Exactly what does Matthew mean when he says that Jesus gave to The Twelve "authority" [that is, *power* plus the *right* to exercise it] "over unclean spirits, to cast them out, and to heal every sickness and every infirmity"? Does he wish to say that by means of, and as a result of, casting out these demons the disciples acquired the authority to heal every sickness and every infirmity? If that is the sense it would almost seem as if every sickness and every infirmity is somehow caused by demons. Now in connection with 9:32 it has already been shown: *a.* that according to the Gospels in certain cases diseases were indeed associated with demon possession, but also

---

[431] See K. Schneider's article on μαστιγόω and related words, Th.D.N.T., Vol. IV, p. 515-519.

[432] That the task assigned to these twelve men was not limited to what is mentioned here in 10:1 is shown in verses 7, 8, 14, 19, 20, 27; cf. Luke 9:2a.

b. that this was by no means always true. At times a physical affliction is ascribed to Satanic influence rather than specifically to demon-possession (Luke 13:16; cf. Job 2:7). Often neither Satan nor his underlings are even mentioned in connection with human illnesses. It is true that in a very general and indirect way every manifestation of human distress, whether physical or spiritual, can be ascribed to Satan, for had Adam as head of the race resisted the temptation these evils would not now be in evidence (Gen. 2:16, 17; 3:3, 6, 19; Rom. 5:17). All this hardly suffices to justify the conclusion: "Matt. 10:1 means *a.* that every sickness and every infirmity is directly caused by demons, and *b.* that the disciples by receiving authority to drive them out acquired the power to heal every disease."

Grammatically it is entirely legitimate to interpret 10:1 differently, namely, that Jesus gave to The Twelve "authority over unclean spirits, so that these men were able and were instructed to cast them out, and he gave them authority to heal every sickness and every infirmity." The shortened manner in which this is expresssed in 10:1 may be considered one of the many instances of abbreviated discourse. [433]

The similarity of 10:1 to 4:23 and 9:35 shows that in faithfully carrying out their assignment The Twelve are truly representing their Master, for they are doing what he himself is doing and what they have been ordered to do. In the same manner Jesus himself represents the Father (John 5:19).

2. Now the names of the twelve apostles are as follows:
first, Simon called Peter, and Andrew his brother; and
James the son of Zebedee, and John his brother;
3. Philip and Bartholomew;
Thomas and Matthew the tax collector;
James the son of Alphaeus, and Thaddaeus;
4. Simon the Cananaean, and Judas Iscariot, the one who betrayed him.

In the New Testament the names of The Twelve are listed four times (Matt. 10:2-4; Mark 3:16-19; Luke 6:14-16; Acts 1:13, 26). Acts 1:15-26 records the manner in which Judas Iscariot was replaced by Matthias. As to the Gospel lists, each begins with Peter (so does Acts) and ends with Judas Iscariot. Even the arrangement within the four references shows but little variation. When theoretically the twelve names are viewed in each case as consisting of three groups of four, the following result is obtained:

In Matthew's summary Andrew's name is listed immediately after that of his brother Peter; the brothers James and John are mentioned next. This completes the first group of four. These four may well have been Christ's first disciples (see N.T.C. on John 1:35-42; and see above on Matt. 4:18-22). The second group of four begins with Philip and Bartholomew (=Nathanael), called to be Christ's disciples immediately after the first group of four (John

---

[433] See N.T.C. on John 5:31.

1:43-51); and concludes with Thomas and Matthew. In the final group the first three names are those of "obscure" disciples, that is, men about whom little (Thaddaeus) or next to nothing (James the son of Alphaeus and Simon the Cananaean) is known; the last name is that of the traitor Judas. Does this obscurity and (in one case) perversity account for the fact that these four are mentioned last? Or are they mentioned last because they were the last to be called? We do not know.

In Mark's list the sequence for the first group of four is the same as in Matthew's with the exception that Andrew is now placed last. In Mark's second four we find "Matthew and Thomas" instead of "Thomas and Matthew." With respect to his last four, Matthew's and Mark's lists are identical.

Luke's *Gospel* list follows Matthew's for the first four names, Mark's for the second four. With respect to the last four names Luke goes his own way, reversing the order of the two middle names as listed in both Matthew and Mark. Besides, he substitutes the name "Judas the son [or: the brother] of James" for Thaddaeus, undoubtedly having in mind one and the same person. Hence, here Luke has the sequence: "James the son of Alphaeus, and Simon the one called the Zealot, and Judas the son [or: the brother] of James, and Judas Iscariot, who became a traitor."

Luke's list in the book of *Acts* has the sequence "Peter and John and James and Andrew," for the first four; "Philip and Thomas, Bartholomew and Matthew," for the second four; and ends with "James the son of Alphaeus and Simon the Zealot and Judas the son of James." The name of Matthias is added in verse 26.

Therefore, not only do the four lists contain the same twelve names (with the exception already indicated: in Acts 1 Matthias instead of Judas Iscariot); they even (again, with exception as noted) have the same names in each group of four.

According to Mark 6:7 Jesus sent out the twelve "two by two." In Matthew, as the "and" *within* each pair and the omission of "and" *between* each pair indicates, the grouping is in pairs: "Philip and Bartholomew; Thomas and Matthew," etc. Exception: "and" also occurs between the first two pairs, perhaps because these are two sets of brothers. The possibility that on the journey Philip and Bartholomew actually traveled together, and so also Thomas and Matthew, Peter and Andrew, etc., must be allowed. Yet, there can be no absolute certainty about this, all the less so because the grouping varies somewhat in the four lists, as has been indicated. At any rate the old rhyme makes it easy to remember the names, and also reminds one of the fact that the men were actually sent out in pairs.

> Peter and Andrew, James and John,
> Philip and Bartholomew,
> Matthew next and Thomas too

451

[or: Thomas next and Matthew too],
James the Less and Judas the Greater,
Simon the Zealot and Judas the Traitor.

As to the individuals that composed this group of twelve, no one is mentioned more often than colorful, impetuous *Peter.* His original name was Simon (or Simeon). He was the son of Jonas (or John). By trade he was a fisherman, with his brother Andrew dwelling first in Bethsaida, afterward in Capernaum. Jesus, by whose grace and influence he was to be gradually transformed from a rather unstable person to a faithful, dependable witness, prophetically changed his name from Simon to Cephas (Aramaic), the same as Peter (Greek: Petros), meaning *rock.* For a description of Peter's character and personality see especially on 4:18-22; 26:58, 69-75; and N.T.C. on John 13:6-9; 18:15-18, 25-27; ch. 21. Two New Testament books are by tradition credited to Peter, namely, the epistles called I and II Peter. As was shown earlier (see pp. 41, 44, 53) the Gospel writer Mark has not unjustly been called "Peter's interpreter." Here in Matt. 10:2 to the name of this disciple, who is variously called Simon, Peter, Simon Peter, and Cephas, is prefixed the word "first." He was indeed the leader of the group. In this connection see on 16:16-19. It is hard to overestimate Peter's meaning for the history of the early church.

It was *Andrew,* also a fisherman, who brought his brother Peter to Jesus (see N.T.C. on John 1:41, 42). For other references to Andrew see above (on 4:18-22); also study Mark 1:16, 29; 13:3; John 6:8, 9; 12:22. See also below under Philip.

James and John, too, were brothers, sons of Zebedee. Matthew mentions these two fishermen not only here and in 4:21, 22 (see on that passage), but also later on (17:1; and cf. 20:20, 21).[434] There are also several references to them in the other Gospels. Because of their fiery nature Jesus called James and John "sons of thunder" (Mark 3:17; cf. Luke 9:54-56). James was the first of the apostles to wear the martyr's crown (Acts 12:2). While he was the first to arrive in heaven, his brother John was in all probability the last to remain on earth. On the life and character of John, considered by many (I believe correctly) as being "the disciple whom Jesus loved" (John 13:23; 19:26; 20:2; 21:7, 20) see N.T.C. on the Gospel according to John, Vol. I, pp. 18-21. Five New Testament books have by tradition been assigned to John: his Gospel, three epistles (I, II, and III John), and the book of Revelation.

Philip was at least for a while a fellow townsman of Peter and Andrew, that is, he too was from Bethsaida. Having himself responded to the call of Jesus, he found Nathanael, and said to him, "The one about whom Moses

---

[434] I fail to understand Lenski's statement that besides Judas Matthew mentions only Peter in the rest of his Gospel; *op. cit.,* p. 378.

wrote in the law and about whom the prophets wrote, we have found, Jesus, son of Joseph, the one from Nazareth" (John 1:45). When Jesus was about to feed the five thousand he asked Philip, "How are we to buy bread-cakes that these (people) may eat?" Philip answered, "Bread-cakes for two hundred denarii would not be sufficient for them so that each might get a little something" (John 6:5, 7). Philip apparently forgot that the power of Jesus surpassed any possibility of calculation. To deduce from this incident the conclusion that Philip was a coldly-calculating type of person, more so than the other apostles, would be basing too much on too little. In the Gospels Philip generally appears in a rather favorable light. Thus, when the Greeks approached him with the request, "Sir, we would see Jesus," he went and told Andrew, and these two, Andrew and Philip, brought the enquirers to Jesus (John 12:21, 22). It must be admitted that Philip did not always immediately understand the meaning of Christ's profound utterances—did the others?—but to his credit it must be said that with perfect candor he would reveal his ignorance and ask for further information, as is also clear from John 14:8, "Lord, show us the Father, and we shall be content." He received the beautiful and comforting answer, ". . . He who has seen me has seen the Father" (John 14:9).

Bartholomew (meaning: son of Tolmai) is clearly the *Nathanael* of John's Gospel (1:45-49; 21:2). It was he who said to Philip, "Out of Nazareth can any good come?" Philip answered, "Come and see." When Jesus saw Nathanael coming toward him he said, "Look, truly an Israelite in whom deceit does not exist." This disciple-apostle was one of the seven persons to whom the resurrected Christ appeared at the Sea of Tiberias. Of the other six only Simon Peter, Thomas, and the sons of Zebedee are mentioned.

The references to *Thomas* combine in indicating that despondency and devotion marked this man. He was ever afraid that he might lose his beloved Master. He expected evil, and it was hard for him to believe good tidings when they were brought to him. Yet when the risen Savior in all his tender, condescending love revealed himself to him it was he who exclaimed, "My Lord and my God!" For more information on Thomas see N.T.C. on John 11:16; 14:5; 20:24-28; 21:2.

Matthew has already been discussed in some detail (see on 9:9).

About *James, the son of Alphaeus,* by Mark (15:40) called "James the Less," which by some is interpreted as meaning "James the younger," but by others as "James small in stature," we have no further positive information. It is probable, however, that he was the same disciple who is referred to in Matt. 27:56; Mark 16:1; and Luke 24:10. If this be correct, his mother's name was Mary, one of the women who accompanied Jesus and stood near the cross. See N.T.C. on John 19:25. It has already been shown that the Alphaeus who was the father of Matthew should probably not be identified with Alphaeus the father of James the Less. See above, footnote 113 on p. 95.

Thaddaeus (called Lebbaeus in certain manuscripts of Matt. 10:3 and Mark 3:18) is in all probability the "Judas not Iscariot" of John 14:22 (see on that passage); cf. Acts 1:13. From what is said about him in John 14 it would seem that he wanted Jesus to show himself to the world, probably meaning: to get into the limelight.

The second *Simon* is called *the Cananaean,* the latter being an Aramaic surname meaning enthusiast or zealot. In fact Luke calls him "Simon the Zealot" (Luke 6:15; Acts 1:13). In all probability this name is here given him because formerly he had belonged to the party of the Zealots, which party in its hatred for the foreign ruler, who demanded tribute, did not shrink from fomenting rebellion against the Roman government. See Josephus *Jewish War* II.117, 118; *Antiquities* XVIII.1-10, 23. Cf. Acts 5:37.

Finally, there was Judas Iscariot, generally interpreted as meaning "Judas the man from Kerioth," a place in southern Judea. The Gospels refer to him again and again (Matt. 26:14, 25, 47; 27:3; Mark 14:10, 43; Luke 22:3, 47, 48; John 6:71; 12:4; 13:2, 26, 29; 18:2-5). He is at times described as "Judas who betrayed him," "Judas one of the twelve," "the betrayer," "Judas the son of Simon Iscariot," "Judas Iscariot, Simon's son," or simply "Judas." It is probably useless to speculate about the reasons which induced Jesus to select this man as one of his disciples. The basic answer may well be embedded in such passages as Luke 22:22; Acts 2:23; cf. 4:28. This man, though thoroughly responsible for his own wicked deeds, was an instrument of the devil (John 6:70, 71). While other people, when they felt that they could no longer agree with or even tolerate Christ's teachings, would simply disassociate themselves from him (John 6:66), Judas remained, as if he were in full accord with him. Being a very selfish person he was unable—or shall we say "unwilling"?—to understand the unselfish and beautiful deed of Mary of Bethany, who anointed Jesus (John 12:1 ff.). He was unable and unwilling to see that the native language of love is lavishness. It was the devil who instigated Judas to betray Jesus, that is, to deliver him into the hands of the enemy. He was a thief; yet it was he who had been entrusted with the treasuryship of the little company, with the predictable result (John 12:6). When, in connection with the institution of the Lord's Supper, the dramatic moment arrived—forever commemorated in Scripture (Matt. 26:20-25; John 13:21-30) and emblazoned in art (Leonardo da Vinci, etc.)—in which Jesus startled The Twelve by saying, "One of y o u will betray me," Judas, though having already received from the chief priests the thirty pieces of silver as a reward for his promised deed (Matt. 26:14-16), had the incredible audacity to say, "Surely not I, Rabbi?" Judas served as guide for the detachment of soldiers and the posse of temple police that arrested Jesus in the garden of Gethsemane. It was by means of perfidiously kissing his Master, as if he were still a loyal disciple, that this traitor pointed out Jesus to those who had come to seize him (Matt. 26:49, 50; Luke 22:47, 48). As to the manner of Judas' self-inflicted demise, see on Matt. 27:3-5; cf. Acts 1:18. What caused this privileged disciple to become Christ's betrayer? Was it injured pride, disappointed ambition, deeply intrenched greed, fear of being put out of the synagogue (John 9:22)? No doubt all of these were involved, but could not the most basic reason have been this, that between the utterly selfish heart of Judas and the infinitely unselfish and outgoing heart of Jesus there was a chasm so immense that either Judas must implore the Lord to bestow upon him the grace of regeneration and complete renewal, a request which the traitor wickedly refused to make, or else he must offer his help to get rid of Jesus? One thing is certain: The shocking tragedy of Judas' life is proof not of Christ's impotence but of the traitor's impenitence! Woe to that man!

What points up the greatness of Jesus is that he took *such men as these,* and welded them into an amazingly influential community that would prove to be not only a worthy link with Israel's past but also a solid foundation for the church's future. Yes, he accomplished this multiple miracle with such men as these, with all their faults and foibles, as described on pp. 246, 247. Even when we leave out Judas Iscariot and concentrate only on the others, we cannot fail to be impressed with the majesty of the Savior, whose drawing power, incomparable wisdom, and matchless love were so astounding that he was able to gather round himself and to unite into *one* family men of entirely different, at times even opposite, backgrounds and temperaments. Included in this little band was Peter the optimist (Matt. 14:28; 26:33, 35), but also Thomas the pessimist (John 11:16; 20:24, 25); Thaddaeus the one-time Zealot, hating taxes and eager to overthrow the Roman government, but also Matthew, who had voluntarily offered his tax collecting services to that same Roman government; Peter, John, and Matthew, destined to become renowned through their writings, but also James the Less, who remains obscure but must have fulfilled his mission.

Jesus drew them to himself with the cords of his tender, never-failing compassion. He loved them to the uttermost (John 13:1), and in the night before he was betrayed and crucified commended them to his Father, saying:

"I have manifested thy name to the men whom thou gavest me out of the world; thine they were, and thou gavest them to me, and they have kept thy word. . . . Holy Father, keep them in thy name which thou hast given me, in order that they may be one, even as we are one. . . . I do not make request that thou shouldest take them out of the world, but that thou shouldest keep them from the evil one. They are not of the world, even as I am not of the world. Consecrate them in the truth; thy word is truth. Just as thou didst send me into the world, so have I also sent them into the world. And for thy sake I consecrate myself, in order that they also may be truly consecrated" (John 17:6-19, in part).

The Charge

5, 6. These twelve Jesus sent out after giving them the following charge: Into any road of the Gentiles do not turn off, and into any city of the Samaritans do not enter, but go rather to the lost sheep of the house of Israel. Though, as just indicated, this group of twelve was to be sent into "the world," that did not happen immediately. Initially these men were told to limit their activity to "the lost sheep of the house of Israel" (see 9:36; 15:24; cf. Jer. 50:6; Ezek. 34:5, 6). With some important exceptions Jesus himself also followed the rule, "To the Jew first, and also to the Greek" (Rom. 1:16; 2:9, 10). Though his teaching was not confined to temple and synagogue, yet for him and his work these retained their basic importance (Matt. 4:23; 13:53; John 18:20). Nevertheless, that the Lord was by no means forgetting the Gentiles has already been made clear (see on chapter 2; 4:23-25; 8:11, 12; cf. John 10:16). But in God's plan it was from Jerusalem that the gospel must spread out among the nations (Gen. 12:3; 18:18; 22:18; 26:4, cf. Acts 3:25; also Isa. 49:6, cf. Acts 13:47; then Isa. 54:1-3, cf. Gal. 4:27; and Amos 9:11, 12, cf. Acts 15:16-18). All this does not subtract one iota from the fact that in principle the nationalism of the Old Testament (with internationalism shining through frequently) is destroyed by the cross, so that today "There is no distinction between Jew and Greek" (Rom. 10:12; cf. John 3:16; I Cor. 7:19; Gal. 3:9, 29; Eph. 2:14, 18; Col. 3:11; and I Peter 2:9). The command given in 10:5, 6 was a temporary restriction which later on would be lifted, as is clearly implied in Matt. 28:19, 20. That the apostles actually obeyed the command regarding the proper sequence in spreading the gospel is clear from Acts 3:26; 13:46.

So then, for the time being the apostles are told not to go outside of Jewish territory nor even to the Samaritans, people of mixed descent and religion (II Kings 17:24; John 4:22), and living between Galilee and Judea. Matthew's recording of this temporary restriction adds force to one of the main purposes of his book, namely, *fully to win the Jews for Christ* (see above, p. 97). It is as if the evangelist (and God through him) were saying to the Jews: "Think of all the privileges y o u have enjoyed, the work that was bestowed upon y o u by prophets and priests. Besides, when Messiah arrived, in fulfilment of the predictions and symbols, he saw to it that y o u were the first to receive the glad tidings. Intensive work to make known salvation through him was carried on first among yourselves. Therefore accept him today as y o u r Lord and Savior!"

Jesus continues: 7. And as y o u go, preach, saying, The kingdom of heaven is at hand. This kingdom theme, proclaimed first by John the Baptist, then by Jesus, and now also by his disciples, has already been explained (see on 3:2; 4:17, 23). Briefly stated it means that the apostles must keep on proclaiming that the dispensation, when through the fulfilment of Messianic prophecy heaven's (i.e., God's) reign in the hearts and lives of men would assert itself more powerfully than ever before, was about to begin, in a sense had even now arrived. The charge continues: **8. Heal (the) sick, raise (the) dead, cleanse (the) lepers, cast out (the) demons; freely y o u received, freely give.** A comparison of 10:8 with 4:23; 9:35 shows that what Jesus means is, "Do and continue to do what I am doing and have been doing." The "authority" to do this had already been imparted to them (10:1). By God's grace they themselves must now apply that power.

There is abundant evidence to show that what is here ordered and predicted actually took place, some of it at once, on this journey or soon afterward, some at a later time, after Christ's resurrection; some through the agency of The Twelve, through their leader Peter, or Peter and John, and some through Paul, who must certainly also be reckoned among the apostles (hence we speak of "The Twelve and Paul"). See the following passages: Mark 6:13, 30; Luke 9:6-10; Acts 3:1-10; 5:12-16; 9:32-43; 14:8-10; 19:11, 12; 20:7-12; 28:7-10. Jesus, moreover, directs The Twelve that they must give their services freely. What they have received freely they must give freely and gladly. There must be no simony of any kind (Acts 8:18-24).

Jesus has told the apostles where to go, what to proclaim, and what to do. He now tells them in what condition they are to set out on their tour: **9, 10. Don't supply yourselves with gold or silver or copper (money) to put into y o u r belts, nor with a traveler's bag, two tunics or (extra) sandals, or a staff. . . .** Only that which is strictly necessary must be taken along on this trip. Accordingly The Twelve must not supply themselves with money, for they will not need it. They must not attempt to acquire such coins as, for example, the gold aureus, the silver denarius, or even the copper assarion. They must not burden their belts with these.

Some have suggested that money was put into a belt by placing it in a little bag or wallet, which, like a sword, could then be attached to the belt. Others point out that the belt was not always or necessarily made of leather (3:4) but often of linen or wool, as was the tunic. By winding or wrapping such a belt around the body a few times its folds would serve admirably as "pockets" for money or other valuables.[435] A knapsack or traveling bag (literally: bag for the road or for traveling) to carry supplies, such as food and clothing, must also be left behind.[436] Moreover, *one* tunic will suffice.

---

[435] A Sizoo, *op. cit.*, p. 52.

[436] The addition "for the road" would seem to indicate that the idea here is "a bag containing supplies or provisions that y o u think y o u might need as y o u are traveling," rather than "a bag for collecting alms." Accordingly, A. Deissmann's idea (*op. cit.*, p. 109) that there is here a reference to "the beggar's collecting bag" should probably be rejected.

An extra one, whether simply for reserve or for extra protection against inclement weather (cf. Mark 6:9) will not be necessary. This warning against taking along "extras" probably carries over to the next item. If so, "Don't supply yourselves with . . . sandals" would mean, "Do not take along an extra pair of sandals. The ones y o u are wearing will suffice." Not only does this interpretation seem to fit the context, it also brings the passage into harmony with Mark 6:9. Besides, barefootedness is in Scripture associated with other ideas, such as reverence in the divine presence (Exod. 3:5), extreme poverty (Isa. 20:2; 15:22), and grief (II Sam. 15:30; cf. Ezek. 24:17). The acquisition of a new staff to replace the old will also not be necessary and here is not even allowed (cf. the Matthew passage with Mark 6:8).

The question will be asked, "Why all these restrictions?" The answer that immediately suggests itself might well be, "Because God will provide. The apostles must place their trust entirely in him." No doubt this is indeed the basic answer. See on 6:19-34, to which add Luke 22:35. Nevertheless, in the present context another thought (not unrelated, to be sure) is added; namely, **for the worker is entitled to his support.** [437] To be sure, from the side of the apostles there should be no greed, no desire for enrichment: what they have received freely must be given away freely (verse 8). This, however, by no means cancels the obligation resting upon those who receive the good tidings. Upon them rests the obligation to supply the needs of these twelve men. This is in line with Scripture everywhere. See especially the following passages: Deut. 25:4; I Cor. 9:7, 14; and N.T.C. on I Tim. 5:18. To every worker God has given the right to partake of the fruits of his work. This includes also physical provision. Very interesting in this connection is Paul's stand on this question. See the ten point summary in N.T.C. on I Thess. 2:9.

It has become clear, therefore, that God is going to provide for these men on their journey, both now and later on, and that he will use the friends of the gospel to carry out his plan. This implies that the apostles, on their part, must carefully select the families that will lodge them. Therefore, it is not surprising that Jesus now adds: 11. **Whatever city or village y o u enter, look for someone there who is deserving, and stay at his house until y o u leave (the place).** It is probably legitimate to suppose that, arrived in any town of whatever size, the missionaries would first of all preach out in the open, at this or that street corner, in the market-place or square (cf. Jonah 3:4); or, if invited to do so, in the synagogue. From the response they receive it would not be difficult to determine who, among the listeners, were "worthy" or "deserving" to provide hospitality to the bringers of good tidings. They might be the kind of people who were waiting for "the consolation of Israel"

---

[437] Literally, "to his nourishment" (or: "food"), but in line with the immediately preceding context the somewhat broader meaning is perhaps intended.

(Luke 2:25) or "the redemption of Jerusalem" (Luke 2:38). Such people could be expected to rejoice in the opportunity to lodge God's messengers. Having found such a home, let the disciples consider it their headquarters until they leave this town for another place. Since The Twelve were traveling two by two, the privilege of helping the cause of the gospel in this manner might be extended to several people.

In the time and region where all this was happening there was a long tradition of hospitality. Social conditions were such that this practice was almost a necessity, due to the fact that travel was not as yet easy, and inns few and far between. Also, the family that offered shelter today might be in need of receiving the same courtesy the following week. In addition to this it should be noted that those among the listeners who were versed in Israelitish tradition—and in view of verses 5 and 6 there were many of them—knew that the Scriptures by means of a long list of noble examples in no uncertain way encouraged the practice of entertaining guests. Among those who had in former years extended hospitality were Abraham (Gen. 18:1-8), Rebekah (Gen. 24:25), Reuel (Exod. 2:20), Manoah (Judg. 13:15), the Shunnamite woman (II Kings 4:8-10), and Job (Job 31:34). This practice continued into the next dispensation. Hence, for the New Testament period add the names of such generous persons as Levi (=Matthew, Matt. 9:10; Luke 5:29), Zacchaeus (Luke 19:5, 10), Martha and Mary (John 12:1, 2), Lydia (Acts 16:14, 15), Aquila and Priscilla (Acts 18:26; Rom. 16:3, 4), Phoebe (Rom. 16:1, 2), Philemon (Philem. 7, 22), Onesiphorus (II Tim. 1:16), and Gaius (III John 5, 6). The Bible regards the spirit and practice of hospitality to be one of the indispensable qualities of the Christian life (Rom. 12:13; I Tim. 3:2; 5:10; Titus 1:8; Heb. 13:2).[438]

Continued: **12, 13. When y o u enter a home pronounce y o u r greeting upon it; and if that home is deserving let y o u r peace come upon it, but if it is not deserving let y o u r peace return to y o u.** Having established themselves in the homes of those who were worthy, the apostles must now go from home to home, bringing the gospel. When they enter any home they must pronounce their greeting upon it. Accordingly, they will use the familiar formula, "Peace to y o u." At that time, as also even today, this was and is a customary greeting (Gen. 43:23; Judg. 6:23; 19:20; I Sam. 25:6; I Chron. 12:18; Ps. 122:8; Dan. 4:1; 6:25; 10:19; Luke 10:5; 24:36; John 20:19, 21, 26). Nevertheless, it makes a great difference who says it. In the mouth of the unthinking person it may be no more than a conventional phrase. Among friends it was and is undoubtedly the expression of a sincere wish. In the present instance, however—and so also in such passages as Luke

---

[438] On the subject of hospitality, including a paragraph showing why it would not be wise for today's missionaries to pagan lands in every detail to try literally to apply the same methods which Jesus here urges upon The Twelve, see the excellent article, "Hospitality," by B. S. Easton, I.S.B.E., Vol. III, pp. 1432, 1433.

24:36; John 20:19, etc.—it is far more than a wish. In the name of their Sender these apostles not only *wish* peace, they actually *bring* it. Just as in the Aaronitic benediction (Num. 6:24-26) the name of Jehovah *was put* upon the children of Israel, so that his blessing would actually result, so it is here. [439] Yet, there was nothing magical about this. The special blessing was for those who by grace were "worthy" to receive it through faith, not for the others. If the home is undeserving "let y o u r peace return to y o u," says Jesus, that is, in that case no blessing will be bestowed. In this connection see the explanation of the fourth beatitude (5:6). Continued: 14, 15. And if anyone will not receive y o u and listen to y o u r words, in going out of that house or of that city shake the dust off y o u r feet. I solemnly declare to y o u, in the day of judgment it will be more tolerable for the land of Sodom and Gomorrah than for that city. After traveling through heathen territory Jews had the custom of shaking the dust off their sandals and clothes before re-entering the Holy Land. [440] They were afraid that otherwise in their own country levitically clean objects might be rendered unclean. What Jesus is saying, therefore, is that even an Israelitish place, be it a house or a city, that refuses to accept the gospel must be considered unclean, as if it were pagan soil. Therefore such a center of unbelief must be treated similarly. Paul and Barnabas did exactly that when a persecution was organized against them in the Jewish district of Antioch in Pisidia (Acts 13:50, 51). A colossal responsibility, a heavy load of guilt, rests on such a place. Jesus says that in the day of judgment the punishment awaiting the land [441] of Sodom and Gomorrah, classical examples of wickedness (Gen. 13:13; 18:20; Jude 7), will be lighter than that which is in store for the city that rejects the gospel. The reason why this is true is clearly stated in Luke 12:47, 48.

It is difficult, if not impossible, to read verses 14 and 15 and not feel that the Lord is already suggesting that the proclamation of the kingdom message will meet with severe opposition. In what now follows, the nature of this opposition and the forms in which it will express itself is more sharply defined, and the apostles are shown how they must cope with it. 16. Look, [442] I am sending y o u out as sheep in the midst of wolves. Cf. Luke 10:3. Sending them out "as sheep" (John 10:11, 14, 27, 28) is wonderful, but "in the midst of" or "among" wolves, vicious and destructive, spells danger. See on 9:36; cf. Ezek. 22:27; Zeph. 3:3; and Acts 20:29. There is comfort, however, in the announcement that *he,* Jesus himself, is sending them. He must have his wise purpose: *a.* that they may there proclaim the

---

439 See N.T.C. on I and II Thessalonians, pp. 43-45.
440 S.BK. I, p. 571.
441 As in 4:15 the word "land" indicates the people who inhabit it. So, here in verse 15, does the word "city."
442 See footnote 133 on p. 131.

gospel of the kingdom; *b.* that by doing so "sheep" may be gathered from among those very people who are now still called "wolves"; *c.* that thus the faith of the apostles may be strengthened; and *d.* that all of this may redound to the glory of God. Besides, the fact that he himself is sending them means that he is very deeply involved in their ministry, for the phrase, "I am sending y o u," means, "I myself am commissioning y o u to be my apostles, that is, my official representatives, [443] so that I will be working through y o u." This certainly implies protection. Come what may, they are under his loving care. If it were not for this they would be helpless, for what can sheep do when they are in the midst of wolves?

In extending this wonderful care Jesus does not, however, exempt them from personal responsibility. So he continues: **Therefore be keen as the serpents, guileless as the doves.** As to the first (cf. Luke 16:8), the serpent is here viewed as the very embodiment of intellectual acumen or shrewdness (Gen. 3:1). The cautiousness and wariness of serpents had become proverbial. The keenness here recommended as a human quality involves *insight* into the nature of one's surroundings, both personal and material, *circumspection, sanctified common sense, wisdom* to do the right thing at the right time and place and in the right manner, a serious attempt always to discover the best means to achieve the highest goal, an earnest and honest search for an answer to such questions as: "How will this word or this action of mine look 'in the end'?" "How will it affect my own future, that of my neighbor, God's glory?" "Is this the best way to handle the problem or is there a better way?" See Eph. 5:15.

This keenness never implies compromise with evil. Jesus teaches that it is man's duty to be not only keen as the serpents but also guileless or innocent (cf. Phil. 2:15) as the doves. As to doves see on Matt. 3:16; cf. Song of Sol. 5:2, "my dove, my undefiled."

An excellent example of those by whom this combination of keenness and innocence is exhibited is the apostle Paul, as his epistles and the book of Acts abundantly indicate. He is, to be sure, "all things to all men" (I Cor. 9:22), carefully selecting his approach to suit each distinct situation. See, for example, Acts 17:22-31 as contrasted with Acts 13:16-41. He is "keen" indeed. What he does as reported in Acts 23:6-8 might even be considered "clever." Yet, he is guileless (Acts 24:16), and exhorts his readers, too, to hold off from every form of evil (I Thess. 5:22) and to live lives that are filled with positive goodness (I Thess. 5:14, 15).

Among others in whom these two characteristics—keenness and guilelessness—are combined are David in his relation to envious King Saul, who is

---

[443] For "I am sending" Jesus might have used the weaker verb πέμπω, but he uses the stronger ἀποστέλλω (cf. ἀπόστολος), and besides makes the expression even more emphatic by fully spelling out the first person singular pronoun "I." He says ἐγὼ ἀποστέλλω: "I myself am sending."

persecuting him (I Sam. 24 and 26); Mordecai, in his reaction to arrogant Haman (Esther 3:2-4; 4:12-14); and Abigail, "a woman of good understanding and discretion," in her dealings with her foolish husband Nabal (I Sam. 25:3).

The connection between verses 16 and 17, far from being abrupt, as some have thought, is in reality natural. Jesus has been speaking about "wolves," that is, evil men who would try to harm the sheep. So he now continues: **17. And beware of men. . . .** Such evil men were certainly present already before Christ's death on the cross and his resurrection. See 8:3; 9:22, 34. Moreover, was not Judas Iscariot one of Christ's disciples, and was it not going to be his purpose to deliver Jesus over to the authorities? And were there not those who were constantly setting traps for the Savior, that they might have a reason to bring a charge against him? See Matt. 12:10; 22:15; cf. John 8:6. Does not hatred toward Jesus imply unfriendliness toward his disciples also? See 5:10-12; 10:24; John 15:20. The basis for Christ's warning is therefore the present, that is, the condition prevailing right now, during Christ's earthly ministry.

In the case of Christ's followers the hatred would be continued and even intensified during the post-resurrection period. Between the persecution which was occurring already, and of which especially Jesus was himself the object, and that of which his disciples were and were to be the objects there was a very close connection, so that the prediction found here in Matt. 10:17 is very natural.

It is in this context that Jesus warns his disciples to "beware of"[444] men. He means, "Be on y o u r guard against" them. Although there is no way of determining exactly what the Lord may have had in mind when he said this, he probably meant that the disciples should watch out for men's evil intentions. Probably one or more of the following items could be arranged under this general idea: *a.* Do not naively entrust yourselves to men; *b.* Do not without good cause make them angry; *c.* Do not fall into the traps of their catch-questions, but pray for grace to give them the appropriate answer; and/or *d.* Do nothing that might enable them to bring a valid charge against y o u (cf. I Peter 4:15, 16). Continued: **for they will hand y o u over to councils, and in their synagogues they will flog y o u.** These councils were probably the local Jewish courts, climaxed in the Jewish supreme court, the Sanhedrin (see on 2:4). It was in the synagogue that those who by the court were convicted of certain definite crimes were scourged.[445]

---

[444] The verb προσέχω (here 2nd per. pl. pres. imperative προσέχετε) has various meanings. Basically it means: to turn (the mind) to, pay attention to; and so be concerned about (Acts 20:28), apply onself to (I Tim. 4:13), be addicted to (I Tim. 3:8), cling to (I Tim. 6:3), and so also: to be on one's guard against (7:15, 10:17, 16:6, 11, 12; Luke 20:46; cf. Matt. 6:1, "Take care that y o u do not").

[445] M.M., p. 604, entry συνέδριον, regard Matt. 10:17 as referring to the local Jewish

Jewish sources contain detailed regulations regarding such scourging. One judge would recite an appropriate passage from Deuteronomy or from the Psalms, a second would count the blows (see Deut. 25:1-3), a third would issue a command before each blow, etc. [446] From the book of Acts (22:19) we learn that Saul (=Paul) of Tarsus caused believers in Christ to receive this horrible punishment. After his conversion he himself was going to be similarly tortured. He was going to write, "From the Jews five times I received forty lashes less one" (II Cor. 11:24). It was the servant of the synagogue ("the attendant," Luke 4:20) who was charged with the responsibility of delivering the blows.

The prediction broadens, as Jesus continues: 18. **On my account y o u will be dragged before governors and kings for a testimony to them and to the Gentiles.** As to "governors," think of such procurators as Pontius Pilate, Felix, and Festus; as to kings, of Herod Agrippa I (Acts 12:1) and of Agrippa II (Acts 25:13, 24, 26). Even Herod Antipas, who technically was not a king, is also given that title at times (Matt. 14:9; Mark 6:14). It was Pontius Pilate who sentenced Jesus to die on the cross, after he had sent him to "king" Herod Antipas (Matt. 27:26; Luke 23:6-12). It was King Herod Agrippa I who killed James (son of Zebedee, and brother of the apostle John). See Acts 12:1. From Acts 25:13 it appears that Paul was brought before King Agrippa II and the procurator Festus. He gave a wonderful testimony as he had also done previously before the procurator Felix. It is understandable that such testimonies were also given before other Gentiles, namely, those who were either present or subsequently heard what had been said. Cf. Phil. 1:12, 13; 4:22. Thus the good news would continue to spread.

Thus, *a.* the initial fulfilment of this prophecy was a matter of the immediate future, as is clear from already existing conditions and attitudes; and *b.* details concerning its subsequent fulfilment are recorded in the book of Acts and in the epistles. See also Rev. 1:9; 2:8-11; 6:9-11; 12:6, 13-17; etc.

What is all-important is the fact that Jesus says this will happen "on my account." When anyone persecutes Christ's disciple he is persecuting Christ himself, a fact that was stamped so indelibly upon the mind and heart of Paul (and through him upon Luke's consciousness) that, however much the accounts of Paul's conversion may vary, the words, "Saul, Saul why do you persecute *me?*" are found in all three (Acts 9:4, 5; 22:7, 8; 26:14, 15). That means that the persecuted one is never separated from Christ's love and from the strength and the comfort he imparts.

---

courts of Justice attached to the synagogue, and so finally to the great council at Jerusalem, the Sanhedrin.

[446] For further details on this see K. Schneider's article on μαστιγόω, in Th.D.N.T., Vol. IV, pp. 515-519.

This comfort is given beautiful expression in verses 19, 20. Now whenever they hand y o u over (to the authorities), do not worry as to how or what y o u should speak, since what y o u should say will be given to y o u in that hour; for it is not y o u who speak, but it is y o u r Father's Spirit (who is) speaking in y o u. Being haled to court is a serious matter. *How* to conduct oneself before judges, including even governors and kings, particularly how to address them, and *what* to say in defense, might well fill these men with apprehension and horror. Very strikingly Jesus says, "Do not worry" (see above, on 6:31); that is, "Whenever worry raises its head knock it down at once." Here, as in the Sermon on the Mount, Jesus forbids not only the habit of worrying but its very beginning. Reason: it will be given to y o u in that hour. This does not mean that the mind of the persecuted apostle is a *tabula rasa* (blank tablet) and that then in some mechanical fashion God will suddenly begin to write words upon that blank space. On the contrary, neither when these witnesses are brought to trial nor when they—think, for example of Matthew, John, and Peter—write books or epistles will their personality be suppressed, or will the previous apostolic training which they received from Jesus be nullified. All this will be enlivened and sharpened and raised to a higher plane of activity. It is in that organic sense that what they must speak will be given to them in that hour. The Father's Spirit will be speaking in them, and that very Spirit, namely, the Holy Spirit, the third person of the Holy Trinity, will "remind them of everything" that Jesus himself said to them (John 14:26). That Spirit was at work already long before Pentecost (Ps. 51:11). But on and after Pentecost he was going to be "poured out" in all his fulness.

That this prophecy, too, was gloriously fulfilled is evident from the speeches of Peter, or Peter and John (Acts 4:8-12, 19, 20, with the effect upon the audience described in 4:13, 14) and from those of Paul (Acts 21:39–22-21; 23:1, 6; 24:10-21; 26:1-23).

Confessing Jesus will create division not only between groups of people—for example, between those, on the one hand, who welcome the disciples and their message, and those, on the other hand, who reject both—but even within the family circle: 21. **Brother will deliver up brother to death, (the) father (his) child, and children will rise up against (their) parents and will kill them.** True, this last clause can be softened somewhat to mean "and will hand them over to be killed" (cf. 26:59; 27:1; Mark 13:12; 14:55); basically, however, this makes little if any difference. The person who unjustly causes someone to be put to death is as guilty as if he had committed the act with his own hand. See II Sam. 11:15, cf. 12:9.

As the wording indicates verse 21 bears some relation to Mic. 7:6. In that passage the prophet complains about the lack of loyalty prevailing among his people, the son dishonoring his father, the daughter rising up against her mother, etc. What Jesus says here, as reported by Matthew, can hardly be considered a "quotation," however. It cuts more deeply. It is a prediction of actual slaughter which, on *his* account, will be occurring within families, one member being opposed to Christ, another in agreement with him. The Christ-hating son will hand over his own brother, to be put to death; the father his child, children their parents.

Recently the terrible words were heard, "I think kids should kill their parents." [447] Now if this means, "because these parents are selfish, unwilling to listen to the cries of the hungry and to share their own substance with them," the sentiment thus expressed, though certainly to be condemned, is not nearly as altogether wicked as is the action predicted and described here in 10:21. As the context—note, "And y o u will be hated"—shows, *here* the meaning is, "Children will rise up against (their) parents and will kill them *because* of the parents' loyalty to Christ." Now it is true that Jesus also teaches what is found in 10:37, 38. But it is one thing to express preference and to do so decisively. It is another to kill the one on whose side we do not wish to be found.

The killing here predicted and condemned results from hatred: **22. And y o u will be hated by all for my name's sake.** . . . The meaning is, "Y o u *will continue* to be hated." [448] The form of the expression may well imply that Jesus was not thinking only of what would happen to The Twelve but also of the persecutions to be endured by their successors in future years, in fact until his return. See on verse 23b. The hatred of which Jesus makes mention here is also described by John (I John 3:13). The words "by all" must not be taken literally as if referring to every man, woman, and child on earth, or even to all those reached by the gospel. When the Lord accuses Israel of having played the harlot "under every green tree" (Jer. 3:6) we immediately understand that this is hyperbole, a perfectly legitimate figure of speech. The same applies to the passage, "All night I make my bed to swim; with my tears I dissolve my couch" (Ps. 6:6). The expression "hated by all" must mean, "by men in general, regardless of rank, station, race, nationality, sex, or age." Is not the same true also with respect to the use of "all" in Mark 1:37; 5:20; 11:32; Luke 3:15; John 3:26; I Tim. 2:1; and Titus 2:11? The words, "for my name's sake" (cf. "for my sake," verse 18) indicate, "for the sake of myself, as I reveal myself in word and deed." Because the world hates Christ it also hates his representatives.

There is comfort, however, in the assurance, **But he that endures to the end, he will be saved.** He who remains loyal to Christ throughout the period of persecution will enter into glory. For himself this period of persecution will last until death delivers him from this earthly scene (John 16:33; II Tim.

---

[447] Quoted in the Princeton Seminary Bulletin, Vol LXII, No. 3, autumn 1969, p. 59.

[448] Periphrastic future passive, probably with durative force, as if to say: this will be going on and on throughout the ages. The original has ἔσεσθε μισούμενοι.

3:12). For the church in general it will last until Christ's return in glory (II Thess. 1:7; Rev. 11:10-12).

The disciples need not despair therefore. Let them work while it is day, making the best possible use of their time. Hence Jesus continues, **23. Now whenever they persecute y o u in this city, flee to the next one. . . . The** Lord lays down a principle here. This rule is to be put into practice by the disciples and by those who will follow them. What must the messengers of good tidings do when a city rejects them and their gospel? To be sure, they must be patient. See Isa. 5:1-7 and Luke 13:6-9. These same passages, however, also teach that there is a limit to God's patience and to that which, in imitation of him, his followers should exercise. Nowhere does the Bible teach that a kingdom worker who, while working in a certain village or town, is being constantly harassed and whose message is being persistently rejected must stay in that same place year after year until he dies. Would not his talents be wasted? Would it be fair to other communities that are crying for help? Let him move out! That the apostles adhered to this principle is clear from many passages (Acts 12:17; 13:46, 51; 14:6, 20; 16:40; 17:10, 14).

With respect to the words that follow there is a wide difference of opinion among commentators: **for I solemnly declare to y o u, y o u will certainly not finish (going through) the cities of Israel before the Son of man comes.** Among the many explanations of this passage there are a few that I would definitely reject:

1. Since we know that the second coming did not occur Jesus must have been mistaken.

Answer: If Jesus was mistaken about this important point how do we know that he was not also mistaken about others? Both doctrine and ethics are thus undermined and destroyed.

2. Matthew misplaced this passage.

Answer: Another "easy" way to get rid of a difficulty. There is no evidence to support this theory.

3. The meaning is: "before the Son of man catches up with y o u."

4. The reference is to the terrible judgment upon the Jews in the years 66-70.

Answer to Nos. 3 and 4: There is nothing in the context that in any way calls for or suggests this explanation.

Something else must be borne in mind. These explanations ignore the fact that in the other Matthew passages in which the coming of the Son of man is mentioned and described the reference is linked with the second coming. It is a coming "in the glory of his Father," "with his angels," "to render to every man according to his deeds" (16:27, 28); a coming when Christ shall "sit on the throne of his glory" (19:28); a coming that will be "visible" (24:27); "sudden and unexpected" (24:37, 39, 44); a coming "on clouds of heaven with power and great glory" (24:30; cf. 25:31; 26:64). It would be strange therefore if from 10:23 any reference to Christ's exaltation which attains its climax in the second coming would be wholly excluded. Besides, as to theory No. 4, this is all the more questionable because here in 10:23 the context (see verses 22b, 28-32) is very definitely one of comfort, not one of terror. The destruction of Jerusalem is predicted not here in chapter 10 but in 22:7; 23:38; see also 24:2, 15 f.

Even so, however, the question may well be asked, "Granted that a reference to Christ's coming in glory cannot be excluded, does 10:23 refer *a.* to the beginning of that process, or *b.* to its culmination? In other words, *a.* was Jesus predicting the manner in which he, as risen Lord, would reveal himself to his immediate disciples (John 20:19-29; see also Matt. 28:16-20); and was he solemnly declaring that this return would occur before they would have finished going through the cities of Israel; or *b.* was he promising that until the very moment of his glorious return upon the clouds of heaven the good news of salvation would be spread not only among other nations but also among the Jews?" Taken in either sense it is a comforting assurance, and this not only for the missionaries themselves, whether The Twelve or their successors, but even for the Jews. For Christ's ambassadors it would mean, "Do not be afraid, I will return to y o u." For Israel it would signify, "I am not through with y o u; y o u r remnant, too, will be saved."

In favor of *a.* is the fact that the starting-point of this solemn declaration would seem to be the *present* situation: the disciples whom Jesus addresses are being sent out here and now, and are being told that if they are persecuted in one city they must flee to the next, to which is immediately added a "for"-clause, stating the reason for this exhortation. Moreover, does not also 10:28b support this reasoning? [449] —On the other hand, as has been established, the very mention of "the coming of the Son of man," an eschatological way of speaking, would certainly point in the direction of *b.* as being the correct interpretation.

Is this, however, an either-or proposition? May not both be right? Is it not possible that Jesus, the Great Prophet, is here unveiling the future, and in so doing is making use of the well-known and firmly established device of "prophetic foreshortening," by means of which before our eyes the widely separated mountain peaks of historic events merge and are seen as *one*? In a sense, *are* they not really one, for are not Christ's resurrection and his return the results of one and the same activity of the Father whereby he glorifies

---

[449] Against this interpretation, according to which a fleeing from city to city may have occurred already before Golgotha and Olivet, it has been argued that not until after Christ's resurrection were the disciples persecuted. But it is hard to reconcile that position with such passages as the following: John 7:13; 9:22, 34; 12:42; 15:20; cf. Matt. 5:10-12; 9:11; 10:14, 16-22; 12:2; 15:1, 2; 19:27-29. If it were true that, from a human point of view, before Christ's resurrection close association with Jesus had been perfectly safe, why did Peter deny his Master?

and exalts his Son as a reward for his accomplished mediatorial work? Also, if it be granted that according to Matt. 24 Jesus makes use of prophetic foreshortening when in vivid colors borrowed from the destruction of Jerusalem by the Romans he paints his coming at the close of history, why can we not have something of similar nature here in 10:23? Easter morning and Pentecost are part of the entire picture!

In the preceding verse Jesus spoke about persecution in store for his disciples. They must not be surprised about this, as if something very strange were happening to them (cf. John 14:29; I Peter 4:12). Says Jesus: **24, 25. A pupil does not outrank his teacher, nor a slave his master. Let the pupil be satisfied to share his teacher's lot, and the slave to share his master's. If (even) the master of the house was called Beelzebul, how much more the members of his household!** Just as it is true that a pupil does not outrank his teacher, nor certainly a slave his master or owner, so it is with respect to The Twelve (or all of Christ's followers) in their relation to Christ, their Teacher and Lord. If Jesus is not *revered,* his disciple will not even be *respected.* Therefore if the enemy treats the pupil or slave with *the same* disdain which he confers upon the superior, that is, if he does not treat the subordinate still worse, let the latter be satisfied.

In Matt. 12:24-27 (cf. Mark 3:22-27; Luke 11:15-20) the Pharisees call Jesus Beelzebul's tool. They say that Beelzebul is the source of Christ's exorcistic power and activity. According to John 8:48 they call Jesus demon-possessed. Here in Matt. 10:25 we are told that they had said that he himself was Beelzebul, [450] that is, that he was the devil in person. If Christ's enemies are bold enough in this vile manner to calumniate Christ, the master of the house (cf. John 13:14; Eph. 3:15; 4:15; Col. 1:18; 2:10), will they not far more readily slander and maltreat "the members of his household," (I Cor. 12:27; Eph. 2:19, 20; 5:30), that is, his disciples?

However, the very fact that they are thus closely associated with Christ, hence also "bound in the bond of life with Jehovah their God" (I Sam. 25:29), should encourage them. Accordingly, they must not be afraid of the enemy but must testify boldly.

---

[450] It was as Baal-zebu*b* (II Kings 1:2, 3, 6; LXX Βααλ μυῖαν), that is, lord of the carrion-fly, and thus also protector against this nuisance, that Baal was worshiped at Ekron. King Ahazia, who sent messengers to inquire of Baal-zebub whether he would recover from the results of his fall, was told that because of this disloyalty to Jehovah he would die. The New Testament passages substitute Beel[=Baal] zebu*l* for -zebu*b*. Beelzebul means "lord of the dwelling." The reason for the change in spelling is not clear. It may have amounted to no more than an accident of popular pronunciation. Another explanation is that there is here a play on words, for -*zebul* resembles *zebel:* dung. Thus, those who despised the Baal of Ekron were able, by means of a slight change in pronunciation, to heap scorn upon him by conveying the thought that he was nothing but a "lord of dung." But, however this may be, in New Testament usage Beelzebul is definitely "the prince of the demons," as a comparison of Matt. 12:24-27 (and parallel passages) with Matt. 9:34 proves. Beelzebul is Satan (cf. 12:26 with 12:27).

Summary of Reasons for Fearless Proclamation
of the Good News:

1. Y o u r enemies cannot prevent y o u r public vindication nor their own public exposure (verses 26, 27).
2. They cannot kill y o u r soul, only y o u r body (verse 28).
3. They can undo neither the Father's will nor his loving care (verses 29-31).
4. "I will confess those who confess me, and deny those who deny me" (verses 32, 33).

Beginning with No. 1 Jesus says 26, 27. **Therefore do not become afraid of them; for there is nothing covered that will not be uncovered, or hidden that will not be made known.** One day whatever is now concealed will be revealed: who these enemies are, what they have done, whom they have persecuted, how they will be punished, etc. Also revealed will be who the righteous are, what they have done, whom they have honored, how precious they are in the sight of God, how they will be rewarded, etc. See Eccl. 12:14; Matt. 12:36; 13:43; 16:27; Luke 8:17; 12:2; Rom. 2:6; Col. 3:3, 4; Rev. 2:6, 23; 20:12, 13. The fact that on that great day Christ's followers will shine forth in all their glory is one good reason why now they must not even begin to be afraid. [451] Therefore the continuation is: **What I say to y o u in the dark, tell it out in broad daylight; what is whispered into y o u r ear, proclaim it on the housetops.** Let them preach openly, frankly, courageously. There were certain basic and important matters which had already been made known to the disciples, for example, "Repent, for the kingdom of heaven is at hand." These things they are to proclaim at *this* time (verse 7). There was no danger that on this very first trip they would talk about things that had not even been whispered into their ears. Though, as we know in the light of later revelation, Christ's death on the cross had indeed been vaguely implied (9:15), this was not understood at the time when the words were uttered. Clearer predictions were to follow (see on verse 38). Even then, however, though Jesus spoke "openly," it frequently happened that what he said failed to register (Matt. 16:22; Mark 8:32; Luke 9:45; 18:34), as if it had been whispered very softly into the ear.

Besides, there was much that could not even be revealed until the resurrection and the outpouring of the Holy Spirit had occurred (John 16:12, 13). Before this had taken place the disciples were not as yet ready for it. This is not difficult to understand, for naturally redemptive *revelation*

---

[451] The distinction between the aorist middle subjunctive φοβηθῆτε in verse 26 and the present middle imperative φοβεῖσθε in verse 28 somewhat reminds one of the two verbs that center around a synonymous theme—that of anxiety—in 6:25 and 6:31, where the sequence is reversed: first present imperative, then aorist subjunctive.

cannot reach its zenith until the redemptive *events*—such as Christ's death on the cross, his burial, resurrection, ascension, etc.—had actually taken place. This may well be one reason why before Christ's resurrection the public disclosure of what happened on the Mount of Transfiguration would have been premature (Matt. 17:9).

In the light of all this it becomes clear that when the disciples are told to tell out in broad daylight what Jesus had told them in the dark, and to proclaim *on*, hence also *from*, the flat roofs what they had heard "in the ear" (thus literally), obedience to this command could not be fully achieved until Easter and Pentecost. To be sure, there was a story to tell even now, a marvelous story indeed, accompanied by deeds of power and compassion. But more, in fact far more, must be reserved until later, when these men would be better qualified. Then, indeed, let them shout in as public a manner as possible (Matt. 28:18-20) what previously had been whispered into their ear. Let them not become afraid, for the truthfulness of the story of God's love revealed in Christ would be fully vindicated and so would its messengers. It would be confirmed in the lives of the sinners transformed into saints. Especially would it be validated on the great judgment day, when all the wicked opposition to it would be thoroughly exposed.

The second reason why whatever could be proclaimed—some things now, others later—must be heralded fearlessly is stated in verse 28. **And do not fear those who kill the body but are unable to kill the soul. . . .** Whatever the enemies may wish to do, there is one thing they cannot do, namely, kill the *psuche*, that is, the soul, that part of man which is immaterial and invisible.

As to the distinction in Biblical usage between *psuche* (soul) and *pneuma* (spirit), from my book *The Bible on the Life Hereafter*, Grand Rapids, 1959, pp. 37-39, I quote the following:

"Nowhere does Scripture teach that man is composed of three parts. Read Gen. 2:7, and you will notice that in the story of man's creation his *twofold* nature is clearly asserted. A long list of passages could be given to indicate that the inspired authors of the Bible were dichotomists. The list would include such passages as Eccl. 12:7; Matt. 10:28; Rom. 8:10; I Cor. 5:5; 7:34; Col. 2:5; and Heb. 12:9 [452] . . . There is only one immaterial and invisible element, though *at least* two names are given to it. Now, it is true that when the Bible is referring to that immaterial element in its relation to the body, to bodily processes and sensations, and in fact to this entire earthly life, with its feelings, affections, likes and dislikes, it *generally* employs the term *soul* (psuche); for example, 'The Jews stirred up the *souls* of the Gentiles' (Acts 14:2). It is also true that when reference is to the same immaterial element considered as the object of God's grace and as the

---

[452] I Thess. 5:23 is no exception to this rule. See N.T.C. on I and II Thessalonians, pp. 141, 142; also in that book the note on pp. 146-150.

subject or worship, the term *spirit* (pneuma) is used most frequently (*always* in Paul when that meaning is intended); for example, 'My spirit prays' (I Cor. 14:14). But the matter is by no means as simple as that. In several instances the two terms *soul* and *spirit* are used interchangeably, with no (or very slight) difference in connotation. Let me give one clear example. It is Luke 1:46, 47: 'My *soul* (psuche) magnifies the Lord, And my *spirit* (pneuma) rejoices in God my Savior.'

"The conclusion therefore is this: When you are talking about man's invisible and immaterial element, you have a perfect right to call it either *soul* or *spirit*. And if anyone, in speaking to you, should maintain that man's *soul* is necessarily his *lower* immaterial substance, not nearly as valuable as his *spirit*, you might ask him whether he does not believe in *soul*-winning, whether he does not also believe that his *soul* is saved, and whether he does not agree that it were better for a man to forfeit the whole world and not lose his *soul*. When you have made your point clear, suggest to him that he and you sing the hymn, 'O *my soul*, bless thou Jehovah!' "

For the various shades of meaning in which in Matthew's Gospel the word "soul" is used, see footnote. [453]

Jesus, then, is warning against the tragic error of being constantly filled with fear because of those who are able to kill the body, as if the body were more important than the soul. He continues: **rather fear him who is able to destroy both soul and body in hell.** It is hardly necessary to add that the pronoun "him" refers to God. By omitting the noun itself more emphasis is placed upon God's character and activity, that is, upon whatever he is and what he is able to do. The word "destroy" is used here in the sense not of annihilation but of the infliction of everlasting punishment upon a person

---

[453] In this Gospel the term ψυχή occurs sixteen times. In 2:20 and twice in 6:25 it is obviously the animating principle of man's physical existence and well-being. In such cases the translation "life" is correct. In our present passage (10:28, twice) it is clearly the immaterial and invisible part of man, as contrasted with the material and visible. In such passages as 10:39 twice; 11:29; 12:18; 16:25 twice; 16:26 twice; and 20:28, due to Semitic influence, the meaning "self" (hence, himself, yourself, yourselves, or even "I," the exact connotation depending on the specific context in each case) deserves serious consideration, especially in the light of parallelisms and parallel passages. In 22:37 ψυχή approaches the meaning of πνεῦμα. It is the human soul or spirit in its relation to God. Finally in 26:38 ψυχή indicates the invisible part of man viewed as the principle of thinking, willing, or desiring. If in such cases there is any distinction between πνεῦμα and ψυχή, it would be that πνεῦμα is used more often in connection with mental, ψυχή in connection with emotional, activity. Thus it is the πνεῦμα that perceives (Mark 2:8), plans (Acts 19:21), and knows (I Cor. 2:11), It is the ψυχή which is sorrowful (Matt. 26:38). The πνεῦμα prays (I Cor. 14:14); the ψυχή loves (Mark 12:30). Also ψυχή is often more general, broader in scope, at times indicating the sum-total of life that rises above the physical; while πνεῦμα is more restricted, frequently indicating the human spirit in its relation to God. In such cases it describes man as the subject in acts of worship or acts related to worship, such as praying, bearing witness, serving the Lord. But these distinctions are not rigid. There is overlapping.

(25:46; Mark 9:47, 48; II Thess. 1:9). As to the word "hell," which here in the original is *Gehenna* (and so also in 5:22, 29, 30; 18:9; 23:15, 33; Mark 9:43-47; Luke 12:5; James 3:6), it generally refers to the abode of the wicked, body and soul, *after* the judgment day. When that same abode is called *Hades* the reference is to the time *before* the judgment day, though Hades also has other meanings in Scripture. [454]

Jesus, then, is saying that there is an everlasting future for both the soul and the body. Neither will ever be annihilated. But everlasting "destruction" is in store for those who reject him. The attempt to save the body so that it may continue to exist here and now for a very brief span of time, while the everlasting interests of the entire person, soul and body, are being neglected, is foolish indeed, like exchanging a minor for a major peril. See Luke 12:13-21. By proclaiming the message of the kingdom courageously the disciples will receive the assurance of everlasting life to the glory of God. In addition, they will be a blessing to their fellowmen. Let them then stand in awe of God. Let them revere him in whose hands they themselves, with soul and body, are everlastingly secure. Let them not be scared of earthly opponents who can accomplish so very little.

To the two reasons for the fearless proclamation of the good news already given a third is now added, in substance amounting to this, "Y o u r enemies can· undo neither the Father's will nor his loving care": 29-31. **Are not sparrows sold two for a cent? Yet not one of them shall fall to the ground without (the will of) y o u r Father. And as for yourselves, the very hairs of y o u r head are all numbered. Therefore do not fear. Y o u are worth more than many sparrows.** Sparrows and other small birds were caught, killed, skinned, roasted, and consumed. They were considered delicacies, as is still the case in certain countries. It is not surprising therefore that they had become an article of commerce, were bought and sold. The price at the time when Jesus spoke these words was "two for an *as* (or: *assarion*)," (cf. 5:26), a Roman copper coin worth only about one-sixteenth of a denarius. We would call it a cent or penny; hence, "two for a penny." For the price of *two* cents an extra sparrow was thrown in; hence, "five for two cents" (Luke 12:6). But even though relatively speaking these sparrows were so cheap, so insignificant in comparison with costlier articles, Jesus assures his disciples, "Not a single sparrow shall fall to the ground *without* y o u r *Father*," thus literally; probably meaning, "without the involvement or the will of y o u r Father." Note that *their* Creator is "y o u r Father." With emphasis [455] Jesus declares that not only the soul and the body (see verse 28) of the disciples

---

454 See my book *The Bible on the Life Hereafter;* on Hades, pp. 83-86; on Gehenna, pp. 195-199.

455 Note position of ὑμῶν at the head of verse 30, and thus immediately after the ὑμῶν of the preceding clause.

are matters of importance to their heavenly Father, but even the very hairs of their head are all numbered; and this in the sense that he both knows how many there are and pays attention to each and to all. Each of these hairs is of some value to him, since it is a hair of one of his children. Therefore apart from his sovereign care and loving heart nothing can happen even to any of these hairs. Here God's general providence with respect to all his creatures and his special providence of which all men are the objects make place for that *very special* watchfulness which he exercises in behalf of those who by virtue not only of creation but also of redemption are his own. Are they not more precious to him than any number of sparrows? There is something unique about the Father's love for those whom he has chosen as his own, something very special. To appreciate the depth and tenderness of 10:31 it should be read not only in its own context but also in the light of other similarly beautiful assurances, namely, those found in Ps. 91:14-16; 116:15; Isa. 49:16; Hos. 11:8; Matt. 11:25, 26; Luke 12:32; John 13:1; 14:3; 17:24; Rom. 8:28; I John 4:19; and Rev. 3:21, to mention only a few.

And now the fourth and final reason for the command that the disciples should herald the gospel of the kingdom without trepidation: 32, 33. **Whoever therefore shall confess me before men, I will also confess him before my Father who is in heaven. But whoever shall deny me before men, I will also deny him before my Father who is in heaven.** The Twelve were being sent out to proclaim the King's message. However, this message must not be coldly objective, not just a recitation of memorized words. The hearts of the disciples must be in their message, that is, they must profess their faith in [456] Christ. Cf. Ps. 66:16. To profess—or "confess"—Christ means to acknowledge him as Lord of one's life, and to do so openly ("before men"), even in the hearing of those who were opposing him. To deny him means to repudiate him, to refuse to acknowledge him as one's own, to disown him. In the second clause of each member of this fine illustration or antithetic parallelism, i.e., in verses 32b, 33b, Jesus promises to confess before his Father in heaven those who have confessed him, and to deny before him those who have denied him. When Jesus confesses a person he claims him as his own and pleads his cause. That this intercessory activity which he as Mediator performs began already during his earthly ministry is clear from such passages as Luke 22:31, 32; John 17:6-11, 15-26. That he is continuing it now is taught in I John 2:1. That he will acknowledge his own on the judgment day is clear from 25:34-36, 40. That, in a sense not exactly the same as in I John 2:1, he never ceases this work in their behalf, in fact that

---

[456] In both of the balancing clauses of verse 32 the verb for confessing (ὁμολογήσει in the first clause; ὁμολογήσω in the second) is followed by the preposition ἐν. This is probably due to Aramaic influence, added proof that Jesus generally spoke in that language. See Gram.N.T., p. 475.

he not only continues to intercede but "ever lives to make intercession for them," is the comforting truth expressed in Heb. 7:25. [457]

On the contrary, that before the Father in heaven he will deny, disown, repudiate those who will have persisted in their denial of him, having never repented of their evil conduct, is taught in Matt. 7:21-23; 25:41-43, 45. For those who during the day of grace repent of their sin there is forgiveness and restoration (Luke 22:62; John 21:15-17).

The fact that among men there will be, on the one hand, those who confess Jesus, and on the other, those who deny him, indicates that the coming of Christ brought division (see verse 21). This thought is expressed in a pithy manner in the words of Jesus as reported in verses 34, 35. **Do not think that I came to bring peace on earth. I did not come to bring peace but a sword. For I came to set a man against his father, a daughter against her mother, and a daughter-in-law against her mother-in-law.** We have here a *mashal;* that is, a paradoxical saying, one that sounds unbelievable! That it is contrary to prevailing opinion is indicated by the opening words, "Do not think that. . . ." Cf. 3:9; 5:17; John 5:45. What Jesus says here causes the one who hears or reads it to startle in shocked disbelief. The natural reaction to the surprising statement would be: "How can this saying be true? Is not Christ 'the Prince of Peace' (Isa. 9:10)? Is he not the One who pronounces a blessing on those who make peace (Matt. 5:9)? If he did not come in order to bring peace how can the following passages be true: Ps. 72:3, 7; Luke 1:79; 2:14; 7:50; 8:48; John 14:27; 16:33; 20:19, 21; Rom. 5:1; 10:15; 14:17; Eph. 2:14; Col. 1:20; Heb. 6:20–7:2? Do not all of them in, the strongest terms proclaim Jesus as the Bringer of peace?"

We should remember, however, that it is the characteristic of many a mashal to place emphasis on one aspect of the truth rather than on a proposition that is universally valid. See on Matt. 5:34, "Do not take any oath at all." The merit of such aphorisms is that they stop a person short and make him think. So here also. A little reflection will soon convince the earnest student of Scripture that there is a sense in which the coming of Christ into this world not only brought division but was even intended to do so. If that had not been its immediate purpose would not *all* men have been lost (John 3:3, 5; Rom. 3:9-18)? Would they not *all* have rushed onward toward their doom? Besides, even in the lives of those who are ultimately saved is it not true that *through many tribulations* they must enter into the kingdom of God (Acts 14:22)? Is not the life of the believer one of Sturm und Drang (storm and stress)? To be sure, *in the end all is peace,* but the

---

[457] See on this entire subject H. H. Meeter, *The Heavenly Highpriesthood of Christ* (doctoral dissertation submitted to the Free University at Amsterdam), Grand Rapids (no date).

same Paul who exclaims, "I thank God through Jesus Christ our Lord" also complains, "Wretched man that I am!" (Rom. 7:24, 25).

In addition, there will be bitter opponents. Here "on earth," that is, during this present dispensation, the followers of Christ must expect "the sword." This word is here used to symbolize the very opposite of peace; hence, "division" (Luke 12:51), resulting in persecution. It is thus that it will become evident who is on the Lord's side and who is not. It is thus that "the thoughts of many hearts will be revealed" (Josh. 5:13, 14; Matt. 21:44; Luke 2:34, 35; 20:18). The entrance of Christ into this world divides in two, splits apart, *cleaves asunder,* and in so doing "sets" or "turns" one person *against* another. [458]

Faith not only creates division between one race and another, one people and another, one church and another; it even brings about division in the family, in fact often the sharpest division of all. In this connection Luke 12:52, 53 mentions "five" family-members all living under the same roof: father, mother, unmarried daughter, married son and his wife (the parents' daughter-in-law). Because of the relation which these various members assume toward Christ there is intense friction between them. Here in Matthew the best interpretation would seem to be that the mother, because of her faith in Christ, is being opposed by the unmarried daughter and by the daughter-in-law; similarly, the believing father by his son.

With allusion to Mic. 7:6 (see on verse 21) a summary of verses 34, 35 follows in verse 36. **A man's enemies (will be) the members of his household.** Among the Biblical illustrations of faith as being in a sense a divider of families are the following, in each of which pair it is the first member that opposes the faith. It is he who is the real personal enemy and must therefore bear the responsibility for the division: Cain versus his brother Abel (Gen. 4:8; cf. I John 3:12); Maacah arrayed against her son Asa (I Kings 15:13); and Nabal opposed to his wife Abigail (I Sam. 25:2, 3, 10, 11, 23-31). In the last two instances the story emphasizes the *reaction* of faith rather than the action of unbelief. See also II Sam. 18:33; Ps. 27:10; and I Cor. 7:12-16.

A choice must be made. It must be the right choice, even if this should mean the alienation of a child from his parents or vice versa: **37. He who loves** [459] **father or mother more than me is not worthy of me; he who loves**

---

[458] Note διχάσαι aor. act. infin. of διχάζω; followed three times by κατά, down on, against.

[459] Note the present participle φιλῶν fr. φιλέω; hence, literally, "the one loving," thus also in verse 37b. The fact that this verb rather than a form of ἀγαπάω is here used has no special significance. It stands to reason that within the family circle love is basically spontaneous natural affection, in which the emotions often play a more prominent role than either the intellect or the will. Though it is true that the object "me," namely Christ, is governed by the same verb, nevertheless the starting-point in the comparison is love within the family. Besides, between φιλέω and ἀγαπάω there is much overlapping. For

son or daughter more than me is not worthy of me. . . . To belong to Christ is a privilege so inestimable that no other relationship can replace it. It is a duty so imperative that no other obligation is more binding. See Acts 5:29. If the choice is between a parent or Christ, the parent's wish, no matter how ardent, should be rejected; if between a child or Christ, the child's wish, no matter how vehement must be overridden. This must be done out of predominating love for Christ. Those who refuse this supreme loyalty to Jesus are "not worthy" of him, that is, not deserving of belonging to him and being honored by him.

Willingness to sacrifice for Christ and his cause must be total. Therefore the words, "He who loves father and mother . . . son or daughter more than me is not worthy of me," are immediately followed by verse 38. **and he who does not take up his cross and follow after me is not worthy of me.** The underlying figure is derived from the then prevailing custom according to which a man who had been sentenced to die by crucifixion was compelled to carry his own cross to the place of execution (John 19:17). Bearing a cross after Jesus thus became a symbol of willingness to endure pain, shame, and persecution for his sake and in his cause. It should be stressed in this connection that the term cross-bearing is not being used properly, that is, in the full Biblical sense, when it is made to refer very generally to any kind of affliction visited upon a person during the course of his earthly life; for example, rheumatism or loss of hearing.

A somewhat similar error must also be guarded against. In speaking of cross-bearing one should be careful not to deprive *Christ's* suffering of its unique value and significance. This is done at times; for example, when the following lines, ascribed to Thomas Shepherd (1665-1739), are misinterpreted:

> Must Jesus bear the cross alone,
> And all the world go free?
> No, there's a cross for everyone,
> And there's a cross for me.

If this is explained to mean that Christ's bitter agony was simply one among many, what is there left of the truth with reference to the vicarious character and infinite value of *his* sacrifice? In the light of full biblical revelation cross-bearing, applied to the believer, can have only one meaning, namely, submissively and in a sense even joyfully "bearing his [Christ's] reproach" (Heb. 13:13; cf. Acts 5:41). This is true of those who, come what may, *follow* where he leads, trust in his redeeming blood, reflect his mind (John 13:15; II Cor. 8:7, 9; Eph. 4:32–5:2; Phil. 2:5; I Peter 2:21); and proclaim him. For "is not worthy of me" see on the preceding verse.

---

the rest, see the lengthy discussion and complete tabulation of these two verbs in N.T.C. on the Gospel according to John, Vol. II, footnote 306 on pp. 494-501.

On the basis of Christ's saying as reported here in verse 38 did the disciples at this time understand that Jesus was going to be literally crucified? Probably not; for, *a.* this passage lays down a principle, teaches a lesson, that has meaning even apart from the assumption of Calvary's cross; and *b.* if even Christ's later clear predictions about his own approaching death on the cross (16:21; 17:22, 23; 20:17-19; and parallel passages in the other Gospels) were not understood by them (see above, on verse 27), is it at all probable that at this earlier stage they interpreted what is reported in verse 38 to refer in any sense to Calvary? To *us* the Calvary reference is clear.

The person who refuses to take to heart the lesson of verse 38 will suffer total loss. For the opposite kind there is a rich reward: verse 39. **He who finds his life shall lose it, and he who loses his life for my sake shall find it.** What does "his life" mean in such a connection? [460] In all probability influenced by the Hebrew idiom, it simply means *himself.* This is clear from passages in which the two terms "life" and "self" are used interchangeably: "The Son of man came to give *his life* a ransom in exchange for many" (Matt. 20:28; Mark 10:45; see also Isa. 53:12 and John 10:11). Now compare ". . . who gave *himself* a ransom for all" (I Tim. 2:6). Even better, for it is closer to the thought of Matt. 10:39, is Luke 9:23, 24: "If any one would come after me, let him deny *himself* and take up his cross daily and follow me. For whoever would save *his life* shall lose it, and whoever loses *his life* for my sake, he shall save it." [461]

Accordingly, and also in the light of parallel passages, Christ's words may be paraphrased as follows: "The person who, when the issue is between me and what he considers his own interests, chooses the latter, thinking that by so doing he is going to 'find' himself, that is, secure a firmer hold on the full life, will be bitterly disappointed. He will lose rather than gain. His happiness and usefulness will shrink and shrivel rather than increase. At last he will perish everlastingly. On the other hand, the one who, confronted with the choice, gives himself away, that is, denies himself out of lòyalty to me, being willing if need be to pay the supreme sacrifice, will attain to complete self-realization. He will have life and will have it more abundantly until at last he will share with me the glory of my return and of the new heaven and earth." Among the passages in which the same or at least a similar thought is expressed, and which shed light on the meaning of Matt. 10:39, are (in addition to Luke 9:23, 24): Matt. 16:26; Mark 8:34-38; Luke 17:32, 33; and John 12:25, 26.

---

[460] For the various shades of meaning of the words ψυχή and πνεῦμα see N.T.C. on I and II Thessalonians, pp. 148-150. See also above, on 10:28, including footnote 453 on p. 471.

[461] I do not agree with the reasoning of Lenski, *op. cit.* p. 406. In order to arrive at the meaning of ψυχή we are not here *exclusively* dependent on Hebrew and/or Aramaic. Context and parallel passages should also be given their due.

Illustration of the two dispositions contrasted in verse 39: a. the lake or sea that has an inlet but no outlet, contrasted with one that has both; b. the raging torrent before it has been dammed, contrasted with that same stream after a dam has been constructed across part of it, producing a useful lake and channels for irrigation.

From the further encouragements found in the remaining verses it becomes evident that this time, in contrast with the Sermon on the Mount (see 7:27), Jesus is going to end his discourse on a positive note: **40. He who receives y o u receives me, and he who receives me receives him who sent me.** Such is the promise for those who, in spite of knowing full well that they will be looked down upon and perhaps even persecuted by their neighbors, etc., welcome and continue to welcome the disciples and their message. They are told that when they accept these men in their true capacity, as fully authorized representatives of Christ, they are accepting Christ himself. Not only this, but since Jesus, in turn, was sent from the Father (15:24; 21:37; Mark 9:37; 12:6; Luke 4:18; 10:16; John 3:17, 34; 5:23, 24, 40; 9:4, 7; 10:36; Gal. 4:4; I John 4:9; etc.), that is, from the loving heart of the very Father who had authorized his Son to commission these disciples (Matt. 28:18-20; John 17:28; 20:21), they, the welcomers, are accepting the Father himself into their hearts, lives, and homes. Is it even possible to imagine a blessing that could be richer than this?

This same promise is spelled out even more definitely in verse 41. **He who receives a prophet because he is a prophet shall receive a prophet's reward.** Literally the original reads, "He who receives a prophet in (the) name of a prophet." But since in English this translation is not very clear, and since we already know (see on 6:9, "hallowed be thy name") that in Scripture the "name" indicates the person himself, and describes *what he is* in his relation to his surroundings, neighbors, etc., we agree with many other translators [462] in rendering the passage: "He who receives a prophet *because he is* a prophet. . . ." The meaning, then, is this: He who welcomes a prophet—not necessarily one of The Twelve but anyone who has the right to proclaim God's truth—and does this not merely out of considerations of politeness or cordiality but very definitely because he regards this messenger to be a prophet indeed, and therefore in welcoming him wishes to welcome his Sender, shall receive the same reward as if he, the welcomer, were himself a prophet.

Lest there be any misunderstanding, as if the reward of grace and glory would be granted only to those who welcomed a specially commissioned messenger, Jesus adds, **and he who receives a righteous person because he is a righteous person shall receive a righteous person's reward.** Here again for

---

462 Beck, Berkeley, Norlie, Phillips, R.S.V., Ridderbos, Twentieth Century, Weymouth.

"because he is" the original has "in the name of." The explanation is similar. The reward is promised because in the man who knocks at his door the welcomer recognizes "a righteous person," that is, one who practices the true religion. The man who devotes his life to the performance of the urgently necessary and eminently noble task of providing lodging for, co-operating with, and encouraging God's traveling children is promised the same reward as are those whom he befriends.

Beautifully Jesus climaxes this discourse by saying: 42. **And whoever gives to one of these little ones even so much as a cup of cold water because he is a disciple, I solemnly declare to y o u, he shall certainly not lose his reward.** With a term of endearment Jesus speaks about "one of these little ones," one who acknowledges his dependence on him and reposes his trust in him. To the world this disciple may be a nobody, insignificant in fame and fortune. Nevertheless, anything that is given to such a disciple is by Jesus regarded as if given to himself. The gift may be as inexpensive as a cup of cold water. It is not the gift as such but rather the motive that matters (25:35, 37, 40; cf. Heb. 6:10). If it be given to the little one "because he is a disciple" [463] the reward will not be lacking.

The quality of the gift and of the giving receives special emphasis. According to what is probably the best reading the act of love is described as giving "a cup of cold water only" (thus literally), meaning "even so much as a cup of cold water." For "I solemnly declare" see on 5:18. Jesus then is saying, "I solemnly declare to y o u that for such a gift the reward will not be lacking." In fact, "he shall *certainly not* [464] lose his reward." What reward? Think of peace of mind now (Matt. 10:13), public acknowledgment by Christ himself at his return (25:34 ff.), and ever afterward all the blessings that are bestowed solely by grace, according to works (16:27).

---

[463] Once more, as twice in the preceding verse, "in the name of."
[464] Very emphatic: οὐ μή.

Outline of Chapter 11

Theme: *The Work Which Thou Gavest Him to Do*

CHAPTER XI

11 1 Now when Jesus had finished instructing his twelve disciples, he went on from there to teach and to preach in their cities.

2 And when John in his prison heard about the activities of Christ he sent word by his disciples 3 and said to him, "Are you the Coming One, or must we look for someone else?" 4 Jesus answered and said to them, "Go and report to John the things which y o u hear and see: 5 (the) blind are gaining their sight and (the) cripples are walking, (the) lepers are being cleansed and (the) deaf are hearing, (the) dead are being raised up and (the) poor are having good news preached to them. 6 And blessed is he who is not repelled by me."

7 When these (messengers) were going away Jesus began to say to the crowds concerning John, "What was it that y o u went out into the wilderness to look at? A reed swaying in the wind? 8 But what did y o u go out to see? A man dressed in soft garments? Surely those who wear soft garments are (to be found) in kings' palaces. 9 But what did y o u go out to see? A prophet? Yes, I tell y o u, even more than a prophet. 10 This is the one it is written:

'Behold, I send my messenger before thy face,
Who shall prepare thy way before thee.'

11 I solemnly declare to y o u, Among those born of women there has not arisen anyone greater than John the Baptist; yet he who is least in the kingdom of heaven is greater than he. 12 From the days of John the Baptist until now the kingdom is pressing forward vigorously, and vigorous men are eagerly taking possession of it. 13 For all the prophets and the law prophesied until John; 14 and if y o u are willing to accept it, he is Elijah who was to come. 15 He who has ears let him hear.

16 "But to what shall I compare this generation? It is like children sitting in the market places and shouting to their playmates,

17 'We played the flute for y o u, and y o u did not dance;
We sang dirges, and y o u did not beat the breast.'

18 For John came neither eating nor drinking, and they say, 'He has a demon.' 19 The Son of man came eating and drinking, and they say, 'Look, a glutton and a drinker, a friend of tax-collectors and sinners.' Yet wisdom is vindicated by her works."

11:1-19 *The Doubt of John the Baptist and the Manner
in Which Jesus Dealt with It*
Cf. Luke 7:18-35

The account of the sending forth of The Twelve as kingdom ambassadors (chap. 10) is followed here in chapter 11 by a report of Christ's words of tribute to the herald of the kingdom, John the Baptist. Actually the chapter begins with the story of John's doubt as reported to Jesus by the Baptist's disciples (11:1-3). Christ's answer, a message to be conveyed to John, is next reported (verses 4-6). Then, to offset any wrong conclusion on the part of the people, as if John were merely a fickle person, a large section (verses 7-19) records the manner in which the Lord extolled the Baptist. The small paragraph in which woes are pronounced on the impenitent cities is basically an outgrowth of the preceding much larger one. Many of the people have not accepted John's testimony, at least have not truly repented. Some, in fact, have even called John "demon-possessed." They have also rejected the testimony of the Son of man (verses 16-19). Accordingly, the cities which had been most highly favored but have nevertheless rejected the good tidings are now denounced (verses 20-24). This denunciation is however more sharply worded than the preceding rebuke. It is also more specific, mentioning certain centers of unbelief by name (Chorazin, Bethsaida, Capernaum). In the unforgettably touching closing words of the chapter (verses 25-30) curse is replaced by blessing, accusation by invitation.

It is clear therefore that the entire chapter forms a unit. It is as it were a pyramid whose large lower section could be labeled "John the Baptist, herald of the kingdom, reassured and extolled." The two smaller units—think of the higher portion tapering toward the pyramid's apex—a. a natural transition (verses 20-24), and b. a striking contrast (verses 25-30)—can hardly be forgotten.

Essentially, however, the theme is far more exalted, for throughout the evangelist is showing his readers the majesty of the Christ. Even while the latter was uttering his remarkable saying, "Among those born of women there has not arisen anyone greater than John the Baptist" (verse 11), was he not proving his own infinitely superior greatness revealed in dealing so wisely and so tenderly with his faltering disciple? Matthew does not even report how the Baptist, when the answer reached him, reacted to it. This, too, confirms what was just stated, namely, that ultimately not John forms the subject of the story but Jesus Christ does, and God through him. "The Work Which Thou Gavest Him to Do," is the theme throughout.

The conclusion of the book of Jonah forms an interesting parallel. Have we not often wondered how Jonah reacted to Jehovah's searching question (Jonah 4:10, 11)? It is not recorded, for the emphasis must be placed on the love of God, not on Jonah. So it is also in Matthew's Gospel, and, in fact, in the Bible throughout.

First, then, we turn to the account describing the manner in which Jesus dealt with the Baptist's doubt. **11:1-3. Now when Jesus had finished instructing his twelve disciples, he went on from there to teach and to preach in their cities. And when John in his prison heard about the activities of Christ he sent word by his disciples and said to him, Are you the Coming One, or must we look for someone else?** At first glance we might feel inclined to

482

criticize the division of the chapter. Would it not have been better to include verse 1 with the preceding paragraph? Does it not form a fitting conclusion to The Charge to The Twelve? It does indeed. But it also definitely introduces chapter 11, for it was exactly the report concerning Christ's activities, his teaching, preaching, etc. in the cities, that contributed toward John's doubt.

Had Matthew been an uninspired author he would undoubtedly have given us a detailed account of "The Experiences of The Twelve on Their First Mission Tour." He would have placed this interesting story immediately after The Charge. But the evangelist is far more interested in Jesus than in the latter's disciples, though, of course, he is also interested in the latter. However, as to them, he takes for granted that the readers will draw the correct conclusion. Even Mark and Luke, who share an equal degree of inspiration with Matthew, have but little to say about the experiences of the disciples. They do say something (Mark 6:12, 13; Luke 9:6), but then immediately continue with the story of Jesus and his love.

Matthew, then, informs us that having finished his charge to the disciples, Jesus went on from there to teach and to preach. The distinction between "teaching" and "preaching" has already been explained (see on 4:23). "In their cities": accordingly, the Great Galilean Ministry is continuing. Though only "teaching and preaching" are mentioned in 11:1, it is clear from verse 5 that a goodly number of "mighty works" were also being performed. It is for this reason that even though in verse 2 the rendering "deeds" or "works" would have been correct, yet in the light of the context "activities" is probably better. This includes teaching and preaching as well as miracles.

According to 4:12 and 14:3, 4 (see on these verses) John the Baptist had been taken into custody by King Herod Antipas. He had been locked up in the gloomy fortress of Machaerus, modern Khirbet Mukâwer, located about five miles east of the Dead Sea and fifteen miles south of its northern tip. The prison was part of one of the Herodian palaces, [465] which explains the possibility of the action recorded in Mark 6:25-28. Though his imprisonment must have been a very grim ordeal, John was allowed to receive visitors. From these he had learned about the activities of Jesus, the very One about whom the Baptist had said so many wonderful things (Matt. 3:11; John 1:15-18, 26, 27, 29-36; 3:28-30). As John saw it, the gracious words that fell from the lips of the Savior and the miracles of mercy he performed did not harmonize with the manner in which he, the Baptist, had pictured him before the public. He had presented him as One who had come to punish and destroy (Matt. 3:7, 10; Luke 3:7, 9). As was pointed out previously (see on 3:10) John's word had been true and inspired, the very "word of God"

---

[465] Josephus, *Jewish War* VII.175; cf. *Antiquities* XVIII.119. See also L. H. Grollenberg, *op. cit.*, Plate 353 on p. 124, and map 34 on p. 116.

(Luke 1:76; 3:2). What Christ's herald missed, however, was this: he failed to discern that this prophecy of doom would go into fulfilment not now but at Christ's second coming. He had not seen the present and the future in true perspective.

John made a very wise decision when, instead of keeping his difficulty regarding Jesus to himself, or talking it over with others but not with the right person, he took it to Jesus. Owing to the fact that the Baptist was himself in prison, so that he was unable to go and see Jesus in person, he sent word by his (the Baptist's) disciples. [466] This does not mean however that the interpretation according to which it was not John himself who doubted but only his disciples who did, and that John now sends these men to Jesus so that the Savior may solve *their* problem, is correct. It is definitely incorrect. Why otherwise would Jesus have said, "Go and report to John"? (verse 4). There is no question about it: It was John himself who had a problem. It was he who wondered whether or not Jesus was "the Coming One." [467]

4-6. Jesus answered and said to them, Go and report to John the things which y o u hear and see: (the) blind are gaining their sight and (the) cripples are walking, (the) lepers are being cleansed and (the) deaf are hearing, (the) dead are being raised up and (the) poor are having good news preached to them. In which sense was this answer reassuring? Is it not true that John already knew all this (verse 2), and that the very fact that he knew it had contributed substantially to his doubt? True indeed, but *the wording* was new. . . . Or was it? It was "new" in the sense that friends who had been reporting Christ's activities to John had not used this type of formulation. On the other hand, the message *as phrased by Jesus* had a familiar ring. It must have reminded John of certain prophetic predictions, namely, Isa. 35:5, 6 and 61:1: "Then the eyes of the blind shall be opened, and the ears of the deaf unstopped; then shall the cripple [or: lame] man leap like a hart, and the tongue of the dumb shall sing for joy. . . . The Spirit of the Lord Jehovah is upon me, because Jehovah has anointed me to preach good news to the poor [or: meek]." It is as if Jesus were tenderly saying to John, "Do you remember these prophecies? This, too, was predicted concerning Messiah. And all this is being fulfilled today, namely, in me." Jesus was going to use Isa. 61 also on another occasion, and again as a prediction fulfilled in himself (Luke 4:16-21).

In connection with these prophetic words and their fulfilment in Jesus two additional facts should be noted: *a.* Isaiah had referred both to miracles and preaching; Christ's message to John also contains a reference to both;

---

[466] Support for the reading "two" of his disciples (δύο instead of διά) is weak. See, however, Luke 7:18.
[467] Cf. J. Sickenberger, "Das in die Welt Kommende Licht," *ThG,* 33 (1941), pp. 129-134. See N.T.C. on the Gospel according to John, Vol. I, pp. 78, 79.

and *b.* the fulfilment in Christ was even better than the prediction, for in the latter not a word had even been whispered with reference to raising the dead. The predictions had to do with healing, cleansing, and preaching good tidings. The fulfilment included all these *and more,* namely, raising the dead. It is interesting to notice that in Luke's Gospel the story of bringing back to life the son of the widow of Nain (7:11-17) immediately precedes the report of John's doubt and of the manner in which Jesus dealt with it (7:18-23).

The message addressed to John the Baptist ends with the words: **And blessed is he who is not repelled by me,** that is, who does not allow anything I do or say to ensnare him, to lure him into sin. See on 5:29, 30. Though the view according to which by means of this admonition John was being rebuked may well be correct, yet if so it was a tender rebuke, one that did not in any respect eclipse the Master's love for his momentarily confused disciple. In fact, rightly considered, the admonition contains a blessing, "Blessed is he. . . ." The Lord treats John as tenderly as he did the man born blind, the woman caught in adultery, Peter, Thomas, etc. In view of the manner in which Jesus immediately proceeds to praise John publicly and to rebuke those who were finding fault both with this herald and with the One to whom he bore witness (verses 7-19), and also in view of such passages as Mal. 3:1, 4:5, 6; Luke 1:15-17, 76, 80; Phil. 1:6, it must be considered certain that the message of Jesus had the desired effect on John. But it is the wisdom and tenderness of Jesus that stand out, and this both in the message of reassurance addressed to John and in the words spoken about John and directed to the crowd that was present.

The latter paragraph begins as follows: **7. When these (messengers) were going away, Jesus began to say to the crowds concerning John, What was it that y o u went out into the wilderness to look at? A reed swaying in the wind?** Here Jesus corrects the erroneous conclusion which some of the people were apt to draw with respect to John because of the question in which he had revealed his doubt concerning the very One whom he had formerly pointed out as the Messiah, that conclusion being that the Baptist was a fickle, vacillating person. In the paragraph taken as a whole the Master is saying that it is wrong to condemn a person on the basis of one deviation from the straight course. In order to form a true opinion about a man his entire life, past as well as present, must be taken into consideration. In the case of John that past had been glorious. The crowd should reflect on the tremendous impact the Baptist had made on them during his earlier appearance in the wilderness of Jordan. "What was it," says Jesus as it were, "that made y o u travel all the way from Galilee to the Judean wilderness? Was it perhaps to look at a man who resembled a reed swaying in [literally: being swayed by] the wind on the banks of the Jordan?" Of course, that could not have been the reason. The person about whom everybody had been talking was like a sturdy oak, not like a trembling reed. Jesus takes for granted that the answer to the question voiced in verse 7 is "Indeed not. We definitely did not go out into the wilderness to look at a reed swaying in the wind." So he continues: **8. But what did y o u go out to see? A man dressed in soft garments?** Again the answer is a firm negative, as Jesus makes clear by continuing, **Surely those who wear soft garments are (to be found) in kings' palaces.** As to John's actual garments see on 3:4. Those who wear "soft" garments are the people without backbone, sycophants who readily kowtow to those in authority and are rewarded with a high office in the king's palace, a position that enables them to wear soft garments in harmony with the high station in life to which they have attained. The people whom Jesus here addresses know very well that John was a totally different individual. Instead of flattering the king he had even rebuked him. So now, instead of enjoying gay palace life he was locked up in a horrid dungeon. Moreover, at the time when the Baptist was still free and preaching in the wilderness the people, by and large, had not even thought of finding fault with his stern message and rustic appearance. At that time John had been a popular hero (3:5). No doubt even afterward many continued to hold him in high esteem (14:5). Yet opinions were beginning to change. What many formerly praised in John, his ascetic manner of life and unsparing warnings, they had now begun to criticize. It is for that reason that Jesus here takes them to task. Continued: **9, 10. But what did y o u go out to see? A prophet?** The Lord answers his own question, and in doing so gives a true appraisal of John: **Yes, I tell y o u, even more than a prophet;** meaning, "Yes, y o u went out to see a prophet, and I assure y o u that he is even more than a prophet."

"More than a prophet" for John not only prophesied (see, for example, Matt. 3:7-12) but was himself also an object of prophecy. He was himself the predicted forerunner of the Messiah. Therefore Jesus continues: **This is the one of whom it is written:**

        Behold, I send my messenger before thy face,
        Who shall prepare thy way before thee. [468]

That Mal. 3:1 refers indeed to John the Baptist as Messiah's herald is clear from the fact that this way-preparer is evidently "Elijah the prophet" of Mal.

---

[468] The phraseology here in Matt. 11:10 strongly reminds one of the LXX rendering of Exod. 23:10, and with respect to the second line also somewhat of Mal. 3:1 in the Hebrew. These three may be rendered into English as follows:

               Matthew 11:10
Behold, I send my messenger before thy face,
Who shall prepare thy way before thee.
           LXX rendering of Exod. 23:10:
And behold I send my messenger before thy face,
That he may guard thee in thy way.
             Mal. 3:1 in the Hebrew:
Behold, I send my messenger,
And he shall make ready a way before me.
Nevertheless, as explained in the text, it is Mal. 3:1 of which Jesus was mainly thinking.

4:5, who, in turn, is John the Baptist, according to Christ's own words as recorded in Matt. 11:14. We are justified in saying, therefore, that this is Christ's own interpretation of Mal. 3:1. Thus interpreted, the meaning, in brief, of Mal. 3:1 must be:

"Take note, I Jehovah, send my messenger, John the Baptist, to be the forerunner of thee, the Messiah. The forerunner's task is to prepare everything—especially the hearts of the people (Mal. 4:6)—for thy coming." The meaning is "to pave the way" for Messiah's *first* coming, but in view of the fact that the first coming and the second coming are as it were two stages whereby God comes to his people in Immanuel, therefore also for his *second* coming. When applied in the latter sense the appellation "my messenger" attains a broader meaning, from which neither John the Baptist nor Christ's apostles nor their successors throughout the new dispensation can be excluded. Though it is true that the immediate context of Mal. 3:1 reaches forward to the final judgment (see especially verses 2 and 3), Matthew very legitimately, as has already been explained, applies the prophecy especially to the first phase of the coming, or, to put it more simply, to the first coming.

It was in a marvelous manner that John the Baptist had fulfilled his task as herald. Hence Jesus is able to continue as follows: 11. **I solemnly declare to y o u, Among those born of women there has not arisen anyone greater than John the Baptist. . . .** As already indicated, John was greater because he was not only a prophet but one whose arrival upon the scene of history had been prophesied. It may well be questioned however whether this is all that Jesus meant when he made the tremendous statement found here in 11:11, introducing it with the impressive formula, "I solemnly declare to y o u," explained in connection with 5:18. Is it not very probable that the Lord was thinking not only of the simple fact that John the Baptist, the herald, arrived in fulfilment of prophecy, but also of the marvelous manner in which this forerunner had fulfilled his task? He had done exactly what a herald must do. First, he had very clearly announced the arrival of Messiah, directing the people's attention to that Great One: "Look, the Lamb of God who is taking away the sin of the world" (John 1:29). Secondly, he had emphasized the necessity of repentance as the only way for the sinner to enter Messiah's kingdom (Matt. 3:2 and parallels; see also Luke 1:76, 77). And thirdly, since it is the duty of the herald to recede to the background when the One whom he has introduced has fully arrived upon the scene, so John had resisted the temptation to call attention to himself. Instead in humility of spirit he had said, "He must increase, but I must decrease" (John 3:30). Now in view of the fact that Jesus himself, in describing the nature of true greatness, always links it with humility (Matt. 8:8, 10, cf. Luke 7:6, 9; Matt. 18:1-5, cf. Mark 9:33-37 and Luke 9:46-48; Matt. 20:26, 27, cf. Mark 10:43-45; Matt. 23:11; and see also Matt. 15:27, 28), is it not altogether probable that he does this also in the present case? This humility, in turn, must be viewed as a gift which John had received from the Holy Spirit. Thus the word of the angel addressed to Zechariah, "He shall be great . . . and filled with the Holy Spirit from his mother's womb" (Luke 1:15) had been and was being fulfilled. Surely, *all* of this—*a.* John not only "the prophet of the Highest" but himself the fulfilment of prophecy, *b.* as such one who in a most humble manner fulfilled his task, *c.* being filled with the Holy Spirit and this from his mother's womb—must be taken into consideration in order to do justice to the full meaning of Matt. 11:11. When that is done it will be clear that the statement is not in any sense an exaggeration.

To this Jesus adds: **yet he who is least in the kingdom of heaven is greater than he.** This cannot mean that John, after all, was not a saved man. Perish the very thought! Rather, the statement must be explained in the light of 13:16, 17, "But blessed are y o u r eyes, because they see, and y o u r ears, because they hear. I solemnly declare to y o u, many prophets and righteous persons longed to see what y o u are seeing, yet did not see it, and to hear what y o u are hearing, yet did not hear it." The one least in the kingdom was greater than John in the sense that he was more highly privileged, for the Baptist in his prison was not in such close touch with Jesus as was this least one. And was it not this very circumstance which had also contributed to the herald's confusion with respect to whether or not Jesus was truly the Messiah? At the very moment when the messengers sent by John submitted his question to Jesus, the latter was busily engaged in the act of healing and restoring (Luke 7:20, 21). Is it not true that actually seeing all this happening before one's very eyes would be more likely to ring memory's bell recalling to mind Isa. 35:5, 6; 61:1 ff. than would a dismal prison atmosphere, with no opportunity even to see, much less to speak to the One about whom the prisoner was thinking? Yes, in a sense the kingdom had already arrived: the afflicted ones were being delivered from their ills, the dead were being raised up, and the words of life and beauty were proceeding from the heart and lips of the Master. But in his sovereign providence, which no one has a right to question, John was not an immediate participant or even a direct witness. Also, he was not to see Calvary nor to experience Pentecost. However, he was not being forgotten or neglected. The message Jesus sent him (11:4-6) was sufficient to reassure him.

But even though John the Baptist was now far away from the scene of action, nevertheless through his earlier emphasis on the necessity of genuine repentance and his pointing to Jesus as the Savior from sin he had been used as an instrument of God in paving the way for blessings to happen, so that Jesus is able again to refer to him favorably as he now continues: **12. From the days of John the Baptist until now the kingdom is pressing forward** vigorously, and vigorous men are eagerly taking possession of it. [469] Truly the work of John the Baptist had not been in vain. He had pointed away from himself toward Jesus, and the crowds had followed Jesus (John 3:26). Was it not an act of kindness and magnanimity on the part of the Lord to give credit to John for what he had formerly done, and especially to extol him thus at this very time when the Baptist had given expression to his uncertainty regarding Jesus? It is true that Christ's drawing power was not dependent on John, not in the least. Nevertheless, in the providence of God and in fulfilment of prophecy John's preaching had contributed toward the result of paving the way for Christ.

The kingdom, says Jesus, ever since the days of John's first appearance upon the scene has been pressing forward vigorously, forcefully. It is doing so now, as is clear from the fact that sick are being healed, lepers cleansed,

---

[469] The passage has led to much discussion and many differences of interpretation. The difficulties center especially around the verb βιάζεται and the cognate noun βιασταί. As to the first, this is third per. sing. pres. indicative of βιάζω and can be either passive or middle. In the New Testament it occurs only here and in the parallel passage Luke 16:16. As a passive and used in an unfavorable sense it could mean "is suffering violence." The entire passage then would read somewhat as follows: ". . . the kingdom is suffering violence, and violent men are seizing it." Along this line, with individual variations, see A.V., A.R.V., N.A.S., Beck, Weymouth, R.S.V., N.E.B. (text). There is nothing in the context that suggests this meaning, which should therefore be definitely rejected. Also construed as passive, but now in a favorable sense, the meaning might be "is being seized eagerly," or "is being taken by storm," followed by "and eager men are seizing it," or "are forcing their way into it." See, for example, Phillips and Williams. This is much better. Nevertheless, it is not entirely satisfactory, since thus interpreted the second line virtually repeats what has already been said in the first. Taking the verb as a middle, and translating it "is pressing forward vigorously," yields a meaning for the entire passage as given in my translation; supported in one form or another also, among others, by Lenski, Ridderbos, and N.E.B. footnote. The two lines express two thoughts, the first relating to the kingdom itself, the second to the men who are eagerly taking possession of it. Yet between the two there is a very close connection. It appears to me that the context fully supports this interpretation.
As to the second verb, namely, ἁρπάζουσιν, this is third per. pl. pres. indicative active, of ἁρπάζω. It occurs several times in the New Testament, always in the sense of *seize* or one of its modifications. Naturally the resultant meaning can be unfavorable; for example, seize someone's property (John 10:28, 29). Not only human beings but also wolves (symbolizing humans) can be snatching thieves (John 10:12). Nevertheless, the intent of seizing something or somebody may not always be unfriendly (see John 6:15, where the indicated action was wrong but not unfriendly). Or, again, the Spirit may "catch" or "snatch" someone away (Acts 8:39, with which compare II Cor. 12:2, 4; I Thess. 4:17; Rev. 12:5). Finally, there may be a seizing which has rescuing as its purpose (Acts 23:10; Jude 23). It is clear from all this that the exact meaning of this verb, whether favorable or unfavorable, depends on its context. Since it has already been established that the first verb βιάζεται is here used in a favorable sense, the conclusion must be that also the second is so used. The same is true with respect to the noun βιασταί, occurring only here in the New Testament. In the present context it cannot mean "violent men" but must mean "vigorous men," or "forceful men," men of courage, fortitude, determination.

the dead raised, sinners converted to everlasting life, all this now as never before. Still, by no means everybody is entering. Many, very many, even now are refusing and resisting. But vigorous or forceful men, people who dare to break away from faulty human tradition and to return to the Word in all its purity, no matter what be the cost to themselves, such individuals are eagerly taking possession of the kingdom; that is, in their hearts and lives that kingship or reign of God and of Christ is being established.

What Jesus here emphasizes is that one cannot sleep his way into the kingdom. On the contrary, entrance into the kingdom requires earnest endeavor, untiring energy, utmost exertion. See also Luke 13:24; 16:16; John 16:33; Acts 14:22. This is true because Satan is mighty, has a large army of helpers, the demons, has learned to use crafty methods (see N.T.C. on Eph. 6:11), and receives aid and support from his fifth column established in man's very heart (I John 2:16). Therefore it takes vigorous men, men who are eager to fight and to conquer, to overcome Satan and thus to take possession of the kingdom, of all the blessings of salvation. The kingdom, then, is not for weaklings, waverers, or compromisers. It is not for Balaam (II Peter 2:15), the rich young ruler (Matt. 19:22), Pilate (John 19:12, 13), and Demas (II Tim. 4:10). It is not won by means of deferred prayers, unfulfilled promises, broken resolutions, and hesitant testimonies. It is for strong and sturdy men like Joseph (Gen. 39:9), Nathan (II Sam. 12:7), Elijah (I Kings 18:21), Daniel and his three friends (Dan. 1:8; 3:16-18), Mordecai (Esther 3:4), the Peter of Acts 4:20, Stephen (Acts 6:8; 7:51), and Paul (Phil. 3:13, 14). And here let us not forget such valiant women as Ruth (Ruth 1:16-18), Deborah (Judg. 4:9), Esther (Esther 4:16), and Lydia (Acts 16:15, 40).

The words of Jesus recorded in verse 12 imply that with John a new period had begun, when the kingdom started to press forward vigorously. That thought is confirmed in verses 13, 14. **For all the prophets and the law prophesied until John; and if y o u are willing to accept it, he is Elijah who was to come.** "All the prophets and the law" indicates "the entire Old Testament," as far as the prophets that wrote books are concerned ending with Malachi, in whose book the coming of Christ and of his herald was predicted. Thereupon prophecy was silent for more than four hundred years. After that came the fulfilment of prophecy in Jesus Christ, but (chronologically speaking) first of all in John the Baptist. In him, accordingly, prophecy was beginning to be fulfilled. It was he who tied together the old and the new dispensation. At least equally important, it was he whose inspired exhortation, if obeyed, would solve the problem of the generation gap, for by means of faith in the Christ whom he proclaimed the hearts of the fathers were turned to the children, and the hearts of the children to their fathers (Mal. 4:5, 6). This John the Baptist, preacher of repentance and faith, was accordingly the Elijah who was to come. Like the Elijah of old, John too was a preacher of repentance. The two resembled each other also in the sudden character of their appearance, the incisiveness of their message, and the simplicity of their life. See on 3:3. True, John was not literally Elijah (John 1:21), but inwardly he was indeed, for "he went forth in the spirit and power of Elijah" (Luke 1:17), and was therefore called Elijah by no one less than Jesus himself (Matt. 17:12). "If y o u *are willing* to accept it," says Jesus, for he knows that accepting this truth was a matter not solely of the mind but also of the will. If the people were but willing to accept John as being truly the prophet of the Most High, then there was hope for them. Therefore Jesus adds: **15. He who has ears let him hear.** Let him listen attentively to the message of salvation as God's gracious reward for repentance and faith. Let him find peace and joy in the One who had been described by John as taking away the sin of the world. In all of Christ's teaching, both on earth and from heaven, it would be difficult to discover any exhortation that he repeated more often, in one form or another, than the one of verse 15 (13:9, 43; Mark 4:9, 23; Luke 8:8; 14:35; Rev. 2:7, 11, 17, 29; 3:6, 13, 22; 13:9; cf. 8:18 in both Mark and Luke). No wonder, for is not lack of receptivity that which, if persisted in, leads directly to the unpardonable sin? For more on this unresponsiveness or unwillingness to hear and to heed see 13:3-9, 18-23. In the present connection it is evident that when Jesus says, "He who has ears let him hear," he was thinking surely not only of what he had said in verse 14, namely, that John was Elijah who was to come, but of the entire contents of verses 7-14. Over against the gradual change of attitude on the part of many with respect to John, Jesus had extolled him. It was not John who was fickle, but rather that large group of individuals who had allowed themselves to be led astray by the Pharisees (Luke 7:30), so that their earlier noisy enthusiasm about John had cooled, in fact had been replaced by hostile criticism. In fact, both John and Jesus had become the butt of their disparaging and insolent remarks (see verses 18, 19). So Jesus continues: **16-19. But to what shall I compare this generation? It is like children sitting in the market places and shouting to their playmates,**

> **We played the flute for y o u, and y o u did not dance;**
> **We sang dirges, and y o u did not beat the breast.**

For John came neither eating nor drinking, and they say, He has a demon. The Son of man came eating and drinking, and they say, Look, a glutton and a drinker, a friend of tax-collectors and sinners.

It is clear that Jesus is here accusing these critics of being childish. There is a difference between being childlike and being childish. The Lord recommends the first (18:1-5 and parallel passages). He condemns the second. The picture he draws is that of children who on those days when no business is being transacted on the market have gathered in its ample spaces in order to play games. Today, however, nothing seems to succeed. Some children begin to play the flute, as an accompaniment not to mourning (9:23) but to merriment (cf. Rev. 18:22). They want to play wedding. Others object. So the players put their flutes away and start to lament pitifully and/or moan a dirge, as they had heard their elders and the professional mourners do. That idea, too, does not go across. In a spirit of desperation they then scold their playmates (literally "the others") for being so unco-operative, a complaint which the others return (Luke 7:32).

We can easily imagine something of this nature happening today. "Let's play wedding," says one child. Others chime in. "Let Mary be the bride, Ruth the maid of honor. I'll be the groom. Bert can be the best man, Peter the father of the bride, Jack will do very nicely for the preacher." "Yes, let's do that," say some of the others, and they start whistling a wedding march. But many voices scream back in disgust, "Not that silly stuff. That's not for us." "Then let's play funeral," says the boy who had been the first to suggest playing wedding, and he adds, "I'll be the funeral director, the pall-bearers are John, Bert, Peter, and Larry. Mike can be the corpse." Dolefully the speaker and some others begin to intone a funeral hymn. But their groaning is drowned out by loud protests: "Cut it out. We want none of this sad stuff." So a petty quarrel develops, in which those who had suggested the games are shouting to their playmates, "Y o u 're never satisfied. Y o u doñ't want to play wedding and y o u don't want to play funeral. What *do* y o u want to play?" The accused hurl back similar charges. [470] All are unhappy, disgruntled, sulky. Weddings are too silly, too glad; funerals, too gloomy, too sad. Not only are the children peevish and quarrelsome, they are also fickle, inconsistent: what they used to get all excited about they now look down upon.

Jesus, then, is saying, "That is the way y o u, Pharisees and y o u r followers, are behaving. Y o u are being childish. Y o u are frivolous and are acting irresponsibly, inconsistently. Y o u are never satisfied. Y o u used to be filled with enthusiasm about John; at least, y o u stood in awe of him and did not find fault with his austerity and call to repentance. But now y o u say, 'He is too harsh and unsociable; his message is too severe. Why, he must be possessed.' But y o u are also turning against me, the Son of man. [471] Y o u are pointing the finger at me and saying, 'Though he demands

---

[470] Because of Luke 7:32, which clearly states that the children shouted "to one another" I cannot join those commentators who make a kind of allegory of this illustration, and, having divided the children into two groups, the complainers and those complained against, then proceed to identify the former (those who did "the piping and the wailing") with those who were *disappointed* with John the Baptist and Jesus; and the latter, with John the Baptist and Jesus. See, for example, Lenski, *op. cit.* p. 429. I agree with Tasker, *op. cit.*, p. 116, when he states, "It is the general characteristics of children at play to which Jesus directs attention." So also H. N. Ridderbos, *op. cit.* p. 22.—For the meaning of the word "generation" (11:16) see on 1:17.

[471] On this title see above, pp. 403-407.

self-denial in others, he himself is a glutton and a drinker, a friend of tax-collectors and sinners. He is too sociable.' "

Jesus points out that in the end such thoroughly unfair and bitter criticism and intolerance will get nowhere. The victory is on the side of truth. He says, Yet wisdom is vindicated [472] by her works. The wisdom of John the Baptist, when he insisted on repentance, and of Jesus, when he held out the hope of salvation even to those with whom many in Israel would have nothing to do, was shown to have been fully justified by what it actually accomplished in the hearts and lives of those who, by sovereign grace, gave the proper response to both of these preachers. John and Jesus each had his distinct mission to perform. Each carried out his assignment. By Jesus, who himself in person was and is "wisdom from God" (I Cor. 1:30), this assignment was carried out flawlessly; by John, by and large superbly. Wisdom's children (Luke 7:35) are all those who were wise enough to take to heart the message of John and of Jesus. Between John and Jesus there was this similarity: both proclaimed the gospel. Even John's message was certainly not without hope (see especially John 1:29). Even when his emphasis was on repentance, his exhortation was hope inspiring. See Matt. 3:7-11. Yet between John and Jesus there was also a contrast, not only the one pointed out here in 11:18, 19, but also this, namely, that while John *proclaimed* the good news, Jesus not only proclaimed it but came into this world that there might be good news to proclaim!

Today we know that to a considerable degree wisdom's vindication has already arrived. For example, has not the designation that was originally intended as a disparaging nickname, "friend of tax-collectors and sinners" become one of the Savior's most hope-imparting and soul-stirring titles? Is this title not being "justified" by thousands upon thousands of lives that have taken it to heart and acted upon it? And will not the full and final vindication arrive on the day of the consummation of all things, and ever afterward?

---

20 Then he began to reproach the cities in which most of his mighty works had been performed, because they did not repent: 21 "Woe to you Chorazin! woe to you Bethsaida! for if the mighty works done in you had been done in Tyre and Sidon they would have repented long ago in sackcloth and ashes.   22 But I tell y o u, for Tyre and Sidon it will be more tolerable in the day of judgment than for y o u.   23 And you Capernaum, will you be exalted to heaven? To Hades you shall descend, for if the mighty works done in you had been done in Sodom it would be standing today.   24 But I tell y o u that for the land of Sodom it will be more tolerable in the day of judgment than for you."

---

[472] In agreement with A. B. Bruce, *The Expositor's Greek Testament*, Vol. I, p. 176, I take the verb ἐδικαιώθη to be a "gnomic" aorist, expressive of what is usual. It has also been called the "proverbial" aorist, or the aorist "of experience."

11:20-24 *Woes Pronounced on Impenitent Cities*
Cf. Luke 10:13-15

The relation between this and the immediately preceding section (verses 1-19) has already been indicated (p. 482). **20. Then he began to reproach the cities in which most of his mighty works had been performed, because they did not repent.** . . . The exact moment indicated by "then" is not given. The contents of the paragraph clearly indicate however that many miracles had already been performed in Capernaum and its neighboring cities. This might point to the latter part of the Great Galilean Ministry. However, if we reflect on the fact that at the very beginning of that ministry Jesus immediately chose Capernaum as his headquarters and began to exhibit his healing power in that city and its vicinity (4:13 ff.) we are led to conclude that such a late date is not even strictly necessary: *either* the middle or the latter part of that period of activity is probably indicated.

Jesus, then, began to reproach the cities in which most of his mighty works had been performed. The verb "reproach" is here used in a sense somewhat different than in 5:11. There it had reference to an unjustifiable action, that of heaping insults upon Christ's disciples; here it indicates the Lord's justifiable denunciation of those who have hardened themselves in sin. We read that Jesus reproached *the cities.* Here again, as in 10:15, the term "city" refers first of all and most of all to the inhabitants. See on 4:15; also footnote 441 on p. 460. A mere topographical entity—streets, buildings, a wall—cannot be expected to "repent," is not held accountable for any deeds, and does not enter into the judgment. It is true, nevertheless, that what is done by the citizens is bound to affect the place where they live (see verse 23; cf. Gen. 19:13, 24).

These "cities" had seen Christ's mighty works, his deeds of power, as the miracles are here called. Such works should have caused them to reflect on their ways and to turn to God in true sorrow for sin, but that had not been the effect (cf. Rev. 9:20, 21). So Jesus continues: **21. Woe to you Chorazin! woe to you Bethsaida! for if the mighty works done in you had been done in Tyre and Sidon they would have repented long ago in sackcloth and ashes.** It is probable that Chorazin and Bethsaida were situated very close to Capernaum, which is mentioned last of all, namely, in verse 23. The ruins of present day Kerazeh, northwest of the Sea of Galilee, and two and one-half miles north of what used to be Capernaum, are all that is left of ancient Chorazin. The Bethsaida here mentioned could be either Bethsaida Julias, located just southeast of the point where the Jordan River, coming from the north, flows into the Sea of Galilee, or else another Bethsaida, situated closer to Capernaum.[473] In view of the mention of Chorazin and Capernaum in

---

[473] For the arguments favoring two Bethsaidas see N.T.C. on the Gospel according to John, Vol. I, pp. 216-218.

this very connection, the latter would seem to be probable. If so, it was the Bethsaida located in the plain of Gennesaret (Mark 6:53), which stretches northwest from the Sea of Galilee. It was the home town of Philip, the place where Andrew and Peter also originally came from (John 1:44). It is easily understood that with Capernaum as his headquarters Christ's mighty deeds would have been performed not only inside this city but also in the nearby towns of Chorazin and Bethsaida. Jesus states that if the mighty works done in the two last-named cities had been done in Tyre and Sidon, these Phoenician cities, situated more northerly, along the eastern shore of the Mediterranean, would have repented long ago. Yet, from Isa. 23 and Ezek. 26-28 one receives the definite impression that the commercial seafarers and colonizers who inhabited these cities were proud, money-mad, and cruel. Amos denounced the Tyrians for selling Israelites into slavery to the Edomites (Amos 1:9). The Phoenicians also sold "the children of Judah and the children of Jerusalem" to the Greeks (Joel 3:6). In the description of pleasure-mad, arrogant, presumptuous "Babylon" of Rev. 17-19 there is much that brings back to mind the heathen center of wickedness and seduction, Tyre. The assertion, therefore, that had Tyre and Sidon been favored in a manner similar to Chorazin and Bethsaida, the people of these Phoenician cities would have repented long ago [474] shows with what revulsion the Lord views those who were far more highly privileged but had remained impenitent. The "woe" pronounced upon them amounts to a curse.

Tyre and Sidon would have repented "in sackcloth and ashes," says Jesus. Since the material of which sackcloth was made was a coarse kind of cloth, dark in color ("black as sackcloth of hair," Rev. 6:12), it was especially appropriate as a symbol of mourning. The sackcloth worn by mourners was actually a kind of shirt, with openings for neck and arms, slit down the front, and cast about the loins. It could be worn over an undergarment (Jonah 3:6) or directly over the skin (I Kings 21:27; II Kings 6:30; Job 16:15; Isa. 32:11). This symbolic reference to sorrow is even strengthened by the addition of "and ashes." Continued: 22. **But I tell y o u, for Tyre**

---

[474] To the question, "If so, then why were not such favors shown to Tyre and Sidon?" I would give the following answer: a. The reference here seems to be to traditional Tyre and Sidon, as described in the prophets. At that time the wonder-working Christ had not yet become incarnate. b. As to the response of these Phoenician cities to Jesus and the apostles see on Matt. 4:24 and 15:21-28 (Mark 7:25-30). See also Mark 3:8; Luke 6:17; Acts 21:3-6. Note prophecies (Ps. 45:12; 87:4). By the second century A.D. a bishopric was established for the people of Tyre and vicinity. The Christian scholar Origen was buried in Tyre's Christian basilica. c. As to whatever remains of the question, "Why were not such favors shown to Tyre and Sidon?" the answer must be Deut. 29:29. Matt. 11:21 was not written to encourage speculative questions but rather to emphasize the fact that the responsibilities of those who have been specifically privileged are greater by far than are those of the people who have not been thus favored.

and Sidon it will be more tolerable in the day of judgment than for y o u. For explanation see on 10:15.

The Lord now turns to the very heart and center of his activity, namely, Capernaum: **23, 24. And you Capernaum, will you be exalted to heaven? To Hades you shall descend....** This city and the work which the Savior performed here, including the miracles, have already been discussed; see on 4:13. The main point now is this: by and large the population of Capernaum had remained impenitent in spite of all the labor of love which Jesus had bestowed upon it. It is for this reason that he now addresses this center of his activity in terms that remind one of Isa. 14:13, 15, where the king of Babylon is pictured as boasting that he will ascend into heaven, and is then described as actually descending into Sheol's lowest depth. In a question full of dramatic emphasis Jesus, accordingly, asks, "And you Capernaum, will you be exalted to heaven?" In other words, "You don't really expect to be exalted to heaven, do you?" As far as the form is concerned, the question is so phrased as to expect a negative answer. [475] This is irony, for Capernaum expects exactly to be thus exalted. Swift as an arrow from a bow comes the answer, "To Hades you shall descend." Note position of Hades (before the verb) in this answer, making this curse-filled prediction all the more emphatic, an emphasis that is lost in many of the renderings. Here (and in the parallel, Luke 10:15), as probably everywhere in the *Gospels,* but not everywhere in the entire New Testament, Hades means "hell." Note how sharply it is contrasted with "heaven." Hades is here the place of torments and of the flame (Luke 16:23, 24). See also on Matt. 16:18. [476] That the utter ruin here predicted for the people of Capernaum also implied the destruction of their city is clear. Similarly, the punishment which was visited upon the people of Sodom and Gomorrah included the loss of their city. Nevertheless, in both cases it is the curse upon the *people* that is primary. It is as a result of their sin that the city, too, is destroyed, not vice versa. In a manner similar to that found in verses 21 and 22 and 10:15, so that no further explanation is even necessary, Jesus concludes this paragraph by saying: **for if the mighty works done in you had been done in Sodom it would be standing today. But I tell y o u that for the land of Sodom it will be more tolerable in the day of judgment than for you.**

---

25 At that time Jesus answered and said, "I praise thee, Father, Lord of heaven and earth, that thou didst hide these things from wise and learned (people) and didst reveal them to babes; 26 yes Father, for such was thy good pleasure. 27 All things have been handed over to me by my Father, and no one knows the Son but the Father, nor does anyone know the Father but the Son and he to whom the Son is willing to reveal (him).

---

475 Note μὴ ὑψωθῇσῃ; see Gram. N.T., p. 917.
476 See the more detailed discussion in my book *The Bible on the Life Hereafter,* Chapter 17, "What Is Meant by Sheol and Hades?," pp. 83-87.

28 Come to me all who are weary and burdened, and I will give y o u rest. 29 Take my yoke upon y o u and learn from me, for I am meek and lowly in heart, and y o u shall find rest for y o u r souls. 30 For my yoke is kindly, and my burden is light."

11:25-30 *The Savior's Tender Invitation*
Cf. Luke 10:21, 22

This oft-quoted paragraph, dear to the heart of every true believer, forms a striking contrast with the preceding one. There withering denunciation, here tender invitation; there the curse, here the blessing: **25, 26. At that time Jesus answered and said.** . . . "At that time," but Matthew does not tell us just when these words of adoration, revelation, and invitation issued from the heart and lips of the Savior. Luke does, however (10:1, 17, 21, 22). They were uttered after the return of seventy men whom Jesus had sent, two by two, into every place where he himself was about to come. Of course, even this is by no means a definite time designation. But it provides a background for the precious saying found in Matt. 11:25-30 and in part also in Luke 10:21, 22. Naturally the seventy had much to report (Luke 10:17), though, as remarked earlier, what *they* reported was not nearly as important as what the Lord says in response. It is to this reaction on the part of Jesus that the evangelists, each in his own way, call attention. See Luke 10:18-22; and compare Matt. 11:25-30. In fact, here as often the very words "answered and said" indicate a reaction or response to a situation, rather than a reply to a question. In the present case Christ's reaction develops into a tender invitation. Since everything in verses 25-27 can be viewed as preparing for the invitation found in verses 28-30, this theme suggests the following subdivisions:

The Thanksgiving That Precedes It

Enthusiastic reports not only about demons that had been expelled (Luke 10:17) but probably also about souls converted (cf. Mark 6:12) cause Jesus to give expression to his gratitude. The connection, however, is not only with the preceding events but also with that which follows in verses 27-30. A gracious invitation is about to be extended. Burdened ones are going to be urged to come to Jesus. Yet no one can come unless the path which in so doing he must tread has been revealed to him (verses 25, 26). Nor would it make much sense to come unless the One who invites knows what those invited need and unless he has whatever it takes to satisfy this need (verse 27). So, with a feeling of serene trust in his Father, an attitude of mind and heart similarly reported of him on another stirring occasion (John 11:41), the Mediator between God and man, himself man (I Tim. 2:5), probably lifting up his eyes to heaven (cf. John 17:1), says, **I praise** [477] **thee, Father,**

---

[477] The verb is ἐξομολογοῦμαι, first per. sing. pres. middle indic. of ἐξομολογέω. Although this is a compound verbal form, a strengthened ὁμολογέω, the compound form

497

Lord of heaven and earth, that thou didst hide these things from wise and learned (people) and didst reveal them to babes. Jesus does not say "Our Father," the form of address found in the prayer which he taught his disciples to pray. He says "Father" (cf. Mark 14:36; Luke 10:21; 22:42; 23:34; John 11:41). Sometimes he is quoted as saying, "(O) my Father" (Matt. 26:39, 42), or as using this expression ("my Father") in speaking *about* his Father (Matt. 6:17; 10:32, 33; 11:27; 12:50; 18:10, etc.; Luke 10:22; 22:29; 24:49; John 5:17; 6:32, 65; 8:19, 28, 38, 49, 54; 10:30, etc.). Even his enemies interpreted this to mean that he was claiming equality with God (John 5:18), in so far a correct interpretation (John 10:30, 38). In the present connection the term was appropriate also for another reason: *his* Father, in a unique, trinitarian, and also Messianic (or mediatorial) sense, is at the same time, though in a different—sometimes called "religious or

---

probably retaining some of its "perfective" force, it must be remembered that frequent use of such a compound tends to obscure the added adverbial idea. See Gram. N.T., p. 563.

The simple (or "simplex") form ὁμολογέω has the meaning "I say the same thing," hence "I agree," or "concede" or "consent" or "admit." Cf. Luke 22:6 (he agreed, consented). In secular Greek usage we also find the same basic meaning "agree" or "admit." Thus in the *Anabasis* (I.vi.7) Xenophon represents Cyrus as saying to Orontas, ". . . as you yourself admit." This basic sense developed into such ideas as "confessing," "solemnly declaring," "committing oneself to an agreement," hence "promising." In the New Testament John the Baptist "admitted" or "confessed, "I am not the Christ" (John 1:20). See also Acts 24:14. Similarly, the heroes of faith "admitted (or "confessed") that they were strangers and pilgrims on earth" (Heb. 11:13). For this meaning "confessing" or "acknowledging" see also on Matt. 10:32. In that passage and in Luke 12:8 Christ's acknowledgment of the believer is the counterpart of the believer's acknowledgment of Christ. Although in Rev. 3:5 the phraseology is different, the thought is about the same. "Confessing" or "acknowledging" Jesus—with or without the addition "to be the Christ," or "the Son of God," or "Lord," or "incarnate"—is also the meaning in John 9:22; 12:42; Rom. 10:9; I John 2:23; 4:2, 3, 15; and II John 7. Similarly I Tim. 6:12 speaks of "confessing the good confession" (thus literally). In a different kind of context "confessing" or "acknowledging" is also the sense in Acts 23:8. Confessing may also be viewed as "saying (or "declaring") openly" (see on Matt. 7:23). Another closely related idea is "confessing one's sins" (I John 1:9). When one "agrees" to do something for someone he is "making a promise" (Matt. 14:7; cf. Acts 7:17). It is not difficult to see that thorough-going, enthusiastic "confessing," so that one joyfully acknowledges his allegiance to another, could lead to the meaning "praising" (Heb. 13:15).

As to the compound form ἐξομολογέω, more usual than the simplex in the LXX, in the New Testament the meaning "confessing one's sins" has already been indicated (see on 3:6; cf. Mark 1:5; James 5:16). Though in Acts 19:18 the object "sins" is not added, it or a synonym seems to be implied. "Confessing" in the sense of "acknowledging" is the idea in Phil. 2:11. Finally, perhaps in the manner already suggested for the simplex form, the compound verb attains the sense "praising" or "giving thanks." The verb has this sense not only here in Matt. 11:25 and its parallel Luke 10:21 but also in Rom. 15:9 and probably 14:11. In the LXX, too, this meaning is amply illustrated.

It would be impossible to maintain that the semantic shifts from one shade of meaning to another have thus been correctly and fully explained. All that can be safely affirmed is that it is not really difficult to understand how it was possible for one verb to attain what superficially viewed might seem to be so many wholly different meanings. Actually these meanings are not very far apart.

spiritual"—sense, the Father of all those who are his children by adoption, all true believers, here designated by the endearing term "babes."

Altogether fitting is also the next title of address, namely, "Lord of heaven and earth." As such, the Father is the sovereign Ruler, whose decisions and dispositions—for example, that he purposely hides certain things from wise and learned people—must not be criticized.

The question is raised, "But how could Jesus actually praise the Father not only for *revealing* matters touching salvation to some, but even for *concealing* them from others?" It is not entirely satisfactory to say: "Jesus meant that salvation transcends human understanding but can be appropriated by the humble heart." By rereading the question it becomes evident that if this is intended as a full answer it is somewhat unsatisfactory. It tries to evade the difficulty experienced when we think of the kind and loving Savior as praising the Father for actually *hiding* from certain individuals knowledge that is essential to their salvation. Perhaps a more satisfactory way of dealing with the question would be: *a.* To admit that in our present state of knowledge it cannot be fully answered. Is not God "the Lord of heaven and earth"? Are not such passages as Deut. 29:29; Job 11:7, 8; Dan. 4:35; and Rom. 9:20 applicable here? *b.* In so far as a *partial* answer is possible, to view this praise of the Father as the thankful recognition of the latter's righteousness shown in punishing those who are "wise in their own eyes" (Prov. 26:5; Rom. 11:25; 12:16), the very opposite of "babes."

The matter becomes easier when we consider the next clause, namely, ". . . and didst reveal them to babes." Physically speaking, "babes" are "sucklings" (Matt. 21:16). They drink milk, not solid food (I Cor. 3:1; Heb. 5:13), and have not yet advanced very far in learning to speak (I Cor. 13:11). It is clear, therefore, that "babes" are those who are conscious of their utter dependence on others. Spiritually, therefore, babes are those who humbly confess their own nothingness, their emptiness and helplessness, and who, being thoroughly aware of their absolute dependence upon the might and mercy of the heavenly Father, betake themselves to him, trusting that from him they will receive whatever is necessary so that, enjoying salvation full and free, they may live lives of gratitude to his glory. It must have become clear by now that the contrast between *a.* "wise and learned" and *b.* "babes" is not that between educated and uneducated people. It is between *a.* Those who imagine that, because of their practical "wisdom" or superior "intellect," they can save themselves, at least to some extent—think of Pharisees and scribes, with their doctrine of meritorious good works—; and *b.* those who realize that they must be saved by grace alone (Eph. 2:8). If this is understood, it will be clear that a highly educated individual can be a "babe," and that a wholly uneducated person can be in the undesirable company of the "wise and learned."

That Jesus would praise the Father for revealing these things to babes is understandable. In the present context the designation "these things" must mean the things concerning the kingdom of God (Matt. 11:12; cf. Luke 10:9, 17), the gospel (Luke 9:6) of repentance, hence of salvation (Mark 6:12). Such praise then is understandable, for if, in order to enter the kingdom or to obtain salvation, looking away from self and leaning on the everlasting arms of God is the path that must be trodden, then the way is opened to educated and uneducated, extraordinarily talented and intellectually retarded, rich and poor, young and old, male and female, slave and free. Truly, the Lord of heaven and earth has provided a glorious solution to the problem of human sin and misery. Is it not worthy of everlasting praise and adoration that the sovereign Ruler, who is self-sufficient and does not need man, is nevertheless willing to reveal the way of salvation to him; yes to humble people of every rank and station? "For thus says the high and lofty One who inhabits eternity, whose name is Holy: I dwell in the high and holy place, with him also who is of a contrite and humble spirit, to revive the spirit of the humble, and to revive the heart of the contrite" (Isa. 57:15).

It is as if the Mediator wishes to linger for a moment on this comforting thought, for in reverence and adoration he now continues, **yes, Father, for** [478] **such was thy good pleasure.** It is comforting to note that throughout the New Testament the good pleasure or delight of the Father, when positively expressed, everywhere else has as its object Christ and/or the work of salvation in connection with him. [479] It seems logical, therefore, to believe that also here (in Matt. 11:26 and in its parallel Luke 10:21) the positive thought of revealing to babes the things pertaining to salvation is uppermost in Christ's mind when he mentions the Father's good pleasure. Says H. Bavinck, "In a certain sense, the fall, sin, and eternal punishment are included in God's decree and are willed by him. But this is true *in a certain sense* only, and not in the same sense as grace and salvation. These are the

---

478 Or, with very little difference in ultimate meaning, "(I praise thee, Father) *that* [instead of "for"] such was thy good pleasure.

479 Sometimes the noun εὐδοκία is used with reference to human delight, good will, pleasure, or resolve (Rom. 10:1; Phil. 1:15; II Thess. 1:11). So it is also with the verb εὐδοκέω (Rom. 15:26, 27; II Cor. 5:8; I Thess. 2:8; 3:1; II Thess. 2:12). When the reference of the noun is to *God's* good pleasure or delight the contexts are as follows: Those with whom God is delighted (literally: "men of [God's] good pleasure," Luke 2:14); God's delight in choosing a people for himself (Eph. 1:5, 9) and in the fact that, by means of the strength imparted by God, believers are working out their own salvation (Phil. 2:13). As to the verb, the action positively expressed, the references are to the Father's delight in the Son (Matt. 3:17; 12:18; 17:5; Mark 1:11; Luke 3:22; II Peter 1:17), to his good pleasure in *a.* giving his children the kingdom (Luke 12:32), *b.* the salvation of his people through the preaching of the gospel (I Cor. 1:21), *c.* revealing his Son in Paul (Gal. 1:15), and *d.* the decision that in Christ all the fulness should dwell (Col. 1:19). Negative references: God is *not* delighted with unbelievers (I Cor. 10:5), with burnt-offerings (Heb. 10:6, 8), and with those who shrink back (Heb. 10:38).

objects of his delight; but God does not delight in sin, neither does he take pleasure in punishment." [480] Cf. Ezek. 18:23, 32; 33:11.

The Claim That Gives Meaning to It

The *way* that leads to salvation has been pointed out (verses 25, 26). It is the way of humble trust in God, or if one prefers, in Jesus Christ. However, another question must now be answered, "Does the One who extends the invitation to accept this salvation *have* what the sinner needs, and does he even *know* what he needs? The answer is implied in verse 27. **All things have been handed over to me by my Father. . . .**

First of all, then, he *has* what the sinner needs. "All things" (cf. John 3:35; 13:3) necessary for the carrying out of the mediatorial task have by the Father been entrusted to the Son. What things? From the preceding chapters it has already become clear that Jesus, the Father's Son, has received authority over Satan (4:1-11) and demons (8:28-32); over human ailments and handicaps (9:20-22; 9:1-8), winds and waves (8:23-27), body and soul (9:1-8), life and death (9:18, 19, 23-26), his own disciples and all other people (ch. 10), to save them (9:13) and to judge them (7:22, 23). From 28:18 we learn that he has been given all authority in heaven and on earth. From other parts of Scripture it is clear that as Mediator he was endowed with the Spirit of Jehovah, that is, with the Spirit of wisdom and understanding, counsel and might, knowledge and the fear of Jehovah (Isa. 11:1, 2). In the heart of the Mediator there is peace (John 14:27; 20:21, 26), light, life, love (John 1:4, 17, 26), and joy (John 15:11; 16:24; 17:23). All these spiritual qualities and many more have been entrusted [481] to him by the Father in order that from him as the Fountain they might flow out to others (John 1:16, 17; 3:16; 6:51; and other passages already mentioned). It has become clear, therefore, that the Mediator *has* whatever is needed to render a human being truly blessed.

---

[480] *The Doctrine of God* (my translation of *Gereformeerde Dogmatiek*, Vol. II, Chapter IV, Over God), Grand Rapids, 1955, p. 390.

[481] According to Lenski the aorist παρεδόθη ("handed over" or "entrusted") refers to the incarnation (*op. cit.*, pp. 440, 441). The tense itself, however, says nothing whatever about the length of time in which the indicated action took place, nor does it tell us when it took place. In the immediately preceding context (verse 26), however, there was a reference to the Father's sovereign *good pleasure* (εὐδοκία) regarding the revelation of the matter of salvation to babes. This *good pleasure* (same word in the original), used in a similar connection, is by Paul linked with the election and foreordination "in Christ" that took place "before the foundation of the world" (Eph. 1:4, 5). What was decided from all eternity was realized in time (Eph. 1:7 ff.). It would seem, therefore, that also here in Matt. 11:27 it is not necessary or even advisable to connect the action indicated by παρεδόθη with one particular moment in Christ's existence, for example, with the incarnation. The entire process—what happened in eternity, at the incarnation, at the baptism, and even later—may well be indicated by the verb. The use of the aorist is no obstacle. See also N.T.C. on the Gospel according to John, Vol. I, p. 125, footnote 64.

He also *knows* what the sinner needs. This follows from the fact that he is able to add: **and no one knows** [482] **the Son but the Father.** So great and so glorious is the heart of this Mediator that none but the Father can fathom its riches of knowledge, wisdom, and love. The very fact that the word "Son" is now used—not "me"—shows that what is being revealed here is the inner relation between Father and Son, a relation that existed from all eternity. When *Paul* speaks about "the treasures of wisdom and knowledge" hidden in Christ (Col. 2·3), about "the fulness of the godhead" dwelling in him (2:9), he immediately applies this theme in a very practical manner by adding, "and in him y o u have attained to fulness" (2:10). It is probable that a similar practical implication is also implied here in Matt. 11:27, as if to say: from a reservoir so inexhaustible that only the Father knows its capacity weary and heavily burdened ones are urged to replenish their needed supplies.

This practical purpose becomes even more clearly evident, it would seem, with the addition of the clause that is the counterpart of the preceding: **nor does anyone know the Father but the Son. . . .** The sinner's inner self and therefore his needs are known to God alone (Ps. 139; Jer. 17:9, 10). Before him every creature is laid bare (Heb. 4:13). Really to know a person means therefore to be able to see him as the Father sees him. Therefore, he who knows the Father knows the sinner and his needs also. It is the Son, the Son alone, who knows the Father, and who therefore also knows the sinner and his needs.

Since the Son knows the Father he, he alone, is able to reveal him, and does reveal him (John 1:18; 6:46; 14:8-11). Therefore to the words "nor does anyone know the Father but the Son" there is added: **and he to whom the Son is willing to reveal (him).** This must not be interpreted to mean that the Son is reluctant to reveal the Father, for just a moment ago (verse 25)

---

[482] The question is whether or not the compound ἐπιγνώσει, occurring twice in this verse, should be interpreted intensively ("really knows" referring to "a knowing that really penetrates," Lenski, *op. cit.*, pp. 440, 441; "fully knows," A. T. Robertson, *Word Pictures*, Vol. I, p. 91). As far as the context is concerned, something can be said in favor of this intensive interpretation: whatever is known by the Father or by the Son is known thoroughly. Also, the compound seems to have this intensive meaning in some other passages, the clearest of which is I Cor. 13:12, where γινώσκω ἐκ μέρους is contrasted with ἐπιγνώσομαι. Lexicons offer little help here. L.N.T., p. 237, opts for the intensive meaning; L.N.T.(A. and G.), p. 291, for the simple sense, that is, without emphasis on the preposition, on the basis of the fact that the parallel passage (Luke 10:22) has γινώσκει, not ἐπιγινώσκει. This argument may not be entirely convincing. The reason why, after some hesitancy, I decided in favor of the simple "knows" is that when the intensive sense is accepted, the passage not only says that the Son thoroughly knows the Father but also that such *thorough* knowledge is possessed by the believer. The simple meaning is also favored by nearly every translator: Wiclif, Tyndale, Geneva, Cranmer, Rheims, A.V., and the moderns. Exceptions: Williams ("perfectly knows") and Rotherham ("doth fully know").—The other meanings of the verb ἐπιγινώσκω (acknowledge, recognize, learn, learn to know, ascertain) do not enter the picture in the present connection.

the Son has been praising the Father for having revealed salvation to his humble children. The words indicate that the salvation of God's children is dependent not upon anything in man but solely upon revelation, and that this revelation, in turn, is based solely upon the will and delight of both the Father and the Son, for not only as to essence but also as to purpose Father and Son are one (John 10:30). From start to finish therefore salvation is based on sovereign grace. Cf. Eph. 2:8.

The Content That Encourages Its Acceptance

The Son *has* and he *knows,* and now he also *offers* and *gives* what is needed by those who are weary and burdened: 28-30. **Come**[483] **to me all who are weary and burdened. . . .** What it means to come to Jesus is clearly described in John 6:35, "He who comes to me will in no way get hungry, and he who believes in me will in no way get thirsty." It is clear from this passage that "coming" to Jesus means "believing" in him. Such faith is knowledge, assent, and confidence all in one. Moreover, faith, being the gift of the Holy Spirit, produces the fruit of the Spirit: love, joy, peace, long-suffering, kindness, goodness, faithfulness, meekness, and self-control (Gal. 5:22; cf. John 14:15; 15:1-17; I John 2:3). It brings forth the works of gratitude, performed in spontaneous obedience to Christ.

It is to the weary[484] and burdened[485] ones that the invitation is extended.

It is they, *all* of them, who are urged to come to Jesus. Specifically whom does Jesus have in mind? Matt. 23:4 provides the answer. The reference is to all those who are oppressed by the heavy load of rules and regulations placed upon their shoulders by scribes and Pharisees, as if only then when in any person's life obedience to all these traditions outbalances his acts of disobedience can he be saved. When in anyone's mind and heart the belief took root that in this way, and *only* in this way, man must earn his way into everlasting life, the result at best was painful uncertainty; more often something worse, namely, clutching fear, gnawing anxiety, rayless despair (cf. Rom. 8:15a).

It stands to reason that Christ's urgent invitation that such weary and burdened ones should come to him is relevant today as well as it was at the time when Jesus walked on earth. It applies to anyone who, for whatever reason, tries wholly or partly to achieve salvation by means of his own exertion. And does not the heart of every sinner, including even the man

---

[483] The word used is δεῦτε (δεῦρο: hither, here, and ἴτε: come), that is, "come here," or simply "come," with "here" implied.

[484] κοπιῶντες, nom. pl. masc. pres. participle from κοπιάω. See on 6:28; also N.T.C. on I and II Thessalonians, p. 134; cf. Gal. 4:11; Eph. 4:28; Phil. 2:16. "Jesus, travel-weary (fatigued as a result of a long journey) was sitting by the spring" (John 4:6).

[485] πεφορτισμένοι, nom. pl. masc. perf. participle pass. from φορτίζω; cf. Luke 11:46.

already reborn but still living here on earth, harbor a Pharisee, at least once in a while?

The promise is: **and I will give you rest.** [486] Such rest is not only negatively absence from uncertainty, fear, anxiety, and despair; positively it is peace of mind and heart (Ps. 125:1; Isa. 26:3; 43:2; John 14:27; 16:33; Rom. 5:1); assurance of salvation (II Cor. 5:1; II Tim. 1:12; 4:7, 8; II Peter 1:10, 11). Continued: **Take my yoke** [487] **upon y o u and learn** [488] **from me.** ... In Jewish literature a "yoke" represents the sum-total of obligations which, according to *the teaching* of the rabbis, a person must take upon himself. This definition accounts for such terms as "yoke of the Torah," "yoke of the commandments," "yoke of the kingdom of heaven," etc. It has already been shown that because of their misinterpretation, alteration, and augmentation of God's holy law, the yoke which Israel's teachers placed upon the shoulders of the people was that of a totally unwarranted legalism. It was the system of *teaching* that stressed salvation by means of strict obedience to a host of rules and regulations. Now here in 11:29 Jesus places his own teaching over against that to which the people had become accustomed. When he says, "Take my yoke upon y o u and learn from me," or "and become my disciples," he means, "Accept my teaching, namely, that a person is saved by means of simple trust in me." Continued: **for I am meek and lowly in heart** [489] .... In explaining the word "meek" as it occurs in 5:5, it was pointed out that the meek person is the one "who finds refuge in the Lord, commits his way entirely to him, leaving everything in the hand of him who loves and cares." See also on 12:19, 20. It is clear that the meek person is peaceful and peace-loving. It is therefore not so strange that the Syriac (Peshitta) New Testament has: "Come to me ... and I will *rest*

---

486 ἀναπαύσω, first per. sing. fut. act. indic. of ἀναπαύω. See also on 26:45. Cf. Mark 6:31; 14:41; Luke 12:19; I Cor. 16:8; II Cor. 7:13; I Peter 4:14; Rev. 6:11. Note Philem. 7: "the hearts of the saints have been rested" or "refreshed." Note the combination of ἀναπαήσονται and κόπων in Rev. 14:13.

487 See S.BK., Vol. I, pp. 608-610; also Rengstorf's article on ζυγός in the N.T. (Th.D.N.T., Vol. II, pp. 898-901).

488 μάθετε, sec. per. pl. aor. imper. of μανθάνω. The learning may be through instruction or through experience; here the stress seems to be on the former ("learn from me") though the latter is not ruled out. See also on 9:13 and 24:32. Modern Greek recognizes both μανθάνω and μαθαίνω. The root of such and similar words, both in Greek and in related languages, including English, is MAN: to think. Thus the Greek New Testament presents (in addition to μανθάνω): ἀμαθής, ignorant; καταμανθάνω, I consider (carefully); μαθητής: learner, disciple; μαθήτρια: woman disciple; μαθητεύω: I become a disciple, I make a disciple; and συνμαθητής: fellow-disciple. English offers: man (who has been called "a thinking animal"), mind, mental, monition, monster, monument, medicine, mathematics, and many others. See also on 13:52 and on 28:19.

489 The heart (καρδία) is the core and center of man's being, the mainspring of dispositions as well as of feelings and thoughts. It is the very hub of the wheel of man's existence, the center from which all the spokes radiate (Prov. 4:23; cf. I Sam. 16:7). All of this also applies to *Christ's* human nature.

y o u . . . for I am *restful* . . . and y o u shall find *rest* for yourselves." This, or something very similar to it, may well have been what Jesus, speaking Aramaic, closely resembling Syriac, said that day to the conscious-stricken multitude. [490] The synonym of "meek" is "lowly" or "humble," as opposed to "proud" (cf. I Peter 5:5).

The result of taking Christ's yoke and becoming his disciple is: and y o u shall find rest for y o u r souls [491] (or "for yourselves"). Such "finding" is "obtaining." Note the parallel: "I will give y o u rest" (verse 28) and "y o u shall find rest" (verse 29). Men can never obtain unless Christ gives. They can never discover what he has not disclosed. Concluded: For my yoke is kindly, and my burden is light. It should never be forgotten that a yoke, literally a wooden frame, was placed upon a person's shoulders in order to make a load or burden easier to carry, by distributing its weight in equal proportions to opposite sides of the body. This, however, did not entirely rule out the possibility that if the burden was very heavy the yoke would not be of sufficient help to the wearer. Consequently even a yoke could be called *heavy* (Acts 15:10). Accordingly, to make the carrying task delightful not only must the *yoke* be well adjusted to the shoulders, not chafing, but also the *burden* must not be too heavy. Symbolically speaking, Jesus here assures the oppressed persons whom he addresses, both then and now, that *his* yoke, that is, the one he urges them to wear, is kindly, [492] and his burden, that is, that which he requires of us, is light. What he is really saying, therefore, is that simple trust in him and obedience to his commands out of gratitude for the salvation already imparted by him is delightful. It brings peace and joy. The person who lives this kind of life is no longer a slave. He has become free. He serves the Lord spontaneously, eagerly, enthusiastically. He is doing what he (the "new man" in him) wants to do. Cf. Rom. 7:22. On the contrary, the attempt to save oneself by means of scrupulous adherence to all the artificial rules and arbitrary regulations superimposed upon the law by scribes and Pharisees (23:4) spells slavery. It produces wretchedness and despair. Therefore, says the Lord, *"Come to me."*

In the study of this marvelous passage (verses 28-30) one fact is generally passed by in silence. It is this: The authoritative advice Jesus gives is not only good for the soul; when heeded it also greatly benefits the body. The rest—peace of heart and mind—which Jesus here provides is the very opposite of the aggravated mental stress that sends so many people to doctors, hospitals, and death. Absence of peace, whether in the form of anxiety or of

---

[490] See W. Jennings, *Lexicon to the Syriac New Testament*, revised by U. Gantillon, Oxford, 1926, p. 6.

[491] For ψυχή see footnote 453 on p. 471.

[492] Greek χρηστός; cf. Luke 6:35. *The New Testament in Modern Greek*, London, 1943, has καλός, in modern Greek meaning *good, kind*, comparable to one of its connotations in Homeric, classical, and Koine Greek.

rancor and vindictiveness (the lust to "get even"), may lead to ulcers, colitis, high blood pressure, heart attacks, etc. The teachings of Christ, if taken to heart, have a curative effect on the entire person, soul and body. [493] He is a complete Savior!

Summary of Chapter 11

After the discovery of the Dead Sea Scrolls many have attempted to link John the Baptist with the Qumran movement. See, for example, *General Bibliography,* under W. H. Brownlee, and J. Daniélou. Among the resemblances that have been pointed out in some of the many books and articles are these: Both (The Baptist and the Qumran community) were associated with the desert in the general vicinity of the Dead Sea. Both were austere. Both emphasized the need of repentance and baptism. Both originated in the priesthood (John's father was a priest). Both reacted vigorously against "the establishment," that is, the recognized authority of Pharisees and Sadducees, etc.

There are certain outward resemblances, and it must be admitted that the Baptist may have been acquainted with the Qumran community. Nevertheless, in connection with certain more or less essential items, he was different. He did not try to keep his doctrines a secret but welcomed multitudes. Not only men but also women went to hear him and were converted (Matt. 21:31, 32). His disciples were not a highly organized group, kept under control by strict rules and regulations and by a rigid code of discipline. Most of all, John proclaimed a Messiah who had already arrived. He said, "Look, the Lamb of God, who is taking away the sin of the world." "I on my part baptize y o u with water with a view to conversion, but he who is coming behind me is mightier than I. . . ."

But though John had spoken with profound conviction about Jesus, there came a moment when he began to have his doubts. See Matt. 11:1-19. So the Baptist sends a few of his disciples to Jesus with the question, "Are you the Coming One, or must we look for someone else?" Probable reasons for his doubt: *a.* He was in a grim and gloomy prison and was not being rescued; *b.* The activities of Jesus, reported to the Baptist, did not seem to harmonize with the manner in which John had described the Messiah.

John had pictured impending judgment (the axe already at the root of the trees), but words of grace were falling from Jesus' lips, and works of mercy were being performed by him. Yet what John had said was correct, based on prophecy. However, he had not been able to distinguish between the first and the second coming. So he expected first-coming fulfilments of second-

---

[493] See S. I. McMillen, *op. cit.,* pp. 60, 62, 67, 70-75, 86. On p. 99 the author refers to this very passage. He quotes verses 28, 29.

coming predictions. Jesus dealt very kindly with him. He directed his attention to that aspect of Old Testament prophecy—promises of healing, deliverance, and restoration—which pertained to the first coming, and he reassured him by showing that right now these good tidings were being gloriously fulfilled. At the same time he defended John before the public, speaking with distinct approval of the work he had done as a herald. Not a reed swayed by every gust of wind was John, nor a flatterer. Had he been a flatterer he would right now have been in the king's *palace* instead of in the king's *dungeon.* The people therefore should take to heart John's preaching of repentance. They should not be like children in the market-place, quickly condemning what they formerly applauded, whether in John or in the Son of man.

In the second section (verses 20-24) Jesus denounced the cities in which most of his mighty works had been performed, because they had not repented. Lesson: judgment will not be easy on privileged impenitents.

In the third section (verses 25-30) withering denunciation is replaced by tender invitation. The return of missionaries with an enthusiastic report is for Jesus the occasion for the utterance of a stirring thanksgiving. He concludes with the tender invitation, "Come to me all who are weary and burdened, and I will give y o u rest. . . ."

Outline of Chapter 12

Theme: *The Work Which Thou Gavest Him to Do*

CHAPTER XII

12   1 Now at that time Jesus on the sabbath went through the fields of standing grain. His disciples were hungry and began to pick heads of grain and to eat them. 2 But the Pharisees saw it and said, "See here, your disciples are doing what is not permitted on the sabbath." 3 He said to them, "Have y o u not read what David did when he and those with him were hungry: 4 how he entered the house of God and ate the consecrated bread, which neither he nor those with him but only the priests were allowed to eat? 5 Or have y o u not read in the law how on the sabbath the priests in the temple break the sabbath, yet are guiltless? 6 And I tell y o u, something greater than the temple is here. 7 However, if y o u had known what this means, 'I desire mercy and not sacrifice,' y o u would not have condemned the guiltless. 8 For the Son of man is Lord of the sabbath."

    9 He went on from there and entered their synagogue. 10 And look, a man with a shriveled hand! "Is it right to heal on the sabbath?" they asked him [Jesus], aiming to bring a charge against him. 11 He said to them, "What man of y o u, if he has a sheep and it falls into a pit on the sabbath, will not grab hold of it and lift it out? 12 Of how much more value is a man than a sheep! Therefore it is right to do good on the sabbath." 13 Then he said to the man, "Hold out your hand." He held it out, and it was restored, sound as the other. 14 But the Pharisees went out and took counsel against him, how they might destroy him.

12:1-14 *The Son of Man*
Asserting His Authority as Lord of the Sabbath
Cf. Mark 2:23—3:6; Luke 6:1-11

Between the close of chapter 11 and the beginning of chapter 12 there is a twofold connection. First, the phrase "at that time" of 12:1 recalls 11:25. Though the words are rather indefinite, they do indicate that the events introduced cannot have been very far removed from each other in time. [494]

---

[494] This would still be true even though what is recorded in 12:1-21 should have taken place shortly *before* the preaching of the Sermon on the Mount. For example, if the sabbath controversies recorded in John 5; Matt. 12:1-14 followed each other in rather close succession and took place in April and early May, and if the preaching of the sermon and the events recorded in chapter 11 occurred sometime during late May-July, Matthew would still be fully justified in describing all such events as having happened "at that season." This may well have been the season "spring to mid-summer of the year A.D. 28." See also A. T. Robertson, *Harmony of the Gospels*, pp. 42-55. And see N.T.C. on the Gospel according to John, Vol. I, p. 188, 189. With reference to this chronology very

And secondly, as to material content, the "burden" of superimposed legalism from which Jesus promised to deliver all who would come to him (11:28-30) receives a double illustration in 12:1-14, which passage implies that a heavy load of sabbath rules and regulations had been placed on the people's shoulders by scribes and Pharisees.

1. **Now at that time Jesus on the sabbath went through the fields of standing grain.** Grain was evidently ripening. This process, varying with the altitude, occurred during a period extending from the spring of the year until mid-summer. In Palestine's warm Jordan Valley barley ripens during April; in Transjordan and the region east of the Sea of Galilee wheat is harvested in August. *Exactly* when it was that Jesus and his disciples went through the fields of standing grain is not stated in the text. The place is even more indefinite than the time. A. T. Robertson's suggestion that the event took place "probably in Galilee on the way back from Jerusalem" may be as good a guess as any.[495] But it is no more than a conjecture.

The translation "fields of standing grain" leans heavily upon the context for its justification. Literally and etymologically the reference is simply to "that which was sown." However, the context shows that when the trip on a path through the grain fields occurred, harvest time had arrived or was soon to arrive.

His disciples were hungry.... This is related by Matthew alone, though also implied by Mark (2:25) and Luke (6:3). No longer being regularly engaged in their earlier occupations it is not surprising that at times the disciples—how many at this time is not indicated—were (or "became") hungry. Jesus, too, experienced not only thirst (John 4:6, 7) but also hunger (Matt. 21:18). This little group was poor, needy, and now also hungry.

For people in such a condition the law had made special provision (Deut. 23:25): "When you enter your neighbor's field of standing grain, you may pick the heads of grain with your hand, but you must not thrust a scythe into your neighbor's standing grain."

What the disciples did to relieve their hunger is related variously in the Synoptics. Mark merely states that they started to pick the heads ("ears") of grain; Matthew: **and began to pick heads of grain and to eat them.** This eating is also *implied* by Mark (2:26). Luke, more complete on this point than either of the others, has, "His disciples began picking and eating the heads of grain, rubbing them with their hands."

---

little can be established with certainty. In its favor are these facts: *a.* John 5:1, 16 suggests that *the first* of the three sabbath controversies took place after "a feast" (probably a Passover, and if so, not the first Passover of Christ's ministry for which see John 2:23); *b.* Luke 6:11, 12 suggests that *the last* of the three controversies was followed by the preaching of the Sermon on the Mount; and *c.* Matt. 12:1 shows that *the second* sabbath controversy took place during the season of ripening grain.

[495] *Harmony of the Gospels*, p. 44.

As to these "heads of grain," some prefer ". . . of wheat."[496] Since by us wheat is generally thought of as most closely related to "the staff of life," so that we think of it first of all in connection with the stilling of hunger, and also since the recorded event must not be dated too early in the year (barley ripens before wheat), it is not difficult to understand that there are those who favor the rendering "wheat." This may well be correct. It is but fair to add, however, that A. T. Robertson, in his *Word Pictures* (see my footnote above) makes allowance for the *possibility* that the grain to which Matthew refers was barley. See John 6:9, 13. Cf. Ruth 1:22; 2:17, 23; 3:2, 15, 17. If we knew more definitely where and when the event related in Matt. 12:1, 2 occurred it would be easier to prove which grain was meant.

To satisfy their hunger and in full accordance with the law of Deuteronomy, as has already been shown, the disciples began to pick the heads and to eat the grain after rubbing it out with their hands. On the part of those who hated Christ and were trying to find some excuse for having him condemned there was an immediate reaction, as is shown in verse 2. **But the Pharisees saw it and said, See here, your disciples are doing what is not permitted on the sabbath.** On the hostile attitude of the Pharisees toward Jesus see what has been said earlier, in connection with 3:7; 5:17-20; 9:11, 34. By means of their hairsplitting legalism these men were constantly burying God's law under the heavy load of their traditions, as has become clear from the explanation of 5:21-48; see also on 15:1-11 and on chapter 23. Filled with envy they were always watching Jesus to see whether something he said or did could be used as a charge against him, so as to destroy him. As to the Pharisees here referred to, whether they had come a great distance—having traveled on his heels, perhaps from Judea back to Galilee, as some think—or were from nearby, one thing is certain: their intentions were not honorable. There was murder in their hearts. See verse 14. Cf. John 5:18; 7:19; 8:40.

Suddenly they confront Jesus, blaming him for allowing his disciples to profane the sabbath. Was not work forbidden on the seventh day (Exod. 20:8-11; 34:21; Deut. 5:12-15)? Had not the rabbis drawn up a catalogue of thirty-nine principal works, subdivided into many minor categories, so that, for example, plucking heads of grain was considered *reaping,* and rubbing out the grain *threshing?*[497] And here were the disciples engaged in these very activities and even enjoying the fruits of their sins: they were *eating* this ill-gotten grain! And Jesus was doing nothing about it. According to the

---

[496] Thus A. T. Robertson, *Word Pictures*, Vol. I, p. 93; cf. same author, *A Translation of Luke's Gospel*, New York, 1923, p. 40. Williams, in his translation of the New Testament, has "heads of wheat," thus rendered also by L.N.T. (A. and G.), p. 773.

[497] According to the Mishna that man is guilty of sabbath desecration who on that day "takes ears of grain equal to a lamb's mouthful" (Shabbath 7:4; cf. 7:2). See also S.BK., Vol. I, pp. 615-618; and A. T. Robertson, *The Pharisees and Jesus*, New York, 1920, pp. 87, 88.

passage now under discussion (cf. Mark 2:24) the charge was leveled against Jesus himself. According to Luke 6:2 it is the disciples who are being accused. Since both were involved there is no real discrepancy here (see also Matt. 10:24, 25; John 15:20).

In his answer Jesus, who elsewhere gave the true, spiritual interpretation of the first and second commandments (Exod. 20:1-6; cf. Matt. 22:37, 38, which summarizes the entire first table of the law), of the third commandment and the ninth (Exod. 20:7; Lev. 19:12; Num. 30:2; Deut. 23:21; cf. Matt. 5:33-37), the fifth and eighth (Exod. 20:12, 15; cf. Matt. 15:3-6), the sixth (Exod. 20:13; cf. Matt. 5:21-26, 38-42), the seventh (Exod. 20:14; cf. Matt. 5:27-32; 19:3-12), and the tenth (Exod. 20:17; cf. Luke 12:13-21; 16:14, 19-31; see also Matt. 22:39, in which the entire second table is summarized), now reveals the true meaning of the fourth commandment (Exod. 20:8-11). Implied in his interpretation, but in this case not stated in so many words, is a condemnation of the false explanation which the rabbis had superimposed upon this commandment and which in the days of Christ's sojourn on earth was being widely propagated by scribes and Pharisees. They were either completely ignoring or else leaving insufficient room in their teaching for the following truths, which also summarize Christ's teaching as now presented.

a. *Necessity knows no law* (Matt. 12:3 and 4)

b. *Every rule has its exception* (verses 5 and 6)

c. *Showing mercy is always right* (verses 7 and 11)

d. *The sabbath was made for man, not vice versa* (Mark 2:27); and

e. *Sovereign Ruler over all, including the sabbath, is the Son of man* (Matt. 12:8; cf. verse 6).

a. *Necessity knows no law*

3, 4. He said to them, Have y o u not read what David did when he and those with him were hungry: how he entered the house of God and ate the consecrated bread, which neither he nor those with him but only the priests were allowed to eat? "Have y o u not read?" As if to say, "Y o u pride yourselves in being the very people who uphold the law and y o u deem yourselves to be so thoroughly versed in it as to be able to teach others; yet are y o u yourselves unacquainted with the fact that even this very law allowed its ceremonial restrictions to be ignored in cases of necessity? Have y o u not read about David and the bread?" This reference is to consecrated bread, showbread, literally "bread of the presence," twelve loaves of bread laid in two rows and displayed on "the table of showbread" before the Lord. The twelve loaves represented Israel's twelve tribes and symbolized the constant fellowship of the people with their God, receiving their bread from him, eating with him, being consecrated to him, and gratefully acknowledging their indebtedness to him by means of this offering.

This bread was changed for fresh loaves every sabbath. The old loaves were eaten by the priests (Exod. 25:30; I Sam. 21:6). The rule was that this "holy" bread was for "Aaron and his sons," that is, for the priesthood, definitely not for everybody (Lev. 24:9). Yet when Ahimelech, functioning in the days of Abiathar the high-priest (I Sam. 21:1-6; Mark 2:26), realized that David and his men were hungry, and became convinced that the man whom God had anointed to be king over Israel (I Sam. 16:12, 13) had undertaken a sacred mission (I Sam. 21:5), he gave him the bread needed by this future king and by his retinue. David, having entered "the house of God," that is, the tabernacle in Nob (I Sam. 21:1; 22:9) ate this bread. If then David had a right to ignore a *divinely ordained ceremonial provision* when necessity demanded this—for, surely, Jehovah's anointed had a right and a duty to maintain himself physically, and so did his hungry attendants! —then would not David's great Antitype, namely, Jesus, God's Anointed in a far more exalted sense, have the right to set aside *a totally unwarranted, man-made sabbath regulation?* The aptness of this historical reference appears all the more clearly when the fact is considered that a parallel is drawn here between, on the one hand, David and his followers, and on the other, Jesus and his disciples. Though, to be sure, during the old dispensation ceremonial laws were instituted to be obeyed, yet it would be hard to prove that even then a higher law—in this case the principle that human life and health must be preserved (Exod. 20:13; Matt. 22:39b; I Cor. 6:19)—could not under certain circumstances invalidate or at least modify an ordinance of lesser significance. *All the more* was there good reason in the case of Jesus and his disciples to ignore a purely rabbinical regulation regarding sabbath observance, a rule resting upon nothing more solid than a misinterpretation and misapplication of God's holy law.

b. *Every rule has its exception*

The principle announced in verses 3 and 4 applies always, sabbath or no sabbath. What David did when he ate the consecrated bread was right and necessary, whether it was done on the sabbath or on any other day of the week. Turning now specifically to God's ordinances regarding the sabbath, Jesus continued, **5, 6. Or have y o u not read in the law how on the sabbath the priests in the temple break the sabbath, yet are guiltless?** On the sabbath the priests were kept very busy (Lev. 24:8, 9; Num. 28:9, 10; I Chron. 9:32; 23:31; II Chron. 8:12-14; 23:4; 31:2, 3), all this in spite of the sabbath commandment found in Exod. 20:8-11; Deut. 5:12-15. What happens in such a case is that a higher law, demanding that everything be done to make possible the worship of God by the people, modifies and restricts the too literal interpretation of the regulation concerning sabbath rest. So also today no one in his right mind will blame a minister for preaching and/or administering the sacraments on the Lord's Day. The trouble with the Pharisees when they found fault with Jesus and his disciples was this, that they not only placed rabbinical tradition on a par with God's written law, which often in practice amounted to elevating it above the written law, but that in addition to this they attached an all but absolute value to specific traditions. Not even the divine law as recorded in the Decalog, says Jesus as it were, was to be applied with such rigidity. Otherwise how could the priests have performed their work on the sabbath?

The remark has been heard: "Every rule has its exception. This is a rule. Therefore it has its exception." The exception in the present case is, of course, *the basic principle* expressed by Jesus in Matt. 22:37-40; Mark 12:29-31; Luke 10:27, whatever be the wording of this principle. That basic principle applies always and everywhere.

In an authoritative manner Jesus adds, **And I tell y o u, something greater than the temple is here.** Meaning: If even an earthly temple, which was but a type, demanded modification of the fourth commandment, literally interpreted, would not its far superior Antitype, namely, Jesus Christ, who was addressing the Pharisees here and now, and in whom "all the fulness of the godhead dwells bodily" (Col. 2:9; cf. John 10:30), have the right to make a similar demand? Surely, something greater than the temple, a treasure infinitely more precious, a gift from heaven immeasurably more valuable, an authority endowed with rights far more magisterial, was speaking to them.

c. *Showing mercy is always right*

Repeating what he had said on another occasion—accordingly for the meaning of the passage see on 9:13—the Lord continues, 7. **However, if y o u had known what this means, I desire mercy and not sacrifice, y o u would not have condemned the guiltless.** That was exactly the trouble with these Pharisees: they lacked pity. They did not love kindness. Therefore the hunger which plagued the disciples of Jesus failed to kindle within the hearts of their critics any feeling of tenderness or eagerness to help. Instead they were condemning the disciples. As to Jesus, they not only condemned him but secretly rejoiced in having discovered another reason, as they saw it, for causing him to be destroyed.

With respect to what the disciples were doing to those heads of grain, these hungry men were entirely "guiltless." In no sense whatever were they transgressing any divine commandment. Yet the Pharisees, these hypocrites, with murder in their hearts, were condemning them. Yes, "them" but especially their Master (cf. James 5:6). If they had only taken to heart the words of Hosea 6:6 they would have known that showing mercy is right on any day of the week, including most certainly the sabbath!

d. *The sabbath was made for man, not vice versa*

This statement of our Lord, in further defense of his disciples, is found in Mark 2:27, where it immediately precedes the words, "Therefore the Son of man is Lord also of the sabbath," paralleled in Matt. 12:8. The sabbath was instituted to be a blessing for man: to keep him healthy, to make him happy, and to render him holy. Man was not created to be the sabbath's slave.

e. *Sovereign ruler over all, including the sabbath, is the Son of man*

In line with the saying of verse 6 ("Something greater than the temple is here"), Jesus concludes this grainfield sabbath controversy by saying, 8. **For the Son of man is Lord of the sabbath.** The conjunction "for" is not difficult to understand. Jesus has just now pronounced his disciples "guiltless." They were indeed without any guilt with respect to the charge made against them by the Pharisees, "for" in picking and (after rubbing out the grain) eating this food they were doing what Jesus allowed and wanted them to do. They were recognizing "his" lordship rather than the lordship of the Pharisees and their oft foolish traditions. The disciples were right in so doing, "for" the Son of man is indeed Lord of the sabbath. They were correct when they placed obedience to him above slavish observance of arbitrary, man-made sabbath ritual. Is not the Son of man—for which term see on 8:20—Lord over all (11:27; 28:18)? Would he not then be Lord of the sabbath also? *Guilty* are those who imagine that they can honor the sabbath while dishonoring its Lord.

Jesus, as Lord of the sabbath, not only honored it by regularly attending the synagogue services on that day but also by at times taking a leading part (Luke 4:16-27). Again, he honored it by performing acts of mercy and healing on that day (12:9-14; Luke 13:10-17; 14:1-6; John 5:9; 7:23; 9:14). Also, he hallowed it by resting in the tomb on that day, thereby sanctifying the grave for his followers (Matt. 27:57-60; Mark 15:42, 46; 16:1; Luke 23:53, 54; 24:1). Moreover he did justice to it by fulfilling its symbolic significance.

During the old dispensation the week began with six days of LABOR. These were followed by one day of REST. Later, by the labor of his vicarious suffering Christ, the great Highpriest, procured for "the people of God" "the eternal sabbath rest" (Heb. 4:8, 9, 14). By faith in him believers even now (in principle!) enter into this REST, which is constantly being followed by their LABOR of love, that is, by their works of gratitude for salvation already obtained for them as a free gift. The order LABOR—REST is therefore changed to REST—LABOR: very appropriately the week now *begins* with the day of REST. In summary, Jesus asserted his authority over the sabbath by interpreting it by word and deed as being a day of true freedom, a day of rejoicing, of rendering service of love to each and to all, and, in and through it all, by worshiping God above everything else!

The truths mentioned above, in items *b, c, d,* and *e,* apply also to the next sabbath controversy. Not so directly item *a,* for it was not immediately apparent that the man with a shriveled hand *needed* to be cured *on the sabbath.* Humanly speaking one might argue that such a restoration of a paralyzed hand could wait until the next day. Here, then, the Pharisees seem to be on safer ground. They jump at the opportunity, not even waiting for Jesus to take the initiative. Note their eagerness: 9, 10. He went on from there and entered their synagogue. And look, a man with a shriveled hand! Is it right to heal on the sabbath? they asked him [Jesus], aiming to bring a charge against him. From the grainfield the action now shifts to the synagogue. It is sabbath. In walks a man with a lame hand. It is moreover his right hand (Luke 6:6). The apocryphal Gospel according to the Hebrews states that the man was a stonemason, who pleaded with Jesus to heal him that he might not have to spend his life as a beggar. Be that as it may, the point is that this is a sabbath, and though there may well have been a difference of opinion between the disciples of Shammai, with their stricter interpretation of sabbath observance, and those of Hillel, with their more lenient view—the more rigorous position prevailing in Jerusalem, the more lenient in Galilee—the rule that only in such cases in which a man's life was actually in danger would it be permissible to heal him on the sabbath was widely endorsed. [498] Would Jesus dare to oppose this rule, by the Pharisees regarded as a well-established and basic principle which must not be violated?

Secretly the opponents hope that by word and/or deed Jesus may trample upon their rule of conduct. Thus basely motivated (see verse 14) they ask him, "Is it right to heal on the sabbath?" Their purpose is "to bring a charge against him." Do they fail to realize that their own wicked motivation is the grossest sabbath desecration of all, a sin so damning that in the sight of the Almighty it constitutes a most grievous charge against *them?* Also, do they fail to realize that Jesus knows their thoughts (Luke 6:8)?

The Lord of the sabbath (see verse 8) orders the man to stand up before the entire assembly (Mark 3:3; Luke 6:8), as if to say to one and all, "Look at him; study his hand, and consider what his condition means to him. Does he not arouse y o u r sympathy?" Next, Jesus answers the question of his critics. He does so by, as it were, turning the tables on them. By means of a counter-question he makes these Pharisees answer their own question: 11, 12. He said to them, What man of y o u, if he has a [499] sheep and it falls into a pit on the sabbath, will not grab hold of it and lift it out? Of how much more value is a man than a sheep! It is safe to infer from the question asked by Jesus that at least at that time and place it was not regarded wrong to rescue a sheep that had suffered such a mishap, regardless of whether the accident occurred on a sabbath or on any other day. That being so, is not a

---

498 See S.BK., Vol. I, pp. 622-629.
499 This may well be an instance of εἰς (here naturally ἕν) having the force of an indefinite article. The meaning need not be, "only one," or "one in distinction from more than one," or "one lone sheep" (Lenski, *op. cit.*, p. 455), but simply "a." See Gram. N.T., pp. 674, 675. However, the rendering "*one* sheep" may be right!

human being of more value than a sheep? If on the sabbath doing good to an animal is allowed, then all the more it is right and proper on that day to show kindness to a man, God's image-bearer!

Must such help be offered only when life is in danger? Jesus does not even enter into this question, except by implication. That implication is very clear: showing mercy is *always* right (see above, p. 512, point *c.*). Ethical conduct is ever far more important than ceremonial obedience. If the Pharisees had only made a more thorough and unbiased study of their own truly sacred scriptures (see for example Mic. 6:6-8) they would have known this! Certainly, because a man is incomparably more valuable in the sight of God than a sheep, **Therefore it is right to do good on the sabbath**, that is, to be a blessing to man, not to remain indifferent to his needs. For this type of argument see also 6:26, 30; 10:29, 31 (cf. Luke 12:6, 7).

These words, "Therefore it is right to do good on the sabbath" must have been spoken with deep earnestness. They may have been uttered both as a positive statement (thus Matthew) and in question form, "Is it lawful on the sabbath to do good or to inflict injury, to save a life or to kill?" (Mark 3:4; cf. Luke 6:9). But if the question form alone was used, did it not imply Christ's affirmation of the thesis that it is indeed right to do good on the sabbath? A real conflict between the Gospel writers cannot be proved therefore. It was Jesus himself who was about to do good to this man. Christ's critics, on the other hand, were harboring thoughts of murder, the murder of the Benefactor (verse 14). Which was best?

Jesus, looking around, studies the faces of his opponents and reads their inner secrets (Luke 6:8, 10). His cheeks are glowing with holy indignation. He is grieved at their hardness of heart (Mark 3:5). No one is able to answer him. The Pharisees cannot very well deny that to do good on any day, and certainly on the sabbath, is right and proper. Yet to admit this openly means surrender for them. So an embarrassed, chilling silence prevails in their ranks (Mark 3:4). With bated breath the rest of the people are also watching, wondering what will happen now. The atmosphere in the synagogue is surcharged with uneasiness on the one hand, expectancy on the other. The man with the "withered" hand is still standing there, in full view of the audience.

Jesus is about to perform the miracle demanded by this situation. He must act *now*, not later. For him to have waited until the following day could easily have been interpreted as an admission on his part that deeds of healing are after all wrong when performed on the sabbath. Such a delay, accordingly, would have compounded error. This must not be. Now is the time. So, after this searching look all around, the Master rivets his attention upon the handicapped man. 13. **Then he said to the man, Hold out your hand. He** held it out, and it was restored,[500] sound as the other. The cure is instantaneous and complete. Subsequent treatments or even check-ups are not required. The right hand is now as sound as the left. It must be emphasized also that the cure took place in connection with the man's act of obedience. Nevertheless, for the miracle itself we must give all the credit and the glory to Jesus, to him alone. He did not touch the man. In fact, not even by means of a single syllable did he order the hand to be cured (contrast Mark 7:34). He merely told the man to stretch out his hand and it was made well. In a manner too mysterious for any mortal to comprehend, the Savior had concentrated his mind on the plight of this poor man, had become filled with compassion, and in the sight of everyone present had willed and performed the cure!

Did this astounding deed of might and mercy convince the Pharisees of their error? Did they now confess their guilt? Not at all. They hated Jesus all the more because of what he had done on the sabbath. As they saw it, imparting health and happiness to a man by removing his handicap was a crime when it was done on the sabbath, but plotting on that same day to destroy the Healer amounted to a meritorious act. **14. But the Pharisees went out and took counsel against him, how they might destroy him.** Had it been possible they would have been glad to kill Jesus right now, for they were filled with rage (Luke 6:11). Two obstacles made it difficult for them to carry out their wicked plan immediately: *a.* the Roman government (John 18:3), and *b.* the spectators. The deeply impressed synagogue audience would not have tolerated any drastic action against Jesus at this time. What could be done in this situation? To find a solution to their problem the Pharisees, those very men who were always boasting about their extraordinary holiness, at times carrying their high opinion of themselves to the very throne of God (Luke 18:11, 12), now consult with . . . of all people, the thoroughly unholy, worldly Herodians (Mark 3:6), a political party that supported Herod's dynasty! Misery makes strange bedfellows, especially when it is linked with envy. Together the two groups now plot how to crush Jesus. See also on 3:7 and on 22:16 (cf. Mark 12:13). These bitter enemies of the Lord should have read and taken to heart Ps. 2.

---

15 Jesus, aware of this, departed from that place. Many followed him, and he healed them all. 16 And he warned them not to make him known, 17 in order that what was spoken through Isaiah the prophet might be fulfilled:

18 "Behold, my servant whom I have chosen;

---

500 ἀπεκατεστάθη third per. sing. aor. indic. pass. of ἀποκαθίστημι. The verb refers to the action whereby something is *set* (ἵστημι) *down* (κατά) or *established* by being delivered *from* (ἀπό) its disturbed condition. In the present context (cf. Mark 3:5; Luke 6:10) ἀπεκατεστάθη means "was restored," "was cured," or "was made well." In a somewhat different sense "restored" is also the meaning in Heb. 13:19. See also on Matt. 17:11 (cf. Mark 9:12).

My beloved, with whom my soul is well pleased.
I will put my Spirit upon him,
And he shall proclaim justice to the Gentiles.
19 He shall not quarrel or shout,
Nor shall anyone hear his voice in the streets.
20 A bruised reed he shall not break,
And a smoldering wick he shall not quench,
Until he leads justice on to victory.
21 And in his name shall the Gentiles hope."

12:15-21 *The Chosen Servant*
Cf. Mark 3:7-12

Since Jesus was fully aware of the murderous intent of his enemies, and since he also knew that the time for his departure from this earth had not as yet arrived, we are not surprised to read: **15. Jesus, aware of this, departed from that place.** But even in his departure he was thinking not only of himself but of those elsewhere for whom he could be a blessing: **Many followed him, and he healed them all.** For explanation see on 4:23-25; 9:35; and 11:5. He did all this for people many of whom were going to reject him. Cf. 11:20-24; John 6:66. As to **16. And he warned them not to make him known,** see the detailed explanation of 8:4, especially points *b.*, *c.*, and *d.* See also on 9:30.

Jesus was not seeking fame. He did not wish to stand out as a worker of miracles. Vain display, earthly glory, matters such as these did not constitute the reason for his incarnation and sojourn among men. They were completely out of harmony with the humble "Servant of Jehovah" of Isaiah's prophecies. This explains verse **17. in order that what was spoken through Isaiah the prophet might be fulfilled.** To prove Christ's unassuming, gentle, and retiring nature a reference to Isa. 42:2, 3 would probably have sufficed, but it is Matthew's desire to quote also the preceding and following context, in order that Messiah's glory may become all the more strikingly evident, and the wickedness of his opponents stand out more clearly by contrast. Accordingly, what is offered here in 12:18-21 is Isa. 42:1-4 as interpreted by Christ's fully inspired apostle Matthew. It is not a word for word reproduction but the result of profound sympathetic reflection. And a careful comparison of the Hebrew original with Matthew's version leaves no doubt about the fact that the former publican had indeed caught the thrust of Isaiah's strikingly beautiful description of the coming Christ.[501]

---

[501] Translated rather literally from the Hebrew original, Isa. 42:1-4 reads as follows:
42:1 "Behold, my servant, whom I uphold,
My chosen, in whom my soul delights,
I have put my Spirit upon him,
He shall bring forth justice to the nations.
2 He shall not cry nor lift up his voice,
Nor cause it to be heard in the street,

Isa. 42:1-4 is the first of four prophecies regarding "the Servant of Jehovah." The others are Isa. 49:1-9a; 50:4-9; and 52:13–53:12 (cf., however, also Isa. 61:1 ff.). Matthew's version begins as follows:

18. Behold, my servant whom I have chosen,
My beloved with whom my soul is well pleased.
I will put my Spirit upon him,
And he shall proclaim justice to the Gentiles.

It is clear from the entire context that when Matthew in his own way quotes Isa. 42:1-4 he refers this prophecy directly to Jesus Christ, God's beloved Son, the Mediator between God and man. Matthew interprets Isa. 42 as Philip the evangelist and as the apostles John and Peter interpreted Isa. 53 (Acts 8:26-35; John 12:37-43; I Peter 2:24). In fact, Isa. 42 cannot be separated from Isa. 53. Because of 42:6, 7 (cf. 9:2, 6) it is simply impossible to intepret Isa. 42:1-4 intelligibly except as referring to and being fulfilled in Christ. Moreover, as to the marvelous things said about "the Servant of Jehovah" in Isa. 49:6; 53 (the entire chapter); and 55:3-5, to whom could such statements refer if not to the Son of God who is also the Son of man? Those who refer such passages to Israel forget that 53:6 draws a sharp distinction between *a.* the people who have gone astray and *b.* the Servant upon whom Jehovah places the burden of their iniquity (see also verses 4, 5, 8, and 12).

Matthew, then, draws a sharp contrast between *a.* Christ's wicked opponents, in this case the Pharisees, who are seeking to destroy him (12:14), and

---

3 A bruised reed he shall not break,
And a languishing wick he shall not quench;
In truth he shall bring forth justice.
4 He shall not languish and not become bruised,
Until he has established justice on earth.
And the coastlands shall wait for his law."

Note the following:

a. In Isa. 42:1a, cf. Matt. 12:18a, although "my servant whom I uphold" was not literally reproduced by Matthew, Isaiah's full expression "my servant, whom I uphold, my chosen, in whom my soul delights" gives Matthew every right to say, "my bloved, with whom my soul is well pleased" (or "my beloved in whom I delight").

b. As to Isa. 42:2b, cf. Matt. 12:19b, there surely is no essential difference between Isaiah's "Nor cause it to be heard in the street" and Matthew's "Nor shall anyone hear his voice in the streets."

c. A moment's reflection proves that Isa. 42:3b, 4a enables Matthew to say (12:20b) "until he leads justice on to victory."

d. The "coastlands" of Isa. 42:4b represent the farthest regions, that is, the nations outside of Israel; hence, correctly rendered by Matthew (12:21) "the Gentiles." And the "waiting" of the Hebrew text is a waiting with confident anticipation, a *hoping* (cf. Matt. 12:21).

Matthew follows the LXX translation when in verse 18 he uses the word παῖς instead of δοῦλος. This, however, makes no essential difference, since παῖς frequently means "servant." See on Matt. 8:6. It is to be noted, however, that Matthew avoids "*Jacob* my servant . . . *Israel* my elect" (LXX), and correctly applies Isa. 42:1-4 directly to Christ.

b. Christ himself, the Father's beloved Son (Matt. 3:17; Luke 9:35; Col. 1:13; II Peter 1:17, 18; cf. Ps. 2:6-12), ever eager to do the will of his Sender (John 4:34; 5:30, 36; 17:4).

It is upon this divine and human Redeemer that the Father pours out his Spirit, and this "without measure" (Matt. 3:16; John 3:34, 35; cf. Ps. 45:7; Isa. 11:2; 61:1 ff.). As a result (Luke 4:18) the Mediator carries out his prophetic activity, namely, that of proclaiming "justice," that which is right, in harmony with the will of God: that sinners repent, come to (that is, believe in) the Savior, find salvation in him, and out of gratitude live to the glory of their Benefactor. See further on verse 21.

In close connection with verse 16 the attitude of the Spirit-filled Mediator between God and man is now pointed out. His frame of mind and heart is the very opposite of that of his enemies:

19. **He shall not quarrel or shout,**
     Nor shall anyone hear his voice in the streets.

The shouting mentioned here is not that of religious rejoicing (Ps. 5:11; 32:11; Isa. 12:6; Zech. 9:9, etc.), nor of battle or victory (Exod. 32:18; Amos 1:14; cf. Josh. 6:20). It rather resembles the raving of "a ruler among fools," as contrasted with "the words of the wise" spoken and received in an atmosphere of blessed quietness (Eccl. 9:17). It is like the riotous screaming which by popular belief was ascribed to the satyr (Isa. 34:14). It is, as the passage (Matt. 12:19) clearly shows, the kind of shouting that is associated with quarreling. Think of the nasty public wrangling among those who have just lost a game, the uproarious fulmination of the demagogue as he stirs up the people in the streets, the boisterous boasting and fighting of the Bacchus parade (see N.T.C. on Gal. 5:21), etc. Completely different is the meek and gentle Savior. See (in addition to Isa. 42:1-4) Isa. 57:15; Zech. 9:9; I Kings 19:11, 12; Matt. 5:7-9; 21:5; Luke 23:34. Continued:

20. **A bruised reed he shall not break,**
     And a smoldering wick he shall not quench. [502]

In a context that speaks of justice being proclaimed to the Gentiles, and of the Gentiles hoping in his name it is well-nigh certain that the terms *bruised* [503] *reed* [504] *and smoldering* [505] *wick* [506] must be taken figuratively, as referring to those from afar, to the weak and helpless, those of little faith, etc. What a contrast between the cruelty of the Pharisees and the kindness of

---

[502] See P. Van Dyk, "Het gekrookte riet en de rookende vlaswiek," GTT, 23 (1923), pp. 155,172.

[503] Greek συντετριμμένον acc. sing. masc. perf. pass. participle of συντρίβω: break, bruise.

[504] Greek κάλαμος (acc. -ον), cf. Latin *calamus*.

[505] Greek τυφόμενον, pres. pass. participle from τύφω: give off smoke, smolder.

[506] Greek λίνον: flax, linen; also anything made of such materials (cf. Rev. 15:6), in the present instance a lamp-wick.

Jesus, between their vanity and his reserve, their love for display and his meekness. *They* plan murder (12:14) and are callous, indifferent to the agony of the handicapped (12:10). "Is it lawful? Is it lawful?" is their constant cry; never, "Is it kind?" *He* is completely different. In fact, so very different that it would be incorrect to interpret the words of verse 20 in a purely negative manner, as if they merely meant to indicate what he would *not* do to those who fear that their faith will fail or that the tempter will prevail. On the contrary, these expressions belong to the figure of speech called "litotes," by means of which a positive truth is conveyed by the negation of its opposite. The real significance of "the bruised reed" which he will not break and of "the smoldering wick" which he will not quench is therefore that he will treat with profound and genuine sympathy, with tender concern, whatever is near to exhaustion. He will impart strength to the weak, to all who while pining away ask him for help. He will heal the sick (4:23-25; 9:35; 11:5; 12:15), seek and save tax-collectors and sinners (9:9,.10), comfort mourners (5:4), cheer the fearful (14:13-21), reassure doubters (11:2-6), feed the famished (14:13-21), and grant pardon to those who repent of their sins (9:2). He is the true Immanuel (see above, on 1:23).

He will never cease to do all this **until he leads justice on to victory**, that is, until at last, at the great consummation, sin and all its consequences will have been banished forever from God's redeemed universe. Then the justice of God (see above, on verse 18) will triumph completely, for "the earth shall be filled with the knowledge of Jehovah as the waters cover the (bottom of the) sea" (Isa. 11:9; cf. 61:2, 3, 11; Jer. 31:34).

It is not surprising therefore that according to the divine plan the time was coming when the command not to make Jesus known (12:16) would be withdrawn. *Israel's* Savior must become "*the world's* Savior" (John 4:42; I John 4:14). The continuation, therefore, is natural: **21. And in his name,** that is, in "Christ as revealed" to the world, **shall the Gentiles hope.** They shall place their firmly anchored (cf. Heb. 6:19) confidence in the Lord Jesus Christ. The period of secrecy (Matt. 12:16) will be gradually replaced by that of wide publicity, when the church fulfils its mission among the Gentiles. [507] A foreglimpse of this era of gospel proclamation and salvation for Gentiles as well as for Jews, predicted but not yet widely realized during the old dispensation (Gen. 22:15-18; Ps. 72:8-11; 87; Isa. 54:1-3; 60:3; Mal. 1:11), can be seen in Matt. 2:1, 2, 11; 8:10-12; 15:21-28; Luke 2:32a; John 3:16; ch. 4; 10:16. For a larger measure of fulfilment see Matt. 28:18-20; Acts 22:21; Eph. 2:11-22. For the final result or "victory" see Rev. 7:9-17.

---

[507] Cf. G. W. Barker, W. L. Lane, and J. R. Michaels, *The New Testament Speaks,* New York, 1969, p. 269.

22 Then a demon-possessed man who could neither see nor speak was brought to him. And he healed him, so that the dumb man spoke and saw. 23 All the people were amazed and said, "Surely, this cannot be the Son of David?" 24 But when the Pharisees heard (this) they said, "This fellow does not cast out demons but by Beelzebul the prince of the demons." 25 Knowing their thoughts he said to them, "Every kingdom divided against itself is on the way to ruin, and no city or house divided against itself shall stand. 26 If Satan is engaged in casting out Satan he is divided against himself; How then shall his kingdom stand? 27 And if it is by Beelzebul that I cast out demons, by whom do y o u r sons cast them out? Therefore they shall be y o u r judges. 28 But if it is by the Spirit of God that I cast out demons, then the kingdom of God has come upon y o u. 29 Or how can anyone enter the strong man's house and carry off his goods unless he first binds the strong man? It is only then that he will ransack his house. 30 He who is not with me is against me; he who does not gather with me scatters. 31 Therefore I say to y o u, every sin and blasphemy shall be forgiven men, but blasphemy against the Spirit shall not be forgiven. 32 And whoever shall speak a word against the Son of man, it shall be forgiven him; but whoever shall speak against the Holy Spirit, it shall not be forgiven him, either in the present age or in the age to come.

33 "Either consider the tree to be good and its fruit good, or consider the tree to be sickly and its fruit sickly, for by the fruit the tree is known. 34 Y o u offspring of vipers. how can y o u speak what is good when y o u yourselves are evil? For out of the abundance of the heart the mouth speaks. 35 The good man from his good inner storehouse brings out what is good, and the evil man from his evil treasure brings out what is evil. 36 But I say to y o u that for every careless word that men shall speak they shall render account on the day of judgment. 37 For by your words you shall be justified, and by your words you shall be condemned."

12:22-37 *Christ's Miracles:*
Proof of Beelzebul's Dominion or of His Doom?
For 12:22-32 cf. Mark 3:19-30; Luke 11:14-23; 12:10.
For 12:33-37 cf. Luke 6:43-45

22. Then a demon-possessed man who could neither see nor speak was brought to him. The adverb "then" is again very indefinite. As in 12:2, 10, and 14 so also here Jesus is in the company of his opponents. A demoniac afflicted with loss of sight and of speech is brought to him. For demon-possession in general and for the relation between it and physical afflictions see on 9:32. **And he healed him, so that the dumb man spoke and saw.** Jesus cured him instantly and completely, so that the man who had been so grievously afflicted was now no longer demon-possessed nor blind nor dumb. Effect upon the spectators: **23. All the people were amazed and said, Surely, this cannot be the Son of David?** The people who witnessed this miracle were utterly astounded. A feeling of amazement coupled no doubt with a measure of fear in the presence of the One who had performed this startling feat took possession of them. If it were not, perhaps, too colloquial, we might say, "They were knocked out of their senses." This, or something approaching it, preserves the flavor of the original. That the attention of the audience, having focused itself on the man who was the recipient of this

523

triple blessing, was soon fixed upon the great Benefactor himself is clear from the question whether the latter might be the Son of David. For the meaning of this title see on 9:27. The question was so phrased that a modified negative answer was expected, somewhat on the order, "No, he is probably not the Son of David . . . and yet, who else could he be, to perform such a miracle?" The question was significant indeed! Perhaps the people's state of mind at this moment might be described thus: the astonishing character of the miracle had convinced them that this Jesus could very well be the Messiah, but they do not dare to give definite vocal expression to this thought, especially because of the presence of Christ's bitter opponents, the Pharisees. Their question can also be rendered, "Could this be the Son of David?" Though the possibility that Jesus might be the Messiah is expressed ever so hesitantly, it is certainly an advance on the more or less neutral, "What kind of person is this?" (8:27).

But though we should guard ourselves against attaching too little significance to the question, we must equally refrain from reading too much into it. It must be borne in mind that even if it should be granted that these people, at least some of them, saw in Jesus the Messiah, the further question would still be, "What kind of Messiah? Merely a deliverer from earthly woes, such as bodily afflictions and handicaps, yes even from demons, possibly also a potential rescuer from the Roman yoke, hence from degradation and oppression, all this. . . . *but not from sin?* Not from the evil underlying all other miseries, namely, man's alienation from God?" The Messianic conception of many of the people, including to some extent Christ's own disciples, was distinctly materialistic, earthly, Judaistic (Matt. 20:21; 23:37-39; Luke 19:41, 42; Acts 1:6; John 6:15, 35-42).

The very suggestion of the possibility, no matter how imperfectly and remotely conceived or presented, that Jesus might be the long awaited One, was poison to the Pharisees; particularly also to the scribes, who had come all the way from Jerusalem (Mark 3:22), no doubt to ensnare Jesus in his words and/or actions. Continued: **24. But when the Pharisees heard (this) they said, This fellow does not cast out demons but by Beelzebul the prince of the demons.** This time, unlike in 12:2, 10, the opponents do not address Jesus directly but slander him behind his back. They basely ascribe his demon expulsions to the power of Beelzebul the prince of the demons. For a discussion of the title Beelzebul (=Satan) see on 10:25, including footnote 450. See also on 9:34. The charge leveled against Jesus by scribes and Pharisees was wicked. It was the result of envy. Cf. Matt. 27:18. They felt that they were beginning to lose their following, and this they were unable to endure. How completely different had been the attitude of John the Baptist (John 3:26, 30). The thoroughly shameful character of the charge becomes apparent also from the fact that it regards Beelzebul not as an evil spirit exerting his sinister influence upon Jesus from the outside; no, Satan is regarded as being inside the soul of Jesus. The latter is said to *have* an unclean spirit (Mark 3:30; cf. John 8:48); in fact, to be himself Beelzebul (Matt. 10:25).

Replying to the charge that he is casting out demons by the power of Beelzebul, Jesus points out that *a.* it is *absurd* (verses 25, 26); *b.* it is also *inconsistent* (verse 27); *c.* it *obscures* the true situation (verses 28-30); *d.* it is *unpardonable* (verses 31, 32); and *e.* it *exposes* the wickedness of those who make it, showing whose sons these blasphemers really are, in the same way in which the good deeds and attitudes of others supply evidence to prove what kind of individuals these good men are inwardly (verses 33-37).

First of all, then, the charge is *absurd.*

25, 26. Knowing their thoughts he said to them, Every kingdom divided against itself is on the way to ruin, and no city or house divided against itself shall stand. If Satan is engaged in casting out Satan he is divided against himself; how then shall his kingdom stand? The slander is ridiculous, thoroughly unreasonable, for if it were true Satan would be opposing Satan. He would be destroying his own work. First, he would be sending out his envoys, the demons, to work havoc in the hearts and lives of men. Afterward, in base ingratitude and suicidal folly, he would be supplying the very power needed for the expulsion of his own obedient servants! Thus he would be breaking down his own empire. No kingdom, city, or household thus divided against itself can maintain itself.

Secondly, it is also *inconsistent.*

27. And if it is by Beelzebul that I cast out demons, by whom do y o u r sons cast them out? Therefore they shall be y o u r judges. There were others besides Jesus and his disciples who claimed to possess the power to expel demons. That occasionally such successful conjuration of evil spirits by the "sons" or disciples of the Pharisees may actually have occurred need not be disputed. See on 7:22. It is, however, not necessary either to prove or to disprove this. The point is: friends and followers of the Pharisees claimed that they possessed this power, and for reasons adequate or inadequate this claim was generally accepted. Naturally *the teachers* of these reputed exorcists were only too eager to accept their share of the credit, that is, to bask in reflected glory. But if the Pharisees were right in doing this, how could they with any kind of consistency oppose Jesus for engaging in the same type of work? Let the "sons" then judge whether or not what their teachers said about the source of Jesus' power to drive out demons was correct. If these sons should deem the charge to be correct, affirming therefore that he was actually expelling demons by the power of the demons, they would be condemning themselves. On the other hand, if they judge the charge to be false they are condemning their teachers and vindicating Jesus. Either way their verdict would be very embarrassing to Christ's opponents.

Another instance of the Master's use of this method of argumentation, by which the enemies lose whether they answer one way or the other, is reported in 21:23-27. On the other hand when *they*—in this case the Pharisees supported by the Herodians—confront Jesus with a dilemma, he not only eludes their trap but also in the process of doing so teaches them a lesson which they, as well as all people everywhere, should take to heart (22:15-22). Jesus is the Master of every situation. So exalted is he!

Thirdly, it *obscures*.

The slander spread by the adversaries was not a slight deviation from a factual presentation but a wicked obscuration. It was the very opposite of the truth, for not by the power of an evil spirit but by the Spirit of God did Jesus cast out demons. How could it be otherwise? **28. But if it is by the Spirit of God that I cast out demons, then the kingdom of God has come upon y o u.** This "if" means "if, as is actually the case." The very fact that Satan's kingdom is being proved vulnerable—for his envoys are being driven out of men's hearts and lives—shows that God's kingdom (see on 4:23) is making its presence felt. It is in the process of gaining the victory over the realm of Satan. It is very clear from this passage that the term "kingdom of God" (Matthew's more usual designation is "of heaven," see above, p. 87) indicates a reality that is not merely future but also present. It is a growing reality, a developing entity, each of its blessings being a harbinger of greater blessings still to come, until the never ending climax is reached in the great consummation, and even then "perfection" will in a sense be progressive. [508] Even now, during Christ's earthly ministry, the sick were being healed, the dead raised, lepers cleansed, demons cast out, sins pardoned, truth spread, lies refuted. Instead of opposing and fighting this kingdom, let men everywhere enter it (7:13, 14; 11:28-30; 23:37; John 7:39).

It is "by the Spirit of God" that Christ's power is thus being manifested on earth. For this title "the Spirit of God" see also 3:16; Rom. 8:9b, 14; I Cor. 2:11b (cf. 2:12b); 2:14; 3:16; 6:11; 7:40; 12:3; II Cor. 3:3 ("the Spirit of the living God"); I Peter 4:14; I John 4:2a. The parallelism in I Cor. 12:3 proves that this "Spirit of God" is the third person of the Trinity, "the Holy Spirit." So certainly also here in Matthew, as a comparison of 12:28 with 12:32 shows.

That this explanation of the source of Christ's power is the only logical one is explained in verse 29. **Or how can anyone enter the strong man's house and carry off his goods unless he first binds the strong man? It is only then that he will ransack his house.** In ordinary life the burglar does not receive willing help from the home owner. Instead, in order to get what he wants the intruder first ties up the owner. Then he burglarizes. Jesus by word and deed is depriving Satan of those values which the evil one regards as his own and over which he has been exercising his sinister control (Luke

---

[508] See the author's book, *The Bible on the Life Hereafter*, pp. 75-78.

13:16). The Lord is casting out Beelzebul's servants, the demons, and is restoring that which through their agency Satan has been doing to men's souls and bodies. Jesus is doing all this because by means of his incarnation, his victory over the devil in the desert of temptation, his words of authority addressed to the demons, his entire activity, he has begun to bind Beelzebul, a process of binding or curtailment of power that was going to be further strengthened by means of his victory over Satan on the cross (Col. 2:15) and in the resurrection, ascension, and coronation (Rev. 12:5, 9-12). He has done, is doing, and will do this through the power not of Beelzebul himself surely but of the Holy Spirit, as he has just said (verse 28). Yes, the devil is being, and is progressively going to be, deprived of his "furniture," that is, of the souls and bodies of men, and this not only through healings but also through a mighty missionary program, reaching first the Jews but later on also the nations in general (John 12:31, 32; Rom. 1:16). Is not this the key to the understanding of Rev. 20:3? [509] Note how also in Luke 10:17, 18 the "fall of Satan as lightning from heaven" is recorded in connection with the return and report of the seventy missionaries.

In this struggle between Christ and Satan neutrality is impossible (so also Mark 9:40; Luke 9:50), as is shown by verse 30. **He who is not with me is against me.** Reason: there are only two great empires: *a.* that of God or heaven, with Christ as Head, and *b.* that of Satan. A person belongs either to the one or to the other. Consequently if he is not in intimate association *with* Christ, he is *down on,* [510] that is, *against,* him. To be "with" Jesus means to gather; to be down on him means to scatter: **he who does not gather with me scatters.**

To be "with" Jesus means to be instrumental in gathering people to be his followers (Prov. 11:30; Dan. 12:3; Matt. 9:37, 38; Luke 19:10; John 4:35, 36; I Cor. 9:22). To be "against" him means to be unwilling to follow him in his mission to gather the lost. It means to leave them in their shepherdless, scattered condition, an easy prey for Satan (see on 9:36; cf. John 10:12).

Fourthly, it is *unpardonable.*

Jesus continues: **31, 32. Therefore I say to y o u, every sin and blasphemy shall be forgiven men, but blasphemy against the Spirit shall not be forgiven. And whoever shall speak a word against the Son of man, it shall be forgiven him; but whoever shall speak against the Holy Spirit, it shall not be forgiven him, either in the present age or in the age to come.**

Every sin of which men sincerely repent shall be forgiven (so also Mark 3:28; Luke 12:10). To be sure, in none of these passages is the condition of repentance mentioned. That it was, however, implied is clear from the very

[509] See my *More Than Conquerors, An Interpretation of the book of Revelation,* pp. 223-229.
[510] In Greek the two prepositions are μετά versus κατά.

527

context (12:41), from 4:17, and perhaps even more specifically from Luke 17:3, 4. See also Ps. 32:1, 5: Prov. 28:13; James 5:16; I John 1:9. This rule holds also with respect to that very heinous sin, namely, blasphemy. In this connection we must be careful, however, to bear in mind that Scripture at times uses this word in a broader sense than we do. Among us "blasphemy" may be defined as "defiant irreverence." In this connection we think, for example, of such crimes as cursing God or the king who reigns by the grace of God, of willful degradation of things considered holy, pulling them down to the realm of the secular, or of claiming for the secular or purely human the honor that belongs to God alone. In Greek, however, a more general sense was also ascribed to the word "blasphemy," namely, the use of insolent language directed against either God *or man*, defamation, railing, reviling (Eph. 4:31; Col. 3:8; I Tim. 6:4). Accordingly, when Jesus assures us that "every (or "every kind of") blasphemy shall be forgiven men," he is using the term "blasphemy" in the most general sense. However, when he makes an exception—"but blasphemy against the Spirit shall not be forgiven"—he is referring to a sin which even in our English language would be considered "blasphemy." See also on 9:3. Cf. Mark 2:7; Luke 5:21; John 10:30, 33; Rev. 13:1, 5, 6; 16:9, 11; 17:3.

Nevertheless, even for all but one kind of defiant irreverence there is forgiveness, as is clear from the fact that Jesus says, "Whoever shall speak a word against the Son of man, it shall be forgiven him." If this were not true how could Peter's sin have been forgiven (Mark 14:71), and how could he have been reinstated (John 21:15-17)? How could Saul (=Paul) of Tarsus have been pardoned (I Tim. 1:12-17)? On the other hand, for "blasphemy against the Spirit," that is, for "speaking against the Holy Spirit" there is said to be no forgiveness, either now or in "the age to come."

In passing, it should be pointed out that these words by no stretch of the imagination imply that for certain sins there will be forgiveness in the life hereafter. They do not in any sense whatever support the doctrine of purgatory. The expression simply means that the indicated sin will *never* be forgiven. As to the doctrine of purgatory, supposedly the place where the souls of those who are not eternally lost pay off the remainder of their debt by suffering punishment for the sins which they committed while still on earth, it is clearly contradicted by Scripture, which teaches that "Jesus paid it all" (Heb. 5:9; 9:12, 26; 10:14; I John 1:7; Rev. 1:5; 7:14).

The question remains, "How is it to be understood that blasphemy against the Holy Spirit is unpardonable?" As to other sins, no matter how grievous or gruesome, there is pardon for them. There is forgiveness for David's sin of adultery, dishonesty, and murder (II Sam. 12:13; Ps. 51; cf. Ps. 32); for the "many" sins of the woman of Luke 7; for the prodigal son's "riotous living" (Luke 15:13, 21-24;); for Simon Peter's triple denial accompanied by profanity (Matt. 26:74, 75; Luke 22:31, 32; John 18:15-18, 25-27;

21:15-17); and for Paul's pre-conversion merciless persecution of Christians (Acts 9:1; 22:4; 26:9-11; I Cor. 15:9; Eph. 3:8; Phil. 3:6). But for the man who "speaks against the Holy Spirit" there is no pardon.

Why not? Here, as always when the text itself is not immediately clear, the context must be our guide. From it we learn that the Pharisees are ascribing to Satan what the Holy Spirit, through Christ, is achieving. Moreover, they are doing this willfully, deliberately. In spite of all the evidences to the contrary they still affirm that Jesus is expelling demons by the power of Beelzebul. Not only this, but they are making progress in sin, as a comparison between 9:11; 12:2; and 12:14 clearly shows. Now, as has already been indicated, to be forgiven implies that the sinner be truly penitent. Among the Pharisees here described such genuine sorrow for sin is totally lacking. For penitence they substitute hardening, for confession plotting. Thus, by means of their own criminal and completely inexcusable callousness, they are dooming themselves. Their sin is unpardonable because they are unwilling to tread the path that leads to pardon. For a thief, an adulterer, and a murderer there is hope. The message of the gospel may cause him to cry out, "O God be merciful to me, the sinner." But when a man has become hardened, so that he has made up his mind not to pay any attention to the promptings of the Spirit, not even to listen to his pleading and warning voice, he has placed himself on the road that leads to perdition. He has sinned the sin "unto death" (I John 5:16; see also Heb. 6:4-8).

For anyone who is truly penitent, no matter how shameful his transgressions may have been, there is no reason to despair (Ps. 103:12; Isa. 1:18; 44:22; 55:6, 7; Mic. 7:18-20; I John 1:9). On the other hand, there is no excuse for being indifferent, as if the subject of the unpardonable sin is of no concern to the average church member. The blasphemy against the Spirit is the result of gradual progress in sin. Grieving the Spirit (Eph. 4:30), if unrepented of, leads to resisting the Spirit (Acts 7:51), which, if persisted in, develops into quenching the Spirit (I Thess. 5:19). The true solution is found in Ps. 95:7b, 8a, "*Today* O that y o u would listen to his voice. Harden not y o u r hearts!" Cf. Heb. 3:7, 8a.

Finally, it *exposes.*

This charge exposes the wickedness of those who make it. It shows whose sons these blasphemers really are. Similarly, the good deeds and attitudes of God's true children prove what kind of individuals these good men are inwardly. It is evident from verse 34 ("offspring of vipers") that also in the present brief paragraph (verses 33-37) Jesus still has the Pharisees in mind. Nevertheless, it is also clear that from the particular he is advancing to the general, that is, from this particular group of people he is making a transition to "the evil man," whether Pharisee or not, versus "the good man," whoever he may be (verse 35). He concludes with an earnest word of warning addressed directly to each individual distinct from the rest; note the change from "y o u" ("I say to y o u," verse 36) to "you" ("For by your words," verse 37).

The paragraph begins as follows: **33. Either consider the tree to be good and its fruit good, or consider the tree to be sickly and its fruit sickly, for by the fruit the tree is known.** Fruit and tree belong together. They must not be separated. Therefore to say that while the deeds of Jesus, such as demon-expulsion, healing the sick, etc., may be beneficial, yet he himself is bad, being a tool of Beelzebul, makes no sense. Who Jesus *is* must be determined by what he *does:* a tree is judged by its fruit. Literally, the original says, "Either *make* the tree good and its fruit good, or *make* the tree sickly and its fruit sickly," where "make" means "consider to be." See also John 5:18; 8:53; 10:33. English usage is similar, for example, "He is not the genius some make him," that is, ". . . some consider him to be." For the rest see on 7:16-20.

Sickly fruit proves that something is wrong with the tree. The Pharisees have produced sickly fruit: blasphemous speech (see verse 24). From sickly trees, that is hearts, nothing better could be expected: **34. Y o u offspring of vipers**—see on 3:7—**how can y o u speak what is good when y o u yourselves are evil?** Since the hub from which all the spokes of their being issue, since the very mainspring of their thinking, feeling, and willing is thoroughly depraved, how would it be possible for their mouth to utter anything but evil? **For out of the abundance of the heart the mouth speaks.** Literally "out of the overflow," the surplus or excess. As a teeming population will overflow into adjoining territory, and a too full cistern into an overflow pipe, so also the overplus of the heart will burst out into speech, as it certainly did in the case of these wicked Pharisees. The opposite is also true: when the heart is filled with good and noble intentions the good man's speech will prove this to be a fact. The rule according to which whatever a man has set his heart on, so that the very core and center of his being is full of it, will sooner or later be disclosed in his speech, holds for good and bad alike: **35. The good man from his good inner storehouse brings out what is good, and the evil man from his evil treasure brings out what is evil.** A person's heart is a reservoir, a storehouse or, as the original literally expresses it, a *thesaurus.* Compare Matt. 2:11 where the word is used to indicate a chest or box from which the wise men took gold, frankincense, and myrrh. [511] What a man brings out of this inner storehouse, whether good or bad, precious or cheap, depends on what he was carrying in it.

This, however, does not offer any excuse for a fatalistic view of life. It does not make it right for a man to say, "I did not make myself, did I? Can I help it that I am what I am, and that I think, speak, and act the way I do?"

---

[511] The same word may also refer to the treasure itself (Matt. 6:19-21; 13:44; Heb. 11:26; Col. 2:3).

On the contrary, Jesus says, **36. But I say to y o u that for every careless word that men shall speak they shall render account** [512] **on the day of judgment.** Every man remains fully responsible for what he is, thinks, speaks, and does, for though it is true that he cannot change his own heart, it is also true that with strength given to him by God he is able to flee to him who renews hearts and lives. The Lord is ever willing and eager to give whatever he demands of men. If men do not receive it, this is *their* fault, not God's (Ps. 81:10; Isa. 45:22; 55:6, 7; Matt. 7:7; 11:28-30; Luke 22:22; John 7:37; Acts 2:23; James 4:2b; Rev. 3:18; 22:17b).

Now if even for every "careless" word--according to the original mere "talk" that does *no* (useful) *work* and is therefore ineffective in producing any good result—men shall render an account on the day of the final judgment, shall they not be called upon to give a satisfactory reason for their false, hurtful, blasphemous words, such as those recorded in 12:24? For the comprehensive character of the final judgment see the list of passages mentioned on p. 469 in connection with the explanation of 10:26.

Emphatically addressing each individual person in the audience, as if that individual were no longer in the group but alone and face to face with the Lord, Jesus, now using the second person singular, concludes and climaxes his words by saying, **37. For by your words you shall be justified, and by your words you shall be condemned.** The judgment passed upon the individual in the final day (see verse 36) is going to be "by," in the sense of "in conformity with," in accordance with," "in harmony with," his words, considered as mirrors of the heart. These words will reveal whether he was a professed believer or an unbeliever; if a professed believer, whether his faith was genuine or faked. To be sure, a man is saved by grace alone, through faith, apart from any works considered as if they have earning power. Nevertheless, his works—this includes his words—supply the needed evidence showing whether or not he was and is a child of God. Moreover, if this judgment turns out favorably, the works, reflecting the man's degree of loyalty to his Maker and Redeemer, figure in the determination of his degree of glory. They figure similarly in establishing the degree of punishment for those who perish. Jesus wants each individual to meditate upon this important truth, that he may be justified (declared righteous in the sight of God) and not condemned.

---

38 Then some of the scribes and Pharisees answered him, saying, "Teacher, we wish to see a sign from you." 39 Answering he said to them, "An evil and adulterous generation is looking for a sign, but no sign shall be given to it except that of Jonah the prophet. 40 For as Jonah was in the belly of the sea-monster three days and three nights so also

---

512 Literally, ". . . every careless word that men shall speak they shall render an account of it, etc." Such an anacoluthon, if one wishes to call it that, is readily understood. See Gram. N.T p. 718. It occurs in Greek and is frequent in Hebrew.

shall the Son of man be in the heart of the earth three days and three nights. 41 Men of Nineveh shall stand up in the judgment with this generation, and shall condemn it, for they repented at the preaching of Jonah; but look, something greater than Jonah is here. 42 The queen of the south shall arise in the judgment with this generation and shall condemn it, for she came from the ends of the earth to listen to the wisdom of Solomon; and behold, something greater than Solomon is here.

43 "Now when the unclean spirit goes out of a man it wanders through waterless places, seeking rest, but does not find it. 44 Then it says, 'I will go back to my house that I left.' It goes and finds it unoccupied, swept clean, and put in order. 45 Then it goes and brings back with it seven other spirits more wicked than itself, and they come and live there. And the final condition of that person becomes worse than the former. So it shall also be with this wicked generation."

12:38-45 *The Craving for Signs Rebuked*

For 12:38-42 cf. Mark 8:11, 12; Luke 11:29-32.

For 12:43-45 cf. Luke 11:24-26.

38. Then some of the scribes and Pharisees answered him, saying, Teacher, we wish to see a sign from you. The Pharisees must have resented their total defeat. Jesus had shown that the report which they were spreading about him (see 12:24) was both wicked and absurd. Also, he had called them "offspring of vipers." So now the Pharisees, who somewhat earlier had allied themselves with the Herodians (Mark 3:6), seek the help of those whom they so highly admire (at least pretended to admire), namely, the scribes, the acknowledged expounders and teachers of the Old Testament and of the traditions that had become linked with it. For more about the sect of the Pharisees and the profession of the scribes see on 3:7; 5:20; and 7:29.

Together these Pharisees and scribes walk up to Jesus and tell him that they wish to see a sign from him. How utterly Judaistic (I Cor. 1:22)! In presenting their request they observe the outward forms of politeness and respect. [513] Yet this politeness was veneer. These men hated Jesus (cf. Luke 11:16). What they were actually saying was that none of the marvelous works of healing which Jesus had so far performed, including the one described in verse 22, was sufficient to show that it was by the power of the Spirit that he had done them. *They* had a different explanation (12:24). At bottom, therefore, their request was insulting and impudent. All the requisite proofs of Christ's claims had already been provided. They had been furnished by means of miracles in connection with which efficacy and

---

[513] It may well be doubted whether the theory is correct according to which the use of the indicative θέλομεν indicates abruptness—"we want from thee" (Lenski), "we want to see" (N.A.S.)—, so that the request would amount to a demand. In keeping with the fact that these men respectfully address Jesus as "Teacher" it would seem to be more probable that *as to form* the request was courteous: "we would see" (A.V. and A.S.V.), "we wish to see" (R.S.V.), "we would like to see" (Williams), renderings that are certainly not out of line with the use of the indicative of the verb θέλω. See L.N.T. (A. and G.), p. 355.

sympathy had embraced each other. Yes, also sympathy, love, grace for poor, lost sinners. But the enemies were interested not in sympathy but in prodigy, not in healing but in that which was appealing, that is, to the senses. The sign must differ from anything done previously. It has to be thrilling, exciting, sensational. Well, what *did* they want? Did they want Jesus to cause the heavenly constellations to change places in the zodiac? Did they want him to make the Bull (Taurus) catch up with the Giant Hunter (Orion)? Must he perhaps blaze his name across the sky in enormous letters of gold? Is he expected to produce in the sky above them a vision of Michael suddenly leaving his celestial abode and coming forth to deliver the Jews from the galling yoke of the Romans? Their demand was wicked, for in addition to being insulting and impudent it was also hypocritical, for they felt sure that what they so politely asked Jesus to do he could not do anyway.

Continued: **39, 40. Answering he said to them, An evil and adulterous generation is looking for a sign, but no sign shall be given to it except that of Jonah the prophet. For as Jonah was in the belly of the sea-monster three days and three nights so also shall the Son of man be in the heart of the earth three days and three nights.** Jesus, far from being deceived by the outward courtesy shown him by these adversaries, discerns their true motive, namely, to curb his influence among the people, and, having exposed what by them would be regarded as failure and inability, to destroy him as a false claimant to Messianic rights and prerogatives (12:14).

It is clear from the words "an evil and adulterous generation" that the Lord is addressing not only the Pharisees and scribes but also their followers. He calls these contemporaries "evil," that is, morally corrupt; also "adulterous," unfaithful to their rightful Husband, Jehovah (Isa. 50:1 ff; Jer. 3:8; 13:27; 31:32; Ezek. 16:32, 35 ff., Hos. 2:1 ff.). See also on Matt. 9:15. It was exactly to such an adulterous generation that the Messiah, according to a rather general Jewish opinion, would make his appearance. [514]

It is not surprising therefore that Jesus refuses to give these enemies, the Pharisees and scribes and their adherents, the sign for which they were asking. He, and the Father in connection with him, will give them his own sign, a sign in which he will triumph completely over them, to their everlasting dismay, namely, the sign of Jonah the prophet, the latter's recovery from "the three days and three nights" in the belly of the sea-monster. See Jonah 1:17—2:1 in the original Hebrew—; 2:10). It is clear that Jesus accepts this Old Testament account as the record of a historical fact. Now the Lord says that similarly the Son of man—for the title see on 8:20—shall be in the heart of the earth, the grave, three days and three nights. The point is that as Jonah was swallowed up by the sea-monster, so he, Jesus, will be swallowed up by the earth; and as Jonah was delivered

---

[514] S.BK. Vol. I, p. 641.

from his imprisonment, so also Jonah's great Antitype would arise from the grave.

Exactly how, in the case of *Jonah,* these three days and three nights were computed Scripture nowhere reveals. Were they three entire days and nights, seventy-two hours in all, or was the period of his stay in the belly of the "fish" one entire day plus parts of two other days? We do not know. We *do* know that in Esther 4:16 the third day cannot have been an entire day (see 5:1, "on the third day," not "after the third day"). See also the apocryphal book Tobit 3:12, 13. To say, therefore, that in order to do justice to Matt. 12:40 Jesus must have been in the grave three entire days plus three entire nights is unreasonable. It is contrary to Jewish usage of such terms.

Nevertheless, again and again—sometimes in small pamphlets—the opinion will be advocated that according to Matt. 12:40 Jesus must have died and been buried on Thursday. This, however, is definitely wrong, for the inspired records tell us that these events took place on Friday, that is, on *Paraskeuē,* this very word being used even in modern Greek to indicate Friday (Mark 15:42, 43; Luke 23:46, 54; John 19:14, 30, 42). Also, if the proponents of this "Jesus was buried on Thursday afternoon" theory demand that "three days" means three entire *days,* their theory will still fall short; and, on the other hand, if, as they see it, a part of a day must be figured as a day, the result is: too many days!

Neither is it *entirely* satisfactory to say that, while Jesus died indeed on Friday and rose again on Sunday morning, the solution is to be found in the fact that, as already proved, the Jews counted a part of the day as equal to a day, and a part of the night as amounting to a night. As far as the "days" are concerned, this would be a satisfactory explanation, but it would still leave us with only two nights, not three.

What then? Some, despairing of a solution, declare that the saying, though having been a part of the Gospel from the beginning, is spurious, never having been uttered by Jesus himself. There is, however, no good reason thus to cut the Gordian knot. The true solution probably lies in a different direction. When we say "the universe," the ancients would say "heaven and earth." So also, should not their expression "one day and one night" be taken to mean one time unit, one diurnal period, [515] a part of one such period being taken as a whole? He was indeed in the heart of the earth three "days-and-three-nights," that is during three of these time units.

In the present passage Christ's prediction with reference to his coming resurrection was still rather veiled. Subsequently the prophecy would be expressed with increasing clarity (cf. 16:21; 20:17-19; Mark 9:31; Luke 9:22; 18:31-33).

The mighty event of Christ's glorious resurrection should cause all men to

---

[515] Cf. the Dutch term "etmaal."

repent. Will they do so? With respect to many of them, those who have been completely hardened (12:24, 31, 32), Jesus does not expect this at all, for these people are far more wicked than those of Nineveh who were called to repentance by Jonah: **41. Men of Nineveh shall stand up in the judgment with this generation, and shall condemn it, for they repented at the preaching of Jonah.** If even Ninevites [516] repented, should not Jews have done so?

Comparison between Those Whom Jesus Addresses,
and Ninevites

As to the scribes and Pharisees and their followers:	As to Ninevites:
a. It is the Son of God himself who addresses them again and again, and bids them to repent (Matt. 4:17; 7:28-30; 11:28-30; 23-37).	a. It was a minor prophet who preached to them.
b. This Christ is completely sinless (12:17-21; John 8:46), filled with wisdom and compassion (Matt. 11:27-30; 15:32; I Cor. 1:24).	b. This prophet was a sinful, foolish, and rebellious person (Jonah 1:3; 4:1-3, 9b).
c. He presents the message of grace and pardon, of salvation full and free (Matt. 9:2; 11:28-30; Luke 19:10; John 7:37).	c. His message was one of doom. Though a call to repentance was certainly implied, the emphasis was on "Yet forty days, and Nineveh shall be overthrown" (Jonah 3:4).
d. This message is being fortified by miracles in which prophecy is being fulfilled (Matt. 11:5; Luke 4:16-21; cf. Isa. 35:5, 6; 61:1-3; John 13:37).	d. There were no miracles or other authenticating signs to confirm Jonah's message.
e. It is being brought to a people who have enjoyed ever so many spiritual advantages (Deut. 4, 7, 8; 19:4; Ps. 147:19, 20; Isa. 5:1-4; Amos 3:2a; Rom. 3:1, 2; 9:4, 5).	e. Jonah's message was addressed to a people with none of the advantages that scribes, Pharisees, and their followers had enjoyed.

---

[516] Not "the" men of Nineveh, as if all of them had repented, but "men of Nineveh." So also in Luke 11:32. It is probable that the very omission of the article emphasizes the nature or character of these people as compared with Jews, as if to say: "Think of it, mere Ninevites repented, then should not y o u have done so?"

Yet Ninevites repented; most of the Israelites do not (John 1:11; 12:37). Less enlightened people obeyed less enlightened preaching, but more enlightened people refuse to obey the Light of the world. The question is asked, "But was this repentance of Ninevites genuine, that is, unto salvation?" The answer, often given, is that it was not, otherwise Nineveh would not have been destroyed. Objection: the destruction of this great city occurred about the year 612 B.C., that is, about a century and a half after Jonah's preaching. It is therefore unjust to charge the Ninevites of Jonah's day with the sins of a much later generation. [517]

Scripture nowhere claims that the repentance of *all* the Ninevites was genuine, but neither does it leave the impression that none of them were saved; rather the opposite. That there were indeed genuine conversions in Nineveh, perhaps many of them, seems to be implied both in the prophetic book and here in Matt. 12:41. The idea that the repentance of Ninevites was not genuine, that it was merely from vice to virtue, is open to three other objections: *a.* if in speaking about the need of repentance in Matt. 1:17 Jesus had in mind genuine sorrow for sin, why not here in 12:41?; *b.* in 11:20-24 (cf. Luke 10:13-15; 11:30) Nineveh is not included in the list of Old Testament impenitent cities; and *c.* if the repentance referred to in Matt. 12:41 is not genuine it is hard to explain the statement, "Men of Nineveh *shall stand up in the judgment* with this generation and shall condemn it." It should be noted that concerning these "men of Nineveh" it does not say, as it does in the case of those of Sodom and Gomorrah, Tyre and Sidon, that in the judgment it will be "more tolerable" for them (10:15; 11:22, 24), but that, like the queen of the south (12:42), they shall stand up in the judgment and shall condemn "this" generation, that is, the generation of the scribes and Pharisees and their followers. Since it is the teaching of Scripture (Dan. 7:22; Matt. 19:28; I Cor. 6:2; Rev. 15:3, 4; 20:4) that God's children are going to participate in the final judgment (for example, by praising God in Christ for his judgments?), this statement of Jesus about the role of certain Ninevites in that Great Assize is understandable if their repentance was genuine.

Again, in words similar to those in 12:6 (see on that passage) Pharisees and scribes are reminded of the greatness of their sin in rejecting and blaspheming the Christ: **but look, something greater than Jonah is here.** This superior greatness was explained above; see the comparison, points *a, b, c,* and *d,* p. 535.

In line with Ninevites, as an example that should put the Pharisees to shame is "the queen of the south," that is "the queen of Sheba." See I Kings

---

517 I agree fully, therefore, with the judgment of F. E. Gaebelein on this subject. See his book, *Four Minor Prophets*, Chicago, 1970, p. 109. For the opposite view see Lenski, *op. cit.*, pp. 433, 481.

10:1-13 (=II Chron. 9:1-9). **42. The queen of the south shall arise in the judgment with this generation and shall condemn it, for she came from the ends of the earth to listen to the wisdom of Solomon; and behold, something greater than Solomon is here.** From ancient times many interesting anecdotes have been circulated with reference to this queen. Whether or not there could be any inkling of truth in them let the investigator judge. The starting point of these stories is factual. This queen did indeed come a very great distance in order to listen to the wisdom of Solomon, to test him with riddles or difficult questions (I Kings 10:1).

According to one of the legends Solomon falls in love with the queen but she refuses his advances. She even tells the king that unless her wishes with respect to this matter are respected she will stay away from the farewell banquet that is to be given in her honor. She makes him promise with an oath. In turn, he makes her swear that she will not take away from the palace anything that has not been given to her. She agrees that if she breaks her oath the king can have his way with her. The banquet is held and the queen takes part, though, according to custom, she does not eat with the men. Her food, however, has been given special treatment. It has been highly seasoned, in order to make her very thirsty.

She retires to her own bedroom for the night, but burning thirst awakes her. She takes a drink from a golden pitcher standing nearby. It had however not been given to her! Suddenly she hears a voice, "You have broken your oath." After a little verbal skirmishing she admits that she has indeed committed a wrong. She, accordingly, releases Solomon from his oath. . . . Sometime later, back in her own country, she gives birth to a son. She names him Ebna El Hakim (son of the wise man).

The question has been asked, "Could this be the reason why in Ethiopia there is a tribe of ancient Jews of unknown origin?" The counter-question might also be asked, "Did the very presence of these Jews perhaps give rise to the legend?" [518]

Other questions have also been asked; for example, did her trip to Jerusalem have something to do with seeking protection for the exports of those goods of her country which on their way to Syria, Phoenicia, etc., must pass through the land of Israel? We are on safe ground, however, when we turn to the account found in the already indicated passages of the inspired records. The queen's curiosity had been aroused. It was a curiosity of the best kind. She had heard about "the fame of Solomon in connection with the name of the Lord." So she came to Jerusalem with an immense

---

[518] For this and other legends—for example, with respect to Solomon as the inventor of the airplane, and to Ebna El Hakim proving his remarkable sharpness by recognizing his father upon seeing him for the first time, even though Solomon, to test him, had assumed the garments of a beggar—see S. Bergsma, *Rainbow Empire*, Grand Rapids, 1932, pp. 194-198, 200, 244.

train of camels bearing spices, gold in great abundance, and precious stones. Solomon gave a satisfactory answer to all her questions. When she had observed his great wisdom, the house he had built, the seating of his servants, the way they were dressed, etc. "there was no more spirit in her. . . . And she said to the king, 'The report was true indeed, which I heard in my own country about your actions and wisdom, but I did not believe it until I came and my own eyes saw it all. Truly, the half has not been told me.' " The queen showered the king with gifts of gold, precious stones, and spices. In return, he also gave her costly presents.

Now one of the most remarkable sayings of this queen, a saying in harmony with the purpose for which she had made the trip (see I Kings 10:1), was her exclamation recorded near the close of the account, "Blessed be Jehovah your God who was pleased to set you on the throne of Israel. Because Jehovah loves Israel forever he has made you king, that you may execute justice and righteousness."

It is in line with all this that we are not surprised to read that here in Matt. 12:42 Jesus declares that in the final judgment this queen, too, shall arise and condemn his wicked contemporaries. In which respect did the queen put these Jews to shame? Note the following:

The scribes and Pharisees and their followers:	The Queen of the South
a. For them the truth is near at hand, within easy reach (Matt. 26:55).	a. She braved the hardships of a lengthy journey over difficult terrain. She probably came from what today is Yemen, in the southwestern part of the Arabian peninsula, on the Asian shore of the Red Sea, opposite Ethiopia (Africa). Her trip must have covered at least twelve hundred miles.
b. They have access to One wiser, better, and greater by far than Solomon.	b. She came to listen to Solomon's wisdom, "in connection with the name of the Lord," even though the truth concerning God was but very imperfectly reflected in Solomon.
c. They *give nothing*, but are plotting *to take away* Christ's very life.	c. She *gave* Solomon of her treasures, an enormous present (I Kings 10:10).
d. They have enjoyed many religious advantages.	d. She had merely heard reports.

e. They have been invited, urged
even, to accept Jesus, and the
truth in him (Matt. 11:28-30; cf.
22:1-5).

Yet *she* came, but *they* refuse.

e. It is not reported that she had
received any invitation at all.

What kind of "religion" do these Pharisees and their followers substitute for the one they have rejected? It is too emphatically a religion of negatives; such as, "Be careful *not* to associate with publicans and sinners, and *not* to break an oath sworn to the Lord. On the sabbath do *not* pick heads of grain; do *not* rub them out in y o u r hands and eat them. On that day do *not* heal anyone unless there is danger that he might die before tomorrow. Do *not* eat an egg laid on the sabbath unless y o u intend to kill the hen." Etc.

There had been a time when the more positive note, "Be converted," sounded by John the Baptist, had gained many followers (Matt. 3:5). A little later the same admonition proceeding from the lips of Jesus (4:17), together with his other very positive teaching, had been greeted with enthusiasm (John 3:26). It may have seemed for a while as if a demon had been driven out of a man, the man representing the Israel of that day. But under the influence of scribes and Pharisees, envious men, the picture was even now rapidly changing. At this very moment these wicked leaders are plotting Christ's destruction (Matt. 12:14). And at last the Jewish people as represented in front of the cross will cry out, "Crucify, crucify." (27:20-23). They will do so prompted by their leaders (John 19:6, 15, 16). The one demon will have been replaced by eight. Cf. 11:7-19.

Understood in this light the illustration which Jesus now uses becomes clear: **43-45. Now when the unclean spirit goes out of a man it wanders through waterless places, seeking rest, but does not find it. Then it says, I will go back to my house that I left. It goes and finds it unoccupied, swept clean, and put in order. Then it goes and brings back with it seven other spirits more wicked than itself, and they come and live there. And the final condition of that person becomes worse than the former. So it shall also be with this wicked generation.**

Many questions immediately arise; for example, "Why is this demon described as wandering through waterless or desert places?" "How is it that it does not find rest there?" "What exactly is meant by these seven other spirits worse than itself?" Etc. Three facts, however, must be borne in mind: *a.* Scripture tells us very little about the peculiarities and customs of demons, and to speculate too presumptuously about such matters would serve no useful purpose. *b.* The Lord is not giving us a discourse on demonology. He wants us to think not so much about these demons as about "this wicked generation" (verse 45, cf. verse 39), as symbolized by the man who was first possessed by one demon, then delivered, and finally repossessed, only this time not by one but by eight demons. *c.* If this illustration is in the nature of a parable, as it well may be, it would be wrong to press every detail as if it were to be interpreted separately and literally. In the case of the parable of the Rich Man and Lazarus (Luke 16:19-31a) rigid insistence on taking each item apart by itself and attaching a figurative meaning to it leads to absurdities. With these principles as a guide the lesson may be reproduced as follows:

Satan is eager to send his demons into human hearts, for them to assume control over these hearts, always in subjection to the prince of evil. For a demon to dwell outside the earth's atmosphere, and especially outside of the human heart where he can carry out his evil designs, is painful, for he is the arch-sadist.

As to the "waterless places" or deserts (see also Isa. 13:21; 34:14; Matt. 4:1; Rev. 18:2), only this: if we are accustomed to associate the good angels with places in which order, beauty, and fulness of life prevail, does it not seem natural to link evil angels with regions where disorder, desolation, and death dominate?

To be delivered from a demon is a blessing. That type of condition, as has been indicated, might well describe Israel during the days of the Baptist's active ministry and shortly thereafter. But in and by itself this does not suffice. To become scared of going to hell, scared, perhaps, even to the point of confessing one's sins and accepting baptism, is not enough. It would only leave the soul *empty:* "unoccupied, swept clean, put in order." Such a condition cannot meet the deepest needs of the human heart. Harmlessness is not the same as holiness. Desisting from wrong differs by a whole heaven from being a blessing. What Jesus demands is the entire devotion of the heart, so that it will render spontaneous thanksgiving to God and for his sake will be a blessing to the neighbor. Nothing less than that is required. A fig tree that produces nothing but leaves is cursed even though it yields no rotten fruit (Matt. 21:19). The man who buries his talent is rejected (25:18, 26-28). Those who during the present life have done nothing for the hungry, thirsty, etc. never enter the halls of glory (25:41-46). Cf. James 4:16. What Jesus wants is a full life of being a positive blessing out of gratitude for salvation by grace alone. He wants nothing less than this.

It is for this very reason that there was bound to be a collision between Jesus and the Pharisees. It was not the positive but the negative aspect of the law that was stressed by most Pharisees in obedience to the rules laid down by the scribes. Jesus was entirely different. So, kindness began to clash with coldness, broadmindedness with clannishness, outgoingness (love) with selfishness, emphasis on the deeper meaning of the law with insistence on the letter. These two—Christ and the bigot—cannot dwell together in unity. Moreover the Pharisees have their many followers among the people in general. But does not Jesus also have his following? Yes, indeed! And, in the eyes of the envious Pharisees, that makes matters even worse. The end is as has already been noted.

The reference to "this wicked generation" in verse 45, a reflection on a similar description of Christ's hostile contemporaries in verse 39, shows that the entire section (verses 38-45; in a sense even verses 22-45; see verse 24) is a unit, belongs together. Have the Pharisees charged Jesus with being linked with Satan (verse 24)? Jesus answers that they and their followers resemble a man who is repossessed by no less than eight demons! Yet throughout it all we cannot fail to detect a summons to conversion (see especially verses 28, 35a, 41, 42).

---

46 While he was still speaking to the crowds, lo and behold, his mother and his brothers were standing outside, seeking to speak to him. 47 And someone said to him, "Look, your mother and your brothers are standing outside, seeking to speak to you." 48 But he answered the one who was telling him (this) and said, "Who is my mother and who are my brothers?" 49 And stretching out his hand over his disciples he said, "Look, my mother and my brothers! 50 For whoever shall do the will of my Father in heaven, he is my brother and sister and mother."

12:46-50 The Mother and the Brothers of Jesus
Cf. Mark 3:31-35; Luke 8:19-21

46. While he was still speaking to the crowds, lo and behold, his mother and his brothers were standing outside, seeking to speak to him. Just why the mother and the brothers of Jesus had arrived at the scene and were trying to contact him has not been revealed. It is possible that Mark 3:21, 22 sheds some light on this. If so, it is also possible that disturbing remarks about Jesus—for example, that his opponents regarded him as being demon-possessed and that even his friends thought that he was out of his mind—induced them, out of natural affection to try to remove him from the public eye and to provide for him a haven of rest and refreshment. Even if this guess as to their motive should be correct, it does not warrant anyone to say, as some commentators do, that Mary and her other children shared the view of the "friends," and were actually of the opinion that the one dear to them was becoming mentally unbalanced.

As to the identity of these brothers of Jesus, this matter has been discussed in connection with 1:25. The names of the brothers are given in 13:55; cf. Mark 6:3.

The fact that Mary and the brothers of Jesus were standing "outside" would seem to indicate that the one whom they were seeking to contact was inside a house, at least during the events recorded in the latter part of chapter 12 (from verse 38 on?), if not even before that. Cf. also Mark 3:19b.

This would also seem to be supported by Matt. 13:1, which describes Jesus as going "out of the house." [519]

This explains the situation described in verse 47. **And someone said to him, Look, your mother and your brothers are standing outside, seeking to speak to you.** [520] Since because of the crowd (Luke 8:19) it was impossible for the new arrivals to get through to Jesus—the house was that full—someone standing near the door conveys the news to Jesus.

Here, then, was one of those interruptions on which comment was made previously. See on 9:20. Here too, as always, far from embarrassing Jesus in any way, it is seized by him as an opportunity to be turned to better spiritual account: **48. But he answered the one who was telling him (this) and said, Who is my mother and who are my brothers?** He wishes to indicate that neither Mary nor these brothers must be permitted to divert him from his appointed task. Cf. 10:37; Luke 2:49; John 2:4; 7:6.

Jesus asks a question. As verses 49 and 50 indicate, what he meant was "Who are those that belong to my spiritual family," to "the household of God" or "of the faith?" He is indicating that spiritual ties are more important than ties of blood. For other references to this spiritual family see John 1:13; Gal. 6:10; Eph. 2:19; and N.T.C. on Eph. 3:15.

Jesus answers his own question. Brief and beautiful, above all very comforting, is that answer: **49. And stretching out his hand over his disciples he said, Look, my mother and my brothers!** It was toward and over his disciples, the inner circle, that he lovingly stretched out his hand. It was to them that he gave this title of honor, "my mother and my brothers"; yes, and "my sisters" too (see verse 50 and cf. Mark 3:35), for in the all-important spiritual family sex makes no difference. Not only does this answer, accompanied by this meaningful gesture, prove what relationship mattered most to Jesus, the physical or the spiritual, it also proved the self-forgetful, marvelous character of his love, for even granting that the designation could have meaning only for those who were his *true* disciples, that is, for those who were doing the will of the Father in heaven (verse 50)—hence, could not have applied to Judas Iscariot!—who were these men? To be sure, *they had left all and followed him!* Yet, they were men "of little faith," weaklings in many respects, as has been shown in connection with 10:2-4. Yet he was not ashamed to call *them* "brothers" (Heb. 2:11; cf. Rom. 8:17, 29). What a

---

519 Another view is that of Lenski, who interprets "the house" of 13:1 to refer to the home of Christ's mother and brothers, and believes that the phrase "standing outside" of 12:46 means "outside the packed crowd." Though this seems to me to be the more unnatural of the two views, the difference is not very important.

520 Is this verse authentic? The textual evidence is inconclusive. Nevertheless what is stated in verse 47 is probably what actually took place, for it furnishes a very natural explanation of the manner in which the information regarding Jesus' mother and brothers was conveyed to him.

commentary Jesus furnishes for a section of Holy Writ that was going to be written by one of his future ambassadors, the apostle Paul (I Cor. 13:4-8a)! Concluded: **50. For whoever shall do the will of my Father in heaven, he is my brother and sister and mother.** The word "for" indicates a connection with the preceding somewhat as follows: "These disciples belong to my family because they are members of that larger group that consists of all those who do the will of my Father in heaven." For the latter phrase ("my Father in heaven") see on 7:21-23.

Note the inclusiveness of this "whoever." It means black and white, male and female, young and old, rich and poor, bond and free, educated and unlettered, drawn from the world of the Jews or from that of the Gentiles. Yet, note also the exclusiveness: those, and those *alone,* who do the Father's will!

It is very natural for Jesus to say "of *my* Father," for he stands in a very peculiar relationship to his Father, being the Father's Son by nature, and thus the Mediator between God and man.

The Father's "will" to which reference is made here is, of course, his revealed will, the will that can be "done" by man, through God's enabling grace. Briefly, that will may be summarized as follows: *a.* that man repents from his sin; *b.* accepts Jesus as his Savior and Lord; and *c.* in the Spirit and out of gratitude lives to the glory of God.

A few of the many passages in which this will of the Father is more fully described are: Matt. 3:2; 4:17; chaps. 5—7; 10:7, 32; 11:28-30; chap 13; chap. 18; 19:4, 5, 9, 14; 22:37-40; 24:42-44; 25:13; parallels in the other Synoptics; John 3:16; 6:29, 40, 47, 48; 13:12-20, 34; 14:1 ff.; 15:4, 12, 16, 17, 27; 16:1 ff. To these may be added such passages in the other New Testament books, as Acts 2:38, 39; 4:12; 16:31; Rom. 12—15; I Cor. 13; II Cor. 6:14-18; 8:7, 8; Gal. 5; Eph. 4—6; Phil. 2:12-18; Col. 3; I Tim. 2:4; Heb. 4:14-16; every chapter in James; I Peter 2:9, 21-25; II Peter 3:9.

Though it must be admitted, of course, that chapter-divisions are by no means infallibly inspired, is it not striking how often the chapters in this Gospel end in a touching climax? See chapters 1, 2, 3, 5, 6, 7, 9, 10, 11, 12, 14, 16, 18, 19, 22, 25, 26, 27, and 28.

Summary of Chapter 12

To all who would *come* to him, that is, to all who would accept him by faith, Jesus (11:28-30) had promised rest, including deliverance from the burden of superimposed legalism. So, in the first section of the present chapter (12:1-14) he shows how acceptance of him and of his doctrine will deliver people from the yoke of man-made sabbath regulations. When, on a certain sabbath his hungry disciples, walking through fields of grain, picked a few heads and ate them after rubbing out the kernels with their hands, the

Pharisees blamed him for his disciples' violation of sabbath rules. But he, by means of a five-point refutation—see pp. 512-515—demolishes their criticism, and declares himself to be Lord of the sabbath. On the sabbath he even heals a man with a shriveled hand. This act of restoration takes place in the synagogue, and in spite of the fact that no danger of loss of life was involved. "It is right to do good on the sabbath" is *Christ's* rule. If it was proper to rescue a *sheep* that on the sabbath had fallen into a pit, how much more should not kindness be shown to a *man* in need of help. Reaction on the part of the Pharisees: they took counsel against him, how they might destroy him.

Even though Jesus had performed a great miracle, and upon departing, many other miracles besides, it was not his desire to become known chiefly as a miracle worker. Acquiring earthly fame was not his goal. Rather, as the next section (verses 15-21) shows, he was "the Chosen Servant" of Isa. 42:1-4, unassuming, gentle, and retiring in nature.

In the next section (verses 22-37) another person in dire need is brought to Jesus. This sorely afflicted one was demon-possessed and could neither see nor speak. On him an astounding triple miracle was performed, so that the people wondered whether Jesus was the Son of David, the Messiah. This angered the Pharisees, who then said that he was casting out demons by the power of Beelzebul (Satan) the prince of the demons. Jesus shows that this charge is absurd and inconsistent, that it obscures the truth, if persisted in is unpardonable, and exposes the wickedness of those who make it. The slanderers are "offspring of vipers," and in the final day will have to answer for their wickedness.

As the next section (verses 38-45) shows, the Pharisees resented this scathing denunciation. In alliance with the scribes, they asked Jesus to show them a sign, as if the miracles which he had already performed did not really amount to much. The Lord tells them that the only sign they can expect is that of Jonah the prophet, namely, his [Christ's] resurrection from the dead on the third day, a sign by means of which he will completely triumph over them. He predicts that in the final judgment men of Nineveh shall condemn them, for these Ninevites repented at the less enlightened preaching of Jonah, whereas they, these scribes and Pharisees, are rejecting the Light of the world. For a somewhat similar reason the queen of the south shall then also condemn this generation.

Under the leadership of the scribes and Pharisees the Jews are going from bad to worse, like a man who, possessed by an evil spirit, is first delivered from this demon but later repossessed by it and by seven other spirits even more wicked than itself.

As the final paragraph (verses 46-50) shows, at this point there is interference by the mother and brothers of Jesus. Their intention seems to have been to remove him for a while from the public. When Jesus, in a house at the time, is informed that his mother and brothers are standing outside wishing to see him, he stretches out his hands over his disciples and says, "Look, my mother and my brothers." He is emphasizing the fact that spiritual ties are more important than physical.

Chapter 13

Theme: *The Work Which Thou Gavest Him to Do*

Seven Kingdom Parables

The Third Great Discourse

CHAPTER XIII

13 1 That day Jesus left the house and was sitting on the seashore. 2 The crowds that gathered about him were so large that he stepped into a boat and sat there, while all the people were standing on the shore. 3 Then by means of parables he told them many things. He said:

"Once upon a time the sower went out to sow. 4 While sowing, some seeds fell along the path. The birds came and gobbled them up. 5 Some fell on rocky ground, where they had little soil. Because they did not have depth of soil they sprang up immediately. 6 But when the sun came up they were scorched, and since they had no root they withered away. 7 Some fell among the thorns. The thorns shot up and choked them. 8 But some seeds fell into good soil. They yielded a crop; some a hundredfold, some sixty, and some thirty. 9 He who has ears let him hear."

10 The disciples approached him and asked, "Why do you speak to them in parables?" 11 He answered, "To y o u it has been given to know the mysteries of the kingdom of heaven but to them it has not been given. 12 For whoever has, to him shall be given, and he shall have abundantly; but whoever does not have, from him shall be taken away even what he has. 13 It is for this reason that I speak to them in parables, because seeing they do not see, and hearing they do not hear and understand. 14 And in their case that prophecy of Isaiah is being fulfilled which says:

'Y o u shall hear and hear, but never understand,
And y o u shall see and see, but never perceive.
15 For the heart of this people has become dull,
And their ears (have become) hard of hearing,
And their eyes they have closed,
Lest they should perceive with their eyes,
And hear with their ears,
And understand with their heart, and turn again,
And I should heal them.'

16 But blessed are y o u r eyes, because they see, and y o u r ears, because they hear. 17 For I solemnly declare to y o u, many prophets and righteous persons longed to see what y o u are seeing, yet did not see it, and to hear what y o u are hearing, yet did not hear it.

18 "Listen, then, to the parable of The Sower. 19 When anyone hears the message of the kingdom but does not grasp it, the evil one comes and snatches away what was sown in his heart. He is the one that was sown along the path. 20 And the one that was sown on rocky ground is he who upon hearing the message immediately accepts it with joy. 21 However, he has no root in himself and lasts but a short while. When affliction or persecution arises on account of the message he immediately falls away. 22 And the one that was sown among the thorns is he who is hearing the message, and then the cares of this present world and the deceitful glamor of riches choke that

message, and it becomes unfruitful. 23 And the one that was sown on the good soil is he who both hears and grasps the message. He bears fruit and yields, in one case a hundredfold, in another sixty, in another thirty.''

24 He presented another parable to them, saying, ''The kingdom of heaven is like a man who sowed good seed in his field. 25 But while men were sleeping his enemy came and sowed tares among the wheat and went away. 26 So when the early grain sprouted and began to fill out, the tares were seen also. 27 Then the owner's servants approached him and said, 'Sir, didn't you sow good seed in your field? Then where did the tares come from?' 28 He said to them, 'An enemy has done this.' The servants said to him, 'Then do you want us to go and gather them?' 29 He said, 'No, lest while y o u are gathering the tares, y o u uproot the wheat along with them. 30 Let both grow together until the harvest. Then at harvest time I will say to the reapers, ''First gather the tares, and tie them up in bundles to burn them up, but gather the wheat into my barn.'' ' ''

31 He presented another parable to them, saying, ''The kingdom of heaven is like a mustard seed which a man took and sowed in his field. 32 It is the smallest of all seeds, yet when it is full-grown it is the biggest of the garden herbs, and becomes a tree, so that the birds of the air come and lodge in its branches.''

33 He told them another parable: ''The kingdom of heaven is like yeast which a woman took and put into three measures of wheat flour, until the whole batch had risen.''

34 All these things Jesus said to the crowds in parables, and without using a parable he was not saying anything to them, 35 that what was spoken through the prophet might be fulfilled:

''I will open my mouth in parables,
I will utter mysteries from ancient times.''

36 He then dismissed the crowds and went into the house. His disciples approached him, saying, ''Explain to us the parable of The Tares of the field.'' 37 He answered and said: ''The one who sows the good seed is the Son of man. 38 The field is the world; the good seed, these are the sons of the kingdom; the tares are the sons of the evil one; 39 the enemy who sowed them is the devil; the harvest is the close of the age; and the reapers are the angels. 40 As the tares, then, are gathered and burned up, so it is going to be at the close of the age. 41 The Son of man shall send his angels, and they shall gather out of his kingdom everything that is offensive and those that perpetrate lawlessness, 42 and shall throw them into the fiery furnace. There shall be weeping and grinding of teeth. 43 Then, in the kingdom of their Father, the righteous shall shine as the sun. He who has ears, let him hear.

44 ''The kingdom of heaven is like a treasure hidden in the field, which a man found and covered up. Then, in his joy over it, he goes and sells all he has and buys that field.

45 ''Again, the kingdom of heaven is like a merchant in search of fine pearls. 46 Having found one pearl of great value, he went and sold all he had, and bought it.

47 ''Again, the kingdom of heaven is like a dragnet that was cast into the sea and gathered up fish of every variety. 48 When it was full the men dragged it ashore, sat down, picked out the good ones for the containers, but threw away the bad. 49 So it shall be at the close of the age. The angels shall come and separate the wicked from the righteous, 50 and shall throw them into the fiery furnace. There shall be weeping and grinding of teeth.

51 ''Have y o u understood all this?'' They answered, ''Yes.'' He said to

them, 52 "Therefore every scribe who has been trained for the kingdom of heaven resembles a head of a household who brings out of his storehouse things new and old."

53 Now when Jesus had finished (telling) these parables he left that place. 54 He came to his hometown and was teaching the people in their synagogue, so that they were astonished. "Where did he get this wisdom?," they asked, "and (the power to do) these miracles? 55 Isn't he the son of the carpenter? Isn't his mother's name Mary, and aren't James, Joseph, Simon, and Judas his brothers? 56 And aren't all his sisters here with us? Where, then, did he get all this?" 57 And they took offense at him. But Jesus said to them, "A prophet is not without honor except in his hometown and in his own family." 58 And because of their unbelief he did not do many miracles there.

13:1-58 *Seven Kingdom Parables*

For 13:1-23 cf. Mark 4:1-20; Luke 8:4-15.

For 13:31-33 cf. Mark 4:30-32; Luke 13:18-21.

For 13:34, 35 cf. Mark 4:33, 34.

For 13:53-58 cf. Mark 6:1-6; Luke 4:16-31.

Introduction

The number and distribution of the parables have already been discussed, and their character has been described. See pp. 21-25. Their purpose was *a.* to reveal, and *b.* to conceal. Among Christ's listeners there were those who by grace had been led to trust in Christ to such an extent that they not only believed what they could readily understand but even that which as yet was mysterious. There were also those who by constant refusal to accept him had hardened their hearts. The life of Jesus, including his words and works, had made it very clear that he was indeed the One whom the prophets had predicted, and that when he taught he was speaking the truth. But the opponents willfully rejected the obvious. So Jesus now, more than ever before, [521] begins to speak in parables, in order *a. to further reveal the truth to those who accepted the mysterious,* and *b. to conceal it from those who rejected the obvious,* both of these purposes being clearly indicated in 13:10-17.

Here in Matt. 13 the Lord teaches precious truths concerning *the kingdom.* For the not always identical meaning of this term see above, pp. 249, 250. In other parables he dwells more fully on the character of *the King himself,* the manner in which he deals with his subjects; as is clear from The Laborers in the Vineyard (Matt. 20:1-16), The Marriage of the King's Son (22:1-14), and The Talents (25;14-30). In still others he describes the character that should be disclosed by *the King's subjects;* thus, The Good Samaritan (Luke 10:29-37) and The Persevering Widow (Luke 18:1-8). These three themes—the kingdom, the King, and the King's subjects—often overlap. So, for example, it can be argued that all three themes are treated in

---

[521] "More than ever before": Matt. 7:24-27 already contains a parable; see also 12:43-45. But extensive use of parables begins here in chap. 13.

the parable of The Tares (Matt. 13:24-30, 36-43): here *the kingdom's* present mixe i character and future consummation in purity and splendor is set forth, as is also *the King's* order to his angels, and *the King's subjects'* duty to be patient with a view to the manner in which he will dispose of all things.

Summary

The Kingdom's

a. Message, how received: The Sower (verses 3-9), explanation (verses 18-23).

b. Present mixed character and future consummation in purity and splendor: The Tares (verses 24-30), explanation (verses 36-43); The Dragnet (verses 47-50).

c. Growth and Development, both outward: The Mustard Seed (verses 31, 32), and inward: The Leaven or Yeast (verse 33).

d. Preciousness: The Hidden Treasure (verse 44); The Pearl of Great Price (verses 45, 46).

Altogether, this material covers thirty-eight verses, that is, about two-thirds of the entire chapter. The remaining twenty verses are devoted to a couple lines of introduction (verses 1 and 2; strictly speaking 1-3a); several verses setting forth the purpose and use of parables (verses 10-17, 34, 35); a description of the true scribe (verses 51, 52); and a brief concluding paragraph (verses 53-58) describing Christ's rejection at Nazareth, showing the bitter and unreasonable opposition to him that had developed. This was one of the two main reasons (reason *b.* mentioned above, namely, to conceal) which had led him to the use of parables. Thus considered, we notice that the entire chapter is a unit.

From 13:1, 2, 36 it is clear that Jesus spoke the first four parables to the multitudes from a boat, a little offshore (Mark 4:1), and that he afterward dismissed the crowds, went ashore and into a home. Here he explained to the disciples the parable of The Sower and the one of The Tares (full title: The Tares among the Wheat), and added three more parables.

Opening Words and The Parable of The Sower

13:1. That day Jesus left the house and was sitting on the seashore. It is clear that the temporary withdrawal (12:15) has ended. By going to the seashore Jesus is able to reach more people than by staying in the house. **2. The crowds that gathered about him were so large that he stepped into a boat and sat there, while all the people were standing on the shore.** On the part of many interest in Jesus had not waned. With them eagerness to hear him had not abated. Was not the prophet from Nazareth most interesting?

Was he not going to establish himself, if he had not even already done so, to be the best teller of fascinating stories? So, from all around, from "every city" (Luke 8:4), the people kept coming.

The multitudes became so vast that Jesus, to escape the crush and the probability of being hampered in his efforts to address the people, stepped into one of several boats that had been beached here. By doing this he was able to address a very large number of people, to speak somewhat at length, and to have speaker and audience face each other. In this region and at this time it was usual for the speaker to sit, for the audience to stand. Continued: **3. Then by means of parables he told them many things.** What these many things were has already been indicated; see above, the summary. It is not necessary to believe that all the parables spoken to the multitudes that day are here recorded (cf. 13:34; John 21:25).

Here, then, follows the first of this series of seven recorded kingdom parables. **He said: Once upon a time the sower went out to sow;** literally, "Behold" or "Lo," or "Look," etc. For a discussion of this little Greek word (and its Hebrew equivalent) see on 1:20, footnote 133. In the present case the focus of attention is not the fact as such that the sower went out to sow, which, after all, was a constantly recurring event familiar to everybody, especially to every farmer, but the entire story. Since among us the introduction "Once upon a time" has about the same interest arousing effect as in this connection the little Greek word (or its Aramaic equivalent) must have had, it has been suggested that this proposed English rendering is legitimate. [522] Continued: **4. While sowing, some seeds fell along the path.** It was customary for wheat or barley to be sown by hand. But it makes all the difference in the world how that seed is received. As this man is sowing, it was unavoidable that a portion of the seed fell along the footpath on which he was walking through the field. Since the place where it fell had not been reached by the plow, and/or many feet had walked here, the soil was too hard for anything to fall "into" it. So the separate seeds remained on the surface, with the result: **the birds came and gobbled them up.** The feathered creatures acted very quickly and greedily. The seeds were snatched *up;* then *down* they went into the alimentary tract; hence literally, "they (the birds) ate them down." **5. Some fell on rocky ground, where they had little soil. Because they did not have depth of soil they sprang up immediately.** It is typical of Palestine—now "Israel" and its surroundings—that a considerable portion of its tillable soil is found on top of layers of rock. In such a situation the seeds, in the process of sprouting, have only one way to go, namely, up. So, instead of first becoming firmly rooted, the seeds described in this part of the parable "sprang up immediately." **6. But when the sun came up they were scorched, and since they had no root they withered**

---

[522] See J. A. Alexander, *The Gospel according to Matthew*, New York, 1867, p. 353.

away. Because these seeds lacked depth of earth, they could not take root; hence, when the sun was risen they were scorched, thus Matthew and Mark. Luke 8:6 supplies the intermediate cause of withering: (for lack of roots) these seeds "had no moisture." No wonder that they were scorched to death. **7. Some fell among the thorns. The thorns shot up and choked them.** This soil was infested with the roots of thorns. Since generally nothing grows faster than that which is not wanted, and each patch of ground had adequate room for only a definitely restricted amount of healthy plant life, it is not surprising that the faster growing weeds were soon choking the very life out of the noble grain. **8. But some seeds fell into good soil. They yielded a crop, some a hundredfold, some sixty, and some thirty.** This soil was fertile. It was neither hard, nor rocky, nor "preoccupied," but good in every way, serving its purpose excellently. The degree of yield was not uniform, however. In some cases one grain or seed produced a hundred grains (cf. Gen. 26:12); in others sixty; in still others thirty.—The admonition of 11:15 (see on that passage) is now repeated, **9. He who has ears let him hear.** Implication: There is more than appears on the surface. The lesson taught here is very important. Let those who have the spiritual capacity to do so ponder this parable, and let them apply its lesson to their lives.

The Purpose of the Parables

10. The disciples approached him and asked, Why do you speak to them in parables? The admonition, "He who has ears let him hear" (verse 9) did not remain unheeded. When four of the seven parables had been spoken, and Jesus was not only back on the shore but "in the house" (13:36), the inner circle of disciples, together with some other loyal followers (Mark 4:10), approached him with the question, "Why do you speak to them in parables?" Why did Matthew depart from the chronological order to insert this question and its answer here at verse 10? Probable answer: *a.* because verses 18-23, in which the very parable (The Sower) is explained which the evangelist has just now recorded is so closely connected with Christ's answer that it might even be considered part of that answer; and *b.* because the thrust of Christ's immediate answer (verses 11-17), to the effect (see II Cor. 2:16) that the gospel is either "a savor of death unto death" (verses 13-15) or "a savor of life unto life" (verses 16,17), harmonizes beautifully with the central lesson taught in that parable (verses 4-7 contrasted with verse 8).

The disciples' question must not be interpreted to imply that the story-form of teaching was a novelty, something introduced by Jesus here and now, and never used before his day. This would contradict the evidence supplied by Judg. 9:7-15; II Sam. 12:1-14; 14:4-17. For this or closely related methods of instruction see also Ezek. 17:1-10; 19:10-14; 23:1-29; 37:1-14. Besides, was not even Matt. 7:24-27 a parable, and had not Jesus at least approached the parabolic form in 11:16, 17; 12:43-45? But never before had he addressed the multitudes so extensively and deliberately in parables as he is doing now. Why?

11. He answered, **To y o u it has been given to know the mysteries of the kingdom of heaven but to them it has not been given.** A "mystery" is something that would have remained unknown had it not been revealed. One of these mysteries now being disclosed is the fact that with the entrance of Jesus upon the scene of history the kingdom of heaven's reign on earth had made its appearance. Another mystery, now being revealed, was the nature of the visible realization of this reign, that is, of this "kingdom," in a sense sometimes (as probably in verses 24-30, 47-50) nearly equivalent to "church," its present mixed character versus its future consummation in beauty and purity. A mere look at the Summary of the parables (above, p. 550) will immediately indicate what were some of the other mysteries. All of these matters are mysteries, for they cannot be perceived by unaided human reasoning. "Unless a man is born anew (or "from above") he cannot see the kingdom of God" (John 3:3).

To the disciples the privilege of, to a certain extent, discerning these mysteries had been *given.* Note "given." It was a matter of pure grace. To be sure there is also a human factor that enters in, as will become clear in the following verses, but at bottom understanding these mysteries is always a matter of grace (I Cor. 4:7; Eph. 2:8). To some this grace is given, to others not. See also on 25:15, and cf. Dan 4:35; Rom. 9:16, 18, 20, 21.

But without in any way bypassing the basic truth concerning the necessity of sovereign grace not only for the impartation of salvation to man but even for his intellectual and spiritual grasp of the truth concerning salvation, it is only fair to add that in the ensuing verses (see especially verses 13 and 15) it is man's responsibility and the use he makes of it that is emphasized. Note the beginning of this line of thought even in verse 12. **For whoever has, to him shall be given, and he shall have abundantly; but whoever does not have, from him shall be taken away even what he has.** In matters spiritual, standing still is impossible. A person either gains or loses; he either advances or declines. Whoever has, to him shall be given. The disciples (exception Judas Iscariot) had "accepted Jesus." With reference to them he was later on going to say to the Father, "They have kept thy word" (John 17:6) and "They are not of the world" (17:16). To be sure, this faith was accompanied by many a weakness, error, and flaw. But the beginning had been made. Therefore, according to heaven's rule, further progress was assured, an advance in knowledge, love, holiness, joy, etc., in all the blessings of the kingdom of heaven, for salvation is an ever deepening stream (Ezek. 47:1-5). Every blessing is a guarantee of further blessings to come (John 1:16): "he shall have abundantly."

On the other hand, whoever does not have, from him shall be taken away even that semblance of knowledge, that superficial acquaintance with ·mat-

553

ters spiritual, which he once had. Is there not an analogy of this in the realm of knowledge on a level below the strictly spiritual? Is it not true that the person who has learned enough music to play a few simple melodies, but not really enough to be able to say, "I have mastered this or that instrument," and then stops practicing altogether, will soon discover that the little skill which he had at one time has vanished? The man who refuses to make proper use of his one talent loses even that (Matt. 25:24-30).

Now if even *neglect* of things valuable is bad, willful rejection is even worse: **13. It is for this reason that I speak to them in parables, because seeing they do not see, and hearing they do not hear and understand.** The growing hostility of the Pharisees, the scribes, and their followers, against Jesus has already been indicated (9:11, 34; 12:2, 14, 24; cf. 11:20-24). This human obduration cannot be left unpunished. When Pharaoh hardens his heart (Exod. 7:22; 8:15, 19, 32; 9:7), Jehovah hardens Pharaoh's heart (9:12, predicted already in 7:3). "He who, having been often reproved, hardens his neck, shall suddenly be destroyed, and that without remedy" (Prov. 29:1).[523] "Seeing they do not see," that is, "Though they outwardly observe the miracles. . ., they do not grasp what, in the light of prophecy, these mighty works tell about me." Similarly, "hearing they do not hear," that is, "Though the sound of my voice penetrates their eardrums, and they catch enough of my meaning to become antagonized, they do not really understand and certainly do not heed, do not take to heart, my instructions, warnings, and invitations." My parables, says Jesus as it were, will therefore lead to further obfuscation. That is the punishment which these people deserve and receive. They have brought it upon themselves!

Such human hardening followed by divine hardening was nothing new. The Pharisees, scribes, and their followers were simply repeating the story of ancient Israel. Then too Jehovah had tenderly and earnestly admonished the people to repent of their evil ways. Then also, in many cases, this striving of the Spirit had been given the cold shoulder. Punishment always followed. See Isa. 5:1-7; Jer. 7:12-15, 25-34; 13:8-14; 29:19, 20; 35:16, 17.

The exile of ancient Israel, a punishment for its hardness of heart, had been a type of that which was now happening to Christ's bitter opponents: **14, 15. And in their case that prophecy of Isaiah is being fulfilled which says:**

> Y o u shall hear and hear, but never understand,
> And y o u shall see and see, but never perceive.
> For the heart of this people has become dull,
> And their ears (have become) hard of hearing,

---

[523] Hence, the fact that Matthew says ὅτι (*because*, in "because seeing they do not see," etc.), while Mark 4:12 and Luke 8:10 have ἵνα (*that* or *in order that*) presents no real problem. It was *because* the willful rejectors refused to see and to hear, that Jesus spoke to them in parables *in order that* they might not see and hear so as to understand.

And their eyes they have closed,
Lest they should perceive with their eyes,
And hear with their ears,
And understand with their heart, and turn again,
And I should heal them.

The quotation is from the vision in which Isaiah received the call to the prophetic office. This vision, in which the prophet saw the glory of Jehovah as reflected in the coming Christ (John 12:41), is found in the sixth chapter of Isaiah, the words here quoted being found in 6:9, 10. Cf. John 12:40 for quotation in part; Acts 28:26, 27 in full. However, the quotation, as spoken by the Lord and recorded by Matthew, does not follow the Hebrew [524] but

---

524   The Hebrew may be rendered as follows:
        "Hear and hear, but do not understand,
        And see and see, but do not perceive
        [Or: "Hear indeed, but understand not,
        And see indeed, but perceive not"],
        Make the heart of this people fat,
        And their ears heavy,
        And shut their eyes,
        Lest they see with their eyes,
        And hear with their ears,
        And understand with their heart,
        And turn again, and be healed."

Essentially there is no difference between the Hebrew original and the LXX translation here used by the Lord. The translation brings the prophecy in line with history. Hence the imperative mood, as addressed directly to Isaiah, but implying nevertheless that what was commanded was also going to happen, is here (in Matthew) replaced by the future indicative ("y o u shall hear," "y o u shall see") and by the aor. subj., with future force (strengthened in both lines by οὐ μή, "but never understand," "but never perceive"). The force of the Hebrew idiom for "hear and hear" is reproduced in Greek by a noun in the dat. sing. plus the verb (hence, ἀκοῇ ἀκούσετε); then for "see and see," by a pres. act. participle plus the verb (hence, βλέποντες βλέψετε).

Similarly, in the next three lines—the anesthetizing of the heart, numbing of the ears, and closing of the eyes—aorist indicatives have been substituted for the Hebrew imperatives, because what Isaiah had by implication predicted had become terrible reality. The verb used here in Matt. 13:15 in connection with the heart literally means (in the active) to make thick or heavy. Here the aor. pass. indic. is used (ἐπαχύνθη). The cognate adjective παχύς occurs in *pachyderm*, thick-skinned animal; for example, the elephant and the rhinoceros. With respect to the ears the line literally reads, "And with their ears they have heard heavily," the adverb βαρέως, cf. adjective βαρύς, reminding one of the *baro*meter, an instrument indicating how heavy is the atmosphere at any certain time and place; hence, an atmospheric-pressure meter. The verb used in connection with the eyes is ἐκάμμυσαν from καμμύω (=κατά and μύω, shut down, close).

It appears clearly both from Isaiah, especially when 6:9, 10 is read, as it should be, in the context of the immediately preceding chapter, and from Matt. 13:13 ("because seeing they do not see . . ."), 13:15 ("for the heart of this people has become dull . . ."), that divine hardening follows human hardening. What we have here in Matt. 13:14, 15 is a further commentary on 12:31, 32, which tells us how the blasphemy against the Spirit is punished. It is because by their own choice the heart of the people has become dull or fat, that it is made dull or fat. It is because by their own unwillingness to listen their ears have become hard of hearing, that they are made even more so. And it is because they

the Septuagint (Greek) translation, with no essential difference (as explained in footnote 524).

The manner in which the quoted words are introduced is unique. Here not the simple "might be fulfilled," (as in 12:17, "in order that what was spoken through Isaiah the prophet might be fulfilled," and cf. 1:22; 2:15, 23; 4:14; 8:17; 13:35; 21:4) but "is being fulfilled" or "is being filled up," [525] as if to stress the fact that Israel's doom, partly realized at the time of the exile, is now being made full in the lives of all those who reject the Lord. That this is so is not God's fault. It is in fact made very clear that for all who in true repentance turn to the Lord there is forgiveness and healing. Note the words, "and turn again and I should heal them." But the point is this: envious Pharisees and scribes, together with their followers, have anesthetized their heart, muffled their ears, and closed their eyes to the works and words of the Lord. Now *because* they have done this (verse 15; cf. verse 13), the result will be as stated in verse 14, "Y o u shall hear and hear, but never understand, and y o u shall see and see but never perceive." As already explained in connection with verse 13, there is a "hearing" which hardly even deserves the name, and a seeing that is a mere caricature of the genuine article.

If the objection should be raised that Jesus, in his reference to Isaiah's prophecy, speaks as if the wicked people's *own purpose*, negatively expressed, is, "lest they should perceive with their eyes, and hear with their ears . . .," whereas, on the other hand, in Isaiah's prophecy it is *God himself* who has decided that such perception, hearing, understanding, turning again, and being saved, shall be impossible for these hardened sinners, the answer is that the two coincide perfectly. It is because the people have decided not to really see, hear, etc., as if this were a dreadful thing to do, that God has decided to punish them by allowing them to have their way! Causing them to be addressed by means of parables is a means to this end.

With respect to Christ's true disciples the very opposite holds: **16. But blessed are y o u r eyes, because they see, and y o u r ears, because they hear.** In close conjunction with 11a and 12a those who are receptive to Christ's message are pronounced *blessed,* the word being used in the same sense as in the beatitudes; see above, pp. 264, 265. The word is not limited in meaning to "how they feel," whether in high spirits or not. In the present connection it means that both in their seeing and in their hearing God's favor is resting upon them. They see and they hear with the organs of faith, hence the great contrast between them and Christ's critics. Not that the disciples are by

---

have deliberately closed their eyes, that these eyes are shut even more tightly. There is therefore no real difference between the Hebrew text, when read in its context, and the version of it uttered by the lips of the Lord and recorded by Matthew. For the rest, see the text.

525 In the other passages here listed (1:22, etc.) the verb is πληρωθῇ; here in 13:14 it is ἀναπληροῦνται, a compound verb that occurs nowhere else in the Gospels.

nature any better than the others. Whatever they have they owe to sovereign grace.

So to them the parables are a great blessing. Being Christ's followers these disciples attach top value to these stories. They meditate upon them. The very fact that they present to the mind vivid images, moving pictures, as it were, makes it easier to store them away in the memory. Also, since the disciples accompany the Master from place to place, they have the golden opportunity to ask him for an explanation of whatever it may be that they do not understand. They also made use of this opportunity. Thus, they asked him to explain to them the parable of The Sower (Luke 8:9) and the one of The Tares (Matt. 13:36). Neither did Jesus always wait until they asked: privately he explained all things to them (13:51, cf. Mark 4:34).

What a wealth of material was that which these men saw, heard, and believed! Says Jesus, 17. **For I solemnly declare to y o u, many prophets and righteous persons longed to see what y o u are seeing, yet did not see it, and to hear what y o u are hearing, yet did not hear it.** See also on 11:11b. For "I solemnly declare" see on 5:18. As to these Old Testament prophets— for example, Samuel, Isaiah—and (other) righteous persons—Noah, Abraham, etc.—they looked forward with longing to the coming Redeemer (Heb. 11:13, 39, 40; I Peter 1:10, 11). They yearned, searched, but got no farther than, "O that thou wouldest rend the heavens, that thou wouldest come down!" (Isa. 64:1).

To be sure, even to the saints of the old dispensation glimpses of the coming glory were given at times, even while these men were still living on earth. Thus, for example, in the birth of Isaac, Abraham by faith saw a guarantee of the fulfilment of the Messianic promise (see N.T.C. on John 8:56), and what a great blessing this was! Similarly, with the eye of faith, a faith greatly strengthened by revelation, Isaiah *in a vision* saw Messiah's glory and spoke of him (John 12:41). Such were indeed inestimable privileges. "Many" longingly looked forward. But none of them, while still on earth, *saw* the incarnate Christ. None witnessed his miracles. None *heard* his words. They all "died in faith, not having received the fulfilment of the promises" (Heb. 11:13; cf. 39). That "better thing" (cf. Heb. 11:40), the fulness of Messianic blessing, had been reserved for believers of the new day.

Explanation of the Parable of The Sower

In this paragraph Jesus explains to his loyal followers the parable found in verses 2b-9: **18. Listen, then, to the parable of The Sower.** As has previously been indicated, the parable was first told, and at a later time explained in response to the disciples' request. If the objection be raised that even on the surface, without any explanation whatever, the parable is quite clear, its meaning obvious, so that any further elucidation is really superfluous, the answer is: *a* that the disciples did not then have the light which we have

557

now; *b.* that sowing and at a later time fruit-bearing, both of which are mentioned in this parable, presuppose a gradual and time-consuming process of development with reference to the kingdom, a process which the disciples, in their oft revealed impatience, may not have expected (especially in view of 3:11, 12); *c.* that by means of his words and works of majesty Jesus had revealed himself to these men as a mighty King, while here in this parable he seems to identify himself with a humble "sower," but can the same person be both?; and *d.* that in this story he seems to assign a considerable degree of responsibility, for success in obtaining spiritual results, to "the soil" on which the seed falls; can he really mean that? To all this it may well be added that even now, among interpreters who have both the parable and Christ's own infallible explanation, complete unanimity as to interpretation is lacking. Nevertheless, this is not the fault of him who had told it, and who now proceeded to explain it as follows: **19. When anyone hears the message of the kingdom but does not grasp it, the evil one comes and snatches away what was sown in his heart.** Although it is nowhere stated in the explanation of *this* parable, yet in that of The Tares Jesus definitely affirms that "he who sows the good seed is the Son of man" (verse 37). And as to the seed, Christ's own explanation is found in Luke 8:11, "The seed is the word [or: message] of God." Is this not clearly implied also in the passage now under study here in Matthew, namely, in the clause, "When anyone hears the message of the kingdom"? See also 13:11, 17b. Of these two things we can be certain, therefore: *a.* the sower is the Son of man, and, by a legitimate extension of the figure (see Matt. 10:40; Mark 4:14), is anyone—whether minister, missionary, evangelist, any believer whoever he may be—who faithfully proclaims the Son of man's message; and *b.* the seed is that message. The comparison of a "word" or "message" of God, or of any word or message whatever, with a seed that is sown or planted has become an idiom in the literature of many people. In Scripture, too, it is by no means confined to this parable. See, for example, John 4:36, 37; I Cor. 3:6; 9:11. To depart from this basic position is to go in a wrong direction in the explanation of this parable.

To these two tenets a third can now be added: *c.* The "ground" or "soil" upon which the seed falls is clearly man's heart. This is definitely implied here in 19a, "what was sown in his heart." In each of the four instances recorded in the parable that "ground" or "soil," that is, that "heart," is different. One might speak of *the unresponsive heart* (verse 19), *the impulsive heart* (verses 20, 21), *the preoccupied* heart (verse 22), and *the good, responsive, or well-prepared heart* (verse 23). Correct is therefore the following: "What, then, is the lesson? The Savior has given us the answer in his own intepretation of the story. The seed is the word of God, or the word of the kingdom; and the soil is human hearts: so that, reduced to a general law, the teaching of the parable is, that the result of the hearing of the gospel always and everywhere depends on the condition of heart of those to whom it is addressed. The character of the hearer determines the effect of the word upon him." [526]

Verse 19a speaks about the unresponsive, insensible, callous heart, the heart of the person who by persistent refusal to walk in the light has become accustomed hardly even to listen to the message as it is being proclaimed. Under the influence of the devil whatever it is that this man hears he immediately thrusts away from himself as if for him at least it contained nothing of importance. Perhaps he does not like the speaker, and/or hates to be reminded of a particular weakness in himself. In any event he does not bother to reflect or meditate upon the meaning of the message. Therefore he does not grasp it. The evil one, who figures so often in the teaching of Jesus (see footnote 297, p. 308), snatches away what was sown in this man's heart.

When Jesus was speaking can he have had in mind, among others, the scribes and Pharisees, who were filled with ill-will toward him, and were always on the lookout to see whether they could catch him in his words so as to prepare a charge against him? But there must have been other persons also who refused to ponder the words of the Master. Some, perhaps, found it inconvenient to take the message to heart; perhaps next time, but not just now (Acts 24:25). Let anyone add his own up-to-date illustrations.

The next line uttered by our Lord has brought about a startling diversity of opinion among translators and commentators. What Jesus said was: **He is the one that was sown along the path.** Other legitimate ways of rendering the original would be, "This is he, etc." (A.V., A.R.V.) or "This is the man, etc." (T.C.N.T.). There are, however, some questionable ways of treating this statement:

a. Perhaps because it is hard to conceive of *a person* being sown, translators have made various attempts to solve this difficulty. One attempt is: "This [or: that] is what is sown. . . ." (Beck, Williams, R.S.V.). However, this ignores the original's reference to a person. [527]

b. Probably in order to avoid this error another comes up with, "This is the one on whom seed was sown" (N.A.S.). With due respect for the general excellence of the work referred to, we may well ask whether in this particular instance the translator has been completely successful. Seed sown on a man, what does that mean? Besides, does the text really say that seed was sown on a man?

c. The third attempt at a solution, while deserving credit for being faithful to the original, errs in *taking literally* the words, "He is the one that was sown along the path." We are told that the seed is indeed "men who

---

[526] W. M. Taylor, *The Parables of Our Savior, Expounded and Illustrated*, New York, 1886, p. 22.

[527] My point is that οὗτος should not be ignored.

have heard the word." [528] But this not only produces a very awkward picture, but besides, as we have seen, fails to do justice to Christ's clear statement that the seed is the word or message.

d. What may well be regarded as the only reasonable procedure is that which sees in these words of Jesus (verse 19b) an illustration of "abbreviated expression." [529] The thought completely expressed would have been somewhat as follows (with the actual words of Jesus in italics): *"He is the one that* in his reaction to the message resembles the reaction of the ground to the seed that *was sown along the path."* [530] In both cases the reaction is the same: the piece of ground upon which this seed falls does nothing about it. It does not welcome or absorb it. So also this person's heart does nothing with the message. When the question is asked, "Why did not Jesus express this thought more fully, instead of using this compressed manner of speaking?," the answer is that for Christ's true followers to whom he gave his explanation that would have been unnecessary. For those who had heard the Master state and imply that the seed meant the word or message, verse 19b was perfectly clear.

20, 21. And the one that was sown on rocky ground is he who upon hearing the message immediately accepts it with joy. However, he has no root in himself and lasts but a short while. When affliction or persecution arises on account of the message he immediately falls away. Here "the one that was sown on rocky ground" is the person who in his reaction to the message behaves as does rocky ground to seed that fell upon it. The reception which the seed received from such a thin layer of soil over a stratum of rock has already been noted (see on verses 5, 6). The tiny seed that never became firmly rooted sprang up quickly and then by the sun was scorched to death. So, says Jesus, it is also with the person here symbolized. Immediately, impulsively, gladly, he as it were jumps up to accept the message. He is thrilled and enthused, may even be sufficiently affected to shed a tear. Once the spell has subsided he seems to have forgotten all about it and returns to his former sinful life. A modern, rather recent, example from actual life: So affected by the sermon was this lady that at its conclusion she

---

[528] G. Campbell Morgan, *The Gospel according to Matthew*, New York, Chicago, London, Edinburgh, 1929, p. 148.

[529] Discussed in some detail in N.T.C. on the Gospel according to John, Vol. I, p. 206.

[530] Says J. A. Alexander, *op. cit.*, p. 361 (commenting on verse *20*, but the same holds for verse 19b), "Every ordinary reader understands without instruction that the (one) sown upon the rocky (places) means those whose character and state are represented by the falling of the seed upon the rock and not that the seed itself represents the person." Similarly H. N. Ridderbos, commenting on this passage, *op. cit.*, p. 258, states that we are dealing here with "a somewhat compressed expression, which more accurately formulated, would have to read somewhat as follows: this is he upon whom the word has the same effect as the seed sown by the wayside." He, too, is of the opinion that even without any further addition the meaning is clear.

fainted. When the visiting preacher, showing concern, stepped up to her, one of the elders, taking him aside, whispered, "She does this little trick every once in a while. In the interval between spells she falls back into her former life again."

For Biblical analogies see 8:19, 20; 19:16-22; and for apostasies after a longer period of seeming loyalty note the cases of Judas Iscariot (26:14-16) and of Demas (II Tim. 4:10). Today's evangelical revival gatherings, undoubtedly sources of blessing for many, add illustrative material. Investigation has established that by no means all those who at the spur of the moment—emotionally affected by the message and personal appeal of the evangelist, as well as by the music and the words of the old familiar hymns—were led to come forward and to sign the pledge card, have remained faithful.

As the very closely related twin causes of such defection Jesus speaks of *affliction,* meaning pressure, probably mostly from the outside in a non-Christian environment, and of *persecution,* actual suffering brought about by the enemy, all on account of the message. By devices such as these the fair-weather adherant is led to apostatize. Literally he "gets caught," "is ensnared," hence, "falls away." [531] The erstwhile adherant, never a *genuine* follower at all, for his confession did not spring from inner conviction, had failed to consider that true discipleship implies self-surrender, self-denial, sacrifice, service, and suffering. He has ignored the fact that it is the way of the cross that leads home.

22. And the one that was sown among the thorns is he who is hearing the message, and then the cares of this present world and the deceitful glamor of riches choke that message, and it becomes unfruitful. This verse describes the case of the man whose heart resembles soil infested with roots and runners of thorns. Such "dirty" soil is a serious threat to the growth of any desirable plant. Similarly a heart filled with worry with respect to the workaday world and beclouded by dreams about riches thwarts any influence for good that might otherwise proceed from the entrance of the kingdom message. Such a heart is preoccupied. It has no room for calm and earnest meditation on the word of the Lord. Should any such serious study and reflection nevertheless attempt to gain entrance, it would immediately be choked off. Constant anxiety about worldly affairs fill mind and heart with dark foreboding. When this person is poor he deceives himself into thinking that if he were only rich he would be happy. When he is rich he deludes himself into imagining that if he were only still richer he would be satisfied, as if material riches could under any circumstances guarantee contentment.

The man in question cannot be richly blessed nor can he be a blessing. The word as it affects him cannot be fruitful. There is nothing wrong with the

---

[531] On the verb used in the original see above, footnote 293, p. 303.

sower. Also, there is nothing wrong with the seed. With the man, however, everything is wrong. He should ask the Lord to deliver him from absorbing cares and dream-world delusions, so that the kingdom message may begin to have free course in heart and life. Then the mind, rescued from gnawing anxieties and delusory fantasies, will be able to reflect meaningfully on such precious passages as Prov. 30:7-9; Isa. 26:3; Matt. 6:19-34; 19:23, 24; Luke 12:6, 7, 13-34; I Tim. 6:6-10; and Heb. 13:5, 6.

Finally, there is the case of the well-prepared heart, the kind of heart symbolized by good soil: **23. And the one that was sown on the good soil is he who both hears and grasps the message. He bears fruit and yields, in one case a hundredfold, in another sixty, in another thirty.** With this kind of person the message of the kingdom falls into good soil, the kind of soil that, negatively speaking, is neither hard nor shallow nor preoccupied; positively speaking, is receptive and fertile.

This type of person hears because he wants to hear. He reflects on what he hears, for he has faith in the speaker. So he reaches a measure of true understanding. He puts the message into practice and bears fruit: conversion, faith, love, joy, peace, longsuffering, etc.

The importance of spiritual fruitbearing, as the mark of the true believer, is stressed even in the Old Testament (Ps. 1:1-3; 92:14; 104:13). This line of thought is continued in the Gospels (Matt. 3:10; 7:17-20; 12:33-35; Luke 3:8; John 15) and in the rest of the New Testament (Acts 2:38; 16:31; Rom. 7:4; Gal. 5:22; Eph. 5:9; Phil. 4:17; Col. 1:6; Heb. 12:11; 13:15; James 3:17. 18).

There is, however, a difference in the degree of fruitfulness. Not all are equally penitent, trustful, loyal, courageous, meek, etc., hence also not all are equally productive in bringing other lives to Christ. In the case of one believer the seed, the message, yields a hundredfold, in another sixty, in still another thirty. [532] In each, however, the seed has fallen upon good soil, and brings forth fruit, to the glory of God.

The Parable of The Tares among the Wheat

24. He presented another parable to them, saying, The kingdom of heaven is like a man who sowed good seed in his field. The parable of The

---

[532] Instead of being translated "in one case . . . in another . . . in another," this modifier has also been correctly rendered "some . . . some . . . some" (A.V., A.R.V., N.A.S.). Cf. entry ὅς, ἥ, ὅ L.N.T. (A. and G.), p. 589, under II.2. The objection presented by Lenski, p. 506, that ὅς is already singular and cannot be split up, does not impress me as being valid, for everyone understands immediately that in each of the instances "the one that was sown . . . he" represents a class, and can therefore very well be "split up." Also his further position that grammar necessitates the sense according to which one and the same individual causes one portion of the word to yield a hundredfold, another sixty, etc. is open to question.

Sower and the one of The Tares among the Wheat were probably explained
to the disciples in close succession (cf. Luke 8:9 with Matt. 13:36). It is not
unlikely that they were also spoken in similar chronological sequence, the
contents of verses 1-9 being immediately followed by that of verses 24-30.
To an extent they are similar in nature: both introduce a sower, a field, seed,
and crop-yield.

There are, however, also striking differences. Though the evil one appears
in the interpretation of both (13:19, 39), he is seen in a different character:
in the first he snatches away the good seed; in the second he is the one who
sows the tares among the wheat. So also in the first all the seed is good; in
the second tares appear among the wheat. Finally, in the first the emphasis is
on the kind of reception given to the seed by the various types of soil; in the
second on the sower, that is, on his command *a.* to the servants long before
harvest-time, and *b.* to the reapers at harvest-time.

"The kingdom of heaven (literally "has become like," hence) *is* like" is an
abbreviated expression. The kingdom itself is not like the man but resembles
the situation on this man's farm at the present time, while the plants are still
developing, and again later on, at the time of the harvest. Both the farm (the
farmer's field with whatever grows on it) and the kingdom in this present age
present a mixture in which the good and the bad are mingled together. In the
end both farm and kingdom are subjected to a cleansing or sifting process,
with the result: purity, beauty, and glory for both. It is in that sense that
"the kingdom of heaven is like a man. . . ."

This man, apparently a wealthy farmer, one who employs several "hands"
to work his farm, sows good seed in his field. Continued: 25. **But while men
were sleeping his enemy came and sowed tares among the wheat and went
away.** What this enemy does is mean, cruel, cowardly, sadistic. He waits until
everybody is fast asleep, so that he will not be seen and caught. Then,
without the least bit of concern for all the labor that has been bestowed on
the field, the expenses incurred, and the hopes inspired, he oversows the
field with tares. By this term is meant an obnoxious weed which in its
earliest stage, while both wheat and tares are still in blade, closely resembles
the nobler grain. The weed's technical name is *lolium temulentum.* This
"bearded darnel" is host to a fungus which, if eaten by animals or man, is
poisonous. The question may be raised, "But would anyone really be base
enough to commit a crime so contemptible?" The answer is that something
very similar—in this case the sowing of charlock over wheat—happened to a
field that belonged to the versatile Dean Henry Alford, as he relates in his
four volumed Greek Testament (London, 1849-61), commenting on this
parable. [533]

---

[533] For other occurrences see R. C. Trench, *Notes on the Parables of Our Lord,* Grand
Rapids, 1948, p. 35.

26. So when the early grain sprouted and began to fill out, the tares were seen also. It was not until the grain began to fill out that the difference between wheat and tares became evident. The servants are struck with alarm. Clearly the relation between them and their master is excellent, so that when he suffers damage he can figure on their sympathy. 27. Then the owner's servants approached him and said, Sir, didn't you sow good seed in your field? The ratio of tares to wheat must have been unusually large. Otherwise these servants would not have been so surprised, for to see some tares among the wheat was, after all, not very strange. What these men see in this field however is altogether different and calls for an explanation. The *real* solution does not even occur to the farm hands. Perhaps they regard the oversowing of good seed with bad a crime so unbelievable that they have dismissed this possibility completely from their minds. Certainly no one would do that, at least not to *their* master! What then? What *was* the source of the trouble? Had the seed even before being sown by the master been contaminated perhaps, having become accidently mixed with that of weeds? But this, too, seems hardly possible, so that, as the original implies by its very wording, to the question, "Sir, didn't you sow good seed in your field?" they expect an affirmative answer, "Yes, I did." Completely baffled they now ask, Then where did the tares come from? Literally, "Then, whence does it have tares?" 28. He said to them, An enemy has done this. The answer is definite. The owner's mind is not filled with any doubt whatever. Nevertheless, he does not mention the culprit by name but wisely limits himself to pointing out that what has happened is not to be accounted for by accidental scattering of kernels from nearby fields or by "contaminated" seeds. No, it was the deliberate deed of an enemy.

With respect to the tares, The servants, ever eager to co-operate, said to him, Then do you want us to go and gather them? The question was not unnatural. "Allow us to pull the tares out before they do any more harm," such is their reaction. 29. He said, No, lest while y o u are gathering the tares, y o u uproot the wheat along with them. The intertwining of the roots of wheat and tares made this a real possibility. And if, at *this* time, before the wheat was fully ripe, it would be pulled out, total loss for all such wheat would result. Therefore the owner continues, 30. Let both grow together until the harvest. Then at harvest-time I will say to the reapers, first gather the tares, and tie them in bundles to burn them up, but gather the wheat into my barn. Not only would the difference between wheat and tares be even more apparent at harvest-time, but then the wheat, even if uprooted, will still serve its useful purpose. Besides, the task of reaping will then be assigned to those who are specialists in that type of work, namely, the reapers. The owner will then order those reapers first to gather the tares with a view to burning them up, and then very carefully to gather the wheat and bring it to its proper place, the storehouse, barn, or granary (on which see also 3:12; 6:26; cf. Luke 3:17).

For the explanation of this parable see on verses 36-43.

The Parables of the Mustard Seed and the Leaven

31, 32. **He presented another parable to them, saying, The kingdom of heaven is like a mustard seed which a man took and sowed in his field. It is the smallest of all seeds, yet when it is full-grown it is the biggest of the garden herbs, and becomes a tree, so that the birds of the air come and lodge in its branches.** As indicated in the summary on p. 550, the two parables of verses 31-33 (The Mustard Seed and the Leaven or Yeast) are a pair, the first referring to the outward, the second to the inward growth of the kingdom of heaven. These two cannot be separated: one might say that it is because of the invisible principle of eternal life, by the Holy Spirit planted in the hearts of the citizens of the kingdom and increasingly exerting its influence there, that this kingdom also expands visibly and outwardly, conquering territory upon territory.

Jesus, then, first of all speaks of a mustard [534] seed (parallels Mark 4:31 and Luke 13:19; see also Matt. 17:20, parallel Luke 17:6). A man sows it in his field. Among seeds sown in a garden it was generally the smallest. Proverbially it indicated anything very minute in its beginning. But though insignificant at first, the mustard seed grows and grows until it becomes a tree so tall that the birds of the air come and lodge (literally "tent") in its branches. [535] Rabbinical literature took cognizance of the size which this "tree" would at times register. [536] Even today mustard grows vigorously in Palestine. It reaches ten feet, sometimes fifteen. In the fall of the year, when its branches have become rigid, birds of many kinds find here a shelter from the storm, rest from weariness, and shade from the heat of the sun, [537] all in all a wonderful place to go tenting! "The kingdom of heaven in its outward manifestation on earth is like that," says Jesus. It is seemingly insignificant in its beginning, but from this small beginning great results will grow.

---

[534] The word σίναπι is of Egyptian origin. Modern Greek uses σινάπι as one of its equivalents for mustard and mustard seed. It also uses ἀβυρτάκι and even μουστάρδα. See entry σίναπι in M.M., p. 575; also *The National Herald English-Greek, Greek-English Dictionary*, entry "mustard," p. 212.

[535] After ὥστε, ἐλθεῖν is aor. infinitive; κατασκηνοῦν is pres. infinitive hence, literally, "so as to come and to go tenting." ..." The indicated result is actual, not merely contemplated. As to κατασκηνοῦν, for the cognate noun κατασκήνωσις see above, on 8:20.

[536] S.BK., Vol. I, p. 669.

[537] They also find delicious food—the small black seeds—which they remove from the pods, but this feature is not included in the parable. For a most interesting description of the action of birds in connection with mustard see A. Parmelee, *op. cit.*, p. 250.

This too was a "mystery" (see on 13:11), in need of clarification or at least of re-emphasis. The disciples, and other adherents in a looser sense, were often impatient. Relatively speaking, the group of Christ's *loyal* followers was so small and so weak that at times they must have almost despaired. They were looking for revolutionary changes right here and now (Matt. 21:8, 9 and parallels; Luke 9:54; John 6:15; Acts 1:6). They may have asked, "Did not John the Baptist point in this direction?" See Matt. 3:11, 12. "Did not the Old Testament contain prophecies concerning the exaltation of Israel, its expansion among the nations, and its cosmic significance during the Messianic age?" See Gen. 22:17, 18; Ps. 72:8-11; Isa. 54:2, 3; chap. 60–62; Jer. 31:31-40; 32:36-44; Amos 9:11-15; Mic. 2:12, 13; 4:1-8; chap. 5; Zech. chap. 2; 8:18-23; etc. But in the thinking of the people these passages if pondered at all were probably often lifted out of their contexts.

There is the additional consideration that this same Old Testament bears testimony to the truth that spiritually great results generally develop from *small* beginnings (Isa. 1:8, 9; 11:1; 53:2, 3; Dan. 2:35b; Ezek. 17:22-24; Zech. 4:10). It would seem that this truth, too, did not always receive the respectful attention it deserved. Yet it is reaffirmed in the New Testament (Luke 12:32; I Cor. 1:26-31). Christ's *rule of grace,* no matter how despised and seemingly insignificant at first, is bound to go forward, "conquering and to conquer." "From vict'ry unto vict'ry his army he shall lead."

Accordingly, to those who first heard it, this parable was saying, "Have patience, exercise faith, keep on praying, and keep on working. God's program cannot fail." It is saying the same thing to those who have come afterward. Only, it is saying it today with even greater force, because the story-illustration is really a prophecy, and this prophecy has already been partly fulfilled! As to this matter of fulfilment see on 24:14.

Now whenever Christ's rule enters human hearts this happens *by implantation from without.* That is one of the important lessons taught by the first three parables. Man can never think or talk or work his way into the kingdom. The poet who wrote,

> By ourselves we cease from wrong,
> By ourselves become we pure,
> No one saves us but ourselves

was wrong. Once established, however, this rule of Christ, through the operation of the Holy Spirit, begins to operate also *from within outward.* More and more thoroughly—though the line of progress is not always straight but often diagonally upward, and even has its ups and downs—that kingship of the Son of man penetrates the various "faculties" (if use of this term is still permissible) of the human soul, with the result that the changed and constantly changing person begins to exert his influence for good not only in his individual and family life but also in "every sphere of life." Sometimes he becomes a blessing by means of the words he speaks or writes or by the motions he makes; at other times it is his very presence or his example of good deeds that counts. Sometimes, but by no means always, the power that proceeds from him operates secretly, mysteriously. The important fact is that art, science, literature, business, industry, commerce, government, these and all the other departments of human thought and endeavor begin to be blessed by this man's activity. The yeast is working! That, briefly, would seem to be the meaning of verse 33. **He told them another parable: The kingdom of heaven is like yeast which a woman took and put into three measures of wheat flour, until the whole batch had risen.**

The "measure" [538] here indicated, though not always and everywhere identical in capacity, is generally held to have averaged about a peck and a half. Three such measures would therefore amount to a huge quantity, not less than an *ephah;* one might say "more than a bushel." But it was not at all unusual for a woman to make so large a batch. Sarah did it (Gen. 18:6). A similar amount is also mentioned in Judg. 6:19 and in I Sam. 1:24. The point of the parable is that yeast once inserted continues its process of fermentation until the whole batch has risen. So also the citizen of the kingdom demands that every sphere of life shall contribute its full share of service, honor, and glory to him who is "King of kings and Lord of lords" (Rev. 19:16). Not as if on a sinful earth, before the return of Christ, this state of perfection will ever become a reality. Scripture clearly reveals that this will not be the case (Luke 17:25-30; 18:8; II Thess. 1:7-10; 2:8). But nothing less than the ultimate realization of this goal can ever be the aim of the believer. He is comforted by the prophecy of Isa. 11:9, "They shall not hurt nor destroy in all my holy mountain; for the earth shall be full of the knowledge of Jehovah, as the waters cover (the bottom of) the sea."

Meanwhile his purpose is not merely to get to heaven when he dies, or only to be an instrument in God's hand to bring others there, but everywhere to bring every thought of whatever kind into submission to, and therefore harmony with, the mind and will of Christ (see II Cor. 10:5), [539] that is, to demand that not only every tongue but also every "domain of life" shall exalt him. Therefore Christ's true follower actively promotes such causes as the abolition of slavery, the restoration of women's rights, the alleviation of poverty, the repatriation, if practicable, of the displaced (if not practicable then help of some other kind), the education of the illiterate, the reorientation of fine arts along Christian lines, etc. He promotes honesty among those who govern and those who are governed, as well as in business, industry, and commerce. He does all this not apart from but in connection

---

[538] Greek σάτα, pl. of σάτον; cf. Aramaic ṣā'thā = Hebrew ṣeʾāh. As to its capacity see S.BK. I, pp. 669, 670.

[539] On that passage see P. E. Hughes, *Paul's Second Epistle to the Corinthians* (*The New International Commentary on the New Testament*), Grand Rapids, 1962, p. 353.

with, in fact as part and parcel of, the evangelization of the world. That this "yeast" of the rule of Christ in human hearts, lives, *and spheres* has already exerted a wholesome influence in thousands of ways, and that this influence is still continuing, is clear to all who have eyes to see. All one has to do is to compare conditions—for example, the treatment of prisoners of war, of women, of workmen, of the underprivileged—in countries where Christ's rule has not yet become acknowledged to any great extent, with those existing in nations where this principle has already been operative for some time on a generous scale.

In the explanation of this parable as presented in the preceding it will have become apparent that an attempt has been made to avoid over-interpretation. (This holds too for the other parables.) For example, those who have tried in this Commentary to find an answer to the question, "To what does the woman who put the yeast into the flour refer?" have received no satisfaction. [540] Nor has any sympathy been shown for interpretations that contradict the context; for example, for the idea that the "leaven" or "yeast" symbolizes a corrupting influence that mars fellowship with God. [541] The argument advanced in favor of the latter position, namely, that everywhere else in Scripture leaven indicates something bad, breaks down immediately. One could, for example, say that in Scripture "the serpent" is generally associated with, and/or is a symbol of, evil (Gen. 3:13; Ps. 58:4; 140:3; Prov. 23:32; Isa. 27:1; Matt. 23:33; II Cor. 11:3; Rev. 12:9, 14, 15; 20:2). But what shall we do with Num. 21:8, cf. John 3:14, where the serpent obviously represents the Son of man; and with Matt. 10:16, which admonishes us to be "keen as the serpents, guileless as the doves"? It is the context in each case that must decide the symbolical meaning, if there be any such meaning. In the present case the yeast clearly represents the kingdom or kingship of heaven, that is, the rule of Christ gladly acknowledged in heart and life, and this is something very good indeed!

Christ's Use of Parables in Fulfilment of Prophecy

34, 35. All these things Jesus said to the crowds in parables, and without using a parable he was not saying anything to them, that what was spoken through the prophet might be fulfilled:
I will open my mouth in parables,
I will utter mysteries from ancient times.
We are told here that at this particular season Jesus, in describing the mysteries of the kingdom (13:11) to the crowds, confined himself to parables. His twofold reason for employing this story method, namely, *revealing* the truths concerning salvation to those who were willing to accept

---

[540] According to Lenski she represents the church, *op. cit.*, p. 514.
[541] For this see G. C. Morgan, *op. cit.*, p. 160.

them, and *concealing* them from those whose hardened hearts rejected them, has already been discussed (13:10-17). By the inspiration of the Spirit, Matthew sees in this use of parables a fulfilment of prophecy, once again focusing the attention upon Jesus as being indeed the Messiah who was to come.

For the introductory formula—"that what was spoken through the prophet might be fulfilled"—see on 1:22. Though in the present case there is no (spoken) "by the Lord" (as in 1:22; 2:15), nor any mention of the name of the prophet (as in 2:17; 3:3; 4:14; 12:17),[542] the fact that "the prophet" was the agent through whom the Lord spoke is clearly implied.

As to the quoted words themselves, these present no real problem. They are taken from Ps. 78:2.[543] The prophet referred to was the psalmist Asaph, also called a "seer" or "prophet" in II Chron. 29:30. The "mystery" which he explains by means of ever so many pithy sayings is that in the history of Israel from its very establishment God carried out his plan and revealed his marvelous attributes. Throughout the psalm the poet speaks about the manifestation of God's power, his marvelous works. He dwells also on the Lord's unfailing and forgiving love (see verses 4-7, 12-16, 23-28, 38, 52-55). Did not Jesus, in an even more unforgettable manner set forth the Father's tender concern (Matt. 5:45-48; 6:4, 6, 8, 26, 30-34; 7:7, 8, 11; 10:20,

---

[542] Textual support for "through Isaiah" is weak.
[543] The original Hebrew can be rendered as follows:
> I will open my mouth with a parable [strictly, a mashal];
> I will utter mysteries [or "riddles"] from of old.

In the first line, "I will open my mouth" presents no problem, as the Greek here fully translates the Hebrew. Matthew, following the LXX translation, uses the plural "in parables." If the Hebrew singular, "with a parable" be viewed as representative, which is probably correct, then either a singular or a plural Greek rendering would do very well. For Matthew the use of the plural would be very appropriate, since Jesus uttered *many* parables.

In the second line the verb ἐρεύξομαι, basically "I will disgorge," but here softened to "I will utter," harmonizes with the Hebrew verb which it represents. From the parallelism it appears that Asaph views the mashal as a "mystery." The word κεκρυμμένα perf. passive participle pl. of κρύπτω, hence, "hidden things," used by Matthew, shows that the evangelist, as well as the psalmist, was thinking of truths that would have remained unknown had they not been revealed. "From ancient times" is, of course, the same as "from of old," which is also a good translation of ἀπὸ καταβολῆς; strictly, "from (the) foundation" or "from (the) beginning." There is considerable doubt about the reading, in Matthew, that adds κόσμου to καταβολῆς, resulting in "from (the) foundation *of the world.*" Was this a scribal addition, influenced perhaps by the frequency of the occurrence of the full phrase in Scripture (25:34; Luke 11:50; John 17:24; Eph. 1:4; Heb. 4:3; 9:26; I Peter 1:20; Rev. 13:8; 17:8)? If "of the world" is authentic, the meaning might be that the mysteries cleared up by Jesus were from eternity determined in God's plan. By itself that is true enough (Eph. 1:4, 11). Nevertheless, this thought is not necessarily implied in Ps. 78:2, nor is there any reference to it anywhere else in that psalm. The psalmist, in a broad sweep, records the history of ancient Israel. He does not go beyond this to eternity or even to the story of creation.

28-32) and his own besides (Matt. 8:3, 16, 17; 9:2, 12, 13, 22, 35-38; 11:25-30; 12:15-21, 48-50)?

The psalmist also shows how, in spite of all this love, many of the people rejected God (verses 8, 10, 11, 17-19, 32, 36, 37, 40-42, 56-58). Did not Jesus, in passages that will live forever, present to his audiences that same regrettable fact (10:16, 22; 11:16-24; 12:38-45; 13:1-7, 13-15)?

Thirdly, Asaph's psalm ends on a climactic, triumphal note, showing how the Lord had chosen David to be Israel's shepherd (Ps. 78:68-72). According to Matthew's Gospel, the Antitype of this shepherd was David's great Son and Lord, namely, Jesus Christ (9:36; 22:41-46; cf. John 10:11, 14, 16, 28), who in his very character as "The Good Shepherd" mirrored the Father (Matt. 18:12-14; cf. Luke 15:3-7; John 14:9).

Finally, even in his style of speaking Jesus was the poet's Antitype, who, by means of the parabolic form, as revealed here in Matt. 13 and elsewhere, carried to new heights of perfection Asaph's highly figurative language (Ps. 78:27, 50: metaphor; verses 45, 48: hyperbole; verse 65: anthropomorphism).

Explanation of The Parable of the Tares among the Wheat

36. He then dismissed the crowds and went into the house. After what has been said about this "house" in the comments on 9:28; 12:46; and 13:1 nothing further by way of explanation is necessary. **His disciples approached him, saying, Explain to us the parable of the tares of the field.** See what has been said before with reference to the disciples asking Jesus to explain parables (on 13:16, 18, 24). The reason they asked for an explanation of this particular parable was probably the same as, or similar to, that which caused them to ask the Master to clarify the parable of The Sower. The Baptist's saying about the *impending* judgment, with the axe lying even now at the root of the trees (3:10-12), may well have seemed to them to be at variance with the long delay, for gradual ripening of wheat and tares, implied in the parable of The Tares. Had not even Jesus himself proclaimed that the kingdom of heaven was "at hand" (4:17)?

Jesus, then, is once again going to impress upon these men that before the final judgment arrives there will be a lengthy period of waiting, during which they must exercise patience. To be sure, the kingdom of heaven had indeed entered a new stage with the coming of the Son of man (11:4, 5). As has been shown in the explanation of 4:17, the declaration, "The kingdom of heaven is at hand" was fully justified. But the disciples must learn that this was not as yet the final act in the drama. The great consummation was a matter for future realization.

37. He answered and said, The one who sows the good seed is the Son of man. For a detailed study of the title "Son of man" see on 8:20. Think of it:

the mysterious "Son of man" of Daniel's prophecy (7:14), to whom, according to Daniel's vision, was to be given "dominion and glory and royal power" was now a humble sower! As such he is constantly sowing the good seed, the kingdom message of salvation through repentance and faith. **38. The field is the world.** In line with such passages as 11:27a; 13:31, 32; 24:14; 28:18, 19, cf. John 3:16; 4:42, the gospel must be proclaimed everywhere, not immediately, to be sure (10:5, 6), but progressively. Not only the minds and hearts of men, without any distinction of race or nationality, must be reached, but every sphere of life must be won for him who is King of kings and Lord of lords (see explanation of 13:33). From the statement, "The field is the world" nothing should be subtracted. Continued: **the good seed, these are the sons of the kingdom,** meaning that the sons of the kingdom, those who gladly own Jesus as their Lord and King, are those in whom the good seed of the gospel bears fruit (see on verses 19 and 23). Similarly, **the tares are the sons of the evil one,** meaning that the sons of the evil one, Satan's children and followers, are those in whom the tares sown by the prince of evil produce a harvest of corruption. This is in harmony with what immediately follows, namely, **39. the enemy who sowed them is the devil,** mentioned again and again in the teaching of Jesus. For further explanation see on 4:1; 5:37b (especially footnote 297 on p. 308); and 6:13b. Continued: **the harvest is the close of the age.** The servants are not allowed to pluck out the tares now. There must be no impatience. Harvesting must wait until the day of the great consummation; **and the reapers are the angels.** For the function to be performed by the angels as reapers see also 24:31; Rev. 14:17-20. Though it is true that according to Rev. 14:14-16 the Son of man himself gathers the grain harvest (the believers), while according to verses 17-20 of that chapter the gathering of the vintage (the unbelievers) is assigned to the angels, this does not mean that there is a conflict between Matt. 24:31 and Rev. 14:14-16. Why would it be impossible for the Son of man, in gathering his elect, to assign a subsidiary function to the angels? **40-42a. As the tares, then, are gathered and burned up, so it is going to be at the close of the age. The Son of man shall send his angels, and they shall gather out of his kingdom everything that is offensive and those that perpetrate lawlessness, and shall throw them into the fiery furnace.** The fire of this furnace is unquenchable. The shame which "those who perpetrate lawlessness," i.e., who defy God's holy law, are going to suffer is everlasting (Dan. 12:2). Their bonds are never ending (Jude 6, 7). They will be tormented with fire and brimstone . . . and the smoke of their torment ascends forever and ever, so that they have no rest day or night (Rev. 14:9-11). Yes, "day and night, forever and ever" (Rev. 20:10; cf. 19:3). The passages in which the doctrine of everlasting punishment is taught are so numerous that one stands aghast that there are people who affirm that they accept Scripture, but who nevertheless reject this doctrine. What is perhaps the most telling argument against the notion that the wicked are simply annihilated but that the righteous continue to live forevermore is the fact that in Matt. 25:46 the same word describes the duration both of the punishment of the former and of the blessedness of the latter: the wicked go away into *everlasting* punishment, but the righteous into *everlasting* life.

Here in verses 40-42a what happens to the tares is presented from the point of view of *a cleansing of the kingdom.* On the day of judgment—but not before!, that is the emphasis here—the kingdom will be purged of all impurities. As to the *spheres* of activity (see on 13:33), whatever in them was offensive or seductive, hence contrary to God's holy law, will in the gloriously transformed universe have been completely removed. Between the perpetrators of lawlessness, who nevertheless, as in 7:22, claim a share in this kingdom, and those who, out of gratitude for salvation freely bestowed, obey God's law, there will then be and forever remain a complete separation.

In the fiery furnace **There shall be weeping and grinding of teeth.** For explanation see on 8:12. **43. Then, in the kingdom of their Father, the righteous shall shine as the sun.** The recipients of grace here will be the recipients of glory there. To be sure, even here and now a measure of glory is bestowed on them. But this glory is generally concealed. But then the prophecy of Dan. 12:3 is going to be fulfilled: "They that are wise shall shine as the brightness of the firmament; and they that turn many to righteousness as the stars forever and ever." Christ's—hence, also their Father's—glory will be reflected in them (I John 3:2, 3; Rev. 3:12). If II Cor. 3:18 is true even here and now, will it not be far more gloriously realized hereafter, in the Father's kingdom?

As a tender, earnest warning to all who listened to this explanation of the parable, the familiar words are added: **He who has ears, let him hear.** See on 11:15. Let him take to heart the meaning of the parable, not only by being attentive, patient, hopeful, and trusting, but also by examining himself, and this to ask not only, "Am I represented by the wheat, or by the tares?" but also, "Have I, in my impatience, forgotten to 'let both grow together until the harvest,' or am I willing to await patiently the decision of the Son of man at harvest-time?"

Notice should be taken of the controversy that has developed among commentators with respect to the question, "In this parable what is meant by the intermixture of wheat and tares, a symbol of 'the kingdom of heaven' in its earthly manifestation? Is the reference here to the commingling of sharply contrasted inhabitants of the earth; for example, Cain and Abel, Haman and Mordecai, Herod the Great and Mary (the mother of Jesus); or does the symbol indicate the dwelling together, *within the church visible,* of sincere Christians and hypocrites?" [544]

---

[544] According to H. N. Ridderbos, *op. cit.,* pp. 265, 266 (cf. his work *De Komst van*

The disagreement, though real, may not actually be as sharp or total as on the surface it may seem to be. The terms "kingdom of heaven" and "church" are probably never exact equivalents. The church is the body of professing believers. It consists of people. On the other hand, as has already been shown (see on 13:33), the kingdom, in its concrete manifestation, refers to that entire complex of people and spheres in which Christ's rule is recognized. In view of this distinction it can be said that the reference in the parable is to the kingdom rather than to the church.

It is also true, however, that in connection with none of the other parables do the terms "kingdom" and "church" approach each other as closely as they do here and in the parable of The Dragnet. The following should be borne in mind:

a. If "wheat" refers to those in whose hearts the good seed is bearing fruit, hence, in general, to the sum-total of true believers, and "tares" are sown *among* the wheat, not alongside of it or on some other field, then is it not natural to think of the intermingling of true and false members within the church visible?

b. In these parables Jesus is shedding needed light on "mysteries" (13:11). Now the circumstance that a Cain and an Abel, a Haman and a Mordecai, etc., are both living on the same earth, and even have dealings with each other, a fact which we must not by means of rashness try to change, can hardly be called a mystery. What is far more of a mystery, however, is that *within the church visible* God allows both the true and the merely nominal Christians to dwell side by side, and that, within the proper bounds of divinely instituted discipline, we must respect this arrangement.

c. We are distinctly told that at the close of the age the Son of man shall gather "out of his kingdom" everything that seduces and those that perpetrate lawlessness. The parable does not say that these are going to be plucked away "from the earth," but "out of his kingdom." How can they be "gathered out" if previously they were not inside, in this case inside the church visible?

It would seem, therefore, that the conclusion must be that, with the reservation already made, the church visible is indeed definitely involved in this parable.

---

het Koninkrijk, p. 298), the reference is to intermixture in the world, not in the church. He is by no means the only one who holds that view. In disagreement with Ridderbos are W. M. Taylor, *op. cit.*, p. 42: R. C. Trench, *op. cit.*, p. 35; S. E. Johnson, *The Gospel according to Matthew* (*The Interpreter's Bible*, Vol. VII), p. 415; A. Fahling, *The Life of Christ*, St. Louis, 1936, p. 304; W. O. E. Oesterley, *The Gospel Parables in the Light of their Jewish Background*, London, 1938, p. 69; and C. Graafland, "Ingaan in het Rijk," *Theologia Reformata* XIII, No. 4 (Dec. 1970), p. 239: "Our conclusion must be that Scripture views the connection between kingdom and church as being much closer than do many theologians in our time."

The lesson taught here is always timely, It was certainly needed by the disciples, who were too eager to expel from their company some of those who did not belong to Christ's regular followers (Luke 9:49, 50), too ready to flare up in anger and quarrelsomeness even against fellow-disciples, members of their own group of Twelve (Matt. 20:24; Luke 22:24). The lesson has been needed by the church ever since. How often have not men of eminent ecclesiastical position tried to drive out of the church those whom, for one reason or another, they did not favor, even though at times the latter may not even have been at fault? How often have not "difficult" members been treated with an impatience for which there was no excuse? Sometime ago when, in connection with a church anniversary, a summary account of that congregation's past had to be prepared, the archivist came across this consistory minute, "It was decided to give sister X the sum of . . . to enable her to take the train to . . .; then we'll be rid of her." Whether rash measures are carried out against large groups or against single individuals really makes no difference as far as the principle is concerned. It is exactly as A. B. Bruce has said, "Christ is not here laying down a rule for the regulation of ecclesiastical practice, but inculcating the cultivation of a certain spirit, the spirit of wise patience." [545] According to Christ's own teaching it is the "spirit" that counts even more than the outward act (Matt. 5:21, 22).

The Scriptural teaching regarding discipline is not hereby overruled. Quite the contrary. If the spirit of loving patience is exercised, personal discipline (I Cor. 11:28), mutual discipline (Matt. 18:15, 16; Gal. 6:1, 2), and church discipline (Matt. 18:17, 18; Titus 3:10, 11; Rev. 2:14-16), will all be strengthened and ennobled. Even in the case of church discipline one of the chief purposes is "that the spirit may be saved" (I Cor. 5:5).

Before proceeding to a discussion of verse 44 one final question should be answered. Does not Christ's explanation of the parable of The Tares among the Wheat indicate that entirely wrong is the well-known rule of parable interpretation, according to which each of these story illustrations has only one *third of comparison,* that is, one main lesson, and we should not assign a separate symbolic significance to each item? What Jesus said was, "The sower of the good seed is . . .; the field is . . .; the good seed, these are . . .; the tares are . . .; the enemy is . . .;" etc. On the basis, therefore, of what Jesus himself did with this parable are we not justified in ascribing separate symbolical significance, for example, to each item in the parable of The Good Samaritan (Luke 10:30-37): the man who went down from Jerusalem to Jericho is Adam, the robbers are the devil and his angels, the priest and the Levite are the law and the prophets, the good Samaritan is Christ, the inn is the church, etc. (Augustine)? The answer is:

a. The parable of The Tares among the Wheat does indeed convey only

---

[545] *The Parabolic Teaching of Christ,* London, 1882, p. 54.

one main lesson, already indicated (see above, p. 572). This lesson is clearly suggested by verses 29, 30, 41-43. So it is also with the other parables. Either the parable itself or its historical setting or the words that introduce it or the conclusion indicates what that lesson is. Thus, in the parable of The Good Samaritan the key is found in Luke 10:25-29, 36, 37 (Do not ask, "Who is my neighbor?" but prove yourself a genuine neighbor to any needy person whom the Lord providentially places in your path); in the three parables of Luke 15, it is found in Luke 15:1, 2, 7, 22-24; in the parable of The Barren Fig Tree, in Luke 13:1-5; in that of The Pharisee and the Publican, in Luke 18:1, 7, 8; etc.

b. The fact that in connection with the parable of The Tares among the Wheat (and also the one about The Sower) *Jesus* interpreted certain items individually, does not give us the right to assume that *we* have the wisdom to do the same with the other parables. In fact, this wrong practice has led to all kinds of wholly arbitrary and conflicting so-called "interpretations."

The Parable of the Hidden Treasure

The three final paragraphs of the series of seven are now recorded. Their place in the entire group, immediately following the explanation of the parable of The Tares among the Wheat, an explanation given to the disciples (verse 36), their very contents, and the conclusion which in verses 51, 52 follows them ("Have y o u understood all this;"), show that they were spoken to the disciples, not to the multitudes at large. Their purpose, accordingly, must have been "to reveal" (verses 10-12a, 16, 17), not also "to conceal" (verses 10-17).

44. The kingdom of heaven is like a treasure hidden in the field, which a man found and covered up. Then, in his joy over it, he goes and sells all he has and buys that field. The attention in this parable is fixed on a man who, while digging in a field, unexpectedly came upon a treasure. The picture is true to life. Due to wars, raids, and the difficulty of finding a secure place to store valuables in houses that offered rather easy access to accomplished burglars (6:19), a home-owner would at times resort to burying in the ground his most durable precious possessions or a portion of them. In the case here described the man who, probably in a chest, had buried his treasure in the ground may have died before informing anyone about his deed. Someone else now owns the field.

So now the digger, suddenly finds it. By what right he was digging in somebody else's field is not stated in the parable. Let us assume that he had this right. One possibility would be that he was a renter. His sense of fairness (or shall we say, fear that he himself might otherwise not escape punishment?) prevents him from scooping up the entire find and running off with it. So he covers up his find. He realizes that in order to claim legal ownership of the treasure he must first of all own the field. So he buys the field, even though in order to acquire the purchase price he must sell all he has. Not in the least does he mind this, so delighted is he to obtain possession of the treasure.

The point of the parable is that the kingdom of heaven, the glad recognition of God's rule over heart and life, including salvation for the present and for the future, for soul and ultimately also for the body, the great privilege of being thereby made a blessing to others to the glory of God, all this, is a treasure so inestimably precious that one who obtains it is willing to surrender for it whatever could interfere with having it. It is the supreme treasure because it fully satisfies the needs of the heart. It brings inner peace and satisfaction (Acts 7:54-60).

An excellent commentary on this parable is Paul's experience as recorded in his autobiographical note: "Yes, what is more, I certainly do count all things to be sheer loss because of the all-surpassing excellence of knowing Christ Jesus my Lord, for whom I suffered the loss of all these things, and am still counting them refuse, in order that I may gain Christ and be found in him" (Phil. 3:8, 9a). Paul had come upon this treasure suddenly, unexpectedly (Acts 9:1-19). Moreover, he was not reading the Bible when it happened. All extraneous ideas—for example, that in this parable the field indicates Scripture—should be dropped. When God leads the sinner to the discovery that causes him to shout for joy he employs all kinds of ways and methods. Think of his dealings with Nathanael (John 1:46-51), with the Samaritan woman (John 4:1-44), with the man born blind (John 9), etc. Of course, the possession of the treasure also implies love for the Word, but rather than loading the parable with subjective allegorical embellishments of individual items, we should grasp its one important lesson: the incalculable preciousness of salvation for those who discover it and obtain possession of it *without even looking for it!*

Also for those who obtain possession of the kingdom *after diligent search* it is the summum bonum (highest good), as is made clear in

The Parable of the Pearl of Great Price

45, 46. Again, the kingdom of heaven is like a merchant in search of fine pearls. Having found one pearl of great value, he went and sold all he had, and bought it. Pearls, generally obtained from the Persian Gulf or from the Indian Ocean, were fabulously priced, far beyond the purchasing power of the average person. Only the rich could afford them. It is said that Lollia Paulina, wife of the emperor Caligula, had pearls gleaming all over her head, hair, ears, neck, and fingers! In addition to the reference to pearls in the present passage see also 7:6; I Tim. 2:9; Rev. 17:4; 18:12, 16; 21:21.

In the passage now under discussion a wholesale merchant, [546] dissatisfied

---

[546] Greek ἔμπορος. Modern Greek still uses the same word; note, however, the

with the pearls he has been able to obtain up to the present, is in search of the very best. His search is successful. When he sees this particular pearl his heart and mind immediately exclaim, "This is it!" There is never any hesitancy. Not only that but he buys it, though, as in the preceding parable (see verse 44b), in order to do this he had to sell all his possessions.

Here, as in verse 44, willingness to surrender for the coveted prize of the glad recognition of the supremacy of God in heart and life whatever might be inconsistent with it is again the main lesson. Money will not buy salvation. It is God's free gift (Isa. 55:1). We can "buy" it only in the sense that we gain rightful possession of it. We do this by grace, through faith in the Lord Jesus Christ, realizing that even that faith is God's gift (see N.T.C. on Eph. 2:8).

As to examples of those for whom discovery of the "one pearl of great price" followed diligent search, it is necessary to make one important reservation, namely, that human life is very complex. It is therefore not easy, perhaps not even possible, to divide all believers whose stories are related in Scripture into two well-marked groups, and to say, "Group A found salvation without even looking for it; group B only after diligent search." In some cases each parable may apply to a certain extent. With that reservation the following concrete examples are offered, allowing the reader to judge whether, and if so in how far, they properly illustrate the parable of The Pearl of Great Price, that is, *discovery after search:* Cleopas and his companion (Luke 24:29), the Ethiopian eunuch (Acts 8:26-38), Cornelius (Acts 10:1-8, 30-33), Lydia (Acts 16:14), the jailer (Acts 16:29-34), and the Bereans (Acts 17:10-12).

The final one in this series of seven kingdom parables was

The Parable of the Dragnet

47-49. Again, the kingdom of heaven is like a dragnet that was cast into the sea and gathered up fish of every variety. When it was full the men dragged it ashore, sat down, picked out the good ones for the containers, but threw away the bad. So shall it be at the close of the age. The angels shall come and separate the wicked from the righteous. . . . Even on the surface and especially in the interpretation the parable resembles that of The Tares among the Wheat. Just as in the field the wheat and the tares were allowed to grow to maturity intermingled, and were not separated until the time of the harvest, so also fish of every variety, both good and bad, are caught in the net, and are not divided into two categories until the net has been drawn ashore. The words of interpretation, "So shall it be at the close of the age"

---

leisurely manner in which the parable is presented: literally "merchant man" (A.V.) or "man that is a merchant" (A.R.V.). As to ἔμπορος, etymologically the word refers to someone who is "in the way," or "on the road." We speak of an *emporium:* market place. Those acquainted with Grimm's Law of consonantal correspondence will see that the word used in the original is related to our *ferry, fare,* etc.

577

occur in connection with each parable (verse 40b, cf. 49a), the function of the angels is essentially the same in both cases (verse 41, cf. 49b), and the lot of the wicked is described in two verses that are identical (verses 42 and 50).

As to the dragnet, for the meaning of this and of the other kinds of nets mentioned by Matthew see on 4:18. Those who listened to Jesus when he told this parable—some of them were fishermen—were, of course, very well acquainted with the business of setting out such a very large net, and allowing it to catch fish of every variety, as the sea-water, teeming with fish, freely splashed through it. They knew what was meant by dragging such a net ashore, then sitting down on the beach and sorting out the fish. Those edible and salable were thrown into buckets or barrels, the rest were discarded. Thus also the gospel of salvation provided by God through faith in Christ is constantly "catching" men (Luke 5:10). However, not all of those that enter the kingdom in its visible manifestation—for all practical purposes we might as well say not all those who enter the church visible—are truly saved. This will become evident in the great day of judgment when the angels will separate the wicked from the righteous.

The question has been asked, "Why did Jesus add this parable?" Does it teach something distinctive, something that had not as yet been touched upon in any of the other parables, particularly in that of The Tares among the Wheat? The search for something "different" is unrewarding. One might, perhaps, point to a phrase like "fish of every variety," and point out that at least this feature had not been mentioned before, and in this connection one might begin to think of the gospel as God's instrument for the gathering of men of every nation, clime, age, social group, degree of education or of intelligence, etc. Or, again, one might point out that in distinction from the twin parable, in which the work of sowing the good seed is explicitly ascribed solely to the sower, here, on the other hand, Jesus is obviously thinking of the many phases of the work of fishermen, and is even going into some detail in describing them. However, in his explanation of the parable (verses 49, 50) the Lord never refers to the idea of "variety," only to the two classes: the good and the bad. And as to the work of the fishermen in its initial phases—the casting of the net, dragging it ashore, and sitting down on the beach—in the explanation this is never taken up again. And as to the final items of their activity—picking out the good fish and discarding the bad—by the Master this is referred symbolically to the activity of *the angels,* exactly as is the reapers' work in the other parable. Honesty compels us to conclude therefore that although the figure used is, of course, quite different, yet when it comes to the most important point, namely, "What is the one important lesson taught by this parable?" there is nothing that is distinctive, nothing that has not already been said! In fact, as already indicated, verse **50. . . . and shall throw them into the fiery furnace. There shall be weeping** and grinding of teeth is an exact duplicate of verse 42; for explanation see on that verse.

But is not this very repetition of the identical idea under another symbol exactly what we should admire most of all? Does it not mean that the Savior is impressing upon his disciples, both for their own good and for the good of those to whom they were to bring the message, the absolute certainty, the irrevocable decisiveness of the coming judgment, in order, as far as possible, to prevent everlasting despair? Does not the fact that from parables about sowers, mustard seed, yeast, hidden treasure and pearls, illustrations with which they and most people were familiar, he now closes his series with one in the realm of fishing, with which the disciples were even more familiar, support this conclusion? Is he not telling them, "What y o u yourselves have been doing many a time, or have seen y o u r fellow-disciples doing, namely, pick out the bad from the good and discard them, will be done once for all by the angels at my order"? Is he not implying, "Therefore warn men everywhere to repent"? And, in the light of what precedes (verses 44-46) is he not, as it were, adding, "In view of the irreversible decisiveness of the coming judgment impress upon men the exceeding preciousness of the kingdom of heaven and the necessity for everyone to take possession of it here and now"?

This view of the situation is in line with Christ's constant emphasis on the finality of the eschatological sentence when once it is pronounced (8:12; 13:4, 50; 25:10, 30, 46; Luke 17:26-37). It is also in line with his urging that men everywhere repent (Matt. 4:17; 9:13) and be constantly on the alert (25:13; Mark 13:35-37; Luke 12:32). Lastly, it is in harmony with what the Gospels tell us about Christ's deeply sympathetic heart (Matt. 9:35-38; 11:28-30; 14:13-18; 15:32; 23:37; etc.).

That the Lord was indeed thinking about the disciples and their task is evident from the words he now uses to picture

The True Scribe

51. Have y o u understood all this? They answered, Yes. By means of his question Jesus gives the disciples the opportunity to ask for more information about the kingdom, in case there should still be matters that are not clear to them. Their answer implies that, as they themselves see it, their insight has been immeasurably deepened.

Now to acknowledge gratefully that one's mind has been enriched is wonderful. It is, however, not enough. What has been received must also be imparted to others. That is the duty and responsibility of the true scribe, as the Master now indicates: **52. He said to them, Therefore every scribe who has been trained for the kingdom of heaven resembles a head of a household who brings out of his storehouse things new and old.** The lesson Jesus here

579

teaches can be applied to every kingdom worker. Is it not particularly fitting in connection with induction into office? The true scribe, then, must be as follows:

a. *He must have received adequate training*

He must have become a disciple or pupil [547] to (or: of) the kingdom of heaven. The Jewish scribe of that day and age has already been described (see on 2:4; 5:20). He was the acknowledged student and teacher of the Old Testament and of the "traditions" that had been superimposed upon it. The inadequacy of his teaching, both as to content and method, has also been noted (see on 7:28, 29).

Now the "scribe" whom Jesus here pictures is not at all like that. He has been trained for—and in matters touching—the kingdom of heaven, that is, the kingdom of salvation full and free, the kingdom all are invited to enter, the kingdom of grace and glory.

b. *In the eyes of God, this kingdom-scribe is rich and important*

Is he not the citizen of the kingdom of heaven, endowed with all the rights and privileges of such citizenship? In fact, is he not even himself the son of the King? Jesus compares him here with "the head of a household." [548]

c. *This implies that he has the responsibility of providing for his household*

This scribe has been provided with a veritable "thesaurus" (see on 2:11; 6:19-21; 12:35; 13:44; 19:21), a treasure, a rich supply of goods. His goods include knowledge of Scripture; hence, of the way of salvation; knowledge of the manner in which out of gratitude men should live to the glory of God; knowledge of how a person may obtain the peace that passes all understanding, the joy unspeakable and full of glory, etc. Would it not be a shame if he did not impart this knowledge to others also, beginning with those who belong to his own household?

d. *He must provide "things new and old"*

The trouble with the Jewish scribe of Christ's day was that he was forever repeating the opinions, fancies, and vagaries of the ancient rabbis (see above, on 7:28, 29). He specialized in that which was "old," and was unable to stir man's soul and to meet his deepest needs. Others there are who are constantly interested in whatever is "new" (Acts 17:21). It has to be the latest. The true scribe is thoroughly acquainted with the old, and builds on it. He does not despise but loves that old Bible, these old doctrines, etc., but he applies

---

[547] Greek μαθητευθείς first aor. passive participle of μαθητεύω. In the intr. this verb means *to become a disciple or pupil;* hence, in the passive *to be instructed, be trained.* Used transitively the meaning is *to make a disciple of, to teach, instruct* (Matt. 28:19; Acts 14:21). Cf. Matt. 11:29.

[548] Greek ἀνθρώπῳ οἰκοδεσπότῃ; note pleonastic use of ἄνθρωπος, as also in verse 45.

all this to new situations, is always ready to receive new light from any source (just so it is really "light"), and, by God's grace, remains ever fresh in his approach, for he drinks from the Fountain of Living Waters (Ps. 46:4; Jer. 2:13; John 4:14; Rev. 22:1, 17b).

The Rejection of Jesus at Nazareth

The reason why inclusion of this paragraph in a chapter covering a series of kingdom parables is justified has already been stated (see p. 550). **53. Now when Jesus had finished (telling) these parables he left that place.** We have followed Jesus from the Capernaum synagogue (12:9) to his temporary departure (12:15), his implied return (12:47), his teaching from a boat near the shore (13:1, 2), and his stay in a Capernaum home (13:36). He now leaves this place. Continued: **54. He came to his hometown and was teaching the people in their synagogue, so that they were astonished.** His hometown was Nazareth, the place where he had been brought up (2:23; Luke 4:16). According to Mark 6:2 and Luke 4:16 it was sabbath. Graphically Matthew pictures Jesus in the act of teaching the synagogue audience: "he was teaching the people." Result: astonishment (cf. 7:28, 29). **Where did he get this wisdom, they asked, and (the power to do) these miracles?** The "wisdom" revealed in his teaching was evident right then and there. As to the miracles, they had had opportunities to hear about them, for ever so many of them had been performed in Galilee (see on 4:23-25; chap. 8; chap. 9; 11:4, 5, 20-23). As these people saw it, however, Jesus was not supposed to reveal such wisdom and such power, for he had not enjoyed any "higher" education, and besides, he was *merely* one of their own: **55, 56. Isn't he the son of the carpenter? Isn't his mother's name Mary, and aren't James, Joseph, Simon, and Judas his brothers? And aren't all his sisters here with us? Where, then, did he get all this?**

The very wisdom which he here revealed and the mighty works which were constantly being reported should have persuaded these townspeople that Jesus was indeed what he claimed to be, namely, the fulfilment of glorious Messianic prophecies (Luke 4:17-21), but their pettiness and probable envy prevented them from admitting the truth. So they begin to run off a list of the speaker's relatives, as if to say, "Who does he think he is anyway? Isn't he the son of the carpenter?" (From this it has been inferred that Joseph was no longer alive.) They recall that Jesus himself used to be a carpenter also (Mark 6:3). Of course, they know Mary very well, and they know Jesus' brothers—James, Joseph, Simon, and Judas—who used to live with him in the parental home. As to the sisters, presumably married, they are still living with their husbands here in Nazareth.—The question, "Were these Jesus' brothers and sisters in the sense that they had issued from the same womb?" has already been answered. See on 1:25.

581

The story is told in far greater detail by Luke (4:16-30). Matthew summarizes the result of the happening, as follows: **57. And they took offense at him.** Or: "were repelled by him." [549] His humble origin was for them a sufficient reason to reject him. **But Jesus said to them, A prophet is not without honor except in his hometown and in his own family.** Other translations, such as that a prophet is always honored except, etc., or never fails to be honored except, etc., or is without honor only in, etc., are not precise. Jesus did not say that a prophet is respected everywhere except in his hometown and family. What he did say was to the effect that wherever it might be that a prophet would be honored, certainly not in his hometown and family. [550] As to this reference to his family, particularly his brothers, it should be interpreted in the light of such other passages as 12:46-50, which, however, is not decisive in indicating the attitude of Jesus' brothers toward him at this time, and especially in the light of John 7:5, and Acts 1:14. It will then be seen that by God's grace unbelief was subsequently changed to faith.

Before leaving this passage it should be pointed out that Jesus here definitely implies that he is indeed a prophet, with the right to be honored as such (cf. Deut. 18:15, 18; Matt. 21:11; Luke 24:19; John 9:17; Acts 3:22; 7:37).

The result of the rejection at Nazareth was: **58. And because of their unbelief he did not do many miracles there.** Because the people of Nazareth rejected him they did not come to him in great numbers to be healed. So the unbelievers were not healed. Some believed and were healed. It is not necessary to go to the extreme of saying that no one was ever miraculously healed by Jesus unless he wholeheartedly believed in him with a faith to which nothing was lacking (see, for example, Luke 17:11-17). On the other hand, it would also be foolish to deny that divinely imparted faith was a great help (Matt. 8:10; 9:22, 28, 29; Mark 9:23), and that stubborn unbelief was a tremendous hindrance!

---

[549] For the verb ἐσκανδαλίζοντο from σκανδαλίζω see on 5:29, 30, especially footnote 293; see also on 11:16.

[550] Thus also H. N. Ridderbos, *op. cit.*, pp. 270, 271.

Outline of Chapter 14

Theme: *The Work Which Thou Gavest Him to Do*

CHAPTER XIV

14 1 At that time Herod the tetrarch heard the news about Jesus, 2 and said to his servants, "This is John the Baptist; he is risen from the dead; that's why these miraculous powers are at work in him." 3 For Herod had arrested John, had bound him and put him away in prison, on account of Herodias, his brother Philip's wife; 4 for John kept telling him, "It isn't right for you to have her." 5 And although he wanted to kill him, he was afraid of the people, because they were holding John to be a prophet.

6 But when Herod's birthday came, the daughter of Herodias danced before them and fascinated Herod, 7 so that with an oath he promised to give her whatever she might ask. 8 She, urged on by her mother, said, "Give me here on a platter the head of John the Baptist." 9 The king was distressed, but on account of his oaths and his dinner guests he ordered it to be given. 10 So he had John beheaded in prison. 11 The head was brought in on a platter and given to the girl, who brought it to her mother. 12 Then John's disciples came, took away the body and buried it; and they went and reported it to Jesus.

14:1-12 Herod's Wicked Birthday Party
and
John the Baptist's Gruesome Death
Cf. Mark 6:14-29; Luke 9:7-9

1, 2. At that time Herod the tetrarch heard the news about Jesus, and said to his servants, This is John the Baptist; he is risen from the dead; that's why these miraculous powers are at work in him.

The phrase "at that time" is very indefinite. In connection with the words, "he (John the Baptist) is risen from the dead" the temporal designation must refer to a period of time extending beyond John's execution, which probably occurred many months after his imprisonment. It is not improbable that the murder of Christ's herald took place in or near the beginning of the year A.D. 29. [551]

A "tetrarch" was originally a ruler of the fourth part of a region, but later the term was used to indicate any prince or governor less in rank than a king (Herod the Great) or an ethnarch (Archelaus). The "Herod" to which

---

[551] For a discussion of the tentative dates during which the various events of Christ's ministry occurred see N.T.C. on the Gospel according to John, Vol. I, pp. 36, 188, 189; also the author's *Bible Survey*, pp. 59-62.

reference is made here, and everywhere in the Gospels except in Matt. 2:1-19 and Luke 1:5, where "Herod the Great" or "Herod I" is indicated, was at this time ruler over Galilee and Perea. He continued in that position from A.D. 4 to 39, when he was banished to Lyons in Gaul. He was the son of Herod the Great by Malthace the Samaritan. Though in the Gospels (and in Acts 4:27; 13:1) he is simply called "Herod," elsewhere (see, for example, Josephus *Jewish War* I.562) his name is frequently given as "Antipas." We may therefore consider his full name to have been "Herod Antipas." The reverse is probably the case with the man who (according to the best text) is called "Philip" here in 14:3 ("his brother Philip's wife"), but who is elsewhere called "Herod," and was therefore probably "Herod Philip." For better understanding of 14:1-12 with reference both to Herod Antipas and John the Baptist what was said earlier in connection with 2:22; 4:12; and 11:1-19, should be consulted. See also the charts on pp. 161 and 189.

It seems somewhat strange that not until now did Herod Antipas hear the news or the reports about Jesus, especially in view of the fact that it was exactly this ruler's own domain that the Lord had chosen as the main sphere of his labors (4:12-16; 11:20-24). The explanation of 14:1 may well be: *a.* that although Herod Antipas had previously heard about Jesus, nevertheless the tidings of his great fame, gained through his unforgettable words and illustrious miracles, had not penetrated the walls of this ruler's residence until now; or *b.* that the palace where Herod Antipas was now staying (Machaerus, described earlier) being in Perea, far to the south, was too far removed from Capernaum and surroundings for the news concerning Jesus to have reached him earlier; or *c.* a combination of *a.* and *b.*

When the tetrarch heard the reports about Jesus he was greatly disturbed. He was impressed particularly with the reports concerning Christ's miracles, the results of mighty energies operating within him. These *works* of Jesus, even more than his *words,* shocked him to such an extent that in his restless, morbid, feverish imagination he saw in Jesus a "John the Baptist Redivivus" (restored to life). He, the guilt-laden superstitious murderer, so informed his servants.

What follows, in verses 3 ff. is an explanation of the fact, already implied in verse 2, namely, that John the Baptist had died. He had not been put to death at once but had first been arrested and imprisoned. The reason for this action against John, and also the reason for the ruler's hesitancy in putting him to death, are given in the account beginning with vss. 3, 4. **For Herod had arrested John, had bound him and put him away in prison, on account of Herodias, his brother Philip's wife; for John kept telling him, It isn't right for you to have her.**

Herodias, as shown on the chart, p. 189, was the daughter of Aristobulus, who was a son of Herod the Great by Mariamne I. She had married her half-uncle (her father's half-brother) Herod Philip, son of Herod the Great by Mariamne II. To this Herod Philip she bore a daughter, who in 14:6 (cf. Mark 6:22) is referred to simply as "the daughter of Herodias," but who by Josephus is called Salome (*Antiquities* XVIII.136). At a later time this daughter was going to marry her half-uncle, Philip the tetrarch (Luke 3:1), thereby becoming both the sister-in-law and aunt of her own mother! It should also be noted that Salome's mother Herodias had a brother who was to become King Herod Agrippa I (see Acts 12:1), and to whom reference will be made later (see p. 590).

Now Herod Antipas, on a visit to Herod Philip, became infatuated with Herodias. The two illicit lovers agreed to separate from their present marriage partners—Herodias from Herod Philip; Herod Antipas from the daughter of Aretas, king of the Nabatean Arabs—and to marry each other. This was done. When John the Baptist heard about this he rebuked Herod Antipas. He did this repeatedly. [552] There was good reason for the rebuke, for such a marriage was incestuous (Lev. 18:16; 20:21). Was it not also adulterous (Rom. 7:2, 3)?

Of course, Herodias knew very well that whenever John rebuked the tetrarch he was also, by implication, denouncing her. So she insisted—by means of constant nagging perhaps?—that John be put to death. As to Herod Antipas himself, his attitude to the accuser was not entirely hateful. In fact, there were certain qualities in John that he admired. See Mark 6:20. Was his admiration due, perhaps, to the very fact that, in sharp contrast with the flatterers usually found in the company of rulers, here was one man who dared to speak his real mind, in other words, who was righteous and holy? Was it John's manly eloquence that caused the tetrarch to hear him gladly? Was it the ruler's conscience that kept the Baptist alive? On the other hand, Herod Antipas had to "put up" with the woman whom he now considered his wife, and whose heart was seething with unmitigated, savage vengeance. Not at all to yield to her wishes seemed impossible. So he compromised. He arrested John, put him in chains, and shut him up in a terrible, deep, and hot dungeon that formed part of the castle-palace at Machaerus. [553]

In addition to the voice of the tetrarch's conscience to which Mark 6:20 by implication calls attention, there was one other reason that prevented him from immediately having John put to death, so that even when he was about to yield to his wife's wishes he did not carry out his plan. That reason is mentioned by Matthew in these words: 5. **And although he wanted to kill him, he was afraid of the people, because they were holding John to be a prophet.** In our estimate of the people's attitude toward John it is well to

---

[552] Note the imperfect tense: ἔλεγεν.
[553] In addition to the sources mentioned in footnote 465 on p. 483 see also the vivid description of this fortress and its prison in A. Edersheim, *op. cit.*, Vol. I, pp. 658-660.

avoid extremes. In the beginning it had been very favorable (3:5, 6; 11:7-9), except among the Jewish religious leaders in Jerusalem (John 1:19-28). Due in all probability to their influence the original noisy enthusiasm about John had cooled, in fact on the part of many had been replaced by hostile criticism (Matt. 11:16-18). But even this adversely critical attitude was by no means unanimous. Besides, various factors may have co-operated to reverse the general opinion once again and to make it more favorable toward the Baptist; for example, *a.* among Christ's followers, the high praise which Jesus had bestowed upon John (Matt. 11:9-11); *b.* among the general populace the sympathy aroused by the Baptist's cruel imprisonment; and *c.* the people's unfavorable attitude toward Herod Antipas, the man who had imprisoned John. Whatever other reasons there may have been, it is a fact that the favorable attitude of the multitude toward John, at least to the extent of regarding him to be (or, after his death, to have been) a prophet, is reported not only here in 14:5 but also in 21:26.

What was it, then, that nevertheless brought about the murder of John the Baptist at the order of Herod Antipas? The answer is given in verses **6-10. But when Herod's birthday came, the daughter of Herodias danced before them and fascinated Herod, so that with an oath he promised to give her whatever she might ask. She, urged on by her mother, said, Give me here on a platter the head of John the Baptist. The king was distressed, but on account of his oaths and his dinner guests he ordered it to be given. So he had John beheaded in prison.**

The day arrived when the birthday of Herod Antipas was celebrated. This gave Herodias the opportunity for which she had been anxiously waiting. There was, of course, a banquet. For women to recline with men at the same table was contrary to the mores of the times (cf. Esther 1:9). However, when the men needed to be entertained, the distaff side was by no means ignored. From the story of Esther we learn that Queen Vashti refused to be so used. Queen Herodias was of a different disposition. She was willing even to have her own daughter used for such a purpose. The queen stood ready to employ whatever means was necessary to wreak vengeance on her enemy, John the Baptist. So, with the hearty consent of Herodias, Salome danced "in the midst of"—here probably to be rendered "before" or "in front of"—the invited male guests. Had her mother, through womanly intuition aided by intimate knowledge of her husband's weaknesses, guessed what was going to happen? Had she even planned it that way perhaps? However that may have been, when things began to work out the way she wanted she was ready to strike. Evidently her daughter was of one mind with her.

It takes but little imagination to surmise what kind of guests a Herod would have invited to such a feast. See Mark 6:21. Those, of course, to whom the gratification of sensual delights meant everything. Cf. Esther 1:3, 10; Dan. 5:1, 4, 23. Were they even sober as they watched Salome go through her rhythmic movements, dancing bewitchingly and seductively? Her glamorous appearance and exotic movements pleased Herod to such an extent that he, losing all sense of propriety and dignity—if he ever had any!—and not suspecting that the words he was about to utter might have serious results, promised under oath to give Salome whatever she might ask, "even to the half of my kingdom" (Mark 6:23). The girl, at the instigation of her mother, answered, "Give me here on a platter the head of John the Baptist." Moreover, she wanted it "immediately" (Mark 6:25). [554]

Herod Antipas was definitely in a quandary. The "king"—the title is used now in a loose, very general sense, for technically this man was not a king and was never to become one—was distressed. His conscience told him that issuing an order for the execution of John was wrong. It amounted to murder. He must also have realized that by doing this he would be heaping upon himself the ill-will of all those people who thought highly of John. On the other hand,

> Heaven has no rage like love to hatred turned,
> Nor hell a fury like a woman scorned
> —Congreve, *The Mourning*
> *Bride*, Act III.

Imagine the scorn Herodias would have poured out upon the tetrarch had he refused to play her game now! But at this point she is not even mentioned. She has done her part and can afford to wait developments. The text however does make mention of the consideration that must have weighed heaviest in the "king's" mental balances, namely, the oaths made publicly and probably also emphatically. How could he ever violate such oaths? [555]

It can be argued that the way out of his predicament would have been for him to say to Salome, "I promised to favor you with a *gift;* I certainly did not promise to commit a *crime.*" Or else, "I promised *you,* not your mother, a gift." Best of all would have been, "I see now that I sinned when I made this promise; hence I retract it." But Herod lacked the courage, humility, and perhaps also the sobriety or clarity of mind, to consider such answers.

---

[554] The noun πίναξ can also be translated "plate" or "dish"; cf. "pine-board." In modern Greek πίναξ means a board or table. The rendering of Mark 6:25b found in the A.V.—"I will that thou give me by and by in a charger the head of John the Baptist"—was undoubtedly excellent in its day, but fails to convey any clear meaning today.

[555] Josephus mentions still another reason that may have influenced Herod in reaching his decision, namely, that with John the Baptist still alive and popular the people might have been willing to follow his advice even if he should urge them to start a political revolt (*Antiquities* XVIII.118, 119). Nothing of the kind is hinted in Scripture. Nevertheless, there may have been some truth in it. It is not in conflict with anything in Matthew's or Mark's text. But we may rest assured that the inspired authors, in stressing the matter of the oaths given before the dinner guests, are stating that which for Herod Antipas really decided the issue.

Of supreme importance to him were the oaths made before the guests, and the necessity not to "lose face" before them.

So the order was issued, and Herod Antipas "had John beheaded in prison." [556] Continued: 11. **The head was brought in on a platter and given to the girl, who brought it to her mother.** It frequently happens that from a banquet dishes are brought to those unable to attend. This, then, was the portion received by the wicked queen. Revenge, how sweet? Rather, how gruesome, and how productive of bitter consequences for both "king" and queen!

As to the results of the tetrarch's action, considered as a whole (rejecting his own wife, marrying Herodias, and murdering John) note the following:

a. *The increased displeasure of many of the Jews*

b. *The wrath of Aretas, the father of Herod's rejected wife*

Aretas bitterly resented what Herod Antipas had done to his daughter. He therefore waged war against him and "in the ensuing battle the entire army of Herod was destroyed" (Josephus *Antiquities* XVIII.114, 116, for both points *a.* and *b.*).

c. *Banishment*

Gaius Caesar, better known to us as Emperor Caligula, who ruled over the Roman empire from A.D. 37-41, soon after his accession promoted the brother of Herodias, namely, Herod Agrippa I (see Acts 12:1), to the rank of king, with all the honors and emoluments pertaining to that high position. This made Herodias very jealous. She begrudged her brother his rise to power and egged her husband on to embark to Rome and seek equal status. For a while Herod Antipas resisted, but he finally gave in. Herod Agrippa I, however, hearing about this, dispatched Fortunatus, one of his freedmen, to Rome, bearing letters showing that even now Herod Antipas was allied with the Parthians in a conspiracy against the emperor. At the very time when the emperor was greeting Herod Antipas he was also reading these letters from Herod Agrippa. Since the tetrarch was unable to disprove the evidence against him which the letters contained, he was deprived of all his powers and condemned to perpetual exile in Lyons of Gaul. His tetrarchy was added to the kingdom over which Agrippa reigned.

As to Herodias? She was with her husband when this sentence was pronounced. When the emperor learned that Herodias was the sister of Agrippa, he, out of consideration for her brother, did not banish her and even allowed her to keep all her personal property. To do her justice it must be stated that whatever spark of virtue was still left in her was shown at this

---

[556] Though in rendering πέμψας ἀπεκεφάλισεν most translators use two verbs ("sent and beheaded"), just why this is needed is not clear, especially because it is well known that in such combinations the idea of "sent" recedes to the background. With N.E.B. I therefore prefer, "he . . . had John beheaded." So also the Dutch Bible (Nieuwe Vertaling): ". . . en hij liet Johannes in de gevangenis onthoofden."

time, for she decided to remain with her husband and to go into exile with him. [557]

The story of John the Baptist is concluded as follows: **12. Then John's disciples came, took away the body and buried it; and they went and reported it to Jesus.** For the disciples of John see on 9:14; 11:1-3; also N.T.C. on John 3:25, 26. In view of the fact that these men had been permitted to visit John in his prison it is not surprising that they were also allowed to provide an honorable burial for his decapitated body. The very fact that these disciples, now that their master had been murdered, reported this to Jesus would seem to indicate that they were on friendly terms with the latter; not only that, but that they believed in him. Does not this also seem to indicate that "the answer Jesus had sent to John (11:14) must thus have satisfied John"? [558] For more on John the Baptist see Summary of Chapter 11, p. 506.

---

13 Now upon hearing this, Jesus withdrew from there privately by boat to a lonely place. But when the crowds heard about it they followed him on foot from the towns. 14 So, as he came out he saw a great multitude. He was moved with compassion for them and healed their sick.

15 And when it was evening the disciples came to him and said, "This is a lonely place, and it is already late in the day; dismiss the crowds, that they may go into the villages and buy food for themselves." 16 But Jesus said to them, "They do not need to go away; y o u give them to eat!" 17 They said to him, "All we have here is five bread-cakes and two fishes." 18 He said, "Bring them here to me." 19 Then he ordered the people to sit down on the grass, took the five bread-cakes and the two fishes, and looking up to heaven gave thanks. He then broke the bread-cakes and gave them to the disciples, and the disciples (gave them) to the people. 20 All ate and were filled. They picked up what was left over of the pieces: twelve baskets full. 21 The number of men who ate was about five thousand, not counting women and children.

14:13-21 *The Feeding of the Five Thousand*
Cf. Mark 6:30-44; Luke 9:10-17; John 6:1-14

It is clear from Matt. 14:1, 2, 12, 13; Mark 6:29-32; and Luke 9:7-10, that at least the following items belong to the interval between the execution of John and the withdrawal of Jesus to a desolate place (Matt. 14:13): *a.* John's burial, *b.* the Baptist's disciples' report to Jesus, *c.* the report of The Twelve to Jesus regarding their mission tour, and *d.* the report to Herod Antipas regarding the works of Jesus, causing the tetrarch to exclaim, "This is John the Baptist; he is risen from the dead; that's why these miraculous powers are at work in him." All of this may well indicate an activity covering several weeks. It is not strange, therefore, that the feeding of the five

---

[557] See the very moving account of this attempt of Herod Antipas and Herodias that failed so dismally, in Josephus *Antiquities* XVIII.238-256.
[558] R. C. H. Lenski, *op. cit.,* p. 544.

thousand, described here in 14:13-21 took place when Passover, probably April of the year A.D. 29, was already approaching, as is clear from John 6:4. The Great Galilean Ministry, probably extending from December, A.D. 27 to April, A.D. 29, is coming to an end. One more year and the Lamb of God will by means of his death on the cross render satisfaction for the sins of all who trust in him.

13. **Now upon hearing this, Jesus withdrew from there privately by boat to a lonely place.** In view of the immediately preceding context it is natural to interpret this passage as indicating that what Jesus heard was the report of the disciples of John the Baptist regarding the death and burial of their leader and the events that had led to his execution. The shocking intelligence of the Baptist's cruel death required reflection and quiet meditation. Besides, the disciples had recently returned from a mission tour. They must have felt the need to be alone with the Master to tell him "all about" what had happened. On the busy, western shores—especially in Capernaum—there was no opportunity for leisure and relaxation. This point is distinctly mentioned by Mark (6:30-32; cf. Luke 9:10, 11). There is no need, therefore, to link the present withdrawal too closely with the terror in the heart of Herod Antipas, as if Jesus, realizing that the time for him to lay down his life had not yet arrived, were fleeing from him. It must be borne in mind that the withdrawal here mentioned was of a very temporary nature. In fact, presently Jesus is back on the western shore once more, at Gennesaret (Matt. 14:34; cf. Mark 6:53), and a little later in the synagogue at Capernaum, where he delivers the discourse on The Bread of Life (John 6:59). The real Retirement Ministry, therefore, begins not at this point but at Matt. 15:21; Mark 7:24; see above, pp. 8, 9.

The statement that Jesus withdrew "privately" does not mean that he crossed the sea all by himself, without his disciples. His disciples were with him (14:15-19, 22). In John 6:3-14 some are even mentioned by name. The statement means that he wanted to get away from the multitude to be alone for a while with his disciples. The lonely or desolate place to which Jesus and his little company withdrew was in the neighborhood of Bethsaida (Luke 9:10), that is in all probability Bethsaida Julias, originally a fishing village located on the northeastern shore of the Sea of Galilee. By the tetrarch Philip it had been rebuilt, strengthened, and named in honor of the daughter of Augustus. [559]

About a mile south of this town there is a little plain of rich silt soil. A hill rises just behind this plain. Jesus went up into this hill (John 6:3; cf. Matt. 14:23). Continued: **But when the crowds heard about it they followed him on foot from the towns.** The people from the various towns and villages,

---

[559] For the reasons in support of the position that it was indeed Bethsaida Julias see N.T.C. on the Gospel according to John, Vol. I, pp. 216-218.

noticing that Jesus had stepped into a boat and was heading for Bethsaida Julias, walked around the northern shore of the lake in order to be with him once more. They were definitely impressed with this Worker of miracles (John 6:2). They were willing to brave any obstacles to be in his company.

14. So, as he came out he saw a great multitude. He was moved with compassion for them and healed their sick. When Jesus came out from the place on the slope of the hill, to which he had already arrived (verse 13), he saw a great multitude. John describes the scene as follows: "Jesus went up into the hill . . . he lifted up his eyes and observed that a vast crowd was coming toward him" (6:3, 5). Luke presents the same idea: "the crowds . . . followed him, and he welcomed them." [560] Instead of addressing this vast crowd as follows, "I came here for rest, quiet, and meditation; so please go home and see me some other time," "he was moved with compassion for them." Another excellent rendering would be, "his heart went out to them." [561] For a fuller discussion of this sympathy see on 8:17 and on 9:36. The needs of people, sick, ignorant, disconsolate, and also hungry (as they were soon to become, verses 15, 16), meant far more to him than his own convenience and ease. So he healed their sick (cf. 4:23, 24; 8:16, 17; 9:35; 11:4, 5), this in spite of a. *his own* need for rest, and b. *their* earthly, materialistic motivations (John 6:2, 15, 26, 66). It must not escape us that by doing this under such circumstances he was also setting an example for the disciples (10:8), and in a sense for the entire church throughout the ages (Matt. 5:43-48; Luke 6:27-36; John 13:14, 15; Eph. 4:32—5:2).

Jesus not only healed the sick but also spent some time in teaching the people (Mark 6:34). All this activity must have taken a considerable amount of time. Almost at once after Jesus from the place where he was had stepped out toward the people, he had asked Philip, testing him, "How are we to buy bread-cakes that these people may eat?" Philip had answered, "Bread-cakes for two hundred denarii would not be sufficient for them so that each might get a little something." So Philip had struggled with this problem, Andrew also. All the time Jesus knew exactly what he was going to do (John 6:5-9). But the disciples were at a loss what to do, and this in spite of all the miracles they had already witnessed. **15. And when it was evening the**

---

[560] See F. W. Groshcide, *Het Heilig Evangelie volgens Mattheus* (*Commentaar op het Nieuwe Testament*), p. 233: "From the remote place to which Jesus had arrived he steps forward and meets the multitude." This is also Lenski's view, *op. cit.*, pp. 545, 546. It certainly seems to be supported by Matthew, Luke, and John, all of whom picture Jesus as disembarking before the arrival of the great multitude. *They* follow. *He* gets there first, goes up the hill, then sees the crowds gathering and goes out to meet them. When three of the four Gospels are in agreement on this point, as they are, it is not wise to overthrow all this and to follow what Mark 6:33b (of which there are many textual variants) may seem to say.

[561] The verb is ἐσπλαγχνίσθη. On the cognate noun see footnote 39, p. 58 of N.T.C. on Philippians.

disciples came to him and said, This is a lonely place, and it is already late in the day; dismiss the crowds, that they may go into the villages and buy food for themselves. Though the sun had not yet set it was becoming late. By means of his miracles and teachings the Lord so captivated the vast crowds that even now they were not leaving. If they were to depart they must be sent away. So the disciples remind their Teacher of the loneliness of the place and the lateness of the hour.

"This is a lonely place," they say. In other words, this is not a city, containing all kinds of places within easy reach where food may be bought; it is a desolate region. To go to any of the surrounding villages in search of food will take time. Besides, "It is already late in the day," or more literally, "The time is already past," referring perhaps to the time when food is generally bought. Accordingly they advise Jesus to send the people away right now in order that they may still try to go to the nearby hamlets to buy food for themselves.

Christ's answer was striking: **16. But Jesus said to them, They do not need to go away; *y o u* give them to eat.** This demand baffles the disciples. Does he mean that their very limited material resources will suffice to feed such a vast multitude? Certainly he cannot mean that! See Mark 6:37; Luke 9:13.

What then does the Master mean when he tells the disciples that they must supply food for this vast multitude? It may be impossible to give a fully satisfactory answer to this question. A few things can be pointed out however.

a. Jesus means that these men must not be so quick to shake off responsibility. They were often ready to do this very thing, and to say, "Dismiss the crowds" (here in 14:15); "Send her [the Syrophoenician woman] away" (15:23). They even "rebuked" the parents who brought their little children to Jesus that he might bless them (19:13). See also Luke 9:49, 50. "Don't bother the Master and don't bother us," was too often their slogan. In the light of this evidence it is safe to say that Jesus wants to remind these men of the fact that simply trying to get rid of people in need is not the solution. It is certainly not God's way of doing things (Matt. 5:43-48; 11:25-30; Luke 6:27-38; John 3:16).

b. He wants them to ask, seek, and knock (Matt. 7:7, 8); in other words, to claim God's promise for themselves, and to go to him who is able to supply every need. He who, when there was a shortage, supplied wine (John 2:1-11), can he not also supply bread?

c. In view of the fact that "bread," as the term is used in this account (see verses 17, 19), while referring to be sure, to that which supplies a physical need, is also symbolical of Jesus as the Bread of Life (John 6:35, 48), is he not also telling these "fishers of men" that they must be the means in God's hand to supply the *spiritual* needs of the people?

594

17. They said to him, All we have here is five bread-cakes and two fishes. It was Jesus himself who told his disciples to see how many bread-cakes they had. "When they knew they said, 'Five, and two fishes' " (Mark 6:38). John's Gospel supplies further details: "One of the disciples, Andrew, the brother of Simon Peter, said to Jesus, 'There is a young lad here who has five barley-cakes and two fishes, but what are these for so many?' " (6:8, 9). For "bread" the original uses a term that should not be rendered "loaves," since this English word has a meaning that is entirely foreign to the sense of the original. What is meant is something that resembles a pancake, flat and round. At times the term used in the original simply means *bread.*

What deserves the emphasis here in verse 17 is that these men are giving an answer not of faith but of near-despair, "All we have here is . . ."; even more literally, "We do not have (anything) here except five bread-cakes and two fishes." Evidently the disciples had not caught the real meaning of the exhortation, "*Y o u* give them to eat." Their Lord is now going to strengthen their faith by means of an unforgettable miracle: **18, 19. He said, Bring them here to me. Then he ordered the people to sit down on the grass, took the five bread-cakes and the two fishes, and looking up to heaven gave thanks. He then broke the bread-cakes and gave them to the disciples, and the disciples (gave them) to the people.** Of all the evangelists Matthew is the only one who reports the order, "Bring them here to me." Implied is, of course, that the five bread-cakes and the two fishes are bought from the lad and brought to Jesus. The Lord then issues another order, namely, for the people to sit down on the grass. This command was easy to obey, since about this time of the year the slopes of the hill must have been covered with grass. So the people reclined against the hillside. According to Mark 6:40 they reclined in groups, by hundreds and by fifties.

By means of this grouping a charming picture is formed: "And they reclined group by group," or possibly even "garden-bed by garden-bed," *if* the basic meaning of the original phrase [562] in the Marcan passage still shines through, which, however, is by no means certain. We may have to be satisfied with the weakened sense "in groups" or "group by group." Nevertheless, there was this strikingly colorful arrangement of people dressed in their bright garments, reclining under the blue vault of heaven, upon the green grass with the Sea of Galilee nearby.

Jesus takes the five bread-cakes and the two fishes. He looks up to heaven. For this lifting heavenward of the eyes in prayer see also Ps. 25:15; 121:1; 123:1, 2; 141:8, 145:15; John 11:41; 17:1; I Tim. 2:8. [563]

Looking up to heaven Jesus "blessed," thus literally. The same verb is also

---

[562] The phrase is πρασιαὶ πρασιαί.
[563] The subject *Prayer Postures* is treated in some detail in N.T.C. on I and II Timothy and Titus, pp. 103-104.

found in the Synoptic parallels (Mark 6:41; Luke 9:16). John, on the other hand, has "having given thanks" (6:11). Solution: "blessed" in this instance means "gave thanks," and can be thus translated. When a person blesses or praises God is he not giving thanks to him? [564] It was the custom of the Jews to thank God before starting a meal. However, since it is abundantly clear from the Gospels that our Lord never spoke as the scribes, that is, that his words were always characterized by freshness and originality (cf. Matt. 7:29), we may well believe that this was true also on the present occasion.

Then from the bread-cakes Jesus begins to break off fragments of edible size. He gives these to his disciples who carry them (in baskets collected here and there from the crowd?) to the people. With the fishes the procedure is somewhat similar.

The striking beauty of the account is heightened by the fact that only a few simple words are used to relate the miracle of the multiplication of the fragments. One might even say that the miracle is implied rather than expressed: **20. All ate and were filled.** Exactly when did the bread and the fish multiply? "Under his hands"? Probably, but even this is not stated. All we really know is that there was plenty bread—in fact, plenty and to spare—for everybody: at some point of time between the breaking of the bread and the reception of the fragments by the people the miracle must have occurred. All—men, women, children—ate and "were filled," that is, "had all they wanted," "were fully satisfied." For the meaning and history of the verb used in the original see footnote 267 on p. 274. **They**—the disciples—**picked up what was left over of the pieces: twelve baskets full.** Wastefulness is sinfulness. Besides, even the rabbis had carefully regulated the manner in which what remained of a meal must be gathered and used. So the people were accustomed to this idea. There were others who needed something to eat: the young lad, if he were still around, the disciples, the poor on the day of tomorrow, Jesus himself. Some people must have taken more fragments than they could eat. When the disciples went back, probably each equipped with a large wicker-basket, they collected not less than twelve baskets full of left-over fragments.

To emphasize the greatness of the miracle the size of the crowd is now indicated: **21. The number of men who ate was about five thousand, not counting women and children.** It is probable that the reason—at least one of the reasons—why the men alone were counted was that they constituted the overwhelming majority. One can hardly imagine that many women to whom the care of the little ones was entrusted would have walked all the way from Capernaum and surroundings to the northeastern shores of the Sea of Galilee. Some of this terrain is marshy and difficult. Not counting women

---

[564] In the present tense, first per. sing. indic. the two verbs are εὐλογέω and εὐχαριστέω.

and children, no less than five thousand had been miraculously fed. Because the people had been arranged in groups of fifty and one hundred the tally must have been easy.

To try to explain or rationalize what happened here is foolish. An example of this attempt is described in N.T.C. on the Gospel according to John, Vol. I, p. 227.

As to the significance of the miracle, the following should be noted:

a. It points beyond itself, that is, from the gift to the Giver. This is clear not only from Mark 6:52 (cf. 8:17-21; Matt. 16:8-11) but also, and especially, from Christ's discourse on The Bread of Life, found in chapter 6 of John's Gospel; see especially verses 35, 48. Jesus is described as the perfect Savior, the One who provides for both body and soul.

b. It also points to Christ as the Fulfilment of Old Testament prophecy, the One to whom the prophets point forward. Had Moses given the Israelites manna (Exod. 16:15)? This was but a shadow of him who was "the real bread out of heaven" (John 6:32). Had Elijah been used by God to see to it that the widow's jar of flour was never empty and that her jug of oil did not diminish (I Kings 17:16)? And did the people remember how through Elisha a hundred men had been fed with twenty barley-cakes, so that there had been something left over (II Kings 4:43, 44)? Here, with Jesus at Bethsaida Julias, were more than five thousand people for whom five bread-cakes and two fishes were more than sufficient. It is not surprising that the people said, "This is really the prophet who is to come into the world" (John 6:14; cf. Deut. 18:15-18). [565]

Yes, the people were filled with enthusiasm—the type of fervor which takes hold of a Jewish mob at the season of Passover. They were ready to proceed posthaste to Jerusalem, holding in their midst their *strong man*, that they might crown him king! But he whose kingdom is not of this world (John 18:36) dismisses this multitude, the disciples also, and proceeds toward the top of the hill, that he may be by himself—alone with his heavenly Father, as will be shown in the next section.

---

22 Then immediately Jesus made the disciples get into the boat and go ahead of him to the other side, till he should send the crowds away. 23 Now after he had sent the crowds away he went up into the hill by himself to pray, and when evening fell he was there alone. 24 But the boat was already many stadia from the land, battered by the waves, for the wind was from the opposite direction. 25 And in the fourth watch of the night Jesus came to them, walking on the sea. 26 Now when the disciples saw him walking on the sea they were frightened and said, "It's a ghost!" And they screamed with fear. 27 At once Jesus spoke to them, "Take courage, it is I; do not be afraid!" 28 Then Peter answered him, "Lord, if it be thou, bid me to come to thee on the water." 29 He said, "Come." So Peter stepped out of the boat, walked on the water, and came toward Jesus. 30 However, when he saw the wind he got scared, and as he began to sink he cried out,

---

[565] See G. E. P. Cox, *The Gospel according to St. Matthew*, London, 1952, p. 103.

"Lord, save me." 31 Immediately Jesus reached out his hand, grabbed him, and said to him, "O man of little faith, why did you waver?" 32 And when they stepped into the boat the wind ceased. 33 Those in the boat worshiped him, saying, "Thou art indeed God's Son."

14:22-33 *Walking on the Water*
Cf. Mark 6:45-52; John 6:15-21

This section pictures separation, storm and stress (verses 22-24), fright (verses 25, 26), reassurance (verse 27), wavering (verses 28-32), and worship (verses 32, 33). The first part (verses 22-27) might be viewed as an elaboration of the theme: *On the Stormy Sea Christ Speaks Peace to His Disciples.* So viewed, there is a description *a.* of the disciples without Jesus (verses 22-24); *b.* of the disciples with the unknown Jesus (verses 25, 26); and *c.* of the disciples with Jesus, whom they now recognize because he speaks peace to them (verse 27).

The description of the disciples without Jesus begins as follows: **22. Then immediately Jesus made the disciples get into the boat and go ahead of him to the other side, till he should send the crowds away.** Why did Jesus wish to send the crowds away? A simple answer would be: by now many of these people have been with Jesus a long time, and are a considerable distance away from their homes; moreover, on the basis of 14:15 it can be added that the region is about to be—or is already—engulfed in darkness. Another very general answer, applicable to many an occasion, suggests itself, namely, the people had to be *sent* home because, having just now witnessed—rather *experienced*—an astounding miracle, they are by no means eager of their own accord to leave the Miracle-worker. There is, however, a more specific reason for the decision of Jesus to dismiss this multitude. It is given in John 6:15: the people "were about to come and take him by force that they might make him king." Jesus, whose kingdom is spiritual, refuses to become involved in any such definitely earthly, Jewish, political scheme.

Being fully aware of the weaknesses of his own disciples, for whom co-operation with the throng in its unholy political planning constituted a real temptation (Matt. 20:20; Acts 1:6), the Lord first of all causes his constant companions to get into a boat and to go ahead of him to the other side. This phrase "to the other side" must mean to the side opposite from Bethsaida Julias.

Accordingly, the disciples, leaving the northeastern shore—sometime between 7:30 and 9:00 P.M.?—start to row (Mark 6:48; John 6:19) toward western Bethsaida (Mark 6:45), in the vicinity of Capernaum (John 6:16, 17) and of the plain of Gennesaret (Matt. 14:34; Mark 6:53).

One reason, perhaps the most important of all, for the dismissal of the disciples and of the crowd, has not yet been mentioned: Jesus wanted to be by himself. He desired to enter into solitary communion with his Father, as

598

is clear from verse 23. Now after he had sent the crowds away he went up into the hill by himself to pray, and when evening fell he was there alone. Far more significance must be attached to these words than is generally done. During his earthly sojourn Jesus spent much time in prayer. He prayed in lonely places, on a hill, in Gethsemane; in the morning, in the evening, sometimes all night (Mark 1:35; 6:46; Luke 5:15, 16; 6:12; 9:18; 22:41, 42; Heb. 5:7; etc.).

Not only did he pray for himself; the recorded prayers of Christ offer abundant evidence that he prayed also for others. The longest of these recorded supplications (John 17) may be divided as follows: a prayer for himself (verses 1-5), for the apostles (verses 6-19), and for the Church Universal (verses 20-26). Matt. 11:25 records a prayer of thanksgiving for those whom he affectionately calls his "babes." He even prayed for his tormentors (Luke 23:34, assuming this passage to be authentic). He made intercession for Simon (Luke 22:31, 32), and for the people who were standing around at Lazarus' tomb (John 11:41, 42). Even now he not only makes intercession but actually lives in heaven for the very purpose of making intercession (Heb. 7:25).

We are on safe ground therefore in maintaining that in the quiet of the evening indicated here in Matt. 14:23 Jesus, in solitary communion with his Father, prayed not for himself alone, but also for his disciples.

The picture of Jesus on the hill praying for himself, his disciples, etc., must not be separated from that of the disciples on the stormy sea: **24. But the boat was already many stadia from the land, battered by the waves, for the wind was from the opposite direction.** John's Gospel mentions twenty-five to thirty stadia, a stadium being about one-eighth of a mile. Hence, the boat had proceeded a distance of "about three or four miles." Now if the distance between the point from which the disciples started to the place where they landed was five miles, as seems probable, then these men were now indeed "in the midst of the sea" (which is one of the variant readings here in 14:24 and the accepted text in Mark 6:47). Then, while it was already dark a storm arose. "And the sea was getting rough, as a strong wind was blowing" (John 6:18). The boat was being "battered" or "distressed" [566] by the waves, says Matthew. Besides, the wind was from the

---

[566] Matthew uses the pres. pass. participle, nom., sing. neut. βασανιζόμενον, from βασανίζω. It reminds us of the centurion's "boy" who was "fearfully tortured" (Matt. 8:6), of the demoniacs who asked Jesus, "Do you come here to torture us before the apointed time?" (8:29), of Lot, who was "distressed" or "vexed" by the lawless deeds of his wicked neighbors (II Peter 2:8); to which can be added the instances of the use of this word in Rev. 9:5; 11:10; 12:2; 14:10; 20:10. Jesus came to heal those who were distressed by—"torments" (Matt. 4:24); the noun βάσανος (cf. our English word "basan-ite") indicating *a.* basically, a touchstone to test gold and other metals; *b.* the instrument of torture by which men—for example, slaves—were tested, i.e., forced to reveal the truth; and *c.* as in 4:24, where it occurs in the plural, *torments* or *acute pains.*

opposite direction; hence, blowing from the west. No wonder that the men were not making any appreciable headway! For a more detailed account of such storms on the Sea of Galilee see above, on 8:24.

If we had only 14:24 the situation would be gloomy indeed: the violent wind from the opposite direction, the darkness, the angry billows, the absence of Jesus! But, as already indicated, we also have verse 23. O that an artist would reproduce this combined scene: the disciples apparently in peril of losing their lives on this stormy sea, but Jesus on that hill interceding for them, undoubtedly including also this petition, that they might be safeguarded against misleading Messianic conceptions and that their lives might be spared so that they would be able to carry out their tasks. Seen from that angle, were not these men perfectly safe after all? And does not this combined picture have many applications for the present day and for every time of trouble and distress?

But Jesus intended to do more for the disciples than pray for them. **25. And in the fourth watch of the night Jesus came to them, walking on the sea.** The fourth watch is from 3 to 6 A.M. (the first being from 6 to 9 P.M., the second from 9 P.M. to 12 midnight, and the third from midnight until 3 A.M.). These many hours—shall we say "between six and ten hours"?—the disciples had been harassed by the elements, and they were still a considerable distance away from their destination. It was then that Jesus came to them, actually walking on the heaving and falling billows. The disciples must discover that they have a Savior who is able not only to still the storm but even to use it as his pathway! For him the very "laws of nature" are means for the effectuation of his purpose. The winds cannot overturn him. Are they not his willing messengers? The waves cannot drown him. Are they not his obedient servants? The disciples however were alarmed because of what they thought they were seeing: **26. Now when the disciples saw him walking on the sea they were frightened and said, It's a ghost! And they screamed with fear.** With the boat heading southwest, the rowers must have been facing northeast. By the little light there was—coming perhaps from the pre-Passover moon intermittently peeping from between the dark clouds—they see, probably not far away from them, what looked like a man coming toward them from the direction of Bethsaida Julias. Of course, it could not be a man, for men cannot walk on water! Of this the boat's occupants are sure. They do not realize how wrong they are. Overcome with fear [567] they scream, "It's a ghost!" They were looking at their Lord and Savior but they thought that they saw an infernal, haunting specter; literally "a phantasm," one of the meanings of this English word being "ghost."

This incident, too, has many applications, for how often do not believers

---

[567] Greek ἐταράχθησαν third per. pl. aor. indic. passive of ταράσσω, a very interesting verb, see on 2:3.

ascribe their unpleasant experiences to the machinations of some sinister power, when in reality they are the manifestations of Christ's loving care? How frequently does not that which at first appears to be a stumbling-block turn out to be a stepping-stone to glory? See Gen. 42:36; 50:20; Rom. 8:28. Continued: 27. **At once Jesus spoke to them, Take courage, it is I; do not be afraid** [or: **stop being afraid**]. The bracing words, "Take courage" or "Be of good cheer," so characteristic of Christ, have been discussed in connection with 9:2; see on that passage. [568] "It is I," hence, it is the very Lord who has chosen y o u as his disciples, has been guiding y o u step by step, and has already given y o u so many proofs of his power and love. So, do not be afraid.

Is it not encouraging how very often in Scripture God—or Jesus Christ—tells his people, "Do not be afraid"? A partial list of passages in which this exhortation is found would be Josh. 1:9; 11:6; II Kings 19:6; II Chron. 20:15; 32:7; Neh. 4:14; Ps. 49:16 (cf. 27:1); 91:5; Isa. 10:24; 37:6; 44:8; Matt. 17:7; 28:10; Mark 5:36; Luke 12:4; John 14:1, 27; Acts 18:9; I Peter 3:14. If even we today receive encouragement from the reading of these many assurances, and thrill when we listen to F. Mendelssohn's "Be not afraid" (from The Elijah), how unforgettably precious must not the comfort have been which the disciples received when by means of this brief command, spoken by the One they adored, they were lifted in one moment from crushing fear to exuberant joy! Moreover, this "Be not afraid" is well-founded. It is firmly anchored in limitless power and infinite, intensely personal love.

The effect of Christ's words upon Peter is now dramatically portrayed: **28. Then Peter answered him, Lord, if it be thou, bid me to come to thee on the water.** Impulsive Peter is immediately ready for action. He trusts and loves the Lord, and therefore desires to be with him. From more than one aspect this trust of Peter merits admiration: *a.* It is the very opposite of the fear which the disciples, not excluding Peter, have expressed a moment ago, when they said, "It's a ghost!" Peter's "if" ("if it be thou") is not that of doubt but amounts to "since." *b.* It implies consciousness of utter dependence on the authority and the power of Jesus. Peter knows that without the Master's permission he will not be allowed to walk on the water, and that apart from Christ's power he will not be able to do so. So he asks that this permission and this power be granted. Peter's action, therefore, starts out as a deed of faith and devotion. Solid evidence of recklessness on his part (see, by contrast, 4:5-7) is completely or at least largely lacking. Also, evidence of boastfulness is absent. We are doing this apostle an injustice when we accuse

---

[568] The verb is θαρσεῖτε, sec. pers. pl. pres. imperat. of θαρσέω. A similar verb is θαρρέω. In the sense in which the latter is a synonym of the one used here in Matt. 14:27 it is found in Heb. 13:6 (in the form θαρροῦντας), in which being courageous is again very closely linked with the presence of the Lord and the help he grants.

him of wishing to "show off" before the others. *c*. It shows that Peter grasped something of the significance of Christ's constant teaching with respect to the very close relationship existing between the Lord and those whom he calls his own. The very thought, "If Jesus can walk on the water, so, with strength imparted by him, can I," is admirable.

We are not surprised therefore that Jesus, without a word of rebuke or criticism, gave permission: **29. He said, Come. So Peter stepped out of the boat, walked on the water, and came toward Jesus.** He walked (literally) "on the waters," idiomatic plural (cf. Gen. 1:2; Deut. 5:8; Josh. 3:13; Ps. 107:23). Perhaps this plural stems from the fact that in such connections the emphasis is not so much on water as contrasted with land or air or fire, as on the vastness of its expanse and the boisterousness of its many waves.

For the idea that before the feet of Peter the waters were smooth [569] I can find no support. The stilling of the storm did not take place until later (see verse 32). Besides, this "smooth water" concept is contradicted by verse **30. However, when he saw the wind he got scared, and as he began to sink he cried out, Lord save me.** Peter "saw the wind," that is, he saw the effect of the wind upon the billows. As long as he concentrated his attention on Jesus all went well. But the moment he took notice of the boisterous winds and the surging waters he became frightened. Had he been *somewhat* over confident? However that may be, his faith, though "little," was not "lost," for as he began to sink [570] he cried to Jesus for help.

A most interesting person, this Peter. He seems to do nothing by halves. When he is good he is very good, when he is bad he is very bad, and when he repents he weeps bitterly. He turns from trust to doubt (14:28, 30), from clear and open profession of Jesus as the Christ to rebuking that very Christ (16:16, 22), from a vehement declaration of loyalty to base denial (26:33-35, 74), from "By no means shalt thou wash my feet ever" to "Not my feet only but also my hands and my head" (John 13:8, 9). See also John 20:4, 6; Gal. 2:11, 12. Nevertheless, by the grace and power of the Lord this "Simon" was transformed into a true "Peter."

The Lord does not disappoint his wavering disciple, who in his distress has cried to him for help: **31. Immediately Jesus reached out his hand, grabbed him, and said to him, O man of little faith, why did you waver?**

Strictly speaking it would not have been necessary for Jesus to reach out his hand to rescue Peter. A simple command would have sufficed. But was not the method which the Lord actually used reassuring? Jesus wanted Peter to feel his love as well as to experience his power. See also on 8:3 and 9:25.

The Lord calls Peter a "man of little faith." For this expression see on 6:30. Doubt or wavering had entered Peter's heart because for a moment he

---

[569] R. C. H. Lenski, *op. cit.*, pp. 556, 557.

[570] Greek καταποντίζεσθαι; literally, "to plunge *down* into *the sea*," a very picturesque word.

had looked away from Jesus, that is, he had failed to rest the eye of his faith upon the Master. He had not sufficiently taken to heart the comfort he should have derived from the presence, promises, power, and love of Christ.

32. **And when they stepped into the boat the wind ceased.** Jesus had just shown that he could make use of the elements of nature. Now he proves that he is also able to cause them to stop their raging. He had done this before (8:23-27). At *that* time the storm was at its height when he was in the boat. He stilled it. *Now* he causes it to cease when he steps into the boat. Either way he is always in full control. So also, through faith his followers are always secure. John 6:21 reports that "all at once the boat was at the land where they were going."

Jesus had walked upon the water. He had even enabled Peter to do likewise. He had rescued Peter. He had stilled the storm. He had done all this *and more!* He had walked upon the water *to them,* to be with them and to comfort them, to strengthen them in their faith. Thus the power and the love of their Lord had been gloriously manifested. The effect of all this is described in verse 33. **Those in the boat worshiped him, saying, Thou art indeed God's Son.** Those in the boat fell at his feet in humble adoration. For the meaning of the verb "worshiped" see on 2:11. [571] By acknowledging Jesus as "God's Son" or as "the Son of God" [572] they confess that they now realize that what the Father had previously declared (3:17; cf. 17:5) and what even the demons had confessed (8:29) was true indeed. They are overwhelmed by the infinite power and love of Jesus, that is, by the fact that he was able to do what he had just done, and was willing to do it—*for them!*

---

34 Having crossed over they landed at Gennesaret. 35 And when the men of that place recognized him, they sent (messengers) to the entire surrounding region; and they brought to him all that were ill, 36 begging him to allow them merely to touch the tassel of his garment; and all who touched were cured.

14:34-36 *Healings in Gennesaret*
Cf. Mark 6:53-56

34. **Having crossed over they landed at Gennesaret.** This is the name of a densely populated and fertile plain south of Capernaum. It measures about 3 miles in length along the Sea of Galilee (also called the Lake of Gennesaret, Luke 5:1), and 1½ miles in width away from the shore. According to

---

[571] In the New Testament the verb προσκυνέω occurs with great frequency in the Gospel according to Matthew, in John 4, and in the book of Revelation; elsewhere its use is scattered.

[572] In the present case either rendering is correct. Titles can be definite even without the article, and it would be difficult to imagine that these Jewish monotheists would have regarded Jesus as being one of many deities. They now see the one and only true God manifested in Jesus.

Josephus the plain produced walnuts, palms, figs, olives, and grapes. As indicated previously, from the landing place Jesus will proceed to nearby Capernaum, but not until he has blessed the people of this region by means of his gracious presence, as is now indicated: **35, 36. And when the men of that place recognized him they sent (messengers) to the entire surrounding region; and they brought to him all that were ill, begging him to allow them merely to touch the tassel of his garment, and all who touched were cured.** The men, rather than the women and children, were the travelers (see also on 14:21). On previous trips away from home—perhaps to Capernaum—these men had become acquainted with Jesus. In all probability they had seen him perform miracles (see 11:23). So they spread the news of Jesus' presence, with the result that they, the people of the surrounding towns and villages, brought to Jesus all those who were afflicted with any sickness whatever, exactly as in 4:24; 8:16. Those who brought their sick also implored Jesus to allow the diseased merely to touch the tassel of his garment (for this tassel see on 9:20, 21); so great was their faith in Jesus—as a Miracle-worker! All who touched were cured. Does this mean that only those who by what is generally called "saving faith" touched Jesus were healed? Not necessarily. The *main* point of the story is not the faith of men—whether of the sick or of those who brought them—but the power and love of Christ, as is evident also from 4:24; 8:16, 17; 9:13, 36; 12:7; 14:14.

Summary of Chapter 14

Though Jesus did not perform many miracles in Nazareth (13:58), he did accomplish a great many elsewhere, so that this news reached even the palace of King Herod Antipas, causing him to exclaim, "This is John the Baptist; he is risen from the dead; that's why these miraculous powers are at work in him" (14:1, 2). Thus the opening section (verses 1-12) of chapter 14 is introduced.

The king was deeply disturbed, for he had murdered the Baptist. It had come about in this way: On a trip to Rome to visit his half-brother Herod Philip, Herod Antipas had eloped with his host's wife, Herodias. When John hears about the incestuous marriage he repeatedly rebukes the king, telling him, "It isn't right for you to have her." Herodias, realizing that her married state is insecure, wants her new husband to kill John. However, the king is afraid of the people, many of whom have high regard for the Baptist. So the ruler compromises by having John imprisoned. At Herod's birthday party Salome, the daughter of Herodias, so fascinates the king by her dancing that with an oath he promises to give her whatever she asks. Prompted by her mother, she asks for the head of John the Baptist. So John is beheaded in prison. His disciples come, remove the body, bury it, and report the entire story to Jesus.

The next paragraph (verses 13-21) implies that the shocking intelligence of the Baptist's cruel death requires reflection and quiet meditation. Besides, The Twelve had recently returned from a mission tour. To give them an opportunity to rest a while from their labors and to tell their Master all that had happened Jesus takes them with him to Bethsaida Julias, located on the northeastern shore of the Sea of Galilee. Arrived there Jesus, looking down from a hill, sees a great multitude. Filled with compassion he heals their sick and teaches. Toward evening the disciples say to him, "The place is lonely and it is already late in the day; dismiss the crowds, that they may go into the villages and may buy food for themselves." Jesus answers, "They do not need to go away; y o u give them to eat." By saying this the Lord impresses upon them their own responsibility with respect to the crowds in need of both physical and spiritual sustenance. Then, by means of five bread-cakes and two fishes (bought from a lad, John 6:9) Jesus, after giving thanks, miraculously feeds five thousand persons, not counting women and children. The disciples pick up what is left over of the pieces of bread: twelve baskets full.

Verses 22-27 show how Jesus, having dismissed the crowds and having ordered the disciples into a boat to go back to the western shore, remains for a few more hours in the region where he had performed the great miracle. Here he goes up into the hill by himself to pray, so that when evening falls he is there alone. The paragraph pictures *a.* the disciples, frightened by a storm and without Jesus; *b.* the disciples with the unknown Jesus; that is, with "someone" who is walking on the water toward them and whom they regard to be a ghost; and *c.* the disciples with Jesus whom they now recognize because he has made himself known to them, saying, "Take courage, it is I; do not be afraid." There follows the episode of Peter walking on the water, then becoming afraid, and in the nick of time being rescued by the Lord. When Jesus and Peter step into the boat the wind ceases. Those in the boat worship Jesus, confessing him to be God's Son (verses 28-33).

In the closing paragraph (verses 34-36) the power and love of the Savior again stand out, as in the fertile plain of Gennesaret, south of Capernaum, he heals all that are brought to him.

Chapter 15:1-20

Theme: *The Work Which Thou Gavest Him to Do*

Ceremonial versus Real Defilement

CHAPTER XV:1–20

15 1 Then Pharisees and scribes came to Jesus from Jerusalem and said, 2 "Why do your disciples transgress the tradition of the elders? For they do not rinse their hands when they eat bread." 3 He answered and said to them, "And why do y o u yourselves transgress God's commandment for the sake of y o u r tradition? 4 For God said, 'Honor your father and your mother,' and 'He who curses father or mother must certainly be put to death.' 5 But y o u say, 'Anyone who says to his father or to his mother, "It's a gift, whatever it be by which I might benefit yo·ı," 6 surely does not have to honor his father.' And y o u have made the word of God null and void for the sake of y o u r tradition. 7 Y o u hypocrites, Isaiah was right when he prophesied about y o u:

> 8 'This people honor me with their lips
> But their heart is far from me.
> 9 But in vain do they worship me,
> Teaching (as their) doctrines precepts of men.' "

10 When he had called the people to him he said to them, "Hear and understand: 11 It is not what goes into the mouth that defiles a man, but it is what comes out of the mouth that defiles a man."

12 Then the disciples approached him and said, "Do you know that the Pharisees were offended when they heard what you said?" 13 He answered and said, "Every growth that my heavenly Father has not planted shall be uprooted. 14 Let them go. They are blind leaders. Now if a blind man leads a blind man both shall fall into a pit." 15 Peter answered and said to him, "Explain the parable to us." 16 He said, "Are y o u also even yet without understanding? 17 Do y o u not know that whatever enters the mouth goes into the stomach and passes into the latrine? 18 But what comes out of the mouth issues from the heart, and that is what defiles a man. 19 For from the heart issue wicked schemes, murders, adulteries, sexual sins, thefts, false testimonies, abusive speeches. 20 These are the things that defile a man, but to eat with unrinsed hands does not defile a man."

15:1-20 *Ceremonial verses Real Defilement*
Cf. Mark 7:1-23

1, 2. Then Pharisees and scribes came to Jesus from Jerusalem and said, Why do your disciples transgress the tradition of the elders? For they do not rinse their hands when they eat bread. "Then" is again very indefinite, meaning no more than, "about this time," or "on one of these days." Pharisees and scribes are mentioned together. For Pharisees see on 3:7; for scribes, on 2:4 and on 7:28, 29; for scribes and Pharisees, on 5:20. It is

607

evident that the opposition against Jesus is increasing in intensity. No longer just the Pharisees (as in 9:11, 12:1) are attacking him but in 12:38 and here in 15:1 we have the combination of the two. Whether there is any significance in the fact that in 15:1 Matthew, contrary to his usual custom (5:20; 12:38; 23:2), mentions the Pharisees before the scribes is not clear. What is significant, however, is that these "Pharisees and scribes" came from Jerusalem (cf. Mark 7:1, 2), probably not meaning that they were local men who originally had been living in that city, but that they were citizens of Jerusalem, law experts and teachers, etc., who, perhaps at the request or suggestion of likeminded friends, had agreed to make a trip to the north, for the purpose of stopping Jesus in his tracks.

The attack is becoming heated and organized. These enemies of Jesus have taken notice of the fact that the latter's disciples do not follow "the tradition of the elders," that is, in the present case the regulations imposed by former rabbis and handed down to the present generation regarding ritual cleansing of the hands before and during meals.

There was a vast mass of opinions and decisions that had been handed down from the past. This "tradition of the elders" was regarded as being equally binding as God's law itself, since, according to the scribes and their followers, they showed what the divine law really meant, that is, how it should be applied to everyday life. The trouble was however that in many cases—not in all; otherwise Jesus could not have spoken the words recorded in 23:2, 3a—these judgments *a.* went far beyond anything demanded by God's law, or *b.* failed entirely to do justice to the real requirements of that law. For *b.* see on 5:20-48. For *a.,* on 12:1-8. Generally *a.* and *b* combine.

What we have here in 15:1, 2 is another instance of "the tradition of the elders" demanding far more than was required in the law.

To be sure, the law of God required holiness (Lev. 19:2). That such holiness implied not only inner renewal but must also be expressed outwardly, and this not only in ethical conduct but also in a ritual sense, so that, for example, *a.* the people must wash their garments when the Lord is about to descend upon Mount Sinai (Exod. 19:2); and *b.* the priests before performing various sacred functions must bathe (Lev. 15:5-27; 16:26, 28; 17:7, 8, 19), is true. It is even true that Aaron and his "sons" were ordered to cleanse their hands before performing their duties in the tabernacle (Exod. 30:17-21), and that under certain specified conditions the law prescribed hand-rinsing for the people in general (Lev. 15:11; Deut. 21:6). But God's law nowhere prescribes ritual hand-rinsing for *everybody* and in connection with *every* meal. This was strictly a "tradition of the elders," unsupported by any divine ordinance. But the Pharisees, whether scribes or not, made it a matter of emphasis (Mark 7:3, 4).

The question may well be asked, "How did this emphasis on matters nowhere prescribed in the law, to the neglect of stressing the essence of the law (Matt. 22:37-40), come about?" The story, in brief, is as follows. The destruction of the temple and the Babylonian captivity had violently shocked the Jews. The God-fearing people among them realized that what had befallen them was the result of departure from Jehovah their God, and that their only hope of reconciliation and restoration was by returning to him with their whole heart (Jer. 29:13). God's law, as revealed in the Pentateuch, must be obeyed so that God's favor may again rest on his people. During the exile men like Ezekiel and Daniel led the way. Soon after the return of the remnant Ezra is described as "a ready scribe in the law of Moses" (Ezra 7:6, 11). New conditions seemed to require new applications of this law. For a while all went well. However, gradually men arose—the Pharisees, described earlier, and especially their scribes—who made the promulgation of regulations, ostensibly based upon the law, their specialty. They delighted in it and made it their hobby. They began to regulate for the purpose of regulating. Highest honor was bestowed upon the most famous rabbis or teachers among them. What they said was passed on from generation to generation. Not only did the scribes, in schools connected with the synagogues, teach the children to read, using the Hebrew Scriptures as the text, but both in synagogue rooms and temple chambers they taught the older "disciples" or "learners" how the law had been interpreted by the famous rabbis of the past.

The method of teaching that was chiefly relied on was that of "repetition." The matter to be learned was repeated *to* the pupil by the teacher, and then to the teacher *by* the pupil. As the regulations and opinions increased in number so also the amount of material to be memorized snowballed year by year, decade by decade, until at last it became so enormous that Rabbi Jehuda, about the year A.D. 200, committed this "tradition of the elders" to writing in what is called the *Mishnah* or *Mishna,* a word formed from a verb meaning *to repeat.* There had been previous attempts to do this, but Jehuda's work was at once recognized as the most complete and successful. The Mishna, accordingly, embraces the entire content of that which was considered important Jewish tradition as far as it had been handed down up to the end of A.D. 200. The rabbis of Palestine during the first two centuries A.D. whose views regarding Hebrew oral tradition are recorded in the Mishna and in other works are called the *tannaim* (from Aramaic *tenā*, to repeat, to teach).

Well known is the fact that the Mishna consists of *a.* the decisions of the sages on ever so many particular cases, as well as *b.* the elucidation of the basic texts of the Pentateuch. All these materials are arranged under six Orders, namely, Seeds, Set Feasts, Women, Damages (or Injuries), Hallowed Things (or Consecrations), and Cleansings (or Purifications). Each Order, in turn, is divided into several subsidiary tracts or treatises, these again into chapters, and the latter into paragraphs. So, for example, one of the tracts of the Order "Cleansings" has something to say about the rinsing of hands.

It was soon discovered, however, that the Mishna, in turn, also stood in need of elucidation and augmentation. So Commentaries—first oral, later written—on the Mishna were produced. The addition to the Mishna is called the *Gemara,* a noun derived from a verb meaning *to complete.* The rabbinical school of Jerusalem, combining the Mishna with its Gemara, produced the Jerusalem or Palestinian Talmud. This word *Talmud* is related to a verb meaning in its simplest form *to learn,* and in the modified (Pi'el) form which concerns us here, *to teach.* The rabbinical school centered in Babylonia produced the much bigger (four times as long) and generally considered more authoritative Babylonian Talmud. When "Talmud" is mentioned without modifying adjective it is the Babylonian work that is generally meant.

The language of the Jerusalem Talmud is Talmudic Hebrew; that of the Babylonian Talmud has been described as "a barbaric commixture of Chaldaic, Hebrew, and other dialects, jumbled together in defiance of all the rules of composition and grammar." [573] For English translations of Mishna and of Talmud see below.

The material found in Mishna and Talmud is by no means uniform in character. It is necessary to distinguish especially between *a. halakah,* pl. *halakoth,* a noun derived from a verb meaning *to go, to walk,* this noun referring therefore to the manner in which one should conduct himself; hence, to the traditional statement of law in its categorical form; and *b. haggadah, pl. haggadoth,* a noun derived from a verb which in one of its forms (*Hiph'il*) means *to tell,* this noun therefore indicating whatever *is told* by way of illustration; that is, all such material that is not halakic in character. Among the *haggadoth* we find legends, folklore, parables, proverbs, and scattered remarks and paragraphs in such fields as philosophy, medicine, natural science, astrology, music, etc. Gems of wisdom are mixed with ideas that by many are regarded, probably correctly, as absurdities. One may find the reading of several pages of the Talmud a rather dreary task. "The Talmud is one of the strangest of the Bibles of humanity. . . . It is drawn from the promiscuous notebooks of students of very diverse attainments and character in which they have scribbled down all the wisdom and all the unwisdom, all the sense and all the nonsense which was talked for centuries in the schools of all kinds of Rabbis" (F. W. Farrar, *History of Interpretation,* p. 91 f.).

Both here and in ancient Jewish literature generally many an explanation of a Bible passage is presented. Such a comment is called a *midrash,* pl. *midrashim,* a noun related to a verb meaning *to search, to examine,* and thus *to elucidate.* The *midrash* may, however, cover an entire book. Thus we

---

[573] B. Pick, *The Talmud, What It Is,* New York, 1887, p. 72.

speak of a Midrash Genesis, meaning a Commentary on the book of Genesis. Such *midrashim* are often mainly homiletical in nature.

Since even the Mishna itself, without Gemara, was not reduced to writing until about the year A.D. 200, it stands to reason that it is not always possible on the basis of its contents to say exactly what were the laws and customs prevailing in the days of Christ's sojourn on earth. It is true that the mention of names of famous rabbis whose opinions are disclosed and whose vital statistics are known or can be approximated, may at times help us to describe the background of the Gospel narrative; but even then, and even when it is taken for granted that the information furnished is correct, it is not always possible to decide whether—and if so, in how far—the information given applies to the particular time and region of Palestine to which reference is made in Scripture.[574] Nevertheless, study of this tannaitic

---

[574] Helpful literature on the subject of Mishna and Talmud in general, and particularly also on the Jewish background of Matt. 15:1 ff. is represented by the following books:

Bacher, W., *Die Exegetische Terminologie der Judischen Traditionsliteratur*, Hildesheim 1965.

Cohen, B., *Everyman's Talmud*, New York, 1949.

Dalman, G., *Aramäisch-neuhebräisches Wörterbuch zu Targum, Talmud, und Midrasch*, Frankfort, 1897-1901.

————, *Christentum und Judentum*, Leipsic, 1898; English translation, *Christianity and Judaism*, Oxford, 1901.

————, *Jesus-Jeshua*, English translation, New York, 1929.

Edersheim, A., *The Life and Times of Jesus the Messiah*, New York, 1897, 1898. On Matt. 15:1 ff. see especially Vol. II, pp. 207-211.

Farrar, F. W., *The Life of Christ*, New York, 1875.

Finkelstein, L., *The Jews, Their History, Culture, and Religion*, New York, 1949.

Ginzberg, L., *A Commentary on the Palestinian Talmud*, New York, 1941, 1967.

Hauck, F., article νίπτω, ἄνιπτος in Th.D.N.T., Vol. IV., pp. 946-948.

Hertzberg, A. (editor), *Judaism*, New York, 1962.

Mishna, The, English translation by H. Danby, London, 1933.

Montefiore, C. G., *Rabbinic Literature and Gospel Teaching*, New York, 1970.

Moore, G. F., *Judaism in the First Centuries of the Christian Era*, Cambridge, 1927-1930.

Pick, B., for title see above, footnote 573.

Popma, K. J., *Eerst De Jood Maar Ook De Griek*, Franeker, 1950.

Robertson, A. T., *The Pharisees and Jesus*, New York, 1920. For Matt. 15:1 ff. see pp. 97-97.

Schürer, E., *Geschichte des jüdischen Volkes im Zeitalter Jesu Christi*, Leipzig, 1886-1890; English translation: *A History of the Jewish People in the Time of Jesus Christ*, Edinburg, 1890, 1891.

Strack, H. L., *Introduction to the Talmud and Midrash*, New York and Philadelphia, 1959.

S.BK., for title see The List of Abbreviations, p. vii.

Talmud, The Babylonian, English translation by M. L. Rodkinson, Boston, 1918.

Trattner, E. R., *Understanding The Talmud*, New York, 1955.

Walker, T., *Jewish Views of Jesus*, New York, 1931.

Yaffe, J., *The American Jews*, New York, 1969. This book shows the influence of The Talmud on the life of American Jews.

To this list should be added the remarks of various commentaries on Matt. 15:1 ff.,

literature is not only helpful but necessary for the understanding of the New Testament. This is true also with respect to Matt. 15:1ff.

In the light of this background literature a few points become clear:

a. The criticism of the Pharisees and scribes, reported here in 15:1, 2, had nothing to do with hygiene. These men did not imply that Jesus was allowing his disciples to eat with physically "dirty" hands. The matter in dispute touched ceremonial purity, not dirt. It did not have anything to do with germs, about which neither the disciples nor their critics knew anything.

b. The translation "wash" in verse 2 and "unwashed" in verse 20, though favored by many, is probably not the best. "According to the Jewish rite the hands were not washed in a basin, but with elevated hand affused from above" (G. Dalman, *Jesus-Jeshua*, p. 117). "What the Pharisees wanted was not the normal cleansing of the hands but the washing, or expressed more accurately, the ritual rinsing[575] of the hands in any case, that is, even though they were clean" (F. W. Grosheide, *op. cit.*, p. 239).

c. The expression "when they eat bread," the latter being the main dish, simply means "when they partake of a meal."

On the basis of the then still unwritten but subsequently written "tradition of the elders" these Pharisees and scribes were of the opinion that any contact with a Gentile, for example by brushing against him on the street or the market-place or by unwittingly touching an object belonging to him, was an impediment to worship in temple or synagogue. That explains their criticism. These men were O so concerned about "the tradition of the elders," far more than about the Word of God. They substituted mere legalism for true piety, outward conformity to tradition for the attitude of heart and mind, and "a torturing scrupulosity for glad obedience" (Farrar).

That this is exactly the criticism leveled against these enemies by Jesus is clear from what follows in verse 3. **He answered and said to them, And why do y o u yourselves transgress God's commandment for the sake of y o u r tradition?** Note the parallel between:

"Why do your disciples transgress the tradition. . . ?"

and

"Why do y o u yourselves transgress God's commandment. . . ?"

The Lord is as it were saying, therefore, "*Y o u* should talk! Granted that my disciples are transgressing tradition, y o u yourselves are transgressing something infinitely more important, namely, God's holy law, which y o u are subordinating to 'y o u r tradition,' the tradition to which y o u erroneously attach paramount importance." See further on 5:20. Continued:

---

and the articles on Mishna and Talmud in encyclopaedias, including those in S.H.E.R.K., Vol. XI, pp. 255-264; its Twentieth Century Extension, pp. 1089, 1090; and S. Zeitlin's in Enc. Britannica, 1969 edition, Vol. 21, pp. 639-645.

[575] *"ritueel afspoelen."*

4. **For God said, Honor your father and your mother, and He who curses father or mother must certainly be put to death.** As to the positive commandment to bestow honor on father and mother see Exod. 20:12; Deut. 5:16; Prov. 1:8; 6:20-22; cf. Mal. 1:6; Matt. 19:19; Mark 7:10-13; 10:19; Eph. 6:1; Col. 3:20. *To honor* father and mother means more than *to obey* them, especially if this obedience is interpreted in a merely outward sense. It is the inner attitude of the child toward his parents that comes to the fore in the requirement that he *honor* them. All selfish obedience or reluctant obedience or obedience under terror is immediately ruled out. To honor implies to love, to regard highly, to show the spirit of respect and consideration. This honor is to be shown to *both* of the parents, for as far as the child is concerned they are equal in authority.

In Exod. 21:17; Lev. 20:9 the death penalty is pronounced on those who curse father or mother, but see also Exod. 21:15; Deut. 21:18-21 and Prov. 30:17.

What did these Pharisees and scribes do with this clear and definite teaching of the Word of God? The answer is given in verses 5, 6. **But y o u say, Anyone who says to his father or to his mother, It's a gift, whatever it be by which I might benefit you, surely does not have to honor his father.** [576] The Pharisees and scribes were telling the children that there was a way to get around the heavy burden of having to bestow honor upon their parents by supporting them. If either father or mother, noticing that a son had something which was needed by the parent, asked for it, all that was necessary was for this son to say, "It's *dōron* (a gift)" or "*corbān* (an offering)," Mark 7:11. Either way, whether the son uses the Greek word *dōron* or the Hebrew *corbān,* he is really saying, "It is consecrated to God," and by making this assertion or exclamation he, according to Pharisaic teaching based on tradition, [577] had released himself from the obligation of honoring his parents—here "father" as also representing the mother—by helping them in their particular need.

It is even possible that a broader interpretation, favored by some, may be correct. If so, the son would be saying, "Whatever it is by which I might benefit you, whether now or in the future, I here and now declare that it is to be considered an offering." Interpreted either way it was a wicked device to deprive parents of the honor due to them. Moreover, what was thus unjustly withdrawn from the parents was not necessarily offered to God at all. The one who shouted, "It's a gift" or "It's an offering" could simply keep it for himself! It is not surprising that Jesus adds: **And y o u have made the word of God null and void for the sake of y o u r tradition.** Or, as the

---

[576] The verse division, with "6" prefixed to "he shall not honor his father" (A.R.V.) is confusing. A better place for this "6" would have been immediately preceding "And y o u have made. . . ."

[577] See S.BK. Vol. I, p. 71 f.

parallel passage (Mark 7:8) has it, "Y o u let go [ignore, neglect] the commandment of God in order to cling to the tradition of men." That this was no exaggeration is clear from the passage in the Talmud, "To be against the words of the scribes is more punishable than to be against the word of the Bible." [578] Exactly opposite was the attitude of Jesus with respect to God's holy law (see on 5:17, 18).

Now when people are corrupt enough to teach the younger generation how to evade the requirements of a very important commandment of the Decalogue, and are doing this while pretending to be very pious and devout, they deserve to be called *hypocrites*. This is exactly what Jesus does in verses 7-9. **Y o u hypocrites, Isaiah was right when he prophesied about y o u:**

> **This people honor me with their lips**
> **But their heart is far from me.**
> **But in vain do they worship me,**
> **Teaching (as their) doctrines precepts of men.**

In addition to what has already been said about this passage (see above, pp. 89) note the following:

First, Matthew cannot have meant that Isaiah in writing Isa. 29:13 was thinking of these Pharisees and scribes. He meant that what the prophet wrote concerning the people of his own day was still very relevant, for both then and now those condemned were honoring God with their lips, while their hearts were far removed from him. History, in other words, was repeating itself.

Secondly, the description given is exact: Pharisees and scribes were constantly honoring God with their lips, that is, outwardly, as is clear from such passages as 6:5; Luke 18:11, while inwardly they were corrupt, their heart being far removed from the very One whom they were praising with their lips. Did not Jesus prove this very fact in the immediately preceding context, in which the manner in which these enemies taught the younger generation how to evade the requirements of the commandment regarding duties toward parents was described?

Thirdly, the designation "hypocrites" (see also 6:2, 5, 16; 7:5; 22:18; 23:28; etc.) was apt, for these enemies pretended to be what they were not: they pretended to be very pious but were actually very wicked.

Fourthly, their worship was "vain," that is futile, neither honoring God nor benefitting either themselves or other men in any way.

Finally, when the heart is estranged from God his Word is exchanged for "precepts of men," merely human "traditions."

Having rebuked the Pharisees and scribes Jesus now turns to the multitude: **10. When he had called the people to him he said to them, Hear and understand. . . .** Evidently the people had been standing at some distance

---

[578] Quoted from the Talmud by A. T. Robertson, *The Pharisees and Jesus*, p. 130.

away, probably out of respect for those who had come to question Jesus about the conduct of his disciples. It seems that the crowd wanted to give the men who had come from Jerusalem every opportunity to interrogate their opponent. So Jesus, turning away from the critics, asks the people to come closer. He has something of great importance to tell them, something that concerns the very essence of religion and ethics, that they may no longer allow themselves to be misled. To emphasize the significance of what he is about to say he prefixes his remarks with the solemn introduction, "Hear and understand." He wants them to listen closely and to ponder thoroughly, so that they will understand properly. Continued: **11. It is not what goes into the mouth that defiles a man, but it is what comes out of the mouth that defiles a man.** What Jesus is saying in such a simple, terse, and axiomatic way has to do with the contemptuous question of the Pharisees and scribes (see verse 2) about the ritual rinsing of hands in connection with meals. According to the men who had come from Jerusalem to find fault with Jesus, unrinsed hands defiled the food and therefore also the eater. Unless ceremonially clean, whatever it was that came into the mouth from the outside defiled a man. Jesus shows that the very opposite is true: not what goes into but what comes out of the mouth defiles a [literally "the"] man! Defilement, in other words, issues from the heart (see verses 18, 19; cf. Mark 7:19-23). That inner storehouse, according to the rule laid down in 12:35, employs the mouth as its instrument for the outward expression of all kinds of thoughts and sentiments that are really defiling.

What Jesus is doing here is placing the emphasis where it belongs, not on that which is physical but on that which is spiritual and abiding, just as he had done previously (see 5:3, 4, 6, 17; 9:13; 12:7, 50). In our own day and age, in which understandably and rightly many warnings are being issued against air pollution and water pollution, Christ's implied warning against the incalculably more ominous evil of mouth pollution and heart pollution is certainly needed.

At this point Christ's disciples come into the picture again: **12. Then the disciples approached him and said, Do you know that the Pharisees were offended when they heard what you said?** Are these disciples referring *a.* to the immediately preceding line, "It is not what goes into the mouth. . . ," a statement which had been addressed to the people; or *b.* to the entire contents of verses 3-9, addressed to the Pharisees and scribes? Some prefer the former. [579] It is, however, very doubtful whether Christ's bitter opponents had heard this rather brief remark that had not even been directed to them. But whether or not they heard it, is it not more reasonable to believe that they took offense at, were repelled by, [580] the very sharp reprimand to

---

[579] So, for example, R. C. H. Lenski, *op. cit.*, p. 571.
[580] Again a form of the verb σκανδαλίζω; see on 5:29, 30, especially footnote 293 on p. 303; see also on 11:6.

which they themselves had been exposed, and in which they had been characterized as "transgressors" and "hypocrites"? My own preference is for *b.* therefore.

It is implied that in the hearing of the disciples the Pharisees had given vent to their hot displeasure. Had the disciples become somewhat afraid? Were they shaken with a measure of awe for those men who by many were regarded as venerable leaders? Were they perhaps fearful of the possible consequences of the sharp rebuke their Master had administered?

However this may have been, one fact stands out: the wrath of the religious leaders had made a deep impression upon the disciples. These Pharisees must have been very indignant, and this perhaps not only because of the fact already stated, namely, that they had been publicly stigmatized as transgressors and hypocrites, but also for a different reason: If the word of God ranked infinitely higher than the tradition of the elders (see verses 3, 6 and 9), and if that judgment as to comparative values took root among the people, these leaders knew that in that case they might as well go home. Was it not exactly this tradition which they had made their hobby, their specialty? So they were offended and repelled, to the extent that because of their own corrupt heart they began to think and to utter wicked sentiments about Jesus.

The disciples having taken cognizance of this bitter resentment on the part of the leaders want Jesus to know about it, so that in his future words and actions he may figure with it. As if the Lord needed their advice!

13, 14. He answered and said, Every growth that my heavenly Father has not planted shall be uprooted. Let them go. They are blind leaders. Now if a blind man leads a blind man both shall fall into a pit. The underlying figure seems to be that of a "growth" or "planting." The original does not here use the word commonly employed to indicate a "plant." It says "planting" or "growth," a growth of any size and found anywhere, whether in a garden, field, vineyard, grove, along a stream, or anywhere else. [581]

God's people may be viewed as a well-watered garden (Isa. 58:11), as God's field or acreage (I Cor. 3:9), as Jehovah's vineyard (Isa. 5:7). The believer is at times compared to a luxuriant tree (Ps. 1:3; 92:12). Under any figure the thought is emphasized that for a planting to thrive God must be the Planter. For human beings to fulfil their task to the glory of God and to enter heaven at last they must have been so firmly rooted that they have

---

[581] Here in 15:13 the original has φυτεία, not φυτόν. In the most comprehensive sense the former is broader than the latter, just as "planting" is broader than "plant." Though neither translation can be called incorrect, both the modifier "every" and the figurative phraseology of Scripture, according to which God is viewed as having planted a garden, field, vineyard, etc., would seem to point to the broader connotation. So also, Ridderbos, *op. cit.*, p. 281, who offers "ieder gewas," i.e., every "growth" or "planting."

become "one plant with" Christ, "grown together" [582] in the likeness of his death and subsequently in the likeness of his resurrection.

However, in the present passage Jesus speaks of growths which his "heavenly Father" (see on 11:25-27; cf. John 5:17, 18) has not planted. Such growths remind us of the tares which the devil planted (Matt. 13:25, 39). They were destined to be uprooted and thrown into the fire (13:30; cf. 3:10, 12; Luke 17:6; John 15:5; Jude 12). That is to happen at the time of the final judgment. Christ's critics belong to this group. Those who place their confidence in them are going to be uprooted along with them. This explains Christ's exhortation to the disciples, "Let them go," thus literally. One might also render his command: "Ignore them," "Pay no attention to them," "dissociate yourselves completely from them."

Following these men will lead to disaster, for as leaders they are "blind," says Jesus. Their blindness, moreover, is of a very tragic kind: *a.* It is *self-inflicted,* the result of hardness of heart (John 3:19). In that respect these Pharisees differ from people afflicted with physical blindness. *b.* It is *self-deluding,* for these would-be guides imagine that they, they alone, are able to see (John 9:40, 41). This deplorable fact points up another striking contrast between them and those who are blind in the literal sense.

How sad is the lot of the person who follows such a leader. The leader is blind and so is the follower. Shall not both fall into a pit? In this connection was Jesus thinking of a pit as the symbol of hell? We can say no more than that this may have been the case.

Jesus has addressed *a.* the Pharisees and scribes (verses 3-9); *b.* the people in general (verses 10, 11); and *c.* his disciples (verses 12-14). He now receives response: **15. Peter answered and said to him, Explain the parable to us.** The term "parable" is here used in the sense of pithy saying, mashal, ⁺he aphorism of verse 11. That Peter was the spokesman for The Twelve is clear from Christ's answer: **16. He said, Are y o u also even yet without understanding?** Jesus seems to be saying, "That others—for example, the Pharisees and scribes, the people in general—do not grasp my teaching (cf. verse 11) is not strange, but that y o u, who have associated with me for so long a period and so closely, *even yet* [583] are without insight into its meaning is inexcusable." We find something similar in John 14:9, "So long a time have I been with y o u, and yet you have not learned to recognize me, Philip?" Continued: **17, 18. Do y o u not know that whatever enters the mouth goes into the stomach and passes into the latrine? But what comes out of the mouth issues from the heart, and that is what defiles a man.** Even the best modern

---

[582] For "one plant with" or "grown together" Rom. 6:5 uses a word, namely, σύμφυτοι, from the same stem as φυτεία and φυτόν.

[583] Greek ἀκμήν adverbial accusative of ἀκμή (point; cf. "acme"); hence, "up to this point (of time)."

science can find no fault with Christ's statement as to what happens to whatever enters the mouth. Whether rather directly, as in the case of such intake as is not assimilated by the body, that is, which does not enter into the formation of new cells, or indirectly, as is true with respect to foods that are assimilated, in view of the fact that anabolism is constantly followed by catabolism, in the end elimination is what happens to whatever enters the mouth. None of it in any way defiles the heart and thus the person. On the other hand, the words that proceed from the lips have their source in the heart, the latter being the core and center of man's being, the mainspring of his thoughts, words, and actions (Prov. 4:23). All these things proceed "from within" (Mark 7:21). The words, if wicked, "defile the man." This point is made even clearer in verse 19. **For from the heart issue wicked schemes, murders, adulteries, sexual sins, thefts, false testimonies, abusive speeches.** As to these "schemes" or "deliberations," the word used in the original gave rise to our English word *dialogue*. Although the dialogue that a person has with himself need not be sinister—see Luke 2:35 in which passage the deliberations referred to are not necessarily bad—yet it is worthy of note that in nearly every passage in which the word is used the activity described is clearly of a sinful nature (Luke 5:22; 6:8; 9:46, 47; Rom. 1:21; 14:1; I Cor. 3:20; Phil. 2:14; I Tim. 2:8). In I Tim. 2:8 these deliberations are associated with "wrath." Here in Matt. 15:19 they are called evil; hence "evil deliberations" or "wicked schemes."

Wicked schemes reveal themselves in wicked words and deeds. Matthew mentions several of these, arranging them more or less according to their sequence in the second table of the Ten Commandments. By no means all of the items mentioned are necessarily associated with spoken words, but all of them come from within, from the heart. The action is from within outward. The manner in which Pharisees and scribes were teaching the younger generation to evade responsibility toward parents (see verses 3-9) furnishes an excellent illustration of a wicked scheme in connection with the fifth [some would say "the fourth"] commandment. The rest of the list is self-explanatory. Mark's list (7:21, 22) is twice as long. The important point is the same in both Gospels, recorded most fully by Matthew in these words: **20. These are the things that defile a man, but to eat with unrinsed hands does not defile a man,** which is a direct answer to the charge made by the enemies (verses 1, 2). Let them therefore pay attention to the things that really matter instead of immersing themselves in ritualistic trivialities. Let them stop making the word of God null and void for the sake of their tradition!

Summary of Chapter 15:1-20

Since the fame of Jesus is spreading, having reached even the palace of the king, and since the variety of miracles is increasing, the feeding of the five thousand having now been added to the many healings, it is not surprising that the Pharisees and scribes are becoming concerned lest they should lose their hold upon the people. So they come from Jerusalem, with sinister purpose. They soon find an issue. Approaching Jesus they demand to know why it is that his disciples neglect ceremonial hand rinsing before meals. They are not talking about washing physically dirty hands, as if the disciples were neglecting this, but about "rinsing the hands," whether they were physically dirty or not, "rinsing" them in any event since they might have touched something or someone considered "unclean." They are referring to a human "tradition."

In his answer Jesus points out that these Pharisees and scribes should refrain from criticizing ("Those who live in glass houses better not throw stones"), since what they themselves are doing is really bad, for they are transgressing *not a man-made regulation* but *God's command* to honor father and mother (Exod. 20:12). "Y o u are telling the children how to evade the obligation of supporting their parents. Y o u are saying to them: 'If y o u r parents want anything from y o u, just tell them: Whatever it is y o u want me to hand over to y o u, is *a gift,* an offering to God.' " The Lord continues, "Y o u have made the word of God null and void for the sake of y o u r tradition." He shows his critics that Isaiah's description of the hypocrites of his own day also applies to them:

> "This people honor me with their lips
> But their heart is far from me.
> But in vain do they worship me,
> Teaching (as their) doctrines precepts of men."

Jesus then points out to them that it is not what goes into the mouth that defiles a man, but it is what comes out of the mouth that defiles him.

When in a fearful mood the disciples say to their Master, "Do you know that the Pharisees were offended when they heard what you said?" he answers, "Every growth that my heavenly Father has not planted shall be uprooted. Let them go. They are blind leaders, etc." Finally, in answer to Peter's request, "Explain the parable to us," Jesus sheds further light on the fact that not what enters the mouth defiles the man, but the evil things that issue from the mouth and in the final analysis come out of the man's heart, constitute that which defiles him.

619

Outline of Chapter 15:21-39

Theme: *The Work Which Thou Gavest Him to Do*

B. The Retirement Plus Perean Ministries

15:21-28   The Faith of the Canaanite Woman Rewarded

15:29-31   Healing Great Multitudes

15:32-39   The Feeding of the Four Thousand

CHAPTER XV:21-39

21 Jesus went away from there and retired to the district of Tyre and Sidon. 22 Then, lo and behold, a Canaanite woman from that region came out, constantly crying, "Take pity on me, O Lord, Son of David; my daughter is severely tormented by a demon." 23 But he did not answer her a word. His disciples came and kept urging him, "Send her away, for she is shouting after us." 24 But he answered, "Only to the lost sheep of the house of Israel was I sent." 25 She, however, came, was falling at his feet and saying, "Lord, help me." 26 He answered and said, "It is not proper to take the children's bread and throw it to the house dogs." 27 "Right, Lord," she said, "but even the house dogs eat some of the scraps that drop from their masters' table." 28 Then Jesus answered and said to her, "O woman, great is your faith! Let it be done for you as you desire." And healed was her daughter from that very moment.

15:21-28 The Faith of the Canaanite Woman Rewarded
Cf. Mark 7:24-30

The theme of the Synoptics, including Matthew, we may conceive to be *The Work Which Thou Gavest Him to Do.* The first division under this theme is *Its Beginning or Inauguration* (1:1–4:11). The second is *Its Progress or Continuation* (4:12–20:34). The first subdivision of this second division, namely, *The Great Galilean Ministry* (4:12–15:20) has now been completed. The second subdivision, *The Retirement plus Perean Ministries,* begins at this point (15:21) and continues through 20:34. [584] Justification for the name of this subdivision and also a brief characterization of its contents are found on pp. 8, 9. *Tentative* dates (certainly is impossible) are as follows: Retirement Ministry A.D. 29, April to October; Perean Ministry A.D. 29, December to A.D. 30, April. For the intervening Later Judean Ministry, A.D. 29, October to December, see especially the Gospel according to John (7:2–10:39).

21. **Jesus went away from there and retired to the district of Tyre and Sidon.** This time Jesus retires or withdraws himself to definitely Gentile territory. It is clear that he leaves the land of Israel. This time it is not a case of "outsiders" coming to him (4:24, 25); he himself goes out to them. But this action of going out to them does not begin immediately. First he enters

---

[584] After arriving at this division independently I discovered that F. W. Grosheide, *op. cit.*, p. 244, also considers 15:21–20:34 a unit.

a house for the purpose of temporary seclusion, but "he could not be hid" (Mark 7:24). 22. Then, lo and behold, a Canaanite woman from that region came out, constantly crying, Take pity on me, O Lord, Son of David; my daughter is severely tormented by a demon. Note first of all *her reverential attitude toward Jesus.* She calls Jesus "Lord" (see on 7:21 and 8:2) and adds "Son of David," honoring him as being indeed the promised Messiah, as has been shown in connection with 9:27 where the same title occurs (see also on 21:9, 15, 16; 22:41-45). The great contrast between the unbelief of the Jews (see the preceding paragraph: 15:1-20) and the faith of this woman, born a Gentile, stands out.

Secondly, consider *her agony.* She is crying out constantly, or "again and again," as the Greek tense implies. The reason for her near despair is the fact that her dear little daughter (cf. Mark 7:25) is demon-possessed. On Demon-Possession see above, pp. 436, 437. Moreover, the child's affliction is very serious, very grievous.

What was Christ's immediate reaction? It is stated in verse 23. But he did not answer her a word. There was absolute silence on his part. He acted as if he had not even heard her. A little later more will be said about this seeming (never real!) indifference on the part of Jesus. Continued: His disciples came and kept urging him, Send her away, for she is shouting after us. The theory according to which the disciples meant, "Grant her request and then dismiss her," is not supported by any solid argument. These men evidently considered this woman, who was constantly crying out after them, an intolerable nuisance (see on 14:15). 24. But he answered, Only to the lost sheep of the house of Israel was I sent. In this connection it is important to take note not only of the fact that Jesus seems to remain adamant in his refusal to help this woman, but also of the fact that neither did he heed the urgent request of his disciples. The latter is sometimes forgotten. Yet, it is very important. One might even say that the Lord's refusal to give heed is aimed at the disciples far more than at the woman. Though the words addressed to her may seem harsh, at least he continues to deal with her. He even breaks his silence and is now talking to her. But as to the suggestion of the disciples, he does not even consider it worthy of an answer! One might also say: Granted that the words of the Lord recorded here in verse 24 were also meant for the ears of the disciples—was this not the very ministry during which, in a special way, Jesus was teaching them?—it remains true that Jesus by his very action as here recorded rejects their urgent request! But he does not reject the woman's request, though it seems as if he does.

Jesus wishes to make it perfectly clear to all concerned that the wide-opening of the doors for the influx of the Gentiles into the kingdom of heaven is a matter that pertains to the future. For the present, in total harmony with 10:5, 6 (see on that passage), his mission is to those whom he tenderly calls "the lost sheep (see on 9:36; 10:6) of the house of Israel."

25. **She, however, came, was falling at his feet and saying, Lord, help me.** The woman's *a.* attitude of reverence and *b.* bitter agony, both of which were mentioned in connection with verse 22, are clear also from verse 25. Matthew vividly pictures her in the act of worshipping Jesus, perhaps even prostrating herself at his feet again and again. [585] A third feature is now added to those already enumerated, namely, *her intense love for her little daughter.* In verse 22 she had spoken about her "daughter." Now, here in verse 25, in the heat of her agonizing appeal she says, "Help *me.*" She and her daughter are inseparable. It is in that sense that we can say that she identifies herself with her child. Is not this one of the chief characteristics of effective intercessory prayer, namely, to so immerse oneself into the trials and afflictions of others that these experiences become in a sense our own? Did not Jesus teach Saul (=Paul) that by persecuting Christ's followers he was persecuting Christ himself? See Acts 9:4; 22:7; 26:14. See also on Matt. 8:17.

For the moment the Lord's answer was anything but encouraging: 26. **He answered and said, It is not proper to take the children's bread and throw it to the house dogs.** The word for "dogs" is not that used in 7:6 (cf. Phil. 3:2). Not the large, savage, and ugly dogs prowling about the garbage thrown into the streets are meant here but the dogs kept in the homes as pets. Jesus had already fixed the attention of the woman upon the fact that he had not been sent to those outside of Israel (verse 24). In the same vein he now adds that it would not be proper to give Israel's blessings—the blessings that belong to "the children"—to those who do not belong to Israel. After all, dogs, no matter how dear to the owner, are not children, and have no right to be treated like children.

This is probably the proper place to take up the question, "Why did Jesus delay so long in giving this poor woman the help she needed so desperately?" The answers that are given to this question vary rather widely. The old answer is "to test her faith." Whether or not this answer satisfies depends on what is meant by testing faith. Another answer is that since only toward the end of the story (verse 28) Jesus becomes willing to grant this woman's emphatic request, he must have changed his mind at the last moment; hence the delay. This answer is unacceptable for the following reasons: *a.* If that had been the case why did he not heed the repeated advice of the disciples to send her away? Also, *b.* No other case is recorded in which Jesus refused to heed an earnest, humble, and sincere appeal for help. For him to have intended from the very start to reject this woman's plea would have been totally unlike Jesus as he is revealed to us in Scripture. After all he is the Lord who spoke the words of 7:7, 8; 11:28-30; John 7:37.

In order to reach the right answer to our question it is probably necessary

---

[585] Note the tense, here as in verse 22, the imperfect.

first of all to take note of the fact that Christ's "delay"—if we may call it that—in granting this woman's request is not unique. It is one of the many instances in which requests are not immediately answered. Abraham and Sarah had to wait a long time before they finally received Isaac (Gen. 21:1-5; Rom. 4:18-21). When "the father of all believers" (Rom. 4:11) was ordered to make Isaac a burnt-offering, it took what must have seemed a very long time indeed before he discovered that his son, whom he loved intensely (Gen. 22:2), was not going to be literally sacrificed. Did not David express dismay because God did not immediately answer his prayers? See Ps. 22:2. And, turning now to the New Testament and calling attention to only a few of the many instances that could be cited, did it not seem as if Jesus was going to arrive at the home of Jairus too late (Mark 5:35)? Did it not for the moment appear to the two blind men as if the Lord was indifferent to their cry (Matt. 9:27, 28)? If Jesus knew exactly what he was going to do about feeding the hungry multitude—and Scripture affirms that he did indeed know this—, then why did he not immediately tell Philip all about it, instead of saying to him, "How are we to buy bread-cakes that these people may eat" (John 6:5, 6)? And why do we read, "So when he [Jesus] heard that he [Lazarus] was ill, *he then remained two days in the place where he was* (John 11:6)?"

In several cases the reason is either plainly stated or at least suggested in the context; for example, "Abraham waxed strong through faith" (Rom. 4:20). Jairus is told, "Fear not, only believe" (Mark 5:36). In connection with Philip we read, "This he was saying to test him" (John 6:6). And in connection with Lazarus, the Lord says to his disciples, "For y o u r sake, that y o u may believe I am glad that I was not present" (John 11:15). Evidently, raising a dead Lazarus would be a more effective means of strengthening faith than healing a sick Lazarus.

The same reasoning should, in all probability, be applied in connection with the Syrophoenician or Canaanite woman. Jesus delayed to heed her request in order to test her faith, that is, to refine it as silver is refined, purified. He wanted to give her faith an opportunity for more glorious expression. He aimed to strengthen it by means of the very answer he had given her in verses 24 and 26; for she would now begin to realize, far better than if he had immediately healed her daughter, what an extraordinary blessing she was receiving.

The more glorious expression of the woman's faith is found in verse **27. Right, Lord, she said, but even the house dogs eat some of the scraps that drop from their masters' table.** To the three things said about her in the preceding a fourth is now added, namely, *her humility.* She does not even resent being compared with a house dog as contrasted with a child. She accepts her inferior position.

Fifthly, note also *her quick-wittedness.* She turns the very word of seeming reproach into a reason for optimism. She transforms impending defeat into jubilant victory. She is saying as it were, "Am I being compared with a house dog? I accept what is implied in this comparison. I not only accept it, I rejoice because of it, for certainly good masters do not allow their pet dogs to starve to death. They permit them to eat the crumbs that fall from the table."

Basic to all her words and actions is, sixthly, *her unswerving God-given faith in Jesus*, whom she has confessed as her Lord and Messiah.

Seventhly and finally we shall ever remember this woman because of *her perseverance*, a quality that can be viewed either by itself or in combination with her faith (hence, her persevering faith).

As to this perseverance the following should be noted. It has been said that Jesus is here departing from the principle that he has himself expressed. He is making an exception—as if this were bad!—to the rule, "Only to the house of Israel was I sent." Well, in a sense, he was making an exception, a marvelous exception indeed (see p. 456), for certainly this woman was a Greek, a Gentile (Matt. 15:22; Mark 7:26). In a different sense, however, this was no exception at all, as will become evident when we consider that she triumphed in spite of *a.* the initial silence of Jesus, *b.* his seeming (never real!) coldness and his words of seeming reproach, and *c.* the indifference of the disciples ("Send her away"). Now was it not a very similar manifestation of determined perseverance in the face of opposition ("I will not let thee go except thou bless me," Gen. 32:26) that changed a "Jacob" into an "Israel" (Gen. 32:28)? This woman, then, was in that sense a true Israelite!

28. Then Jesus answered and said to her, "O woman, great is your faith! Let it be done for you as you desire." And healed was her daughter from that very moment. Divine love is so infinite and marvelous that it even praises a human being for exercising a gift—in this case faith—with which this very divine love has endowed her, and which apart from that divine activity could not have gone into action at all.

The praise which this woman receives cannot fail to remind us of the eulogy with which Jesus lauded the centurion (8:10). Here as well as in 8:10, 11 is there not a prediction of the fast approaching wide-opening of the door for the reception of the Gentiles into the kingdom of heaven?

Note also that the blessing bestowed on the woman cannot even be conceived of apart from that with which her daughter was favored. When the woman received what she desired this implied that the daughter likewise was given what she needed. The latter was healed immediately and completely! Moreover, these blessings did not rob "children" of their "bread."

---

29 Jesus left that place and went along the Sea of Galilee. He climbed a hill and was sitting there. 30 Large crowds came to him, having with them (the) lame, blind, crippled, those lacking the power of speech, and many others. They laid them down at

Jesus' feet, and he healed them, 31 so that the people were astonished when they saw (the) dumb speaking, (the) crippled restored, (the) lame walking, and (the) blind seeing; and they glorified the God of Israel.

15:29-31 *Healing Great Multitudes*
Cf. Mark 7:31, 37

29. Jesus left that place and went along the Sea of Galilee. He climbed a hill and was sitting there. Both in Matthew and in Luke there is no time indication. How long Jesus stayed in the district of Tyre and Sidon is not known. Even the place to which the Lord now wended his way is only very vaguely described. All we read is that "he went along the Sea of Galilee." He spent at least three days on the eastern or southeastern, the less densely populated, shore of the sea. So much is clear from verse 32 and from Mark 8:2. Cf. Matt. 4:25. Here, then, near the sea, Jesus climbed a hill, [586] on which (not necessarily on its very top) he is pictured as sitting down. Continued: **30, 31. Large crowds came to him, having with them (the) lame, blind, crippled, those lacking the power of speech, and many others.** Soon the news of Christ's arrival began to spread throughout the entire Decapolis (League of Ten Cities), described in connection with 4:25. As had happened before so also now, from the entire region roundabout people flocked to Jesus bringing their afflicted relatives, friends, and neighbors. The crowds knew that Jesus was able to help in every need, it mattered not whether people were merely sick (14:35, 36), sick and/or demon-possessed (4:24; 8:16), or, as catalogued here in 15:30, 31, mainly handicapped, that is, blind, crippled, etc., Jesus was willing and able to heal them all. **They laid them down at Jesus' feet, and he healed them.** The very simplicity of the account makes it all the more touching. As far as the record goes no questions were asked as to whether a person happened to be Gentile—this was Gentile territory—or Jew. There is nothing at all to indicate whether the handicapped individual had already accepted Jesus as his personal Lord and Savior (which seems improbable) or whether perhaps he or his sponsor "believed" in him only as a worker of miracles. All that mattered was that this man or woman or child needed help, and that Jesus was able and was eager to provide this help, this healing—**so that the people were astonished**

---

[586] It is true that here in 15:29, as well as in 5:1; 8:1; Mark 3:13, the original uses the definite article and speaks of τὸ ὄρος. There is a difference however. In the case of 5:1, etc. the place indication, though not precise, is far more definite than in 15:29. We know that the hill to which reference is there made was in the vicinity of Capernaum (see 8:5; cf. 7:1). Similarly we know that "the hill" from which Jesus saw and went forth to meet the large multitude which he fed, as recorded in Matt. 14, Mark 6, Luke 9, and John 6, was in the close vicinity of Bethsaida (Luke 9:10). Here, however, in 15:29, nothing is definite. Therefore it makes little difference whether in the present passage one wishes to retain the full force of the definite article and to translate "*the* hill" or simply "*a* hill."

when they saw (the) dumb speaking, (the) crippled restored, (the) lame walking, and (the) blind seeing.

It all happened at once. This was not a case of *one* astounding miracle; no, miracles were being performed on every side, wherever one might look. That many of the people on whom these miracles were being performed were Gentiles by birth is clearly implied in the manner in which their thanksgiving and praise is described: **and they glorified the God of Israel.** This certainly reads as if it means that they ascribed honor to the God who originally was not theirs but the God of another people. Something truly wonderful was happening. There had been a time when many people from this region made a trek to Galilee to be healed by Jesus (4:23, 25). But now the Prophet from Galilee had actually come nearer to them. What a blessing!

In this connection it is certainly unnecessary to construct arguments in defense of Christ's manifestation of mercy toward those who for the most part were Gentiles by birth. For example, to say that Jesus had a right to work among these people because the Decapolis was considered part of Galilee and therefore belonged to the Jewish domain, [587] so that in performing his ministry of mercy among them the Lord was not really violating the principle expressed in 15:24, [588] is, to say the least, unnecessary. To include all of these people in the group designated "the lost sheep of the house of Israel," is not this stretching the meaning of that designation somewhat beyond its proper limits?

When during an Alpine avalanche a rescue team is sent out to save the life of a skier, the order to do this mentioning *only* that one person; but the team, having arrived at the scene, saves not only his life but also that of three others, are not the rescuers lauded for having done this? So also the rule expressed in 15:24 must not be construed as a restriction so rigid and confining that Jesus would not have been able by word and deed to provide a foreglimpse of the entrance of the Gentiles into the kingdom of heaven. If that had been the case he could not have healed the centurion's servant (8:5-13). Or shall we say that the centurion's request was granted because he happened to be living on Jewish soil and therefore belonged to "the lost sheep of the house of Israel"? This would be impossible. In fact in the very context he is viewed as a forerunner of those who shall come from east and west, and not as belonging to "the children of the kingdom." Nevertheless, his prayer was answered!

Were the people of the Decapolis, etc., given instruction in the way of life, the mysteries of the kingdom of heaven? This is not recorded. Nevertheless, I

---

[587] R. C. H. Lenski assigns this territory to Herod Antipas; R. V. G. Tasker (*op. cit.*, pp. 152, 153) to "Herod (!) Philip." This combination of originally ten cities, forming a trade, commerce, and defensive alliance, seems to have been to a great extent answerable directly to the governor of Syria (Josephus, *Antiquities* XIV.74-76).

[588] Along this line Lenski, *op. cit.*, p. 583.

would join Lenski in opining that we can hardly imagine that the Lord would have spent three days (verse 32) with these crowds without ever teaching them "about *the God of Israel* and his kingdom of salvation." [589]

Applicable to verses 29-31, as well as to similar passages (especially 14:34-36) are the words of E. H. Plumptre:

> Thine arm, O Lord, in days of old
> Was strong to heal and save;
> It triumphed o'er disease and death,
> O'er darkness and the grave.
> To thee they went: the blind, the dumb,
> The palsied, and the lame,
> The leper with his tainted life
> The sick with fevered frame.
>
> And lo, thy touch brought life and health,
> Gave speech and strength and sight;
> Lo, youth renewed and frenzy calmed
> Owned thee, the Lord of light.
> And now, O Lord, be near to bless,
> Almighty as of yore,
> In crowded streets, by restless couch,
> As by Gennesareth's shore.

32, Then Jesus summoned his disciples and said to them, "I am moved with compassion for the multitude, because already for three days they have remained with me and have nothing to eat. I do not want to send them away hungry, lest they collapse on the way." 33 And the disciples said to him, "Where in this uninhabited region would we get bread enough to feed such a crowd?" 34 Jesus asked them, "How many bread-cakes do y o u have?" They answered, "Seven, and a few small fishes." 35 So, having ordered the people to take their places on the ground, 36 he took the seven bread-cakes and the fishes, and having given thanks he broke them and kept giving them to the disciples, and the disciples (kept giving them) to the people. 37 All ate and were filled. What was left over of the pieces they picked up, seven hampers full. 38 The number of those who ate was four thousand men, not counting women and children. 39 Now after he had sent the crowds away he stepped into the boat and came to the region of Magadan.

15:32-39 *The Feeding of the Four Thousand*
Cf. Mark 8:1-10

32. Then Jesus summoned his disciples and said to them, I am moved with compassion for the multitude, because already for three days they have remained with me and have nothing to eat. I do not want to send them away hungry, lest they collapse on the way. A human being in need or a crowd in need always filled the heart of Christ with *compassion* (on which see

---

[589] *Op. cit.*, p. 583.

footnote 425, p. 439). See, for example, 9:36; 14:14; 20:34. Also, he wants his disciples to be similarly affected (cf. 14:16, 18, 19; cf. John 6:5). So he summons them and reveals to them that his heart is going out to the multitude. In this connection it must not be overlooked that, as indicated earlier, this is the very ministry during which Jesus in a special way gave instruction to his disciples.

A strange thing was happening in this Gentile region. The crowds would be with Jesus in the morning hours and also in the afternoon. When it became time to go home they, instead, would stay on. Evidently they did not wish to miss out on any of Christ's marvelous deeds. They were still there the next day, and even the next. Finally their food supply had dwindled down to nothing. If under these circumstances they should be dismissed they might well collapse [590] on the way, so the Lord informs his disciples. This must not happen. Continued: **33. And the disciples said to him, Where in this uninhabited region would we get bread enough to feed such a crowd?** The uninhabited region, evidently to the east or southeast of the Sea of Galilee, was a desolate place, a veritable wilderness (cf. Mark 8:4; II Cor. 11:26; Heb. 11:38). To say that the disciples meant, "Where would *we* get bread enough for this crowd, but what *we* cannot do *thou* canst do," and that these men show that they have taken to heart the lesson of the feeding of the five thousand, and therefore deserve credit for their question, seems somewhat unnatural. The more usual interpretation, namely, that the disciples were at a loss what to do about the situation, is certainly far more in keeping with the impression which their words make upon the average reader. Besides, this second interpretation is in harmony with 16:8-10. **34. Jesus asked them, How many bread-cakes do y o u have?** They answered, **Seven and a few small fishes.** This strongly reminds one of 14:17. To say that what the Lord is about to do is less important than the feeding of the five thousand, because this time it took more bread-cakes to feed less people, is an error. Humanly speaking it is just as impossible to cause seven bread-cakes and a few fishes to be sufficient for four thousand than to make five bread-cakes and two fishes enough for five thousand. It takes a miracle to do either.

The reason for Christ's question, which required a detailed answer, was probably this, that the complete and accurate knowledge of the (humanly speaking) totally inadequate supply would make the miracle stand out all the more strikingly.

The miracle itself is now related: **35, 36. So, having ordered the people to take their places on the ground, he took the seven bread-cakes and the fishes,**

---

[590] ἐκλυθῶσι, 3rd, per. pl. aor. subj. passive of ἐκλύω. In the passive this means *to have one's strength loosened or relaxed;* hence, *to give out, to be weakened to the point of utter exhaustion,* and thus, *to collapse.*

and having given thanks he broke them and kept giving them to the disciples, and the disciples (kept giving them) to the people. With a few minor exceptions this is the same as what is found in 14:19; hence, for explanation see on that passage. Exceptions: *a.* The phrase "on the grass" of 14:19 is replaced by "on the ground." It is later in the season now. The grass has withered away. *b.* There is no mention now of "looking to heaven," but that is understood. *c.* A different verb is substituted for the action of the host—generally the father of the family bit in this case Jesus—in invoking the blessing upon the food, but, as was pointed out previously (see on 14:19), the two verbs are synonymous. *d.* The substitution of "kept giving" for "gave" [591] makes the present account even more vivid than the former.

The greatness of the miracle is shown in the next two verses. To bring out their almost verbal resemblance to 14:20, 21 (see on that passage for explanation), the two accounts will be placed side by side:

14:20, 21	15:37, 38
All ate and were filled. They picked up what was left over of the pieces: twelve baskets full. The number of men who ate was about five thousand, not counting women and children.	All ate and were filled. What was left over of the pieces they picked up: seven hampers full. The number of those who ate was four thousand men, not counting women and children.

Note the twelve *baskets* of broken pieces that were picked up in connection with the feeding of the five thousand, as compared with the seven *hampers* filled with such pieces that were collected now. [592] There is, after all, a difference between "a basket," be it ever so strong, and "a large basket" or "hamper." One can easily carry a baby in a basket, but it took nothing less than a hamper to lower Paul from the wall (Acts 9:25). Once this point is grasped it also becomes clear that it is not at all sure that after the feeding of the four thousand less broken pieces were picked up than after that of the five thousand. The *seven hampers* may have contained no less bread than the *twelve baskets.*

Is the account of the feeding of the four thousand a near-repetition of the earlier miracle, so that had it been omitted entirely from Holy Writ we should not have been the poorer for this omission? Definitely not. Two

---

591 Matt. 14:19 has the aorist ἔδωκεν; 15:36 the imperfect ἐδίδου.

592 In 14:20 the Greek uses the plural of the noun κόφινος, a wicker-basket. Cf. the parallel passages Mark 6:43; Luke 9:17; and John 6:13. The same word is also used in Matt. 16:9 ("how many baskets") and its parallel Mark 8:19. The distinction between this word and σπυρίς (or σφυρίς) is maintained consistently in the New Testament. Hence, both Matt. 15:37 and its parallel Mark 8:7 use the plural of the word σπυρίς, a hamper. And (in contrast with Matt. 16:9; Mark 8:19) both Matt. 16:10 and Mark 8:20 refer to hampers. "Hamper" is also a good translation of the word as used in Acts 9:25.

additional points are now made clear: *a*. Jesus is able not only *to perform* but also *to repeat* his mighty works. He is always ready to help; and *b*. His sympathy is shown not only to the people of the covenant but even to those outside of it.

The story concludes with the words: **39. Now after he had sent the crowds away he stepped into the boat and came to the region of Magadan.** Having been amply fed, the crowds are now sent home. Besides, the people must not be given an opportunity to give concrete expression to erroneous and dangerous deductions (see John 6:15 in connection with the feeding of the five thousand). The Lord then stepped into "the boat"—the one in which he had arrived on the east side of the sea, though this boat was not mentioned earlier—and crossed over to the region of Magadan, or, as a variant reading has it, "Magdala" (cf. A.V.). Mark 8:10 has "Dalmanutha." Since the crossing must now have been from the eastern to the western shore of the Sea of Galilee, and since south of the Plain of Gennesaret a cave bearing the name "Talmanutha" was found, it would seem that it was at or near this spot on the western shore of the sea that Jesus landed. This interpretation also enables us, without great difficulty, to obtain an intelligible view of Christ's further travels, namely, recrossing the sea to the northeastern side (i.e., to Bethsaida Julias), and from there proceeding to the villages of Caesarea Philippi (see Mark 8:13, 22, 27).

Summary of Chapter 15:21-39

For a long time—perhaps from December of the year 27 to April of the year 29—Jesus had labored mostly in and around Galilee. Now at last the Great Galilean Ministry is ended. Jesus retires to the district of Tyre and Sidon. The Retirement Ministry has begun. It will probably last until about October of the same year. Jesus, then, has now definitely entered Gentile territory. Then (verses 21-28), lo and behold, a Canaanite woman from that region approaches him. She is constantly crying, "Take pity on me, O Lord, Son of David; my daughter is severely tormented by a demon." From the manner in which she addresses Jesus her reverential attitude toward him is evident. She must have heard about him. She is agonizing over her daughter's dire affliction. She does not seem to resent the Master's initial silence, the constant urging of the disciples for her curt dismissal, the remark of Jesus, "Only to the lost sheep of the house of Israel was I sent," nor even his *seemingly* insulting statement, "It is not proper to take the children's bread and throw it to the house dogs." Her humility must be admired. Also her intense love for her daughter, with whom she identifies herself in the most inseparable union, so that the child's suffering is her (the mother's) suffering; its needs, her needs. Note, "Lord, help *me*." In spite of all obstacles she perseveres, turning the very word of seeming reproach into a reason for optimism: "Even the house dogs eat some of the scraps that drop from their masters' table." The end is victory, the triumph of her God-given faith. "Let it be done for you as you desire," says Jesus. "And healed was her daughter from that very moment." Had Jesus come to save the lost sheep of the house of Israel? Well, here was a true Israelite! See Gen. 32:26.

In the next few verses (29-31) we are shown that Jesus spent at least three days (cf. verse 32) on the eastern or southeastern shore of the Sea of Galilee. From the entire surrounding region people bring their handicapped relatives, friends, and neighbors. They lay them at Jesus' feet. He heals all, regardless of whether they are men or women, young or old, Jews or Gentiles. The crowds are astonished, and they glorify "the God of Israel." This very designation may indicate that a good many of them were not Israelites by race.

The final paragraph (verses 32-39) narrates the feeding of the four thousand. On the eastern or southeastern shore of the Sea of Galilee, Jesus, sympathizing with a huge crowd that has been with him three days and has nothing left to eat, tells his disciples, "I do not want to send them away hungry, lest they collapse on the way." The disciples, at a loss what to do about the situation—they evidently have not taken to heart the lesson of the feeding of the five thousand—answer, "Where in this uninhabited region would we get bread enough to feed such a crowd?" In answer to his question they inform their Master that they have only seven bread-cakes and a few small fishes. For these hungry people Jesus then performs a miracle that is similar in many respects to that of the feeding of the five thousand. Seven hampers full of broken pieces are left after everybody has had plenty to eat. The very fact that Jesus was able to repeat his miracles shows his greatness. The fact that, as this second miraculous feeding indicates, his sympathy goes out to Gentiles as well as to Jews, enhances its significance, proving that "the love of God is broader than the measure of man's mind; and the heart of the Eternal is most wonderfully kind" (F. W. Faber).

Outline of Chapter 16

Theme: *The Work Which Thou Gavest Him to Do*

CHAPTER XVI

16 1 Now the Pharisees and Sadducees came and, tempting him, asked him to show them a sign from heaven. 2 But he answered and said to them, "In the evening y o u say, 'Fair weather, for the sky is red'; 3 and in the morning, 'Bad weather today, for the sky is red and lowering.' Y o u know how to interpret correctly the appearance of the sky, but the signs of the times y o u cannot interpret. 4 An evil and adulterous generation is looking for a sign, but no sign shall be given it except that of Jonah." And having left them, he went away.

16:1-4 Renewed Craving for Signs and Renewed Rebuke
Cf. Mark 8:11-13; Luke 12:54-56

Now that Jesus has arrived once more on the western, more densely populated, and more Jewish (though still ethnically "mixed") side of the Sea of Galilee, another confrontation of himself and his bitter opponents is not surprising. Had these enemies been anxiously waiting for his arrival so that they could begin their sinister attack? We read: 1. **Now the Pharisees and Sadducees came and, tempting him, asked him to show them a sign from heaven.** Had they heard about his miracles of providing food for the hungry and physical restoration for the handicapped on the eastern side of the sea? Was it this that had nourished afresh their ever-present envy? As before (see on 12:38) so also now the sign-value of Jesus' miracles, the idea that these marvelous works indicated that he had been sent by God, was challenged.

The Pharisees could not very well deny his extraordinary powers but they tried hard to convince themselves and others that these were nothing but black magic, straight out of hell. Besides, were they not merely "earthly" signs? What they are once again asking for is "a sign *from heaven.*" Let him cause manna to drop from the sky, as (according to their view) Moses had done (Exod. 16; cf. John 6:32). Or, like Joshua, by means of prayer let him cause the sun and the moon to stand still (Josh. 10:12-14). Or again, as in the days of Deborah and Barak, let him make the stars to fight for Israel (Judg. 5:20). Or, in imitation of Samuel, let him, by means of a fervent petition, draw down a thunderstorm to discomfit the "Philistines" of his own day, that is, the Romans (I Sam. 7:10). Let him at least not lag behind Elijah whose imploration brought an instantaneous response of "fire from heaven" (I Kings 18:30-40).—As if, had he done any of these things, or anything of a similar sensational nature—see on 12:38, 39—these bitter foes, driven by envy, would not have ascribed also such a sign to Beelzebul as its source! See Luke 16:31.

This time (contrast 12:38, 39) we are told specifically that the purpose of the enemy was *to tempt* Jesus, to put him to the test, in the hope and with the expectation that he would fail, and would thus be publicly discredited.

There is another difference between 12:38, 39 and the present account. This time, as Matthew not only states but repeats and stresses (16:1, 6, 11, 12), the Pharisees are joined by the Sadducees in their efforts to expose Jesus to public embarrassment and loss of face. The marked contrast between these two parties and the reason why they were able, nevertheless, to form a united front against Jesus, have already been indicated; see pp. 201-204. This very combination of forces shows that the effort to destroy the One whom they considered their enemy was becoming more and more determined. The Pharisees, single-handedly most of the time (9:3, 11, 34; 12:2, 14, 24, 38; 15:1; but see also 12:14; cf. Mark 3:6), had frequently attacked Jesus. But now we see Pharisees *and Sadducees* allied against him.

In asking for a sign from heaven did these men not realize that *the* sign from heaven was standing right in front of them? See Matt. 24:30; Luke 2:34. Had he not already provided abundant proof of the genuine character of his mission? Had he not done so by word and deed, in fulfilment of prophecy? See Matt. 11:4-6.

2, 3. But he answered and said to them, In the evening y o u say, Fair weather, for the sky is red; and in the morning, Bad weather today, for the sky is red and lowering. Y o u know how to interpret correctly the appearance of the sky, but the signs of the times y o u cannot interpret. [593] Jesus rebukes these men because they pay far more attention to constantly changing weather conditions than to events that usher in epoch-making historical changes. Did not the coming into this world of the Son of man, with his emphasis on the power, grace, and love of God, rather than on man-made—often silly—regulations, and with his exhibition of power over everything, including even disease, death, demons, and destructive storms, foretell the downfall of legalistic Judaism? Did it not spell the rise of a church gathered out of both Jews and Gentiles and consisting of all those who believed in salvation by grace through faith and in a life of gratitude to

---

[593] The fact that Vaticanus, Sinaiticus, Old Syrian and Coptic texts omit these verses has been explained as the result of mental assimilation of the phraseology of one passage to that of another (that other one being 12:38, 39; cf. Mark 8:11, 12), an explanation that deserves consideration. Also, there are those who believe that texts originating in Egypt omit verses 2 and 3 because a red morning sky does not there herald rain. Since it is easier to explain the omission of these verses than their addition, the conclusion that they were probably authentic is warranted. Omitting them would result in what is left (16:1, 4) being virtually nothing but a repetition—except for the reference to the Sadducees and the words "tempting him"—of 12:38, 39, an improbable supposition.

God and of service to man? Was not this coming and that manifestation of power and grace a clear prediction both of the doom of Satan and of the significant strengthening of the kingdom that can never be destroyed? Were these critics utterly blind? Could they not read the handwriting on the wall? Did they not understand that their days, including their quibbling about nonessentials, were numbered, and that the gospel that was being proclaimed by the Prophet from Galilee, even the Son of God, would begin to spread and spread until it covered the earth? But no, the signs of the *times* [594] do not seem to interest them. *They* prefer to concentrate on the weather!

Along with ever so many people who observe the sky, these Pharisees and Sadducees knew how to differentiate between and judge correctly [595] the varying aspects of the sky. They knew that in their country a bright red evening [596] sky was a frequent indicator of a clear tomorrow, [597] the cloud masses and mists having moved to the west. "When the sunset is clear, there's nothing to fear." On the other hand when, during the night, the wind, coming from the west, that is, from the Mediterranean, had driven clouds and vapors across the country, so that at dawn the eastern sky was a brilliant red mixed with threatening bands of darkness, they knew that a rainy or stormy day might well be in the offing, for, "When clouds move down and turn dark gray, one may expect a stormy day." Of course, all such predictions are subject to many variables: vision may be obscured and distorted by dust clouds, winds may change (John 3:8), etc., but by and large the weather predictions made by Pharisees and Sadducees were correct. How deplorable that these men were majoring on minors!

As to their request for a sign, as if none had been given, Jesus answers: **4. An evil and adulterous generation is looking for a sign, but no sign shall be given it except that of Jonah.** By means of that sign, Christ's atoning death and glorious resurrection from the grave, he would triumph completely over them, and would prove himself to be the Messiah (Rom. 1:4). This was going to be the "sign" of his complete victory over all his enemies (Matt. 26:64; Mark 14:62) and a forecast of his triumphant return upon the clouds of heaven (Phil. 2:9-11; 3:20; Rev. 1:5, 7). For the rest, see the explanation of 12:39, where these same words are found.—For "generation" see on 1:17.

What a sign this death and resurrection would be for the Pharisees, who were constantly planning Jesus' death, with no fear that he would ever be

---

594 Note καιρῶν. Jesus is speaking about epoch-making periods in history, not about time viewed as a change from the past into the present into the future, mere duration. See R. C. Trench, *Synonyms of the New Testament*, par. lvii, on χρόνος versus καιρός.

595 Note διακρίνειν pres. act. infinitive of διακρίνω.

596 The adjective ὄψιος, α, ον means *late*. Here we have ὀψίας, with ὥρας understood; hence, *in the evening*. The word πρωΐ is an adverb of time meaning *early*.

597 The term εὐδία, "fair weather," is derived from εὐ and Ζεύς, gen. Διός, Zeus being considered the ruler of the air and the sky; hence, of the weather.

able to conquer death; and for the Sadducees, who did not even believe in any resurrection! **And having left them, he went away.** They are abandoned to their fate, the destiny they, by their hardness of heart, have chosen for themselves.

---

5. And when the disciples went to the other side they forgot to take along bread. 6 Jesus said to them, "Look out for and be on y o u r guard against the yeast of the Pharisees and Sadducees." 7 They began to reason among themselves, saying, "It's because we didn't take any bread." 8 When Jesus noticed this he said, "Why do y o u reason among yourselves, y o u men of little faith, that y o u have no bread? 9 Do y o u still lack understanding, and do y o u not remember the five bread-cakes for the five thousand and how many baskets y o u picked up? 10 Or the seven bread-cakes for the four thousand and how many hampers y o u picked up? 11 How is it then that y o u do not understand that I was not talking to y o u about bread but (said to y o u), 'Be on y o u r guard against the yeast of the Pharisees and Sadducees?' " 12 Then they understood that he had not told them to be on their guard against yeast used in bread but against the teaching of the Pharisees and Sadducees.

16:5-12 *The Yeast of the Pharisees and Sadducees*
Cf. Mark 8:14-21

5. **And when the disciples went to the other side they forgot to take along bread.** Jesus and his disciples had spent a little while on the western shore of the sea (15:39). Now they recross the same body of water, this time going back to the east or northeast side. As they "went" [598] or "started out" (Beck's rendering), they forgot to buy bread. One solitary bread-cake is all they had with them in the boat (Mark 8:14). Continued: 6. **Jesus said to them, Look out for and be on y o u r guard against the yeast of the Pharisees and Sadducees.** The Master is still thinking about his recent experience with these two groups (see verses 1-4). Since these two had combined in their assault against him he speaks of them as if they were not two but one, *one* definite article preceding "Pharisees and Sadducees." Well, they were indeed one, namely, in the basic principle that governed their lives as shown in their effort to attain "salvation" or "security" by their own efforts. Religion in both cases was outward conformity to a certain standard. They were one in "dislike of single-hearted devotion to truth and righteousness." [599] They

---

[598] The original uses the word ἐλθόντες (masc. pl. aor. participle of ἔρχομαι) which may, however, mean "having gone" as well as "having come." In the present context "went" must therefore be considered a legitimate rendering; cf. Mark 8:13, "went away [or: departed] to the other side." See also Luke 15:20: "and he went to his father."

Though there are those who interpret the original as meaning that the disciples forgot to buy bread after arriving on the eastern side, yet the more usual view, namely, that in starting out on the western side they forgot to buy bread, deserves the preference, since the staff of life was much more readily obtainable on the heavily populated western than on the eastern side.

[599] A. B. Bruce, *The Synoptic Gospels*, p. 220.

were one, accordingly, in their philosophy of life and therefore also basically in their teaching. Thus, although the outwardly pious Pharisees may be contrasted with the worldly Sadducees, yet when the Pharisees were teaching the younger generation how to evade the requirement of honoring their parents (15:3-9) were they not just as "worldly" as the Sadducees?

It is against this teaching of the Pharisees and Sadducees that Jesus is here earnestly warning his disciples. He calls their teaching "yeast," for like an increasingly penetrating principle it influenced their own as well as other lives. In view of the fact that the disciples had already heard the parable of the yeast "which a woman took and put into three measures of wheat flour, until the whole batch had risen" (13:33), there was really no good reason for misunderstanding what Jesus meant.

Nevertheless, the disciples misunderstood it: **7. They began to reason among themselves, saying, It's because we didn't take any bread.** They interpreted "yeast" literally, and thought that Jesus was warning them against accepting any bread from Pharisees and Sadducees. Here, then, we have another instance of what was happening repeatedly, namely, that human minds, by nature superficial, failed to grasp the deep and often figurative meaning of Christ's sayings. For other instances of erroneously literal interpretation see John 2:19, 20; 3:3, 4; 4:13-15; 6:51, 52; 11:11, 12.

The disciples, in saying, "It's because we didn't take any bread," were guilty also of another error, as is clear from Christ's reaction as recorded in the following verses. They thought that the Lord was very displeased with them for having forgotten to buy bread; at least, they were worried about this lack of bread-cakes. Note how in verses 8-10 Jesus reflects on this irresponsible worry; in verse 11, on the misinterpretation of his words of warning. **8-10. When Jesus noticed this he said, Why do y o u reason among yourselves, y o u men of little faith, that y o u have no bread? Do y o u still lack understanding, and do y o u not remember the five bread-cakes for the five thousand and how many baskets y o u picked up? Or the seven bread-cakes for the four thousand and how many hampers y o u picked up?** Again, as before—see on 6:30; 8:26; and for the singular see 14:31—Jesus calls the disciples "men of little faith," that is, men who were not sufficiently taking to heart the comfort which they should have derived from the presence, promises, power, and love of their Master, and were not applying to the present situation the lessons received in the past. The Lord reminds them of the time when five bread-cakes more than fed five thousand, and of that other occasion when seven bread-cakes more than sufficed for four thousand. Do the disciples remember how many "baskets" full of broken pieces were collected afterward in connection with the first miracle, and how many "hampers" in connection with the second? For the distinction between "baskets" and "hampers" see footnote 592 on p. 630.

The failure of the disciples to apply to the present situation the lesson of the multiplication, not once but twice, of the bread-cakes was certainly inexcusable. But when it is argued, as has happened, that this part of the story is so unnatural as to warrant the conclusion that it is also unhistorical, the answer is that such behavior, though inexcusable, is after all not entirely inexplicable. The idea that a few rolls will suffice for only a few people is so deeply embedded in the human mind that the presence of anxiety when only a single one is available must not be regarded as impossible or unnatural. Besides, for the person who accepts God's Word as true there is no insuperable difficulty in believing that the event as here recorded took place in every detail as recorded.

As to the misinterpretation of Christ's words of warning the story continues as follows: **11. How is it then that y o u do not understand that I was not talking to y o u about bread but (said to y o u), Be on y o u r guard against the yeast of the Pharisees and Sadducees?** If the disciples had reflected on the fact that concern with reference to bread *for a small company,* though understandable, was totally out of place on the basis of the fact that Jesus with a few bread-cakes had twice fed *thousands,* with plenty of bread left on both occasions, their minds would have turned in a different direction in attempting to interpret the Master's warning with respect to "the yeast of the Pharisees and Sadducees." "I was not talking to y o u about bread," says Jesus, "but I was warning y o u to beware of the yeast of the Pharisees and Sadducees." The result of Christ's explanation, an explanation recorded only by Matthew, was favorable: **12. Then they understood that he had not told them to be on their guard against yeast used in bread but against the teaching of the Pharisees and Sadducees.** Finally, the light dawned on them so that they understood [600] that Jesus was warning them against *the teaching* of the Pharisees and Sadducees.

---

13 Now when Jesus arrived in the district of Caesarea Philippi he asked his disciples, "Who do the people say that the Son of man is?" 14 They said, "Some (say) John the Baptist; some, Elijah; and others, Jeremiah, or one of the prophets." 15 "But y o u," he asked, "Who do y o u say that I am?" 16 Simon Peter answered and said, "Thou art the Christ, the Son of the living God." 17 Jesus answered and said to him, "Blessed are you, Simon Bar-Jonah, for it is not flesh and blood but my Father who is in heaven who has revealed this to you. 18 And I say to you, you are Peter, and upon this rock I will build my church, and the gates of Hades shall not overpower it. 19 I will give to you the keys of the kingdom of heaven, and whatever you shall bind on earth shall be bound in heaven, and whatever you shall loose on earth shall be loosed in heaven." 20 Then he gave the disciples strict orders not to tell anyone that he was the Christ.

---

[600] The word συνῆκαν is the aor. active indic. of συνίημι. The meaning "to set together," hence, "to understand," reminds us of our own expression, "to put two and two together." Instances of the use of this verb in the New Testament: In Matthew it is u ed also in 13:13, 14, 15, 19, 23; 15:10; 17:13. There are several instances of its use in Mark. Luke has it in both of his books. So does Paul in Rom. 3:11; 15:21; II Cor. 10:12; Eph. 5:17.

16:13-20 *Peter's Confession and Christ's Reply*
Cf. Mark 8:27-30; Luke 9:18-21

Jesus continues to instruct his disciples. During this Ministry of the Retirement he has already *by example* taught them to help those in need, whether Jew or Gentile (15:21-39); and *by precept* to be on their guard against the teaching of the Pharisees and Sadducees (16:1-12). Of course, this teaching was simply a continuation of that which had been given earlier, but could now be imparted with greater emphasis since the Master was spending more time alone with his disciples. Beginning with 16:13 he is going to teach them matters concerning himself. As *King* he is in complete control of every situation, as he shows throughout; as *Prophet,* he is about to set forth that he is indeed the long expected Messiah, and that as such, in fulfilment of prophecy he must suffer, be put to death, and rise again, truths which before had been conveyed to the disciples in a veiled manner only (10:38; 12:40) but were now going to be revealed to them clearly. Now was the right time, for as *Highpriest* the Son of man will soon be bringing himself as an offering "in exchange for many" (20:28; Mark 10:45).

To bring about the right atmosphere of quietness, serenity, and privacy, the Lord decides to go with his disciples to "the district of Caesarea Philippi": **13. Now when Jesus arrived in the district of Caesarea Philippi he asked his disciples, Who do the people say that the Son of man is?** If "the other side" to which the little company had arrived previously (16:5) was anywhere in the neighborhood of Bethsaida Julias, then from there almost straight north to Caesarea Philippi was a distance of approximately twenty-four miles. By Philip the tetrarch this place had been enlarged, beautified, and named in honor of Caesar Augustus. Near it was a sanctuary to the pagan god Pan, which gave rise to the name *Paneas* to mark the general site where Caesarea was subsequently located. The very designation *Pan* is still reflected in *Bāniyās*, as it is called today. It is located near the northern tip of that small section of S.W. Syria that is now occupied by Israel. To distinguish Caesarea to which reference is made here in 16:13 from its namesake, the far more important seaport south of Mt. Carmel, and to indicate its founder, it was called Caesarea *Philippi.*

Situated near one of the sources of the Jordan River, with 9,232 feet high majestic Mt. Hermon, snow-covered throughout most of the year, in the immediate background, it was truly a landscape of unforgettable pictur-esqueness, [601] a place exactly suited to the purpose for which Jesus wished

---

[601] The following sources shed further light on this: H. La Fay, "Where Jesus Walked," *National Geographic,* Vol. 132, No. 6 (December, 1967), pp. 739-781, with map supplement of "The Lands of the Bible Today"; L. H. Grollenberg, *op. cit.,* maps 2, 34, plate 360; E. G. Kraeling, *op. cit.,* p. 389; W. Ewing, art. "Hermon" in I.S.B.E., Vol. III, p. 1378; and Viewmaster Travelogue Reel No. 4015, Scene 1, "The River Jordan, Palestine."

to use it, namely, for prayer (Luke 9:18) and for imparting instruction to his disciples.

Having been strengthened through fellowship with his heavenly Father, Jesus now asks his disciples, "Who do the people say that the Son of man is?" For a detailed study of the term "Son of man" see on 8:20. The disciples knew that "Son of man" was their Master's self-designation, which explains why both Mark 8:27 and Luke 9:18 record the question in the form ". . . that *I* am." Already Jesus knew that at the appropriate moment, that is, after the disciples' reply, he would ask an even more important question, the one found in verse 15. What had been veiled heretofore must now come out into the open, not as yet for announcement to the general public, but so that the disciples may know who this Jesus really is and what is going to happen to him. Then, when the dramatic events do actually take place these men will not remain as thoroughly perplexed as would have been the case had they not been pre-informed about them (cf. John 14:29; 16:1, 4, 33).

Continued: **14. They said, Some (say) John the Baptist; some, Elijah; and others, Jeremiah, or one of the prophets.** They graciously omit that some identified Jesus with Beelzebul (10:25). This omission may also be explained by the fact that Jesus was not asking what envious scribes and Pharisees thought of him but what name the people in general applied to him. The answer was that some were of the opinion that Jesus was John the Baptist, brought back to life (cf. 14:2). Others held him to be Elijah. Now, although John had gone forth in the spirit and power of Elijah (Luke 1:17), and was therefore going to be called "Elijah" by no one less than Jesus himself, as Matthew's next chapter indicates (17:12), yet he was not literally Elijah, and it was the literal, personal forerunner Elijah whom many of the Jews expected and confused with Jesus, partly as a result of their misinterpretation of Mal. 4:5. These first two groups seem to have viewed Jesus as a forerunner of the Messiah.

Still others identified Jesus with Jeremiah, as another forerunner perhaps? Did they imagine that, in the person of Jesus, Jeremiah had returned in order to bring back the tent, the ark, and the altar of incense, which, according to a legend recorded in II Macc. 2:4-8, that prophet had hid in a cave? Finally, there were those who considered Jesus to be neither the Messiah nor even his forerunner but simply one of the prophets "risen again" (Luke 9:19).

And now the far more important question: **15. But y o u, he asked, Who do y o u say that I am?** On a previous occasion (see on 14:33) the disciples had already exclaimed, "Thou art indeed God's Son." Had this been merely a momentary reaction to a mighty miracle, the giving vent to a conviction that had just as quickly disappeared? Or had the truth that Jesus was indeed the Messiah, the very Son of God, become permanently lodged in their hearts and minds?

In the original enormous stress is placed on "But *y o u.*" This personal pronoun, second person plural, stands at the very head of the question. It appears first as a word all by itself, and is then included again as an element in the verb. In the translation an attempt has been made to retain this tremendous emphasis. Salvation is a very personal matter. The people all around us may have their various opinions about Jesus, but what do *we* think of him? That is the question.

It must be borne in mind that this question had been addressed to all these men, not just to one of them; hence, "y o u," not "you." Accordingly when *one* of the Twelve now answers it, he does so as the spokesman for the entire group, and the answer which Jesus gives him must therefore also be regarded as not being altogether without significance for the group. **16. Simon Peter answered and said, Thou art the Christ, the Son of the living God.** The personality of Peter and his position of leadership has received earlier comment (see on 4:18-22; 10:2; 14:28, 29). In the present passage note:

a. Probably to add solemnity and clarity to the record of the event this disciple's full name is here used: "Simon Peter." This appellation is the usual one in *John's* Gospel, but not in the Synoptics. It occurs in Luke 5:8, in connection with another context of deep emotion and humble reverence.

b. In the Gospels and in the book of Acts Peter frequently represents The Twelve, as is clear not only from the present context but also, among others, from Matt. 15:15, 16; 19:27, 28; 26:35, 40, 41; Luke 8:45; 9:32, 33; 12:41; 18:28; John 6:67-69; Acts 1:15; 2:14, 37, 38; and 5:29. Nevertheless, his identity is not lost. It is Peter who speaks and Peter who is going to be addressed in verses 17-19.

c. Even before this time Peter had made soul-stirring declarations concerning Jesus (Luke 5:8; John 6:68, 69), but the present profession of faith is the most complete of them all.

d. As to definiteness, in this concise statement, containing only ten words, the original uses the definite article no less than four times.

e. When Peter declares Jesus to be "the Christ" he means the long awaited Anointed One, the One who as Mediator was set apart or ordained by the Father and anointed with the Holy Spirit, to be his people's chief Prophet (Deut. 18:15, 18; Isa. 55:4; Luke 24:19; Acts 3:22, 7:37); only Highpriest (Ps. 110:4; Rom. 8:34; Heb. 6:20; 7:24; 9:24); and eternal King. (Ps. 2:6; Zech. 9:9; Matt. 21:5; 28:18; Luke 1:33; John 10:28; Eph. 1:20-23; Rev. 11:15; 12:10, 11; 17:14; 19:6).

f. Peter's declaration that Jesus is "the Son of the living God" can mean no less than that in a unique sense, a sense not applicable to any mortal, Jesus is, was, and always will be the Son of that God who not only is himself the only living One, over against all the dead so-called gods of the pagans (Isa. 40:18-31), but also is the only source of life for all that lives.

Immediate, definite, warm, and commendatory is Christ's response to

Peter's confession: 17. Jesus answered and said to him, Blessed are you, Simon Bar-Jonah, for it is not flesh and blood but my Father who is in heaven who has revealed this to you. The literature on the interpretation of 16:17-19, as a whole or in part, is vast.[602] The designation "Simon Bar-Jonah," that is, "Simon, son of Jonah" (or: "of John," John 1:42), was for the person addressed a reminder of what he was by nature, simply a human son of a human father. He was a man who of himself could not have contributed anything worthwhile, just one human being among many. This reminder is going to be followed shortly (verse 18) by an affirmation of that which by grace this same Simon Bar-Jonah had become, namely, a worthy bearer of the name "Cephas" (Aramaic) or "Peter" (Greek).

Jesus pronounces this "Simon Bar-Jonah," alias "Peter," *blessed,* pouring into this word all the depth of meaning which it has in the beatitudes (see on 5:1-3). Naturally, all who agree with Peter are also blessed.

In continuing his address to Peter, Jesus emphasizes that "flesh and blood," that is, merely human calculation, cogitation, intuition, or tradition, could never have produced in this disciple's heart and mind the insight into the sublime truth that he had just now so gloriously professed. On the expression "flesh and blood" see also N.T.C. on Gal. 1:16 and on Eph. 6:12. It was, says Jesus, "my Father who is in heaven" who had disclosed this truth to Simon Bar-Jonah and had enabled him to give buoyant expression to it. To this disciple, and to all those similarly minded, he, this Father in heaven, had "revealed" it (11:25, 26); and this not necessarily directly, by whispering something into the ear, but by blessing to the heart the means of grace, not the least of these means being the lessons which issued from the words and works of Jesus.

In speaking about (or *to*) the One who sent him, not only the eternal essence-relationship but certainly also the warmth of love existing between the persons of the Holy Trinity are disclosed by Christ's preference for the designation *"my* Father." In several passages his use of this phrase is

[602] Among periodical articles are the following, to mention only a few:

Allen, E. L., "On this Rock," *JTS,* 5 (1954), pp. 59-62.

Dell, A., "Zur Erklärung von Matthäus 16:17-19," *ZNW,* 17 (1916), pp. 27-32.

Easton, Burton S., "St. Matthew 16:17-19," *ATR,* 4 (1921, 1922), pp. 156-166; also on the same subject and in the same periodical, 5 (1922, 1923), pp. 116-126.

Jansen, J., "Het Vraagstuk van de sleutelmacht," *GTT,* II (1910), pp. 308-322.

Oulton, J. E. L., "An Interpretation of Matthew 16:18," *ET,* 48 (1936-37), pp. 525, 526.

Seitz, O. J. F., "Upon this Rock: A Critical Re-examination of Matt. 16:17-19," *R.E., JBL* 69 (1950), pp. 329-340.

Slotemaker de Bruine, J. R., "De Sleutelmacht," *TS,* 22 (1904), pp. 23-43.

Soltau, W., "Wann ist Matt. 16:17-19 eingeschoben?" TSK, 89 (1916), pp. 233-237.

Tottenham, C. J., " 'The Gates of Hell' (Matt. 16:18)," *ET,* 29 (1917-18), pp. 378, 379.

Vardapet, E., "The Revelation of the Lord to Peter," *ZNW,* 23 (1924), pp. 8-17.

Votaw, C. W., "Peter and the Keys of the Kingdom," *BW,* 36 (1910), pp. 8-25.

Warren, J., "Was Simon Peter the Church's Rock?" *EQ,* 19 (1947), pp. 196-210.

recorded (11:27; 20:23; 25:34; 26:39, 42, 53). In a number of instances the fuller appellation "my Father (who is) in heaven" is used (in addition to 16:17 see also 7:21; 10:32, 33; 12:50; 18:10, 19), or else "my heavenly Father" (15:13; 18:35).

Jesus continues: 18. **And I say to you, you are Peter, and upon this rock I will build my church.** . . . . The interpretation of this passage varies widely. As I see it, the first three of the following views must be rejected, the fourth one appreciated, the fifth adopted:

1. The passage is unauthentic. It must have been inserted or interpolated, *"eingeschoben"* (W. Soltau), at a later time. It was written, perhaps, to enhance the authority of Peter. It is hard to believe that Jesus himself ever spoke these words. Neither Mark nor Luke has them.

Answer. Since the passage is found in the best and earliest manuscripts as well as in those of later date it cannot be dismissed so lightly. Was it not natural for Jesus, with the cross so near, to have made predictions and issued orders concerning the future of the church? As to Mark's omission of the praise which Jesus bestows upon Peter because of the latter's confession, it should be borne in mind that Mark was, according to reliable tradition, "Peter's interpreter," and that it is reasonable to suppose that Peter, the fiery post-resurrection preacher, who had become a humble man, in telling the story of Jesus downgraded his own contribution to the memorable event described in 16:13-20. So his interpreter, Mark, does the same. And Luke, as so often, follows Mark's account.

2. This passage (especially 16:17-19) proves that Peter was the first pope. "The pope is crowned with a triple crown, as king of heaven, of earth, and of hell." He wields "the two swords, the spiritual and the temporal." [603] "The Catholic Church teaches that our Lord conferred on St. Peter the first place of honor and jurisdiction in the government of his whole church, and that same spiritual authority has always resided in the popes, or bishops of Rome, as being the successors of St. Peter. Consequently, to be true followers of Christ all Christians, both among the clergy and laity, must be in communion with the See of Rome, where Peter rules in the person of his successor." [604]

Answer. The passage does not support any such bestowal of well-nigh absolute authority on a mere man or on his successors.

3. The expression *this rock* "does not signify the apostle Peter," since "Jesus had already finished with Peter." [605]

Answer. Throughout verses 17-19 Jesus is addressing someone whom he indicates by using the second person singular personal pronoun. The phrase

---

[603] These statements can be found in H. M. Riggle, *Roman Catholicism*, Anderson, Ind. and Kansas City, Mo., 1917, pp. 51, 52, quoted from Roman Catholic sources.

[604] Cardinal J. Gibbons, *The Faith of our Fathers*, New York, 1871, p. 95.

[605] R. C. H. Lenski, *op. cit.*, p. 605.

645

"to you" (Greek σοί) occurs once in each of these three verses, in harmony with the pronoun "you" (σύ) in verse 18 ("You are Peter"), and with the use of the second person singular form of the verbs in the statements: "You are blessed" (verse 17), "you are Peter" (verse 18), and "you shall bind . . . you shall loose" (verse 19). According to verse 17 that person is "Simon Bar-Jonah"; according to verse 18, "Peter." It is natural to assume that the subject of "you shall bind" and "you shall loose" (verse 19) is still Peter. It is hard to believe, therefore, that when Jesus said, "And upon this rock I will build my church" (verse 18) he "had already finished with Peter."

4. Jesus purposely uses two Greek words which, though not identical, are closely related in meaning. What he said was, "You are *petros,* and upon this *petra* I will build my church," meaning, "You are a rock, and upon the rocky ledge (or: cliff) of the Christ, 'the Son of God the living' who was revealed to you and whom you confessed, I will build my church." If Jesus had intended to convey the thought that he was going to build his church on Peter he would have said, "and on you I will build my church." When it is argued that the Lord spoke these words in Aramaic and that in that language the two words *petros* and *petra* were the same, the answer is that we do not know enough about Aramaic to make this assertion. We have the inspired Greek text and we must be guided by that.[606]

Evaluation. The argument sounds rather convincing and, in fact, as I see it, has some merit. Granted that Jesus generally addressed his audiences in Aramaic, it still cannot be proved incontrovertibly that in that language *petros* and *petra* were represented by one and the same word. It is also true that in certain contexts *petra* may differ in meaning from *petros.* What I like especially about the theory is this, that those who advocate it are deeply concerned about the danger that the man Peter or even his confession, viewed apart from God's revelation, shall be considered the rock upon which the church is built.

My inability to accept the theory in its entirety is based on the following:

a. On the basis of what is known about Aramaic it must be regarded as very probable that the same word was used in both cases. The question will be asked, "Then why not the same word in Greek?" Answer: for the simple reason that *petra,* the common word for *stone* or *rock,* being feminine, had to be changed to a masculine—hence to *petros*—to indicate the name of *a male person, Peter.* As to *petros* and *petra* differing in meaning, this is not always true. A very frequent meaning of *petra* is *rock* or *stone.* It does not

---

[606] Along this line with individual variations, R. C. H. Lenski argues (*op. cit.,* pp. 605-607, in addition to the statement to which reference was made in the preceding footnote and which was answered in point 3, above); thus, in general, also L. Boettner, *Roman Catholicism,* Philadelphia, 1962, pp. 105, 106; and F. W. Grosheide, *op. cit.,* pp. 255, 256.

always mean "rocky ground," "rocky ledge," or "rocky cliff." See the entries *petra, petros* in L.N.T. (A. and G.), p. 660.

b. Even in Greek, regardless of whether one translates *petra* as *rock* or as *rocky ledge* Jesus is saying, "You are *Rock* and on THIS *rock*—or *rocky ledge*—I will build my church." The word THIS makes reference to anything else than the immediately preceding *petros* very unnatural. In the sentence, "You are Margaret [meaning *pearl*] and on *this* pearl I am about to bestow a favor," it would be very difficult to interpret "this pearl" in any other sense than as referring to Margaret, even though the word "pearl" has more meanings than one. It indicates a gem but can also refer to a kind of printer's type. It would be rather unnatural to conclude that "this pearl" had reference to something that someone had said to Margaret or had shown her, or to something she had just said.

5. The meaning is, *You are Peter, that is, Rock, and upon this rock, that is, on you, Peter, I will build my church.* Our Lord, speaking Aramaic, probably said, "And I say to you, you are *Kepha'*, and on this *kepha'* I will build my church."[607] Jesus, then, is promising Peter that he is going to build his church *on him!* I accept this view.

Having said this, it is necessary to qualify this interpretation as follows. Jesus promises to build his church:

a. Not on Cephas as he was by nature but on him considered as a product of grace. By nature this man was, in a sense, a weakling, very unstable, as has been indicated; see p. 602. By grace he became a most courageous, enthusiastic, and effective witness of the truth which the Father had revealed to him with respect to Jesus Christ, the Son of the living God. It was in that sense that Jesus used Peter in *building*—gathering and strengthening—his church.

b. Not on Cephas considered all by himself, but on Cephas as "first (Matt. 10:2) among equals," that is, on "Peter taking his stand with the eleven" (Acts 2:14). The authority which in 16:19 is entrusted to Peter is in 18:18 given to The Twelve (see also John 20:23). In fact, in the exercise of this authority the local congregation must not be ignored (18:17).

When the Lord spoke the words recorded here in 16:18, 19 he certainly did not mean that Peter could now begin to "lord it" over the other disciples. The others did not understand it in that way (18:1; 20:20-24), and Jesus definitely rejected any such interpretation (20:25-28; cf. Luke 22:24-30). If Peter himself had conceived of his own authority or that of others as being that of a dictator, how could he have written the beautiful passage I Peter 5:3?

c. Not on Cephas as the primary foundation. In the primary or basic sense of the term there is only one foundation, and that foundation is not Peter

---

[607] Cf. B. M. Metzger, *The New Testament, its background, growth, and content*, p. 139.

but Jesus Christ himself (I Cor. 3:11). But in a secondary sense it is entirely legitimate to speak of the apostles, including Peter, as the church's foundation, for these men were always pointing away from themselves to Jesus Christ as the one and only Savior. Striking examples of this are found in Acts 3:12 and 4:12. In that secondary sense Scripture itself refers to the apostles as the church's foundation (Eph. 2:20; Rev. 21:14).

In this connection emphasis should also be placed on the fact that in the passage now under consideration Jesus speaks of himself—not of Peter—as the Builder and Owner of the church. He says, "*I* will build *my* church."

The figure of a building to represent the church is found also in such passages as I Cor. 3:9; Eph. 2:21, 22; I Peter 2:4, 5. Little by little the building goes up. It increases in strength, beauty, and usefulness, its members being considered "living stones." In building his church Jesus makes use of Peter and of the other apostles. In fact, he makes use of all the living members of the church to accomplish this purpose.

The expression "my church" refers, of course, to the church universal, here especially to the entire "body of Christ" or "sum-total of all believers" in its New Testament manifestation, wherever it is truly represented on earth (cf. Acts 9:31; I Cor. 6:4; 12:28; Eph. 1:22, 3:10, 21; 5:22-33; Col. 1:18; Phil. 3:6). It is a great comfort that Jesus considers this church "his very own." Did he not come from heaven in order to purchase his church "with his own blood" (Acts 20:28)?

The history of the early church as recorded in the first twelve chapters of the book of Acts abundantly proves that Christ's prophecy regarding Peter was fulfilled. Or, phrasing it differently, it confirms the given interpretation.

In that large section of Acts the name of Peter occurs more than fifty times. Here it is found everywhere except in chapters 6 and 7, which contain the story of Stephen. Let me stress once again that I am not referring to Peter as he was in himself, nor to that apostle acting all by himself, but to him as Christ's instrument for the establishment of his church in its New Testament manifestation, and taking his stand as one of The Twelve.

During that very early period (before Paul comes mightily to the fore, in Acts 13-28) Peter was the most powerful and effective human link between Jesus and the church, the most influential means of the latter's inward and outward growth.

It was Peter who preached the sermon on Pentecost, as a result of which no less than three thousand people were converted (Acts 2:41). It was again through the testimony of Peter and John (3:11; 4:1), chiefly of Peter (3:12), that two thousand were subsequently added to the membership (4:4). Other events in which Peter took a leading part were: the election of Matthias to take the place of Judas Iscariot (Acts 1:15-22), the healing of the lame begger (Acts 3:4-6), and the heroic proclamation of Jesus Christ before the Sanhedrin (4:8-12, 29). See also 5:15; 8:20; and chapters 9 and 10.

It has been pointed out earlier that in every listing of The Twelve Peter's name occurs first of all.

Besides, according to reliable tradition, was not Mark "Peter's interpreter"? And was not Mark's Gospel, in turn, one of the main sources used by Matthew and Luke in writing their Gospels?

Add Peter's epistles, in which he so beautifully sets forth the meaning of Christ's life and death (see especially I Peter 2:21-25). Christ's prophecy was fulfilled in the labors of Peter. The One whom Peter describes as "the Shepherd and Overseer of our souls" (I Peter 2:25), "the Chief Shepherd" (I Peter 5:4) had said to this apostle, "Feed my lambs," "Shepherd my sheep," "Feed my dear sheep" (John 21:15, 16, 17). That there were also sheep that did not belong to the Jewish fold (John 10:16) was going to be vividly impressed upon Peter (Acts 10:9-16, 34-48; 11:17, 18). Though in the life of this apostle there was a momentary, sad departure from the implications of the great principle "that they all may be one" (John 17:21), there is every reason to believe that Peter took Paul's reprimand to heart (see N.T.C. on Gal. 2:11-21). He labored on faithfully until at last the Lord delivered him—according to John 21:18, 19 and early tradition (I Clement, chap. 5) *by means of martyrdom*—from this earthly scene and bestowed upon him the promised inheritance (I Peter 1:4). Christ's prophecy, "You are Peter, and upon this rock I will build my church" had been amply fulfilled by means of his witness-bearing.

Continued: **and the gates of Hades shall not overpower it.** For the argument showing that in the Gospels "Hades" means "hell" see on 11:23, 24. Besides, those who favor the meaning "the realm of the dead" experience great difficulty in their attempt to show in what sense the gates of that realm are striving to overpower the church, and are failing in their assault. When Hades is interpreted as indicating "hell" the assurance given here by the Lord can be readily understood. "Gates of hell," by metonymy represents Satan and his legions as it were storming out of hell's gates in order to attack and destroy the church. What we have here is an oft-repeated promise of the victory [608] of Christ's church over the forces of evil. See John 16:33; Rom. 16:20; Eph. 6:10-13; Rev. 12:13-16; 17:14; 20:7-10.

Misuse is often made of this passage, as if Jesus meant, "Do not be concerned about the doctrinal purity of the denomination or congregation to which y o u belong. Have I not promised to see to it that the gates of hell shall never prevail against the church?" As if Jesus promised that this or that

---

[608] Note "shall not overpower." This rendering does justice to the real as well as the etymological meaning of the verb which occurs here in the form of the 3rd per. fut. indic. of κατισχύω. In the only other New Testament passages in which it occurs (Luke 21:36; 23:23) the meaning is slightly different.

particular *denomination* or *local congregation* would never lose its doctrinal purity! The real meaning of "church" as here used has already been indicated. Jesus promised that he would always cause *his people* to triumph over the devil and his army. This promise is given not to lukewarm Laodiceans but to "Christian soldiers." In the midst of the battle their consolation is:

> Crowns and thrones may perish,
>   Kingdoms rise and wane,
> But the Church of Jesus
>   Constant will remain;
> Gates of hell can never
>   'Gainst that Church prevail;
> We have Christ's own promise,
>   And that cannot fail.
>   —Sabine Baring-Gould

The words addressed to Peter, as representing the group, are continued in verse 19. **I will give to you the keys of the kingdom of heaven. . . .**

The one who "has the keys" (cf. Rev. 1:18; 3:7) of the kingdom of heaven determines who should be admitted and who must be refused admission. Cf. Isa. 22:22. That the apostles as a group exercised this right is clear from the entire book of Acts. *All* did this on an equal basis (4:33): there was no boss or superintendent. Nevertheless, as has already been shown, the influence of Peter was outstanding. By means of *the preaching of the gospel* he was opening the doors to some (Acts 2:38, 39; 3:16-20; 4:12; 10:34-43), closing them to others (3:23).

In answer to the question, "How is the kingdom of heaven opened and shut by the preaching of the holy gospel?" the Heidelberg Catechism (Lord's Day 31, Answer to Question 84) states: "By proclaiming and openly witnessing, according to the command of Christ, to believers, one and all, that, whenever they receive the promise of the gospel by a true faith, all their sins are really forgiven them of God for the sake of Christ's merits; and on the contrary, by proclaiming and witnessing to all unbelievers and such as do not sincerely repent that the wrath of God and eternal condemnation abide on them so long as they are not converted. According to this witness of the gospel God will judge, both in this life and in that which is to come."

Discipline was also exercised by The Twelve, and here again the role played by Peter is emphasized (5:1-11). Somewhat later Paul, too, very effectively used both keys: the preaching of the gospel and the exercise of discipline. The former requires no proof, for it is evident from all of his epistles as well as from chapters 13–28 of the book of Acts. As to the latter, discipline, both the shutting and the opening or at times reopening of the door, are beautifully illustrated, respectively, in Cor. 5:1-5 and II Cor. 2:8. As the first passage indicates, the shutting took place with a view to reopening. Paul, moreover, did not act apart from the church but in conjunction with it (I Cor. 5:3, 4).

Though "church" in Matt. 16:18 and "kingdom" in verse 19 may not be identical in meaning, the latter also here being perhaps the broader concept, nevertheless A. T. Robertson's question (*Word Pictures,* Vol. I, pp. 133, 134) whether Jesus does not here (verse 19) mean the same thing by "kingdom" that he did by "church" in verse 18, is definitely in order. Excommunication from the visible church is possible (18:17; I Cor. 5:5a; Titus 3:10); so is exclusion from the kingdom (8:12).

From the manner in which, with divine approval, the apostles carried out their ministry and asserted their authority it would appear, therefore, that the rather popular view, according to which the term "the keys of the kingdom of heaven" refers to the preaching of the gospel and the exercise of discipline, is correct.

From such passages as Matt. 11:30; 15:19, 20; Acts 15:10; Gal. 5:1; Col. 2:14, 16, 20-23; Rev. 2:24, it is very clear that it was not the purpose of Jesus and of the apostles after him to replace one kind of hierarchical despotism (that of Jewish hair-splitting legalism) by another. Nevertheless, in order that the Christian's way of life might be clearly understood and discipline properly exercised certain basic principles of conduct had to be set forth. It is in this connection that Jesus continues: **and whatever you shall bind on earth shall be bound in heaven, and whatever you shall loose on earth shall be loosed in heaven.** It is immediately clear that these words are still addressed to Peter. "It is unmistakable that Peter is described as exercising *on the earth* the power of the keys of the kingdom."[609] But see also 18:18. The very wording—note "whatever," not "whoever"—shows that the passage refers to things, in this case beliefs and actions, not directly to people. *Binding* and *loosing* are rabbinical terms, meaning *forbidding* and *permitting.* Naturally if a person continued to do or to believe what was forbidden, refusing to repent, he would be disciplined; conversely, if he repented from his evil way, he would be forgiven: the "ban" would be lifted.[610] Hence, indirectly the passage also has implications with respect to the good standing, or lack of good standing, of church members, as a comparison of Matt. 16:19 with John 20:23 indicates.

The assurance is given that whatever Peter, representing The Twelve (Matt. 16:19), or The Twelve (John 20:23), ultimately whatever the church (Matt. 18:18), binds on earth shall be and shall definitely remain bound in heaven; and similarly whatever Peter (etc.) looses on earth shall be and definitely remain loosed in heaven.[611]

---

[609] N. B. Stonehouse, *The Witness of Matthew and Mark to Christ,* p. 235.

[610] See S.BK. *op. cit.,* I, pp. 738, 739.

[611] Notice the use of perfect passive participles δεδεμένον and λελυμένον, after the copula ἔσται in each clause. To read these forms as periphrastics and then to interpret

It should hardly be necessary to add that such authority over faith and morals, and consequently also over the membership, can be exercised only when this is done in thorough harmony with the teachings of Jesus, or, phrasing it differently, with the Word of God. Jesus definitely condemned any arbitrary binding and loosing, such forbidding and permitting, such excluding and admitting or re-admitting, as amounts to a transgression of the commandment of God (15:1-20; 23:13). When a person is unjustly excommunicated the Lord welcomes him (John 9:34-38).

Peter, as spokesman for The Twelve, had confessed Jesus to be the Christ (verse 16). In logical relation with this is Christ's warning found in verse **20. Then he gave the disciples strict orders not to tell anyone that he was the Christ.** The people would have interpreted the term "Messiah"="Christ" in the political sense (cf. John 6:15). This might have fanned the flames of enthusiasm about him, as a potential Deliverer from the Roman yoke, to such an extent that the opposition and envy roused by such widespread attention might have brought his public ministry to an untimely end. This must not happen. When an open announcement must finally be made to the Jewish religious authorities Jesus himself will make it (Matt. 26:63, 64). We should also bear in mind that it would not have been proper for Jesus, during the days of his humiliation, to encourage *public* acclaim. That must be postponed until after his death and resurrection (Matt. 17:9; Luke 9:21, 22). See also on 8:4. The very fact of this death, followed by resurrection and ascension, will shed light on the character of his messiahship (Acts 2:36; I Peter 1:3).

---

21 From that time Jesus began to say plainly to his disciples that he must go away to Jerusalem, and suffer many things from the elders and chief priests and scribes, and be killed, and on the third day be raised up. 22 And Peter took him aside and began to rebuke him, saying, "Mercy on thee, Lord, this shall never happen to thee!" 23 But he turned around and said to Peter, "Get out of my sight, Satan. You are a trap to me, for you are looking at things not from God's point of view but from men's."

24 Then Jesus said to his disciples, "If anyone wishes to come behind me, let him deny himself, take up his cross, and follow me. 25 For whoever would save his life shall lose it, but whoever loses his life for my sake shall find it. 26 For what good will it do a man if he gains the whole world and forfeits his life, or what shall a man give in exchange for his life? 27 For the Son of man shall come in the glory of his Father, with his angels, and then shall he render to each according to his deeds. 28 I solemnly declare to y o u that there are some of those that are standing here who shall not taste death until they see the Son of man coming in his royal dignity."

---

them as meaning that such beliefs and actions (and the persons who either keep clinging to them or abandon them) shall have been *previously* "bound" or "loosed" in heaven yields a very difficult and unnatural sense.

16:21-28 *The First Prediction of the Passion and the Resurrection*
Cf. Mark 8:31–9:1; Luke 9:22-27

Previously, in veiled utterances, Jesus had predicted his death (9:15), and even his death and resurrection (12:39, 40; 16:4). Now there was going to be a change. We see the Anointed One, as our chief Prophet, in plain unfigurative language foretelling his own demise; as our merciful Highpriest, preparing to lay down his life, that he might "take away the sin of the world" (John 1:29); and throughout it all, as our eternal King, being in complete control of every situation, so that the plan of God Triune, made before the foundation of the world, was being carried out in every detail, yet in such a manner that all the human agents who took part in carrying out this plan—elders, chief priests, scribes, the common people, the soldiers, the presiding judge, the betrayer, etc.—were fully responsible for their actions (Luke 22:22; Acts 2:23).

21. **From that time Jesus began to say plainly to his disciples that he must go away to Jerusalem, and suffer many things from the elders and chief priests and scribes, and be killed, and on the third day be raised up.** "From that time," because Jesus had now told the disciples that he accepted Peter's confession as being the result of the Father's revelation. Accordingly, he had made clear to The Twelve that he was indeed the long expected Messiah. Therefore the next lesson was now very definitely in order. He must now convey to this little company the shocking truth, which at first seemed entirely unbelievable, that *this Messiah must suffer and be killed!* To be sure, Jesus added "and the third day be raised up," but it is doubtful whether the first clear announcement of the resurrection even fully registered in the disciples' minds, so utterly painful and inconceivable did the news of their Master's fast approaching suffering and death seem to them.

Stranger still, this suffering will be climaxed in Jerusalem, that is, in the very place known from of old as "the holy city," "the city of the Great King" (4:5; 5:35).

Note: he *must* go to Jerusalem to suffer and to die, etc. He must satisfy the demands of the law, that is, he must pay the penalty for his people's sin, in perfect obedience to his Father's will, and in fulfilment of prophecy (20:28; Mark 10:45; Luke 12:50; 13:33; 22:37; 24:26, 27, 44; John 1:29; II Cor. 5:21; 17:4; and last but not least Isa. 53). He "must" do what he himself also wanted to do (John 10:11; II Cor. 8:9; Gal. 2:20).

Here in Jerusalem, the place to which Jesus will soon be wending his way, the Sanhedrin sits "enthroned." There was an earlier reference to this body (see on 2:4), but now (16:21) not only its chief priests and scribes are mentioned but also its elders, so that here we have the full listing of all the units that constituted this highest Jewish tribunal. In ancient Israel the

653

"elders" were the heads of tribes or heads of a tribe's main subdivisions. In fact, every city or town of any importance began to have its elders. When the Sanhedrin came into existence the more prominent local elders became members of this august body, jointly with the chief priests and the scribes. What Jesus is saying, then, is this, that Israel's very leaders, who should have been the foremost to honor and worship the Christ, were going to afflict him and put him to death.

Note also the lack of gruesome details in this, the first of the three lessons on the cross. All Jesus says at this time is that he must suffer "many" things. He knows that the little group has already received such a shock that it cannot now bear to hear more (cf. John 16:12). For the references to the two lessons that were to follow see p. 9.

The Lord added, "and the third day be raised up." Although the present passage does not mention the remaining items that belong to Christ's exaltation, verse 27 refers to the glorious return. If this *implies* the ascension and the coronation (the sitting down at the Father's right hand), as it seems to do, then in this paragraph (verses 21-28) Jesus is giving us a complete summary of the steps that belong to his exaltation. It is clear that "the third day" must be interpreted as shown previously (see on 12:40), a part of a day being counted as a day.

That not only now but even later the disciples did not grasp just what Jesus meant by this resurrection on "the third day"—whether, for example, the resurrection to which reference was made belonged to the general resurrection at the close of the world's history—is clear from 17:9, 10. Shall we say then that these words of Jesus were futile, since they were not understood? Not at all. Because of the very fact that the disciples did, after all, hear these predictions, and heard them not just once but with increasing clarity three times in the three lessons on the cross, it was possible, after the resurrection, for the angel(s) and for the resurrected Lord himself to refer to them (Matt. 28:6; Luke 24:6-8, 45, 46). Those reminders served, as it were, to pull the rope that caused the bell of memory—a memory deeply rooted in the subconscious area—to ring forth, so that faith was strengthened (cf. John 16:4).

22. And Peter took him aside and began to rebuke him, saying, Mercy on thee, Lord, this shall never happen to thee. If in verse 16 we saw Peter at his best, were it not for the event recorded in 26:69-74 we would be ready to say that we see him here at his worst. For a summary of Peter's vacillations see on 14:30. We assume that Peter had been walking behind the Master. Now he tries to pull Jesus aside and begins to rebuke [612] him. Jesus had not

---

[612] Greek ἐπιτιμᾶν, pres. act. infin. of ἐπιτιμάω. 8:26 speaks of rebuking wind and sea; 17:8, a demon; 17:18, parents who were trying to bring their little ones to Jesus. Sometimes the word is used in a slightly different sense, namely, to strictly forbid, to

as yet turned around to face Peter. Peter *began* to rebuke: he did not get very far. "Mercy on thee, Lord," is about as literal a translation as is possible in English. Peter meant, "May God be merciful to thee, for this must not, shall not happen." For a somewhat similar expression see II Sam. 20:20; 23:17; I Chron. 11:19 ("Far be it from . . . me . . ."). For Peter the very idea of messiahship, which he had just now ascribed to Jesus, excluded that of suffering and death, violent death at that!

The reaction of Jesus to Peter's rash, though well-meant, action is described in verse 23. **But he turned around and said to Peter, Get out of my sight, Satan.** Now Jesus turns around so as to face Peter. The latter had spoken his words in the hearing of all. Verses 24-28 seem to imply that Christ's answer, too, was heard by all. Literally Jesus said to his erring disciple, "Get *behind* me. . . ." However, this rendering is rather ambiguous, and has even been interpreted to mean that the Lord was merely telling Peter that he has committed a breach of etiquette when he grabbed hold of Jesus and tried to pull him aside, and that he must now assume his previous position in the lineup and start walking behind Jesus again. Also, it should be borne in mind that a somewhat similar expression (4:10, *exactly* identical according to a variant reading) is far more forceful than such a literal rendering might seem to indicate. The true interpretation, as I, along with many others, see it, is this, that the Lord recognizes that Satan is using Peter as his agent in an attempt to seduce Jesus to try to obtain the crown without enduring the cross (see on 4:8, 9). So Jesus, in speaking to Peter, is actually addressing Satan, or if one prefers, is addressing whatever in Peter has been perversely influenced by the prince of evil. What is needed here, accordingly, is a translation like "Be gone, Satan," or "Get out of my sight, Satan."

Jesus continues: **You are a trap to me, for you are looking at things not from God's point of view but from men's.** Jesus immediately recognizes the "trap"[613] Satan is setting. Not for a moment does he entertain the devil's suggestion. He knows that he is being confronted by the same tempter who at a previous occasion tried to inveigle him with a false promise (4:8, 9). So with finality he rejects the implied inducement to sin. By doing so he is himself carrying out the advice he gave to others, namely, not to dilly-dally with sin but to take drastic action against it (5:29, 30).

Literally Jesus said, "You are not thinking the (things) of God but the (things) of men." From God's point of view it was necessary for the Savior to suffer, die, rise again, etc., in order to save his people. From the human point of view the two concepts *Messiah* and *suffering* were wholly incompatible. Peter, allowing himself to be influenced by Satan, was speaking from

---

warn against (12:16; 16:20; cf. 20:31). Basically the verb means to award a τιμή (penalty) ἐπί (upon).

613 For σκάνδαλον see footnote 293 on p. 303.

the foolishly human point of view when he said, "Mercy on thee, Lord, this shall never happen to thee." He did not realize that he was asking for his own eternal damnation. How quickly the "rock" of verses 16-18 had become "a stone of offense." By God's grace he did not remain such but became a most effective preacher of the very cross which he is here trying to dismiss forever from his own and from the Master's consciousness. The transforming power of the Holy Spirit in the heart and life of Peter produced such a remarkable result that among all the inspired writers there is none who at a later time more clearly set forth the pre-ordained necessity of Christ's atoning death. See Acts 2:23; 3:18; 4:1` 12; I Peter 1:11; 2:21-24 (cf. Isa. 53:4-8).

Jesus now turns to the entire little group of disciples, and shows them that the inevitable law of Christian life is that the servant is not above his master: what happens to Christ, though it is indeed unique, must nevertheless be reflected also in his followers: 24. **Then Jesus said to his disciples, If anyone wishes to come behind me, let him deny himself, take up his cross, and follow me.** Christ's death will be of value only to those who are willing to die to sin and self. Since verses 24 and 25 closely resemble 10:38, 39 the reader is referred to the explanation there. A few additional words may be in order. By doing justice to the tenses of the verbs in the original verse 24 may be paraphrased as follows: "If anyone wishes to be (counted as) an adherent of mine, he must once and for all say farewell to self, decisively accept pain, shame, and persecution for my sake and in my cause, and must then follow and keep on following me as my disciple."

To deny oneself means to renounce the old self, the self as it is apart from regenerating grace. A person who denies himself gives up all reliance on whatever he is by nature, and depends for salvation on God alone. He no longer seeks to promote his own predominantly selfish interests but has become wrapped up in the cause of promoting the glory of God in his own and in every life, and also in every sphere of endeavor. The best commentary on Matt. 16:24 is Gal. 2:20: "I have been crucified with Christ; and it is no longer I who lives, but Christ who lives in me; and that (life) which I now live in flesh I live in faith, (the faith) which is in the Son of God, who loved me and gave himself up for me." Denying self means subjecting oneself to Christ's discipline.

The expression "take up his cross" refers to the cross that is suffered because of union with Christ. One "follows" Christ by trusting in him, walking in his footsteps (I Peter 2:21), obeying his commandments out of gratitude for salvation through him, and being willing even to suffer in his cause. Only then, when he is willing and ready to do this can he truly be Christ's disciple, his adherent.

Continued: 25. **For whoever would save his life shall lose it, but whoever loses his life for my sake shall find it.** This is the grand paradox of 10:39 and similar passages. It is held by some that the substitution of "save" here in 16:25 for "find" in the first clause of 10:39 ("He who finds his life shall lose it")[614] makes the present passage even fuller and more forceful, as if, in distinction from merely trying to "find" his life, that is, attaining to what he considers a richer, happier life, the man described in 16:25 puts forth every effort to "save," that is, "rescue" his self, and having done so, to cling to it by every possible means. Whether this distinction can be sustained is debatable. In view of the fact that in both passages the antonym is "lose," it may well be that the difference between "finding" and "saving" is very slight. At any rate we may be sure that in both cases the person who is condemned is the selfish person, the individual who is turned in upon himself and the one who is commended is the outgoing person, the one who, for the sake of the love of Christ shown to him, now in turn loves the Lord and all those whom the Lord wants him to love, and who, in the process of doing this is even willing to suffer extreme personal affliction and, if need be, even death. That person's life shall be marvelously enriched, says Jesus.

A few examples of the persons here condemned: envious Cain (Gen. 4:1-8; I John 3:12), greedy Ahab and Jezebel (I Kings 21), haughty Haman (Esther 3:5; 5:9-14), vengeful King Herod I (Matt. 2:3, 16), perfidious Judas Iscariot (Matt. 26:14-16; Luke 22:47, 48). See also the story of "the rich young ruler" (Matt. 19:16-22).

A few examples of those here commended: self-negating Judah (Gen. 44:18-34), noble Jonathan (I Sam. 18-20), the Good Samaritan of the parable (Luke 10:29-37), men like Epaphroditus (Phil. 2:25-30) and Onesiphorus (II Tim. 1:16; 4:19), who were willing to risk everything for the sake of Christ's cause, and humble, self-sacrificing Paul (Rom. 9:3; Gal. 4:19, 20; 6:14). In all of these the spirit of Jesus Christ himself was reflected (II Cor. 8:9).

With an earnest appeal that his disciples may always be willing to lose their lives for the sake of Christ's cause, Jesus continues: **26. For what good will it do a man if he gains the whole world and forfeits his life, or what shall a man give in exchange for his life?** It is clear from verses 25 and 26 that even though verse 24 places man before a choice he himself must make, and God does not make for him, that nevertheless the Lord, in his infinite tenderness and love, encourages man to make the right choice. Whoever thinks only or even mainly of his own ease, comfort, popularity, prestige, opulence, etc., lacks love, outgoingness. It is love that causes the soul to expand, imparts riches, usefulness, joy, satisfaction. Love for the Lord does this, and love for his children, his causes, his kingdom; in a sense even love for the enemy, that he may be saved. So, if a person should gain the whole

---

[614] Another difference is: 10:39 has two aorist participles: "the finder" . . . "the loser," while 16:25 has relative clauses.

world—when Jesus said this, was he thinking of the offer which the devil once made him? (4:8, 9)—and in the process of doing so should "forfeit" (lose the right to possess) his own life or soul, that is, "should lose or forfeit *himself*" (Luke 9:25), what good will such an exchange do him, for "What shall a man give in exchange for [615] his life?"

That *love* does indeed mean *life* is clear from such passages as I Cor. 13; Gal. 4:19, 20; Phil. 1:21; I Thess. 3:8. And that nothing whatever can be given in exchange for life is also evident. Selfishness causes the soul to contract; love makes it expand, enriches it, fills it to overflowing with assurance, peace, joy, etc. To know that one is loved, and then to love in return, and in showing this love to recognize no boundaries among men beyond which love cannot go, that is life. Jesus, who spoke the words of 16:24-26 knew that he was the object of the Father's love (Matt. 3:17; 17:5, 23, 24). He, in turn, loved the Father, loved his own, loved the world, prayed even for his enemies. No wonder that his own soul was filled with life, peace, joy, etc. He wants his disciples, and everyone, to choose between love and selfishness, between life and death. He wants them to make the *right* decision. Cf. Exod. 32:26; Josh. 24:15; Ruth 1:16, 17; I Kings 18:21; Heb. 11:25.

Between verses 24-26, on the one hand, and verse 27, on the other, there is a much closer connection than is often realized. That connection is somewhat as follows: Do not seek to possess the whole world. That will mean loss. Leave the matter of receiving a reward to the Son of man. He at his coming will reward every man according to his deeds: **27. For the Son of man shall come in the glory of his Father, with his angels, and then shall he render to each according to his deeds.** For "Son of man" see on 8:20. The Father will reward this Son of man, the One who from suffering attains to glory, in achieving salvation for his people. The Father will impart his own glory to him and give to him his own angels (cf. Dan. 7:10) to be his brilliant retinue (Matt. 25:31). The glory of the Son of man is revealed also in this very fact, that he will be the Judge who will render to each man according to his deeds.

Entrance into or exclusion from the new heaven and earth will depend on whether one is clothed with the righteousness of Christ. Apart from Christ there is no salvation at any time (Acts 4:12; cf. John 3:16; 14:6; I Cor. 3:11). Salvation is wholly by grace, through faith (Eph. 2:8).

Nevertheless, there will be degrees of punishment and also degrees of glory. Note the expression "many stripes . . . few stripes" (Luke 12:47, 48), and see also Dan. 12:3; I Cor. 3:12-14.

---

615 The Greek has ἀντάλλαγμα (cf. Mark 8:36, 37). As the parallelism indicates, ἀντί strengthens the idea of *exchange*, one object being traded, as it were, for another. See the author's doctoral dissertation, *The Meaning of the Preposition ἀντί in the New Testament*, p. 76.

The degree of glory or of punishment will depend on two considerations: a. What amount of "light" (knowledge) has this person received? (Rom. 2:12).

b. How has he used the light which he has received? (Luke 12:47, 48). Has he been faithful? And if so, in what measure? Has he been faithless? And if so, to what extent? This will be evident from his *works*. These works will show both *whether or not* a person is a genuine believer in Christ, and also to *what extent* he has used or abused the light which he received (Rev. 20:13; then I Cor. 3:12-14). Hence the passage under consideration says, "Then shall he render to each according to his deeds."

Jesus concludes his remarks with the following solemn prediction: **28. I solemnly declare to y o u that there are some of those that are standing here who shall not taste death until they see the Son of man coming in his royal dignity.** As to "I solemnly declare" see on 5:18. It introduces a very important statement. The difficulty which many readers have experienced with this passage can be avoided by bearing in mind that Jesus did not say, "Some of those that are standing here shall not taste death until the Son of man shall come in the glory of his Father, with his angels," but, ". . . until they see the Son of man coming in his royal dignity." To "taste death" means to experience it, that is, to die. For the term "Son of man" see on 8:20. That the coming of the Son of man "in his royal dignity," a coming whose date is so clearly fixed in the mind of Jesus that he is able to add that some of the men whom he addresses are going to see it before they die, cannot refer to the second coming is clear from 24:36 (cf. Mark 13:32), where Jesus specifically declares that the date of *that* coming is unknown to him.

To be sure, the "coming to render to each according to his deeds" (verse 27) and the "coming in his royal dignity" or literally "in his kingship"[616] (verse 28) are closely related. They are not identical, however. Here in 16:27, 28, as well as in 10:23 (see pp. 467, 468, where this subject is discussed in greater detail) Jesus is making use of "prophetic foreshortening." He regards the entire state of exaltation, from his resurrection to his second coming, as a unit. In verse 27 he describes its final consummation; here in verse 28 its beginning. Here, then, he is saying that some of those whom he is addressing are going to be witnesses of this beginning. They are going to see the Son of man coming "in his royal dignity," that is, coming in majesty, to reign as king. Is not he the One who was destined to rule as "King of kings and Lord of lords" (Rev. 19:16)? Here in Matt. 16:28 the reference is in all probability to: *a.* his glorious resurrection, *b.* his return in the Spirit

---

[616] In addition to "kingdom" the Greek word βασιλεία also has this abstract meaning "kingship," "royal reign" or "royal dignity," whichever of these suits the context best (cf. Matt. 6:10; Luke 17:21; I Cor. 15:24).

on the day of Pentecost, and in close connection with that event, *c.* his reign from his position at the Father's right hand, a rulership that would become evident in the history of the post-Pentecost church as described in the book of Acts.

Again and again these great happenings (*a., b.,* and *c.,* just mentioned) are in Scripture associated with the ideas of power, kingship, exaltation, and coronation, as anyone can see for himself by studying such passages as Acts 1:6-8; 2:32-36; Eph. 1:19-23; Phil. 2:9; Heb. 2:9; I Peter 1:3; and Rev. 12:10.

As a result of Jesus' resurrection and return in the Spirit on the day of Pentecost changes so vast would begin to take place that, as outsiders saw it, the world would be turned "upside down" (Acts 17:6). Momentous events were about to occur: the "becoming of age" of the church, with spiritual illumination, love, unity, and courage prevailing within its ranks as never before, the extension of the church among the Gentiles, the conversion of people by the thousands, the presence and exercise of many charismatic gifts (Acts 2:41; 4:4, 32-35; 5:12-16; 6:7; 19:10, 17-20; I Thess. 1:8-10). All of these things certainly justified the prediction that the Son of man would be coming "in his kingship," that is "in his royal dignity."

Jesus predicts that this will take place during the lifetime of some of those whom he is now addressing. That too was literally fulfilled. By no means all of those who heard the Lord make this prediction lived or were present to see its plenary fulfilment. Judas Iscariot never saw any of it. Thomas was not present with the other disciples on the Sunday evening of the day of the resurrection. James, the brother of John, saw only the beginning of the wonderful period described in the book of Acts (see Acts 12:1). Some of the apostles were absent when certain important events took place (John 21:2). The transfiguration (Matt. 17:1-8), at which occasion "our Lord Jesus Christ . . . received from God the Father honor and glory" (II Peter 1:17; "majesty" also, verse 16) is by some regarded as included in the prediction made in 16:28. It was witnessed by only three of the apostles. But whether it be included or not, sufficient other evidence has been mentioned to show that the prediction of Jesus was literally and gloriously fulfilled.

Summary of Chapter 16

As to verses 1-4, after the miraculous feeding of the four thousand Jesus recrossed the lake to spend a few days on the western shore. Again, as before (12:38), his marvelous works are challenged, even though only by implication. Again, as before, the opponents demand that he perform a sign. This time, too, they are told that the only sign they can expect is that of Jonah (see on 12:39). And this time, as before, those asking for the sign are called "an evil and adulterous generation."

As to the differences: *This* time the challengers specifically ask for a sign "from heaven," even though that was probably also their intention previously. The second difference is that this time the Pharisees combine with *the Sadducees* in asking for a sign. Finally, this time Jesus rebukes his adversaries because while they know how to interpret weather signs, they cannot interpret the far more important "signs of the times "

With Christ's entrance into the world vast changes were beginning to occur: ever so many demons were being driven out; the sick, in great numbers, restored to health; the handicapped delivered of their handicaps. legalism exposed; salvation by grace taught and accepted; men welcomed into the kingdom of light and love; such love, all around—even for enemies—advocated and exemplified; God's kingdom ushered in on earth. Nevertheless, the enemies of the truth were opposing all this. They continued to cling to their old ways and theories.

While crossing back to the eastern or northeastern side of the lake the disciples discover (verses 5-12) that they had forgotten to buy bread. Jesus said to them, "Be on y o u r guard against the yeast of the Pharisees and Sadducees." The disciples, interpreting these words literally, think that he is displeased with them because they had forgotten to bring bread. Do they not remember the two miracles of feeding large multitudes with, respectively, five bread-cakes and seven bread-cakes? The disciples finally understood that he had not told them to be on guard against yeast used in bread but against the teaching of the Pharisees and Sadducees.

In the next paragraph (verses 13-20), which describes what took place in the vicinity of Caesarea Philippi, Jesus asks his disciples, "Who do the people say that the Son of man is?" When they answer, "John the Baptist . . . Elijah . . . Jeremiah . . . one of the prophets," he asks, "But y o u, who do y o u say that I am?" Simon Peter answers, "Thou art the Christ, the Son of the living God." Jesus pronounces him blessed, adding, "You are Peter, and upon this rock will I build my church, and the gates of Hades shall not overpower it." For explanation of verses 17-20 see above, pp. 644-652.

In his first prediction (in plain language) of his approaching suffering, death, and resurrection (verses 21-28) Jesus spares his disciples the gruesome details of the bitter trial that awaits him, rebukes the rebuker (Peter), emphasizes that a true disciple is one who does not seek but denies himself, and points to the fact that the way of the cross leads to glory. The Son of man's own glory will not become fully evident until the day of the second coming. Yet a beginning of that glory—think of the resurrection, Pentecost, the rapid and vigorous extension of the early church—will be seen by some of those whom Jesus is addressing right here and now.

Outline of Chapter 17

Theme: *The Work Which Thou Gavest Him to Do*

CHAPTER XVII

17 1 Six days later Jesus took with him Peter and James and John his brother, and led them up a high mountain (to be) alone (with them). 2 And he was transfigured before them; his face shone like the sun, and his clothes became white as the light. 3 And look, there appeared to them Moses and Elijah, engaged in conversation with him. 4 Then Peter spoke up and said to Jesus, "Lord, how good it is for us to be here! If you wish, I will make three shelters, one for you, one for Moses, and one for Elijah." 5 While he was still talking a bright cloud suddenly covered them, and a voice from the cloud was saying, "This is my Son, the Beloved, with whom I am well pleased; listen to him!"

6 Upon hearing this the disciples fell on their faces and were terribly frightened. 7 Then Jesus approached, touched them, and said, "Get up and do not be afraid." 8 And when they raised their eyes they saw no one but Jesus only.

9 And when they were coming down the mountain Jesus warned them, saying, "Never tell anyone what y o u have seen, until the Son of man is raised from the dead." 10 The disciples asked him, saying, "Then why do the scribes say that first Elijah has to come?" 11 He answered and said, "Elijah is coming and is going to restore everything. 12 But I say to y o u that Elijah already came, but they failed to recognize him, and treated him as they pleased. Similarly the Son of man is about to suffer at their hands." 13 Then the disciples understood that he had spoken to them about John the Baptist.

17:1-13 *The Transfiguration of Jesus on a High Mountain*
Cf. Mark 9:2-13; Luke 9:28-36

The exaltation of Jesus, from resurrection to second coming, is foreshadowed in the transfiguration, recorded here in 17:1-13; especially in verses 1-8. This transfiguration served the twofold purpose of: *a.* preparing the Mediator to face with courage his bitter trial, by reminding him of the Father's constant love (17:5) and of the glory that would follow his suffering (Heb. 12:2); and *b.* confirming the faith of Peter, James, and John—and indirectly of the entire church afterward—in the truth that had been revealed to and confessed by Simon Peter, as spokesman for The Twelve (Matt. 16:16).

1. **Six days later Jesus took with him Peter and James and John his brother, and led them up a high mountain (to be) alone (with them).** The expression "six days later" is not in conflict with Luke 9:28, "about eight

663

days after these sayings." Luke may have included both the day of Peter's confession and that of Christ's transfiguration when he wrote as he did; besides, he does not intend to be precise, for he says "*about* eight days." Matthew and Mark may have used the exclusive method of time computation, referring only to the six intervening days.

Most of the events pertaining to Jesus' sojourn on earth could be safely witnessed by all the twelve disciples. There were others, however, that took place in the presence of only three of these men. Exactly why this was we can only guess. Did Jesus allow only three disciples to enter the room where the resurrection of the daughter of Jairus took place (Mark 5:37; Luke 8:51), because the presence of the entire group would not have been in accord with proper decorum and might have disturbed the child when she reopened her eyes? Was the Master's Gethsemane agony too sacred to be witnessed by more than three of the disciples (Matt. 26:37; Mark 14:33), and was it for this reason that even then it was "witnessed" by these three to only a very limited extent? And is it possible that the transfiguration, described here in Matt. 17 and its parallels, could have only three disciples as eye-witnesses (Matt. 17:1; Mark 9:2; Luke 9:28), because otherwise the injunction mentioned in Matt. 17:9 would have been more difficult to enforce? Such may have been the reasons, but we do not know.

Neither do we definitely know why Peter, James, and John were the ones chosen. Some say, "Because these were the three disciples most capable to understand and sympathize." [617] Others, "Because these were among Jesus' first disciples." [618] See on 4:18, 21; also N.T.C. on John 1:35-37, 40, 41. Both of these answers may be true; at least, may contain an element of truth.

That Peter was among the three does not surprise us, in view of Matt. 16:16-19. It is entirely possible that John's spiritual affinity with His Master—he was "the disciple whom Jesus loved" (John 13:23; 19:26; 20:2; 21:7, 10)—accounted for his inclusion in this innermost circle. But what about James, John's brother? Was it not considerate of the Lord to grant to him, who was going to be the first of The Twelve to seal his testimony with his blood (Acts 12:2), the privilege of being included among the three intimate witnesses?

These are considerations that may well be taken into account in considering the question, "Why these three?" Nevertheless, it must be frankly admitted that the answer to this question, as also the answer to the previous one, has not been revealed. It is easier to understand why there had to be witnesses at all, namely, so that, when the proper time arrived, they could

---

[617] A. B. Bruce, *Synoptic Gospels*, p. 228.
[618] H. N. Ridderbos, *op. cit.*, p. 24.

testify to the church concerning the things they had seen and heard. Besides, see Deut. 19:15; Matt. 18:16; John 8:17; II Cor. 13:1; I Tim. 5:19.

It is impossible with certainty to identify "the high mountain" to which Jesus brought the three. Some say, "It was Mount Tabor." However, in view of the fact that there was at that time a city or fortress on top of that mountain it is not easy to see how the Lord and these three men could here have found the privacy they were seeking. Mount Hermon is favored by others. However, when Jesus and the three descend from the mountain he is met by "a great multitude," including scribes (Mark 9:14). This seems to indicate that "the Mount of Transfiguration," as it can safely be called, was not in the far north, populated mostly by Gentiles. A far more logical place is *Jebel Jermak* (or . . . *Jermuk*) in Upper Galilee, the highest elevation in that entire region, rising 4,000 feet above the Mediterranean Sea, affording a beautiful view in all directions. From this mountain it was but a relatively short distance to Capernaum, which Jesus seems to have reached soon afterward (17:24; Mark 9:28, 33). We are, of course, not certain that this was "the high mountain" to which Matthew refers, but at least it fills all the requirements.[619]

2. **And he was transfigured before them; his face shone like the sun, and his clothes became white as the light.** Some are of the opinion that an actual metamorphosis took place.[620] Now metamorphoses come in various shapes and degrees. A radical example would be that of an outraged girl changing into a nightingale, or that of a boastful woman into a stone (both examples taken from Ovid, *Metamorphoses*). Milder illustrations would be the trans-

---

[619] This location is favored also by W. Ewing in his article *Transfiguration, Mount of*, I.S.B.E., Vol. V, p. 3006; and by E. G. Kraeling, *op. cit.*, p. 390. He mentions *Jebel Kan'an*, north of Capernaum, as another possibility.

[620] The verb μετεμορφώθη, generally rendered "was transfigured," is the one from which our English words "metamorphose" and "metamorphosis" are derived. We are told that the *morphe* element in the Greek word "always denotes the essential form," and that therefore in the present case this essential form was changed. Jesus, then, underwent a metamorphosis: his human nature begins to make use of its divine attributes. "The whole body of Jesus for a brief time was allowed to shine with the light and refulgence of its heavenly divinity" (R. C. H. Lenski, *op. cit.*, pp. 632-634). Now it is true that in certain contexts *morphe* or *form* refers indeed to the inner, essential, and abiding nature of a person or thing, while *schema* or *fashion* points to his or its external, accidental, and fleeting bearing or appearance; and that especially when, as in Phil. 2:6, 8; Rom. 12:2, these two are used side by side, we do well to mark this distinction. See N.T.C. on Phil. 2:6, 7a. This does not mean, however, that in every context a verb that is based on the *morphe* stem must refer to an actual change of substance, a metamorphosis. Words have histories, become adaptable to all kinds of situations, and there is no reason whatever why in the present case this verb may not indicate *change of appearance* instead of change of nature or essence. Besides, the context—"his face shone like the sun, and his clothes became white as the light"—does not prove that a change of essence or of nature took place, though it is true that the change in outward appearance here indicated *may* have been due to glory *from within* irradiating Christ's whole being.

formation of a caterpillar into a butterfly, or of a tadpole into a frog. The context here in verse 2 does not point in any such direction.

It is necessary, however, also to guard against the opposite extreme, [621] as if Christ's altered appearance was simply due to an exalted state of mind, and as if Moses and Elijah appeared only in a vision (with an appeal to verse 9, but see on that passage).

All the passage under consideration really tells us is that, while the little group was on the mountain, the disciples, who had been sleeping but were now fully awake (Luke 9:32), saw clearly that a change of appearance came over Jesus, so that not only his face began to shine like the sun but even his clothes became white and radiant with dazzling light. The source of the sudden, extraordinary brightness is not indicated. Some imagine that it was all due to the setting sun (in which case the disciples must have become "heavy with sleep" rather early!); others, to the divine glory bursting forth from within; and still others, to Christ's exalted state of mind brought about by the fact that he had been in communion with his heavenly Father (Luke 9:29). How this could have affected his clothes is either skipped or else the sun is brought in to take care of that difficulty. Since no explanations are given in the text it is probably best to omit all speculation, and to postpone further elucidation until we reach verse 5. Continued: 3. **And look, there appeared to them Moses and Elijah, engaged in conversation with him.** This was a visible, objective appearance of these two men. For comparable manifestations, perceptible to the senses, see Gen. 18:1, 2; 19:1; Judg. 13:3; etc.

How did the disciples know that these two visitors from the other world, who suddenly appeared upon the scene, were Moses and Elijah? Did they introduce themselves? Did the disciples gather this information from the words spoken by each in his conversation with Jesus? Had the appearance of the two been transmitted to the disciples by tradition, whether oral or written, so that for this reason it was easy to distinguish between the two? Was it divinely revealed to them? Did they know it intuitively? Or, last but not the least fanciful, was Moses carrying in his hand a copy of the law, and did Elijah descend from heaven to the mount in his fiery chariot? All we know, and need to know, is that in a manner not revealed to us the three disciples recognized the two visitors.

As to Moses, we know that he had died and had been buried (Deut. 34:5, 6). Had his body subsequently been disinterred and translated to heaven, and does Jude 9 indirectly support this theory? Or was his body still buried, and did God equip his soul with another body to be used just for this occasion? As to Elijah, we know that he never died, but was bodily translated to heaven (II Kings 2:11).

---

[621] See A. B. Bruce, *Synoptic Gospels,* pp. 228-230.

So, here they are: Moses and Elijah, appearing "in glory," probably meaning, "surrounded with heavenly brightness," and speaking with Jesus about his "exodus" or departure, which he was to accomplish in Jerusalem (Luke 9:31). That the word "departure" has reference to the Lord's bitter suffering and especially to his death needs no proof. See also II Peter 1:15. The question has been asked, "Does it include the resurrection?" The question is, however, not very important, for even if the word in and by itself should not be that inclusive, is it conceivable that the heavenly visitors spoke with Jesus about his death without even mentioning his victory over death? Matthew, however, does not touch upon the topic of conversation between Jesus and the two. He merely states that the two were "engaged in conversation with" or "conversing with" Jesus.

Why just these two? Leaving aside all useless speculation, the simplest and best answer still seems to be that Moses and Elijah represented respectively the law and the prophets, both of which Jesus had come to fulfil (Matt. 5:17; Luke 24:27, 44).

4. **Then Peter spoke up and said to Jesus, Lord, how good it is for us to be here! If you wish, I will make three shelters, one for you, one for Moses, and one for Elijah.** The trouble with Peter was that too often he spoke first and did his thinking afterward, if at all. So also here. Still, we should not be too hard on him, for he had just been awakened out of his sleep and did not know what he was saying (Luke 9:32, 33). Also, he certainly does not evince any selfishness: he wants to make *three* shelters, not four (including one for himself) or six (also one for James and one for John).

Nevertheless, his suggestion was foolish. As if Jesus and the two visitors had no other means of protecting themselves against the cold. Besides, would branches and shrubbery—let us suppose that they were immediately available—provide sturdy protection, had it been needed?

It might be said in Peter's favor that he at least submits the suggestion to the Lord, so that the latter may decide. On the other hand, this apostle's very desire to prolong the glory-scene shows that he had not yet fully taken to heart what Jesus had taught him (see on 16:23-25). From suffering, from the cross, whether for Jesus or for himself, he wishes to stay far removed.

Peter's question did not even receive an answer; either that, or else: the answer was included in the action reported in verse 5. **While he was still talking a bright cloud suddenly covered them...** In Scripture the presence of God is often indicated by the mention of a cloud. In several cases, as also here, it is a bright, white, or luminous cloud (cf. Exod. 13:21; 16:10; 40:35; I Kings 8:10, 11; Neh. 9:19; Ps. 78:14; Ezek. 1:4; Rev. 14:14-16). The disciples saw that this cloud of diffused light covered Jesus, Moses, and Elijah. Continued: **and a voice from the cloud was saying, This is my Son, the Beloved, with whom I am well pleased; listen to him.** The explanation has already been given, for, with the exception of "listen to him," the identical words were spoken also at Jesus' baptism. See on 3:17. At that occasion the words were heard by Jesus and by John the Baptist; whether also by others is not definitely stated. Here, in connection with the transfiguration, these words were heard by Jesus and the three disciples: Peter, James, and John, who are urged to keep on listening to the words of the Father's beloved Son, and to take them to heart.

It has been pointed out previously, in connection with verses 1 and 2, that many questions with respect to Christ's transfiguration cannot be answered. *One* thing is clear, however. When we put together into a composite picture all that has been definitely revealed—such as, Christ's radiant countenance, his white garments, the resplendent visitors, the bright cloud, and the love-revealing voice—the total impression is exactly that which Peter, inspired by the Holy Spirit, subsequently summarized in these words, "We were eye-witnesses of his majesty. . . . He received honor and glory from God the Father" (II Peter 1:16, 17). All in all, therefore, the transfiguration of Jesus was both for himself and for the disciples who witnessed it a definitely positive, encouraging, glorious experience. It was the Father who, in his great love for the Son, clothed him with glory and encouraged him with a bracing re-affirmation of continued delight, in order that this might sustain him in his fast approaching agony. It was this same Father who simultaneously strengthened Peter, James, and John in their faith, enabling them to be worthy and exuberant witnesses. [622]

For the moment, however, the voice from the cloud startled the disciples: **6. Upon hearing this the disciples fell on their faces and were terribly frightened.** The night, the luminous cloud—visible manifestation of the presence of God—the sudden voice coming out of the cloud, all these combined to fill the hearts and minds of the three men with fear and trembling. In the presence of that which is holy and filled with majesty sinful men become frightened (Gen. 3:10; Judg. 6:22; 13:22; Isa. 6:5; Dan. 8:17; 10:9; Hab. 3:16; Rev. 1:17a). Says Calvin, commenting on this verse, "God intended that the disciples should be struck with this terror, in order to impress more fully on their hearts the memory of this vision." Continued: **7. Then Jesus approached, touched them, and said, Get up and do not be afraid.** Jesus loves these men. So, to comfort them he walks up to them and tenderly touches them (see on 8:3; and cf. Rev. 1:17). He tells them to arise and to stop being afraid.

---

[622] The interpretation offered by the theologian-philosopher K. Schilder—*Christ in his Suffering* (translated from the Dutch), Grand Rapids, 1938, pp. 26-34—is different. That author was of the opinion that Jesus had taken Satan along with him to the mountain, and that what occurred there was a temptation for the Mediator, a link in the chain of his humiliation. Jesus was enveloped with the aureole of the glamor of Moses and Elijah. He shone with light reflected from them. While Schilder's work furnishes worthwhile reading material, I believe that II Peter 1:16, 17 points in the opposite direction and that the temptation theory cannot be proved.

The words "Be not afraid" in one form or another are found throughout Scripture, showing that God is love (Exod. 14:13-15; Josh. 1:5-7; 11:6; II Kings 19:6; Neh. 4:14; Isa. 40:9; 43:1-7; Matt. 14:27; 28:10; Mark 5:36; Acts 18:9; Rev. 1:17b, 18). How this cheerful *negative* saying, "Be not afraid" reminds us of its *affirmative* complement, "Take courage" (for which see on 9:2). Such exhortations are either empty or meaningful, either flippant or strength-imparting. When they are uttered by him who is able and eager to supply whatever is needed in any circumstance of life they really help! **8. And when they raised their eyes they saw no one but Jesus only.** The Lord not only tells these men not to be fear-filled; he also removes the reason for their fear. He sees to it that the strangeness, brilliance, and majesty of the scene is not prolonged beyond what they can bear. Result: when Peter, James, and John take hold of themselves and raise their eyes, the bright cloud, together with the heavenly visitors, has vanished, so that the disciples see no one but Jesus. Even he does not scare them, for the dazzling brightness has left him. The event has ended. Its memory remains.

The scene changes: **9. And when they were coming down the mountain Jesus warned them, saying, Never tell anyone what y o u have seen, until the Son of man is raised from the dead.** The reason for this warning has already been given (see on 16:20). The injunction, "never tell *anyone*" naturally implies, "not even the other nine disciples." Every danger of a premature public proclamation must be avoided. When the proper time arrives, that is, after the Son of man's resurrection, the story of the transfiguration can, will, and must be proclaimed. The very fact of the resurrection will shed the necessary light on it.

Jesus said, "never tell anyone *what y o u have seen.*" In the present context this is a much better rendering than "Tell *the vision* to no man" (A.V. and several others). That translation is very ambiguous: it suggests that the transfiguration may not have been historical; that perhaps it never really happened at all, except in the mind of the three apostles. Even an objective vision, one that is not the product of subjective imagination but of divine revelation, as were the visions which the apostle John was going to receive on the island of Patmos, will not do in the present case. The statement: "He [Jesus] was transfigured" (verse 2) and Peter's commentary (II Peter 1:16, 17) rule out the "vision" idea in any form whatever. What the three men had seen was as real as was the voice which they had heard. Moreover, although it is true that the word used in the original frequently does have the meaning "vision" (Acts 9:10; 10:3, 17, 19; 11:5; 12:9; 16:9, 10; 18:9), that is not always the case. See the footnote for further information on this point. [623]

---

[623] The fact that in the present case τὸ ὅραμα means "what has been seen" or "what y o u have seen" is also confirmed by the verbal forms found in the other Gospels (see Mark 9:9: "he charged them not to tell anyone what they had seen"; cf. Luke 9:36). Besides, Acts 7:31, using the same noun ὅραμα, cannot mean that Moses at the burning

Christ's injunction produced the following reaction: **10. The disciples asked him, saying, Then why do the scribes say that first Elijah has to come?** There are several interpretations of this question. In view of the immediately preceding context the simplest would seem to be this: Jesus just now had spoken about his resurrection from the dead, implying his imminent death. But not only does it seem strange to the disciples that Messiah would have to die at all (cf. 16:22), what bothers them also is that such a death would, as they see it, leave Messianic prophecy unfulfilled. Are not the scribes constantly saying that according to Mal. 4:5, 6 (3:23, 24 in the Hebrew Bible) Messiah's coming would be preceded by that of Elijah? They were probably even using this prophecy to prove that Jesus could therefore not be the Christ, for Elijah had not yet returned. Now the disciples, by means of their spokesman, have already confessed Jesus to be Messiah (16:16), but the non-fulfilment of prophecy with respect to the sequence of the two comings—first Elijah's, then Christ's—puzzles them; for even though the Tishbite (I Kings 17:1) obviously has not yet reappeared upon the scene of history, "turning the heart of the fathers to the children, and the heart of the children to their fathers," Jesus, the Messiah or Christ, not only has already arrived but even declares that he is about to die. In view of Malachi's prediction how is this possible? [624]

In answering the question of the disciples and solving their problem Jesus first of all declares that the scribes were right in maintaining that Elijah's coming would precede Christ's: **11, 12a. He answered and said, Elijah is coming and is going to restore everything.** Though Christ's denunciation of the scribes could at times be sharp and cutting (5:20; 12:39; 15:3, 7; 23:13, etc.: the seven woes), he never went to the extreme of condemning all their teachings (see on 23:2, 3a). Here he is saying that the view of the scribes with respect to the sequence of the two comings—first Elijah's, then Messiah's—was correct; as was also their theory that Elijah had been called in order to bring about a restoration; and their conviction that Elijah's coming

---

bush merely saw a vision. On the contrary, "he wondered at the sight [the spectacle, that which he saw.] " L.N.T. (A. and G.), entry ὅραμα, p. 580, fails us here. L.N.T. (Th.) and H. G. Liddell and R. Scott are to be preferred in this particular instance.

[624] Other explanations: There is, first of all, that advanced by C. R. Erdman, *op. cit.*, p. 139, and by A. T. Robertson, *Word Pictures*, Vol. I, p. 141. As they see it, the disciples are thinking of Elijah's appearance on the mount of transfiguration, and are saying, in effect, "How is it that Jesus arrived before Elijah did, whereas according to prophecy Elijah should have come first?" Objection: this very brief appearance of the Tishbite could hardly have been regarded by these men as a fulfilment of Malachi's prophecy.

W. C. Allen, *op. cit.*, p. 186, thinks that the disciples are virtually asking, "Why death in view of the restorative work of a forerunner?" Evaluation: This may well be part of the explanation, but does it do justice to the difficulty which, according to verse 10, confronted the three, that difficulty being one pertaining to *the sequence* in which according to Malachi's prophecy the two comings (Elijah's and Messiah's) had to occur?

is a divine "must," because ordered in God's eternal plan and predicted by God's prophet.

Nevertheless, the scribes were making a mistake, and so were these three men, for it was the literal Elijah whose return they expected, the Tishbite in person. So, secondly, Jesus directs the attention of Peter, James, and John to the "Elijah" to whom Malachi actually was referring, and who had already arrived: **But I say to y o u that Elijah already came.** . . . Jesus was thinking of John the Baptist, whose arrival had preceded his (Christ's) own, and who in a worthy manner had been his forerunner, paving the way for his own ministry.

In order to understand the sense in which the Baptist was not Elijah, as also the sense in which he was indeed Elijah, all that is necessary is to combine the following three statements:

a. "When the Jews sent priests and Levites to him [i.e., to John the Baptist] and asked him, 'Are you Elijah?' he said, 'I am not' " (John 1:19, 21).

b. Jesus said, "And if y o u are willing to accept it, he [John the Baptist] is Elijah who was to come" (Matt. 11:14; cf. 11:10).

c. "He [the promised child; hence, John the Baptist] shall go before his face in the spirit and power of Elijah" (Luke 1:17; cf. 7:27).

Summary: Malachi's prophecy had actually been fulfilled, not, to be sure, literally but figuratively, namely, in John the Baptist, who, because he went forth in the spirit and power of Elijah, deserved to be called "Elijah."

There is a slight difficulty that must still be cleared up. The question may be asked, "But is it true that John the Baptist had brought about a restoration sufficiently important to satisfy the requirements of Mal. 4:6 and Matt. 17:11?"[625] In answering this question it should be pointed out, first, that the number of those people for whom, by God's grace, John became a great blessing, must have been considerable (See Matt. 3:5, 6; 14:5; Acts 19:3). Nevertheless, as Matt. 17:12b indicates, the emphasis should not be placed on the number or quantity of people affected, but on the thoroughgoing character or quality of the change which John, as God's servant, demanded and was instrumental in bringing about; a turnabout of heart, mind, and life so radical that for those experiencing it all things, including the relation between parents and children, would indeed become new. Viewed in this light Mal. 4:6 and Matt. 17:11 no longer present any great difficulty.

---

[625] Ancient Jewish interpreters gave a variety of interpretations to the restoration (*apokatastasis*) which the literal (as they saw it) Elijah was to bring about; for example, he would promote peace in the family (Mal. 4:6a), would establish harmony between God and man, would restore the tribes of Israel, etc. For Jewish source material on all this see J. Jeremias, article 'Ηλ(ε)ίας in TH.D.N.T., Vol. II, pp. 933, 934.

12b. **But they failed to recognize him, and treated him as they pleased.** By and large the people did not take to heart the preaching of the Baptist, completely failing to recognize in him the fulfilment of prophecy (Matt. 11:16-18), though they probably continued to regard him as a great man, "a prophet" (21:26). The religious leaders of the Jews turned against him (21:25). Herod Antipas killed him (14:3, 10). Instead of asking, "How does *God* want us to treat John the Baptist?" they did to him whatever *they* pleased. Jesus adds, **Similarly the Son of man is about to suffer at their hands.** The same combination—the people in general, the religious leaders, the political authorities—was about to afflict and kill Jesus. The mob was going to exclaim, "His blood be on us and our children" (27:25). In demanding that Jesus be crucified the people were going to co-operate with their leaders (27:20-23). From John 19:11 it is clear that Pilate too was going to heap guilt upon himself, though in lesser degree than the Jewish leaders. And so was Herod Antipas (Luke 23:11), the very man who had ordered the Baptist's execution. The entire world of unbelief was about to combine against Christ (Acts 4:27, 28). [626]

When Jesus assured the three that "Elijah" had already come, and had been rejected and killed, 13. **Then the disciples understood that he had spoken to them about John the Baptist.** In view of the fact that this was not the first time that Jesus had identified the Baptist with the "Elijah" whose return had been predicted (see on 11:14), and that, as has been shown previously, the two—namely, the Tishbite and the Baptist—resembled each other in many ways, the truth finally dawned on the three men that their Master had been speaking to them about John the Baptist. Except for the fact that they still experienced difficulty in understanding why the Messiah had to be afflicted and killed, and were in the dark about the resurrection, their problem, the one mentioned in verse 10, was now solved.

---

14 And when they came to the crowd a man approached him and kneeling before him said, 15 "Lord, take pity on my son, for he is an epileptic and suffers severely; for he often falls into the fire and often into the water. 16 And I brought him to your disciples but they couldn't cure him." 17 Jesus answered and said, "O faithless and perverse generation, how long shall I be with y o u; how long shall I put up with y o u? Bring him here to me." 18 And Jesus rebuked the demon, and it came out of him, and from that very moment the boy was cured. 19 Then the disciples came to Jesus privately and said, "Why could we not cast it out?" 20 He said to them, "Because of y o u r little faith; for I solemnly declare to y o u, if y o u have faith as a mustard seed, y o u shall say to this mountain, 'Move from here to there,' and it shall move; and nothing shall be impossible to y o u."

---

[626] For a more detailed discussion see my paperback, *Israel and The Bible,* chap. 1, "Who Killed Jesus?," pp. 7-15.

17:14-20 *The Healing of an Epileptic Boy*
Cf. Mark 9:14-29; Luke 9:37-43a

Raphael's painting, *The Transfiguration,* [627] on which that famous artist worked himself to death, dramatizes the contrast between that which had taken place on the summit of the mountain and what was happening in the plain below. Only, Raphael has united the two scenes that must have occurred at a considerable distance from each other and a day apart (Luke 9:37). But in bringing the two scenes together Raphael rendered a real service, emphasizing exactly what the Synoptists also seem to stress, namely, the tremendous contrast between the glory above (represented by the upper half of Raphael's masterpiece) and the shame and confusion below (the lower half). Above is the light, below are the shadows.

Nevertheless, there is also similarity: on the summit the Father, in spoken words, had reaffirmed his love to his only, his beloved Son; in the plain a father agonizingly intercedes in behalf of his only child (Luke 9:38), a son grievously afflicted. We are shown how the great, unique Only Son, in his infinite love, revealed his power and compassion to this other only son and to the latter's father, the man who uttered the heart-rending cry: **14, 15. And when they came to the crowd a man approached him and kneeling before him said, Lord, take pity on my son, for he is an epileptic and suffers severely....** This story is found in all three Synoptics, but it is Mark who has given us the most complete account. Luke too supplies certain details not found in the others. Matthew tells us that when Jesus with his three disciples had descended to the plain they saw *a.* a crowd, *b.* a man from this crowd stepping up to Jesus and kneeling down in front of him, and *c.* (implied) this man's son. In verse 16 the nine disciples who had been left behind when Jesus with the three ascended to the summit are also brought into the picture. Mark 9:14 adds the scribes, who were arguing with the nine disciples, probably mocking the nine because they had been unable to heal the boy.

The man who with reverence and humility is kneeling down before Jesus is in deep agony, for his only child is an epileptic. [628] The poor child "had it bad," suffered severely: **for he often falls into the fire and often into the water.** He had to be watched all the while; even so, terrible accidents, such as falling into the fire and into the water, would occur again and again, endangering his very life. Symptoms of epilepsy, such as foaming at the mouth, having convulsions, and teeth-grinding, are added in the other Gospels (Mark 9:18, 20, 26; Luke 9:39). The condition was even more grave than this, for in addition to being an epileptic this boy was also deaf and

---

[627] See A. E. Bailey, *op. cit.,* pp. 240-246; C. P. Maus, *op. cit.,* pp. 250-252.
[628] Greek σεληνιάζεται. For a defense of the rendering "is an epileptic" instead of "is a lunatic" or "is moon-struck" see on 4:24.

dumb (Mark 9:25). Worst of all, these afflictions had been brought about by "a spirit," that is, the boy was demon-possessed (as Matthew finally states in 17:18; the other evangelists much earlier in their separate accounts: Mark 9:17, 18, repeated in verses 20, 22, 25, 26, 28, 29; Luke 9:39, 40, 42). Demon-possession has been discussed in connection with 9:32.

It was the pity or compassion of the Lord to which the tempest-tossed father appealed. He did not doubt the fact that Jesus was indeed filled with mercy and kindness. That is why he pleaded, "Lord, take pity on my son." On the other hand, the man's faith in Christ's *power* needed strengthening (Mark 9:22-24).

Next, the deeply distressed father said to Jesus: 16. **And I brought him to your disciples but they couldn't cure him.** Evidently he had brought his boy to the nine disciples in the hope that Jesus was with them, for from the very beginning it had been his purpose to seek the Savior's help, not that of the disciples (Mark 9:17). However, when he noticed that Jesus was not among them he had asked the disciples to heal the boy. After all, these men had been commissioned by their Master to cast out unclean spirits and to heal every sickness and every infirmity (Matt. 10:11). That they had also been doing this is evident from Mark 6:13, 30; Luke 9:6-10. This time, however, something had happened that had never occurred previously, as far as the record shows: the disciples had not been able to cure the lad.

And now Christ's reaction: 17. **Jesus answered and said, O faithless and perverse generation, how long shall I be with y o u; how long shall I put up with y o u?** When from the dazzling splendor of the transfiguration Jesus descended to the pitiable situation below he, by means of this exclamation, gave expression to his pain and indignation. The fact that he directed his complaint to the "generation" shows that he cannot have been thinking only of the nine disciples who had failed in this emergency. He was evidently deeply dissatisfied with his contemporaries: with the father, who lacked sufficient faith in Christ's healing power (Mark 9:22-24); with the scribes, who, instead of showing any pity, were in all probability gloating over the disciples' impotence (Mark 9:14); with the crowd in general, which is pictured in the Gospels as being generally far more concerned about itself than about others (John 6:26); and, last but not least, with the nine disciples, because of their failure to exercise their faith by putting their whole heart into persevering prayer (Mark 9:29).

To a greater or lesser extent all were faithless, lacking in the exercise of true, warm, enduring faith, a faith operating effectively. By and large the minds and hearts of these people were "perverted," that is twisted and degenerate, turned in the wrong direction, away from undivided trust in God. When Jesus adds, "How long shall I be with y o u; how long shall I put up with y o u?" he shows that in view of his own trust in the heavenly Father, a confidence that was faultless, and in view of his own love which was infinite and tender, it was painful for him to "put up with" (the exact meaning of the original) those who lacked these qualities or who failed to exercise these virtues in a sufficient degree. His ministry had lasted almost three years by now. He was longing for the end.

By means of the heart-warming and positive command, **Bring him here to me,** Jesus gave the perfect example of proper behavior during annoying and distressing circumstances. In what he was about to do he revealed not only his power but also, as always his love. The result was: **18. And Jesus rebuked the demon, and it came out of him, and from that very moment the boy was cured.** A detailed account of the rage of the demon in being ordered to leave the boy, of the father's prayer for increase of faith, of the boy's final spasms followed by complete physical relaxation and deathlike stillness, and of the manner in which Jesus grasped his hand and lifted him up, is found in Mark 9:20-27; to which Luke 9:43 adds a description of the effect of the cure on the multitude: "And all were astonished at the majesty of God."

A little later the Lord had entered the house (see on 9:28). **19. Then the disciples came to Jesus privately and said, Why could we not cast it out?** The question was natural, for, as shown earlier, the disciples had met with success in casting out demons; so, why not this demon? **20. He said to them, Because of y o u r little faith....** [629] They had not sufficiently taken to heart the comfort they should have derived from the assurances which their Lord had given them (7:7-10; 10:8), and had not persisted in prayer. When the demon did not immediately leave they should not have stopped praying. On the subject of little faith see also 6:30; 8:26; 14:31; and 16:8. Continued: **for I solemnly declare to y o u, if y o u have faith as a mustard seed, y o u shall say to this mountain, Move from here to there, and it shall move....** For "I solemnly declare" see on 5:18. A mustard seed (see 13:31, 32), though at first very small, yet, because of its uninterrupted and vital contact with its nourishing environment, grows and grows until it becomes a tree so tall that the birds of the air come and lodge in its branches. Accordingly, "faith as a mustard seed" is the kind of trust in God which does not immediately give up in despair when its efforts do not meet with immediate success. It maintains its uninterrupted and vital contact with God and therefore continues to pray fervently, knowing that God at his own time and in his own way will bestow the blessing. Such faith links its possessor with the inexhaustible and infinite resources of God's power, wisdom, and love. It operates in harmony with God's revelation in his Word. Consequently, its prayers are not motivated by sinful desires, and it does not tempt God. It is therefore able to remove mountains.

---

[629] On the basis of manuscript evidence this reading must be retained, instead of "Because of y o u r unbelief."

This must not be understood literally but figuratively, in harmony with: *a.* Christ's very frequent use of figurative language, a striking example of which was given in the preceding chapter (16:6-12), and another in the present (17:12, 13); *b.* the well-known figure of speech found in Zech. 4:7, "What are you, O great mountain? Before Zerubbabel you shall become a plain," referring to the mountain of difficulties that would disappear; and *c.* the words which immediately follow here in Matt. 17:20: **and nothing shall be impossible to y o u.** No task assigned by the Lord is going to be impossible to perform when the person who receives the mandate is and remains in trustful contact with God. No burden will then be too heavy to bear. "With God all things are possible" (19:26). "I can do all things through him who infuses strength into me" says Paul (Phil. 4:13).

The words, "But this kind never comes out except by prayer and fasting," cf. **verse 21** in A.V., are lacking in the best manuscripts and were probably inserted from Mark 9:29.

---

22 Now while they were moving about together in Galilee Jesus said to them, "The Son of man is about to be delivered into the hands of men, 23 and they shall kill him, and on the third day he shall be raised up." And they were deeply distressed.

17:22, 23 *The Second Prediction of the Passion*
and the Resurrection
Cf. Mark 9:30-32; Luke 9:43b-45

22, 23a. Now while they were moving about together in Galilee Jesus said to them, The Son of man is about to be delivered into the hands of men. . . . This is the second prediction of the Passion. For all three see p. 9. It has been shown that the transfiguration and the cure of the epileptic boy probably occurred in Galilee. Here, in verse 22, we are told that the second announcement concerning Christ's impending suffering was made while Jesus and The Twelve were moving about together [630] in Galilee. From this it is also clear that The Ministry of the Retirement or Withdrawal, during which Jesus spent much time away from the crowds and with his disciples, instructing them, is still continuing: they—Jesus and The Twelve—were moving about *together;* hence, not in public; or, as the parallel passage, Mark 9:30, puts it, "He would not have anyone know it."

This second announcement adds certain details to the one found in 16:21:

---

[630] Textual evidence seems to support συστρεφομένων rather than ἀναστρεφομένων. The word συστρεφομένων is the gen. pl. participle, pres. middle of συστέφω. In the active voice the meaning is to turn together, to gather, collect (Acts 28:3); hence, here in the middle voice the sense is probably "were moving about together." This meaning, though not entirely certain, fits the context, is also in harmony with the cognate noun συστροφή: a gathering, concourse (as in Acts 19:40), and brings the passage into harmony with Mark 9:30.

a. Here (contrast 16:21) the emphasis is not on the necessity but on the certainty of the coming passion.

b. The humiliation to which the impending bitter experience will subject Jesus is here emphasized: he who is the glorious Son of man (see on 8:20) is going to be "delivered" into the hands of men; that is, he, the exalted One, will be given or handed over from one to another, as if he were a mere thing or toy. He will be delivered into the hands of the persons mentioned in the first prediction: elders, priests, and scribes: the Sanhedrin, and by them to Pilate. Note contrast between "Son of man and . . . men," mere "men," viewed as wicked, corrupt. Continued: **and they shall kill him.** Nothing was going to prevent these wicked men from doing away with their enemy.

Here, as in 16:21, the resurrection on the third day is also mentioned: **23b. and on the third day he shall be raised up.** See on 16:21. As before, so also now, the disciples do not know what to make of this prediction. They understood neither the necessity and certainty of the passion nor the announcement of the resurrection on the third day. Cf. Mark 9:32a: "But they did not understand the saying." Their total reaction to the second prediction, taken in its entirety (17:22, 23a) was: **And they were deeply distressed.** Since they did not know what was meant by being raised up, this part of the prediction was not able to turn their sorrow into joy. They were very, very sad. Besides, as Mark 9:32b adds, "They were afraid to ask him." See also Luke 9:45.

---

24 And when they had come to Capernaum the collectors of the double-drachma tax came to Peter and said, "Doesn't y o u r teacher pay the double-drachmas?" 25 He said, "Yes, he does." And when he [Peter] came into the house Jesus spoke first to him, saying, "What do you think, Simon? The kings of the earth, from whom do they collect toll or tax, from their sons or from foreigners?" 26 When he answered, "From foreigners," Jesus said to him, "Then the sons are exempt. 27 But that we may not ensnare them, go to the sea and throw in a hook; then take the first fish that comes up, open its mouth and you will find a stater. Take that and give it to them for me and for yourself."

17:24-27 *The Payment of the Temple Tax*

24. And when they had come to Capernaum the collectors of the double-drachma tax came to Peter and said, Doesn't y o u r teacher pay the double-drachmas? Jesus and The Twelve had been absent from Capernaum for a long time, traveling from place to place away from the large Jewish crowds, as has been shown. They had visited the neighborhood of Tyre and Sidon and the district of Caesarea Philippi. Three of the disciples had been with Jesus on the Mount of Transfiguration. And even after the descent from that elevation, the party had not immediately re-entered Capernaum. But now they were back in the place where Jesus had his headquarters and where Peter also lived. So, the tax-collectors arrive!

However, the story told by Matthew—by him alone—has nothing to do with taxes exacted by Rome. It concerns redemption money, the ransom price—"a ransom for his soul"—which every Israelite, twenty years and over, was by the Lord ordered to pay, and which was used for the maintenance of the sanctuary (Exod. 30:12-14; 38:26; II Chron. 24:6, 9; cf. Josephus *Antiquities* XVIII.312; *Jewish War* VII.213). It amounted to half a shekel, equal in value to the *didrachma* or *double-drachma.* The drachma, a Greek silver coin, was about equal in value to a Roman denar(ius). It amounted to a workman's average daily wage. Consequently the double-drachma was the amount a man would generally earn for two day's work. Since this temple tax was paid in Jewish coin the money-changers profited by making a small charge for exchanging foreign money for Jewish.

Now it was this double-drachma or half shekel which neither Jesus nor Peter had as yet paid, perhaps due to absence from Capernaum. So the collectors approach Peter. Why did they not go directly to Jesus? It may have been because they did not wish to embarrass the Master. They may have approached Peter, instead of one of the other disciples, because they regarded him as the leader of The Twelve, or simply because they knew that he at least would be able to answer their question. Speaking to Peter they call Jesus "y o u r teacher," the teacher recognized as such by The Twelve, and by many others besides. There was nothing strange about that title used with respect to Jesus (see also 8:19; 9:11). The Lord certainly deserved it in every way.

"Doesn't y o u r teacher pay the double-drachma?" We have no right to assume that any adverse criticism was intended. These tax-collectors probably knew that on many questions—such as fasting, sabbath-observance, handling food with hands that had not been ceremonially rinsed, etc.—Jesus and the Pharisees disagreed. The collectors probably did not distinguish sharply, as Jesus did, between things commanded in the law and human regulations superimposed upon the law. Accordingly, they may well have been of the opinion that for some reason or other Jesus did not pay the double-drachmas, the half-shekels.

25. He said, Yes, he does. Peter does not hesitate for a moment. He may have remembered what Jesus had said regarding the law of God (5:17, 18). Also, he may have been present on other occasions when the Lord paid the tax.

The conversation between Peter and the tax-collectors seems to have taken place on the street. Peter now proceeds on his way, intending to relate his experience to Jesus, and therefore to go to the house where the latter was staying at this time (for this house see on 9:28). He must have been hardly prepared for the surprise he received when Jesus himself opens the conversation and shows that he already knows whatever Peter was about to tell him. **And when he [Peter] came into the house Jesus spoke first to him, saying, What do you think, Simon? The kings of the earth, from whom do they**

678

collect toll or tax, from their sons or from foreigners? Jesus "antici-pated"⁶³¹ Peter, got ahead of him. That apostle received the same kind of a surprise that Cleopas and his companion were going to receive on the Sunday evening of the resurrection (Luke 24:33, 34). In that case "the eleven . . ." were the ones who spoke first. As to Christ's penetrating knowledge see John 1:47, 48; 2:25; 21:17. Cf. Ps. 139; Heb. 4:13.

By asking Simon, "From whom do they [the kings of the earth] collect toll [on goods] or tax [on their persons],⁶³² from their sons or from foreigners?" the Lord wishes to make it very clear that, strictly speaking, he is not under any obligation to pay this tax. The members of the king's family are not taxed but are maintained by the taxes paid by others. Frequently kings will not even tax their own citizens, but will gather tribute from conquered nations. **26. When he answered, From foreigners, Jesus said to him, Then the sons are exempt.** Was not Jesus the Son of God by nature? Was not the temple "his Father's house" (Luke 2:49; John 2:16)? Was he not, in fact, "greater than the temple" (Matt. 12:6)? And as to Peter? Was he not a son by adoption? Continued: **27. But in order not to ensnare them, go to the sea and throw in a hook; then take the first fish that comes up, open its mouth and you will find a stater. Take that and give it to them for me and for yourself.** Jesus means, "We must not cause others to become *ensnared* in sin."⁶³³ After all, the paying of this tax was not a merely human regulation but a divinely instituted requirement. Besides, had he and Peter not paid this tax it would have been interpreted as lack of interest in, and want of esteem for, the temple; perhaps even as irreverence. That must not be. So out of the Father's vast resources Jesus is going to take what is needed to pay the temple-tax for himself and for Peter.

Simon must go to the sea. He does not have to cast any net; a mere hook will suffice. The first fish that comes up will have a *stater,* that is, a *four-drachma* coin, in its mouth. That coin, amounting to a shekel, will be exactly sufficient for Jesus and Peter. They will secure freedom from debt—that is, that which by the general public might be considered a debt—*in exchange for* that stater.

Needless to say, that is exactly what also happened. One stands in awe before this miracle. A careful reading of the entire account indicates the following with respect to Jesus Christ: his penetrating knowledge (verse

---

⁶³¹ The verb used is προέφθασεν, third per. sing. aor. indic. of προφθάνω, the only occurrence of this word in the New Testament. See, however, II Clement 8:2.

⁶³² The word τέλη refers to indirect taxation, duty, or custom, gathered at custom-houses by τελῶναι, "publicans."
The next word, κῆνσος, was loaned from the Latin "census." The names of those who were obliged to pay it were written on a roll; hence our "census."

⁶³³ The word σκανδαλίσωμεν is first per. pl. aor. subj. active of σκανδαλίζω. See footnote 293 on p. 303.

25a), consciousness of sonship (verse 25b), considerateness (verse 27a), authority even over the sea and its denizens (verse 27b), and generosity (verse 27c).

Summary of Chapter 17

"I solemnly declare to y o u that there are some of those that are standing here who shall not taste death until they see the Son of man coming in his royal dignity" (16:28). There are interpreters who believe that by means of the transfiguration recorded in chapter 17 these words occurring at the close of chapter 16 are beginning to be fulfilled. However that may be, according to 17:1-13 six days after Peter's glorious profession of faith in Jesus as being the Messiah, the latter takes with him Peter, James, and John to a high mountain, so that after Christ's resurrection (see 17:9) the three will be able to bear witness concerning the things which they now are about to see and hear. While on this mountain Jesus is transfigured before their eyes, so that his face shines like the sun and his clothes become radiant with dazzling light. Suddenly Moses and Elijah, surrounded with heavenly brightness—the one probably representing the law, the other the prophets—also appear. They are speaking to Jesus concerning the departure which, in fulfilment of law and prophecy, he will accomplish at Jerusalem (Luke 9:31). Impulsive Peter, not knowing what he is saying, suggests that he be allowed to make three shelters, one for Jesus, one for Moses, and one for Elijah. Suddenly a cloud of diffused light covers Jesus, Moses, and Elijah. As previously at baptism so now also a voice is heard, saying, "This is my Son, the Beloved, with whom I am well pleased; listen to him." The frightened disciples fall on their faces, but by Christ's touch they are delivered from their fear and at his command they arise. When they raise their eyes they see no one but Jesus only. During the descent from the mount Jesus clears up the mystery concerning John the Baptist being Elijah whose coming, in fulfilment of prophecy, had preceded Christ's own.

What a contrast (verses 14-20) between the glory on top of the mount and the misery, shame, and confusion below! Having descended to the valley Jesus and the three are looking at a distraught father whose demon-possessed, epileptic, only son the nine disciples, because of their lack of enduring faith and prayer, had not been able to heal. Probably gloating over this failure scribes are arguing with the nine (Mark 9:14). A crowd of curiosity seekers is looking on. "O faithless and perverse generation, how long shall I put up with y o u?" Jesus cries. He adds, "Bring him here to me," and instantly cures the lad. The Master then explains to his disciples how it was that they had failed, adding that if they have faith like a mustard seed they will be able to carry out any task assigned to them.

Verses 22, 23 contain the second clear prediction concerning Christ's approaching passion and resurrection, with emphasis on the certainty and humiliating character of the coming ordeal.

Jesus and his disciples had been away from Capernaum—a tax collecting center—for a long time. So the temple tax had not yet been paid. "Doesn't y o u r teacher pay the double-drachmas?" It was the question put to Peter by the collector of this tax. Peter answers, "Yes, he does." When Peter is at the point of telling Jesus what has happened, the latter speaks first and shows that he already knows. He also knows where the tax money for both himself and Peter can be obtained, namely, from the mouth of the very first fish which Peter, ordered to the sea, is going to catch. For the light which verses 24-27 shed on Jesus see pp. 679, 680.

Chapter 18

Theme: *The Work Which Thou Gavest Him to Do*

Kindness toward the Little Ones
and
The Forgiving Spirit toward All

The Fourth Great Discourse

CHAPTER XVIII

18 1 At that moment the disciples came to Jesus, asking, "Who then is greatest in the kingdom of heaven?" 2 So he called to himself a little child, had him stand in the midst of them, 3 and said, "I solemnly declare to y o u, unless y o u turn and become like the little children, y o u will never enter the kingdom of heaven. 4 Therefore whoever becomes humble like this little child, he is the greatest in the kingdom of heaven. 5 And the person who in my name welcomes one such little child as this, welcomes me.

6 "But whoever causes one of these little ones who believe in me to sin, it is better for him that a heavy millstone be hung around his neck and he be drowned in the depth of the sea. 7 Woe to the world because of its temptations. [634] For temptations must come, but woe to the man who is responsible for the temptation. 8 And if your hand or your foot lures you into sin, cut it off and fling it away from you. It is better for you to enter life maimed or lame than with two hands or two feet to be thrown into the everlasting fire. 9 And if your eye lures you into sin, pluck it out and fling it away from you. It is better for you to enter into life with one eye than with two eyes to be thrown into the hell of fire.

10 "Be careful that y o u do not scornfully look down upon a single one of these little ones, for I say to y o u that in heaven their angels always see the face of my Father who is in heaven. 12 What do y o u think? If a man has a hundred sheep and one of them goes astray, will he not leave the ninety-nine in the mountains, [635] and does he not go in search of the wandering one? 13 And if he actually finds it, I solemnly declare to y o u that he rejoices over it more than over the ninety-nine that have not gone astray. 14 So also it is not the will of y o u r Father in heaven that one of these little ones should perish.

15 "Now if a brother sin against you, go and show him his fault while you are alone with him. If he listens to you, you have won your brother. 16 But if he does not listen (to you), take one or two other persons with you, in order that by the mouth of two witnesses or three every matter may be established. 17 If he refuses to listen to them, tell the church. And if he refuses to listen even to the church, let him be to you as the foreigner and the tax-collector. 18 I solemnly declare to y o u, whatever y o u shall bind on earth shall be bound in heaven, and whatever y o u shall loose on earth shall be loosed in heaven. [636] 19 Again I say to y o u, if on earth two of y o u agree about anything that they may ask, it shall be done for them by my Father who is in heaven. 20 For where two or three are gathered in my name there am I in the midst of them."

---

[634] Or: its enticements, allurements, traps, snares, pitfalls.

[635] Or: on the hillside.

[636] Or, instead of "bind" and "loose," one might render this: "forbid" and "permit," and so also in 16:19.

21 Then Peter came up and said to him, "Lord, how often shall my brother sin against me, and I forgive him? Up to seven times?" 22 Jesus answered, "I say to you, not up to seven times, but up to seventy times seven. 23 That is why the kingdom of heaven is like a king who wished to settle accounts with his servants. 24 Now when he had begun to settle (accounts), there was brought to him one (servant) who owed him ten thousand talents. 25 But since he did not have the means to pay his debt his master ordered him to be sold, along with his wife and children and all that he had, and payment to be made. 26 So the servant fell prostrate at his master's feet, saying, 'Have patience with me, and I will pay you everything.' 27 The heart of that servant's master was moved with pity, and he let him go free and forgave him the debt. 28 But that same servant, as he went out, came upon one of his fellow-servants, who owed him one hundred denarii. He grabbed him (by the throat) and started to choke him, saying, 'Pay whatever it is you owe!' 29 So that fellow-servant fell at his feet and was begging him, saying, 'Have patience with me, and I will pay you.' 30 But he was and remained unwilling, and instead had him thrown in jail until he should pay what was owed. 31 Now when his fellow-servants saw what had happened they felt very sad, and went and reported in detail to their master all that had occurred. 32 Then his master, having summoned him, said to him, 'You wicked servant; all that debt I forgave you when you begged me. 33 Should you not also have had mercy on your fellow-servant, even as I had mercy on you?' 34 And filled with wrath his master handed him over to the torturers until he should pay the entire debt. 35 So also shall my heavenly Father do to y o u if each of y o u does not heartily forgive his brother."

18:1-35 *Kindness toward Little Ones and the Forgiving Spirit toward All*

For 18:1-5 cf. Mark 9:33-37; Luke 9:46-48.
For 18:6-9 cf. Mark 9:42-48; Luke 17:1, 2.
For 18:10-14 cf. Luke 15:3-7.
For 18:15-20 cf. Luke 17:3.
For 18:21-35 cf. Luke 17:4.

Connection

That there is a close *temporal* connection between this chapter and the preceding paragraph (the temple tax) is clear from the words, "At that moment" (literally, "in that hour," 18:1). Evidently Peter had now been joined by the other disciples, all of them grouped around the Savior at his home or lodging place (see on 9:28) in Capernaum (17:24; Mark 9:33).

There is probably also a *material* or *thought* connection. In the last few chapters Matthew has been mentioning Peter far more often than any of the other disciples (14:28, 29; 15:15; 16:16-18, 22, 23; 17:4, 24-27). It was Peter who had walked on the water. It was Peter who had asked Jesus to explain his saying regarding ceremonial versus real defilement. It was to Peter that Jesus had addressed the words, "You are Peter, and upon this rock will I build my church." On the Mount of Transfiguration it was again Peter who was the most vocal of the three accompanying disciples. The tax-collectors, wishing to know whether or not Jesus customarily paid the temple tax, had singled out Peter, evidently thinking that he, rather than anyone else, would have the answer. And it was Peter who by the Lord was ordered to catch the fish with the coin in its mouth. In fact, while Matthew mentions Peter only a few times in the earlier part of his Gospel, and in the final section only in chapter 26 (mainly in the story of Peter's denial), in chapters 14—19 his name (Peter, Simon, Simon Peter) occurs at least a dozen times. Matthew, moreover, reported what was actually happening. It is not surprising, therefore, that the question would arise in the minds of the other disciples, "Could it be that in Christ's kingdom Peter is, or is going to be, after Jesus himself the most important person?"

Nevertheless, they were not sure that this question would receive an affirmative answer. There were the following facts to offset the idea of Peter's superior importance: a. he had been sharply rebuked by Jesus (16:23); b. not only Peter but also James and John had been with Jesus on "the Holy Mount" (17:1); and c. Peter's suggestion that three shelters be built on that mount had not even received an answer (17:4, 5), as the sons of Zebedee knew very well. So, perhaps Peter was not the greatest after all. But if not Peter, who then?

The question of these disciples was by no means an innocent one. In their favor it must be granted that implied in their very question was the faith that Jesus was indeed King, and that his kingdom—whatever might be its nature—was going to become publicly and gloriously manifested. Nevertheless, the men who were constantly discussing the matter of rank and priority in the kingdom were not free from sinful ambition. Otherwise, why would they have been ashamed of themselves when Jesus asked, "What were y o u discussing on the way?" (Mark 9:33, 34).

Now it was in answer to the question "Who is greatest?" that Jesus said, "Unless y o u turn and become like the little children, y o u will never enter the kingdom of heaven" (18:3).

However, it is not merely the lesson of trustful humility that the Master is here teaching his disciples. The sinful yearning to be greater than one's fellowmen and to rule over them is not a merely passive attitude. It is a very active drive. Therefore also its opposite and antidote can be nothing less than the similarly active effort to love all, that is, not only *to become like* the children but also *to love* them and *to protect* them; indeed, to exercise this same loving attitude toward *all*, gladly forgiving *all*.

Summary

The chapter must be considered a unit. [637]

---

[637] I can see no reason to adopt the view of H. W. Ridderbos, *op. cit.*, Vol. II, pp. 38, 39, that Matthew combined several sayings of Jesus, spoken at different occasions, into

Under the general heading or title *Kindness toward the Little Ones and the Forgiving Spirit toward All* the subdivisions with their main teachings may be summarized as follows:

Be Kind to the Little Ones:
Become like them (verses 1-5)
Guard them, preventing them and yourselves from falling into temptation (verses 6-9)
Regard them highly; and if they wander away, go and find them and bring them home (verses 10-14).

Show the Forgiving Spirit toward All:
Church Discipline should be a matter of last resort: "If a brother sins against you, go and show him his fault while you are alone with him, etc." The steps in discipline (verses 15-20).
The Parable of the Unmerciful Servant (verses 23-35), in answer to Peter's question, "Lord, how often shall my brother sin against me, and I forgive him? Up to seven times?"

1. *Be Kind to the Little Ones*

a. Become like them

1. At that moment the disciples came to Jesus, asking, Who then is greatest in the kingdom of heaven? In the light of Mark 9:33, 34 it is evident that Matthew abbreviates. In all probability the disciples had not intended to reveal to Jesus what they had been discussing on the way to his home. But the Lord knew, and wanted them to make a clean breast of it. For other instances of Christ's penetrating knowledge see 17:25; John 1:47, 48; 2:25; 21:17; but see also Mark 13:32; (cf. Matt. 24:36). So Jesus asked, "What were y o u discussing on the way?" Embarrassed silence followed. Then they came out with it: they had been "arguing" (Luke 9:46) about rank or status, and their question had been as it was even now, "Who then is greatest [638] in the kingdom of heaven?"

It seems strange that almost the first recorded result of Christ's second announcement (17:22, 23a) of his rapidly approaching departure in Jerusalem should have been the disciples' "quarrelling for the lead" [639] in the kingdom. How quickly their sorrow (17:23b) caused by Christ's prediction

---

one discourse. Solid proof for this position has not been supplied. For the most part the ideas follow one another very naturally. If in a few cases the connection should not be immediately clear room must be left for the possibility that the evangelists did not have the space to report everything (John 20:30; 21:25).

[638] Here the adjective μείζων, though literally "greater," clearly has the sense of a superlative, as in I Cor. 13:13: "greatest of these is love." The last example also shows that this comparative form does not always need to be preceded by the definite article to be equal in force to a superlative. On the substitution of a comparative form for a superlative, in Koine Greek, see Gram. N.T., pp. 281 and 667.

[639] See A. Maclaren, *Expositions of Holy Scripture,* Vol. III (on chapters 18-28), Cincinnati and New York (no date), p. 1.

of his deep humiliation had given way to their craving for exaltation! Yet, such men as these Jesus had chosen to be his disciples! For such as these—see also p. 246 f.—he was going to lay down his life! When we consider this we see more clearly the greatness and sovereign (by men wholly unmerited) character of God's electing love. Cf. Ps. 103:14; 115:1; Ezek. 16:1-14; Dan. 9:7, 8; I John 4:19; and N.T.C. on Eph. 1:4.

2-4. **So he called to himself a little child, had him stand in the midst of them. . . .** What Jesus *did* at this occasion revealed not only his thorough understanding of the nature of the kingdom and of the way of entering it, but also his tenderness toward the little ones. What he *said* deserved all the praise that has ever been ascribed to it, and far more than that. But was not the amazing glory of the Mediator's soul revealed also in his restraint, that is, in what he did not do and did not say? He did not even scold his disciples for their callousness, their insensibility with respect to his approaching agony, the non-lasting character of their grief, their quickness in turning the mind away from him to themselves, their selfishness. All this he passed by, and addressed himself directly to their question.

It is pleasing to note the frequency with which the presence of children around Jesus and/or his love for them is mentioned in the Gospels. See Matt. 14:21; 15:38; 18:3; 19:13, 14 (cf. Mark 10:13, 14; Luke 18:15, 16); 21:15, 16; 23:37 (cf. Luke 13:34). Undoubtedly children felt attracted to Jesus, wanted to be with him. Whenever he wanted a child there was always one present, ready to do his bidding, to come when he called him. So also here. To speculate who this child was is useless. The point is that this was indeed a child, endowed with all the favorable and amiable qualities generally associated with childhood in any clime and at any time.

The Lord calls this little one to his side, and places him "in the midst of" all these "big" men, perhaps in such a position that the child faced them while they were arranged in a crescent before him. The child was not afraid, for it stood by the Lord's very side (Luke 9:47), and was then taken up in his arms (Mark 9:36), where he would feel perfectly at ease and able to look up into the face of Jesus.

The Master looked at his disciples **and said, I solemnly declare to y o u, unless y o u turn and become like the little children, y o u will never enter the kingdom of heaven.** What he meant was this: "Y o u have been arguing about the question who will be greatest in the kingdom of heaven, as if y o u were sure of already being in it and of being destined for its future manifestation in glory. But if y o u continue in y o u r present state of mind and heart, each of y o u being eager to be higher than his fellows and to lord it over them, y o u will be excluded; y o u will then most certainly [640] not even enter it."

---

[640] Note οὐ μή, strengthening the negation.

Jesus demands that the disciples *turn,* that is, that they *be converted* from their worldly ambition, their coarse selfishness. Of course, they cannot do this in their own power. They must pray the prayer found in Jer. 31:18, "Turn thou me, and I shall be turned; for thou art Jehovah my God." Only when the divine act of causing a person to be reborn (born "from above") has taken place, is conversion, as an act in which man himself takes part, even possible (John 3:3, 5).

That this turning—from self to God; from sin to grace—implies "becoming like the little children" is clear from the juxtaposition of the words, for Jesus said, "unless y o u turn and become like the little children, etc." This poses the question, "Exactly what did he mean when he *solemnly declared* (see on 5:18) that with a view to entrance into *the kingdom of heaven* (see on 4:23; 13:43) the disciples must become like the little children?'"

Among the favorable qualities which we generally associate with the little ones the following are perhaps the most outstanding: simplicity, frankness, obedience, unpretentiousness, humility, trustfulness. The fact that they are weak, very limited in strength and knowledge, and that they do not deny this, endears them to us. All of these traits may well have been in the mind of the Savior when he told the disciples that if they wanted to enter the kingdom of heaven they must become like the little children. Nevertheless, it is especially *humility* or, if one prefers, *humble trustfulness* (see verse 6: "who believe in me") which the Savior emphasizes in the present passage. This is evident first of all from the preceding context, which requires that the disciples' striving to be the greatest make place for willingness to be the least; then also from the immediately following passage (verse 4); note the words: "whoever becomes humble like this little child"; and finally, from such parallels as 20:20-28; 23:11, 12; Mark 9:35, 42; Luke 18:14; 22:24-30. See also John 13:1-20 and I Peter 5:5, 6. Salvation, whether in its initial, continuing, or final stage, must always be accepted as an undeserved gift, even the faith by means of which it is accepted being also a gift. See N.T.C. on Eph. 2:8. Thus all human boasting is excluded (Rom. 3:27). God alone receives the glory.

Christ's negative statement (verse 3) implies the positive:**Therefore whoever becomes humble like this little child, he is the greatest in the kingdom of heaven.** It was a reaffirmation of a lesson Jesus had been teaching right along. He had taught it by means of the first four beatitudes (see on 5:3-6). He had stressed it in connection with the praise which he had heaped upon the centurion (8:5-13) and upon the Canaanite woman (15:27, 28). He was constantly teaching it by means of his own example (Matt. 12:15-21; 20:28; 21:5; Luke 22:27; John 13:1-20; cf. II Cor. 8:9; Phil. 2:5-8). And now there was *this* humble little child, still looking trustfully into the eyes of the Master! Let the disciples—yes, let everyone (note "whoever")—then become like this child. Let them learn that the only way to ascend is to descend. Do they wish to become great? Then let them become little! Do they wish to rise? Then let them sink! Do they wish to rule? Then let them serve! Or, as a Dutch poem (*Te worden als een kindeke*), of which I here offer my free translation, has it:

> Make me, O Lord, a child again,
> So tender, frail, and small,
> In self possessing nothing, and
> In thee possessing all.

> O Savior, make me small once more,
> That downward I may grow,
> And in this heart of mine restore
> The faith of long ago.

> With thee may I be crucified—
> No longer *I* that lives—
> O Savior, crush my sinful pride
> By grace which pardon gives.

> Make me, O Lord, a child again,
> Obedient to thy call,
> In self possessing nothing, and
> In thee possessing all.

5. And the person who in my name welcomes one such little child as this, welcomes me. That the truth here expressed applies not only to the lambs of the flock but also to all who by grace have become like them was made clear in 10:40 (see on that passage). By welcoming *any* of those who belong to Jesus Christ, no matter how insignificant he may appear to the world roundabout, we are welcoming Jesus Christ himself, for it is impossible to separate the Lord from those whom he considers his own (Acts 9:4, 5; 22:7; 26:15; Rom. 8:35-39).

> b. *Guard them, preventing them and yourselves*
> *from falling into temptation*

Accordingly, Jesus continues: **6. But whoever causes one of these little ones who believe in me to sin, it is better for him that a heavy millstone be hung around his neck and he be drowned in the depth of the sea.** Here the Savior places the negative (not welcoming the little ones but causing them to sin) over against the positive (welcoming them) of the preceding verse. It is clear that the Lord is speaking about possibilities that may, and often do, arise when some "worldly" (see verse 7) person, whether within or outside of the visible church, commits the grave sin of trying to lead one of God's true children astray. He is saying that even if the sin be planned against *only* *one* of those so precious in God's sight, physical death for such a planner—yes, death of the most gruesome kind—would be preferable. [641]

The evil to which Jesus here refers, namely, causing someone else, one of God's dear children, to sin, clearly refers to placing in his path enticements to do wrong, traps, beguiling allurements, [642] as is clear from verse 7.

Jesus, then is saying that it is preferable for such an evil person that a heavy (literally *donkey-drawn*) millstone be hung about his neck and he be drowned in the depth of the sea (literally "that he be plunged down into the sea, [643] into the sea of the sea"); that is, that with this heavy millstone around his neck, making drowning doubly sure, he be taken far away from shore to the place where the splashing waters of the turbulent sea or ocean are very deep, and that he there be plunged into this watery grave from which return is absolutely impossible.

The millstone of which Jesus speaks is the top-stone of the two between which the grain is crushed. The reference is not to the handmill but to the much heavier stone drawn by a donkey. [644] In the middle of the top-stone, whether of a handmill or of a donkey-drawn mill, there is a hole through which grain can be fed so as to be crushed between the two stones. The presence of this hole explains the phrase "that a heavy millstone *be hung around his neck.*" [645]

To summarize, what Jesus is saying in verses 1-6 is this, that, instead of striving to become greatest in the kingdom of heaven (verse 1), in the process of attempting this hurting others instead of guarding them (verse 6), the disciples should rather learn to forget about themselves and to focus their loving attention upon Christ's little ones, upon the lambs of the flock and upon all those who in their humble trustfulness (or trustful humility) resemble these lambs. By welcoming them they will be welcoming their Lord (verse 5). This they will learn to do if they themselves also become like the little children, even like this little one whom Jesus has taken into his arms. That is the only way to greatness in the kingdom of heaven (verses 2-4).

On the subject of *a.* hurting others by leading them into temptation (verse

---

[641] The verb συμφέρω (here συμφέρει: third per. sing. pres. indic.) means basically *to bring together;* hence, to help, to be profitable or advantageous. When it is associated with an alternative—as here, the alternative in this case being *a.* refraining from carrying out the plan and instead suffering gruesome physical death (verse 6), or *b.* carrying it out and therefore facing "the everlasting fire" (verse 8), "the hell of fire" (verse 9)—the meaning *be preferable, be better than* results. See also Matt. 5:29; 19:10; John 11:50; 18:14.

[642] In connection with the verb σκανδαλίζω (here σκανδαλίσῃ third per. sing. aor. subj. active) see above, footnote 293 on p. 303.

[643] For the verb καταποντίζω (here καταποντισθῇ, third pers. sing. aor. subj. passive, as is κρεμασθῇ) see footnote 570 on p. 602.

[644] See A. Deissmann, *op. cit.*, p. 81.

[645] See F. F. Bishop, *Jesus of Palestine*, London, 1955, p. 163.

7, cf. verse 6), or *b.* allowing oneself to be misled (verses 8, 9) Jesus continues as follows: **7. Woe to the world because of its temptations.** Those who tempt others to sin and do not repent of this terrible evil show that they belong to "the world," to mankind alienated from the life of God. [646] Not all of these people upon whom this prophetic curse—the very opposite of a beatitude (5:3-12)—is pronounced are necessarily to be thought of as being from the start outside the kingdom, when the latter concept is taken in its broadest sense. Even the disciples themselves must be on their guard, as Jesus has shown just now (see verses 3, 6), lest they should belong to "the world" that strives to lure God's children into sin. The seriousness of committing this sin appears from the fact that it was through temptation that sin entered the human realm (Gen. 3:1-6) and is still spreading (I Tim. 6:9; James 1:12). Temptation is of the devil, the great tempter (Matt. 4:1; John 8:44; I Peter 5:8), whose "wiles" are many (see N.T.C. on Eph. 6:11). The substance of the curse pronounced upon the world is indicated in verse 8 ("the everlasting fire") and verse 9 ("the hell of fire").

It is, however, impossible in this present realm of sin to put an end to every temptation, every enticement to sin: **For temptations must come. . . .** It is of the very nature of sin that it spreads. It would be easier to stop water hyacinths from clogging the waterways of Florida than to prevent temptations from clogging the tracks of the human race, including even the church. But though it is impossible to eradicate temptations, by God's grace it is possible to prevent oneself from belonging to the company of the tempters. Hence Jesus adds, **but woe to the man who is responsible for the temptation,** or, more literally, "through whom the temptation comes." Neither God's eternal decrees nor the facts of history offer any excuse for the terrible sin of enticing others to do wrong. See Luke 22:22; Acts 2:23.

By God's grace it is also possible to overcome temptations in one's own life: **8, 9. And if your hand or your foot lures you into sin, cut it off and fling it away from you. It is better for you to enter life maimed or lame than with two hands or two feet to be thrown into the everlasting fire. And if your eye lures you into sin, pluck it out and fling it away from you. It is better for you to enter into life with one eye than with two eyes to be thrown into the hell of fire.** The admonition found in 5:29, 30 is here repeated, with slight variations; for example, here in 18:8, 9 the reference to hand and foot is followed by that to the eye; in 5:29, 30 the reverse order is followed, the foot is not even mentioned, and instead of "eye" we find "right eye." So also here in 18:8, 9 the punishment is described as being thrown into the everlasting fire . . . into the hell (Gehenna) of fire; in 5:29,

---

[646] For the various meanings of the word κόσμος see N.T.C. on the Gospel according to John, Vol. I, footnote 26 on p. 79. In Matt. 18:7 meaning (4), perhaps even the closely related meaning (6), is probably indicated.

30 it is pictured as being thrown into or going down into hell (Gehenna). Finally, here in 18:8, 9 it is made very clear that the Gehenna of everlasting fire is the very opposite of "life," that is, "life everlasting" with God in heaven (cf. the contrast pictured in Matt. 25:46). But it is not upon these minor details that we should especially fix our attention but upon the central meaning which is the same in both places. See, therefore, the explanation of 5:29, 30.

Drastic action is necessary to overcome temptation, action made possible by prayer (Matt. 6:13; 26:41). The promise of victory is given in such passages as Matt. 7:7; I Cor. 10:13; Heb. 2:18; James 1:12.

It may seem as if Jesus has wandered away from the subject of guarding his "little ones," and not tempting them to sin. In reality, however, he has not, for is not taking drastic action against the temptations by which Christ's disciples themselves are assailed one of the best methods of preventing themselves from enticing others? As to these "little ones," Jesus further exhorts his disciples as follows:

> c. *Regard them highly; and if they wander away,*
> *go and find them and bring them home.*

10. Be careful that y o u do not scornfully look down upon a single one of these little ones, for I say to y o u that in heaven their angels always see the face of my Father who is in heaven. At the root of all self-exaltation lies sinful pride, a looking down, or, as the Greek literally expresses it, a *thinking down* upon others. The proper attitude is that conveyed so touchingly by Paul: "in humble-mindedness each counting the other better than himself" (Phil. 2:3).

The words of Jesus are very emphatic. He warns the disciples *constantly to see to it* not to make *even a single one* of those whom he considers his own the object of scorn or disdain, of belittlement or contempt.

Much has been written about the words, "for I say to y o u that in heaven their angels. . . ." As to "for," this is easily explained as introducing the reason why no one must despise a single one of these little ones. And as to "I say to y o u," this probably means, "I declare to y o u with all the authority at my command. I solemnly affirm."

Now as to the "saying" itself, on its basis some have affirmed that each of God's children has his own "guardian angel" who remains with him for life, protecting him from harm and helping him in various ways. [647] In this precise form, however, the theory has no solid Scriptural support. Passages to which an appeal has been made do not really confirm the theory. So, for example, Gen. 48:16 does not refer to a created angel (see the context, verse 15). Dan. 3:28 must be explained in the light of 3:25. As far as text and

---

[647] See S.BK. I, pp. 781 ff.; III, pp. 48 ff.; 437 ff.; Th.D.N.T., Vol. I, pp. 82, 86.

context are concerned this "angel" or "son of the gods" who had been sent
for the protection and encouragement of Daniel's friends remains a sublime
mystery, and for that very reason can render no service in defense of the
above-mentioned theory. The "angel" who was with Daniel in the lions' den
(Dan. 6:22) is said to have been *God's* angel (an angel sent by God), not
Daniel's in the sense of being an angel who remained with and took care of
the prophet at all times. And as to Acts 12:15, the apostles' outcry—"It is
his angel"—at the appearance of Peter, who had been imprisoned and
securely guarded, but now suddenly stood before them no longer bound,
must probably be ascribed to overwhelming amazement coupled with a
measure of superstitious fear. [648] In Heb. 1:14 the service which angels
render to God's children is ascribed in very general terms. Not a word is said
about each believer having his own guardian angel. Finally, even the apocryphal book Tobit (see especially 5:4 ff.; 12:5), if it refers at all to Raphael as
"guardian angel" in the sense defined above, can hardly be regarded as a
dependable basis for this doctrine. It may reflect a belief pertaining to
Zoroastrianism. So much for the "guardian angel" notion.

Other interpreters, in their explanation of Matt. 18:10, advocate the view
that Jesus is saying that the esteem in which "the little ones" are held in
heaven is so high that "the most exalted angels" had been commissioned by
his Father to watch over them and to protect them. [649] In favor of this view
it has been argued that the words "for in heaven their angels always see the
face of my Father who is in heaven" are probably based on a custom
prevailing at the time in Eastern courts, where the men who were said to
"stand before the king" and to "see his face" (cf. I Kings 10:8; II Kings
25:19) were officers who enjoyed their sovereign's special favor, were near
him, were privileged to enjoy close fellowship with him, constantly awaiting
his orders. They were the men who were said to "sit first in the kingdom"
(Esther 1:14). If this line of reasoning is followed, then Jesus is saying to his
disciples, "Do not regard as unimportant those who by 'my Father in
heaven'—on this touchingly beautiful phrase and other similar ones see pp.
287, 326, 378, 543—are regarded so highly that he has appointed his
most illustrious angels, those who as it were stand nearest to his throne and
constantly rejoice in his glorious presence, to keep watch over them."

It is not entirely certain that this Eastern custom actually underlies
Christ's words. Either way, however, the difference in resultant meaning is
not very substantial. Two qualifications must, however, be borne in mind: *a.*
the meaning cannot be "*only* his highest angels," for this would bring the

---

[648] On this passage see F. F. Bruce, *Commentary on the Book of The Acts* (*The New
International Commentary on The New Testament*), Grand Rapids, 1964.

[649] Thus A. Maclaren, *op. cit.*, on this passage. See also C. R. Erdman, *op. cit.*, p. 147,
who similarly opines that the angels who protect the little ones are nearest to God's
throne.

passage into conflict with the rest of Scripture, in which angels rushing to the defense and consolation of God's children are by no means always characterized as *only* the most exalted ones (cf. Ps. 91:11; Heb. 1:14); but rather as "his angels, *including* even the highest ranking ones" (cf. Dan. 12:1; Luke 1:26); and *b.* the modifier "their" (in the phrase "their angels") must not, with some interpreters [650] be explained as indicating the angels of those *only* who are young in years, for that view fails to do justice to the contextual transition from the expression "the little children" to "those who become like the little children" (see especially verses 3 and 4). The little children are *included,* to be sure!

What, then, can be regarded as the correct interpretation? I have not been able to find any better explanation of the passage than that offered by Calvin in his Commentary on *A Harmony to the Evangelists Matthew, Mark, and Luke.* He interprets the words of Jesus to mean, "it is no light matter to despise those who have angels for their companions and friends. . . . We ought therefore to guard ourselves against despising their salvation, which even angels have been commissioned to promote. . . . The care of the entire Church is committed to angels, to assist each member as his needs require."

To this, A. Kuyper [651] adds two significant thoughts: *a.* Matt. 18:10 does not emphasize that the angels speak to God in our behalf but rather that God through his angels takes care of his chosen ones; and *b.* nevertheless, the care and watchfulness bestowed upon God's children by the angels is not of a merely mechanical or arbitrary character. On the contrary, as is clear from such passages as Luke 15:10 ("There is joy in the presence of the angels over one sinner who repents") and 16:22 ("Lazarus was carried by the angels into Abraham's bosom"), the angels bear the needs of God's children on their very hearts, are deeply interested in them, and love them. To this I would add: Do not also such passages as Dan. 10:11; Luke 2:13, 14; I Peter 1:12; and Rev. 5:11, 12 point in the same direction?

According to Scripture

ANGELS ARE:

A ttendants of Christ (II Thess. 1:7), their exalted Head (Eph. 1:21; 22; Col. 2:10)

B ringers of good tidings concerning our salvation (see on Luke 2:14; 24:4; Acts 1:11; I Tim. 3:16)

C horisters of heaven (Luke 15:10; I Cor. 13:1; Rev. 5:11, 12)

D efenders of God's children (Ps. 34:8; 91:11; Dan. 6:22; 10:10, 13, 20; Matt. 18:10; Acts 5:19; II Thess. 1:7-10; Rev. 12:7), though the latter outrank them and will judge them (I Cor. 6:3; Heb. 1:14)

E xamples in obedience (Matt. 6:10; I Cor. 11:10)

---

650 E.g., W. C. Allen, *op. cit.,* p. 196.
651 See his book *De Engelen Gods,* Kampen, 1923, pp. 280, 281.

F riends of the redeemed, constantly watching over them, deeply interested in their salvation, and rendering service to them in every way, also
in executing the judgment of God upon the enemy (Matt. 13:41;
25:31, 32; Luke 15:10; 16:22; I Cor. 4:9; Gal. 3:19; II Thess. 1:7; I
Peter 1:12; Heb. 1:14; Rev. 20:1-3)
The words, "For the Son of man is coming to save that which was lost,"
cf. verse 11 in A.V., are lacking in the best manuscripts and were probably
inserted from Luke 19:10.

The fact that God is indeed a loving Father, One who tenderly cares for
his flock, using angels and other means to carry out his gracious designs,
introduces the parable of *The Lost Sheep*. In a more extended form this
parable is found also in Luke 15:3-7. There, in view of the introduction that
mentions the grumbling of the Pharisees and the scribes because Jesus
welcomed sinners, and in view of the appended lesson in verse 7, which
makes mention of "ninety-nine righteous persons," it is clear that a figurative meaning must be assigned to these ninety-nine. This is not difficult, and
it is surprising that the question, "Who are the ninety-nine?" has resulted in
so much difference of opinion.

However, in Matt. 18 this question need not be faced, for here *all* the
emphasis is on the *one* sheep that got lost. The ninety-nine are mentioned
only as a kind of background, making the attention devoted to the one
wandering sheep stand out all the more clearly.

Jesus says, 12. **What do y o u think?** This can be regarded as a device to
arouse the undivided attention of the listeners, eliciting their immediate and
complete agreement with that which Jesus is about to say, namely, **If a man
has a hundred sheep and one of them goes astray, will he not leave the
ninety-nine in the mountains, and does he not go in search of the wandering
one?** [652] The fact that at least some people in the audience were well

---

[652] Note the vivid character of the portrayal. First we have a future more vivid (third
class) conditional sentence, introduced in the protasis by ἐάν followed by γένηται, third
per. sing. aor. subjunctive of γίνομαι ("If a man has" or "have") and by πλανηθῇ, third
per. aor. subj. passive of πλανάω ("Goes"—or go—"astray"; cf. "planet," wandering star).
The expectation is aroused, and is sharpened by the question demanding assent from the
audience. The future contingency becomes present to the mind of the listener who, as it
were, sympathizes with the one sheep that is wandering away. What is to be done? The
apodosis supplies the answer, implied in a question: "Will not the shepherd leave the
ninety-nine in the mountains?"
The negative οὐχί followed by the appropriate third per. sing. fut. indic. active
(ἀφήσει) of ἀφίημι ("will he not leave") is now used. The listeners immediately grasp that
the shepherd will indeed go out, leaving the ninety-nine. "Having gone," says Jesus (using
πορευθείς, aor. participle of πορεύομαι), creating another situation which must lead to
still another action, namely, "does he not seek" (ζητεῖ, third per. sing. present indic. act.
of ζητέω) the wandering one (τὸ πλανώμενον, acc. sing. neut. pres. pass. participle of
πλανάω)?" Combining the aor. participle, the verb, and the pres. participle results in:
"Does he not go in search of the wandering one?" In verse 13 another future more vivid
conditional sentence, in the protasis beginning similarly with ἐὰν γένηται, in this case

acquainted with the idea of Jehovah being his people's Shepherd (see especially Ps. 23) must have driven the meaning home immediately. On this general subject and the use Jesus makes of it elsewhere, showing that also in this respect he and the Father are one, see what has been said previously in connection with 9:36; also N.T.C. on the Gospel according to John, Vol. II, pp. 97-132. Certainly the shepherd would leave the ninety-nine in the mountains and would go in search of the one wandering sheep. That is exactly what Jehovah is constantly doing. Is not this also exactly what Jesus himself came to do? Is it not also what the disciples should be doing, instead of focusing their attention upon their own future greatness (verse 1)?

Continued: **13. And if he actually finds it, I solemnly declare to y o u that he rejoices over it more than over the ninety-nine that have not gone astray.** Jesus says "if," for there are times when a straying sheep cannot be found. It may have been devoured by a wolf, or it may have perished for some other reason. So also not all those who belong to the church visible and for a while were *outwardly* walking in the way of the Lord, but who afterward show that they do not love the Lord, can be reclaimed. On the other hand, if the shepherd actually finds the wandering sheep he will rejoice over it more than over the ninety-nine that have not gone astray. He rejoices not only because he has found what he had lost. With him it is not a matter merely of recovering a material loss. Far from it! If he has a real shepherd's heart he rejoices also and especially in the joy of the sheep.

Christ's statement is not a question, nor even a mere statement; it is a very solemn pronouncement, introduced by "Amen (see on 5:18), I say to y o u." The joy over the rescue of that one sheep is greater than that over the ninety-nine. The elation over being a benefactor is greater than that of being a mere possessor!

Jesus continues: **14. So also it is not the will of y o u r Father in heaven that one of these little ones should perish.** In close connection with the preceding verses we must conclude that what Jesus is asserting so very emphatically is that the Father in heaven is definitely interested in each of his sheep, yes, even in each of his wandering sheep. By sending his Son into the world he is rescuing sheep that have gone astray. In this the Father *delights*. See Luke 15:7, 20, 22-24. So does the Son. See Matt. 9:12, 13; Luke 19:10; John 10:11, 14. In this kind of work the disciples too should be engaged. See Matt. 9:36—10:1; John 4:35.

It is indeed a very comforting truth that is here revealed. That it is God's revealed will that not a single one should perish but that all be saved, that

---

followed by εὑρεῖν αὐτό; hence, "And if he gets to find it" (thus literally), leads to an apodosis which is not, as in verse 12, a question to be answered by the audience, but a very strong and solemn assertion, as is shown by ἀμὴν λέγω ("I solemnly declare"), see on 5:18.

this is his *delight,* is the doctrine of Scripture throughout. In line with this see the following passages: Deut. 5:29; Ps. 81:13; Isa. 45:22; 48:18; Ezek. 18:23, 32; 33:11; Matt. 11:28, 29; John 7:37; II Peter 3:9; Rev. 22:17. See also on Matt. 9:37, 38 and 23:37 (cf. Luke 13:34). [653]

Reclaiming love implies forgiveness. So the next sub-topic is:

2. *Show the Forgiving Spirit toward All*

a. *Church Discipline should be a matter of last resort: "If a brother sins against you, go and show him his fault while you are alone with him. . . ." The steps in discipline.*

15. **Now if a brother sin against you, go and show him his fault while you are alone with him.** Jesus has been warning against the evil of tempting others to sin. Instead of becoming the cause of someone else's ruin every follower of the Lord should make it his business to find the sheep that has gone astray and to bring it back to the fold. But suppose the shoe is on the other foot. Suppose I myself am not the sinner, the one who causes others to become ensnared in sin, but instead the one sinned against, what then? In answering this question the Lord starts out by saying, "Now if a brother sin against you. . . ."

Much discussion has centered around the phrase "against you." Did Matthew actually write this? Did Jesus actually say this? Or must the phrase be omitted in view of the fact that some of the best and oldest manuscripts omit it? Those who are interested in the textual details should see the footnote. [654] My own opinion is as follows: retention or omission of *the*

---

[653] Excellent material on this general topic is found in J. Murray and N. B. Stonehouse, *The Free Offer of the Gospel,* Phillipsburg, 1948; and also in A. C. De Jong's doctoral dissertation, *The Well-Meant Gospel Offer,* published in Franeker, no date; and in L. Berkhof, *Systematic Theology,* pp. 397, 398. I disagree with Lenski's statement (*op. cit.,* p. 676) that verse 14 excludes the idea of reprobation. One must distinguish between God's secret (decretive) and his revealed will. Mysteries remain, to be sure. But is not the very fact that God foresaw the obstinate rejection (on the part of many) of his intense and yearning love a factor in explaining, in whatever small degree, the decree of reprobation? See Isa. 5:1-7. On reprobation itself see Luke 22:22. For both election and reprobation see Rom. 9. The best I have read in elucidation, as far as possible, of the doctrine of reprobation is found in H. Bavinck, *The Doctrine o God,* Grand Rapids, 1955, pp. 396, 397.

[654] Naturally the A.V., basing its translation on the Textus Receptus, retains the phrase. For the rest, Lenski writes that the phrase is "textually very strongly assured" (*op. cit.,* p. 678), while F. W. Grosheide in his *Commentaar op het Nieuwe Testament, Het Heilig Evangelie volgens Mattheus,* Kampen, 1954, p. 282, regards the words "against you" as not belonging to the text, adding, "they are lacking in Sinaiticus and Vaticanus." H. Ridderbos, *op. cit.,* p. 45, in his comments rejects the phrase, but in a footnote adds a qualification, namely, "if the reading of some manuscripts—'if a brother has sinned against you'—is not the right one." In modern English translations among those who retain the phrase are Williams, Beck, R.S.V., and Phillips. Among those who reject it in their texts are N.A.S., N.E.B., and The Jerusalem Bible.

If the matter is to be decided only on the basis of external textual criticism the phrase must probably be rejected. But that surely would not be a safe rule to follow. Wisely, I

phrase is not the big question. Even though the words as such are left out and the text simply reads, "Now if a brother sins, go and show him his fault while you are alone with him," would not the admonition to have a *private* interview with the erring brother somewhat favor the assumption that the sin referred to was also of a *private* character? Passages such as I Cor. 5:1-5 and Gal. 2:11-14 (see N.T.C. on the last reference) show how sins that are not of a strictly private nature should be handled. Cf. I Tim. 5:20. Also, does not the context favor the retention of the phrase "against you," whether expressed or implied? Note verse 21, "Then Peter came up and said to him, 'Lord, how often shall my brother sin *against me*, and I forgive him?' " It seems as if he were saying, "I know now what I must do when my brother sins against me, but *how often* must I do this?" What may well be the strongest argument is derived from the parallel passage, Luke 17:3, 4. There in verse 3 the phrase "against you" is omitted, but is nevertheless clearly implied, as verse 4, which has it, indicates. It is my judgment, therefore, that the words "against you" may well have been in the original text, but that even if they were not actually there, they are implied. [655] Nevertheless, although Jesus is here speaking about private offenses, the underlying requirement of showing love and the forgiving spirit toward all makes it reasonable to state that whenever the interests of the Church demand or even allow it, the rule of Matthew 18:15 should also be applied to public sins. However, the qualification, "Whenever the interests," etc. is important! Gal. 2:11-14 must not be ignored! See John Calvin on that passage.

The word *sin* ("Now if a brother sin against you") is of a very general nature, so that the meaning of the entire conditional clause is this, "If a member of the Christian fellowship obviously misses the mark, so that his conduct toward you is clearly not in keeping with the demand of God's holy law, as expressed in 7:12; 22:39; Mark 12:31. . . ."

The second and concluding clause is, "Go and show him his fault. . . ," [656] Jesus means that the offended brother should in the spirit of brotherly love go and show the sinner his fault, and this not—certainly not most of all—for the purpose of receiving satisfaction for a personal grievance, but rather in the interest of the offender, that he may repent, and may seek and find forgiveness. Whether the offended brother should make only one personal visit or should go more than once is not stated, and may depend on circumstances. To spare the honor of the brother who has sinned Jesus adds that such an interview with the offender must take place "while you are

believe, Greek N.T. (A-B-M-W) retains the words, though placing them in brackets and giving them a "considerable doubt" rating.

[655] See also W. C. Allen, *op. cit.*, p. 199, the fine print textual note on Matt. 18:15.

[656] For a detailed discussion of the meaning of the verb ἐλέγχω (here ἔλεγξον, second per. sing. aor. active imperative) see N.T.C. on the Gospel according to John, Vol. II, footnote 200 on pp. 324, 325 (on John 16:8).

alone with him," literally, "between you and him alone," that is, privately. There must be a tête-à-tête, a brotherly "face-to-face" confrontation. The Dutch and the Germans frequently use an expression which, literally translated into English, is (a meeting) "between four eyes."

If he listens to you, you have won your brother, Jesus continues, in similar loving vein. You have (meaning *will have*) won your brother: you will have been an instrument in God's hand in saving your brother for the kingdom. Cf. Prov. 11:30; I Cor. 9:19-22; Gal. 6:1; I Peter 3:1.

The admonition of verse 15 is all the more appropriate because the brother who has been sinned against is, after all, also himself a sinner, one who should at all times first of all examine himself (7:3, 4; I Cor. 11:28; cf. Ps. 139:23, 24). *Self-discipline*, which if properly performed always leads to humiliation, must precede and accompany *mutual discipline. Church discipline*, viewed negatively, is a matter of last resort. The objection to this line of exegesis might be that in Matt. 18 Jesus proceeds at once to mutual discipline, never even mentioning self-discipline. But is this true? See 18:8, 9; one might even say, see 18:1-14. A sermon based on Matt. 18:1-20, and having as its theme *Christian Discipline*, and its "points" or sub-headings *self-discipline, mutual discipline,* and *church discipline*, would follow the trend of Christ's discourse.

Jesus continues: **16. But if he does not listen (to you), take one or two other persons with you....** "If the sinner refuses to admit his guilt and to repent, do not immediately give up," says Jesus as it were. For his own sake continue to work with him. The heart of the One who uttered the words of 23:37 and the parable of The Barren Fig Tree (see especially Luke 13:8) is being openly displayed here in all its wooing love and patience.

The offended brother is urged to revisit the offender. He must carefully choose and take along with him one or two—exactly how many is left to him—other persons. How wise this admonition! The Lord Jesus Christ, foreseeing the church's future course, is stipulating a method of disciplinary procedure that merits whole-hearted admiration and obedience. Anyone, in later years, reading these rules in their entirety (see especially verses 15-17), must be struck by their wise and practical character. For example, a church member who is of the opinion that he has a cause of complaint against his brother, reading these rules, and noticing that if he fails in his private attempt he must then ask one or two others to go with him, will probably ask himself, "Is my case really so serious that I can get one or two other persons of sound judgment to go with me; or am I, perhaps, making a mountain out of a mole-hill?"

The main reason, though, necessitating taking along one or two others is stated in the words quoted from Deut. 19:15: **in order that by the mouth of** two witnesses or three every matter [657] may be established. [658] Cf. John 8:17; II Cor. 13:1; I Tim. 5:19; Heb. 10:28.

Questions must be asked and answered. If it is agreed by the two or three—the person who claims to have been wronged plus the witness(es) whom he has with him—that a substantial wrong was really committed, firm but brotherly persuasion must again be used to convince the sinner of his error and to bring him to repentance and confession. It may be easier for two or three persons to succeed in this task than for one. It is implied, of course, that also in the present situation, if the effort of the visitors is crowned with success the sinner will have been won.

But the possibility remains that he will not be won. In that case the matter will subsequently have to be reported to the church. The person(s) who accompanied the offended brother will then be able to confirm the latter's assertion that the matter is indeed as stated by him: that firm but brotherly methods were used to try to persuade the erring one of his fault and to bring him to repentance and confession, but that these efforts failed. This shows the reason why the visit by two or three must follow the private call.

Accordingly, if these two or three do not succeed, the next step, now duly prepared for, regrettably is in order: 17. **If he refuses to listen to them, tell the church.** "Church" must here be taken in the sense of "the locally organized fellowship of believers." On the basis of the principles which Jesus himself laid down, the New Testament carefully avoids two extremes into which some in later years have fallen. On the one hand the extreme of minimizing the office and authority of apostles and elders is guarded against. See Matt. 10:1, 40; Acts 15:6; 20:28a; I Thess. 5:12, 13; I Tim. 5:17; Heb. 13:17. On the other hand, the extreme of belittling the high standing, in the eyes of God, of the entire congregation, as if it lacked maturity; as if the body of all believers, whether conceived *locally* (*as here in 18:17*), denominationally, or universally, had no real "say" in matters of discipline or otherwise; and as if it were the privilege of the ecclesiastical authorities to rule arrogantly, as so many "little tin gods" (see I Peter 5:3 in Phillips' translation; cf. III John 9.)

In the latter connection the following passages merit careful study:

---

[657] Though the meaning of ῥῆμα is basically "spoken word," "saying" (Matt. 12:36; 27:14), along with its Hebrew equivalent it acquires the secondary meaning *thing, matter, event.*

[658] The Hebrew text of Deut. 19:15 literally reads, "Upon the mouth [i.e., upon the testimony proceeding from the mouth; hence, upon the evidence] of two witnesses or upon the mouth of three witnesses the matter shall stand." The Septuagint inserts "all" (πᾶν ῥῆμα: everything). Clearly Matthew's slight variation is not of any material nature. The rule as expressed in Hebrew was meant to apply to *every* case. And Matthew's "by the mouth of two witnesses or three" is identical in meaning to the fuller Hebrew phrase.

besides I Peter 5:3 also Matt. 18:1-4 (see the explanation given above); 20:20-28; Acts 15:22 ("Then it pleased the apostles and the elders *together with the whole church . . .*"); 20:28b. To be sure, the church "authorities" must take the lead. So also here (see verse 18 the apostles—in later times the elders—must now be informed about the disciplinary matter which so far has. not been resolved. But when the proper time arrives, should they not in turn ask the congregation as a whole to be remembered in prayer, along with all the individuals concerned, so that the Lord may provide wisdom and grace in this important matter? Is it not even possible that the consistory or session can think of someone outside its own immediate group, a very wise, experienced, and saintly member of the church, who might render assistance? Certainly not *all* the wisdom resides in "elders," "sessions," "consistories," "presbyteries," "classes," "special" or "general assemblies" or whatever they may be called. Without in any way shirking their own responsibilities or laying aside their own authority, should not the overseers recognize the *entire* body of believers (here locally organized) in all important matters? Is not this the clear meaning of, "Tell the church"?

Jesus continues: **And if he refuses to listen even to the church, let him be to you as the foreigner and the tax-collector.** Not as if Jesus despised or would have nothing to do with foreigners and tax-collectors. As to his attitude toward non-Israelites see 8:11; and toward "publicans" see 9:10-13. But just as foreigners and tax-collectors who are still unconverted must be considered as being as yet outside the kingdom of God, so also this impenitent person must now be viewed as being in the same class. Because of his own stubbornness he has lost his right to church membership, and it has now become the church's painful duty to make this declaration—in order that even this severe measure of exclusion may, with God's blessing, result in the man's conversion (I Cor. 5:5; II Thess. 3:14, 15). Note: "*even* to the church," indicating the honor the Lord bestowed upon the church (Matt. 16:18 "my church," cf. Acts 20:28b; Eph. 1:23), and the grievous character of rejecting its admonition.

Lack of discipline is a curse to any church. There must be rules regarding faith and conduct. To be sure the church has no right to regiment the life of its members, so that freedom is thrown out of the window, Pharisaism revived, and the Colossian heresy (Col. 2:20, 21) repeated. But there are, after all, certain broad principles, clearly stated in Scripture, and epitomized in such well-known passages as Matt. 5:43-45; 10:32, 33; 11:28-30; 16:24, 25; 22:37-40; John 13:34; Rom. 10:9; 12:1, 2, 21; 13:14; I Cor. 14:1a, and many, many others; principles which, as it were, summarize the whole of God's will for man's life. It is the privilege and the duty of the church to set forth these principles and to demand that its members strive, with the help of God's Spirit, to apply them to their everyday living and thinking. Gross and continued violations without subsequent repentance cannot be toler-

701

ated. It is the duty of the church as a whole and as represented by those who by the Lord have been appointed to rule over it *to bind,* that is, to *forbid* violation of these principles, and *to loose,* that is, *to permit* whatever is in harmony with them. The right of *exclusion* or *excommunication* from the church and, upon repentance, of *readmission* into the church is implied. It is for this reason that Jesus, speaking now in the plural and referring to the apostles as a group (these men in turn representing the church), repeats what he had previously (16:19) said in the singular, to Peter. He says: **18. I solemnly declare to y o u, whatever y o u shall bind on earth shall be bound in heaven, and whatever y o u shall loose on earth shall be loosed in heaven.** The solemn introduction—see on 5:18—indicates that the Lord regarded and still regards discipline, as described in 18:15-18, to be a very important matter. Its neglect means the ultimate destruction of the church as a powerful means of spreading the light of the gospel among its members and among the unsaved. See Rev. 2:5. There should be no doubt about the fact that, as in John 20:23 (note the expression "the disciples" in verse 20 and "the twelve" in verse 24) these words were addressed to the disciples or apostles.

Continued: **19. Again I say to y o u, if on earth two of y o u agree about anything that they may ask, it shall be done for them by my Father who is in heaven.** Note in verse 18 and again in verse 19 the combination "earth . . . heaven." In both cases there is perfect harmony between that which by a conscientious church is done on earth and that which takes place in heaven, the former action preceding the latter. According to verse 18 the dicipline exercised on earth is confirmed in heaven; according to verse 19 the prayer offered on earth is answered by Christ's "Father in heaven." On this phrase ("my Father . . .") and similar ones, see pp. 287, 326, 378, 543.

In line with the preceding context the symphonious asking to which verse 19 refers, though covering a large territory—note *"anything* that they may ask"—relates especially to prayer for wisdom in dealing with matters of discipline. The assurance is given that even though at a certain place the fellowship of believers consists of only two person, even these two, when in agreement with each other, can definitely figure on the guidance for which they have made request. It should hardly be necessary to add that such a prayer must be in keeping with the characteristics of true prayer which Jesus reveals elsewhere. It must be the expression of humble, childlike faith (7:11; 17:20; 18:3; cf. 21:22). It must be marked by sincerity, absence of ulterior motives (6:5), by perseverance (7:7), and by love for all concerned (5:44). It must be in subjection to God's sovereign will (6:10b), "not as we will, but as thou wilt" (cf. 26:39). It must be in Christ's name (see verse 20; cf. John 15:16).

In confirmation of the words of verse 19 (notice "for") Jesus continues: **20. For where two or three are gathered in my name there am I in the midst** of them. The expression "two or three" is a development of "two" in the preceding verse. The Lord again assures his disciples that the gathering of believers for prayer and worship need not be one of "crowding worshipers." Even two or three will receive a blessing as long as they gather in his name, that is, in close fellowship with him; hence, with his atoning work as the basis of their approach to God, at his direction, and in harmony with that which he has revealed concerning himself. For the concept "name" see also on 6:9; 7:22; 10:22, 41, 42; 12:21; 18:5.

The promise is, "There am I in the midst of them." The expression "Jehovah ("God" or "I") in the midst of you ("her," "us")" is in Scripture generally associated with the impartation of strength, direction, protection, and consolation: "to help, to comfort, and to bless." See such passages as Ps. 46:5; Isa. 12:6; Jer. 14:9; Hos. 11:9; Zeph. 3:5, 15, 17; Zech. 2:10. Similar is "I am ("will be") with you" (Gen. 28:15; Deut. 31:6; Josh. 1:5; Judg. 6:16, etc.). We can safely conclude therefore that in the present passage the meaning is the same. It is in that favorable sense that Jesus is spiritually in the midst of his people gathered for prayer and worship.

Most comforting is also the fact that Jehovah—and this holds also for Jesus Christ—though great and infinite, in his tender love condescends to that which is small, weak, humble, and by the world generally despised (Judg. 6:15, 16; 7:7; Ps. 20:7; Isa. 1:8, 9; 57:15; Zeph. 3:12; Matt. 18:10; Luke 12:32; I Cor. 4:11-13). This explains "where *two or three* are gathered, etc." See also on Matt. 1:23, p. 141.

The Parable of The Unmerciful Servant

1. Occasion: Peter's Question and Christ's Summarizing Answer

21. Then Peter came up and said to him, Lord, how often shall my brother sin [659] **against me, and I forgive** [659] **him? Up to seven times?** In the present context the adverb "then" probably means "shortly afterward," since there would seem to be a close connection between the matter presented in verse 15 ("Now if a brother sin against you. . . .") and Peter's question ("How often shall a brother sin against me. . . ?").[660] Peter, then, realizes that he must forgive the brother who has sinned against him, that is,

---

[659] Both ἁμαρτήσει, third per. sing. of ἁμαρτάνω, and ἀφήσω, first per. sing. of ἀφίημι, are deliberative future indicatives. Note αὐτῷ, dative of the person whose sin is forgiven. In Greek, as often in English, the accusative of the sin itself is implied.

[660] The adverb τότε can hardly be appealed to in support of the idea that an entirely new subject begins here. That adverb has a wide variety of meanings, as any lexicon will show. Naturally those commentators who favor the idea that verse 15 refers to sin in general (not sin "against you") and who are therefore also of the opinion that in each instance public sin, too, must be dealt with according to the three "steps" mentioned in Matt. 18, see only a remote connection between verse 15 and verse 21. The opposite view seems to the present author to be more natural. See also pp. 697, 698.

that he must take the initiative in bringing about complete reconciliation; but *how often* must he reveal this merciful attitude, this disposition of sweet reasonableness? Must he forgive "up to seven times?"

Peter may have been of the opinion that Jesus would praise him for his bigheartedness. If so, his expectation was not fulfilled. There was something wrong with Peter's approach. It smacked of rabbinism. It sounded as if the forgiving spirit were a commodity that could be weighed, measured, and counted; as if it could be parceled out little by little up to a certain well defined limit, when further distribution would have to stop.

22. **Jesus answered, I say to you, not up to seven times, but up to seventy times seven.** Jesus, though in manner of expression falling in line with Peter's quantitively worded question, completely destroys that apostle's underlying assumption. He takes the two perfect numbers—ten and seven—multiplies them together, and then once again multiplies the result by seven. [661] He does this to show that the spirit of genuine forgiveness recognizes no boundaries. It is a state of heart, not a matter of calculation. One might as well ask, "How often must I love my wife, my husband, my children?" as to ask, "How often shall I forgive?". Everyone immediately senses that when Jesus said, "up to seventy times seven times," he did not mean "exactly four hundred ninety times, but not four hundred ninety-one." Clearly what he meant was, "Forgive without ever stopping. Be kind toward your brother . . . *always.*"

2. *The Parable Proper*

a. *A king shows mercy to his servant by canceling his huge debt.*

Jesus continues by telling a parable, a story-illustration: 23. **That is why the kingdom of heaven is like** [662] **a king** [663] **who wished to settle accounts** [664] **with his servants.** Here "that is why" means: because the matter is as stated in verse 22, therefore in the realm of God's grace through Christ the principle that the forgiven person must *always* be ready, in turn, to reveal the forgiving spirit to others, may be illustrated as follows. For the meaning of the term "the kingdom of heaven" see on 4:23; 13:43.

The "servants" with whom the king is about to settle accounts must have been high officials, probably satraps or provincial governors, whose duty it was to collect the royal taxes in their several domains, and to deliver these large sums to the king at the proper time. They could not have been

---

[661] Whether or not there is here an allusion to Gen. 4:24, either in Hebrew or in the Septuagint, cannot now be determined.

[662] Greek ὡμοιώθη. Whatever name may be given to this aorist, it means "has become like; hence, *is like.*" See also on 13.24; 22:2.

[663] The original has ἀνθρώπῳ βασιλεῖ, pleonastic use of ἄνθρωπος. Cf. 11:19; 13:45, 52; 21:33; 22:2.

[664] Note συνᾶραι aor. infinitive of συναίρω: to take up together; hence, to settle. The word λόγος (here acc. λόγον) is used in the sense of *reckoning, account;* cf. 12:36; 25:19.

"slaves," though the word used in the original frequently has that meaning. One by one the servants were summoned to appear before the king.

Continued: 24. **Now when he had begun to settle (accounts), there was brought to him one (servant) who owed him ten thousand talents.** An Attic talent, the kind probably meant here, amounted to no less than six thousand denarii or denars. At the rate of six denars a week (a denar for each working day, cf. 20:2, 13) it would take a laborer a thousand weeks to earn just *one* talent. To *earn* it! To *save* that amount in older to pay a debt would, of course, take much longer. But even if a laborer were able to save all the money he earned he could not expect during his lifetime to accumulate even ten talents. If a satrap earned a hundred times as much as a common laborer his total *income*—not savings—during his lifetime would hardly amount to a thousand talents. But this man already owes the king ten thousand! How did he come to owe so large a sum? Had he been pre-empting the king's treasury, that is, the tax money that had been collected from the province and should have been kept in a safe place until the king asked for it? Had he been using for his own purpose and squandering vast amounts collected over many years? The parable does not answer this question. It is unimportant. The point is: when he appeared before the king he was penniless; in fact, he was burdened with a debt of no less than ten thousand talents! If a talent be figured at a thousand dollars—bearing in mind today's "inflation" it would probably be worth much more—the total amount owed would be equal to ten million dollars, a debt impossible to pay off. Continued: 25. **But since he did not have the means to pay his debt his master ordered him to be sold, along with his wife and children and all that he had, and payment to be made.** It is often pointed out by commentators that the selling (into slavery) of insolvent debtors was nothing unusual in those days, *and is even mentioned in Scripture.* The first part of this assertion is true and requires no further comment. The following passages are generally listed in proof of that which appears in italics: Exod. 22:3; Lev. 25:39, 47; II Kings 4:1; Neh. 5:5; Isa. 50:1; Amos 2:6; 8:6. These passages do indeed prove the point, provided that such *mention* not be confused with unqualified *approbation.* The facts are as follows: Exod. 22:3 speaks of a man who had incurred his debt through burglary. Lev. 25:39 describes what amounted to mild indenture or voluntary apprenticeship. II Kings 4:1 does not countenance enslavement but merely reports it. In Neh. 5:5 (see also verse 6) enslavement for debt is condemned. Isa. 50:1 indicates that not God had sold Israel but by means of its iniquity Israel had sold itself. Finally, Amos 2:6; 8:6 *condemn* the selling of insolvents. [665]   Outside of the country of the Israelites the practice of selling those who were unable to pay their debts was common, and it is to

---

[665] For more on this subject see N.T.C. on Colossians and Philemon, Appendix "Scripture on Slavery," pp. 233-237.

this that the parable refers. So by royal decree this official, his family, and all his possessions are ordered to be sold. The proceeds must go *toward* paying the debt. The words used in the original (pay, payment) indicates that the debtor must "*give back*" what he owes: he must "pay off" his obligation in full. Of course, this was actually impossible. The amount that was to be placed in the king's treasury, the full proceeds of the sale, would be but a drop in the bucket. So huge was the debt!

The king had pronounced the sentence, but it had not yet been carried out. What happened next is recorded in verse **26. So the servant fell prostrate at his master's feet, saying. . . .** The servant is completely crushed by the realization of the severity of his impending punishment. He does not deny that he owes the huge amount, neither does he try to explain how he got into this terrible predicament. He was probably well aware of the fact that excuses would have been useless. It is important to note also that he does not offer to make at least a down-payment on his debt. The implication is clearly this: he makes no such offer for the simple reason that he has nothing! "Having prostrated himself" (thus literally; see on 2:11) he begged, **Have patience** [666] **with me, and I will pay you everything.** He must have known that this promise was absolutely incapable of fulfilment. What a man will not do to escape from a horrible situation!

The result of the prayer for mercy was as follows: **27. The heart of that servant's master was moved with pity, and he let him go free and forgave him the debt.** For "was moved with pity" see on 9:36. It was out of sheer compassion that the master granted this servant far more than he had asked, completely canceling his huge debt [667] and releasing him from punishment.

b. *That servant refuses to cancel his fellow servant's petty debt.*

The story takes a turn here. It is no longer the compassion of the king or master that holds our attention but the cruelty of the forgiven servant whose enormous debt had been canceled and whose sentence had been remitted: **28. But that same servant, as he went out, came upon one of his fellow-servants, who owed him one hundred denarii.** The very servant to whom such marvelous mercy had been shown, upon his departure from the king's presence happens to meet a fellow-servant who owes him one hundred denars. Compared with the huge debt mentioned earlier this was a mere

---

[666] The verb used is μακροθύμησον, second per. sing. aor. imperative of μακροθυμέω. As to the cognate noun and its synonyms, Scripture speaks of the μακροθυμία, longsuffering (patience with respect to persons) of *God* (Rom. 2:4; 9:22; I Tim. 1:16; I Peter 3:20; II Peter 3:15) and of *men* (II Cor. 6:6; Gal. 5:22; Eph. 4:2; Col. 3:12; etc.). It also refers to *God's* ἀνοχή, forbearance, clemency, suspense of wrath (Rom. 2:4; 3:26); and of *man's* (not God's) ὑπομονή endurance, stedfastness, perseverance (patience with respect to things): Luke 21:19; Rom. 5:3 f.; II Cor. 6:4; I Thess. 1:3; II Thess. 1:4; etc. On the distinctions between these three synonyms see also R. C. Trench, *op. cit.*, liii.

[667] Literally "canceled the loan for him," but in view of the preceding context τὸ δάνειον ἀφεῖκεν αὐτῷ must here mean "absolved him from his debt."

trifle. The one hundred denars amounted to one six-hundred-thousandth ($\frac{1}{600,000}$) part of the canceled sum. Now what does the man who had been so kindly treated do to his fellow servant? **He grabbed him (by the throat) and started to choke** [668] **him, saying.** ... It should be noted that he *started* this cruelty of grabbing by the throat, etc., even before *speaking* to his fellow servant. Then he said to him, **Pay whatever it is you owe!** [669]

The reaction of the fellow-servant was almost—not exactly—the same as had earlier been that of the first servant: 29. **So that fellow-servant fell at his feet and was begging him, saying, Have patience with me, and I will pay you.** So similar was this second plea (verse 29) to the first (verse 26) that it must have brought back to the mind of the man whose hand was on the throat of his neighbor what he himself a few moments earlier had been doing and saying. There are a few slight changes: *a.* the substitution of "fell" (literally "having fallen") for "fell prostrate" or "fell and was worshiping"; and *b.* the omission of "all," for the smallness of the sum rendered "all" inappropriate in the present case. To these two differences may be added a third, touching not upon the wording but upon the changed situation: *c.* in the previous case the promise, "And I will pay you everything" was bombast. The present "And I will pay you" is far more realistic.

Far from permitting the near-echo of his own words to fill him with pity, so that he would now be happy to welcome the opportunity to treat others as he had himself been treated, the first servant reacts as recorded in verse 30. **But he was and remained unwilling,** [670] **and instead had him thrown in jail** [671] **until he should pay what he owed.** Because of the smallness of the debt he was not legally permitted to sell his fellow servant into slavery, but was legally permitted to have him sentenced to prison and forced labor, to work off his debt. [672]

c. Result: Upon this cruel servant the king reimposes the former sentence, even adding to it.

31. Now when his fellow-servants saw what had happened they felt very

---

[668] Note ἔπνιγεν, imperfect (probably inceptive or inchoative) of πνίγω (cf. πνέω, πνεῦμα and other Greek words referring to wind or air).

[669] The original is not easy to translate. Note εἴ, "pay what you owe" is hardly adequate. The more literal, "Pay if you owe anything" might be interpreted to mean that the first servant was not sure whether his fellow servant owed him anything, which obviously cannot be the meaning, because it implies: *a.* that the first servant knew very well that his fellow servant owed him something, and also *b.* that he may not have known just how much it was.—Another possible rendering would be, "If you owe something, as you know very well that you do, then pay it!"

[670] Note the imperfect οὐκ ἤθελεν, implying that he not only refused once but persisted in his refusal to show mercy.

[671] Here what is literally "having gone away he threw [or: put] him in jail" is probably idiomatic for "he had him jailed." Cf. footnote 556 on p. 590.

[672] Note ἀποδῷ, third per. sing. futuristic aor. subjunctive of ἀποδίδωμι. On the subject of imprisonment for debt see A. Deissmann, *op. cit.*, pp. 270, 330.

sad. . . . For sadness see on 17:23. In the present case for whom did these servants feel sad? Naturally for the king whose splendid magnanimity had been so grossly insulted and whose example had been treated with such contempt. No doubt also for the fellow servant whose plea—an appeal probably justifiable, at least understandable—had been so curtly and pitilessly refused. Continued: **and went and reported in detail to their master all that had occurred.** They are convinced that they must tell the king the whole story. Was not his honor at stake? Besides, must not the ingratitude and insensitiveness of the first servant be duly punished?

Continued: **32, 33. Then his master, having summoned him, said to him, You wicked servant; all that debt I forgave you when you begged me.** Note the vividness of "You wicked servant," or as we would say today, "You scoundrel" or "villain." The original is very emphatic. It places the words "all that debt" at the very beginning of what follows after "You wicked servant." This brings out the emphasis better than do the renderings that disregard word order. The immensity of the debt thus stands out, and so do the amazing character of the generosity that had been shown, and the baseness of the first servant's refusal to allow this noble spirit to govern his actions.

Jesus continues: **Should you not also have had mercy on your fellow-servant, even as I had mercy on you?** "Should you not. . . ?" means, "Was this not your *lasting obligation*?"[673] It was this man's duty not only to be filled with unceasing gratitude but also to let his master's mercy of which he, the servant, had been the recipient, be and remain a pattern or example of his own feeling and conduct toward his fellow men.

The striking character of the portrayal is also enhanced by the contrasted use of the spelled out personal pronouns; literally: "I forgave *you* when you begged *me*. Should *you* not also have had mercy on *your* fellow servant, even as *I* on *you* had mercy?" In the original, as in the renderings, the question is so phrased that the answer "Yes" is expected.

Continued: **34. And filled with wrath his master handed him over to the torturers until he should pay the entire debt.** As to divine wrath see on 3:7; also N.T.C. on John 3:36 and on Eph. 2:3. As to human wrath and its synonym "anger" see N.T.C. on Eph. 4:31.[674] Upon hearing what has happened the king, filled with settled indignation, revokes his earlier clemency. The punishment ordered in verse 25 is now carried out. In addition, the unmerciful servant is handed over to "the torturers," a word occurring only here in the New Testament.[675] These were officials appointed by the

---

[673] Note ἔδει, imperfect of δεῖ, impersonal; cf. δέω.

[674] Here in Matt. 18:34 the verbal form ὀργισθείς, aor. pass. participle of ὀργίζω is used.

[675] See, however, footnote 566 on p. 599 for the verbal form.

courts to torture those who had committed atrocious crimes. Cf. Rev. 9:5; 18:7. The words "until he should pay the entire debt" definitely imply, "Which he will never be able to accomplish."

In reading this touching story one immediately senses that it is indeed a parable. The lesson "those who refuse to show mercy will receive everlasting punishment" is but thinly veiled. It is clearly stated in the final, interpretative, verse 35. So also shall my heavenly Father do to y o u if each of y o u does not heartily forgive his brother. For the meaning see on 6:12b, 14, 15. [676] This, then was Christ's answer to Peter's question (18:21).

Positively stated the one and only main lesson of the parable is this: *Prompted by gratitude the forgiven sinner must always yearn to forgive whoever has trespassed against him, and must do all in his power to bring about complete reconciliation.*

Many subsidiary lessons are implied, as follows:

a. We are all God's debtors (verse 23; cf. Rom. 3:23).

b. None of us is able to pay either his own or his brother's debt (verse 25; cf. Ps. 49:7; Rom. 3:20).

c. Nevertheless, this debt must be paid (verses 23, 24; cf. Gen. 2:17; Rom. 3:19; 5:18).

d. By means of Christ's atoning sacrifice the debt has been paid for all who believe in him (verse 27; cf. 20:28; Rom. 3:24; II Cor. 5:21).

e. Only then can men be certain that their debts are canceled if they themselves also cancel the debts of those who are indebted to them; that is, only then can they experience the assurance of forgiveness if they are eager to forgive the sins that have been committed against them (verse 35; cf. 6:12, 14, 15; Eph. 4:32).

f. It should not be too difficult for those who have been forgiven to forgive in turn, for what they owe God is infinitely more than what men owe them (verses 32, 33; cf. II Cor. 9:15).

g. The unforgiving person is destined for everlasting punishment (verses 34, 35; cf. Rom. 1:31, "unmerciful").

h. When the question is asked, "Who must take the first step toward reconciliation: the one who inflicted injury, or the one who suffered injury?" the answer is "Both" (verse 35; Matt. 5:23, 24; cf. Col. 3:12-14).

With the telling of this parable Christ's *Retirement Ministry* ends. For *The Later Judean Ministry* (probably October to December of the year A.D. 29) see especially John 7:2–10:39.

---

[676] In 6:14, 15 note "y o u r heavenly Father . . . y o u r Father." Here in 18:35 "my heavenly Father." For the latter phrase and those related to it see pp. 287, 326, 378, 543, 644.

Outline of Chapter 19

Theme: *The Work Which Thou Gavest Him to Do*

CHAPTER XIX

19 1 Now when Jesus had finished these sayings he departed from Galilee and came to the region of Judea beyond the Jordan. [677] 2 Great crowds followed him, and he healed them there. 3 Then Pharisees came up to him and tempted him by asking, "Is it lawful for a man to divorce his wife for any reason whatever?" 4 He answered and said, "Have y o u not read that from the beginning the Creator made them male and female, 5 and said, 'For this reason a man shall leave his father and his mother, and shall cleave to his wife, and the two shall be one flesh'? 6 It follows that no longer are they two but one flesh. What therefore God has joined together, let not man separate." 7 They said to him, "Why then did Moses command to give her a divorce certificate and to divorce her?" 8 He said to them, "It was because of y o u r hardness of heart that Moses allowed y o u to divorce y o u r wives, but from the beginning it has not been that way. 9 But I tell y o u that anyone who divorces his wife except on (the ground of her) infidelity, and marries another, involves himself in adultery." 10 His disciples said to him, "If such is the case of a man with respect to his wife, it is better not to marry." 11 He replied, "Not all men can accept this statement, but only those to whom it is given. 12 For there are eunuchs who were born thus: they were that way from their mother's womb; and there are eunuchs who were made eunuchs by men; and there are eunuchs who made themselves eunuchs in the interest of the kingdom of heaven. The one who is able to accept it, let him accept it."

19:1-12 *Teaching about Divorce*
Cf. Mark 10:1-12

Here Matthew's account of what may be called *The Perean Ministry* begins. It covers chapters 19 and 20. As the approximate period within which it took place we would suggest December of the year 29 to April of the year 30. Neither Matthew nor any of the other evangelists give us a full biography. See John 20:30, 31; 21:25. In fact, writing a biography of Jesus was not at all their purpose. They are not reproducing a diary or attempting to give us a day by day chronicle (see above, p. 9). From the many incidents they might have covered they select only a few. Each Gospel-writer selects in accordance with his own specific purpose. It should also be borne in mind that during the period of his trans-Jordanic activities the Lord may well have made more than one trip to the west side of the

---

[677] Or: to the boundaries of Judea, beyond the Jordan.

river, that is, perhaps to Bethany. In any event it is clear that toward the ministry's close we find that he has recrossed Jordan and is now in the Jericho (of Judea) region (20:29-34).

The time indications in chapters 19 and 20 are sometimes rather indefinite; see 19:1; 20:17, 29. Any attempt to construct a perfect "Harmony," so that at a glance one can see exactly in what order the various events recorded in Matthew, Mark, Luke, *and John,* occurrred, is doomed to failure. On the other hand, the general trend of direction is clear enough. Note: "he departed from Galilee" (19:1); "(he) came to the region . . . beyond the Jordan" (same verse); "Jesus was going up to Jerusalem" (20:17, 18); and "they went out of Jericho" (20:29). In the next section, chapter 21 ff., the events relating to the Week of the Passion are introduced by "And when they approached Jerusalem" (21:1).

1. **Now when Jesus had finished these sayings he departed from Galilee and came to the region of Judea beyond the Jordan.** See the alternate translations suggested in footnote 677. Whether, with some, one thinks of *Judea* as in those days extending politically somewhat beyond (that is, to the east of) the Jordan; or, with others, one interprets the evangelist as saying that Jesus went to the Perean or trans-Jordanic region, "bounded by Judea," in either case we find the Lord, together with his disciples (verse 10), as being now no longer in the North—i.e., in Galilee and its surroundings—where *The Great Galilean and Retirement Ministries* had taken place, but in the region east of the Jordan.

The text does not say that from Capernaum (17:24) Jesus, having departed from Galilee, *immediately* started his ministry in Perea. All we can safely affirm is *a.* that Jesus soon after he had finished the discourse recorded in chapter 18 entered the region east [678] of Jordan; [679] and *b.* that the events selected for narration by Matthew lead straight from Galilee to Jerusalem, and from Jerusalem's temple, via the various stations of *The Passion Week* (Mt. of Olives, Bethany, Gethsemane, house of Caiaphas, Judgment Hall, Pilate's Palace, Golgotha), to the tomb, from which the Lord arose gloriously. See 19:1; 20:17, 18, 29; 21:1, 10, 12, 18, 23; 23:37; 24:1, 3; 26:6, 36, 57; 27:3, 11, 27, 33, 60; 28:1 ff. There is no mention of any return to Galilee—except after the resurrection (28:16).

The words "Now when Jesus had finished these sayings" (18:1) are found also, either in this exact form or slightly altered by reason of the preceding context, at the conclusion of each of the preceding discourses (see 7:28; 11:1; 13:53), and again at the close of the final discourse (see 26:1). The inference drawn by some, namely, that Matthew, imitating Moses, who

---

[678] Is Lenski's "westward," *op. cit.,* middle of p. 706, a printer's error?

[679] Since Mark 10:1 also lends itself to at least two different interpretations it cannot be of much help in establishing the exact sequence of events.

wrote five books, wanted to divide his Gospel into five parts, or even that he wanted to present exactly five—no more, no less—discourses which our Lord delivered, is open to serious question. It can only be defended by supposing that the closely knit and uninterrupted sayings called *The Seven Woes* (chap. 23) are either no discourse at all or should be linked with Christ's sermon on *The Last Things* (chaps. 24 and 25) as forming one unit. It is not clear how either of these propositions can be successfully defended. See further on 24:1. Matthew surely had other methods of showing that a discourse was ended than the one indicated here in 19:1. He did not need to say, "Now when Jesus had finished these sayings." He could also say, "And Jesus left the temple" (24:1).

Continued: 2. **Great crowds followed him, and he healed them there.** This, then, is the second part of what we have called *The Retirement and Perean Ministries*. Together with *The Great Galilean Ministry* it belongs to the division to which we have given the name: "The Work Which Thou Gavest Him to Do. Its Progress or Continuation." See the Outline, p. 99.

It deserves attention that in its general character this *Perean Ministry* (chaps. 19, 20) in certain respects resembles *The Great Galilean Ministry* (4:12—15:20) more closely than it resembles *The Retirement Ministry* (15:21—18:35). No longer does Jesus generally withdraw himself from the multitudes. In fact, as is evident from 19:2, 13; 20:29, 31 (cf. Mark 10:1, 13, 46; Luke 18:15, 36, 43), great multitudes assemble to hear him. He heals their sick, just as he had done previously in and around Galilee (4:23-25; chaps. 8 and 9; 11:5, 6, 21, 23; 12:15, 22). Always he was ready to heal, and his love overleaped every boundary. The motive which caused him to reveal his power and love to so very many people is stated beautifully in such touching passages as 8:17 and 9:35-38.

There were those, however, whose hearts were not melted by Christ's love. It would almost seem as if the more he loved, the more they hated. We have met the Pharisees before (3:7; 5:20; 9:11, 34; 12:2, 14, 24, 38; 15:1; 16:1) and have become acquainted with their characteristics and their increasing hostility toward Jesus. So here they are again. Whether Matthew is referring to Perean Pharisees, or to Judean Pharisees who, having heard that Jesus was not very far away, have crossed over into Perea, is not very important. The point of emphasis is that, whoever they were, they were as hostile as ever. Note their sinister purpose: 3. **Then Pharisees came up to him and tempted him by asking, Is it lawful for a man to divorce his wife for any reason whatever?** This *temptation* (cf. 16:1; 22:35) was, as often, a kind of trap. Answered either way, so the Pharisees thought, Jesus would be in difficulty. The situation was as follows: Among the Jews there was a difference of opinion as to what Moses had taught with respect to the problem of divorce. He had written, "When a man takes a wife and marries her, if then she finds no favor in his eyes because he has found *'erwath dābhār* in her, and he writes her a bill of divorce . . ." (Deut. 24:1). But what is meant by *'erwath dābhār*? [680] Does it mean "a scandalous thing"? Other guesses are "some indecency," "something improper," "improper behavior," "something offensive," "a shameful thing" (LXX), etc. According to Shammai and his followers the reference was to unchastity or adultery. According to Hillel and his disciples the meaning was far broader. They emphasized the words, "If then she finds no favor in his eyes," and accordingly would allow divorce for the flimsiest reasons, so that the husband could reject his wife if she accidentally served him food that had been slightly burned, or if at home she talked so loud that the neighbors could hear her. If Jesus endorsed the more strict interpretation, favored by Shammai, he would be displeasing the followers of Hillel. Moreover, there seem to have been very many who agreed with Hillel's "liberal" opinion. Even the disciples may have shared this view; see verse 10. [681] Besides, if the Lord sided with Shammai the Pharisees might have accused him, though not justly, of being inconsistent when he nevertheless consorted with sinners and ate with them.

On the other hand, if Jesus endorsed the lax—"anything will do as ground for divorce"—interpretation, what would the disciples of Shammai think of him? Would not the more serious and conscientious people charge him with tolerating moral looseness? And what would the female part of the population think of him?

Jesus does not avoid the question. In verse 9 his specific answer is recorded. The question was, "Is it lawful for a man to divorce his wife *for any reason whatever?*" The implied answer is going to be, "No, not for any reason whatever, but *only for marital unfaithfulness.*" However, before Jesus even gives this answer he shows that the underlying emphasis of the question is wrong. Why all this talk about the possibility of divorce, as if to say, "If this marriage does not work out I can always divorce my wife"? Why not go back beyond Deut. 24 to God's marriage ordinance recorded in such passages as Gen. 1:27 and 2:24? **4-6. He answered and said, Have y o u not read that from the beginning the Creator made them male and female, and said, For this reason a man shall leave his father and his mother, and shall cleave to his wife, and the two shall be one flesh?** [682] **It follows that no longer are they two but one flesh.**

---

[680] The word is derived from a verb meaning basically *to be naked, bare*. According to Brown, Driver, Briggs, *Hebrew and English Lexicon of The Old Testament*, Boston and New York, 1906, p. 789, the meaning of *'erwath dābhār* is probably *indecency, improper behavior*.

[681] See also Josephus *Antiquities* IV.253.

[682] The quotation from Gen. 2:24, "For this reason . . ." differs in no essential from the original Hebrew. According to Matthew (also Mark 10:7) Jesus said "the two" (so also the LXX in Gen. 2:24), where the Hebrew simply has "they." But "they" means "the two" in this instance, as the context clearly indicates. Furthermore, the LXX spells

"Have y o u not read?" As if to say, "Y o u people who are always boasting about y o u r knowledge of the law, have y o u not even read Gen. 1:27 and 2:24?" One is reminded of Gal. 4:21. See N.T.C. on that passage. Well then, if the Pharisees are acquainted with Gen. 1:27 they know that even though Adam was created before Eve, he was at once created male; hence, with a view to intimate union with Eve, who was created later on from the very body of Adam, and as a female. Each, accordingly, was made for the other, with the definite purpose of joining together *one* man to *one* woman. Those who are eager for divorce ignore this fact.

Add to this Gen. 2:24, where God ordains that for this very reason—that is, because the union between the two was intended to be so intimate and they were designed for each other (see both Gen. 1:27 and 2:23)—a man shall leave his father and his mother, and shall do this with a view to a more intimate and more lasting attachment, namely, "and shall cleave to his wife, and the two shall be one flesh"; yes, "no longer two but one flesh," says Jesus.

It is clear that Jesus viewed Gen. 2:24 (in combination with Gen. 1:27) as a divine ordinance, and not as a mere description of what generally takes place on earth. And since one is not doing injustice to the Hebrew original of Gen. 2:24 by bringing out this divine institution idea in the translation—hence "a man shall leave . . . and shall cleave," not merely "a man leaves and cleaves"—what good reason can there be for not expressing it? On this passage (Gen. 2:24), therefore, the translation adopted by A.V. and A.R.V. is to be preferred to some of the more modern versions.

That Jesus did indeed so regard marriage, namely, as an indissoluble union, a union until death parts the two, a definitely divine institution that must not be tampered with, is clear from the following: *a.* Otherwise his argument would lose its force; *b.* the audience hardly needed to be told that it is customary for men to get married; and *c.* this is in line with the words immediately following, namely, **What therefore God has joined together, let not man separate.**

This does not mean that a man is committing a sin by not getting married. Rather, it means that those who decide to marry must view marriage as a divine institution, a state in which they must so conduct themselves that true union—sexual, to be sure; note "shall cleave to his wife," but also intellec-

---

out the possessive pronoun "his" after both "father" and "mother" (the exact equivalent of the Hebrew suffix "his" with both nouns); Mark 10:7 has "his" only after "father," and Matthew omits these possessives entirely. Are they not already implied in the prefixed definite articles? Both Mark and the LXX use the preposition πρός before the accusative.form γυναῖκα, where Matthew says the same thing by substituting the noun in the dative for the preposition plus noun in the accusative. Finally, the Septuagint and Mark use the compound form of the verb "and shall cleave," where Matthew uses the simple form. The meaning is identical all around.

tual, moral, and spiritual—is not only established but more and more firmly cemented.

It was God who made this union possible (Gen. 1:27); God also who issued the command, "Be fruitful . . ." (Gen. 1:28). It was he, again, who said, "It is not good that man should be alone; I will make him a help fit for him" (Gen. 2:18). It was also God who brought Eve to Adam, to be the latter's wife (Gen. 2:22). Indeed, from every angle, it was God who established marriage as a divine institution (Gen. 2:24; Matt. 19:5, 6). Marriage is therefore indeed "an honorable estate." Therefore, let not man separate what God has joined together! [683]

So accustomed to talking about divorce and neglecting the divine marriage ordinance have the Pharisees become, that even now they refuse to take to heart Christ's exposition of Gen. 1:27 and 2:24. They prefer by far to emphasize the possibility of divorce: 7. **They said to him, Why then did Moses command to give her a divorce certificate and to divorce her?** The reference is, of course, to Deut. 24:1-4. See what has been said about this in connection with 5:32. 8. **He said to them, It was because of y o u r hardness of heart that Moses allowed y o u to divorce y o u r wives, but from the beginning it has not been that way.** It is one thing to say to a man, "If you don't like your wife, go right ahead and divorce her." It is an entirely different matter to say, "If you are convinced that you have a good reason to reject your wife, you must at least provide her with a bill of divorce. Besides, you better carefully consider what you are about to do; for if you subsequently regret what you have done it may very well be impossible for you to regain what you have lost." As pointed out earlier, Moses had done everything in his power to discourage divorce. It was only because of the stubbornness of the people that Moses had made a concession! In this *concession* of Deut. 24 the Pharisees are far more interested than in the *institution* of Gen. 1:27; 2:24. So Jesus points back once more to the original marriage ordinance, that is, to the way it had been "from the beginning." See above on verses 4-6.

Jesus now declares that whoever divorces a faithful wife, and adds to his sin by marrying someone else, thereby rendering reconciliation with the woman to whom he had been married impossible, involves himself in—or: commits—adultery. The form of the statement of verse 9 is such that it is at the same time an answer to the question of verse 3, "Is it lawful for a man to divorce his wife *for any reason whatever?*" Jesus said, 9. **But I tell y o u that anyone who divorces his wife except on (the ground of her) infidelity,** [684]

---

[683] See also W. A. Maier, *For Better Not for Worse*, St. Louis, 1935, pp. 80, 81; and N.T.C. on Eph. 5:22-33.

[684] The term πορνεία ("fornication") is very broad in meaning. In its widest sense it indicates immorality or sexual sin in general (15:19; Gal. 5:19), illicit (often clandestine)

and marries another, involves himself in adultery. Such marital unfaith-fulness is an attack upon the very essence of the marriage bond. In the present instance the wife is herself "putting asunder" what God has joined to-gether. As far as the record goes, this is the only ground Jesus ever mentioned for giving the innocent person—in the present case the husband, but see footnote 295 on p. 305—the right to divorce his wife and marry again.

The Pharisees have again been defeated. For the present they have been silenced. By an appeal to "Moses," to whom they had referred (verse 7), Jesus had proved them wrong. They disappear from the scene. Jesus enters a house, where we find him in the company of the disciples. The Pharisees are no longer mentioned (Mark 10:10). Now it is the disciples' turn to speak. They do not deny what Jesus had said, but reveal that they are struggling with a difficulty. These men seem to have been so impressed by the lax ideas about marriage that were current at that time, that Christ's words about marriage as a divine institution that must be kept inviolate had come as somewhat of a surprise to them, perhaps even as somewhat of a disappoint-ment. Jesus loved these men, and appreciated their willingness to sacrifice for his sake (see verse 28). Nevertheless, in some respects they were still weak, far away from the goal (see pp. 246 f.), as is evident from verse 10. **His disciples said to him, If such is the case** [685] **of a man with respect to his wife, it is better** [686] **not to marry.** Yes, "better" or "more profitable." They, along with many other people of that day and age—and of today!—seem to have been obsessed by the idea, "What can I get out of marriage *for myself?*" Their question should have been, "How can a man use this marvelous institution for the benefit of his wife, himself, his children-to-be, his fellow men, and God's kingdom?" These men did not as yet fully understand that the spirit of love, service, and sacrifice, the very attitude of their Master (20:28; Luke 22:27), must be applied to *every* relationship of life, also to that of marriage. See Eph. 5:22-33.

---

relationships of every description, particularly unlawful sexual intercourse (John 8:41). In Paul's epistles the word occurs frequently. In addition to Gal. 5:19 see also I Cor. 5:1; 6:13, 18; 7:2; II Cor. 12:21; Eph. 5:3; Col. 3:5; I Thess. 4:3. In the book of Acts it occurs a few times; also several times in Revelation. In the latter book, as in the Old Testament (LXX), it may at times be used figuratively, to indicate departure from the Lord, who was considered his people's "husband." Hence, in such passages (see, for example, Hos. 6:10 and Rev. 19:2) it has at times been translated "whoredom," "harlotry," or even "idolatry." By reason of the context it is clear that here in Matt. 19:9, as also in 5:32, the reference is to the infidelity of a married woman.—As to the other word, a form of the verb μοιχάω, see on 5:32, where also the verb μοιχεύω is explained in the light of its context.

[685] With αἰτία compare the Latin *causa* when that word is used in the sense of *case* or *relationship.*

[686] See footnote 641 on p. 690.

11. He replied, Not all men can accept this statement, but only those to whom it is given. Among commentators there is a difference of opinion as to the connection of thought. In verses 11 and 12 is Jesus making a comment on his own words, found in verses 4-6, 8, 9, or is he referring to the remark of the disciples, recorded in verse 10? Probably to both, that is, to the entire situation that has now developed. The Lord has quoted and explained the divine ordinance of marriage. The disciples have replied, "If such is the case . . . then it is better not to marry." So Jesus now shows that there is actually no reason for despair. To be sure, not all men can accept his statement—spoken word, talk, declaration; cf. 15:12; 19:22—with reference to marriage as a divine institution of the highest significance for man, one that must not be violated in any way. For this teaching not all men *have room* [687] in their hearts and lives. To properly fulfil the responsibilities of marriage requires grace. This grace is God's gift. Without this divine help true, God-glorifying marriage is impossible.

The disciples have suggested that it might be better not to marry. Rather, Jesus implies, let a man ask for the gift of God's grace so that he will be able, properly motivated, to enter the wedded state. Nevertheless, apart entirely from this consideration, there still are situations which make it either impossible or inadvisable for a man to marry. There is that much truth in the observation of the disciples.

Jesus is about to mention three situations, each of which applies to a special group. The three have in common: abstinence from the relationships commonly associated with the married state. Truly, what Jesus has said about life within the married state is not applicable to all. **12. For there are eunuchs who were born thus: they were that way from their mother's womb; and there are eunuchs who were made eunuchs by men; and there are eunuchs who made themselves eunuchs in the interest of the kingdom of heaven.** The first group consists of those who are eunuchs because of a congenital defect. The second refers to physically castrated men. This deplorable condition was brought upon them by other men. See II Kings 20:18; Esther 2:14. Such eunuchs frequently were chosen to serve as keepers of the harem. That at times they attained to important positions is clear from Acts 8:26-39. The third class can also be called "eunuchs," though the word is now used in a figurative sense. These men are not impotent. They could marry and fulfil all of their responsibilities in that state, if they so desired. Their abstinence from marriage is of a purely voluntary character. They are eunuchs or celibates "in the interest of the kingdom of heaven." Being fully aware that, in the course of spreading the gospel, situations will develop that are marked by tremendous hardship and sore distress, but nevertheless being filled with eagerness to spread the message of salvation far

---

[687] The basic meaning of χωρίζω is *to have room for, to hold;* cf. John 2:6.

and wide, these men, of their own accord—not because of any divine or human decree—decide not to marry. Cf. I Cor. 7:26. That is their privilege. They are not thereby raised to a higher degree of holiness, as if in the eyes of God the state of celibacy as such would give them extra credit. Such a doctrine is entirely foreign to Scripture, which everywhere exalts the married state (Gen. 1:27, 28; 2:24; 9:7; 25:67; Ps. 127:3, 4; 128:3, 8; John 2:1-11; Eph. 5:22-33; I Tim. 5:14), and even pictures it as a symbol of the beautiful love relationship between Christ the Bridegroom, and the Church the Bride (Eph. 5:32; Rev. 19:7). But if Paul wishes to remain unmarried, let him do so. If Cephas prefers to take his wife along in his travels (I Cor. 9:5), he, too, has a right to do this.

Having finished his teaching on *a.* marriage (verses 4-6, 8, 9, and to some extent 11) and on *b.* refraining from marriage (verse 12 and to some extent verse 11), Jesus adds, **The one who is able to accept it, let him accept it.** Here, again, as in verse 11, when Jesus speaks about "accepting" or "receiving" what he has said, he is not referring merely to intellectual comprehension, but to that plus making room for this teaching in heart and life. He exhorts each of his disciples to carry his words into practice!

---

13 Then little children were brought to him, that he might lay his hands on them and pray. The disciples rebuked (those who brought) them. 14 But Jesus said, "Leave the little children alone and stop hindering them from coming to me, for to such belongs the kingdom of heaven." 15 And he laid his hands on them and went away from there.

19:13-15 *Jesus and the Children*
Cf. Mark 10:13-16; Luke 18:15-17

13. Then little children were brought to him, that he might lay his hands on them and pray. Although the adverb "then" does not necessarily mean "immediately afterward," yet the connection between *a.* marriage, ideally described by Jesus in the immediately preceding paragraph, and *b.* childre·:, is so close that we like to think of the present paragraph as setting forth an event that took place immediately after the discussion about the wedded state, while Jesus was still in "the house."

Children! How Jesus loved them! See on 18:2-4. It is not at all surprising therefore that certain followers of Jesus brought their little ones to him, so that he might lay his hands on them, blessing them and praying for them. How big were these little ones? There are those who, basing their theory on the fact that the word used in the original for "little children" is in the New Testament by no means confined to those very young in years (for proof see John 21:5; I John 2:18, 3:7), believe that those who were brought to Jesus were children of elementary school age or even older. However, Luke 18:15 informs us that these "little children" were actually "infants." See Luke

719

1:44 (an unborn babe). Cf. I Peter 2:2. They—or at least many of them—must have been "carried" to Jesus in the arms of their parents. [688]

Continued: **The disciples rebuked (those who brought) them.** They re-buked [689] not the children, of course, but their parents, or more generally all who brought them, probably mostly mothers and fathers; in a few cases perhaps sisters or nurses. Were the disciples standing at the doorway and were they with angry gestures shooing away all those who approached the house carrying children in their arms? Was their reasoning, "Jesus must not be bothered; he has things to do that are far more important than blessing babies"? 14. **But Jesus said, Leave the little children alone and stop hindering** [690] **them from coming to me, for to such belongs the kingdom of heaven.**

The reaction of the disciples was rather characteristic, as has been pointed out earlier (see on 14:15, 16). Yet, this attitude was sinful. It would appear that those who brought their children to Jesus were properly motivated in doing so. They were not superstitious, that is, they did not ascribe some kind of magical potency to Jesus' touch. Had that been the case the Lord would have rebuked them. He does nothing of the kind. To be sure, he was "indignant" (Mark 10:14), not at the parents, but at the disciples! It is to them that he says, "Leave the little ones alone." The meaning of the verb is indeed "Let (them) be." [691]

The reason Jesus gives for ordering the disciples to stop hindering the little ones from coming to him is: "for to *such*—that is, to them and to all those who in humble trustfulness are like them (see on 18:2-4)—belongs the kingdom of heaven." For "kingdom of heaven" see on 4:23; 13:43. In the present case the verse means that *in principle* all blessings of salvation belong even now to these little ones, a fact which was to be realized progressively here on earth and perfectly in the hereafter.

15. **And he laid his hands on them and went away from there.** The laying on of the hands was the symbolical act which indicated and accompanied the actual blessing that was then and there bestowed upon these babes. Mark 10:16 informs us that lovingly the Master had taken them into his arms. We

---

[688] Probably "parents" is better here than specifically "mothers," since in the latter case, at the end of verse 13, αὐταῖς (as in Phil. 4:3) would have been expected rather than αὐτοῖς.

[689] ἐπετίμησαν; see footnote 612 on p. 654.

[690] Although it is not true that in each occurrence the negative present imperative must be translated "*Stop* (a certain action)," in the present case, by reason of the immediately preceding context (the disciples were actually hindering the little ones from coming to Jesus), "stop hindering" reproduces the sense of the original adequately. Another equally good translation would be, ". . . do not try to prevent them." There is a slight difference between Matt. 19:14 and its parallels, Mark 10:14 and Luke 18:16. In the latter two cases the text, correctly translated, reads, "Let the little children come to me. . . ." However, there is no essential difference.

[691] Ἄφετε second per. pl. aor. imper. active of ἀφίημι; cf. 27:49.

do not read that Jesus also prayed for them, though this, too, had been included in the wish of the parents when they brought their little ones to Jesus (verse 13). From this omission some have concluded that the Lord, in the consciousness of his own equality with the Father (John 10:30), did not feel that he needed to ask the Father to bestow a blessing upon these babes. He himself could bless them. But was not prayer, including certainly intercession, characteristic of the Savior in his state of humiliation? See Matt. 11:25, 26; 14:19; 15:36; Luke 6:12; John 11:41, 42; ch. 17. And even in the state of exaltation is he not always living to make intercession for his own (Heb. 7:25)? Surely, it is not necessary for the evangelists to spell everything out in detail! The parents had carried their little ones to Jesus for him to lay his hands on them, and, praying for them, to bless them. We believe that Jesus satisfied their desire to the full!

The fact that the Lord regarded these little ones as being already "in" the kingdom, as being even now members of his church, must not escape our attention. He definitely did not view them as "little heathen," who were living outside of the realm of salvation until by an act of their own they would "join the church." He regarded them as "holy seed" (see I Cor. 7:14). It must be borne in mind that those who brought their little ones to Jesus must have had faith in him. This faith may not as yet have been very far advanced—is ours?—but it had made sufficient progress so that these people believed that the Master was far more than a Physician for those who were physically ill. We do not receive the impression that these infants were sick or dying. Yet they were brought to Jesus that he might bless them. This he did, in line with all the assurances of divine favor for believers *and their seed* (Gen. 17:7, 12; Ps. 103:17; 105:6-10; Isa. 59:21; Acts 2:38, 39, to mention only a few).

In the work of salvation it is always God who is first, never man. See John 3:3, 5; 6:37; I John 4:19. How wonderful that in later years parents would be able to say to their child, now arrived at the age of understanding, "Think of it, when you, my child, were just a suckling, Jesus took you into his arms and blessed you. Then already you were the object of God's tender love. And he has been with you ever since. What, then, is your response?" On the basis of such passages as Matt. 19:13-15 (and parallels)—and see also those mentioned at the close of the preceding paragraph, to which add Acts 16:15, 33; I Cor. 1:16; Col. 2:11, 12—the belief that since the little children of believers belong to God's church and to his covenant, baptism, the sign and seal of such belonging, should not be withheld from them, must be regarded as well-founded. In later years, through parental instruction, the divine blessing earlier received becomes a mighty incentive to wholehearted personal surrender to Christ. Such individual commitment is, of course, necessary (Josh. 24:15; Matt. 10:32, 33; 11:28-30). God's earnest and challenging invitation, "Give me your heart" (Prov. 23:26), must be answered by:

721

Take my life and let it be
Consecrated, Lord, to thee;
Take my hands and let them move
At the impulse of thy love.

Take my love, my God, I pour
At thy feet its treasure store;
Take myself, and I will be
Ever, only, all for thee.
                         —Frances R. Havergal

The very prohibition, "Stop hindering the little children from coming to me," implies, "Let them come to me." It means, "As the children grow older, let the parents do all in their power to bring them to the point of voluntarily accepting their great Benefactor, Jesus Christ, to be their Savior and Lord."

The objection might be advanced, "How was it possible for Jesus to say even now that these sucklings were already citizens of his kingdom, heirs of salvation? Did he not know that at least some of them might in later years turn their backs upon him? Why this distinctly *positive* approach?" The answer is that, as is plainly indicated in many of the references given on pp. 720,721, the Lord as a rule gathers his church from the circle of believing parents and their children. Just as Jesus said many wonderful things about The Twelve (10:29, 30, 40; 19:28, etc.) without always immediately adding, "I exclude Judas," so also it must be understood here (19:13-15) that those little ones who in later years reject the Lord and persist in this unbelief are not saved.

Having blessed the infants Jesus left the house, perhaps even the place (village or town) where he was.

---

16 And look, a man came up to him and asked, "Teacher, what good thing shall I do that I may possess everlasting life?" 17 He answered him, "Why are you asking me concerning that which is good? One there is who is good, and if you wish to enter into life, keep the commandments." 18 "Which ones?" he asked. Jesus said to him, "You shall not kill, You shall not commit adultery, You shall not steal, You shall not bear false witness, 19 Honor your father and your mother, and You shall love your neighbor as yourself." 20 The young man said to him, "All these things have I observed; what do I still lack?" 21 Jesus said to him, "If you wish to be perfect, go and sell your possessions and give (the proceeds) to the poor, and you will have treasure in heaven; and come, follow me." 22 But when the young man heard this word he went away sorrowful, for he had much property.

23 And Jesus said to his disciples, "I solemnly declare to y o u, it will be hard for a rich man to enter the kingdom of heaven. 24 Again I tell y o u, it is easier for a camel to go through the eye of a needle than for a rich man to enter the kingdom of God." 25 Now when they heard this they were profoundly shocked and said, "Then who can be saved?" 26 Fastening his eyes on them Jesus said, "With men this is impossible, but with God all things are possible."

27 Then Peter answered and said to him, "Look, we have left everything and followed thee; what then shall we have?" 28 And Jesus said to them, "I solemnly assure y o u that in the restored universe, when the Son of man shall be seated on the throne of his glory, y o u who have followed me shall also be seated on thrones, (on) twelve (of them), judging the twelve tribes of Israel. 29 And everyone who has left houses or brothers or sisters or father or mother or children or fields for my name's sake shall receive a hundredfold, and shall inherit everlasting life. 30 But many that are first shall be last, and (many) last first."

19:16-30 *The Peril of Riches*
and
The Reward of Sacrifice
Cf. Mark 10:17-31; Luke 18:18-30

16. And look, a man came up to him and asked. . . . Although Matthew is very indefinite with respect to the time when the event recorded in 19:16-30 occurred, the parallel account in Mark (see 10:16, 17) leaves the distinct impression that it took place immediately—at least very soon—after the bestowal of a blessing upon the little children. If so, then Christ's views on marriage, children, and material possessions follow each other in a sequence that commends itself as being very logical. "And look," says Matthew, fixing the attention of the reader on something that was indeed quite remarkable. See footnote 133 on p. 131. What was this extraordinary happening? This, that suddenly, right on the open road, as Jesus and his disciples were journeying through Perea, a man came up to the Master with a question that was preying upon him and to which he eagerly desired the answer. It was a very important question, having to do with salvation.

The person who came up to Jesus had many things going for him:

He was rich, young, and prominent;
Clean, keen, and reverent.

He was *rich* (Matt. 19:22), that is, in earthly material possessions. He was *young* (Matt. 19:20), probably not more than forty years of age, perhaps much younger (see N.T.C. on I Tim. 4:12). He was *prominent* (Luke 18:18), being called "a ruler," probably one of the officials in charge of the local synagogue (see on Matt. 9:18), a man of high reputation. This was true all the more because he was *clean* (Matt. 19:20), a man of excellent outward behavior, a virtuous individual. He was *keen,* eager. He had a problem on his heart and mind. He had not found that which would put his soul at rest. Being anxious to solve that problem he "ran up" to Jesus (Mark 10:17). Finally, he was *reverent,* shown by the fact that he "knelt before" Jesus, as the reference in Mark's Gospel indicates.

He asked: **Teacher, what good thing shall I do that I may possess everlasting life?** As to essence the question is the same in all three Gospels. The slight differences—*a.* "Teacher" in Matthew; "Good Teacher" in Mark

723

and Luke; *b.* "What good thing" in Matthew; "what" in Mark and Luke; and *c.* "that I may possess" in Matthew; "that I may inherit" in Mark and Luke—do not change the substance of the story. They indicate that each Gospel-writer had his own style. A document can be fully inspired and inerrant without being pedantically precise. The evangelists are not reeling off a recording. What each of them is doing is reproducing the happening in his own characteristic manner. For this we should be thankful. It makes the combined account that much more interesting. Besides, it is surely not to be supposed that *all* the words of Jesus spoken at each occasion were written down. It is entirely possible that in the course of the conversation with the young man, the latter, in addressing the Lord, used both forms of address, "Teacher" and "Good Teacher." And so also in connection with the other slight differences: an evangelist has the perfect right to substitute a synonym for the actual word that was spoken, as long as this synonym conveys the same meaning.

What *is* important is that this young man realized that he had not as yet attained everlasting life, not even in principle. It was this that had made him restless, ill at ease. By going to Jesus he went to the right source. Just how well the young man understood the nature of "everlasting life," we do not know. If "life" means active response to one's environment, then everlasting life must mean never-ending, active response to the best environment of all, namely, the heavenly. It is fellowship with God (John 17:3). Other beautiful descriptions are: "the love of God shed abroad in our hearts through the Holy Spirit" (Rom. 5:5), "the light of the knowledge of the glory of God in the face of Jesus Christ" (II Cor. 4:6), "the peace of God that surpasses all understanding" (Phil. 4:7), and "joy unspeakable and full of glory" (I Peter 1:8). Life everlasting is another name for "salvation."

Now the fact that this young man was in search of salvation must be appreciated. He was not so engrossed in earthly pleasures that he no longer cared for the things pertaining to God. However, he was making a tragic mistake. It is clear from his very question—"What good thing shall I do . . ." —that he believed in salvation by works. This becomes even clearer when verse 16 is read in the light of verse 20. Now since the essence of good works, to the glory of God, is found in the Ten Commandments, and since these commandments were there for all to read, both in complete form (Exod. 20; Deut. 5) and in summary (Deut. 6:5; Lev. 19:18) we are not surprised to read: **17. He answered him, Why are you asking me concerning that which is good? One there is who is good, and if you wish to enter into life, keep the commandments.** Certainly what God demands in his law is good, for God himself is the Highest Good. Why ask Jesus about "that which is good" when God the Father has so clearly revealed it? If the enquirer

724

thinks that he will be able to obtain everlasting life by doing good, let him then by all means keep the commandments. [692]

The commandments! But has not the young man been observing every one of them? Let the Master be specific: 18, 19. Which ones? he asked. Jesus said to him, **You shall not kill, You shall not commit adultery, You shall not steal, You shall not bear false witness, Honor your Father and your mother, and You shall love your neighbor as yourself.** [693] Just why it was that in all three accounts "Honor your father and your mother" is made the last of the regular Decalog commandments we do not know. Was there a special reason why in this particular case Jesus placed this commandment at the very close (except for the summary in Matthew)? Neither do we know why Jesus mentioned only the commandments of the second table. To the many guesses I wish to add one more: It was not necessary for Jesus to include the commandments relating to man's duty with respect to God; for, failure to observe the second table implies failure to observe the first: "He who does not love his brother whom he has seen cannot love God whom he has not seen" (I John 4:20).

That the young man's attitude toward keeping the commandments was of a superficial character, not at all in harmony with Christ's deeply spiritual

---

[692] With reference to the rather widely varying passage in Mark (10:18, "Why do you call me good? No one is good but God alone"), on which there is a vast literature, I would refer especially to N. B. Stonehouse, *Origins of the Synoptic Gospels*, chap. 5, "The Rich Young Ruler," pp. 93-112; and to B. B. Warfield, *Christology and Criticism*, chap. 3, "Jesus' Alleged Confession of Sin," pp. 97-145. The charge that Matthew purposely changed Mark's narrative because he took exception to Mark 10:18 on doctrinal grounds, as if according to that passage Jesus would be implying that he himself is neither God nor good, is open to the following objections: *a.* Luke does not modify Mark at this point, as 18:19 shows. Evidently he saw no doctrinal difficulty. *b.* As has been shown, see pp. 58-60, Mark pictures Jesus as being not only fully human but also fully divine, does justice to all his moral and spiritual perfections, and nowhere ascribes to him sin in any form whatever. *c.* Mark's account with reference to the rich young ruler is somewhat more detailed than that of the other synoptists. It must not be supposed that any of the three Gospel-writers who report this event reproduced *all* the words of Jesus. Hence, variety should cause no surprise.—For the meaning of Mark 10:18 see Commentaries on that Gospel.

[693] The differences between the manner in which these commandments are reproduced in Matthew, Mark, and Luke are of a minor character. Matthew alone represents Jesus as having, at the close, summarized the commandments of the second table. Luke reverses the more usual order (Exod. 20:13, 14; Deut. 5:17, 18; Matt. 19:18; Mark 10:19) of the sixth and seventh commandment, so that his Gospel reads, "You shall not commit adultery, You shall not kill." Cf. Rom. 13:9. Mark inserts "You shall not defraud" between the ninth commandment ("You shall not bear false witness") and the fifth ("Honor your father and your mother"). This insertion may be considered a combination of the last two commandments of the Decalog. Therefore, whatever reason Matthew and Luke may have had for omitting this item of Christ's words, it cannot have been a doctrinal one. "You shall not defraud" truly reflects Exod. 20:16, 17.

and penetrating interpretation (for which see 5:21-48), is clear from his reaction: **20. The young man said to him, All these things have I observed; what do I still lack?** Here superficial smugness is struggling with deep discontent. This young man tries to make himself believe that all is well; yet on the inside he is pathetically perturbed. Has he really loved his neighbor as himself? Why then this lack of peace of mind and heart that had made him run up to Jesus with the anxious question, "What do I still lack?" Did his inward monitor echo the truth expressed in 5:20; cf. Rom. 2:15b? Was that why, though he tried hard to believe in his own virtue and respectability, he was actually feeling ill at ease? He seems to be saying, "What additional good deed must I be doing over and above all those very many that I have already done, for 'from my youth' (Mark 10:20; Luke 18:21) I have observed God's law?"

Jesus, looking upon him, loved this young man who was kneeling before him (Mark 10:21). Not only did he appreciate his "regard for virtue and for good outward behavior" (Canons of Dort, Third and Fourth Heads of Doctrine, article 4), but he must also have pitied him because of the struggle which he was experiencing (Matt. 9:36-38; 11:28). But Jesus also knew that there was something terribly wrong with this rich young ruler. His material possessions enslaved him (see verses 22, 23). Did he really love his neighbor *as himself?* He did not. Was he actually willing to follow all the way where God, through the voice of Jesus Christ, would direct him? He was not, as is evident from what follows: **21. Jesus said to him, If you wish to be perfect, go and sell your possessions and give (the proceeds) to the poor, and you will have treasure in heaven....** The question may be asked, "But by thus instructing the young man was not Jesus endorsing the 'salvation by good works' doctrine?" Should he not rather have told him, "Trust in me?" The answer is that "Trust completely in me" was exactly what the Lord was telling him, for certainly without complete confidence in and self-surrender to the One who was issuing the order the rich young ruler could not be expected to sell all he had (Luke 18:22) and give the proceeds to the poor.

Did this young man really wish to be "perfect," fully mature (see on 5:48 and cf. N.T.C. on Phil. 3:15)? This was the test. If he sustains it he will have "treasure in heaven." The reference is to all those blessings that are heavenly in character, are in full measure reserved for God's child in heaven, and of which we experience a foretaste even now. For more about this concept see on 6:19, 20. It is important to note that Jesus added, **and come, follow me.** Such "following," to be accompanied by and to prepare for active witness-bearing, would imply that the young man must learn to "deny himself and take up his cross" (16:24), and would therefore no longer be able to devote himself to the service of Mammon. The reply was tragic: **22. But when the young man heard this word he went away sorrowful, for he had much property.** He was "sorrowful" (cf. 14:9; 17:23; 18:31; 26:22, 37). "His countenance fell" (Mark 10:22; cf. Gen. 4:6). Placed before the choice of either surrendering to Jesus or clinging to his material wealth he chooses the latter.

The demand which Jesus had made on this bewildered man was suited to his particular circumstances and state of mind. The Lord does not ask every rich person—for example Abraham (Gen. 13:2), or Joseph of Arimathea (Matt. 27:57)—to do exactly this same thing. There are those opulent individuals who, speaking by and large, are living for themselves. What they contribute to the cause of others is wholly out of proportion to what they keep for themselves. There are other wealthy persons, however, who are willing to go all out in helping others, including even the ungenerous (Gen. 13:7-11; 14:14); and who, motivated by gratitude, are constantly building altars and bringing offerings to God (Gen. 12:8; 13:18; 15:10-12; 22:13).

According to Scripture two men were asked to make a sacrifice. The one was Abraham (Gen. 22:1, 2); the other, the rich young ruler. The sacrifice Abraham was asked to make was by far the most enormous. By means of his willingness to make the sacrifice Abraham proved the genuine character of his faith. He "believed in Jehovah, and he reckoned it to him for righteousness" (Gen. 15:6; cf. James 2:21-23). The rich young ruler, though asked to make a much smaller but still considerable sacrifice, refused, thereby proving that he did not have the faith whereby salvation is accepted as God's free gift. Abraham placed his trust in God; the young man, in his riches. That was the difference. See I Tim. 6:17.

The young man "had much property." He had it; it had him, holding him tightly in its grasp. In connection with this fact note the continuation: **23, 24. And Jesus said to his disciples, I solemnly declare to y o u, It will be hard for a rich man to enter the kingdom of heaven. Again I tell y o u, it is easier for a camel to go through the eye of a needle than for a rich man to enter the kingdom of God.** For the solemn introduction see on 5:18; for the meaning of the concept "kingdom of heaven" or "of God" see on 4:23; 13:43. A comparison of verses 23, 24 with verse 25 shows that the disciples understood "entering the kingdom" to mean "being saved." Another near equivalent, as verse 16 shows, is "obtaining everlasting life." With great emphasis, therefore, Jesus is saying that "a rich man with difficulty shall enter the kingdom of heaven" (thus literally). Difficult? Yes, so difficult that it will even be "impossible." Note the climactic arrangement of the thought in verses 23, 24. It is, of course, entirely impossible for a camel to pass through the eye of a needle. Yet, even this, says Jesus, impossible as it is, would be easier than for a rich man to enter the kingdom of God. [694] To

---

[694] Note "kingdom of God" in verse 24; cf. 12:28. Matthew's far more usual designation is "kingdom of heaven," as in verse 23. See also pp. 249 f. The same entity is indicated by either designation.

explain what Jesus means it is useless and unwarranted to try to change "camel" into "cable"—see on 23:24 where a real camel must have been meant—or to define the "needle's eye" as the narrow gate in a city wall, a gate, so the reasoning goes, through which a camel can pass only on its knees and after its burden has been removed. Such "explanations" (?), aside from being objectionable from a linguistic point of view, strive to make possible what Jesus specifically declared to be impossible. The Lord clearly means that for a rich man in his own power to try to work or worm his way into the kingdom of God is impossible. So powerful is the hold which wealth has on the heart of the natural man! He is held fast by its bewitching charm, and is thereby prevented from obtaining the attitude of heart and mind necessary for entrance into God's kingdom. See on 6:24; cf. I Tim. 6:10. It should be noted that Jesus purposely speaks in absolute terms. A moment ago we used the phrase "in his own power." Though in view of verse 26 this qualification does not need to be retracted, yet it should be pointed out that here in verse 24 Jesus does not thus qualify his assertion. He speaks in absolute terms in order all the more to impress upon the minds of the disciples that salvation, from start to finish, is not a human "achievement." The fact that "man's extremity is God's opportunity" is reserved for later (see verse 26).

The reaction on the part of the disciples was as follows: **25. Now when they heard this they were profoundly shocked, and said, Then who can be saved?** The disciples' amazement, according to Mark 10:24 already present after Christ's declaration found in verse 23 (i.e., Matt. 19:23; Mark 10:23), increases to the point where these men are "knocked out of their senses"; see on 7:28. As in 7:28 so also here in 19:25 the tense of the verb shows that their state of bewildered astonishment was not just a momentary experience but lasted for a while. They drew the conclusion that if what Jesus had said was true then no one could be saved. To reach this conclusion they probably reasoned that though not all men are rich yet even the poor yearn to become wealthy; hence, all men, rich and poor alike, trust in riches; hence, cannot be saved.

The beautiful and reassuring answer is found in verse 26. **Fastening his eyes on them Jesus said, With men this is impossible, but with God all things are possible.** In this dramatic moment the eyes of Jesus, as he fixed them on his disciples, must have been filled with deep earnestness and tender love. When he now tells them, "With men this is impossible," he means exactly that. At every point, beginning, middle, end, man is completely dependent on God for salvation. Of himself man can do nothing. If he is to be saved at all he must be born again or "from above" (John 3:3, 5). Even when by faith—God-given faith! (Eph. 2:8)—he reaches out to God, yet in order to do this he must be enabled and supported every day, hour, minute, and second by God's omnipotent grace. For the religion of the rich young ruler (see verses 16, 20), which was the religion current among the Jews of that day and age, there is no room here. Not only Pelagianism but even Arminianism stands condemned.

Glory be to God, however: there is a way out. What is impossible with men is possible with God, with whom all things are possible. It is he who, through Christ, is able to save to the uttermost (Heb. 7:25). His grace extends even to the determined and relentless persecutor Saul of Tarsus (Acts 9:1; 26:9-11; I Cor. 15:8-10; Gal. 1:15, 16; I Tim. 1:15). Just how, through the Mediator, this salvation is brought about, Jesus has already begun to reveal (Matt. 16:21; 17:22, 23). He will continue to do so with increasing clarity (see 20:17-19; especially 20:28; 26:26-29).

Peter is still thinking about the words which the Master had addressed to the rich young ruler (see verse 21). Jesus had asked him to sell all he had and give the proceeds to the poor, promising that if he did this he would have treasure in heaven. So Peter "answers," that is, he reacts to that statement (that demand plus promise) of Jesus, as follows: **27. Then Peter answered and said to him, Look, we have left everything and followed thee; what then shall we have?** Had The Twelve not done exactly what Jesus had asked the young man to do? Had they not "left everything" and followed Jesus? The answer, then, would seem to be obvious, namely, that The Twelve would have treasure in heaven. Nevertheless, Peter seems not to have been entirely certain about this, for the Master had also declared that with men it is impossible to be saved, and that it is God, he alone, who imparts salvation (verses 23, 24, 26).

Peter and the other disciples receive a very comforting answer. It is in the nature of a reassurance (verses 28, 29), and is followed by a warning (verse 30 and 20:1-16). **28. And Jesus said to them, I solemnly assure y o u that in the restored universe, when the Son of man shall be seated on the throne of his glory, y o u who have followed me shall also be seated on thrones, (on) twelve (of them), judging the twelve tribes of Israel.** For the solemn introduction see on 5:18; for "Son of man" see on 8:20, pp. 403-407. What a wonderful promise this is, especially when we consider how lacking in perfection were the men to whom it was given. See on 10:2-4. Jesus assures these twelve disciples—excluding Judas, but since he would be replaced the number twelve is still correct—that even though it is God who is the sole Author of their salvation, they themselves will be richly rewarded for the sacrifice they have made and are making. The fact that God delights in bestowing upon his children the reward of grace is clearly established in Holy Writ (Gen. 22:15-18; Ps. 25:12-15; Dan. 12:3; Matt. 5:1-12; 10:32, 41, 42; 11:28-30; 25:34-40; Luke 12:32, 37, 43, 44; 19:17-19; I Cor. 3:14; 9:17; Col. 2:18; 3:24; II Thess. 1:7-10; Heb. 10:35; 11:6, 26; II John 8; Rev. 2:7, 10, 17, 26-28; 3:5, 10-12, 21; 22:12). Many, many other passages from both the Old and the New Testament could easily be added, for "God is love" (I John 4:8).

The reward to which Jesus refers in the present passage was definitely promised to The Twelve. A broader promise, given to all believers, follows in verse 29. Turning then to the first of these promises, it is to be noted that it pertains to the position of The Twelve in "the regeneration," that is, in what we would call "the restored (or: renewed) universe," "the new heaven and earth" described in such passages as Isa. 65:17; 66:22; II Peter 3:13; Rev. 21:1-5. The time when this promise will be fulfilled is definitely indicated as being the day "when the Son of man shall be seated on the throne of his kingdom"; in other words the reference is clearly to the period beginning with the day of Christ's return for judgment (see on 25:31-46; cf. on 16:27, 28). Ranged, as it were, *around* that throne (cf. Rev. 4:4) there will be twelve other thrones. Upon these thrones The Twelve apostles will be seated, judging—probably in the sense of reigning over, being resplendent above (cf. Dan. 12:3; Matt. 20:21; Rev. 3:21)—"the twelve tribes of Israel."

What is meant by these "twelve tribes of Israel"? In all probability the term refers to the restored new Israel. Whether, as such, it indicates the total number of the elect gathered out of the twelve tribes of the Jews from the beginning to the end of the world's history (cf. Rom. 11:26), or even *all* the chosen ones of both the Jews and the Gentiles (cf. Gal. 6:16), in either case it must refer to those who have been regenerated, for into the reborn universe to which 19:28 refers nothing unclean will ever enter (Rev. 21:27). The Twelve, who have followed Jesus here, having remained loyal to him in his trials (Luke 22:28), are going to receive the special reward that among all the members belonging to the new Israel they will be pre-eminent in reflecting the glory of their Lord and Savior. Those who have been closest to Jesus here will also be closest to him there. See also II Tim. 2:11, 12; Rev. 3:21; 20:4.

The general promise, the one intended for all true followers of the Lord, is found in verse 29. **And everyone who has left houses or brothers** [695] **or sisters or father or mother or children or fields for my name's sake shall receive a hundredfold, and shall inherit everlasting life.** With this compare 10:37. This promise is for all who have in life chosen Christ above everybody and everything else, even above their nearest relatives and most cherished possessions. They have made the sacrifice, says Jesus, "for my name's sake," explained in Mark 10:29 as meaning "for my sake." The "name" of Jesus indicates Jesus himself as he has revealed himself. See also on 6:9; 7:22; 10:22, 41, 42; 12:21.

These loyal followers of the Lord are going to receive "a hundredfold," that is, they will be reimbursed "many times over" (Luke 18:30). For "hundredfold" see also Gen. 26:12 and Matt. 13:8. Even in the present day

---

[695] Luke 18:29 has "house or wife," but in Matt. 19:29 the words "or wife" (after "or mother") lack sufficient manuscript support.

and age (note Mark 10:30; Luke 18:30), that is, before the great day of judgment, and for each believer before his death, these loyal followers receive the blessings indicated in such passages as Prov. 15:16; 16:8; Matt. 7:7; John 17:3; Rom. 8:26-39; Phil. 4:7; I Tim. 6:6; Heb. 6:19, 20; 10:34; I Peter 1:8. In spite of the persecutions which they will have to endure, they will even be able to enjoy their material possessions ("houses . . . lands," Mark 10:30), far more than the ungodly enjoy theirs. Reason? See Isa. 26:3; contrast 48:22. For the sake of Christ has it become necessary for his followers to forsake close relatives? New "relatives" will now be theirs (Matt. 12:46-50; Rom. 16:13; I Cor. 4:15), for they now belong to "the family of God" (see N.T.C. on Eph. 3:15).

When Esau boasts about having "enough" or "much," Jacob—rather "Israel"—answers that he has "all" or "everything" (Gen. 33:9-11 in the original Hebrew and in the Septuagint). With this compare Paul's exuberant testimony (I Cor. 3:22, 23). These treasures are real. Otherwise how shall we account for Paul's triumphant outbursts of optimism (II Cor. 4:7-18; 12:9; Phil. 4:10-13)?

Jesus adds, "and shall inherit everlasting life." As meant here this blessing pertains to "the age to come" (Mark 10:30; Luke 18:30). For the concept "everlasting life" see on verse 16. All the spiritual blessings that are bestowed upon God's children in the present life "in principle" will be theirs "in full measure" in the hereafter. On and after the day of Christ's return in glory material blessings will be added to the spiritual. [696] They shall *inherit* them, in the present context implying that *a.* they are freely given to them, not earned by them; *b.* the gift is based upon justice: they were earned *for* them and are therefore theirs by right; and *c.* they are theirs forever.

To the apostles and to believers in general Jesus has given rich promises. Does this mean now that the pledged blessings will be theirs regardless of how they conduct themselves? Not at all. It is only in the way of trust and obedience that the promised goods are delivered to the children of God (Phil. 2:12, 13; II Thess. 2:13).

When Peter said, "Look, we have left everything and followed thee; what then shall we have?" (verse 27), was his question the product of holy curiosity, or, in whatever slight degree, of a mercantile spirit? The division of opinion among commentators in their attempt to answer this question is most interesting. Some, in their zeal to defend Peter against every charge, go so far as to say that those who distrust Peter's motives are judging others by their own ethical standards. Others go to the opposite extreme and regard Christ's sayings, the one reported in verse 30, as also the parable immediately following (20:1-16), to be inexplicable unless Peter's worldly motivation be

---

[696] On this subject see the author's *The Bible on the Life Hereafter*, pp. 49-78, 205-217.

taken into account. May not the best procedure be the following: A man is innocent unless his guilt can be established beyond any reasonable doubt. Accordingly, we have no right to charge Peter with anything wrong. On the other hand, it is also true that his question, though purely motivated, may have occasioned the warning that is found in the verse we are about to consider. Jesus may well have meant something on this order: "Peter, your question, 'What then shall we have?' is right and proper. Nevertheless, since it is so easy to fall into the error of expecting a reward based on supposed merit, I must warn you, so that you may not be caught unawares." Besides, is it not possible that the undoubtedly mercantile attitude of the rich young ruler (verse 16) may have caused Jesus to issue a needed warning?

It should not escape our attention that the words of verse 30. (as well as those of verses 28 and 29) are not addressed to Peter alone but to all the disciples: **But many that are first shall be last, and (many) last first.** We are reminded of the words of Jehovah addressed to Samuel, "Jehovah does not see as man sees; man looks on the outward appearance, but Jehovah looks on the heart" (I Sam. 16:7). The "first" are those who because of their wealth, education, position, prestige, talents, etc., are highly regarded by men in general, sometimes even by God's children. But since God sees and knows the heart many of these very people are by him assigned to a position behind the others; in fact, some may even be altogether excluded from the halls of glory. Cf. Matt. 7:21-23.

There does not seem to be any good reason for saying that Jesus meant that *all* of those who "shall be last" are going to be lost or outside the kingdom. Fact is: not only are there degrees of suffering in hell (Luke 12:47, 48), there are also degrees of glory in the restored universe (I Cor. 15:41, 42). There will be surprises however. Not only will many of those who are now regarded as the very pillars of the church be last, but also many who never made the headlines—think of the poor widow who contributed "two mites" (Mark 12:42), and Mary of Bethany whose act of loving lavishness was roundly criticized by the disciples (Matt. 26:8)—shall be first on the day of judgment (Mark 12:43, 44; Matt. 26:10-13). The disciples, who were constantly quarreling about rank (18:1; 20:20; Luke 22:24) better take note!

Summary of Chapter 19

In Matthew's Gospel Christ's ministry "beyond the Jordan" (19:1), often called his Perean Ministry, begins here and continues to the end of chapter 20. It is probable that not much more than three months elapsed between its beginning and the day of the crucifixion. Chapter 19 indicates the Master's teaching on three related subjects: *a.* marriage and divorce, *b.* children, and *c.* material possessions.

As to marriage and divorce (verses 1-12 both in Matt. 19 and in Mark 10) some Pharisees asked Jesus, "Is it lawful for a man to divorce his wife for any reason whatever?" In asking this question—with sinister intent, to lead Jesus into a trap—they are taking their cue from *the Mosaic concession* of Deut. 24. Jesus however points back to *the divine institution* of marriage, as recorded in Gen. 1:27; 2:24; and accordingly declares, "What therefore God has joined together let not man separate. . . . Anyone who divorces his wife except on (the ground of her) infidelity and marries another involves himself in adultery." When his disciples answer, "If such is the case of a man with respect to his wife, it is better not to marry," Jesus replies that grace is needed to properly fulfil one's marriage responsibilities: "Not all men can accept this statement, but only those to whom it is given." He adds that there are indeed situations which make it either impossible or inadvisable for a man to marry. He mentions three kinds of eunuchs: *a.* the congenitally defective; *b.* the physically castrated; and *c.* the voluntary abstainers (in the interest of the kingdom of heaven). In the latter case "eunuchs" is used in a figurative sense.

In the short paragraph about Jesus and the children (verses 13-15) Jesus says to the disciples, who were trying to prevent the little ones from being brought to Jesus, "Leave the little children alone and stop hindering them from coming to me, for to such belongs the kingdom of heaven." It was an important lesson not only for the disciples then, but for all parents, educators, and children (when arrived at the years of discretion) both then and now.

In the section on the peril of riches and the reward of sacrifice (verses 16-30) a rich young ruler is described as asking Jesus, "Teacher, what good thing shall I do that I may possess everlasting life?" This young man seems to be convinced that he has already observed the entire law, but wonders whether perhaps there is an additional good work he must perform in order to be saved. His understanding of what is involved in obedience to God's law is very superficial. When Jesus tells him that in his particular case the required love toward the neighbor means that he must sell all his goods and give the proceeds to the poor, the young man, deeply disappointed, departs. He was not willing to entrust himself and all his belongings to Jesus. This causes the Master to say to his disciples, "I solemnly declare to y o u, it will be hard for a rich man to enter the kingdom of heaven. . . ." When they ask, "Then who can be saved?" he answers, "With men this is impossible, but with God all things are possible." In answer to Peter's question Jesus assures the disciples that in view of their voluntary sacrifice a rich reward awaits them in the restored universe; in fact, a reward of grace, both here and in the hereafter, is given to all who have made sacrifices for Christ's sake. Only, they must be on their guard lest the mercantile spirit gains the mastery over them; for, "Many that are first shall be last, and (many) last first."

Outline of Chapter 20

Theme: *The Work Which Thou Gavest Him to Do*

CHAPTER XX

20 1 "For the kingdom of heaven is like an owner of an estate who went out early in the morning to hire workmen for his vineyard. 2 And having come to an agreement with the workmen for a denarius a day he sent them into his vineyard. 3 And he went out about the third hour and saw others standing in the market-place with nothing to do. 4 He said to them, 'Y o u go into the vineyard too, and whatever is right I will give y o u.' 5 So they went. And he went out again about the sixth hour and the ninth, and did the same thing. 6 Then about the eleventh hour he went out and found other men standing about, and he said to them, 'Why do y o u stand here all day doing nothing?' 7 They said to him, 'Because nobody has hired us.' He said to them, 'Y o u go into the vineyard too.' 8 So when evening had come, the owner of the vineyard said to the foreman, 'Call the workmen and pay them their wages, beginning with those (that came) last and ending with the first.' 9 And when those came who (had been hired) about the eleventh hour, each one received a denarius. 10 And when those who (had been hired) first came, they expected to receive more, but each of them also received a denarius. 11 They took it and began to grumble against the owner of the estate, 12 saying, 'These late-comers have worked (only) one hour, yet you have put them on a par with us, who have endured the arduous toil and the sweltering heat of the day.' 13 But he answered one of them, 'Friend, I am not doing you an injustice; didn't you come to an agreement with me for a denarius? 14 Take what is yours and go home. I want to give this late-comer as much as I give you. 15 Don't I have the right to do as I please with what is mine? Or are you envious because I am generous?' 16 So the last shall be first, and the first last."

20:1-16 *The Parable of the Laborers in the Vineyard*

1. For the kingdom of heaven is like an owner of an estate who went out early in the morning to hire workmen for his vineyard.

The very use of "for" as well as the modified repetition of 19:30 in 20:16 show that the parable that begins here is meant as an elucidation of the immediately preceding rule: "But many that are first shall be last, and (many) last first." One might say, "There should have been no chapter division between 19:30 and 20:1." When Jesus says, "the kingdom of heaven is like an owner of an estate . . ." he means something like this, "What happens when the reign of God in its final phase—see on 4:23; 13:43—is unfolded, on judgment day, may be compared to what took place, in the following story-illustration, between an owner of an estate and his employees, when the latter at day's end received their 'reward' for the work they had accomplsihed."

The "owner of an estate" is literally "a house-lord."[697] He is here pictured as a wealthy man, one who owns an estate consisting of a homestead plus a large vineyard. This vineyard is the object of his special care. It requires the labor of many hands. The very fact that Jesus here links the concept "kingdom of heaven" with "house-lord" or "owner of an estate" (cf. 13:27; 21:33; 24:43) shows that he calls attention immediately to the fact that God is the "owner" of all, and therefore also the sovereign Disposer of men's destinies. Of course, even the very term "kingdom *of heaven*" or "*of God*" stresses the same thought: the right to rule is his, not ours. Salvation in all its phases is his free gift. It is not the product of human effort.

Now although this estate-owner has a "steward" or "foreman" (verse 8), to whom he has assigned the care of the vineyard and the oversight over those who labor in it, he himself takes such interest in it that he goes out at dawn of day to hire [698] workmen.

2. **And having come to an agreement with the workmen for a denarius a day he sent them into his vineyard.** The point to note in this connection is that a conversation apparently takes place between the owner and these prospective employees. Whether or not there was any haggling the parable does not state. It is entirely possible that when the owner proposed "a denar(ius) a day" the unemployed men immediately consented, realizing that this was the standard daily wage for both soldier and laborer. Of course, there may have been some arguing about terms. One point, however, is clear: these men who consent to go into the vineyard and to do the work that is required of them are definitely working for wages, not also for the joy of working at such a good place for such a noble owner and for such a worthy purpose. The one and only thing mentioned with reference to these laborers in verse 2 is that the estate-owner "came to an agreement" (cf. 18:19), made a wage contract, with them! So, imbued with this mercenary spirit, these men go off to work in the vineyard.

Due to constant fluctuation in the value of money—one year a dollar or a pound will buy much more than another year—it is well-nigh impossible to express in up-to-date terms what a denar(ius) today would be worth. Some say sixteen (American) pennies or cents; others, seventeen cents, etc. For the understanding of the parable it is sufficient to know that for that day and age a denar (shall we, with A.R.V., say "shilling"?) a day was considered fair

---

[697] Even more precisely, "a man, a house-lord." This is another instance of the pleonastic use of ἄνθρωπος. See footnote 663 on p. 704.

[698] Note μισθώσασθαι middle aor. infin. of μισθόω: literally "to engage for μισθός (wages)."

remuneration for a day's work. Moreover, in the present case both employer and employees must have considered it fair, for they *agreed* on it.

Since the vineyard must have been large and in need of constant attention, and/or since just at this particular time much work by many hands was urgently necessary, we are not surprised that the owner wanted more workmen: **3. And he went out about the third hour and saw others standing in the market-place with nothing to do.** At 9 A.M. he goes—perhaps "returns"—to the place where the unemployed generally gathered, namely, the market-place, and saw others standing "without work," [699] thus literally. **4. He said to them, Y o u go into the vineyard too, and whatever is right I will give y o u.** It should be noted that these men do not enter into any wage agreement with the owner. They trust him, thoroughly convinced that when he promises to give them whatever is right he will do exactly that. **5. So they went. And he went out again about the sixth hour and the ninth, and did the same thing.** Both at noon and at 3 P.M. the owner returns to the marketplace and hires more workers. They were glad to be hired so that they would be able to work, even if it be only part of the day. With respect to them the owner "did the same thing." Does this simply mean that he hired them or also that to them too he said, "Whatever is right I will give y o u"? Taken either way, they offer no objections. They ask no questions but with joy of heart go to work.

The day wears on until it is 5 P.M., an hour before quitting time: **6, 7. Then about the eleventh hour he went out and found other men standing about, and he said to them, Why do y o u stand here all day doing nothing? They said to him, Because nobody has hired us. He said to them, Y o u go into the vineyard too.** What a gracious man this estate-owner is. It is clear that he is interested not only in his vineyard but also in the unemployed. He hires them when they, and everyone else, must have thought that for such men as these all hope of working in the vineyard on that day was baseless. What a strange thing to hire men at 5 o'clock P.M., for one hour's work! There is no bargaining. Gladly the men accept the invitation to enter the vineyard. Have they not made plain to the owner that the only reason for their standing about in the market-place, doing nothing, was that nobody had hired them?

Finally, quitting time arrives. Then something even stranger happens, as is apparent all the way from verse 8 through verse 15. In these eight verses we find the first surprise at the end of verse 8. **So when evening had come, the owner of the vineyard said to the foreman, Call the workmen and pay them their wages, beginning with those (that came) last and ending with the first.** "When evening had come!" Here the real meaning, the one main lesson,

---

[699] In the New Testament certain sparkling sayings have ἔργον (work) as their point of departure. See N.T.C. on II Thess. 3:11; I Tim. 5:13.

begins to come through; for this evening of the day indisputably points to the evening of the world's and of the church's history, the great day of the final judgment and of the manifestation of God's kingdom in all its glory. See the context, 19:28. We are beginning to be told what will happen when that day arrives.

It is tempting to indulge in allegorizing, and, with some commentators, to see in the command of the *owner* to the *foreman*, "Call the workmen and give them their wages," a symbolical indication of the fact that "the Father judges no one, but has committed all judgment to the Son" (John 5:22). The owner, then, would symbolize the Father; the foreman, Jesus Christ. It is very questionable, however, whether such a procedure is legitimate, especially since from verses 11-15 the foreman has moved out of the picture entirely! It is far better, therefore, to accept the fact that this figure of the foreman, and much more besides, belongs to the parable, not to the lesson to be learned from it. It makes the story more interesting and vivid.

Wages were generally paid when the working day was done (see Lev. 19:13; Deut. 24:15). What is strange, though, is that the foreman is told that when he calls the workers to pay them he must first pay those who had started to work last of all, at 5 P.M.; next, those who had begun at 3 o'clock, and so on until he finally paid those who had started first. Clearly this surprising order is in harmony with the rule laid down in verse 16 (cf. 19:30): the last are going to be first, and the first last. Besides, those who had come first must be given an opportunity to see what happened at the close of the day to those who had come later. Had the far more usual rule "first come first served" been applied, those first-comers would have taken their money and gone home before seeing what happened to the others.

Were the men who had been working since early dawn disappointed by being paid last of all? Undoubtedly, but there is another unwelcome surprise awaiting them: **9, 10. And when those came who (had been hired) about the eleventh hour, each one received a denarius. And when those who (had been hired) first came, they expected to receive more, but each of them also received a denarius.** When the late-comers receive an entire denar for just one hour's work, the first-comers expect to receive more than had been agreed upon between themselves and the owner. But each of them receives exactly the same amount as did each of the late-comers: one denar. Thus not only do they get paid last but also they receive less than by now they had come to expect. On the other hand, those who had worked only one hour receive a glad surprise: a whole denar for an hour's work! Nothing is said about those who had been hired at 9 o'clock, noon, and 3 o'clock. We may assume that they are satisfied—perhaps even more than satisfied—with what they receive. But they are no longer mentioned.

The disappointed men take their money and give vent to their feelings: **11, 12. They took it and began to grumble against the owner of the estate,** saying, These late-comers have worked (only) one hour, yet you have put them on a par with us, who have endured the arduous toil and the sweltering heat of the day. During the distribution of the wages the owner is himself also present. The employees readily understand that it is he, rather than the foreman, to whom they must bring their complaint if they have any. And, indeed, the early arrivals have a complaint. We are told that they "began to grumble," or "were grumbling." The very tense of the verb (imperfect) shows that the emphasis is either on the beginning of their act or else on its persistence. The word used in the original [700] is an onomatopoeia, that is, a sound-imitation, as are our equivalents: *mutter, mumble, murmur, grumble*.

The nature of their grumbling, moreover, showed what kind of men they were. They did not say, "You have put us on a par with the late-comers," but "you have put them on a par with us." In other words, they were not only dissatisfied with what they themselves had received; they were also— perhaps *especially*—envious of what had been given to the others! [701] They talk about the "arduous toil" [702] and the "sweltering—or scorching—heat" [703] which they have borne.

Their grievance amounts to this therefore: "In spite of the fact that we have worked much longer than these late-comers, and have toiled under conditions that were far more oppressive, look what you did *for them,* how generously you treated *them.*"

The main reason for their sullen dissatisfaction is that others, though last, were made to be first, and that they themselves, the first, had been made last. But for this dissatisfaction they were themselves to blame, their sin being a triple one: *a.* the mercantile spirit that had marked them from the very beginning; *b.* their failure to recognize the rights of the owner; and *c.* loathsome envy. Note how in that exact order this threefold root of their unhappiness is now exposed: 13-15. **But he answered one of them, Friend, I am not doing you an injustice; didn't you come to an agreement with me for a denarius? Take what is yours and go home. I want to give this late-comer as much as I give you. Don't I have the right to do as I please with what is mine? Or are you envious** [704] **because I am generous?** [705] This triple expo-

---

[700] ἐγόγγυζον.

[701] D. A. Schlatter, in his *Erläuterungen zum Neuen Testament*, Stuttgart, 1908, p. 223, states, in *explanation* of the parable, "To harbor within oneself envy over against others because God reveals his grace to them . . . what a depth of depravity is revealed by this kind of disposition."

[702] According to the context this seems to be the correct English equivalent of βάρος (basically "burden") here. See also N.T.C. on Galatians for both βάρος (footnote 176, p. 234 of that Commentary) and the verb βαστάζω (footnote 171, p. 232).

[703] The noun καύσων is found also in Luke 12:55 ("It is going to be a scorcher," that is, a very hot day) and in James 1:11 ("The sun arose with its scorching heat.") Compare the verb καίω, to light, burn.

[704] Literally, "Is your eye evil. . . ."

[705] It is clear also from I Peter 2:18 (note the synonyms) that at times ἀγαθός means *kind, generous.*

sure is here represented as a heart-to-heart address—earnest, disapproving, yet not entirely unfriendly—by the owner to one of the complainers, probably one who represented all the others. The refutation of the complaint was complete and crushing. All that was left for the grumbler was to take his denarius and go home.

In harmony with the explanation given it is now possible to state that the real point of the parable is clearly implied in verse 16. **So the last shall be first, and the first last.** [706]

The "point" or main lesson of the parable is therefore this: *Do not be among the first who become last.* This may be subdivided as follows: *a.* Avoid falling prey to the work-for-wages spirit with respect to matters spiritual (besides 20:2, 13 see also the context, 19:16, 22, and what was said in connection with 19:27). *b.* Do not fail to recognize God's sovereignty, his right to distribute favors as he pleases (in addition to 20:14b, 15a see again the context, 20:23). *c.* Be far removed from envy (see not only 15b but also the general context, 18:1; 20:20-28). Was not each disciple's yearning to be the greatest a next-door neighbor to gruesome soul-destructive envy?

In this parable Jesus is not condemning his audience. He is not taking back anything of the promise found in 19:28, 29. It is exactly in the way of sanctification (II Thess. 2:13), which includes also heeding this admonition, that the promise of 19:28, 29 is fulfilled, as are also all the other promises. But neither is he erasing 19:30. On the contrary, he is confirming it in a form suitable to the present parable, so that the reference to the last who become first is now mentioned first, for it was exactly the generosity extended to the last that had aroused the envy of the complainants. [707]

---

[706] The addition, "for many be called, but few chosen" (A.V.) is not based upon the best Greek text.

[707] Having now presented an explanation of this parable, what is the author's estimate of the views of some of the other commentators? For titles of their works see the Bibliography at the end of this volume. In this note (with one necessary exception) only the *pages* will be indicated.

John Calvin, pp. 410-312, points out that according to this parable God calls freely whomsoever he pleases, and grants to those whom he calls whatever rewards he deems suitable. Calvin definitely rejects the idea that those called first represent the Jews; those called last the Gentiles.

This very idea, or something closely resembling it, is however advocated by R. Knox, p. 43, who claims that any interpretation which ignores this view becomes intolerably flat and almost meaningless. Since there is nothing in the text or context to suggest this Jew-Gentile contrast I agree with Calvin and many others on this point. It is only fair to state that Knox presents much valuable material, and is easy to read.

Zahn, pp. 605, 606, points out—correctly, I believe—that according to the teaching of this parable those who boast about remuneration as if it were a right, and who envy their fellows, do not remain unpunished. Also, as he sees it—again, I agree—the parable commends those who went to work fully confident that the owner would reward them generously.

Schlatter—see also above, footnote 701, p. 739—points out, p. 223, that according to this parable those alone are the recipients of grace who do not begrudge others the

17 And as Jesus was going up to Jerusalem he took the twelve disciples aside and on the road he said to them, 18 "Listen, we are now going up to Jerusalem, and the Son of man shall be handed over to the chief priests and scribes; and they shall condemn him to death, 19 and hand him over to the Gentiles, to mock and to scourge and to crucify (him); and on the third day he shall be raised up."

20:17-19 *The Third Prediction of the Passion
and the Resurrection*
Cf. Mark 10:32-34; Luke 18:31-34

17. **And as Jesus was going up to Jerusalem he took the twelve disciples aside and on the road he said to them. . . .** Here we have the third and final prediction of the Passion and the Resurrection. For the first see 16:21; for the second, 17:22, 23; for all three in Matthew and its parallels in Mark and

blessing of receiving it. I find his comments—many of them of a very practical nature and always presented in a lively style—most interesting and instructive.

J. A. C. Van Leeuwen, p. 138, in his unique manner, offers some worth-while sidelights: *a.* on 20:12: in their envy those who complain even neglect to address their employer politely; *b.* on 20:15: if the complainer looks darkly (or: askance) at the employer because of the latter's generosity shown to the late-comers, so much the worse for that complainer! What was said about Schlatter can also be truly said about Van Leeuwen: his style sparkles!

Though I find much of Lenski's material worthy of hearty endorsement, yet his treatment of the present parable is to me not wholly satisfactory. On pp. 742-759 he allegorizes so generously—the steward is Christ; the denarius means temporal blessings; the laborers hired last are inexcusable idlers; etc.—that, because of this, the main lesson of the parable does not stand out with sufficient clarity. Also, his statement, p. 750, that the expression "now evening having come" (20:8) is no indication of the final judgment or of the end of each person's individual life, will probably find few supporters. Does not the parable show exactly what will take place "in the end," namely, "when the Son of man shall be seated on the throne of his glory" (19:28, closely connected with 19:30, which, in turn, introduces 20:1-16)? See also 13:40-43, 49, 50; 25:31-46.

As I see it, what is the weak point in Lenski's treatment is the strong point in the interpretation presented by H. N. Ridderbos, Vol. II, pp. 69-73. That author avoids all unnecessary allegorization and, as I see it, places the emphasis where it belongs.

F. W. Grosheide, pp. 300-303, in his own succinct and sparkling manner, points out that the parable stresses the freedom and sovereignty of God in imparting the reward of grace, no one being entitled, because of what he did or imagines he did, to receive anything from God.

R. C. Trench, in his *Notes on the Parables of Our Lord*, pp. 61-66, commenting on Matt. 20:15b—"Is thine eye evil, because I am good?"—points out that Scripture represents envy as being expressed by the eye (Deut. 15:9; I Sam. 18:9). He also rightly shows that the parable teaches men to refrain from priding themselves on their deeds, as if these would give them a claim on God's blessings.

W. M. Taylor, pp. 104-120, is certainly correct when, in his refreshing and very valuable treatment of this parable, he points out, as some other interpreters have also done, that what the employer is said to have done when he paid the late-comers as much as the early arrivals would lead to disaster if applied to labor and industry generally. He also states, however, that it truly represents *God's* dealings with men. As he sees it, the parable condemns the disposition of the hireling—think of the older brother (Luke 15:25-30)—that seeks to deal with God on the basis of so much work for so much pay. All of this I heartily endorse.

741

Luke see p. 9. As the second prediction added certain particulars to the first, so this third announcement is more detailed than those that preceded it. We now learn that not only was the Sanhedrin going to cause Jesus to suffer, as even the very first prediction had already declared, and not only was he going to be *delivered over* to that body, which action had been stipulated in the second announcement; but also that *a.* this highest court of the Jews, after condemning Jesus to death, would *b.* hand him over to the Gentiles, with the result that *c.* they, in turn, would mock (Mark 10:34 has "mock and spit upon") and scourge him, and that *d.* his death would be by crucifixion. The climax is glorious, just as in the first two predictions: "and on the third day he shall be raised up."

Shall we say, then, that as the Lord drew nearer to Jerusalem, the details of his rapidly approaching passion began to stand out more vividly in his own human consciousness? Shall we add, however, that another reason why these announcements became more and more detailed was that in his infinite love the Master wished to spare his disciples, breaking the news to them bit by bit in the realization that they would not have been able to endure the full story all at once? See John 16:12. There is probably some truth in both of these suggestions. As to the reason why there were predictions at all, see John 14:29; 16:4.

The time and place indication is very indefinite: "as Jesus was going up to Jerusalem." Combining verse 1 with verse 29 we are probably correct in assuming that the third prediction was made while Jesus and his disciples were on their way to Jerusalem via Jericho.

In view of 19:2 it is not surprising that in addition to The Twelve there were also others who followed Jesus. Since the Lord knew that it would not be wise to make the announcement of his suffering and death to all those followers (see on 16:20), he took the twelve disciples aside, so that in private he might give them this detailed information.

He said to them: **18, 19. Listen, we are now going up to Jerusalem, and the Son of man shall be handed over to the chief priests and scribes; and they shall condemn him to death, and hand him over to the Gentiles, to mock and to scourge and to crucify (him); and on the third day he shall be raised up.**

As to "listen," showing that an important statement is about to follow, see footnote 133, p. 131.

For an explanation of the term "Son of man," Christ's self-designation, in which he often describes himself as the One who, according to God's decree and prophetic prediction, moves from a humble beginning to exaltation at the Father's right hand, and who, in reality, was glorious from the beginning, see on 8:20, pp. 403-407.

The expression "the chief priests and scribes" here replaces the fuller designation of the first prediction, "the elders and chief priests and scribes" (16:21). In both cases the reference is to the Sanhedrin of the Jews.

The prediction that the members of this supreme court would condemn Jesus to death indicates that there was going to be a trial, and that at this trial the death penalty would be pronounced upon Jesus. The fulfilment is described in 26:57, 59-66; 27:1; Mark 14:53-64; Luke 22:66-71.

Since the Romans did not allow the Jews to carry out the death sentence, the Jewish authorities were going to hand Jesus over to the Gentiles, that is, in the present case to Pilate and those who carried out his commands. Fulfilment: see 27:2; Mark 15:1; Luke 23:1.

Jesus also predicted that these Gentiles would mock him. Fulfilment: 27:31; Mark 15:16-20. For the mockery by Herod see Luke 23:11.

The scourging of which Jesus speaks was definitely in connection with the crucifixion that was to follow, as is clear from the fulfilment, for which see 27:26. Scourging, however, was not always a prelude to crucifixion. On this see 10:17; Luke 22:16, 22; II Cor. 11:25; Heb. 11:36.

The prediction, in all three cases, ends on a note of triumph: the resurrection on the third day. For this see on 12:39, 40. Fulfilment: Matt. 28:1-10; Mark 16:1-8; Luke 24:1-12; I Cor. 15:1-20.

Mark 10:32, in language filled with pathos, depicts the disciples' state of mind as they followed Jesus on his way toward Jerusalem, and as they listened to this third prediction of his fast approaching suffering, death, and resurrection. These men were filled with amazement and anxiety. Luke 18:34 emphasizes that they were also thoroughly bewildered, not being able to digest the words spoken by Jesus.

---

20 Then the mother of the sons of Zebedee came to him with her sons. She was kneeling before him and asking him to do her a favor. 21 He said to her, "What do you wish?" She said to him, "Say that these two sons of mine shall sit one at thy right and one at thy left in thy kingdom." 22 Jesus answered and said, "Y o u do not know what y o u are asking for yourselves. Are y o u able to drink the cup that I am about to drink?" They said to him, "We are able." 23 He said to them, "My cup y o u shall drink, but to sit at my right and at my left is not for me to grant, but is for those for whom it has been prepared by my Father." 24 Now when the ten heard (what had happened) they were angry at the two brothers. 25 But Jesus called them (all) to him and said, "Y o u know that the rulers of the Gentiles lord it over them, and their great men keep them under their despotic power. 26 Not like that shall it be among y o u; rather, whoever wishes to become great among y o u let him be y o u r servant, 27 and whoever wishes to be first among y o u let him be y o u r humble attendant; 28 just as the Son of man did not come to be served but to serve, and to give his life as a ransom in the place of many."

20:20-28 *The Request of the Mother of the Sons of Zebedee*
Cf. Mark 10:35-45

Jesus had been emphasizing that in his kingdom greatness is measured by the yardstick of humility (18:1-4), that salvation belongs to the little ones and to those who have become like them (19:14), that trusting fully in the Lord, denying oneself, and giving instead of getting, is the mark of his true followers (19:21). He had taught that eagerness to labor for the Master without always asking, "What is there in it for me?" is the characteristic of the last who in the final days are going to be first (19:30; 20:16). James and John, the sons of Zebedee, had heard all this. But had they taken it to heart?

One might be inclined to ask, "How was it possible that, in spite of all this teaching about humility and service, teaching constantly reinforced by the example of Christ himself (12:15-21; Luke 22:27), the mother of these two disciples comes to Jesus with her two sons, and asks him to assign to them, next to himself, the two highest positions in the kingdom?" But is it not true that, speaking in general, more than nineteen hundred years of gospel proclamation have not succeeded in teaching men the lesson of self-denial and willingness to be least in the kingdom? Besides, it would be unfair to this mother if we failed to grant that in some respects her request was to her credit.

Her story begins as follows: **20. Then the mother of the sons of Zebedee came to him with her sons.** There is nothing precise about "then," nor does Matthew state exactly where the event took place. From a comparison of verse 18 with verse 29 we may, however, conclude, with a fair amount of probability that it occurred on the way to Jerusalem via Jericho. And as to the time? The third and by far the most detailed prediction of Christ's imminent ordeal has just been recorded (verses 18, 19). The present story (verses 20-28) concludes with another very pointed reference to the cross (verse 28). It would seem, therefore, that the request of this mother was made soon after the third lesson on the cross had been delivered and very shortly previous to the week of the passion.

Who was this "mother of the sons of Zebedee"? Why is she not simply called "Zebedee's wife"? As to the last question, Zebedee, still definitely alive and active in 4:21 (cf. Mark 1:20), may have died. It is also possible that the designation results from the fact that this mother's request concerns her sons, not her husband. We simply do not know. As to the first question, though certainty is lacking here also, the theory that she was Salome, the sister of the Mary who was the mother of Jesus, and that she was accordingly an aunt of Jesus, so that James and John, her sons, were his cousins, can be called a reasonable inference from a comparison of three Gospel references (Matt. 27:56; Mark 15:40; and John 19:25). For further details see on 27:56.

From Mark 10:35-41 it is very clear that the request which this mother is about to make is definitely also the request of her sons. In fact, Mark does not even mention the mother, and even Matthew, though telling us that the request was made by the mother, represents Jesus as directing his answer to the sons (verses 22, 23). To conclude from this that Matthew contradicts Mark at this point is wholly without justification. Mother and sons were in perfect agreement. Together they came to Jesus.

Continued: **She was kneeling before him and asking him to do her a favor.** Literally: "(The mother . . . came to him . . .) kneeling before [708] (him) and asking something from him." Very respectfully she waits until Jesus encourages her to state her request, to make it definite: **21. He said to her, What do you wish? She said to him, Say that these two sons of mine shall sit [709] one at thy right and one at thy left in thy kingdom.** Her request is evidence of her faith. It was a remarkable faith. The basis for it may well have been the saying of Jesus reported in 19:28, according to which he promises that one day he would be seated on the throne of his glory, and that each of The Twelve would then also be seated on a throne. She believes that this is actually going to happen. She is convinced of this in spite of the fact that right at this moment there is very little to show that events are moving in that direction.

Nevertheless, she was guilty of confusing earthly realities with heavenly, as if what generally happens on earth, when men who, after a tremendous struggle, have finally reached the top, will then from their lofty perch look down upon and hold down all those below them, also applied to the kingdom of heaven. She wanted *her* sons, and not Andrew or Philip—not even Peter!—no, no one but her two sons, James and John, to occupy the two pre-eminent positions. She was ignoring all that Jesus had said so clearly in 18:1-4 and 20:1-16. We can hardly imagine that her own sons had not reported this teaching to her. "So big!" was still her slogan, if not for herself, at least for her sons. She probably thought that her request must be made *now,* without any delay, because the kingdom of God in all its glory might be established at any moment (Luke 19:11). Besides, if our assumption that she was probably Jesus' aunt should be correct, this family relationship may also have encouraged her to make her request. But even if this should not be correct, at least she knew very well that within the largest circle of Christ's followers there was another, smaller circle, namely, The Twelve; that concentric with these two, but still smaller, was the circle of The Three; and finally, that two of these three were her own sons, James and John. Now then, if the

---

[708] For a detailed study of the verb προσκυνέω, from which this nom. sing. fem. pres. participle προσκυνοῦσα is derived, see pp. 171, 391. It has been variously rendered: "dropping to her knees," "kneeling," "bowing low," followed in each case by "before" with "him" understood.

[709] καθίσωσιν third per. pl. ao: subjunctive of καθίζω.

reign of God in all its splendor should be established next month or perhaps even next week, and Jesus should be enthroned in majesty, should not her sons be seated at his right and left? Was not this the way of kings and other dignitaries? See Exod. 17:12; II Sam. 16:6; I Kings 22:19 (II Chron. 18:18); Neh. 8:4.

So she may well have reasoned. But, as already indicated, there was too much of sin, too much of self, mingled with this reasoning. She was leaving out of account the teaching of Jesus concerning true greatness; also that concerning the sovereignty of God (20:14b, 15a, 23b).

22. Jesus answered and said, Y o u do not know what y o u are asking for yourselves. [710] **Are y o u able to drink the cup that I am about to drink?** As the original indicates, and as is also clear from the A.V., but not from most modern translations, which are very confusing at this point, in his answer Jesus addresses more than one person. He uses the plural, which means that either he is now speaking to James and John (cf. Mark 10:38), or to these two and their mother. Since the two apostles were in full agreement with their mother, so that they themselves had actively supported her in this request, making it also their own petition, and since these two were most directly concerned with its gratification, it is understandable that Jesus in his answer should especially have them in mind. Jesus, then, reminds them that they do not understand what their request really involves. They forget that a prayer for glory is a prayer for suffering; in other words, that it is the way of the cross, that alone, that leads home. So he asks them whether they are able to drink the cup that he is about to drink. In the idiom of the Old Testament and of those conversant with its literature "drinking a cup," i.e., its contents, means fully undergoing this or that experience, whether favorable (Ps. 16:5; 23:5; 116:13; Jer. 16:7) or unfavorable (Ps. 11:6; 75:8; Isa. 51:17, 22; Jer. 25:15; Lam. 4:21; Ezek. 23:32; Hab. 2:16). Jesus, too, spoke of his cup of bitter suffering (Matt. 26:39, 42; Mark 14:36; Luke 22:42). And for the New Testament see also Rev. 14:10; 16:19; 17:4; 18:6. Are these disciples, then, willing to become partakers of his suffering, that is, of the suffering for his name and his cause (10:16, 17, 38; 16:24; II Cor. 1:5; 4:10; Gal. 6:17; Phil. 3:10; Col. 1:24; I Peter 4:13; Rev. 12:4, 13, 17)? **They said to him, We are able.** On the favorable side we can at least credit them with a considerable measure of loyalty to their Master. Nevertheless, the future would prove that they were at this moment too self-confident. See 26:31, 56.

Christ's reaction to this positive assertion of the two men, and his final answer to the request is found in verse **23. He said to them, My cup y o u shall drink, but to sit at my right and at my left is not for me to grant, but is for those for whom it has been prepared by my Father.** Both the martyrdom

---

[710] Note the distinction between αἰτοῦσα active (20:20) and αἰτεῖσθε middle (20:22). On this distinction see Gram.N.T., p. 805.

of James (Acts 12:2) and the banishment of John to the island of Patmos (Rev. 1:9) are here foretold. These two future happenings were part of the suffering for Christ's sake that would be experienced by these disciples. However, as to the request itself, Jesus points out that the degrees and positions of glory in his kingdom have been determined in the Father's eternal decree. They cannot now be altered by the Mediator. See Matt. 24:36; 25:34; Luke 12:32; Acts 1:7; Eph. 1:4, 11.

When the ten other disciples heard what had happened, what was their reaction? 24. **Now when the ten heard (what had happened) they were angry** [711] at the two brothers. The report of the occurrence filled the remaining disciples with indignation. They probably felt that James and John, by asking for these positions of pre-eminence, had been plotting against *them*. It seems that they, too, had not yet taken to heart the lesson of 18:1 ff. They probably wanted these highest posts for themselves. This indicates that the spiritual attitude of the ten was not any better than that of the two. How easy it is to condemn in others what we excuse in ourselves. It takes a Nathan to make this clear to us (II Sam. 12:1 ff). Cf. Rom. 2:1.

It should not escape our attention that even though the attitude of all these twelve men must have caused the Lord much sorrow of heart, since it showed that even now, in spite of all his messages, they had not yet put into practice this part of his teaching, he reacts very gently. Is he not the tender Shepherd who loves his sheep? So, first he calls The Twelve to himself. Then calmly and earnestly he reproves and admonishes them: 25. **But Jesus called them (all) to him and said, Y o u know that the rulers of the Gentiles lord it over them, and their great men keep them under their despotic power.** That, says Jesus as it were, is the way of worldly people. They spend all their energies in order to get to the top; and, once having reached that peak, they cause all others to feel the weight of their authority. It would sound awkward to translate the Greek as follows: ". . . the rulers of the Gentiles lord *down* upon them and their grandees wield power *down* upon them," but that is nevertheless the sense of the saying. These worldly rulers, once "arrived," often think of themselves alone, and cause all their subjects to quail under the crushing weight of their power. Their rule, in other words, is oppressive. Continued: 26, 27. **Not like that shall it be** [712] **among y o u;**

---

[711] The form ἠγανάκτησαν is the third per. pl. aor. indic. of ἀγανακτέω. Besides its occurrence here in 20:24 (Mark 10:41), it is also found in 21:15 for the Jewish leaders' displeasure with Jesus; in 26:8 (Mark 14:4) for the disciples' attitude toward Mary of Bethany; in Mark 10:14, for Christ's anger when babes were being prevented from reaching him; and in Luke 13:14, of the ruler of the synagogue, because Jesus healed on the sabbath. These references show that in all these instances, except one, being angry was the result of sin. In the case of Jesus it was the result of love, his own love for the little ones. See also N.T.C. on Eph. 4:26.

[712] The preferred reading ἔσται has imperative force: "it shall not be," "must not be"; hence, "do not let it be." See Gram.N.T., p. 943.

rather, whoever wishes to become great among y o u let him be y o u r servant, and whoever wishes to be first among y o u let him be y o u r humble attendant. Essentially this is the teaching of 18:1 ff. See also 10:39; 16:24, 25; Luke 9:23, 24. The form given to it is new and refreshing. It is an unforgettable paradox. Jesus is saying that in the kingdom over which he reigns greatness is obtained by pursuing a course of action which is the exact opposite of that which is followed in the unbelieving world. Greatness consists in self-giving, in the outpouring of the self in service to others, for the glory of God. To be great means to love. See John 13:34; I Cor. 13; Col. 3:14; I John 3:14; 4:8; I Peter 4:8. Were not the following the list is incomplete—truly great? Was not childlike faith in God coupled with loving service to men (according to the rule of Gal. 6:10), characteristic of them all?

> Abraham (Gen. 13:8, 9; 14:14-16; 15:6; 18:22-33; 22:15-18)
> Moses (Exod. 32:32)
> Joshua (Josh. 24:14, 15)
> Samuel (I Sam. 7:5)
> David (Ps. 23; 103)
> Jonathan (I Sam. 23:16)
> Nehemiah (Neh. 1:4 ff.)
> The commended centurion (Matt. 8:5-13)
> Barnabas (Acts 4:36; 11:22-26)
> Stephen (Acts 6:8)
> Paul, Silas, and Timothy (I Thess. 1:1, 9; 2:1-12)
> Epaphroditus (Phil. 2:25-30; 4:18)
> Epaphras (Col. 1:7, 8; 4:12, 13)
> Luke (Col. 4:14)
> Ruth (Ruth 1:16-18)
> Hannah (I Sam. 1:27, 28)
> Abigail (I Sam. 25:18-42)
> The "great woman" of Shunem (II Kings 4:8-10)
> Naaman's servant-girl (II Kings 5:1 ff.)
> Mary, the mother of Jesus (Luke 1:38, 46-55; Acts 1:14)
> Elizabeth (Luke 1:39-45)
> The "generous" widow (Luke 21:1-4)
> Mary and Martha (John 11:1, 2; 12:1-8)
> Dorcas (Acts 9:36-42)
> Lydia (Acts 16:14, 15, 40)
> Priscilla and Aquila (Acts 18:26)

It is the inverted pyramid, the believer being at the bottom—being the *servant*, the *humble attendant* [713] of all others—that symbolizes the position

---

[713] It is clear that in verses 26, 27 the two words διάκονος and δοῦλος are synonyms.

of the Christian as, with simple trust in God and love for all men, he continues on his way to the mansions of glory. In doing this is he not following in the footsteps of his Lord and Savior? See Luke 22:27; John 13:34, 35.

In fact, that is the very thought which Jesus stresses, as he continues: **28 ... just as the Son of man did not come to be served but to serve, and to give his life as a ransom in the place of many.** Cf. Mark 10:45. This has always rightly been regarded as one of the most precious of Christ's sayings. Note "just as," clearly indicating that Christ's humiliation in the place of, and for the benefit of, his people, must be both their example and their motivation. He is "the Son of man," the fulfilment of the prophecy of Dan. 7:14. For a detailed study of the concept "Son of man" see on 8:20; pp. 403-407. In himself and from all eternity he is the all-glorious One. Yet he humbles himself. He becomes incarnate, and this not with the purpose of being served but of serving. See also on 9:13. Study II Cor. 8:9; Phil. 2:5-8; and see N.T.C. on I Tim. 1:15.

The service which it was the Son of man's purpose to render is described in the words: "to give his life as a ransom in the place of many." "In the place of" or "in exchange for" must be considered the right translation here. [714] The passage is a clear proof of Christ's substitutionary atonement. A *ransom* was originally the price paid for the release of a slave. Jesus, then, is saying that he came into this world to give his life—that is, himself (see I Tim. 2:6)—in exchange for many. The conception of Christ's death on the cross as the price that was paid, a price far more precious than silver or gold, is found also in I Peter 1:18. With this compare I Cor. 6:20; 7:23.

The phrase "a ransom for many" is in all probability an echo of Isa. 53:11, as the entire surrounding phraseology would seem to indicate. Now in Isa. 53 the idea of substitution predominates: see verses 4, 5, 6, 8, and 12. See also Matt. 26:28. It is, of course, perfectly true that this ransom "in the place of" and "in exchange for" many immediately implies that benefit accrues to the many. The two ideas "in the place of" and "for the benefit of" blend into one. How can we even for a moment entertain the idea that a

---

The temptation is, with many others, to translate them "servant" and "slave." However, in the course of history the ideas of lack of freedom, unwilling service, cruel treatment, etc., have become so closely attached to "slave" that, together with other translators, I too find it impossible to accept this translation as truly representing what Jesus had in mind *in the present context*. Far better, it would seem to the present author, is therefore the rendering (for the pair): "minister . . . servant" (A.V., A.R.V., Berkeley Version). My only reason for suggesting still another English equivalent is that today the term "minister" is very often understood in the technical sense of *clergyman*. For διάκονος see also N.T.C. on the Gospel according to John, Vol. I, p. 119; and N.T.C. on I and II Timothy and Titus, footnote 67 on p. 135; and for δοῦλος, N.T.C. on Philippians, p. 44.

[714] See the author's doctoral dissertation, *The Meaning of the Preposition ἀντί in the New Testament*, Princeton Seminary, 1948.

ransom "in the place of" many would not be for their benefit? Besides, the very context states in so many words that by means of this ransom the Son of man *serves* the many. He rescues them from the greatest possible bane, namely, the curse of God upon sin; and he bestows upon them the greatest possible boon, namely, the blessings of God for soul and body throughout all eternity. See Isa. 53:10; Rom. 4:25; II Cor. 5:20, 21; Titus 2:14; I Peter 1:18, 19.

Who are the "many" in the place of whom and for whose benefit the Son of man came to give his life as a ransom? The answer is as follows:

"my people" (Isa. 53:8)	"the church" (Eph. 5:25)
"his people" (Matt. 1:21)	"the church of God" (Acts 20:28)
"the sheep" (John 10:11, 15)	"God's elect" (Rom. 8:32-35)

There are passages, however, which, taken out of their context, seem to teach that Jesus came to this earth in order to pay the ransom for every individual living on earth in the past, present, and future. As soon as these passages are interpreted in the light of their contexts it immediately appears that this is not the meaning. Rather, the river-bed of grace has broadened. The church has become international, and it is in that sense that "the grace of God has appeared, bringing salvation to all men" (Titus 2:11; cf. I Tim. 2:6). For more on this point see N.T.C. on the Gospel according to John, Vol. I, pp. 98, 99; and N.T.C. on I and II Timothy and Titus, pp. 93, 94. Male and female, rich and poor, old and young, Jew and Gentile, slave and free, the Lord gathers his church from all of these classes. He is truly "the Savior of the world" (John 4:42; I John 4:14; cf. I Tim. 4:10).

A few more points must not be overlooked. First, and in connection with the immediately preceding, it is clear that Scripture in its doctrine of salvation is perfectly consistent. There is no conflict between the Father and the Son and the Holy Spirit. These three are really One. Those, and those alone, whom the Father has chosen (Eph. 1:3, 4), the Son came to ransom (John 6:39; 10:11, 15). No one shall snatch them out of his hand (John 10:28). These same ones also—no less, no more—are led and sealed by the Holy Spirit (Rom. 8:14, 16; Eph. 1:13). Thus the doctrine of the Holy Trinity is wholly maintained.

Another point that must be stressed is that the very wording of our passage (Matt. 20:28), namely, "to give his life as a ransom," indicates that Christ's death for his own must be considered *a voluntary self-sacrifice*. It was not forced upon the Mediator. He laid down his life of his own accord. See, again, John 10:11, 15. That fact gives to this death its atoning value.

Finally, the ransom price was paid not (as Origen maintained) to Satan, but to the Father (Rom. 3:23-25), who also himself, together with the Son and the Holy Spirit, had made arrangements for the salvation of his people (John 3:16; II Cor. 5:20, 21). [715]

The context must not be overlooked. Here in Matt. 20:28 Jesus is teaching that his own willingness to humble himself to the point of giving his life as a ransom for many must be reflected in The Twelve (see verse 20: the two sons of Zebedee; and verse 24: the ten); and, by extension, in all his followers. To be sure, Christ's own sacrifice is unique. It alone has atoning value. Consequently it cannot be duplicated. But in his own small degree and manner every follower of Christ must, by God's grace, show that love to others. He who believes John 3:16 must not forget to practice I John 3:16b! Such is the law of the kingdom.

---

29 Now as they were going out of Jericho a large crowd followed him. 30 And look, two blind men, sitting by the wayside and hearing that Jesus was passing by, cried out, "Lord, take pity on us, Son of David." 31 The crowd warned them to be quiet, but they shouted all the louder, "Lord, take pity on us, Son of David." 32 So Jesus stopped and called them. "What do y o u want me to do for y o u?" he asked. 33 They said to him, "Lord, (we desire) that our eyes may be opened." 34 Jesus, moved with compassion, touched their eyes, and immediately (the men) regained their sight and followed him.

20:29-34 *The Healing of the Two Blind Men at Jericho*
Cf. Mark 10:46-52; Luke 18:35-43

The Jericho of Jesus' day and its present-day ruins lie somewhat to the south of Old Testament Jericho. The city which Matthew mentions here in 20:29 was located about fifteen miles northeast of Jerusalem. Since Jerusalem was about 3,300 feet higher in altitude than Jericho, this fact sheds light on Luke 10:30: "a certain man was *going down* from Jerusalem to Jericho." Herod the Great—and later also Archelaus, his son—had strengthened and beautified this city, giving it a theater, amphitheater, villas, and baths. Even before the reign of Herod I it was already "a little paradise," with its palm trees, rose gardens, etc. Its winter climate was delightful, making it a winter-residence fit for a king. Had not Mark Antony given it to Cleopatra, the Egyptian queen, as a token of his affection? [716]

However, it was not with the beauty and splendor of Jericho that Jesus was chiefly concerned, as he travels now, with his little company, from Perea southwestward, across the Jordan; and thus via Jericho to Jerusalem—and the cross. Though an indescribably heavy burden is resting upon his own

---

[715] An excellent book on this subject is that by L. Berkhof, *Vicarious Atonement through Christ*, Grand Rapids, 1936. For other titles on the same subject see Select Literature on p. 179 of Berkhof's volume.
[716] See above: pp. 159, 162, 163, 165; also Josephus *Antiquities* XV. 53, 96; XVI. 143, 145, 320; XVII. 160, 173, 194, 202, 254, 274, 340; XX. 248; and L. H. Grollenberg, *op. cit.*, Plates 308-310 on p. 110; see also Index, pp. 153, 154.

heart (20:17-19; cf. Luke 12:50), he has not lost his sympathy with the needs of others.

Before entering upon the exegesis of verses 29-34 it is, however, necessary to say a word about the little paragraph as a whole. It has proved to be a feast for *a.*, on the one hand, *harmonizers;* and *b.*, on the other, *detractors.* The trouble is that Matthew speaks of *two* blind men, while Mark and Luke make mention of *one,* whom Mark calls Bartimaeus. Also, according to Matthew and Mark the miracle occurred as Jesus and his disciples were leaving Jericho; Luke, as he drew near to Jericho.

As to the first difficulty, is it possible that Mark, who was Peter's interpreter, had heard only the story of Bartimaeus? Of course, this is not really a solution; it simply pushes the problem back a little, from Mark (and Luke, who presumably had read Mark) to Peter. On the other hand, the problem is not at all serious. There is no real contradiction, for neither Mark nor Luke tells us that Jesus restored sight to the eyes of *only* one blind man. For the rest, it must be admitted that we do not have the answer: we do not know why Mark wrote—and Peter, let us suppose, had spoken—about Bartimaeus and not also about the other blind man.

As to the second problem, among the solutions that have been offered are the following: *a.* There were two Jerichos: Jesus therefore could have performed the miracle while he was leaving the one and entering the other; *b.* One blind man was healed as Jesus entered Jericho, another as he left; *c.* Jesus entered the city, had passed through it, and was now leaving it. While he was *going out* of the city he saw Zacchaeus up in the tree, and told that little publican to come down. So, with Zacchaeus he *re-entered* the city to lodge at the tax-collector's home for the night. According to the proposed solution it was during this re-entry of the city that the miracle took place. Hence, Matthew and Mark can say that it was performed while he was leaving the city; Luke, as he drew near to it.

All three solutions are open to objections, however. As to solution *a:* in an account which presents so much resemblance—compare, for example, Mark's account with that of Luke—it would be very strange, indeed, if the name "Jericho" meant two different things. As to *b.* this does not solve anything, for Mark and Luke are clearly speaking about the same blind man, "Bartimaeus, the son of Timaeus." Nevertheless, according to Mark this man had his eyesight restored "as Jesus was leaving Jericho"; according to Luke, as he "drew near to Jericho." And as to *c*, it does not explain why, as this view presupposes, the word "entered" would have the meaning "re-entered from the other side."—Other solutions are not any better: for example, that the blind man was sitting by the roadside begging, as Jesus entered the city from the east; that he then kept on following Jesus all the way through the city until finally, while Jesus was leaving the city, he cured him. The best answer is, There is, indeed, a solution, for this "Scripture," too, is inspired. However, *we do not have that solution!*[717]

Turning now to the story itself, as Matthew tells it, we notice that the material covered by its indicated theme, The Healing of the Two Blind Men at Jericho, may be distributed under these headings: 1. their wretched conditon (verses 29, 30); 2. their added difficulty (verse 31a); 3. their commendable persistence (verse 31b); and 4. the marvelous blessing which Jesus bestowed on them (verses 32-34).

1. *Their Wretched Condition*

29, 30. **Now as they were going out of Jericho a large crowd followed him. And look, two blind men, sitting by the wayside and hearing that Jesus was passing by, cried out, Lord, take pity on us, Son of David.** As Passover was approaching we are not surprised that a large crowd, probably from Galilee and from Perea, was following Jesus. Outside the city, Jesus having now passed through from east to west, two blind men were sitting by the wayside. This is not the first time Matthew has recorded the cure of two blind men (see on 9:27-31). Nevertheless, one can hardly speak of a "doublet" in this connection, for in *every* verse of 20:29-34 there is at least one item with respect to which the story here recorded differs from that in the previous passage, as any reader can see for himself by placing the two accounts side by side.

Although the blind men cannot see Jesus, they hear the bustle of the crowd, and upon enquiry learn that Jesus is passing by. They then immediately begin to cry out, "Lord, take pity on us, Son of David." As this same cry had also been uttered by the two blind men of 9:27-31, I shall simply refer to the explanation there given. As there explained, the term "Son of man" must be taken in its Messianic sense. This does not mean that these men already at that time had a full appreciation of the spiritual character of Jesus' messiahship. Not at all. It does, however, indicate that they were among the few who were able to give a better answer to the question, "Who do the people say that the Son of man is?" than was given by the people in general, according to 16:13, 14.

These two blind men, then, are imploring Jesus to take pity on—that is, to show mercy to—them. Their situation was indeed deplorable. Not only were they blind but, if for a moment we may cull an item of information from the accounts in Mark and Luke, they were beggars. For their sustenance they had to depend on the generosity of the crowd.

---

[717] S. V. McCasland, in his article "Matthew Twists the Scriptures," *JBL* (June, 1961), pp. 143-148, states (on pp. 146, 147, that "according to Mark there was only one blind man; but when Matthew tells the same story, the one blind man becomes two." This is manifestly unfair. Mark nowhere states that there was *only* one blind man!

2. Their Added Difficulty

31a. The crowd warned them to be quiet. . . . Just why the crowd did this we do not know. Possible answers: *a.* The people were in a hurry to get to Jerusalem and did not want Jesus to be stopped by these beggars; *b.* they deemed this yelling to be out of harmony with the dignity of the person addressed; *c.* they were not as yet fully ready to hear the idea "Jesus is the Son of David, the Messiah" publicly proclaimed (see on 8:27; 12:23); and *d.* they knew that their religious leaders would not appreciate this.

3. Their Commendable Persistence

31b . . . but they shouted all the louder, Lord, take pity on us, Son of David. That was to their credit. They realized that if help was going to come from any source, it would have to come from the Son of David.

4. The Marvelous Blessing Which Jesus Bestowed on Them

32-34. So Jesus stopped and called them. What do y o u want me to do for y o u? he asked. **They said to him, Lord, (we desire) that our eyes may be opened. Jesus, moved with compassion, touched their eyes, and immediately (the men) regained their sight and followed him.** The time has arrived when Jesus no longer forbids this public acclaim (contrast 8:4; 9:30; 17:9). Within just a few days he will, by means of his suffering on the cross, show to all who are willing to see, in what sense he is indeed the Son of David. The character of his messianic office—in simple language: how he saves—will then become evident, though the majority will still refuse to accept the truth.

Jesus reveals himself here as being not only all-powerful but also superlatively merciful. Very tenderly he asks these men to tell him, here in public, just what it is they desire of him. They are beggars. Are they asking for alms? Their answer is the expected one: "(We desire) that our eyes be opened." We are then once more specifically assured that Jesus not only granted them their wish, but that he did this because he was "moved with compassion." His *heart* was in the act. For the concept "compassion" see N.T.C. on Philippians, footnote 39 on p. 58. In line with this "compassion" was the tender "touch." For this see on 8:3, pp. 391f. Immediately and completely their sight was restored. All is light now, and this, we may be sure, not only physically—what a joy and what a riches was even this!—but also, at least to a certain extent, spiritually. Their confidence in Jesus had been rewarded.

This very miracle may well have contributed its quota to the enthusiasm with which the multitude would soon be acclaiming Jesus in connection with his triumphal entry into Jerusalem. It did not mean, however, that the people now recognized in him the *real* Messiah, the one of Isa. 53.

Thus, on a note of glory, ends the second large division of Matthew's Gospel.

Summary of Chapter 20

The parable (verses 1-16) that begins here is an elucidation of the immediately preceding rule: "But many that are first shall be last, and (many) last first." The owner of an estate goes to the market-place early in the morning to hire laborers for his vineyard. He reaches an agreement with them for a denar a day, and sends them into the vineyard. At 9 A.M., 12 noon, and 3 P.M. he hires more laborers, promising them, "Whatever is right I will give y o u," an assurance which these men accept without any haggling. Even at 5 o'clock he sends some more laborers into his vineyard. They too are glad to go, no questions asked. At quitting time the owner orders the foreman to pay the men their wages, but strangely adds, "beginning with those hired last." Stranger still: all the men must be given the same wage: one denar. Those hired first complain to the owner, for, in view of what those hired last had received, they (those hired first) had expected more. They envy the late-comers. The owner reminds them of the fact that they had *agreed* to work for a denar a day. He rebukes them for their mercantile spirit, their failure to recognize the right of the owner to do with his own money whatever he pleases, and their loathsome envy. For the spiritual lessons to be drawn from this parable see p. 740.

The next paragraph (verses 17-19) contains the third prediction of Christ's approaching passion and resurrection. It is far more circumstantial than either of the preceding, describing several of the details of the bitter trial Jesus is about to undergo.

In both of these paragraphs (verses 1-16; verses 17-19) eager service, willingness to sacrifice for the sake of others, without always asking, "What is there in it for me" has been stressed. How slow are people to learn this lesson! This appears from the paragraph (verses 20-28) that tells about the request of the mother of the sons of Zebedee. She kneels down in front of Jesus with the request, "Say that these two sons of mine shall sit one at thy right and one at thy left in thy kingdom." Her sons, James and John, join their mother in asking this favor. Jesus points out that *a.* the "greatness" for which they yearn requires sacrifice; *b.* not he but the heavenly Father has determined the degree of glory each of the ransomed shall receive; and *c.* only by forgetting all about greatness and instead dedicating one's life to God in humble service in the interest of others, after the example of Christ, can true greatness be obtained. The unique sacrifice of Christ is stressed in the meaningful passage, "the Son of man did not come to be served but to serve, and to give his life as a ransom in the place of many."

The closing paragraph (verses 29-34) describes what happened when Jesus with his disciples was traveling from Perea in a southwestern direction, across the Jordan, and thus via Jericho toward Jerusalem and the cross. As he was going out of Jericho two blind men, sitting by the wayside, cry out, "Lord, take pity on us, Son of David." Their wretched condition consists in this that they are not only blind but also beggars. Their added difficulty is that the huge crowd following Jesus tells them to keep still. Their commendable persistence appears from the fact that instead of being quiet they cry all the louder. Finally, the marvelous blessing which Jesus bestows on them becomes evident in that not only are they healed but they are treated with marvelous compassion and tenderness.

.

The Work Which Thou Gavest Him to Do

Its Climax

or

Culmination

Chapters 21:1–28:20

Outline of Chapter 21

Theme: *The Work Which Thou Gavest Him to Do*

A. The Week of the Passion

CHAPTER XXI

21 1 And when they approached Jerusalem and came to Bethphage, to the Mount of Olives, Jesus sent two disciples, 2 saying to them, "Go into the village opposite y o u, where at once y o u will find a donkey tied up and a colt with her. Untie them and bring them to me. 3 And if anyone says anything to y o u, y o u shall say, 'The Lord needs them,' and immediately he will let them go." 4 This happened in order that what was spoken through the prophet might be fulfilled,

5 "Say to the daughter of Zion,
Look, your King is coming to you,
Meek, and mounted on a donkey,
Even upon a colt, the foal of a pack-animal."

6 So the disciples went and did as Jesus had directed them. 7 They brought the donkey and its colt, and laid upon them their outer garments, on which he took his seat. 8 Most of the crowd spread their outer garments on the road; others were cutting branches from the trees and were spreading them on the road. 9 Then the crowds that were walking in front of him and those that were following (him) began to shout,

"Hosanna to the Son of David;
Blessed (is) the One coming in the name of the Lord;
Hosanna in the highest."

10 And when he entered Jerusalem the entire city was stirred up, saying, "Who is this?" 11 The crowds kept answering, "This is the prophet Jesus, from Nazareth of Galilee."

21:1-11 *The Triumphal Entry into Jerusalem*
Cf. Mark 11:1-11; Luke 19:28-38; John 12:12-19

The week of The Passion, which was followed by the Resurrection, begins here. Matthew has informed us that Jesus left Perea, crossing the Jordan and at Jericho restoring sight to two blind men. From Jericho the little party wended its way toward Jerusalem, as Matthew had also reported (20:17, 18). On reasonable grounds it may be assumed that Bethany—the home of Simon the leper, Lazarus, Mary, and Martha—was reached before sunset on Friday, that on the sabbath (Friday sunset to Saturday sunset) Jesus enjoyed the sabbath-rest with his friends, that on Saturday evening a supper was given in his honor, and that the next day, being Sunday, the triumphal entry into Jerusalem occurred. [718]

---

[718] For proof of the fact that this chronology is at least reasonable see N.T.C. on the Gospel according to John, Vol. II, pp. 171-173.

This Triumphal Entry was an event of outstanding significance. Note the following:

1. By means of it Jesus deliberately evokes a demonstration. He fully realizes that, as a result, the enthusiasm of the masses will enrage the hostile leaders at Jerusalem, so that they will desire more than ever to carry out their plot against him.

2. Jesus forces the members of the Sanhedrin to change their time-table, so that it will harmonize with his (and the Father's) time-table. The enthusiasm of the crowds with respect to Jesus will hasten the crisis.

3. By means of this Triumphal Entry Jesus fulfils the Messianic prophecy of Zech. 9:9. When the people hail him as the Son of David, i.e., the Messiah, he does not try to restrain them.

4. However, he also shows the crowds what kind of Messiah he is, namely, not the earthly Messiah of Israel's dreams, the One who wages war against an earthly oppressor, but the One who came to promote and establish "the things that make for peace" (Luke 19:42), lasting peace: reconciliation between God and man, and between a man and his fellow man. Accordingly, Jesus enters Jerusalem mounted on a colt, the foal of an ass, an animal associated not with the rigors of war but with the pursuits of peace, for he is the Prince of Peace (Isa. 9:6). But the people in general, their minds filled with earthly ideas concerning the Coming One, did not understand or appreciate this. In hailing him as the Messiah, the people were right; the Pharisees, chief priests, and scribes (Matt. 21:15, 16; Luke 19:39, 40) were wrong. But in expecting this Messiah to reveal himself as a political, earthly Messiah the Hosanna shouters were as wrong as were their leaders. Those who in every way rejected Jesus were committing a crime, but those who outwardly "accepted" and cheered him were also doing him a gross injustice, for they did not accept him for what he really was. Their tragic mistake was committed with dire results for themselves. It is not surprising therefore that Luke pictures a weeping King in the midst of a shouting multitude (19:39-44), nor is it strange that, a little later, when the crowds begin to understand that Jesus is not the kind of Messiah they had expected, they, at the urging of their leaders, were shouting, "Crucify (him)!"

In order to be able to appreciate Matthew's account of this Triumphal Entry and the immediately following events (21:1-17) it is probably best first of all to see the story in outline form. Piecing together the different accounts (Synoptics and John) the following summary results:

Sunday

1. Matt. 21:1-3, 6, 7a; Mark 11:1-7a; Luke 19:28-35a; John 12:2, 12:

As Jesus takes his departure from Bethany he sends two of his disciples into a small village, Bethphage. He gives them detailed instructions in order to enable them to fetch from there a young donkey on which he plans to ride into Jerusalem. Matthew points out that there were two animals involved, a colt and its dam, but it appears later that Jesus makes use only of the colt. The disciples succeed in carrying out Christ's command.

2. Matt. 21:4, 5, 7b; Mark 11:7b; Luke 19:35b; John 12:14, 15:

The disciples throw their garments on both of the animals, and when it becomes clear that Jesus wishes to ride upon the colt, they assist him in mounting it. Jesus starts riding toward Jerusalem. Both Matthew and John see in this event a fulfilment of the prophecy of Zech. 9:9.

3. Matt. 21:8; Mark 11:8; Luke 19:36:

Most of the people who accompany Jesus from Bethany spread their outer garments on the path. Others cut branches from the trees and with these pave the way before him.

4. John 12:1, 12, 13a, 18:

Meanwhile the caravan of pilgrims that had arrived in Jerusalem previously and had heard that Jesus had raised Lazarus from the dead and was on his way toward the city, come pouring out of the eastern gate to meet him. With fronds cut from palm trees they proceed on their way to welcome the Messiah.

5. Matt. 21:9; Mark 11:9, 10; Luke 19:37, 38; John 12:13b:

As the two throngs meet, the enthusiasm mounts. The accompanying multitude includes the following: The Twelve, a throng from Bethany, pilgrims from Galilee and Perea, and even some hostile Pharisees.

Descending the western slope of the Mount of Olives, and drawing near to Jerusalem, everyone (with the exception of the hostile Pharisees) starts to shout "Hosanna to the Son of David. . . ."

6. John 12:17:

Those who had witnessed the resurrection of Lazarus continue to bear testimony. Result: the excitement reaches a climax.

7. Luke 19:39, 40:

The Pharisees, beside themselves with envy as they listen to this cheering, appeal to Jesus to stop it: "Teacher, rebuke your disciples!" Jesus answers: "I tell y o u, if these were silent, the very stones would cry out."

8. Luke 19:41-44:

When, of a sudden, the city comes into view, Jesus, fully realizing that much of the praise which he had been receiving is shallow and is based upon the identification of himself with an expected earthly, political Messiah, breaks into loud weeping. Before his prophetic eyes there arises the vision of Jerusalem as a besieged city, a city surrounded by Roman legions. In a wail of bitter lamentation he cries, "Would that even today you, yes you yourself, had known the things that pertain to peace! but now they are hidden from your eyes. . . ."

9. Matt. 21:10, 11; Mark 11:11, 12:

As Jesus enters Jerusalem the entire city is stirred. Everybody who had remained behind, on seeing someone approaching surrounded by a huge crowd and riding into the city on a donkey, asks, "Who is this?" The answer comes back, "This is the prophet Jesus, from Nazareth of Galilee." In the evening Jesus returns to Bethany with his disciples.

Monday and Later

10. Matt. 21:12-14; Mark 11:15-17; Luke 19:45-47:
Jesus cleanses the temple and (according to Matthew) heals the blind and the lame.

11. Matt. 21:15, 16:
The children in the temple begin to shout, "Hosanna to the Son of David." The chief priests and the scribes, in their fury, ask Jesus: "Do you hear what these are saying?" Jesus answers, "Yes, have y o u never read: 'From the mouth of babes and sucklings thou hast prepared praise for thyself'?"

12. John 12:19:
The Pharisees, filled with the spirit of frustration, envy, and rage, say to each other, "Y o u see that y o u are gaining nothing. Look, the world has gone after him."

13. Matt. 21:17:
When evening falls Jesus and The Twelve again retire to Bethany for the night.

14. John 12:16:
Not until Jesus had been glorified did the disciples, looking back and revolving all these things in their minds, realize that the Triumphal Entry was the fulfilment of prophecy.

Of the fourteen elements that enter into the composition of this harmonized story Matthew has eight (items 1, 2, 3, 5, 9, 10, 11, and 13). In listing these fourteen items it is not claimed that the order in which they were presented is necessarily in each instance the exact chronological sequence in which they occurred. However, the order as here presented is probably not far removed from the actual facts of history.

1, 2. (see No. 1 on p. 760) And when they approached Jerusalem and came to Bethphage, to the Mount of Olives, Jesus sent two disciples, saying to them, Go into the village opposite y o u, where at once y o u will find a donkey tied up and a colt with her. Untie them and bring them to me. On this Sunday, starting out from Bethany, a village located on the eastern slopes of the Mount of Olives and about two miles east of Jerusalem (John 11:18), Jesus and his disciples were nearing Bethphage ("house of unripe figs"). The Mount of Olives is a rounded ridge to the northeast of Jerusalem. At its highest point it rises to a height of over 2600 feet above sea level, about 250 feet above the hill on which the temple was built. The "mountain" or "hill" has four peaks, known (from north to south) as Karem, Ascension, The Prophets', and (Mount of) Offense. When the second and third, separated by only a shallow depression, are counted as one, there are three summits, the second, when thus counted, being sometimes called "Mt. Olivet proper." Between the western slope of Mt. Olivet and the city is the valley of the winter-brook Kedron. See N.T.C. on John 18:1. It may well have been from the eastern slope of the Ascension summit that Jesus sent two of his disciples. The exact location of Bethphage is no longer known, but it must have been close to (northwest of?) Bethany, as a comparison of 21:1 with Mark 11:1; Luke 19:29, seems to indicate. "Go into the village opposite (or: over against) y o u" can without any difficulty be interpreted as meaning "just ahead of y o u." [719]

The two disciples were told that at the very entrance of the village (Mark 11:2), hence "immediately" after coming to it, they would find a donkey tied up and its colt with her. In view of the fact that Mark and Luke mention only the colt, critics see another "Gospel contradiction" here. It is held that Matthew a. misinterpreted Zech. 9:9, as if the prophet meant ". . . upon a donkey *and* upon a colt . . ."; and b. changed Mark's account, by substituting two animals for one, and picturing Jesus as riding on two asses at the same time (Matt. 21:7b), in harmony with the prediction. Answer: a. Matthew, the Jew, was probably better acquainted with Hebrew parallelism than his critics. He knew that the Hebrew conjunction allowed the translation "even" as well as "and." Neither was he completely dependent upon Mark's Gospel. Was he not one of The Twelve? Moreover, would it have been an act of kindness toward the colt to separate it from its dam, and to do so before Jesus was riding upon it? And b. Verse 7 literally reads, "They brought the donkey and the [or: and its] colt, and laid upon them the [meaning: their] outer garments, and he sat on them." The closest antecedent of "them" is "outer garments," not "the donkey and the colt." Besides, must we actually suppose that the evangelist was foolish enough to picture Jesus as riding on two animals at the same time? Verse 7b certainly allows the translation: "and laid upon them their outer garments, on which he took his seat." [720]

Just how it was that Jesus knew about this colt and its dam—whether through union of his divine and human nature, or simply through informa-

---

[719] For more information on the Mount of Olives, Bethphage, and Bethany see M. C. Tenney (editor), *The Zondervan Pictorial Bible Dictionary*, articles "Bethany" (p. 107), "Bethphage" (p. 112), and "Olives, Mount of" (pp. 607, 608); and L. H. Grollenberg, *op. cit.*, maps 24 (p. 96), 33 (p. 115), and 34 (p. 116); plates 192 (p. 69) and 326 (p. 113).

[720] For a statement of the position of those who charge Matthew with twisting the Scripture see S. V. McCasland, *op. cit.*, p. 145. For an excellent refutation of the view that Matthew here deliberately altered the narrative see R. V. G. Tasker, *The Gospel according to St. Matthew*, Grand Rapids, 1961, p. 198.

tion which he had received in a very natural way from the owners—we do not know. One thing we do know, namely, that when he orders the two disciples to untie the animals and to bring them to him, he is exercising his right of requisitioning whatever he needs for the fulfilment of his mediatorial task.

This is made even clearer in verse 3. (also included in No. 1 on p. 760) **And if anyone says anything to y o u, y o u shall say, The Lord needs them, and immediately he will let them go.** Note especially that Jesus is here using the title "Lord" to designate himself (see Matt. 11:27; 28:18). It is clear, therefore, that this epithet was not an invention of the early church after Christ's departure. It was not something borrowed from a non-Christian culture. It came from the very mouth of Jesus! [721] Note also "the" Lord, not merely "y o u r" Lord; rather, the Lord of all, with the right to claim all for his own use. Jesus predicts that when his claim, by mouth of the two men, is asserted, the owners will immediately release the animals. These owners must have been friends and followers of the Lord.

Before Matthew even informs his readers how the two disciples fared, he marks this event as a fulfilment of prophecy: 4, 5. (No. 2, p. 761) **This happened in order that what was spoken through the prophet might be fulfilled,**

> **Say to the daughter of Zion,**
> **Look, your King is coming to you,**
> **Meek, and mounted on a donkey,**
> **Even upon a colt, the foal of a pack-animal.** [722]

---

[721] J. G. Machen, *The Origin of Paul's Religion*, 1947, pp. 296, 297, makes proper use of this argument to bolster his position that Paul's "religion" was derived from Jesus himself.

[722] The main variations from the original Hebrew (Zech. 9:9) are:

a. Matthew omits "righteous and victorious is he." The idea "riding on to victory" is certainly implied in this event, for the evangelist is describing Christ's "triumphal entry." Cf. Ps. 45:4; Rev. 6:2; 17:14. Nevertheless, the emphasis is on the manner in which this victory is obtained, namely, through peaceful methods, for the Rider is described as meek. Does this perhaps account for the omission?

b. Instead of "riding," Matthew follows the LXX and writes "mounted."

On the other hand, Matthew approaches the Hebrew more closely than does the LXX, in the following respects:

a. He first describes the animal on which Jesus was mounted as "a donkey," where the LXX has "a pack-animal" or "beast of burden."

b. "In the last of the four lines he, like the Hebrew but unlike the LXX, describes the animals as "a colt, the foal of a pack-animal."

Taken in its entirety (all four lines) the passage does not in any essential differ from its original in Zech. 9:9. This is true especially because the Greek conjunction (at the beginning of the fourth line), like the Hebrew, can be translated "even" as well as "and." In the present case "even" is, of course, correct.

For "in order that . . . might be fulfilled" see on 1:22, 23, p. 133. [723]

The daughter of Zion is Jerusalem, that is Israel, only "the true Israel" being able to understand the significance of this Triumphal Entry, and even then not fully until later. Cf. John 12:16. "Look, your King is coming to you" is the joyful message addressed to the daughter of Zion. This King differs in certain very important respects from other kings:

a. This is "*your*" King, your very own. He is not a foreign king or a king bent on his own aggrandizement at the expense of the people, but One who had been commissioned to seek and to save. He "is coming to you," that is, *to benefit you.*

b. In line with this is the fact that this King is meek, gentle, peaceful, gracious. See on 11:29; 12:19, 20: 20:25-28; John 13:14, 15, 34, 35; 19:36, 37. This also explains why he is mounted on an unbacked ass (Mark 11:2b), not on a high-spirited war steed, or on a prancing white stallion.

c. This King is not the fulfilment of men's dreams but of a specific Messianic prophecy: Zech. 9:9. See also Isa. 6:6. He is both great and humble, exalted and lowly. He is the One who in this very act is riding . . . to his death, and thus to victory, a victory not only for himself but also for his true people, those who believe in him.

6, 7. (No. 1 and 2, pp. 760f.) **So the disciples went and did as Jesus had directed them. They brought the donkey and its colt, and laid upon them their outer garments, on which he took his seat.** Everything happened exactly as Jesus had predicted. The disciples found the colt and its dam at the place described by the Master. When they were in the process of loosing them from their hitching post, the owners objected. However, the answer, "The Lord needs them" (verse 3; cf. Luke 19:31, 34) resulted in immediate and wholehearted compliance. The animals were brought to Jesus. He solves their problem—namely, "Which animal is the Rider going to use?"—by taking his seat, with the assistance of the disciples (Luke 19:35), upon the coats that had been laid on *the colt.* He then starts to ride away. What happened to the dam is not stated.

8. (No. 3, p. 761) **Most of the crowd spread their outer garments on the road; others were cutting branches from the trees and were spreading them on the road.** In a way the crowd was following the example of the disciples. If the latter considered it proper to remove their coats so that Jesus could sit upon them, why should not the multitude also throw down coats and tree branches before the feet of the pack-animal? Besides, were they not honoring Jesus as King? If something of this nature had been done for King Jehu

---

[723] For a brief review of Zechariah's prophecies see N.T.C. on the Gospel according to John, Vol. II, p. 190; and the author's *Bible Survey,* pp. 283-286.

(II Kings 9:13), should it not most certainly take place to honor the Messiah-King?

9. (No. 5, p. 761) **Then the crowds that were walking in front of him and those that were following (him) began to shout,**

      Hosanna to the Son of David;
      Blessed (is) the One coming in the name of the Lord;
      Hosanna in the highest.

As to *"Hosanna to the Son of David,"* it should be noted that "Hosanna" means "save now," or "save, pray." The attitude of the people toward God was perhaps about as follows: "We beseech thee, O Lord, save now, grant victory and prosperity at this time, since because of thy goodness the appropriate moment has arrived." Hence, in this "Hosanna" exclamation, the two elements: supplication and adoration, or if one prefers: prayer and praise, are combined. It is clear that the source of 21:9 is Ps. 118 (LXX Ps. 117), which from beginning to end is filled with prayer and praise; see especially verses 22-26a. It is in essence a Hallel Psalm, one of the series Ps. 113-118, sung at Passover. See N.T.C. on the Gospel according to John, Vol. I, p. 121. It is also one of the six Psalms most often quoted or referred to in the New Testament; the others being Pss. 2; 22; 69; 89; and 110. Ps. 118 is distinctly Messianic. It speaks about the stone rejected by the builders but destined to become the cornerstone. See on Matt. 21:42; cf. Mark 12:10; Luke 20:17; Acts 4:11; and I Peter 2:7. Note the words immediately following "Hosanna," namely, "to the Son of David," and cf. II Sam. 7:12, 13. See further on Matt. 9:27-31; 12:23; 15:22; 22:42-45.

There were two crowds: one from Bethany that followed Jesus; and one from Jerusalem which, having arrived there mostly from Galilee, and having gone forth to meet Jesus, had then turned around so as to walk in front of him. In connection with Jesus, these two crowds are making God the object of their prayer and praise.

As to *"Blessed (is) the One coming in the name of the Lord,"* this is a quotation from Ps. 118:26. Combined with "the Son of David," as here in Matt. 21:9, it must refer to Jesus as the Messiah. It was deplorable, however, that by far the most of these people did not go one step farther: they should have combined Ps. 118 with Isa. 53 and with Zech. 9:9; 13:1. Then they would have recognized in Jesus the Messiah who saves his people *from their sins* (Matt. 1:21).

Finally, as to *"Hosanna in the highest,"* this shows that Messiah was regarded as a gift from God, the One who dwells in the highest heaven and is worthy of the prayers and the praises of all, including even the angels. One cannot help thinking of Ps. 148:1, 2 and of Luke 2:14.

10, 11. (No. 9, p. 761) **And when he entered Jerusalem the entire city was stirred up, saying, Who is this?** When the people who had stayed behind in Jerusalem had their first glimpse of the approaching throng and heard the joyful Hosanna shouts in honor of the central figure, their curiosity was aroused. Their excitement became contagious, until the entire city was as it were electrified, or, as the Greek has it, *was shaken.* [724]

"Who is this?" the people asked. Now Jesus was no stranger to Jerusalem and its temple (John 2:14; 5:14; 7:14, 28; 8:20, 59; 10:23; 18:20). But no one expected *him* to come riding into the city in the midst of a multitude singing his praises. This accounts for their question. Continued: **The crowds kept answering, This is the prophet Jesus from Nazareth of Galilee.** When those who accompanied Jesus repeatedly gave this answer, everybody learned who was entering the city; for, first of all, Jesus was known—and rightly so—as "a prophet." According to the New Testament he was thus designated by the people in general (Mark 6:15; Luke 7:16; John 6:14; 7:40); by the woman of Samaria (John 4:19); by Peter (Acts 3:22, 23, quoting Deut. 18:15); and by Stephen (Acts 7:37, also quoting Deut. 18:15). He used this same title in reference to himself (Matt. 13:57; Luke 13:33; John 4:44). The Pharisaic refusal to honor him with this title (Luke 7:39) seems not to have been very effective. He was, and is, indeed a prophet, for he revealed and reveals the will of God to man. Note how in the present connection he is represented both as the fulfilment of prophecy (21:4, 5, 9) and as being himself a—yes "the"—prophet (21:11).

The further description was also very appropriate: "Jesus from Nazareth" or "Jesus, the Nazarene" was a designation used, in referring to Jesus, by a demoniac (Mark 1:24; Luke 4:34), Bartimaeus (Mark 10:47; Luke 18:37), a portress (Mark 14:67; cf. Matt. 26:71), an angel (Mark 16:6), the apostle Philip (Luke 24:19), the temple police (John 18:5, 7), Pilate (John 19:19), Peter (Acts 2:22, 3:6; 4:10; 10:38), false witnesses (Acts 6:14), Paul (Acts 26:9), and even by the exalted Christ himself (Acts 22:8). The full combination "the prophet Jesus from Nazareth" is reflected in the words used by Cleopas and his companion to describe the One whom they thought they had lost (Luke 24:19).

Finally, "of Galilee." Was it with pride in their tone of voice that especially those in Christ's company who had come from Galilee, as pilgrims to attend the Passover, stressed this fact, as if to say, "he is *our own* prophet"? Had not Jesus performed most of his miracles and spent most of his time in Galilee? Did these pilgrims recount some of the mighty works which Jesus had done among them, just as the friends from Bethany "kept on testifying" about the resurrection of Lazarus (John 12:17)? This is very well possible.

---

[724] For the cognate noun see on 8:24. The verb used here (21:10) is ἐσείσθη, third per. sing. aor. indic. passive of σείω, to shake (cf. Heb. 12:26), but here used in figurative sense *was stirred up, became upset with emotion.* For the literal sense: *to be shaken by the wind* see Rev. 6:13; for *earthquakes,* Matt. 24:7; 27:54; 28:2, etc.

This "prophet Jesus, from Nazareth of Galilee" was the One, therefore, who was being enthusiastically proclaimed on this, his last Sunday on earth before the crucifixion, as being "the Son of David, the Blessed One, coming in the name of the Lord," that is, not only at God's command but as God's voice to the people.

---

12 And Jesus entered the temple and drove out all those who were buying and selling in the temple. He turned upside down the tables of the money-changers and the seats of those selling doves. 13 And he said to them, "It is written,

'My house shall be called a house of prayer';

but y o u are making it a robbers' den." 14 And the blind and the lame came to him in the temple, and he healed them. 15 But when the chief priests and the scribes saw the wonderful things that he did, and the children (who were) shouting in the temple, "Hosanna to the Son of David," they became angry, 16 and said to him, "Do you hear what these are saying?" "Yes," Jesus said to them, "Have y o u never read,

'From the mouth of babes and sucklings thou hast prepared
praise for thyself'?"

17 And he left them and went out of the city to Bethany, and spent the night there.

21:12-17 *The Cleansing of the Temple*

Cf. Mark 11:15-19; Luke 19:45-48; and for earlier cleansing, John 2:13-22

Jesus spent Sunday night at Bethany (Mark 11:11). The story continues, describing what happened afterward, beginning on Monday (but *not immediately* on that day; see on verses 18-22): 12. (see No. 10, p. 762) **And Jesus entered the temple. He drove out all those who were buying and selling in the temple, and turned upside down the tables of the money-changers and the seats of those selling doves.** Jesus entered the outer enclosure of the Jerusalem sanctuary, the section open not only to Jews but also to Gentiles, hence called "the Court of the Gentiles." What a sorry spectacle greets his eyes, ears, and even nostrils! He notices, as had happened also in the early part of his ministry, [725] that this court—hence, the temple—was being desecrated. It resembled a market-place. Business was booming, lucrative too. Some men were selling oxen and sheep. At this time of the year, with passover so close at hand and pilgrims crowding into the court from everywhere, there were many buyers. They paid high prices for these sacrificial animals. True, a worshipper could bring in an animal of his own choice. But if he did that he was taking the chance that it would not be approved. The temple merchants had paid generously for their concession, which they had bought from the priests. Some of this money finally reached the coffers of sly, wealthy Annas and of clever Caiaphas. It is therefore understandable that the tradesmen and the priestly caste were partners in this business. As

---

725 The attendant historical circumstances and the literary contexts of the two temple cleansings (Matt. 21:12-17 and John 2:13-22) differ so widely that the attempt to equate the two has not met with any success.

Jesus enters he notices the hustle and bustle of all the buyers and sellers; also the noise, filth, and stench produced by all the animals. Could this, in any sense whatever, be called *worship?*

Also in evidence were the money-changers, sitting cross-legged behind their little coin-covered tables. In the temple area foreign money was not accepted in payment. Also, the temple tax of half a shekel (Exod. 30:13; see on Matt. 17:24-27) had to be paid in Jewish coin. And money was needed to fulfil the various rites of purification (Acts 21:24). So, the money-changers would exchange foreign money, carried especially by those who came from foreign lands, for Jewish money, charging a small fee for the favor. This business, too, was profitable. It presented abundant opportunity for cheating the unsuspecting pilgrim.

And then there were the vendors of pigeons and turtledoves, probably standing near the "seats" or "benches" on which the crates filled with doves were piled. Not everybody was able to buy even a lamb. So, in connection with purification, "two turtledoves or two young pigeons" could be substituted (Lev. 12:6, 8; Luke 2:24). However, by now conditions had deteriorated to such an extent that even the poor were often being grossly overcharged. Imagine having to pay at least $4 for a pair of doves worth not much more than a nickel. [726]

It is not difficult to picture the righteous indignation that must have flashed from the eyes of Jesus when he drove out all—both the buyers and the sellers—who were engaged in this nefarious business, and overturned the tables of the money-changers and the seats of those selling doves. Whether also at this time, as in the first temple cleansing, he made a whip out of cords that were lying around and then let fly with that scourge, we do not know. One thing is certain: Jesus revealed himself as being indeed Lord of the temple (cf. 12:6). This is clear also from the words he spoke: 13. **And he said to them, It is written,**
My house shall be called a house of prayer;
but y o u are making it a robbers' den.

The first part of this statement is quoted from Isa. 56:7b, which reads, "My house shall be called a house of prayer for all peoples." The final phrase "for all peoples" is reproduced neither in Matt. 21:13 nor in Luke 19:46, but only in Mark 11:17 ("Is it not written, 'My house shall be called a house of prayer for all the nations'?"). It is clear from this that the temple was intended to be the place where God met with his people, a sanctuary for quiet, spiritual devotion, meditation, and fellowship, in connection with sacrifice. See I Kings 8:29, 30, 33; Ps. 27:4; 65:4; cf. I Sam 1:9-18. The second part of the statement is Christ's own comment, in which he contrasts

---

[726] For this and many other details, with references to Jewish sources, see A. Edersheim, *op. cit.,* Vol. I, pp. 367-376.

the divine ideal for worship as described in Isa. 56:7b with the present situation, a condition that reminded him of Jer. 7:11, which he quotes. In the days of Jeremiah, too, as is proved by that prophet's famous Temple Discourse, the Jews were oppressing aliens, stealing, murdering, etc. Nevertheless, they continued to offer their sacrifices in the temple; as if such merely formalistic worship of Jehovah would do any good, and as if the very presence of the temple would protect them from the outpouring of God's wrath. It was then that Jeremiah had said, "Do not trust in lying words, saying, 'The temple of Jehovah, the temple of Jehovah, the temple of Jehovah is this, ... Has this house that is called by name, become a den of robbers in y o u r eyes?" In the days of Christ's sojourn history was repeating itself: the temple had again become "a cave of thieves," an allusion, perhaps, to the rocky caves in the hills of Judea, where thieves and robbers would often assemble.

It has been objected that this story, as recorded in the three Synoptics, and the similar one, referring to the beginning of Christ's public ministry and recorded by John, cannot be true, for certainly the temple police would have interfered with Christ's action. However, note the following:

a. Right at this moment—think of the Triumphal Entry—Jesus was so popular that the Jewish authorities did not immediately dare to touch him (21:26, 46; cf. 26:5; Mark 11:32; cf. 14:2; Luke 20:6; cf. 22:2).

b. So unpopular was the temple trade, because of the greed of those who conducted it, that three years before the destruction of Jerusalem the people in an uprising against it swept away "the bazaars of the sons of Annas," as the temple market was called. In this connection Philip Schaff draws an interesting parallel between the first century temple-cleansing (the one of John 2:13-22) and the sixteenth century Reformation. He states, "Jesus began his public ministry with the expulsion of the profane traffickers from the court of the temple. The reformation began with a protest against the traffic in indulgences which profaned and degraded the Christian religion." [727]

c. The majesty of Christ's person—"the godhead veiled in flesh"—must not be discounted.

d. Nevertheless, the Jewish authorites did afterward question Jesus concerning the source of his right to do "these things." See on verse 23. Cf. John 2:18.

The lessons taught by this cleansing of the temple can be summarized as follows:

a. Jesus punished degradation of religion and insisted on reverence.

b. He rebuked fraud, in the present connection especially "religious" (?) racketeering, and demanded honesty.

---

[727] *History of the Christian Church*, New York, 1916, Vol. VI, p. 146.

c. He frowned upon indifference toward those who desired to worship God in spirit and truth, and by declaring that the temple must be a house of prayer *for all peoples* (Mark 11:17) gave his endorsement to the wonderful cause of Christian Missions. Cf. I Kings 8:41-43; Matt. 28:19.

d. By means of all this he glorified his heavenly Father. Was not the temple his Father's house?

14. And the blind and the lame came to him in the temple, and he healed them. What a scene! While some people are expelled, others are welcomed. Jesus has not changed any. He is still the Good Shepherd. So, when the blind and the lame come to him right here, *in the temple,* his eyes, a moment ago flashing with the fire of holy indignation, fill with tender compassion. He did not say, "Come back some other time. I am not now in the mood for healing y o u." On the contrary, the Great Physician is standing there in the midst of overturned tables, scattered coins, and knocked down benches, manifesting his healing power and marvelous compassion to those in need. None of those who came to him went away disappointed.

15, 16a. (see No. 11 on p. 762) **But when the chief priests and the scribes saw the wonderful things that he did, and the children (who were) shouting in the temple, Hosanna to the Son of David, they became angry and said to him, Do you hear what these are saying?** Finally the chief priests and the scribes gather enough courage to do something about Jesus. For both groups, representing respectively the Sadducees and the Pharisees, see on 2:4; 3:7; for the scribes see also on 5:20; 7:28, 29; 15:1, 2; and chap. 23. How it was that men who differed so widely in their views on religion could unite against Jesus has already been explained. See pp. 201-204. What irked them at this particular moment was the following combination of facts: *a.* the cleansing of the temple; *b.* the miracles performed on the blind and the lame; and last but not least, *c.* the shouting of the children, repeating yesterday's joyful outburst by their parents, etc., "Hosanna to the Son of David." Was not this blasphemy? And that right here in the temple! That they, these very enemies of Jesus, were themselves guilty of blasphemy because of the desecration of the temple which they had allowed and to some extent even encouraged, and because of the murderous design in their hearts against him, they did not acknowledge. But these children must be stopped! What they are doing is terrible, and even more reprehensible is the fact that Jesus is allowing this to continue. Apparently he approves of it. Such was their reasoning. That was why they—whether as a group of individuals who happened to be on the scene, or as men who had been officially delegated by the Sanhedrin [728] —became angry. [729] That is also why, motivated by envy (27:18), they asked, "Do you hear what these are saying?"

---

[728] Note similarity between 2:4 and 21:15 as to designation of combined group.
[729] For the verb ἠγανάκτησαν see footnote 711, p. 747.

That these children were shouting "Hosanna" should not have surprised them at all. Are not children imitators? Besides, as has been shown—see on 18:2—Jesus was the children's Friend. In all probability *their* hosannas were far more pure in spirit than those of the older people. It is hard to imagine that the hearts and minds of children were as filled with chauvenistic dreams as were those of the middle-aged and the elderly. **16b. Yes, Jesus said to them.** He affirms that he hears what the children are saying, and implies his approval. Continued: **Have y o u never read.** . . . Cf. 12:3, 5; 19:4; 21:42; 22:31. Then, quoting Ps. 8:2 (8:3 according to the Hebrew and the LXX),

> **From the mouth of babes and sucklings thou has prepared**
> **praise for thyself?**

Jesus is quoting these words according to the LXX version. [730] He is telling the chief priests and the scribes that children sometimes speak the truth; better still, that God takes even the incoherent prattle of babes and sucklings, in order out of such material to prepare praise for himself. [731] The implication is: God is also using for his own glory the shouts of the children who are now saying, "Hosanna to the Son of David." If those who heard Jesus give this answer were listening carefully, they must have realized that in a veiled manner he was here affirming what he is going to declare openly in 26:63, 64.

17. (see No. 13 on p. 762) **And he left them and went out of the city, to Bethany, and spent the night there.** As he had done the previous evening so also now Jesus returned to Bethany. The rendering "spent the night" is broad enough to include either of two possibilities: *a.* he spent the night with his friends in their hospitable home (see 26:6-13; cf. Luke 10:38-42; John 11:3; 12:1-8); or *b.* he lodged out in the open somewhere in or near the village; cf. Luke 22:39. [732]

---

18 Now in the morning, when he was returning to the city, he was hungry. 19 And seeing a fig tree by the side of the road he went up to it and found nothing on it but leaves. He said to it, "Never again let there be fruit from you!" And the fig tree withered at once. 20 And when the disciples saw (it) they were astonished and said, "How did the fig tree wither at once?" 21 But Jesus answered and said to them, "I solemnly declare to y o u, 'If y o u have faith and do not doubt, y o u shall not only do what was done to the fig tree, but even if y o u say to this mountain, 'Be lifted up and thrown into the sea,' it shall be done. 22 And whatever y o u ask for in prayer, believing, y o u shall receive."

---

[730] Although it is true that where the LXX and Matt. 21:16 have "praise," the Hebrew word basically means "strength," "bulwark," yet even this Hebrew word can mean "praise," as the context in Exod. 15:2 and in other passages indicates.

[731] The verb κατηρτίσω second per. sing. aor. indic. of καταρτίζω, *to put in order, prepare:* nets (4:21); *to restore* (Gal. 6:1), *to complete* (I Thess. 3:10), here in the middle voice means *thou hast prepared* [or *perfected*] *praise for thyself.*

[732] Basically this aorist ηὐλίσθη from αὐλίζομαι means *lodged in an open court-yard;* then, *lodged out in the open,* or simply *spent the night, lodged, stayed.* The meaning of the noun αὐλή (cf. Latin, *aula*) also varies rather widely and in certain passages is disputed. See N.T.C. on the Gospel according to John, Vol. II, pp. 104, 391.

21:18-22 *The Cursing of the Fig Tree*
Cf. Mark 11:12-14, 20-24

That the Gospel writers were not mere copyists but independent authors, each using his own method, appears very clearly in the present instance. Since part of the Fig Tree story occurred on Monday and part on Tuesday (Mark 11:11, 12, 19, 20), with the cleansing of the temple taking place (on Monday) between these two parts, it is clear that this story could be handled in two ways: *a.* chronologically or *b.* topically. Mark follows the first method, describing the first part of the Fig Tree story, the part that took place on Monday morning, in 11:12-14; then, the cleansing of the temple, later that same day, in 11:15-19; and finally, the second part of the Fig Tree story, the part that happened on Tuesday morning, in 11:20-24. Matthew, on the other hand, uses the second method. He wishes to tell the entire story all at once, in one connected and uninterrupted account. In doing this he does not come into real conflict with Mark, for his (Matthew's) time indications are very indefinite. For example, he says, "Now in the morning" (21:18), but does not indicate which morning. He does not say, "on the following day" (as he does in 27:62). Also, when he begins to report the second part of the Fig Tree story he simply says, "And when the disciples saw it . . ." (21:20). He does not indicate on what day this conversation between Jesus and his disciples took place. It is Mark who makes it very clear that what Matthew states in 21:18, 19 occurred on Monday; and what Matthew says in 21:20-22, on Tuesday. Each of these two methods (chronological and topical) has its merits. The combination of the two is something to be thankful for.

18. Now in the morning, when he was returning to the city, he was hungry. If it was at the home of his friends that Jesus had spent the night of Sunday to Monday, it is not clear why he should be hungry on this Monday morning. Had he arisen very early, before breakfast (cf. Mark 1:35)? We simply do not know. How thoroughly human is this Jesus, how close to us: even becoming hungry at times!

19a. And seeing a fig tree by the side of the road he went up to it and found nothing on it but leaves. The fig tree is the first common fruit tree whose presence on earth is clearly implied in Scripture (Gen. 3:6, 7). It was and is not only a fruit tree but also a shade tree (I Kings 4:25). It is characteristic of Palestine (Deut. 8:8; Num. 13:23), and today is found not only in most of the lands of the Mediterranean, where its fruit is called "the poor man's food," but in an area extending also all the way east to northern India. In the United States figs are grown in California, Texas, Louisiana, and other southern states.

773

In the region referred to here in Matthew, the early or smaller figs, growing from the sprouts of the previous year, begin to appear at the end of March and are ripe in May or June. The later and much larger figs that develop on the new or spring shoots are gathered from August to October. It is important to point out that the earlier figs, with which we are here concerned, begin to appear simultaneously with the leaves. Sometimes, in fact, they even precede the leaves.

Passover (about April) was at hand. Accordingly, the time when either the earlier or the later figs are ripe had not yet arrived. It was therefore "not the season for figs" (Mark 11:13). But Jesus, being hungry, notices—even from a distance (also Mark 11:13) that this particular tree, growing by the side of the road, was something special. It had leaves, was probably in full foliage, and could therefore be expected to have fruit. So Jesus went up to it.

We are confronted with a mystery here: the secret of the interaction between Christ's human and his divine nature. According to his divine nature Jesus was—and is—omniscient. That even during the days of Christ's humiliation this divine nature at times communicated its knowledge to the human nature is clear from such passages as Matt. 17:27; Mark 9:33, 34; John 1:47, 48; 2:25. That this did not always happen appears not only from the present passage (Matt. 21:19) but also from 24:36 (Mark 13:32). Jesus, then, went up to this fig tree to see whether he could find any fruit on it. He found nothing but leaves! **19b. He said to it, Never again let there be fruit from you! And the fig tree withered at once.** On the spot, as the original states, the tree began to lose its luster, the process of withering beginning in the roots (Mark 11:20).

It is impossible to believe that the curse which the Lord pronounced upon this tree was an act of punishing it, as if the tree as such was responsible for not bearing fruit, and as if, for this reason, Jesus was angry with it. The real explanation lies deeper. The pretentious but barren tree was a fit emblem of Israel. See Luke 13:6-9 (cf. Isa. 5). Jesus himself would interpret the figure the next day (Tuesday); see on 21:43. In fact, the disciples did not even have to wait until the next day for the explanation: The pretentious fig tree had its counterpart in the temple where on this very day (Monday), as has already been noted, a lively business was being transacted so that sacrifices might be made, while at the same time the priests were plotting to put to death the very One apart from whom these offerings had no meaning whatever. Plenty of leaves but no fruit. Bustling religious (?) activity, but no sincerity and truth. In cursing the fig tree and in cleansing the temple Jesus performed *two* symbolic and prophetic acts, with *one* meaning. He was predicting the downfall of unfruitful Israel. Not that he was "through with the Jews," but that in the place of Israel an international and everlasting kingdom would be established, a nation bringing forth not just leaves but fruits, and gathered from both Jews and Gentiles.

20. And when the disciples saw (it) they were astonished and said, How did the fig tree wither at once? The next day (Tuesday, according to Mark 11:20, as already explained) the disciples noticed that the fig tree in such a very short time—only twenty-four hours—had completely withered. They, especially Peter (Mark 11:21), gave expression to their astonishment. 21, 22. But Jesus answered and said to them, I solemnly declare to y o u, If y o u have faith and do not doubt, y o u shall not only do what was done to the fig tree, but even if y o u say to this mountain, Be lifted up and thrown into the sea, it shall be done. And whatever y o u ask for in prayer, believing, y o u shall receive. "This mountain" is the Mount of Olives; "the sea" is the Dead Sea. For this mountain to be cast into the sea, taken literally, would mean a sudden plunge of about 4,000 feet altogether. Now there would be no sense in even trying, by faith concentration, to dump Olivet into the sea. The dramatic figure, in the light of its context, which speaks of *faith* and *prayer,* must mean therefore that no task in harmony with God's will is impossible to perform to those who do not doubt. [733]

We should not try in any way whatever to minimize the force of this saying and to subtract from its meaning. Both in the physical and in the spiritual sphere the apostles had already been doing things that would have been considered just as "impossible" as causing a mountain to be lifted up and thrown into the sea. Had not Peter "by faith" walked on the water? See Matt. 14:29. Did not The Twelve exclaim, "Lord, even the demons are subject to us in thy name"? (Luke 10:17). A few days later was not Jesus going to make the promise, "I most solemnly assure y o u, he who believes in me, the works that I do will he do also, and greater (works) than these will he do, because I am going to the Father" (John 14:12)? See also Acts 2:41; 3:6-9, 16; 5:12-16; 9:36-43; 19:11, 12. In fact, does not the entire book of Acts prove that what Jesus said here in verses 21 and 22 was true? For the rest, since verse 21 closely resembles 17:20, see on that passage; and for verse 22 see on 7:7, 8; 18:19.

---

23 Now when he had entered the temple and was teaching there, the chief priests and the elders came up to him with the question, "By what authority are you doing these things, and who gave you this authority?" 24 Jesus answered and said to them, "I too have a question to ask y o u; if y o u give me the answer, I will tell y o u by what authority I do these things: 25 The baptism of John, where did it come from, from heaven or from men?" They were reasoning among themselves, "If we say, 'From heaven,' he will say to us, 'Why, then, did y o u not believe him?' 26 But if we say, 'From men,' we are afraid of the people, for they all consider John a prophet." 27 So they answered Jesus, "We do not know." He, in his turn, said to them, "Neither do I tell y o u by what authority I do these things."

---

[733] διακριθῆτε 2nd per. pl. aor. pass. subjunctive of διακρίνω: *to be of a divided mind, at odds with oneself.* Cf. Mark 11:23; Rom. 4:20; etc.

21:23-27 *Christ's Authority: Question and Counter Question*
Cf. Mark 11:27-33; Luke 20:1-8

23. Now when he had entered the temple and was teaching there, the chief priests and the elders came up to him with the question, By what authority are you doing these things, and who gave you this authority? Jesus was teaching, no doubt, in one of the "porches," "porticos" or "halls" of the temple. These porches were beautiful and huge. They were covered colonnades that ran all around the inside of the wall of the vast temple complex. Or, to put it differently, these halls were bounded on the outside by the temple wall, on the inside by the Court of the Gentiles. Most splendid and widest of them all was "the Royal Porch" (Stoa Basilica)—built where according to tradition the palace of Solomon used to be—consisting of four rows of columns, 162 in all, forming three vast halls, on the south side of the temple complex. Famous also was Solomon's Porch on the east side (John 10:23; Acts 3:11; 5:12). [734]

While Jesus was teaching and "preaching the gospel" (Luke 20:1) in one of these places, "the chief priests and elders" (thus Matthew), "the chief priests and the scribes and the elders" (Mark 11:27; cf. Luke 20:1), came up to Jesus. See on 2:4 and 16:21 for a description of these three groups. Again, as in 21:15, it is impossible to say definitely whether these groups were acting on their own initiative or as a delegation sent by the Sanhedrin, though in the present instance—because they ask Jesus about his *authority*— the latter seems probable. Their question is clear. They want to know by what authority Jesus was doing these things, that is, who had given him this right. They were saying, "Show us your credentials!" It was an attempt to embarrass Jesus. If he admitted that he had no credentials the people could be expected to lose respect for him. On the other hand, if he considered himself authorized to do the things he had been doing, was he not arrogating to himself rights that belonged only to God? Could he not then be accused of being guilty of blasphemous behavior? By not assaulting him directly, for example by having him arrested, they reveal that they are afraid of him because of his following.

But what do they mean by "these things"? They must have been referring to recent or present activities, that is, to things he had done on Sunday or on Monday, or to what he was doing on this Tuesday. Among commentators there is general agreement that the cleansing of the temple was included in "these things." This opinion is undoubtedly correct (cf. John 2:18). But was

---

[734] Cf. A. Edersheim, *The Temple*, London, 1908, see especially frontispiece diagram and pp. 42-45; L. Halberthal, *The Plan of the Holy Temple of Jerusalem*, colored print with accompanying description, Montreal, Canada. A copy was obtained at Pavilion of Judaism at Expo, 1967; and T. Kollek and M. Pearlman, *Jerusalem, A History of Forty Centuries*, New York, 1968, pp. 99-106.

this the only thing to which these enemies of Jesus referred? There is a wide difference of opinion among commentators. Some would include Sunday's royal entry into Jerusalem. Others say, "No," for the ovation he received at that time was not his own doing. Over against this stands the fact that he did not at all oppose the hosannas of his disciples and of the children (see 20:16; Luke 19:39). The royal entry may therefore have been included in "these things." And if we bear in mind the fact that Christ's enemies ascribed his miracles to the power of Beelzebub operative within him, even the deeds of kindness to the blind and the lame may have been included. However, the context in Luke would seem to indicate that it was especially the teaching in the temple and the preaching of the gospel there that must have irked the Jewish leaders. To say, with some, that the chief priests, elders, etc., could not have had this in mind because "any rabbi had a right to teach" misses the point: these Jewish dignitaries certainly did not want "the gospel" preached there!

24, 25a. **Jesus answered and said to them, I too have a question to ask y o u. If y o u give me the answer, I will tell y o u by what authority I do these things: The baptism of John, where did it come from, from heaven or from men?** By means of this counter question Jesus was by no means evading the question that had been asked him, for an honest and correct answer to *his* question would unmistakably have pointed to himself as the Greater One whom John had proclaimed, and would therefore have meant that Jesus' right or authority to do these things had come from God. It was while John was baptizing that he had proclaimed Jesus as being his superior (3:11, 12; cf. John 1:26, 27), and it was soon after the Lord's baptism by John that the latter had described Jesus as "the Lamb of God who is taking away the sin of the world" (John 1:29).

By means of Christ's question his enemies had been driven into a corner. Obviously they did not want to answer, "The baptism of John had a heavenly source," for they knew very well that the reply would be, "Why, then, did y o u not believe him?" On the other hand, were they to come out with what was probably that which most of them believed, or at least wanted to believe, namely, that the baptism of John was from men, the general public—perhaps especially the crowds of pilgrims that had come from Galilee—would become definitely hostile toward them, and might even stone them (Luke 20:6). Did not these people consider John a prophet? So these dignitaries start reasoning among themselves as to what to answer. Their decision was dishonest, though not surprising. They do not say, "We don't want to answer that question," which would at least have been honest, but "We do not know."

Having given this background, verses 25b-27 require no further explanation. **They were reasoning among themselves, If we say, From heaven, he will say to us, Why, then, did y o u not believe him? But if we say, From men, we**

777

are afraid of the people, for they all consider John a prophet. So they answered Jesus, We do not know. He, in his turn, said to them, Neither do I tell y o u by what authority I do these things.

---

28 "Now what do y o u think (of the following)? A man had two sons. He went to the first and said, 'Son, go and work in the vineyard today.' 29 But he answered and said, 'I will not.' Afterward, however, he repented and went. 30 Then he went to the other and said the same thing. That one answered, 'I will, sir,' but he did not go. 31 Which of the two did what the father wanted?" They answered, "The first." Jesus said to them, "I solemnly declare to y o u that the tax-collectors and the prostitutes are getting into the kingdom of God ahead of y o u. 32 For John came to y o u in the way of righteousness, and y o u did not believe him; but the tax-collectors and the prostitutes believed him. Yet when y o u saw this, y o u did not even repent afterward so as to believe him."

21:28-32 *The Parable of the Two Sons*

As verse 32 indicates, this parable is closely connected with the immediately preceding account. The attitude of the authorities to John the Baptist, verses 24-27, is the link. The inexcusable character of this attitude is here set forth. **28-30. Now what do y o u think (of the following)? A man had two sons. He went to the first and said, Son, go and work in the vineyard today. But he answered and said, I will not. Afterward, however, he repented and went. Then he went to the other and said the same thing. That one answered, I will, sir, but he did not go.** [735] In order to do justice to the *point* or *thrust* of the parable it is probably best to refrain from changing it into an allegory. One should not ask, "What does the vineyard, etc. represent?" The story should be allowed to proceed as Jesus told it. He himself, in verses 31b, 32, will make the application.

We note, therefore, that the father of two sons asks one of them to go to work in "the vineyard." It is not necessary to give "the" the meaning "my." Imagine a similar situation today. Is it not natural for a father to assume that not only he himself but also his sons would be sufficiently interested in that precious plot to regard it as the family's vineyard, not just his own? The lad's answer, "I will not," or "I won't," "I don't want to," also has a modern ring. Children have not changed much over the centuries. Happily, however, that even applies to the boy's further reaction: subsequently "he repented [736]

---

[735] The textual evidence showing whether the son who refuses and later repents comes first (as reflected in A.V., R.S.V., Beck, etc.), or whether the order should be reversed (N.A.S., Phillips, N.E.B., etc.), is about equally divided. It makes little difference which order is followed. To me it seems somewhat more natural that Jesus would save to the end the reference to the son who promised much but accomplished nothing, in order to connect the illustration with his stern condemnation (verses 31b, 32) of the chief priests and elders.

[736] Much has been written about the word μεταμέλομαι, *to become a care to one afterwards*, the nom. sing. masc. aor. participle μεταμεληθείς of which is here used. It is clear that no deeply religious sense can be assigned to the word as used in verse 29

and went." For one reason or another he regretted his earlier flat refusal. He rues his blunt, negative reply and goes to work.

With the same request the father then goes to his other son. The latter's reaction is the exact opposite. His response, "I will, sir" (literally "I, sir") has the flavor of ready and eager compliance, but it leads to nothing: he did not go.

Jesus now turns to his audience: those who had gathered about him in the temple, particularly the chief priests and the elders (see 23) and asks, **31a. Which of the two did what the father wanted? They answered, The first.** The answer was so obvious that, were they to reply at all, this was the only possible way to do it. The "application" is driven home with tremendous force: **31b, 32. Jesus said to them, I solemnly declare to y o u**—for this see on 5:18—**that the tax-collectors and the prostitutes are getting into the kingdom of God ahead of y o u. For John came to y o u in the way of righteousness, and y o u did not believe him; but the tax-collectors and the prostitutes believed him. Yet when y o u saw this, y o u did not even repent afterward so as to believe him.** The tax-collectors, for reasons stated in connection with 5:46—see on that passage—were despised by the Jewish people, especially by their leaders. They were considered in a class with prostitutes or whores, women of ill fame (cf. Luke 15:30; I Cor. 6:15; 6:16; Heb. 11:31; James 2:25; Rev. 17:1; etc.). Matthew uses this term "prostitutes" only here in 21:31, 32. For the related noun (5:32; 19:9) see footnote 684 on p. 716. Tax-collectors by means of their greed and extortion, prostitutes by means of their gross immorality, had said "I will not" to God's demand. They were like the first son in this parable. Afterward, however, as a result of the preaching of John the Baptist—see the present passage and Luke 3:12—many "publicans" had become converted. We now learn (21:32) that prostitutes, too, probably in considerable numbers, had responded favorably to John's message. They had been impressed with

---

(contrast verse 32). On the other hand, even in verse 29 it has a favorable connotation, for otherwise it could not serve as a basis for its occurrence in verse 32: there must be a link between the parable and its lesson. Only the verbal form is used in the New Testament, not the cognate noun μεταμελεία. Also, in the New Testament the verb occurs only five times (21:29, 32; 27:3; II Cor. 7:10; and in a quotation from Ps. 110:4, Heb. 7:21). It should be compared with its synonym μετανοέω, discussed in connection with 3:2. While the idea of repentance or regret is certainly implied in both verbs, μετανοέω goes much farther, as has been indicated, while μεταμέλομαι stops here; that is, here the emphasis is on the negative and retrospective. While heart, mind, and will are all deeply involved in μετανοέω, it is especially the emotional element that is stressed in μεταμέλομαι. For that reason, too, μεταμέλομαι is not used in the imperative. The regret of which this verb speaks *may* have value for eternity, leading to—and being an element of—full-fledged faith (see verse 32), but the word as such does not necessarily imply this. Judas "repented" and then hanged himself (27:3-5). He experienced remorse. On μεταμέλομαι see also W. G. Chamberlain, *op. cit.,* pp. 27-34; R. C. Trench, *Synonyms of the New Testament,* par. lxix; and L. Berkhof, *Systematic Theology,* p. 482.

John's "way of righteousness": his own righteous conduct coupled with the righteous conduct which he, as God's prophet, demanded of the people, namely, that they repent, etc. [737]

It is worthy of note, in this connection, that *women*, too—not only men—must have repented at the teaching of John. More and more the gate of the kingdom was being opened also to them (see 27:55, 56; Mark 16:9; Luke 7:36-50; 23:27 ff.; John 4:7 ff.; 11:1 ff.; 12:1 ff.; Gal. 3:28). These penitent tax-collectors and prostitutes had said, "We will not," but afterward had repented, so as to believe.

On the contrary, the religious leaders of the Jews, men who were deemed to be well at home in God's law, and *outwardly* behaved in such a manner as if they were constantly saying, "Yes, Lord, we will do whatever thou dost require of us, and we will go wherever thou dost want us to go," *did not do* and *did not go*. It was concerning them that Jesus was going to declare, "They say, and do not" (23:3). Cf. Exod. 19:8; 32:1 ff.; Isa. 29:13. They had rejected John (3:7-10), and even the conversion of the publicans and prostitutes through his preaching had failed to change their minds and hearts. They were like the second son therefore. Having rejected the Baptist, they were now in the process of planning the murder of the One whom he had proclaimed. And by answering, "The first" (the first son did what the father wanted), they had condemned themselves! So the tax-collectors and the prostitutes were getting into the kingdom of God ahead of these leaders; that is, *they* were obtaining the blessings of the kingdom, from which the hostile chief priests and elders and their followers were by their ôwn choice being excluded. For the term "kingdom of God" (usually in Matthew "kingdom of heaven") see on 4:23; 13:43.

Though this parable of the Two Sons, found only in Matthew, is perhaps not as well-known as many of the others, it is by no means less important. In fact, a more important lesson than the one taught here is scarcely imaginable. That lesson is, of course, this: *the doing of the will of God is the one thing needful.* Is not that the teaching of both the Old and the New? See I Sam. 15:22; Ps. 25:4; 27:11; 86:11; 119 passim; 143:10; Isa. 2:3; Jer. 21:33; Matt. 7:21-27; 28:20; John 15:14; Acts 5:29. And the will of God is that men should everywhere be converted and acknowledge Jesus Christ as Lord and Savior, to the glory of God Triune (Matt. 3:2; 4:17; 11:28-30; John 3:16, 36; I Cor. 10:31; II Cor. 10:5). As for the Mediator's own relation to the will of his Sender, did he not say, "My food is to do the will of the One who sent me, and to accomplish his work" (John 4:34)?

---

[737] For analogous figurative uses of the word "way" (way of life, teaching, religion, the Christian religion) see Acts 9:2; 19:23; 22:4; 24:22; I Cor. 4:17; II Peter 2:2. Cf. also the two "ways" in Ps. 1 and in Matt. 7:13, 14, the exact meaning in any specific passage to be determined in the light of the context in each individual case.

33 "Listen to another parable. There was an owner of an estate who planted a vineyard. He set a fence around it, dug a winepress in it, and built a watch-tower. Then he leased the vineyard to share-croppers, [738] and went abroad. 34 When the time approached to harvest the grapes, he sent his servants to the share-croppers to collect his (share of the) fruit. 35 But the share-croppers took his servants, and beat up one, killed the other outright, and stoned a third. 36 Again he sent other servants, more in number than the first group, but they treated these the same way. 37 Finally he sent to them his son, saying, 'They will have regard for my son.' 38 But when these share-croppers saw the son they said to each other, 'This is the heir; come on, let's kill him and get possession of the inheritance (that would have been) his.' 39 So they took him, cast him out of the vineyard and killed him. 40 When therefore the owner of the vineyard arrives, what will he do to those share-croppers?" 41 They said to him, "He will bring those dreadful scoundrels to a dreadful end, and will lease the vineyard to other share-croppers, who, when the fruit is ripe, will give him his share."

42 Jesus said to them, "Have y o u never read in the Scriptures,
'The stone which the builders rejected
This became the cornerstone;
By the Lord was this done
And it is wonderful in our eyes'?

43 "Therefore I tell y o u that the kingdom of God shall be taken away from y o u, and shall be given to a nation producing its fruit. [44 And he who falls against this stone will be dashed to pieces; but when it falls on anyone it will crush him]."

45 Now when the chief priests and the Pharisees heard his parables, they realized that he was speaking about them. 46 But although they wanted to arrest him, they were afraid of the crowds, who considered him to be a prophet.

21:33-46 *The Parable of the Wicked Tenants, and Its Sequel*
Cf. Mark 12:1-12; Luke 20:9-19

Between the parable of the Two Sons (verses 28-32) and that of the Wicked Tenants there are certain resemblances, also certain differences. As to the first: *a.* both parables mention a vineyard; *b.* in both parables Jesus had in mind the leaders of the Jews, whom he condemns. As to the second: *a.* the parable of the Wicked Tenants is much longer and more detailed than that of the Two Sons; for example, the figure of the vineyard is far more prominent in the parable which we are about to study; *b.* although also this second parable has one main lesson, clearly brought out in verses 40-43, nevertheless it approaches an allegory far more closely than does the first; and *c.* the first parable stresses the rejection of John the Baptist by the leaders; the second, the rejection, not only by the leaders but by the entire people, of the Father's beloved Son (cf. Luke 20:13), whose forerunner John had been.

33. **Listen to another parable. There was an owner of an estate who planted a vineyard. He set a fence around it, dug a winepress in it, and built a watch tower. Then he leased the vineyard to sharecroppers and went abroad.**

---

[738] Or "tenants"; literally "workers of the soil."

For "owner of an estate" see on 20:1, including footnote 697. This man reserved a portion of his ground for a vineyard. He planted vines in that plot, enclosed it with a fence or hedge as a protection against thieves and animals, and equipped it with a winepress and a watch-tower. The winepress generally consisted of two excavations dug into the earth and lined with stonework, or hewn out in a cliff. The upper cavity, wide and shallow, served as a receptacle for the grapes. Here they were crushed by the feet of the grape-treaders (cf. Isa. 63:2, 3). Through a pipe the juice would run into the lower, narrow and deep compartment. Afterward it was put into jars (cf. Hag. 2:16). The watch-tower may have been constructed from the very stones that had been gathered when the ground set aside for the vineyard was cleared (cf. Isa. 5:2). A watchman had to be stationed in such a tower to warn of any danger from pillagers, jackals, and foxes (Song of Sol. 2:15). The tower could also be used for storage.

When the owner had thus fully prepared his vineyard he leased it to share-croppers, that is, to tenants or lessees who, as the parable itself clearly indicates (cf. verse 34 with Mark 12:2; Luke 20:10), had to give the owner a definite amount of the vintage. Having made this arrangement the owner "went away from home," that is, "went abroad."

34. When the time approached to harvest the grapes, he sent his servants to the share-croppers to collect his (share of the) fruit. These "servants" must be distinguished from the "tenants" or "share-croppers." The latter are the vine-growers with whom the owner has made a contract, amounting to this: "I will let y o u manage this vineyard and harvest its crop for yourselves provided that at the time of the vintage y o u give me this or that definite portion of the grapes." The servants, on the other hand, were commissioned by the owner to collect and carry to their master's home the portion of the fruit that belonged to him. Having been delegated by him, it follows that they were invested with his authority. They made their demand or request "in his name."

35, 36. But the share-croppers took his servants, and beat up one, killed another outright, and stoned a third. Again he sent other servants, more in number than the first group, but they treated these the same way. The tenants proved to be wicked men, scoundrels, dishonest and cruel. When the servants asked for the portion of the grape-harvest to which the owner had a legal claim, they were refused. Not only that, but one servant was beaten, another was killed outright, and still another was slowly stoned to death. [739]

---

[739] A distinction will have to be made between "killed" and "stoned." Otherwise tautology results. This can be avoided in one of two ways: *a.* by translating as I have done ("killed outright and stoned," cf. R. Knox's New Testament Translation, supported also by R. V. G. Tasker) or *b.* by conceiving of the stoning as only partial, resulting in a rendering such as, "killed another, and threw stones at a third." This, too, is possible, for not all stoning resulted in death. See Acts 14:19, 20; II Cor. 11:25.

One might have expected that the owner would have responded most vigorously to the cruel treatment his servants had received, treatment which at the same time was an insult to himself. But he did not. He decided to give the share-croppers another chance to do their duty. So again he sent servants, more in number than the first time. However, these were treated similarly.

The parable now reaches a dramatic climax: 37-39. **Finally he sent to them his son, saying, They will have regard for my son. But when these share-croppers saw the son they said to each other, This is the heir; come on, let's kill him and get possession of the inheritance (that would have been) his. So they took him, cast him out of the vineyard and killed him.** It might be argued that at this point the story goes way beyond the boundaries of reason, that in the ordinary course of life no proprietor whose rights had been so rudely trampled upon would have been generous enough to give the criminals still another chance, and certainly that he would not have delivered over his own dear son to the whims and wiles of those who had bludgeoned his servants. This must be granted. But then, it should be borne in mind that this is *a parable.* Moreover, as will be shown later (see on verse 42), it is a parable depicting *sin most unreasonable* and *love incomprehensible!* Considered in this light, the story is one of the most beautiful and touching ever told.

The word "finally" [740] is full of intense emotion and pathos. The owner has a son, a beloved son, his only child (see Mark 12:6). Besides that son there is no longer anyone else he can send. That son is his one and all. He is all there is left, the owner's last word. So he sent his son, thinking, "They will be ashamed of hurting my son. They will respect him." [741] He spared not his own son! But what happens? When these wicked tenants see his son approaching they begin to plot. They enter into a consultation with each other. Accordingly, what they are going to do to him is not a matter of impulse. On the contrary, it is "malice aforethought," the result of wicked deliberation, of corrupt, selfish scheming. It is premeditated murder. They reason as follows: "This is the heir. When we kill him, there will be no other heir to worry about. So the inheritance which he would have obtained will be ours." In their sinister folly they forget that the owner, the son's father, is still alive, and will certainly wreak vengeance. How blatantly foolish is sin!

---

[740] ὕστερον is here used adverbially and as a superlative: "last of all." Cf. 22:27; 26:60; Luke 20:32.

[741] The verb is ἐντραπήσονται third per. pl. fut. indic. passive of ἐντρέπω, with active or middle sense, something like: "they will turn themselves about, being ashamed of hurting"; hence, "they will stand in awe of," "will have respect or regard for." German: "*Sie werden sich vor meinem Sohne scheuen.*" Dutch (Nieuwe Vertaling): "*Mijn zoon zullen zij ontzien.*"

How absurd! "He who dwells in the heavens will laugh. The Lord will hold them in derision" (Ps. 2:4).

The villains carry out their wicked plan. When the son arrives they take him, cast him out of the vineyard and kill him. [742]

The story is finished. Jesus has told it but has not yet explained it. First, he elicits a reaction from his audience (verses 40, 41). The explanation—which is at the same time the application—will follow like a crash of thunder (verses 42, 43). Do we perhaps have an Old Testament parallel in the procedure followed by Nathan when he addressed David? Note: a. Nathan's parable (II Sam. 12:1-4); b. David's reaction (verses 5 and 6); c. the explanation and application: "You are the man! . . ." (verses 7-12). While Nathan was telling the story, David was unaware that the prophet was, in a concealed manner, talking about him. So also it is *possible* that the chief priests and Pharisees, among others, were at first unaware of the fact that they themselves were "the wicked tenants."

In any event what now happens is this: these enemies of the Lord begin to condemn *themselves:* **40, 41. When therefore the owner of the vineyard arrives, what will he do to these share-croppers? They said to him, He will bring those dreadful scoundrels to a dreadful end, and will lease the vineyard to other share-croppers, who, when the fruit is ripe, will give him his share.** These concluding lines closely parallel the close of the preceding parable. In both cases Christ's question is followed by an answer from the audience, which, in turn, is followed by a sentence of condemnation pronounced by Jesus upon those who have just given a correct reply (cf. verses 31, 32 with verses 40-43).

It may be objected that those whose answer, as recorded in the parable of The Two Sons, had led to a stinging retort can hardly have been the same individuals who also in connection with this new parable risk giving a reply to Christ's question. But here there are several possibilities: a. as already suggested, they *may* have been unaware of the fact that also in this parable

---

[742] In footnote 35, under *h,* p. 38, reference was made to the fact that Mark 12:8 has the order "killed him and cast him out of the vineyard," instead of "cast him out of the vineyard and killed him" (Matt. 21:39; Luke 20:15). Is this an essential difference, due, let us say, to a later stage of theological understanding in Matthew and Luke? Would it not be more simple to say that in this passage Matthew and Luke are giving us the historical sequence, while in Mark's parallel passage the climactic order is presented, meaning: "They killed him, and this in the most shameful manner, casting him out of the vineyard as an accursed one"? There is, then, no real conflict between Mark and the others. The figure refers to the death of Christ of course. Whether he was crucified inside the gate or outside the gate must have been a matter of common knowledge. The answer cannot very well have been a product of later theological reflection. Mark (15:22 ff), Matthew (27:33 ff.), Luke (23:33 ff.) and John (19:17 ff.) all bear witness to the fact that Jesus was led outside the gate, being crucified on Calvary or Golgotha, a place which until the reign of King Herod Agrippa I was outside the wall. See L. H. Grollenberg, *op. cit.,* notation in connection with plate 373 on p. 130.

Jesus was talking about *them; b.* those who now reply may have been other persons belonging to the same group; *c.* the fact that the answer was so obvious may have made it almost impossible not to reply; and *d.* those who answered may even have expected and welcomed a scathing retort, in order that it might help them to carry out their plan to destroy Jesus! See verses 45, 46.

Among the Jews audiences were used to being asked to reply to questions asked by teachers. This question-and-answer method was employed by the rabbis to hold the students' attention and to increase their interest in the subject that was being discussed. On the present occasion Christ's question was the expected one, for after hearing about the terrible wickedness of the share-croppers everyone was wondering how they would be punished.

As to the answer Jesus receives, note the sound repetition (paranomasia) [743] : "He will bring those dreadful scoundrels to a dreadful end." As a matter of course, those who answer add that the vineyard will be leased to other share-croppers, men who will meet their obligations when the time of the vintage has arrived.

Then suddenly the thrust of the parable is driven home: **42, 43. Jesus said to them, Have y o u never read in the Scriptures,**

> The stone which the builders rejected
> This became the cornerstone;
> By the Lord was this done,
> And it is wonderful in our eyes?

Therefore I tell y o u that the kingdom of God shall be taken away from y o u, and shall be given to a nation producing its fruit.

"Have y o u never read . . .?" As if to say, "Y o u people who are always boasting about y o u r knowledge of the Word, have y o u not even read Ps. 118 (LXX 117):22, 23? The quotation as here reproduced is from the Septuagint, which, in turn, for this passage very faithfully renders the Hebrew original. It will be recalled that the parable reached its climax when the wicked tenants were described as casting the owner's son out of the vineyard and killing him. They had utterly *rejected* not only the servants but even the son! They had done this in order to enrich themselves. The son was gone now, so they thought, so his inheritance would be theirs. Jesus now surprises them by reminding them about this passage from the psalms. Here a very similar transaction had been described: builders had *rejected* a stone; meaning: leaders, prominent men, had rejected, despised, scoffed Israel. Nevertheless, Israel had become in a very true sense the head of the nations

---

[743] This striking feature of the original is not retained in the A.V., nor in several modern-English translations. It is, however, nicely reflected in (among others) the following versions, each in its own way: Latin, Weymouth, A.R.V., N.A.S., N.E.B., Dutch (both Staten Vertaling and Nieuwe Vertaling), Swedish, Frisian, and South African.

(Ps. 147:20). This, moreover, had not happened because of Israel's own intrinsic moral and spiritual excellence or because of its power. On the contrary, by the Lord this wonderful thing had been accomplished. Jesus now shows that the words of Ps. 118 reach their ultimate fulfilment in "the owner's son," that is, in himself, the *true* Israel. He is that stone that was being rejected by the chief priests, scribes, and their followers; at Calvary, by the nation as a whole ("Crucify, crucify!"). See John 1:11. But something marvelous was going to happen: *the rejected stone would become the cornerstone:* Christ crucified would rise again triumphantly. And what about the nation, namely, the old unconverted Israel, the rejectors of the Messiah? "From y o u," says Jesus, the "kingdom of God," that is, the special kingdom privileges—the special standing in the eyes of God which this people had enjoyed during the old dispensation, to which had now been added the blessed words and works of Jesus—"will be taken away." Why? Because they had not lived up to their obligations. They had been like the share-croppers who at the time of the vintage had refused to render to the owner that portion of the vintage that was his due. So, in the place of the old covenant people there would arise—was it not already beginning to happen?—"a nation producing its fruit," a church international, gathered from both Jews and Gentiles.

Briefly, therefore, the thrust—the one main lesson—of the parable can be expressed in the words of Ps. 2:12: "Kiss [or: pay homage to] the Son, lest he be angry, and y o u perish in the way; for soon shall his wrath be kindled. Blessed are all those who take refuge in him."

As to the separate items in this parable, it has now become clear that:

a. *The vineyard* reminds us immediately of Israel. See Isa. 5:1-7, on which the parable is clearly based. Notice the mention of the vineyard, the fence or hedge, the winepress, and the watch-tower in both. Also cf. Deut. 32:32; Ps. 80:8-16; Isa. 27:2, 3; Jer. 2:21; Ezek. 15:1-6; 19:10; Hos. 10:1. Nevertheless, not the nation as such but "the special advantages and opportunities which were given to the people as the chosen seed, and in virtue of God's covenant with them" (W. M. Taylor, *The Parables of Our Savior,* p. 140) is what is signified, for we are told that the vineyard "will be given to a nation producing its fruit."

b. *The one who planted and owns the vineyard* is God.

c. *The wicked share-croppers or tenants* are Israel's leaders: chief priests, scribes, elders, and all their followers; hence, the nation as a whole.

d. *The servants* who were sent to collect the portion of the vintage that could be rightfully claimed by the owner, and who were treated shamefully, are the prophets. The treatment they received has been described in some detail in connection with the explanation of 5:12b; see on that passage.

e. As already indicated, *the owner's son* is Jesus Christ himself. An additional word, in conclusion, should be said about Jesus as "the stone which the builders rejected." [744] Other references to this stone (in addition to Ps. 118:22, 23 and the present passage, Matt. 21:42) are Isa. 28:16; Acts 4:11; Rom. 9:33; Eph. 2:20; and I Peter 2:6. The cornerstone of a building, in addition to being part of the foundation and therefore *supporting* the superstructure, *finalizes* its shape, for, being placed at the corner formed by the junction of two primary walls, it determines the lay of the walls and crosswalls throughout. All the other stones must adjust themselves to this cornerstone. Such is the relation of Christ to his church. By his glorious resurrection, ascension, and coronation he has become highly exalted, and from his place at the Father's right hand sends out the Spirit to dwell in the hearts of his followers and to rule over the entire universe in the interest of the church, to the glory of God Triune.

[44. **And he who falls against this stone will be dashed to pieces; but when it falls on anyone it will crush him.**] The textual support for the inclusion of this passage is not very strong. Besides, as everyone can see for himself, if Matthew wrote it he would in all probability have added it after verse 42. The passage is probably an interpolation from Luke 20:18. It is thoroughly inspired but was probably not written by the former publican. The meaning of the verse may be briefly summarized as follows: anyone who opposes Christ is going to be "pulverized" (cf. Matt. 3:12). If Christ strikes him with his judgment, the person so stricken will be crushed.

45. **Now when the chief priests and the Pharisees heard his parables, they realized that he was speaking about them.** The reference is to the men also mentioned earlier (see on verse 23). If some of them had in the beginning not fully understood that even in the parable of The Two Sons there had been a reference to them—think of the second son—, they surely could not fail to understand that the parable of The Wicked Tenants was directed at them. They knew very well that *they* and *their* followers were rejecting Jesus. Besides, in verse 43 Jesus had used the second person plural ("I tell y o u that the kingdom of God shall be taken away from y o u...."). Perhaps, at the moment when this became clear to them, they may also have understood that in the parable that preceded it Jesus had been speaking especially to *them*. The result? 46. **But although they wanted to arrest him, they were afraid of the crowds, who considered him to be a prophet.** They would have liked to arrest Jesus on the spot, but they remembered the hosannas shouted in his honor, the popularity he enjoyed especially among the pilgrims that had come down from Galilee and among those who had witnessed the resurrection of Lazarus. To be sure, the people in general even

[744] See the following: F. F. Bruce, *op. cit.,* pp. 99, 100; G. H. Whitaker, "The Chief Cornerstone," *Exp,* Eighth Series (1921), pp. 470-472; J. M. Joffatt, "Three Notes on Ephesians," Eighth Series (1918), pp. 306-317; and F. G. Selwyn, *The First Epistle of St. Peter,* London, 1946, pp. 268 ff.

now did not honor Jesus for what he really was, the Messiah who had come to lay down his life as an atonement for sin (cf. Isa. 53), but by far the most of them considered him to be at least "a prophet." See 21:11. And that sufficed to keep the leaders from taking any radical measures against him before further careful planning.

Summary of Chapter 21

The Week of the Passion begins with the triumphal entry into Jerusalem on Sunday (21:1-11) and the cleansing of the temple on Monday (verses 12-17). For a brief summary of these two events see above, items 1, 2, 3, 5, 9, 10, 11, and 13, on pp. 762-772. The paragraph on the cursing of the fig tree follows in verses 18-22. This took place on Monday (even before the cleansing of the temple). The tree started to wither immediately. Yet the full effects were not visible until the following day. A chronological arrangement of these events is found in Mark 11:12-25. While Mark separates the two parts of the fig tree story, the first occurring *before,* the second the following day, hence *after* the temple cleansing, Matthew keeps the two parts together, telling it as one story. It was (Monday) morning, and Jesus was hungry. Though it was not yet the season for figs (Mark 11:13), this particular fig tree growing by the side of the road looked promising, for it was in foliage, indicating that it might have at least some early figs. But when Jesus went up to it he saw that it had nothing but leaves. So he cursed it, saying, "Never again let there be fruit from you." Result: it withered. Having cursed the fig tree Jesus cleansed the temple. The unfruitful fig tree, as Isa. 5 and Matt. 21:43 (cf. also Luke 13:6-9) show, symbolizes unfruitful Israel. By means of what the Lord did to the tree and to the temple he was predicting Israel's downfall. The disciples were astonished that the tree had withered so quickly. Jesus assures them that no task done in harmony with God's will is impossible for those whose faith does not waver.

When Jesus was teaching in the temple the chief priests and the elders asked him, "By what authority are you doing these things, and who gave you this authority?" (verses 23-27). Just what "things" they were referring to is not entirely certain, though all or most of the following must have been included: the triumphal entry, the cleansing of the temple, teaching and preaching the gospel there, and performing miracles. Christ's heavenly origin had been clearly set forth by John the Baptist. But the chief priests, elders, and scribes had not accepted John's testimony. However, by many of the common people John was regarded as having been a prophet. So Jesus asks a counter question, namely, "The baptism of John, where did it come from, from heaven or from men?" This question greatly embarrassed the leaders, for the reason indicated in verses 25, 26. So they answered, "We do not know." Jesus replied, "Neither do I tell y o u by what authority I do these things."

In the parable of The Two Sons (verses 28-32), the first of whom, having refused the father's request that he work in the vineyard, afterward repented; and the second of whom had promised much but accomplished nothing, Jesus pictured respectively penitent sinners and impenitent leaders.

In the parable of The Wicked Tenants (verses 33-46), who not only refused to give the owner his share of the vintage but even abused the servants who came to collect it, killing some of them, and who in the end murdered even the owner's beloved son, resulting in their own terrible destruction, Jesus pictured the Jews, as represented by their leaders. Though they had killed the prophets and were about to crucify Jesus, he at last would triumph over them, as predicted in Ps. 118:22, 23.

Outline of Chapter 22

Theme: *The Work Which Thou Gavest Him to Do*

CHAPTER XXII

22 1 Jesus responded and spoke to them again in parables, saying, 2 "The kingdom of heaven is like a king who gave a marriage feast for his son. 3 He sent his servants to summon those who had been invited to the wedding, but they were not willing to come. 4 He tried again and sent other servants, saying, 'Tell the invited guests, Look, I have prepared my banquet, my steers and fattened cattle have been butchered, and everything is ready; come to the wedding.' 5 But they paid no attention to it and went off, one to his farm, another to his place of business. 6 The rest grabbed the servants, treated them shamefully, and murdered them. 7 So the king's wrath was kindled, and having despatched his troops he destroyed those murderers and set fire to their city.

8 "Then he said to his servants, 'The wedding is ready, but those that were invited did not deserve the honor. 9 Therefore go to the country crossroads, and as many people as y o u can find invite to the wedding.' 10 And those servants went out on the roads and gathered all they could find, good and bad alike; and the wedding hall was filled with guests.

11 "Now when the king went in to view the guests he saw there a man who was not wearing a wedding robe. 12 He said to him, 'Friend, how did you get in here without a wedding robe?' But he was speechless. 13 Then the king said to his attendants, 'Bind him hand and foot and throw him into the most distant darkness; there shall be weeping and grinding of teeth.' 14 For many are called, but few chosen."

22:1-14 *The Marriage Feast of the King's Son*

It has already been shown (p. 22) that this parable is peculiar to Matthew's Gospel. It must not be confused with that of the Great Supper (Luke 14:15-24).

The little group of three parables of which The Marriage Feast is the last is arranged climactically. Not only will those who disobey God's command and reject his messenger (John the Baptist) never enter the kingdom if they continue in this state of impenitence (see the parable of The Two Sons, 21:28-32); and not only will the dreadful scoundrels who maltreat and murder God's ambassadors (the prophets) and even kill his only Son be brought to a dreadful end, while the privileges and opportunities of which they could have taken advantage are given to others (see the parable of The Wicked Tenants, 21:33-44); but far more definitely, the "city" of these impenitents will be destroyed by fire (A.D. 70), and the Gentiles will come pouring into the church. By no means all of them are blessed with everlasting life however. That inestimable blessing is only for those who wear the wedding robe (22:1-14).

The parable of The Royal Marriage is divided into three easily recognizable parts: *a.* the rejected invitation (verses 1-7); *b.* the filled wedding hall (verses 8-10); and *c.* the missing wedding robe (verses 11-14). For various titles given to this parable see p. 23.

1. Jesus responded and spoke to them again in parables, saying. . . . No question had been asked. Nevertheless the verb "answered" or "replied" is used, or else "responded." The last may well be the best, for though Jesus was not answering a question, he was responding to a situation, the attitude present within the hateful and embittered hearts of his enemies (21:45, 46). Once more, as so often previously, he is going to show them the inexcusable nature of this impenitence and the terrible result to which it leads. The phrase "in parables" probably means "by means of a parable" or "by means of figurative language." It is not necessary to press the use of the plural here. This plural is most likely idiomatic. The mere possibility, however, must be granted that there is a reference here to that which the author regards as being, from a certain angle, more than one parable. Yet, he can hardly have been thinking of the further parables found in chapters 24 and 25, for these did not follow immediately, and besides, were spoken to a more restricted audience, the disciples. If, as is only remotely possible, the author was actually thinking of more than one parable, could he have been referring to the fact that the present story illustration is really three parables rolled into one? Continued: **2. The kingdom of heaven is like a king** [745] **who gave a marriage feast for his son.** For "kingdom of heaven" see on 4:23; 13:43. The expression "is like" has been explained in the comments on 20:1. Also, in connection with 8:11, 12 it has been shown that the blessedness of the Messianic kingdom in its final phase—if one prefers: the joy to be experienced in the new heaven and earth where the reign of God in Christ will be exuberantly acknowledged by all the partakers—is often pictured under the symbolism of guests reclining together on couches at a table loaded with food, and communicating with each other and with the host in a spacious banqueting hall flooded with light.

That here in 22:1 ff. this feast is described as a *marriage* feast is also in keeping with Christ's earlier teaching and with many other passages in both Old and New Testament, as has been shown in connection with 9:15; see on that passage.

In the references to this feast the original at times uses the plural (verses 2, 3, 4, 9), at times the singular (verse 8), with little, if any, difference in

---

[745] "a certain king" (A.V.). This is another instance of the pleonastic use of ἄνθρω-πος; see footnote 663 on p. 704.

meaning. [746] The plural may have arisen from the fact that a celebration lasting several days (seven, according to Judg. 14:17) must have included many festive activities.

It is by no means certain that a figurative sense must also here be ascribed to the word "his son," as if the reference were to Jesus Christ. If this had been the case, would not this "son" have played a far more prominent role in the parable? He actually does assume such prominence in 21:37-40. But in 22:3-14, the son is never mentioned again. We must conclude, therefore, that the only—at least the main—reason why "a king" and "his son" are here mentioned is to emphasize the fact that this is indeed a very important marriage feast. It is a *royal* feast.

3, 4. He sent his servants to summon those who had been invited to the wedding, but they were not willing to come. He tried again and sent other servants, saying, Tell the invited guests, Look, I have prepared my banquet, my steers and fattened cattle have been butchered, and everything is ready; come to the wedding. These verses strongly remind one of the parable of The Wicked Tenants. In both parables the patience and persistence shown by the Sender is stressed.

This marvelous longsuffering of "the king," in the present parable, reveals itself in the fact that *a.* he first issues a "call" or general invitation; *b.* then he sends servants earnestly summoning the invited ones to come; and *c.* when the latter are unwilling to come he sends other servants, instructing them to present an even more urgent, moving appeal: all things are now ready, and there is no lack of food: butchered steers and fatted cattle!

That it was not unusual among the Jews first to send out a general invitation and then later to invite those that had been called appears not only from Esther 5:8; 6:14, but also from "the boast of the men of Jerusalem that no one of them went to a banquet unless he were twice invited." [747] In this parable, however, there were in all not less than *three* invitations!

With respect to the symbolical meaning of these three there is a wide difference of opinion. Most of the interpretations proceed from the assumption—which, in view of the resemblance of this parable to that of The Wicked Tenants, may well be correct—that a separate figurative meaning must be assigned to each of the three invitations. Assuming, then, that this assumption is correct, what is the meaning of each invitation?

---

[746] Do not we also speak of *wedding festivities* (plural) and *a wedding feast* (singular)? In our language even the word "wedding," used all by itself, can refer either to the solemnization of the marriage or to that plus the attendant festivities. The Dutch language avoids this ambiguity by differentiating between *huwelijk* (cf. *huwelijksvoltrekking, h.inzegening*) and *bruiloft*, the latter word alone referring to the festivities on the day when a marriage materializes or on the anniversary of that day.

[747] P. A. Micklem, *St. Matthew, with Introduction and Notes*, London, 1917, p. 210.

The "call" or first invitation for Israel to walk in the ways of the Lord did not *originally* reach that nation through any prophet, whether Moses, Samuel, Elijah, Isaiah, or any other. According to Scripture's own representation, that call came *directly* from God. It was God who called Abraham (Gen. 12:1 ff.; 13:14-18; 15:1-6; 17:1-21; 22:11-18), Isaac (Gen. 26:24); and Jacob (Gen. 28:13-15; 32:22-28; 46:2 ff.). It was God who called Moses (Exod. 3). And it was God whose voice Israel heard and who made a covenant with the people (Deut. 4:9-13, 32-36). Cf. Isa. 42:6; 43:1; 45:4; Hos. 11:1; Ezek. 16:1-14.

The "servants" sent first naturally suggest the Old Testament prophets, just as in the preceding parable (21:34, 35), for it was through Moses and Elijah, through Isaiah, Jeremiah, and all the other prophets, that God next addressed Israel. I can see no good reason to interpret these "servants" differently here than in the parable of The Wicked Tenants.

In general what was the reaction of the people who had received the call and the first special invitation? They were unwilling to come (Ps. 95:10; Isa. 1:2-15; 5:4; Jer. 7:25, 26; etc.).

The second group of servants naturally suggest John the Baptist, Jesus himself, and his "disciples" (twelve, seventy, Stephen, Paul, etc.).

But we should not spend too much time on details which, after all, do not touch the main point. That central thought, as has already been indicated but must here be repeated, is the patience of God, symbolized by the king. It is God who first calls, and then invites those who had been previously called. It is God who, when they refuse, does not even then immediately pour forth his wrath upon the obstinate refusers but makes still another urgent appeal. For further references to this divine patience and delight in imparting salvation to men see Jer. 7:13, 25; 11:7; 25:3, 4 passim; Ezek. 18:23, 32; 33:11; Luke 13:6-9; Rom. 2:4; 9:22; I Tim. 1:16; I Peter 3:20; II Peter 3:15.

The reaction of the invited guests to what may be called the third and most insistent invitation is related in verses 5, 6. **But they paid no attention to it and went off, one to his farm, another to his place of business. The rest grabbed the servants, treated them shamefully, and murdered them.** Two attitudes are indicated here: *a. indifference,* that is, far more interest in earthly matters than in heavenly, in material things than in spiritual, in the farm and the place of business than in the invitation to accept salvation full and free for soul and body throughout all eternity (for a parallel thought see Luke 14:18-20; 17:26-28); and *b. active hostility:* grabbing the servants, treating them shamefully, and even murdering some of them. Cf. Matt. 21:35, 36.

The fact that persecution of God's messengers had already occurred, was actually taking place, and was going to be the order of the day also during the years immediately following is clear from several passages. What had been the reaction of many, especially of the leaders, to John the Baptist? See Matt. 3:7-9; 11:18, 19; 21:25. What was—and was going to be—their attitude to Jesus? See Matt. 12:24; 16:21; 20:18; 21:38, 39; 27:20, 22; John 1:5-11; 5:18; 6:66. And to the disciples? See Matt. 10:16, 22, 25; John 16:33; Acts 4:3; 7:58-60; 8:1; 12:1-3; etc.

There is a limit to God's patience (Gen. 6:3; Prov. 29:1; Dan. 5:22-31; Matt. 21:40-44; Luke 13:9; Rev. 2:21, 22): **7. So the king's wrath was kindled, and having despatched his troops he destroyed those murderers and set fire to their city.** It appears that the invited guests had a city of their own. Dropping the figure, it is clear that the reference is to Jerusalem. Its destruction (A.D. 70) is here clearly predicted. See also 21:40-43; 23:37, 38; 24:1, 2, 15 ff; Luke 19:41-44.

As to the fulfilment, Jerusalem was taken by Titus, son of the emperor Vespasian (A.D. 69-79). The temple was destroyed. It is believed that more than a million Jews, who had crowded into the city, perished. As a political unit Israel ceased to exist. As a nation specially favored by the Lord it had reached the end of the road even long before the beginning of the Jewish War.

An ex-combatant and eye-witness, Josephus, almost immediately after the struggle between the Jews and the Romans had ended, began to write his *History of the Jewish War.* On the whole his narrative may be described as trustworthy, although a definitely pro-Roman bias cannot be denied. Of the seven "books" into which this work is divided one should read especially books IV-VI. A few excerpts from Josephus may illumine the fulfilment of Matt. 22:7, and thus also the passages itself:

"That building [the temple at Jerusalem], however, God long ago had sentenced to the flames; but now in the revolution of the time-periods the fateful day had arrived, the tenth of the month Lous, the very day on which previously it had been burned by the king of Babylon. . . . One of the soldiers, neither awaiting orders nor filled with horror of so dread an undertaking, but moved by some supernatural impulse, snatched a brand from the blazing timber and, hoisted up by one of his fellow soldiers, flung the fiery missile through a golden window. . . . When the flame arose, a scream, as poignant as the tragedy, went up from the Jews . . . now that the object which before they had guarded so closely was going to ruin" (VI. 250-253).

"While the sanctuary was burning . . . neither pity for age nor respect for rank was shown; on the contrary, children and old people, laity and priests alike were massacred" (VI. 271).

"The emperor ordered the entire city and sanctuary to be razed to the ground, except only the highest towers, Phasael, Hippicus, and Mariamne, and that part of the wall that enclosed the city on the west" (VI. 1).

The first act in the drama has ended. The parable's portion to which we gave the name "the rejected invitation," has been concluded. Here follows the second part, namely, "the filled wedding hall": **8-10. Then he said to his servants, The wedding is ready, but those that were invited did not deserve the honor. Therefore go to the country crossroads, and as many people as y o u can find invite to the wedding. And those servants went out on the roads and gathered all they could find, good and bad alike; and the wedding hall was filled with guests.** The king's plan, that his son shall have a good wedding, cannot be foiled. His will cannot be thwarted. In view of the fact that the former invitees have proved themselves unworthy—here probably litotes for "very wicked"—not deserving the honor that had been conferred upon them, let others be brought in. Let the servants, then, go out to the country, to the places where the main streets leading *out* of the city stop and *divide* (branch off) into side streets. [748] From all of these crossings or outlets let the servants pick up as many people as they can find, never mind whether the newly invited ones are in good standing with their fellow citizens or not.—The servants do as they had been instructed.

The meaning is clear. When the Jews who had been invited refuse to accept Christ, other people in great numbers are brought in. These others are mostly from the Gentiles (cf. 8:11, 12; 21:41), though Jews are not hereby excluded. The fact that both good and bad are brought into the kingdom or visible church has been explained in connection with the parable of The Dragnet; see on 13:47-50.

The fact that through the sacrifice of Christ and the leading of the Spirit salvation is now for *all,* entirely regardless of race, nationality, sex, social standing, etc., and that no nation—whether British, Jewish, Dutch, Swedish, German or whatever—has any *special* standing before God is clear also from such other passages as Matt. 28:19; Luke 24:47; John 10:16; Rom. 10:12, 13; I Cor. 7:19; Gal. 3:9, 29; Eph. 2:14, 18; Phil. 3:2; Col. 3:11; etc. What is probably the most comforting statement of all, in the present passage, is the one at the close of verse 10: "and the wedding was filled with guests."

We might feel that the parable, already in a sense a double one, could have ended here. For an excellent reason it does not. "Good and bad alike" had entered the wedding hall, so we have been assured. It is now made clear, however, that this "good and bad" has reference only to human standards of judgment. It does not mean that in the final analysis those who in God's eyes are and remain "bad" are destined for the joys of the new heaven and earth. Verses 11-14, "the missing wedding robe," will make this clear. This closing paragraph begins as follows: **11. Now when the king went in to view the**

---

[748] Justice is thus done to both of the prefixes (διά and ἐκ here ἐξ) of the compound διέξοδοι, as well as to its base.

[749] For the verb θεάομαι (here aor. infin. θεάσασθαι) and its synonyms see N.T.C. on the Gospel according to John, Vol. I, footnote 33 on p. 85.

guests he saw there a man who was not wearing a wedding robe. The king went in to view the guests, to feast his eyes on them. [749] As his eyes move from one person to the next, suddenly his countenance darkens; his smile is replaced by a frown, for he is looking at a man who is not wearing a wedding garment.

At this point the question may well be asked, "What else could the king expect?" Do not verses 8-10 create the distinct impression that these guests had been rushed from streets and street corners to the wedding hall, where the food was standing *ready*? Is not the "solution" proposed by some interpreters, namely, that before coming to the wedding all except one of the newly invited individuals had first gone home to change clothes, a kind of subterfuge? It must be borne in mind that most of these people were probably drawn from the underprivileged ranks. Cf. Luke 14:21-23. It is a question whether they even owned what today would be called "Sunday clothes," or that they had the money to buy them. Besides, even if they did, there had been no time either to make or to purchase such costly robes.

There is only one solution, as far as I can see, that will help us out of this difficulty. It is an old one. Until someone offers something better it must stand. It is that, by the command of the king and from his bountiful supplies, at the very entrance of the wedding hall a wedding robe had been offered to each guest. All except this one person had accepted the robe. This one man, however, had looked at his own robe, had perhaps lightly brushed it off with his hand, and had then told the attendant, "My own robe is good enough. I don't need the one you're offering me." Then, in an attitude of self-satisfaction and defiance, he had marched to the table, where he was presently reclining; or from which, when the king entered, he, along with the other guests, had just now arisen.

The objection to this theory is that nowhere in text or context is there any mention of this offer of a wedding robe to entering guests. We do know, however, *a.* that in all probability guests such as these did not themselves have such a robe and could not have obtained it in any other way; *b.* that the king expected each guest to be decked in a robe fit to be worn to a royal wedding; *c.* that the man who lacked this robe was not able to offer any excuse for not having one (verse 12); *d.* that among the many scriptural passages which have been cited by those who favor the idea of an offered robe there are at least a few that may well be considered applicable, by way of analogy, to the present situation: "He said to the man in charge of the wardrobe, Bring out the vestments for the servants of Baal" (II Kings 10:22); "Let us be glad and triumphant, and let us give him the glory, for the wedding of the Lamb has come, and his bride has made herself ready: *fine linen was given her to wear,* bright and clean, for fine linen indicates the righteous deeds of the saints" (Rev. 19:7, 8; cf. Isa. 61:10); and *e.* that historical evidence indicating that in the Near East even in post-biblical times a person who wished to enter the king's presence was required to wear a robe sent to him by the monarch is not completely lacking. [750]

Proceeding on the assumption, therefore, that such a garment had been offered to each guest and that the king expected the offered robes to be accepted and worn, his speech and action with respect to the man who had treated the royal order with contempt is not surprising: **12, 13. He said to him, Friend, how did you get in here without a wedding robe? But he was speechless. Then the king said to the attendants, Bind him hand and foot and throw him into the most distant darkness; there shall be weeping and grinding of teeth.** In order to give the man an opportunity to justify himself if he can do so, the king addresses him in a not unfriendly manner, and pauses for a reply. But the man, realizing that he has no ground to stand on and that any excuse would be useless, is reduced to utter silence. [751] The result is that the king orders him to be bound hand and foot and to be cast into a region of total darkness, a darkness that is in sharp contrast with the light that fills the wedding hall. For "there shall be weeping and grinding of teeth" (thus also in 8:12; 13:42, 50; 24:51; 25:30; Luke 13:28) see on 8:12.

Great emphasis is placed on the man's own responsibility and guilt. Does this mean now that the others—those who did accept the robe and are wearing it—have themselves to thank for their deed of obedience? Not at all: **14. For many are called, but few chosen.** The gospel call goes forth far and wide. It reaches ever so many. Most of them are like the man in the parable: they hear but do not heed. In comparison with those many that are lost there are but few that are saved, that is, few that are chosen from eternity to inherit life everlasting. Salvation, then, in the final analysis, is not a human accomplishment but the gift of God's sovereign grace. Cf. Luke 12:32; John 6:39, 44; Eph. 1:4.

The question is asked, "Just what is meant by the wedding robe, apart from which everlasting blessedness is impossible?" Passages illustrating the figurative use of a *robe* or *garment* are found in both the Old and the New Testament. See Job 29:14; Ps. 132:9; Isa. 11:5; 61:10; Rom. 13:14; Gal. 3:27; Eph. 4:22, 24; Col. 3:8-14; Rev. 19:8; to mention only a few. The charge to put on such a robe cannot mean that a person should base his hope for salvation on his own goodness or moral fitness, for this would be contrary to all of Scripture's teaching (Job 9:2; Isa. 64:6; Rom. 3:9-18, 23, 24; Eph. 2:8; Rev. 7:14). Does this mean, then, that the wedding garment is to be limited to "the imputed righteousness which is ours by faith"? [752] Not

---

[750] On this last point (*e.*) see W. M. Taylor, *op. cit.*, pp. 155, 156.

[751] Note ἐφιμώθη 3rd per. sing. aor. indic. passive of φιμόω; active in verse 34 and in I Peter 2:15, *put to silence*. The verb is used in I Cor. 9:9; I Tim. 5:18 with respect to the *muzzling* of oxen; in Mark 1:25; Luke 4:35, as a command addressed to demons, "*Be silent*"; and in Mark 4:39, as a similar order directed to the raging sea.

[752] See Lenski, *op. cit.*, p. 834.

at all. God not only *imputes* but also *imparts* righteousness to the sinner whom he pleases to save. Although these two must be distinguished, they must not be separated. Careful study of those passages in Scripture (see above: the list beginning with Job 29:14) that mention the robe with which the sinner must be clothed makes it clear that not only guilt must be forgiven but also the old way of life must be laid aside and the new life to the glory of God must take its place. Briefly, the sinner must, by God's grace, "put on Christ" (Gal. 3:27). There must be a complete turnabout, a thorough-going renewal or "conversion," exactly as Jesus himself had taught (Matt. 4:17), and as the apostles after him were going to teach.

The one thought of the parable, then, is this: "Accept God's gracious invitation, lest while others enter into glory you be lost. But remember that membership in the visible church does not guarantee salvation. Complete renewal (including both justification and sanctification), the putting on of Christ, is what is necessary."

---

15 Then the Pharisees went and plotted how they might trap him in what he said. 16 And they sent to him their disciples along with those of the Herodians, saying, "Teacher, we know that you are truthful and that you truthfully teach God's way, and court no man's favor, for you are impartial. 17 Tell us then what you think: Is it lawful to pay a poll-tax to Caesar, or not?" 18 But Jesus, aware of their wickedness, said, "Why put me to the test, y o u hypocrites? 19 Show me the poll-tax coin." So they brought him a denarius. 20 He said to them, "Whose likeness and inscription is this?" 21 "Caesar's," they replied. Then he said to them, "Then render to Caesar what is due to Caesar, and to God what is due to God." 22 Now when they heard it, they were astonished, and they left him and went away.

23 That same day some Sadducees, who deny that there is a resurrection, approached him with the question, 24 "Teacher, Moses said, 'If a man dies childless, his brother, as next of kin, must marry the widow and raise up children for his brother.' 25 Now seven brothers were (living) among us. The first got married, died, and having no children left his wife to his brother. 26 The same thing happened also to the second and to the third, down to the seventh. 27 Last of all the woman herself died. 28 In the resurrection, therefore, to which of the seven shall she be wife? for they all had her." 29 Jesus answered and said to them, "Y o u are deceiving yourselves, because y o u know neither the Scriptures nor the power of God. 30 For in the resurrection they neither marry nor are given in marriage, but are like angels in heaven. 31 Now concerning the resurrection of the dead, have y o u not read what was spoken to y o u by God:

32 'I am the God of Abraham and the God of Isaac and the God of Jacob'? He is not the God of the dead but of the living." 33 And when the crowds heard it, they were astounded at his teaching.

34 Now when the Pharisees heard that he had silenced the Sadducees they gathered together. 35 And one of them, a law expert, asked him a question, testing him: 36 "Teacher, which is the great commandment in the law?" 37 He answered him,

"You shall love the Lord your God with all your heart and with all your soul and with all your mind.

38 This is the great and first commandment. 39 And a second is like this:

You shall love your neighbor as yourself.

40 On these two commandments depend the whole law and the prophets."

41 Now while the Pharisees were gathered together, Jesus asked them, 42 "What is y o u r opinion of the Christ? Whose son is he?" They said to him, "David's." 43 He said to them, "How then does David, in the Spirit, call him Lord, saying:
44 'The Lord said to my Lord,
   Sit at my right hand
   Until I put your enemies under your feet'?
45 "If David then calls him Lord, how is he his son?" 46 And no one was able to say a word in reply, nor from that day on did anyone dare to ask him another question.

22:15-46 *Captious Questions and Authoritative Answers*
also
Christ's Own Question
verses 15-22	Cf. Mark 12:13-17; Luke 20:20-26
verses 23-33	Cf. Mark 12:18-27; Luke 20:27-40
verses 34-40	Cf. Mark 12:28-34
verses 41-46	Cf. Mark 12:35-37; Luke 20:41-44

Is it lawful to pay a poll-tax to Caesar, or not?

15. Then the Pharisees went and plotted how they might trap him in what he said. Earlier on that very day Jesus had, by means of a counter-question, defeated the leaders (21:23-32), and had even exposed them as being murderers (21:39; 22:7). However, this did not bring them to repentance. Instead of crying, "O God, be merciful to us, sinners" (cf. Luke 18:13), they became all the more determined to kill Jesus. Yet, they are afraid to attack him personally. They fear the people. So they go into collusion and in an underhanded way plot how they may trip him up [753] in what he says.

16. And they sent to him their disciples along with those of the Herodians. Instead of confronting Jesus themselves these Pharisees send some of their students. Did they think, perhaps, that Jesus might be more sympathetic toward these younger men, and that for this very reason it might be easier to trap him? Also, either these leaders themselves or their disciples—but in the latter case, at the leaders' suggestion—persuade some other young men, disciples of the Herodians, to go with them. What a strange combination: *a.* Pharisees, who were—or made believe that they were—very concerned about keeping God's law, and *b.* partisans of the Herod family, who cared very little about the divine commandments. These two groups unite against Jesus. Each has its own reason for wishing to get rid of the prophet from Nazareth. Did not his teaching imply a denunciation of the self-righteousness of the first group and of the worldlimindedness of the second? Besides, the Herodians cannot have been happy with Jesus' *royal* entry into Jerusalem, nor

---

[753] παγιδεύσωσι 3rd per. pl. aor. subjunctive of παγιδεύω, to set a παγίς (trap, snare); cf. πήγνυμι, *to make fast, fix.* The English words *fasten, fang, compact* may be related to this.

the Pharisees with his entry as the "Son of David," the Messiah. Also, both envy Jesus because, as they see it, his influence over the people is becoming too pronounced.

There was still another reason why the combination "disciples of the Pharisees along with those of the Herodians" was clever. That reason has to do with the question which the young enquirers were going to ask Jesus, "Is it lawful to pay a poll-tax to Caesar, or not?" The answer which the Herodians would have given was, "Yes, by all means." The very position and prestige of King Herod Antipas and his partisans depended, to a not inconsiderable extent, upon the payment of tribute. Hence they favored the tax, and, together with it, the political *status quo.* The Zealots, a party not mentioned here, were bitterly opposed to the tax, and declared that they recognized only one Master, even God. [754] They were even willing to go to war in defense of this principle. The Pharisees took a similar, though somewhat less fanatic, position. In general, their hatred for the Herodians was even greater than that for the Romans. But they resented having to pay taxes to a foreign ruler, and this all the more because that ruler demanded honors and laid claim to titles that belonged to God alone. In the eyes of strictly "religious" Pharisees the emperor who demanded this tribute was a blasphemer.

The tribute to which the present passage refers was a capitation tax which, after the deposition of Archelaus (A.D. 6), was collected by the procurator from every adult male in Judea, and was paid into the imperial treasury. "Is it lawful for the Jew to pay this poll-tax?" If Jesus answers "Yes," he could well be alienating not only the Zealots and Pharisees but every devout and freedom-loving Jew. If he answers, "No," he exposes himself to the charge of treason (cf. Luke 20:20; 23:2). So, also for this reason it was clever to arrange for a mixed committee, consisting of young Pharisees and Herodians, to question Jesus.

This committee must have received detailed instructions as to just how to approach the Master. We can hardly imagine that the flattering introduction by means of which they preluded their question was original with them. They came to Jesus ... saying, **Teacher, we know that you are truthful and that you truthfully teach God's way, and court no man's favor, for you are impartial.** They recognize him as a "teacher" in Israel. Moreover, they say, as it were, "You are a teacher on whom the people can depend, for, as everybody knows, you yourself are reliable, and you faithfully expound to the people the 'way' [755] or will of God." They continue (literally): "and not is it a care to you concerning no one," probably meaning, "And you do not allow yourself to be influenced by anyone's opinion," or, "And you are not

---

[754] Josephus *The Jewish War* II. 117, 118; *Antiquities* XVIII. 23.
[755] For "way" see on 21:32.

afraid of anyone," or, "And you court no one's favor." They conclude their introduction by saying (again literally according to a Greek and Hebrew idiom), "For you do not look at the face of men," in other words, "You are impartial." See I Sam. 6:7; also N.T.C. on Gal. 2:6. Thus these "spies" (Luke 20:20) veil their real intention, which was to trap Jesus in a statement which he was expected to make. They hide their purpose under a cloak of flattering compliments. Then, as if they were enquirers searching sincerely for information, they spring their question: 17. **Tell us then what you think: Is it lawful to pay a poll-tax to Caesar, or not?**

One hardly knows what to admire more in Christ's reaction, whether it is his penetrating insight into the hearts and motives of men (see verse 18), or his marvelous mental alertness in so quickly giving an answer that establishes a principle whereby every person should be guided in his search for the proper relationship to both the earthly and the heavenly kingdom (verses 19-21): 18. **But Jesus, aware of their wickedness, said, Why put me to the test, y o u hypocrites?** Jesus had used this word "hypocrites" before (see on 6:2, 5, 16; 7:5; 15:7). He is going to use it again (several times in chapter 23; then also in 24:51). It suited the present situation exactly, for a hypocrite says one thing but means something else. He *pretends* to do one thing but *intends* to do another. He is play-acting, dissembling. He is hiding his real face *under* a mask. Jesus adds, 19. **Show me the poll-tax coin.** [756] **So they brought him a denarius.** A denarius or denar was a Roman silver coin, about equal in value to a Greek drachma. Its standard weight was 60 grains. For further information with respect to it see on 5:26, footnote 290; and on 17:24; 18:28; 20:2, 9, 10, 13. Because of the large caravans of pilgrims streaming into Jerusalem from various parts of the empire, to attend the Passover, it must have been easy to produce a denarius immediately. That this coin was also widely circulated among the Jews of Palestine and was very well known among them appears from the many references to it in the Gospels.

Jesus, then, is holding this denar in his hand. By this very act of asking for it and having it in his hand he is directing the attention of the spectators to it; i.e., to the head shown on the coin and to the legend accompanying it. He does so even more by the question he is about to raise. The Herodian disciples are perhaps asking themselves, "Is he going to belittle the image or the writing on this coin, and is he going to forbid using the coin for paying the tax? If he does, we've got him." And the students of the Pharisees may have been thinking, "Aside from the horror of actually being required to pay

---

[756] Note νόμισμα, in which one can detect the word νόμος law; hence, money or coin which by law entered into common use; currency; and κήνσου, gen. of κήνσος, tax or tribute; in this case poll tax. For this word see on 17:25, footnote 632 on p. 679. The entire expression therefore means "coin by which the tribute or poll tax is paid," "poll tax coin." The denarius was in fact minted with a view to the poll tax.

this tribute money, isn't the very appearance of the 'image' on the coin a transgression of the second commandment? And isn't the legend blasphemous? If he endorses the use of this kind of money for the purpose of supporting the self-glorifying foreign oppressor, will not all enthusiastic nationalists run away from him?"

Whether the coin dated from the reign of Augustus or of Tiberius, either way the emperor is ascribing glory to himself. A denarius from the reign of Tiberius pictures on its *obverse side* the head of the emperor. On the *reverse side* he is seated on a throne. He wears a diadem on his head and is clothed as a highpriest.

The inscriptions, with abbreviations as shown, and with V representing our present U, are as shown:

Obverse	*Reverse*
TICAESARDIVI AVGFAVGVSTVS	PONTIF MAXIM
Translated:	Translated:
TIBERIUS CAESAR AUGUSTUS	HIGHEST PRIEST
SON OF THE DIVINE AUGUSTUS	

All eyes are on Jesus, and the tension must have been tremendous when **20, 21. He said to them, Whose likeness and inscription is this? Caesar's, they replied. Then he said to them, Then render to Caesar what is due to Caesar, and to God what is due to God.** Explanation:

a. He was not evading the issue, but was clearly saying, "Yes, pay the tax." Honoring God does not mean dishonoring the emperor by refusing to pay for the privileges—a relatively orderly society, police protection, good roads, courts, etc., etc.—one enjoys. Cf. I Tim. 2:2; I Peter 2:17. Thus, no truthful charge of sedition could be made against Jesus.

b. He was qualifying his "yes" answer by stating that the emperor should be paid (given back) only what was *his due*. Hence, the divine honor which the emperor claimed but which is due to God alone must be refused. [757] How could the Pharisees find any fault with that? Besides, this word was a warning to all—from the most exalted emperor to the subject lowest in rank—not to claim undue honors. Cf. II Kings 18:19—19:37 (II Chron. 32:9-23; Isa. 36, 37); Dan. 4:28-32; 5; Acts 12:20-23.

c. By adding "and to God what is due to God" Jesus was stressing the fact that all the service, gratitude, glory, etc. due to God should be constantly and gladly accorded to him. Nothing must be withheld. See, for example, Ps. 29; 95; 96; 103-105; 116; John 17:4; Rom. 11:33-36; I Cor. 6:20; 10:31; 16:1, 2; II Cor. 9:15. One does not give God what is his due by plotting to

---

[757] A Deissmann (*op. cit.*, p. 252) correctly observes that in this passage Jesus showed no disrespect to the emperor but by distinguishing so sharply between Caesar and God made a tacit protest against the worship of the emperor.

destroy his beloved Son! But this was exactly what these spies and their teachers were trying to do.

d. By drawing a distinction between "what is due to Caesar" and "what is due to God" Jesus was rejecting the very claim of Caesar, a claim made on the coin and otherwise, to the effect that his was not only a physical kingdom but also a spiritual (note: "Pontifex Maximus," i.e., "Highest Priest"). Cf. John 18:36. Naturally God is Sovereign over all (Dan. 4:34, 35). The emperor, to be sure, should be respected and obeyed whenever his will does not clash with the divine will. See Rom. 13:1-7. But when there is a clash the rule laid down in Acts 5:29 must be followed.

By means of this answer Jesus had discomfited his enemies. We are not surprised to read: **22. Now when they heard it, they were astonished.** They had not expected this kind of an answer. In spite of themselves they were filled with awe and wonder. Cf. John 7:46. Were they converted? They were not. We read: **and they left him and went away.**

In the resurrection whose wife shall she be?

23, 24. That same day some Sadducees, who deny that there is a resurrection, approached him with the question, Teacher, Moses said, If a man dies childless, his brother, as next of kin, must marry the widow and raise up children for his brother. The Sadducees now make their onslaught against Jesus. See also 16:1, and N.T.C. on John 11:49. Their beliefs, denial of the immortality of the soul and of the resurrection of the body, relation to the Pharisees, etc., have been discussed in connection with 3:7; see on that passage. They were the worldly people of their day, and often behaved in an uncouth manner. In view of the fact that they are going to poke fun of the doctrine of the resurrection, it is understandable that they come all by themselves. The Pharisees, since they as well as Jesus believed in the resurrection, could not have joined them in this attack. The Sadducees approach Jesus "that same day," the day which in Matthew begins at 21:20 and probably continues until 26:5, a remarkable day indeed, the Tuesday of Passion Week.

The Sadducees begin their attack with the phrase, "Moses said." The reference to the great law-giver, Moses, must serve to add weight to their argument. It should be borne in mind that this sect regarded the Pentateuch as being higher in value than the other books of the Old Testament. They now make Deut. 25:5, 6 the springboard of their question. In that passage the law of "levirate [758] marriage" is given to Israel. According to this law, if a wife loses her husband before any male child has been born, the brother of that husband—or else the nearest of kin—must marry the widow, so that the

---

[758] *Levirate* is from the Latin *levir* (for devir; cf. Greek δαήρ), a husband's brother; hence, brother-in-law.

first child born of this marriage may be counted as a child of the deceased, and the latter's line may not die out. Disobedience to this command was frowned upon (Deut. 25:7-10). Half-hearted obedience, so that a man was willing to marry the widow but not to raise offspring by her since such a child could not be counted as his own, was in the case of Onan punished with death (Gen. 38:8-10). For an interesting application of the law of levirate marriage see Ruth 4:1-8. To what extent this law was still being obeyed during Christ's sojourn on earth is not clear.

The Sadducees, then, make use of this commandment in order to show how thoroughly absurd, as they see it, is belief in the resurrection of the body. Whether the story which they are about to relate was a report of an actual event, as some commentators believe, let the reader judge for himself. I, for one, am inclined to believe that they fabricated it. They say: **25-28. Now seven brothers were (living) among us. The first got married, died, and having no children left his wife to his brother. The same thing happened also to the second and to the third, down to the seventh. Last of all the woman herself died. In the resurrection, therefore, to which of the seven shall she be wife? for they all had her.** Provided that their basic assumption—namely, that married life continues in the hereafter—was correct, two husbands would have been sufficient to prove their point. But seven makes the story more interesting and might also make belief in the resurrection seem even more absurd. Think of it: when the dead arise, this woman—husband-killer?—will have seven husbands! Of course, that cannot, must not, be. She is allowed to have only one, but which one?

29. Jesus answered and said to them, Y o u are deceiving yourselves, [759] **because y o u know neither the Scriptures nor the power of God.** Had they known the Scriptures, they would have known that there is nothing in Deut. 25:5, 6 that makes it applicable to the life hereafter, and they would also have known that the Old Testament in various passages teaches the resurrection of the body (more on that in connection with verses 31, 32). And had they recognized the power of God (Rom. 4:17; Heb. 11:19), they would have understood that God is able to raise the dead in such a manner that marriage will no longer be needed (for more on this see verse 30).

Proof for the statement that the basic premise of the argument which the Sadducees have been advancing is erroneous and that they have failed to figure with the power of God is furnished in verse **30. For in the resurrection they neither marry nor are given in marriage, but are like angels in heaven.** The glorious resurrection body—Jesus says nothing about the resurrection of the wicked—is going to be immortal. Since there will be no death,

---

[759] Or: "Y o u are mistaken." The verb πλανάω, in the active: *to cause to wander;* here πλανᾶσθε, with middle sense, reminds one of a *planet* or *wanderer*. A grossly mistaken person is mentally *wandering*.

the race will not have to be reproduced. Marriage, accordingly, will be a matter of the past. In not marrying and not being given in marriage the blessed will therefore resemble the angels, for they too do not marry. The saved will be like the angels *in this one respect;* yes, like the angels whose very existence the Sadducees also deny (Acts 23:8), and this in spite of the fact that the Pentateuch, accepted by them, teaches their existence (Gen. 19:1, 15; 28:12; 32:1)! Does not verse 30, taken in its entirety, and in connection with what is known of the beliefs of the Sadducees, prove that these men know neither the Scriptures nor the power of God?

Although the Sadducees ridicule a wonderful truth accepted and taught by Jesus, namely, that of the resurrection of the dead, he does not refuse to impart needed instruction to them on this very subject: **31, 32. Now concerning the resurrection of the dead, have y o u not read what was spoken to y o u by God:**

I am the God of Abraham and the God of Isaac and the God of Jacob? He is not the God of the dead but of the living. "Have y o u not read?" says Jesus (cf. 12:3, 5; 19:4; 21:16, 42). Certainly those who try to base their argument on Scripture (Deut. 25:5, 6) should know Scripture! They should be acquainted with Scripture as a whole, not just with one passage, which they then misapply. Now it is true that the Sadducees did not have the New Testament, which mentions the resurrection (whether of Jesus himself or of his people, or even of all the dead) again and again (Matt. 12:39, 40; 16:21; 17:22; 20:19; 21:42; 25:31 ff.; 28:1-10; Mark 16:1-8; Luke 24; John 5:28, 29; 11:24; 20; 21; Acts 2:24-36; 4:10, 11; 17:31, 32; Rom. 1:4; I Cor. 15; Phil. 3:20, 21; I Thess. 4:16; I Peter 1:3; Rev. 20:11-15, to mention but a few of all the many passages in which this doctrine is taught). But even the Old Testament is not lacking in references to the bodily resurrection. Clearest, perhaps, are Ps. 16:9-11 (interpreted by Peter in Acts 2:27, 31) and Dan. 12:2. Worthy of consideration are also Job 14:14; 19:25-27; Ps. 17:15; 73:24-26; Isa. 26:19; Ezek. 37:1-14; Hos. 6:2, 13:14 (cf. I Cor. 15:55); passages which, though not always directly teaching the resurrection of the body, may well imply belief in this truth. Take for example, Ps. 73:24-26, which clearly teaches the blessed after-death existence of the believer's soul in heaven. Does not this very existence of the soul in the intermediate state demand the resurrection of the body? Two facts certainly point in that direction: *a.* the creation of man as "body and soul" (Gen. 2:7), and *b.* this very passage, "He is not the God of the dead but of the living." Note also that Abraham surely believed in the possibility of a physical resurrection (Heb. 11:19).

Jesus, however, refers to another passage, namely, Exod. 3:6, "I am the God of Abraham. . . ," and implies that since God is not the God of the dead but of the living, the conclusion is that Abraham, Isaac, and Jacob are still alive, and are awaiting a glorious resurrection.

Attempts have been made to rob Christ's argument of its value. It has been said, for example, that the expression, "the God of Abraham" simply means that while Abraham was on earth he worshiped Jehovah. However, a study of the context in which Exod. 3:6 and all similar passages (see Gen. 24:12, 27, 48; 26:24; 28:13; 32:9; 46:1, 3, 4; 48:15, 16; 49:25; etc.) occur, quickly proves that the One who reveals himself as "the God of Abraham . . ." is the unchangeable, eternal covenant God who blesses, loves, encourages, protects, etc. his people, and whose favors do not suddenly stop when a person dies but go with that person beyond death (Ps. 16:10, 11; 17:5; 73:23-26).

Another fact must be mentioned in this connection. The men with whom this immutable Jehovah (Exod. 3:6, 14; Mal. 3:6) established an everlasting covenant (Gen. 17:7) were Israelites, not Greeks. According to the Greek (and afterward also the Roman) conception, the body is merely the prison-house of the soul. See N.T.C. on I and II Thessalonians, pp. 110, 111. The Hebrew conception, product of special revelation, is entirely different. Here God deals with man as whole, not only with his soul or merely with his body. On the contrary, when God blesses his child he enriches him with physical as well as spiritual benefits (Deut. 28:1-14; Neh. 9:21-25; Ps. 104:14, 15; 107; 136; and many similar passages). He loves him body and soul. He is going to send his beloved Son in order to ransom him *completely*. The body, accordingly, shares with the soul the honor of being "the sanctuary of the Holy Spirit" (I Cor. 6:19, 20). The body is "for the Lord, and the Lord for the body" (I Cor. 6:13). God loves the entire person, and the declaration, "I am the God of Abraham and the God of Isaac and the God of Jacob" (note the triple occurrence of the word "God," mentioned separately in connection with each of the three to stress personal relationship with each) certainly implies that their bodies will not be left to the worms but will one day be gloriously resurrected. The burden of proof is entirely on the person who denies this. See also H. W. Robinson, *The People and the Book*, Oxford, 1925, p. 353 f.

33. And when the crowds heard it, they were astounded[760] **at his teaching.** The people were filled with awe and wonder. They knew that Jesus had again triumphed gloriously over his opponents.

Which is the great commandment in the law?

34. Now when the Pharisees heard that he had silenced the Sadducees they gathered together. Jesus had *silenced* (see on verse 12) the Sadducees. His victory must have pleased the Pharisees, for the latter, as well as Jesus, believed in a bodily resurrection, the doctrine denied by the Sadducees. Yet, from another viewpoint many of the Pharisees cannot have been too pleased,

---

[760] For the verb ἐξεπλήσσοντο see on 7:28.

for they did not want their enemy's influence with the general public to be strengthened. So, once again they assembled themselves [761] around Jesus in order to test him. This time, however, they do not, as in verse 15, send some of their disciples and some disciples of the Herodians to Jesus, but quiz him more directly, that is, through one of their own number and rank: **35, 36. And one of them, a law expert, asked him a question, testing him: Teacher, which is the great commandment in the law?** When Matthew wishes to say something about an expert in, and teacher of, the Mosaic law, taken in its broadest sense, he uses the word *scribe* to indicate such a person (see on 2:4; 7:28, 29). So does Mark. Luke uses both *scribe* and *law-expert* ("lawyer"). Here, for once—it is the only exception—Matthew writes *law-expert* [762] (cf. Zenas, Titus 3:13). Just why he makes this exception is not known. It may have been simply for stylistic variation. Another possibility is that Matthew wishes to tell us that here was a law-expert who really deserved the title. However, this may be, we receive a favorable impression of this man, not only because he asked a worthwhile question, for which Jesus does not rebuke him in any way (contrast verse 18), but also because he of his own accord approvingly repeats Christ's answer, for which he receives praise (see Mark 12:32-34). [763] Having learned from many previous passages how very hostile the Pharisees and scribes were toward Jesus (9:3; 15:1, 2; 16:21; 20:18; 21:15, 16; 22:15), and how he, in turn, condemns them, a fact of which we shall be reminded seven times over in chapter 23, we find it surprising that this not unfriendly—shall we say "noble"?—law-expert or scribe was chosen to represent the Pharisees in testing Jesus. Was it because they did not really know this man? Was he hostile at first and did he become deeply impressed by Christ's answer, so that he then and there experienced a change of mind toward this Teacher? Or does the reason for the Pharisees' selection of this man to represent them lie even deeper: they did indeed know him rather thoroughly, and sent him, thinking, *"him* Jesus will not suspect, and we may still be able to trip up our enemy because of the *answer* he will give"? We do not know.

The question asked by this law-expert was one that could be expected from him and from the men he represented. The rabbis, devoted to hairsplitting legalism, carried on lengthy debates about the commandments, arguing whether any particular one was great or small, heavy or light. For details see on 5:19 and on 15:1 ff. It was natural, therefore, that they often

---

[761] συνήχθησαν 3rd per. pl. aor. indic. passive of συνάγω, here probably with middle sense: *gathered (themselves) together, assembled themselves.* From the same verb is also συνηγμένων (verse 41), gen. pl. perf. passive participle: *having gathered themselves together, were gathered together.*

[762] The text, however, is not entirely certain. Some textual authorities omit the word.

[763] Luke 10:25-28 is a parallel only in a secondary sense. It parallels the summary of the law. But the circumstances are different and so is the story itself.

debated the question, "Which [764] —of the 613 commandments, 248 of them positive, 365 negative—was "the great," here in the sense of a superlative, "the greatest," [765] one.

To this question Jesus gives an unforgettably beautiful reply:

37-40. He answered him,

You shall love the Lord your God with all your heart and with all your soul and with all your mind.

This is the great and first commandment. And a second is like this:

You shall love your neighbor as yourself.

On these two commandments depend the whole law and the prophets.

Jesus here teaches that:

a. The whole duty of man, the whole moral-spiritual law, can be summed up in one word: *love*. Cf. Rom. 13:9, 10; I Cor. 13.

b. This love should be directed toward God (Deut. 6:5) and toward man (Lev. 19:18). In the Sermon on the Mount the obligation to love is set forth in greater detail (see especially 5:43-48; chapter 6; and 7:1-12).

c. Heart, soul, and mind must co-operate in loving God. The *heart* is the hub of the wheel of man's existence, the mainspring of all his thoughts, words, and deeds (Prov. 4:23). The *soul*—the word used in the original has a variety of meanings (see footnote 334 on p. 349)—is here probably the seat of man's emotional activity; the *mind,* not only of his purely intellectual life but also of his disposition or attitude. In the Hebrew original (and also in the LXX) of Deut. 6:5 the reading is "heart, soul, and might (or: power)." Mark 12:30 has "heart, soul, mind, and strength." Cf. Luke 10:27. No essential difference is intended. We must not begin to over-analyze. What is meant in all these passages is that man should love God with all the "faculties" with which God has endowed him.

d. Man must use all these powers to the full; note triple "all ... all ... all," or "whole ... whole ... whole." The point is that God's whole-hearted love must not be answered in a half-hearted manner. When God loves, he loves the world; when he gives, he gives his Son, hence himself. See N.T.C. on John 3:16. He gives him up; he spares him not. Greater love is impossible (John 15:13; Rom. 5:6-10; II Cor. 8:9). Surely, *the response* to such love must not be less than that indicated in Rom. 11:33-36; I Cor. 6:20; II Cor. 9:15; Eph. 5:1, 2; Phil. 2:1-18; Col. 3:12-17.

e. This commandment is called the great(est) because it epitomizes the

---

[764] The translation "what kind of?" is probably an unnecessary overrefinement. The adjective ποῖος, generally "(of) what kind?" (Rom. 3:27; I Cor. 15:35; I Peter 1:11; etc.), at times simply has the meaning "which?" or "what?" See also Acts 23:34.

[765] Not only the comparative μείζων (18:1; see footnote 638 on p. 686) can have the sense of a superlative, but so can also the positive μέγας, here fem. μεγάλη. Cf. John 7:37. In the New Testament the superlative μέγιστος is found only in II Peter 1:4, and there in the sense of "very great."

most excellent response to the Most Wonderful Being, and is basic to all other genuine love.

f. "A second commandment which is similar to it" resembles the first, because it too requires love. Moreover, this love toward the neighbor, who is God's image-bearer, flows forth from the love toward God (I John 4:21; see also 5:43; 7:12; 19:19).

g. This twofold command (love for God and for the neighbor) is the peg on which the whole "law and the prophets" hang. Remove that peg, and all is lost, for the entire Old Testament, with its commandments and covenants, prophecies and promises, types and testimonies, invitations and exhortations, points to the love of God which demands the answer of love in return.

What is y o u r opinion of the Christ?

41, 42. Now while the Pharisees were gathered together, Jesus asked them, What is y o u r opinion of the Christ? Whose son is he? At first glance there seems to be no connection between this paragraph and the immediately preceding one. We are not told that the Pharisees of verse 41 were those of verse 34. Matthew does not even tell us where the present confrontation took place. Mark informs us, however, that it occurred in the temple (12:35). Cf. Matt. 21:23; Mark 11:27; Luke 20:1.

Nevertheless, over against this vagueness as to some of the circumstances, it is but fair to state that there is, after all, a probable link between this paragraph and the immediately preceding one. Verse 34 informs us that the Pharisees "gathered themselves together," presumably (see the context) around Jesus; verse 41 states, "Now while the Pharisees were gathered together." See footnote 761 on p. 808. In all probability, therefore, Jesus is still in conversation with the same audience.

Upon this very reasonable assumption the words of Jesus here in verse 41 ff. gain added significance. Just a moment ago, in his summary of the law, Jesus has placed all the emphasis on *love*, as being the fulfilment of the Decalog. And now he is putting this love into practice by directing the attention of his audience to faith in himself, for apart from such faith—and from the right conception about the Christ—no Pharisee (or anyone else) can be saved (11:28-30; John 14:6; Acts 4:12). Although we know that most of those to whom the Master's question was addressed continued to harden themselves (see chapter 23; 26:3, 4, 47, 57; 27:41, 62-64), is it not possible that the man to whom Jesus had said, "You are not far from the kingdom" (Mark 12:34) was brought completely into the kingdom when he pondered Christ's question? Not all Pharisees and scribes were equally bad. Not all the Jewish leaders permanently rejected Jesus. See Matt. 27:57; Luke 23:50, 51; John 19:38, 39. But regardless of all this, nothing can detract from the fact that Jesus, in causing this kind of audience (remember 22:15!) to come face to face with the most important question ever asked, is revealing his marvelous love. He is conversing with these men publicly *for the very last time,* [766] and therefore asks the most important question of all.

"What is y o u r opinion of the Christ? Whose son is he?" Cf. 16:13. It is clear that the Master is referring to himself when he says "the Christ." The question is, however, so phrased (namely, in the third person) that the Pharisees are able to give a ready answer without affirming that Jesus is himself the Christ. In fact, the idea that Jesus would be the Christ was repugnant to them. The expected *Messiah* (of which "Christ" is the Greek translation) was, indeed, the Son of David. This they knew, and this they taught (Mark 12:35; John 7:42). Moreover, in so far they were correct, for that is the teaching of Scripture (II Sam. 7:12, 13, Ps. 78:68-72; 89:3, 4, 20, 24, 28, 34-37; Amos 9:11; Mic. 5:2; etc.). But hearing *Jesus* called "the Son of David," how they hated that! See Matt. 12:23, 24; 21:15, 16.

There was one more thing which these Pharisees knew. It was this, that Jesus had made no objections to the title "Son of David." He had rebuked neither the disciples nor the children when they, by implication, had called him this. However, the air must be purified. The earthly ideas attached to the concept "Son of David" or "Messiah" must be removed. Cf. John 18:36. The time has arrived to prepare the audience for the idea that the title "Son of David" means more than was generally realized. The Pharisees must learn that David's Son is also David's *Lord.* Not only is he man; he is also God!

Very wisely, in this instruction of the Pharisees, Jesus proceeds from the known to the unknown; that is, from that which they are willing to admit to that which is going to puzzle them. When he asks them, "What is y o u r opinion of the Christ? Whose son is he?" they said to him, David's.

43-45. He said to them, How then does David, in the Spirit, call him Lord, saying:

> The Lord said to my Lord,
> Sit at my right hand
> Until I put your enemies under your feet?

If David then calls him Lord, how is he his son?

Explanation:

a. The quotation is from Ps. 110 (LXX 109):1. Between, on the one hand, the original Hebrew text faithfully reproduced in the LXX Greek text, and, on the other, Matthew's version, there is no *essential* difference. Whether, with the Hebrew and the LXX, one says, "until I make your enemies a (foot)stool for your feet"; or, with Matthew (recording the words of Jesus) "Until I put your enemies under your feet," in both cases the figure that results is that of an enemy lying before a person in the dust, so

---

[766] In chapter 23 Jesus spoke to the crowds and to his disciples (23:1). Also to the scribes? See on 23:13. He did not *converse* with them.

that the conqueror's feet can be placed upon his neck. Cf. Josh. 10:24. Complete triumph over every foe is assured *by* "the Lord" *to* "the Lord."

b. Jesus ascribes this psalm (110) to David, and asserts that the latter wrote it "in the Spirit," that is, "by inspiration."

c. By saying, "What is y o u r opinion of the Christ? . . . David calls him Lord," Jesus is stating that the One whom David calls Lord is the Christ. In other words, Jesus is declaring that Ps. 110 is a Messianic Psalm. It was so regarded also by Peter (Acts 2:34, 35), by Paul (I Cor. 15:25), and by the author of the Epistle to the Hebrews (1:13; cf. 10:13). [767]

d. In this psalm David is making a distinction between YHWH (Jehovah) and 'Adonai (for both of these see on 6:9). YHWH, then, is addressing David's 'Adonai; or, if one prefers, God is speaking to the Mediator. He is promising the Mediator such pre-eminence, power, authority, and majesty as would be proper only for One who, as to his person, from all eternity was, is now, and forever will be God. See Eph. 1:20-23; Phil. 2:5-11; Heb. 2:9; Rev. 5:1-10; 12:5.

e. Nevertheless this same exalted Lord is David's *son* (II Sam. 7:12, 13; Ps. 132:17). That *Jesus* satisfies this description is clear from Matt. 1; Luke 1:32; 3:23-38; Acts 2:30; Rom. 1:3; II Tim. 2:8; Rev. 5:5. This Christ is therefore both David's son and David's Lord. He is both human and divine, both man and God.

f. The words, "If David then calls him Lord, how is he his son?" do not mean, "the Messiah cannot be David's son," but must mean, "cannot be David's son *merely* in the sense of his descendant." He is far more than that. He is the root as well as the offspring of David (Rev. 22:16; cf. Isa. 11:1, 10).

It is as if Jesus were saying to the Pharisees, "Y o u have found fault with me for accepting the praises of those who called me 'the Son of David.' Bear in mind, then, that I am the Son of David in the most exalted sense, for David himself called me 'my Lord.' Therefore whoever rejects me is rejecting David's Lord." Yet, Jesus is not as yet *openly* telling the enemies that *he* is indeed the Christ. That will come a little later. See 26:63, 64.

g. It is comforting to know that not only according to 21:42 (see on that passage) but also according to the present passage Jesus a few days before his most bitter agony was fully aware that the way of the cross would for him lead home, to the crown!

46. And no one was able to say a word in reply, nor from that day on did anyone dare to ask him another question. Also in this final confrontation between Jesus and his enemies, who had tried to trip him up, Jesus had

---

[767] According to S.BK., Vol. IV., p. 452 ff. the Messianic character of this psalm was also accepted by the rabbis.

vanquished these foes so completely that rebuttal had become impossible. In fact, no one even dared to quiz him any more.

Summary of Chapter 22

This chapter has two main parts: (1) the parable of The Marriage Feast of the King's Son (verses 1-14), and (2) Captious Questions and Authoritative Answers (verses 15-46). The first part consists of the last of a little group of three parables. It follows the parable of The Two Sons (21:28-32) and that of The Wicked Tenants (21:33-43). In unmistakable symbolism the third story illustration predicts not only the entrance of so-called "undesirables" into the kingdom (22:9, 10)—as did the first of the three parables (21:31)—and the destruction of those formerly favored (22:3-7a)—as did the second parable (21:41)—but also the burning of the foes' city (verse 7b). The ancient covenant people's loss of special standing and their replacement by a much larger group consisting of people gathered from everywhere is either taught or implied in all three parables.

A king gives a marriage for his son. He sends out invitations, and subsequently servants to call those who had been invited. Since even then no one seems to be willing to come he sends other servants, this time with the urgent appeal, "Look, I have prepared my banquet, my steers and fattened cattle have been butchered, and everything is ready; come to the wedding." When all of these entreaties are met by indifference and even by acts of hostility, the king destroys the murderers and sets fire to their city.

The monarch, insisting that the wedding hall shall be filled with guests— what a marvelous insight this trait affords into the loving heart of God!— sends his servants to gather all they could find, good and bad alike.

However, when he enters the hall he sees a man who, without any excuse, is not wearing a wedding robe. That man is cast into the most distant darkness. Sovereign love does not cancel human responsibility. To be saved one must "put on Christ" (Rom. 13:14; Col. 3:12-17).

As a person travels through this life (verses 15-46) there are especially three questions he should ask himself. In ascending order of importance they are: *a.* "What is my duty toward the government?" (cf. Rom. 13); *b.* "If I die shall I live again?" (cf. Job 14:14); and "What shall I render to the Lord for all his benefits toward me?" (Ps. 116:12). Differently phrased these questions were put to Jesus. His answers were: *a.* "Render to Caesar what is due to Caesar, and to God what is due to God," a statement with which neither the most emperor-loving Herodian nor the strictest Pharisee could find fault; *b.* "God is not the God of the dead but of the living," implying both immortality and bodily resurrection; and *c.* (amounting to) "You shall love the Lord your God with your whole being, and your neighbor as yourself." Spontaneous love is law's fulfilment.

Jesus himself asked the most important question, "If by David (Ps. 110:1) the Christ is called 'Lord,' how is Christ David's son?". Is Jesus Christ merely the final item of a line of descent; in other words, is he merely the proper subject for argumentation and debate? Or is he indeed our "Lord," whom to love and to serve is life everlasting?

Chapter 23

Theme: *The Work Which They Gavest Him to Do*

The Seven Woes

The Fifth Great Discourse

CHAPTER XXIII

23   1 Then Jesus spoke to the crowds and to his disciples, 2 saying, "The scribes and the Pharisees sit in the chair of Moses; 3 therefore everything they tell y o u, do and observe, but do not do according to their deeds; for they say (things) but do not do (them). 4 They tie up heavy burdens, and lay them on men's shoulders, but they themselves are unwilling to move them with so much as a finger. 5 They do all their deeds to attract the attention of the people; for they widen their phylacteries and enlarge their tassels; 6 they love the place of honor at the banquets, the chief seats in the synagogues, 7 the formal salutations in the market-places, and to have the people address them as 'rabbi.' 8 But as for yourselves, do not let the people call y o u 'rabbi,' for One is y o u r Teacher, and all of y o u are brothers. 9 And do not call anyone on earth y o u r father, for One is y o u r Father, the One in heaven. 10 And do not let the people call y o u leaders; for One is y o u r Leader, namely, Christ. 11 He who is greatest among y o u shall be y o u r servant. 12 Moreover, whoever exalts himself shall be humbled, and whoever humbles himself shall be exalted.

     13 "Woe to y o u scribes and Pharisees, hypocrites! because y o u shut the kingdom of heaven in men's faces; for y o u yourselves are not entering, nor do y o u permit those to go in who are trying to enter.

     15 "Woe to y o u, scribes and Pharisees, hypocrites! because y o u travel about on sea and land to make a single proselyte, and when he has become one, y o u make him twice as much a son of hell as y o u are yourselves.

     16 "Woe to y o u, blind guides! that say, 'Whoever swears by the temple, that amounts to nothing; but whoever swears by the gold of the temple, he is bound by his oath.' 17 Y o u blind fools, for which is more important: the gold, or the temple that sanctifies the gold? 18 And [who say], 'Whoever swears by the altar, that amounts to nothing; but whoever swears by the offering upon it, he is bound by his oath.' 19 Y o u blind men, for what is more important: the offering, or the altar that sanctifies the offering? 20 Therefore he who swears by the altar, swears by it and by whatever is on it; 21 and he who swears by the temple, swears by it and by him who dwells in it; 22 and he who swears by heaven, swears by the throne of God and by him who sits on it.

     23 "Woe to y o u, scribes and Pharisees, hypocrites! because y o u tithe mint, dill, and cummin, but have neglected the more important requirements of the law: justice and mercy and faithfulness; but these y o u should have kept, without neglecting the others. 24 Y o u blind guides, who strain out the gnat but swallow the camel!

     25 "Woe to y o u, scribes and Pharisees, hypocrites! because y o u clean the outside of the cup and of the dish, but inside they are full of extortion and intemperance. 26 You blind Pharisee, first clean the inside of the cup, so that the outside of it may also become clean.

     27 "Woe to y o u, scribes and Pharisees, hypocrites! because y o u resemble whitewashed tombs, which, while they appear beautiful on the outside, on the inside are

full of dead men's bones and all kinds of filth. 28 Similarly y o u too outwardly seem to people to be righteous, but inwardly y o u are full of hypocrisy and lawlessness.

29 "Woe to y o u, scribes and Pharisees, hypocrites! because y o u build the tombs of the prophets and decorate the monuments of the righteous, 30 and y o u say, 'If we had lived in the days of our fathers, we would not have taken part with them in (shedding) the blood of the prophets.' 31 So y o u are testifying against yourselves (in acknowledging) that y o u are sons of those who murdered the prophets. 32 Go ahead then, and make full the measure (of the guilt) of y o u r fathers.

33 "Y o u snakes, y o u offspring of vipers! how are y o u going to escape being sentenced to hell? 34 Therefore, look, I am sending y o u prophets and wise men and scribes. Some of them y o u shall kill and crucify, and some y o u shall flog in y o u r synagogues and pursue from town to town, 35 that upon y o u may come (the guilt of) all the righteous blood shed on the earth, from the blood of righteous Abel to the blood of Zechariah, son of Barachiah, whom y o u murdered between the sanctuary and the altar. 36 I solemnly assure y o u, all these things shall come upon this generation.

37 "Jerusalem, Jerusalem, who kills the prophets and stones those that are sent to her! how often would I have gathered your children together as a hen gathers her brood under her wings, but y o u would not! 38 Behold, y o u r house is left to y o u a deserted place. 39 For I tell y o u, from now on y o u shall certainly not see me until y o u shall say, 'Blessed is he who comes in the name of the Lord.' "

23:1-39 *The Seven Woes*
For 23:1-36 cf. Mark 12:38-40; Luke 20:45-47
For 23:37-39 cf. Luke 13:34, 35 [768]

Introduction and Summary

This discourse clearly consists of three parts. After a few introductory words (23:1-3a) in which Jesus states that to the extent in which the scribes and the Pharisees truly interpret the teaching of Moses they must be obeyed, he warns the people and his disciples not to imitate the conduct of these leaders, because in several respects they fail to practice what they preach. The three parts are: *a.* a description of the sins of the scribes and the Pharisees (verses 3b-12); *b.* the Seven Woes pronounced upon them (verses 13-36); and *c.* Christ's moving Lament over impenitent Jerusalem (verses 37-39).

In the first paragraph Jesus tells his audience that these law-experts and their adherants fall short in three respects: they lack sincerity, sympathy, and humility. They are insincere, for they pile heavy loads on men's shoulders, precept upon precept, but when it comes to themselves they are unwilling to move these burdens with so much as a finger. They are unsympathetic, for they do not try to lighten men's loads. Contrast

---

[768] In agreement with A. T. Robertson (*Word Pictures*, Vol. II, pp. 192, 193) room must be left for the possibility that Jesus spoke closely similar words (Lament over Jerusalem) both during the week of the Passion (Matt. 23:37-39) while in Jerusalem, and earlier (Luke 13:34, 35) while in Perea. If the words were indeed spoken at two different occasions, Luke 13:34, 35 parallels Matt. 23:37-39 only in a modified sense.

11:28-30. Finally, they are show-offs, as is evident from the manner in which they try to impress men with their piety. They make very conspicuous those articles of their apparel—prayer-cases and tassels—which the Lord had prescribed as reminders of his law. They make these articles more obvious by widening the straps of the tie-on cases and by enlarging the tufts that hang down from the four corners of their outer garments. They love the places of honor at festivals and in synagogues, and they yearn to be addressed as "rabbi." Jesus exhorts his followers to reveal the opposite attitude, reminding them that vanity is punished, humility rewarded.

In the second paragraph Jesus pronounces his Seven Woes upon the scribes and the Pharisees. He denounces them because they:

S hut the door of the kingdom in men's faces (verse 13);

C orrupt proselytes, after having, with great effort, won them over to the Jewish religion (verse 15);

R everse the truth regarding the oath, as if the gold of the temple were more important than the temple; and the gift upon the altar, than the altar, so that swearing by the temple and by the altar would not be binding (verses 16-22);

I nvert values, as if tithing small flavoring herbs were of greater significance than practicing justice, mercy, and faithfulness, and as if straining out the gnat were obligatory even though it meant swallowing the camel (verses 23, 24);

B oost ritual, as if the ritualistic cleansing of cup and plate were to be preferred to exercising *a.* honesty in obtaining what goes into these, and *b.* self-control in consuming the contents (verses 25, 26);

E xternalize religion, as if outward appearance were an adequate cover for sham and crime (verses 27, 28); and

S wagger about their superior goodness, as if they were better than their ancestors, who killed the prophets (verses 29-32).

For all these sins judgment is pronounced upon them (verses 33-36).

With a Moving Lament over impenitent Jerusalem, an outpouring of grief, contained in the third paragraph, Jesus closes this, his last, *public* address. There is going to be one more discourse (chaps. 24, 25), but that will be directed to the hearts and ears of the disciples, and will therefore not be public. Here, in verses 37-39, Jesus exclaims, "Jerusalem, Jerusalem . . . how often would I have gathered your children together as a hen gathers her brood under her wings, but y o u would not." He predicts that their house—the city of Jerusalem—would be doomed to utter desolation and ruin, and that after Passion Week they will not again see him until at his glorious return they, along with everybody else, would proclaim, whether joyfully (if believers) or ruefully (if unbelievers), "Blessed is he who comes in the name of the Lord." Cf. Phil. 2:10, 11, and see N.T.C. on that passage.

1-3. **Then Jesus spoke to the crowds and to his disciples, saying, The scribes and the Pharisees sit in the chair of Moses; therefore everything they tell y o u, do and observe.** . . . Note that 23:1 reads, "*Jesus* spoke." 24:1 informs us that after Jesus had spoken he left the temple. Nowhere in chapter 23 does anyone interrupt the words reported in verses 2-39 of this chapter. The natural inference is that chapter 23 is Matthew's presentation of a connected and uninterrupted discourse delivered by our Lord. That it was delivered in the temple also seems to be implied. See 21:23; 24:1. Between 21:23 and 24:1 there is no evidence to show that Jesus left the temple precincts. See also Mark 12:35. Here again, therefore, as in connection with previous discourses, I fail to agree with the theory of those who hold that at least to a certain extent chapter 23 is a Matthean composition. [769] I believe that Jesus did at times deliver discourses or sermons, and that chapter 23 is the record of one of these. What we have here is not merely a number of scattered "sayings of Jesus," uttered by him at different times and places and subsequently gathered and unified by the editor, "Matthew." To be sure, some of the words found in this chapter were also spoken at other occasions, as the Gospel according to Luke indicates; but this does not take away the fact that the evangelist leaves us with the distinct impression that the Lord delivered at least the six discourses reported respectively in chapters 5–7, 10, 13, 18, 23, and 24, 25. This does not in any way cancel the fact that the present discourse, in the form in which we have it, was reported by the ear-and-eyewitness Matthew, as he, in accordance with his own characteristic personal qualities, handed it down to us. But he wrote under the guidance of the Holy Spirit, so that what he has given us is a report in every aspect reliable, that is, reproducing from start to finish the sense of the Lord's own message. Cf. II Peter 1:19-21.

"Jesus spoke . . . to the crowds and to his disciples." As to scribes and Pharisees, whenever in this first paragraph there is any reference to them— repeatedly throughout verses 2-7—that reference is always in the third person. In the entire paragraph (verses 2-12) they are never addressed directly. If from this fact anyone wishes to draw the conclusion that they are no longer present, or, if present, then only sparsely, he can hardly be blamed. In any event it is not to them but to the Passover pilgrims and to The Twelve that Jesus is here represented as addressing himself.

As pointed out earlier, the scribes were the acknowledged expounders and teachers of the Old Testament. The Pharisees professed to follow their teaching. Scribes, too, were generally Pharisees, but by no means every Pharisee was a scribe. For the characteristic weaknesses of the scribes and the Pharisees see on 5:20; 7:28, 29; and 15:1, 2. The increasing hostility of scribes and Pharisees toward Jesus is clear from such passages as 9:3, 11, 34;

---

[769] See H. N. Ridderbos, *op. cit.*, Vol. II, p. 129.

12:2, 14, 24; 15:1; 16:1; 19:3; 21:45, 46; 22:15. They considered Jesus to be in league with Beelzebul, to be a blasphemer, one who was deceiving the multitudes and should not be allowed to live.

Because of this situation it may seem somewhat strange that Jesus is now telling the assembled crowds and his disciples that they should do whatever the scribes and Pharisees tell them to do. The proposed solution, namely, that a sharp distinction must here be made between *teaching* and *telling,* as if Jesus meant, "Do whatever the scribes and the Pharisees *tell* y o u to do, but not whatever they *teach* y o u to do," is too subtle to be satisfactory. The following should, however, be borne in mind:

a. Christ's statement must not be interpreted absolutely, as if without any qualification whatever the precepts of the scribes and the Pharisees were to be obeyed. If that had been the meaning, Jesus would here be contradicting himself. See 5:21-48; 15:3-11.

b. The context sheds light on the meaning. Not only did every synagogue probably have a special seat, called "Moses' chair," assigned to the most famous scribe of the town or village where the synagogue was located, [770] but in a sense the scribes and Pharisees as a body could be described as occupying that chair. It was their business, especially that of the scribes, to teach the people the will of God as it had been revealed to Moses. Though these men were often mistaken, though they refused to see the fulfilment of prophecy in Jesus, and though by accepting the "traditions of the fathers" and even augmenting this mass of subtle distinctions and burdensome regulations they were often burying the law of God, it remains true nevertheless that on several points they—in distinction from the Sadducees and the Herodians—were telling and teaching the truth. See on 3:7. They believed, for example in the divine decree and providence, in human responsibility, in the immortality of the soul, the resurrection of the body, the existence of angels, etc. Their views on the canon, too, were far more biblical than those of others. What Jesus must have meant, therefore, was that whenever the scribes and the Pharisees faithfully interpreted "Moses," their instructions should be obeyed.

c. The fact that before Jesus pronounces "woes" upon his bitter opponents, who are planning to kill him, he first has something good to say about their teaching should increase our reverence and love for him. Also, it should be borne in mind that not all the scribes and the Pharisees were necessarily hostile to Jesus. Simon invited him to dinner (Luke 7:36). Certain Pharisees warned him about physical danger (Luke 13:31). The scribe or law-expert referred to in Matt. 22:35 (cf. Mark 12:32-34) approved of Jesus' summary of the law and was praised by him. See also Luke 10:25-28. After Christ's

---

[770] See E. L. Sukenik, *Ancient Synagogues in Palestine and Greece,* London, 1934, pp. 57-61.

resurrection another very distinguished Pharisee, Gamaliel (Paul's teacher), prevented the Jewish authorities from carrying out their plan to slay the apostles (Acts 5:33-40).

Though this is true, it is also a fact that by and large the scribes and Pharisees were enemies of Jesus, and were guilty of all the sinister qualities for which Jesus is about to condemn them. It was their conduct, even more than their teaching, which Jesus here denounces, as he continues . . . **but do not do according to their deeds; for they say (things) but do not do (them).** Cf. 7:21-23. This is explained especially in verses 4 and 23.

4. They tie up heavy burdens, and lay them on men's shoulders, but they themselves are unwilling to move them with so much as a finger. Jesus had already made reference, though indirectly, to these heavy burdens (11:28-30). See also Acts 15:10, 28. They consisted of the many regulations by means of which the ancient rabbis, and the scribes and Pharisees after them, had buried the law of God and deprived men of their liberty and peace of mind; ordaining, for example, that plucking heads of grain amounted to reaping, hence was forbidden on the sabbath (12:1, 2); that (according to the opinion of the stricter scribes and Pharisees) healing a person on the sabbath was wrong unless that person's life were in immediate danger (12:9-14); and that ritual hand-rinsing in connection with every meal was required of everybody (15:1, 2). Cf. John 5:9, 10, 16, 18; 9:14, 16. The heaviest burden of all was the fear, encouraged by these leaders, that a man's good deeds must outbalance his evil deeds if he is to be saved. Jesus points out that, as far as they themselves were concerned, these scribes and Pharisees had mastered the art of avoiding burdens. That they would at times show others how to bypass obligations, even when these duties were assigned by the law of God itself, has already been shown (15:3-6). We may be sure, therefore, that what they would at times do for others they would be even more eager to do for themselves. Is it reasonable to suppose that men who "neglected the more important requirements of *the law*" (verse 23), would permit themselves to be at all times hamstrung by their own burdensome *regulations?* [771]

In verse 4 Jesus has described the lack of sincerity or consistency that characterized scribes and Pharisees, and also their lack of human sympathy. Then, too, they lacked humility: **5-7. They do all their deeds to attract the**

---

[771] There is also another interpretation of this verse, according to which it would mean that the scribes and the Pharisees, having laid heavy burdens on men's shoulders, were unwilling to adjust these burdens. See R. V. G. Tasker, *op. cit.*, p. 219. However, it would appear to me that the very prominent and forward position of αὐτοί, stressing the contrast between burdened men, on the one hand, and the scribes and Pharisees *themselves*, on the other, favors the interpretation given above. So does probably also verse 3. "They *say* but do not *do*." As to the expression "are unwilling to move them with so much as a finger," this does not necessarily imply "in order to adjust them." It can also indicate "in order to lay them on their own shoulders."

attention of the people; for they widen their phylacteries and enlarge their tassels; they love the place of honor at the banquets, the chief seats in the synagogues, the formal salutations in the market-places, and to have the people address them as rabbi. For the expression "to attract the attention of the people" see on 6:1. Illustrations of the manner in which the scribes and the Pharisees tried to harvest praise for themselves are now given. The following examples are in addition to those already furnished in 6:2-18.

a. They widened their phylacteries. By "phylacteries" are meant the small leather cases, boxes, or capsules holding slips on which were written passages from the law: Exod. 13:3-10, 11-16 (memorializing God's glorious deed in delivering Israel from Egyptian bondage and instituting the Passover); Deut. 6:4-9 ("Hear O Israel, Jehovah our God is one Jehovah, and you shall love Jehovah your God with all your heart. . ."); and Deut. 11:13-21 (how Jehovah will reward obedience to his law, and how children should be instructed in his ways: "Y o u shall teach them to y o u r children, speaking of them when you sit in your house. . ."). One of these capsules was fastened to the forehead, the other to the left arm (near the heart!), during prayer. This is still the practice of the members of the orthodox Jewish faith. It is based on Exod. 13:9, 16; Deut. 11:18. These phylacteries, then, were reminders to observe God's law, that is, to do so out of gratitude for his marvelous deeds in the interest of his people. As happens with so many of those "reminders," among the superstitious they degenerate into charms to protect the wearer against harm and danger, particularly against demons.

What verse 5 is saying is that the scribes and the Pharisees were in the habit of widening the straps by means of which these phylacteries were tied to the forehead and to the left arm. Making these thongs broader would cause them to stand out, so everyone could see what a law-observing and devout man was wearing them!

b. They also enlarged or lengthened their tassels—see on 9:21—and this for the same reason, namely, to make also these reminders of God's law more conspicuous, so that others, seeing these scribes and Pharisees, would honor them for their marvelous devotion, their celestial piety.

c. They loved the place of honor at the banquets and the chief seats in the synagogues. Vanity and ostentatious display go hand in hand. Jesus issued a warning against this very sin of seeking the best seat at a banquet or dinner (Luke 14:8). James condemned the sin of assigning the best seat in the meeting-place to the rich, while telling the poor man to stand or else to sit on the floor near someone's footstool (2:2, 3). The best seats in the synagogue were those in front of the raised platform, on which stood the prayer leader and the reader of the Scriptures. Thus seated, a person had the double advantage of being near the person reading or leading in prayer, and of facing the congregation and thus being able to see everybody. Besides, being ushered to such a seat was regarded as a mark of honor.

d. Th·y yearned for the formal salutations in the market-places. Though the word used in the original can indicate a friendly spoken greeting, or a written message of regards (I Cor. 16:21; Col. 4:18; II Thess. 3:17), it has here a more formidable connotation, as the immediate context indicates. What the men who were here rebuked were always looking and longing for was not a mere token of friendliness but rather a demonstration of respect, a public recognition of their prominence: they wanted to be addressed as "rabbi," a word derived from the Hebrew and literally meaning "my lord," but subsequently used in addressing those who had attained a high reputation as teachers of God's law.—For such honors as these the scribes and Pharisees whom Jesus had in mind were hungering and thirsting.

Over against this vice of pomposity, so characteristic of many a Pharisee or scribe, Jesus commends the virtue of humility: **8-10. But as for yourselves, do not let the people call y o u rabbi, for One is y o u r Teacher, and all of y o u are brothers. And do not call anyone on earth y o u r father, for One is y o u r Father, the One in heaven. And do not let the people call y o u leaders; for One is y o u r Leader, namely, Christ.** Those who think that Jesus is here condemning the idea of an apostolic office are clearly mistaken. Was it not the Master himself who instituted the office? See 10:1, 5, 40; 18:18; John 20:21-23. Cf. Acts 1:15-26; 6:1-6; 13:1-3; 14:23; 20:28; Rom. 1:1; I Cor. 1:1; 9:1, 2; II Cor. 1:1; 12:12; Gal. 1:1; Philem. 8, 9. In the light of both the preceding and the following context the statement is justified that what Jesus is here condemning is the yearning for rank, for special recognition above one's fellow members. He is declaring that he alone is their Teacher. "The Father in heaven" alone is their Father; Christ alone, their Leader. It is not wrong, of course, to address one's immediate male ancestor as "father." However, here in 23:9 Jesus is not speaking about physical or earthly fatherhood, but about fatherhood in the spiritual sphere.

The warning was necessary. Many a Jew must have envied the man who was called "rabbi" (loosely translated, "teacher"); or, if a member of the Sanhedrin was addressed as "father" (Acts 7:2); or, if already departed from this earthly scene, having left behind him an illustrious memory, was referred to by the same title (Rom. 4:12; I Cor. 10:1; James 2:21). The epithet "leader" or "guide," ascribed perhaps—this is not certain—to a beloved and highly honored teacher, sounded alluring. So Jesus is saying that the attention of his followers must not be fixed on human titles and distinctions but on God in Christ, worthy of all reverence, praise, and honor.

The objection may be raised, however, that Paul, by implication, calls himself the "father" of the Corinthians and of Timothy, and even the "mother" of the Galatians (respectively in I Cor. 4:15; I Tim. 1:2, and Gal. 4:19). However, to state a fact is one thing; to yearn for distinctions and honors above one's fellowmen, and unrelated to the glory that is due to Christ, is something different. It is the latter that Jesus condemns. It is clear from the Corinthian context that it was only "in Christ Jesus" that Paul had begotten the Corinthians through the gospel. So also it was only in a secondary sense that Paul could call himself Timothy's father. He calls Timothy "(my) genuine child *in faith,*" and, according to Paul's teaching, faith is God's gift (Eph. 2:8). As the context makes very plain (see I Tim. 1:12), Paul thanks Christ Jesus for having enabled him to be of service. Finally, also in the Galatian passage the emphasis is not on Paul but on Christ: "My dear children, for whom I am again suffering birth-pangs *until Christ be formed in y o u.*" There is therefore nothing in any of these passages that can be considered to be in conflict with Matt. 23:8-10.

As for Christ's followers in their relation to each other, all of them are "brothers" (23:8b), members of one spiritual family. See N.T.C. on Eph. 3:14, 15. Therefore no one has a right to look down on any of the others. Remember Phil. 2:3! The spirit of the Pharisees, who considered themselves to be far more worthy of respect and honor than that crowd of ignoramuses, "the rabble that does not know the law" (John 7:49), is here condemned.

In the same vein Jesus continues: 11. **He who is greatest among y o u shall be y o u r servant,** virtually repeating the words of 20:26, 27 (see on that passage). 12. **Moreover, whoever exalts himself shall be humbled, and whoever humbles himself shall be exalted.** With minor variations this proverb occurs in Scripture again and again (Job 22:29; Prov. 29:23; Luke 14:11; 18:14; James 4:6; I Peter 5:5). As to self-centered ambition and vanity, "Before downfall goes pride; and before stumbling, a haughty spirit" (Prov. 16:18). Was not this the experience of Sennacherib (II Chron. 32:14, 21), of Nebuchadnezzar (Dan. 4:30-33), and of Herod Agrippa I (Acts 12:21-23)? On the other hand, as to humility, God himself promises to dwell with the person who is "of a contrite and humble spirit" (Isa. 57:15). What more glorious exaltation can one desire? Examples: the commended centurion (Matt. 8:8, 10, 13), the humble Syrophoenician woman (15:27, 28), and the penitent tax-collector (Luke 18:13, 14). Jesus Christ himself is both the cause of his disciples' humility (Phil. 1:6; 4:13, 19), and their example in humility and in rendering willing service (Matt. 20:25-28; Luke 22:27; John 13:1-15; Phil. 2:5-8). The present passage (Matt. 23:11, 12) should be compared to all similar teaching in this Gospel. In addition to 20:26, 27 (already mentioned) see also 5:5; 11:29; 12:18-21; 18:1-4; 19:14. Cf. Luke 22:27; John 13:1-15; Phil. 2:5-8; James 4:6, 10; I Peter 5:5. When all these passages are studied it will become clear that apart from humility there is no salvation and no life to the glory of God. Christ's teaching on humility is one of the most important and constantly recurring subjects in the entire New Testament. Without fear of successful contradiction one can say that humble trust in God and grateful eagerness to carry out his will is stressed throughout Scripture. "Where then is the glorying [or boasting]? It is excluded!" (Rom. 3:27).

Here begin The Seven Woes. Why did Jesus utter them? Probably because his soul was deeply stirred by the impenitence of so many of the scribes and Pharisees, and this in spite of all the evidences he had furnished of the fulfilment of Messianic prophecy in himself. Also, because he knew that they had so many followers among the people. His heart and mind were filled with sorrow when he thought of this. He knew that exposing his opponents was in the interest of the people. Add one more fact: this was going to be Christ's final public address, hence his last opportunity personally to warn the people against these enemies of the truth. So he must make the best use of it.

As to the nature of these woes, they must be regarded as denunciations. Any softer way of describing them fails to do justice to the exclamation "hypocrites!" (six times) and "blind guides!" (once), and to such passages as verses 15, 17, 28, 33, and 35. But they are also expressions of sorrow, as the sequel (verses 37-39) clearly indicates. These two designations—denunciations and expressions of sorrow—are not necessarily self-contradictory. See I Sam. 3:15-18; 15:13-31; II Sam. 12:7-13.

The seven woes are addressed to the "scribes and Pharisees." Does this necessarily mean that these men were present? How do commentators deal with this question? *a.* Several completely avoid it; *b.* according to H. A. W. Meyer they are present but keeping themselves in the background; *c.* according to R. C. H. Lenski they are present, and Jesus hurls his fearful woes into their faces; and *d.* according to F. W. Grosheide they are no longer present, so that the seven woes must be considered a figure of speech, or, as others have described them "a rhetorical apostrophe."

Certainty in reaching a conclusion is perhaps impossible. My reasons for leaning toward Grosheide's position are as follows: *a.* The presence of the Pharisees during the incident related in 22:34-40 is definitely stated; so is also their presence immediately afterward (22:41-46); but in chapter 23 their presence is nowhere mentioned; *b.* 23:1 states that Christ's address was delivered before an audience consisting of "the crowds and his disciples"; *c.* throughout the first twelve verses the scribes and the Pharisees are referred to in the third person, as if they were not present; their sudden reappearance at verse 13, without a word being mentioned about this, would be strange; *d.* the figure of speech called *apostrophe* (*the turning away* from the immediate audience—presently from the people in general and from the disciples—in order to address a person or persons, a thing or things, living or dead, and not present) is by no means rare but abounds in the Hebrew prophets, the oriental mind being "notably given to express thoughts and feelings in this emotional style"; [772] and *e.* is not even Christ's lament over impenitent

---

[772] M. S. Terry, *Biblical Hermeneutics*, Grand Rapids, no date, p. 252. For proof see II Sam. 18:33; Isa. 14:12 ff.; 22:1, 2; 23:1 ff.; Mic. 1:2 ff.; Matt. 11:20-24; Rev. 18:10, 14, 20.

Jerusalem, at the close of this very chapter (verses 37-39) in the nature of an apostrophe?

In six of these seven woes Jesus calls the scribes and Pharisees "hypocrites." Immediately afterward (verse 33) he styles them "snakes . . . offspring of vipers," which, in the final analysis, does not differ materially from "hypocrites." To determine just what is meant by this term "hypocrites" it is well to review its use in other Matthean passages. Does the evangelist merely mean that Christ's enemies opposed him because they did not know any better? Or does he mean that they willfully and wickedly slandered him; that is, that they were dishonest, were fighting their own inner convictions? The use of the word in 6:2, 5 favors the latter meaning, for in these passages men are described who, while pretending to be generous toward the poor and to be praising God in prayer, are actually intending to garner honor for themselves. According to 6:16 they are putting on an act when in fasting they artificially disfigure their faces so as to appear very sorry for their sins, while what they are really after is praise from men. In 15:7, 8 they honor God with their lips, while their hearts are far from him. In 22:18 they are called hypocrites because they are addressing Jesus with words of flattery though their real purpose is to trip him up, so that a formal charge may be leveled against him. Finally, the "servant" mentioned in 24:51 never told his master that during the latter's absence he, this servant, was going to get drunk and to beat up his fellow-servants. We are told that his portion would be with "the hypocrites." The only conclusion we can arrive at, therefore, is that also here in chapter 23 the hypocrite is the man who pretends to be better than he really is. He is *a fraud, a deceiver, a phony, a wolf in sheep's clothing, a snake in the grass.*

In the first of the seven woes Jesus reproves the scribes and the Pharisees because, though pretending to be door-openers, they actually shut the door of the kingdom of heaven in men's faces: 13. **Woe to y o u, scribes and Pharisees, hypocrites! because y o u shut the kingdom of heaven in men's faces; for y o u yourselves are not entering, nor do y o u permit those to go in who are trying to enter.** For the meaning of the concept "kingdom of heaven" see on 4:23; 13:43. In the present case, as frequently, it is perhaps best not to define this concept too narrowly. It may here be described as the reign of God in Christ that begins on earth in human hearts and lives and is perfected in the hereafter.

The denunciation views the matter of entering the kingdom from the aspect of human responsibility. It would be wrong, therefore, to draw the conclusion that Jesus is saying that the scribes and Pharisees are stronger than God, that is, that they are able to thwart or frustrate God's design. What is probably meant is simply this, that these leaders, in addition to not themselves entering by accepting Jesus as their Lord and Savior, are exerting a sinister influence on other men, resulting in apostasy from Christ, in the sense of John 6:66. They are deceivers of men, genuine followers of Satan (Gen. 3:1, 4, 5). They are false prophets. Cf. Num. 15:1, 2; II Chron. 18:15; Rev. 2:14, 15, 20.

They accomplished their purpose by opposing Jesus, so that those who allowed themselves to be influenced by them concluded that they must also oppose him. Specifically, the scribes and Pharisees fought Jesus by means of *a. their teaching,* that is, by proclaiming the doctrine of work-righteousness. Think of their many rules and regulations directly contrary to the doctrine of grace and freedom in Christ. By such teaching they took away from the people "the key of knowledge" (Luke 11:52; cf. Hos. 4:6). They also fought Jesus by means of *b. their conduct.* The result upon those who associated with them was as indicated in I Cor. 15:33.

In the second woe Jesus rebukes his opponents because they do more harm than good to those whom they win over from heathendom. **15.** [773] **Woe to y o u, scribes and Pharisees, hypocrites! because y o u travel about on sea and land to make a single proselyte, and when he has become one, y o u make him twice as much a son of hell as y o u are yourselves.** The years during which the incarnation and the earthly ministry of Christ took place were pre-eminently marked by missionary activity carried on by the Jews. [774] This is not strange. In fact, the Jewish religion, in contrast with all kinds of pagan cults, had never been exclusivistic. The following passages prove that from the very beginning it was the will of God that strangers should have a share in the blessings of salvation: Gen. 22:18; Exod. 12:49; Lev. 19:34; I Kings 8:41-43; Ezra 6:21; Ps. 72:8-17; 87; Isa. 54:2, 3; 56:3-8; 60:1-3; Jer. 39:15-18; Joel 2:28-32; Amos 9:11, 12; Zech. 8:23; Mal. 1:11. It is true that the prophet Jonah was anything but mission-minded. But for that very sin God rebuked and punished him (Jonah 4).

Over against pagan idolatry and immorality, such activity whereby the religion of the one true God was made known to those in darkness was a great blessing. Moreover, by means of the open synagogue, the translation of the Hebrew Old Testament into Greek—we are thinking now especially of the Seputagint (LXX) translation—the very life and habits of devout Israelites, their songs, testimonies, etc., the Gentiles had been greatly blessed, so that many had turned away from their former wicked practices and superstitions, and had begun to attend the synagogues. During the apostolic age this very opportunity of meeting and addressing people of pagan origin who through such Jewish missionary activity had *arrived at* or *to* the worship of

---

[773] Verse 14. about "devouring widows' houses and for a pretence making long prayers" does not have sufficient textual support. It is probably an interpolation from Mark 12:40. Cf. Luke 20:47.

[774] See G. F. Moore, *Judaism in the First Five Centuries of the Christian Era,* Cambridge, 1927-1930, Vol. I, pp. 323-353. Cf. L. Finkelstein, *The Jews, Their History, Culture and Religion,* two volumes, New York, 1949, Vol. I, pp. 76, 77, 104.

Jehovah, and were therefore called *proselytes* (see the present passage; also Acts 2:10; 6:5; 13:43), became a boon for the spread of the good tidings of salvation in Christ.

In dealing with the concept "proselytes" one has to be very careful, however. These people did not all belong to one and the same category. They did not all accept the Jewish religion "hook, line, and sinker." Some are called "worshipers of God" (Acts 16:14; 18:7) or simply "worshipers," devout persons (Acts 13:50; 17:4, 17). They had given up their heathen practices and had become sufficiently sympathetic toward the religion of the Jews to attend the synagogue. It was especially from among such "proselytes of the gate" that many (for example, Lydia) were reached by the gospel and turned to Christ. Others, however, proceeded much farther in changing from paganism to the religion of the Jews. Though it was impossible for them to become Jews *by race,* they did become Jews *in religion;* in fact, to such an extent that by means of baptism and the bringing of a sacrifice—and in the case of men by being also circumcised—and by promising to submit to all the commandments, including all the rabbinical regulations, they were accepted into the Jewish community, as "proselytes of righteousness," "new men" and "new women." They were even given new names.

Now we may be sure that when Matt. 23:15 tells us that the scribes and the Pharisees "compassed sea and land to make a single proselyte" it is the latter kind of proselyte to which reference is made. It was not the purpose of the Pharisees merely to change a Gentile into a Jew; no, he must become a full-fledged, legalistic, ritualistic, hair-splitting Pharisee, one filled with fanatical zeal for his new salvation-by-works religion. As Jesus implies, soon this new convert would even out-Pharisee the Pharisees in bigotry, for it is a fact that new converts frequently outdo themselves in becoming fanatically devoted to their new faith. [775] This explains why Jesus can say, "and when he has become one [a proselyte], y o u make him twice as much a son of hell as y o u are yourselves." "A son of hell" is a typically Hebrew way of saying "a person belonging to, worthy of, and bound for hell." "When Jesus saw in the Pharisees the annulment of God's sovereignty and the enthronement of man-made righteousness, he as the obedient Servant of God could only speak in truthful assessment as to what they were doing to themselves and their converts among the Gentiles." [776]

In the third woe Jesus shows how the religious leaders of the Jews were turning the truth regarding the oath upside down: 16-22. **Woe to y o u, blind guides! that say, Whoever swears by the temple, that amounts to nothing; but whoever swears by the gold of the temple, he is bound by his**

---

[775] I agree on this point with Tasker, *op. cit.,* p. 220.

[776] R. R. De Ridder, *The dispersion of the people of God,* doctoral dissertation submitted to the Free University at Amsterdam, and published at Kampen, 1971. The quotation is from pp. 121, 122.

oath. Y o u blind fools, for which is more important: the gold, or the temple that sanctifies the gold? And [who say], Whoever swears by the altar, that amounts to nothing, but whoever swears by the offering upon it, he is bound by his oath. Y o u blind men, for what is more important: the offering, or the altar that sanctifies the offering? Therefore he who swears by the altar, swears by it and by whatever is on it; and he who swears by the temple, swears by it and by him who dwells in it; and he who swears by heaven, swears by the throne of God and by him who sits on it. After the rather detailed exegesis of 5:33-37 it would be superfluous to say much about its parallel here in 23:16 22. The main implication of both paragraphs is the same: "Let there be truth in heart and life. Then flippant oaths will disappear." Both paragraphs also place emphasis on the fact that even oaths by heaven, earth, Jerusalem, a person's head (chap. 5), or by the sanctuary, the altar, heaven (chap. 23), are binding. In the final analysis every oath is an oath "by God," and therefore binding.

The present paragraph (23:16-22), in distinction from the one in chapter 5, shows how stupid and absurd it is to say that an oath by the sanctuary (*the inner temple,* consisting of "the holy place" and "the holy of holies") amounts to nothing, but that an oath by the gold of the sanctuary is binding; that an oath by the altar is not valid; but one by the gift on the altar, valid. Naturally it is the greater, in the present case the sanctuary and the altar, that lends sacredness to the lesser; that is, respectively, to the gold of the sanctuary and to the gift on the altar; just as, for example, the "office" of the president of the United States is greater than the person who happens to be elevated to it at any particular point in history. But whether one swears by the sanctuary, by its gold; by the altar, by its gift; by heaven, or by God's throne, in the final analysis all such oaths are "by God" who owns all and controls all.

The present paragraph accordingly emphasizes that the scribes and the Pharisees, in *reversing* palpable truths, as if the gold were superior to the temple; the gift, to the altar, so that oaths by the latter of each pair would not be binding, reveal themselves as being blind and foolish, guides that are dangerous, hence not to be trusted and followed. [777]

In the fourth woe Jesus returns to the introductory words of the first and second woes. He accuses the scribes and Pharisees of inverting values, as if

---

[777] To distinguish sharply (see Lenski, *op. cit.,* p. 883) between the aor. participle ἁγιάσας in verse 17 and the present participle ἁγιάζον in verse 19, as if Jesus meant to bring out a temporal distinction between, on the one hand, the gold decorations that were associated with the sanctuary from the very beginning, and, on the other, the gift received right now, that is, whenever the priest places it on the altar, is probably not justifiable. It assumes that we know what kind of gold is meant. But that is exactly what we do not know. Is the reference to gold ornamentation, to gold utensils, gold coins, other gifts or offerings of gold? We do not know. It is probably best to regard ἁλιάσας as a timeless aorist, and to treat ὀμόσας in verses 20-22 similarly.

tithing small aromatic herbs were of greater significance than practicing the "heavier" (thus literally) demands of the law: 23, 24. **Woe to y o u, scribes and Pharisees, hypocrites! because y o u tithe mint, dill, and cummin, but have neglected the more important requirements of the law: justice and mercy and faithfulness. . . .** On the one hand these men scrupulously observed the tithing ordinance of Lev. 27:30-33; Deut. 14:22-29. In fact, as was usual with them, they even overdid it, by giving to the Lord the tenth portion of the small aromatic herbs which they grew in their gardens, and requiring their followers to do likewise. As they saw it, the "sweet-smelling" mint, the well-known dill, and the small, tender seeds of cummin (or cumin), all three of this series being used to flavor food, [778] must by all means be tithed! Now in the law of Moses not a word is said about tithing these. However, if a person had reminded these scribes and company of this fact, they would immediately have answered, "But does not the law definitely demand that 'all the increase of your seed' be tithed?" To the mind of a scribe or Pharisee this would have amounted to an unanswerable argument in favor of their position. However, careful examination of *the context* shows that what the law really meant—at least emphasized—was that, as far as products of the field were concerned, the three "great" crops of the land, namely, grain, wine, and oil, should be tithed. Scribes and Pharisees were always illegitimately over-extending or over-stretching the law. Was not that exactly what they also did with respect to fasting, hand-rinsing, sabbath-observance, etc.?

However, they committed even a far greater sin: their inflexible insistence on tithing mint, dill, and cummin was coupled with neglect of the more important requirements of the law, namely, justice and mercy and faithfulness. They stressed human regulations at the expense of divine ordinances! It is upon this point that all the emphasis is placed here in verses 23, 24.

As to the triad "justice and mercy and faithfulness," it would be difficult to find a better commentary than the one offered in Mic. 6:8, "He has shown you, O man, what is good; and what does Jehovah require of you, but to do justly, and to love mercy, and to walk humbly with your God?" So interpreted we see immediately that the combination *justice* and *mercy* means the exercise of fairness and helpfulness with respect to the neighbor. This so often was the exact opposite of the attitude of the scribe and Pharisee toward the common people of their generation (see on verse 25), and had also been lacking in the Israel of Micah's day, as is clearly indicated in Mic. 2:2, 9; 3:2, 3. We shall have no trouble therefore in explaining these concepts when we examine them in the light of their specific contexts. In Micah's day the Lord's "controversy" was pre-eminently with the leaders:

---

[778] Also as medicines or medical ingredients; see the articles on *mint, dill, and cummin* in H. N. and A. L. Moldenke, *Plants of the Bible*, Waltham, 1952; and in W. Walker, *All the Plants of the Bible*, New York, 1957.

the prophets, priests, and princes. Therefore Micah denounced idolatry and hollow ritualism. So also Christ's controversy is with the leaders, whose similar hollow ritualism he condemns. There is also this further parallel between Mic. 6:8 and Matt. 23:23, that in both cases not only the duty a man owes to his neighbors is emphasized (for this see also Zech. 7:8-10; Col. 3:12, 13), but in the same breath also his obligation toward *God:* walking humbly with him, being and remaining faithful or loyal to him. Such *faithfulness* cannot exist apart from *faith* in God!

Jesus adds: **but these y o u should have kept, without neglecting the others.** This addition has led to conflicting interpretations. As I see it, two extreme positions should be avoided. On the one hand we should not interpret this to mean that, after all, Jesus is here endorsing the tithing of mint, dill, and cummin. If he were saying this, would he not be defeating his very argument? Besides, the parallelism in verse 24 shows that the Lord is subjecting such overly conscientious tithing to scorn and is comparing it to filtering out a gnat but swallowing a camel! On the other hand, it is not necessary, it would appear to me, to draw the conclusion that since these words seem to be out of line with Christ's doctrine of freedom and with his entire argument against the scribes and Pharisees, he cannot have uttered them; so that, consequently, they must be regarded as a marginal note which, without any justification, was by a legalistic scribe subsequently inserted into the text. What Jesus probably meant was this: "These, that is, God's ordinances with respect to tithing, y o u should have observed, without neglecting the weightier matters of the law: justice, mercy, and faithfulness." As long as the divinely enacted ceremonial ordinances had not been blotted out (Col. 2:14), that is, as long as Jesus had not as yet died on the cross, the law with respect to tithing was still valid. The reference here is to *God's* law, as actually found in Lev. 27:30-33; Deut. 14:22-29 (and a few other places), not to man-made over-extensions of God's law. Such totally unwarranted misapplications and misuses of the law had, of course, never been justified.

When the question is asked, "What principles does the New Testament contain to guide the believer in the financial contributions toward kingdom causes which he should make, and by gratitude feels impelled to make, the answer would be as follows: *a.* he should give systematically and proportionately, that is, in proportion to his ability (I Cor. 16:2); and *b.* he should give generously and cheerfully (II Cor. 9:7).

Jesus adds: **Y o u blind guides, who strain out the gnat but swallow the camel.** This is not an entirely new thought. It is simply another and very impressive way of repeating the same denunciation and stressing the same truth. By tithing mint, dill, and cummin, while ignoring justice, mercy, and faithfulness, these enemies of Christ were indeed straining out [779] a gnat

---

[779] Not "which strain *at* a gnat" (A.V.)!

(unclean, Lev. 11:42), while gulping down a camel (also unclean, Lev. 11:4)! It is perhaps unnecessary to add that this is figurative language, the type of style Jesus is using repeatedly (see also 5:13, 29, 30, 39; 7:3-6; 8:22; 12:43-45; 18:8, 9; 21:21; etc.). The meaning is: they were paying no attention to the really important requirements of God's law but spending all their thought and energy on that which was totally unimportant. No wonder that Jesus prefaces his metaphor by calling these men "blind guides." To be blind is sad enough; but, while in this condition, to serve as a guide, that is disastrous for all those who allow themselves to be guided by such willfully blind men.

The fifth woe is closely related to the fourth. It does not begin by fixing our attention on food but rather on vessels—cups and dishes—in which consumables are served: **25, 26. Woe to y o u, scribes and Pharisees, hypocrites! because y o u clean the outside of the cup and of the dish, but inside they are full of extortion and intemperance.** For the ceremonial rinsing of vessels see on 15:1-20; also N.T.C. on John 4:9b and on Gal. 2:11-13. See also what is said about the "tradition of the elders" touching this subject (Mark 7:4b). It is clear from the entire context that when Jesus speaks about "the outside of the cup and dish" he has in mind the entire cup and dish, in distinction from what was put into them. What the Lord is saying, then, is that his opponents pay far more attention to ritualistic cleansing of these vessels than to a. the origin of the things that go into them and b. the manner in which the contents are consumed. The cup and the dish may have been made ever so clean ceremonially and physically, but if what they contain was obtained by means of extortion how can this compliance with a tradition avail the scribes and the Pharisees? These men were *harpies,* as the Greek original clearly indicates. They were rapacious, greedy and grasping. Jesus undoubtedly has reference to something very definite when he said this, though it is not easy to determine just what it was. Luke 16:14 may be of some help. It shows that the accused were not *philanthropists,* "lovers of men" but (pardon the word) *philargurists,* "lovers of money." They were the kind of people who "devoured widows' houses" (Mark 12:40; Luke 20:47). Does this mean that to funds under their control and from which they could draw, these men asked widows to contribute more than could be reasonably expected of them? Think of Luther's battle against indulgences and, even more to the point, of C. Chiniquy's chapter, "The Priest, Purgatory, and the poor Widow's Cow." [780]

Not only were the scribes and the Pharisees guilty because of the manner in which they obtained the contents of cup and dish—and their clothes, houses, gold and silver, etc.—but also because of the manner in which they

---

[780] *Fifty Years in the Church of Rome,* New York, Chicago, Toronto, 1886, pp. 41-48.

used whatever they had obtained. They were guilty of *intemperance.* [781] They were probably not as conspicuous in this trait as were those coarse materialists, the Sadducees. After all, one can expect scribes and Pharisees to be refined! Yet, even among the scribes and the Pharisees there must have been a generous sprinkling of guzzlers.

Jesus, continuing his rhetorical apostrophe, now turns to the individual Pharisee. For a moment he uses the singular instead of the plural, doing this to enhance the effect of his message: **You blind Pharisee, first clean the inside of the cup, so that the outside of it may also become clean.** Meaning: outward conformity to the traditions of the elders, in the present case by thoroughly cleaning the outside of cup and dish, will never bring about inner purity of heart. By the grace of God the inside must be purified first. When that has been done one need not bother about outward ceremonial cleansing. The man who fails to see this is *blind,* willfully so!

Also between the fifth woe and the sixth there is a close relationship, as even the occurrence of the words "outside" and "inside" in both of these woes indicates. Jesus is about to point out that the sin of his opponents is that they externalize religion, as if outward appearance were an adequate cover for shame and crime. **27, 28. Woe to y o u scribes and Pharisees, hypocrites! because y o u resemble whitewashed tombs, which, while they appear beautiful on the outside, on the inside are full of dead men's bones and all kinds of filth.** Passover was just around the corner. This meant that the pilgrims, streaming into Jerusalem from every direction, near the city saw many a whitewashed tomb. With powdered lime dust a few weeks earlier the burial places had been made to look spick-and-span, neat and trim. They had been made conspicuous, lest any pilgrim should render himself ceremonially "unclean" by inadvertently coming into contact with a corpse or a human bone. See Num. 19:16; Luke 11:44. Yet, on the inside such graves were full of dead men's bones and all kinds of dirt and debris. **Similarly,** says Jesus, **y o u too outwardly seem to people to be righteous, but inwardly y o u are full of hypocrisy and lawlessness.** See also Acts 23:3. For proof of the hypocrisy of which Jesus speaks see 6:1-8, 16:18; 15:1-20; 16:1-12; 22:15-18, and, in 23:1-36, all that precedes and follows the present passage. What really counts, as far as God is concerned, is what a man is on the inside,

---

781 Some regard ἀκρασία to be a synonym of ἁρπαγή. That theory has something attractive about it and may even be correct. The rendering then becomes "extortion and graft," or something similar. In favor of this translation is the fact that the two words are then expressing *one* idea. It remains true, nevertheless, that the literal meaning of ἀκρασία is *want of power* (over self), hence *lack of self-control,* and therefore *self-indulgence* or *intemperance.* In the only other instance of its New Testament occurrence (I Cor. 7:5) the word has this meaning. In II Tim. 3:3 ἀκρατής means *unrestrained,* and in Rev. 14:10 *undiluted.*

morally and spiritually (cf. I Sam. 16:7). The "lawlessness" here mentioned is not the condition of being without law but that of despising God's law.

The seventh woe shows that in spite of their inner perversity these men boast about their superior goodness. But their murderous designs against those who warn them prove that they are the opposite of what they claim to be: 29-32. **Woe to y o u, scribes and Pharisees, hypocrites! because y o u build the tombs of the prophets and decorate the monuments of the righteous, and y o u say, If we had lived in the days of our fathers, we would not have taken part with them in (shedding) the blood of the prophets.** Building such tombs may indicate erecting new structures—large imposing tombs or mausoleums—over the places where the prophets had been buried. The verb can also refer, however, to the enlargement or keeping in repair of older structures. It is thought by some that the tomb of the prophet Zechariah at the base of the Mount of Olives was, in some sense, being *built* during Christ's earthly ministry. That David's tomb was being kept in honor is clear from Acts 2:29. Such elaborate tombs were at the same time monuments or memorials in honor of the dead. On the basis of that interpretation "tombs" and "monuments" would be synonyms (cf. II Kings 23:17); so would "the prophets" and "the righteous." There could also be *monuments* distinct from *graves*. In Gen. 35:20 we read about "the pillar of Rachel's grave."

The hypocrisy which Jesus signalizes refers to the fact that these very scribes and Pharisees who occupied themselves with the task of thus honoring the prophets, at the same time were making plans to murder the greatest Prophet of all! See 12:14; 16:21; 17:23; 20:19; 21:38, 39, 46; 22:15. Yet, they were saying, "If we had lived in the days of our fathers, we would not have co-operated with them in murdering the prophets." Whether the boasters realized it or not, their statement implied, "We are sons of murderers." And the evil intention of their hearts proved that they themselves too were indeed murderers. They were not only sons of murderers but *typical* sons: the blood of their murdering fathers was still in their veins. It was exactly as Jesus said: **So y o u are testifying against yourselves (in acknowledging) that y o u are sons of those who murdered the prophets.** He continues: **Go ahead then, and make full the measure (of the guilt) of y o u r fathers.** This rhetorical exhortation reminds one of John 13:27, "What you [Judas] are doing, do it faster." The Lord is as it were saying, "Since y o u have hardened yourselves against all warnings, the responsibility is now entirely y o u r s. Because of the baseness of y o u r hearts, the crime y o u have planned can no longer be averted. Carry it out therefore, and suffer the punishment."

The discourse or oration now proceeds toward its momentous climax, as Jesus pronounces upon these men hardened in sin the judgment that can no longer be avoided: 33. **Y o u snakes, y o u offspring of vipers! how are y o u** going to escape being sentenced to hell? Literally ". . . how shall y o u escape [782] the condemning judgment of Gehenna?" For "y o u offspring of vipers" see on 3:7. John the Baptist had added, "Who warned y o u to escape from the approaching (outpouring of) wrath?" For the meaning of "hell," here literally "Gehenna," see on 10:28. And for "judgment" see on 5:22. What Jesus is saying, therefore, is that escape for these often warned but obdurate impenitents is now no longer possible. Continued: **34-36. Therefore, look, I am sending y o u prophets and wise men and scribes.** The passage must be interpreted in the light of *a.* its context; see especially verses 31, 32; and *b.* the parallel passage, Luke 11:49. As to *a.*, the context indicates that in verses 34, 35 Jesus is showing how the scribes and Pharisees, together with all their followers, are proving and are going to prove that they are indeed typical sons of their fathers, who murdered the prophets. History is being repeated. The measure of the fathers' guilt is being, and is going to be, made full. As to *b.*, Luke 11:49 shows that what Jesus is saying in Matt. 23:34, 35 was also what Jehovah in his wisdom had declared concerning the sins of those who would kill his ambassadors, and concerning the judgments that would be visited upon them. In other words Jesus, in saying "*I*—very emphatic—am sending y o u prophets. . . ," is declaring that in making this statement he joins his voice to that of the God who inspired the Old Testament prophets. Although it is true that, in this exact form verses 34, 35 occur nowhere in the Old Testament or in any other written source known to us, *in essence* what we have here is also found in the Old Testament; for example, in Jer. 7:25-29. In that passage, too, the Lord stated the same three facts found here in Matt. 23:34, 35. A side by side comparison will show that this is true:

<table>
<tr><td align="center">Jer. 7:25-29</td><td align="center">Matt. 23:34, 35</td></tr>
<tr><td align="center">a.</td><td align="center">a.</td></tr>
<tr><td>"I have sent to y o u all my servants, the prophets.</td><td>"I am sending y o u prophets, and wise men, and scribes.</td></tr>
<tr><td align="center">b.</td><td align="center">b.</td></tr>
<tr><td>"Yet the people did not hearken to me, nor inclined their ear, but made their neck stiff. They did worse than their fathers.</td><td>"Some of them y o u shall kill and crucify, and some y o u shall flog in y o u r synagogues and pursue from town to town. . . .</td></tr>
<tr><td align="center">c.</td><td align="center">c.</td></tr>
<tr><td>"Jehovah has rejected and forsaken the generation of his wrath."</td><td>". . . that upon y o u may come all the righteous blood shed on the earth, from the blood of Abel to the blood of Zechariah. . . ."</td></tr>
</table>

---

[782] φύγητε, 2nd per. pl. aor. subjunctive (here deliberative) of φεύγω.

In both cases the prophetic voice, the refusal to heed it, and the punishment are mentioned. It is as it were a timeless story. The decision or decree to pour final wrath upon all those who harden their hearts was made not only in the days of Jesus' sojourn on earth, nor only in the days of Jeremiah and the other prophets, but all the way back in God's eternal plan.

As to the further details here in Matt. 23:34, 35, the prophets are all those who truly declare the will and mind of God to the people: Moses, Elijah, Isaiah, Jeremiah, the prophets and teachers mentioned in Acts 13:1, 2, Agabus, etc. The greatest prophet of them all is Jesus. But were not all the apostles also, in a sense, *prophets?* Were they not also *wise men,* those who, filled with wisdom from God, preached Christ, who himself is "the wisdom of God"? See I Cor. 1:23, 24, 30. And as to the apostles—substituting Matthias for Judas, and adding Paul—were they not also *scribes?* See on 13:52 for proof that the term "scribes" is at times used in a favorable sense, to indicate those who are well-versed in the gospel and are able to impart it to others; sometimes (think of Matthew, John, and Paul) even in written form. Though Jesus himself did not write anything that was transmitted to us, did he not inspire all the *true* scribes? The very fact that where Matthew has "prophets and wise men and scribes" Luke writes "prophets and apostles" shows that it would be wrong for us to try to distinguish here between three different groups, as if some of the Lord's ambassadors during the old or new dispensation were prophets, some wise men, and still others scribes. In the present context the three different terms simply view God's emissaries from three different angles.

Continued: **Some of them y o u shall kill and crucify, and some y o u shall flog in y o u r synagogues and pursue from town to town.** Fulfilment: as to "kill and crucify," or "kill, even crucify," think of Jesus himself (27:31, 35); and of Peter (John 21:18, 19). As to "flog" or "scourge" (see on 10:17), think of those who at the suggestion of Paul before his conversion were thus cruelly treated (Acts 22:19; 26:11); and consider Paul himself, after his conversion (II Cor. 11:24). And with respect to "pursued from town to town" (see on 10:23), recall the passage: "I [Paul before my conversion] persecuted them even all the way to foreign cities" (Acts 26:11).

It is indeed remarkable how literally this prophecy was going to be fulfilled. The book of Acts bears testimony to this fact. The Jews were always on the heels of the Christian missionaries. They never tired of pursuing them: at Pisidian Antioch (Acts 13:45, 50), Iconium (14:2), Lystra (14:19), Thessalonica (17:5), Berea (17:13), Corinth (18:12; 20:3), Jerusalem (21:27; 23:12), and Caesarea (24:1-9).

God allows all this to happen. In fact, his own *purpose* is being realized in all of this, both in the reward given to those persecuted (Rom. 8:28, 37; II Cor. 4:17, 18), and in the punishment of the persecutors. As to the latter, Jesus continues: **that upon y o u may come (the guilt of) all the righteous** blood shed on the earth, from the blood of righteous Abel to the blood of Zechariah, son of Barachiah, whom y o u murdered between the sanctuary and the altar. I solemnly assure y o u—see on 5:18—all these things shall come upon this generation.

First of all a matter touching the text must be briefly investigated. It concerns "Zechariah, son of Barachiah, whom y o u murdered...." The reference is undoubtedly to the Zechariah whose courageous testimony and cruel death are recorded in II Chron. 24:20-22. The reason why Jesus says "from Abel to Zechariah" is that according to the arrangement of the books in the Hebrew Bible *Genesis* (hence "Abel") comes first, *Chronicles* (hence "Zechariah") last. What Jesus is saying then is that the blood of all those righteous men whose murder stories, from first to last—that is, from Abel to Zechariah—are recorded in Scripture (the Old Testament) is charged to "this generation" (cf. Luke 11:50), the Jewish people, particularly Christ's own contemporaries. See on 1:17.

So far there is no difficulty in understanding the text. The real problem is that here in Matthew the murdered Zechariah of II Chron. 24:20-22 is called "son of Barachiah," but Chronicles calls him "the son of Jehoiada the priest." Also, the minor prophet Zechariah, of a much later date, was indeed "the son of Berechiah" (Zech. 1:1). I shall not weary the reader with the enumeration and discussion of all the proposed solutions. Among them all the three best may well be the following:

a. As is true of so many other persons mentioned in Scripture, so also here: the father of the murdered man had two names, Jehoiada and Barachiah (or Berechiah).

b. As happens more often in Scripture, "father" (II Chron. 24:22) means "grandfather." Those who favor this theory claim that it is supported by the statistics regarding the persons who are prominently mentioned in the account (see especially II Chron. 24:1, 2, 15).

c. Into an early copy of Matthew's Gospel, at 23:35, a copyist who remembered the name of the father of the minor prophet erroneously and without any warrant inserted "son of Barachiah." [783]

On the basis of none of these three proposed solutions is the fully inspired author of this Gospel charged with any error. Any of the three may be correct. Nevertheless, with Ridderbos, I believe that *c.* is the most simple.

Returning now to the explanation of the passage, it means, "Y o u shall do all these things—kill, crucify, flog, pursue—in order that it may become crystal clear that the sentence pronounced upon y o u was thoroughly justified." Thus the river of blood, from Abel to Zechariah, is followed by

---

[783] Lenski, after saying that Luther already had the solution—namely, theory *a.*—mentions also theory *b*, and permits us to choose between these two. Grosheide regards theory *b.* as very well possible. H. N. Ridderbos favors *c.*

the river of fire, the fire of God's wrath and punishment. This wrath was poured out upon the Jewish people because in murdering the Christ and persecuting his ambassadors they showed that they were of one mind with those in bygone days who had murdered the prophets. Moreover, all these terrible crimes had been committed in spite of repeated warnings and earnest invitations to repent. Think, for example, of the manner in which Cain had been admonished earnestly and even tenderly (Gen. 4:6, 7). Nevertheless, he went right ahead and murdered his brother Abel. And think also of the kindness that had been bestowed upon King Joash by Jehoiada the father of Zechariah. In spite of this it was at the command of Joash that Zechariah, God's true and faithful servant, had been murdered. Moreover, this deed of cruelty had been committed *in the immediate vicinity of the sanctuary!* — Between Abel and Zechariah ever so many other righteous men had been similarly treated. See on 5:12. Even Jesus, the very climax of God's love, was about to be murdered also; in fact, by many had already been rejected. And, as has been indicated, the same was in store for the "prophets, wise men, and scribes" of the New Testament era. Result: the Jews cease to be in any special sense the people of God. Jerusalem falls (A.D. 70) amid indescribable horrors.

Christ's final public address fittingly closes with a moving lament, in which are revealed both his solemn tenderness and the severity of divine judgment on all who have answered such marvelous compassion with contempt. The lamentation begins as follows: **37. Jerusalem, Jerusalem, who kills the prophets and stones those that are sent to her! how often would I have gathered your children together as a hen gathers her brood under her wings, but y o u would not!** [784]

This outpouring of grief is addressed to "Jerusalem" because this city, being the capital, Israel's very heart and center, symbolizes the spirit or attitude of the nation as a whole. Intense emotion, unfathomable pathos, finds its expression in the repetition of the word *Jerusalem*. Cf. "altar, altar" (I Kings 13:2), "Martha, Martha" (Luke 10:41), "Simon, Simon" (Luke

---

[784] In this passage ἀποκτείνουσα and λιθοβολοῦσα are fem. sing. present active participles; hence (the one or she) *killing* and *stoning*; ἀπεσταλμένους is acc. pl. masc. perf. passive participle of ἀποστέλλω: *those having been sent or commissioned*, with the implication "by God"; ἠθέλησα is first per. sing. aor. indic. of ἐθέλω: (how often) *did I yearn*, followed by the double compound infinitive ἐπισυναλαλεῖν *to gather to myself*. Later in this passage the same verb occurs in connection with a bird; hence (as a hen) *gathers to herself*. The noun ὄρνις (cf. "ornithology") basically means *bird*, and as such can refer to either a cock or a hen. By reason of the action ascribed to it, the reference here seems to be to a hen. The noun νοσσία is related to νέος; hence, *new ones, young ones, brood*. With πτέρυξ, *wing*, (here acc. plural πτέρυγας) compare πέτομαι *to fly*. English *pinion, pen, feather*, etc., are related to it. Note also how the singular "Jerusalem" finally expands into the plural οὐκ ἠθελήσατε.

22:31), and such multiple repetitions as "O my son Absolom, my son, my son Absolom! if only I had died for you, O Absolom, my son, my son!" (II Sam. 18:33); and "Land, land, land, hear the word of the Lord" (Jer. 22:29; cf. 7:4). That the nation was indeed guilty of killing and stoning God's official ambassadors has already been established; see on 5:12. Proof for "How often would I have gathered your children to myself" is found first of all in the Gospel according to John (2:14; 5:14; 7:14, 28; [8:2]; 10:22, 23). Incidentally, this statement of Jesus also shows that even the Synoptics, though stressing Christ's work in and around Galilee, do bear testimony to the extensive labor which Jesus had performed in Jerusalem and vicinity. Bearing in mind, however, that Jerusalem represented the nation, it should be pointed out that Christ's sympathy and yearning love had by no means been confined to the inhabitants of this city or even of Judea. It had been abundantly evident also in the northern regions. See Matt. 9:36; 11:25-30; 15:32; Luke 15; etc.

The simile Jesus uses is unforgettable. A chicken hawk suddenly appears, its wings folded, its eyes concentrated on the farmyard, its ominous claws ready to grasp a chick. Or, to change the figure, a storm is approaching. Lightning flashes become more frequent, the rumbling of the thunder grows louder and follows the electrical discharges more and more closely. Raindrops develop into a shower, the shower into a cloudburst. In either case what happens is that with an anxious and commanding "cluck, cluck, cluck!" the hen calls her chicks, conceals them under her protecting wings, and rushes off to a place of shelter. "How frequently," says Jesus, "I have similarly yearned to gather y o u. But y o u refused to come." Did they really think that his threats were empty, his predictions of approaching woe ridiculous?

The result of these constant refusals, this hardening of heart, is described in verses **38, 39. Behold, y o u r house is left to y o u a deserted place. For I tell y o u, from now on y o u shall certainly not see me until y o u shall say, Blessed is he who comes in the name of the Lord.** [785] Y o u r house does not merely indicate "y o u r temple," but "y o u r city." Nevertheless, the temple is certainly included. For fulfilment see on 22:7. Cf. Deut. 28:24, 37, 45; I Kings 9:7; Luke 21:20, 24, 28. In the modifier "from now on" the word "now" must here be interpreted to include the immediately following days. The meaning is that after this week of the passion Jesus will not again publicly reveal himself to the Jews until the day of his second coming. Except for a brief transition period (Acts 13:46), the day of *special* opportunity for the Jews is past. At Christ's return upon the clouds of glory "every

---

[785] On ἰδού see footnote 133, p. 131. ἀφίεται, third per. sing. pres. indic. passive of ἀφίημι, *to send away, let alone, leave*; ἔρημος, *lonely, desolate, deserted*; cf. *hermit*; εὐλογημένος, nom. sing. masc. perf. passive participle with present meaning (past action resulting in continuing present state), *blessed.*

eye shall see him" (Rev. 1:7). "Blessed is he who comes in the name of the Lord" (see on 21:9; Luke 19:38) will then be on every lip. Those who will have repented before they died will then, at that glorious coming, proclaim Christ joyfully; the others ruefully, remorsefully, *not* penitently. But so majestic and radiant will be Christ's glory that all will feel impelled to render homage to him. Cf. Isa. 45:23; Rom. 14:11; Phil. 2:10, 11. For the rest, this passage must be understood in the light of 8:11, 12, including footnote 379 on p. 397.

Chapters 24 and 25

Theme: *The Work Which Thou Gavest Him to Do*

The Last Things

The Sixth Great Discourse

CHAPTERS
XXIV–XXV

24 1 Jesus left the temple and was walking away when his disciples approached him to call his attention to the buildings of the temple. 2 He answered them, "Do y o u see all this? I solemnly assure y o u, there shall not be left here one stone upon another that shall not be thrown down."

3 And as he was sitting on the Mount of Olives the disciples came to him privately, saying, "Tell us, when shall this happen, and what (shall be) the sign of thy coming and of the end of the age?"

4 Jesus replied, "Take care that no one misleads y o u. 5 For many shall come in my name, saying, 'I am the Christ,' and shall mislead many. 6 And y o u are going to hear about wars and rumors of wars, but watch out; do not be disturbed, for such things must happen, but that is not yet the end. 7 For (one) nation shall rise up in arms against (another) nation, and (one) kingdom against (another) kingdom, and there shall be famines and earthquakes in various places, 8 but all these things are (only) the beginning of birth pains. 9. Then y o u shall be handed over to tribulation and y o u shall be put to death, and y o u shall be hated by all the nations for my name's sake. 10 And then many shall fall away, [786] betraying and hating each other. 11 And many false prophets shall arise and shall mislead many; 12 and because lawlessnesss shall increase, the love of the majority shall grow cold. 13 But he that endures to the end, he shall be saved. 14 And this gospel of the kingdom shall be preached in the whole world as a testimony to all the nations, and then shall come the end.

15 "Now when y o u see 'the desolating sacrilege,' which was spoken of through Daniel the prophet, standing in the holy place—let him who reads understand—, 16 then let those in Judea flee to the hills; 17 let him who (happens to be) on the housetop not go down to get the things out that are in his house; 18 and let him who is in the field not go back to get his coat. 19 But woe to those who are pregnant and to those who nurse babies in those days! 20 Pray that y o u r flight may not occur in winter or on the sabbath; 21 for then there shall be great tribulation, such as there has never been since the beginning of the world until now, and as there shall never be again. 22 And if those days were not cut short no one would be saved. But for the sake of the elect those days shall be cut short. 23 At that time if anyone should say to y o u, 'Look, here (is) the Christ!' or 'There (he is)!,' do not believe (him); 24 for false Christs shall arise and false prophets, and shall perform great signs and miracles, so as to mislead, if possible, even the elect. 25 See, I have told y o u ahead of time. 26 So, if they shall say

---

[786] Or: "be trapped, be ensnared"; see on 5:29, 30; 18:6, 8, 9; footnote 293 on p. 303.

to y o u, 'Look, he is in the wilderness,' do not go out there; 'Look, he is in the inner rooms,' do not believe (them). 27 For as the lightning goes out from the east and flashes clear to the west, so shall be the coming of the Son of man. 28 Wherever there is a corpse, there the vultures will gather.

29 "Immediately after the tribulation of those days,

The sun shall be darkened,

And the moon shall not give her light,

And the stars shall fall from the sky,

And the powers of the heaven shall be shaken.

30 And then the sign of the Son of man shall appear in the sky, and then

All the tribes of the earth shall mourn,

and they shall see

The Son of man coming on the clouds of the sky, with power and great glory; 31 And he shall send forth his angels with a loud trumpet blast, and they shall gather his elect from the four winds, from one end of heaven to the other.

32 "Now from the fig tree learn this lesson: as soon as its branch becomes tender and puts forth leaves, y o u know that summer is near. 33 So also y o u, when y o u see all this, know then that it is near, at the very gates. 34 I solemnly declare to y o u that this generation shall certainly not pass away until all this takes place. 35 Heaven and earth shall pass away, but my words shall never pass away.

36 "But about that day and hour no one knows, neither the angels of heaven nor the Son, but the Father only. 37 And as (were) the days of Noah, so shall be the coming of the Son of man. 38 For just as men were in those days before the flood, eating and drinking, marrying and giving in marriage, until the day Noah entered the ark, 39 not recovering their senses until the flood came and swept them all away, so also shall be the coming of the Son of man. 40 Then two men shall be in the field; one is taken, one left behind. 41 Two women (shall be) grinding with a hand-mill; one is taken, one left behind. 42 Be on the alert, therefore, because y o u do not know on what day y o u r Lord is coming. 43 But this y o u do know, that if the owner of the house had known at what watch of the night the burglar would arrive, he would have been on the alert, and would not have allowed his house to be broken into. 44 Therefore y o u also, be ready, for at an hour when y o u do not expect (him), the Son of man comes.

45 "Who then is the faithful and sensible servant whom the master has put in charge of his household employees, to give them food at the proper time? 46 Blessed is that servant whom his master at his coming shall find so doing. 47 I solemnly assure y o u that he shall set him over all his possessions. 48 But if that servant be wicked, and shall say in his heart, 'My master is taking his time,' 49 and shall begin to beat up his fellow-servants, and shall eat and drink with drunkards, 50 the master of that servant shall arrive on a day when he does not expect him, and at an hour he does not figure on, [787] 51 and shall cut him to pieces and assign him a place with the hypocrites; there shall be weeping and grinding of teeth.

25 1 "Then the kingdom of heaven shall be comparable to ten girls, who took their lamps and went out to meet the bridegroom. 2 Five of them were foolish, and five sensible. 3 For the foolish, having taken their lamps, took no oil with them; 4 but the sensible took oil in their vessels with their lamps. 5 Now when the bridegroom was taking his time, they all grew drowsy [788] and (soon) were sleeping.

---

[787] Or: he does not know.
[788] Or: nodded.

6 But at midnight there was a shout, 'Here comes the bridegroom! Go out to meet him!' 7 Then all those girls awoke and trimmed their lamps. 8 And the foolish said to the sensible, 'Give us some of y o u r oil, because our lamps are going out.' 9 But the sensible girls answered, 'There may not be enough for both us and y o u. Y o u better go to those who sell (it), and buy (some) for yourselves.' 10 However, when they were on their way to buy, there came the bridegroom! The girls who were ready went in with him to the wedding, and the door was shut. 11 Later the other girls came also, saying, "Sir, sir, open the door for us.' 12 But he replied, 'I solemnly declare, I do not know y o u.' 13 Keep on the alert, therefore, because y o u do not know the day or the hour.

14 "For (it is) like a man going abroad, who called his servants and placed his property in their hands. 15 To one he gave five talents, to another two, and to another one, to each according to his ability; then he went abroad. 16 At once the man who had received the five talents went and put them to work and gained five more. 17 So also the man (who had) the two gained two more. 18 But the man who had received the one (talent) went off, dug a hole in the ground, and hid his master's money. 19 Now a long while afterward the master of those servants came and settled accounts with them. 20 He who had received the five talents came forward, brought five additional talents, and said, 'Master, five talents you placed in my hands; look, an additional five talents I have gained.' 21 His master said to him, 'Well done, good and faithful servant. Over a small amount you have been faithful, over much I am going to put you in charge; come, share your master's happiness.' 22 He (who had received) the two talents also came forward, and said, 'Master, two talents y o u placed in my hands; look, an additional two talents I have gained.' 23 His master said to him, 'Well done, good and faithful servant. Over a small amount you have been faithful, over much I am going to put you in charge; come, share your master's happiness.' 24 Also he who had received the one talent came forward and said, 'Master, I always knew that you were a hard man, reaping where you did not sow, and gathering where you did not scatter; 25 so, being afraid, I went away and hid your talent in the ground; look, (here) you have what is yours.' 26 But his master answered and said to him, 'You wicked and lazy servant! did you know that I reap where I did not sow, and gather where I did not scatter? 27 Then you should have invested my money with the bankers, and upon my return I would have received what was mine plus interest. 28 Take the talent from him and give (it) to the one who has the ten talents. 29 For to everyone who has shall (more) be given, and he shall have plenty; but from him who does not have, even what he has shall be taken away. 30 And fling the useless servant into the most distant darkness; there shall be weeping and grinding of teeth.'

31 "When the Son of man comes in his glory, and all the angels with him, then he shall sit on the throne of his glory; 32 and before him shall be gathered all the nations, and he shall separate them from each other, as the shepherd separates the sheep from the goats; 33 and he shall put the sheep at his right and the goats at his left. 34 Then the King shall say to those at his right: 'Come, y o u who are blessed by my Father, inherit the kingdom prepared for y o u since the founding of the world; 35 for I was hungry, and y o u gave me to eat; I was thirsty, and y o u gave me a drink; I was a stranger, and y o u welcomed me; 36 in need of clothes, and y o u clothed me; I was sick, and y o u looked after me; I was in prison, and y o u came to see me.' 37 Then the righteous shall answer, saying, 'Lord, when did we see thee hungry and feed thee, or thirsty and give thee a drink; 38 and when did we see thee a stranger and welcome thee, or in need of clothes and clothe thee; 39 and when did we see thee sick or in prison and come to thee?' 40 And the King shall answer them, 'I solemnly assure y o u, whatever y o u did for one of these brothers of mine, (even) for one of the least, y o u did it for me.' 41 Then he shall also speak to those at his left (saying): 'Depart from me, y o u

accursed ones, into the everlasting fire prepared for the devil and his angels; 42 for I was hungry, and y o u did not give me to eat; I was thirsty, and y o u did not give me a drink; 43 I was a stranger, and y o u did not welcome me; in need of clothes, and y o u did not clothe me; sick and in prison, and y o u did not look after me.' 44 Then they too shall answer, saying, 'Lord, when did we see thee hungry or thirsty or a stranger or in need of clothes or sick or in prison, and did not wait on thee?' 45 Then he shall answer them, saying, 'I solemnly assure y o u, whatever y o u did not do for one of the least of these, y o u did not do for me.' 46 And these shall go away into everlasting punishment, but the righteous into everlasting life."

24:1—25:46 *The Last Things*

For most of 24:1-44 cf. Mark 13:1-37; Luke 21:5-36. For 24:37-51 cf. also Luke 12:37-48; 17:26, 27, 34, 35. Matt. 25 has no true parallel in the other Gospels. Luke's parable of The Pounds (19:11-27) is not a true parallel to Matthew's parable of The Talents (25:14-30). See also p. 23. There are, however, certain resemblances.

Introduction and Summary

A few points are worthy of special notice:

1. This is next to the longest of Christ's six discourses. The evangelist Matthew devotes far more space to it than does Mark or Luke; though much of chapter 24 is paralleled in the other Synoptics, and they, in turn, contain a few passages not found in Matt. 24. The sermon is generally known as "Christ's Eschatological Discourse" or "Discourse on the Last Things." To indicate more clearly its material content one might also use the caption "Watchfulness Urged in View of The Son of Man's Return as Judge and Rewarder."

2. The effort to combine it with chapter 23, making chapters 23-25 one discourse, in order, by means of this manipulation, to reduce the six discourses to five—comparable to the five books of Moses!—cannot succeed, for the address found in chapter 23 was delivered in the temple; the one recorded in chapters 24, 25, on the Mount of Olives. The former had as its audience the crowds and Christ's disciples; the latter, the disciples alone. The themes, too, are entirely different, as has been indicated.

3. The prophetic material found in this sixth discourse has reference not only to events near at hand (see, for example, verse 16) but also to those stretching far into the future, as is clear from 24:14, 29-31; 25:6, 31-46. Cf. Luke 21:24.

4. By the process of prophetic foreshortening, by means of which before one's eyes the widely separated mountain peaks of historic events merge and are seen as one, as has been explained in connection with 10:23 and 16:28, two momentous events are here intertwined, namely, *a.* the judgment upon Jerusalem (its fall in the year A.D. 70), and *b.* the final judgment at the close of the world's history. Our Lord predicts the city's approaching catastrophe

as a type of the tribulation at the end of the dispensation. Or, putting it differently, in describing the brief period of great tribulation at the close of history, ending with the final judgment, Jesus is painting in colors borrowed from the destruction of Jerusalem by the Romans. [789]

The now rather popular view according to which chapter 24, including even such an exalted passage as 24:30, which pictures "the Son of man coming on the clouds of the sky, with power and great glory," limits itself to the woes that were to come upon the Jewish people in the year A.D. 70, is open to the following objections:

a. If we thus restrict the meaning Jesus did not answer the question of the disciples. To study the contents of that question we must not refer only to the Gospel of Mark (13:4) and that of Luke (21:7) but also to Matthew (24:3). This gives us the total picture. Included in the question of the disciples were these words: ". . . what (shall be) the sign of thy coming and of the end of the age?" Now if in the entire discourse which follows Jesus never speaks about his eschatological coming at the close of the world's history, he did not answer their question.

b. We are clearly told, Matt. 24:29, that the tribulation to which that passage refers "immediately" precedes the appearance of "the sign of the Son of man in heaven."

Jesus emphasizes that no one—"neither the angels of heaven nor the Son, but the Father only"—knows the day and the hour when this great event will take place (verse 36). Does he merely mean to say that no one knows when Jerusalem will be destroyed? In verse 37 we read: "And as (were) the days of Noah, so shall be the coming of the Son of man." Is the destruction of the face of the earth by means of the flood a type merely of Jerusalem's fall, or is it a type of "the passing away of heaven and earth" to which reference is made in verse 35? Not only the immediate context but also II Peter 3:5-7 furnishes the answer (cf. also Luke 17:20-37).

c. Our Lord continues his discourse in chapter 25. The two chapters belong together. If the lofty language of 24:29-31 refers to nothing more momentous and final than Jerusalem's destruction in the year A.D. 70, then by the same process of reasoning the very similar words of 25:31-46 must be given this restricted interpretation. Observe the parallel: in both cases the Son of man appears in great glory, and the people ("his elect"—"all nations") are gathered before him. But 25:46 proves without possibility of successful contradiction that the end of the age has been reached. The moment has arrived when "these—the goats; i.e., the wicked—shall go away into everlasting punishment: but the righteous into everlasting life."

It is not claimed, of course, that any exegete is able completely to untangle what is here intertwined, so as to indicate accurately for each

---

[789] Thus also F. W. Grosheide, *op. cit.*, pp. 355, 356; C. R. Erdman, *op. cit.*, p. 192, and many others.

individual passage just how much refers to Jerusalem's fall, and how much to the great tribulation and second coming.

5. The main emphasis in both chapters is on the necessity of always being on the alert, active for the Master, faithful to him. See especially 24:4, 23, 25, 42, 44-51; and the entire chapter 25.

The two chapters contain ten easily recognized parts or paragraphs:

1. In verses 1-3 *the occasion* that gave rise to this discourse is described. That occasion was as follows: In harmony with what Jesus had already implied in 23:38 he now, having left the temple, in reply to the disciples' expression of amazement about the grandeur of that building predicts its total destruction. Arrived on the Mount of Olives the disciples ask him when this shall happen and what shall be *the sign* (note the singular) of his coming and of the end of the age. They evidently think that the end of the temple means the end of the age (or "world").

2. In his answer Jesus first of all—verses 4-14—predicts various coming events: the arrival of false Christs and false prophets, wars and rumors of wars, famines, earthquakes, persecution, apostasy, lawlessness, and the chilling of mutual love. He declares that all of this shall be only *the beginning of woes or birth pains.* The "end" about which the disciples have inquired "is not yet." More definite is the fact that the gospel shall be preached in the whole world. "And then shall come the end."

3. If the world-wide preaching of the gospel may be considered the first of two definite preliminary signs, then *the great tribulation,* described in verses 15-28, is the second. Occurring immediately before the appearance of "the sign of the Son of man in the sky" and his glorious (second) coming (see verses 29, 30), it is foreshadowed by woes in store for Jerusalem. These woes, too, are followed by one definite sign, namely, the appearance of "the desolating sacrilege," that is, Jerusalem compassed with armies (Luke 21:20) carrying idol images of their emperor upon their standards. This would be the sign or signal for those in Judea to flee to the hills. However, the destruction of Jerusalem is not the end of the age. Believers must not be deceived by cries such as, "Look, here (is) the Christ," or "There." As far as the second coming is concerned, no one will have to call attention to it, for it will be sudden and everywhere visible, resembling an abrupt lightning flash seen from one horizon to the other. That coming of the Son of man is going to occur when it *must* occur, because morally and spiritually mankind will have deteriorated to such an extent that it will resemble carrion ready to be devoured by vultures.

4. The sun shall be darkened, the moon shall not give her light, the stars shall fall from the sky, etc. Then suddenly there is *the sign,* the *one* sign about which the disciples had asked, "the Son of man appearing in the sky." The glorious character of this appearance is convincing proof that this is

848

indeed the Messiah of prophecy and that "the wedding of the Lamb" with his bride, the church, is about to take place (cf. Eph. 5:32; Rev. 19:7). With a loud "trumpet blast" the angels shall gather his elect from everywhere (verses 29-31).

5. *A lesson from the fig tree* is found in verses 32-35, and may be paraphrased thus: "As soon as its branch becomes tender and puts forth leaves, y o u know that summer is near. So also y o u, my disciples, when y o u see all this—the series of events climaxed by the appearance of 'the desolating sacrilege'—will know that the fall of Jerusalem and its temple is near, even at the gates." As for the Jews in general, Jesus predicts that this generation or kind of people shall not pass away until "all this"—events stretching all the way to the appearance of the Son of man and his coming on the clouds of the sky—*takes place*. Jesus adds, "Heaven and earth shall pass away, but my words shall never pass away."

6. *The necessity of being ready always, in view of the unknown day and hour of Christ's coming* is stressed in verses 36-44. At the time of the flood people did not expect sudden disaster. So they continued to live as if nothing would ever happen, paying no attention to their spiritual calling. Then suddenly the flood came and swept them away. By no means is Jesus at his return going to welcome every person to his loving embrace. One is taken, the other left behind. The disciples should therefore always be on the alert, just as a home-owner would be on the alert all the time if he knew that a burglar was going to try to break into his house but did not know exactly when this would occur.

7. *Such readiness means faithfulness,* loving and loyal service to the Master. This truth is set forth by means of the parable of *The Faithful and Sensible Servant* (who is rewarded) *versus The Unfaithful and Wicked Servant* (who is punished); see verses 45-51.

8. and 9. The parable of *The Five Foolish and The Five Sensible* (or The Five Thoughtless and The Five Thoughtful) *Girls* (25:1-13) and that of *The Talents* (verses 14-30) re-emphasize the proper manner of awaiting Christ's return. However, each does this in its own way: the first stressing *preparedness;* the second, adding to this *faithfulness.*

10. *The Son of man's coming in his glory, to judge all the nations,* is pictured in verses 31-46, under the symbolism of a shepherd who puts the sheep on his right, the goats on his left. Those on the right, subsequently called "the righteous" (verses 37, 46), shall be rewarded with everlasting life. The loving service which by grace they have spontaneously rendered to Christ's brothers, even to the least of them, hence, to Christ himself, shows that their faith was genuine. So also the lack of this loving service proves the opposite for those on the left, the wicked, who are condemned to everlasting punishment.

1. *The Occasion*

24:1. Jesus left the temple and was walking away when his disciples approached him to call his attention to the buildings of the temple. It is Tuesday, a few days before the Passover Lamb is going to offer himself as an atonement for the sins of his people. In all probability it is late afternoon of this very busy and memorable day. Jesus left the temple and is in the act of walking away from it when his disciples approach him with the purpose of calling his attention to the beauty and massiveness of their sacred edifice: "Teacher, look, what (huge) stones, what (magnificent) buildings!" The reason why just at this particular moment these men are thinking of the temple is that Jesus had just told them, "Behold, y o u r house is left to y o u a deserted place." Though it is reasonable to believe that the expression "y o u r house" meant Jerusalem, the temple was certainly included. It is as if the disciples were saying, "Is it really true that also this glorious structure is going to be entirely deserted by and by?" **2. He answered them, Do y o u see all this? I solemnly assure y o u, there shall not be left here one stone upon another that shall not be thrown down.** For "I solemnly assure y o u" see on 5:18. The meaning of the solemn statement is probably: not only is this building complex going to be *deserted,* it shall be completely *destroyed,* the hyperbolic figure "not one stone upon another" indicating the totality of its destruction. For fulfilment see on 22:7.

3. And as he was sitting on the Mount of Olives the disciples came to him privately, saying, Tell us, when shall this happen, and what (shall be) the sign of thy coming and of the end of the age? A little while afterward Jesus is sitting on the Mount of Olives. We can imagine how, looking across the valley, a truly fascinating view disclosed itself to the eyes of the little company. There was the roof of the temple bathed in a sea of golden glory. There were those beautiful terraced courts and also those cloisters of snowy marble which seemed to shine and sparkle in the light of the setting sun. And then to think that all this glory was about to perish! The minds of the disciples reeled and staggered when they pondered that mysterious and awesome prediction.

All this glory! "Beautiful for elevation, the joy of the whole earth, is Mount Zion . . . the city of the Great King. . . . Walk about Zion, and go round about her: count her towers. Mark well her bulwarks. Consider her palaces" (Ps. 48:2, 12, 13). This surely was true no less with respect to the greatly enlarged and lavishly adorned temple which King Herod I had started to build. See above p. 159. "Nor has there been, either in ancient or modern times, a sacred building equal to the temple, whether for situation or magnificence." [790] Rabbinic literature is not particularly favorable to Herod.

---

[790] A Edersheim, *The Temple,* London, 1908, p. 28.

Nevertheless, concerning Herod's temple it states, "He who never saw Herod's edifice has never in his life seen a beautiful building." [791]

We can picture the disciples riveting their eyes on "Jerusalem's pride," in deep silence and sorrow meditating on the words of doom spoken by Jesus. Finally that silence is broken by four of the men: Peter, James, John, and Andrew (Mark 13:3). Stepping up to Jesus they ask, "Tell us, when shall this happen, and what (shall be) the sign of thy coming and of the end of the age?" The very form in which the question is cast—the juxtaposition of the clauses—seems to indicate that, as these men (spokesmen for the rest of The Twelve) interpret the Master's words, Jerusalem's fall, particularly the destruction of the temple, would mean the end of the world. In this opinion they were partly mistaken, as Jesus is about to show. A lengthy period of time would intervene between Jerusalem's fall and the culmination of the age, the second coming. Nevertheless, the disciples were not entirely wrong: there was indeed a connection between the judgment to be executed upon the Jewish nation and the final judgment on the day of the consummation of all things. As has already been indicated, the first was a type, a foreshadowing or adumbration, of the second.

The point has been raised, "How could the disciples, to whom Christ's repeated predictions of his coming death and resurrection meant so little (16:21, 22; Mark 9:32; Luke 9:45; 18:34), ask about his (second) coming?" A distinction must be made, however, between *thoroughly understanding* a thing and *being emotionally interested* in it. The disciples, to be sure, failed to fathom Christ's predictions concerning a resurrection from the dead, but if anything of that nature was going to happen, so that Jesus would rise again and would then go to his Father and sit on the throne, they wanted to know more about this; perhaps especially also because their Lord had promised that he would return to them and that they, too, would sit on thrones (19:28; 23:39). For the term "coming" or "parousia" see on verse 27.

Though it must be freely admitted that this is not a thorough explanation of their condition of mind, it may clear up the situation to some extent. At any rate, the question they asked was the occasion that gave rise to their Master's famous eschatological discourse.

2. The Beginning of Woes or Birth Pains

4-12. **Jesus replied, Take care that no one misleads y o u. For many shall come in my name, saying, I am the Christ, and shall mislead many. And y o u are going to hear about wars and rumors of wars, but watch out; do not be disturbed, for such things must happen, but that is not yet the end. For (one) nation shall rise up in arms against (another) nation, and (one) kingdom against (another) kingdom, and there shall be famines and earth-**

---

[791] Baba Batra 4a.

quakes in various places, but all these things are (only) the beginning of birth pains. Then y o u shall be handed over to tribulation and y o u shall be put to death, and y o u shall be hated by all the nations for my name's sake. And then many shall fall away, betraying and hating each other. And many false prophets shall arise and shall mislead many; and because lawlessness shall increase, the love of the majority shall grow cold.

Jesus now proceeds to correct their mistaken inference. He shows them that "not everything that seems to be a sign of the end of the world is in reality such a sign." In other words, there are also signs which only in a very general sense are deserving of that name. Whenever these separate happenings are interpreted as being infallible indications that the end of the age is immediately in sight, they deserve the name "mistaken signs." Thus, Jesus predicts the coming of false Christs—individuals who will say: "I am the Christ.'—and false prophets, who shall mislead many. Those who persist in being misled show that they never belonged to Christ's true flock (I John 2:19; cf. I Cor. 11:19). There have always been false prophets, deceivers. Their victims begin to oppose God's laws. This "lawlessness" shall increase, with the natural result: division within the family circle, decrease in love for each other, exactly as Jesus had previously predicted (cf. 24:12 with 10:34-37). It is not necessary to name any of the false prophets. They were present in connection with Jerusalem's fall, but they did not cease to be in evidence after that great catastrophe of A.D. 70. The disciples must not be led astray by them (24:4). Their claims should be rejected. Moreover, the very fact that they never vanish from the earth during this entire dispensation clearly shows that their appearance and work can never constitute a sign in the restricted sense of the term.

This also holds true with respect to "wars and rumors of wars" (24:6). When Jesus speaks these words, the Roman empire has been enjoying a long era of peace. But about four decades later political turmoil will upset the great realm from one end to the other, so that Rome will see four emperors in one year: Galba, Otho, Vitellius, and Vespasian. But these violent revolts and insurrections cannot by any stretch of the imagination constitute definite indications that the Lord will return immediately. This is evident at once when one considers the fact that wars and rumors of war did not cease with Jerusalem's fall. Throughout the centuries the prophecy attains fulfilment: "nation shall rise against nation, and kingdom against kingdom" (verse 7a). One author counted three hundred wars in Europe during the last three hundred years. And these wars are increasing in intensity. It is perfectly clear that when any particular war is singled out as a help for "date-fixers" another "mistaken sign" has been produced.

Jesus also speaks about "famines and earthquakes in various places" (verse 7b). As was true with respect to other predicted events, so it is here. These disturbances in the physical realm are indeed foreshadowings and portrayals of that which, on a much more extensive and intensive scale, will take place in the realm of nature at the end of the age; but except in that very general sense they cannot be correctly termed signs. Not any single one of them could ever give anyone the right to make predictions with reference either to the date of Jerusalem's fall or to the time of the Parousia (Christ's second coming). It is true that during the period A.D. 60-80 famine, pestilence, fire, hurricane, and earthquake ravaged the empire, as Renan points out in *l' Antichrist*. Vesuvius erupted violently in the summer of 79, destroying Pompeii and its surroundings. But, as is already clear from the preceding sentence, these catastrophes were not limited to the decade preceding the fall of Jerusalem in the year 70. Moreover, throughout the centuries there have been violent earthquakes. For example: On Nov. 1, 1755, 60,000 people perished at Lisbon, Portugal; in 1783 the great Calabrian earthquake occurred with the death of an estimated 30,000; in 1857 the Neapolitan earthquake took more than 12,000 lives. There was also the Charleston earthquake in 1886; the Assam in 1897; the one in California in 1906, which destroyed a considerable section of San Francisco; the one in Messina in 1908; in Avezzano, Italy in 1915; several in Turkey, from 1939 until very recently; the one that shook Kansu Province, China, in 1920; the one that hit Japan, in 1923, wrecking parts of Tokyo and Yokohama; those in Chile, in 1939, 1960, and even more recently; the devastating earthquake in Peru, 1970; etc. Ancient historians and philosophers—such as Thucydides, Aristotle, Strabo, Seneca, Livy, and Pliny—describe similar seismic phenomena in their days. And as early as the year 1668 Robert Hooke wrote his work bearing the title, *Discourse on Earthquakes*. A certain author counted no less than seven hundred disturbances of this nature, great and small, which had occurred in the nineteenth century!

It is hardly necessary to add to this that not only false Christs and false prophets, wars and rumors of war, earthquakes and famines occur in every age throughout the history of the church, but so do also persecutions and defections, to which Jesus refers in verses 9, 10, 12, and 13. The saying has been verified in every century: "And y o u shall be hated by all nations for my name's sake," that is, because of y o u r vital connection with me. See also on 6:9; 7:22; 10:22, 41, 42; 12:21. The very expression "all nations" clearly shows that Jesus is not thinking solely of what happens during the life-time of the apostles.

Now with respect to events such as these described Jesus says in verses 6 and 8, "Do not be disturbed, for such things must happen, but that is not yet the end. All these things are (only) the beginning of birth pains." They mark the beginning, says Jesus. They do not mark the end. Therefore, do not be alarmed.

In spite of this clear warning which our Lord gave to his disciples, many present-day church members are filled with admiration for the minister or

evangelist who speaks learnedly about "The Signs of the Times," and strives
to show his audience that this or that terrible battle, serious earthquake, or
devastating famine "on the basis of prophecy" is the infallible "sign" of
Christ's imminent return.

To be sure, the events here indicated have significance. They are stepping
stones leading to the final goal. By means of them the end of the age is both
foreshadowed and brought closer, and God's eternal plan is being carried
forward. Moreover, when we realize that toward the end of the present
dispensation the indicated disturbances will occur together (24:33), will
probably be more numerous, extensive, and fearful than ever before (24:11;
cf. Luke 21:11, 25, 26), and are going to take place in connection with the
great tribulation that shall usher in the parousia (Matt. 24:5-9), we may
conclude that it would not be unreasonable to call *the final outbreak* of
these terrors "concurrent or accompanying signs."

Jesus continues: 13. **But he that endures to the end, he shall be saved.** As
in 10:22 so also here the meaning is: he who, in spite of all these disturbances and persecutions, remains loyal to Christ shall enter into glory. For
himself the period of persecution and trial will last until death delivers him
from this earthly scene (John 16:33; II Tim. 3:12). For the church in general
it will last until Christ's return in glory (II Thess. 1:7; Rev. 11:10-12).

In verses 4-12 Jesus has been speaking about a series of events which,
taken by themselves, do not definitely indicate "the end" about which the
disciples had inquired. Suddenly there is a change from "but that is not yet
the end" to "and then shall come the end." Perhaps we may regard "he that
endures to the end" of verse 13 as the transition, since in saying "the end"
the mind easily moves from the contemplation of the close of any believer's
individual life, to the consummation of the world's history. At any rate, it is
clear that the Lord did not forget the question of the disciples. Having
warned them against paying undue attention to such constantly repeated
disturbances which in large measure can be called "false signs," he now says:
14. **And this gospel of the kingdom shall be preached in the whole world as
a testimony to all the nations, and then shall come the end.** He does not say,
"Then *immediately*," reserving this word "immediately" for verse 29, but
simply "then." This "then" may well be taken as covering more territory
than "immediately afterward" would have done. The final bitter attack
against God's people, called "the great tribulation" (verse 21), of very brief
duration (verse 22), as well as the actual coming of the Lord upon the
clouds, is probably included in this reference to "the end." What Jesus is
saying, therefore, is that the concluding events of the world's history are
going to be preceded by the preaching of the kingdom gospel "to all the
nations." That, as he saw and predicted it, such worldwide gospel proclamation would not be a matter of a few weeks, months or even years, but would
range over a much longer period of time, many centuries, can be regarded as

certain. The essence of that gospel is summarized in such passages as 3:2; 4:17, 23; 11:28-30; 26:6, 7; John 3:16; cf. Rom. 1:17; 3:24; II Cor. 5:20, 21. It is definitely the gospel of "the kingdom," that is, of the reign of God in heart and life, by grace and through faith. For more on this one and only gospel—its power, author, emphasis, message, etc.—see N.T.C. on Philippians, pp. 81-85.

It is hardly necessary to point out that there is here no promise that "every person will receive a chance to be saved." Jesus is speaking about *the nations* of the world. He is saying that each of these nations at one time or another during the course of history will hear the gospel. This gospel will be a *testimony:* its acceptance or its rejection will be decisive. There is no promise here of any second chance. Whatever each nation or people does with the *present* gospel proclamation will have final results. It is instructive to compare these words of our Lord with Rev. 11. In that chapter the witnesses go forth and prophesy "a thousand two hundred and threescore days." Finally, their testimony is finished. Then, after a very brief period of persecution (called symbolically "three days and a half"), they are translated to heaven. Similarly also in Rev. 20 the nations receive their great opportunity (so that the dragon cannot deceive them) during the thousand year period. Then, "for a little time" Satan is loosed out of his prison. This, in turn, is followed by the appearance of the Christ upon "a great white throne." It is therefore clearly evident that the program of history is the same in all three chapters (Matt. 24; Rev. 11; 20).

A brief survey of the progress of missions from the earliest period until the present day will convince anyone that the days in which we are now living are significant indeed! By and large the gospel has been spreading "from the rising of the sun to its setting." One author estimates that by the close of the Apostolic Period the total number of Christian disciples had already reached half a million. [792] During this early period one missionary towers above all the rest, namely, Paul. Farther and farther westward he brought the gospel. He finally reached Rome as the Lord's prisoner. But even his imprisonment is a help rather than a hindrance to the spread of the good news. He states: "Now I want you to know, brothers, that the things that have happened to me have in reality turned out to the advantage of the gospel, so that it has become clear to the whole praetorian guard and to all the rest that my bonds

---

[792] R. H. Glover, *The Progress of World-Wide Missions,* New York, 1925, p. 39. Another very valuable source for the study of missionary progress is *The Evangelical Missions Quarterly,* published by Evangelical Information Service, Wheaton, Ill. Further: *Frontier,* Wrexham, England; *De Heerbaan,* Amsterdam; *INFA NEWS,* Ridgefield Park, N. J.; *East Asia Missions,* Philadelphia; *Africa Now,* New York; and *Church Growth Bulletin,* Pasadena, Cal. See also the article, "Expansion of Christianity (Modern)" in Twentieth Century extension of S.H.E.R.K., Vol. I, pp. 412-417; and the article "Religion" in *Britannica, Book of the Year* 1971, pp. 634-652.

are for Christ" (Phil. 1:12, 13). During the next period, 100-313 (death of John to Constantine) the gospel continues to penetrate the then-known world, and this in spite of many persecutions (Trajan to Diocletian). This is, indeed, very remarkable especially in the light of the fact that no less than 174,000 martyrs were buried in a single great tomb, namely, the catacombs of St. Sebastian in Rome. From Constantine to Charlemagne, 313-800, the tidings of salvation are carried to the countries of *Western* Europe by such famous heroes of the cross as Ulfilas, Patrick, Columba, Augustine, Willibrord, and Boniface. Meanwhile, Mohammedanism banishes the light of the gospel from many lands of Asia and Africa. Next comes the period of the Middle Ages, from Charlemagne to Luther, 800-1517. Norway, Iceland, and Greenland are evangelized, and the Eastern Slavs turn to Christianity in a body. The Crusades, expeditions originally intended to wreak vengeance upon the Mohammedans, turned out to be a hindrance as well as a help to the propagation of the truth. During the period 1517-1792 many missionary societies originate, and the gospel is carried still farther *westward.* Think of John Eliot, the apostle to the North American Indians, and those that follow in his footsteps. And so we come to the modern period, 1792 to the present. It is in the year 1792 that William Carey at a ministerial conference proposes the discussion of the theme "The duty of Christians to attempt the spread of the gospel among heathen nations." On May 31 of that year this truly great man preaches his famous missionary sermon based on Isa. 54:2, 3. As a result of the enthusiasm which he arouses missionaries are sent to faraway countries so that India, southeastern Asia, China, Japan, Korea—nations that are reached by traveling from America across the great Pacific in a *westerly* direction—receive the gospel.

The work has not been completed. Even today it can hardly be said without qualification that the heart of Africa, of Asia, and of South America has been thoroughly penetrated. But it cannot be denied that the prophecy of our Lord is approaching fulfilment. Consider this important fact: seventy years ago the Bible (as a whole or in part) had been translated into only 300 languages; today into about 1400 languages and dialects. And the work is still continuing; in fact, more vigorously than ever, many forces combining to bring it about.

It must not be supposed, however, that the world is going to get better and better right along, until the very moment of Christ's arrival. If the preaching of the gospel to all the nations may be called *the first preliminary sign* of Christ's return, *the second preliminary sign* is now going to be pointed out. As already shown, it will cover a much shorter period of time. Cf. Rev. 20:3. In this connection it must also be stressed that in all probability the close of the gospel age and the beginning of the great tribulation overlap. As has also been shown—see p. 847—in describing the brief period of great tribulation at the close of history, ending with the final judgment, Jesus is painting in colors borrowed from the destruction of Jerusalem by the Romans. This must be borne in mind as we now study:

3. The Great Tribulation

15, 16. Now when y o u see 'the desolating sacrilege,' which was spoken of through Daniel the prophet, standing in the holy place—let him who reads understand—, then let those in Judea flee to the hills. . . . Jesus had said, "Behold, y o u r house is left to y o u a deserted place. . . . I solemnly assure y o u, there shall not be left here one stone upon another that shall not be thrown down" (23:38; 24:2). The disciples had reacted with the question, "Tell us, when shall this happen, and what (shall be) the sign of thy coming and of the end of the age?" (24:3). As to the erroneous implication of that question, as if the fall of Jerusalem and its temple would be immediately followed by the end of the age, Jesus has set the disciples straight on that. He has shown that many disturbances will occur and that a lengthy period of gospel proclamation is going to intervene before the day of his coming arrives. As to the first part of the question, considered all by itself, "When shall this—destruction of Jerusalem and its temple—be?" Jesus answers it now, but in such a way that the answer suits more than one event in history. To begin with, it was appropriate for the days immediately referred to by Daniel; see especially Dan. 11:31; 12:11. In accordance with that prophet's prediction Antiochus Epiphanes (175-164 B.C.), unaware that he was indeed fulfilling prophecy, and being thoroughly responsible for his own wicked deed, erected a pagan altar over the altar of burnt-offering, thus polluting the house of God. This had happened long ago. Nevertheless, Jesus says, "Now when y o u see 'the desolating sacrilege,' " showing that he is telling the disciples that a divine oracle may apply to more than one historical situation: the sacrilege that results in the desolation of city and temple takes place more than once in history. Let the man who reads Daniel's prophecy understand this! Just as in the past the holy places of the Lord had been desecrated, so it will happen again. And it did indeed take place when the Roman armies, with the image of the emperor upon their standards, an image and an emperor worshipped by them[793] laid siege to the city of Jerusalem (Luke 21:20). But just as the pagan altar and the swine offered upon it in the very temple of Jehovah in the second century B.C. pointed forward to the idolatrous legions of Rome, so these in turn foreshadowed the great and final violation by the antichrist of all that is sacred. It is for this reason that in verses 29-31 Jesus is able to say, "Immediately after the tribulation of those days, the sun shall be darkened, and the moon shall not give her light. . . . And then the sign of the Son of man shall appear in the

---

[793] See Josephus *Jewish War* VI.316.

sky . . . and then they shall see the Son of man coming on the clouds of the sky, with power and great glory."

Returning now to the second application of the prophecy, namely, to the days just previous to Jerusalem's fall (A.D. 70), when the Roman armies would arrive and desecrate "the holy place," that is, the soil which, together with its "holy city" and "holy Temple," had been historically consecrated to the Lord, Jesus warns his followers that when this occurs those in Judea should "flee to the hills." Cf. Luke 21:20. They must not try to enter Jerusalem, thinking that the Lord would never allow it to be taken. Instead those who are still in the city and have a chance to get out must do so at once; those dwelling in the Judean countryside must join them in fleeing to the hills.

As to the fulfilment, we know that the Jews in general rushed *into* Jerusalem, resulting in a horrible blood bath. [794] But what happened to the Christians? Did they heed Christ's exhortation to flee to the hills? According to many commentators they did, and finally found refuge in Perean Pella. To substantiate their opinion these commentators appeal to the statement of Eusebius: "On the other hand, the people of the Jerusalem church were commanded by an oracle given by revelation before the war to those in the city who were worthy of it to depart and dwell in one of the cities of Perea which they called Pella" (*Eccl. Hist.* III.v.3). According to Epiphanius the exit from the city and flight to Pella began just before the Romans laid siege to Jerusalem (Ag. Her. XXIX.7). Scholars who have made a special study of the early history of the Jerusalem church doubt this fourth century A.D. report. They tell us that *a.* in order at this time to get to Pella, believers would have had to break their way through lines of Roman soldiers; *b.* the people left in Pella were filled with bitter hatred against all Jews, including Christian Jews; *c.* Pella could not have provided housing for all the refugees; and *d.* if the escape had been attempted at a slightly earlier date, the Christians would have fallen into the hostile hands of the fanatical Jewish freedom-fighters. [795]

Pella is nowhere mentioned in Scripture. With reference to the extent to which believers obeyed the Lord's instruction to flee "to the hills"—he did not say "to Pella"—there is no reliable information. Let us hope that many obeyed his kind and urgent warning, which continues as follows: **17, 18. let him who (happens to be) on the housetop not go down to get the things out that are in his house; and let him who is in the field not go back to get his coat.** The man who is on the flat roof, from which by an outside ladder he is able to descend in order as quickly as possible to flee to the hills, must not,

---

[794] Josephus refers to the city's overcrowded condition (*Jewish War* VI.420).

[795] See, among others, H. Mulder, "Wederkerige assistentie en vervreemding van kerken in de nieuwtestamentische tijd," *De Heerbaan*, 4 (1971), pp. 265-269; and, by the same author, *Geschiedenis van de palestijnse kerk (tot 638)*, Kampen, no date, pp. 46-48.

after descending, go into the house to rescue his goods. Similarly, the laborer, dressed only in his tunic, and thus working in the field, must not go back from the field into his house, but must immediately take off for the hills. Delay, in either case, might mean being captured, turned back, or perhaps even being killed.

The sympathetic heart of our Lord, revealed on so many previous occasions as recorded in this Gospel (8:17; 9:13, 36; 11:25-30; 12:7, 30; 15:32; 19:13-15; 23:23, 37), is deeply affected by two additional considerations: *a.* the plight of women, and *b.* travel difficulties during the winter and on sabbaths: **19. But woe to those who are pregnant** [796] **and to those who nurse babies** [797] **in those days!**

In this connection it should be borne in mind that this tender concern for women with babies was revealed by Christ in days when women were often looked down upon. The words uttered came from the lips of the same Son of man who showed special kindness to widows (Mark 12:42, 43; Luke 7:11-17; 18:1-8; 20:47; 21:2, 3); to women who were, or had been, living in sin (Luke 7:36-50; John 4:1-30); and, at the time of his own crowning agony, to his own mother (John 19:26, 27). It is to him that also the women of today should turn for help and comfort!

20. Pray that y o u r flight may not occur in winter or on the sabbath. . . . Even in that climate the winter has its cold days. Moreover, it is the rainy season. Snow, especially in the hills to which Jesus had ordered his followers to flee and even lower down, could not be entirely ruled out (cf. I Macc. 13:22). Traveling on the sabbath was difficult. To be sure, even the rabbis permitted flight on the sabbath when a person was in danger of losing his life. And Christ's own teaching on the subject of sabbath observance (Matt. 12:11; Mark 2:27) was sufficiently generous to make allowance for escape on that day. But the many man-made rules and regulations by means of which the scribes and the Pharisees had created the impression that man was indeed made for the sabbath would have resulted in refusals on the part of many a strict observer to help those in need. So the Lord urges his disciples to pray that they may not have to flee in winter or on the sabbath. [798]

From what immediately follows it is evident once again that for Jesus the transition from the second to the third application of Daniel's prediction was as easy as that from the first (the tribulation experienced by God's people during the reign of Antiochus Epiphanes) to the second (the distress in connection with the fall of Jerusalem): **21, 22. . . . for then there shall be**

---

[796] ἐν γαστρὶ ἔχειν (*to have in the womb*) is idiomatic for to be *pregnant*.

[797] θηλαζούσαις is dat. pl. fem. pres. participle of θηλάζω (cf. Mark 13:17; Luke 21:23), literally *to give suck, give the breast.* Cf. θηλή: *breast.*

[798] Mark (see 13:18), writing for a different public, not hampered by Jewish restrictions, did not have to retain what Jesus says here with reference to traveling on the sabbath.

great tribulation, such as there has never been since the beginning of the world until now, and as there shall never be again. And if those days were not cut short no one would be saved. But for the sake of the elect those days shall be cut short. As to the "great tribulation" to which Jesus here refers, care should be exercised. Rev. 7:14 also speaks about a "great tribulation." Are these two the same? The answer is: they are not. As the context in Rev. 7 indicates, the word is used there in a far more general sense. Because of his faith every genuine child of God experiences tribulation during his life on earth. See John 16:33; cf. Rom. 8:18; II Cor. 4:17; II Tim. 3:12. But Jesus is here speaking about a tribulation that will characterize "those days," a tribulation such as has never been and never again shall be, *a very brief period of dire distress that shall occur immediately before his return* (see verses 29-31). It is the period mentioned also in Rev. 11:7-9; 20:3b, 7-9a. For the sake of God's chosen ones—see N.T.C. on Eph. 1:4—in order that not all might have to die a violent death, the days of this final tribulation shall be cut short. [799] Herein, too, the love of God is made manifest. It should hardly be necessary to add that justice is not done to the concept of this tribulation, which immediately precedes "the end" of the world's history and which surpasses any other distress in its intensity, if it is referred solely to the sorrows experienced during the fall of Jerusalem.

Jesus continues: **23, 24. At that time if anyone should say to y o u, Look, here (is) the Christ! or There (he is)!, do not believe (him); for false Christs shall arise and false prophets, and shall perform great signs and miracles, so as to mislead, if possible, even the elect.** In connection with Jerusalem's fall but certainly also with the end of the age there will be those who claim that the Christ has already arrived, and will even point to the place where he has landed. Jesus warns his disciples not to believe these deceivers. Some of them (the pseudo-Christs) pretend to be Christ; the rest (the pseudo-prophets) say that this or that other person is the Christ. By means of a mighty display of *a.* "signs"—supernatural feats which point away from the performers to their enabler—, and of *b.* "wonders" or "marvels"—the same astonishing performances viewed now from the aspect of their unusual character and their effect on the spectators—these deceivers shall try *to mislead*, [800] *if possible*, even the elect. For "the elect" see N.T.C. on Eph. 1:4. The implication is that to successfully mislead God's elect, so that until the day of their death they would permit themselves to resemble wandering stars, is impossible. See N.T.C. on Phil. 1:6. The comforting little sentence, only three words in the original, **25. See, I have told y o u ahead**

---

[799] κολοβοθήσονται, 3rd per. pl. fut. indic. passive of κολοβόω, *to cut short, curtail.* Our English word *halt*, in the sense of *lame*, is related to it, since it refers to a person whose walking ability has been cut short or curtailed.

[800] For πλανάω see on 18:12, 13.

of time—literally: "See I-have-foretold y o u"—reminds us of Christ's similar sayings in John 13:19; 14:29; 16:4. Lovingly the Master provides for his disciples. When the fiery trial arrives they must never be able to say, "How strange and unexpected! Why did not the Lord prepare us for this? Why did he not warn us?" Having been forewarned, the disciples will not be unduly disturbed when the prediction is fulfilled. In fact, their faith in Jesus will even be confirmed. 26. **So, if they shall say to y o u, Look, he is in the wilderness, do not go out there; Look, he is in the inner rooms, do not believe (them).** [801] Some, with reflection on John the Baptist (3:1), may point to the wilderness as the place where the Messiah is to be found. Others, to the inner rooms, as if the Christ were only for a few initiates, the Head of a private fraternity, revealing himself to no one else. In fact, the very opposite is the truth. It will not be necessary in that day to go in search of the Christ, as if he were to be found in some arid waste or some dark corner. Fact is: 27. **For as the lightning** [802] **goes out from the east** [803] **and flashes clear to the west, so shall be the coming of the Son of man.** For *Son of man* see on 8:20; pp. 403-407.

A word should be said about the important term "coming," in Greek *parousia*. It is sometimes used in the non-technical sense of *a. presence;* see I Cor. 16:17; II Cor. 10:10; Phil. 1:26; 2:12; or of *b. coming, advent,* or *arrival* (II Cor. 7:6, 7; II Thess. 2:9). In other passages—see especially Matt. 24:3, 27 (the one now under study), 37, 39; I Cor. 15:23; I Thess. 2:19; 3:13; 4:15; 5:23; II Thess. 2:1, 8; James 5:7, 8; II Peter 1:16; 3:4, 12; and I John 2:28—the term refers to *the return or advent of the Lord, his coming in order to bless his people with his presence.* This meaning may be viewed as a modification of the sense: "the arrival" or "the visit" of the king or emperor. [804] The sense of the comparison, then, is this, that just as a lightning flash is so brilliant that from one end of heaven to the other it is clearly visible, so Christ's coming shall be such that "every eye shall see him" (Rev. 1:7).

As to the time of this coming, and one of its reasons, note verse 28. **Wherever there is a corpse, there the vultures will gather.** Cf. Job 39:30, "Where the slain (lie) there is he"; also Luke 17:37. Vultures swoop down upon *a carcass.* When morally and spiritually the world has degenerated to such an extent that it resembles carrion, in other words when the Lord judges that the world's cup of iniquity is full (cf. Gen. 15:16; Rev. 14:18),

---

[801] For ἔρημος (*wilderness*) see on 23:38; for ταμεῖον *inner room,* on 6:6.

[802] ἀστραπή here *lightning;* so also in 28:3; Luke 10:18; 17:24; and in Rev. 4:5; 8:5; 16:18; but in Luke 11:36 *shining brightness.*

[803] For ἀνατολή see on 2:1, 2. Here in 24:27 it is coupled with *the west,* that is, the place of the *going down* or *setting* of the sun.

[804] See A. Deissmann, *op. cit.,* p. 368.

then, and not until then, Christ shall come to condemn that world. Then his coming is a divine necessity.

The final "tribulation" to which the wicked will subject God's children is that which will ripen the world for judgment. So it is immediately after that severest of all trials that the Son of man arrives.

4. *The Sign and The Coming*

In view of the fact that what now follows is deeply rooted in prophecy, and must be interpreted in the light of the style that is characteristic of that type of literature, the most significant Old Testament references (and a few from the New) will at once be shown:

29-31. Immediately after the tribulation of those days,

> The sun shall be darkened,
> And the moon shall not give her light,   Isa. 13:10; Ezek. 32:7; Joel 2:10b; 2:31 (=3:4 Heb.); 3:15 (=4:15 Heb.); Rev. 6:12.

> And the stars shall fall from the sky,   Isa. 34:4b; Rev. 6: 13.

And the powers of the heavens shall be shaken,   Isa. 34:4b; Joel 2:10a; Hag. 2:6, 21; Luke 21:25, 26; Rev. 6:13.

And then the sign of the Son of man shall appear in the sky, and then

> All the tribes of the earth shall mourn,   Zech. 12:10, 12; Rev. 1:7.

and they shall see

> The Son of man coming on the clouds of the sky with

power and great glory;   Dan. 7:13, 14; Matt. 16:27; 26:64.

> And he shall send forth his angels with a loud trum-

pet blast,   Isa. 27:13; Matt. 13: 41; 16:27; I Cor. 15: 52; I Thess. 4:16; II Thess. 1:7.

> And they shall gather his elect from the four winds,
> from the one end of heaven to the other.   Deut. 30:4; Zech. 2:6.

862

The picture is very vivid. While the earth is drenched with the blood of the saints in the most terrible tribulation of all time, all at once the sun becomes darkened. Naturally the moon now also ceases to give her light. The stars deviate from their orbits and race to their doom; they "fall from heaven." The powers of the heaven are shaken. Terrifying sounds are heard. There is "the roaring of the sea and the billows," causing perplexity among men. People faint with fear and with foreboding of what is beginning to happen to the world (Luke 21:25, 26).

In connection with this apocalyptic picture strict literalness must be avoided. Until this prophetic panorama becomes history we shall probably not know how much of this description must be taken literally and how much figuratively. That at least some of it must be taken literally is clear from II Peter 3:10. There will indeed be a "new heaven and earth" (Rev. 21:1). The great change that will take place may be described as follows:

a. The universe will have been purged completely by *a great conflagration* (II Peter 3:7, 11, 12).

b. Closely linked with this conflagration there is going to be a *rejuvenation*. The fire will not completely destroy the universe. It will still be the same heavens and earth, but gloriously renewed as explained in II Peter 3:13; Rev. 21:1-5. Not only shall God's children "go to heaven," but heaven will, as it were, come down to them; that is, the conditions of perfection that will obtain in heaven will be found throughout God's rejuvenated universe.

c. This wonderful transformation can also be viewed as a *self-realization,* a mighty change whereby the organic realm attains to self-expression and complete liberty. This thought is brought out most beautifully in Rom. 8:18-22. In this passage the apostle states that at present creation is subjected to "vanity." Now this word "vanity" does not at all have the meaning which we commonly attach to it. The word as used here in the original does not mean "shallow pride," or "saucy airs." It has no reference to ambitious display, as when we say: "What a vain fellow." It means *futility,* lack of effectiveness. Compare the expression: "Vanity of vanities, saith the Preacher; all is vanity" (Eccl. 12:8). It indicates that at present, as a result of man's sin, nature does not come to self-realization or self-expression. Its potentialities are cribbed, cabined, and confined. It is subject to arrested development. Though it aspires, it is not able to achieve. Though it blossoms, it does not reach the point of bearing fruit. It may be compared to a very powerful man, a world champion boxer or wrestler, but chained in such a manner that he cannot make use of his tremendous physical prowess. The curse of plant disease decimates the crops. The loss is estimated in millions of dollars for each separate disease.

What a glorious day that will be when all the restraints which are due to sin will have been removed. And when this wonderful creation will finally be "coming into its own," attaining unto "the glorious liberty of the children of God," and no longer subject to "futility."

d. Finally—and this follows from the preceding—this transformation will include *harmonization*. At present nature can be described as "raw in tooth and claw." Peace and harmony are lacking. But then all nature, gloriously transformed, will, as it were, sing a symphony. There will be concord and harmony everywhere. There will be variation, to be sure, but a most delightful blending of sounds so that the total effect will be unity. And the prophecy of Isa. 11:6-9 will reach its *ultimate* fulfilment:

"And the wolf shall dwell with the lamb, and the leopard shall lie down with the kid, and the calf and the young lion and the fatling together; and a little child shall lead them. And the cow and the bear shall feed; their young ones shall lie down together; and the lion shall eat straw like the ox.... They shall not hurt or destroy in all my holy mountain; for the earth shall be full of the knowledge of Jehovah, as the waters cover the sea."

Observe, moreover, that the convulsions described here in Matt. 24 do not blot out the human race. Today, by means of sensational books and articles, we are being told that this or that frightfully destructive bomb will completely wipe out humanity. There are also scientists who tell us that the sun will gradually lose its mass—hence its gravitational pull—and that as a result the earth will recede farther and farther away from the solar orb and from its heat. Cold winds accompanied by blinding snow will cause the human race to freeze to death. According to another theory, however, some day a celestial body—call it a "star" or a "star-fragment"—will come whizzing toward our planet. Before it even touches the earth, buildings and homes everywhere will be a sea of flames, and everybody will be roasted to death. But according to the passages which we are now studying (also according to I Thess. 4:17) there will still be people on earth when Jesus returns! The souls already in heaven will regain their bodies and will quickly join God's children who are still on earth.

Suddenly light streams down from heaven. The sign appears. Just what is meant by this one great final sign by which believers will know that Jesus is about to take his children to himself? Some have thought that a special mark or emblem will appear in the sky; for example, a huge cross. But there is nothing that in any way suggests this. Far more probable is the view that the very appearance of the Son of man upon clouds of glory is itself the sign, the one, great, final sign from the point of view of the earth. Christ's brilliant self-manifestation will be a sign that he is about to descend in order to meet his people while they ascend to meet him in the air. This explanation gains some support from the fact that while Matthew says, "And then the sign of the Son of man shall appear in the sky (or: in heaven)," Mark and Luke leave out the word *sign*, and simply say, "And then shall they see the Son of man coming in clouds with great power and glory" (or: "in a cloud with power and great glory"). Remember also that the Lord told his disciples that not wars and rumors of wars, famines and earthquakes would mark the immediate end for Jerusalem, but that the actual visible appearance of hostile armies laying siege to Jerusalem would indicate that its desolation would be at hand (Luke 21:20). In both cases, therefore, we are dealing with a sudden visible spectacle.

But when Jesus appears in majesty, surrounded by a multitude of angels, upon clouds of glory, this will be to his people a sign in still another respect. It will not only mean that now "The Wedding of the Lamb" will most certainly take place, but it will also mean that this Jesus is indeed the Messiah of prophecy; for, the glorious manner of his appearance will correspond exactly with that which was predicted concerning the Messiah (Dan. 7:13, 14; cf. Matt. 26:64). This glory which will mark his appearance will be a sign, a definite proof, of God's delight in his Son and of the justice of the cause of him who was once the Man of sorrows and acquainted with grief.

In fulfilment of Zechariah's prophecy all the tribes of the earth shall then mourn. Conscious of their own lost condition they shall beat their breasts, frightened by the display of the majesty of the Christ in all his glory, fulfilling Daniel's prophecy! The terror of the wicked, to which reference is made in Zech. 12:10, 12; Rev. 1:7, is graphically described in Rev. 6:15-17.

The positive or comforting aspect of Christ's return is again emphasized by means of the words, "And he shall send forth his angels . . . and they shall gather his elect. . . ." See on 13:41. Note also "with a loud trumpet blast."

It is clear that the Lord's return will be heard as well as seen. This is clear unless one should adopt the principle of interpretation that these passages about the second coming convey no meaning whatever. There are, indeed, interpreters who, in view of the fact that the Bible at times employs figurative language, take the position that we can know nothing at all about these eschatological events. To them these precious paragraphs in which the Holy Spirit reveals the future convey no meaning whatever. But this is absurd. Scripture was written to be understood, and when it states "He shall send forth his angels with a loud trumpet blast"; "the Lord is going to descend from heaven with a shout, with the voice of the archangel, and with the trump of God," it certainly must mean at least this: that a reverberating sound will actually pervade the universe. It is not necessary to think of an actual, literal trumpet. What forces of nature the Lord will use to produce this sound has not been revealed. One fact cannot be doubted: for believers this sound will be full of cheer. It will announce the coming of the One whom they joyfully hail as "King of kings and Lord of lords" (Rev. 19:16). It will be the fulfilment of the trumpet ordinance found in Lev. 25, and will proclaim liberty throughout the universe for all the children of God, their everlasting jubilee.

Now, according to Scripture, when the trumpet sounds, great events are going to happen in rapid succession. The angels gather the elect from the four winds, that is from everywhere. For what purpose? See 25:31-40. The Biblical picture is as follows:

When the Lord begins to descend, the souls of the redeemed leave their heavenly bodies. The saints still living on earth at the moment of Christ's return are changed in a moment, in the twinkling of an eye (I Cor. 15:52), and *all* the saints—those raised and those changed—now go forth to meet the Lord (I Thess. 4:17) to be forever with him. It is a doctrine of great comfort. See also Phil. 3:20, 21; II Tim. 4:8; Titus 2:13; Rev. 19:6, 7.

5. *A Lesson from The Fig Tree*

32, 33. Now from the fig tree learn this lesson: as soon as its branch becomes tender and puts forth leaves, y o u know that summer is near. So also y o u, when y o u see all this, know then that it is near, at the very gates. In Isa. 34:4, one of the passages in which the language of verses 29-31 is probably rooted, the convulsions in the realm of nature—the sky disappearing as a scroll when it springs shut (cf. Rev. 6:14) and the starry hosts falling from heaven—are compared with "leaves falling from the fig tree." Could this be the reason why, as recorded by Matthew, Jesus, having a moment ago spoken about the shaking of the powers of the heavens, symbolized by a fig tree that is shaken by a gale, now draws a lesson from this very tree? There must have been some reason why it is especially the fig tree about which the Master now begins to speak, for what is said here with respect to this tree might also have been spoken about ever so many other trees; in fact, about "all" the others (Luke 21:29), with the exception of the evergreens.

However that may be, the "lesson"—in the original the word "parable" occurs, but that term is here used in the very general sense of an "instructive comparison"—is clear: the tender branch and the young leaves indicate the approach of summer. There can be no question about that. Jesus now states that when "all this" (literally "all these things") is seen, "it" is near, at the very gates. "All this" must refer to the fulfilment of the various predictions *in so far as this fulfilment could be witnessed by the disciples;* note "when y o u see all this." It was with reference to Christ's prediction that not one stone of the temple was going to be left upon another that the men had asked, "Tell us, when shall this happen?" See verse 3. With reference to the rise of false Christs, wars and rumors of wars, famines and earthquakes, etc., events which did indeed begin to happen already before and in connection with the fall of Jerusalem, Jesus had said, "But *all these things* are (only) the beginning of birth pains" (verse 8). It is natural, therefore, to interpret 33 as meaning that when the disciples see "all this," for some of them including even the fulfilment of the prediction regarding the "desolating sacrilege" (verse 15) as far as that prediction was fulfilled in their own day, then "it," namely, the fall of Jerusalem and its temple, must be considered as being near; in fact, at the very gates.

In words that have given rise to much controversy Jesus continues: **34, 35. I solemnly declare to y o u that this generation shall certainly not pass away until all this takes place. Heaven and earth shall pass away, but my words shall never pass away.** For "I solemnly declare" see on 5:18. It is evident that these words are spoken with marked emphasis and impressive solemnity. The question, however, is, "Just what does Jesus mean when he says, "this generation," and "all this" or "all these things"? The notion that "this generation" refers either to *a.* all mankind, or *b.* all believers, can be dismissed without much argumentation. Not only could such a remark be considered somewhat superfluous and therefore inconceivable as coming from the mouth of the Lord, but both of these interpretations are also out of line with the context. There is still another view that must be rejected, namely, "Before they die, the people living today are going to witness all these things, including even my coming on the clouds of the sky." If that is the meaning, then Jesus was mistaken. But in view of verse 14 it is unreasonable to believe that Jesus could have meant anything of the kind.

There are, however, two interpretations that are worthy of serious consideration. According to the first, Jesus meant, "This generation shall not pass away until the events culminating in the fall of Jerusalem have occurred," not necessarily meaning, "Everybody now alive will still be around by the year A.D. 70," but simply, "The generation of our contemporaries shall not have died out by that time: some are still going to be alive." In support of this interpretation one or more of the following arguments are usually presented: *a.* the term "this generation" elsewhere indicates "the people (specifically, the Jews) *living today*"; *b.* if "all this" of verse 33 refers to the events leading up to the fall of Jerusalem, why should not the identical expression in verse 34 have the same meaning?; and *c.* is not 16:28 a parallel passage?—It is not surprising that by the force of these arguments many[805] have become convinced that this is indeed the meaning.

However, the interpretation thus offered is not without its difficulties, some of which are rather serious. Therefore S. E. Johnson (*Interpreter's Bible*), commenting on this passage, states that its exact force "is uncertain"; and F. W. Grosheide, *op. cit.,* pp. 369, 370 rejects this interpretation, as does also Lenski, *op. cit.,* pp. 929, 930.

As to the arguments summarized above in its defense, the following counter arguments can be advanced:

---

[805] As is clear from A. B. Bruce, *Synoptic Gospels,* p. 296; A. Plummer, *op. cit.,* p. 338; G. L. Murray, *Millennial Studies,* Grand Rapids, 1948, p. 110; H. Bavinck, *Gereformeerde Dogmatiek,* third edition, Kampen, 1918, Vol. IV, p. 765. This line of reasoning, with variations, can also be found in the works of De Wette, Meyer, Luther, Starke, Lisco, Erdman, Robertson, etc.

As to *a*. By no means has it been established that the term "this generation" must be limited to contemporaries. It can also refer to "this kind of people"; for example, the Jews, at any time or in any age. Worthy of consideration in this connection are such passages as Deut. 32:5, 20; Ps. 12:7; 78:8; etc., where the LXX uses the same word as is here rendered "generation," but evidently with a meaning that goes beyond "group of contemporaries." Thus even in the New Testament (see Acts 2:40; Phil. 2:15; Heb. 3:10), though the starting point may well be a reference to the people of that particular day, this may not be the entire meaning. So also probably here in Matt. 24:34.

As to *b*. This argument may not be as decisive as it sounds. The point is: *the verbs differ:* "when y o u see all this" is not the same as "until all this *takes place.*" Jesus does not necessarily mean that his disciples shall see all that has been predicted and is going to take place.

As to *c*. The same reasoning applies to 16:28. That passage, too, refers to that which "some of those that are standing here" *shall see*. That is not necessarily as broad an expression as is "all this" or "all these things" that "shall take place." It is not true, therefore, that 16:28 is an exact parallel of 24:34.

My reasons for leaning toward the view that here in verse 34 the Lord is declaring that the Jewish people shall not pass away until all the things which he has been predicting—events stretching all the way to, and including, the glorious second coming—have taken place, are the following:

First, as has already been indicated, the word "generation" may refer to "a kind of people or race," in this case the Jews.

Secondly, in the preceding verses the centuries have already been spanned (see especially verses 9 and 14). Though the immediate disciples of Jesus are not going to "see" all this, yet these things—namely, the church being hated by all the nations, the gospel being preached throughout the world, etc.— belong to that which will "take place."

Thirdly, the disciples had asked two questions, the first pertaining to the destruction of Jerusalem and its temple, the second with respect to Christ's return. Would it not seem natural that verse 33 is part of the Master's answer to the first question; and that verse 34 is his reply to the second?

Fourthly, the immediately following context, "But about that day and hour no one knows," etc. (verse 36), refers to the day of Christ's return upon the clouds with power and great glory, as has been shown (see p. 847). The further context (verses 37-39) also points to that same eschatological event (cf. Luke 17:26-30; II Peter 3:1-13).

Fifthly, the words of verse 35 also refer to the consummation of all things.

Finally, it is wrong to say that the idea "the people of the Jews will not be completely wiped out but will still be on earth when the Lord returns" was a matter that could be taken for granted, and hence was not in need of a solemn declaration. On the contrary, it might have seemed rather natural that those who, in spite of all their special privileges, rejected and crucified their own Messiah, would be wiped out as a nation. That this would not happen, but that, on the contrary, this people would continue to exist and that in every age their remnant, as well as that of the non-Jews, would be saved, was certainly worthy of special mention. At least Paul, by divine direction, was of that opinion (Rom. 11:1, 2, 25, 26); and because of the wonderful chain of events which this manifestation of God's mercy would bring about, breaks out into a doxology (Rom. 11:33-36). [806]

The majestic statement, "My words shall never pass away," deserves emphasis, for the abiding character of Christ's message, over against the transient nature even of "heaven and earth" in their present condition, is the foundation on which faith can build. See also Isa. 40:8; John 15:7; Col. 3:16; I Peter 1:24, 25.

6. *The Necessity of Being Ready Always, in View of the Unknown Day and Hour of Christ's Coming*

36. But about that day and hour no one knows, neither the angels of heaven nor the Son, but the Father only. The series of events that shall precede Christ's return has been described. The precise moment of that great event has however not been indicated. Neither could it have been, for that moment is known to the Father alone, and it has not pleased him to reveal it. The angels, though standing in a very close relationship to God (Isa. 6:1-3; Matt. 18:10), and though intimately associated with the events pertaining to the second coming (13:41; 24:31; Rev. 14:19), do not know the day nor the hour. Nor, in fact, does the Son himself, viewed from the aspect of his human nature. See also on 21:19. The Father, he alone, knows. This proves the futility and sinfulness of every attempt on man's part to predict the date when Jesus will return, whether that imagined date be 1843, 1844, more precisely Oct. 22, 1844, the autumn of 1914, or any later one. See Deut. 29:29. Curiosity is wonderful. For nosiness, intrusiveness, impertinence there is no excuse.

37-39. And as (were) the days of Noah, so shall be the coming of the Son of man. For just as men were in those days before the flood, eating and drinking, marrying and giving in marriage, until the day Noah entered the ark, not recovering their senses until the flood came and swept them all away, so also shall be the coming of the Son of man. The very suddenness of the coming points up the necessity to guard against unpreparedness and carelessness. During the days of Noah—that is, when this "preacher of righteousness" was building the ark (Gen. 5:32—7:5) and warning the people

---

[806] See the author's paperback, *Israel and The Bible*, Grand Rapids, 1968, pp. 32-52.

(II Peter 2:5)—they refused to take to heart what he was doing and saying. They were unconcerned. They continued to live "as always," eating and drinking, marrying and giving in marriage.

.. The question might be asked, "What is wrong with these activities, or with 'buying and selling, planting and building,' as in the similar days of Lot (Luke 17:28-30)?" The answer is, "Nothing at all." In fact, by means of them men are able to glorify God (I Cor. 10:31). But when the soul becomes entirely wrapped up in them, so that matters such as these become ends in themselves, and spiritual tasks are neglected, they are no longer a blessing but have become a curse. They have become evidences of gross materialism, false security, and often cold selfishness.

The men of Noah's day did not in time recover their senses. They failed to realize[807] their perilous situation until it was too late. Suddenly the *cataclysm*—the word used in the original—came. For them it was indeed a "washing down," which is the basic meaning of the word. The flood carried or swept them all away. Similarly sudden and disastrous for the wicked shall be the "coming" (see on verse 27) of the Son of man. For the latter concept see on 8:20, pp. 403-407. The nature of the punishment that awaits the unprepared on that day is described in 25:46.

40, 41. Then two men shall be in the field; one is taken, one left behind. Two women (shall be) grinding with a hand-mill; one is taken, one left behind. It is clear that once this final day arrives, every opportunity still to be saved is gone forever. The door is shut. See on 25:10. The Lord arrives. Of two men engaged in the same kind of work, probably even toiling next to each other in the field, *one* is taken. By the angels he is gathered to be forever with the Lord. *The other* is left behind, assigned to everlasting perdition. The same thing happens in the case of two women who at that very moment are grinding[808] with a hand-mill (cf. Exod. 11:5), made of two round, flat stones, with a handle near the edge of the upper stone. This mill must not be confused with the much larger one worked by donkey-power (see on 18:6). The lesson is the same: *one* of the two is taken, *the other* left behind. The One who takes is the Son of man himself through the agency of angels.

The lesson is clear: **42. Be on the alert, therefore, because y o u do not know on what day y o u r Lord is coming.** *To be* (constantly) *on the alert* or *watchful*—a Greek word from which the proper name Gregory (the watchful or vigilant one) is derived—means to live a sanctified life, in the consciousness of the coming judgment day. Spiritual and moral circumspection and forethought are required; preparedness is necessary. The watchful person has his loins girded and his lamps burning (Luke 12:35). It is in that condition

---

807 οὐκ ἔγνωσαν: third per. pl. aor. act. indic. of γινώσκω.

808 ἀλήθουσαι nom. pl. fem. pres. participle of ἀλήθω.

that he looks forward to the coming of the Bridegroom. For more on this subject of watchfulness and its implications see N.T.C. on I and II Thessalonians, pp. 124, 125. Note that Jesus refers to himself as "y o u r Lord." So glorious, powerful, and clothed with authority and majesty is he; also, so condescending, so closely united with those whom he is pleased to call his own, and who are loyal to him. Cf. Isa. 57:15. Let them therefore persevere in being vigilant.

"Y o u do not know on what day y o u r Lord is coming." 43. But this y o u do know, that if the owner of the house had known at what watch of the night the burglar would arrive, he would have been on the alert, and would not have allowed his house to be broken into. For the watches of the night see on 14:25. The comparison of the Lord's coming with that of a night burglar is also found in I Thess. 5:2-4; II Peter 3:10; and Rev. 3:3; 16:15. That unpreparedness is inexcusable is stressed in I Thess. 5:2-4. That the coming is in fulfilment of a promise, will result in catastrophic changes, and should be an incentive to santified living, is the teaching of II Peter 3:10. And that for the impenitent the sudden arrival is a source of terror, but for the vigilant a reason for joy, is brought into the foreground by the passages from the book of Revelation.

Common to all these passages is the idea of the suddenness and unexpectedness of the coming, and consequently the danger of unpreparedness on the part of those for whom that *parousia* has significance. The very fact that the owner of the house does not know when the thief is coming—for had he known this, he would have been on the alert at that particular time—makes it necessary for him to be on his guard at all times. For the same reason, with a view to the coming of the Lord everyone should always be on the alert. Since this coming is a matter of finality, affording no further opportunity for repentance, the exhortation is now repeated in slightly different language, namely, 44. Therefore y o u also, be ready, for at an hour when y o u do not expect (him), the Son of man comes. To be "ready" is synonymous with: to be "alert" or "on the alert," prepared in mind and heart. Here, too, as in verse 42, because of the tense used in the original "Be ready at all times" interprets the sense of the original.

7. Such Readiness Means Faithfulness

45. Who then is the faithful and sensible servant whom the master has put in charge of his household employees, to give them food at the proper time? Let every disciple answer the question for himself. The very word "then" indicates the connection with the immediately preceding; as if to say, "such readiness implies faithfulness." Jesus now presents the parable of *The Faithful and Sensible versus the Unfaithful and Wicked Servant.* Cf. Luke 12:42-46.

When, along with many other interpreters, I call this story-illustration a parable, I do so with the qualification that again and again reality as it were rises to the surface, so that it is not always easy to see exactly where figurative language makes way for plain statement of fact. So masterfully and inextricably are the two interwoven.

A safe presupposition is that a master of a number of "servants" or, if one prefers, "slaves," is about to leave on a journey. Before he leaves he places his most trusted underling in charge of all the other household employees. In this capacity this newly appointed household manager not only supervises the work of all the helpers but also and specifically takes care that they are well provided for. Some [809] are of the opinion that Jesus was thinking especially of his disciples, considered as office-bearers, and so, by extension, of all ministers and pastors of the churches to be organized during the entire new dispensation. But we cannot be certain about this. After all, the duty of faithfulness applies not only to leaders but also to followers. Doing the will of the Master and caring for those in need, whether this need be material, spiritual, or both, is certainly the task assigned to all. Now upon the faithful and sensible (cf. 25:2, 4, 8, 9) servant a special beatitude is pronounced: **46. Blessed is that servant whom his master at his coming shall find so doing.** Such "blessedness" (see above, pp. 264, 265) means that the servant upon whom the words of approval, congratulation, and cheer are pronounced is the object of his master's special favor, is a delight to him. Moreover, the clause "whom his master shall find *so doing*" shows that the proper attitude on the part of the one who awaits the master's return is active service in the interest of those whom the master has entrusted to him. When the figure is interpreted, this means that the proper spirit in which believers should eagerly await as Savior the Lord Jesus Christ (Phil. 3:20) is not the feverish nervousness of certain Thessalonians (II Thess. 2:1, 2; 3:6-12), nor the nauseating lukewarmness of the Laodiceans (Rev. 3:14-22), but the active faithfulness of the Smyrniots (Rev. 2:8-11). Continued: **47. I solemnly assure y o u**—see on 5:18—**that he shall set him over all his possessions.** Just as in the parable the master, upon his return, rewards his faithful servant by setting him over all his possessions, so also Jesus himself at his glorious coming shall bestow upon all his faithful ones a high degree of glory and honor. Cf. 25:21, 23, 34-40; Luke 19:17, 19. Does not Christ's promise also imply the assignment of certain specific tasks in the life hereafter, each task a matter of pure delight and satisfaction, and each in harmony with the individuality of the person for whom it is marked out?

And now the other side of the picture: **48-51. But if that servant be**

---

[809] Cf. Lenski, *op. cit.*, p. 936.

wicked, and shall say [810] in his heart, My master is taking his time, [811] and shall begin to beat up his fellow-servants, and shall eat and drink with drunkards, the master of that servant shall arrive on a day when he does not expect him, and at an hour he does not figure on, and shall cut him to pieces and assign him a place with the hypocrites. The wicked servant here described is marked by the following characteristics:

a. *Carelessness.* He is saying something "in his heart," that is, to himself. Now what a man says to himself is often even more important than what he says openly. See Prov. 23:7; Matt. 9:3, 21; Luke 12:17; 15:17-19. But within the secret precincts of his own being this particular man is conversing wickedly, irresponsibly. We are reminded of I Peter 3:20; II Peter 3:4. He is saying, "A long, long time is going to elapse before the master returns. In the meantime let me have some worldly fun."

b. *Cruelty.* A sadistic fellow is this servant. He begins to beat up his fellow-servants. Many reasons have been given for the expression "(if that servant) *begins to*, [812] etc." My own suggestion is that the context explains the word: the wicked man does not get very far, for suddenly and when least expected the master returns (verse 50).

c. *Carousing.* Note: "(and if he shall, or shall continue to) eat and drink with drunkards." [813]

Suddenly the master arrives, altogether unexpectedly. He causes the wicked servant or slave to be "dichotomized," that is, to be cut in pieces. Cf. Luke 12:46, inflicting upon him the punishment appropriate for "hypocrites" (see on 23:13). A hypocrite he was indeed, for he had accepted and then betrayed the confidence which his master had placed in him. When he was appointed, he had done nothing to disabuse his superior of the idea, "This man will be a faithful and sensible household manager." Yet he had proved to be the very opposite. The reference to "cutting to pieces" may be a reminder of the cruel treatment which in those days was accorded to slaves who disappointed their masters. For the reality that corresponds to the figure here used see on 25:46a. In line with this reference to the severity of

---

[810] To avoid thought confusion I, along with many others, have given a rendering which is *ad sensum* rather than strictly *ad verbum.*

[811] This rendering is about as close as one can come to the meaning of the Greek word χρονίζω; cf. χρόνος, *time.* Cf. 25:5; Luke 12:45; Heb. 10:37.

[812] ἄρξηται third per. sing. aor. subj. middle of ἄρχω.

[813] These present subjunctives are no longer dependent on "begins to," but, in co-ordination with "shall say" (verse 48) and "shall begin" (verse 49a), are governed by "if" (ἐάν). This fine distinction does not come out clearly in certain translations. Nevertheless, it is of some importance. By now the wicked servant has been eating and drinking with drunkards for some time, and he *continues* (note *present* tense) to do so. He has *begun to* abuse his fellow-servants. Then suddenly the "lord" or "master" arrives!

the punishment are also the closing words: there shall be weeping and grinding of teeth. As explained earlier (see on 8:12; cf. also 13:42, 50; 22:13; 25:30; and Luke 13:28), this weeping is that of inconsolable, never-ending wretchedness, and utter, everlasting hopelessness. The accompanying grinding or gnashing of teeth denotes excruciating pain and frenzied anger.

The lesson of the parable, therefore, is this "Be and remain actively loyal to the Master, sensibly and joyfully carrying out the task assigned by him, in the interest of those who are precious to him."

8. *The Parable of the Five Foolish and the Five Sensible Girls*

25:1. **Then the kingdom of heaven shall be comparable to ten girls who took their**[814] **lamps and went out to meet the bridegroom.** As is clear from a comparison of 25:13 with 24:42, 44, there is a close connection between this parable and the immediately preceding one. Both emphasize the need of being prepared at all times for the coming of the Bridegroom, Jesus Christ. For the meaning of "comparable to" see on 20:1. As the ten "virgins" of the parable were under obligation to be well-prepared to meet the bridegroom, so all those who profess Jesus as their Lord and Savior should be ready to receive him when at his glorious return he ushers in "the kingdom of heaven"—on which see 4:23; 13:43—in its final phase.

Exactly how the going out to meet the bridegroom fits into the entire picture of a typical Jewish wedding[815] is not explained in the text. One might ask, for example, "Who are these girls? Bridesmaids? Daughters of friends and neighbors of the bride? Is it their intention to meet the bridegroom when the latter, having taken his bride from her parental home, is conveying her to, and is now approaching, his own home, where the festivities are to be held?[816] Where are these young ladies when they hear the shout, 'Here comes the bridegroom! Go out to meet him'? Somewhere out in the open, along the road, where they had been sleeping? At the home of the bride? Or, of the groom? Or, of some friend?"

In defense of any of these implied theories the reader can find at least one commentator. It would be tiresome to discuss all the pros and cons in each case. Instead of doing this, therefore, I shall simply state my own position. If anyone chooses to differ he is welcome to do so. The fact that Scripture does not answer these questions would seem to indicate that they are not of supreme importance. By spending too much time on them one is apt to

---

[814] Here ἐαυτῶν probably simply means "their." As in 21:8; Luke 11:21; 12:36, it seems to be used in the place of the possessive pronoun.

[815] For the various elements of such a wedding see my book, *More Than Conquerors*, pp. 215, 216.

[816] In that case these girls would be going out "to meet the bridegroom and the bride," as a few textual variants represent the situation. But the preponderance of textual evidence omits "and the bride."

forget the main lesson: *Preparedness is essential, for the time is coming when getting ready will no longer be possible; the door will be shut.*

On the basis of the fact that the bridegroom takes a long time in arriving (cf. 24:48; 25:19), and is therefore presumably coming from a distant place, I shall assume that the interested parties have already taken care of the preliminaries. Why should the bridegroom still have to fetch the bride from her home? The best Greek text has nothing whatever to say about the bride being with the bridegroom in the arriving procession! Never is the bride even mentioned! Hence, is it not more reasonable to assume that the bride is already at the place where the wedding is to be held, which then is either her own parental home or else the home of the groom? Since the latter was more usual, I shall assume it.

On this assumption the situation is as follows: It is evening. The guests, the bride, and the ten girls—call them "bridesmaids" if y o u wish—have all gathered at the home of the groom (either his own new home or that of his parents). Everything is ready—except that *the bridegroom has not yet arrived!*

Why there were exactly ten girls we do not know. This may have been customary, or "ten" may simply be a round figure. The idea that it is symbolical and indicates "the complete number of those who belong to the church on earth" cannot be proved. Besides, it is perhaps not wise to allegorize so generously. We are definitely told, however, that these young ladies have taken their "lamps," probably meaning: devices equipped with oil receptacles and wicks, and in characteristic procession-style held aloft (like "torches") by means of wooden poles. The statement, "and went out to meet the bridegroom" must be understood proleptically. The matter is here set forth in summary before being described in detail. The actual "going out" to meet the bridegroom is not intimated until verse 10 is reached. Even then it is only implied, and, as will be seen, strictly speaking applies to only five of the bridesmaids, though originally all ten had the intention to go out to meet the bridegroom.

The bridesmaids are divided into two groups: **2-4. Five of them were foolish and five sensible. For the foolish, having taken their lamps, took no oil with them; but the sensible took oil in their vessels with their lamps.** The ten are alike in ever so many respects. All intend to meet the bridegroom and to escort him to the place where the festivities are to be held. All have lamps. All are expecting the bridegroom to come before another day has arrived, but none of them knows at what hour he is coming. All are looking forward to taking part in the marriage feast. When the bridegroom lingers, all these ten girls fall asleep, a sleep from which all are suddenly aroused (verses 5 and 6).

But though the ten resemble each other in so many outward points, their dissimilarity is even more striking. It is basic. It is what really counts: five were foolish, five sensible. The foolishness of the first group consisted in the fact that they were totally unprepared to meet the bridegroom; for, though they had taken lamps, *they had taken no oil.* That is what the text plainly indicates. Says A. T. Robertson, "Probably none at all." A. Edersheim, "The foolishness of the five virgins therefore consisted . . . in *the entire absence of personal preparation* [his italics], having brought no oil of their own in their lamps." Lenski, "The foolish brought no oil at all—that was their folly." [817] They had lamps but no oil. They were careless, not forward-looking, guilty of inexcusable and senseless neglect, shortsighted, thoughtless. The sensible girls, on the contrary, were equipped with a generous supply of oil. [818] They were fully prepared.

5. Now when the bridegroom was taking his time, they all grew drowsy and (soon) were sleeping. The temptation is to attach an allegorical meaning to this verse, as if it were a reference to the debilitation of the church. But is it not better to follow the example of the Master, and to wait with the application until the end (verse 13) of the story has been reached? We cannot blame these girls for having become sleepy, so that they nodded and presently were fast asleep. After all, the excitement caused by dressing up for the wedding, taking their lamps, making the trip to the home where they now were waiting, wondering every moment whether the groom (accompanied by a procession?) would soon come in sight, again and again being disappointed, etc., all this had been exhausting. Besides, the expected one was staying away so long, much longer than anyone had expected.

It should be borne in mind, however, that the nodding and the sleeping took place in the very home to which the ten had come, not outside, somewhere along the road!

6. But at midnight there was a shout, Here comes the bridegroom! Go out to meet him! We are not told who did the shouting. It may have been done by the young fellows who, let us suppose, accompanied the bridegroom. Or else, by some of the guests who had remained awake and from some dark place in or near the house had been quietly looking down the lane. Had they almost given up hope? It was already midnight! When the approach of the long awaited one was at last announced—he may still have been a considerable distance away from the house—what a shout must have been raised!

7, 8. Then all those girls awoke and trimmed their lamps. And the foolish said to the sensible, Give us some of y o u r oil, because our lamps are going out. All the girls, now fully awake, trim their lamps. They try to make them look bright and beautiful by lighting them. For a moment all is well. A wick

---

[817] Respectively, *Word Pictures*, Vol. I, p. 196; *The Life and Times of Jesus The Messiah*, Vol. II, p. 457; *op. cit.*, pp. 942, 944.

[818] This is true whether one interprets the term ἀγγείον-είοις (in the New Testament occurring only here; but see the related word in 13:48) to refer to the oil receptacles that were part of the lamps (thus A. Edersheim) or to separate oilcans (thus A. T. Robertson). H. N. Ridderbos, *op. cit.*, Vol. II, p. 164, leaves room for either possibility. I agree.

that is not yet completely dry can burn brightly a few seconds. After that, however, since the foolish girls had taken no oil with them, their lamps begin to flicker and sputter and die down, resulting in their owners' agonizing appeal to their wiser partners, "Give us some of y o u r oil, because our lamps are going out." We must not suppose that the ten lamps had been burning all through the evening. In the case of the five foolish girls that would have been impossible, for they had taken no oil with them. But even the idea that the five lamps of the sensible girls had been burning all this time, on top of their poles, *inside* the house, would appear to be rather unreasonable. Besides, a house where a feast was about to be held would have illumination of its own. No, as far as the parable is concerned, now for the first time this night five lamps are burning brightly, and are about to be carried outside the house.

The answer to the pathetic request of the foolish girls is given in verse 9. **But the sensible girls answered, There may not be enough for both us and y o u.** Instead of finding fault with these girls because of their heartlessness, we must try to understand their situation. Wedding processions generally move slowly. Besides, this is midnight. Not only must the girls go out to meet the bridegroom; they must also escort him back to the house with their lamps still brightly burning all the time. Their reply is therefore not unreasonable. It is rather "in character," showing forethought, a further manifestation of the same careful planning they had done when they had filled their lamps with oil. [819]

When they now add, **Y o u better go to those who sell (it) and buy (some) for yourselves,** this need not be interpreted as a saucy (or "sassy") remark. They may actually have thought that somewhere a bazaar might still be open, or if not, that it might be possible to awaken the bazaar keeper in order to buy some oil from him. That any attempt of this kind would be entirely futile was for the senseless girls to discover: **10. However, when they were on their way to buy, there came the bridegroom. The girls who were ready went in with him to the wedding, and the door was shut.** Certain passages of Scripture are filled with pathos, with a deep feeling of tragedy. Think, for example, of II Sam. 18:33, "O my son Absolom, my son, my son, Absolom. . . ." So also the "never agains" at the close of the six lines of Rev. 18:21-23a. And so here also: when the bridegroom comes, those who are ready enter. The others never get in, for when they arrive they discover that the door is shut. Cf. Luke 13:25.

At this point the parable gradually leaves us, and the reality begins to surface, until in verse 13 the parable has completely disappeared, having served its purpose. **11, 12. Later the other girls came also, saying, Sir, sir,**

---

[819] Shall we say that their refusal was all the more justifiable if the "vessels" mentioned in verse 4 were not *extra* oil flasks? See footnote 818.

open the door for us. But he replied, I solemnly declare, I do not know y o u. "Too late, too late, ye cannot enter now." We may call this reality. We may also describe it as being contrary to reality. Both would be correct. It is surely contrary to reality that an earthly bridegroom would exclude such girls. But it is indeed reality that the Lord Jesus Christ, at his glorious coming, will exclude all those who by then are still not converted. It is to them that he will say, "I do not know y o u," that is, "I do not recognize y o u as belonging to those whom I am pleased to call my own." See 7:21. "The Lord knows those who are his" (II Tim. 2:19). He "knows" Abraham (Gen. 18:19), Moses (Exod. 33:12, 17), those who take refuge in him (Nah. 1:7). See also John 10:28, 29; Rom. 8:28, 29. By virtue of his sovereign grace the Lord from eternity acknowledged them as his own. Consequently in time he made them the recipients of his special love and fellowship (in the Spirit). To those who have not surrendered their lives to him—*for that is what readiness means*—he says, "I do not know y o u." There must be no delay, for once he has returned, the door of grace is irrevocably closed!

The one altogether obvious lesson is therefore: **13. Keep on the alert, therefore, because y o u do not know the day or the hour.** See on 24:36, 42, 44, 50.

Having now studied the parable, and having fixed our attention upon its main lesson, namely the necessity of constant preparedness, hearts and lives ever consecrated to the Lord in the here and now, we are entitled to ask, "In keeping with this main application, what are some of the ancillary truths taught here?" Probably the following:

a. All who profess to believe in the Lord Jesus Christ are alike in many respects; especially in this, that all are on their way to meet the Bridegroom, Jesus Christ. See Matt. 25:1.

b. The resemblances are, however, superficial. There is an essential difference. By no means all who read the Bible, attend and even belong to a church, sing the songs of salvation, make public profession of faith, even preach in Christ's name, are going to share in the blessings of Christ's return. *Some are sensible.* Religion with them is not sham and pretense. They believe in being prepared by faith in the Savior and lives dedicated to him and therefore to God Triune. *Others are foolish.* "They have a form of piety but deny its power" (II Tim. 3:5; cf. Matt. 7:22, 23). Unprepared they travel on—to meet the Judge. See Matt. 25:2-4.

c. A long span of time will elapse between the first and the second coming. See Matt. 25:5; and on 24:9, 14; 25:19.

d. The return of the Lord will be sudden, visible, and audible. See Matt. 25:6; and on 24:31.

e. Preparedness is not transferable from one person to another. See Matt. 25:7-9; also Ps. 49:7; Prov. 9:12; Gal. 9:12.

f. For those who are *not ready*—that is, for those unsaved before they die, and for those who in their unsaved condition survive on earth until Christ's return—there is no "second chance." See Matt. 25:10-12; also 7:22, 23; 10:32, 33; 24:37-42; 25:34-46; II Cor. 5:9, 10; Gal. 6:7, 8; II Thess. 1:8, 9; Heb. 9:27.

g. Therefore—and in view of the fact that the moment of Christ's return is unknown—watchfulness at all times is required. See Matt. 25:13; also Ps. 95:7, 8; II Cor. 6:2.

Whether or not the "oil" in this parable has a symbolical meaning is not certain. *If* it does, it would point to the Holy Spirit, through whose transforming and enabling power men are *prepared* to welcome the Bridegroom. See Matt. 25:2-4; and cf. Isa. 61:1; Zech. 4:1-6; II Thess. 2:13.

9. *The Parable of The Talents*

The material here presented may be divided as follows:

a. How a business man, about to go abroad, distributed his talents among his servants (verses 14, 15).

b. What use they severally made of them (verses 16-18).

c. The reckoning that took place when the "master" returned (verses 19-27).

d. The lesson here taught (verses 28-30).

The first point is introduced as follows: 14. **For (it is) like a man going abroad, who called his** [820] **servants and placed his property in their hands.** This is clearly an instance of "abbreviated expression," for which see N.T.C. on the Gospel according to John, Vol. I, p. 206. The meaning is in all probability that what happens in "the kingdom of heaven" (see verse 1) in its final manifestation resembles the outcome of the story concerning the talents.

The beginning of the parable pictures a propertied individual who is about to leave on a journey. Cf. 21:33. Before he does so he entrusts his belongings to his servants. In the present parable it is not a vineyard that he entrusts to them but *money* (verse 27), specifically "talents." 15. **To one he gave five talents, to another two, and to another one, to each according to his** [821] **ability; then he went abroad.** Basically a "talent" is a measure of weight. So, for example, Rev. 16:21 speaks of hailstones weighing a talent (125 Roman pounds) each. The same word "talent" is, however, also used to indicate a unit of coinage. The value differed from one place and time to another, and also with the metal that was used, whether copper, silver, or gold. It has already been pointed out (see on 18:24) that an Attic talent amounted to no less than six thousand denars. It would take an ordinary laborer almost twenty years to earn one. It is clear, therefore, that in the present parable we

---

[820] Acc. pl. of ἴδιος, which here, as frequently, is used for the gen. of αὐτός.
[821] Or in this case "his own," "his respective."

are dealing with a rich businessman. Naturally he does not want his money to lie idle during his absence. It must be used so that he may make a profit. The owner of all this wealth is not only rich but also sagacious. He realizes that not all servants (or "slaves") have equal business skill. So, figuring with each man's ability, he lets one servant have five talents, another two, and another one. Then he goes on his way.

As to what use the three severally made of the entrusted wealth, the parable continues: **16, 17. At once the man who had received the five talents went and put them to work and gained five more. So also the man (who had) the two gained two more.** Prompted undoubtedly by the orders they had received from their master, by the confidence he had placed in them, and by the knowledge that one day they would have to give an account to him, the first and the second servants used the entrusted sums so effectively that in each case the amount doubled. **18. But the man who had received the one (talent) went off, dug a hole in the ground, and hid his master's money.** The third servant did not care to be bothered by the task that had been assigned to him. So he dug a hole in the ground and buried the talent there. It was not unusual for treasures to be buried in the ground. See 13:44. What motivated this man in deciding to do this? Was it love for his master, lest some burglar might come along and steal what belonged to the absent one? Was it timidity perhaps, a feeling of inferiority strengthened by the consideration that less had been entrusted to him than to the others? From verses 24-27 we learn that it was neither of these, but rather unjustified suspicion and laziness.

When the master returned, a reckoning took place: **19. Now a long while afterward the master of those servants came and settled accounts with them.** This matter of settling accounts between servants and their master has been mentioned also in another parable; see on 18:23; cf. 21:34; Luke 19:15. It was ever the duty of servants to bear in mind this day of their master's return, when there would be a reckoning. Did the slothful servant think that his master would never return? How thoroughly irresponsible his action; or shall we say "lack of action"? Well, in a sense, both. Note especially that the return of the master occurred "a long while afterward," an expression that will be taken up again when the parable's figurative meaning is pointed out. See *d.* on p. 884.

20-23. He who had received the five talents came forward, brought five additional talents, and said, Master, five talents you placed in my hands; look, an additional five talents I have gained! His master said to him, Well done, good and faithful servant. Over a small amount you have been faithful, over much I am going to put you in charge; come, share your master's happiness. He (who had received) the two talents also came forward, and said, Master, two talents you placed in my hands; look, an additional two talents I have gained. His master said to him, Well done, good and faithful

servant. Over a small amount you have been faithful, over much I am going to put you in charge; come, share your master's happiness. The first servant, in bringing his report, hands the master two bags full of money, each containing five talents. Here the story becomes very vivid. This should not be lost in the translation. Note therefore the emphasis on the exact number of talents that had been entrusted to him. The words "five talents" are placed at the very head of the clause (after the term of address, "Master"). This is followed by the subject-predicate "you placed in my hands (or: entrusted to me)." In the next clause the parallel object, "an additional five talents," again precedes the subject-predicate, which in this case is, "I have gained." But, to make the story even more vivid, between the two clauses occurs the word "look" (for which see footnote 133 on p. 131). The man's eyes are sparkling. He is bubbling over with enthusiasm, is thoroughly thrilled, and, as it were, invites the master to start counting!

"Well done," answers the master. This can also be translated, "Excellent," or "wonderful." When the master now adds, "Over a small amount you have been faithful," we wonder, perhaps, whether this was not a gross understatement. Certainly in those days five talents could hardly be considered "a small amount!" To justify the expression we need not immediately resort to the figurative meaning. We can, for the time being, stay right with the story as such, and find the solution in the fact that what the master was telling this servant was that, in comparison with the even weightier responsibilities with which he would be charged in the future, those which he had shouldered so nobly were but small. Note also that the servant is called "good" and "faithful." In the eyes of the master this man had proved himself to be thoroughly reliable. Accordingly, he was going to have a share in the master's feast.

It is gratifying to notice that when the next servant, his countenance beaming with equal joy, steps forward, hands the master two talents and then another two, and with the substitution of "two" for "five" in both clauses, makes the same speech, he receives identical praise. Has he not also doubled the amount? Has he not also added 100 percent to that which had been entrusted to him? He too, therefore, had been "good" and "faithful," just as excellent as the first servant. Such moral soundness and such loyalty was what counted. He too, therefore, was going to share his master's joy. We can picture a party at which the three—the master and these two good and faithful servants—tell each other what has happened, rejoice because of the business enterprises that have been carried forward so successfully, but especially share each other's joy. Each man is happy because so are the others.

The time has arrived for the third servant to bring his report: 24, 25. **Also he who had received the one talent came forward and said, Master, I always** knew [822] that you were a hard man, reaping where you did not sow, and gathering where you did not scatter; so, being afraid, I went away and hid your talent in the ground. . . . In order to invent an excuse for his own dereliction of duty this fellow has the audacity to accuse his master of being "hard," [823] that is unrelenting, harsh, merciless, stern, one who exacts more than he has a right to exact. When the servant tells his master, "You are reaping where you did not sow, and gathering where you did not scatter," [824] he is lying. This particular employer was not at all like Pharaoh who without giving the Israelites straw demanded that they make as many bricks as heretofore (Exod. 5:7, 8); or like Rehoboam who said, "My father chastised y o u with whips, but I will chastise y o u with scorpions" (I Kings 12:11). *This* master, in assigning tasks, had mercifully figured with each man's capacity. And as to whether he at all sowed and scattered, the answer is that he certainly did, namely, when he distributed his talents among the three servants. So now he had every right to reap and gather.

What the wicked servant is saying, then, amounts to this, "If in doing business with the talent which you entrusted to me I had lost it, you would have demanded it of me nevertheless. That's the kind of man you are. I was afraid, therefore. That fear was not really my fault but yours. You made it so that the only thing I could do was to dig a hole in the ground and hide the talent." Then, calling his master's attention to the bag holding the money, he adds, **Look, (here) you have what is yours;** as if to say, "I did not keep anything back. You should be thankful that I kept it intact, and that I now return to you whatever is yours."

By no means is the master satisfied with this lame excuse and this groundless accusation: **26, 27. But his master answered and said to him, You wicked and lazy servant! Did you know that I reap where I did not sow, and gather where I did not scatter? Then you should have invested my money with the bankers, and upon my return I would have received what was mine plus interest.** This man was wicked because he deliberately misrepresented both his master and himself. He falsely accused his master of being cruel. He also lied, namely, when he said, "Look (here) you have what is yours," for he actually owed his employer not only that one talent but also whatever it would have earned had he been faithful. But instead of admitting his guilt, he acts as if the master should have given him credit for having been so cautious and for having returned the entire talent intact. This shows that he was indeed an utterly wicked and selfish individual. His master, moreover,

---

[822] first per. sing. aor. act. ind. of γινώσκω, indicating *experimental* knowledge; hence, here "I always knew" (Phillips) can be considered a good translation.

[823] σκληρός, *hard,* cf. *arteriosclerosis:* hardening of the arteries.

[824] Note the balancing of the verbal forms, the positive pres. act. participles θερίζων and συνάγων contrasted with the negative sec. per. sing. aor. act. indicates οὐκ ἔσπειρας and οὐ διεσκόρπισας.

is as it were saying to him, "Your own words convict you; for if you were so sure that I was 'hard,' you should have exerted yourself all the more. The least you could have done would have been to put my money in the bank, so that, upon my return, I could have received it back with interest."

Literally the master said, "You should have invested my money with *the bankers.*" These "bankers" or "benchers" [825] were the men who displayed their coins on the "trapezas" or "benches." They were money-exchangers and bankers all in one. For a small fee they exchanged money, and they also paid interest [826] on money that was deposited with them. Naturally, as is the case with present-day bankers, the money invested with them was by them loaned out at a higher rate of interest. In passing, a safe inference would seem to be that Jesus, who tells this parable, is not opposed to responsible capitalism. Profit promotes employment and makes possible helping those in need, etc.

But helping others was about the last thing this man thought of. He was not only wicked but also lazy, guilty of the very sin against which again and again Scripture hurls its thunderbolts (Prov. 6:6, 9, 10; 10:5; 13:4; 15:19; 18:9; 19:15, 24; 20:4, 13; 21:25; 23:21; 24:30, 31; 26:16; Eccles. 10:18; II Thess. 3:11; Heb. 6:11). Wickedness and laziness are allies, not as if the wicked person is always lazy or slothful, but the lazy one is certainly wicked. In the original the combination is unforgettable, for the words used for "wicked" and "lazy" rhyme; cf. "pernicious and unambitious." While the other two servants had been busily at work, figuring out ways in which, by honest means, they would be able to multiply their master's capital, this wicked and lazy fellow had dug a hole, little realizing that in a sense he was digging it for himself!

What follows also belongs, in a way, to *the reckoning* that took place when the master returned. Yet, one can also consider it separately, for here again, as in other parables, the truth which Jesus wishes to teach his disciples, the real *point* of the story-illustration, comes to the surface. The lesson here taught is expressed as follows: 28-30. **Take the talent from him and give (it) to the one who has the ten talents. For to everyone who has shall (more) be given, and he shall have plenty; but from him who does not have, even what he has shall be taken away.** The master issues a command. To whom? To other servants present at the scene, as in Luke 19:24 ("to those who stood by")? Though the answer to this question is not given, the command itself is very clear. The talent must be given to the first servant, the one who had increased to ten talents the five that had been entrusted to

---

[825] τραπεζίτης = *banker*, from τράπεζα, *bench, small table* (cf. 21:12) equipped with four feet or legs (τέτρα-πέζα: four-footed).

[826] The Greek word τόκος, *interest*, is related to τέκνον, *child*, and to τίκτω, *to bear, to bring forth.*

him. In this connection the principle already announced in 13:12 is now repeated. A superficial glance at the rule here expressed might cause sharp disagreement and perhaps even resentment. One might ask, "What? Does Jesus here actually justify taking from the poor in order to give to the rich?" In the light of the entire context and of other passages—such as 10:39; 16:26; Mark 8:34-38; Luke 9:23, 24; 17:32, 33; and John 12:25, 26—one soon discovers the true meaning. It is this: the man who through diligent use of the opportunities for service given to him by God has by divine grace surrendered himself to the Lord, to love and to help others (Luke 10:29-37; Gal. 6:10; I Thess. 5:15), and who in so doing has enriched himself, shall by continuing in this course become more and more abundantly rich. On the other hand, from the person who has become poor, because he has never given himself, even whatever little he once had shall be taken away. For the rest, see on 13:12. There follows, in words strongly reminiscent of 8:12, and of 22:13, **And fling the useless servant into the most distant darkness; there shall be weeping and grinding of teeth.** For the second part (weeping and grinding of teeth) see also 13:42; 24:51; and Luke 13:28. For the complete thought see on 8:12.

The point of the parable, then, is this, *Let everyone be faithful in using the opportunities for service which the Lord has given him.* These opportunities, bestowed upon each according to his (God-given) ability, should, out of gratitude to God, be improved in such a manner that the glory of God Triune is advanced, his kingdom extended, and his "little ones" benefited. *Negligence is punished; diligence, rewarded.*

A few subsidiary points may be noted:

a. Whatever we have, whether opportunities or ability to use them to advantage, belongs to God. We *possess.* God *owns.* What we have is still "his property." We are stewards. See Matt. 25:14; also Luke 16:2; I Cor. 4:1, 2; 5:19, 20; I Peter 4:10.

b. The Lord grants us opportunities for service in accordance with our ability to make use of them. Accordingly, since not all men have the same ability, therefore not all have the same, or an equal number of, opportunities. In the day of judgment the number (of opportunities for service, "talents") will not matter. The question is only, "Have we been faithful in their use?" See Matt. 25:15, 16, 19-23; also 7:24-27.

c. Not only *committing* murder, adultery, theft, etc. is wrong, but so is also *omitting* good deeds to the glory of God. See Matt. 25:18, 26; also 25:41-45; James 4:17.

d. Jesus did not expect to return immediately. He knew that a relatively long time would elapse before his return. See Matt. 25:19; also 24:9, 14; 25:5; II Thess. 2:2, 3; II Peter 3:4-9; Rev. 20:1-3; 7-11.

e. Everything should be done with a view to the day of reckoning that is coming. "How will this wish, thought, word, or deed, look on the day of the final judgment?" is the question that should constantly be asked. See Matt. 25:19; also 25:35-45; Eccles. 12:14; Luke 12:47, 48; Rom. 2:16; II Cor. 5:10; Rev. 20:13.

f. Though, in the light of their meaning for eternity, our responsibilities here and now are very important, they will be surpassed by those in the life hereafter. See Matt. 25:21, 23.

g. To share the Master's own joy and the joy of all the saved is the glory of the life hereafter. See Matt. 25:21, 23; also II Tim. 4:8; and N.T.C. on Eph. 3:15.

h. Instead of being true to his trust, a wicked and lazy person will offer excuses. See Matt. 25:24-30; also 7:22, 23; 25:44, 45; Luke 13:26, 27. None will avail.

10. *The Son of Man's Coming in His Glory to Judge All the Nations*

What follows is not really a parable, though it does contain parabolic elements. It is a very dramatic, frequently symbolic, description of the last judgment: **31. When the Son of man comes in his glory, and all the angels with him, then he shall sit on the throne of his glory. . . .** Cf. 24:30b, 31. In both cases the glorious coming of the Son of man, accompanied by angels, is described. The Son of man—for this title see on 8:20, pp. 403-407—is here represented as seated upon "the throne of *his glory.*" The symbol indicates a most glorious throne, that is, a throne characterized by external splendor, brightness, brilliance, or radiance, corresponding with the internal and essential splendor of its Occupant's attributes. [827]

Somewhere in the renewed universe this throne or center of majesty and judgment will be established. Where will that be? Some place it on the earth (cf. Job 19:25; Zech. 14:4). Whether the passages to which reference is made actually prove this is another question. Two possible objections against the idea of the throne being on earth might be: *a.* In the book of Revelation the throne of God and of the Lamb is generally in the upper regions, not on earth; and *b.* Would there be room *on earth* for all the generations that have ever lived, so as to stand *together* before the throne of judgment? But if not on earth, why not in the air? (This still would not prevent the Son of man from "standing upon the earth" *after* the judgment). We know at any rate that at Christ's return believers will be caught up in clouds, to meet the Lord *in the air* (I Thess. 4:17). Why would it be impossible that believers go forth joyfully to meet their Lord and Savior, while at the same time the wicked are driven before the judgment-throne?

One thing is certain. It will be a very glorious throne. God, through the Mediator Jesus Christ, will be Judge. Of course, in the outgoing divine works (such as creation, providence, redemption, judgment) all three persons of the

---

[827] For the concept δόξα see N.T.C. on Philippians, footnote 43 on pp. 62, 63.

Holy Trinity co-operate. Nevertheless, from our present passage it is clear that the honor of judging was conferred on Jesus Christ as Mediator, that is, as a reward for his accomplished mediatorial work. See also Dan. 7:13; Joel 3:2 (Heb. 4:2); Matt. 13:41; 16:27; 26:64; 28:18; John 5:22, 27; Phil. 2:9, 10.

Associated with the Son of man in the judgment will be the angels. They are mentioned here not only because, by forming Christ's train, they enhance his glory, but also because they are given a task to perform. They will gather the wicked before the judgment throne and cast them into the furnace of fire (13:41, 42; 24:31; II Thess. 1:7, 8; Rev. 14:17-20). That the angels will also gather the elect from the four winds and bring them to their Judge-Savior, is clear from Matt. 24:31.

This gathering of both the saved and the unsaved, and their separation, are described in verse 32. . . . **and before him shall be gathered all the nations, and he shall separate them from each other, as the shepherd separates the sheep from the goats.** . . . Clearly, then, the judgment described concerns everybody, the entire human race. It is as universal here as in Rev. 20:11-15. None are excluded, neither the wicked nor the righteous. "All the nations" indicates all people indiscriminately; not, for example, the "nations" as contrasted with "the Jews," as if the essence of the Grand Assize would be to discover how this or that "nation" had treated the Jews!

Those gathered before the throne are persons, individuals, without any regard to their nationality; hence, "all the nations." And in the case of any given individual what matters is whether he has during his earthly life given evidence of his faith in the Lord Jesus Christ; therefore, of a life in harmony with Christ's commands and example. See verses 34-46.

On the basis of this determination the Judge separates those gathered, as a shepherd separates the sheep from the goats. Cf. 13:40-43; and 13:49, 50. Though sheep and goats during the day often intermingle, yet when the shepherd calls the sheep, the goats do not respond. Sheep probably symbolize those who trust in—that is, "follow"—the Savior, are meek, and obedient (cf. John 10:3, 4, 27); goats, those who are belligerent, unruly, and destructive (cf. Ezek. 34:17-19; Dan. 8:5, 7, 21. The manner in which anyone standing before the Son of man has treated his people, that is, all those saved by grace regardless of nationality, race, etc., determines whether he is a sheep or a goat.

33. . . . **and he shall be put the sheep at his right and the goats at his left.** [828] Being thus placed, each person knew immediately that he was *a.* saved, or *b.* condemned. That believers, too, are standing before the throne is clear not only from the very description—"all the nations . . .

---

[828] *Right* and *left* are plurals in the original; hence, literally, "from the right parts of his body" and "from the left parts of his body."

sheep ... goats"—but also from such passages as John 5:28, 29; Rom. 14:10; I Cor. 3:13; II Cor. 5:10. Yet believers do not "come into judgment," are not condemned (John 3:18; 5:24). In fact, in the passage that immediately follows (see verses 34-40) not a single one of their sins is even mentioned, only their good deeds.

The objection is often heard, "The final judgment is entirely unnecessary and superfluous, for long before that time the reprobate will already know where they will spend eternity, and so will also the elect. Is it not true that when a person dies, his soul immediately enters heaven or hell? So, what possible purpose would a final judgment serve?"

However, this reasoning is faulty. Note the following facts which show that the final judgment, at the last day, is indeed necessary:

a. The *survivors*—that is, those individuals who will still be living on earth when Jesus returns—have not yet been assigned either to heaven or to hell. Hence *they* at least must still be judged.

b. But the final judgment is necessary not only for them but for everyone. This is true because the exact degree, or measure of weal or woe which anyone will receive *in soul and body* throughout eternity has not yet been designated. Up to the moment of the final judgment all those who have died have been in heaven or hell *with respect to their souls only.*

c. The righteousness of God must be publicly displayed, that he may be glorified.

d. The righteousness of Christ and the honor of his people must be publicly vindicated. When the world in general last saw Jesus, he was hanging on a cross, *as if* he were a criminal! This estimate—as if he were a malefactor condemned for his own personal crimes—must be reversed. All men must see him whom they have pierced. They must behold him in his glory—with his people "on his right hand."

34. Then the king shall say to those at his right, Come, y o u who are blessed by my Father, inherit the kingdom prepared for y o u since the founding of the world. . . . Since the Son of man is clothed with "all authority" (11:27; 28:18; cf. Eph. 1:22), he is called "the King" (cf. John 18:36; Rev. 19:16). To be at the King's right means to hear from his lips, "Come." They are welcomed to close, loving, and abiding fellowship with their Savior, the Judge and King. No greater blessing can be imagined (Ps. 17:15; 73:23-25). They are those who have been and, as the tense of the original implies, are abidingly the blessed of—or: those blessed by—the Father, who bestowed upon them *salvation,* that is, who delivered them from the greatest evil, sin and all its consequences, and placed them in possession of the greatest good, right standing before him and all it implies.

They hear the joyful words, "inherit the kingdom." For "kingdom" see on 4:23, 13:43. Since this is the judgment day, the kingdom in its final phase is meant here. These blessed ones, who were already heirs *by right* now also become heirs *in fact,* and this in the full sense of the term. All the promises of salvation full and free are now about to be fulfilled in them everlastingly and ever progressively; all this in and through Christ (Rom. 8:17). For the implications of the term "inherit" see on 5:5.

It is surely wonderful and comforting to observe that before the good deeds of these "sheep" are mentioned (verses 35, 36) emphasis is first of all placed on the fact that the basis of their salvation, hence also of these good deeds, is their having been chosen from eternity: *the kingdom had been prepared for them,* and this not just recently, but *"from the founding* (or: *foundation) of the world."* Whether this phrase *(from,* etc.) is used or *before,* etc. (Eph. 1:4), the result is the same: "from eternity." The good pleasure of God Triune, his sovereign grace, is the foundation of their salvation. Their good works are the fruit, not the root, of grace. This must be borne in mind throughout the study of verses 35, 36. To God alone be the glory!

Having pointed this out, Jesus, predicting and describing the words of welcome which he himself will one day use, is now able to continue: **35, 36 . . . for I was hungry, and y o u gave me to eat; I was thirsty, and y o u gave me a drink; I was a stranger, and y o u welcomed me; in need of clothes, and y o u clothed me; I was sick, and y o u looked after me; I was in prison, and y o u came to see me.** Throughout his ministry, by means of precept and example, Jesus had stressed the necessity of feelings and works of love, mercy, and generosity (5:7, 43-48; 8:17; 9:36; 11:28-30; 12:7, 20, 21; 14:16, 34-36; 15:32; 18:1-6, 22, 35; 19:13-15; 20:28; 22:9, 37-39; 23:37). So it is altogether natural that this is what he expects of his followers. Now those who are here called blessed have shown kindness to the Son of man while he was still in the state of humiliation, "rejected of men." Therefore all the more they will be called "blessed" when he returns in glory. All these kindnesses y o u have shown *to me,* says the King when he returns in glory. The combination "I . . . me" occurs six times in succession.

What is deserving of special attention is the fact that in each case of need—I was hungry, thirsty, a stranger, etc.—and of satisfaction of this need—y o u gave me to eat, etc.—*it is the faithful discharge of humble duties pertaining to day by day living, that is given as the reason for the words of congratulation and approbation, and for the cheering invitation to come in and take possession of the blessings of the kingdom in its final stage.* What Jesus is saying is, "In y o u r daily life and conduct, in what are often called 'the little things of life,' y o u have furnished proof that y o u are my true disciples. Therefore I call y o u blessed." This shows that in the kingdom of heaven there is room, plenty of room, for people who have not in the technical sense prophesied in Christ's name, have not cast out demons, and have not done "many mighty works" in his name. In fact, for those who *boast* about such "great accomplishments" there is no room (7:22, 23). It is

Christ's unpretentious but sincere follower, who honors him in the common things of life, that is here pronounced blessed.

That these people are indeed genuine children of God is clear from their reaction to the words of the Son of man, the King: 37-39. **Then the righteous shall answer, saying, Lord, when did we see thee hungry and feed thee, or thirsty and give thee a drink, and when did we see thee a stranger and welcome thee, or in need of clothes and clothe thee, and when did we see thee sick or in prison and come to thee?** Thoroughly unaware are these people of ever having performed any good deeds—which was exactly what made these deeds so good! It seems strange to them that they who had accomplished so little should now receive the ultimate accolade, a bestowal of praise uttered by the One who was their Lord and King. Note also that they are called "the righteous." To limit this term as here used entirely to the forensic sense [829] would seem to be impossible. Certainly the forensic sense is basic. But righteousness of imputation cannot be separated from that of impartation. Justification goes hand in hand with sanctification. In the present context the emphasis may well be on conduct that is in conformity with the law of God, deeds that are pleasing to him.

The astonishment expressed by these followers of the Lord was that borne of service spontaneously, gladly, gratefully, and humbly rendered, and then completely forgotten. Their utterance of surprise receives a memorable reply: **40. And the King shall answer them, I solemnly assure y o u,**—see on 5:18—**whatever y o u did for one of these brothers of mine, (even) for one of the least, y o u did it for me.** The very close connection between Christ and his genuine followers is shown here, as also in 10:25, 40, 42; Mark 13:13; John 15:5, 18-21; Acts 9:4, 5; 22:7; 26:14, 15; II Cor. 1:5, 10; Gal. 2:20; 6:17; Col. 1:24; Rev. 12:4, 13. Cf. Prov. 19:17. Whatever was done for Christ's disciples, out of love for Christ, is counted as if done for Christ. Note especially "for one of these brothers of mine," a marvelous word of condescending love, made even more glorious by the addition of "(even) for one of the least." The reference is to the little favor to one of Christ's little ones, one who will never be mentioned in the headlines, the little favor almost instantly forgotten by the doer, but by the little one's Lord and Savior remembered throughout all the coming ages, and mentioned on the day of the final judgment! Wonderful!

Jesus now also addresses those on the left, and in doing this he shows that not only human beings but even angels are judged. Cf. 8:29; II Peter 2:4; Jude 6; Rev. 20:10, 14, 15: **41. Then he shall also speak to those at his left (saying): Depart from me, y o u accursed ones, into the everlasting fire prepared for the devil and his angels. . . .** This passage describes the punish-

---

[829] See Lenski, *op. cit.*, pp. 971, 972. He claims that the adjective is never used in any but a forensic sense.

ment of the wicked as consisting of: *a.* separation ("Depart from me"); *b.* association ("prepared for the devil and his angels"); *c.* fire ("into the everlasting fire"), to which may be added *d.* (see verse 30) darkness ("into the outer darkness").

It must be borne in mind that hell's most dreadful torment is for those who, though they knew the way, rejected it (Luke 12:47, 48). First of all, then, hell means *separation.* The wicked will hear the terrible words, "Depart from me, y o u accursed," which is the opposite of "Come, y o u blessed." Besides 25:41 see also 7:23; Luke 13:27. They will "go away" into everlasting punishment (25:46). Their dwelling-place will be "outside" the banquet hall, the wedding feast, the shut door (8:11, 12; 22:13; 25:10-13). Within is the bridegroom. Within are also all who accepted the invitation before it was too late. Outside are the sons of the kingdom who, having spurned the gracious summons, are knocking at the door in vain (Luke 13:28). Outside are dogs (Rev. 22:15). The wicked are cast down—down—down—into the bottomless pit (Rev. 9:1, 2; 11:7; 17:8; 20:1, 3). Thus they sink away endlessly from the presence of God and of the Lamb.

Secondly, hell means *association,* the most gruesome togetherness of all. The wicked will dwell forever with the devil and his angels, for whom the everlasting fire was prepared.

Thirdly, then, hell is the place of *fire,* of *the flame.* This is the language of Scripture throughout (Isa. 33:14; 66:24; Matt. 3:12; 5:22; 13:40, 42, 50; 18:8, 9; Mark 9:43-48; Luke 3:17; 16:19-31; Jude 7; Rev. 14:10; 19:20, 20:10, 14, 15; 21:8). This fire is unquenchable. It devours forever and ever.

Fourthly, hell is the abode of *darkness* (8:12; 22:13), the place where evil spirits are kept "in everlasting chains under darkness" (Jude 6). For the impenitent the gloom of darkness has been preserved forever (Jude 13).

This description gives rise to questions: *a.* "How is it possible for the wicked to be sent away from (or: to depart from) God?" Is not God omnipresent? (Ps. 139:7-12). Answer: Although God is indeed everywhere, that presence is not everywhere a presence of love. It is from this presence of love, patience, and warning that the wicked are finally banished forever. *b.* If hell is the place of fire, of the flame, of burning, how can it also be the abode of darkness?" Answer: Burning and darkness are not necessarily mutually exclusive. For example, by a certain form of radiation a person may be seriously burned while he is in a dark room. It has happened. We also speak of burning thirst and of burning fever. It is therefore possible that in some literal, semi-literal, at least physical, sense hell can be the place of burning even though it is also the abode of darkness. Moreover, the term "everlasting fire" here in 25:41 may be used mainly as a symbol. At least, the physical sense does not exhaust its meaning. Everlasting fire has been prepared for the devil and his angels, yet these are *spirits.* Also, Scripture frequently associates two other concepts with that of fire, namely, divine

890

wrath and human anguish (Deut. 32:22; Ps. 11:6; 18:8; 21:9; 97:3; 140:10; Jer. 4:4; Amos 1:4, 7, 10, etc.; Nah. 1:6; Mal. 3:2; and Rev. 14:10, 11). See also on Matt. 27:45, 46.

As a statement of the reason why the wicked are consigned to everlasting fire the sixfold "I was . . ." of verses 35, 36 is now repeated, the last two items being condensed into one, so that we now have a fivefold description of Christ's condition. Each of the five items is followed by the dismal "and y o u did not . . ." instead of by the joyous "y o u gave me . . . y o u welcomed me . . ." of verses 35, 36: **42, 43 . . . for I was hungry, and y o u did not give me to eat; I was thirsty, and y o u did not give me a drink; I was a stranger, and y o u did not welcome me; in need of clothes, and y o u did not clothe me; sick and in prison, and y o u did not look after me.** It should be noted that all these sins are negative. Not a single sinful deed—such as idolatry, murder, adultery, theft, etc.—is mentioned. Only sins of omission are enumerated, sins of neglect. Cf. Heb. 2:3. This neglect proves that these people have not believed in the Son of man. For this unbelief, thus demonstrated, they are condemned.

In abbreviated form the wicked now ask the same question as that asked by the righteous (vss. 37-39): **44. Then they, too, shall answer, saying, Lord, when did we see thee hungry or thirsty or a stranger or in need of clothes or sick or in prison, and did not wait on thee?** It cannot be proved that any special significance should be attached to this abbreviated form. The question in both cases is essentially the same. In both cases it is an utterance of astonishment. Nevertheless, the root of the question reveals a sharp contrast. In the case of the righteous we are dealing with astonishment borne of service gratefully rendered, and then completely forgotten. In the case of the wicked the expression of surprise, if not actually feigned, is rooted in self-delusion, the product of unbelief. Continued: **45. Then he shall answer them, saying, I solemnly assure y o u, whatever y o u did not do for one of the least of these, y o u did not do for me.** Because of the close connection between Christ and his genuine followers—see on verse 40—whatever was not done for Christ's disciples is counted as if not done for Christ. Final result: **46. And these shall go away into everlasting punishment, but the righteous into everlasting life.** Cf. Dan. 12:2. Common to the concept "everlasting" in both of these cases is the idea "without end." "There is going to be an enduring separation. Punishment and life are everlasting. There will be no change" (F. W. Grosheide). Contrary to A.V.—"everlasting . . . eternal"—the adjective must be rendered by the same word in both of these balanced and co-ordinate clauses; hence, either "eternal . . . eternal" or "everlasting . . . everlasting." Along with Williams, Beck, Goodspeed, and Norlie I prefer the latter. See Isa. 66:24; Mark 9:48, "where their worm does not die and the fire is not quenched"; Rev. 14:11, "the smoke of their torment goes up forever and ever." Note also the sixfold "no more at all" of Rev. 18:21-23.

Similarly, with respect to God's children, "They shall hunger no more, nor thirst any more" (Rev. 7:16). Nowhere—not even in Rev. 10:6—does Scripture support the notion that either after death or after the judgment day there will be no more time. Nowhere does Scripture eternalize or deify the inhabitants of the coming aeon. [830] And since here in 25:46 the same adjective is used in both clauses, the word to be used in the translation should make clear in which respect the two, namely, punishment for the wicked and life for the righteous, are the same. They are the same in this one respect, namely, that they last on and on and on, without ever coming to an end.

Having said this, it must now immediately be emphasized that qualitively there is, of course, a vast difference between the punishment and the life. In connection with "life" this has been shown above; see on 19:16; cf. N.T.C. on John 3:16. Briefly, "life" in the expression "everlasting life" (or "life everlasting") means salvation full and free. On the contrary "punishment" in the phrase "everlasting punishment" (or "punishment everlasting") means damnation and all this implies. [831]

With this important word of instruction, prediction, warning, and consolation, the last of Christ's six discourses, as reported by Matthew, is ended.

---

[830] For more on this see my book, *The Bible on the Life Hereafter*, pp. 72-74.

[831] The idea that since κόλασις, comes from κολάζω: *to prune* (as a tree), and so *to restrain, discipline*, and since αἰώνιος basically means *agelong*, hence the hope of ultimate salvation for everybody is here taught, is worthless. Words have histories. "Punish" seems to be the meaning in Acts 4:21. In II Peter 2:9 the punishment on the day of the final judgment is indicated. I John 4:18 teaches that fear has to do with punishment. And as to αἰώνιος, if we limit the duration of the punishment, then why not also that of the life? But this hardly anyone wishes to do. Also, though it is true that αἰώνιος may indicate either "without beginning" (cf. Rom. 16:25; II Tim. 1:9), or "without end" (Matt. 18:8; 25:41), or both (Heb. 9:14), this does not help us in the present context, which, as has been shown, must be interpreted in the light of parallel passages, and therefore means "without end."

Outline of Chapter 26

Theme: *The Work Which Thou Gavest Him to Do*

CHAPTER XXVI

26 1 It came about that when Jesus had finished all these words, he said to his disciples, 2 "Y o u know that after two days the Passover is held; then the Son of man is handed over to be crucified." 3 Then the chief priests and the elders of the people assembled in the palace of the highpriest named Caiaphas, 4 and plotted by some trick to take Jesus into custody and kill him. 5 But they went on to say, "Not at the Festival, lest there be a riot among the people."

26:1-5 *God's Counsel versus Man's Collusion*
Cf. Mark 14:1, 2; Luke 22:1, 2

1, 2. It came about that when Jesus had finished all these words, he said to his disciples, Y o u know that after two days the Passover is held; then the Son of man is handed over to be crucified. The formula, "When Jesus had finished all these words," or something similar, has been discussed in connection with 19:1. See on that passage. The expression "holding" or "celebrating" the Passover obviously refers here to the eating of the Passover lamb on Thursday, the fourteenth of the month Nisan (see Exod. 12:6, 7). The entire Festival of Unleavened Bread lasted seven additional days; that is, until the twenty-first of the month. It is clear, therefore, that when Jesus reminds his disciples that "after two days" the Passover would be held, Tuesday—that very memorable day on which so many events transpired and so many words were spoken (beginning at 21:20)—is not yet over. The disciples knew, of course, when the Passover would be held. They also knew, at least should have known, that Jesus was going to be crucified, for this he had predicted again and again. See above, p. 9. Something new is added when Jesus now designates the very day when this being handed over for crucifixion would take place, namely, during the night from Thursday to Friday, with the crucifixion itself to occur on Friday.

It is not only the precise prediction, indicated by the prophetic present tense ("is handed over") that arrests our attention, but also the implied determination on the part of the Son of man—for this title see on 8:20, pp. 403-407—that the counsel of God shall stand (Isa. 53:10; Luke 22:22; Acts 2:23; 3:18; 4:28), and that he himself shall, in accordance with that counsel, actually "lay down" his life (John 10:11, 15). Apart from this *voluntary* sacrifice salvation for sinners would be impossible.

895

The clash between God's counsel and man's collusion is indicated in 26:3-5; 27:1, 35, 50, 62. These passages clearly show that while the Jewish authorities insisted that the arrest, trial, and death of Jesus must not take place during the Festival, the divine decree that it would indeed happen at that particular time triumphed. Even in and by itself this victory of God over every wicked design of man is a source of comfort for every believer (Isa. 46:10; Eph. 1:11, 12). Moreover, was it not also very appropriate that *the type,* namely, the slaying of the Passover lamb, and *the antitype,* the crucifixion of the Lamb of God, who was taking away the sin of the world (John 1:29), should follow each other in such close succession?

The narrative relating how vain men tried to overthrow God's eternal plan and to vent their fury on Jesus begins as follows: **3-5. Then the chief priests and the elders of the people assembled in the palace of the highpriest named Caiaphas, and plotted by some trick to take Jesus into custody and kill him.** The envy of the leaders had been aroused by Christ's miracles, climaxed by the raising of Lazarus from the dead, causing many people to believe in Jesus (John 11:45-53). The wrath of these same religious authorities had been further uncorked by the triumphal entry's effect upon the crowds (Matt. 21:1-11), the cleansing of the temple (21:12, 13, 23), parables which they knew were meant for them (21:45), and the discourse by means of which "the seven woes" were pronounced against the scribes and Pharisees (chap. 23).

Consequently the Sanhedrin, here indicated by two of its three groups— "the chief priests and the elders"—held a meeting. No doubt the third group, consisting of "the scribes" (see on 2:4 and 16:21), was also represented. The plan to put Jesus to death did not originate at this meeting. That purpose was of long standing (12:14; 21:38; cf. John 5:18, 7:1, 19, 25; 8:37, 40; 11:53). What is *now* decided is how to carry out this plan. The leaders agree on a scheme to take Jesus by surprise, by trickery. Were they even now devising the kind of plot in which Judas would play an important role? But see on verses 14-16. However that may have been, one thing is certain, their presiding officer was not going to restrain them from using questionable methods to attain their end.

Who was this presiding officer? His name was *Caiaphas* ("Joseph who was called Caiaphas," says Josephus). The exact meaning of the name Caiaphas is not known, though it has been interpreted as *physiognomist* (expert in the art of reading character in the lineaments of a person's face or form) or, by a slight modification of this interpretation, fortune-teller, prophet. See John 11:49-51. Having been appointed to the highpriesthood by Valerius Gratus, the predecessor of Pontius Pilate, in the year A.D. 18, he was going to be deposed by Vitellus, the successor of Pontius Pilate, in the year A.D. 36. Caiaphas was the son-in-law of Annas, who was highpriest from A.D. 6-15. See Josephus *Antiquities* XVIII. 35, 95.

That Caiaphas was a rude and sly manipulator, an opportunist, who did not know the meaning of fairness or justice and who was bent on having his own way "by hook or by crook," is clear from the passages in which he is mentioned (Matt. 26:3, 57; Luke 3:2; John 11:49; 18:13, 14, 24, 28; Acts 4-6). He did not shrink from shedding innocent blood. What he himself ardently craved, for selfish purposes, he made to look as if it were the one thing needful for the welfare of the people. In order to effect the condemnation of Jesus, who had aroused his envy (Matt. 27:18), he was going to use devices which were the product of clever calculation and unprecedented boldness (Matt. 26:57-66). He was a hypocrite, for in the night trial, at the selfsame moment when he was filled with inner glee because he had found what he considered a ground for Christ's condemnation, he tore his priestly robe as if overcome by profound sorrow! Such was Caiaphas.

Leadership in hatching insidious plots could be expected from such a man. Judged by worldly standards both he and his father-in-law Annas—on whom see N.T.C. on the Gospel according to John, Vol. II, p. 388—were very clever individuals. The meeting, moreover, took place "in the palace [832] of Caiaphas," a probable reference to the spacious and sumptuous residence, one wing of which may have been occupied by Annas, another by his son-in-law. [833] Just why it was held here and not at the more usual place, namely, "the hall of hewn stone" on the south side of the great temple court, is not indicated. One guess would be: because secrecy was required. This sounds reasonable. Besides, old Annas may have considered it more convenient for himself to have the meeting right in or near his own home! Or, one other possibility, those who were to attend the meeting may have known that it would last on into the night, when no meetings were allowed within the temple complex.

It is entirely in line with the spirit of these clever manipulators to read: **But they went on to say, Not at the Festival, lest there be a riot among the people.** The plotters knew that especially among the thousands of Galileans attending the festivities lasting eight days Jesus had many friends and adherants, people who in case of any action against their Leader might make trouble for the authorities. So it was decided to wait with the arrest, etc. until the followers of Jesus were no longer around. That this part of the plan miscarried was due to the fact that, because of the unexpected help offered by one of Christ's own disciples (verses 14-16), events took a much more rapid course than had been anticipated.

"Not at the Festival," said the plotters. "At the Festival," said the

---

[832] This, rather than "open courtyard" (26:69), seems to be the meaning of αὐλή here. The inner court of the palace, with servants passing in and out, would not have suited the scheming and plotting that was taking place. See also footnote 732 on p. 772.

[833] Here again, for the evidence pointing in this direction I must refer to N.T.C. on John, Vol. II; this time see p. 391.

Almighty; "after two days," echoed Jesus. His words and those of the conspirators seem to have been spoken at the same time, for the context seems to imply that here, for once, the full temporal sense must be given to the opening word of verse 3, "Then." The divine decree always wins; in the interest of the kingdom, and to God's glory (Ps. 2:4; 33:10, 11).

---

6 Now when Jesus was in Bethany, at the home of Simon the leper, 7 there came to him a woman having an alabaster jar of very precious perfume, which she poured on his head as he was reclining at table. 8 But when the disciples saw (this) they were indignant. "Why this waste?" they said, 9 "for this perfume could have been sold at a high price, and (the money) given to the poor." 10 But when Jesus perceived it he said to them, "Why are y o u bothering this woman? For it is a beautiful thing she has done to me; 11 for the poor y o u always have with y o u, but me y o u have not always. 12 For when she poured this perfume on my body, she did it to prepare me for burial. 13 I solemnly assure y o u, wherever this gospel is preached in the whole world, also what she has done shall be told in memory of her."

26:6-13 *The Anointing at Bethany*
Cf. Mark 14:3-9; John 12:1-8

Though the fact that Jesus would be handed over to be crucified "after two days" was news for The Twelve, it cannot be said that among Christ's true followers there was no one who had a presentiment of his impending death. See 26:12. The story begins as follows: **6, 7. Now when Jesus was in Bethany, at the home of Simon the leper, there came to him a woman having an alabaster jar of very precious perfume, which she poured on his head as he was reclining at table.** There is no conflict between this account and John 12:1, "Now six days before the Passover Jesus came to Bethany. . . ." The time indication in Matt. 26:2, "after two days" does not apply to the anointing at Bethany (verses 6-13). At verse 6 Matthew begins to tell a new story. To do so he must go back a few days, to the preceding Saturday evening, when a supper was given at Bethany in honor of Jesus. Present at this supper were at least fifteen men: Jesus, The Twelve, Lazarus (John 12:2), and a certain Simon, mentioned only here (Matt. 26:6) and in Mark 14:3. The idea readily suggests itself that the supper (or "dinner" if one prefers) was prompted by love for the Lord, specifically by gratitude for the raising of Lazarus and for the healing of Simon, the man who had been a leper, is still called "Simon the leper," but had presumably been healed by Jesus. It was at the home of this Simon that the dinner was given. From John 12:2 we learn that Martha, the sister of Mary and of Lazarus, was serving, while Lazarus was one of those reclining with Jesus.

While the guests, according to the custom prevailing in that region, were reclining at table, "there came to him a woman." That this woman was Mary of Bethany we learn from John 12:3. [834] She has taken a position behind the reclining Jesus. In her hand she holds "an alabaster jar of very precious perfume," that is, a jar of white (or perhaps delicately tinted) fine-grained gypsum. It is filled with "perfume" or "ointment," characterized as being "very precious" (Matt. 26:7), "very costly" (Mark 14:3). In fact, the perfume had been extracted from pure nard (John 12:3). The same passage also informs us that there was a large quantity of this precious and very fragrant extract, not less than a Roman pound (twelve ounces)! Suddenly she purposely breaks this jar and pours its contents over Jesus. According to Matthew and Mark she pours it on his *head* (cf. Ps. 23:5); according to John she anoints his *feet*. There is no conflict, for Matthew and Mark clearly indicate that the perfume was poured over Christ's *body* (Matt. 26:12; Mark 14:8). Evidently there was enough for the entire body: head, neck, shoulders, and feet. Simon's house was filled with fragrance.

The true meaning of what happened here will never be grasped until it is realized that when Mary was pouring out her perfume, she was also pouring out her heart, filled with genuine religious love, gratitude, and devotion. The vessel in which the perfume was stored generally had a rather long and narrow neck. This bottle could have been opened or even broken at the top in such a manner that the perfume would have trickled out. But that would not have satisfied Mary. So she broke it in such a manner that the ointment came gushing out over Jesus.

The rest of the paragraph describes the reaction on the part of *a.* the disciples (verses 8 and 9), and *b.* Jesus (verses 10-13). **8, 9. But when the disciples saw (this) they were indignant. Why this waste? they said, for this perfume could have been sold at a high price, and (the money) given to the poor.** John 12:4-6 (see N.T.C. on this) supplies further details, showing that it was the treasurer of The Twelve, namely Judas Iscariot, who voiced the strongest objection, and who quickly calculated the value of the gift, assessing it at three hundred denarii, for which, he implies, it should have been sold, the money to be given to the poor. But Matthew and Mark make it clear that the other disciples chimed in. With one exception, wherever Mary looked she met angry glances, shocked disapproval. That the native language of love is lavishness they did not understand. Noble people, these disciples, especially Judas, the protector of the simple way of life, the defender of the poor! But see John 12:6.

It is almost beyond belief that the disciples should, by implication, mark as lacking in sufficient sympathy for the poor a most generous hostess; in fact one who together with her sister was in the habit of showing hospitality

---

[834] This story must not be confused with that of "the sinful woman" of Luke 7. For the arguments in favor of *rejecting* this identification theory see N.T.C. on the Gospel according to John, Vol. II, pp. 174, 175.

to them and to their Master whenever *these poor people* (Matt. 8:20), in need of constant help (27:55, 56), were in the neighborhood. It is even more amazing when one considers that at this very hour these adverse critics, the disciples, were being entertained at the home of one of Mary's friends! "He is ungrateful who denies that he has received a kindness which has been bestowed upon him; he is ungrateful who conceals it; he is ungrateful who makes no return for it; most ungrateful of all is he who forgets it" (Seneca, *De Beneficiis* III.1). Moreover, in view of all that Jesus had already done for them, was doing for them, and was going to do for them, should not these men have been happy that Mary was in this marvelous manner honoring *their* Benefactor?

It is not surprising that Jesus rushes to Mary's defense: **10, 11. But when Jesus perceived it he said to them, Why are y o u bothering this woman? For it is a beautiful thing she has done to me; for the poor y o u always have with y o u, but me y o u have not always.** Jesus did not want his disciples to worry about the perfume, as if it had been wasted, nor did he desire that they concentrate their attention exclusively upon the poor. He is saying, as it were, "Consider what Mary has done *for me.*" Not that the Master was unconcerned about the needs, both physical and spiritual, of those to whom help and mercy should be shown. Far from it, as the following passages indicate: Matt. 5:7; 6:2-4; 12:7; 19:21; Luke 6:20, 36-38; 21:1-4; John 13:29. On this subject, as well as on all others, his teaching was in line with the rest of special revelation (Exod. 23:10, 11; Lev. 19:10; Deut. 15:7-11—was he not in a sense quoting Deut. 15:11?—Ps. 41:1; Prov. 14:21b, 31; 19:17; Isa. 58:7; Jer. 22:16; Dan. 4:27; Amos 2:6, 7; and for the New Testament see II Cor. 8:1-9; Gal. 6:2, 9, 10; II Thess. 3:13; James 5:1-6). But there would be many more opportunities to attend to the cause of Christian charity or benevolence. On the contrary, the opportunity to show love and honor to Jesus in the state of humiliation had almost vanished. Gethsemane, Gabbatha, and Golgotha were just around the corner. What Mary had done was therefore right, beautiful even, for it was prompted by thankfulness of heart. It was also unique in the thoughtfulness it revealed. Moreover, it was regal in its lavishness. Last but not least, it was marvelous in its timeliness.

As to the latter Jesus continues: **12. For when she poured this perfume on my body, she did it to prepare me for burial.** On this difficult passage much has been written. As some see it, Jesus is saying that Mary, without realizing it herself, had anointed Jesus for his impending death and burial. [835] Now it must be admitted that this interpretation makes sense: God's purpose is often accomplished through the deeds of human beings,

---

[835] See, for example, A. H. McNeile, *The Gospel according to St. Matthew*, London, 1915, p. 375.

even though the latter are unaware of what is actually happening. Besides, Mary may not have known that her Master's death was so close at hand. On the other hand, the fact should not be overlooked that Mary of Bethany was perhaps the best listener Jesus ever had. The woman who now *anointed* Jesus' feet was the same one who had previously been *sitting* at his feet (Luke 10:39). If even the enemies of Jesus knew about the predictions Jesus had made concerning himself (27:63), can we not assume that Mary knew fully as much? If so, is it not probable that the thought had occurred to her, "This may well be the last opportunity I shall ever get to bestow a kindness upon Jesus; and when, according to his own prediction, his enemies kill him, will his friends be accorded the privilege of anointing his body?" The view, accordingly, that Mary's *conscious* purpose was to prepare Jesus for burial must not be ruled out. For more detail on this see N.T.C. on the Gospel according to John, Vol. II, pp. 178-180.

Jesus concludes his defense of Mary as follows: **13. I solemnly assure y o u**—see on 5:18—**wherever this gospel is preached in the whole world, also what she has done shall be told in memory of her.** As already indicated, it was now Saturday evening, the day before the triumphal entry. Then on Tuesday Jesus was going to make the astounding prediction that the gospel of the kingdom would spread throughout the world (Matt. 24:14). But before that announcement is even made, he *now,* that is three days earlier, solemnly promises that wherever the joyful story concerning Jesus is told there the deed of Mary will march hand in hand with it. The memory of Mary's noble act must be kept alive. The Master will not allow it to be forgotten.

This, of course, is a lesson for all time. The gospel and Mary's beautiful deed, the message of salvation and the response of gratitude for salvation received, these two must never be separated.

---

14 Then one of the twelve, named Judas Iscariot, went to the chief priests   15 and said, "What are y o u willing to give me if I hand him over to y o u?"
And they weighed out for him thirty pieces of silver.   16 And from then on he was looking for an opportunity to hand him over.

26:14-16 *The Agreement between Judas and the Chief Priests*
Cf. Mark 14:10, 11; Luke 22:3-6

In sharp contrast with Mary's manifestation of loyalty stands forever Judas' deed of disloyalty: **14, 15. Then one of the twelve, named Judas Iscariot, went to the chief priests and said, What are y o u willing to give me if I hand him over to y o u?** For a description of Judas and a discussion of the reasons which may have prompted him to commit the deed of treachery which from this moment on is linked forever with his name see on 10:2-4, pp. 454, 455. The word "then," as so often in Matthew, is again rather indefinite. It seems reasonable, nevertheless, to conclude that the agreement between Judas and the chief priests occurred not only after the Saturday evening supper (verses 6-13) but even after the Tuesday meeting of the Sanhedrin (verses 3-5). In order to allow enough time for Judas to work out his plans it is probably correct to say that he went to the chief priests immediately or almost immediately after their recorded session. Not before, for it is clear from verses 3-5 that the decision reached at the meeting was still rather indefinite. They agreed by means of some trick or strategem to take Jesus into custody, not during the festival however. The exact nature of their dark device seems not to have been clear even to themselves at that time. They were hoping that something would turn up, or someone would show up. After all, everybody knew that they were seeking the help of the public in arresting Jesus (John 11:57). Did Judas arrive on Tuesday evening, just as the members of the Sanhedrin were leaving, and did they then quickly re-assemble? We do not know.

"One of the twelve," that was the tragedy. One cannot help thinking of Ps. 41:9, "Even my bosom friend, in whom I trusted, who ate my bread, has lifted up his heel against me." In fact, Scripture itself (John 13:18) encourages us to look in this direction in order to sense something of the depth of this man's sin and of his responsibility.

"What are y o u willing to give me if I hand him over to y o u?" Naturally the chief priests "were glad" (Mark 14:11) when they heard these words. Here, just when they were in a quandary, thinking perhaps that the crowds of Jewish Passover pilgrims were rather solidly on the side of Jesus, this man—one of the twelve closest companions of him whom they considered their enemy—volunteers his services! The chief priests must have considered this an answer to their prayers. **And they weighed out**[836] **for him thirty pieces of silver.** Right there, on the spot, the deal was finalized, the money paid. This is not in conflict with "promised to give him" (Mark 14:11). Luke 22:5, 6a solves the puzzle: "they came to an agreement with him, to pay him money. He consented." The implication is, "So they paid." We can perhaps picture the situation as follows:

Judas: "What are y o u willing to give me if I hand him over to y o u?"

The chief priests: "We promise to give you thirty pieces of silver as soon as you agree to deliver him into our hands."

Judas: "I agree."

The chief priests, after weighing out the money: "Here are the thirty silver coins." Judas takes them and departs.

This interpretation is in harmony with the psychology of the situation.

---

[836] As various commentaries and also L.N.T. (A. and G.), p. 383, clearly indicate, the verb ἔστησαν 3rd per. pl. aor. indic. of ἴστημι, basically "set" or "fixed," can be interpreted to mean either "offered" or "weighed out" (on the scales). For the reasons given in the text I accept the latter meaning as being the correct one.

The chief priests would not have allowed their golden opportunity to pass by unheeded. They knew very well that if Judas had the money "in his pocket" he would not have dared to back out before committing the deed. Besides, if it is Matthew's intention that the words regarding the thirty pieces be interpreted as a fulfilment of the prophecy of Zech. 11:12, as is probably true, they must have the meaning "they weighed out for him," for that is their connotation in that prophecy, as Zech. 11:13 makes clear.

As to the price paid, namely "thirty pieces of silver," these *pieces* were tantamount in value to tetradrachmas or Hebrew shekels. Thirty of these, figured at 64-72 cents each, add up to (a sum) slightly more or less than $20. But with money values, both then and now, constantly fluctuating, it is impossible to determine with any exactness what this would amount to in present currency. For a price of a slave, gored by an ox, the Savior was sold to his enemies. See Exod. 21:32. For such a pitiful sum [837] Judas betrayed the Master!

With the money already in his possession, Judas now feels obliged to go into action. We are therefore not surprised to read: **16. And from then on he was looking for an opportunity to hand him over.** That opportunity would come his way very soon.

---

17 Now on the first day of the Feast of Unleavened Bread the disciples came to Jesus, saying, "Where do you want us to get the Passover supper ready for you to eat?" 18 He said, "Go to the city, to So-and So, and say to him, 'The Teacher says, My time is near; at your house I am going to celebrate the Passover with my disciples.'" 19 So the disciples did as Jesus had instructed them, and prepared the Passover meal.

20 When it was evening Jesus was reclining at table with the twelve. 21 And while they were eating he said, "I solemnly assure y o u that one of y o u shall betray me." 22 Filled with deep distress they, one by one, began to say to him, "Surely not I, Lord?" 23 But he answered and said, "He who has dipped his hand into the bowl together with me, he shall betray me. 24 The Son of man goes as it is written concerning him, but woe to that man by whom the Son of man is betrayed. It would have been better for that man if he had not been born." 25 Judas, who was betraying him, said "Surely not I, Rabbi?" He said to him, "You said (it)!"

26:17-25 *The Passover*
Cf. Mark 14:12-21; Luke 22:7-14, 21-23; John 13:21-30

Finally the morning of the fourteenth of Nisan arrived. When, as sometimes happens, the term "Festival of Unleavened Bread" is taken in its broadest sense, even the day on which occurred the eating of the Passover lamb is included. We are not told where Jesus and his disciples spent Wednesday, the day between the announcement recorded in verse 2 (Tuesday), and the Passover, verses 17-25 (Thursday). [838] We read: **17. Now on**

---

[837] For more on coins, etc. see on 10:29; 17:24, 27; 18:24, 28; and 20:9, 10. For the thirty pieces of silver see on 27:3-10.
[838] Luke 21:37 may give a hint, but this is not certain.

the first day of the Feast of Unleavened Bread the disciples came to Jesus, saying, Where do you want us to get the Passover supper ready for you to eat? Nothing is said about the purchase of a lamb. We may probably assume that this had been attended to a few days earlier. See Exod. 12:3. Further preparations had to be made however. During the afternoon the lamb must be killed in the forecourt of the temple (cf. Exod. 12:6). A room of sufficient size must be obtained, and everything in connection with this room and its furniture must be arranged. Besides, purchases must be made: of unleavened bread, bitter herbs, wine, etc. The lamb must be made ready for use, the sauce must be prepared. Since it was now Thursday morning, there can be no delay. **18. He said, Go to the city, to So-and-So . . .** Mark 14:13 informs us that these instructions were given to "two of his diciples." Luke 22:8 supplies the names "Peter and John." Both of these Gospels also supply a more detailed description of Mr. "So-and-So," without naming him, however. Is the indefiniteness of the three accounts due to the fact that not until later in the day must Judas know where the Passover will be kept, so that Jesus may indeed observe it with his disciples, and the plan of God regarding the subsequent events may be fully carried out? However this may be, the two apostles are told that upon entering the city (Jerusalem) they will be met by *a man* carrying a pitcher of water. Ordinarily not a man but a woman or a girl would be doing this; hence, this man with a jar of water, probably carrying it on his head, will be rather conspicuous. The disciples will have no difficulty singling him out from the crowd. Jesus instructs them to follow this man into whatever house he enters, and then to bring Christ's message to the master or owner of that house: **and say to him, The Teacher says, My time is near; at your house I am going to celebrate the Passover with my disciples.** It was the rule in Israel that if anyone at this time had space available it must be given free of charge to whatever family or group wished to make sacred use of it. Besides, this particular person, the owner of the house, may well have been one of Christ's followers, who accordingly would be glad to accommodate the Master and his disciples. [839]

The words, "My time is near," clearly indicate Christ's consciousness of the fact that he was accomplishing the work which the Father had given him to do. Every detail of this task had been marked out in the eternal decree, so that for each event there was a stipulated moment. See John 2:4; 7:6, 8, 30; 8:20; 12:23; 13:1; 17:1; and the climax: 19:30. The "time," to which Jesus refers here (Matt. 26:18), must not be limited to the hours of the Passover but should be interpreted in a somewhat broader sense, "the time appointed

---

[839] According to Zahn this man was John Mark's father, then still alive. See Mark 14:51, 52; Acts 12:12. Grosheide also calls attention to this possibility, but does not necessarily endorse it. His—as well as my—position is: we do not know. This holds also with respect to the theory that the man carrying the pitcher was John Mark himself. All such embellishments are nothing but speculation.

to me to bring to its conclusion the task of redemption assigned to me by the Father."

19. So the disciples did as Jesus had instructed them, and prepared the Passover meal. Christ's detailed prediction was literally fulfilled. The disciples are met by the man carrying the pitcher, etc. They make all the necessary preparations. The exact prediction and its precise fulfilment reminds one of similar occasions when the omniscience pertaining to Christ's divine nature seems to have conveyed information to his finite and by no means omniscient (see on 24:36) human mentality (17:27; John 1:48; and perhaps Luke 19:29, 30, but see on its parallel, Matt. 21:1, 2).

20, 21. When it was evening Jesus was reclining at table with the twelve. And while they were eating he said, I solemnly assure y o u—see on 5:18—**that one of y o u shall betray me.** According to John's Gospel (13:1-20) Jesus has already washed the feet of his disciples, giving them a lesson in humility. Afterward he startles them by telling them that one of them is going to betray him (13:21-30). The pointing out of the betrayer occurred, according to our passage, "while they were eating," that is, after the meal had been proceeding for some time. For the elements that pertained to the Passover meal, as far as possible chronologically arranged, see N.T.C. on the Gospel according to John, Vol. I, p. 121. The reference in "while they were eating" is probably to item *f.* on that page. In the same commentary see also p. 242.

"One of y o u!" It came as a bolt from the blue. It was a stunning blow. What! Did the Master actually mean to say that one of their own number was going *to hand him over* to the authorities, for them to deal with as they pleased? Why, it was almost unbelievable—Yet, the One who never told an untruth and whose very name was "the Truth" (John 8:46; 14:6) was saying this; so it must be true.

Christ's shocking announcement evoked three responses, in the form of questions, as follows: *a.* a question of *wholesome self-distrust,* "Surely not I, Lord?" That was the reaction on the part of all the disciples with the exception of Judas Iscariot. In Matthew's Gospel the question is found in 26:22, Christ's answer in verses 23, 24. There was also *b.* a question of *loathsome hypocrisy,* "Surely not I, Rabbi?" That, probably after considerable hesitation, was Judas' reaction. For both his question and Christ's answer see Matt. 26:25. Finally, there was *c.* a question of *childlike confidence,* "Lord, who is it?" That was the way in which John, prompted by Peter, expressed himself. The question in this form, the events relating to it, Christ's response, and the disciples' reaction to that response, are recorded only in John 13:23-30, which also in verse 30 mentions the traitor's departure. Therefore for *c.* read N.T.C. on the Gospel according to John, Vol. II, pp. 245-250.

Here in Matthew, therefore, we are dealing only with *a.* and *b.*

As to *a.* the question of wholesome self-distrust, note verse 22. **Filled with deep distress they, one by one, began to say to him, Surely not I, Lord?** Eleven hearts—those of The Twelve minus Judas Iscariot—are filled with misgiving. Each of these eleven men feels that he could not possibly be the one meant by the Lord—and yet one never can tell. And so, one by one, each of them, caught with a certain dread of himself, asks, "Surely not I, Lord?" As to its form in the original, the question expects a negative answer, the kind of answer each ardently hopes the Master will give. **23. But he answered and said, He who has dipped his hand into the bowl together with me, he shall betray me.** It is clear that Jesus did not immediately allay the fear of these men or cure their self-distrust. Nor did he at once satisfy their suddenly aroused curiosity. Were not all the twelve disciples dipping morsels of food into the bowl filled with a broth consisting of mashed fruit (probably dates, figs, and raisins), water, and vinegar? Judas surely was not the only man doing this. What the Lord is doing, therefore, is this: he is emphasizing the base character of the betrayer's deed. He is saying, "Think of it, my betrayer is a man who is sharing his meal with me." Jesus was himself the Host. All the others were eating *his* food. That very fact, especially in the Near East, a region where accepting someone's hospitality and then injuring him, was considered most reprehensible, should have tied the hands of all. It should have made it impossible for any of The Twelve to take any action against their Host. Think of Ps. 41:9.

The answer given by Jesus here in verse 23 served the following purposes:

(1). It was a warning for Judas. Let Judas ponder what he is doing. "I know your designs, Judas," the Master seems to be saying. The revelation of this detailed knowledge should have put Judas on guard even at this late hour to return those thirty pieces of silver! Yes, in God's incomprehensible and all-comprehensive decree there is room even for solemn admonitions given to those who ultimately are lost. You ask, "How is that possible?" I answer: "I do not know, but the fact remains, nevertheless." If one does not want to accept the idea of warnings even for reprobates, he misses something of the meaning of this account. The serious character of the implied admonition increases the guilt of Judas. Before one is ready to deny the possibility of earnest warnings even for the reprobate, he should study Gen. 4:6, 7; Prov. 29:1; Luke 13:6-9, 34, 35.

(2). It rivets the attention upon the depth of Christ's suffering. In a treacherous and humiliating manner he, the Lord of glory, is being handed over to his enemies. It is very important that we see this. Our reflection on the account of Christ's Passion should not become lost in all kinds of details regarding Judas and Peter and Annas and Pilate. It is, after all, the story of *his* suffering. It centers in *him,* and we must never forget to ask how all these things affected *him!*

(3). It showed, once again, that Jesus was in full control of the situation.

He was not taken by surprise. He knew exactly what was happening and what was going to happen, the very details.

(4). It furnished an opportunity to the disciples *to examine themselves.* This point is often passed by. It is, nevertheless, very important. By giving the answer that is recorded here in Matt. 26:23 Jesus did not identify the betrayer, and exactly by not identifying him the Lord was actually doing all a favor. He knew that self-examination would be the very best exercise for men such as these (remember Luke 22:24!). Let each disciple be filled with grave misgivings, with wholesome self-distrust. These men need time for self-examination.

Jesus continues: **24. The Son of man goes as it is written concerning him, but woe to that man by whom the Son of man is betrayed. It would have been better for that man if he had not been born.** Cf. Mark 14:21; Luke 22:22. For "Son of man" see on 8:20, pp. 403-407. Jesus, the One who via the path of humiliation attains to glorification, and in fact was glorious from the very beginning, *goes,* that is, lives on earth, suffers, dies, all this not as a victim of circumstances, but "as it is written concerning him," hence as predicted by the prophets (Isa. 53, etc.) and established in God's eternal decree. It was necessary for the Master to emphasize this truth once again, for it was so very difficult for the disciples to reconcile themselves with the idea of a Messiah who would die. Besides, when, on the day of tomorrow— by Jewish reckoning "today"—he dies on the cross, let the disciples reflect on this solemn statement, that they may know that this death does not mean the triumph of his enemies but rather the realization of God's gracious, sovereign, and ever victorious plan.

However, nowhere in Scripture does predestination and prophecy cancel human responsibility. So also here: the expression "Woe to that man by whom the Son of man is betrayed" fully maintains the guilt and establishes the doom of the traitor. Not to have been born would have been better for such a man. But he was born, and is in the process of committing the gruesome deed. Therefore the entire statement, "It would have been better for that man if he had not been born" is an expression of unreality—a situation that can be changed only if Judas, who remains fully responsible, still repents. We know that he did not repent. Hence he faces everlasting damnation (25:46). What makes his guilt all the heavier is the fact that he not only planned the treachery and took the next step—volunteering to deliver Jesus to the enemy—and the next—accepting the thirty pieces of silver—but even now, in spite of Christ's impressive warnings, goes right ahead.

As to *b.,* the question of loathsome hypocrisy, note verse 25. **Judas, who was betraying him, said, Surely not I, Rabbi?** Thus speaks the man who has the blood-money on his person! Was he thinking, "Perhaps Jesus does not really know; perhaps he is only guessing. Besides, if I don't imitate the others, I'll be exposing myself. So I better put on a bold front"? It may be significant, however, that *he* does not say "Lord," as did the others, but "Rabbi." Did his real self momentarily rise to the surface when he made this change? Jesus shot back the answer. **He said to him, You said (it)!** Yes, Judas, you yourself are the man! And after this reply and the additional word, "What you are doing, so do it faster" (John 13:27), Judas, into whose heart Satan has entered, rushes out of the room and into the night (John 13:30), with night in his heart. [840]

---

26 While they were eating, Jesus took bread, gave thanks, and broke it. He then gave it to his disciples and said, "Take, eat; this is my body." 27 Then he took the cup and gave thanks. He gave it to them, saying, "All of y o u drink from it; 28 for this is my blood of the covenant, which is poured out for many for the forgiveness of sins. 29 But I tell y o u that from now on I will certainly not drink from this fruit of the vine until the day when I am drinking it new with y o u in my Father's kingdom." 30 And when they had sung a hymn they went out to the Mount of Olives.

26:26-30 *The Institution of the Lord's Supper*
Cf. Mark 14:22-26; Luke 22:15-20; I Cor. 11:23-25

26. While they were eating, Jesus took bread, gave thanks, and broke it. At this point Passover passes over into the Lord's Supper; for it was while, toward the close of the Passover meal, the men were all eating freely (see on verse 21) that Jesus instituted the new sacrament that was to replace the old. A few more hours and the old symbol, being bloody—for it required the slaying of the lamb—will have served its purpose forever, having reached its fulfilment in the blood shed on Calvary. It was time, therefore, that a new and unbloody symbol replace the old. Nevertheless, by historically linking Passover and Lord's Supper so closely together Jesus also made clear that what was essential in the first was not lost in the second. Both point to him, the only and all-sufficient sacrifice for the sins of his people. Passover pointed forward to this; the Lord's Supper points back to it.

Having taken from the table a thin slice or sheet of unleavened bread, Jesus "gave thanks" and then started to break up the slice. Though the original, in referring to the prayer, uses one word in verse 26 (literally

---

[840] According to this view Judas did not partake of the Lord's Supper. Thus also Lenski, *op. cit.,* p. 1001; A. T. Robertson, *Word Pictures,* Vol. I, p. 208; H. N. Ridderbos, *op. cit.,* Vol. II, p. 186. When *The Belgic Confession,* article 35, states, "even as Judas . . . indeed received the sacrament," must not this line, unless it is deleted, be referred to the sacrament of the Passover? Judas did indeed—at least to some extent—partake of that sacrament. And the main emphasis of this article, namely, "The ungodly indeed receives the sacrament to his condemnation, but he does not receive the truth of the sacrament" can be fully maintained. In the sense indicated, it applied to Judas also.—The problem regarding Luke 22:21, which might seem to imply that Judas too received the Lord's Supper, is solved, as I see it, by Lenski, *Interpretation of Luke's Gospel,* Columbus, 1934, p. 662.

"having blessed"; cf. Mark 14:22), and another in verse 27 ("having given thanks"; cf. Mark 14:23)—the first participial form occurring in connection with the bread, the second in connection with the cup—there is no essential difference. Both Luke (22:19) and Paul (I Cor. 11:24) read "having given thanks" where Matthew and Mark read "having blessed." It is not incorrect therefore, in both Matt. 26:26 and 27, to adopt the rendering, "Jesus . . . gave thanks." For more on this see on 14:19. The words which the Lord used in this thanksgiving have not been revealed. To try to reconstruct them from Jewish formula prayers would serve no useful purpose. How do we even know that our Lord availed himself of these prayers?

The *breaking* of the bread, to which reference is made in all four accounts, must be considered as belonging to the very essence of the sacrament. This becomes clear in the light of that which immediately follows, namely, **He then gave it to his disciples and said, Take, eat; this is my body.** To interpret this to mean that Jesus was actually saying that these portions of bread which he handed to the disciples were identical with his physical body, or were at that moment being changed into his body, is to ignore *a.* the fact that *in his body* Jesus was standing there in front of his disciples, for all to see. He was holding in his hand the bread, and giving them the portions as he broke them off. *Body* and *bread* were clearly distinct and remained thus. Neither changed into the other, or took on the physical properties or characteristics of the other. Besides, such an interpretation also ignores *b.* the fact that during his earthly ministry the Master very frequently used symbolical language (Matt. 16:6; John 2:19; 3:3; 4:14, 32; 6:51, 53-56; 11:11). It is striking that in *all* of the instances indicated by *these* references the symbolical or figurative character of our Lord's language was disregarded by those who first heard it! In *each* case also, the context makes clear that those who interpreted Christ's words literally were mistaken! Is it not high time that the implied lesson be taken to heart? Finally, there is *c.*: when Jesus spoke of himself as being "the vine" (John 15:1, 5), is it not clear that he meant that what a natural vine is in relation to its branches, which find their unity, life, and fruit-bearing capacity in this plant, *that,* in a far more exalted sense, Christ is to his people? Is it not clear, therefore, that the vine *represents* or *symbolizes* Jesus, the Genuine Vine? Thus also he calls himself—or is called—the door, the morning star, the cornerstone, the lamb, the fountain, the rock, etc. He also refers to himself as "the bread of life" (John 6:35, 48), "the bread that came down out of heaven" (John 6:58). So, why should he not be, and be represented and symbolized by, "the broken bread"? Accordingly, the meaning of "the broken bread" and the poured out wine is correctly indicated in a Communion Form which represents Christ as saying: "Whereas otherwise you should have suffered eternal death, I give my body in death on the tree of the cross and shed my blood for you, and nourish and refresh your hungry and thirsty souls with my crucified body and shed blood to everlasting life, as certainly as this bread is broken before your eyes and this cup is given to you, and you eat and drink with your mouth in remembrance of Me." [841]

It was the desire of our Lord, therefore, that by means of the supper, here instituted, the church should remember his sacrifice and *love* him, should reflect on that sacrifice and embrace him by *faith,* and should look forward in living *hope* to his glorious return. Surely, the proper celebration of communion is a loving remembrance. It is, however, more than that. Jesus Christ is most certainly, and through his Spirit most actively, present at this genuine feast! Cf. Matt. 18:20. His followers "take" and "eat." They appropriate Christ by means of living faith, and are strengthened in this faith.

Having said all this, it will not be necessary to expatiate to any great extent on verses 27, 28. **Then he took the cup and gave thanks. He gave it to them, saying, All of y o u drink from it; for this is my blood of the covenant,** ⁓ **which is poured out for many for the forgiveness of sins.**

Note the following:

a. Not much significance should be attached to the fact that Mark speaks of "a" cup, for in the parallel accounts Matthew's text varies, while Luke and Paul both use the definite article; hence "the cup." At the Passover it was customary to drink several cups of diluted wine. Since, as has been shown, the Lord's Supper was linked with the last part of the Passover, it is clear that the cup here mentioned reflects the final drinking that occurred at this feast. Hence both Luke and Paul speak of "the cup *after* supper." The emphasis, moreover, is never on the container. All the stress is on its contents, the wine (see on 26:29), as symbol of Christ's blood.

b. By ordering "all" his true disciples to drink this wine, the unity of all believers in Christ is stressed. Moreover, the practice of having one person, a priest, drink "for all" is hereby condemned.

c. In all four accounts a relation is established between Christ's *blood* and his *covenant.* As reported by Matthew and Mark, Jesus said, "my blood of the covenant." The expression goes back ,to Exod. 24:8. See also the significant passage Lev. 17:11. And note: "Apart from the shedding of blood there is no *remission*" (Heb. 9:22; cf. Eph. 1:7); therefore also no *covenant,* no *special relation of friendship* between God and his people. Reconciliation with God always requires blood, an atoning sacrifice. And since man himself is unable to render such a sacrifice, a *substitutionary* offering, accepted by faith, is required (Isa. 53:6, 8, 10, 12; Matt. 20:28; Mark 10:45; John 3:16; 6:51; Rom. 4:19; 8:32; II Cor. 5:20, 21; Gal. 2:20; 3:13; I Peter 2:24). Thus

---

[841] *Form for The Lord's Supper,* belonging to the Liturgy of the Christian Reformed Church. See *Psalter Hymnal* (Centennial Edition), *Doctrinal Standards and Liturgy of the Christian Reformed Church,* Grand Rapids, 1959, p. 94 of the Liturgical Forms.

the covenant comes into being. Scripture refers again and again to God's covenant with his people. The Lord established it with Abraham (Gen. 17:7; Ps. 105:9); hence, also with all who share Abraham's faith (Gal. 3:7, 29). [842]

d. Jesus says that his blood is poured out "for *many*," not for all. Cf. Isa. 53:12; Matt. 1:21; 20:28; Mark 10:45; John 10:11, 14, 15, 27, 28; 17:9; Acts. 20:28; Rom. 8:32-35; Eph. 5:25-27. Nevertheless, "for *many*," not for just a *few*. Cf. John 1:29; 3:16; 4:42; 10:16; I John 4:14; Rev. 7:9, 10.

In both Matthew and Mark Jesus indicates that this is *certainly* the very last time that he is going to be with his disciples at this kind of supper. By means of this saying and its implications, he both predicts his imminent death and instructs them, and their followers throughout the ages, to continue until his return (cf. I Cor. 11:26) this manner of remembering him: **29. But I tell y o u that from now on I will certainly not drink** [843] **from this fruit of the vine until the day when I am drinking** [843] **it new with y o u in my Father's kingdom.** By speaking of "the fruit of the vine" Jesus undoubtedly refers to wine. Note close relation between "vine" and "wine" in Isa. 24:7. See also Num. 6:4; Hab. 3:17. At this time of the year (April), and under conditions then prevailing in Judea, it is hard to think of anything but fermented grape juice, that is, *wine,* the kind of wine used at Passover; hence, diluted or paschal wine. [844]

By saying "until the day when I am (or: shall be) drinking it new with y o u in my Father's kingdom" Jesus in all likelihood means "until in the kingdom—see on 4:23; 13:43—of *my Father*—a favorite phrase with Jesus; see pp. 287, 326, 378, 543, 644—I shall enter into everlasting, festive fellowship with y o u." Then both passover and eucharist will reach their fruition (Luke 22:16). See also on 19:28.

We see, therefore, that communion not only points back to what Jesus Christ has done for us but also forward to what he is still going to mean for us. "Drinking new wine in my Father's kingdom" in all probability must be

---

[842] For more on this "covenant," its one-sidedness or two-sidedness, the relation of "covenant" to "testament," etc., see N.T.C. on Galatians, p. 134 (including footnote 98) and on Ephesians, pp. 129, 130; also the author's book, *The Covenant of Grace,* Grand Rapids, 1932.

[843] First πίω, 1st per. sing. aor. subjunctive of πίνω; then πίνω, 1st per. sing. present subjunctive ("when I am drinking," or "shall be drinking").

[844] See the article by B. S. Easton, "Wine, Wine Press," I.S.B.E., Vol. V, pp. 3086-3088, noting particularly the Jewish sources on p. 3087. See also Seesemann's article on οἶνος Th.D.N.T., Vol. V, pp. 162-166, in which the author contends, correctly I believe, that the very term "fruit of the vine" was borrowed from Judaism and indicates wine; and note the sources indicated in his footnote 17 on p. 164. While maintaining that in our present-day observance of communion we should retain all the essential elements of the sacrament as instituted by Christ, does this mean that if anything but actual wine is used in the celebration of the Lord's Supper, the sacrament is thereby rendered invalid, as Lenski (*op. cit.,* p. 1007) argues? Should not the *main* emphasis be placed on "the thing signified"?

interpreted as a symbol for the glorious reunion and never-ending festivities awaiting the children of God in the hereafter. Cf. Isa. 25:6; Rev. 19:19; and see also on Matt. 8:11.

30. **And when they had sung a hymn they went out to the Mount of Olives.** "When they had hymned," says the original. Since, as has been shown, the Lord's Supper was the natural outgrowth of the Passover, it is probable that the hymns of praise that were lifted up to God were Pss. 115–118. These are songs of praise, thanksgiving, and trust, as anyone can see by reading them. They not only constituted a fitting conclusion to the blessings enjoyed but also a most appropriate preparation for the ordeal that was about to begin. For the entire subject of songs appropriate for the home as well as for public gatherings see N.T.C. on Eph. 5:19 and on Col. 3:16. When the meeting had been thus concluded, Jesus and his disciples, no longer twelve but eleven, went to the Mount of Olives; for which see on 21:1; 24:3. Specifically, they crossed the Kedron and entered the Gethsemane grove, located at the foot of that mountain. See 26:36; cf. John 18:1.

---

31 Then Jesus told them, "This very night all of y o u shall become untrue to me, for it is written,

'I will strike down the shepherd,
And the sheep of the flock shall be scattered.'

32 But after I have been raised, I will go ahead of y o u to Galilee." 33 But Peter answered him, "Even though all may become untrue to you, I will never become untrue." 34 Jesus said to him, "I solemnly declare to you: this very night, before the rooster crows, you shall deny me three times." 35 Peter said to him, "Even if I have to die with you, I will certainly not deny you." Similarly spoke also all the (other) disciples.

26:31-35 *Peter's Denial Foretold*
Cf. Mark 14:27-31; Luke 22:31-34; John 13:36-38

31. **Then Jesus told them, This very night all of y o u shall become untrue to me, for it is written,**

I will strike down the shepherd,
And the sheep of the flock shall be scattered.

Though "Then" may again be rather indefinite, the most natural interpretation is that what is reported here took place on the way from the Upper Room to Gethsemane. It must have been rather late in the evening—eleven o'clock perhaps? [845] —when Jesus and the eleven men who were with him wended their way toward the garden. That adds meaning to the expression, "this very night." In "all of y o u shall become untrue to me," the basic

---

[845] Think of all the dramatic happenings that took place in the Upper Room, as recorded in the Synoptics, and add to this the discourses recorded in John 14-16, plus the Highpriestly Prayer (John 17) and the closing hymns. Also, in spite of the period of the full moon, those who went to capture Jesus carried lanterns and torches (John 18:3). Besides, when Judas had left, it was already "night" (John 13:30).

meaning of the verb that is used is, as always, "become trapped" or "ensnared." See footnote 293 on p. 303. In connection with Jesus, and because of their own weakness, these men would be lured into sin, in this specific case probably referring to "becoming untrue" to their Master. [846] This would happen to *all* of them, says Jesus.

There are three significant "all's" in this story. Taken together and fathomed in their depth and in connection with the attitude of Jesus toward these men, they reveal human weakness as contrasted with divine strength. Note:

"*All* of y o u shall become untrue to me" (verse 31).

All protest that this will never happen (verse 35).

"They *all* left him and fled" (verse 56).

Nevertheless, *all* of these eleven were saved men, so regarded by the Lord in his bounteous, forgiving love (26:29; cf. John 17:6, 14, 16). *Not one* of them perished (John 17:11).

In this momentary lapse of the disciples—the failure to show their loyalty this night—Jesus sees the fulfilment of the prophecy of Zech. 13:7. The application of the prophecy to Jesus and his disciples does not present any great difficulty. It is true that in the context of Zechariah's prophecy the one who smites the shepherd is not mentioned. An order is simply issued, namely, to strike down the shepherd. On the other hand, the entire context refers repeatedly to Jehovah as being the Actor. It is he who "will turn, bring, refine, try, hear, say." Accordingly, Jesus was entirely justified in saying, "for it is written, '*I* will strike down the shepherd.' " Interpreting this in the light of prophecy and of the New Testament, we can say that it was Jehovah himself who "laid upon" the Mediator "all our iniquities" (Isa. 53:6). It was he who "struck him down," "bruised him," "put him to grief," "made his soul an offering for sin." Cf. Acts 8:32-35. It was God the Father who "spared not his own Son" (Rom. 8:32).

As indicated (see verse 56), the sheep were scattered. They fled—were going to flee—in every direction. The beauty in all this is not only that Jesus loved them all the same, but also that this very prediction would serve the purpose of bringing the scattered sheep together again, once they reflected on the fact that their Master had lovingly forewarned them.

Jesus continues, 32. **But after I have been raised, I will go ahead of y o u to Galilee.** Another revelation of love is this, for here, even before these eleven men have become scattered, they already receive the assurance that they will be regathered. In clear and unfigurative language Jesus again speaks about his being raised from the dead. He assures them that, having been raised, he will go ahead of them to the very region, Galilee, where their

---

[846] Thus interpreted the sense is not far removed from that which the verb has in 11:6 and 13:57; see on these passages.

homes were, and—what is even more significant—where their Lord had originally called them to himself. Immediately after Christ's resurrection a messenger from heaven is going to remind the disciples of this promise (28:7), and so, at his own direction, will the women, with the instruction that they must therefore go and meet the Lord in Galilee (28:10). It was indeed in Galilee that the risen Savior met with these eleven men (28:16), with seven of them (John 21:1-23), and with more than five hundred of his followers (I Cor. 15:6).

Peter now reflects on Christ's prediction recorded in verse 31: **33. But Peter answered him, Even though all may become untrue to you, I will never become untrue.**

At the moment Peter said this he meant every word of it. His desire to be and remain loyal to Jesus, come what may, must not be questioned. However, the very language he used proves that he committed at least three closely related errors. He revealed a threefold weakness. First of all, he treated the word of Jesus, previously spoken (see verse 31) with *disbelief.* "All of y o u shall become untrue to me," the Master had said. "Not true," was essentially Peter's response, though he did not use these very words. But secondly, he also made himself guilty of *disdain:* with respect to his fellow disciples he revealed an attitude of unwarranted superiority. In the original the pronoun "I," "Even though all . . . *I* never," is very emphatic, not only because it is spelled out separately—not just part of a verbal form—but also because it heads the concluding clause of the conditional sentence. The apostle, therefore, was mentally drawing a comparison. He was as it were saying, "Matthew, the former publican, might perhaps stoop down to that low moral level of abandoning the Master in his hour of affliction. My former fishing partners, James and John, might also conceivably fall into this trap. In fact, I wouldn't even put it past my own brother Andrew . . . but *not I.*" In reality he does not even say "not," but "*never,*" which is stronger. But basic to his disbelief and disdain was a very dangerous *distention* or *swelling.* Colloquially we speak about the "swelled head." Peter had an inflated opinion of himself. He was guilty of overconfidence, conceit.

He should have known better. As a child he must have received instruction in what we now call the Old Testament. However, he was not taking to heart the lesson which the stories of other boasters, such as Goliath (I Sam. 17:44, 51), Benhadad (II Kings 20:11, 21), Sennacherib (II Chron. 32:14, 19, 21), Haman (Esther 5:11, 12; 7:10), and Nebuchadnezzar (Dan. 4:30-33) should have taught him; nor was he applying to himself the inspired counsel found in such precious passages as Prov. 16:18; 26:12. Worst of all, he was ignoring Christ's constant emphasis on the necessity of humility (see on Matt. 18:1-6) and his prediction, which was after all a warning, that all would become untrue to him.

In response Jesus now sharpens the prediction of a moment ago: **34. Je-**

sus said to him, I solemnly declare to you: this very night, before the rooster crows, you shall deny me three times. In comparison with verse 31 we notice that the present prediction *a.* is introduced in a more solemn and impressive manner, "I solemnly declare"—see on 5:18—and *b.* is far more specific, being addressed to just one person, Peter; indicating even more precisely when it will be fulfilled, namely, "before the rooster crows," that is, before dawn; and describing the nature of the disloyalty trap into which that disciple will fall, namely, "deny me three times." Rooster-crowing served as a time indication. Mark 13:35 shows that it marked the third of the four "watches." These were: evening: 6-9, midnight: 9-12, rooster-crowing: 12-3, and morning: 3-6. That the reference is to the second part of the 12-3 period is clear from Mark 14:30. However the mention of the crowing of the rooster refers not only to the time, but also to the actual crowing.

We see Jesus here as *the great Prophet*. Though Peter did not know his own heart, Jesus not only knew it but also revealed it. Note the detailed character of this knowledge: *three times*. We see Jesus also as *the great Sufferer*. How what he foresaw must have grieved him. Finally, we see him as *the great Savior*. The reference to the crowing of the rooster does double duty: *a.* It indicates the shallow character of Peter's boast. Within just a few hours, yes, *even before dawn,* Peter will publicly disown his Master! Yet, *b.* this very rooster-crowing is also a means of bringing Peter back to repentance, for Christ's reference to it becomes firmly embedded in his mind, so that at the appropriate moment this hidden memory will suddenly pull the rope that will ring the bell of Peter's conscience. See Matt. 26:74; Mark 14:72; Luke 22:60; John 18:27.

The disciple who by the Lord had been singled out for this specific prediction persists, however, in his profession of unswerving loyalty: **35. Peter said to him, Even if I have to die with you, I will certainly not deny you.** His boast grows louder and louder. He speaks more and more emphatically—note "certainly not"—and even vehemently (Mark 14:31). If need be, he is willing even to die *with* (Matt. 26:35; Mark 14:31; Luke 22:33) and *for* (John 13:37) Jesus! **Similarly spoke also all the (other) disciples.** They were swept off their feet by Peter's mighty boasts. They must have felt that they could not very well promise less than Peter, their leader. With respect to this "all" (the others) see above, on verse 31.

It would seem as if Jesus allows Peter to have the final say, for the Master does not again answer his erring disciple. Nevertheless, also in the present case Jesus proves that he is the Alpha and the Omega, the first and the last. Had he not already prayed for Simon (Luke 22:31, 32)? And at the conclusion of the sad story was he not going to answer Peter by means of a tender, meaningful, marvelous look (Luke 22:61), to be followed after his (Christ's) resurrection by a private visit (Luke 24:34; I Cor. 15:5), and an unforgettable public restoration (John 21:15-17)?

915

36 Then Jesus went with his disciples to a place called Gethsemane, and said to them, "Sit here, while I go over there and pray." 37 And he took with him Peter and the two sons of Zebedee, and began to be filled with sorrow and anguish. 38 He said to them, "I am overwhelmed with sorrow to the point of death. Stay here and keep awake with me." 39 And going a little farther he threw himself face down to the ground in prayer, saying, "My Father, if it is possible, let this cup be spared me; nevertheless, not as I will but as thou wilt." 40 And he came to the disciples and found them sleeping, and said to Peter, "So, were y o u men not able to stay awake with me for a single hour? 41 Keep on the alert and keep on praying, that y o u may not enter into temptation. The spirit is eager but the flesh is weak." 42 Again, for the second time, he went away and prayed, "My Father, if it is not possible that this (cup) be spared me except I drink it, thy will be done." 43 He came again and found them asleep, for their eyes were heavy with sleep. 44 So he left them, went away again, and prayed the third time, saying the same thing. 45 Then he comes to the disciples and says to them, "Sleep on now and take y o u r rest."

"Behold, the hour is at hand, and the Son of man is being betrayed into the hands of sinners. 46 Get up! Let us be going. Look, my betrayer is near."

26:36-46 *Gethsemane*
Cf. Mark 14:32-42; Luke 22:39-46

In Gethsemane Jesus agonized

36. Then Jesus went with his disciples to a place called Gethsemane, and said to them, Sit here, while I go over there and pray. Out of the eastern gate, located north of the temple, Jesus and his disciples proceed along the road that crosses the winter brook Kedron (see N.T.C. on John 18:1). They continue to a point near the place where this road divides into three branches, each leading to the Mount of Olives. Somewhere near this fork was a grove called Gethsemane, in all probability meaning "oil-press." It must have been a secluded spot, fenced in and containing some olive trees and perhaps a grotto used in the fall of the year for an olive oil-press. Was the owner of the grove a follower of Jesus? That would almost seem so, for Jesus went there often with his disciples (John 18:2). It was therefore a quiet place, a place to teach, pray, rest, and sleep.

At or near the entrance of the grove Jesus leaves eight of his disciples. **37. And he took with him Peter and the two sons of Zebedee. . . .** Also at other occasions these same three men were selected by the Master to be with him. Why just these three? See on 17:1. Is it not remarkable that on two occasions Jesus bestowed this honor not only on James and John but also on *Peter* when this very disciple had just sinned grievously against the Master by sharply contradicting him? See 16:22, cf. 17:1; and 26:33, 35, cf. 26:37. This is one more indication of the tenderness and the forgiving love of the Savior.

That Jesus would take some of his disciples with him into the grove is not strange. Being human himself, he stood in need not only of food, drink, clothing, shelter, and sleep, but also of human fellowship. Cf. Heb. 4:15. He needed these men. Even more, they needed him! Continued: . . . **and began to be filled with sorrow and anguish.** All the waves and the billows of distress came pouring over his soul. Cf. Ps. 42:7b. Why this terror and dismay? Was it because he knew that even now Judas was approaching—or preparing to approach—in order to deliver him to his enemies? Was it because he was painfully aware that Peter would deny him, that the Sanhedrin would condemn him, Pilate sentence him, his enemies ridicule him, and the soldiers crucify him? No doubt all that was included. However, as the story develops we notice that it was especially this one thought, namely, that he, a most tender and sensitive soul, is more and more being driven into isolation. Many of the people have already left him (John 6:66). His disciples are going to forsake him (Matt. 26:56). Worst of all, on the cross he will be crying out, "My God, my God, why hast *thou* forsaken me?" (27:46). Did he, perhaps, here in Gethsemane see this tidal wave of God's wrath because of our sin coming? Cf. Isa. 63:3.

> It was alone the Savior prayed
> In dark Gethsemane;
> Alone he drained the bitter cup
> And suffered there for me.
> Alone, alone, He bore it all alone;
> He gave himself to save his own,
> He suffered, bled, and died alone, alone.
> —Ben H. Price

38. He said to them, I am overwhelmed with sorrow to the point of death. Stay here and keep awake with me. To be sure, he had been a curse-bearer throughout the days of his humiliation, but now he was becoming overwhelmed with the curse; and this consciousness would not again leave him until he was able to say, "It is finished" (Gal. 3:13). He knew that he was giving his life as a ransom for many (Matt. 20:28; Mark 10:45); that he, the sinless One, was being made "sin," that is, the object of God's wrath (II Cor. 5:21). Is it any wonder then that he said to his three closest disciples, "Stay here and keep awake with me?" The sorrows of death—not just physical death but eternal death in the place of his people—were coming upon him, now more than ever before. That is why he speaks of "sorrow to the point of death."

In Gethsemane Jesus agonized and prayed

The agony continues and even intensifies. But now the story of Christ's praying (already briefly introduced in verse 36) is added to that of his agonizing. **39. And going a little farther he threw himself face down to the ground in prayer, saying, My Father. . . .** The Master wishes to be undisturbed during his prayer. Hence, he now leaves even the three behind. Yet not far behind, for he desires to retain contact with them. Having arrived at a suitable spot, he casts himself face down to the ground, in the spirit of deep reverence and awe before his heavenly Father, the sorrow and anguish meanwhile continuing and even growing moment by moment. He addresses the Object of his prayer in the most intimate manner, saying, "My Father." For this and related expressions see pp. 287, 326, 378, 543, 644. For prayer postures and their significance see N.T.C. on I and II Timothy and Titus, pp. 103, 104. He continues . . . **if it is possible, let this cup be spared me; nevertheless, not as I will but as thou wilt.** "This cup," see on 20:22. Luke 22:43 relates that there came "an angel from heaven to strengthen him." This may well be considered an answer to his prayer, for though the cup was not taken away, he was given strength to take it to his mouth and drink it until it was empty. The same evangelist in the next verse also states that "being in agony he prayed more earnestly; and his sweat became like great drops of blood falling down upon the ground."

The nature of the cup has already been indicated (see on verse 37). Jesus now prays that it may be spared him, that is, that it may pass him by. The completely sinless, in fact exemplary nature of the prayer appears from the fact that the main clause "Let this cup be spared me," is introduced by the subordinate clause, "if it is possible," which, in turn, is elucidated by the words, "nevertheless, not as I will but as thou wilt." Jesus is submitting himself entirely to the will of his Father.

Never shall we, who do not even know how our own soul and body interact, be able to grasp how the human nature of Christ, in these solemn moments, related itself toward the divine, or vice versa. To the intense suffering, experienced in Christ's human nature, was given infinite value by means of the union of this human to the divine nature, within the second person of the Holy Trinity. Therefore his suffering, from first to last, was all-sufficient, that is, sufficient for the sin of the whole world.

After the first prayer Jesus returned to the three men who had been exhorted to keep awake: **40. And he came to the disciples and found them sleeping, and said to Peter, So, were y o u men not able to stay awake with me for a single hour?** Sleeping at this hour, probably past midnight, was natural, especially after the exciting experiences in the Upper Room (the washing of the disciples' feet, the revelation that one of The Twelve was going to betray his Master, the departure of Judas, the institution of the Lord's Supper) and afterward ("All of y o u shall become untrue to me," Peter's protest, etc.). Nevertheless, these men should have stayed awake. They could have, had they only prayed for strength to do so. Though Christ's gentle reprimand concerned all three—note the plural—yet it was addressed particularly to Peter, no doubt because in the matter of pledging his loyalty and even boasting about it he had taken the lead. Jesus continues, **41. Keep on the alert and keep on praying, that y o u may not enter into** temptation. The context clearly indicates that here a slightly different meaning must be assigned to the same Greek word that was used also in verses 38, 40. "Keep (or: stay) awake" becomes "Keep on the alert," or "Remain watchful." The reason for the change is the clause "that y o u may not enter into temptation." A person may be wide awake physically and may still succumb to temptation, but if he remains awake spiritually, that is, if with heart and mind he remains "on the alert" or "watchful," he will overcome temptation. The temptation for the disciples was to become untrue to Jesus. We already know that they, definitely including Peter, did not remain alert, did not make earnest work of prayer, and therefore did, indeed, succumb to temptation. Jesus adds: **The spirit is eager but the flesh is weak.** If in this nightly hour Jesus experienced the weakness of his own human nature, hence the need of prayer, we may be sure that this was far more seriously true in the case of the disciples. In the present passage "spirit" indicates man's invisible entity viewed in its relation to God. As such it is the recipient of God's favor and the means whereby man worships God. See further on 10:28, including footnote 453 on p. 471. "Flesh," as here meant, is the human nature considered from the aspect of its frailty and needs, both physical and psychical. See N.T.C. on Philippians, p. 77, footnote 55. Cf. Isa. 40:6; I Cor. 1:29; Gal. 2:16. This use of "flesh" must not be confused with that according to which "flesh" indicates the human nature regarded as the seat of sinful desire (Rom. 7:25; 8:4-9; etc.). To the disciples, borne down with sleep, it was a battle between their "spirit" which was eager to do what was right and thus to remain "on guard" against temptation, and their "flesh" which, because of its weakness, was prone to yield to Satan's desires.

42. **Again, for the second time, he went away and prayed, My Father, if it is not possible that this (cup) be spared me except I drink it, thy will be done.** Again Jesus retires to the place of solitude. From his sleepy disciples he could expect no help. Again he prays. Though both prayers—the one of verse 39 and that of verse 42—are the same in essence, there is a difference in emphasis. The main clause is no longer, "Let this cup be spared me," but "Thy will be done," a petition identical in wording and meaning with the one Jesus had himself taught his disciples (Matt. 6:10b). What is happening, then, is that by his own very painful and distressing experience Jesus is "learning" what it means to be obedient, and is revealing this obedience in a progressively glorious manner. [847]

43. **He came again and found them asleep, for their eyes were heavy with sleep.** Their drowsiness had once again gained the victory over their desire to stay awake and remain on the alert. "Their eyes were heavy with sleep," for their hearts had not been filled with prayer. So, all alone Jesus must fight the

---

[847] See the excellent treatment of Heb. 5:8 by F. F. Bruce, *op. cit.*, pp. 102-104.

battle. No help of any kind does he receive from men, not even from The Twelve, now reduced to eleven; in fact, not even from the select three within that small group. From Mark 14:40 it would appear that the Master spoke to the three, but because their eyes were heavy with sleep they barely heard what he said. At least, they were unable to answer him coherently. **44. So he left them, went away again, and prayed the third time, saying the same thing.** Again, therefore, he is all by himself, in communion with his Father, whom he loves and who loves him; and again the prayer, though referring also to the cup, gives expression to the Son's *chief* desire, namely, that his Father's will be done, come what may.

In Gethsemane Jesus prayed and kept watch

With respect to the final two verses of this section there is a great diversity of opinion among commentators. With very slight alteration I have adopted the rendering of verse 45a that is found in A.V. and A.R.V.: **45a. Then he comes to the disciples and says to them, Sleep on now and take y o u r rest.** The problem is that the very next verse begins with the words "Get up! Let us be going." This raises the question, "How would it be possible for Jesus in one breath to be saying, "Sleep on now and take y o u r rest. . . . Get up! Let us be going"? The two statements seem to contradict each other. Many solutions have been proposed, two of the most popular ones being discussed in the footnote. [848]

The explanation that appeals to me most is the following: [849] What marvelous compassion! The Shepherd, who has been asking the disciples to watch with him, is now tenderly keeping vigil over them. His own victory having been won, perfect peace has been restored to his own heart. He has been strengthened through prayer. To be sure, the three men had failed him.

---

[848] *a.* This is irony, perhaps even satire. A cross section of this view translates 45a somewhat as follows, "As far as I am concerned, go right ahead now and sleep, y o u dreadful sleepers. I do not need y o u any longer." Along this line Lenski, *op. cit.*, p. 1024; cf. Robertson, *Word Pictures*, Vol. I, p. 214.

Objection: Is this in line with Christ's character as revealed in the Gospels? Besides, was not the occasion too serious for irony?

b. This is a question: "Are y o u still sleeping?" Or, it is an exclamation, "Y o u still sleeping!" Note the word "still" in both of these attempts. Along this line most modern English translators.

Objection: Lenski—*op. cit.*, p. 1024—has pointed out—I believe correctly—that τὸ λοιπόν does not mean "still." Grosheide—*op. cit.*, p. 403—states, "λοιπόν makes it impossible to regard καθεύδετε, to which it belongs, as a question."

[849] With individual variations—some placing a break between verses 45 and 46; others, after the word "rest"—this construction of the meaning of the passage can also be found in the following: G. C. Morgan, *op. cit.*, p. 304; A. Edersheim, *Life and Times of Jesus the Messiah*, Vol. II, p. 541; J. Bishop, *The Day Christ Died*, New York and Evanston, 1957, p. 215; and R. C. Foster, *Studies in the Life of Christ, The Final Week*, Grand Rapids, 1966, p. 181.

But never, no never will his love fail them! What we have here, accordingly, is one of the most touching pictures in the Gospels, and one, moreover, that is entirely in harmony with the sympathetic character of the Savior as mentioned, described, or implied in many other passages of this Gospel (4:23, 24: 5:43-48; 6:15; 8:16, 17; 9:2, 13, 36-38; 10:42; 11:28-30; 12:7, 17-21; 14:14-16, 27, 34-36; 15:28, 32; 18:1-6, 10-14, 21, 22, 35; 19:13-15; 20:25-28, 34; 21:14; 22:9, 10; 23:37; 25:40; 28:10).

The vigil was of short duration. After just a little while Jesus could see the approaching band. He now rouses the three men by saying: **45b. Behold, the hour is at hand, and the Son of man is being betrayed into the hands of sinners.** For "Behold" or "Look," or "Listen," see footnote 133 on p. 131. For "Son of man," with emphasis here on Christ's afflicted human nature, see on 8:20, pp. 403-407. He continues: **46. Get up! Let us be going.** Going where? Away as far as possible from the approaching band? Fleeing? No, the very opposite: going forward to meet those who have come to arrest him. Jesus adds, **Look, my betrayer** (Judas Iscariot) **is near.**

---

47 While he was still speaking, look, Judas, one of the twelve, came, and with him a big crowd (armed) with swords and clubs, from the chief priests and elders of the people. 48 Now he who was betraying him had given them a sign, saying, "The one I kiss is the man; grab him." 49 And he stepped up to Jesus at once and said, "Hello, Rabbi," and kissed him fervently. 50 Jesus said to him, "Friend, for this are you here?" Then they came, laid their hands on Jesus, and arrested him. 51 And look, one of those who accompanied Jesus stretched out his hand and drew his sword. He struck the highpriest's servant and cut off his ear. 52 Then Jesus said to him, "Put your sword back in its place, for all who take tne sword shall perish by the sword. 53 Or do you think that I cannot call on my Father, and at once he will put at my disposal more than twelve legions of angels? 54 How then would the Scriptures be fulfilled (which say) that it must happen this way?" 55 At that time Jesus said to the crowds, "As against a robber [850] y o u came out, with swords and clubs, to seize me. Every day I was sitting in the temple, teaching, and y o u did not arrest me. 56 But all this has taken place in order that the Scriptures of the prophets may be fulfilled." Then all the disciples left him and fled.

26:47-56 *The Betrayal and the Seizure of Jesus*
Cf. Mark 14:43-50; Luke 22:47-53; John 18:3-12

In the present paragraph we are told about *a.* the Onslaught of the Treacherous (Judas and his band), *b.* the Defeat of the Defenders (the disciples, who left Jesus and fled, as he had predicted), and *c.* the Triumph of the Captive (Jesus, who offered himself willingly).

47. While he was still speaking, look, Judas, one of the twelve, came, and with him a big crowd (armed) with swords and clubs, from the chief priests and elders of the people. When Jesus had exposed Judas at the Passover supper, that traitor must have hurried off to the chief priests, etc., the men

---

850 Or: insurrectionist, revolutionary.

who had hired him. Was he afraid that once his treachery became known the alarm would spread and from everywhere friends of Jesus—think especially of the many from Galilee, now in the city—would gather in his defense? "Act quickly," he must have told the Jewish authorities, preferably by night, when no crowds are around. Act tonight." The authorities had been waiting for him. So busy were they with this plot to destroy Jesus that, as explained in N.T.C. on the Gospel according to John, Vol. II, pp. 401-404 (on John 18:28), they had not yet partaken of the Passover meal. The probable whereabouts of Jesus had to be ascertained; a posse had to be organized; the temple police must be notified; permission must be obtained, whether from Pilate, which in view of 27:62-65 seems probable, or from the Roman "chiliarch," so that a group of soldiers could accompany the temple police; all the members of the Sanhedrin must be alerted; Annas must not be left in the dark; lanterns, swords, and clubs must be collected; the need of secrecy must be emphasized to all those who are "in" on this; etc., etc.

Finally, then, all is in readiness. Now to find Jesus. Judas did not know for certain where the group might have gone after leaving the Upper Room, but since Gethsemane was the place often visited by the Master and his disciples (John 18:2), the traitor was able to make a good guess, one that proved to be correct. So, while Jesus was still talking to the three disciples, Judas was seen entering the grove. "Judas, one of the twelve," says the text, to emphasize the terrible character of the crime this man was committing. See on verse 14. Since he was "one of the twelve," it would be impossible to mention all the privileges that had been bestowed upon him during the many days, weeks, and months he had spent in Christ's immediate company. Such confidence had the other eleven reposed in this same Judas that they had even made him their treasurer. And now he was proving himself totally unworthy of all these honors and advantages, of all this trust. A shameless, disgusting quisling he had become, a wretched turncoat, one who for the paltry sum of thirty pieces of silver was delivering over to the enemy the greatest Benefactor whose feet ever trod this earth, even the Mediator, both God and man, the Lord Jesus Christ.

No one knows exactly how the crowd that accompanied Judas was arranged, if it be even correct to speak about any order or arrangement. If any guess be permissible it would be as follows:

In front Judas. This, at least, seems rather well established. The crowd is said to be "with him." Besides, he is the one who is going to "step up to Jesus" (verse 49), to point him out to the others. The highpriest's personal servant, Malchus, must also have been near the front (26:51; Luke 18:10) and so were also probably the temple police, Levites (26:55; cf. John 18:3). The detachment of soldiers, together with their commander cannot have been far away (John 18:3, 12). John 18:3 mentions a "cohort," probably obtained from the tower of Antonia, situated at the northwest corner of the temple area. Though a cohort at full strength consisted of six hundred men (the tenth of a legion), the Roman authorities would probably not have depleted their garrison to that extent. At any rate, the band must have been rather large. Perhaps somewhat farther toward the back were members of the Sanhedrin (Luke 22:52). Whether any others were present we cannot be certain. Even Matt. 26:55 does not necessarily imply this.

The force that had been commissioned to capture Jesus was well equipped. The men carried swords and clubs. As to the first, these were probably the short swords carried by the heavily armed Roman soldier. See N.T.C. on Ephesians, p. 279, including footnote 177. The clubs or cudgels, we may assume, were in the hands of the temple police. Absolute certainty in such matters is not possible. Words have histories, which in the present case means that the term used in the original for "swords" may at times have a more general meaning. It was not always used to distinguish these weapons from the broadswords. Also, we cannot be entirely certain that none but soldiers carried swords. Did not even Peter have a sword? See verse 51. All we really know is that those who came to arrest Jesus carried swords and clubs. Their distribution is not definitely indicated, though it is natural to think of soldiers equipped with swords. The Gospel of John also mentions "torches and lanterns." Torches and lanterns—to search for the Light of the world. And it was full moon! Swords and cudgels—to subdue the Prince of Peace. For the Man of Sorrows the very sight of this band of ruffians, which considered him their quarry, meant indescribable suffering.—And to think that the men who were supposed to be leaders in Israel, highly religious and devout, together composing the Sanhedrin—here indicated by the two groups "chief priests and elders"—had sent this force. Instead of welcoming Jesus as the long-expected Messiah, they were sending a posse to capture him, with the ultimate purpose of having him brought before the authorities that he might be sentenced to death! For the concept *Sanhedrin* see on 2:4 and on 16:21.

Now if all these soldiers and temple police, with their swords and clubs, indicated that those who had assigned to these men the task of seizing Jesus held him to be a revolutionary, one who might wish to make trouble for the Roman government and set up an earthly kingdom of his own, they were certainly mistaken. Not even once during his ministry did Jesus give any encouragement to this idea. The very opposite was the case. See 26:51-54; cf. Luke 22:49-51; John 6:15; 18:10.

48, 49. Now he who was betraying him had given them a sign, saying, The one I kiss is the man; grab him. And he stepped up to Jesus at once and said, Hello, Rabbi, and kissed him fervently. Jesus had come out from among the trees in the grove and was now standing in front of the band (26:46; cf. John 18:4). As he did this, Judas performed that act which has caused all later generations to recoil with horror at the mere mention of his name. Embracing Jesus, he kissed him—probably fervently or repeatedly [851] —and greeted him, saying, "Hello (or: Hail), Rabbi!" It was a prearranged sign, whereby the symbol of friendship and affection was made the sign to grab Jesus. **50. Jesus said to him, Friend, for this are you here?** [852] Cf. "With a kiss are you betraying the Son of man?" (Luke 22:48). The purpose of this word addressed in an earnest but not unfriendly way—note even now "Friend" (cf. 20:13; 22:12)—to Judas was probably: *a.* to reveal to the traitor the meanness of his deed; *b.* to show him that the Master was not being deceived but thoroughly understood the reason for this embrace; and *c.* even at this point to warn the traitor. If anyone should raise the objection that in view of the fact that from all eternity the deed of Judas, too, was included in the divine decree (Luke 22:22), so that a warning or admonition was now impossible, the answer would be that this decree does not exclude but includes all such warnings. Was not Cain's deed also included in the decree? Nevertheless, he was warned, earnestly and tenderly (Gen. 4:6, 7). As happened in the case of Cain, so also here: Judas does not take the warning to heart, but allows matters to proceed as they had been planned. **Then they came, laid their hands on Jesus, and arrested him.** For details see John 18:4-9 and N.T.C. on those verses. It is clear from John 18:3, 12 that the arrest was made by *a.* the soldiers and their chiliarch (commander) and *b.* the temple guards. Gentiles and Jews combine against Jesus. Cf. Acts 4:27. John's Gospel, moreover, makes it perfectly clear that before allowing himself to be bound Jesus demonstrated his power over his captors, proving that he voluntarily surrendered himself to them, in line with John 10:11b, 15b. In this capture it was the Captive who triumphed!

51. And look, one of those who accompanied Jesus stretched out his hand and drew his sword. He struck the highpriest's servant and cut off his ear. By this time the other eight disciples too have rejoined Jesus. See verse 56 and cf. Luke 22:49. At this point Peter goes into action. Although the incident is related in all four Gospels, only John mentions the names of the two persons who (in addition to Jesus himself) figured most prominently in it. When John published his Gospel it was no longer possible to punish the assailant. Hence, in John's Gospel the assailant's name and that of the person attacked could be mentioned.

The "one who accompanied Jesus" was Simon Peter. Emboldened perhaps

---

[851] It is a well-known fact that the prefixes in such compounds as the one here used—κατεφίλησεν—often lose their intensive force. Nevertheless, the use of the simple form of the verb in verse 48—φιλήσω first per. sing. aor. subjunctive of φιλέω—contrasted with the compound form in the next verse, probably points to the strengthened connotation in this second case.

[852] In Josephus *Jewish War* II.615, "he proceeded to carry out ἐφ'ὅ παρῆν" obviously means "that for which he had come." The nearby similar ἐφ ὅ πάρει probably has the same meaning.

by the marvelous triumph of Jesus over the men who had come to capture him—at first the would-be captors, at the word of Jesus, "I am the One for whom y o u are looking" had lurched backward and fallen to the ground— and impelled by his own previous boast (verses 33, 35), Simon drew his short sword from its scabbard. Having drawn it, he sprang at Malchus (John 18:10), the servant of the highpriest, and—probably because the servant saw what was coming and quickly jumped aside—cut off his ear. Peter probably still believed that the Messiah must not die. Cf. 16:22.

Christ's reaction to this rash act is described most fully here in Matthew's Gospel. But see also John 18:11. Matthew states: **52-54. Then Jesus said to him, Put your sword back in its place, for all who take the sword shall perish by the sword. Or do you think that I cannot call on my Father, and at once he will put at my disposal more than twelve legions of angels? How then would the Scriptures be fulfilled (which say) that it must happen this way?** Luke 22:51 relates that Jesus touched the servant's ear and healed him. According to Matthew's record, then, Jesus told Peter to sheathe his sword, and this for the following reason:

a. Use of the sword for this purpose was *unprofitable,* definitely harmful— for Peter and for all who might think of following his example: "All who take the sword shall perish with the sword." This proverbial saying must not be interpreted in an absolute, unqualified sense, as if use of the sword were always wrong. See Gen. 9:6; Rom. 13:4. But rashly swinging the sword, without even being willing to wait for Christ's answer to the question, "Shall we strike with the sword?" (Luke 22:49) is always wrong, and will mean retribution for the one who does it. See also Rev. 13:10.

b. Also, it was wholly *unnecessary.* He who is able, in answer to his request, to receive immediately from the Father twelve times six thousand angels, rushing to his defense, certainly does not need the help of a few weak disciples. What Jesus implies is this: Since I am not appealing to "my Father"—again, as in 26:39 that beautiful appellation—to send me these angels, it is clear that I am determined to lay down my life as a voluntary sacrifice.

c. Finally, it was *unenlightened,* failing completely to figure with prophecy and the necessity that it be fulfilled. Jesus must drink the cup which the Father gave him (John 18:11; cf. 19:11). In the garden, in answer to his prayers, he has found perfect peace. He is fully determined to drink this cup, and to do so in fulfilment of such prophecies as Ps. 22:1 ff.; 69:20, 21; Isa. 53; Jer. 23:5, 6; Zech. 13:1, etc. If Peter had had his way, how then would these passages of Scripture be fulfilled? And how would all the symbols of the Old Testament, pointing forward to the Suffering Servant, be fulfilled?

55. At that time Jesus said to the crowds, As against a robber y o u came out, with swords and clubs, to seize me. Every day I was sitting in the temple, teaching, and y o u did not arrest me. Right then and there Jesus, though bound, addressed the crowds. The venerable members of the Sanhedrin were also present (Luke 22:52). Of course, they had no business being here during this sacred night, but were so anxious to see whether their sinister plot against the enemy would succeed that they were actually to be seen among this crowd. See N.T.C. on the Gospel according to John, Vol. II, pp. 403, 404. Jesus, then, pointed out to the crowds—to all those who had come to arrest him and all those who gloated over his capture—how cowardly and perfidiously they were behaving. They had come out against him with an army, as if he were a highwayman or, as the text can also be rendered, an insurrectionist, a revolutionary. In reality he was and had been a quiet, peaceful Prophet, sitting day by day in the temple, teaching the people. His life had been an open book. Had he been guilty of any crimes, those in charge of law and order would have had every chance to seize him.

If anyone wishes to know what kind of person this Jesus had proved himself to be during the slightly more than three years of his public ministry, let him read such passages as 4:23-25; 11:25-30; 12:18-21; Luke 24:19; Acts 2:22. To say, as some, in commenting on Matt. 26:55, have done, that he was "harmless" is putting it too mildly. He was and is, "the Savior of the world" (John 4:42; I John 4:14), the world's greatest Benefactor. How absurd and hypocritical it was for the foe in the hour of darkness to pounce upon this Good Shepherd, from whom no one who heeded his message had anything to fear, and who even taught people to love their enemies! See Matt. 5:44.

By addressing the crowds in this manner Jesus was in reality doing them a favor. He was exposing their guilt. Is it not true that it takes confession of guilt to bring about salvation? Though it is a fact that by far the most of those who heard Jesus speak these words hardened themselves in sin, we have no right to conclude that the message, together with other messages that followed (for example, the seven words from the cross, Peter's Pentecost address, etc.), was completely ineffective. See, for example, Acts 6:7. The impression left upon us by these words of our Lord is that they were spoken in a calm and earnest manner. To be sure, Jesus rebukes, but at the same time he is even now seeking the lost, that he may save them. He continues: **56. But all this has taken place in order that the Scriptures of the prophets may be fulfilled.** Had it not been for God's eternal decree with respect to man's salvation, a decree reflected in the prophets (Isa. 53:7, 10, 12; Jer. 23:6; Dan. 9:26; Zech. 11:12; 13:1; etc.), these captors could have accomplished nothing at all! **Then all the disciples left him and fled.** All alone Jesus must suffer and die. For further comments see above, on verse 31.

---

57 Now those who had seized Jesus led him away to Caiaphas the highpriest, where the scribes and the elders were assembled. 58 But from a considerable distance Peter was

following him until (he came) to the courtyard of the highpriest; and having entered he sat down with the officers to see the outcome. 59 Now the chief priests and the entire Sanhedrin were seeking to obtain false testimony against Jesus, so that they might put him to death; 60 but they did not find (any), though many false witnesses came forward. But at last two came forward 61 and declared, "This fellow said, 'I am able to destroy the temple [853] of God, and in three days to rebuild it.' " 62 And the highpriest arose and said to him, "You don't answer? What are these men testifying against you?" 63 But Jesus remained silent. And the highpriest said to him, "I adjure you [854] by the living God that you tell us whether you are the Christ, the Son of God." 64 Jesus replied, "You said (it), but I tell y o u, from now on y o u shall see

the Son of man
sitting at the right hand of the Power
and coming on the clouds of heaven."

65 Then the highpriest tore his robes, saying, "He has blasphemed. What need do we still have of witnesses? Look, now y o u have heard his blasphemy. 66 What do y o u think?" They answered, "Deserving of death is he." 67 Then they spat in his face and struck him with the fist. Others slapped him 68 and said, "Prophesy to us, Christ, who was it that hit you?"

26:57-68 *The Trial before the Sanhedrin*
Cf. Mark 14:53-65; Luke 22:54, 55, 63-65, 67-71; John 18:24 [855]

To understand Matt. 26:57-68 and that which follows in chapter 27 it is necessary to bear in mind that Jesus had to undergo two trials. The first has often been called the ecclesiastical trial; the second, the civil. The first contained three stages, and so did the second. The three stages of the so-called ecclesiastical trial were: *a.* the preliminary hearing before Annas (John 18:12-14, 19-23); *b.* the trial before the Sanhedrin, that is, before Caiaphas and the scribes and the elders (Matt. 26:57); and *c.* the trial before the same body just after daybreak (Matt. 27:1). The hearing before Annas, described only by John, must not be confused with the trial before Caiaphas. See the argument in N.T.C. on the Gospel according to John, Vol. II, pp. 385-388. The three stages in the trial before the civil authorities were: *a.* the trial before Pilate, *b.* that before Herod, and *c.* that before Pilate resumed. Just as it is true that the preliminary hearing before Annas is found only in John's Gospel, so also Christ's appearance before Herod is recorded only by Luke (23:6-12).

In our present paragraph (Matt. 26:57-68), therefore, it is assumed that the preliminary hearing before Annas has been held. 57. **Now those who had seized Jesus led him away to Caiaphas the highpriest, where the scribes and the elders were assembled.** Perhaps for one of the reasons mentioned above

---

[853] Or: sanctuary.

[854] Or: "I charge you on oath."

[855] Luke 22:66; 23:1 do not belong here but parallel Matt. 27:1, 2; Mark 15:1. John 18:12-14, 19-23 do not belong here either but describe Christ's preliminary hearing before Annas.

(see on 26:3-5) this meeting again is held in the palace of Caiaphas the highpriest. Whether such a session is described as attended by "the chief priests and scribes" (2:4), "the chief priests and the elders" (26:3), "the scribes and the elders" (here in 26:57), or "the elders and chief priests and scribes" (16:21), the reference in each of these cases is probably to the Sanhedrin in Jerusalem.[856] Jesus, then, is sent "bound" to Caiaphas the highpriest and those who were assembled with him. Cf. John 18:24. **58. But from a considerable distance Peter was following him until (he came) to the courtyard of the highpriest; and having entered he sat down with the officers to see the outcome.** Though all the disciples had fled, two—Peter and "another disciple"—soon rallied and began to follow the band that was leading Jesus to the highpriest's palace. In the case of Peter, "following Jesus" was probably prompted, in part, by the loud boasts he had uttered, as recorded in verses 33 and 35; in part also, by sheer curiosity, as the text states. How this disciple secured admission to the palace is described in John 18:15, 16. See N.T.C. on the Gospel according to John, Vol. II, pp. 388-392. Peter, then, having been allowed to enter the palace by its outer gate, walked through the archway that led to the unroofed courtyard, where he sat down with the palace servants and the temple guards (policemen). By this time most of the soldiers, having delivered their prisoner, had probably returned to the fortress of Antonia. The record of Peter's first denial, which here in verse 58 is merely introduced, is found in verses 69, 70; cf. Mark 14:54, 66-68; Luke 22:54-57; and John 18:15-18. The story now returns to Christ's trial before the Sanhedrin.

59, 60a. Now the chief priests and the entire Sanhedrin were seeking to obtain false testimony against Jesus, so that they might put him to death; but they did not find (any), though many false witnesses came forward. Probably this trial took place in a large upper room of that wing of the palace where Caiaphas lived. The question might be asked, "But why have a trial at all, since the Sanhedrin had decided a long time ago that Jesus must be put to death (John 11:49, 50), an agreement which very recently had been reconfirmed (Matt. 26:4)?" Answer: the verdict must be made official and reasons must be formulated, so that the sentence that subsequently will be based upon it can be justified before the Jews, and so that the indispensable co-operation of the Gentiles—especially of Pilate—can be obtained.

For the absolutely sinless One to be subjected to a trial conducted by sinful men was in itself a deep humiliation. To be tried by *such* men, under *such* circumstances made it infinitely worse. Greedy, serpent-like, vindictive

---

[856] See, however, P. Valentin, "Les Comparutions de Jesus devant le Sanhedrin," *RSR* 59 (2, '71), pp. 230-236. According to the author, during the night Jesus is taken to Annas, then to Caiaphas, who is surrounded by some members of the Sanhedrin and some scribes. Not until the next morning (Luke 22:66) is Jesus led to the entire Sanhedrin. Does this view do justice to the expression "the entire συνέδριον" here in verse 59?

Annas (see on John 18:13), rude, sly, hypocritical Caiaphas (see on John 11:49, 50), crafty, superstitious, self-seeking Pilate (see on John 18:29); and immoral, ambitious, superficial Herod Antipas; these were his judges!

In reality, the entire trial was a farce. It was a mis-trial. There was no intention at all of giving Jesus a fair hearing in order that it might be discovered, in strict conformity with the laws of evidence, whether or not the charges against him were just or unfounded. In the annals of jurisprudence no travesty of justice ever took place that was more shocking than this one. Moreover, in order to reach this conclusion it is not at all necessary to make a close study of all the technical points with reference to Jewish law of that day. It has been emphasized by various authors that the trial of Jesus was illegal on several technical grounds, such as the following: *a.* No trial for life was allowed during the night. Yet, Jesus was tried and condemned during the hours of 1-3 A.M. Friday, and executed on the Feast, which was forbidden. According to Pharisaic law, no hearings in a case involving capital punishment could even be initiated on the eve of a major festival like Passover. No conviction was allowed at night. To execute a sentence on the day of one of the great feasts was contrary to the established regulations. [857] *b.* The arrest of Jesus was effected as a result of a bribe, namely, the blood-money which Judas received. *c.* Jesus was asked to incriminate himself. *d.* In cases of capital punishment, Jewish law did not permit the sentence to be pronounced until the day after the accused had been convicted.

Such and similar points of law have been mentioned again and again and used as arguments to prove the illegality of the entire procedure against Jesus of Nazareth. Attempts have also been made to refute them, one by one. The hair-splitting casuistry of rabbinic law had discovered all kinds of ways to circumvent its own regulations. All Caiaphas had to do was to say that the trial of Jesus at this time and under these conditions was in the interest of the people and of religion. [858]

To any fair-minded individual it must be evident at once that all these legal technicalities were but so many details. They do not touch the heart of the matter. The main point is nothing less than this: *it had been decided long ago that Jesus must be put to death* (see on 11:49, 50). *And the motive behind this decision was envy.* The Jewish leaders just could not "take" it that they were beginning to lose their hold upon the people and that Jesus of

---

[857] See Mishna, *Sanhedrin* IV.1.

[858] See G. Dalman, *Jesus-Jeshua*, New York, 1929, pp. 98-100. S. Rosenblatt, who in his article, "The Crucifixion of Jesus from the Standpoint of Pharisaic Law," *JBL* 75 (Dec. 1956), pp. 315-321, denies the account of the trial of Jesus as presented in the Gospels, nevertheless admits (p. 319) that "although the details of the trial given in the New Testament were definitely contrary to Pharisaic law, a way of removing an undesirable enemy is usually found when the will is there." That is exactly the point.

Nazareth had denounced and exposed them publicly. They were filled with rage because the new prophet had laid bare their hidden motives, and had called the temple court from which they derived much of their profit *a den of thieves.* On the surface, the dignified chief priests, elders, and scribes might try to put on an act by the seeming imperviousness of their demeanor; underneath they were vengefully nettled, convulsively agitated. They were thirsting for blood!

Hence, this is not a trial but a plot, and the entire plot is *their own. They* devised it, and *they* see to it that it is carried out. *Their* officers take part in the arrest of Jesus. *They* themselves were present! *They* seek the witnesses—*false* witnesses, of course—against Jesus, in order that *they* may put him to death (Matt. 26:59). *They* all condemn him as being deserving of death (Mark 14:67). "*They* (by means of *their* underlings) bind him and lead him away" (Mark 15:1). *They* deliver him to Pilate (John 18:28). Before Pilate *they* stir up the people to get Barabbas released in order that Jesus may be destroyed (Matt. 27:20). *They* intimidate Pilate, until at last the latter delivers Jesus up, to be crucified (John 19:12, 16). And even when he hangs upon the cross, *they* mock him, saying, "He saved others, himself he cannot save" (Mark 15:31).

Hence, this in reality is no *trial* at all. *It is murder.* Church History offers other sad examples of leaders who were cast out by judges who were filled with envy, and who themselves instigated the witnesses (*false* witnesses, of course!), in order that certain men whom *they* (the leaders) hated might be thrown out. The day of judgment will reveal some startling matters! But among all the travesties of justice, none even begins to compare with the one in which the *heavenly* Highpriest, Jesus Christ, stood before the *earthly* highpriests, Annas and Caiaphas. For the spotlessly Holy One to be arrayed before such wicked scoundrels, *that* was suffering!

Now in order to arrive at a verdict that would "hold up," there must be witnesses. Probably some preliminary work had been done to obtain them. However, when the witnesses started to testify it was soon discovered that, though there were many, not even two of them agreed (Mark 14:56). Yet, such agreement was absolutely necessary. A person could not be condemned to death on the basis of the testimony of just one witness. See Num. 35:30; cf. Deut. 17:6; 19:15; Matt. 18:16; I Tim. 5:19; Heb. 10:28. **60b, 61. But at last two came forward and declared, This fellow said, I am able to destroy the temple of God, and in three days to rebuild it.** The allusion is to the veiled saying of Jesus reported in John 2:19, "Break down this temple [or: sanctuary], and in three days I will raise it up." The Jews who had first heard it had misinterpreted it, as if it referred to nothing else than the physical structure which Jesus had just cleansed. But these two false witnesses, in addition, twisted the saying itself, as if the Lord had declared that he himself was going to destroy the temple. According to their testimony, then, Jesus was a defamer of the temple. In later days a similar false charge would be leveled against Stephen (Acts 6:14) and against Paul (Acts 21:28).

62, 63a. **And the highpriest arose.** . . . Of course, Jesus could have exposed the totally unwarranted character of the accusation. He could have shown that it was both a misinterpretation and a distortion of what he had said. But he knows very well that the purpose of this trial is not to vindicate the right, but rather to cause the wrong to triumph. So he remains silent. This irritates Caiaphas. That presiding officer has taken it upon himself to go way beyond presiding over a meeting. Instead, he is using this session of the Sanhedrin as a tool for the realization of his own pronounced intention (John 11:49-50) to destroy Jesus. So, visibly agitated, he rises from his seat and said to him, **You don't answer? What are these men testifying against you?** As if to say, "A serious charge is this. It certainly requires an answer!" **But Jesus remained silent.** He is again fulfilling the prophecy of Isa. 42:1-4; Matt. 12:18-21; and even more specifically, of Isa. 53:7 ("He opened not his mouth"). See also I Kings 19:11, 12; Isa. 57:15; Zech. 9:9; Matt. 5:7-9; 21:5; Luke 23:24. For similar behavior on the part of Jesus on this day—it is already Friday—see Matt. 27:12, 14; Luke 23:9b; John 19:9b. But not only was he fulfilling prophecy; he was in so doing also suffering intensely because of this assault on himself—"the Truth"—by Satan, "the father of the lie" (John 8:44).

When it seemed as if the trial would turn out to be a failure, Caiaphas all of a sudden leaps to the rescue by as it were waiving all secondary considerations and asking the main question, the one which had been on the minds of the leaders for a long time. Matthew reports this dramatic development in these words: **63b. And the highpriest said to him, I adjure you by the living God that you tell us whether you are the Christ, the Son of God.** That was the clincher, the decisive question. Did this question suddenly suggest itself to his mind, or had he thought of it previously and kept it in reserve, to be used if necessary? Did it, perhaps, have a divine origin? In passing, it might be observed that this idea cannot be entirely discarded (note John 11:51). If it was heavenly in origin, the highpriest himself, not heaven, would still be fully responsible for his sinister motive in asking it.

In order to emphasize the ominous gravity of the question and the impossibility of refusing an answer, the highpriest places Jesus "under oath," the weightiest oath of all, namely, "by the living God." He demands a clear and straightforward reply to the question, "Do you really claim to be the long-expected Messiah?" Now it cannot be said that up to this time Jesus had never revealed himself as such. In his conversation with the Samaritan woman had he not very definitely declared himself to be indeed the Messiah? See John 4:25, 26. Had he not defended those who addressed him as "the Son of David" (Matt. 21:15, 16)? Had he not, by implication, referred to himself as "the stone rejected by the builders but made the cornerstone"

(21:42)? Had he not pointed to himself as "the Son of man" destined one day to judge all men (25:31-46)?

All of this is true. But it could be argued that a declaration made in Samaria did not necessarily reach the Jews; that Matt. 21:15, 16 was not a direct claim but only a reflection on an exclamation made by others; that Matt. 21:37-39; 21:42 are parabolic, hence not direct; and that the term "Son of man" was not interpreted in the same way by everybody. It can even be added that there were definite reasons why during the earlier part of his ministry Jesus did not *openly* declare to the Jews, "I am the Messiah." See on 8:4; 9:30; 17:9. They would certainly have misunderstood it. See John 6:15. But now that the events that were happening with reference to him were making it clear that his messiahship was that of the Suffering Servant, as he had himself declared again and again to his disciples (12:40; 16:21; 17:22, 23; 20:18, 19; John 3:14), the moment had also arrived to come forth with a very clear statement, made before the highest authorities of the Jewish nation. Accordingly, when Caiaphas asked what he must have considered a question that would drive his enemy into a corner, he was actually in the providence of God giving the Son of man the opportunity for which he was looking.

We are not surprised therefore that, without the least hesitancy, in answer to the highpriest's question, "Are you the Christ, the Son of God?" **64. Jesus replied, You said (it).** In other words, "Yes indeed!" That this is actually the meaning of Christ's answer is clear from 26:25, which allows no other interpretation. [859] Jesus immediately reminds the highpriest and all those present that though right at this moment he is their prisoner, the period of his humiliation will soon be ended. By means of his very suffering he, "the Son of God" who is also "the Son of man"—for which see on 8:20, pp. 403-407—will attain to glory: **but I tell y o u, from now on y o u shall see**

> **the Son of man**
> **sitting at the right hand of the Power**
> **and coming on the clouds of heaven.**

That is the way in which Daniel had seen the coming Redeemer (Dan. 7:13, 14). It was thus that David sang of him (Ps. 110:1), and thus also that Jesus had himself described himself (see on Matt. 16:27; 22:41-46; 24:30), be it previously only to his disciples. Jesus is looking down history's lane. He sees the miracles of Calvary, the resurrection, the ascension, the coronation at the Father's right hand ("the right hand of the Power," that is, "of the Al-

---

[859] According to the Synoptics (Matt. 27:11; Mark 15:2; Luke 23:3), the only recorded word that issued from the lips of Jesus and was addressed *to Pilate* was, "You said (it)." Nevertheless, Paul states that, before Pilate, Jesus made "the good [noble or beautiful] confession" (I Tim. 6:13). Unless the apostle is referring also to a tradition preserved and after Paul's death recorded by the apostle John (John 18:37; 19:11), which is possible, he also is ascribing a positive meaning to the expression "You said (it)."

mighty"), Pentecost, the glorious return on the clouds of heaven, the judgment day, all rolled into one, manifesting his power and glory. On the final day of judgment he, even Jesus, will be the Judge, and these very men—Caiaphas and his partners—will have to answer for the crime they are now committing. Christ's prophecy is also a warning!

65. **Then the highpriest tore his robes, saying, He has blasphemed.** Here the hypocrisy of the highpriest becomes very clear. He acts as if he is overwhelmed with grief, though he could have shouted for joy. The man puts on a real show. He tears his highpriestly robe, [860] and says, "He has blasphemed," using the word "blasphemed" in its gravest sense: unjustly he has claimed for himself the prerogatives that belong to God alone. See on 9:3. Not that claiming to be the Messiah would in and by itself constitute blasphemy. But representing oneself as the fulfilment of Daniel's prophecy, that is, as the One who, coming with the clouds of heaven, would receive *a.* authority to judge all the nations, and *b.* everlasting dominion (see Dan. 7:13, 14); such a claim—and it was indeed this claim that Jesus was making—could be made only by God! Hence, either *a.* Jesus was indeed divine, "the Son of God," in the fullest sense of that term, or else *b.* he was guilty of blasphemy, punishable by death (Lev. 24:16). Caiaphas has chosen the second alternative, as we could have expected him to do. At the same time he is hardly able completely to conceal his elation. Bubbling over with excitement, like an explorer who after many dreary and disappointing weeks suddenly sights land, he exclaims, **What need do we still have of witnesses? Look, now y o u have heard his blasphemy,** as if to say, "We've got him now. Why continue the search for witnesses when all of us are witnesses?" He adds, 66. **What do y o u think?** So jubilant is he and so sure of himself that now for once he is willing to give the others an opportunity to express their opinion. In another situation he would, instead, have told them, "Y o u don't know anything" (John 11:49). But this is different. The others, glad that a solution of their problem had at last been found—and perhaps anxious to enjoy a few hours of sweet slumber; it is nearly three A.M. (see on verse 34)—quickly agree. **They answered, Deserving of death is he.** The verdict was unanimous (Mark 14:64). We assume that one member was absent (Luke 23:50, 51). There may have been others.

This unanimous *verdict* was not as yet a formal *sentence*. Declaring a person guilty and sentencing him are two different matters. In order to create at least a semblance of legality, a short period of time must elapse between these two actions. As was pointed out earlier, according to existing regulations that interval should have been a day. But as the Sanhedrists see it, such a prolonged delay would have been too dangerous. It could have given the friends of Jesus enough time to organize a revolt in his behalf. *Now*

---

[860] In spite of Lev. 10:6; 21:10? But commentators are not agreed on the question whether this prohibition was absolute in its application.

is the time to act. Early in the morning the Sanhedrin will have to be convened once more. See on 27:1. That will be for the purpose of sentencing. And even that action will not be final. It must still be approved by Pilate, the governor.

67a. Then they spat in his face and struck him with the fist. Verse 67a emphasizes the *cruelty* that followed the reaching of the verdict. What follows in 67b, 68 stresses the *mockery*. Of course, even that mockery was cruel! The cruelty was perpetrated by those who had captured Jesus and were now holding him (Luke 22:63). Temple police and palace guards had not yet left.

The face which these underlings—with the wholehearted permission and co-operation of their utterly selfish, sadistic, and envious superiors—now covered with their spittle was the one that had smiled upon large throngs of people whom he instructed to love even their enemies. It was the face which used to break into a smile at the approach of a child. It had been in the habit of beaming graciously upon publicans who became penitents. It could glow with righteous indignation when the Father's house was being desecrated, or when the widow's rights were violated, her needs ignored. In days gone by, it had become overspread with gladness when something good could be said about a friend. Above all, it was the face that mirrored the heart of the heavenly Father in all his holiness, displeasure with sin, and—last but not least—love and tenderness. It was into this face that these men were spitting! Surely, unless by the miracle of God's grace they should still repent, they would, on this day of the ultimate fulfilment of the prophecy (26:64) of him who was now a prisoner, be saying to the mountains and to the rocks, "Fall on us and hide us from *the face* of the One who sits on the throne and from the wrath of the Lamb."

The wretches—for that's what they were—even struck this (voluntarily) helpless victim with their fists. —And now cruelest, perhaps, of all: **67b, 68. Others slapped him and said, Prophesy to us, Christ, who was it that hit you?** They "covered his face" (Mark 14:65); they "blindfolded him" (Luke 22:64). Then they slapped him again and again, and as each one did this he would say, "You are the Christ, are you? Well, then you must know who I am. Tell me, will you?" They were playing a game at his expense. The game was their wicked variety of *Blind Man's Buff.* Throughout it all, however, it was he that was triumphing. This very cruelty and mockery was for him a firm attestation of being indeed the Messiah, the Father's beloved Son in whom prophecies—those uttered by others—Ps. 22:6, 7; Isa. 50:6—and by himself—Mark 10:34; Luke 18:32—were being fulfilled.

Isaiah was right: "He was despised and rejected by men" (53:3). He was right again when he continued, "But he was wounded for our transgressions, he was bruised for our iniquities." Hallelujah, what a Savior!

69 Now Peter was sitting outside in the courtyard when there came up to him a servant-girl, saying, "You too were with Jesus of Galilee." 70 But before everybody he denied (it), saying, "I don't know what you're talking about." 71 Now when he had gone out toward the gateway, another girl saw him and said to the people who were there, "This fellow was with Jesus the Nazarene." 72 Again he denied with an oath, (saying), "I don't know the man." 73 A little while later those who were standing around came up to Peter and said, "Certainly you also are one of them, for your accent gives you away." 74 Then he began to call down a curse on himself and to swear, "I don't know the man." At once a rooster crowed. 75 And Peter recalled the word spoken by Jesus, "Before a rooster crows you shall deny me three times." And he went outside and wept bitterly.

26:69-75 *Peter's Threefold Denial*
Cf. Mark 14:66-72; Luke 22:56-62; John 18:15-18, 25-27

The theme "Peter's experiences, words, and deeds during the night of Christ's betrayal and shortly afterward" would provide material for several sermons. The "points" might be: Peter's boast, Christ's prediction concerning him, his boast repeated and strengthened, his failure in Gethsemane, his three denials, his bitter tears, and his restoration.

The present paragraph contains the story of Peter's three denials, the last one followed by bitter tears. For a somewhat different arrangement of these denials in the Gospel according to John see N.T.C. on that Gospel, Vol. II, pp. 388-390.

The background of the first denial has already been indicated; see above on 26:58, where the parallel passages for this denial are also listed. The story is continued here in 69. **Now Peter was sitting outside in the courtyard when there came up to him a servant-girl, saying, You too were with Jesus of Galilee.** It would seem that the very moment when Peter had entered the palace the portress, viewing him from her nook in the vestibule, had her suspicions. The fact that she had admitted him at the request of John seemed to indicate that Peter too was a disciple of Jesus. The uneasiness that could be read on his face confirms her suspicions. So, about to be relieved by another gate-keeper, she walks toward Peter, who has already entered the open courtyard. She fixes her eyes on him (Luke 22:56). Then, stepping even closer, she says to him, "You too were with Jesus of Galilee." That the words she uses are reported somewhat differently in John's Gospel presents no difficulty. It must not be taken for granted that either—or any—Gospel, all by itself, reports all the words spoken by this girl. Her accusing jabber may have included the following lines: "You surely are not also one of this man's disciples, are you?—Why, I'm sure you were also with Jesus of Galilee." **70. But before everybody he denied (it), saying, I don't know what you're talking about.** Here, too, "I am not" of John 18:17 combines very easily with what is found in Matt. 26:70. Peter evidently has been floored. The unexpectedness and boldness of the servant-girl's incriminating statement catches him off guard. In spite of all his loud and repeated promises of unswerving loyalty to Jesus, boasts made only a few hours earlier (26:33, 35), he is now thoroughly frightened. One might say: he panics. Evidently he had failed to take to heart Christ's admonition (26:41).

The second denial follows very closely upon the first. **71. Now when he had gone out toward the gateway, another girl saw him and said to the people who were there, This fellow was with Jesus the Nazarene.** See also Mark 14:69, 70a and Luke 22:58. It seems that in his frustration as a result of the first embarrassment, Peter tried to get out of the building. He had been in the roofless courtyard, among the palace servants and temple guards, warming himself by the fire (Mark 14:54), but now things are becoming "too hot" for him. He is probably afraid that at any moment an underling may grab him and make him a prisoner. Perhaps the thought occurs to him, "What will happen to me if they find out that I'm the man who slashed off the ear of Malchus?" So he must try to escape from the palace as quickly as possible.

However, the portresses are unwilling to let him out. He gets no farther than the entranceway or vestibule which via the gate leads to the road. Several people are standing around. It would seem that the portress who is about to go off duty has already told the news about Peter to the girl who has come to relieve her. So both of these girls (cf. Matt. 26:71 and Mark 14:69) now say to those who are standing around, "This fellow was with Jesus the Nazarene." The constant reference to "of Galilee," "the Nazarene" may imply scorn, but this is by no means certain. See on 2:23 and also on John 1:46. At least one male bystander chimes in with what the girls are saying (Luke 22:58). **72. Again he denied with an oath, (saying), I don't know the man.** Note "the man," as if Jesus were a complete stranger to him. This time Simon is beside himself with rage and frustration. He does something that he had not done during the first denial. *With an oath* he begins to deny his connection with Jesus. Forcefully he maintains, "I don't know the man." Christ's oath (26:63, 64) and Peter's (26:72, 74), what a contrast! The former confirms the truth; the latter sanctions the lie!

Having been refused exit, Peter returns to the open courtyard. An hour elapses (Luke 22:59). It would seem, therefore, that the first two denials took place during Christ's appearance before Annas. Now the situation changes somewhat: Jesus has been brought before Caiaphas and the entire Sanhedrin. Christ's first trial before this body is almost over.

73. A little while later those who were standing around came up to Peter and said, Certainly you also are one of them, for your accent gives you away. During the interval of an hour the news about Peter has been spreading. Now the palace servants and the officers, the men who are standing around the fire with Peter, begin to tell him that he is one of Christ's disciples, and that

his very brogue identifies him as a Galilean. [861] A comparison of the Gospel accounts shows that some people are talking *to* Peter; others, *about* him. Accusations are flying in from every side. This was enough to get anyone excited, especially excitable Simon! As if all this were not enough, a relative of Malchus blurts out, "Did I not see you in the garden with Jesus?" For this story see N.T.C. on the Gospel according to John, Vol. II, pp. 399, 400.
74a. Then he began to call down a curse on himself and to swear, I don't know the man. He must have said something like, "May God do this or that to me if it be true that I am or ever was a disciple of Jesus." He stands there invoking upon himself one curse after another. And the louder this Galilean talks, the more, without realizing it, he is saying to all those standing around, "I'm a liar."

In his infinite and tender mercy the Lord, who in his sovereign providence controls all things, comes to the rescue: **74b, 75. At once a rooster crowed. And Peter recalled the word spoken by Jesus, Before a rooster crows you shall deny me three times.** From Luke 33:61 we gather that at the very moment when the rooster crowed   at least very nearly at that moment, someone is looking straight into Peter's eyes. It is Jesus, his face very likely still covered with spittle, and black and blue because of the blows it has received. It seems that the Master, his trial ended, is being led across the court to his prison cell, from which within a few hours he will be led once more before the Sanhedrin.

When Peter hears the crowing of the rooster, and sees Jesus looking at him, with eyes so full of pain, yet also of pardon, his memory of Christ's warning prediction (verse 34) is suddenly awakened. **And he went outside and wept bitterly.** How it came about that Peter is at last permitted to leave the palace is not stated. Can it have been because now the attention of all the underlings, and perhaps of everybody else, is fixed upon *Jesus?* However that may be, Peter goes out and weeps as only Peter can weep: bitterly, profusely, meaningfully, his heart being filled with genuine sorrow for what he has done.

How deceitful is man's heart! It is "exceedingly corrupt. Who can know it?" (Jer. 17:9). See also II Kings 8:13; cf. verse 15. Think of it: "Thou art the Christ, the Son of the living God."—"I don't even know the man."

How Christ must have suffered! No doubt much more because of these denials by a highly favored disciple and friend than because of the blows and the mockery inflicted on him by his declared enemies. See Ps. 55:12-14.

How God's pardoning grace and the Savior's forgiving love are here revealed! See Isa. 1:18; 53:6; 55:6, 7.

---

[861] A. T. Robertson, *Word Pictures*, Vol. I, p. 220, mentions difficulty with the pronunciation of gutturals as a characteristic of Galilean speech. G. Dalman, *op. cit.*, p. 24, simply states that Peter's language "may in some details have been somewhat different."

Summary of Chapter 26

Chapter 25 closed with the indication of a sharp contrast between the wicked, headed for everlasting punishment, and the righteous destined for everlasting life. That contrast is again strikingly revealed at the beginning of chapter 26: the rulers plotting Christ's death (verses 1-5) are placed over against Mary of Bethany, pouring her precious perfume—the evidence of her love and devotion—on Christ's head (verses 6:13).

As the Outline on p. 894 indicates, chapter 26 may be divided into ten paragraphs, as follows (for references see the indicated outline):

1. "Not at the Festival," said the plotters. "At the Festival" (Passover), said the Almighty, echoed by Jesus. And so it happened.

2. In connection with Mary's generous, thoughtful, and timely deed we are shocked by the disciples' inexcusable criticism, "Why this waste?" What is especially striking is the emphatic manner in which Jesus rushes to her defense with the words, "Wherever this gospel is preached in the whole world, also what she had done shall be told in memory of her."

3. Mary receives the Master's everlasting praise. Judas receives thirty pieces of silver—and even this for only a few days at the most. "Blessed assurance" was Mary's portion. "Gnawing remorse" was the traitor's reward.

4. This was the Passover that ended all meaningful Passovers. It was during this Passover meal that Jesus pointed out the betrayer. He did it, however, in such a remarkable manner that all the disciples were given an opportunity to examine themselves. Divine sovereignty and human responsibility are beautifully joined in Christ's saying, "The Son of man goes as it is written concerning him, but woe to that man by whom the Son of man is betrayed."

5. Toward the end of the meal Jesus instituted what became known as "the Lord's Supper." For its meaning see pp. 908-912.

6. Jesus predicted that all his disciples would become untrue to him. All protested, professing their unflinching loyalty. But in Gethsemane Christ's prediction was verified: they all left him and fled. At the Supper the leader in promising unswerving faithfulness was Peter. It was to him that Jesus said, "This very night, before the rooster crows, you shall deny me three times." Paragraph 10 shows that this was exactly what happened.

7. In Gethsemane Jesus *a.* agonized, *b.* agonized and prayed, *c.* prayed and kept watch. As to his prayers, by a change in the *main* clause—from "Let this cup pass from me" to "Thy will be done"—Jesus, the ever sinless One, reveals his obedience in a progressively glorious manner. Cf. Heb. 5:8.

938

8. What is especially significant is the fact that Jesus allows himself to be seized, bound, and led away. The "Victim" is "Victor" (John 10:11, 15; 16:33b). His life is an "offering" which he renders (Isa. 53:10).

9. Before the Sanhedrin Jesus, in answer to the highpriest's question, definitely and under oath declares himself to be the Messiah, who, after his death, will rise triumphantly from the grave (implied). Enthroned in heaven, he will rule over all his enemies and gloriously return one day upon the clouds of heaven, in fulfilment of Daniel's prophecy. "Then the highpriest tore his robes, saying, 'He has blasphemed. What need do we still have of witnesses?' . . . They answered, 'Deserving of death is he.' " Mockery and cruelty follow.

10. A brief summary of the story of Peter's Threefold Denial has been suggested on p. 935.

Outline of Chapter 27

Theme: *The Work Which Thou Gavest Him to Do*

CHAPTER XXVII

27 1 Early in the morning all the chief priests and the elders of the people took counsel against Jesus to put him to death.   2 And having bound him they led him away and handed him over to Pilate the governor.

27:1, 2 *The Sanhedrin's Decision to Put Jesus to Death*
Jesus Brought before Pilate
Cf. Mark 15:1; Luke 22:66; 23:1; John 18:28

1. **Early in the morning all the chief priests and the elders of the people took counsel against Jesus to put him to death.** From about three o'clock until daybreak Jesus must have been held in imprisonment somewhere in the palace of Caiaphas. Then "early in the morning"—for the reason already stated (see on 26:59, 60, 66)—the Sanhedrin is convened once more. A few minutes may have sufficed, since the verdict, "Guilty of blasphemy and therefore worthy of death" had already been agreed upon. Besides, Jesus must be rushed off to Pilate before the crowds know what is going on. So, very quickly Jesus is sentenced to death. 2. **And having bound him they led him away and handed him over to Pilate the governor.** The *binding* had occurred also earlier (John 18:12, 24). Jesus had to be led before Pilate because the Sanhedrin had no right, without Rome's approval, to carry out its decree (John 18:31).

John 18:28 states that Jesus was led to *the governor's residence* or *praetorium.* The language used in Luke 23:7 makes it well-nigh impossible to believe that Herod's palace is meant. The reference must be to the fortress of Antonia at the northwest corner of the temple area. Pilate had rooms in this fortress, in close proximity to the garrison (Mark 15:16), though his main residence was in Caesarea.

Pontius Pilate was the fifth governor of the southern half of Palestine. He was "governor" in the sense of being *procurator,* ruling over an imperial province, and as such directly responsible to the emperor. Although he had been endowed with civil, criminal, and military jurisdiction, he was under the authority of the legate of Syria.

From the sources that have come down to us [862] we may conclude that he was not a very tactful person. Once he caused soldiers who were under his command to bring with them into "the holy city" of Jerusalem, ensigns with their images of the emperor. To the Jew this was sacrilege. None of the procurators who preceded him had done this. When he threatened with death those who had come to petition him for the removal of these idolatrous standards they called his bluff, and he yielded. At another time he used the temple-treasure to pay for an aqueduct. When a crowd complained and rioted, he ordered his soldiers to club them into submission. The incident which finally led to his removal from office was his interference with a multitude of fanatics who, under the leadership of a false prophet, were at the point of ascending Mt. Gerizim in order to find the sacred vessels which, as they thought, Moses had hidden there. Pilate's cavalry attacked them, killing many of them. Upon complaint by the Samaritans, Pilate was then removed from office. He started out for Rome in order to answer the charges that had been leveled against him. Before he reached Rome, the emperor (Tiberius) had died. An unconfirmed story, related by Eusebius, states that Pilate "was forced to become his own slayer."

From the Gospels we gather that he was *proud* (see N.T.C. on John 19:10); and *cruel* (Luke 13:1). He was probably just as *superstitious* as his wife (Matt. 27:19). Above all, as all the accounts of the trial of Jesus before him indicate, he was a *self-seeker*, wishing to stand well with the emperor. He thoroughly hated the Jews who, as he saw it, were always causing him trouble upon trouble. That he was *utterly* devoid of any remnant of human sympathy and any sense of justice cannot be proved. In fact, there are passages which seem to point in the opposite direction. At any rate, though his guilt was great, it was not as great as that of Annas and Caiaphas, cf. John 19:11.

---

3 When Judas, who had betrayed him, saw that Jesus was condemned, he was seized with remorse and returned the thirty pieces of silver to the chief priests and the elders, 4 saying, "I have sinned by betraying innocent blood." But they said, "What is that to us? That's your problem." 5 And after he had thrown the pieces of silver into the temple [863] he departed. Then he went off and hanged himself. 6 But the chief priests took the pieces of silver and said, "It is not permissible to put these into the temple treasury, since it is blood money." 7 So they took counsel and bought with them the Potter's Field, as a burial place for foreigners. 8 Therefore to this day this field has been called the Field of Blood. 9 Then was fulfilled what had been spoken through the prophet Jeremiah, saying,

---

862 These sources are, first of all, *The Gospels;* then Philo, *De Legationem ad Caium* XXXVIII; Josephus *Antiquities* XVIII.55-64; 85-89; Josephus *The Jewish War* II.169-177; Tacitus *Annals* XV.xliv; and Eusebius, *Ecclesiastical History* I.ix, x; II.ii, vii. See also G. A. Müller, *Pontius Pilatus der fünfte Prokurator von Judäa*, Stuttgart, 1888; and P. L. Maier, *Pontius Pilate*, New York, 1968.
863 Or: sanctuary.

"And I took the thirty pieces of silver, the price for the man whose price was set, on whom the children of Israel had set a price, 10 and I gave them for the field of the potter, as the Lord had directed me."

27:3-10 *Judas' Death by Suicide*
Cf. Acts 1:18, 19

3, 4a. **When Judas, who had betrayed him, saw that Jesus was condemned, he was seized with remorse and returned the thirty pieces of silver to the chief priests and the elders, saying, I have sinned by betraying innocent blood.** Exactly when it was that Judas was seized with remorse is not indicated, but the text leaves the impression that it was immediately after he knew that Jesus had been sentenced to death. He may have rushed to the chief priests and elders at the very moment when the procession was forming to lead Jesus to the praetorium.

Judas was seized with remorse. He, in a sense, "was sorry afterward." See on 3:2 and on 21:28-30, especially footnote 736 on pp. 778, 779. He was burdened with self-reproach. Not that he now, had the opportunity been given, would have confessed his sin to the Savior and begged his forgiveness. A *basic* change of heart and mind he did not experience. But the feeling of guilt and fear of what might be the result for himself made it impossible for him to face the future. So, to the chief priests and elders—not necessarily the Sanhedrin still in session, for nothing is here said of their being assembled— he rushes in order to return to them the thirty pieces of silver, while he sobs, "I have sinned by betraying innocent blood."

We should not form too favorable an opinion of this self-reproach of Judas. Origen (*Against Celsus* II.xi) was of the opinion that the traitor's sorrow, exceeding great, was the result of the teaching of Jesus. We are rather of the opinion that it resembled the sentiment of Cain as expressed in Gen. 4:14. But however that may be, the chief priests and elders were not ready to co-operate with the betrayer. One is reminded of Benedict Arnold, another traitor. The reward he received from the British was of a very temporary character. He was hated by those whom he had betrayed and disliked even by the British whom he had favored. He died in poverty. So it was also in the case of Judas. How did his "friends" of a moment ago react to his "confession"? We read: 4b. **But they said, What is that to us? That's your problem.** [864] It must have been with sublime unconcern, with scorn and loathing, that they uttered these words. Judas had served their purpose. They wanted to have no further dealings with him; nor did they, at this particular moment, want to have anything to do with his blood-money. In despair Judas now goes to the temple. 5. **And after he had thrown the pieces**

---

[864] Literally, "*You* must see (to that)." Note emphatic σύ, followed by volitive future indicative ὄψῃ, amounting to an imperative.

of silver into the temple he departed. The flinging away of these coins is the action of a desperate man. Exactly where in the temple they landed is not certain. Some interpreters are of the opinion that the silver was hurled into *the sanctuary*, comprising the Holy Place and the Holy of Holies. According to this theory the traitor flung the bag with its silver into the entrance of the Holy Place. They base this conclusion on the fact that the original uses a word for "temple" which really means "sanctuary." However, words have histories. Thus, for example, in John 2:19 (see N.T.C. on that passage and on Matt. 26:60b, 61) the same word "sanctuary" is used. Nevertheless, probably the entire temple, including the courts, is indicated; otherwise the Jews could not have said, "Forty-six years this sanctuary has been in the process of building." It is rather immaterial whether, in translating this word, [865] one uses "sanctuary" or "temple" as an English equivalent, just so it is understood that "sanctuary" does not always have to refer to the inner shrine but can also have a broader meaning. When this is granted, it becomes clear that Judas did not necessarily fling the silver pieces into the Holy Place. He may, in fact, have intended to donate them to "holy causes." Shall we add, "thus, in a small measure, as he may have thought, to compensate for his terrible crime"? Whatever his intention may have been, verse 6 would seem to lend support to the theory that Judas threw the pieces into "the Treasury." [866] Against the wall in the Court of Women stood thirteen trumpet-shaped chests in which the people deposited their gifts—assessments and free donations—for various religious causes. Hence, using the part for the whole, this court was sometimes called "the Treasury" (John 8:20). We can picture Judas, emotionally upset, flinging these pieces, either singly, more probably still in his bag, into this court. If the string of the bag was loose, did the silver pieces ring loudly on the stone floor and scatter in every direction? Were Judas' clothes torn and his eyes filled with alarm? [867] Having returned the money, the traitor departed. The verb used in the original probably has the meaning generally assigned to it, namely, depart, go away, leave, withdraw. See also 2:12, 13, 14, 22; 4:12; 9:24; 12:15; 14:13. In view of its prefix, and the deed which the traitor was about to perform, some believe that in this instance it means, "went to a higher place." But that is by no means certain. Then he went off and hanged himself. Why this should be regarded as in conflict with Luke's account: "Falling headlong, he burst open in the middle and all his bowels gushed out" (Acts 1:18) is not clear. If he hanged himself from a tree located on a high cliff, above a valley,

---

[865] ναός in distinction from ἱερόν.

[866] So also H. N. Ridderbos, *op. cit.*, p. 217.

[867] See especially Rembrandt's painting, *Judas Returning the Thirty Pieces of Silver* (read what is said about this in R. Wallace and the editors of Time-Life Books, *The World of Rembrandt*, 1606-1669, New York, 1968, p. 47); and see E. Armitage's *The Remorse of Judas* (A. E. Bailey, *op. cit.*, pp. 331-334).

and if then the rope broke and the traitor fell on rocky ground, the result could very well have been as pictured in the book of Acts. Of course, this attempt at harmonization may be erroneous. There could be another and better explanation, but at least there is no reason whatever to cry, "Discrepancy."

6. **But the chief priests took the pieces of silver and said, It is not permissible to put these into the temple treasury, since it is blood money.** This sounds as if these *priests,* charged with the care of the temple, are saying, "What Judas intended cannot be done. To use such tainted money for sacred purposes would be illegal." Cf. Deut. 23:18. It must not be put into the "*qorbana*" (Aramaic), or *temple* treasury. [868] The very thought of "blood money" is repugnant to these "holy" (?) men. The fact that they themselves had in a sense "created" this kind of money did not seem to bother them in the least. When it came to meticulous fulfilment of the law in matters, even rather minor matters, that did no harm to what they regarded as their own personal interests, these men could be very conscientious. On matters far more important, such as "justice and mercy and faithfulness" (23:23), they were not nearly as scrupulous. They did not mind at all to pay out blood money in order to be able to lay hands on their enemy, Jesus, and to murder him! In this respect these priests resembled the scribes and the Pharisees. See on 15:3 ff.; 23:23, 24.

The result of their deliberation regarding the thirty pieces of silver is recorded in verse 7. **So they took counsel and bought with them the Potter's Field, as a burial place for foreigners.** They decide to use this money for a cause not directly connected with the temple and its maintenance or with any other strictly religious project. Instead, they used it for the purchase of "the Potter's Field," "the Acre of Ceramics." This term probably indicates a field from which potters (or a potter) used to obtain their (his) clay, but which had become depleted as a source of further supplies, and had therefore been offered for sale. The priests, then, intend to transform this plot into a burial place for strangers. They were probably thinking especially of Jews living outside the Holy Land and coming to Jerusalem to attend one of the great festivals, and then overtaken by death, without any friends or relatives who were able to provide a funeral for them. In this way the blood money, having been already used for the murder of the Friend of the poor, could now also serve as a help for the poor themselves in their ultimate need!

But if the priests thought that by means of this "good deed" they would be able to cleanse their hearts and hands, they were mistaken. In the future this field would be called the Field of Blood, cf. *ḥaqel dᵉma'* (*Akel dama,* Acts 1:19): 8. **Therefore to this day this field has been called the Field of Blood.** The meaning here is evidently that the place was called "the Field of

---

[868] So also in Josephus *Jewish War* II.175.

Blood" because it was purchased with blood money. The name of the field would then be a continuing testimony against Judas, the priests, and all who had agreed with them. There are those (for example, A. T. Robertson, *Word Pictures*, I, p. 224) who interpret Acts 1:8 to mean that the field derived its name from the circumstance that Judas' blood was shed there. *If* the passage in Acts really implies this, there is still no conflict with Matt. 27:8, for the two reasons are not irreconcilable. Since the fourth century A.D. a location has been assigned to this field, namely, south of the city, in the Valley of Hinnom near the latter's junction with the Kedron (or Kidron) Valley.

In a passage on which much labor by many commentators has been spent Matthew continues: **9, 10. Then was fulfilled what had been spoken through the prophet Jeremiah, saying,**

And I took the thirty pieces of silver, the price for the man whose price was set, on whom the children of Israel had set a price, and I gave them for the field of the potter, as the Lord had directed me. Note: "*I* took . . . *I* gave," a reading followed also by Ridderbos. Cf. Zech. 11:13.

The problem is that nowhere in the prophecy of *Jeremiah* is there any mention of "the thirty pieces of silver, the price for the man whose price was set. . . ." On the other hand, in *Zech.* 11:12, 13, we read, "And I said to them, 'If it is good in y o u r eyes, give me my wages; but if not, let it go.' So they weighed as my wages thirty shekels of silver. Then the Lord said to me, 'Throw it to the potter,'[869] the lordly price at which I was appraised by them. So I took the thirty shekels of silver, and I threw them into the house of the Lord to the potter."

It appears that the people of Zechariah's day had a low opinion of Zechariah as a shepherd, and accordingly paid him only thirty pieces of silver for his labors. So the prophet is directed by the Lord to go to the house of the Lord and to throw these thirty pieces to the potter whom he will meet there. The question, "To what extent must this prophecy be interpreted literally, to what extent figuratively?" need not detain us. See commentaries on Zechariah. For our present purpose it is only necessary to note the following points of resemblance between Zech. 11:12, 13 and Matt. 27:9, 10:

a. The labor of Jesus, as well as that of Zechariah, was held in low esteem by many of those who were the objects of it.

b. As the "lordly" price—this is irony—of thirty shekels was paid to Zechariah, so Jesus was betrayed for the same paltry sum. These thirty pieces of silver were the price which the children of Israel set on Zechariah, and subsequently on Jesus.

---

[869] By a slight change in spelling the Hebrew word for "potter" becomes "treasury." So, for example, R.S.V. twice in Zech. 11:13. I can, however, not see any sound reason for this change. The potter is definitely in the picture both in Zechariah's prophecy and in Matthew.

c. As the thirty pieces at which the labor of Zechariah had been appraised were thrown to the potter—at the Lord's command (Zech. 11:13; cf. Matt. 27:10b)—so also the thirty pieces for which Jesus was betrayed landed at last in the hands of the potter.

d. In both cases also the "throwing" of the pieces took place in the house of the Lord. Cf. Zech. 11:13 with Matt. 27:5.

Up to this point there is agreement between Zechariah's prophecy and its fulfilment in connection with Jesus. The problem, however, is that Matthew says "Jeremiah," not Zechariah. Instead of bothering the general reader with various theories which I, the author of this Commentary, reject, I refer to the footnote for a brief enumeration of solutions which I cannot accept, so that those who are interested may study them. [870]

My own solution, to the extent in which I deem a solution to be possible, is as follows. First of all, the close connection of Matt. 27:9, 10 with the prophecy of Zech. 11:12, 13 cannot be denied. Secondly, Zechariah's prophecy, taken by itself, does *not fully* satisfy the requirements of Matthew's fulfilment passage. One might ask, "Where in Old Testament prophecy is there mention of a plot of ground, used for burial purposes, which became known as 'the Field of Blood,' because innocent blood had been shed?" It is such a plot to which Matthew, according to the context, is

---

[870] I cannot accept the following:

(1) The Jews used to divide the Old Testament into three parts: the Law, the Psalms, and Jeremiah." The title "Jeremiah," accordingly, had reference to the entire book of the prophets, including Zechariah. It is for this reason that Matthew, though quoting from Zechariah, can write "Jeremiah." Thus Lenski, *op. cit.*, p. 1063. *Objection:* The source on which this theory is based cannot be regarded reliable. Besides, the manner in which the inspired authors divide the Old Testament has been indicated in footnote 279 on p. 288.

(2) In the original "through the prophet" (Matt. 27:9) stood alone. "Jeremiah" was added by an early copyist. Thus A. Carr, *The Gospel according to St. Matthew*, Cambridge, 1901, p. 302. *Objection:* The textual evidence in support of the omission is weak. See Gk. N.T. (A-B-M-W).

(3) A. H. McNeile, *op. cit.*, pp. 407, 408, suggests three possibilities: First, "Jeremiah" was written by mistake for "Zechariah." Such a mistake was easily made. Jeremiah's purchase of a field (Jer. 32:6 ff.) and his visit to the potter's house (18:2 f.) may have contributed to it. *Objection:* Neither of these passages says anything about a potter's field. Jer. 18 refers to Jeremiah's visit to the potter's house but says nothing about his field. Jer. 32 speaks about the purchase of a field but says nothing about a potter. Hanamel, from whom the field was purchased, was almost certainly not a potter. Secondly, McNeile suggests that the words to which Matthew makes reference may have occurred in an apocryphal writing of Jeremiah. However, after offering this suggestion the author virtually rejects it. Thirdly, the occurrence of the word "Jeremiah" in Matt. 27:9 may have been a clerical slip due to the misreading of an abbreviation. *Objection:* Though it is admitted that in the original such a slip would indeed be possible, especially in this particular case, nevertheless, as will be shown, Matt. 27:9, 10 reminds one too strongly of what is indeed found in *Jeremiah* to make this solution seem reasonable.

These are by no means the only proposed solutions. But I have not seen any others that appear even on the surface to be more credible.

clearly referring. Yet nothing of the kind is mentioned in Zechariah. It is described, however, in Jeremiah,[871] chapter 19. Note all the resemblances: Judah and Jerusalem have shed innocent blood (Jer. 19:4; Matt. 27:4). Chief priests and elders are mentioned prominently (Jer. 19:1; Matt. 27:3, 6, 7). A potter is mentioned (Jer. 19:1, 11; Matt. 27:7, 10). Topheth, that is, the valley of Hinnom—the very valley where, according to tradition, the Potter's Field was located—has its name changed to "the Valley of Slaughter," which is about the same as "the Field of Blood" (Jer. 19:6; Matt. 27:8; cf. Acts 1:19). And this valley becomes a well-known "burial place" (Jer. 19:11; Matt. 27:7).

As has already been implied, the solution is not complete. That Jeremiah actually *bought* a potter's field (Matt. 27:10) is not stated in Jer. 19 nor anywhere else in the Old Testament. Did Matthew derive this bit of information from oral tradition? It is clear, however, that in many other respects Matthew's passage reflects Jer. 19.

What Matthew does, therefore is this: he combines two prophecies, one from Zechariah and one from Jeremiah. Then he mentions not the minor prophet but the major prophet as the source of the reference. This mentioning of only one source when the allusion is to two is not peculiar to Matthew. Mark does this also. Thus Mark 1:2, 3 refers first to Malachi, then to Isaiah. Nevertheless Mark ascribes both prophecies to "Isaiah," the major prophet. And similarly the quotation found in II Chron. 36:21 is drawn from Lev. 26:34, 35 and from Jer. 25:12 (cf. 29:10), but is ascribed only to "Jeremiah." We are safe, therefore, in allowing the words "through the prophet Jeremiah" (Matt. 27:9) to stand, just so we realize that the background of the passage is actually both Jeremiah and Zechariah, and that the first part of the quotation resembles a passage from Zechariah even more strongly than any from Jeremiah.

The main point to bear in mind, however, is that also in the suicide of the traitor and the purchase of a field with his blood money prophecy is again being fulfilled, and God's plan is being carried out.

---

11 Now Jesus stood before the governor. And the governor questioned him, saying, "You are the king of the Jews?" Jesus replied, "You said (it)." 12 And when he was being accused by the chief priests and the elders, he made no answer. 13 Then Pilate said to him, "Don't you hear how many accusations they are bringing against you?" 14 But he gave no answer, not even to a single charge, so that the governor was exceedingly astonished.

---

[871] As already indicated (see footnote 870 (3)), not in Jer. 18 or 32, but in Jer. 19. F. W. Grosheide (*op. cit.*, p. 420) mentions chapter nineteen but also Jer. 18:2-12; 32:6-9. Best of all, as far as my research goes, is R. W. Gundry, *op. cit.*, pp. 122-127.

27:11-14 *Jesus Questioned by Pilate*
Cf. Mark 15:2-5; Luke 23:2-5; John 18:33-38

The story started in verses 1 and 2—"Jesus Brought before Pilate"—is now resumed. Since several elements enter into the narrative represented by the two sections, "Jesus Questioned by Pilate" (Matt. 27:11-14) and "Jesus Sentenced to Die" (27:15-26), and since the other Gospels, too, make their distinct contributions, it may be helpful before presenting an interpretation of these two sections of Matthew's Gospel, first of all to give a brief summary of events. Combining the Gospel accounts, one gains the impression that from the start almost to the finish Pilate did everything in his power to get rid of this case. He had no love for the Jews. He hated to please them and to grant their request with respect to Jesus. Yet, on the other hand, deep down in his heart he was afraid of them and of the possibility that they might use their influence to hurt him. Up to a point he is willing to do what justice demands, but only up to a point. When his *position* is threatened, he surrenders.

As indicated, from the start he wanted to avoid the necessity of making a definite decision regarding Jesus. So, first he tries to return the prisoner to the Sanhedrin, "Take him yourselves, and judge him according to y o u r own law," he says (John 18:29-31). When the members of that body make clear to Pilate that they desire nothing less than the prisoner's *death,* and when they then are made to understand that to secure their objective definite charges will have to be made against Jesus, they quickly present three of them: *a.* he perverts the nation; *b.* he forbids us to pay tribute to Caesar; and *c.* he claims that he himself is king (Luke 23:2). In reality these three charges amounted to *one:* "This man is a revolutionary, a seditionist, a politically dangerous person." Pilate could not afford to allow such an alleged claim to kingship to remain unexamined. *It is at this point that our present section, "Jesus Questioned by Pilate" (Matt. 27:11-14), takes up the story.*

Having examined Jesus on this point, Pilate returns a verdict of "Not guilty." However, the answer of the Jews is, "He stirs up the people, teaching throughout all Judea, from Galilee even to this place" (Luke 23:5). The mention of Galilee is music to Pilate's ears, for to him it means that he may be able to turn the case over to the tetrarch Herod Antipas, now in Jerusalem (Luke 23:6-12). When also this does not bring about the result which Pilate had in mind, he tries to escape from his difficult situation by meeting the Sanhedrin halfway, that is, by suggesting that Jesus be first scourged and then released (Luke 23:13-16). When this proposal is also rejected, the procurator tries to get rid of his problem by making a very peculiar and wholly unwarranted use of his custom at a festival to permit the Jews to choose a prisoner of their nationality to be set free. *Here begins*

949

Matthew's next section, "Jesus Sentenced to Die" (Matt. 27:15-26; cf. Mark 15:6-15; Luke 23:13-25; John 18:19—19:16.

Pilate offers the Jews the opportunity to choose between Barabbas and Jesus, as if the latter were already a man condemned by the Roman government. But, contrary to his hope and expectation, the people, urged on by their leaders, choose Barabbas. The result is that Pilate, after more desperate attempts to force them to accept his earlier proposal that Jesus be scourged and then set free, etc. (compare verses 16 and 22 of Luke 23, but see also John 19:1-11) finally surrenders. Capitulating to the wishes of the people who are screaming, "If you release this man, you are no friend of the emperor" (John 19:12), he sentences Jesus to be crucified. By publicly washing his own hands the corrupt judge tries to appease his conscience and to place all the blame upon the crowds.

With this brief outline in mind, we are now ready to return to Matthew's account: 11. **Now Jesus stood before the governor.** Pilate, having probably been informed by the soldiers on guard duty that a prisoner had been brought by a Sanhedrin delegation which refused to enter the Praetorium, went out to them. Standing on a gallery or porch over the pavement in front of his temporary residence, he asked the Jewish rulers to present the indictment. When, after some dilly-dallying, as indicated above, the Jews finally present their accusation—Jesus' alleged claim to kingship—the governor simply could not afford to ignore this charge, not with suspicious Tiberius in the saddle at Rome! So he re-enters his residence in order to examine Jesus. As Matthew's story opens here at verse 11 Jesus is standing in front of Pilate. **And the governor questioned him, saying, You are the king of the Jews?** By the Sanhedrin Jesus had been accused of blasphemy (26:65, 66), and had been declared "deserving of death." Before Pilate, however, the Jewish leaders did not immediately present this charge. They must have been of the opinion—and rightly so—that a more definitely political accusation would have a better chance to be considered legally valid from the aspect of Roman jurisprudence. Besides, they may have felt that a strictly religious charge would make little impression on a pagan. This does not mean, however, that they have altogether discarded the idea of ever bringing this religious indictment to the attention of the governor. They did in fact do this very thing (John 19:7), but for the present they hold it in abeyance.

When Pilate now asked Jesus, "You are the king of the Jews?" he asked it because he felt that for his own protection—as already explained—he had to do this, and not because he himself believed the charge. How *could* he believe it? The situation was entirely too ridiculous, too unreal. As if Jews, grievously vexed by the yoke of the oppressor and yearning for the time when they would be able to shake it off and once again enjoy victories under their own kings, would be so very displeased with one of their own countrymen who supposedly was of one mind with them and was even willing to be their leader, that for this reason, out of love for Rome, they wanted him to be crucified! No, Pilate could not believe that. Besides, he already knew the real reason why they hated Jesus and had him arraigned. See Verse 18. But, as explained, Pilate feels that he has to ask the question. **Jesus replied, You said (it).** That this was no evasive answer, as if Jesus meant, "That is what *you* are saying, but *I* have never said that," has already been shown. See on 26:25, 64; also N.T.C. on John 18:37.

12. **And when he was being accused by the chief priests and the elders, he made no answer.** The substance of these charges may be gathered from Luke 23:2, 5; see above, p. 949. For reasons already enumerated (see on 26:62, 63a) Jesus did not answer. 13, 14. **Then Pilate said to him, Don't you hear how many accusations they are bringing against you? But he gave no answer, not even to a single charge, so that the governor was exceedingly astonished.** This is virtually a repetition of 26:62b, 63, but takes place before a different judge. The silence on the part of Jesus, a silence even after Pilate had urged him to speak, amazed the governor. He is confronted with a double contrast: *a.* Between Jesus and ever so many other accused persons who had appeared before him, and had probably been very vocal and excited in defending themselves; and *b.* between the boisterous, troublesome, aggressive person as Jesus had been pictured by the chief priests and the elders; and the quiet, dignified, serene individual who was now standing before him.

---

15 Now at a feast it was customary for the governor to release to the crowd any one prisoner whom they wanted. 16 There was at that time a notorious prisoner, named Barabbas. [872] 17 So when they were assembled Pilate asked them, "Whom do y o u want me to release to y o u, Barabbas or Jesus who is called Christ?" 18 For he knew that because of envy they had handed Jesus over to him. 19 Now while he was occupying the Judicial Bench, his wife sent him a message, saying, "Don't have anything to do with that righteous man; for this very day I have suffered much in a dream because of him." 20 Now the chief priests and the elders persuaded the crowds to ask for Barabbas and to have Jesus executed. 21 So when the governor asked them, "Which of the two do y o u want me to release to y o u?" they said, "Barabbas." 22 Pilate said to them, "Then what shall I do with Jesus, who is called Christ?" They all answered, "Let him be crucified!" 23 But he said, "Why, what wrong has he done?" All the louder they were screaming, "Let him be crucified!" 24 So when Pilate saw that he was not getting anywhere, and that on the contrary a riot was starting, he took water and washed his hands in front of the crowd, saying, "Innocent am I of the blood of this man. That's y o u r problem." 25 All the people answered, "Let his blood be upon us and upon our children." 26 Then he released Barabbas for them. But he had Jesus flogged, and handed him over to be crucified.

27:15-26 *Jesus Sentenced to Die*
Cf. Mark 15:6-15; Luke 23:13-25; John 18:19–19:16

Matthew, probably omitting certain incidents reported elsewhere, as has been shown, continues as follows: 15. **Now at the feast it was customary for**

---

[872] Another reading has "Jesus Barabbas" both here and in verse 17.

the governor to release to the crowd any one prisoner whom they wanted. Whether the reference here is to any of the great religious festivals or exclusively to the Passover is not clear, though the idea of setting a prisoner free would seem to be most appropriate in connection with Passover, the commemoration of the deliverance of the Israelites from the house of bondage. One thing is clear: Pilate at this particular moment is most willing to grant the request of the people (Mark 15:8) that, according to custom, a prisoner be released; for, as he sees it, this may be the way he can get Jesus off his hands. **16, 17. There was at that time a notorious prisoner, named Barabbas.** [873] **So when they were assembled Pilate asked them, Whom do y o u want me to release to y o u, Barabbas or Jesus who is called Christ?** This too was suffering for Jesus, the thoroughly sinless One, to be treated as if he were in a class with Barabbas, who was a condemned robber or insurrectionist [874] (John 18:40), a man who had committed murder in an insurrection (Mark 15:7; cf. Luke 23:19).

It seems altogether probable that Pilate expected the multitude to choose *Jesus.* After all, the echoes of their hosannas in honor of the prophet from Galilee had scarcely died. If five days ago "the whole world" applauded him—and Pilate was not completely ignorant of this; cf. Matt. 27:18; Mark, 15:9, 10—would the people now turn against him? Were there not some who called him "Christ"? Would even the ardent patriots among them prefer a violent man to Jesus, a man in whom Pilate could find no evidence of any crime? See on verse 23. Pilate realizes that he is playing off the people against the leaders. By this time the crowds had begun to swell, and not the leaders only but the people in general were given the opportunity to select a prisoner for release. The governor, moreover, would be happy to triumph over these leaders, all the more in this particular case, **18. For he knew that because of envy they had handed Jesus over to him.** For a word study on the concept *envy* see N.T.C. on I and II Timothy and Titus, p. 388, where one can also find several Biblical illustrations of this sinful characteristic. Envy is the displeasure aroused by seeing someone else having what you do not want him to have. So, for example, the leaders envied Jesus because of his fame and following, his ability to perform miracles, etc.

Surely, now Pilate is going to have his way. Why, even *the leaders* cannot with any consistency ask for the release of a proved, condemned, violent, murderous insurrectionist, since just a little while ago they have accused Jesus of insurrection, a man whose guilt in this respect has not even been proved; in fact, has been disproved.—And as to *the crowds,* Pilate "knows"

---

[873] The reading "Jesus Barabbas," both here and in verse 17, has weak textual support. Unless one is persuaded by the argument of Origen that for reasons of piety this name "Jesus" which originally belonged to the bad man was omitted in many important manuscripts, there is no solid ground for retaining this double appellation.

[874] λῃστής, as in 26:55; see footnote 850 on p. 921.

how *they* will vote! So once again Pilate is ready to ask the question of verse 17. . . . And then there is a sudden interruption. The next two verses should be read together. At least to a considerable extent they explain what otherwise would seem very strange, namely, the contents of verse 21. **19, 20. Now while he was occupying the Judicial Bench, his wife sent him a message, saying, Don't have anything to do with that righteous man; for this very day I have suffered much in a dream because of him. Now the chief priests and the elders persuaded the crowds to ask for Barabbas and to have Jesus executed.**

Pilate was sitting on his official chair on the platform, reached by steps, in front of the praetorium. [875] His wife Claudia Procula, or simply Procla—was that her *real* name?—has had a dream, a kind of nightmare. That she dreamt about Jesus is not strange. Did not everybody in Jerusalem know about Jesus, and is it not even possible that she had been awakened by the procession which, so early in the morning, had brought a prisoner to the praetorium? Besides, though neither she nor her husband were regularly living in Jerusalem, nevertheless it seems rather natural that the procurator, who already knew certain facts about the attitude of the Jewish leaders toward Jesus (see verse 18), had conveyed some of this information to her. Perhaps after the early morning disturbance she had fallen asleep again (note "this very day"). And then, in the providence of God, according to which Jesus must die for the salvation of his people, this woman dreams. The content of her dream has not been revealed. All we really know is that it was a very alarming experience. Did she perhaps see Jesus standing in front of her husband? Did she receive an impression of his innocence, even better: of his righteousness? And was she overwhelmed with agony when her husband was about to sentence him to be crucified? These things have not been revealed. But something of the kind must have occurred. Otherwise, why would she have rushed a message to her husband, "Don't have anything to do with that righteous man. . ."?

Did this woman become a Jewish proselyte and afterward a Christian? The Coptic church honors her memory; the Greek church includes her name in the calendar of saints. But such honors prove nothing.

Was she really giving good advice to her husband? In a certain sense she certainly was doing exactly that, for by means of her message she was urging her husband not to condemn Jesus, whom she called "that righteous man." The inclusion of this story in the Gospel of Matthew is therefore one more piece of evidence attesting the righteousness of our Lord, which makes it possible for him to be the Savior. For more about this see on verse 23. As far

---

[875] For further details on this see N.T.C. on the Gospel according to John, Vol. II, p. 420.

as this woman's advice was good, it can also be considered a divinely directed warning addressed to Pilate.

There is, however, another side to the story. Her advice cannot be called wholly good. She was urging her husband *not to have anything to do* with Jesus. Now this was what he himself was constantly attempting, namely, not to have anything to do with the accused; that is, to dodge his responsibility as a judge. But that was wrong. He should have been brave enough and fair enough not only to pronounce Jesus "Not guilty," which, in fact, he did again and again, but also *to acquit him!* His wife's advice, though good to a certain extent, could have been much better. And the beautiful stories about her are merely legends. When Christ returns he will not shy away from *his* duty as a Judge. That is our comfort. See Matt. 25:31 ff.; II Tim. 4:8.

While Pilate was being kept busy with the message from his wife, the chief priests and the elders took full advantage of the interruption and used it to persuade the crowds to ask for Barabbas and to have Jesus executed. Did these wretched leaders remind the people that by choosing Jesus they would be playing into the hands of their deadly enemy Pilate? Did they recount all the crimes which Pilate had previously committed against the Jewish nation? And did they intimidate those who at first were inclined to choose Jesus? If they did, it would not have been the first time; see John 7:13; 9:22; 19:38; nor would it be the last; see John 20:19; Acts 4:18.

Accordingly, *we* are not as surprised as the governor must have been. **21. So when the governor asked them, Which of the two do y o u want me to release to y o u? they said, Barabbas.** The procurator must have been fully confident that the people would answer, "Jesus." But with one voice they shout, "Barabbas." What follows is one of the most dramatic and also in a sense precious passages in all of Scripture. **22. Pilate said to them, Then what shall I do with Jesus, who is called Christ?** Pilate was desperate. He did not want to sentence Jesus to death. Yet, it was becoming more and more clear to him that this by now had become the desire of the fickle multitude. When the prophet of Galilee was still healing the sick, raising the dead, cleansing the lepers, holding the multitudes spellbound by means of his marvelous discourses, he was popular. When he rode into Jerusalem, he was applauded. But now that he is seemingly helpless, and the leaders have used their strongest arguments to persuade the people to demand his crucifixion, they turn their backs on him. As to Pilate, when he asked, "Then what shall I do with Jesus?" his immediate answer should have been, "I shall pronounce him innocent and therefore I shall order his immediate and definite release." In fact, the judge should not even have asked the question at all. He knew the answer.

Hymnology has caught the deeper meaning, the broader application. See "Jesus is standing in Pilate's hall," by an anonymous author; also "What will you do with Jesus?" by N. Norton. There are those who think that the words "Jesus, who is called Christ" indicate that the man whose release the people demanded was "Jesus, who is called Barabbas," or simply "Jesus Barabbas." Although the possibility must be granted, more probable, it would seem to me, is the theory that the words "who is called Christ" were added not for the mere sake of identification but rather to stress the vast difference between *a.* Barabbas, the criminal; and *b.* Jesus, by some even then considered "the Anointed." Even Pilate, though a heathen, sensed something of the vast difference between the two. **They all answered, Let him be crucified.** It should be borne in mind, however, that not the people in general but their leaders had started the shouting (27:20). The guilt of the leaders was greater than that of the people as a whole, though they too were surely guilty. **23. But he said, Why,** [876] **what wrong has he done?** That was one way of saying, "He has done no evil, has committed no crime." It is rewarding to count the number of times the governor uttered the words, "I do not find any crime in him," or something similar. In addition to the present passage see also 27:24; Mark 15:14; Luke 23:4, 13-15, 22; John 18:38; 19:4, 6. Even when due allowance is made for parallel (duplicate) passages, the fact remains that Pilate stresses and constantly re-iterates the truth that in Jesus there is no cause of indictment. And by means of Pilate it was God himself who declared his Son's complete innocence, his perfect righteousness. Nevertheless, in a few more moments this same Pilate is going to succumb to the persistent clamor of the Jews, and is going to sentence Jesus to die the accursed death of crucifixion. "No guilt in him . . . no guilt in him . . . no guilt in him . . . no guilt in him. . . . So then he handed him over in order to be crucified." Thus reads the sacred record. But how could a righteous God permit this? There is only *one* solution. It is found in Isa. 53:6, 8, "Jehovah has laid on him the iniquity of us all. . . . He was cut off out of the land of the living for the transgression of my people to whom the stroke was due." Cf. Gal. 3:13.

In answer to Pilate's question the people did not even say, "He did this" or, "He did that." They followed what must have been for them the easier course: **All the louder they were [or: kept on] screaming, Let him be crucified.** Over and over again these terrible words are yelled until they become a monotonous refrain, an eery, ominous chant: "Let him be crucified. . . . Let him be crucified. . . ." The crowd has become a riotous mob, an emotion-charged screaming rabble.

24. So when Pilate saw that he was not getting anywhere, and that on the contrary a riot was starting, he took water and washed his hands in front of

---

[876] By no means does γάρ always mean *for* or *because.* It can also be strongly confirmatory or exclamatory: Yes, indeed! Certainly! There! What! Why! (cf. John 7:41; Acts 8:31; I Cor. 9:10; 11:22; Gal. 1:10; Phil. 1:18).

the crowd, saying, Innocent am I of the blood of this man. [877] The governor noticed that he was not getting anywhere, and that matters were getting worse instead of better. The people were becoming more and more clamorous and excited. A riot or turbulence [878] was developing. So in front of everybody Pilate, having ordered water to be brought to him, washes his hands in token of his (pretended) innocence. Whether or not such an action had this symbolic meaning among the Romans is not definitely known. But the Jews must have understood it immediately. Cf. Deut. 21:6, 7; Ps. 26:6; 73:13. Moreover, if there were any that did not understand, they must have quickly grasped the meaning, for the governor added a verbal explanation, saying "Innocent [879] am I of the blood of this man." It is evident that Pilate—even if he merely said "of this man" and not (as a variant has it) "of this righteous man"—was implying that, as he saw it, Jesus was innocent. The judge was saying, as it were, "Since I do not at all believe that Jesus is guilty of any crime, I refuse to assume any responsibility for his death by crucifixion. I am free from the guilt of shedding his blood." Once more, therefore, as on several occasions during this trial (see on verse 23), the innocence of Jesus is being proclaimed. So far, so good. But when Pilate disclaims any responsibility for the murder that is about to be committed, he makes himself guilty of an act of cowardice, untruthfulness, and dishonesty. And when he adds, **That's y o u r problem**; literally, "*Y o u* must see (to that),*" he is again making an unsuccessful attempt to shift responsibility away from himself, and uttering what, at best, was only a half-truth. To the extent in which he was saying, "It is y o u r *and therefore not my* responsibility," he was telling a lie, for it most certainly was his duty as a judge to pronounce a just verdict and, in the present case, to acquit the accused. But to the extent in which Christ's suffering and death were being brought about by the Jewish leaders and their followers, what Pilate said was the truth. To bear the burden of this guilt was indeed in large measure their problem. In God's providence the very expression with which the leaders had reproached Judas (see on verse 4 above) was now cast in their own teeth.

How did those who heard Pilate's declaration of innocence react to his words? The answer is found in verse 25. **All the people answered, Let his blood be upon us and upon our children.** It seems as if they said this flippantly, light-heartedly. Also, they said it unanimously: "*all* the people." The Israel of that day was hereby rejecting the Christ, and in the same breath accepting full responsibility for doing this. In such passages as II Sam. 1:16; 3:28, 29; Acts 18:6 someone (David, Paul) is saying that others (an Amale-

---

[877] According to another reading, "of this righteous man," which, if original, would be an echo of the expression used by Pilate's wife (verse 19).

[878] Note similarity between the Greek θόρυβος and the English *trouble, turbulence*.

[879] Greek ἀθῷος, that is, without penalty, clear, scot-free.

kite, Joab, the Jews) must bear the guilt that attached to their deed(s). In each case the man who utters the statement is doing what Pilate did in verse 24; with this difference, however, that the governor *unjustly* tried to shift responsibility away from himself, while David and Paul were justified in fixing it where it actually belonged. But here in 27:25 the people are loading themselves with responsibility for their attitude and action regarding Jesus. Though they do not realize it, they are in fact pronouncing a curse upon themselves, even involving in this curse their own posterity.

By means of openly rejecting the Messiah, the Jewish people cease to be in any special sense the people of God. See Heb. 10:29. This does not mean that God is through with the Jews. No, also with respect to them it remains true that "a remnant shall be saved," and this throughout the ages, for "God is love," hence not merely toward the end of the world's history. By means of this interpretation justice is done both to the goodness and to the severity that characterize God's attitude toward the Jews. See Rom. 11:22. For the rest see on Matt. 8:11, 12.

As Matthew summarizes the story, the sentence is now ready to be pronounced. It has already been indicated that John adds certain significant details (19:1-11) and also shows (19:12) what finally brought about the complete moral discomfiture of Pilate and the sentencing to death of Jesus. There is no conflict between Matthew's account and that of John. The fact is simply this, that at this point John gives us a more complete account. **26. Then he released Barabbas for them.** This was in accordance with the governor's implied promise (see Matt. 27:17, 21). **But he had Jesus flogged, and handed him over to be crucified.**

The Roman scourge consisted of a short wooden handle to which several thongs were attached, the ends equipped with pieces of lead or brass and with sharply pointed bits of bone. The stripes were laid especially on the victim's back, bared and bent. Generally two men were employed to administer this punishment, one lashing the victim from one side, one from the other side, with the result that the flesh was at times lacerated to such an extent that deep-seated veins and arteries, sometimes even entrails and inner organs, were exposed. Such flogging, from which Roman citizens were excempt (cf. Acts 16:37), often resulted in death.

One can picture Jesus after the scourging, covered with horrible bruises and lacerations, with wales and welts. It is no surprise that Simon of Cyrene was compelled to bear the cross after Jesus had carried it a short distance (27:32; Luke 23:26; John 19:16, 17). Scourging was hideous torture. [880] It must, however, be borne in mind that the suffering of the Man of Sorrows was not only intense but also vicarious:

"He was wounded for our transgressions, he was bruised for our iniquities;

---

[880] See Josephus *Jewish War* II.306; Eusebius, *Ecclesiastical* History IV.xv.4.

the chastisement of our peace was upon him; *and with his stripes we are healed*" (Isa. 53:5; 1 Peter 2:24). Sometime after Jesus had been flogged in the manner described, but not immediately afterward, as the next section will show, Pilate handed him over to be crucified.

---

27 Then the governor's soldiers took Jesus into the governor's headquarters, [881] and gathered around him the whole band. [882] 28 And they stripped him, threw a scarlet robe around him; 29 and having woven a crown of thorns they set it on his head, and a stick in his right hand. Then they knelt in front of him and mocked him, saying, "Hail, king of the Jews." 30 And having spit on him they took the stick and hit him on the head again and again. 31 When they had finished mocking him, they took off his robe, put his own clothes on him (again), and led him away for crucifixion.

27:27-31 *The Mockery*
Cf. Mark 15:16-20; John 19:2, 3

27. Then the governor's soldiers took Jesus into the governor's headquarters, and gathered around him the whole band. The soldiers, as many as were available—note "the entire cohort," though this does not necessarily mean a full cohort of six hundred men—now gather around Jesus in order to make sport of him. They desire to gratify their sadistic urges. They wish to have some fun with this "King of the Jews." These soldiers, though Roman in the sense that they were in the service of the Roman government, were probably recruited from the province of Syria; and if so, were able to converse in the Aramaic language, spoken also by the Jews, and were acquainted with Jewish ways. They probably regarded Jesus as a fake claimant to the royal throne, a person who deserved nothing better than to be mocked.

To say that this mockery had been ordered by Pilate (thus Lenski) is unwarranted. Nowhere does the record support that interpretation. It was Pilate who had ordered the *scourging*. Though it is true that he could and should have prevented the mockery, and was therefore partly responsible for it, we have no right to say that he ordered it.

For a correct view of this mockery it is necessary that we see it not only in its separate parts, but also as a whole. Matthew mentions seven items some of which can also be found in Mark and/or in John. The soldiers, having taken Jesus inside

	Matthew	Mark	John
disrobed him	27:28a		
robed him	27:28b	15:17a	19:2b
crowned him	27:29a	15:17b	19:2a

---

[881] Literally, the praetorium.
[882] Or: cohort.

	Matthew	Mark	John
sceptered him	27:29b		
adored him	27:29c	15:18	19:3a
spat on him	27:30a	15:19b	
hit him	27:30b	15:19a	19:3b

The mockery in general, and particularly the last two items, should be compared to what Jesus had already endured in the house of Caiaphas, just a few hours earlier. See Matt. 26:67, 68; Mark 14:65; Luke 22:65-65.

In summary, the entire picture is as follows. The soldiers, having stripped Jesus of his outer garments, throw a "royal" robe around him. Since a king must wield a scepter, they thrust a stick into his right hand. Then, one by one, they kneel down in front of him in mock adoration, saying, "Hail, king of the Jews." They spit on him and hit him on the head with his own "scepter."

28-30. **And they stripped him, threw a scarlet robe around him; and having woven a crown of thorns, they set it on his head, and a stick in his right hand. Then they knelt in front of him and mocked him, saying, Hail, king of the Jews. And having spit on him they took the stick and hit him on the head again and again.** And now the separate items:

a. *They disrobed him*

This had been done once before, just before he was scourged. How terribly it must have hurt him when the robe had been cast around his scourged body. And now again they strip him of his outer garments in order that in sheer mockery they may take the next step:

b. *They robed him*

They throw around Jesus what was probably a discarded and faded soldier's mantle, of a scarlet [883] hue, representing the royal purple. Cf. Matt. 27:28b: "scarlet" with Mark 15:17a and John 19:2b: "purple." Again, how throwing this around the scourged Savior must have hurt him!

c. *They crowned him*

Somewhere in the vicinity of the praetorium the soldiers find some thorny twigs. Whether the plant from which they obtained these twigs was the *Spina Christi* or *Palinrus Shrub*, as some think, is not known. It has been pointed out by botanists that few countries of the size of Palestine have so many varieties of prickly plants. The identity of the species is of little importance. Far more significant is the fact that thorns and thistles are mentioned in Gen. 3:18 in connection with Adam's fall. Here in Matt. 27:29a and its parallels Jesus is pictured as bearing the curse that lies upon nature, in order to deliver nature and us from it. With fiendish cruelty the soldiers, having

---

[883] Greek κοκκίνη in the nominative; (here accusative -ην); cf. Latin *coccineus*, scarlet-colored.

made a "crown" out of these thorny twigs, press it down upon Christ's head. It represented not an imperial wreath but a crown such as would be appropriate for a "king of the Jews." Those who were engaged in this bit of fun wanted to mock Jesus. They also wanted to torture him. The crown of thorns satisfied both purposes. Rivulets of blood must have started to run down his face, neck, and other parts of his body. [884] Did his molesters realize that they were doing this to him who is "King of kings and Lord of lords"?

d. *They sceptered him*

Having forced Jesus to sit down, in his right hand they now place a sturdy reed, for a king must have a scepter. Matthew is the only evangelist who reports this incident.

e. *They adored him*

Of course, this was cruel mockery. A soldier would drop to his knees in front of Jesus and say, "Hail, king of the Jews!" Then another would take his turn, and still another, until all had shared in this fun. [885]

f. *They spat on him*

They descend to a level lower than the beasts. Gleefully—for they're having fun—each soldier, when his turn comes around, after getting up from his knees spits into the face of God's only begotten and beloved Son!

g. *They hit him*

It is clear that all of these elements that pertain to the mockery belong together. This is especially true with respect to points *e., f.,* and *g.* Before any of these mockers vacates his position in front of Jesus, he removes the stick from the hand of the victim and strikes him on the head with it, as if to say, "What a king you are! One that gets hit over the head with his own scepter!" And as the fiend hits Jesus, the thorny spikes are driven deeper into the flesh.—One look at any plant representing a species of what is still known as "the crown of thorns," thriving not only in what is now called Israel but also in Florida and many other parts of the United States and other countries, will deepen the impression of the sadistic brutality that was taking place here. And even this was not all, for, as John 19:3b informs us, the mockers not only repeatedly used *the stick* on Jesus but also slapped him with their hands. They did all this to him who had already been scourged!

31. When they had finished mocking him, they took off his robe, put his own clothes on him (again), and led him away for crucifixion. Finally they have all had their turn. According to John 19:4 ff. Pilate now enters into the

---

[884] One of the best artistic representations is, perhaps, Guido Reni's "Ecce Homo." See A. E. Bailey, *op. cit.,* opposite p. 335.

[885] Matthew's text varies between ἐνέπαιξαν aorist, and ἐνέπαιζον imperfect, with the probability that the first is correct. Mark 15:18, "They *began to salute* him," and John 19:3a, "They *kept marching up* to him" show that this fiendishly cruel sport must have taken considerable time.

picture again. He brings Jesus out before the crowd, the sorely afflicted one still wearing the thorny crown and the purple robe. A pathetic spectacle is exposed to the view of the public: blood-streaked Jesus, covered with gashing wounds. "Look! The man!" says the governor, in order to arouse the people's sympathy and to testify once again that he, Pilate, finds no crime in him. But this effort on the part of the judge fails as tragically as have all the previous ones. When the chief priests and the officers see Jesus they cry out, "Crucify . . . crucify!" They now use their final argument, the one which up to this time they have held in abeyance, namely, "We have a law, and according to that law he ought to die, because he made himself the Son of God." Having re-examined Jesus and all the while still trying to release him, Pilate finally surrenders when he hears the cry, "If you release this man, you are no friend of the emperor." That was the bombshell. The governor, functioning all the while as judge, sits down on his tribunal, which stood on the Stone Pavement "Gabbatha," and sentences Jesus to die.

The soldiers' game having ended somewhat earlier, these men now remove their victim's royal accouterments and put his own clothes on him again. Then they lead him away to be crucified.

32 Now while they were coming out (of the city) they came upon a man of Cyrene, Simon by name. Him they forced to bear his cross. 33 And when they came to a place called Golgotha, that is, Place of the Skull, 34 they offered him wine to drink, mixed with gall; but when he had tasted it he refused to drink. 35 And having crucified him they divided his garments by casting lots. 36 And sitting down they were keeping watch over him there. 37 And they put above his head the indictment [886] against him which read:

THIS IS JESUS THE KING OF THE JEWS

38 Then there were crucified with him two robbers, one on his right and one on his left. 39 And those who passed by were blaspheming him, shaking their heads, 40 and saying, "You who destroy the temple [887] and in three days rebuild it, save yourself if you are the Son of God, and come down from the cross." 41 Similarly also the chief priests mocking (him), along with the scribes and the elders, were saying, 42 "Others he saved, himself he cannot save; king of Israel is he; let him now come down from the cross and we will believe in him.

43 He has placed his trust in God.
Let him deliver (him) now if he desires him;
for he said, 'I am God's Son.'" 44 And the robbers also who had been crucified with him reviled him in the same way.

27:32-44 *Calvary: the Crucifixion of Jesus*
Cf. Mark 15:21-32; Luke 23:26-43; John 19:17-27

Though the center of interest is always on Jesus himself, what *he* did, said, or endured, our attention is here also fixed upon five subsidiary persons or groups:

886 Or: accusation, charge.
887 Or: sanctuary.

a. *Simon of Cyrene* renders a service to Jesus (verse 32).

b. Arrived at Golgotha *the legionaries* or soldiers offer Jesus drugged wine, which he refuses. Having crucified him between two robbers, and having affixed a label above his head, they cast lots for the division of his clothes. Beneath the cross they sit down, keeping guard (verses 33-38).

c. *Bypassers* blaspheme (verses 39, 40).

d. *Scribes* (and their companions) scoff (verses 41-43).

e. *Robbers* revile (verse 44).

The paragraph that could be captioned *"Women* weep" is not found in Matthew but in Luke 23:27-31. [888] Luke also pictures the multitudes deeply moved (23:48).

With the exception of verse 32, the entire section (Matt. 27:32-44) relates what happened to Jesus from nine o'clock A.M. (cf. Mark 15:25) until noon (cf. Mark 15:33) on (Good) Friday.

Simon of Cyrene

In reality what is said in verse 32 might also have been included under the next heading, because Simon did not act of his own accord. By the soldiers he was forced to do what he did. But since the New Testament and early tradition place such emphasis on him and (probably) his family, a separate caption is given to verse 32. **Now while they were coming out (of the city) they came upon a man of Cyrene, Simon by name. Him they forced to bear his cross.** As was customary and according to law, the execution was carried out outside the city (Exod. 29:14; Lev. 4:12, 21; 9:11; 16:27; Num. 15:35; 19:3; cf. John 19:20; Heb. 13:12, 13). Those condemned to be crucified had to carry their own cross. Commentators are divided on the question whether this refers to the crossbeam alone, the upright having already been set in place on Golgotha, or to the entire cross. Since there is nothing in text or context that suggests otherwise, it is here assumed that the latter position—the entire cross—is correct.

In the light of the fact that the title or indictment was written above Christ's head (verse 37), it is well-nigh certain that artists are correct in their

---

[888] Throughout this section there is a very close parallel between Matthew and Mark. Luke's account, too, parallels the other two Snyoptics to a considerable extent. However, Luke, while saying nothing about those that passed by, adds that the military joined in the mockery and offered Christ vinegar (23:36, 37; cf. John 19:29, 30). Besides the paragraphs already referred to, about the weeping women and what Jesus said to them, and about the deeply moved multitudes, Luke also tells the touching story of the robber who repented (23:39-43). He records the first two words from the cross (23:34, 43). John, having reported that Jesus went out bearing the cross for himself (19:16, 17)—he says nothing about Simon of Cyrene—gives a more detailed account of the superscription and the controversy with reference to it (19:19-22), and of the division of the garments (19:23, 24). In his coverage of the women standing by the cross (19:25-27) he records the third word from the cross (19:27). He omits all reference to mockery and jeering.

preference for the dagger-type or Latin cross: ✝ . For the reasons why death by crucifixion must be considered a curse see N.T.C. on the Gospel according to John, Vol. II, p. 425.

Jesus, too, carried his own cross (John 19:16, 17), but not for long. Sheer physical exhaustion made it impossible for him to carry it very far. Consider what he had already endured within the last fifteen hours: the tense atmosphere of the Upper Room, the betrayal by Judas, the agonies of Gethsemane, the desertion by his disciples, the torture of a totally hypocritical trial before the Sanhedrin, the mockery in the palace of Caiaphas, the denial by his most prominent disciple, the trial before an unjust judge, the terrible ordeal of being scourged, the pronunciation of the death sentence upon him, and the seven-itemed abuse by the soldiers in the praetorium! Humanly speaking, is it not a wonder that he was able to carry the cross any distance at all?

When Jesus succumbed beneath his load, the legionaries, exercising their right of "requisitioning" or "making demands on" people (see on Matt. 5:41), forced Simon, a man from Cyrene—located on a plateau, ten miles from the Mediterranean Sea, in what is now Libya (west of Egypt)—to carry Christ's cross for the rest of the distance. The theory that Simon could not have been a Jew, because he gave his sons Greek names (Mark 15:21), is without merit, since many Jews followed that practice. Besides, in Cyrene there was a large colony of Jews (Acts 2:10; 6:9; 11:20; 13:1). The further speculation that the man must have been a farmer, because on this particular Friday morning he came "from the country" (Mark 15:21), is also without any basis. Even today many people besides farmers have business or social connections in the country. Some even live there!

The following reconstruction, though not certain, is however probable. Simon, a Jew, has come to Jerusalem to attend one of the great festivals (in this case Passover), as was the custom of many Jews, including those from Cyrene (Acts 2:10). There was even a Cyrenian synagogue in Jerusalem (Acts 6:9).

Now on this particular Friday, returning to the city from a visit to the country, Simon is pressed into service by the soldiers who are leading Jesus to Calvary, perhaps (but this is by no means certain) along the Via Dolorosa (Sorrowful Way), and are just now coming through the gate out of the city. So—reluctantly at first?—Simon carries Christ's cross, arrives at Calvary, and witnesses what happens there. The behavior of Jesus and his words from the cross leave such an impression on Simon that he becomes a Christian. Subsequently he and his family are living in Rome. He may have been living there before, but in any event he was a Cyrenian by birth. (Among the early Christians there were many Cyrenians, Acts 11:19; 13:1.)

Mark, writing to the Romans, mentions "Simon, the father of Alexander and Rufus," as if to say, "people with whom y o u, in Rome, are well acquainted." Paul, in his letter to the Romans (16:13), writes, "Greet Rufus, outstanding in the Lord, and his mother and mine." Evidently the mother of Rufus—hence, the wife of Simon—had rendered some motherly service to Paul.

If this reconstruction is factual, then the service which Simon rendered, though initially "forced," turned out to be a genuine blessing for himself, his family, and many others.

The Legionaries

33-38. And when they came to a place called Golgotha, that is, Place of the Skull, they offered him wine to drink, mixed with gall; but when he had tasted it he refused to drink. And having crucified him they divided his garments by casting lots. And sitting down they were keeping watch over him there. And they put above his head the indictment against him which read:

THIS IS JESUS THE KING OF THE JEWS

Then there were crucified with him two robbers, one on his right and one on his left.

Just where was Golgotha and why was it called "Place of the Skull"? For the discussion of these questions the reader is referred to N.T.C. on the Gospel according to John, Vol. II, pp. 425, 426. The wine which the soldiers offered to Jesus and which he refused is described by Matthew as "mixed with gall," that is, with something bitter. The evangelist was probably thinking of Ps. 69:21a, and if so, correctly regarded what was now happening as a fulfilment of that Old Testament passage. According to Mark 15:23 the bitter substance was myrrh. Having tasted this mixture, Jesus refused to drink it, no doubt because he wanted to endure with full consciousness all the pain that was in store for him, in order to be our perfect Substitute.

"And having crucified him," writes Matthew, with marvelous restraint. There is no detailed description here of the manner in which the nails were driven through hands (or wrists) and feet, etc. In the original only two words are used, "having-crucified him." After all, Scripture does not place *all* the emphasis on that which Jesus suffered physically, but on the fact that he himself, in both soul and body, was made an offering for sin, laid down his life. See Isa. 53:10. Cf. Matt. 27:46; John 10:11, 15.

Having crucified him, the legionaries divided his garments by casting lots. In all probability by means of the throwing of dice the four pieces—headgear, sandals, belt, and outer garment—are divided among the four (John 19:23) soldiers. The seamless tunic, all of one piece, woven all the way from top to bottom, is also put into the lottery, all of this in accordance with the prophecy of Ps. 22:18 (LXX Ps. 21:19), though this reference to fulfilment is not found in Matthew but in John 19:23, 24. See N.T.C. on that passage for further details.

The soldiers, having accomplished all this, sit down, and keep watch over Jesus, that no one may either further molest him or try to rescue him. This act of keeping Jesus under strict surveillance is significant. Does it not bear witness to the fact that Jesus really *died* on Calvary?

The next two actions of the soldiers, here described, are probably not mentioned in chronological order. It is very doubtful that the author wishes to convey the idea that the legionaries, having crucified Jesus and having divided his garments, *afterward* attached to the upright above his head the board on which his name and the reason for his crucifixion were written. Nor do we have to assume that everything relating to Christ's crucifixion had been completed before the two robbers were nailed to crosses. The indictment board had undoubtedly been attached much earlier. And it is probable that while four soldiers were nailing Jesus to the cross, two other groups of four each were doing the same to the two robbers.

As to the *indictment* or *charge*—called a *title* in John 19:19, a *superscription* in Mark 15:26 and Luke 23:38—for details see N.T.C. on the Gospel according to John, Vol. II, pp. 427-429. Though no two Gospels report this "notice" or "label" in exactly the same manner, there is no contradiction. It hardly needs to be mentioned that it was Pilate, not the soldiers, who "wrote" it, that is, that it was he who was responsible for the wording (John 19:22), in three languages: Aramaic, Latin, and Greek. It could be read as an accusation, "This is Jesus, who was crucified because he claimed to be King of the Jews," but also as a title, "This is Jesus who is King of the Jews." The Jewish leaders desired to have the ambiguity removed. For reasons of his own Pilate refused. If we bear in mind that by means of this very cross Jesus actually won the victory (John 12:32) we shall understand that he is indeed King over all, including the Jews.

The two men who were crucified with Jesus were "robbers," or, as the word can also be translated "revolutionaries" (see on 26:55; 27:16). With a view to Luke 23:33 ("two malefactors" or "criminals"), "robbers" is probably the best rendering here. It was a gross injustice that Jesus was crucified between these two men, as if he himself were also a criminal. Nevertheless, it was also an honor. Did he not come to seek and to save the lost (Luke 19:10)? Was he not "the Friend of publicans and sinners (Matt. 11:19)? See also N.T.C. on John 3:16 and on I Tim. 1:15.

Bypassers

39, 40. And those who passed by were blaspheming him, shaking their heads, and saying, You who destroy the temple and in three days rebuild it, save yourself if you are the Son of God, and come down from the cross. In rapid succession Matthew now describes how three groups—bypassers, scribes, etc., and robbers—reacted toward Jesus. First, then, the bypassers (or passers-by). The word "bypasser" literally translates the Greek original, conveying its meaning exactly. If, as some believe, Calvary even then was located at the conjunction of roads—cf. the Church of the Holy Sepulchre—then the expression "the bypassers" begins to make real sense. Not everyone belonged to the multitudes (Luke 23:48) that were going *to* Calvary that day, to watch everything that happened there from beginning to end. There were also those who merely "passed by." On their way elsewhere they stop long enough to take in the scene. They center their attention on the One nailed to the central cross, about whom they have heard so much already. They shake their heads in contempt and arrogance. Cf. Ps. 22:7b; Isa. 37:22. Then they begin to hurl abuse at him. They are actually *blaspheming* him, as the original states. For the meaning of this word and its cognates see on 12:31, 32, and note that here in 27:39 it is used not in a general sense, but in its most terrible sense of mocking the very Son of God. This is nothing short of "defiant irreverence."

The words which they use will bear this out. As they shake their heads they are saying, "You who destroy the temple and in three days rebuild it. . . ." They too, therefore, as well as the two false witnesses of 26:60, 61, have picked up the slanderous misquotation plus misinterpretation of Christ's saying (John 2:19), and have accepted it as if it were the very truth. They are now using it, and adding, "Save yourself if you are the Son of God, and come down from the cross." Here they are proving that they completely reject Christ's own confession concerning himself (see on 26:63-66), made only a few hours earlier. They consider it a joke. Scornfully they exclaim that the way for the crucified One to prove his claim to being the Son of God will be for him to descend from the cross. They imply that it is weakness that keeps him there. Actually, however, it was strength, the strength of his love for sinners. But these bypassers have made up their minds to defy the testimony of all the miracles, all the mercy shown to those in need, all the marvelous discourses, yes, the entire beautiful life of the Son of God on earth. All of this they have rejected. They prefer to jeer, to blaspheme!

Chief Priests, Scribes, and Elders

41-43. Similarly also the chief priests mocking (him), along with the scribes and the elders, were saying, Others he saved, himself he cannot save; king of Israel is he; let him now come down from the cross and we will believe in him.

He has placed his trust in God.

Let him deliver (him) now if he desires him;

for he said, I am God's Son.

So delighted were the members of the Sanhedrin with the fact that their archenemy was now hanging on a cross that they—these chief priests, scribes, and elders (see on 16:21)—lose every bit of dignity, and join the bypassers in giving expression to their contempt of Jesus. "Similarly," writes Matthew, and in several respects the words of the leaders were indeed similar to those of the ones who passed by. Both mock. Both are convinced that the victim's remaining on the cross was due to his weakness, his utter inability to rescue himself. Both ridicule the claim that he is, in some special sense, "the Son of God." Both bid him to prove his claims by coming down from the cross.

Nevertheless, there is also a rather striking difference. The bypassers had addressed Jesus directly, using the second person singular. See verses 39, 40. But not once in the narrative of Christ's crucifixion—whether in Matthew, Mark, or Luke—do the leaders address Jesus directly. Each time they talk *about* him, to each other. They never talk *to* him. So thoroughly do they hate him. Matthew and Mark relate that these Sanhedrists, in their conversation with each other about their enemy, *mocked* him. And so they did indeed! Luke uses a different word, however, He shows that this mockery was of the worst possible kind. Their ridicule was mingled with hatred and envy. Says Luke, "They turned up their noses at him," [889] that is, they *sneered;* they *scoffed* (23:35).

When they now say, "others he saved; himself he cannot save," they did not deny that the miracles he had performed in the interest of others were real. Not at all. They had admitted their genuine character before (John 11:47). Only, they had ascribed his power to perform them to Satan (Matt. 9:34). The conclusion they draw is that now that Beelzebub is not able and/or willing to help him any more, he is completely powerless. They too refuse to admit that it was the power of his love for sinners that kept him on that cross.

With derision they refer to the fact that he had claimed to be "king of Israel." Well, he did indeed make that claim (27:11). Moreover, he had accepted the honor implied in similar titles when others bestowed that honor on him (21:16). In fact, he had even ascribed to himself royal authority over a realm wider by far (11:27; 25:34), and he was going to do this again (28:18). But these leaders were deliberately misrepresenting him; for whenever, either in word or action, the people had tried to make of him an earthly king, a ruler who had come to deliver the Jews from the yoke of the Romans, he had quickly walked as far as possible away from that error. See John 6:15; cf. 18:36.

Basest of all was their attack upon the claim of Jesus that in a very unique sense he was the Son of God. He had indeed made this assertion again and again. See pp. 378, 497, 498, 644. Nothing, no nothing was dearer to him

---

[889] Luke's verb is ἐξεμυκτήριζον, 3rd. per. pl. imperfect indicative of ἐκμυκτηρίζω. Cf. μυκτήρ, *nose.*

than that relation of intimacy between himself and the Father (Matt. 11:27; John 10:30; 16:32; 17:5, 24). And now these adversaries, by alluding to the words of Ps. 22:8b, are implying that his heavenly Father has lost all interest in him, and that his trust in God is now futile. Otherwise, so they argue, God would deliver him, would enable him to step down from the cross. They imply that God's failure to do this can mean only one thing, namely, that his assertion, "I am God's Son," is an untruth.

When the enemies of the author of Ps. 42 asked him, "Where is your God?" they meant, "Your God, if he exists at all, is useless. Your faith has no solid foundation." He confesses that this attack of his adversaries affected him as if a sword had been thrust into his bones (Ps. 42:10). Now the relation between the psalmist and his Lord was intimate and sweet. Nevertheless, how incomparably more intimate and vital was not the relation between the Father and his only-begotten Son! How, therefore, this foul attack of the leaders must have hurt the Mediator!

Robbers

44. And the robbers also who had been crucified with him reviled him in the same way. Bypassers and Sanhedrists were agreed that if Jesus wanted to prove that he was indeed what he claimed to be he should save himself. The robbers are carried away by this argument. They too in the same manner begin to revile him. It must be emphasized that according to the plain language of Scripture *both* robbers were at first heaping abuse on Jesus in this manner. The language of one of these men is reported in Luke 23:39. He said, "Aren't you the Christ? Save yourself and us." Even the military joined in this type of mockery (Luke 23:36, 37). The insults were coming from almost every side. Legionaries, bypassers, chief priests, scribes, elders, robbers, and multitudes of other spectators deride him.

In the midst of it all Jesus remains silent. He offers not one word of rebuke. Peter puts it beautifully when he says, "who, while being reviled, did not revile in return; while suffering, never threatened, but continued to entrust himself to him who judges righteously; who himself bore our sins in his body on the cross, that we might die to sin and live to righteousness; for by his wounds y o u were healed" (I Peter 2:23, 24).

Is it not possible—probable even—that this calm and majestic behavior of our Lord, coupled with the prayer, "Father, forgive them, for they do not know what they are doing" (Luke 23:34), was used by God as a means to lead one of these two robbers to repentance? For that story see Luke 23:39-43.

---

45 Now from the sixth hour there was darkness over all the land until the ninth hour.
46 And about the ninth hour Jesus cried out with a loud voice, saying,

"Eli, Eli, lema sabachthani?''
that is
"My God, my God, why hast thou forsaken me?''
47 When some of those who were standing there heard this, they were saying, "He's calling Elijah.'' 48 And immediately one of them ran, took a sponge, filled it with sour wine, put it on a stick, and gave him a drink. 49 But the rest were saying, "Hold off, [890] let us see whether Elijah is coming to rescue him.'' 50 And Jesus, having again cried out with a loud voice, yielded up his spirit. 51 And look, the curtain of the sanctuary was torn in two from top to bottom, the earth quaked, the rocks were split, 52 and the tombs were opened. And many bodies of the saints who had fallen asleep were raised; 53 and having left their tombs, after his resurrection they went into the holy city and appeared to many. 54 Now when the centurion and those with him who were guarding Jesus saw the earthquake and the things that were happening, they were frightened and said, "Surely, this was God's Son.''
55 Now watching from a distance there were many women who had followed Jesus from Galilee, ministering to his needs. 56 Among them were Mary Magdalene, Mary the mother of James and Joses, and the mother of the sons of Zebedee.

27:45-56 *Calvary: the Death of Jesus*
Cf. Mark 15:33-41; Luke 23:44-49; John 19:28-30

What follows in these verses (45-56) shows what transpired at Calvary from noon ("the sixth hour") until three o'clock ("the ninth hour"), as verses 45, 46 indicate.

Darkness

45. Now from the sixth hour there was darkness over all the land [891] **until the ninth hour.** From nine o'clock until noon Calvary had been a very busy place. The soldiers had performed their various tasks, as was shown in verses 33-38. Bypassers had blasphemed. Chief priests, scribes, and elders had scoffed. Robbers had reviled, though one of them had repented. Jesus had uttered his first three words. Then, at twelve o'clock, something of a very dramatic character takes place. Suddenly the land becomes dark. Cf. Amos 8:9. The very fact that this darkness is mentioned shows that it must have been intense and unforgettable. Moreover, it occurred when least expected, at high noon, and lasted three hours.

Much has been written about this darkness. What caused it? How extensive was it? Did it have any meaning? As to the first, very little information is given. We are safe in saying, "God brought it about.'' But when the further question is asked, "By what means?'' a completely satisfactory answer cannot be given. A sudden thunderstorm, even if it lasted three hours, would not have covered the entire country and would probably not have been singled out for special mention. A black sirocco storm from the desert is not

---

890 Or: "Let be.'' Cf. 19:14.
891 Or: earth.

generally known to cause such darkness. To be sure, Luke 23:44, 45 may seem to supply the answer for which we are looking. Does it not say, "the sun being eclipsed"? But, first of all, the reading is not entirely certain. There are several variants. Secondly, granted that "eclipsed" is the right word, this cannot refer to an eclipse in the technical, astronomical sense, for that is impossible at the time of Passover (full moon). Besides, such an eclipse would hardly last three hours! But if the term be taken in a broader sense, namely, "darkened," we are back to where we were: darkened by what? The best answer may well be to regard what happened here as a special act of God, a miracle, and to enquire no further as to any secondary means.

How extensive was it? Here, too, we must abstain from giving a definite answer. It will not do to say that when the light of the sun is shut off half of the globe must be darkened. The light of the sun could be shut off for a certain country or region. See Exod. 10:22, 23. Luther, Calvin, Zahn, Ridderbos, etc. prefer the translation "land" for 27:45. It has been remarked that if the darkness was very extensive, reaching far beyond India, records would have been preserved in secular literature. Well, one might refer, in this connection, to Origen (*Against Celsus* II.33) who alludes to a statement by the Roman historian Phlegon, who supposedly mentioned both the darkness and the earthquake. Tertullian, too, writing to his pagan adversaries and mentioning this darkness, states, "which wonder is related in y o u r own annals and is preserved in y o u r archives to this day." But it is impossible to ascertain the value of such references. Here too, therefore, it is probably best to refrain from giving a definite answer. Even if the translation "land" instead of "earth" should be correct, which may well be the case, the fact must not be ignored that the darkness "covered *all* the land," and was therefore very extensive.

As to the third question, "Did it have any meaning?" here a positive answer is certainly in order. Yes, it did have a very important meaning. The darkness meant judgment, the judgment of God upon our sins. his wrath as it were burning itself out in the very heart of Jesus, so that he, as our Substitute, suffered most intense agony, indescribable woe, terrible isolation or forsakenness. Hell came to Calvary that day, and the Savior descended into it and bore its horrors in our stead. How do we know that this answer is correct? Note the following:

a. Darkness in Scripture is very often a symbol of judgment. See Isa. 5:30; 60:2; Joel 2:30, 31; Amos 5:18, 20; Zeph 1:14-18; Matt. 24:29, 30; Acts 2:20; II Peter 2:17; Rev. 6:12-17.

b. With a view to his impending death the Savior had himself stated that he was giving and was about to give his life as "a ransom for many" (Matt. 20:28; 26:28; Mark 10:45).

c. The agony suffered by our Lord during these three hours was such that he finally uttered the explanatory words of verse 46, to which we now turn:

The Cry of Agony

46. And about the ninth hour Jesus cried out with a loud voice, saying,
Eli, Eli, lema sabachthani?
that is
My God, my God, why hast thou forsaken me?

The link between the darkness and the cry is very close: the first is a symbol of the agonizing content of the second. This, then, is the fourth word from the cross, the very first one reported by Matthew and Mark. [892] It issued from the mouth of the Savior shortly before he breathed his last.

In the Gospels what happened between twelve o'clock and three o'clock is a blank. All we know is that during these three hours of intense darkness Jesus suffered indescribable agonies. He was being "made sin" for us (II Cor. 5:21), "a curse" (Gal. 3:13). He was being "wounded for our transgressions and bruised for our iniquities." Jehovah was laying on him "the iniquity of us all," etc. (Isa. 53).

To be sure, this happened throughout the period of his humiliation, from conception to death and burial, but *especially* in Gethsemane, Gabbatha, and Golgotha.

The question has been asked, "But how could God forsake God?" The answer must be that God the Father deserted his Son's human nature, and even this in a limited, though very real and agonizing, sense. The meaning cannot be that there was ever a time when God the Father stopped loving his Son. Nor can it mean that the Son ever rejected his Father. Far from it. He kept on calling him "*My* God, *my* God." And for that very reason we may be sure that the Father loved him as much as ever.

How, then, can we ascribe any sensible meaning to this utterance of deep distress? Perhaps an illustration may be of some help, though it should be added immediately that no analogy taken from things that happen to humans on earth can ever begin to do justice to the Son of God's unique

---

[892] The address, "Eli, Eli" is Hebrew. See Ps. 22:1 (22:2 in the original). In Matt. 27:46 "Eli, Eli" follows the Grk. N.T. (A-B-M-W) text. The rest—"lema sabachthani"—is Aramaic. The Hebrew line in Ps. 22 is *Eli, Eli, lama azabtani*. But it is reasonable to assume that Jesus spoke these words entirely in one language. If this language was Hebrew, the first two words may have sounded somewhat like the name of the prophet *Eliya* (Elijah), shedding some light on verse 47. However, as N.N. indicates in its textual apparatus, the variant *Eloi, Eloi* has strong textual support in Matthew. See also Mark 15:34. The *possibility* must be allowed, therefore, that here, as so often, it is Mark who is giving the words in the exact form (Aramaic) in which Jesus uttered them, while Matthew—if Grk. N.T. (A-B-M-W) is correct—represents a text which links the passage directly with the Hebrew of Ps. 22, and with the words of mockery, "He is calling Elijah." Certainty as to which text is correct in Matthew—whether "Eli, Eli" or "Eloi, Eloi"—is perhaps impossible.

experience. Nevertheless, the illustration may be helpful in some slight degree. Here, let us say, is a child that is very sick. He is still too young to understand why he has to be taken to the hospital, and especially why, while there, he may have to be in the Intensive Care Unit, where his parents cannot always be with him. His parents love him as much as ever. But there may be moments when the child misses the presence of his father or mother so much that he experiences profound anguish. So also the Mediator. His soul reaches out for the One whom he calls "my God," but his God does not answer him. Is not that exactly the manner in which the cry of agony is interpreted in the context of Ps. 22? Note:

"My God, my God, why hast thou forsaken me?
Why art thou so far from helping me, and from the words of my groaning?
O my God, I cry in the daytime, but thou answerest not;
And by night, but I find no rest."

For the Sufferer with a superbly sensitive soul this terrible isolation must have been agonizing indeed. This all the more in view of the fact that only several hours earlier he had said to his disciples, "Note well, there comes an hour—yes, it has arrived—when y o u will be scattered, each to his own home, and y o u will leave me alone. *Yet I am not alone, for the Father is with me* (John 16:32)." And a little later he had added, in his touchingly beautiful Highpriestly Prayer, "And now Father, glorify thou me in thine own presence with the glory which I had with thee before the world existed" (John 17:5). And now the Father does not answer, but leaves him in the hands of his adversaries. Reflect again on all the abuse and the suffering Jesus had already endured this very night. Is it any wonder that he now cries out, "My God, my God, why hast thou forsaken me?" His God and Father would not have abandoned him to his tormentors if it had not been necessary. But it *was* necessary, in order that he might fully undergo the punishment due to his people's sins.

The Mockery
and
The Sympathy

47-49. When some of those who were standing there heard this, they were saying, He's calling Elijah. And immediately one of them ran, took a sponge, filled it with sour wine, put it on a stick, and gave him a drink. But the rest were saying, Hold off, let us see whether Elijah is coming to rescue him. It was with a loud voice that Jesus had uttered the fourth word from the cross. Those who heard it must have understood, even though not all recognized the words as fulfilment of prophecy, the prophecy of Psalm 22, of which here at Calvary so many passages had already been, or were being, fulfilled (see verses 1, 2, 7, 8, 12-14, 16-18). But so loud and clear was the voice that there could be no mistake about *what* Jesus just now had said. At least, all those who knew Aramaic and Hebrew understood. And recent discoveries are proving that—in addition to understanding Aramaic and possibly Greek—the Jews, many of whom were present here, were more familiar with Hebrew than was previously supposed.

What is described, then, here in verses 47 and 49, is the mockery of those heartless persons who tried to make others believe that they had heard Jesus cry to Elijah for help. Of course, they knew better. But the resemblance between "Eli"—especially if the pronunciation sounded like *Eliya*—and the name of the Old Testament prophet was so close that by the perverted minds and lips of these blasphemers a joke could be made of it. Moreover, was it not a Jewish belief that Elijah would introduce the Messiah and live beside him for a while as his assistant and as the rescuer of those who were about to perish?

But though these mockers were having their fun, there was One who had heard the cry of anguish and immediately answered it. That was God the Father, who right here and now put an end to the brunt of his Son's anguish, so that the Sufferer was permitted to seek some relief for his parched lips and throat, this too in fulfilment of Ps. 22, this time verse 15. So Jesus utters the fifth word, "I am thirsty" (John 19:28). Immediately someone—no doubt a soldier, acting under order of the centurion—took a sponge, filled it with sour wine or vinegar, the kind of cheap wine which the soldiers drank and which was good for quenching thirst—put the sponge on a stick, and brought it to the mouth of Jesus. For details on this see N.T.C. on the Gospel according to John, Vol. II, p. 435.

Not all men standing near the cross that day were equally hardened. Whoever it was that gave the order that was here being carried out—it has been assumed that it was the centurion—was showing genuine sympathy. But this was by no means the sentiment of all. The heartless ones continued their jesting. "Hold off" (or: "Let be"), said they, "Let us see whether Elijah is coming to rescue him." Among the mockers there were also soldiers (Luke 23:36, 37).

Death

50. And Jesus, having again cried out with a loud voice, yielded up his spirit. Note "with a loud voice," showing that the Sufferer did not just allow his life to ebb away. He did not die as a result of physical exhaustion but voluntarily. He *gave* his life, *poured it out, laid it down* (Isa. 53:12; John 10:11, 15), or, as here, *yielded* it. He knew exactly what he was doing when he thus offered himself as a substitutionary sacrifice. This is clear from his two last words: the sixth, "It is finished" (John 19:30), meaning that the work which the Father had given him to do had now been accomplished; that he had now given his life as a ransom for many (Matt. 20:28); and the seventh, "Father into thy hands I commend my spirit" (Luke 23:46), proving that he had fully regained the consciousness of the Father's loving presence and was entrusting his spirit to the Father's loving care. The Father welcomed it to glory, and on the morning of the resurrection restored his Son's spirit to his body, nevermore to die. It is comforting to know that when Jesus went to Paradise he did not go alone, but carried with him the soul of the penitent robber (Luke 23:43).

Signs

The darkness lifted (27:45). The substitutionary death of Jesus brings light (salvation) to a world lost in sin, that is, to all those who accept him by means of a living faith. There were also other signs, those that are distinctly mentioned here in verses **51-53. And look, the curtain of the sanctuary** [893] **was torn in two from top to bottom.**

a. *The curtain torn*

On the basis of Heb. 6:19; 9:3; and 10:20 it is natural to think of this curtain as the inner one, "the second veil," the one that separated the Holy Place from the Holy of holies. This inner curtain is the one described in Exod. 26:31-33; 36:35; II Chron. 3:14. As pictured in these passages, strands of blue, purple, and scarlet were interwoven into a white linen fabric, in such a manner that these colors formed a mass of cherubim, the guardian angels of God's holiness, symbolically as it were barring the way into the holy of holies. A description of the curtain in the Herodian temple is given in Josephus, *Jewish War* V. 212-214.

At the moment of Christ's death this curtain was suddenly sliced in two from top to bottom. This happened at three o'clock, when priests must have been busy in the temple. How did it come about? Not through natural wear, for in that case there would probably have been rents all over, and the tearing would more likely have been from the bottom up. Nor is it at all probable that Matthew is trying to convey the idea that this splitting in two of the curtain was caused by the earthquake. Had that been his intention, would he not have mentioned the earthquake before the tearing of the curtain? What happened must be regarded as a miracle. Any secondary means that may have been used to effect it are not mentioned, and it would be futile to speculate. As to the symbolic significance, this is made clear by two considerations: first, it occurred exactly at the moment when Jesus died; secondly, it is explained in Heb. 10:19, 20: through the death of Christ, symbolized by the tearing of the curtain, the way into "the holy of holies," that is, heaven, is opened to all those who take refuge in him. For

---

[893] In the present case, since we know that there was a curtain that pertained to the sanctuary—the inner shrine—not to the entire temple complex, the rendering "sanctuary" would seem to be preferable to "temple."

the practical lesson see Heb. 4:16. More may be implied, but by limiting the interpretation to this we are on safe ground.

b. *The earth quaking, rocks split, tombs opened*

There appears to be a very close connection between these three, the second and the third of the signs mentioned here probably resulting from the first: **the earth quaked, the rocks were split, and the tombs were opened.** This shows that the death of the Savior had—and still is having—significance for the entire universe. So much at least is clear. There is going to be a new heaven and a new earth (Rev. 21:1), which apart from Christ's atoning death would not have been possible. See N.T.C. on Col. 1:20; cf. Rom. 8:21; II Peter 3:13. Other ideas—such as, that the stones were now crying out because no disciple, standing near the cross, was praising the Savior (cf. Luke 19:40); that Calvary's earthquake answered Sinai's, as if to say, "The curse pronounced upon sin at Sinai is now removed"—are too speculative to be of any great value. It was God who at the moment of Christ's death caused the earth to quake.

This earthquake was great, for deep fissures were formed in the rocks, and even the tombs were opened.

c. *Saints raised*

And many bodies of the saints who had fallen asleep were raised; and having left their tombs, after his resurrection they went into the holy city and appeared to many. With reference to this mysterious event there are ever so many different interpretations. For some that I cannot accept see the footnote. [894] Who these saints were is not stated. The following is clear, however:

---

[894] Unacceptable to me are the following:

a. There may not have been any real resurrection at all. God may simply have temporarily taken some of these bodies out of the earth and shown them to many people. (F. W. Grosheide, *op. cit.*, p. 439). Objection: The text says "were raised," and "they went."

b. This resurrection occurred in connection with, or a little later than, Christ's *resurrection.* (H. N. Ridderbos, Vol. II, p. 241). Objection: If so, this would be the only one of these signs that was postponed until (or: until after) Christ's resurrection. The others all occurred at the moment of Christ's death. The meaning of the passage seems to be that *all* happened at or near the moment of Christ's *death.*—I Cor. 15:20 offers no basis for rejecting the view that these saints were raised *before* Christ arose, for the triumphant death and resurrection of Jesus remain the legal basis for the glorious resurrection even of these saints. Besides, the comparison in I Cor. 15:20, taking its point of departure in Christ's resurrection, looks to the future, the second coming: in relation to all believers who will *then* arise, Jesus is the firstfruits.

c. These saints were not raised with immortal bodies (W. R. Nicholson, *The Six Miracles of Calvary*, Chicago, 1928, pp. 43, 44). Objection: If their resurrection was like that of Lazarus, who died again, then the expression "they *appeared* to many" requires explanation. Also, in that case, the resurrection of these saints would not be a true foretoken of the glorious resurrection at Christ's return. Accordingly, it would then not truly symbolize the significance of Christ's death for our future bodily resurrection.

First, this was a real resurrection, not an appearance of corpses.

Secondly, it occurred at the very moment of Christ's death and, together with the other signs, pointed to the significance of that death.

Thirdly, it is true that the original can be construed in either of two ways, depending on how we parse the phrase "after his [Christ's] resurrection"; whether we conceive the sense to be "having left their tombs after his resurrection," or "after his resurrection they went. . . ." But is it reasonable to believe that these saints, with glorious resurrection bodies, remained in the darkness and corruption of the tombs from Friday afternoon until Sunday morning? The meaning is, in all probability, that these saints were raised and left their tombs at the moment of Christ's death. Not until after Christ's resurrection did they enter Jerusalem and did they appear to many. Where they were from the moment when they left their graves until they appeared to many in what is still called "the holy city" (!) is not explained, just as also the whereabouts of Jesus during the intervals between his post-resurrection appearances is nowhere indicated.

Fourthly, everything seems to point to the fact that these saints did not again die. It must be that after they appeared to many for some small period of time, God took them—now body and soul—to himself in heaven, where their souls had been previously.

Finally, this sign, too, like those described in verse 51, 52a, is prophetic. It shows that Christ's death guarantees our glorious resurrection at Christ's return.

Summarizing the significance of these signs, it can be said that they indicate the meaning of Christ's death for God's children of every clime and nation: ready access to God's throne and to his heavenly sanctuary through the death of Jesus; the inheritance of a marvelously rejuvenated universe; and a glorious resurrection, to a life never to be followed by death. Then, too, all of these signs emphasize the majesty of the Person who gave his life as a ransom for many. Particularly, they stress the rich significance of his death.

For more on the meaning of Christ's cross and of glorying in it see N.T.C. on Galatians 6:14.

The centurion

54. Now when the centurion and those with him who were guarding Jesus saw the earthquake and the things that were happening, they were frightened and said, Surely, this was God's Son. Nature seems generally to be indifferent to human suffering. But here, as this centurion sees it, even nature responded to what happened to Jesus. The earthquake is specifically mentioned. But there is added, "and the things that were happening," or "and what took place." The reference is no doubt to the effects of the earthquake as far as visible on Calvary; hence, the splitting of the rocks and the opening of the tombs. The intense darkness and its disappearance at three o'clock may also have been included. When the man saw all this he was visibly affected to the point of "fearing greatly," that is, being frightened. Never had he seen anything like this.

However, the centurion had seen more than this: he had seen how Jesus had been conducting himself in the midst of all the wicked taunts and mockeries. Specifically he had heard how the Jewish leaders, speaking among themselves, had scoffed at Jesus' claim that he was the Son of God. See on verse 43. Had he also, perhaps, heard how Pilate had examined Jesus with respect to this very point (John 19:7 ff.)?

The centurion, then, combines all these impressions. This legionary was in all likelihood not a Jew. His heart had not been hardened against Jesus, as had the hearts of many of the Jews, especially of their leaders. So, when all was over he is heard to exclaim, "Surely this was God's Son." Whether by this time his knowledge of Christ had advanced to the point where he confessed Jesus to be in a unique sense "the" Son of God, has not been revealed. As far as Greek grammar is concerned, it gives us no information on that point. [895] Legend says that this man became a Christian. Let us hope that it was true. Luke states that the centurion "glorified God and said, 'Certainly, this was a righteous man.' " There is no contradiction here. He may very well have said both.

Matthew informs us that not only the centurion but even the soldiers under him were similarly affected. Here, again, there is no contradiction. It is true that the soldiers had been mocking (Luke 23:36). But that was before the earthquake had occurred, with its effect on rocks and tombs. The men who had crucified Jesus may certainly have changed their minds. Did not one of the robbers also mock at first and then repent? According to Luke 23:48 even the multitude in general was at last deeply impressed and "returned smiting their breasts."

Ministering Women

55, 56. Now watching from a distance there were many women who had followed Jesus from Galilee, ministering to his needs. Among them were Mary Magdalene, Mary the mother of James and Joses, and the mother of the sons of Zebedee. John 19:25 states that these women were standing "near" the cross of Jesus. Matt. 27:55; Mark 15:40; and Luke 23:49 picture them as watching "from a distance." Did they, perhaps, stand far off at first, and did they draw closer later on when they were convinced that the soldiers would not harm them?

---

[895] The Greek has no definite articles here, but simply says υἱός. On the other hand, with proper nouns and titles, forms without the article can still be definite. They may be either definite or indefinite.

As to the identity of the women here mentioned—only a few of the *many* are mentioned by name—it is very well possible that the two lists (Matt. 27:56; Mark 15:40) indicate the same three persons. If this be true, the three would be: *a.* Mary Magdalene, so named in both lists; *b.* Mary the mother of James and Joses = Mary the mother of James the Less and of Joses; and *c.* the mother of the sons of Zebedee = Salome. In fact, it is even possible that the list in John 19:25 has reference to the same individuals plus Mary, the mother of Jesus. John's list in all probability refers to four women, not three. Is it not possible that the reason why John mentions the presence of Christ's mother, but Matthew and Mark do not, was that the author of the fourth Gospel, in distinction from the others, describes the situation as it was before the disciple whom Jesus loved had taken Mary to his home (John 19:27)? The three other women mentioned in John's list would then be the same as those referred to in Matthew and Mark; namely, *a.* his [Christ's] mother's sister = Salome = the mother of the sons of Zebedee; *b.* Mary the (*wife* probably) of Clopas = the mother of James the Less and of Joses; and *c.* Mary Magdalene. For more on this and on the references to the four in the New Testament see N.T.C. on the Gospel according to John, Vol. II, pp. 431, 432.

Taking the three names according to the order given here in Matthew we note that "Mary Magdalene" was from Magdala, located on the southwestern shore of the Sea of Galilee. The Lord had delivered her from a bad case of demon-possession (Luke 8:2). She is the Mary who, after Christ's resurrection, "stood at the tomb weeping" when Jesus, whom she took to be the gardener, appeared to her (John 20:11-18). She is definitely *not* the sinful woman of Luke 7. About "Mary the mother of James and Joses" we know only that, together with Mary Magdalene, she was present also at Christ's burial (Matt. 27:61; Mark 15:47; cf. Luke 23:55), and was one of the women who went out very early on Sunday morning to anoint Christ's body (Matt. 28:1; Mark 16:1). In that same group of women was also "the mother of the sons of Zebedee" (cf. Mark 16:1). We have met her before. See on Matt. 20:20, 21.

Notable women were these, and this for at least three reasons:

a. With the exception of John none of the other disciples who belonged to the group of twelve is reported to have been present at Calvary, but these women were present! They displayed rare courage.

b. We are distinctly told that they were women who had followed Jesus from Galilee and had been in the habit of ministering to his needs. They had given evidence of hearts filled with love and sympathy.

c. Being witnesses of Christ's death, burial, and resurrection appearance, they were qualified witnesses of facts of redemption on which, under God, the church depends for its faith.

57 When evening fell, there came a rich man from Arimathea, named Joseph, who himself had become a disciple of Jesus; 58 this man approached Pilate and asked for the body of Jesus. Then Pilate ordered that it be given (to him). 59 So Joseph took the body, wrapped it in a clean linen cloth, 60 and laid it in his own new tomb, which he had hewn out in the rock; and he rolled a big stone in front of the entrance of the tomb and departed. 61 Mary Magdalene and the other Mary were there, sitting across from the tomb.

27:57-61 *The Burial of Jesus*
Cf. Mark 15:42-47; Luke 23:50-56; John 19:38-42

57, 58. When evening fell, there came a rich man from Arimathea, named Joseph, who also himself had become a disciple of Jesus; this man approached Pilate and asked for the body of Jesus. Then Pilate ordered that it be given (to him). As has been indicated, Jesus died at three o'clock in the afternoon. According to the ancient Hebrew way of speaking there were "two evenings" (cf. Exod. 12:6 in the original). The first "evening" which we would call "afternoon" began at 3 P.M., the second at 6 P.M. Something of this is probably reflected in the phrase "When evening fell," for we cannot imagine that Joseph of Arimathea, a Jew, would have approached Pilate on Friday, 6 P.M., asking for the body of Jesus when the sabbath was beginning. Much sooner than this he must have started to make preparations. It was against the law to leave a dead body on a tree overnight (Deut. 21:23). This would have been all the more reprehensible if by doing so, the body would be hanging on a tree or cross on the sabbath. Moreover, this was the sabbath of the Passover week. Great, indeed, was that sabbath (John 19:31)! Besides all this, as has been pointed out earlier (see on Matt. 9:23, 24), it was customary to bury a person very soon after death had occurred. For all these reasons it is clear that if the body of Jesus was going to be buried at all, it had to be done now, that is, sometime before 6 P.M.

But who was going to take care of this? The disciples, let it be borne in mind, had fled (Matt. 26:56). To be sure, John had retraced his steps and had even been standing among the spectators at Calvary, but not for long (John 19:27). The care of Mary, the mother of Jesus, had been entrusted to him and he had taken her to his home. He did, however, return to Calvary, for he saw the spear thrust (John 19:35), but we can well understand that he had had no time to make preparations for Jesus' burial.

It is at this point that Joseph of Arimathea enters into the picture. What kind of a man was he? He was *rich*. Therefore when he provides a tomb for Jesus, the prophecy of Isa. 53:9 goes into fulfilment. He was also "a good man and righteous," a man who, though he was a member of the Sanhedrin (Luke 23:51; cf. Mark 15:43), had not consented to the verdict pronounced against Jesus by that body. The Arimathea from which he came was probably the ancient Ramathaim-zophim, situated somewhat over twenty miles northwest of Jerusalem, or fifteen miles straight east from Joppa.

Only *secretly* had he been a disciple of Jesus (John 19:38). He may have been afraid that if he should do anything in the interest of Jesus, he would be dismissed not only from the Sanhedrin but even from the synagogue. See on John 7:13; 9:22; 20:19. But now, as the fruit of Christ's love for him, this man has suddenly become very courageous. It was a bold act on his part to ask for the body of Jesus (Mark 15:43), for in all probability he was not a relative of Jesus; and besides, his fellow-Sanhedrists would now discover the real nature of his loyalty.

According to all that we read about this man in the Gospels, he was anything but a schemer, a secret plotter. It need hardly be added that Jesus, too, was the very opposite of a conniver. He was—and is—himself *"the Truth"* and therefore the hater and denouncer of all hypocrisy. [896]

The governor, having been assured by the centurion that Jesus had really died (Mark 15:44), granted Joseph's request. So he returns to Calvary, where the body is given to him.

59, 60. So Joseph took the body, wrapped it in a clean linen cloth, and laid it in his own new tomb, which he had hewn out in the rock; and he rolled a big stone in front of the entrance of the tomb and departed. For the interpretation of this passage, of which there is a virtual parallel in the Fourth Gospel, see the detailed explanation in N.T.C. on John 19:40-42.

61. Mary Magdalene and the other Mary were there, sitting across from the tomb. See above, on verses 55, 56. "The other Mary" must be "Mary the mother of James and Joses." They saw how the body of Jesus was carried into the new tomb which Joseph, who owned the garden in which it was located, had hewn out in the rock. It was a tomb that had never been used. The women also observed how a big stone had been rolled in front of the entrance of the tomb. Having seen all this, they departed.

62 Next day, the day after the Preparation, [897] the chief priests and the Pharisees went in a body to Pilate, 63 saying, "Sir, we remember that while yet alive that impostor said, 'After three days I arise.' 64 Therefore order that the grave be made secure until the third day, lest his disciples come, steal him, and tell the people, 'He was raised from the dead,' and the last deception will be worse than the first." 65 Pilate said to them, "Take a guard; go, make it as secure as y o u know how." 66 So off they went and made the grave secure by putting a seal on the stone in the presence of the guard.

27:62-66 The Guard Stationed

The story about the guard begins here (27:62-66). It is continued in 28:2-4, and is brought to completion in 28:11-15. A fine Easter sermon could have as its theme:

[896] That is why I cannot see how H. J. Schonfield's, *The Passover Plot,* New York, 1965, see especially pp. 156-161, can be regarded as being a credible representation.

[897] In modern Greek "Preparation" is "Friday." Therefore "the day after" would mean Saturday.

"What happened to the Guard
Requested by the Leaders"

The "points" or "divisions" could be as follows: 1. The Guard Posted (or: Stationed); 2. The Guard Scattered; and 3. The Guard Bribed.

62. Next day, the day after the Preparation, the chief priests and the Pharisees went in a body to Pilate. . . . Almost, but not entirely correct are the lines, describing the Saturday immediately following "Good Friday":

Matthew has nothing to relate
Of that one day of dreadful gloom;
Luke has no further word to state.
The stone had sealed the Master's tomb.

With respect to Matthew these lines are in error. What he relates about Saturday is, in fact, very significant. It seems that the Pharisees, who were always insisting on strict sabbath observance, had found an excuse for what they were doing this Saturday morning. It is also remarkable that this time—different than the day before—nothing is said about any hesitancy on their part in connection with entering the praetorium. Since in their hatred for Jesus, chief priests and Pharisees were united, it is really not very surprising that these two groups co-operate in expressing their concern to the governor with reference to Christ's promise that on the third day he would rise from the dead. Even though the chief priests, being Sadducees, did not believe in the resurrection, the issue at present is not really any question regarding the factuality of that article of faith. The point is: neither the chief priests nor the Pharisees want to lose their hold on the people!

63. Continued . . . **saying, Sir, we remember that while yet alive that impostor said, After three days I arise.** Note the sharp contrast. As they see it, Pilate deserves to be addressed as "Sir," but Jesus is "that impostor" (or: "deceiver"). They remember, then, that Jesus has said, "After three days I arise." It is remarkable that while the disciples failed to understand Christ's predictions regarding his resurrection (Mark 8:31; 9:31; cf. 10:33), even when these were uttered in very clear, unfigurative language (Mark 9:32), the Pharisees and their associates did understand and did remember them, even though *to them* they had been couched in veiled phraseology (12:40; 16:4).

Their request, then, is as follows: **64. Therefore order that the grave be made secure until the third day, lest his disciples come, steal him, and tell the people, He was raised from the dead, and the last deception will be worse than the first.** The Jewish leaders desire that Pilate shall issue an order for soldiers under his control to guard the grave until the third day. In a way, this was a very clever move. These men are not sure about their own ability to restrain the disciples from stealing the body of Jesus, and then spreading the rumor that he had arisen from the dead; but they are sure that the authority of the governor appointed by Rome will not be defied. But in another way, this was a stupid move. It was stupid first of all because just

981

about the last thing the disciples were thinking about was Christ's series of predictions regarding a resurrection. Their mental state has been described in N.T.C. on the Gospel according to John, Vol. II, pp. 468-471. The move of these leaders was even more stupid because they could and should have known that no force on earth would be able to prevent the fulfilment of Christ's predictions.

"The last deception will be worse than the first." Granted, for a moment, that they were right about Jesus being merely an impostor, then their reasoning about the first versus the last deception was valid. For surely a man will have more faith in a person whom he regards as having first died and then risen again, thereby proving his greatness, than in one who has not yet died but claims to be the Messiah.

"Ill doers are ill deemers." It is exactly because these leaders are themselves such dishonest people (see 28:11-15) that they mistrust Christ's disciples.

65. Pilate said to them, Take a guard; go, make it as secure as y o u know how. Although the verbal form used in the original, instead of being rendered "Take" or "Have" (a guard), can also be translated "Y o u have" (a guard), which would mean, "Y o u yourselves have a temple guard. Make use of that guard," 28:14 makes clear that Pilate is speaking about the guard under his own control. For this reason—and this is not the only one [898] —we must translate as we did.

Pilate, who has recently refused a favor asked by the Jewish authorities (John 19:21, 22), is perfectly willing to yield to them on a matter as trivial—as he sees it—as this.

66. So off they went and made the grave secure by putting a seal on the stone in the presence of the guard. The chief priests and the Pharisees rejoice in the fact that their request has been granted. Nevertheless, they wish to be very sure that Pilate's promise will be carried out to the full. So, off to Joseph's garden they go, that they may see the guard with their own eyes.—The guard is posted. In the presence of these soldiers who have been ordered to keep this tomb under their surveillance, so that no one will tamper with it, a cord covered with clay or wax on which an official seal has been impressed is affixed to the stone at the grave's entrance. Surely, no one will dare to break this seal or to move this stone.

We see the exceedingly heavy stone, the seal, the guard. "Have a guard; go, make it as sure as y o u can."—"He that sits in the heavens shall laugh. The Lord will have them in derision" (Ps. 2:4). The words "in the presence of the guard" may also be rendered, "posting the guard."

In the providence of God even the sinister plan of these suspicious leaders was overruled for good. It will mean that not the disciples of Jesus but the

---

[898] The temple-guard would have no authority outside of the temple.

frightened members of the very "watch" for which the leaders had made request will be the first to announce to them the marvelous events that happened in Joseph's garden.

Summary of Chapter 27

For the nine paragraphs into which chapter 27 may be divided and for their references see p. 940.

1. Very early in the morning the Sanhedrin condemned Jesus to death, but since that body lacked authority to carry out this sentence Jesus was ordered to be bound and thus, as a prisoner in chains, was led away to Pilate the governor.

2. Was it when Judas saw Jesus being led away that his conscience smote him? It must have occurred either then or very shortly afterward. When he tried to return the thirty pieces of silver to the chief priests and elders they refused this blood money. So, into the temple—perhaps The Treasury—he hurled it. Then away he went and hanged himself.

The conscience of the Jewish hierarchy, though sufficiently elastic to harbor murderous designs against Jesus, was unable to tolerate putting blood money into the treasury, even though this very place may well have been the source from which it had been obtained in the first place, and even though the chief priests themselves had created this blood money. So, to satisfy their scruples, they bought with it the Potter's Field, as a burial place for foreigners; unwittingly thereby fulfilling which prophecy? Jeremiah's? Zechariah's? See pp. 946-948.

3. and 4. See the summaries on pp. 949, 950.

5. See the summary on pp. 958, 959.

6. Calvary, from 9 A.M. until noon: see the summary on pp. 961, 962.

7. Calvary from noon until 3 P.M. There was darkness over all the land, a darkness symbolical of the curse upon sin which Jesus was bearing. At 3 P.M. he cried out with a loud voice, "Eli, Eli, lema, sabachthani." He felt himself forsaken of God, in the sense explained (as far as "explanation" is possible) in Ps. 22. To compare Christian martyrs, who though tortured went singing to their death, with Jesus, who cried out in agony, is unfair. *He* died "forsaken, that *we* might never be forsaken!" A remarkable difference indeed! When, having fully accomplished whatever had been assigned to him, Jesus died, various signs occurred. The curtain of the sanctuary was torn from top to bottom (explained in Heb. 10:19, 20). The earth quaked, rocks split, graves were opened, showing that Christ's death had significance even for the realm of nature (Rom. 8:21; Rev. 21:1). Saints who had been buried near Calvary arose and sometime later appeared to many in Jerusalem, pointing forward to the glorious resurrection of believers on the day of Christ's return. The centurion exclaimed,

"Surely, this was God's Son." Several noble women were watching from a distance. For their identity and the reasons why they must be regarded as noble see pp. 977, 978.

8. The burial of Jesus did not take place in secret. Joseph of Arimathea, a man of unblemished character, wrapped the body in a clean linen cloth, and *while women watched* laid it in his own rock-hewn grave.

9. On Saturday, the day after Christ's death, the chief priests and the Pharisees secured from Pilate a guard, so as to prevent any body-snatching or tampering with the grave. The theme "What Happened to the Guard Requested by the Leaders" begins at this point. It continues and is brought to completion in chapter 28. For the present (chapter 27) the guard is stationed at the tomb and the stone is sealed.

What is the meaning of the cross? See N.T.C. on Galatians 6:14.

Outline of Chapter 28

Theme: *The Work Which Thou Gavest Him to Do*

B. The Resurrection

CHAPTER XXVIII

MATTHEW 28:1

28 1 Now after the sabbath, at dawn on the first day of the week, Mary Magdalene and the other Mary came to look at the tomb. 2 Suddenly there was a violent earthquake, for an angel of the Lord came down from heaven, stepped forward, rolled away the stone and was sitting on it. 3 His appearance was like lightning, and his garment white as snow. 4 And for fear of him the guards shook and became like dead men. 5 The angel, answering, said to the women, "Don't y o u be afraid, for I know that y o u are looking for Jesus, who was crucified. 6 He is not here, for he has been raised, just as he said. Come, see the place where he lay. 7 Then go quickly and tell his disciples, 'He has been raised from the dead, and look, he is going ahead of y o u into Galilee; there y o u shall see him.' Now I have told y o u." 8 So they departed quickly from the tomb with fear and great joy, and ran to report to his disciples. 9 And suddenly Jesus met them and said, "Good morning." They approached, took hold of his feet, and worshiped him. 10 Then Jesus said to them, "Do not be afraid; go, tell my brothers to go to Galilee; there they shall see me."

28:1-10 *The Lord Risen; The Guard Frightened; The Women Surprised*
Cf. Mark 16:1-8; Luke 24:1-12; John 20:1-10

1. **Now after the sabbath, at dawn on the first day of the week, Mary Magdalene and the other Mary came to look at the tomb.** The sabbath has come and gone (Mark 16:1). It is now Sunday morning at dawn. It is definitely the first day of the week. [899] It was then that Mary Magdalene and "the other Mary," that is "Mary the mother of James and Joses" (27:56, 61) came to look at the tomb. Matthew abbreviates. As in 27:61 so also here he mentions only these two. Mark adds Salome (16:1). Luke adds Joanna, and indicates that there were others (24:10). Though at this point John 20:1 mentions only Mary Magdalene, even that Gospel implies that other women had accompanied her (note 20:2: "*We* do not know"). There is no conflict between John's story about Mary Magdalene, and

---

[899] It makes little difference whether one conceives of the Greek plural for *sabbath* as referring *to the day* or to an entire *week* (the time from one day of rest to another). If the first is meant, then the idea is that this was the first day counting from the sabbath-day; hence, the first day after the sabbath-day. If the second is meant, the result is still the same; the day indicated is then not the last of the week but the first. In either case Sunday is meant.

Matthew's about several women. [900] Nor is there any conflict about the time when the women's trip to the tomb took place. John 20:1 states, "while it was still dark," Mark 16:2 "when the sun was risen," Matthew 28:1 "at dawn," Luke 24:1 "at early dawn." Probable solution: although it was still dark when the women started out, the sun had risen when they arrived at the tomb.

They came "to look at the tomb." Here too Matthew summarizes. We must remember that Joseph of Arimathea and Nicodemus had already wound linen bandages around the body, strewing in a mixture of myrrh and aloes. However, the dead body had not as yet been anointed. Sometime after 6 P.M. on Saturday evening—hence, "when the sabbath was past"—the women had bought whatever was necessary to anoint the body. So now, very early Sunday morning, they come to the tomb to do this, in order to prevent rapid decomposition (Mark 16:1; Luke 24:1).

It is true that they should have paid more attention to the Lord's repeated prediction that he would rise again on the third day. On the other hand, while we may criticize their lack of sufficient faith—a lack which they shared with the male disciples—let us not overlook their exceptional love and loyalty. They were at Calvary when Jesus died, in Joseph's garden when their Master was buried, and now very early in the morning, here they are once more, in order to look at the tomb; that is, to see to it that everything is in good order, and to anoint the body. Meanwhile, where were the eleven?

Mark 16:3 informs us that on the way toward the tomb the women were worried about the stone. They said to each other, "Who will roll away the stone for us from the entrance of the tomb?" But suddenly they saw—probably at a turn in the path—that the heavy stone had already been removed (Mark 16:4). What had happened? Matthew by divine inspiration, answers as follows: 2. **Suddenly there was a violent earthquake, for an angel of the Lord came down from heaven, stepped forward, rolled away the stone and was sitting on it.** In connection with the presence of the Lord, his mighty redemptive acts, and the manifestation of his anger poured out upon the enemies of his people, Scripture makes frequent mention of the occurrence of earthquakes. The earthquake means as much as, "Listen, the Lord is speaking!" See Exod. 19:18; Num. 16:31; I Kings 19:11; Job 9:6; Ps. 18:7; 68:8; 77:18; Isa. 3:13; 5:25; 13:13; 24:18; 29:6; Jer. 10:10; 49:21; Joel 2:10; Nah. 1:5; Hag. 2:6; Rev. 6:12; 8:5; 11:13-19. Appropriately there had been an earthquake at the moment of Christ's death (Matt. 27:51); and there will probably be numerous fearful earthquakes in connection with Christ's second coming. See above, on 24:7. So also now, in connection with Christ's

---

[900] For a possible harmony see N.T.C. on the Gospel according to John, Vol. II, p. 448, middle of page.

resurrection, there suddenly [901] occurred a "great" or "violent" earthquake.

The reason for the quake was the descent from heaven of God's special messenger, an angel. He stepped forward and must have taken the stone completely out of its groove and turned it over on its side. Result: the heavy slab was lying flat on the ground and the angel was sitting upon it, to symbolize Christ's triumph.

The women did not see this happen. They saw only the result. Not even the "witnesses of the resurrection" (cf. Acts 1:22), saw Jesus rise from the grave. They did however, at one time or another, see the risen Christ, which was indeed a mighty proof of his resurrection.

Why did the angel have to remove the stone? Not to enable Jesus to make his way out of the tomb—for see John 20:19, 26—but to enable the women (Mark 16:5) and also Peter and John (20:6-8) to enter it.

With reference to the angel, Matthew continues: 3. **His appearance was like lightning, and his garment white as snow.** The marvelous radiance of his countenance gave proof of his descent straight from heaven. The sparkling luster of his garment indicated his holiness. Compare, in this connection Dan. 7:9; Matt. 17:2; Rev. 1:16; 10:1; 12:1; 20:11.

The story about the guard—see on 27:62-66—is now continued, The Guard Scattered: 4. **And for fear of him the guards shook and became like dead men.** The original uses words derived from the same root to describe both the action of the earth and of the guard, so that the rendering might be: "Suddenly there was a violent earth*quake* . . . the men on guard *quaked*. . . ." So overcome with fright were they that if anyone had been present at the scene he could hardly have guessed what was shaking more: the earth or the members of the guard! The latter were knocked unconscious. For a while they lay there in a condition of utter powerlessness and discomfiture, motionless as if dead. From verse 11 it appears that when they finally "came to" they were no longer an organized unit, for not "all" of them but only "some" came into the city, etc.

The stone, the seal, the guard! What a sense of security all this had given to the chief priests and the Pharisees. Yet, in the sight of heaven all this show of strength spelled clumsy, fantastic futility. In Joseph's garden the Almighty was laughing (Ps. 2:4). He uttered his voice and the earth melted. See also Ps. 46:6; 48:4-8.

By means of the resurrection of Christ from the grave, and the mighty earthquake that appropriately accompanied it, "the Father of our Lord Jesus Christ" not only laughed in the faces of the plotters who had requested this guard; he also smiled benignly upon all his dear children, for what he was actually saying was this: "I have accepted my Son's sacrifice as a complete ransom for the sins of all who take refuge in him." See Rom. 4:25. And the

---

[901] Greek ἰδού; see footnote 133 on p. 131.

watchers? No thanks to them, and notwithstanding the machinations of those who had asked for them, they were becoming tools in the hands of God for the confirmation of his truth. See on verse 11.

Christ's resurrection was the work of the Triune God. The Father raised him from the dead (Rom. 6:4; Gal. 1:1; I Peter 1:3). So did the Spirit (Rom. 8:11; and see N.T.C. on I Tim. 3:16). And the Son took back the life which he had laid down (John 10:18; cf. 2:19, 21; 11:25). For the comfort of believers, these three are and always will be *One.*

The story of the guard will be continued at verse 11. For the present Matthew returns to the women: **5, 6. The angel, answering, said to the women, Don't y o u be afraid, for I know that y o u are looking for Jesus, who was crucified.** Luke 24:2 and John 20:12 speak of "two" angels; Matthew and Mark, of only *one.* Why this difference? Some answer, "Although two angels were actually present, one alone was the speaker." But this will hardly do, for according to Luke both of the "two men in dazzling apparel" addressed the women. So do also the two "angels" in John's account. The reason for the difference has not been revealed to us. There is, of course, no contradiction, for neither Matthew nor Mark states that there was *only* one angel.

"Don't y o u—very emphatic in the original—be afraid," says the angel. In other words, "Don't y o u be like others who were scattered in every direction, and some of whom y o u may even have met." Why do not these women need to be afraid? Why must they *stop their weeping and rejoice instead?* [902] The angel answers, "for I know that y o u are looking for Jesus the crucified." In other words, "Y o u have no reason to fear, for y o u are the loyal friends of Jesus. Yes, y o u have remained loyal to him even though the world despised and crucified him. It was to show that loyalty that y o u came here this morning."

We might have expected a different message, for example, a stern rebuke, in view of the fact that these women showed by their action that they had not taken seriously enough Jesus' prediction of rising on the third day. But no, all this is passed by—though not completely. A mercifully veiled rebuke—better, a gentle admonition, a loving reminder—comes at the very end of the angel's message: **He is not here, for he has been raised just as he said.** "Just as he said." The angel does not even say, "just as he said *again and again and again.*" See above p. 9. It is as if the angel is saying, "In view of y o u r

---

[902] To say that in negative commands the present imperative means that an action, already going on, must be stopped, is hardly sufficient. It is true that in many cases of this nature a prohibition to stop doing what one is already doing is indeed implied. So undoubtedly also here (Luke 24:5). But that certainly is not the full meaning. "Don't y o u be afraid" not only means "Stop doing what y o u are already doing," but also, "Do the very opposite. This is a day of cheer, a day to rejoice with joy unspeakable and full of glory."

marvelous courage and loyalty, y o u r lack of sufficient faith is hereby forgiven." Moreover, it must be borne in mind that the heavenly messenger did not create this message. It was given to him, as a comparison between verses 5 and 10 clearly shows. Reassuringly, the angel adds, **Come, see the place where he lay.** According to Mark 16:5, by this time the women were already inside the tomb. But the angel bids them come even closer, so that they may see whatever there is to be seen; for example, not only the empty tomb—"He is not here"—but also "the linen bandages lying there, and the sweatband not lying with the linen bandages but folded up in a place by itself" (John 20:7). They must convince themselves that everything is orderly in this tomb. No disciple has been here to remove the body, nor has an enemy pillaged the tomb. In either case the bandages would no longer have been present. The women—just like Peter and John that same morning—must see that the Lord, restored from death to life, had himself removed the bandages and the sweatband, had provided for himself a garment such as is worn by the living, had calmly and majestically put everything in its place in the tomb, and had then departed from the tomb gloriously alive.

For the church to believe that Jesus rose from the dead is fine, but it is not enough. It should also consider *what kind of Savior* it was who rose from the dead. Is he still the same loving Redeemer who before he died healed the sick, cleansed the leper, raised the dead, comforted the mourning, pardoned and died for the sinner who accepts him by a living faith? Careful study of the resurrection account answers this question with a thunderous affirmative.

As if to make this even clearer, the angel continues, 7. **Then go quickly and tell his disciples, He has been raised from the dead, and look, he is going ahead of y o u into Galilee; there y o u shall see him.** The marvelous message must be imparted. It must be proclaimed everywhere by those who at one time were, and soon will again be, The Twelve. Therefore they themselves must hear the glad news. They must get to know that Christ's repeated prediction, "I am going to rise again on the third day" has now become a fact. Not only that, but for further confirmation of their faith, they must be told that the promise of Matt. 26:32, "But after I have been raised, I will go ahead of y o u into Galilee" is also going to be fulfilled. It is there, in the very region (4:15, 16) where death and darkness once ruled supreme, but where the Light of the world had performed most of his work, that he again will meet with his disciples. Galilee! That region of rejection, but also of acceptance; of hardship, but also of joy; of unbelief, but also of faith, must rejoice once more. See further on 26:32. **Now I have told y o u,** the angel adds, as if to say, "Now *y o u* have heard the glad tidings, and know what to do. So now it is y o u r responsibility."

Objection: "But Jesus' first appearance to his disciples did not occur in Galilee but in Jerusalem. These men did not have to wait until they had arrived at last in Galilee, but were going to see the risen Savior this very evening." Answer: this simply shows that God—or if one prefers, that the risen Savior—is even better than his promises.

But what about Peter, who had bragged in such unrestrained language about his loyalty, but had broken his promises so shamefully, must he also be told? "Yes," says "the young man," that is, the angel, "Go, tell his disciples *and Peter*" (Mark 16:7).

8. **So they departed quickly from the tomb with fear and great joy, and ran to report to his disciples.** That fear and joy can go together is clear from Ps. 2:11. Moreover, was it not natural for these women to be struck with fear at the sight of such a brilliant angel and upon receiving the news of so great a mystery: Jesus risen from the dead? Also, was it not equally natural for them to rejoice when they heard that Jesus, whose loyal friends, disciples, and subjects they were, had conquered Death? Note also that in the struggle between fear and joy, the latter triumphed, for the adjective "great" modifies only "joy," not "fear." These women did not walk. They *ran* to tell the tidings. Luke 24:9 reports that the women fulfilled their mission. How was their report received by the apostles? Answer: it was not believed (Luke 24:10, 11). It began to spread, but by and large was not accepted as true (Mark 16:13; Luke 24:22-25).

However, though the disbelief that was going to greet the women everywhere would not be pleasant, their present joy, great as it was, was going to become even greater: 9. **And suddenly Jesus met them and said, Good morning. They approached, took hold of his feet, and worshiped him.** To put them at ease Jesus used an ordinary greeting when he met them, one that can perhaps be best rendered "Hello," or "How do y o u do?" or "Good morning." See also 26:49; 27:29. Immediately they recognized him, fell down before him, taking hold of his feet and worshipping him. He was real, even physical ("his feet"). He was Jesus, no one else, the very Jesus whom they had known for a considerable time, and to whom they had rendered valuable service.

The question has been raised, "But why did not *Jesus* appear first of all to the eleven? Why first to the women?" Or, going back a little: "Why did *the angel* appear to the women, not to Peter and John?" We do not have the answer. Could it be that the special recognition accorded to the women was a reward for their singular ministry of love and loyalty?

Jesus, too, has a message for these women. It is essentially the selfsame message which they have already received from the angels (see 5a, 7b), showing that in the realm of the sinless there is perfect harmony. If there is any difference, the words now spoken are even more touching: 10. **Then Jesus said to them, Do not be afraid; go, tell my brothers to go to Galilee; there they shall see me.** "My brothers," not: "those habitual quarrelers, those men who promised to remain loyal to me no matter what would happen, but who when the crisis arrived left me and fled; those men who, with one exception, were not even present at Calvary when I was laying down my life for them." None of that. Instead, "my brothers," those whom I acknowledge as members of my family, those who share the inheritance with me, those whom I love. Cf. Matt. 12:49; 25:40; Rom. 8:16, 17, 29; Heb. 2:11, 12. See also N.T.C. on Eph. 3:14, 15. For the rest, Jesus virtually repeats the message of the angel, telling the disciples to go to Galilee, and promising that they shall see him there.

---

11 Now while they were going, some of the guards came into the city and reported to the chief priests all that had happened. 12 And when they had assembled with the elders and taken counsel, they gave the soldiers a considerable sum of money, 13 instructing them, "Say, 'His disciples came during the night and stole him away while we were sleeping.' 14 And if this (report) should reach the governor's ears, we will persuade him and keep y o u out of trouble." 15 So they took the money and did as they had been instructed. And this story has been widely spread among the Jews, to this very day.

28:11-15 *The Guard Bribed*

11. **Now while they were going, some of the guards came into the city and reported to the chief priests all that had happened.** Two paragraphs in connection with the guard placed at Christ's tomb (a story found only in Matthew's Gospel) have already been discussed. How it was that the guard was posted in Joseph's garden, and how the soldiers belonging to it were frightened and scattered has been shown (respectively, in 27:62-66 and in 28:3, 4). Now follows the concluding paragraph, describing how the guard was bribed. The women were on their way to spread the truth about the resurrection. The soldiers were going to allow themselves to be used to hush the truth and to hold forth the lie (verses 12-14).

Note: "some of the guards," apparently not all; at least, not all at once. The guard had been scattered, perhaps in every direction. There are those who think that a few of the men were brave enough to bring a report to the authorities; while the rest held back, somewhere outside, wondering how their representatives would fare, and anxiously awaiting their return. However that may have been, some did indeed bring in a report. That they reported to the chief priests, in charge of the temple, and not directly to Pilate, is not strange; for by saying, "Take a guard," Pilate had temporarily placed these men under the authority and supervision of the chief priests.

These men, then, told the chief priests what had happened, that is, what they themselves had seen and experienced: the sudden descent of a flaming angel, the earthquake; perhaps even the removal of the stone from the entrance of the tomb and together with it the breaking of the seal.

The result was that the Sanhedrin—here indicated by two of its three groups; see on 2:4 and 16:21—hastily met in formal session: **12-14. And when they had assembled with the elders and taken counsel, they gave the** soldiers a considerable sum of money, instructing them, **Say, His disciples came during the night and stole him away while we were sleeping. And if this (report) should reach the governor's ears, we will persuade him and keep y o u out of trouble.** We do not read that the Sanhedrin rejected the soldiers' report in utter disbelief. Neither is it correct, however, to say that the Sanhedrin believed it. One fact is certain: this body did not want to have the people believe what the soldiers had just now reported. It was afraid that any such news would readily be linked with the idea of a resurrection from the grave, and that this belief, in turn, would cause the people to lose confidence in their leaders, who had been chiefly responsible for the murder of Jesus.

So the Sanhedrists pass a resolution containing three items, namely, to give the soldiers: *a.* a large sum of money; *b.* a story to spread; and *c.* assurance of freedom from punishment. As to *a.* the sum had to be large, for the admission that they, the men on guard duty, had been sleeping instead of watching, would not reflect honor on themselves. As to *b.* the story "his disciples . . . stole him" would explain why the tomb was empty, and would hopefully counteract belief in a resurrection. And as to *c.* what had happened at Calvary—see Matt. 27:23-26; cf. John 19:12, 13—had strengthened the Sanhedrin's conviction that Pilate could be bent according to its will. [903] "We will *persuade—*or *satisfy—*him," says the council.

As to the Sanhedrin, it may seem strange that a body of such dignitaries and clothed with such high authority would actually resort to this crookedness. But is it so strange that men who had committed murder now also resort to lying in order to cover up what they had done?

The soldiers' reaction is described in verse 15. **So they took the money and did as they had been instructed.** From the point of view of expediency or (seeming) self-interest, this must have looked to them as the best course to follow. Though it was painful to admit that they had been sleeping at their post, yet by agreeing to do as they had been directed, they gained the promise of protection by the Sanhedrin, and a considerable sum of money besides.

Matthew concludes this account by stating: **And this story has been widely spread among the Jews, to this very day.** To the very day that Matthew was writing these words this false rumor was being circulated among the Jews. Justin Martyr (probable dates A.D. 114-165) writes, "You have sent chosen and ordained men throughout the whole world to proclaim that a godless and lawless heresy had sprung from one Jesus, a Galilean deceiver . . . whose disciples stole him by night from the tomb" (*Dialogue*

---

903 In verse 14 τοῦτο most naturally refers back to the report which the soldiers are ordered to spread (verse 13). Therefore the rendering "And if this (report) should reach the governor's ears," seems natural and best, rather than "come to a hearing before the governor," favored by Lenski, *op. cit.,* p. 1145.

with Trypho 108). Even today, late in the twentieth century, this false rumor is still being spread. [904]

We feel sure, however, that Matthew is not recording this merely to tell an interesting story about "The Guard, Stationed, Scattered, and Bribed." As was indicated earlier, he was writing to the Jews, though he was aiming also for the conversion of a much wider circle. What he is doing in conveying this truthful account found in 27:62-66; 28:3, 4, 11-15, is this: he is showing how utterly ridiculous is the denial of Christ's resurrection; in other words, how well-founded is the true account of what happened in Joseph's garden. That is why, as I mentioned in the beginning, this theme can be turned into an inspiring Easter message.

Let us, then, for a moment try to recall the concrete situation that must have resulted from the spread of the rumor that the disciples had come by night and stolen the body. Let us try to picture what may have happened:

Monday morning, presumably the day after the rumor of the stolen body had begun to spread, one of these guards, let us suppose, is being stopped by a friend who says to him, "What is this we hear about the tomb being empty, and the body missing?" Answer: What actually happened was that his disciples came during the night and stole him away while we were sleeping." "O," says the inquirer, "then that explains it." He continues on his way, satisfied that the problem has been solved. He tells all his friends and relatives about it. Many of them also believe the rumor.

However a little farther along this same guard meets someone else, who asks him the same question. He receives the same answer. But this man is not entirely satisfied with it. As in disbelief he stares at the soldier and asks, "Do you really mean to stand there and tell me that all of y o u twelve men—or whatever was the number—remained asleep when some Galilean fishermen entered the garden, and that while they were busily engaged in removing and turning on its side the heavy slab, entering the tomb, and carrying out the corpse, none of y o u men even so much as woke up? Some sleepers y o u must be!"

A third person enters into conversation with the same soldier. His retort is: "What kind of guards are y o u people, that y o u actually allowed all this to happen? I have always learned that guards were supposed to stay awake."

Finally, the real bombshell! This person, after looking at the watchman in sheer unbelief for a long time, says to him, "Would you please repeat that? I don't know whether I understood you the first time." So very slowly the soldier repeats, "His disciples came during the night and stole him away while we were sleeping." The man answers, "Do you really want me to believe that? You said that you yourself and all the other .men who were

---

[904] H. J. Schonfield, *op. cit.,* pp. 163-165.

supposed to be on guard were sleeping. Well, if you were *sleeping,* then how do you know what happened? If you were sleeping, you didn't see anybody enter the garden and carry away the body. You are merely guessing. I, too, will give my solution of the problem of the empty tomb. It is far more reasonable than yours. It is this: the tomb is empty because Jesus arose triumphantly. He is my Savior and my Lord." Here ends this illustration.

The trouble with all the *so-called* solutions of the problem of the empty tomb is that not one of them is reasonable even on the surface. The stolen body, the swoon theory (according to which Jesus did not really die), mass hallucination, etc., etc., all are absurd. On the other hand, the faith of the Christian, "He lives, he lives, and because he lives I too shall live," is reasonable, true, and satisfying. Not only that, but as already indicated, "He is still the same wonderful Savior, filled with holiness, kindness, and forgiving love for all those who, by sovereign grace, take refuge in him."

16 So the eleven disciples went to Galilee, to the mountain where Jesus had directed them to go. 17 And when they saw him, they worshiped him, but some doubted. 18 Then Jesus came nearer and spoke to them, saying, "All authority has been given to me in heaven and on earth. 19 Go, therefore, and make disciples of all the nations, baptizing them in(to) the name of the Father and of the Son and of the Holy Spirit; 20 teaching them to observe all that I have commanded y o u; and remember, I am with y o u day in day out until the close of the age." [905]

28:16-20 *The Great Claim; The Great Commission; The Great Comfort*
Cf. Mark 16:14-18; Luke 24:36-49; John 20:19-23; Acts 1:9-11

16. So the eleven disciples went to Galilee, to the mountain where Jesus had directed them to go. Note "eleven." Judas has gone to "his own place" (Acts 1:25). These eleven went to Galilee, for that is where Jesus had promised to meet them (26:32), and where the women, upon the instruction of the angel and of Jesus himself (28:7, 10) had directed them to go. In the previous references no mention was made of any mountain. Whether this can be explained by assuming that such passages as the ones already mentioned— 26:32; 28:7, 10 and their parallels in Mark—give us an abbreviated account of what was spoken, or whether the risen Savior had indicated this mountain at one of his other appearances, we do not know.

What we do know is that it was certainly kind of the risen Savior to meet with his disciples at a place in the neighborhood of where their homes were, and where many friends and fellow believers were living. This mountain must have been a place of picturesque scenery and subdued quietness—away from the turmoil of the busy cities and villages. Above all, a scene of tender reminiscences, both for Jesus himself and for his followers, reminding them of what had happened earlier; perhaps on this particular elevation, perhaps

[905] Or: the consummation of the age. Or: the end of the world.

on others (Matt. 5:1; 14:23; 15:29; 17:1; Mark 3:13; John 6:3, 15). It was on a mountain that Jesus had called his disciples; it was also on a mountain that he would take his leave from them.

About a dozen appearances of the risen Christ are recorded in Scripture. See the list, together with references, in N.T.C. on the Gospel according to John, Vol. II, p. 477. It is very well possible that the present appearance to the eleven coincides with, or is part of, the appearance to "the five hundred brothers" (I Cor. 15:6), the majority of whom were still alive when Paul wrote I Corinthians.

When the Lord ascended to heaven this event occurred not in Galilee but from the Mount of Olives, near Jerusalem. For that story one must turn to Luke 24:50, 51; and to Acts 1:4-11. Except for the summarizing statement in the disputed portion of Mark's Gospel (see Mark 16:19), the *story* of the ascension is found only in the writings of Luke. But the *fact* itself is confirmed by ever so many passages (e.g., John 6:62; 14:2, 12; 16:5, 10, 16, 17, 28; 17:5; 20:17; Eph. 1:20-23; 4:8-10; Phil. 2:9; I Tim. 3:16; Heb. 1:3; 2:9; 4:14; 9:24; Rev. 12:5).

Returning then to Galilee, and to the account of the last appearance of Jesus that is recorded in Matthew's Gospel, and may have taken place very shortly before the ascension, we read: **17. And when they saw him, they worshiped him, but some doubted.** When the disciples suddenly saw Jesus they fell down before him in the act of worship. [906] Some, however, doubted. From the very beginning the disciples had difficulty believing that Jesus had actually risen from the dead (Luke 24:10, 11). When ten finally believed it, one (Thomas) was still unconvinced. He, too, became convinced (John 20:24-29). Must we believe that shortly before the ascension there were still a few of the disciples who disbelieved the fact of Christ's resurrection? Probably not. Of that fact all, no doubt, were by this time thoroughly convinced. However, another question was whether *this* man, who suddenly appears to them here in Galilee, was the risen Christ. Was he perhaps someone else?

Many solutions have been offered with respect to this problem. Could it be that the most simple one is also the best, namely, that at first this mysterious person appears to them from a considerable distance? He then steps closer, and the doubt disappeared, though this is not recorded in so many words. What we read is: **18. Then Jesus came nearer and spoke to them, saying. . . .** Jesus steps forward, so that they may be able to see and hear him better. Then follows the great claim, the great commission, and the great comfort.

---

[906] The verb is προσεκύνησαν, third per. pl. aor. indic. of προσκυνέω. In the Gospel according to Matthew this verb occurs again and again (2:2, 8, 11; 4:9, 10; 8:2; 9:18; 14:33; 15:25; 18:26; 20:20; 28:9, 17). It indicates dropping to one's knees in worship or in worshipful adoration. See especially on 2:11; 8:2; and 14:33.

The Great Claim

All authority has been given to me in heaven and on earth. Cf. Dan. 7:14;
Matt. 16:28; 24:30; 26:64. Jesus is here claiming all power and right to
exercise it. When he says, "To me has been given" we naturally interpret this
to mean that he is referring to a gift he has received as Resurrected Mediator.
One might add: "as a reward upon his accomplished mediatorial work, the
atonement which he rendered." But did he not make a somewhat similar
claim long before his death and resurrection? See 11:27. Not only this, but
did he not, even during the days of his humiliation, exercise power over
every sickness, including leprosy, and over hunger, demons, winds and waves,
human hearts, death even? Did he not prove this on many occasions? True,
but there is, nevertheless, an important difference. Before his triumph over
death the enjoyment of that gift was always in some way curtailed. For
example, he must tell the leper not to make known that he was cured (8:4).
The blind men whose eyes were opened receive a similar order (9:30). He is
kept from calling on the Father to send legions of angels to rescue him
(26:53). To be sure, he himself does not desire this help, but self-restraint is
also restraint. He does indeed raise from the dead the daughter of Jairus, the
son of the widow at Nain, and Lazarus. At the moment of his death some
saints are raised. But though all of this was indeed astounding, it is not the
same as actually exercising unlimited power over both heaven and earth,
having it proclaimed everywhere without any restriction, and then at the end
of the age raising *all* the dead, and judging *all* men. It is the investiture of the
risen Christ with such unrestricted, universal sovereignty, that Jesus now
claims and which, especially within a few days that is after his ascension to
heaven, he is beginning to exercise. That is the reward upon his labors (Eph.
1:19-23; Phil. 2:9, 10; Rev. 5; etc.).

Why does Jesus make known this claim? Answer: so that when he now
commissions his apostles to proclaim the gospel throughout the world, they
may know that moment by moment, day by day, they can lean on him. Is
not this the clear teaching of such precious passages as John 16:33; Acts
26:16-18; Phil. 4:13; and Rev. 1:9-20? Not only this, but these apostles and
those that follow afterward must demand that everyone, *in every sphere of
life,* shall joyfully acknowledge Jesus as "Lord of lords and king of kings"
(Rev. 17:14). "The Great Claim" is therefore a fitting introduction to:

The Great Commission

**19, 20a. Go, therefore, and make disciples of all the nations, baptizing
them in(to) the name of the Father and of the Son and of the Holy Spirit;
teaching them to observe all that I have commanded y o u.** We might say
that this passage is of such fundamental significance that something should
be said about each word or combination of words.

"Go"

This stands in rather sharp contrast to "Go not" of 10:5. Cf. 15:24. It is clear that the particularism of the pre-resurrection period has now definitely made place for universalism. Not as if Jesus has changed his mind. It is very clear from the story of the non-Jewish wise men (2:1-12), who came to worship the newborn King, and from such other passages as 8:11, 12; 15:28; 21:43; 22:8-10, that from the very beginning the evangelization of the world was included in the purpose of God. See also John 3:16; 10:16. Matthew too, as has been pointed out, had nothing less than this in mind. But as was stated in connection with 10:5, "In God's plan it was *from Jerusalem* that the gospel must spread out among the nations." Cf. Acts 1:8. Therefore the divinely instituted order was, "To the Jew first, and also to the Greek" (Rom. 1:16). The time to make earnest preparations for the propagation of the gospel throughout the world had now arrived.

"Go" also implies that the disciples—and this holds for God's children in general—must not concentrate all their thought on "coming" to church. They must also "go" to bring the precious tidings to others. Of course, they cannot "go" unless they have first of all "come," and unless they keep coming as well as going. They cannot give unless they are willing to receive.

"Therefore"

This has already been explained in connection with "The Great Claim." Briefly it means: Go, a. because y o u r Lord has so ordered; b. because he has promised to impart all the needed strength; and c. because he is worthy of the homage, faith, and obedience of all men.

"Make Disciples"

Literally the original says, "Having gone, therefore, make disciples. . . ." In such cases the participle as well as the verb that follows it can be—in the present case must be—interpreted as having imperative force. "Make disciples" is by itself an imperative. It is a brisk command, an order.

But just what is meant by "make disciples"? It is not exactly the same as "make converts," though the latter is surely implied. See above on 3:2; 4:17. The term "make disciples" places somewhat more stress on the fact that the mind, as well as the heart and the will, must be won for God. A disciple is *a pupil, a learner.* See on 13:52. Also, see on 11:29 for words related to it in the English language.

The apostle, then, must proclaim the truth and the will of God to the world. It is necessary that sinners *learn* about their own lost condition, God, his plan of redemption, his love, his law, etc. This however, is not enough. True *discipleship* implies much more. Mere mental understanding does not as yet make one a disciple. It is part of the picture, in fact an important part, but only a part. The truth learned must be practiced. It must be appropriated by heart, mind, and will, so that one *remains* or *abides* in the truth. Only then is one truly Christ's "disciple" (John 8:31).

Not every person who presents himself as a candidate for church membership should immediately be accorded all the rights and privileges pertaining to such membership. There are expositors who place all the emphasis on "The wedding-hall was filled with guests" (Matt. 22:10). They forget verses 11-14.

"Of All the Nations"

See above, under the heading "Go."

"Baptizing Them in(to) the Name of the Father and of the Son and of the Holy Spirit"

The main verb is "Make disciples." Subordinate to this are: *a.* baptizing them, and *b.* teaching them. In such a construction it would be completely wrong to say that because the word *baptizing* precedes the word *teaching,* therefore people must be baptized before they are taught. It is rather natural that baptizing is mentioned first, for while a person is baptized once (ordinarily), he continues throughout his life to be taught.

The concepts "baptizing" and "teaching" are simply two activities, in co-ordination with each other, but both subordinate to "make disciples." In other words, by means of being baptized and being taught a person becomes a disciple, with the understanding, of course, that this individual is ready for baptism and is willing to appropriate the teaching. —The context makes very clear that Jesus is here speaking about those who are old enough to be considered the objects of preaching. He is not here speaking about infants.

To be ready for baptism requires repentance (Acts 2:38, 41). It requires "receiving the word" (Acts 2:41). This also shows that a certain amount of teaching must precede being baptized.

The baptizing must be into the name—note the singular: *one* name; hence *one* God—of the Father and of the Son and of the Holy Spirit. A *name,* as indicated previously—see on 6:9; 7:22; 10:22, 41, 42; 12:21—represents the one who bears it. "Being baptized into the name of," therefore means "being brought into vital relationship with" that One, viewed as he has revealed himself.

Should we baptize "in" or "into"? The debate on this has already lasted many years. [907] Now since even in English—at least in conversational style—

---

[907] Lenski (*op. cit.*, p. 1155) very definitely rejects "into," as if it were an absolutely settled matter that this must be rejected. The matter, however, is not nearly as simple as all that. It is a well-known fact that in Koine Greek εἰς often means ἐν, but that does not prove that it *always* must have that meaning. Whether or not it does depends on such matters as whether in any particular passage it is based on Semitic usage, the kind of verbs and nouns with which it is used, etc.

"in" frequently has the sense of "into"—"Children, come in the house"—a decision on this point may not be quite as important as some try to make it. Nevertheless, all things considered, I believe "into" is defensible. Neither "into" nor "in" is necessarily wrong. A good case can be made for either. But when we say, "I baptize . . . in the name of," this could be understood to mean, "I baptize at the command of," or "on the authority of," which certainly is not what is meant. I Cor. 1:13 seems to mean, "Were y o u baptized into the name of Paul?" Similarly verse 15, ". . . baptized into my name." Cf. I Cor. 10:2. And so here in Matt. 28:19, "into the name of the Father and of the Son and of the Holy Spirit" makes good sense. [908]

Not as if the rite of baptism *as such* brings a person into vital union with the Father, Son, and Holy Spirit. But, according to Scripture the following are true: *a.* circumcision was a sign and a seal of the righteousness of Christ accepted by faith (see Rom. 4:11 in its context); *b.* baptism took the place of circumcision (Col. 2:11, 12); *c.* therefore baptism, too, must be regarded as a sign and a seal of the righteousness of Christ accepted by faith.

Accordingly, when through the preaching of the Word a person has been brought from darkness into light, and confesses the Triune God, Father, Son, and Holy Spirit, to be the one Object of his faith hope, and love, then the sacrament of baptism is the sign and seal that God the Father adopts him as his son and heir; that God the Son washes his sins away by his precious blood; and that God the Holy Spirit dwells in him, and will sanctify him; actually imparting to him that which objectively he already has in Christ, and at last bringing him from the Church Militant into the Church Triumphant.

Baptism, therefore, is very important. The one who submits to it, if sincere, is proclaiming that he has broken with the world and has been brought into union with the Triune God, to whom he intends to devote his life.—For "Infant Baptism" see on 19:15.

"And Teaching Them to Observe All That I Have Commanded Y o u"

As already remarked, this teaching both precedes and follows baptizing. The early church insisted that before the person to whom the gospel had been proclaimed be admitted to membership he give evidence of genuine repentance and of knowledge of the basics of Christianity. "The early church was interested in edification as well as evangelism, in sanctification as well as conversion, in church government as well as preaching." [909]

---

[908] For this argument see H. Bietenhard, art. ὄνομα and related words, Th.D.N.T., Vol. V, p. 275; L. Berkhof, *Systematic Theology*, p. 625. Does not this make Acts 19:3 easier to explain?

[909] G. W. Knight, III, *The Faithful Sayings in the Pastoral Epistles*, doctoral dissertation presented to the Free University at Amsterdam, Kampen, 1968, p. 148. Justin Martyr (about A.D. 114-165) states, "As many as are persuaded and believe that what we

That such teaching should not stop when a person has been baptized is clear from the words, "teaching them to observe all that I have commanded y o u." Think of:

a. All of Christ's marvelous discourses.

b. All of his parables; both *a.* and *b.* including ever so many "commands," whether implied or expressed. Among them are:

c. Precious "sayings," such as: "Abide in me . . . love each other . . . also bear witness" (John 15:4, 12, 27); "Love y o u r enemies" (Matt. 5:44); "Deny yourself, take up your cross, and follow me" (Luke 9:23).

d. Specific predictions and promises or assurances: "He who comes to me will in no way get hungry, and he who believes in me will in no way get thirsty" (John 6:35); "In the world y o u have tribulation; but be of good courage. I have conquered the world." Notice the implied directives for Christian conduct.

e. Add to this: the lessons on the cross, hypocrisy, proclaiming the gospel; on prayer, humility, trust, the forgiving spirit, the law.

f. And is not even the narrative of Christ's sojourn on earth—the account of his healing, traveling, suffering, death, resurrection, etc.—full of implied "commands"?

"Teaching them to observe all that I have commanded y o u," what an order! First of all for the eleven and for all ordained teachers; but certainly in a sense also for the entire church, the whole membership. Every true member is a witness-bearer.

In view of the fact that after Christ's ascension there was some hesitancy on the part of Christian leaders to proclaim the gospel to the Gentiles (see Acts 10:14, 28; 11:1-3, 19; Gal. 2:11-13), there are those who believe that either the Great Commission is itself a myth, or else the church quickly forgot about it. They contend that in the book of Acts, the epistles, and the book of Revelation no trace of its influence can be detected.

How can we be so sure of this? Do not the following passages testify to the possible influence of, among other factors, the Great Commission? See Acts 2:38, 39; 3:25; 4:12; 10:45; 11:1, 18; 13:46-49; 14:27; 15:7-11, 12, 13-19; 17:30; 19:10; 21:19, 20a; 22:15, 21; 26:15-20; 28:28; Rom. 1:5, 14-16; 11:32; Gal. 2:9; 3:28; Eph. 3:8, 9; Col. 3:11; I Tim. 1:15; Rev. 7:9, 10; 22:17.

---

teach and say is true, and undertake to be able to live accordingly, are instructed to pray and to entreat God with fasting, for the remission of their sins. . . . Then they are brought by us to where there is water . . ." *First Apology*, chap. 61. Another very early writing called *The Didache or Teaching of The Twelve Apostles* is generally held to be in part a statement of the rules of Christian conduct that was to be taught to those who were looking forward to being baptized.

The Great Comfort

20b. and remember, [910] **I am with y o u day in day out until the close of the age.** Cf. John 14:23; Acts 18:10. There is no vagueness about this assurance. It has been called a promise; it is *a fact.* Note the emphatic introduction: "Remember," or "Take note," "Pay close attention," "Look." The pronoun "I," included in the verb, is also written as a separate word and is very emphatic, as if to say, "No one less than I myself am with y o u." "With y o u" not just "forever" but "all the days," or "day in day out." Think of these days following each other one by one, each with its own trials, troubles, and difficulties, but each day also accompanied by the assurance, "My grace is sufficient for you. I will never leave you or forsake you." This continues on and on until the close or consummation of the age. And even then there is nothing to fear; see Matt. 25:31-40.

At the beginning, in the middle, and at the end of Matthew's Gospel, Jesus Christ assures the church of his constant and comforting presence:

1:23
See p. 133

"Behold, the virgin shall conceive and give birth to a son, and his name shall be called Emmanuel, which, translated, is 'God with us.' "

18:20
See p. 702

"For where two or three are gathered in my name there am I in the midst of them."

28:20

"And remember, I am with y o u day in day out until the close of the age."

Reflection on Chapter 28
Because of Christ's glorious resurrection we know
that our

R ight to heaven has been secured (Rom. 8:1).
E arthly house is to be exchanged for the heavenly (II Cor. 5:1).
S ins are forgiven (Rom. 4:25).
U nion with the church above has begun (Eph. 3:14).
R equests are being heard and answered (Eph. 3:20).
R edeemer has triumphed; hence, so shall we triumph (John 16:33).
E nergies are being constantly replenished (Phil. 4:12, 13).
C hrist is living evermore to intercede for us (Heb. 7:25).
T rials are understood and attended to (Heb. 4:15).
I mmortality (glorious) is guaranteed (John 14:19).
O blations are being accepted (Phil. 4:18, 19).
N ames are written in heaven (Luke 10:20).

---

[910] Or: *note well.* For the meaning and translation of ἰδού see footnote 133, on p. 131.

SELECT BIBLIOGRAPHY

On the Synoptic Problems and Related Subjects

Hawkins, J. C., *Horae Synopticae*, Oxford 1909.

Stonehouse, N. B., *Origins of the Synoptic Gospels*, Grand Rapids, 1963.

On the Reliability of the Gospels

Bruce, F. F., *Are the New Testament Documents Reliable?* Grand Rapids, 1954.

Hughes, F. E., ed., *Creative Minds in Contemporary Theology*, Grand Rapids, 1966.

Kistemaker, S., editor and co-author, *Interpreting God's Word Today*, Grand Rapids, 1970.

Ridderbos, H. N., *The Authority of the New Testament Scriptures*, Philadelphia, 1963.

Stonehouse, N. B. and Woolley, P., editors and co-authors, *The Infallible Word*, Grand Rapids, 1958.

On the Text of the New Testament

Metzger, B. M., *The Text of the New Testament*, Oxford, 1964.

On Introduction to the New Testament

Barker, G. W., Lane, W. L., and Michaels, J. R., *The New Testament Speaks*, New York, 1969.

Berkhof, L., *New Testament Introduction*, Grand Rapids, 1915.

Metzger, B. M., *The New Testament, its background, growth, and content*, New York and Nashville, 1965.

Commentaries on Matthew

Bruce, A. B., *The Synoptic Gospels* (*The Expositor's Greek Testament*, Vol. I), Grand Rapids, no date.

Calvin, J., *Commentary on a Harmony of the Evangelists, Matthew Mark, and Luke* (tr. of *Commentarius in Harmoniam Evangelicam, Opera Omnia*), Grand Rapids, 1949 ff.

Lenski, R. C. H., *Interpretation of Matthew's Gospel*, Columbus, 1932.

Stonehouse, N. B., *The Witness of Matthew and Mark to Christ*, Philadelphia, 1944. Though not strictly a commentary, the book sheds light on many passages of Matthew's Gospel.

Tasker, R. V. G., *The Gospel According to St. Matthew* (*Tyndale New Testament Commentaries*), Grand Rapids, 1961.

For those who are able to read Dutch:

Grosheide, F. W., *Het Heilig Evangelie Volgens Mattheus* (*Commentaar op het Nieuwe Testament*), Kampen, 1954.

Ridderbos, H. N., *Het Evangelie naar Mattheüs* (*Korte Verklaring der Heilige Schrift*), Kampen, 1952.

On The Sermon on the Mount

Lloyd-Jones, D. M., *Studies in the Sermon on the Mount*, Grand Rapids, 1959.

MATTHEW

On The Parables

Taylor, W. M., *The Parables of our Savior, Expounded and Illustrated*, New York, 1886.

On Quotations from the Old Testament

Gundry, R. H., *The Use of the Old Testament in St. Matthew's Gospel*, Leiden, 1967.

GENERAL BIBLIOGRAPHY

Aalders, G. Ch., *Het Boek Daniël (Korte Verklaring)*, Kampen, 1928.

Abbott, E. A., *The Fourfold Gospel*, Cambridge, 1913.

Albright, W. F., "The Names *Nazareth* and *Nazoraean*," *JBL*, 65 (Dec. 1946).

Alexander, J. A., *The Gospel According to Matthew*, New York, 1967.

Alford, H., *Greek Testament*, London, 1849-61.

Allen, E. L., "On this Rock," *JTS*, 5 (1954).

Allen, W. C., *A Critical and Exegetical Commentary on the Gospel According to S. Matthew (The International Critical Commentary)*, New York, 1910.

Allis, O. T., "The Alleged Aramaic Origin of the Fourth Gospel," *PTR*, 26 (1928).

Anderson, S. E., *Our Dependable Bible*, Grand Rapids, 1960.

Ante-Nicene Fathers, ten volumes, reprint, Grand Rapids, 1950, for references to Clement of Alexandria, Irenaeus, Justin Martyr, Origen, Tertullian, etc.

Argyle, A. W., "Evidence for the View that St. Luke used St. Matthew's Gospel," *JBL*, 83 (Dec. 1964).

Armstrong, O. K. and M. M., *The Indomitable Baptist*, Garden City, N.Y., 1967.

Baarda, T. J., *De Betrouwbaarheid van de Evangeliën*, Kampen, 1967.

Bacher, W., *Die Exegetische Terminologie der Jüdischen Traditions-literatur*, Hildesheim, 1965.

Bailey, A. E., *The Gospel in Art*, Boston, 1946.

Baird, W., "What is the Kerygma," *JBL*, 76 (Sept. 1957).

Barker, G. W., Lane, W. L., and Michaels, J. R., *The New Testament Speaks*, New York, 1969.

Bartina, S., "¿Casa o caserio? Los magos en Belen (Matt. 2:11; 10:12-14)," *EB* (March-April 1966).

Bartsch, H. W., ed., *Kerygma and Myth* (tr. of *Kerygma und Mythos*), London, 1957.

Bavinck, H., *Gereformeerde Dogmatiek*, Kampen, 1918.

————, *The Doctrine of God* (tr. of *Gereformeerde Dogmatiek*, Vol. II, "Over God"), Grand Rapids, 1955.

Bergsma, S., *Rainbow Empire*, Grand Rapids, 1932.

Berkhof, L., *New Testament Introduction*, Grand Rapids, 1915.

————, *Vicarious Atonement Through Christ*, Grand Rapids, 1936.

————, *Systematic Theology*, Grand Rapids, 1949.

Berkouwer, G. C., *Dogmatische Studiën* (the series), Kampen, 1949, etc.

Bisek, A. S., *The Trial of Jesus Christ*, Chicago, 1925.

Bishop, F. F., *Jesus of Palestine*, London, 1955.

Bishop, J., *The Day Christ Died*, New York and Evanston, 1957.

Boettner, L., *Roman Catholicism*, Philadelphia, 1962.

Bornkamm, G., *Jesus of Nazareth* (tr. of *Jesus von Nazareth*), London and New York, 1961.

Bornkamm, G., Barth, G., and Held, H. J., *Überlieferung und Auslegung im Mattäus-evangelium*, Wageningen, 1965.

Bouman, J., "Son of Man," *ET*, 59 (1948).

Brownlee, W. H., "John the Baptist in the New Light of Ancient Scrolls" in K. Stendahl, *The Scrolls and the New Testament*, New York, 1957.

Bruce, A. B., *The Parabolic Teaching of Christ*, London, 1882.

————, "The Baptism of Jesus," *Exp*, 5th ser. 7 (1898).

————, *The Training of the Twelve*, Garden City, New York, 1928.

————, *The Synoptic Gospels* (*The Expositor's Greek Testament*, Vol. I), Grand Rapids, no date.

Bruce, F. F., *Are the New Testament Documents Reliable?*, Grand Rapids, 1954.

————, *Commentary on the Book of The Acts* (*The New International Commentary on the New Testament*), Grand Rapids, 1964.

————, *The Epistle to the Hebrews* (*The New International Commentary on the New Testament*), Grand Rapids, 1964.

Bultmann, R., *From Tradition to Gospel* (tr. of *Die Formgeschichte des Evangeliums*), New York, 1935.

————, *Jesus and the Word* (tr. of *Jesus*), New York, 1951.

————, *The Theology of the New Testament* (tr. of *Theologie des Neuen Testaments*), New York, 1951.

————, *The History of the Synoptic Tradition* (tr. of *Die Geschichte der synoptischen Tradition*), New York and Evanston, 1963. A popular abridgement of this work is *The Study of the Synoptic Gospels* (see under Grant, F. C.).

————, *Jesus Christ and Mythology*, London, 1958.

Bundy, W. E., "The Meaning of Jesus' Baptism," *JR*, 7 (1927).

Burney, C. F., *The Aramaic Origin of the Fourth Gospel*, Oxford, 1922.

Burrows, M., *The Dead Sea Scrolls*, New York, 1956.

————, *More Light on the Dead Sea Scrolls*, New York, 1958.

Butler, B. C., *The Originality of St. Matthew*, Cambridge, 1951.

Calvin, J., *Commentary on a Harmony of the Evangelists, Matthew, Mark, and Luke* (tr. of *Commentarius in Harmoniam Evangelicam, Opera Omnia*) Grand Rapids, 1949 ff.

Carr, A., *The Gospel according to St. Matthew*, Cambridge, 1901.

Carson, A., *Baptism in its Mode and Subjects*, London, 1844.

Ceram, C. W., *Gods, Graves, and Scholars*, New York, 1968.

Chamberlain, W. D., *The Manner of Prayer*, Philadelphia, 1943.

————, *The Meaning of Repentance*, Philadelphia, 1943.

Chapman, J., *Matthew, Mark, and Luke*, London, 1937.

————, *The Four Gospels*, London, 1944.

Chiniquy, C., *Fifty Years in the Church of Rome*, New York, Chicago, Toronto, 1886.

Cohen, B., *Everyman's Talmud*, New York, 1949.

Colwell, E. C., *The Greek of the Fourth Gospel*, Chicago, 1931.

Cox, G. E. P., *The Gospel according to St. Matthew*, London, 1952.

Cribbs, F. L., "St. Luke and the Johannine Tradition," *JBL*, 90 (Dec. 1971).

Dalman, G., *Aramäisch-neuhebräisches Wörterbuch zu Targum, Talmud, und Midrasch*, Frankfort, 1897-1901.

————, *Christianity and Judaism* (tr. of *Christentum und Judentum*) Oxford, 1901.

————, *Jesus-Jeshua, Studies in the Gospels*, New York, 1929.

Dana, H. E. and Mantey, J. R., *A Manual Grammar of the Greek New Testament*, New York, 1950.

Dana, Mrs. W. S., *How to Know the Wild Flowers*, New York, 1922.

Daniélou, J., *Les Manuscripts de la Mer Mort et les Origines du Christianisme*, Paris, 1957.

MATTHEW

Davey, J. E., *The Jesus of St. John*, London, 1958.

De Beus, C. H., "Achtergrond en inhoud van de uitdrukking 'de Zoon des Menschen' in de synoptische evangeliën," *NedTT*, 9 (1954-55).

——, "Het gebruik en de betekenis van de uitdrukking 'De Zoon des Menschen' in het Evangelie van Johannes," *NedTT*, 10 (1955-56).

Deissmann, A., *Light from the Ancient East*, New York, 1922.

De Jong, A. C., *The Well-Meant Gospel Offer* (doctoral dissertation), Franeker, no date.

Dell, A., "Zur Erklärung von Mattäus 16:17-19," *ZNW*, 17 (1916).

De Ridder, R. R., *The Dispersion of the People of God* (doctoral dissertation), Kampen, 1971.

De Solages, B., *A Greek Synopsis of the Gospels, a New Way of Solving the Synoptic Problem*, Leiden, 1959.

Dibelius, M., *From Tradition to Gospel* (tr. of *Die Formgeschichte des Evangeliums*), New York, 1935.

Dodd, C. H., *The Parables of the Kingdom*, London, 1935.

Dupont-Sommer, *The Jewish Sect of Qumran and the Essenes, New Studies on the Dead Sea Scrolls*, London, 1954.

Easton, B. S., "St. Matthew 16:17-19," *ATR*, 4 (1921, 1922)

——, "St. Matthew 16:17-19," *ATR*, 5 (1921, 1922)

Edersheim, A., *The Life and Times of Jesus the Messiah*, New York, 1897.

——, *The Temple*, London, 1908.

Elderkin, G. W., *Archaeological Paper VII: Golgotha, Kraneion, and the Holy Sepulchre*, Springfield, Mass., 1945.

Emden, C. S., "St. Mark's Use of the Imperfect Tense," *BTr* (July 1954).

Erdman, C. R., *Exposition of the Gospel according to Matthew*, Philadelphia, 1920.

Evans, W., *From the Upper Room to the Empty Tomb*, Grand Rapids, 1934.

Ewald, G. H. A., *The Prophets of the Old Testament* (tr. of *Die Propheten des Alten Bundes*), London, 1875-81.

Fahling, A., *The Life of Christ*, St. Louis, 1936.

Farrar, F. W., *The Life of Christ*, New York, 1875.

Farrer, A. M., "On Dispensing with Q," in D. E. Nineham (ed.) *Studies in the Gospels, Essays in memory of R. H. Lightfoot*, Oxford, 1955.

Finkelstein, L., *The Jews, their History, Culture, and Religion*, New York, 1949.

Flynn, L. B., *Did I Say That?*, Nashville, 1959.

Foster, L., "The 'Q' Myth in Synoptic Studies," *The Seminary Review* Vol. X, 4 (Summer 1964).

Foster, R. C., *Studies in the Life of Christ*, Grand Rapids, 1966.

Funk, R. W., "The Wilderness," *JBL* (Sept. 1959).

Gaebelein, F. E., *Four Minor Prophets*, Chicago, 1970.

Gaechter, P., *Das Matthäus Evangelium*, Wien-München, 1962.

Gibbons, J., *The Faith of our Fathers*, New York, 1871.

Gibson, J. M., *The Gospel of St. Matthew* (*The Expositor's Bible*), Grand Rapids, 1943.

Gilmour, S. M., *The Gospel according to St. Luke* (*The Interpreter's Bible*), New York and Nashville, 1952.

Ginzberg, L., *A Commentary on the Palistinian Talmud*, New York, 1967.

Glover, R. H., *The Progress of World-Wide Missions*, New York, 1925.

Goodspeed, E. J., *New Solutions of New Testament Problems*, Chicago, 1927.

MATTHEW

————, *New Chapters in New Testament Study*, New York, 1937.

————, *Matthew, Apostle and Evangelist*, Philadelphia and Toronto, 1959. Whenever this author's name is mentioned without designation of specific book title, the reference is to this work.

Graafland, C., "Ingaan in het Rijk," *TR* (Dec. 1970).

Grant, F. C., Editor and Translator, *Form Criticism*, includes *The Study of the Synoptic Gospels* by R. Bultmann, and *Primitive Christianity in the Light of Gospel Research* by K. Kundsin, New York, 1934.

————, *The Gospel of St. John*, New York and London, 1956.

Greijdanus, S., *Bijbelsch Handboek*, Kampen, 1935.

————, *Het Heilig Evangelie naar de Beschrijving van Lucas (Kommentaar op het Nieuwe Testament)*, Amsterdam, 1940.

Groenewald, E. P., *Die Evangelie volgens Markus (Kommentaar op die Bybel, Nuwe Testament)*, Praetoria, 1948.

Grollenberg, L. H., *Atlas of the Bible*, New York, etc., 1956.

Grosheide, F. W., *Het Heilig Evangelie Volgens Mattheus (Commentaar op het Nieuwe Testament)*, Kampen, 1954.

Gundry, R. H., *The Use of the Old Testament in St. Matthew's Gospel* (doctoral disseration), Leiden, 1967.

Halberthal, L., *The Plan of the Holy Temple of Jerusalem*, Montreal, 1967.

Harnack, A., *History of Dogma* (tr. of *Lehrbuch der Dogmengeschichte*), London, 1895-1900.

————, *What is Christianity?* (tr. of *Das Wesen des Christentums*), London, 1901.

————, *The Origin of the New Testament* (tr. of *Die Entstehung des Neuen Testaments*), London, 1925.

Hawkins, J. C., *Horae Synopticae*, Oxford, 1909.

Hendriksen, W., *The Covenant of Grace*, Grand Rapids, 1932.

————, *The Meaning of the Preposition ἀντί in the New Testament* (unpublished doctoral dissertation), Princeton, 1948.

————, *Bible Survey*, Grand Rapids, 1961.

————, *Israel and the Bible*, Grand Rapids, 1968.

————, *More Than Conquerors, An Interpretation of the Book of Revelation*, Grand Rapids, 1970.

————, *The Bible on the Life Hereafter*, Grand Rapids, 1971.

Henry, C. F. H., "Where Is Modern Theology Going?" *Christianity Today*, 11 (March 1, 1968).

Hertzberg, A., ed., *Judaism*, New York, 1962

Hibbard, F. G., *Christian Baptism*, New York, 1842.

Hills, E. F., *The King James Version Defended*, Des Moines, 1956.

Holdsworth, W. W., *Gospel Origins*, New York, 1913.

Hooke, R., *Discourse on Earthquakes*, 1668.

Hughes, P. E., *Paul's Second Epistle to the Corinthians (The New International Commentary on the New Testament)*, Grand Rapids, 1962.

Hughes, P. E., ed., *Creative Minds in Contemporary Theology*, Grand Rapids, 1966.

Huizenga, L. S., *Unclean! Unclean!*, Grand Rapids, 1927.

Jansen, J., "Het Vraagstuk van de sleutelmacht," *GTT*, 2 (1910).

Jeremias, J., "The Theological Significance of the Dead Sea Scrolls," *CTM*, 39 (Aug. 1968).

MATTHEW

Johnson, M. C., *The Purpose of the Biblical Genealogies*, Cambridge, 1969.

Johnson, S. E., *The Gospel According to St. Matthew* (*The Interpreter's Bible*), New York and Nashville, 1951.

Jones, G. V., *Christology and Myth in the New Testament*, London, 1956.

Kähler, M., *Der soganannte historische Jesus und der geschichtliche, biblische Christus*, Munich, 1956.

Kalland, E. S., *The Deity of the Old Testament Messiah, with Special Reference to his Fulfilment in Jesus of Nazareth* (unpublished doctoral dissertation), Gordon College of Theology and Missions, 1942.

Kellersberger, E. R., "The Social Stigma of Leprosy," reprinted in pamphlet form from *The Annals of the New York Academy of Sciences*, 54 (1951).

Kerr, J. H., *An Introduction to the Study of the Books of the New Testament*, Chicago, New York, Toronto, 1892.

Key, A. F., "The Giving of Proper Names in the Old Testament," *JBL* (March 1964).

Kilpatrick, G. D., *The Origins of the Gospel according to St. Matthew*, Oxford, 1946.

Kistemaker, S., editor and co-author, *Interpreting God's Word Today*, Grand Rapids, 1970.

Knight, G. W. III, *The Faithful Sayings in the Pastoral Epistles* (doctoral dissertation), Kampen, 1968.

Knox, R., *A Commentary on the Gospels*, New York, 1952.

Kollek, T. and Pearlman, M., *Jerusalem, A History of Forty Centuries*, New York, 1968.

Kraeling, E. G., *Rand McNally Bible Atlas*, New York, Chicago, San Francisco, 1966.

Kuyper, A., Sr., *De Engelen Gods*, Kampen, 1923.

LaFay, H., "Where Jesus Walked," *National Geographic*, Vol. 132, 6 (Dec. 1967).

Lange, J. P., *Matthew* (*Commentary on the Holy Scriptures*), Grand Rapids, no date.

Lenski, R. C. H., *Interpretation of St. Matthew's Gospel*, Columbus, 1932. Whenever this author's name is mentioned without designation of specific book title, the reference is to this work.

————, *Interpretation of Luke's Gospel*, Columbus, 1934.

Lloyd-Jones, D. M., *Studies in the Sermon on the Mount*, Grand Rapids, 1959.

Loeb Classical Library, New York (various dates), for The Apostolic Fathers, Eusebius, Josephus, Philo, Pliny, Plutarch, Strabo, etc.

Ludlum, J. H., Jr., "More Light on the Synoptic Problem," and "Are we Sure of Mark's Priority?" *Christianity Today* (Respectively Nov. 1 and 24, 1958; Sept. 14 and 28, 1959).

Macartney, C. E., *Of Them He Chose Twelve*, Philadephia, 1927.

Machen, J. G., *The Virgin Birth of Christ*, New York and London, 1930.

————, *The Origin of Paul's Religion*, Grand Rapids, 1947.

Maclaren, A., *Expositions of Holy Scriptures*, Cincinnati and New York, no date.

Maier, P. L., *Pontius Pilate*, Garden City, New York, 1968.

Maier, W. A., *For Better Not for Worse*, St. Louis, 1935.

Manson, W., *Jesus the Messiah*, Philadelphia, 1946.

Maus, C. P., *Christ and the Fine Arts*, New York, 1959.

McCasland, S. V., "Matthew Twists the Scriptures," *JBL* (June 1961).

McMillen, S. I., *None of These Diseases*, Westwood, N. J., 1963.

McNeile, A. H., *The Gospel according to St. Matthew*, London, 1915.

Meeter, H. H., *The Heavenly Highpriesthood of Christ* (doctoral dissertation), Grand Rapids, no date.

MATTHEW

Metzger, B. M., compiler, *Index to Periodical Literature on Christ and the Gospels*, Grand Rapids, 1962.

———, *The Text of the New Testament*, Oxford, 1964.

———, *The New Testament, Its Background, Growth, and Content*, New York and Nashville, 1965.

Micklem, P. A., St. *Matthew, with Introduction and Notes*, London, 1917.

Milligan, G., *The New Testament Documents*, London, 1913.

Mishna, The, Engl. tr. by H. Danby, London, 1933.

Mitchell, B., "What Philosophical Problems Arise from Belief in the Resurrection?" *Th*, 70 (1967).

Moldenke, H. N. and A. L., *Plants of the Bible*, Waltham, 1952.

Montefiore, C. G., *The Synoptic Gospels*, London, 1927.

———, *Rabbinic Literature and Gospel Teaching*, New York, 1970.

Montgomery, J. A., "Some Aramaisms in the Gospels and Acts," *JBL*, 46 (1927).

———, "Torrey's Aramaic Gospels," *JBL*, 53 (1934).

Moore, G. F., *Judaism in the First Five Centuries of the Christian Era*, Cambridge, 1927-1930.

Morgan, G. C., *The Gospel According to Matthew*, New York, etc., 1929.

Mulder, H., *De Eerste Hoofdstukken van het Evangelie naar Lukas in hun Structurele Samenhang* (doctoral dissertation), Delft, 1948.

———, "De Datum Der Kruisiging," *GTT* (1951).

———, "Het Synoptisch Vraagstuk," *Exegetica*, Delft, 1952.

———, *Gids voor het Nieuwe Testament*, Kampen, 1962.

———, "Matthäus' Appel an die Bevölkerung Jerusalems " *BG* (July-Sept. 1966).

———, "Wederkerige assistantie en vervreemding van kerken in de nieuwtestamentische tijd," *De Heerbaan*, 4 (1971).

———, *Geschiedenis van de palestijnse kerk (tot 638)*, Kampen, no date.

Mulder, J. D., "Mental Diseases and Demon Possession," *The Banner* (March 24, 31, April 7, 14, 1933).

Müller, G. A., *Pontius Pilatus der fünfte Prokurator von Judäa*, Stuttgart, 1888.

Murray, G. L., *Millennial Studies*, Grand Rapids, 1948.

Murray, J., and Stonehouse, N. B., *The Free Offer of the Gospel*, Phillipsburg, N.J., 1948.

Murray, J., *Christian Baptism*, Philadelphia, 1952.

Nicholson, W. R., *The Six Miracles of Calvary*, Chicago, 1928.

Oesterley, W. O. E., *The Gospel Parables in the Light of their Jewish Background*, London, 1938.

Orr, J., *The Virgin Birth of Christ*, New York, 1924.

Osterhoff, B. J., *Feit of Interpretatie*, Kampen, 1967.

Oulton, J. E. L., "An Interpretation of Matthew 16:18," *ET*, 48 (1936-37).

Paddock, W. & P., *Hungry Nations*, Boston and Toronto, 1964.

Parker, P., "The Meaning of 'Son of Man,' " *JBL*, 60 (1941).

Parmelee, A., *All the Birds of the Bible*, New York, 1959.

Pauck, W., *Harnack and Troeltsch: Two Historical Theologians*, Oxford, 1968.

Perowne, S. H., *The Life and Times of Herod the Great*, New York, 1956.

Petrie, C. S., "The Authorship of 'The Gospel according to Matthew': a Reconsideration of the External Evidence," *NTStud*, 14 (Jan. 1967).

Pick, B., *The Talmud, What It Is*, New York, 1887.

MATTHEW

Plummer, A., *The Gospel according to St. Luke* (*International Critical Commentary*), New York, 1910.

————, *An Exegetical Commentary on the Gospel according to St. Matthew*, Grand Rapids, 1953.

Popma, K. J., *Eerst De Jood Maar Ook De Griek*, Franeker, 1950.

Rhine, J. B., *New Frontiers of the Mind*, New York and Toronto, 1937.

Riddle, D. W., "The Aramaic Gospels and the Synoptic Problems," *JBL*, 54 (1935).

Ridderbos, H. N., *Zelfopenbaring en Zelfverberging*, Kampen, 1946.

————, *De Komst van het Koninkrijk*, Kampen, 1950.

————, *Het Evangelie naar Mattheüs* (*Korte Verklaring der Heilige Schrift*), Kampen, 1952. Whenever this author's name is mentioned without designation of specific book title, the reference is to this work.

————, *The Authority of the New Testament Scriptures*, Philadelphia, 1963.

————, "Rudolph Bultmann," *Torch and Trumpet*, 9 (Nov. 1965).

Ridderbos, J., *Jesaja* (*Korte Verklaring*), Kampen, 1952.

Riggle, H. M., *Roman Catholicism*, Anderson, Ind. and Kansas City, Mo. 1917.

Robertson, A. T., *Studies in the Epistle of James*, New York, 1915.

————, *The Pharisees and Jesus*, New York, 1920.

————, *A Harmony of the Gospels for Students of the Life of Christ*, New York, 1922.

————, *A Translation of Luke's Gospel*, New York, 1923.

————, *Word Pictures in the New Testament*, New York and London, 1930.

Robinson, H. W., *The People and the Book*, Oxford, 1925.

Ropes, J. H., *The Synoptic Gospels*, Cambridge, 1960.

Rosenblatt, S., "The Crucifixion of Jesus from the Standpoint of Pharisaic Law," *JBL*, 75 (Dec. 1956).

Roux, H., *L'Evangile du Royaume, Commentaire sur l'Évangile selon saint Matthieu*, Geneva, Switzerland, no date.

Runia, K., "The Third Day He Rose Again," *CT*, 11 (March 17, 1967).

Sanders, E. P., *The Tendencies of the Synoptic Tradition*, Cambridge, 1969.

Sandmel, S., *Herod, Profile of a Tyrant*, Philadelphia and New York, 1967.

Schaff, P., *History of the Christian Church*, New York, 1916.

Schlatter, D. A., *Erläuterungen zum Neuen Testament*, Stuttgart, 1908.

Schniewind, J. *Das Evangelium nach Matthäus* (*Das Neue Testament Deutsch*), Göttingen, 1960.

Schilder, K., *Christ in his Suffering* (tr. of *Christus in Zijn Lijden*), Grand Rapids, 1938.

Schoeps, H. J., *Die jüdischen Prophetenmorde Aus frühchristlicher Zeit*, Tübingen, 1950.

Schoneveld, J., *Salomo*, Baarn, no date.

Schonfield, H. J., *The Passover Plot*, New York, 1966.

Schultze, H., "Demon Possession," *The Banner* (Sept. 2, 1932).

Schürer, E., *History of the Jewish People in the time of Jesus* (tr. of *Geschichte des jüdischen Volkes in Zeitaltar Jesu Christi*), Edinburg, 1892-1901.

Schwartz, H., *Das Verständnis des Wunders bei Heim und Bultmann*, Stuttgart, 1966.

Schweitzer, A., *The Quest of the Historical Jesus* (tr. of *Von Reimarus zu Wrede*, Edinburg, 1910.

————, *The Mystery of the Kingdom of God* (tr. of *Das Messianitäts und Leidensgeheimnis*), New York, 1914.

————, *My Life and Thought*, London, 1933.

————, *The Psychiatric Study of Jesus* (tr. of *Die psychiatrische Beurteilung Jesu*), Boston, 1948.

MATTHEW

Scott, E. F., *The Literature of the New Testament*, New York, 1940.

Seitz, O. J. F., "Upon this Rock: A Critical Re-examination of Matthew 16:17-19," *R.E.*, *JBL*, 69 (1950).

Selwyn, F. G., *The First Epistle of St. Peter*, London, 1946.

Shepherd, M. H., "Are Both the Synoptics and John Correct about the Date of Jesus' Death?" *JBL*, 80 (June 1961).

Sickenberger, J., "Das in die Welt Kommende Licht," *ThG*, 33 (1941).

Simcox, C. E., *The First Gospel, Its Meaning and Message*, Greenwich, Conn., 1963.

Sizoo, A., *Uit De Wereld van het Nieuwe Testament*, Kampen, 1946.

———, *De Antieke Wereld en het Nieuwe Testament*, Kampen, 1948.

Slotemaker de Bruine, J. R., "De Sleutelmacht," *TS*, 22 (1904).

Smith, M., "Notes on Goodspeed's *Problems of New Testament Translation*," *JBL*, 64 (Dec. 1945).

Soltau, W., "Wann ist Matt. 16:17-19 eingeschoben?" *TSk*, 89 (1916).

Stalker, J., *The Trial and Death of Jesus Christ*, New York, 1894.

Stevens, G. B., *The Theology of the New Testament*, New York, 1925.

Stonehouse, N. B., *The Witness of Matthew and Mark to Christ*, Philadelphia, 1944.

———, *Paul Before the Areopagus*, Grand Rapids, 1957.

Stonehouse, N. B. and Woolley, P., editors and co-authors, *The Infallible Word*, Grand Rapids, 1958.

———, *Origins of the Synoptic Gospels*, Grand Rapids, 1963.

Strack, H. L., *Introduction to the Talmud and Midrash*, New York and Philadelphia, 1959.

Streeter, B. H., *The Four Gospels*, New York, 1925.

Sukenik, E. L., *Ancient Synagogues in Palestine and Greece*, London, 1934.

Swainson, C. A., *The Greek Liturgies*, London, 1884.

Talmud, The Babylonian (Engl. tr.), Boston, 1918.

Tasker, R. V. G., *The Gospel According to St. Matthew* (*Tyndale New Testament Commentaries*), Grand Rapids, 1961.

Taylor, W. M., *The Parables of our Savior, Expounded and Illustrated*, New York, 1886.

Tenney, M. C., *The New Testament*, Grand Rapids, 1953.

Terry, M. S., *Biblical Hermeneutics*, Grand Rapids, no date.

Thiessen, H. C., *Introduction to the New Testament*, Grand Rapids, 1943.

Thompson, G. H. P., "The Son of Man: The Evidence of the Dead Sea Scrolls," *ET*, 72 (1960-61).

Torrey, C. C., *The Four Gospels, A New Translation*, New York and London, 1933.

———, *Our Translated Gospels*, New York and London, 1936.

———, *Documents of the Primitive Church*, New York and London, 1941.

———, "The Aramaic of the Gospels," *JBL*, 61 (1942).

———, *Lengendary Lives of the Prophets*, Philadelphia, 1946.

Tottenham, C. J., " 'The Gates of Hell' (Matt. 16:18)," *ET*, 29 (1917-18).

Trattner, E. R., *Understanding The Talmud*, New York, 1955.

Trench, R. C., *Notes on the Parables of our Lord*, Grand Rapids, 1948.

———, *Synonyms of the New Testament*, Grand Rapids, 1948.

Trueblood, E., *The Humor of Christ*, New York, Evanston, London, 1964.

Valentin, P., "Les Comparutions de Jesus devant le Sanhedrin," *RSR*, 59 (2, '71).

Van Dyk, P. "Het gekrookte riet en de rookende vlaswiek," *GTT*, 23 (1923).

Van Leeuwen, J. A. C., *Het Evangelie van Mattheus*, Gronigen, Den Haag, 1918.

MATTHEW

Vardapet, E., "The Revelation of the Lord to Peter," *ZNW*, 23 (1924).

Von Hagen, *The Roads That Led to Rome*, Cleveland and New York, 1967.

Vos, G., *The Self-disclosure of Jesus*, New York, 1926.

————, *The Teaching of Jesus Concerning the Kingdom of God and the Church*, Kampen, 1950.

Votaw, C. W., "Peter and the Keys of the Kingdom," *BW*, 36 (1910).

Walker, T., *Jewish Views of Jesus*, New York, 1931.

Walker, W., *All the Plants of the Bible*, New York, 1957.

Wallace, R. and the editors of Time-Life Books, *The World of Rembrandt*, New York, 1968.

Warfield, B. B., *Christology and Criticism* New York, 1929.

————, *The Inspiration and Authority of the Bible*, Philadelphia, 1948.

————, *Biblical and Theological Studies*, Philadelphia, 1953.

Warren, J., "Was Simon Peter the Church's Rock?" *EQ*, 19 (1947).

Weidenschilling, J. M., *Studies in the Gospel according to St. Matthew*, St. Louis, 1948.

Weiss, J., *Die Predigt Jesu vom Reiche Gottes*, Göttingen, 1893.

————, *Die Idee des Reichs Gottes in der Theologie*, Giessen, 1900.

Whitaker, G. H., "The Chief Cornerstone," *Exp*, Eighth Series (1918).

Willoughby, C. A., *A Critical and Exegetical Commentary on the Gospel according to Matthew*, Edinburgh, 1907.

Wilson, E., *The Scrolls from the Dead Sea*, New York, 1955.

Wolff, M., "De Samenstelling en het Karakter van het groote συνέδριον te Jeruzalem voor het jaar 70 Na Chr.," *TT*, 51 (1917).

Wood, H. G., "The Priority of Mark," *ET* (Oct. 1953).

Wrede, W., *Das Messiasgeheimnis in den Evangelien*, Göttingen, 1901.

————, *Paul* (tr. of *Paulus*), Boston, 1908.

————, *The Origin of the New Testament* (tr. of *Die Entstehung der Schriften des Neuen Testaments*), London and New York, 1909.

Wright, G. E., *Biblical Archaeology*, London and Philadelphia, 1957.

Wurth, G. Brillenburg, *De Bergrede en Onze Tijd*, Kampen, 1933.

Yaffe, J., *The American Jews*, New York, 1969.

Young, E. J., *The Prophecy of Daniel*, Grand Rapids, 1949.

————, *Studies in Isaiah*, Grand Rapids, 1954.

————, "The Virgin Birth," *The Banner* (April 15, 1955).

————, "The Teacher of Righteousness and Jesus Christ," *WTJ*, 18 (May 1956).

————, *Thy Word Is Truth*, Grand Rapids, 1957.

Zahn, Th., *Das Evangelium des Matthäus*, Leipzig, 1910.